BOMP! 2

BORN IN THE GARAGE

Mike Stax and Suzy Shaw

BOMP! • UT PUBLISHING

CREDITS

EDITORS:
Mike Stax and Suzy Shaw

ESSAYS BY:
Ken Barnes
Alec Palao
Jon Savage
Suzy Shaw
Mike Stax
William Stout

VINTAGE WRITING BY:
Billy Altman, Cary Baker, Glenn A Baker, Lester Bangs, Ken Barnes, Joel Bernstein, John Blair, Mitch Cohen, David Johnson, Lenny Kaye, Jeff Lind, Richard Meltzer, Peter Menkin, Phast Phreddie Patterson, Lennart Persson, Dick Rosemont, Mike Saunders, Greg Shaw, Bill Small, Mike Thom, Greg Turner, Ron Weiser, and a cast of dozens.

VINTAGE ARTWORK:
Jonh Ingham, Jay Kinney, Tim Kirk, WilliamStout, Dean Torrence & several others.

FRONT COVER BY WILLIAM STOUT.

Back cover collage based on artwork by Dean Torrence and Diane Zincavage. Layout by Patrick Boissel and Geoff Crowe.

Special thanks to Patrick Boissel and Geoffrey Weiss for their invaluable assistance in the making of this book.

© 2009 BOMP / UT Publishing.

No part of this book may be reproduced by any means, in any media, electronic or mechanical, including motion picture film, video, photocopy, recording or any other information retrieval system without prior permission in writing from the publishers.

ISBN: 0-9778166-2-1

ABOUT OUR COVER ARTIST

WILLIAM STOUT was born in Salt Lake City, and raised in Reseda, California. At 17 he won a full California State Scholarship to the Chouinard Art Institute (California Institute of the Arts). During the summer of 1968 he tried to attend every Shrine Expositional Hall concert. A self-confessed Anglophile, he also attempted to catch as many of his favorite English groups as he could in small clubs, before they broke big. After he began his professional career that same year as a magazine illustrator, he became an assistant to Russ Manning on the *Tarzan of the Apes* Sunday & daily newspaper comic strips.

He worked with Harvey Kurtzman and Will Elder on *Little Annie Fanny* for *Playboy* in 1972 before becoming a graphic collaborator with the Firesign Theatre. In 1976 Stout began work as the art director for *BOMP!* He created Rhino Records' original Rocky Rhino mascot and subsequently drew and painted a number of their LP covers. That year also saw Stout's first movie poster. He ultimately worked on the advertising for over 120 films. He has also worked on over 35 feature films including both *Conan* films, *Men In Black*, *Predator*, *Return of the Living Dead* and *Pan's Labyrinth*.

Beginning in 1987, Stout worked for Walt Disney Imagineering, and went on to become one of the world's top theme park designers. In late 1995, Steven Spielberg chose Stout as his senior concept designer for GameWorks. Stout oversaw the concepts, design, and execution of the first three facilities (Seattle, Tempe & Ontario). Stout worked in 1998/99 as the lead designer for Kansas City's Wonderful World of Oz theme park. He designed the wrought iron gates and their Peter Pan-themed sculptural elements for Michael Jackson's NeverLand.

He is currently writing and compiling his most requested book, a volume on all of his music-related art. He resides in Pasadena, California with his perfect wife. Occasionally they are visited by their two brilliant sons.

CONTENTS

FOREWORD *by Alec Palao* 5	**METANOIA #11** 113
INTRODUCTION *by Jon Savage* 7	**WHO PUT THE BOMP #9** 115
R.I.A.W.O.L.: The Roots of Rock Fandom *by Mike Stax* 13	R.I.A.W.O.L / Editorial *by Greg Shaw* 116
REVERBERATIONS *by Ken Barnes* 25	Ahead of his Time: Gene Vincent *by Ron Weiser* . 118
THE BOOTLEG CONNECTION *by William Stout* 31	Feedback 122
GREG SHAW MINUS *by Suzy Shaw* 33	**METANOIA #12** 126
WHO PUT THE BOMP #2 41	**WHO PUT THE BOMP #10-11** 129
KARNIS BOTTLE'S METANOIA #3 42	R.I.A.W.O.L / Editorial *by Greg Shaw* 130
WHO PUT THE BOMP #3 43	Liverpool *by Greg Shaw* 131
LIQUID LOVE #1 45	The Beatles *by Greg Shaw* 133
LIQUID LOVE #3 46	Swinging Blue Jeans *by Ken Barnes* 133
METANOIA #4 47	Liverpool Left Overs *by Greg Shaw* 134
LIQUID LOVE #6	The Hollies *by Mike Saunders & Ken Barnes* 135
Whither Rock? *by Greg Shaw* 48	Wayne Fontana & Mindbenders *by M. Saunders* .. 136
WHO PUT THE BOMP #4 53	Freddie & the Dreamers *by Ken Barnes* 137
R.I.A.W.O.L / Editorial *by Greg Shaw* 54	Dave Clark Five *by Mike Saunders* 138
METANOIA #5 57	The Kinks *by Greg Shaw* 139
METANOIA #6 58	The Nashville Teens *by Ken Barnes* 139
WHO PUT THE BOMP #5 59	British R&B *by Greg Shaw* 140
R.I.A.W.O.L / Editorial *by Greg Shaw* 60	Pretty Things *by Ken Barnes* 141
Feedback 62	Downliners Sect *by Greg Shaw* 142
METANOIA #7 63	The Yardbirds *by Greg Shaw* 142
METANOIA #8 64	The Paramounts *by Greg Shaw* 143
Snazzy Leather Company *by Peter Menkin* 68	Gary Farr & the T-Bones *by Greg Shaw* 143
WHO PUT THE BOMP #6 69	Shel Talmy & Pop Art Rock *by Greg Shaw* 143
R.I.A.W.O.L / Editorial *by Greg Shaw* 70	Sorrows, Don Fardon & Miki Dallon *by GS* 144
Prelude to the Morning of An Inventory of the 60's *by Greg Shaw* 72	Small Faces *by Ken Barnes* 144
Juke Box Jury *by Greg Shaw* 74	The Who *by Mike Saunders* 146
Feedback 75	The Troggs *by Greg Shaw* 147
ALLIGATOR WINE 77	The Easybeats *by Ken Barnes* 148
Pretentious Essay of the Month No. 1 *by GS* 79	Rockin' Around the World *by Greg Shaw* 149
METANOIA #9 83	Novelties *by Greg Shaw* 150
ROCK, YOU SINNERS! 85	The Scene *by Greg Shaw*: 151
WHO PUT THE BOMP #7 87	Pirate Radio in the UK *by Greg Shaw* 152
R.I.A.W.O.L / Editorial *by Greg Shaw* 88	R&R TV in America *by Billy Altman* 153
Kinks Kompendium *by Greg Shaw* 90	Summary / Last Words *by Greg Shaw* 156
A Sam Goody's Discography *by 'Sam Swanson'* ... 95	Feedback 158
Feedback 98	**WHO PUT THE BOMP #12** 161
WHO PUT THE BOMP #8 101	The Beat / Editorial *by Greg Shaw* 162
R.I.A.W.O.L / Editorial *by Greg Shaw* 102	Reverberations *by Ken Barnes* 163
Feedback 104	The Standells *by Greg Shaw* 164
Meltzer on the Troggs *by Richard Meltzer* 110	Sky Saxon & the Seeds *by Ken Barnes* 166
METANOIA #10 111	The GNP-Crescendo Story *by Greg Shaw* 169
	The Leaves *by Ken Barnes* 170

The Knickerbockers *by Bill Small & Ken Barnes*	171
The Beau Brummels *by Bill Small*	172
Autumn Records *by Greg Shaw*	173
Sounds of the Sixties, Part 1:	
The Bay Area *by Greg Shaw*	174
Juke Box Jury Junior *by Greg Shaw*	178
Feedback	179
Fadeout / Overdubs: Errata & Addenda	183
WHO PUT THE BOMP #13	**185**
Reverberations *by Ken Barnes*	186
The Return of Flamin' Groovies *by Greg Shaw*	187
Weird World of Beatle Novelties *by Ken Barnes*	192
Juke Box Jury Junior *by Greg Shaw*	195
Sounds of the Sixties, Part 2:	
Michigan *by Dick Rosemont*	197
Feedback	204
Fadeout/Overdubs: Errata & Addenda	207
WHO PUT THE BOMP #14	**209**
Editorial *by Greg Shaw*	210
Reverberations *by Ken Barnes*	211
The Birth of Surf *by Greg Shaw*	212
Dick Dale: The Man Who Invented	
Surf Music *by John Blair*	213
Surfin' in the San Joaquin	
by Bill Smart & John Blair	214
The Tony Hilder Story &	
Discography *by John Blair & Bill Smart*	214
California Surf Instrumentals Discography	216
Beatle Novelties Addendum	217
Introduction to Dutch Rock *by Ken Barnes*	218
Roky Erickson Interview *by Greg Turner*	223
International Artists & Discography *by GS*	224
Sounds of the Sixties, Part 3: Boston & New	
England *by D. Johnson & J. Bernstein*	225
Juke Box Jury Junior *by Greg Shaw*	231
Errata & Addenda / Michigan Revisited	232
Feedback	233
WHO PUT THE BOMP #15	**235**
The Beat / Editorial *by GS*	236
Reverberations *by Ken Barnes*	237
The Shangri-Las: Psychodrama in	
the Suburbs *by Mitch Cohen*	238
Sawyer & Burton *by Ken Barnes*	241
Juke Boy Jury Junior *by Greg Shaw*	242
Surf Roots	243
Dave Edmunds: The Rockfield Rebel *by GS*	244
Sound on Sound: The Rockfield Story *by GS*	246
Sounds of the Sixties, Part 4:	
Chicago *by Cary Baker & Jeff Lind*	249
Ides of March & Cryan Shames *by Mike Thom*	251
The Dunwich Story *by Cary Baker & Jeff Lind*	252
Feedback	255
Overdubs: Errata & Addenda	256
BOMP! #16	**257**
The Beat / Editorial *by Greg Shaw*	258
Reverberations *by Ken Barnes*	260
The Jack Nitzsche Story *by Ken Barnes*	261
Punk Rock of Mexico *by Phast Phreddie*	264
Sounds of the Sixties, Part 5:	
Sweden *by GS & Lennart Persson*	270
Feedback	275
Overdubs: Errata & Addenda	278
BOMP! #17	**279**
Reverberations *by Ken Barnes*	280
Overdubs: Errata & Addenda	281
Fadeout	282
BOMP! #18	**283**
The Vanda-Young Story *by Glenn A Baker*	284
The Role of the Producer in Powerpop *by GS*	286
BOMP! #19	**293**
The Beat / Editorial *by Greg Shaw*	294
The Aesthetics of Psychedelic Music	
by Phast Phreddie	295
Feedback	296
Fadeout	298
BOMP! #20	**299**
The Beat / Editorial *by Greg Shaw*	300
Fanzines *by Gary Sperrazza*	302
BOMP! #21	**303**
Feedback	304
BOMP! #22	**305**
The New Psychedelia *by Greg Shaw*	306
Garage Band Nation *by Greg Shaw*	307
The Corby Story according to Kim Fowley	309
Feedback	311

FOREWORD by ALEC PALAO

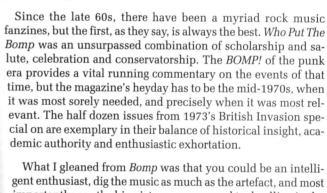

I can clearly recall the first time I met Greg Shaw. It was around 1983, and like the many who looked to Greg as a garage guru of sorts, he and I had been corresponding by mail for a couple of years. He mentioned he was coming to London, and so a rendezvous was arranged at Rock On, Ted Carroll's late lamented vinyl hostelry.

Having virtually memorized most of Greg's writing in *Bomp* by that point—often from dog-eared photocopies, as originals were rarely to be spotted in the UK—I was expecting somebody akin to a college professor, or at least an American businessman, perhaps in JR-styled suit and tie. In strode a youthful-looking, soft-spoken blonde chap sporting a T-shirt, an unblinking stare and a limp handshake. Not yet used to the "mellow intensity" of the Californian mindset, I was taken aback to say the least. But after a night's drinking at the University of London Union—he stuck to a glass of white wine, while myself and Joe Foster got ever more blotto on subsidized student pints—Greg revealed a wicked line in gossip, especially in the face of the drunken interrogation he was undergoing from yours truly. What struck me immediately, apart from his graciousness, was Greg's continued passion for rock 'n 'roll in all its arcane glory, the same passion that flowed from his pen in the pages of *Bomp*.

GREG SHAW

Since the late 60s, there have been a myriad rock music fanzines, but the first, as they say, is always the best. *Who Put The Bomp* was an unsurpassed combination of scholarship and salute, celebration and conservatorship. The *BOMP!* of the punk era provides a vital running commentary on the events of that time, but the magazine's heyday has to be the mid-1970s, when it was most sorely needed, and precisely when it was most relevant. The half dozen issues from 1973's British Invasion special on are exemplary in their balance of historical insight, academic authority and enthusiastic exhortation.

What I gleaned from *Bomp* was that you could be an intelligent enthusiast, dig the music as much as the artefact, and most importantly, see the big picture - as opposed to dwelling in the myopic, drooling demi-monde of moldie-oldie collector fandom. *Bomp* took a sci-fi aficionado's perspective, one that avoided the snobbery of the holier-than-thou rock literati of *Rolling Stone, New Musical Express*, et al, yet was capable of articulate theory rather than escapist daydreaming.

And so I got it: the simultaneous love of rockabilly and Abba; the tacit celebration of independent spirit wherever it had arisen in the past, or had just resurfaced; and of course an endearingly misguided hope that the rock scene would somehow eventually return to the innocent excitement of the mid-60s. The writing was erudite, and by the mid-70s largely bereft of the gonzoid daddie-oh-ism of other fanzines, though not without humour. It is the remarkable prescience of Shaw's editorials that strikes me still, particularly those from the 1974 and 1975 issues, where he eloquently expounded upon the necessity of the cyclical renewal process in rock and pop.

Shaw may have provided the impetus, but *Bomp* had a capable crew, both of volunteers, and of regular and semi-regulars like Lisa Fancher, Gene Sculatti and others. Ken Barnes, in particular, had a way of writing about obscure records in his Reverberations column that would send an impecunious youngster like myself, stranded across the ocean in those eBay-less days, into paroxysms of frustration and envy. Ken's Seeds article in the Summer '74 issue is still the only sensible article ever devoted to that crazy phenomenon, and with his eventual departure, *Bomp* was that much lesser.

Once I moved to the US, we kept in irregular contact, and Greg was unfailingly supportive of my fanzine and, subsequently, archival efforts, and always deferential, telling me after seeing one of my bands, "that reminded me of the Daily Flash at the Avalon in '66." He surely knew which buttons to push. In later years, I often wondered why someone so smart would take such a cavalier attitude to repackaging rock 'n' roll, in both presentation and legality, but Greg's catalogue of reissues was, for the most part, memorable. The liner notes by "Nigel Strange," the mocking "Boy Looked At Roky" treatise, even the compiler credit of "Bill Fold and E.Z. Munny" was hilarious—but it was the music that mattered, and more than anything else, those initial *Pebbles* volumes had a solid role in defining '60s punk as a vital tributary of rock 'n' roll. Later series like *Highs In The Mid-Sixties* and *Rough Diamonds* were more logical, focusing on the parochialism that Greg accurately felt was intrinsic to the make-up of American rock. It's easy to dismiss the embarrassing quality of some of these releases now, but their basic premise was to promote an inclusive, intelligent way of viewing rock's past that, like *Bomp* the magazine, brought everything together.

Re-reading *Who Put The Bomp* is like consulting an oracle, where discographies are ancient runes, and the fragments of commentary, pearls of an ancient, knowing wisdom. For this writer at least, they will remain forever inspirational. Not long into our initial correspondence all those years ago, Greg offered my band a slot on an upcoming *Battle Of The Garages* collection, with the caveat, "there'll be no royalties, of course." Of course! Greg, you can have my royalties—it's the least I can do for your setting me on the right path.

•

> **Re-reading Who Put The Bomp is like consulting an oracle, where discographies are ancient runes, and the fragments of commentary, pearls of an ancient, knowing wisdom.**

Above: The first edition of Pebbles Vol. 1.

Below left: The Choir and the Yardbirds, December 1966. L to R: Jom Bonfanti, Jim McCarty, Keith Relf, Wally Bryson, Jimmy Page, Dave Burke, Chris Dreja, Dann Klawon, Dave Smalley.

ALEC PALAO is a British-born writer, musician, archivist and full-time rock'n'roll fanatic, championing the more esoteric—yet no less worthy—nooks and crannies of pop, R&B and soul for as long as he can remember. As a reissue producer, he has compiled and annotated over two hundred packages, principally for Britain's Ace Records, including the critically acclaimed *Nuggets From The Golden State* series and the Zombies' *Zombie Heaven* box. Recently nominated for a Grammy for assembling Rhino's *Love Is The Song We Sing* set, Palao is also an unabashed groupie, frequently joining his heroes (and heroines), such as the Chocolate Watchband, Sharon Tandy, Beau Brummels and Flamin' Groovies, on stage.

INTRODUCTION by JON SAVAGE

The Trashmen

The needle slips onto the hissy vinyl. There's a slight pre-echo, as the record is cut so loud, and then a voice from the other side comes in: 'uh well everybody's heard about the bird…' Sticking on the last word like a scratched record (or, twenty years hence, a vocal sample), drummer/ singer Steve Wahrer drives the band like an out-of-control hot rod until everything suddenly stops.

"Surfin' bird" Wahrer intones in his deepest "Wipe Out" voice before descending into glossolalia of the most extreme kind: dribbling, retching, forcing the sounds out of his throat. But he can't exorcise this particular demon: he takes in a breath, drenched in reverb and echo, and he's off again, foot to the floor: 'uhpapapapapapapapaummowmowmemow….'

Released at the end of 1963, "Surfin' Bird" is one of the most extreme records in an extreme genre: it takes the reverb, cow-pasture drums and bizarre, sloganeering vocalese ("Wiiiiiiiiipe Out!") of the Surf genre and pushes it way beyond. It's just a string of stupid words, bathroom noises, abrasive kitsch, but at the same it's cosmic in its fidelity to the big bad beat.

"Surfin' Bird" made the US top ten in January 1964, and was poised to move higher when the Beatles arrived. It peaked at number four, and that was it: the sound-alike follow-up, "Bird Dance Beat," while scarcely a drop in quality, just grazed the top 30. Then the Rivingtons—those pioneers of cosmic nonsense—sued for the track's similarities to "Papa-Oom-Mow-Mow."

As if one could patent mania. "We're going to *rock* to the Bird Dance band," Wahrer sang on "Bird Dance Beat," and those classic Trashmen singles are two early pinnacles of what would later be called Frat Rock, which came out of Surf Music before it mutated with the British Invasion, Soul and Folk Rock into the malign virus known as Punk Rock. (The categories are advisory).

Greg Shaw (born late January 1949) was fourteen when he heard "Surfin' Bird." In his book, *This Is Your Brain On Music*, neuroscientist Daniel Levitin cites that very year as the age of key receptivity to music: "part of the reason we remember songs from our teenage years is because those years were times of self-discovery, and as a consequence, they were emotionally charged."

"In general," he continues, "we tend to remember things that have an emotional component because our amygdala and neurotransmitters act in concert to 'tag' the memories as something important. Part of the reason also has to do with neural maturation and pruning: it is around fourteen that the wiring of our musical brains is approaching adult-like levels of completion."

In the 21st century, at the age of fifty-two, Greg conducted an interview about his influences with the Italian magazine *Fun House*, pegged to the release of the second *Nuggets* box: "one of my favourite phases of 60's garage was 1963, when nobody had ever heard of England, and songs like 'Louie Louie' and 'Surfin' Bird' were drawing on 50's R&B to create something new."

He felt that this was a lost future: "the 'surf' label just provided a convenient catch-all term. There were probably hundreds of groups recording music in this vein, yet who remembers any of them now? Still, it was happening at the same time that the Beatles were starting to get their sound together, and if they hadn't a whole new music might've developed here."

From his early adolescence, Greg Shaw was a fan: he first applied his rigorous methodology—lists, rankings, canonization—to science fiction. Then he was transported by the San Franciscan scene that was happening all around him: the result was *Mojo Navigator*, which contained great interviews with the Doors, Country Joe and the Fish, Big Brother and many more.

The last issue (number 14) contained a review from Monterey, the moment when the SF hippie subculture began to go admass. In retrospect, Greg felt that psychedelia had been a failure: when it "died out after less than two years," he wrote in *Liquid Love 6*, "it had already done its damage. It had effectively destroyed the development of white mid-sixties- rock & roll."

Mojo Navigator reported on a scene as it happened, but Greg began to feel drawn back—initially to the late sixties Rock'n Roll Revival: "there was an instinctive grasping out for roots, for some music that was real, meaningful and satisfying." The early seventies were a near total void: "there was no college radio, no fanzines, no indie record labels….no local bands, for the most part."

The first issues of *Who Put The Bomp*—named after the 1961 hit by Barry Mann that satirized Doo Wop scat vocalese—almost exclusively covered Rock & Roll[1]. There was a great Rob Finnis article about Sun Records, as well as editorials about the power of fanzines and the difficulty of finding old records—this in the period before the simultaneous availability of 20th century recorded sound.

But that wasn't enough. Greg was always writing manifestos: lists of groups and eras to canonize, forgotten moments to bring into the light. Over thirty or so years, his vision remained constant: youth music should be by and for youth; it should not be manufactured but should contain enough reality that its target teen audience could recognize their own lives reflected.

Youth music had to be Pop, because Pop=popular music. If it wasn't, or didn't aim to be, then it lost its connection with the listener. It should be easy enough to play – encouraging a new generation of kids to pick up instruments. It should be exciting, earthy, strange; it should take you somewhere different from where you started; and most of all, it should rock.

In the sixth issue of *Who Put The Bomp*, he wrote a brilliant mission statement, "Prelude To The Morning Of An Inventory of the 60's." It was only a few seasons into the new decade, but to him and a few other fellow-travelers—Lester Bangs, Lenny Kaye, Greil Marcus, Ed Ward, Dave Marsh, Gene Sculatti, Jonh Ingham and more—it was as though the previous decade had never happened.

Greg's cartography began with 1954-56: "the Golden Age of rock & roll" that was his first love. Among his favorites from the period, as Suzy Shaw remembers, were "Ain't That A Shame" and "Blueberry Hill" by Fats Domino, "Bird Dog" by the Everly Brothers, and a trio by Buddy Holly – "That'll Be The Day," "Words of Love" and "Not Fade Away."

Next came Surf music, a true American people's music that "arose to meet the cultural needs of a teenage scene" that "suited the times and groups sprang up everywhere to play it." (Indeed, Surf remains a powerful and almost forgotten influence on '60s Garage and Psych: like Skiffle for the Beatles' generation and Punk in the 1970's, it provided an easy entry point for young musicians).

Passing through instrumental groups and the NW Scene (the Wailers, the Sonics), Greg gave full value to the Brit invasion: "the first wave of hard rockers included the Beatles, the Stones, the Kinks, the Who, the Yardbirds, Them." These in turn had a huge influence on the next generation of American groups: "the Beau Brummels, Love, the Turtles, the Byrds…many more."

As well as mentioning the Shadows of Knight and the Remains, Greg also cited several groups who would become garage staples: "the Count Five, the Standells, the Syndicate of Sound, the Chocolate Watchband, the Seeds….the Oxford Circle." As he concluded: "I have never seen a decent discography for any of the groups mentioned thus far."

So he ended with a plan—a long article about the Kinks, followed by a British Invasion issue, then proper attention paid to the surf groups and the girl groups: "let's get this done before the sands of time drift any deeper." And this is how it happened over the next five years or so, as *Who Put The Bomp* gained an influence that could never have been predicted: it changed pop culture.

A quick run-through the issues tells the story. *WPTB 7* had the promised Kinks Kompendium. From its multi-leveled cover art in, Issue 8 (Fall-Winter 1971) may be, as Johan Kugelberg suggests, the single most perfect fanzine ever published. As well as sev-

Mojo Entmooter, 1969, with one of Greg's favorites, Fats Domino, on the cover.

1. Billy Miller and Miriam Linna would later extend this period of WPTB with their great fanzine, *Kicks* (1984ff).

> *It was all coalescing around 1966 and crystallizing around the word 'punk'.*

eral pieces about 'The Roots of English Rock', it also featured Lester Bangs' justly infamous rant: "James Taylor Marked for Death, or What We Need is a Lot Less Jesus and a Whole Lot More Troggs."

Reacting against the sanctimony of the singer-songwriter genre—"punk America is dying"—Bangs called for a directly teen aesthetic: songs about acne, hormones, beer and sundry other unattractive problems. Entranced by the Troggs, he imagined his perfect punk nirvana: *'let's say, East L.A., in 1966 natch, blasting down the streets in a souped up shitcan with some zit-grinning buddies drinkin the cheapest wine you could fine while "Wild Thing" crashes and lunges right thru the radio loud as it'll go out the open windows so everybody can hear it and looking around sonnybitch they all do every car bulbous with noise and rollicking with drunk kids just graduated from high school or out for the summer anyway and taut as high-tension wires just straining out of their bucket seats champing at the bit bursting up into summer like swimmers coming up from a dive to break the surface shoot half out of the water and grin at the sun. It's that kind of a song...'*

It was all coalescing around 1966 and crystallizing around the word 'punk'. It wasn't just Bangs: other writers were playing around with the word and recalling that perfect pop teen moment—of Count Five, the Yardbirds, ? & the Mysterians[2]. And it wasn't just *BOMP* either, as in 1972 Lenny Kaye produced the first great artifact of that fanzine era: the double album compilation, *Nuggets*.

Nuggets played like an issue of *WTPB*, with—in most cases—THE killer track from groups like the Standells, the Vagrants, Mouse and the Traps, the 13th Floor Elevators (to most people then, a mystical, long-forgotten name), the Seeds, the Barbarians, and many others. It was a revelation when it came out into a hard rock desert, with the MC5 gone and the Stooges quiescent.

In his sleeve notes, Kaye gave a pretty good summary of the WPTB aesthetic: "the name that has been unofficially coined for them—'punk rock'—seems particularly fitting in this case, for if nothing else they personified the berserk pleasure that comes from being onstage outrageous, the relentless middle finger drive and determination only offered by rock'n roll at its finest." Right on!

Nuggets helped to make a minority taste much more public: the word punk entered critical terminology, while the idea of a basic, earthy kind of white music gained currency. Greg got to review the album in the January 4, 1973 issue *Rolling Stone*, of all places, and boosted it to the max: "Punk Rock at its best is the closest we came in the '60s to the original rockabilly spirit of Rock'n Roll."

Thus encouraged, Greg and *WPTB* became more ambitious. Issue 10-11 broke new ground with the comprehensive British Invasion issue: a great montage cover, and fantastically detailed articles. The depth of letters at the back—correspondents included Simon Frith, *Zigzag*'s Jeff Cloves and Adny Shernoff—showed that the message was spreading through the US and to the UK.

The next few developed on this promise: Issue 12 was a super-cool punk rock issue, with the Standells, the Leaves, the Beau Brummels and the Seeds, while No 13 mixed the usual historical researches with articles about current groups that somehow had the spirit: the Hollywood Stars and—the great white hope for a few seasons—the Flamin' Groovies.

And thereby lay a story. Just before that issue hit the stands, Greg released the first 45 on BOMP Records—instantly recognisable with its red and dayglo yellow artwork. Backed with a Paul Revere & the Raiders cover ("Him Or Me"), "You Tore Me Down" was a reject from the group's abortive 1972 LP sessions, but sounded like a clarion call in 1975: a quickening of the pulse.

The first BOMP 45, The Flamin' Groovies: "a clarion call in 1975."

The next few issues in 1975-6 kept up the standard—with ever more features, ever more detail—but Greg Shaw began to find himself in a peculiar position. What he had hoped for was beginning to happen: anyone with correctly tuned antennae knew it. Like many prophets, Greg saw his vision become reality, but he was also in danger of being swept away by the speed of change.

The new generation saw psychedelia and its corruption—the ersatz hippie culture that smeared all over the media in the mid seventies—as a huge aberration. In 1976, they harked back to 1966, vaulting over the interim: the Sex Pistols covered the Small Faces' "Understanding," while the Buzzcocks detourned the Troggs "I Can't Control Myself" ("this kind of feeling could destroy a nation").

In theory the activities of the early British and the New York punks—especially the

---

2. For a trace of the word 'punk' through time, go to Punk Etymology on the site jonsavage.com One of my favourite entries comes from Mark Shipper's perfect liner notes for the 1973 Buckshot Records Sonics' comp, *Explosive*: quoting Wayne Davis (looking up from his copy of the April issue of *Leather Thighs Monthly*) on the all-important chimera of authenticity: "It's like if delta blues oughta be played by old black men, and if fag rock oughta be played by real queers, then it stands to reason that punk-rock oughta be played by punks!"

Ramones, anglophiles[3] and Herman's Hermits fans who covered early '60s classics like "Let's Dance" and "California Sun"—were a total vindication of Greg's hard work and uncompromising attitude. The people's uprising that he had called for was beginning to happen: "crude, teenage punk music."

Greg had always been very supportive of other fanzines and writers: *WPTB* had long been a standard around which the loners and outsiders—hard rock fans all—had gathered in the early to mid '70s. Now that these outsiders and loners were getting attention, record deals and—in the UK at least—national publicity and top ten hits, he felt that he should get part of the action.

So *WPTB* became a different beast as 1976 turned to 1977. Not only did it begin, like the early days of *Mojo Navigator*, to cover a scene as it happened—and in this it was hobbled, to some extent, by its periodic appearance, as things happened so fast—but it also attempted to shape the culture. The Power Pop issue (#18, March 1978) was a case in point.

This went hand in hand with the development of the BOMP label, which began to release current acts—Southern California punk groups like the Weirdos and the Zeros, one-offs like Snatch—as well as vintage Stooges off-cuts (including the monumental "I'm Sick of You," with a riff stolen from the Yardbirds' "Happenings Ten Years Time Ago"—1966 on the point of catastrophe).

The Stooges' "I'm Sick Of You": "1966 on the point of catastrophe."

All was not plain sailing. Like the Ramones, Greg underestimated the inertia of the American music industry and the media's hostility towards anything within one hundred miles of Punk—even if sweetened as Power Pop. America wasn't Britain, and there would be no top ten Punk Rock hits until over a decade later, when Nirvana broke through.

Greg had been a lone voice, crying in the hard rock wilderness, and in the same way *WPTB* had had a special position. Now he and the magazine were one of many writers and publications clamouring for space and bickering about who was what, when why how and where. *WPTB* lost its focus and began to trend hop: would the future be Devo, Talking Heads or the Knack? It closed in early 1980.

The BOMP label and its off-shoots continued, of course, releasing the Weirdos' great "Who? What? When? Where? Why?" EP and acid punk 45s by the Last and the Lipstick Killers. In early 1979, Greg began what would one of his most lasting ideas: the *Pebbles* series that, taking off from where *Nuggets* started, introduced a whole new generation to the delights of 60's garage.

This was typical Greg: the legality might have been sketchy, but the intention and the execution were inspired. This was where most people first heard classic '60s records like the Third Bardo's "I'm Five Years Ahead of My Time," "Feathered Fish" by the Sons of Adam, the Bees' "Voices Green and Purple," and of course "Green Fuz" by Randy Alvey & the Green Fuz.

With *Pebbles*, Greg returned to the founding *WPTB* impulse. He was, above all, a fan and it is a condition of fandom that you want to spread the word, which then hits other receptive people, who then become fans, who then spread the word, which then hits other receptive people, who then... Enthusiasm is the key, and it is very contagious.

As he editorialized in *WPTB* #16 (Winter '76/77), "something about this magazine seems to make people want to express their innermost feelings about rock & roll and what it means about their lives. Nothing strange about it: *BOMP* is written by and for people who take the music seriously and relate to it on a deeper, more emotional level than, say, your average Kraftwerk[4] fan."

And listening to "Green Fuz" or "You Treat Me Bad," it was easy to reconnect with the primal drive that links all rock fans: that two chord epiphany, that bump-and-grind that hits your pelvis and makes you move. Greg's "Prelude to an Inventory of the 60's" ended with a little line drawing that said it all: "rock & roll: DIRTY IT'S DIRTY DIRTY DIRTY!" Forget that at your peril.

---

3. Who picked up on the basic teen thrust of glam: check out the Sweet, Bay City Rollers and Bowie references on "The Ramones"

4. I would beg to disagree with Greg only on his choice of example. Kraftwerk are brilliant and have rabid, engaged fans.

WRITER'S NOTE:

The first BOMP I ever saw was the British Invasion issue, which bowled me over with its graphics, detail and its enthusiasm. It came at the point when UK companies like United Artists and Decca were beginning to reissue Brit Beat and Brit R&B records—an inspirational genre still underestimated in its simplicity, directness, and power, and which sounded great in 1973/4.[5]

I bought all the subsequent issues I could find: the Standells and the Groovies' covers particularly come to mind. When it came time for me to move from fandom to participation and produce a fanzine—*London's Outrage*—in late 1976, *WPTB*, along with Brian Hogg's *Bam Balam* and Mark Perry's *Sniffin' Glue*, was a major inspiration.

As Brit Punk gathered steam, I met and corresponded with Greg. He invited me to contribute a montage for his UK issue (#17, November 1977)—which is reproduced on page 190 of Suzy Shaw's and Mick Farren's book *BOMP!: Saving the World One Record At A Time*. He also sent me records, some of which—like Iggy & the Stooges' *Kill City*—I reviewed for *Sounds*.

Over thirty years later, I'm looking at a letter that he sent me in the high summer of Punk, July 1977. The yellow paper is still dayglo, and Greg's comments about the vexed relationship between the US and the UK are still cogent: "I don't think it's good for the UK kids to be so scornful of America—we can't help it if our country isn't falling apart. We identify very strongly with the English kids."

Greg was a believer: "I've been most interested in helping develop the scene here so that in effect really is revolutionary; I want to see thousands of local bands making records and pushing rock 'n' roll to its furthest limits." This is how I would like to remember him, as he concludes: "from one rock & roll obsessive to another." Once you've heard the pied piper, you will follow him for the rest of your days. •

London's Outrage, 1976.

JON SAVAGE is a writer and broadcaster. After graduating from Cambridge he published a fanzine called *London's Outrage*, and worked for *Sounds, Melody Maker* and *The Face*. His first book, *The Kinks: The Official Biography* was followed by *England's Dreaming*, the award-winning history of the Sex Pistols, punk and Britain in the late seventies. He regularly writes for *The Observer* and *Mojo*, and his television credits include the BAFTA winning Arena documentary, *The Brian Epstein Story*. His recent compilation CDs include *England's Dreaming, Meridian 1970* and *Shadows of Love*. He lives in Anglesey, Wales.

5. And that was also heavily sourced by Dr.Feelgood – by far the best live band in the country at that time.

PHONOGRAPH RECORD MAGAZINE

8824 BETTY WAY, WEST HOLLYWOOD, CALIFORNIA 90069

Box 7112
Burbank, CA
91510
Jan. 7, 1974

Dear Harvey,

Thanks for your long and appreciative letter. It's good to know some people out there are sensitive to the things we're trying to do--it's for people like yourself that we go to all the trouble; and it is a lot of trouble, not nearly compensated by the amount of financial return. But it is a lot of fun as well, and as long as people appreciate it, we'll keep busy.

I'll try to respond to some of your many questions. I didn't really decide to become a rock writer, I've been one since I was 15. I had a professional rock magazine in San Francisco for a year before Rolling Stone started--in fact Jann Wenner used to come around to my apartment to pick up pointers while he was still writing for a college paper. So I go back a long ways and it's just a sort of instinct with me, I guess. Over the years I've built up a lot of contacts that I can call on when I need more detailed info for Bomp articles (strangely enough the record companies are the last place where information is likely to be obtained) and between my record collection and that of Ken Barnes we have an extremely comprehensive record library. I also do a lot of buying and trading by mail, and whenever I get a spare hour I usually go out hunting for junk records.

The Record Research book is very useful, even tho it includes only the small percentage of records that actually made the charts. It doesn't list B-sides, however.

Besides the Kinks, did you know Nicky Hopkins also played on records by the Troggs, Cyril Davies, Lord Sutch (his first group, ca. 1959), Neil Christian, and countless more? Also that he had a solo album and a single of "Mr. Pleasant" released in 1967? Also, did you know that when Gene Pitney got Marianne Faithfull knocked up Marianne would've married anyone just to make it legit? She asked P.J. Proby and anybody else she could find, including Kim Fowley (according to Kim). Aside from the fact he was balling Marianne, tho, I don't know of any other reason he played on the Stones' first album, except that he and Spector and Nitzsche happened to be around at the time.

Best,

Greg Shaw   (over)

R.I.A.W.O.L.* by MIKE STAX

* ROCK IS A WAY OF LIFE:
Greg Shaw and the Roots of Rock Fandom

Greg Shaw was a prolific—some might even say obsessive—fanzine publisher. Before the winter of 1971 he'd published, by his own reckoning, "something like 300 of them," and this voracious outpouring of print would continue through various mutations and refinements until the beginning of the 1980s.

Greg's fanzines came in a variety of different formats. In the beginning there were the science fiction and J.R.R. Tolkien-themed zines, simple mimeographed affairs, run off by hand and distributed via the US Postal Service to a small number of like-minded sci-fi fanatics and hobbit-obsessed hippies, anxious to share minutiae about Middle Earth. Shaw's Tolkien zine *Entmoot* was highly regarded by Frodo fans at the time, not only for its content (poetry in Elvish, anyone?) but for its look—Shaw's mimeograph and stencil-making skills were considerable and his experiments with collage and different colored inks and paper led to some original and 'trippy' effects.

Science fiction fandom had a lineage dating back to the 1930s, and Greg amassed a collection of hundreds of sci-fi pulps and fanzines, obsessing over their contents through countless re-readings. His passion was such that the zines themselves became more important to him than the work they discussed. In his own fanzines he'd often lament the passing of what he saw as a kind of 'golden age' of sci-fi fandom, an age all but forgotten whose work he and his friends could never hope to surpass. "I've always upheld the belief that fifties fandom was something of a fannish climax, and that after that the overall quality of fandom has diminished considerably," he wrote in 1970. Decades later fans would say much the same thing about another 'golden age' of fandom: the rock 'n' roll fanzine explosion of the 1970s. That particular explosion sent reverberations through the music scene that continue to this day. And it was Greg Shaw who lit the fuse.

Science fiction wasn't Shaw's only obsession. He was as passionate about Elvis as he was Elvish, and it was inevitable that his interest in rock 'n' roll would spill over into his fanzine publishing activities. In the summer of 1966 Shaw—in collaboration with David Harris—launched his first rock 'n' roll magazine, *Mojo Navigator*. It would run for 14 issues until the end of 1967, functioning less as a fanzine and more as a kind of newsletter for the Bay Area music scene. The zine included interviews with acts like the Doors, the Grateful Dead, the Blues Magoos and Country Joe & the Fish, as well as music news, and reviews of the latest underground rock releases.

After the demise of *Mojo Navigator*, Greg and Suzy Shaw moved from San Francisco to the small town of Fairfax, where Greg took a job with the post office. In January 1968 he launched a new fanzine, *Mojo Entmooter*, in an edition of about 500. The name was a derivation of two earlier Shaw zines, *Mojo Navigator* and *Entmoot*. In his editorial Greg explained that his new fanzine would be "experimental" in nature, and although the emphasis would be primarily on music he would also welcome material relating to Tolkien, science fiction and fandom in general. Although the 24-page debut issue included some interesting material, such as a feature on Elvis Presley by Kurt von Meier (reprinted from the *New York Free Press*), and a lengthy review of the first Deviants album, *Mojo Entmooter* quickly fizzled out. The second and final issue, published in April 1969, was a garish visual experiment that looked like it might have been knocked out over the course of one very stoned afternoon tinkering with the mimeograph machine. So ended the first era of Greg Shaw's publishing career—an era that will some day get a book of its own.

As the 1970s dawned it was time for a new beginning. While the first years of the seventies were in many ways a musical wasteland—at least as far as teenage rock 'n' roll went—it was fertile soil for the emergence of a new and vital publishing sub-culture: rock fandom, a movement spearheaded by Greg Shaw and *Who Put the Bomp* magazine. Greg Shaw's pivotal role in the evolution of that sub-culture is traced here in the pages of *BOMP!*

2: BORN IN THE GARAGE via reprints of the best and most interesting material from Shaw's many publications during the years 1970-1981.

Reprinting every issue of *Who Put the Bomp* and *BOMP!* magazines in their entireties would require a book several inches thick, so it was necessary to cherry-pick what we felt was the most interesting and representative material. The first BOMP! book, *Saving the World One Record At A Time* already included many pages of reprinted material, so we avoided duplication wherever possible, with a few notable exceptions. Without question, *BOMP*'s greatest strength was always its seminal coverage of '60s-era music: British Invasion, surf, girl groups, psychedelia and especially garage rock. Some of the research in this field by Greg Shaw, Ken Barnes and other *BOMP* writers remains unsurpassed, and many of their insights into the era and its music are still valid today. Accordingly, we decided to reprint as much of this material as possible, including many of Greg's meticulously detailed discographies and label listings, all of which remain valuable resources to collectors and historians. We've augmented all of these reprints with plenty of previously unpublished material.

The fanzine's "Feedback" section also yielded reams of fascinating material in the form of readers' letters, including commentary by the likes of Lester Bangs, Lenny Kaye, Richard Meltzer, Dave Marsh, Kim Fowley, and even Gene Simmons of Kiss. (Simmons was an old friend of Greg's from the sci-fi/Tolkien days. At one time there were dozens of letters from Gene in the files, but they have vanished, probably sold by Greg.)

In the early years of *Who Put the Bomp*, Greg continued to publish other, smaller fanzines of a more personal nature, notably *Karnis Bottle's Metanoia* and *Liquid Love*. In these he wrote of his and Suzy's day-to-day lives, their interactions with friends and neighbors, and of his efforts to launch *Who Put the Bomp* as the first self-described 'rock fanzine'. These 'personal zines' were usually published in mimeographed editions of 50 or less and distributed through Amateur Press Associations or APAs. The concept of APAs dated back to the turn of the century, but was adopted in the late '30s by science fiction fans with the formation of the Fantasy Amateur Press Association (FAPA). Since then dozens of fan APAs had sprung up, all operating around the same basic concept. Membership to any given APA was usually restricted to 50 or less members (the most popular ones had waiting lists), each member was required to produce and mail out a small magazine to the other members weekly, monthly, annually, or whatever the agreed schedule was. The magazine or fanzine (sometimes just a single sheet, but often much larger) would consist of comments on the previous mailing, along with newly composed material: essays, reviews or whatever. In the days before communication with like-minded souls was just a mouse-click away, APAs were an effective social networking platform for aspiring writers, publishers or just fans who wanted to share their passion and knowledge.

Written in a more intimate, unguarded style than his usual work, Shaw's APA zines provide a fascinating glimpse behind the scenes, as well as giving us new insights into his personal life, opinions and beliefs. Some of the most entertaining excerpts are reprinted here. Sequenced chronologically, along with the best of *WPTB* and *BOMP!* magazines, they tell a larger story, of the birth and evolution of rock fandom in the 1970s.

What follows over the next few pages is a fanzine bibliography of sorts, an issue-by-issue guide to Greg Shaw's 1970s fanzine output, and the contents of this book.

WHO PUT THE BOMP #1
Circa January 1970
Number of pages: unknown

The first issue of *Who Put the Bomp* was distributed via the newly formed Rock Enthusiasts Amateur Press (or R.E.A.P.), which at its start had a membership of just 13, most drawn from the world of comic fandom. Hardly the makings of a rock 'n' roll revolution. Interestingly, REAP was started up not by Shaw but by Louis Morra, who invited Greg to become a member. Each member produced their own mimeographed rock zine, so *Who Put the Bomp* first entered the world right alongside now forgotten texts like *Harvest*, *Soup*, *Wind*, *Word Chimes of Rock*, and *Noise* (the latter Greg deemed his favorite of a "terrible" batch). Sadly, no copies of *WPTB #1* are known to exist, but likely it was around 2-6 pages in length and not illustrated.

KARNIS BOTTLE'S METANOIA #1
Ca. February/March 1970
Number of pages: unknown

The first issue of Shaw's chatty 'personal' zine ("available free to anyone who's interested") appeared soon after the first *WPTB*. No copies appear to have survived. Around the same time he was also finishing up a *Best of Entmoot* magazine in an edition of 500. Evidently, in the early '70s fanzine

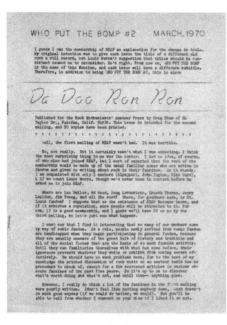

world hobbits ruled over rockers by quite a margin. Thankfully, this would change.

WPTB #2 (Da Doo Ron Ron)
March 1970 (6 pages)

As Shaw explains, his original idea was to give each issue a different title taken from an old rock 'n' roll record. When Louis Morra pointed out that this might be confusing he elected to stick with the title *Who Put the Bomp*, although each issue would have a different sub-title (for a short while anyway), this one being *Da Doo Ron Ron*.

Throughout his career, Shaw always seemed to have one eye on the larger picture, and the future historical context of anything he was involved in. He was hyperconscious of whenever new territory was being charted—even if it really wasn't. In his opening editorial here Shaw observes that: "...to the best of my knowledge the printed discussion of rock music on an amateur basis has no precedent to speak of, except for a few scattered articles in various obscure fanzines of the past five years. So it's up to us to discover what's worth doing and what's not, and until then—anything goes." Some pretty dramatic posturing for someone writing for an audience of 13 readers with stated aspirations of having 20 by its third issue.

The rest of *WPTB #2* includes discussion of promo records and songs not found of official releases (most of this in response to the contents of *Noise*). Harkening back to his *Mojo Navigator* days, Shaw also gives mention of live recordings of the Trips festival and the Acid Test, and extols the virtues of the Mystery Trend and Daily Flash. He also professes a dislike of Led Zeppelin, theorizing that they would be a much better group if Keith Relf was their singer instead of Robert Plant.

METANOIA #2
April 1970 (14 pages)

The second issue of "Fairfax Fandom's Finest Fanmag" was a relatively substantial 14 pages, spiced up with some crude graphics by Jay Kinney and Jonh Ingham. In it Greg relates his recent experiences at a Science Fiction convention, and reviews bootleg LP of early Stones and Dylan material. The most interesting article though is James Wright's "Rough Rider: Memoirs of a Railroad Bum" relating his adventures hopping freight trains around the country.

METANOIA #3
May 1970 (12 pages)

Karnis Bottle's Metanoia really began to settle into its groove with Issue #3, which led off with a short piece by Shaw about his everyday life in Fairfax and his neighbors. Stories about Greg and Suzy's unusual neighbors would dominate future issues of the fanzine. In the letters section Len Bailes comments on the problems some sci-fi fans seem to have with rock fandom. "I never saw any dichotomy between liking sf and digging rock," responds Shaw, "but then I always dug rock & roll at least as much as science fiction. The people who're really having problems adjusting are the ones who completely despised rock a few years ago, being into jazz and folk snobbery."

In his "Platter Chatter" review column Greg rips the new albums by Hendrix, Ringo and David Axelrod, finding Ringo's *Sentimental Journey* album particularly appalling ("This is a terrible record. I don't know what audience Ringo is trying to reach, but it couldn't be a large one").

WPTB #3 (Whenever A Teenager Cries)
May 1970 (8 pages)

By its third outing *WPTB* boasted a print run of 50 copies. The subtitle was taken from one of Greg's favorite girl group records by Reparata & the Delrons. He leads off with an enthusiastic endorsement of the Remains ("a forgotten group that I think merits more attention"), a strong indicator of the future direction of the zine. Shaw's writing in this issue has a new-found passion. One gets the sense that he's finally found his niche. Evidently, he had grander plans for *WPTB* because he announces here that the next issue will be expanded into a "genzine" [a 'general' distribution fanzine rather than a 'closed circle' APA mailout] of about 30 pages. The vision was becoming clearer.

LIQUID LOVE #1
May 15, 1970 (2 pages)

While he worked on the first 'genzine' version of *WPTB*, Shaw's APA-related zine writing continued unabated. *Liquid Love* was a simple one-sheet, distributed via the "Apa L." which was now up to its 262nd mailing. Shaw's involvement with the Apa L. dated back to its 40th distribution back in 1965, as he explains in his opening missive (reprinted in this book), a recollection of his entrance into the world of fandom.

LIQUID LOVE #2
May 25, 1970 (2 pages)

Shaw continued to roll out *Liquid Love* every two weeks for the next half a year. The content was wide-ranging, but music-related topics cropped up regularly, along with discussions of fandom in general. Probably pressed for time, Shaw often inserted material from *Metanoia* into *Liquid Love*.

LIQUID LOVE #3
June 3, 1970 (2 pages)

An unusual issue as Greg wrote his piece from the hospital, where he was recuperating from complications from a bout of bronchitis and hyper-ventilation. Maybe the pressures of compulsive zine publishing were taking a toll on his health? Or maybe not. Suzy remembers Shaw's persistent health issues has more to do with the fact that he was an insulin dependent diabetic who loved to eat entire chocolate cakes, paying little attention, as usual, to the consequences.

METANOIA #4
June 1970 (18 pages)

His recent illness and hospitalization notwithstanding, Shaw's publishing schedule continued unabated. The summer of 1970 was a particularly prolific season for him. *Metanoia #4* was the first to feature a proper, fully-illustrated cover, a line-drawing by John D Berry of Greg lolling in a chair before his mimeo machine, records and fanzines strewn on the floor around him. "I just want to bask in the aura of fannishness," reads the caption. Although billed as the June 1970 issue, *Metanoia #4* actually appeared in mid-July. "Future historians will never know the difference," Greg wrote, only half-jokingly, "and I will not abandon my Chronology!" In deference to Greg, we, the future historians, have not abandoned it in this book either—June 1970 it is.

LIQUID LOVE #4-5
June 1970 (2 pages)

Liquid Love #4 is missing from the Bomp archives (as are several others), but we surmise that it appeared as scheduled in mid-June. Issue #5 included a few interesting remarks about Greg's music taste: "My definition of rock & roll extends as far as it always has: not very," he wrote. "My own favorite type of music is hard rock, and since hardly anyone is playing it anymore (with a few magnificent exceptions, like the Stones and the Who), I've been retreating into the past (and my record collection) a lot lately (meaning the last couple of years)." This retreat into the past would be reflected in the upcoming issue of *Who Put the Bomp*.

LIQUID LOVE #6
July 2, 1970 (4 pages)

The current poor state of rock and its uncertain future was obviously preying on Shaw's mind a great deal at the time, and his thoughts on the subject were outlined in an eloquent four-page essay "Whither Rock" taking up the entire sixth issue of *Liquid Love*. "Whither Rock?" was Shaw's lengthiest and most thoughtful treatise to date, but it reached just a small circle of people at the time. *Liquid Love #6* was distributed only at Westercon 23, a sci-fi fan convention held in Santa Barbara at the beginning of July. (Naturally, it's included in its entirety here).

WPTB Vol 2 #1 ("Whole #4")
July-Aug 1970 (24 pages)

The first 'real' issue of *Who Put the Bomp* was deemed "Volume 2, No. 1 (Whole No. 4)" but subsequent issues would abandon the second volume notion and continue with the "whole" numbering system. Like previous issues, it was distributed through REAP, but was also for sale to the general public for the remarkably fair price of 35 cents. 200 copies were circulated. Shaw's opening editorial was proudly titled "R.I.A.W.O.L." which stood for "Rock is a Way of Life" (although the meaning of the acronym would not be revealed for several more issues). In it he boldly declared that, "*Who Put the Bomp* is rock & roll's first *fanzine*, by definition a thing produced and written by amateurs, for little or no profit, out of love for their hobby … *Who Put the Bomp* is devoted to the appreciation of music, and nothing else," he added. "Because so little really good rock & roll is being made nowadays, we'll be delving into the past frequently." And delve into the past they did. *WPTB #4* was focused primarily on 1950s era rock & roll, centered on a lengthy piece on Sun Records by Rob Finnis, along with Shaw's reviews of several Sun reissues. Other reviews included the Who's new *Live at Leeds* album, and the first appearance of "Juke Box Jury" featuring a rundown of various obscure 45s. The direction of "rock & roll's first fanzine" would shift somewhat in the months and years ahead.

METANOIA #5
July 1970 (16 pages)

Little Richard screamed from the cover of *Metanoia #5*, which included an amusing account of a visit to *Rolling Stone*'s offices in San Francisco where Shaw dropped off copies of the new *WPTB* and saw his old friend Jan Wenner for the first time in several years. Presumably Wenner hadn't read Shaw's recent comments about *Rolling Stone* in *Metanoia #4*, in which he called the magazine "embarrassing." The chasm that separated *Rolling Stone* from Shaw's newly launched *WPTB* was a vast one. While Wenner epitomized the careerist, corporate future of rock music publishing, Shaw continued to champion the amateur, grass roots values represented by rock fandom. In fact, when Harry Warner predicted (in this is-

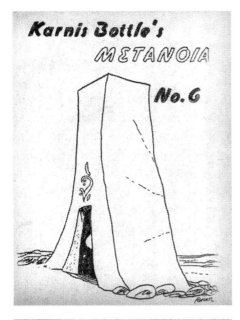

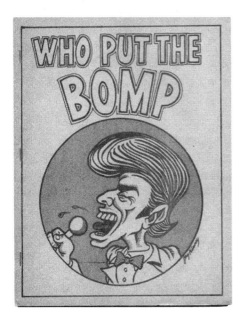

sue) that low-cost office copy machines would some day make the mimeograph approach obsolete, Greg scoffed in reply that "the whole suggestion sounds rather fakefannish to me. A fanzine on…Xerox paper…just wouldn't seem fannish."

LIQUID LOVE #7-9
Ca. July/August 1970 (each 2 pages)

Greg continued with *Liquid Love*. Issues 7 and 8 (now lost) appeared in July, while #9 was sent out at the beginning of August. In it Greg reprinted the story of his meeting with Jan Wenner at the Rolling Stone offices (see *Metanoia* #5), and also described his recent experience of being hooked up to an "Alphaphone," a device that apparently allowed the user to listen to his or her own brain beta waves. The concept obviously appealed to Greg as both a sci-fi lover and a long-time hippie.

METANOIA #6
August 1970 (18 pages)

This issue included the story of a recent fire at the Shaws' Fairfax cottage. Fortunately the fire was extinguished before it could do too much damage. Other personal stories included troubles with Suzy's Snazzy Leather wear business, and also a pleasant account of an afternoon rock concert in a nearby parking lot.

LIQUID LOVE #10-12
Ca. September/October 1970 (each 1-2 pages)

Issue #10 is no longer with us. Issue #11 includes a piece on the effects of marijuana and Shaw reveals that its overuse by his co-editor was a major contributing factor to the demise of *Mojo Navigator*. Meanwhile #12 delves into the area of electro-magnetic propulsion, space travel, UFOs and other non rock 'n' roll related topics.

WPTB #5
October 1970 (36 pages)

Shaw's trusty mimeo machine cranked out Issue #5 in the fall of 1970, a fat 36-pager with a pompadoured rockabilly singer on the cover. In his R.I.A.W.O.L. editorial Shaw expressed disappointment that the 200 copies of #4 only inspired five or six letters from readers. The APA fanzine format generated a constant back and forth discussion that continued from issue to issue, and Greg thrived on this kind of communication. To him that was what fandom was all about—a continuous cycle of shared passion and information. The 'genzine' scene was a different world where readers generally took a more passive role. Greg was having none of it. Fandom was about communication and he would get his readers to participate even if he had to badger them to do so. Eventually *WPTB* (and *BOMP!* after it) would have the liveliest and most engaging letters sections around. One person who did write in this time was Lenny Kaye. "To see something combining my two loves—fanzines and rock 'n' roll—into a really fine done whole is nothing short of great," he wrote. To today's readers a concept as simple as a fanzine about rock 'n' roll inevitably begs the question: "Why did nobody think of it before?" The answer being that, well, *somebody* had to think of it first.

Issue #5 was still a little unfocused all in all, with a lengthy piece about the availability of cut-out singles and how and why records get deleted, an article on black gospel groups, and the usual round of record and book reviews. It also included a handy checklist to indicate whether or not you were and rock 'n' roll 'trufan' (reprinted in *BOMP!: Saving the World One Record At A Time*).

METANOIA #7
Oct-Nov 1970 (20 pages)

Alongside more nutty neighbor stories and assorted record and fanzine reviews, in *Metanoia #7* Greg informed his readers that at the age of 21 he was finally learning how to drive, and also made mention of how busy he'd been putting together the next issue of *WPTB*. "*WPTB* is bringing me into contact with a whole nother fandom … Rock fandom is a lot more extensive than I once thought, and it's beginning to come together and achieve some semblance of self-awareness, just as SF fandom did in the late 30s. There's a lot to be done there, and I look forward to being involved with it."

LIQUID LOVE #13
Ca. Oct-Nov 1970 (1 page)

A peek at Shaw's record listening habits: "…since Suzy doesn't like any kind of music, I only listen for a couple of hours each day in the afternoon or when she goes somewhere, and with that little time I usually find myself playing records from among my 30 or so favorite albums—hard rock at full volume. (I use music to give me energy more than anything else.) The other 500 or so albums are lucky to get played once a year." (Incidentally, Suzy objects to Greg's contention that she wasn't a music lover: "I love music and always have!" she insists. "Greg was probably having a fit about not being able to play it 18 hours a day."

LIQUID LOVE #14
Ca. Nov 1970 (3 pages)

Number 14 of *Liquid Love* appears to be the last. In it Greg expresses his dissatisfaction with APA L and the fact that he was considering dropping out. Evidently he did. Most of his three pages are given over to a reprint of the house fire story from *Metanoia #6*.

METANOIA #8
Feb 1971 (26 pages)

Due to the demands *WPTB* was making on his time, *Metanoia #8* was several months later. Rather than attempt to continue it as a monthly, Greg announced that beginning with this issue it would now be "officially 'irregular'." The issue boasted some wild Jay Kinney cover art featuring a rabid rock 'n' roll band in full swing at a prom dance. The editorial (printed in full in this book) gives some interesting insights into Greg's *WPTB* activities. His writing on this subject exudes a confidence and hunger for success that borders on arrogance—a trait less obviously found in his better-known work. The rest of the contents were as varied as ever, with more neighbor tales, and an article about Suzy's leather business. Shaw also makes some rather pertinent remarks about what he sees as the demise of Science Fiction fandom. He also uses cutting sarcasm to address some harsh criticism he and some of his clique were getting from another section of the SF fan community. "Well, it's finally come out," sneers Shaw. "The boys and I figured nobody'd catch on to our insidious plot to infiltrate the top fanzines and even the prozines and remove all mention of science fiction from them, until it was too late."

WPTB #6
Spring 1971 (42 pages)

With its sixth issue the direction of the magazine finally came into clear focus. In his editorial Shaw explained that he wanted to shift his attention to the music of the mid-'60s as '50s era rock 'n' roll was already being studied in-depth elsewhere. "That's cool with me anyway," he adds, "because the second cycle of rock & roll, which took place in the mid-sixties, is of much greater interest to me." At this early date the subject was still, he points out, "really an untouched field" so there was much to write about. He goes on to reveal his plans for a special Surf/Hot Rod music issue and a British Invasion issue—both would come to pass in the years ahead. Shaw also emphasized the importance of the "lettercol" which he envisioned as "a breeding ground for discussion." This, too, would come to pass. Greg Shaw's vision was at last finding real clarity.

Shaw continued to set the stage for that vision with a two-page article titled "Prelude to the Morning of an Inventory of the '60s." In it he mentions his interest in the lesser-known American groups of the era like the Shadows of Knight, Chocolate Watchband, the Standells (mistakenly identified as a San Jose group) and Peter Wheat & the Breadmen, groups that would eventually be re-categorized as '60s punk' or 'garage', but which at the time were simply referred to as 'hard rock.' This was still uncharted territory and even Shaw still viewed these groups with a certain residual disdain. "I admit that most of this music was pretty bad compared to the rock & roll of the 50s," he writes, "but a lot of it was good in its way and it deserves more attention than it's gotten so far." This condescending attitude would soon be forgotten and Greg would become one of the genre's fiercest champions.

This issue also included other rumblings of a new interest in mid-60s rock with a report that Lenny Kaye was working with Elektra Records on a series of reissues compiling "forgotten great singles of the mid-late sixties" from various regions of the country. After some modification, the concept would become the seminal *Nuggets* collection, which was released the following year.

The rest of the issue included a piece on Del Shannon by Mike Saunders, along with reviews of various rock magazines and records old and new. Aside from Shaw's editorial, most of the action was to be found in the "Feedback" section, which included letters from Dave Marsh, Lenny Kaye and Lester Bangs.

ALLIGATOR WINE
April 1971 (8 pages)

Shaw's APA activities continued as a sideline to his ambitions with WPTB. *Alligator Wine* appeared around the same time as *WPTB #6* as part of the first mailing of Frank's APA. Organized by Shaw's friend Jonh Ingham, Frank's APA was essentially a re-branding of the now defunct REAP, the APA that had spawned the first few issues of WPTB. The aim, Greg explained, was to create an active forum primarily for rock critics, adding that he hoped it would "spawn essays and discussions of the type not intended for the general public, but only for other critics and people in a position to put ideas into effect and make things happen." Ah, how sweet to be the new elite.

The eight-page issue included a rundown of the current rock press, an article about Fats Domino, and "Pretentious Essay of the Month," a lengthy screed about the current state of the music scene and where it all might be heading. The latter was a topic Shaw would return to repeatedly over the

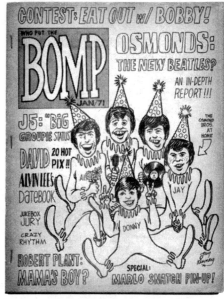

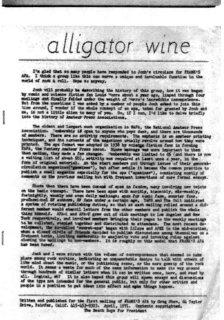

years, and would invariably include the confident prediction that a new teenage rock 'n' roll revolution was on the horizon, if not already upon us. This particular article tried to have it both ways: most of today's music was dire but also we're "in the midst of a rock & roll renaissance." He laid the blame for the poor state of much of the music scene squarely at Jann Wenner's feet, his theory being that Wenner saw himself as "a molder of public taste" and the current prevalence of mellow "acoustic troubadours" was due to *Rolling Stone* pushing solo artists at the expense of the "good rock & roll" that was still out there for anybody to find if they only looked hard enough. The thesis undoubtedly had some merit, and clearly it helped motivate Shaw and like-minded writers to kick against mainstream tastemakers like Wenner and rally the cause of 'real' rock & roll. "If we can put our energy into those corners of the music world where The Spirit is stirring, it won't do any harm at all," Shaw concluded. "Might even help things along." (Suzy adds that Jann Wenner was very helpful with Bomp book #1, so from his end any kind of feud is settled.)

METANOIA #9
April 1971 (32 pages)

Shaw was on fire in the Spring of 1971. *Metanoia #9* was his third zine of the season, and it was also the biggest yet of this particular title. His opening editorial radiated optimism: "Everything's coming up roses" for WPTB he announced, going on to explain that Warner Bros would be funding the next issue ("out of the goodness of their hearts"—yeah, sure) and that 9,000 copies would be printed ("not on my mimeo"). Alongside the usual neighborhood and family tales, the issue also gave some background into Shaw's recent dealings with the music biz bigwigs, describing a recent trip he and Jonh Ingham made to LA, visiting various record companies and attending a Faces show at the Forum. Mention is also made of Shaw's bootleg dealings (see William Stout's story elsewhere in this tome for more on that).

ROCK, YOU SINNERS!
June 1971 (8 pages)

Greg's contribution for the second mailing of Frank's APA was named after a 1956 song by Art Baxter. Of particular interest this time is mention of a Standells article he's working on for an upcoming book. In all likelihood this was the same piece that would eventually appear in WPTB #12. "Treating the Standells will necessarily bring in the whole issue of raunchrock, the essence of rock & roll, the importance of naïve enthusiasm, and provably force me to prove my contention that 1966 was rock & roll's greatest year," he wrote. Later in the issue Shaw despaired at the state of the current music scene and the popularity of Grand Funk in particular.

WPTB #7
Summer 1971 (32 pages)

As explained above, this issue of *WPTB* was printed and distributed by Warner Bros. Their mailing list of 8,000 all received free copies, while a further 1,000 were sold and distributed by Shaw and his colleagues. The highlights of the first non-mimeo issue include a big article on the Kinks by Shaw, discussing some of their lesser-known '60s tracks, and an amusing piece about how to sell all the free records you get as a rock critic (the article was credited to one 'Sam Swanson', supposedly a pseudonym for a well-known rock critic—precisely who, we've not been able to establish, but Lenny Kaye, Ed Ward, Ken Barnes and Dave Marsh have confirmed it's not them). The issue also boasted an allegedly humorous piece by Greil Marcus positing some kind of Crickets-Buddy Holly-Bob Dylan connection. (reprinted in *BOMP! Saving the World One Record At A Time*). Laugh? I thought I'd never start.

WPTB #8
Fall-Winter 1971 (88 pages)

It was back to the trusty mimeo machine for *WPTB #8*, which at 88 pages was, Greg commented, the biggest fanzine he'd put out to date. In addition to the 88 numbered mimeo pages there were also several pages of printed advertising and illustrations, including a foldout poster. All in all a mighty impressive issue. More so because it also included Lester Bangs' glorious, notorious 24-page piece on the Troggs, "James Taylor Marked For Death." Much has already been written on this amazing piece of writing, so no further explanation is needed (you can find the full article in its original form in *BOMP: Saving the World One Record At A Time*). Less well-known, though, is Richard Meltzer's Troggs piece, which appeared in the same issue, and which is reprinted here for (we think) the first time. The nuclear explosion of Bangs' piece put the rest of the issue in the shade somewhat, but the theme this time was English rock 'n' roll of the 1960s, kicking off with a worthwhile piece by Shaw on the "roots" of English rock (i.e. before the Beatles). This was followed by decent if unspectacular articles on Georgie Fame, Zoot Money, Johnny Kidd, the Shadows and a lengthy bit about Cliff Richard. The English rock theme would be revisited with more depth and panache with the classic British Invasion issue two years later.

As for the success of the Warner Bros campaign the previous issue, Shaw reported that of the 8,000 free issues mailed out last time they'd picked up just 50 new subscribers, though more were trickling in. "It only proves there are at least 7,885 people who don't know a good thing when they see it," he wrote, adding: "welcome to the elite!" The "elite" who subscribed to WPTB as of this issue now numbered close to 1,000.

Of note: Page 7 marked, I believe, the first appearance of the words "punk rock" in the context of describing, in Greg's words "white teenage hard rock of '64-66 (Standells, Kingsmen, Shadows of Knight, etc.)."

METANOIA #10
November 1971 (20 pages)

A sketch of Suzy by local artist Joel Belsky graced the cover of the tenth issue of *Metanoia*. Shaw had been so busy with WPTB that it had been more than half a year since the last *Metanoia*, and in his opening editorial he admits that he'd considered shelving it altogether until he was informed of a vacancy on the roster of the esteemed granddaddy of science fiction APAs, FAPA. Shaw had been on the waiting list for this particular APA for "something like eight years" so he didn't hesitate to jump on board with *Metanoia*. Along with a big letters section, the issue included an interesting piece about the Shaws' gradual acceptance into their Fairfax neighborhood (reproduced for your enjoyment in this book), as well as report on the 1971 Westercon.

METANOIA #11
February 1972 (14 pages)

Metanoia continued on its new three-month schedule as part of FAPA. In issue #11 Shaw wrote about the emergence of rock fandom and his role in it, drawing comparisons with the science fiction fandom scene of the late '50s (remember he was writing for the FAPA crowd now). Shaw's words convey the high level of excitement he was evidently feeling as the new movement gathered momentum: "...I always got the impression from the old [sci-fi] fanzines that there was a sort of sustained, giddy group inspiration among the active fans of the period, wherein a great article would only spark other writers to even greater heights of brilliance. I now know that such a thing can be, for I have experienced it. To be a *part* of some large creative gestalt like that—there is no comparable experience."

WPTB #9
Spring 1972 (60 pages)

WPTB #9 was supposed to be Part Two of the "English Invasion," but as there was still much work to do on that subject, Shaw decided instead to clear out some old material from his files and do a '50s rock & roll/rockabilly issue. This meant that he had to do some hasty back-pedaling regarding his comments on that subject in Issue #6. "I remember stating once that the fifties had been so thoroughly mined and sifted through that I saw little point in concentrating our attention on them," he wrote, swallowing mighty gulps of crow. "Well, it turns out I was less than totally correct." One can almost imagine the catcalls from the crowd. Nevertheless it was a solidly enjoyable issue, highlighted by a brilliant piece on Gene Vincent by Ronnie Weiser that crackles with almost as much energy as Gene & the Blue Caps' early records. Comparing the playing of lead guitarists Cliff Gallup and Johnny Meeks, Weiser writes, "[Meeks'] playing is not as bim-bam-boom as Gallup's, but is more insistent: if I may use this analogy, Gallup is like death through violent explosion, while Meeks is death by slow and painful torture!!!" Rock 'n' roll fan writing at its purest and best.

The letters section centered around the fallout from Lester Bangs' Troggs piece in the previous issue with opinions sharply divided. "I'm convinced that he wrote his sickening tribute to the Troggs with a pencil tied to his penis," contended one disgruntled reader.

METANOIA #12
May 1972 (18 pages)

Back in *Metanoia* world, Greg revealed that he had recently taken a two-week jaunt around the South, combing stores and warehouses for rare records. His finds on these early excursions would later provide the basis for the *Pebbles* albums, and many of them would crop up in the pages of future issues of WPTB. Also of interest here is Shaw's embarrassed confessions about his time as a follower of the Cosmic Consciousness cult: "[The cult leader] had me believing that he had been to Mars, and received visits by his saucer friends all the time, out on his farm. He spoke a gibberish that I was convinced had to be Martian." For someone so intelligent, Shaw was oddly susceptible to nonsense like this, even in later years. (Suzy writes hilariously about this topic in *BOMP! Saving the World One Record At A Time*.)

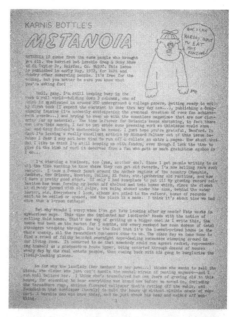

METANOIA #13
Ca. August 1972

Just a few pages of *Metanoia #13* survive in the Bomp vault and it appears to have been the last issue. Shaw's ambitions with *Who Put the Bomp* and his freelance writing work for various other publications were now taking up more and more of his time, and his APA activities apparently ceased. All his energy in 1973, he wrote, would be devoted to *WPTB*. His stated goals were to increase circulation to about 10,000, and attract $1,200 worth of advertising per issue. "That's a pretty high goal," he admitted, "but I'm confident we can do it and really anxious to try."

WPTB #10-11 (a.k.a. Vol 3, No 1)
Fall 1973 (56 pages)

More than a year appears to have passed without Greg Shaw publishing a single fanzine, genzine, prozine or even a two-sheet APA zine, but in the autumn of 1973 he roared back with a "special double issue." *WPTB #10-11* was also designated Volume 3, Number 1—marking the beginning of another new era. No more mimeo; the long-awaited second part to the "English Invasion" issue was a bonafide 'prozine' utilizing typesetting instead of typewriter, and professional offset printing. So much material had been gathered for the issue that Shaw was forced to use some extremely small fonts in order to fit it all in 56 pages. This factor, combined with the yellowing of the cheap newsprint paper, made reproduction a little challenging for this book. Nevertheless, we've included a large chunk of this issue, as it is, to quote Patrick Boissel "a fucking classic!"

With this issue Ken Barnes came on board as co-editor and he would be a crucial presence in the years that followed. His byline is all over this particular issue, including some of the major highlights. His chapter on Freddie & the Dreamers is one of the funniest pieces ever to appear in the magazine, and he also contributes insightful articles on the Hollies and the Pretty Things, among others. Shaw's chapter on Shel Talmy and "Pop Art Rock" is also significant as it was here that many people read for the first time about groups like the Creation, John's Children and the Eyes, later to be hailed as masters of the as-yet-unnamed freakbeat genre. What was somewhat mystifying though was Greg's contention that the Yardbirds with Jeff Beck were somehow inferior to the Clapton-era band.

The issue covered a lot of ground. Not only were there individual piece on dozens of British groups, there was also articles on the '60s pop music press, Britain's pirate radio stations, and rock 'n' roll TV in America. In many cases the writers were venturing into uncharted territory, and factual errors crept in from time to time when supposition or guesswork took the place of solid research, but *WPTB #10-11* was still a groundbreaking effort for its time.

WPTB #12
Summer 1974 (32 pages)

With Issue #12 *Who Put the Bomp* began to establish a distinctive look and a solid format that would serve it well for the next two years. Shaw's editorial, now re-titled "The Beat," would open each issue, followed by Ken Barnes' "Reverberations," in which the co-editor enthused about his recent vinyl discoveries. Greg wrote about his own finds in the "Juke Box Jury Junior" column. Other regular sections included record and fanzine reviews, and the ever popular "Feedback" pages. Jay Kinney was now the zine's Art Director and his hip comic book-style graphics headed up each of these columns, and also graced the front and back covers of #12. This issue shifted the focus from the UK to the USA with stories on some of the most popular American garage bands of the mid-60s. Greg's long-promised Standells article finally saw the light of day and didn't disappoint (by now he'd figured out they weren't from San Jose). Ken Barnes did an equally fine job with his piece on the Seeds, the first to show any kind of respect for this oft-misunderstood group. Barnes also covered the Leaves and contributed to Bill Small's Knickerbockers article. Small also handled the Beau Brummels, while Shaw kicked in with an Autumn Records sidebar. The issue also saw the first of a series of pieces on different regional scenes, an excellent overview of the Bay Area scene by Greg, accompanied by listings for labels like World United, Diplomacy, Scorpio and Jaguar.

At 32 pages the issue was rather slim compared with its predecessor, but the printing quality and overall look and feel were a big improvement.

WPTB #13
Spring 1975 (48 pages)

The first issue of 1975 continued with the same format, while attempting to bridge the gap between the '60s and the '70s by featuring several new or at least current acts. Greg had fallen under the spell of the Flamin' Groovies and they were given front cover status as well as a lengthy feature charting their ten-year career and trumpeting their supposedly imminent breakthrough. In the article (reprinted here) and his opening editorial (reprinted in *Saving the World One Record At A Time*) Shaw wrote of his absolute conviction that a new pop or "teenage rock & roll" revival was underway, with bands like the Raspberries and the Groovies leading the way. While Shaw's passion was infectious, his predictions, as usual, proved to be overly optimistic. 1975 would *not* be the Flamin' Groovies' year.

The issue also included an article on Beatles novelties, an overview of Cameo Records, Kim Fowley's Hollywood Stars, and a piece on the rockabilly reissue scene (again, reprinted in the first *BOMP!* book). The highlight, though, was Dick Rosemont's quite exhaustive piece on the Michigan scene in the '60s.

WPTB #14
Fall 1975 (48 pages)

Issue #14 was the surf music issue (billed as "A Bomp Beach Bonanza"), and featured the magazine's first color cover. By now *WPTB* was starting to attract advertisers, some tailored to the mag's format (Pye Records for the Troggs), others laughably incongruous (the new live album by Grand Funk, a band Greg loathed). Still, money was money, and Shaw happily cashed their checks. The surf music coverage included a fine essay by Shaw on "The Birth of Surf," an interview with Dick Dale by John Blair, and pieces by Blair and Bill Smart on the San Joaquin Valley surf scene and producer Tony Hilder. In the years ahead Blair would be acknowledged as the world's foremost expert on surf music, publishing the definitive *Illustrated Discography of Surf Music* (now in its 4th edition) and also heading up Jon & the Nightriders, who recorded for Bomp Records. This issue also included a groundbreaking feature by Ken Barnes about Dutch rock of the 1960s, giving excellent groups like Q65 and the Motions their first real coverage outside of the Netherlands. Also of interest were Greg Turner's interview with Roky Erickson, which included a good sidebar piece on the International Artists label, and Part Three of the 'Sounds of the Sixties" series, which covered Boston and New England. Starting with this issue, the editors also launched their "Encyclopedia of British Rock," an ambitious A-Z discography slated to run (one letter at a time) for the next umpteen issues. This project was scrapped just a few issues later when it reached the letter 'F' so we've elected not to include any of it in this book.

WPTB #15
Spring 1976 (48 pages)

In 1976 *WPTB* switched to a glossy format with a full-color cover. The "Gala Girl Issue" featured Cherie Currie on the cover, and inside the Runaways were hyped to the max in a story by Lisa Fancher. The girl group theme continued with articles on the Shangri-Las, Lesley Gore, Jackie DeShannon and songwriters Lori Burton and Pam Sawyer (memorably crowned "The Glycerine Queens of Mascara Rock").

Greg had traveled to the UK with the Flamin' Groovies in September and October of the previous year, and the trip yielded an article on Dave Edmunds and his Rockfield studio, where the Groovies recorded. The group's newly released *Shake Some Action* was also afforded a full-page review (surprise, surprise: Greg *loved* it!). The Encyclopedia of British Rock crawled forward to Part One of 'B', while Sounds of the Sixties shifted its focus to the Chicago scene with Cary Baker, Jeff Lind and Mike Thom all contributing interesting material, along with acres of discographies and label listings. (Billed as Part Three of the series, Chicago was in fact Part Four; evidently the editors had already lost count).

BOMP! #16
Fall 1976 (64 pages)

With Issue #16, *Who Put the Bomp* became simply *BOMP!* magazine. It was the first step in a process of reinvention that would see the magazine's focus shift away from the '60s and towards the kind of new music that the editors felt embodied the *BOMP!* spirit (a somewhat nebulous concept that might involve any given permutation of "pop," "punk" or "teenage rock 'n' roll"). Shaw's editorial wrestled with this concept and what the future direction of the magazine might be. While Greg had some well-defined ideas, there was also a sense that he was holding a moistened fingertip to the winds of change before deciding which way to proceed.

The big scoop this time was an interview by Jim Pewter with the famously reclusive Brian Wilson (see *BOMP!: Saving the World One Record At A Time*), but deeper revelations could be gleaned from Ken Barnes' chat with Jack Nitzsche, which took a fascinating trawl through the arranger-producer's '60s discography. Another highpoint was a hilarious piece on '60s punk records from Mexico by Phast Phreddie, editor of the seminal *Back Door Man* 'zine. While all the records in the article were real, the rest of the 'facts' were made up, and the entire piece was a sharp satire on the WPTB style, complete with copious footnotes. The fifth installment Sounds of the Sixties shifted its focus to Sweden (although the editors stuck to their new counting system, designating it Part Four). The article also gave Greg an excuse to devote a page to one of his favorite 'new' groups, ABBA (we've spared you the pleasure). The editors' attempts to bridge the divide between the old and new music with pieces on Dwight Twilley, the current Boston and New York scenes, Eric Carmen

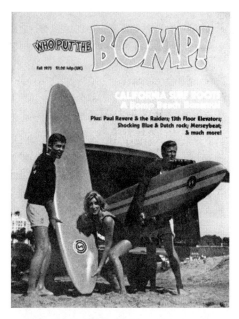

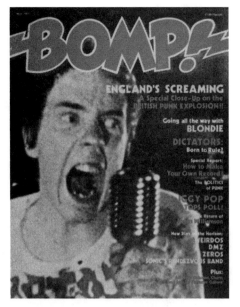

and Flo & Eddie. Change was definitely in the air.

BOMP! #17
November 1977 (64 pages)

A year passed; a year in which the rock 'n' roll scene was turned on its head by the explosion of punk rock. After numerous false starts, Shaw's long predicted rock 'n' roll revolution had finally come to pass, except it wasn't spearheaded by Dwight Twilley, the Runaways, the Raspberries, or even the Flamin' Groovies; it was headed up the Ramones and the Sex Pistols. It took Greg and the *BOMP!* team longer than expected to grasp the situation and reboot the magazine accordingly. Gary Sperrazza (previously editor of the *Shakin' Street Gazette*) was brought in as managing editor, and Ken Barnes became one of four contributing editors (Alan Betrock, Gregg Turner and Gene Sculatti were the others), leaving Greg once more as the sole editor and publisher. *BOMP! #17* was a new beast entirely The logo was the same, but one only has to compare the faces on the covers of #16 and #17 to know that something big had gone down. On one, the big, benign, bearded face of a middle-aged Brian Wilson, open-shirted, furry-chested. On the other: a screaming, bug-eyed Johnny Rotten. Welcome to the new world.

Shaw had seen the Pistols at London's 100 Club back in May 1976. He'd seen the writing on the wall, but he'd not taken in the full picture. Now he was late for the party. Nevertheless he jumped onto the punk bandwagon with both feet, eager to position *BOMP!* on the frontlines of the new movement. "Everything that's happened in the New Wave can be traced directly back to the efforts of rock fandom," he contended in his editorial. By rock fandom, of course, he meant ME, Greg Shaw. But there was something a little shrill and panicked in his tone. Certainly 'rock fandom' in a broader sense (meaning not just Greg Shaw but an entire new breed of rock fans, writers and zine publishers) had helped to set the stage for punk and new wave, but that was just one of many factors that caused the movement to come to a boil at this particular moment in time.

The new *BOMP!*, it was explained, would drastically cut back on rock history and concentrate instead on covering the crop of bands riding the new wave. Accordingly, #17 contained a detailed report on the English punk scene (see the first *BOMP!* book), alongside articles and reviews of bands like the Zeros, the Weirdos, DMZ (all of whom would make records for the BOMP! label), the Dictators, Sonic's Rendezvous Band, and Iggy & the Stooges (who up to now, surprisingly, hadn't ever rated more than a few lines in *WPTB* or *BOMP!*). Even Shaw's Juke Box Jury Junior column featured only new releases. Most long-time readers were favorably disposed towards the punk and new wave scene, but they were still left wondering what on earth had happened to their favorite fanzine. For the most part, the contents of *BOMP! #17* were interesting and well-written, but they weren't much different to what you could read in any of a dozen other music publications. Where *WPTB/BOMP!* had once been unique and special, it was now just another face in an increasingly trendy crowd.

BOMP! #18
March 1978 (72 pages)

The new look magazine's promised bi-monthly schedule didn't come to pass, so it was March 1978 before the next issue appeared. By now the punk movement had lost much of its steam, so when #18 appeared billed as a special "Power Pop" issue the scent of desperation was unavoidable. *BOMP!* now appeared to be hopping from one bandwagon to the next, in the hope of eventually being on the winning team. In actual fact, the Power Pop issue had been in the works for some time, and was in many ways closer to the true spirit of *BOMP!*—or at least to Shaw's personal music tastes, the two were inseparable. He made his case quite convincingly in the magazine's title piece (see the first *BOMP!* book), which traced the lineage of the genre from the Who and the Easybeats through the Move and the Equals, Sweet and the Raspberries, to the Ramones and the Jam. Other angles were covered by Ken Barnes' overview of the glitter rock era (also in the first *BOMP!* book), and scene reports that championed new pop acts like Alex Chilton, the Pleasers, Generation X, 20/20, the Shoes and Pezband. The issue's highlight, though, was an extensive piece on Vanda and Young and the Easybeats by Australian rock historian Glenn A Baker (naturally we've included it in this book).

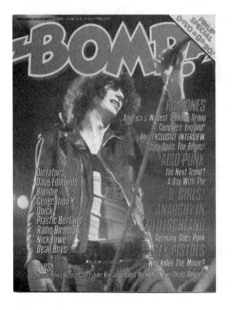

BOMP! #19
October/November 1978 (64 pages)

The new wave format continued with #19, featuring Joey Ramone on the cover and boasting "Pinup Special: Devo A Go-Go." Oh boy. Greg attempted to clearly define the magazine and its changing face in an opening manifesto, but the piece lacked his usual eloquence, probably because he didn't really quite know what *BOMP!* was anymore. "We're historians helping to make history," he posited, "...a magazine for today because it encompasses yesterday and tomorrow." Er...whatever. In the end the magazine would be judged on its content, and Issue #19 was not a high-water mark. Pam Brown's Ramones interview was amusing enough (see the first *BOMP!* book), but the endless regional scene reports were becoming increasingly tedious, and the self-consciously cute teen magazine-style color photo spread of the B-Girls seemed creepily out of place. The issue was saved by Greg's classic "Acid Punk" article (reprinted in the first *BOMP!* book), and Phast Phreddie's piece on "The Aesthetics of Psychedelic Music."

BOMP! #20
January 1979 (48 pages)

By #20 Greg was clearly having regrets about the change in format. In his editorial he acknowledges "the New Wave recession." "A spirit of disenchantment is certainly in the air, and for a lot of valid reasons," he writes. He feels the movement has been neutered by its own success, and that the slide is an unavoidable side effect of a larger problem with the entertainment industry and its effect on our mass culture. The piece turns into something of a pep talk on how the slide can be averted, advocating the strengthening of underground channels that can operate independently from the mainstream. Sensible stuff. The article goes on to make some remarkably prescient statements regarding future technology and its effects on music consumption: "Imagine 20 years from now, if every teenager could sit in his bedroom with a computer screen and terminal (and stereo speakers attached) and call up anything he wanted, from Billy Ward & the Dominoes to Ed Banger & the Nosebleeds—see what they looked like, read extracts from fanzines and historians who wrote about them, cross-referenced to other artists and sources, and above all to hear the music, and maybe even see film footage if any exists." At the beginning of 1979 this sounded like science fiction, or just another Greg Shaw pipe dream, but the Internet, Google, music downloads and YouTube would all come to pass—most of them in less than 20 years.

The rest of the issue: a Nick Lowe interview, Sylvain Sylvain, Throbbing Gristle, scene reports, discographies of Stiff and Sire, and the Encyclopedia of British Rock reached 'F' (it would be discontinued thereafter).

BOMP! #21
March 1979 (48 pages)

That Issue #21 featured a Talking Heads cover story and a free Police bumper sticker should have been indication enough that the mag was in its death throes. Shaw's editorial was generally upbeat and he was cautiously optimistic about what lay ahead, but reading between the lines it was evident that fanzine publishing was no longer where his heart lay, and probably hadn't been for some time. There was no announcement that the magazine would fold, it just did. Shaw's energy would be directed instead into his already active Bomp and Voxx labels.

BOMP! #22
1981 (unpublished)

Just four months after Issue #21, Shaw confessed in a personal letter to reader Al Quaglieri that the magazine had taken a wrong turn: "You might as well be one of the first to know. I am planning to change *BOMP* back to the kind of magazine it was a few years ago, before punk. I've grown so disenchanted with the current punk scene, it just isn't the fun that '60s rock and collecting fandom used to be. I intend to print more discographies, label listings, etc., limited only by the time I have for research these days, which is hardly any." It was another two years before Shaw had the new issue in the bag, but the layout was completed and ready to be sent to the printer some time in 1981. The issue was to include an interview with Sky Saxon, a story on the Barracudas, a big piece on Minnesota in the '60s, reissue reviews and lots of discographies and garage band listings. Sadly, the issue was shelved for financial reasons, and it wasn't until years later that the original artboards (or most of them) were discovered in the Bomp warehouse by Geoffrey Weiss. Most of the issue was reprinted in *BOMP! Saving The World One Record At A Time*, but the best of the rest is included here—complete with paste-up lines and Greg's last-minute crossings-out, etc. Amateur in spirit, fueled by the true fervor and obsession of fandom, the issue had a free spirited sense of fun that Shaw had lost somewhere back in the late '70s. For all intents and purposes *BOMP* was born in the garage, and it was in the garage that the magazine would be reborn—well, almost. •

MIKE STAX is the editor and publisher of *Ugly Things* magazine, focusing on the greatest, overlooked bands and music of the 1960s and other "wild sounds from past dimensions." He has co-authored two books for his own UT Publications, and worked as a writer, editor and consultant on several music biographies and reference books. He has also provided liner notes for dozens of reissues, including the track-by-track liners for the first two acclaimed *Nuggets* box sets on Rhino Records. His work has appeared in numerous magazines and periodicals. He is also the lead singer for the Loons. Born in England, he now lives in San Diego, California with his wife and son.

REVERBERATIONS by KEN BARNES

Nineteen-seventy-one was an eventful year. My girlfriend Terry and I decided to get married and forsake the comforts of a communal Saratoga, California, household for a three-room apartment in nearby San Jose. This meant giving up a number of lifestyle advantages, including the nightly poker games that were my chief source of income, sufficient to purchase food and the occasional album, if I was able to paste a purloined 49c sticker on a full-price record.

It also meant dissolving our ties to the Open Door, an enterprise founded by one of my college roommates set on exploiting the potential million-dollar market for threaded meditation devices labeled "mandalas." And, saddest of all, it meant the end of the household's resident garage band, the Savage Cabbage, which rehearsed sporadically a repertoire consisting of Fleetwood Mac's "The Green Manalishi," "I'm Not Like Everybody Else" by the Kinks, "I'm Eighteen" by Alice Cooper, the Troggs' "I Can't Control Myself," Tommy James's "Draggin' the Line" (the last two being my own vocal showcases, hampered somewhat by a nagging inability to play bass and sing simultaneously), Fontella Bass's "Rescue Me," and my original contribution, "Do the Ching," a rockabilly–styled rip-off of "High School Confidential" inspired, sort of, by the gnomic Chinese oracle the I Ching.

On the plus side, however, we got a car (a '57 Chevy, no less … and no more) as a wedding gift, and both of us secured actual employment, Terry as a shoe salesperson at the Emporium just a block away and I as a bilingual clerk for a social workers' unit (my speaking

solely English somehow didn't enter into the hiring decision). The job brought in enough discretionary income for me to start combing record and thrift stores from Redwood City to Santa Cruz (prior to this temporary bout of solvency I had maybe a couple hundred 45s and albums accumulated since 1965), and afforded me sufficient leisure time to pursuing my literary dream of becoming a published rock critic.

Technically, I already had achieved that lofty status, having answered an ad in a late 1970 edition of the University of California at San Diego's newspaper, *The Triton Times*, reading "Rock Critic Wanted," and—although not enrolled as a student—with a lengthy treatise on Pink Floyd's *Atom Heart Mother* nabbed the prize (the chance to write album and concert reviews for free and all the records the editor was willing to surrender to me, which turned out to be very few). But I had my sights set on higher goals and, armed with a handful of *CREEM* rejection slips from Dave Marsh and Lester Bangs, I could tell I was on my way.

More to the point of *this* lengthy treatise, I made contact with Greg Shaw sometime in late 1971. He was one of the rock writers I looked up to, along with the aforementioned Marsh and Bangs and their *CREEM* cohorts, *Rolling Stone* stars such as Greil Marcus and the arch-mage of attitude, John Mendelssohn, and many more. By 1971, Greg was writing in those magazines, as well as Boston's *Fusion* and LA's *Phonograph Record Magazine*. Greg's work seemed authoritative, clear, direct, yet not impersonal. I didn't know about his pioneering mid-'60s work with *Mojo Navigator*, but in '71 he was doing everything I wanted to do. And, I learned, he had a fanzine too.

As best I can reconstruct the circumstances, I must have seen a mention or ad for *Who Put the Bomp* in one of the mags I devoured, and sent away for a copy. As any rock obsessive of the period would have been, I was gobsmacked by *Bomp*, and when I saw some sort of house ad inviting readers to get in touch and, by the way, let Greg know their favorite artists, I did not hesitate to respond by the next mail. I duly gushed over the zine and appended a voluminous list of favorite acts including every garage band I had heard over the radio in suburban LA, Santa Barbara and San Jose, and every British group I had heard, read about, or purchased a precious import 45 by from Heanor Record Centre in the UK.

Probably because that voluminous list included everything from the Creation to the Chocolate Watchband to the Bees (of "Voices Green and Purple" fame, purchased on impulse at a small store in my hometown of Arcadia, California, where they, or their label, were based, because I thought the picture sleeve looked cool), Greg was impressed enough to write me back.

In an age in which a like-minded enthusiast can be cybernetically friended instantly, it's hard to convey what it was like to establish contact with someone like Greg (or, as happened shortly thereafter, thanks to Greg, *The Rock Marketplace/New York Rocker* publisher Alan Betrock or early *Navigator/Crawdaddy* contributor Gene Sculatti). Most of the historically minded music fans were still steeped in the '50s. Greg was quite knowledgeable in that area, and thanks to unceasing raves from the Savage Cabbage's keyboardist, Jimmy Carleson (and Terry's new gig at a jukebox one-stop), I had learned enough to get by on the '50s stuff and was already fairly clued in to pop and R&B from the early '60s, when I started listening to the radio. But '60s rock fandom (or scholarship) was nearly nonexistent—Lenny Kaye was just assembling the *Nuggets* anthology (which would come out in 1972)—so it bordered on the miraculous to encounter someone who knew and raved about the Seeds or the Shadows of Knight or even the Velvet Underground. (I remember Greg seemed stunned that I, not a member of the critical elite, had discovered their records anyway and had seen them in San Francisco in 1969.)

This Velvets dialogue took place on the occasion of my first actual meeting with Greg, sometime in early 1972 at a *Bomp* "collating party." This fannish ritual, which Suzy Shaw will be describing elsewhere, had the goal of assembling the various pages of the new *Bomp* issue in the proper order, thanks to the labor of a number of invited guest collators, but it was also a pretext for a party. Greg would invite local writers and friends, plus any visiting rock-writer dignitaries, and it was a rare chance to meet people known only as bylines. At this one, eminent *Rolling Stone* editor/writer Ed Ward was there, and that's where I met (and hit it off instantly with) Sculatti.

Greg wasn't quite what I imagined. Sometimes he avoided your gaze; sometimes he fixed you with laser-focused intensity. And he initially seemed kind of … cold. Not what I was expecting from the guy who communicated so eloquently his boundless musical enthusiasm and gave the similarly inclined the good news that there were others who felt the same way you did.

But the apparent chill was a consequence of the unease Greg (and countless other writers) felt about social interactions, a trait that helped drive him toward communicating his enthusiasms in fanzines and other writing in the first place. It evaporated once you hit upon a topic of consuming interest, which at this soiree consisted mainly of establishing mutual musical reference points. He'd light up if you shared his enthusiasm for a (then) little-known artist and wax positively messianic if you hadn't yet heard one of his faves.

I drove back to San Jose in a delirious state (non-chemically induced) to my drab workaday existence. Fortunately, my incessant bombardments of unsolicited record reviews were starting to hit their targets, and I was getting published sporadically in *Phonograph Record Magazine* and *Fusion* and even (thrill of thrills for a record fanatic) getting on a few label promo mailing lists.

Then, around the turn of 1973, a startling proposal came from Greg. He had moved to LA in 1972 at the behest of Martin R. Cerf, editor/publisher of *Phonograph Record Magazine* (*PRM* for short). Marty was a publicist at United Artists Records and a former editor of an amateurish but amusing music rag called *World Countdown*. He somehow convinced UA that it would be a smart imaging move to sponsor a rock magazine—but not your everyday in-house vehicle designed to promote the label's acts. Instead this mag would cover all rock and pop, regardless of label (although UA artists were not underexposed), use the leading writers around the country to contribute reviews and features, and be given away free in markets where a local rock station could be inveigled into "sponsoring" it (i.e., distributing it to record stores and other appropriate venues).

Marty was soon overwhelmed by coordinating the logistics of this effort and, having gotten to know Greg when the latter started writing for *PRM*, secured him a position in UA's

> **Sixties rock fandom was nearly nonexistent so it bordered on the miraculous to encounter someone who knew and raved about the Seeds or the Shadows of Knight or even the Velvet Underground.**

publicity department in which he could share the editorship of the magazine, work on other select projects (like the pioneering Legendary Masters reissue series) and continue to publish *Bomp*. This deal was catnip for Greg; he and Suzy found a house in Toluca Lake (a short drive over the hill from UA's Sunset Blvd. headquarters) and he dived headfirst into the music industry.

But even split with Marty, the UA and *PRM* duties added to the desire to make *Who Put the Bomp* grow proved a heavy burden. The solution: bring in yet another person. Greg proposed that I move down to LA and become his co-editor at *Bomp*. It was a fanzine, so of course there was no money he could offer at this point, but I could probably get even more work at *PRM* and in any case the entire industry was there, just ripe for the picking. How could the steady but mundane jobs Terry and I held down compare? We packed up the whole cat and caboodle (my burgeoning record collection) and in February 1973 moved to a tiny apartment just across the Burbank line from Greg's place.

Fortune sometimes favors the young and foolish, and the UA connection snared Terry a secretarial job that paid nearly $100 a week. And, true to Greg's word, I was quickly enmeshed in the PRM operational structure, becoming assistant editor, a position whose duties mainly consisted of typesetting the monthly issues, as soon as I learned to do a passable job of it. I was richly rewarded for mastering this task: Marty paid me exactly of zero extra money, but continued to pay me for my reviews and stories, and I did get to do a lot more of both. And I was immersing myself in what I felt was my chosen calling.

Marty was a fascinating character. Rather obviously gay (though in considerable denial), he grew up in distant LA suburb Canoga Park working as a teenaged record store clerk, then moved to Hollywood, collaborating on a few songs with Kim Fowley (including a Seeds single!). I got along with him immediately because, like me, he'd been one of those kids who devoured the *Billboard*, *Record World* and *Cash Box* record charts, and he worshipped the 45 rpm single. His home office contained a sizable collection of them, rigorously ordered by label and number (that is, Bell #45,103 would be followed by Bell #45,104) rather than the usual grouping-by-artist method. (Greg might have done this, too, along with various chunks of 45s organized by genre.)

Marty generated a million ideas and theories, 75% or more impractical or preposterous, but was capable of shrewd insights (preserved in his exuberant singles-review columns in *PRM*) and the occasional master stroke—the existence of *PRM* itself, though plagued by spotty distribution and insufficient finances (especially after UA pulled the plug and it went independent), was a considerable entrepreneurial triumph.

He was primarily a fan, of artists and of writers, and although he sometimes attempted to dictate an esthetic *PRM* party line (resulting in perhaps-excessive praise for the likes of Harriet Schock), he was receptive to new writers and novel ideas, encouraging oddball features such as Mark Shipper's brilliant parody review column, "Pipeline," and my eccentric collaboration with ex-Turtles Howard Kaylan and Mark Volman (aka Flo & Eddie), "Blind Date," a takeoff on a British pop-paper staple in which artists were played unidentified records and asked to identify and comment on them. He also encouraged the constant "surf music/glam/teen pop/insert-trendy-genre-here is-coming-back" manifestos that Greg in particular was inclined toward.

For Greg, Marty was a mentor—a bit younger, but far more experienced in the ways of the biz and more of a hustler (at the beginning, anyway). Greg absorbed the mechanics and atmosphere of the then-wide-open record scene and soaked up all the input Marty could impart, but at the same time—and I'm speculating a bit here, since both have passed on—was always convinced he was a lot smarter than Marty and—if Marty would only see the light and surrender his stubbornly held supreme status, which Marty was not about to do—Greg could create a much more successful empire out of *PRM*. Which might have been

Below: Ken Barnes (right) with Flo & Eddie and Greg Shaw.

true, had Greg shared Marty's inexhaustible capacity for schmoozing and other essential attributes of the '70s music business.

Marty always had something new on the boil, one example of which, in mid-1973, was a project to create a trade publication on the order of *Billboard* but aimed specifically at radio. The prime mover in the enterprise was a former radio programmer named Bob Wilson, but Marty was responsible for some of the original concepts, and introduced Wilson to a crop of *PRM* contributors including Sculatti (as editor), Shipper (as production director) and his ace typesetter, me. Greg stayed out of it, I lasted about eight weeks, Sculatti a few months more, but Shipper thrived, bringing in a more skilled production crew (headed by the principals of fabled LA garage revivalists the Droogs) and making sure everything ran smoothly. The publication, known as *Radio & Records*, became highly successful; Marty got—as usual—nothing for his part.

R&R didn't pan out for me, but there was no end of new experiences to savor. An interesting crew of music enthusiasts set up shop around this time. Sculatti had moved down from the Bay Area ahead of me, and had made fast friends with Shipper, who had relocated a few years before from Michigan and had dazzled the rock-fanzine world with the funniest zine yet seen, *Flash*. Shipper was living for a time at the Van Nuys home of Ronny Weiser, the Italian-immigrant rockabilly fanatic who published the *Rollin' Rock* zine and recorded superannuated rockabillies on the label of the same name (Rollin' Rock, not Superannuated Rockabillies) with as much authenticity, savage passion and slappin' bass as he could scare up. The painfully withdrawn but brilliant writer/drummer Mike Saunders moved to town from Arkansas. He, Sculatti and Shipper would later assemble the hilarious one-off fanzine satire *Brain Damage*, unmercifully mocking most of the extant rock critics.

There was a golden opportunity to meet most of those writers not resident in LA, when in May 1973 the first and last Rock Writers Convention took place in Memphis, Ardent Records (home of Big Star) having been convinced that flying in dozens (hundreds?) of writers to put together a trade organization (nothing much came of that) was a good idea. Not being the outgoing type, I hung around overmuch with Greg and Marty and didn't mingle as much as I should have, but it was still an eye-opener.

Back in LA, there were live shows to check out, albums to hear and record shops and thrift stores to loot, plus plenty of time-consuming labor between *PRM* and the long-in-gestation British Invasion issue of *Bomp*, the first under my co-editorship. But the best times with Greg were spent spinning records over the period of a couple of years. Suzy and Terry became pretty good friends quickly and would hang out, and I would walk the few blocks to Greg's place with a sack full of my latest acquisitions. Greg would have a pile of whatever he'd picked up, and we'd spend an afternoon playing the discs (almost always 45s), comparing, speculating as to their arcane connections, and trying to one-up each other. (Greg, owing to superior connections in the collecting community, usually came out on top.)

I'd play some obscure Southern California garage cruncher, Greg would introduce me to a freakbeat classic from the UK, I'd pull out one of the Dutch '60s ravers I'd begun accumulating, he'd counter with a Swedish stunner, I'd change pace with a girl-group delight, he'd rummage up something mind-boggling from Australia. Glam, surf, pre-Beatles pop, it all took its turn (though not, regrettably, soul or country, neither of which Greg seemed big on—although he had good blues and New Orleans collections—and both genres I didn't come to value until a bit later). It was an amazing education and a great time, and the sessions spawned a lot of *Bomp*'s survey features on music from various countries or of specific styles.

Mark Shipper's *Flash*, June-July 1972: "The funniest zine yet seen."

I remember less well the actual work required to assemble the issues of *Bomp* on which I actively collaborated. The amount of research and knowledge and insight poured into those issues still impresses me upon rereading the excerpts in this volume, although all of it has been substantially surpassed by more recent zines—*Kicks*, *Ugly Things* and the like—and more above-ground publications such as *Mojo*. I cringe at the deplorable lack of information I exhibited in some of my *Bomp* pieces, but others make for pretty good jumping-off points for future scholars, and I enjoyed writing the "Reverberations" columns (which were an attempt to conjure the experience of those record-sharing sessions with Greg in print form).

Distractions multiplied, however. Greg got fired up by his crusade to conquer the world with the Flamin' Groovies (understandable to anyone who hears "You Tore Me Down" and "Shake Some Action" for the first time). He adopted Seymour Stein of Sire Records (which eventually put out three Groovies albums) as his new mentor, and the Bomp label became an increasing preoccupation.

The Sire association also generated the History of Rock anthology series, which Greg captained and sometimes annotated. I did a volume myself (the Turtles' *Happy Together Again*, a natural given the ongoing *PRM* "Blind Date" partnership), and particularly enjoyed collaborating with Greg on the *History of British Rock* series' inserts, an affectionate but slightly barbed parody of the British pop weeklies of the '60s called *Memory Maker*.

Sire also funded a series of quickie rock biographies under Greg's editorship. Six were published; Greg whipped one up on Elton John and I spent a lot of time writing an astonishingly superficial volume on the Beach Boys.

Alan Betrock, Greg Shaw and Ken Barnes, 1975. (Photo: Isa Langsam)

Another tantalizing but stillborn collaboration involved Shipper and Sculatti plus Greg and me in a quasi-pirate radio venture, assembling a radio show called *Shakin' Street* that uneasily mixed satire and parody (Shipper and Sculatti's part) with rock nuggets from the past and present (Greg's and my role). At least one show was aired, but as the broadcast facility didn't quite cover the whole of the apartment building where the studio was located, it had little lasting impact. (Sculatti went on to adapt the format for his brilliant *The Cool and the Crazy* public radio collaboration with Ronn Spencer and his current Internet radio treasure, *Atomic Cocktail*.)

I spent more time at *R&R*, where Shipper had brought me back on as a part-time typesetter, working my way toward more significant editorial duties. Neither Greg nor I spent as much time at *PRM*, which wound down slowly under Marty's increasingly erratic leadership. And my involvement with *Bomp* eroded.

A key factor in this gradual winding-down was Terry's and my move from Burbank to Glendale in 1975—still a short freeway hop away from Toluca Lake but certainly not within walking distance. So the casual record-sharing afternoons became scarcer, and my *Bomp* contributions (which continued until 1977, I think) were done strictly solo. (One exception: the extensive Jack Nitzsche interview, conducted at Greg's house with an unusually receptive subject, likely Greg's and my last collaboration.)

Nothing was ever said specifically; we tacitly agreed that I was no longer realistically co-editing *Bomp*, and I faded away. I adapted elements of "Reverberations" to a singles column in *New York Rocker*, founded by Alan Betrock as sort of a fanzine/prozine hybrid and brought to professional fruition by Andy Schwartz. After a brief and less-than-illustrious stint in Casablanca Records' publicity department, I landed a full-time gig at *R&R*.

Greg continued with *Bomp* the magazine, but the label and, later, the Bomp Records store in North Hollywood took up most of his time. I rarely saw him there, though, and strangely – although I'm sure we attended some of the same shows – never seemed to bump into him around town, not even at collectors' meccas such as the monthly Sunday morning-turned-Saturday night Capitol record swaps and their successors. The last time I saw him for any significant amount of time was in the early-to-mid-'80s, at a lunch in Glendale with Sculatti, during which Greg tried to convince us that Black Flag-style hardcore punk was about to conquer the world. The last time I caught a glimpse of him was in the Brian Jonestown Massacre/Dandy Warhols documentary *Dig!*, when he and his quondam managerial clients BJM plotted a disturbance outside a *College Media Journal* convention. This seemed like a puzzling goal to pursue, but then I had no idea about what Greg had been up to since about 1985.

Neither had many other people, and, really, that's Suzy's story to tell. What will stay with me is the warmth and clarity and insight of Greg's writing; the way he, more than anyone, inspired generations of rock archivists and enthusiasts; and the memory of those indolent Toluca Lake afternoons sharing those newly discovered 45s. •

EPILOGUE:

Terry Barnes rose from her secretarial position at UA to gigs at Casablanca and Ariola America Records, eventually becoming a vice president at Motown. She runs her own marketing business. We divorced in 1990.

The Savage Cabbage disbanded in 1971, leaving behind no recordings whatsoever (luckily). **The Open Door** became a successful crafts distribution business, employing its founder, Cabbage guitarist **Mark Jansen** (later an entrepreneur and writer in Los Gatos, CA), and Cabbage keyboardist **Jimmy Carleson**, later a prominent hobby-business sales rep based in New York City. The other Cabbage principal, guitarist **Gerry Lee**, became a doctor in Auburn, CA.

Alan Betrock left the world of music fanzines after launching *Jamz*, *The Rock Marketplace* and *New York Rocker*. He recorded and helped launch Blondie, Marshall Crenshaw and the Violent Femmes, and compiled several books on pulp magazines. He was in bad health for several years and died in 2000.

Gene Sculatti worked at Warner Bros. Records and CBS Television, was Specials Editor at *Billboard* for a number of years, and compiled the cultural anthologies *Catalog of Cool* and *Too Cool* as well as co-writing a history of Bay Area rock. He hosts the *Atomic Cocktail* Internet radio show weekly at luxuriamusic.com.

Suzy Shaw took over the administration of the Bomp label when Greg's interests took a new tack. They eventually divorced, but she expanded the empire and keeps it running.

Marty Cerf went into artist management after *PRM* folded in the late '70s, working with such artists as John Cougar Mellencamp and Billy Squier. He died in circumstances unknown to me.

Radio & Records became the pre-eminent radio trade publication. It was eventually purchased by *Billboard*'s parent company, Nielsen, and folded in June 2009.

Mark Shipper became *R&R*'s editor, and wrote the hilarious Beatles history parody *Paperback Writer*, later becoming a comedy writer.

Ronny Weiser still keeps the rockabilly faith and continues to run Rollin' Rock Records (*www.myspace.com/rollinrockrecords*), based at "Rancho Ronny" in Las Vegas.

Mike Saunders was a principal in the cult punk group Angry Samoans, cut a number of records as Metal Mike, and recently retired as an accountant in Hayward, California. He still proposes sweeping, endlessly debatable theories about rock, teen pop, and punk via e-mail.

Greg died in 2004. His legacy — hundreds of publications and websites inspired by him directly or indirectly, thousands of reissues of neglected music, millions writing about music as if their lives depend on it – survives and thrives.

KEN BARNES was a co-editor and longtime contributor to *Who Put the Bomp* and *BOMP!* magazines, and assistant editor of *Phonograph Record Magazine*. He also worked for Radio & Records, where (the second time around) he became Senior VP & Editor, remaining until 1994. He later worked on the pioneering music website Music Central at Microsoft and was music editor at *USA Today* for 10 years. He and his second wife, Kristi, now live with the much-expanded record collection in Seattle.

THE BOOTLEG CONNECTION by WILLIAM STOUT

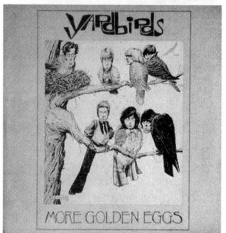

In the mid-1970s I created approximately 45 bootleg record album covers for the company known as Trademark of Quality. For the uninitiated, there were basically two kinds of bootleg LPs: live concert recordings and unreleased or rare/obscure studio recorded tracks. Bootleg records were not counterfeit versions of legitimate releases; those were known as "counterfeit" or "pirated" LPs (counterfeiting was primarily a Mafia domain).

Greg Shaw helped TMQ with a couple of their releases. I was a huge Who and Yardbirds fan. I assisted in the compiling of a couple LPs worth of rarities from those two groups. Greg loaned me some pristine 45s for the mastering of the some of the B-sides, foreign singles and other rarities for their inclusion in our LP collections.

Greg helped us to assemble the Yardbirds bootleg *More Golden Eggs*, furnishing us with some very obscure foreign Yardbirds releases and a couple of other items. This was the first 'semi-legitimate' bootleg. I found out Yardbirds lead singer Keith Relf was living in Burbank at the time (he was rehearsing and recording with his band Armageddon), so I contacted him. In exchange for paying his rent that month, we did a song-by-song taped interview, with Keith commenting on each of the LP's tracks and on the history of the Yardbirds. The photo of Keith on the back cover (and his signature) were from that interview session. The interview was included with the bootleg as a five-page insert.

Because the company's name was Trademark of Quality" I kept pushing them to live up to their name. At first, my black and white covers were printed on separate sheets and sandwiched between the cardboard sleeve and the shrink-wrap. I eventually convinced them to print the art directly on the blank cardboard sleeve. The Bob Dylan *Melbourne, Australia* LP became the first bootleg with a color cover.

Who's Zoo was a double LP with rare studio tracks and TV appearances. Greg provided us with copies of the rarest Who tracks for that release. I designed and illustrated a full color cover and a black and white back cover for *Who's Zoo*. When I returned Greg's records and brought him his copy of *Who's Zoo* he got very excited.

Greg held the LP up and, in gleeful admiration, exclaimed, "It looks just like a *real record!*"

When The Who's John Entwistle saw the TMQ bootleg of *Who's Zoo*, it made him realize how much rare Who stuff was out there. He immediately put together *Odds & Sods* as a result. When the *Odds & Sods* CD version was about to be released, the Who asked my permission to use one of my bootleg covers as the image on the CD's picture disc.

The Rolling Stones' Bill Wyman included one of my TMQ Stones covers in a book of his with a nice caption expressing his praise for my artistic effort. Neil Young just licensed the two Neil Young bootleg covers I did for TMQ. They're both included in his huge new 10-disc box set.

Funny world, ain't it? •

WILLIAM STOUT was the one-time art director for *BOMP!* magazine. His full biography can be found on page 2 of this book.

WHO PUT THE BOMP - AUCTION LIST #3   CLOSING DATE: MAY 1, 1974

THE FOLLOWING RECORDS AND OTHER ITEMS ARE BEING OFFERED TO THE HIGHEST BIDDERS.
ALL RECORDS ARE VISUALLY GRADED AND ARE ON ORIGINAL LABELS EXCEPT AS NOTED.
DESCRIPTIONS ARE GIVEN FOR THOSE TO WHOM SOME RECORDS MAY BE UNFAMILIAR. RECORDS
MAY BE RETURNED FOR A FULL REFUND IF NOT SATISFIED. IN GENERAL THERE ARE NO MIN-
IMUM BIDS, ALTHOUGH I RESERVE THE RIGHT TO REJECT ANY I CONSIDER UNSUITABLE. SOME
MINIMUM BIDS ARE GIVEN TO HELP BIDDERS ASCERTAIN THE BASIC RARITY OF CERTAIN ITEMS.
THESE FIGURES REPRESENT PRICES PAID IN PREVIOUS AUCTIONS, AND SHOULD BE USED AS A
GUIDE TO SUCCESSFUL BIDDING. ONLY WINNING BIDDERS WILL BE NOTIFIED. A BID CAN BE WITHDRAWN AT
ANY POINT PRIOR TO THE CLOSING DATE. BIDDERS HAVE AN OBLIGATION TO PAY FOR RECORDS
THEY HAVE WON. WHEN BIDDING, KEEP IN MIND HOW MUCH YOU CAN AFFORD TO PAY. POST-
AGE AND HANDLING WILL BE ADDED TO WINNING BIDS AT COST, AS WILL INSURANCE. I ASSUME
NO RESPONSIBILITY FOR PACKAGES NOT INSURED. OVERSEAS BIDDERS MAY SPECIFY AIRMAIL,
AGAIN AT COST.

SEND ALL BIDS TO: GREG SHAW, P.O. BOX 7112, BURBANK, CALIF. 91510 USA

WHEN BIDDING, LIST NUMBER AND ARTIST'S NAME. EXAMPLE:

859. KI NUMBERS - $1257.69
934. JUDY COLLINS - $.04   DON'T FORGET THE NUMBERS. BIDS WITHOUT THEM
                                CANNOT BE ACCEPTED.
THE ABOVE EXAMPLES ARE FICTICIOUS. BIDS BELOW $1.00 ARE NOT RECOMMENDED.
THE FOLLOWING GRADING AND ABBREVIATIONS ARE USED:

M - MINT: NEW OR AS NEW
VG - SOME MARKS, BUT PLAYS FINE   WOL - WRITING ON LABEL, INITIALS, X'S
G - WELL USED, BUT LOTS OF PLAY LEFT   CO - CUT OUT, B-B HOLE PUNCHED IN LABEL
F - BADLY SCUFFED AND SCRATCHED   DJ - PROMOTION COPY
P - BARELY PLAYABLE   PS or PIC SLEEVE - PICTURE SLEEVE
                                           SL - STICKER ON LABEL
PLUS AND MINUS SIGNS INDICATE INTERMEDIATE CONDITION

SECTION ONE: ENGLISH. THESE RECORDS ARE U.S. PRESSINGS BY ENGLISH ARTISTS, EXCEPT AS NOTED.

1. ANIMALS   House of the Rising Sun/Talkin Bout You-G
2.   See See Rider/She'll Return It - M
3. ARGENT   Help Me Girl/That Aint Where It's At - VG
4. ARRIVAL   Hold Your Head Up/same - M DJ
5. BABY BUGS   He's Misstra Know-It-All/same Epic 11052 - M DJ
6. CHRIS BARBER   Bingo/Bingo's Bongo Bingo Party - VJ 594 - DJ-d (NOVELTY)
7. BEATLES   Petite Fleur/Wild Cat Blues - Laurie 3022 - G
8.   Atco 6308 - Sweet/Nobody's Child - G
9.   Atco 6308 - Aint She Sweet/Nobody's Child - G-crack-M press
10.   Swan 4152 - She Loves You/I'll Get You - M-DJ (rare)
11.   Swan 4152 - without"Don't Drop Out" - VG- (rare)
12.   Swan 4152 - as above, M - (5% tear on label)
13.   Swan 4152 - regular issue - G/VG
14.   VJ 581 - From Me To You/Please Please Me - VG
15.   Tollie 9001 - Twist & Shout/There's a Place - M
16.   Tollie 9001 - as above, M-
17.   Tollie 9008 - Love Me Do/P.S. I Love You - M
18.   Capitol 72133 (Canadian) Please Mr. Postman/Roll Over Beethoven - VG
19.   Capitol 2134 - Lady Madonna/The Inner Light - M/VG
20.   Apple 0006-04084- Get Back - VG (foreign pressing)
Various Capitol and Apple releases available at $1 in G or better condition, subject to availability.

21. BEATLES   1969 Fan Club Message - M w/cover FROM BRITISH FAN CLUB
The following Beatle records are all in VG condition, in picture sleeves.
22.   Swan 4152 - She Love You/I'll Get You
23.   Capitol 5112 I Want to Hold Your Hand/I Saw Her Standing There
24.   Capitol 5222 A Hard Day's Night/If You Should Have Known Better
25.   Capitol 5235 And I Love Her/If I Fell
26.   Capitol 5327 I Feel Fine/She's a Woman
27.   Capitol 5476 Help!/I'm Down
28.   Capitol 5498 Yesterday/Act Naturally
29.   Capitol 5587 Nowhere Man/What Goes On

30. BEATLE-ETTES   Only Seventeen/Now We're Together - Jubilee 5472 - M
31. DAVE BERRY   Latisha/Do I Still Figure In Your Life - London 20038-M
32. CILLA BLACK   Step Inside Love/same - Bell 726 - VG (CO)
33. COLIN BLUNSTONE Caroline Goodbye/same - Epic 10683 - M-DJ
34.   I Dont Believe in Miracles/same - Epic 10948 - M-DJ
35.   Say You Dont Mind/same - Epic 10668 - M-DJ
36. BONZO DOG BAND Canyons of Your Mind/Urban Spaceman - UA 50809 - M
37.   Slush/King of Scurf - UA 50943-M-DJ
38.   Slush/same - UA 50943 - M
39. DAVID BOWIE   Let's Spend The Night Together/same RCA 0026 - M DJ
40.   The Jean Genie/same - RCA 0838 M-DJ
41.   Suffragette City/Starman - RCA 0719 - M DJ PIC SLEEVE
42.   Space Oddity (long)/(short) RCA 0876 - M DJ PIC SLV
43.   SPECIAL PROMOTIONAL EP Space Oddity/Moonage Daydream/Life
                    on Mars/It Aint Easy - RCA SP-103-M-DJ-PIC SLV-NEVER AVAIL-
                    ABLE TO PUBLIC
44. BRINSLEY SCHWARZ Nightengale/Silver Pistol - UA 50915-M
45.   As above, but with special annotated pic. sleeve by John
                    Mendelsohn contains complete history of group.
46. ANDY BOWN   Open Your Eyes/Oh James - Mercury 73292 - M-DJ
47. BRONX CHEER   Pale Shadow of His Former Self/same Mercury 73295- M-DJ
48. ARTHUR BROWN   Late Date/Hold On To Me - Pye 65,007- M-DJ
49. CHAD & JEREMY   I Put A Spell on You/Nightmare - Track 2582 VG (good; like Mingo J
50.   Summer Song/
51.   If I Loved You/Donna Donna- WA 1027- VG
52. CHICORY TIP   Good Grief Christian/same Epic 10984 - VG
53.   What's Your Name/same - Epic 10889 - M-DJ
54.   Cigarettes, Women & Wine/same - Epic 11047 - M-DJ
55. DAVE CLARK FIVE Anyway You Want It- Epic 9739 - VG
56.   Everybody Knows/Inside & Out - Epic 10265- VG/G
57.   Please Tell Me Why/Look Before You Leap- Epic 10031 - M-DJ
58.   Come Home/Your Turn To Cry - Epic 9763- VG
59.   Red/and Blue/Concentration baby - Epic 10244 M-DJ (rare)
60. (pic. sleeve)   A Little Bit Now/You Dont Play Me Around - Epic 10209 M-DJ
61.   Try Too Hard/All-Night Long Epic 10004 VG-WL
62. DAVE CLARK AFRIENDS Rub It In/same Epic 10894 M-DJ (scarce)
63. COCHISE   Love's Made a Fool of You/Words of a Dying Man UA 50756 M
64.   UA Miniature LP-Swallow Tales- 5 songs, liners-M (collectors item)
65. CREAM   Anyone for Tennis/Pressed Rat & Warthog - Atco 6575 M-CO rare
66.   Badge/What a Bringdown - Atco 6668- M
67. DAKOTAS   The Cruel Surf/The Millionaire - Liberty 55618 M-DJ ('63 hit)
68. SPENCER DAVIS GROUP Keep on Running/High Time Baby - Atco 6400 M-CO
69.   Gimme Some Lovin'/Blues in F - UA 50108 - M
70.   I'm A Man/Can't Get Enough of It - UA 50108 - M
71. SPENCER DAVIS   Rainy Season/same - UA 50993-M-DJ
72.   Voter Registration Spot - UA SP 78 (rare, radio station promo)
73. LYNSEY DE PAUL   Sugar Me/No Storm In a Teacup. MAM 3625 - M
74. DICK & DEE DEE Some Things Just Stick In Your Mind/When Blue Turns To Grey..
                    MB 5627 G/T - DJ (rare Jagger/Richards tune on A side)
75. DONOVAN   Universal Soldier- Hickory 1338 - VG
76. RAY DORSET   Cold Blue excursion/I Need It - Pye 65,008 - M-DJ
77. EASYBEATS   Heaven and Hell - UA 50187 - VG (great record, rare!)
78. DAVE EDMUNDS   Blue Monday/I'll Get Along - MAM 3611 - M
79.   I'm Comin Home/Country Roll - MAM 3609 - M

80. ELEC. LIGHTORCH. 1053B Overture/Battle of Marston Moor - UA50914 - M
81.   Roll Over Beethoven/Queen of the Hours -UA173 - M
82.   Roll Over Beethoven (special remix/re-edit) - M (special yellow label radio station)
83. SCOTT ENGEL   Blue Bell/Paper Doll - Orbit 511 - G/F
84. ADAM FAITH   It's Alright/I Just Dont Know- Amy 913 M (fine raver)
85. MARIANNE FAITHFULL Sister Morphine/Something Better - London 1022- M (rare!)
86.   Tomorrow's Calling/Counting - London 20012 - M
87.   Come And Stay With Me - London 9731 - M (purple & white)
88.   Go Away From My World - London 9802 - M
89.   This Little Bird/Morning Sun - London 9759- M
90.   Tomorrow's Calling Is This What I Get For Loving You - London
                    20020 - M (Ronettes song)
91. FAMILY   Burlesque/The Rockin R's - UA 50951 - M
92.   Seasons/In My Own Time - UA 50632 - M DJ
93.   My Friend The Sun/same -UA 171 - M- DJ
94. CHRIS FARLOWE   Out of Time/Baby Make It Soon - MGM 13567 - G/VG
95. GARY MR & T-BONES Give All She's Got/Don't Stop & Stare - Epic 9832 - G - DJ
96. FLEETWOOD MAC   Oh Well Pt. 1/Oh Well Pt. 2 - Reprise 883 VG
97. FLOWER POT MEN In A Moment of Madness/Young Birds Fly - Duran 85051 M-press
98. WAYNE FONTANA & It's Just A Little Bit Too Late/Long Time Comin' Fontana 151
99. MINDBENDERS   Game Of Love/One More Time - Fontana 1509 - VG M
100. FORTUNES   Here It Comes Again/Things I Should've Known - Press 9796 M
101. FREE   I'll Be Creepin' A&M 1172 - M-DJ (diff. from album version)
102. FRUGAL SOUND   Norwegian Wood/Cruel To Be Kind - Red Bird 052 - M- FJ (RA)
103. GENESIS   Nursery Cryme EP - 3 Cuts, 21 min, w/pic slv.inner notes to
104. GENE PACEMAKERS Girl On A Swing/Way You Look Tonight - Laurie 3354 - VG
105. GRAPEFRUIT   Elevator/Yes - Equinox 70005- M
106. GROUNDHOGS   Split-UA Miniature LP- w/ photos, liners etc. Promo only, PIC SLV
107. NOEL HARRISON Cheryl's Going Home - London 20017 M - PIC SLV
108. HAWKWIND   Silver Machine/Seven By Seven - UA 50949 - M-DJ (not on LP pushing line, LB, d)
109.   Silver Machine/Seven By Seven - UA 35381 - U.K. Pressing on
                    great flourescent picture sleeve - M
110.   Sonic Attack - special 1-sided British promo pressing-very
                    as above, in custom canvas sleeve with stenciled lettering
111.   Urban Guerrilla/same - UA 314-M (DJ hard to find, withdrawn)
112.   Ejection/Catch A Falling Starfighter (as Captain Lockheed
                    The Starfighters) - UA 314- M-DJ (rare,few pressed, not on LP
113.   Hurray On Sundown/Master of the Universe/Silver Machine/
                    Orgone Accumulator - special promo only 2-single 7" album
                    with illo and U.S 1973 tour dates. Songs all edited for pres-
                    Entire package manufactured, in England for American radio
                    clusively. Only 500 made. Illustrated double sleeve: MIN: $4
115.   It's Good News Week/Afraid of Love - Parrot 9800 M
116. HEDGEHOPPERS   Shades of Blue/Daydreaming of You-Kapp 849 - M-DJ 'Group
117. ANONYMOUS   included Capaldi & Mason, who wrote A-side ca.'65- very nice
118. HELLIONS   Strange Affair/same - UA 50973 - M DJ
119. HELP YOURSELF Our Fairy Tale - Fontana 1618 - M-CO
120. THE HERD   The Baby/same Epic 10842 - M - Pic Sleeve
121. HOLLIES   Gasoline Alley Bred - Epic 10677 - VG- DJ
122.   Survival Of the Fittest/same - Epic 10716 - M - DJ
123.   Hey Willy/Row The Boat Together - Epic 10754 - VG
124. HONEYCOMBS   Have I The Right?- Interphon 7707 - G/VG
125.   I Can't Stop/I'll Cry Tomorrow- Interphon 7713 -M
126.   as above, PIC SLV
127. MARCUS HOOK ROLL Natural Man/Boogalooing Is Far Wooing - Capitol - M -DJ
     BAND   (1973 classic - ex-Easybeats-already a collectors item.)
128. HOT CHOCOLATE Rumours/same - Bell 390-M-DJ
129. HULLABALOOS   I'm Gonna Love You/Party Doll - Routette 4587 - G-CO
130. IDLE RACE   Here We Go Round the Lemon Tree/My Fathers Son -Sun-Liberty 55997
                    (Ultra rare, nd on any LP, Jeff Lynn's group before Move
                    American single--not released in England
131. IRON CROSS   Little Bit of Soul - Spark 7 M (great remake of Music
                    Explosion)
132. IVY LEAGUE   Tossing and Turning/Graduation Day-Cameo 377 - M
133.   as above, DJ
134. JOHN'S CHILDREN Smashed! Blocked! - White Whale 239 - G (Marc Bolan's form)
                    group: Great mod-rocker: MIN: $5)
135. PYTHON LEE JACKSON In A Broken Dream/same - GNP 449- M - d (Rod Stewart)
136. MURRAY KELLUM I Dreamed It was a Beatle - MOC 658 M - dj (fantastic novel
137. KINKS   Long Tall Sally/I Took My Baby Home - Cameo 308-M-DJ
                    (one of the most sought after collectors Items of the 60's
                    the Kinks first record, later reissued on Cameo 345. This
                    is the original, on black and white label. In original sleeve
                    never played. MIN $15)
138.   You Really Got Me/It's All Right - Reprise 347 - G
139.   Come On Now/ Tired of Waiting For You- Reprise 347-G
140.   Well Respected Man/Such A Shame - Reprise 420 - VG/G
141.   Victoria/Brainwashed-Reprise 863-VG
142.   Lola/Mindless Child of Motherhood - Reprise 930 - M
143. KATHY KIRBY   The Way of Love - Parrot 9775 - M (original version)
144.   Wonderful Feeling of Love - Parrot 9775 - M (original version)
145. BILLY J KRAMER I'll Keep You Satisfied (Lennon McCartney/I Know-Liberty5)
                    M-DJ- rare
146.   Bad To Me/Little Children - Imperial 66027 - G-VG
147. LINDISFARNE   Lady Eleanor/Down - Elektra 45799 - M - DJ
148. DICK LORD   Like Ringo - Atco 6331 - VG (rare Beatle novelty)
149. LULU & LUVERS Shout/Forget Me Baby - Parrot 9678 - M
150.   as above, DJ
151. JACKIE McCAULEY Shout/When He Touches Me-Parrot 4021 M
152. MAGIC CHRISTIANS It's Alright/Turning Green - Pye 65,002 M DJ
153. MANFRED MANN   Come and Get It - Ascot UR 3006 - M (Trevor Burton, Gary Wright
154.   Sha La La/John Hardy - Ascot 2165 - G/VG
155. MERSEYBEATS   My Name Is Jack/There Is a Man - Mercury 72282 - VG-CO
156.   I Think of You/Mister Moonlight - Fontana 1862 M-DJ
157. MINDBENDERS   Groovy Kind of Love/Love is Good - Fontana 1541 - VG
158.   Ashes to Ashes/You Dont Know About Love-Fontana 1555 M-CO
159.   As above, DJ
160. MONTANAS   Difference of Opinion/You've Got To Be Loved-Independence
                    M-VG, (great Dylan-like punk/psychedelic pop sound)
161.   Ciao Baby/Anyone There- MGM 9 1021 - M - DJ (scarce)
162. MOVE   Chinatown/Down On The Bay- MGM 14332 - M (rare long ver-
                    sion; released illegally and withdrawn after one day: issue
                    edited later on UA- MIN $4)
163.   Flowers In The Rain/Lemon Tree - A&M 984 - M-CO
164.   Fire Brigade/Walk Upon The Water - A&M 914 M-CO
165.   as above, DJ
166.   Chinatown/Down On The Bay - UA 50876 - M - DJ
167.   California Man/Ya - UA 50928 - M - DJ
168.   California Man/Do Ya - UA 50928 - M
169.   Do Ya/Do Ya - UA 50926 M - DJ
170.   Tonight/Tonight - UA 202 M-DJ (special yellow label radio
                    station reserve - remixed to sound better on air..only
                    500 pressed)
171.   Tonight/Marge - UA 202 - M
172. MUD   Crazy/Crazy - Bell 415 M - DJ
173.   In The Summertime/ Might Man - janus 125 - VG
174. MUNGO JERRY   You Don't Have To Be In The Army/O'Reilly - Pye 65,003 - M - DJ
175.   Open Up/Going Back Home - Pye 65009 - M - DJ - WL
176.   Lady Rose/same - Bell 123 - M - DJ - WL
177.

GREG SHAW MINUS by SUZY SHAW

The exodus from the Haight Ashbury had begun by the late '60s, as the hippie movement degenerated, as movements tend to do, into merely a fashion statement and a haircut. The "weekend hippies" were rapidly moving in, along with a large number of Hell's Angels, attracted no doubt by the well-advertised "free love," half naked chicks and easily obtained drugs. And as a bonus they could also have a really good time kicking some hippie ass, something that I saw them doing with great delight on many occasions.

So the original hippies were making their exit, either going back to New York or "goin-up-the-country," as the song says. The Country was Marin County, just across the bridge from San Francisco, and at that time the rent was cheap, the vibe was mellow and the communes were many. I was always a country girl at heart and we jumped at the chance to move out of the city to the sleepy town of Fairfax, 20 minutes out of the city, in the shadow of Mount Tamalpais.

Our quiet street was populated mostly with elderly original residents and some newer arrivals, such as ourselves, escaping the city. It was an interesting group, to say the least. Two doors up we had Doris the Duck Lady, as Greg and I called her, with a loud voice, which sounded, as you may expect, like a quacking duck. Doris was in her late 40s and shaped a bit like Humpty Dumpty (no offense to Humpty), but imagined herself to be quite the hottie, dressed in skintight mini-skirts and revealing blouses, cleavage overflowing, and sporting florid make up. I think if John Waters had met up with her she would have been a superstar. Her husband Don worked in the timber business and rarely spoke, and when he did it was in a low growl, once muttering to me "I cut my toe off with a chain saw today, I just stuck it back in my sock." I didn't dare ask for details.

Hippy Christmas, everybody. Suzy and Greg Shaw, December 1968.

Across the street was Johnny and Ethel, a couple in their 90's who had been "living in sin" for decades and had installed an extra door in the house so that they could pretend that it was really two houses and that they were not living together, although the doors opened into the same room. They could barely walk, let alone have sex, but they never ceased making lurid remarks to one another, complete with winks and leers. (I guess the not being married part was pretty hot stuff for them.) I became good friends with them and helped them out when I could, and in return they would tell me tales of their wild youth.

Our immediate neighbor, Vern, was a hippie-hating, gun-toting, flag-waving alcoholic, (an ever-popular combination) who spent part of his time hitting on me and the rest kicking down my flowerbeds and once even lighting our house on fire (it didn't do much damage, fortunately). We weren't really very convincing hippies, I didn't take drugs at all and mostly just worked really hard and gardened, but try as I might Vern never did forgive us for Greg's hairdo. Vern was clearly not a happy man, and eventually barricaded himself in his house with a shotgun to his head, and after a few very exciting hours of police activity killed himself.

His house was later taken over, after a good cleaning I assume, by Virginia, a good natured pot smoking nymphomaniac in her 30s who was mildly paralyzed by polio and had only half of her face working properly. This had not made her at all shy, however, and she would spend her evenings cruising the local bars and bringing home whatever she happened to find on the barstool next to her. She could hardly believe her good fortune when she discovered that we often had young, reasonably attractive men staying with us, as the rock critics passing thru town would frequently stay at our cottage. She would spring into action the moment our guests arrived, lounging on her porch in a short dress with no underwear, smoking a pipe full of pot, and holding a can of beer, just in case the first two offerings were not enough persuasion. It wasn't unusual to wake up in the morning and find that our visitor had strayed over to Virginia's for the night.

Greg was nothing short of fascinated by the never ending soap opera, and started a column called "Neighbor Stories" in his zine *Metanoia*, which he was publishing at the same time as he was putting out the first issues of *Who Put the Bomp*. He was honing his writing skills and our neighbors were perfect fodder. The stories were quite a popular feature, and the likes of Lester Bangs and Richard Meltzer anxiously awaited each the new issue to see what drama had unfolded on Taylor Drive since the last issue.

In addition to his writing and publishing, Greg was working nights as a mail sorter for the post office, a common hippie job, since they didn't care if you had long hair and looked like a weirdo as long as you could sort mail. Greg rather enjoyed the job, as he had an obsession with specialty magazines, and he was fascinated with the huge variety of them that passed through his hands at the post office. He often brought home issues that he found especially interesting. I can recall one called *Hod Carrier's Monthly* that he giggled about for days. I pointed out that as far as I knew it was a federal offense to take home other people's mail, but he was of the opinion that they would be getting another issue very much like it soon enough, and simply ignored me, as he usually did in matters of taking a little walk on the wild side of the law.

Fortunately his days at the post office were soon to be over. As luck would have it, right there on Taylor Drive was a very nice hippie couple who had decided to move to a commune and give up their earthly possessions, quite a trendy thing to do at the time. (Although I'll bet a year later they wished they had their stuff back.) When they were leaving town they came to say goodbye, bringing me all of the tools and supplies that they had used for their previous business. They had been making leather vests and purses and selling them to some local stores, making a good living at it too, and they showed me the basics and told me where to sell the finished items. In no time at all we were in business, selling our elaborately fringed brightly colored goods to tourists, rock stars, and the local hippies, and making enough extra money for Greg to quit his post office job and devote more time to his writing and publishing.

Greg was also writing for several other publications at the time, including *Rolling Stone* and *Crawdaddy*. Greg had known Jann Wenner long before the beginnings of *Rolling Stone*. Jann was a guest at Greg's apartment on many occasions, and knew the same crowd of rock critics that Greg did. Jann had hired an editor for the rock section, and Greg had gone to the Rolling Stone offices to meet with him. His name was Ed Ward.

"I ran into Greg when I was working at *Rolling Stone*," remembers Ed, "and Jann Wenner assigned me a story on fanzines. I had an inkling of what fanzines were, since I'd been a science-fiction fan years ago, and knew fanzines played a part in that world, but I wasn't quite sure what a rock fanzine would be. I found out soon enough: I went up to Greg and Suzie Shaw's house in San Anselmo [sic] and spent the afternoon talking with them about *Who Put The Bomp*."

Ed wrote the fanzine article and staff photographer Annie Leibovitz was dispatched to our house in Fairfax to take pictures of Greg and I, and the photo and article appeared in *Rolling Stone* in August 1970.

The relationship between Greg and Jann eventually turned somewhat adversarial, the inevitable conflict between the big business approach to publishing that Jann was so successful with and the fannish angle that Greg embraced. Jann had begun showing up to gigs in a chauffeured Mercedes limo, which didn't go over too well with most of the rock writers. But Jann thought Greg was a talented writer and did not allow their quibbles to prevent him from writing articles for *Rolling Stone*. Ed Ward quickly became one our best friends and a frequent guest at our "collating parties."

Most of you probably don't know what a collating party is, but in those days, zines like *Who Put the Bomp* were produced on a mimeograph (there is a nice picture of Greg and his mimeograph to the right for those of you who wish to view this item of antiquity) a hand-cranked machine with a drum to which a stencil was attached, one stencil for each page of the magazine. The stencil was created on the typewriter, and images could also be laboriously added by hand. The crank would be turned and a page would be ejected, joining its smudgy counterparts in a stack until you had reached the desired number of pages. Then the next stencil was attached to the drum and the process would begin again. After the pages were dry they would be run back through for the second side. Sometimes you wanted three colors on the page, and you'd have to cut three stencils and run it through

> *In those days, zines like Who Put the Bomp were produced on a mimeograph, a hand-cranked machine with a drum to which a stencil was attached, one stencil for each page of the magazine.*

A young Greg Shaw and his trusty mimeograph.

three times, a long and tedious process. When at long last all of the pages were ready for assembly it was a fandom tradition to have a collating party, and the invitations would go out to the neighbors, friends, and in our case the local rock critics ... "Collating Party at Greg Shaw's House!"

It wasn't hard to get rock critics to show up if food and beverages were offered, and I was in charge of getting together the tempting snacks and making what became known as "Suzy Burgers," a humungous pile of ground meat and grilled onions on a toasted bun, an extremely popular item with the starving writers. After the crowd was well fed, and a little or a lot drunk, the pages of the magazine would be laid out all over the house, using every surface from the bed to the kitchen table, and the attendees would circle slowly around the tiny cottage, trying not to get potato chip grease on the pages or spill their beers, gradually assembling the magazines. It was a lively event, with everyone from Ken Barnes, Lester Bangs, Gene Sculatti, Richard Meltzer and Greil Marcus showing up, collating the pages while they discussed their favorite bands and enthused over their recent record bin finds.

Suzy Burgers for everybody! Another collating party on Taylor Drive, ca. 1971.

Record collecting was an obscure activity at the time, and the thrift store bins were bulging with rare records, usually priced at a nickel or so regardless of what they were, as the storeowner wasn't likely to know one from the other. The records were so cheap and plentiful that the collectors would often merely load up the car and figure out what they had bought later. Greg often came home with piles of dusty vinyl, which he would research later to see if he already had the item or if it was anything of interest.

This technique let to a considerable surplus, to say the least, (records were soon inhabiting every corner of the cottage, much to my dismay) and he began trying to cut down on the overload by listing a few records for sale here and there in the back of his zines. The price was generally not more than you paid, usually about .10 cents, and your "customers" were friends and people you knew well. Greg enjoyed listing the titles and getting the checks, but that's pretty much where his interest ended. Sending out the merchandise was quite another matter, and this was frequently delayed until he felt like packing the stuff up and going to the post office, which turned out was not very often. Packaging was a problem as well, as Greg wasn't much on condition to begin with. He considered it not only unimportant, but in fact viewed the quest for perfect vinyl with great disdain as an affectation of sorts.

Being more of a historian than a collector, he often said that he hated collectors. All that really mattered to him was getting the general information about the record—it was meant to be played once for the purposes of knowing what type of music it was. If a record was so shattered that it had to be scotch-taped together (this was not unheard of in his collection) it was at least useful for knowing the label, title and catalogue number, and he would file it away with the others without hesitation. So legendary was the generally horrendous condition of his vinyl that certain record dealers still use a grading system to this day that starts with "Mint" and ends with "Greg Shaw Minus."

Thus it was no surprise that Greg had not the slightest qualm about merely tossing a customer's order into a paper grocery bag, stapled at the top to keep the records from spilling out (that's if you were lucky). The odds of a buyer getting what they wanted or having the vinyl arriving unbroken were quite slim. This was bad enough when you were dealing with friends, but the mailing list had begun to branch out to include the general public. These newcomers had the annoying habit of not only insisting that they receive the exact records that they had paid for, but getting them in one piece, and soon enough the angry letters and threats began pouring in. Never one to be bothered by such minor details, or the law (federal, state and local!), Greg simply ignored the whole mess, continuing as he had before, until the registered letters from the Post Office began arriving and the government was actually preparing to file charges. I was nothing short of terrified, and in a move that was to be oft repeated in our lives together, my choice seemed to be between going to prison or to take over that part of the business. And so mail order slid over to my side of the game board for once and for all.

We stayed in Fairfax until 1972, living a quiet life, me spending my days turning out goods for the leather business and working on the then-tiny mail order, and Greg publishing his magazines and writing, often helping me with the leather business when he had the time. And then one day we got a phone call that would be the start of a new life for us.

One of the many magazines that Greg had been writing for was *Phonograph Record Magazine* in Los Angeles, Marty Cerf was the editor and he liked Greg's writing and his ideas. Marty was calling to offer him a job as the editor of PRM and the Assistant Head of Creative Services for United Artists Records, and he wanted Greg to move to Los Angeles and start as soon as possible. (See Ken Barnes' story for more juicy details of the UA days.) The decision to take the job and leave Fairfax was already made for us in a way, as our house had just been put up for sale, and we were going to have to move anyway. (We had declined to buy the property as we thought $3,000 was way too much. What morons we were, that property is probably worth millions today!) So we packed it all up and moved off to Los Angeles.

Greg and I settled into LA and the new job, and eventually I started helping out at PRM too, running the magazine subscription department, proof reading, and handling the phones. PRM was an extremely lively place to be, all of us working at an insane pace, and there were visitors coming and going all day. Most of the UA musicians would come in to say hello if they were in the building, and it was not usual for me to find Johnny Rivers, Tina Turner or John Fogerty perched on my desk talking to Marty. PRM soon outgrew the small space at U.A. and separate offices were obtained a few blocks away in the Max Factor building on Hollywood Boulevard, just across from the Roosevelt Hotel.

Marty Cerf.

Out from under the watchful eye of the UA executives, Marty was free to do whatever he liked with the space, and before long he was virtually living there, sleeping on the couch in the waiting room and installing a TV so that he could watch his favorite shows at night. It wasn't that he needed to live there, he had a house, but work was his life and saw no reason to waste time driving home. He shared his house in West Los Angeles with his pretend girlfriend, Thaan, an impossibly thin elf-like girl who was fond of the LA club scene and taking speed. Marty was clearly gay, and so was she, but it seemed important to him for people to think he was a ladies man, so everyone played along so as not to hurt his feelings.

He also rented out the storage room in the new offices to his friend Dan Bourgoise (an article of his appears in this book), who was starting a music publishing company. I think it was more of a favor to Dan than a moneymaking ploy, as Dan had just started his business and needed a workspace. The tiny room was supposed to be half storage and half Dan's office, but I would often see Marty scurrying down the hall with an armful of magazines knocking on Dan's door and saying, "I just need to put these in the corner, sorry!" until poor Dan's head could barely be seen above the stacks. Seeing Dan try to conduct a meeting in the cramped space was absolutely hilarious. I once showed the legendary Del Shannon to Dan's 'office' and watched him try to make his way through the stacks to the single chair, with Dan peering out from his magazine-piled desk trying to find an angle from which he could see Del. Fortunately Dan had a good sense of humor and a calm demeanor and found it all quite amusing, but moved out and got a proper office before too long, going on to become the biggest music publisher in Los Angeles, handling such artists as Iggy Pop, Bobby Fuller, Mose Allison, Johnny Cash and many more. He also became one of our best friends and handled the publishing for us when Greg started the Bomp label. Del Shannon became a good friend of ours too, and I still have some nice postcards that he sent me, but sadly he committed suicide in 1990. Dan recently sold Bug and retired.

Marty also brought in his nearly full-time record filer, Montreal John. John was the go-to guy for record filing among the Hollywood collectors, which was lucky for John, as I couldn't really imagine him doing anything else. He was entirely psychotic, convinced that he was an Indian living on the astral plane, and his appearance was quite startling as well. Dressed in rags and Indian jewelry, John had huge mats of hair hanging to his waist, his teeth had never been brushed, and his eyes were wild and unfocused, visible behind thick broken glasses that were barely held together with scotch tape. Conversations with John had nothing to do with the previous sentence, and a simple question like "How are you, John?" would bring on a rambling discussion of the wisdom of Running Bear. He filed all day though, cackling and giggling to himself over the apparently amusing record labels, occasionally breaking into hysterical, snorting whoops of laughter when one was particularly funny.

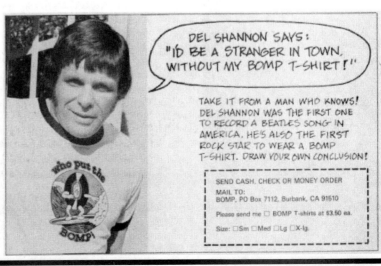

Rodney Bingenheimer was there nearly every day too, he had a column in PRM and Marty had given him a section of the office to use and a dedicated phone number known as the "The Rodney Hot Line." Rodney never did quite get the

> *Greg's style was full speed ahead and worry about the consequences later, and every day brought a whirlwind of both the fantastic creativity that this book and a thousand articles chronicle, and the fallout from Greg's staunch refusal to play by the rules.*

hang of the office phones though, and he eagerly punched in to whatever line was ringing with his cheerful "Rodney Hot Line!" at the same time that I had picked up the same line announcing "Phonograph Record Magazine." The confused caller would then have to wait until Rodney and I had worked it all out. Kim Fowley and Rodney were fast friends and Kim would come in to take Rodney off to Denny's on Sunset Strip to hold their daily court (neither one of them would eat anywhere else), and ogle the endless parade of wannabe actresses passing by the window. (Be sure to see Rodney's movie *Mayor of Sunset Strip* if you haven't already.)

So PRM became a home away from home for our little family of freaks, weirdoes, and misfits, and Greg and I were there a lot, often working late and having dinner with Marty or watching a little TV with him when we were all too tired to work. At that time a soap opera called "All My Children" had somehow become popular with the younger set, and Greg and Marty were hooked on it. Every day at noontime the lights in the reception room would go off and we would curl up on the couch, sometimes joined by Rodney, to eagerly ooh and aah over the latest adventures of Erica Kane and her assorted love interests. Visiting musicians would be startled to open the very corporate looking office door and find a darkened room with shadowy figures watching TV, and would usually say "oh, excuse me!" and make a confused exit, assuming that they were in the wrong place. Marty would have to chase them down the hall and blame the soap opera on me.

The office was made all the livelier as Marty was a bit of a speed freak, probably initially taking it to cope with the huge work load and then finding it hard to work without it. He was already pretty hyper to begin with, and the speed pushed him to a whole new level of non-stop ideas. He was brilliant but after about a week without sleep most of his concepts were seriously unworkable, if not completely crazy, and we would have to try to talk him out of whatever grand plan he had come up on his latest speed binge. He would eventually crash and sleep for four days nonstop, leaving Greg and I to cope with the business until he woke up refreshed and ready to start again.

PRM folded in 1978 and we lost touch with Marty for many years, so I was thrilled to get a call from him in the '90s. My happiness quickly faded when he began speaking, however. He rambled incoherently for nearly an hour, without me getting a word in edgewise, raving wildly about the government and assorted conspiracy theories, and then hung up. I heard later that he died of AIDS, but don't know for sure. It was a tragic ending for such a creative and intelligent man, and I wish we could have helped him. He was a good friend and gave Greg his start. Greg often referred to him as "the godfather." I miss him.

Who Put the Bomp for sale, ECHO convention, 1975. Greg cosies up with Janis Schact, while Suzy sells the wares.

Greg continued to expand the "Bomp Empire" as he called it, with me dutifully following along in the wake of the hurricane that was Greg Shaw, helping with whatever I could and cleaning up the mess, both literal and figurative. Greg's style was full speed ahead and worry about the consequences later, and every day brought a whirlwind of both the fantastic creativity that this book and a thousand articles chronicle, and the fallout from Greg's staunch refusal to play by the rules, or even acknowledge that there were rules, for that matter.

Those of you who have read virtually all of my stories in the first Bomp book (and this one) will know that doing that which is known as business with Greg generally didn't turn out all that well. Two years ago when Patrick and I were in a meeting with our art director for the first book he commented, "Those are very funny stories, but aren't there any other kind of stories about Greg? They are mostly about Greg defying authority and getting into trouble!" Patrick and I were momentarily stunned into confused silence, as if somebody had asked why we kept using the word "wet" when describing water, and in a sitcom-worthy moment we shouted in unison, "NO!!!!!"

The end results of Greg's incredible body of work are all that most people are familiar with, and rightfully so, but we were more involved in the long, painful process of getting there. Greg didn't need my help with signing bands or writing for the magazine, but he needed me (and later Patrick) to make it happen, and I would arrive at Bomp every morning not wondering if anything was wrong, it was, but rather if the problem of the day would be infraction, insult, misdemeanor or felony, as Greg gleefully and fearlessly bulldozed his way through life and his various enterprises.

But, fortunately, the mail order division was of no real interest to Greg. He had soured on it early on, after his exasperating experiences with the nitpicking fanatics that expected to get what they paid for, and mail order became a stable part of Bomp that was largely exempt from Greg's grand plans, 90 percent of which were destined to go very, very wrong.

157 editions of the print catalogue were eventually published before we finally made the switch to all on-line ordering, seemingly a little late in the game, but I knew my customers well, and a surprisingly large number of them are even now vigorously opposed to computers, some bragging that they don't have one and never will. One customer adds proudly that he doesn't even have a cordless phone. Forced to say a final goodbye to their beloved printed catalogues, many of the long-time customers devised elaborate systems of ordering off line, some seemingly far more technologically challenging than just making the order on the cart, such as taking pictures of their on-screen order and mailing the photos to me. To this day some of my little darlings are hanging on to that last print edition, (published in 2004) making copies of it and sending in orders for product long gone. Our pal Jello Biafra is one of the last of the holdouts, calling every now and then to inquire as to if I have finally relented and decided to do another xeroxed catalogue, hating the computer and longing for the good old days of smudgy print.

Above: The Bomp team, ca. late '70s.
L to R: Diane Zincavage, Paul Grant,
Suzy Shaw, Greg Shaw and Lisa Fancher.

I would imagine that most mail order businesses have a "crazy customer" file of some sort, but the Bomp archive of wacky letters is nearly a book in itself. In fact it has been suggested that I turn it all over to Feral House for just that purpose. The main feature of interest are the hundreds of letters, dating back as far as 1980, from a customer who developed schizophrenia and began writing us lengthy letters, sometimes as many as 10 a day, becoming convinced that everyone from Madonna to Belinda Carlisle was not only singing about him but was right there at "Bomp CD place." His letters are tragic but fascinating, usually starting out with a scrawled list of people and entities that he is not—"I am not God and I am not the devil and I am not Jesus"—and then after clearing up that issue would list some of his favorite foods ("tuna fish sandwiches the RIGHT way with tuna on one bread and mayo on the other bread!), or instructing me to "Please have Madonna get this!" and asking her to discuss their future together… "If I moved to California or NY on a bus I don't know if I could be guaranteed work, but you want me, Madonna, right?" Other times he rambles on about topics such as "the devil fooled me that Anna Nicole Smith is Belinda Carlisle in other lifetimes, but that is lies." Once he included a page long list of women he wanted to have sex with that included me, Kathy Ireland, a couple of the Bangles, and, inexplicably, Joan Rivers and Ivanka Trump. I hadn't gotten any letters from him for a few years and was beginning to wonder what happened to him (I've never once replied to him), but a new letter arrived last month, and he now wants to makes it clear that he is not God, not Jesus, not the Father, and not Miley Cyrus. Man, that chick is REALLY famous!

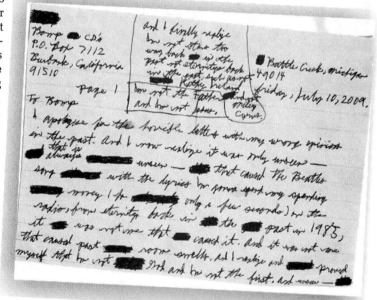

We also get a fair number of letters and e-mails from frantic wives, convinced that their husbands are spending the last of the family nest egg on their vinyl fetish. "PLEASE don't let my husband buy any more stuff. PLEASE stop! PLEASE!! He will spend everything!!!" Probably, but hey, if he doesn't get it from me, he'll just get it somewhere else.

And so mail order has been far from the dull enterprise it might seem; in fact for me it's a non-stop adventure, each day bringing me new pen pals and tales of life and adventure from far away. One day it will be a Russian sailor who supervises a geological vessel (I thought he'd be a big beardy guy with a parrot on his shoulder, but he's a Radio Moscow loving psych-head who looks like an LA surfer!) another day will bring e-mailed photos from an absolutely adorable 21-year girl in Brazil who just discovered BOMP and loves the Dead Boys (we trade cat pictures and she tells me stories of her life as an aspiring artist). Some have eventually become very close friends that I hear from nearly every day, like my brilliant and funny Aussie artist pal Kara-Lynne who cheers me up when I'm down and makes me laugh with her hilarious e-mails, and our friend Tim Frueh in Dayton who

Greg Shaw in Bomp's San Fernando Valley office, ca. 1980s.

is always there to offer his support and well informed advice on everything from our labels to our ad campaigns.

Some customers come in person to meet me and to view the legendary Bomp warehouse, nearly a museum in and of itself and fascinating to see, the walls decorated with albums covers, fliers from the Bomp store, rare posters, and assorted other items of interest from our long history. Many of our overseas friends plan their visits long in advance, like the French teacher who has promised to bring her entire class to Bomp on their trip to America next year. Other visitors live right here in LA and just pop in to say hello, shop, or pick up their orders.

One frequent visitor was eventually nicknamed "Captain Strange" (for reasons that will become clear) and he would stay for hours, reading the backs of the CD and album covers to himself in a loud whisper and laughing out loud from time to time. We tried to keep his visits short, but he didn't take a hint easily. One day Patrick had one of his visiting bands assembled in the warehouse, discussing their plans for the future and their contract. It slowly dawned on Patrick as he spoke that one of the band members he was addressing seemed oddly unfamiliar—even though he was standing with the others, listening attentively and nodding his head eagerly in agreement with Patrick's proposals. Patrick stopped mid-sentence and asked him "Wait, who are YOU?!" It was the Captain, who had happily joined in on the band meeting. I think that was the last time we let him in the warehouse.

And of course, aside from the mail order business the labels are still running, but my man Patrick has generously agreed to taken over the operations of that end of the business for me (he kind of had no choice, since I don't have a clue), and brilliantly so, I might add. That Bomp is still here at all is entirely his doing, and any fan of Bomp, me especially, owes him a big thanks! His own label Alive is going strong, and his roster includes the Nerves, the Breakaways, the Black Keys, Thomas Function, Brian Olive, Nathaniel Mayer, and more. Check his site for the latest at: *www.aliveenergy.com*

After Greg's tragic death in 2004 we had an extremely difficult time recovering from the shock of losing someone who we thought of not just as our partner but part of our family. Greg had been ill for a long time due to his life of excess, and sadly he and I had stopped speaking for several years before his death, communicating only by e-mail. The word "enabling" had been thrown at me many times as regards my dealings with Greg, and I had begun to worry that I was doing him more harm than good, and he was very angry at me for finally taking a stand and refusing to bail him out (once again, literally and figuratively) of his increasingly complex troubles. The news of his death hit us hard; it was unimaginable that he was gone, in spite of our recent disagreements. Patrick and I were devastated and we could have used a break to recover from the shock, but his latest wife (whom I had never met, she had been married to Greg for less than a year) was a very young girl who suddenly found herself in the midst of incredible chaos, and she called me in tears, saying "Greg told me that if anything happened to him I should call you and that you would straighten everything out." Will do, Greg, one more time....

We were about to be plunged into the mess to end all messes—Greg really outdid himself for the grand finale, I have to say! I won't bore you with the details, but at long last the dust has begun to settle, and the lawyers are gone—most of them anyway—and Bomp still stands. We miss Greg, of course, we don't go a day without wishing he were still here SO THAT WE COULD MURDER HIM (just kidding) and that we could have ended our life together on a positive note.

Greg's creative side can't be matched, but his business style (more anti-business, if truth be told) left much to be desired, and we've tackled the seemingly endless task of making the wrongs right. Patrick has taken charge of straightening out the convoluted legal entanglements, and we've recently managed to make peace with Iggy and James Williamson after all these years. Iggy has been amazing, he could have buried us, but he's been cheerful and sweet and funny, forgiving the past and willing to start fresh. And James recently sent me an e-mail saying, "Because of you guys, I'm feeling good about Bomp again after all these years. I'm sure we'll get something else going." Nothing could have made me happier, and I think Greg would have liked it, too.

In closing I just want to thank all of you who care enough about what I do and about Bomp to be reading this, and a special heartfelt thanks goes out to Mike Stax, who has put in an enormous amount of work producing a book that is beyond my wildest expectations. His epic piece listing all of the zines is jaw-dropping and is not only entertaining and funny but will certainly be of use for the history buffs. Mike and I had a great time working together and I can't imagine doing another volume without him. (We're already tossing around ideas for the next edition!)

And thanks to our friend Bill Stout who generously did the cover for practically nothing because he thought it would be fun. (He'll be working with Patrick on some album covers in the near future.) And of course thanks to all of the writers whose work appears here, especially Ken Barnes who seems to have written half the book! His work in the early Bomp mags keeps it all together. And lots of love to Alec Palao for his brilliant piece, and to Jon Savage for coming through with an excellent intro that explains it all. And most of all our deepest gratitude to Geoffrey Weiss, who is always there for us with his friendship, advice, and support.

Come and visit us if you're in town, and check in on the latest news at bomp.com, we've always got something new going on. I'll be here… •

Above : Bomp Christmas card, 1976, and, below, ca. 1980s.

Left: Suzy at the Fairfax house, ca. 1970.

SUZY SHAW has been at the heart of the Bomp Empire since its humble mimeograph machine beginnings in 1970. Almost 40 years later Bomp continues to thrive, headed up by Suzy and husband Patrick Boissel.

WHO PUT THE BOMP #2   MARCH, 1970

I guess I owe the membership of REAP an explanation for the change in title. My original intention was to give each issue the title of a different old rock & roll record, but Louis Morra's suggestion that titles should be consistent caused me to reconsider. He's right. From now on, WHO PUT THE BOMP is the name of this fanzine, and each issue will have a different subtitle. Therefore, in addition to being WHO PUT THE BOMP #2, this is also:

Da Doo Ron Ron

Published for the Rock Enthusiasts' Amateur Press by Greg Shaw of 64 Taylor Dr., Fairfax, Calif. 94930. This issue is intended for the second mailing, and 50 copies have been printed.

: :

Well, the first mailing of REAP wasn't bad. It was terrible.

No, not really. But it certainly wasn't what I was expecting. I think the most surprising thing to me was the roster. I had no idea, of course, of who else had joined REAP, but I sort of expected that the rest of the membership would be made up of the usual familiar names who are active in fandom and given to writing about rock in their fanzines. As it stands, I am acquainted with only 3 members (Alpajpuri, John Ingham, Mike Ward), 4 if we count Louis Morra, though we'd never been in contact before he asked me to join REAP.

Where are Len Bailes, Ed Reed, Doug Lovenstein, Creath Thorne, Jerry Lapidus, Jim Young, and all the rest? Where, for goodness sake, is St. Louis fandom? I suppose that as the existence of REAP becomes known, and if it achieves a reputation, more people will be attracted to it. For now, 13 is a good membership, and I guess we'll have 20 or so by the third mailing, so let's just see what happens.

I must say that I find it interesting that so many of our members come by way of comic fandom. As a rule, people newly arrived from comic fandom are handicapped when they begin participating in general fandom, because they are usually unaware of the great bulk of history and tradition and all of the social forces that are the basis of so much fannish activity. Until they can familiarize themselves with what has come before, their ignorance prevents whatever they write or publish from coming across effectively. We should have no such problems here, for to the best of my knowledge the printed discussion of rock music on an amateur basis has no precedent to speak of, except for a few scattered articles in various obscure fanzines of the past five years. So it's up to us to discover what's worth doing and what's not, and until then—— anything goes.

However, I really do think a lot of the fanzines in the first mailing were poorly written. I don't feel like putting anybody down, which doesn't do much good anyway (if we could do better, we would). But you'll be able to tell from whether I comment on your zine if I liked it or not.

KARNIS BOTTLE'S
METANOIA #3

"FAIRFAX FANDOM'S FINEST FANMAG!"

This is the third of an infinite series of unpublished METANOIAs to obtain a relatively corporeal existence, due to the efforts of GREG SHAW, of 64 Taylor Dr., Fairfax, Calif. 94930. Copies available free to anyone who thinks he deserves one, as well as to the long-suffering members of my Permanent Mailing List. As long as I have the time and energy, this wonderful magazine will continue to appear monthly, but don't panic if I get a bit behind. MAY, 1970.

FAIRFAX FANDOM??? Yes, there is a fandom in Fairfax, though to the best of my knowledge METANOIA is the only fanzine currently being produced here. Actually, for a town of 7,500, Fairfax has quite a few fans. Our local bookstore, The New Albion (which specializes in SF) is run by Hal Bertram and his wife, who have been fans for over 20 years. Their assistant, Jeff Yates, is a fan and collector, who even attended the St. Louiscon. If that's not enough, one of the clerks at our little post office, Bill Barnes, is a fan too. What a scene! Aside from all that, a lot of our casual acquaintances are sf enthusiasts, who freak out when they first see my book collection and start telling me how they've been reading sf for years. Quite a few of them knew about fanzines before meeting me, interestingly enough. A group of them showed up at the recent SFCon and really had a ball. It was strange to see our freaky friends acting like neos, saying things like "Wow, is that really Poul Anderson?" Sometimes I think the whole world must be full of secret fans. Anyway, there's no truth to the rumor that Fairfax is bidding for the 1988 Westercon. '94, maybe.

Speaking of Fairfax, it's now Spring here (for the benefit of our South American readers). Actually, it's been spring since the end of last autumn, which occurred in early January, except for a couple of weeks or rain and cold weather inbetween. Ironically, since the "official" First Day of Spring it's been rather cold and windy, but on the whole the last four months have been beautiful. All the trees and flowers put out their buds as far back as February, and we were afraid a sudden frost would catch them unawares, but it never materialized. Our garden is blooming joyfully, and Suzy is having the time of her life puttering in it.

Last year we didn't pay any attention to the garden, but this year we've cleared out all the weeds, broken up all the rocky clay soil, added all kinds of conditioners, sent away for seeds, and started everything from scratch. We have flowers all around, and some vegetables in the back. I must admit I haven't shown as much interest in the garden as I should. I can't force myself to be interested, but I'm becoming more so as time goes by. Meanwhile, Suzy is learning, learning, learning.

We had a rather unusual experience recently. All the houses in the neighborhood (which belong mostly to very old people) are surrounded by profusions of flowers and foliage, except for that of our neighbor on the right. He is a man of about 70 who is drunk all the time. His house is a plain little wooden box set in a completely naked plot of land. He has poured plant poison on his land for years so nothing would grow, and has also poisoned lots of flowers and even trees on our property which happened to extend an inch or so over the boundary. A couple of weeks ago Suzy decided to erect a small fence to keep the local dogs from desecrating our seedlings, so we bought some stakes and some chicken wire and spent all day stringing it around our yard. Then we went away for an hour.

When we got back, imagine our surprise to find the fence completely gone! Wire, stakes, everything, disappeared. We thought of the old man immediately and went over and knocked on his door. We caught a glimpse of him thru the window, hiding under his kitchen table, so we kept knocking for quite a while before giving up. Finally we went home and talked about it for a long time, then went back and left a little note on his door that went something like this:

"Dear neighbor, we're sorry your life is so empty that you feel the need to steal our fence to get us to pay some attention to you. We hope that when you've had time to consider what you've done you will return our fence. Any time you want to talk to somebody we would be more than glad to be your friends. Love, Suzy and Gregory."

The next day we saw him in the yard and asked him very politely about the fence. He said he'd never seen it, wasn't home, somebody must have ripped us off. We pointed out that whoever it was had also gone to considerable trouble to remove some very heavy (100 lb.) cement blocks and left behind our brand new shovel, but he just mumbled. It was plain he'd have enjoyed it if we'd gotten mad and called the police, he probably had an answer ready for anything we could accuse him of, and the whole thing would have thrilled him.

We didn't feel like putting any energy into his bad trip, though, so we pretended the incident never happened. We continued exchanging "Good morning"s in the yard, borrowing his tools, etc. Then a couple of days ago he took a trellis we'd put in for our morning glories, which was within a foot of his property line, stomping the seedlings in the process. We knocked on his door again, he hid under the table again, the whole ridiculous thing.

And there the score stands for now, until the next time he gets plastered and strikes out against the world, conveniently represented by our garden.

It sure is a funny world, sometimes.

"If I show that I can conquer this galaxy, I'll get a promotion!"
—quoted from a TIME TUNNEL T.V. show

The Fairfax cottage, 1970.

LEN BAILES (Box 474, 308 Westwood Plaza, Los Angeles, Calif. 90024)

I got the second issue of Metanoia today and really liked reading it, especially the pages from James Wright. They are so starkly fucking real that they leave a heavy imprint on the mind... especially since the last stuff I saw from Wright was years ago in the Cult and seems to have been written by a totally different person. If he is over-dramatizing then all I can say is that he could write a fantastic novel, but it seems too vivid for that.

Far out on "I'm Ready". I didn't know what to make of the song when I heard it, so I assumed it was from the new 16-track demo that Dylan made with The Band in December. (There's something Rolling Stone never picked up on. I'll bet that's one thing Greil Marcus doesn't have a copy of.) The singing style on "I'm Ready" sounds a lot like the way Dylan sang "One Too Many Mornings" with Cash, so I was taken in.

I liked your SFCon report and fanzine reviews. I still haven't made a synthesis in my own head between the science fiction fan type person I was a few years ago and the music freak I am today, and I read with interest contributions from people who seem to have gotten these (to me) separate trips together.

It still gives me a very pleasant feeling to think of Phillip K. Dick, and The Grateful Dead, and Sam Delaney and Paul Williams and John Lennon and realize that I am not the only person who knows them all... People in Los Angeles tend to be compartmentalized like the city itself. I really dug talking to Bob Lichtman and you at SFCon.

I envision a rock album called CONAPT, and record buyers who would understand. Someone told me that upon meeting John Lennon, the first thing Paul Williams did was give him a copy of Dune. "Jesus and Hitler and Richard the Lionheart..." maybe it all does turn out to be the same thing.

((Yes, I think it's coming to that. Every freak I meet who finds out I'm an sf fan immediately wants to go into a whole rap about it with me – and they can never believe it when I tell them how stodgy the real science fiction fans are. ## I didn't know you knew John Lennon, or didn't you mean it that way? # I never saw any dichotomy between liking sf and digging rock, but then I always dug rock & roll at least as much as science fiction. The people who're really having problems adjusting are the ones who completely despised rock a few years ago, being into jazz and folk snobbery. # In a sense, one reason we were all sf freaks years ago is that it was a way to get high, not in the same way as being drunk, which was all the term 'high' meant to us then. Now that 'getting high' is commonly accepted as an end in itself, science fiction is becoming more popular among young people, and music, drugs, etc. are being explored by fans. I think this accounts for a lot of what's happening. You'll notice that hippies who read a science fiction book don't do it because they like to read -- very few of them do -- they'll tell you it's because the book is "a trip." # As a matter of fact, James Wright's essay was not intended for fanzine publication. He asked me to make suggestions and to help him find a professional market for the piece or an expanded version of it. I printed it to get some more opinions, and yours is gratefully appreciated.))

WHO PUT THE BOMP #3   MAY, 1970

Published for the Rock Enthusiasts' Amateur Press by Greg Shaw of 64 Taylor Dr., Fairfax, Calif. 94930. This issue is intended for the third mailing. Press run is 50 copies.

As I type this, I'm listening to an album by a group called THE REMAINS, a forgotten group that I think merits more attention. At the very least, they should be familiar to members of this organization. So, for what they're worth, here are my thoughts on THE REMAINS. They were a Cambridge group, originally called BARRY AND THE REMAINS, after Barry Tashian, the leader, vocalist, and guitarist of the group. They got a contract with Epic, put out a few singles, one of which, "Diddy Wah Diddy" made the national charts. Then they accompanied the Beatles on their 1966 U.S. tour, and as a result of widespread favorable reviews, their first and only album, The Remains (Epic BN 26214) was released. It's really an excellent rock & roll album, considering the fact that it's a first effort. If the group hadn't broken up, I think they would have gone on to do some fine things. My favorite songs on the album are the fast rockers, "Heart", "Don't Look Back" (a very good song which a couple of local groups have done) "You Got a Hard Time Coming" and "Time of Day". Also of interest is their version of "Lonely Weekend", the song Charlie Rich wrote and had his biggest hit with on the Sun label, a long time ago. For simple unadulterated rock and roll songs, all 2-3 minutes long, with clean, classic arrangements and hard, imaginative guitar work, I recommend this album

"WHENEVER A TEENAGER CRIES"

as one of musical and historical interest, to anyone who enjoys the type of rock & roll I do. I ought to mention a couple of 45s by THE REMAINS that I've picked up in the promo bins. The flip of "Don't Look Back" has "Mr. Right Now" an early song that was not included on the album. (EPIC 5-10060) Another single has "But I Ain't Got You" a song that is so similar to the song of the same title done by THE YARDBIRDS and THE ANIMALS that it fooled me for awhile. They do it in a slowed-down folk rock style, maybe because they were conscious of the similarity and wanted to make it less noticable The flip is "I Can't Get Away From You", a good rocking song, but not memorable. (Epic 45 5-9872). I recall an article about a year ago on THE REMAINS. Thot it was in Crawdaddy or Hit Parader, but I can't find it there, and I'll be damned if I'll go through 2 years worth of Rolling Stones to find it. The gist of the article, which may have been by Jon Landau, is that the best work of THE REMAINS resides on some tapes and acetates that have never been and aren't likely to ever be released on record. There are also lots of facts and reminiscences about the groups early days. Too bad I didn't find it; I could probably have padded this into a 3-page article with the extra information.

* * * * *

The scholars in our midst will recognize "Whenever a Teenager Cries" as the one and only hit by REPARATA AND THE DELRONS (with Hash Brown and his Orchestra) in the early sixties. The flip is "He's My Guy", and it's not much better or worse than the A-side. Just another forgotten corny record, but it did have some good lyrics. (World Artists 1036) I would appreciate hearing from anyone who knows of any other records by REPARATA AND THE DELRONS, and where they are today. Reparata had a pretty good voice, I wouldn't be surprised if she's still in the business.

Easy Rider 1 (Scott Duncan) I dig folk rock too. I like everything The Byrds have done, especially the first couple of albums. Remember The Beau Brummels? How about the early Turtles? The original Grass Roots were into a good folk-rock sound too. Even P.F. Sloan and Barry McGuire and... Sonny & Cher! Another thing The Byrds and The Everly Bros. (please spell their name right!) have in common is the excellence of their vocal harmonies. On that score a lot of Beach Boys material could also fall into the same category. :: Billy Mundi is one of the finest studio drummers I know of. In '66 he played in San Francisco with a group called Thorinshield, and they sounded great. Played some songs based on Tolkien, too. Their album, recorded without Mundi, was a bomb. He's played with too many other groups to list (or even remember). :: I'm rather surprised to find I agree with most of your comments on groups. Not that my list wouldn't be completely different, but of the groups you mention my judgments are about the same. For someone not into rock that much, your assessments of the various records are very good, if rather brief. I agree that The Who Sell Out is a vastly underrated album. A great group that was widely ignored was The Spencer Davis Group, and I'm glad you mentioned them. They made some excellent records even after Winwood left, such as "On the Green Light."

Easy Rider 2 (Scott Duncan) I always liked Buffalo Springfield too, though I don't think they ever equalled their first album. I had occasion to see them in concert before most people ever heard of their name. It was in early 1966 and The Byrds were doing a tour of college campuses. With them on the tour were The Dillards and... an unknown rock group from Canada that wasn't even mentioned on the posters. I went with some friends to the College of San Mateo auditorium. "Eight Miles High" was just starting to slip down the charts and we all thought it was one of the finest rock & roll records we'd ever heard. The rest of the kids, though, seemed to be more interested in The Dillards; they laughed too much at the silly jokes, applauded too long, and called them back for an undeserved encore. Buffalo Springfield came on next and nobody liked them. Their songs ended to slight applause and a few boos. My companions thought they were really terrible too, but I rose to the band's defense. "Sure they're lousy musicians," I said, "but they have a lot of good original songs. They might be all right someday." I would have forgotten all this by now if it hadn't been a mere 6 months or so later that "For What It's Worth" was released, enabling me to associate the name Buffalo Springfield with that group of kids I'd seen with The Byrds. On that night, incidentally, The Byrds gave the only really great performance I've ever seen them deliver, even though they were greeted mostly by indifference. McGuinn was positively brilliant. Dillards, pfaugh.

I was never too fond of The Buffalo Springfield on record after their first album, but I considered them a great live act. They played The Avalon and the Fillmore a few times in late '66- early '67, did a lot of jamming with San Francisco musicians. I remember one 2-hour set they did at Fillmore, starting around midnight, during which they were joined by members of many groups, including Quicksilver, Moby Grape, and The Airplane. There wasn't much singing; they did songs everybody knew and let each other take long solos. There weren't many people there -- I think it was a private party or something -- and everyone was having a splendid time. I recall being very impressed with the guitar playing ability of one member of the Springfield, who in the light of what I know today must have been Neil Young.

* * * * *

So ends another issue of Who Put the Bomp. Nextish, #4, will be expanded into a genzine format, and available for public consumption. Tell your friends! It will be about 30 pages, profusely illustrated. It will be included in REAP if REAP still exists. Mailing comments will be published spparately. :: Glory be. No sooner had I run off the first page of this issue than Rolling Stone came out with a put-down of a new album by... guess who... Reparata and the Delrons. I saw them on "Scene 70" last week too, and the host, Clay Cole, said they were Very Big in Europe. Whaddaya know.

LIQUID LOVE #1

Intended for the 262nd distribution of Apa L. Written and published by Greg Shaw, 64 Taylor Dr., Fairfax, Ca. 94930 May 15, '70

It gives me a kind of funny feeling to be writing my first Apa L zine since Grunion 73, almost five years ago. It's been a long five years for me, and for the world too for that matter, yet LASFS seems oddly the same. A few old faces (names) moved away or disappeared, a few new ones whose zines are pretty much the same as those put out by the LASFS neos of 1965.

For the sake of those who haven't already fallen off their chairs at Kals at the sight of my name, a brief introduction: I was a member of Apa L from the 40th to the 73rd distributions. This was in '65 and '66, during my first fannish incarnation as a goshwow neofan. I was a fairly successful neo, putting out 5 issues of a popular genzine and 4 issues of Entmoot, a Tolkien fanzine that I'm told is still well thought of in some quarters. Circumstances (like the beginning of the Haight-Ashbury scene and the prospect of publishing a rock & roll prozine instead of fanzines, all of which I found infinitely more exciting than fandom) caused my gafiation, from which I surfaced briefly in early in '69, but which I'm really only emerging from now.

The LASFS occupies a special place in my heart. At the age of 15, as I was beginning to get involved in fandom, I was a rather frustrated kid. My family and the other kids Didn't Understand Me, so I turned to fandom for the relationships I needed. The LASFS, naturally, filled the bill ideally. Here was a ready-made social system into which I could fit and be accepted, even respected to a degree. Though I lived near San Francisco, my parents allowed me to go to Westercons, all of which seemed to be in Southern California at that time. I usually stayed with fans in LA for a couple of weeks in addition to attending the con, and on one occasion I even flew down to spend my Christmas vacation in LA and attend the LASFS Christmas party, confusing my parents no end.

It was those months as a sort of commuting member of LASFS that exposed me to the best things fandom has to offer, and some of the worst. Some of the finest people I've ever known were met in Los Angeles fandom. So it is partly nostalgia for those starry-eyed days when fandom was all Joy and Magic, and partly the desire to maintain certain relationships beyond the once-a-year meeting at conventions that brings me back to Apa L. I don't know how long I'll be staying this time, but for now you're stuck with me.

My current fanac includes publication of a monthly personalzine which usually runs about 12-14 pages called Karnis Bottle's METANOIA. Copies are available for a show of interest, such as a postcard. The first issue had a detailed account of how I live and what I do these days, as well as an introduction to my wife of 3 years, Suzy. I also publish a rock & roll fanzine called Who Put the Bomp.

Some comments on Distribution 260:

Gnomenclature 24 (Greg Chalfin): I don't know much about movies, but I know I saw one on TV a few weeks ago that doesn't seem to be on your list. The title was "Gammera" and it concerned the efforts of a giant, fire-breathing turtle to destroy the world, starting with Tokyo. Also, though seemingly intended for children, the Japanese series of movies based on the adventures of a character named "Starman" are really hilarious.

From Sunday to Saturday (Don Fitch): All the larger communes do have their own newspapers, mostly for distribution inside the group, to let people know what jobs need done, experiences of members, and often poetry & creative writing. Some, like the Hog Farm, Libre, and Harbinger, have published newspapers for outside distribution. I've heard rumors of a zine distributed only to communes consisting of solutions to common problems and such. The smaller groups, tho, are very reluctant to let anybody know of their existence, for fear of hordes of unwanted visitors. An apa limited to self-sustaining communities would be a good idea. Might happen someday.

LIQUID LOVE   ...published under rather peculiar circumstances for Greg Shaw, 64 Taylor Drive, Fairfax CA 94930

for Apa-L #264 by //////// Alpajpuri, his faithful companion and wonderdog. Wednesday 3 June 1970. PajPress X. What some people won't do to stay in an apa--

---

Dear Paj,   1 June 1970:

I'm writing this from the hospital--

No, don't rush off to send a telegram to Locus -- it's really a rather minor complaint. You'll recall from past correspondence that I have been ill to one degree or another the past month or so -- well, it got out of hand and here I am. I don't know how interested you are in the gory details, but I've got nothing better to do so I might as well fill you in. (Hope you can read my handwriting -- it's not very good to begin with and I'm writing this in bed besides.) ((Fortunately for all of us, I am experienced with codes and cyphers. -Paj.)) It started 4 weeks ago with a cold which I didn't take seriously, and developed into bronchitis, at which point I dropped by the hospital for a prescription, not having a family doctor. I got one and it fixed me up in a week or so, but I was so weakened (had been sick 3 weeks by now) that hyper-ventilation set in. Hyper-ventilation is where you're short of breath, panting, pulse racing -- not very pleasant. So we went back to the hospital, where an intern told me it was all psychological and prescribed some phenobarbitol. I gave him the benefit of the doubt because it fit in with some problems I already knew I had, and I achieved some success with some techniques I knew,

"gregory in hopspittle"

but hardly was that cleared up when asthma set in. This time I was really sick and the doctors decided to keep me here a week or so to get over it.

This presents some problems, not the least important to me is what to do about Apa-L. I enjoyed the latest disty immensely and cannot face the prospect of missing the next one. Therefore, I'm going to have to Impose on you. If you don't mind, there are several things you could do to get me a copy of 264. You could swipe a copy from under Fred's nose ((fat chance)) -- you could publish this letter by way of explanation along with the mailing comments I'm gonna write here -- or if the mcs go too long, just them. Don't worry about me, anybody -- I'll be out of here soon and am enjoying the vacation -- I'm catching up on a lot of reading.

Distribution Comments on Apa-L 263:

<u>B-Roll Negative</u> 40 (Ted Johnstone) Yeah, there sure is a lotta crap in the field. The only way is to check the various theories against your own personal experiences and observations. I think you'd enjoy the book I mentioned. :: The alphaphone being advertised in <u>Psychology Today</u>, <u>Whole Earth Catalog</u> and elsewhere isn't as good as the one my friends are putting out -- they call themselves Aquarius Productions and their thing isn't on the market yet -- but it amplifies both alpha and beta waves. It's really funny the way you can put one on and hear a different sound for everything that goes on in your mind -- you get a sort of non-verbal understanding of the relationships between the different mental processes -- maybe you could even learn to make music with it! :: I don't think anyone can afford to buy one except those people who spend $500 for a weekend at Esalen, but the thing to do is get your local school to order one. Maybe the LASFS would be interested. :: Why don't you put your address in Apa-L??

(over)

METANOIA 4

"I JUST WANT TO BASK IN THE AURA OF FANNISHNESS."

KARNIS BOTTLE'S, THAT IS...

A couple of months ago I sent away $10 for all the back issues of Fusion, only 3 of which are unavailable. As Rolling Stone has gradually slid over the past 2 years from 'great' to 'good' to 'disappointing' to 'poor' and finally, with the last 4 or 5 issues, to 'embarrassing', I've become more and more interested in this outspoken and frequently experimental publication from Boston. Fusion is the last bastion of the Crawdaddy! style of writing, but unlike the old Crawdaddy! it also provides a lot of valuable information about music and records, as well as some brilliant writing on occasion. I won't attempt to review 35 issues of Fusion, but I do suggest you check it out. It has suffered a slight decline from last year also, but it's still the best rock mag I know of (Big Fat, which started off with 2 great issues, has gone down the drain in 5). Their regular contributors include ex-fans Lenny Kaye and Joe Pilati.

Fusion 21 (11/14/69) was a special issue on 'the Great Divide', examining the differences in life-style, weltanschauung, and preferences in rock and rock writing between young people in California and those in the East and the rest of the country. I thought it was a very perceptive and necessary discussion. Included was a history of the San Francisco rock scene by John Kreidl, editor of Boston's Vibrations magazine. Kreidl's piece was surprising to me not only because I wasn't aware he'd been in San Francisco during that period but also because of the unexpected clarity of his understanding of what went on here in those days and his avoidance of most of the usual misconceptions that writers from other parts of the country have about San Francisco rock. In the midst of Kreidl's article I happened upon a paragraph that took me completely by surprise with some unexpected egoboo:

"Mojo-Navigator, the original rock magazine from San Francisco was far more representative of the spirit of 1967 than Rolling Stone is. Rolling Stone didn't kill this small publication, it just, apparently, died in 1968 due to an editorial squabble between Greg Shaw and its other editors. But Greg, to me, was tuned in to the mood of 1967. Rolling Stone, on the other hand, seems more out of the minds of slick San Francisco and its hip bankers and hipsters who believe in selling the San Francisco image. It's a kind of West Coast Billboard that seeks to export its image. It, I think, reflects San Francisco, rather than the spirit of rock. For this reason, historials interested in the cultural revolution of 1967, will have to check out Mojo-Navigator. Greg, last I heard, had started another publication, called Mojo-Entmooter. The spirit of '67 lives on. Footnote: Mojo belonged to UPS. Rolling Stone doesn't."

One reason I found his comments so surprising is that when I first discovered Vibrations I sent them a complete back file of Mojo and a letter; all I got back was one copy of their current issue with a note: 'letter follows'. No letter ever came. I assumed they didn't like Mojo. I guess Kreidl must've seen a copy of Mojo-Entmooter somewhere with the explanation of what happened to Mojo. Are any of you responsible?

Lester Bangs and Lisa Robinson at a party, 1971.

LIQUID LOVE 6 GREG SHAW 64 TAYLOR DR. FAIRFAX, CA.

Published for the 268th distribution of Apa L, to be distributed at Westercon 23 in Santa Barbara, on July 2, 1970.

WHITHER ROCK?

Dan Goodman brings up an interesting question in Apa L 266: "What do you think comes after rock? Something will, you know. The next bohemian generation will have its own music; which may be partially derived from rock but will likely bear no closer resemblance than rock does to jazz or folk."

It's a good question and it deserves an answer. Or at least some attention. To begin with, I question the assumption that musical trends originate with 'bohemians'. The folk craze of the early sixties is the only example I can think of that might qualify, and who can be sure how it started? Sure the beats dug folk, but wasn't that after the clean-cut college kids in the East started getting into it? I heard one theory that because popular music (R&R) was so rancid in those years ('59-'63) people were ready to assimilate folk on a mass scale, jazz (the only other 'honest' musical form around) being too esoteric by then. I myself am of the "the time was right so it happened" school. :: At the risk of stating the obvious, I'll point out that every other development in American popular music can be traced directly to black people, who have never had a sizeable bohemian generation, as I understand the term (though the black life style is certainly relaxed enough to appear bohemian to many rigid whites).

There's also the question of whether there will be a next bohemian generation, as Dan implicitly suggests. At times I doubt if there is even a current bohemian generation. As far as I'm concerned, the last time it was clear who was a bohemian and who wasn't was in 1966. As soon as the mass media picked up on the 'hippie' thing and high school (and even subteen) kids began adopting the appearance, habits, opinions, etc. of the fantasy media hippies, bohemian or 'hip' (a more convenient term) culture ceased to exist.

The way I understand the concept of what a bohemian is, it can't exist except as an alternative to something else. If everyone's a bohemian, then nobody is. Right? And I think that's where we're heading right now. Of course I don't mean to imply that the masses are really becoming hip, because they're not. The classic image of the bohemian is that of a sensitive, introverted, intellectual individualist. People like this seem to be getting scarcer (for better or worse -- I make no judgment) but the point is that the outward trappings of the way of life traditionally affected by these people have been adopted on a mass scale by young people in this country, making it impossible to tell the 'real' hip people from the mob. And since a true individualist would not stand for being part of a mob, he'd be likely to (a) go off by himself somewhere, or (b) start looking straight again and confine his deviations to the inside of his head. Both these alternatives are coming into use now.

The conclusion, of course, is that since hip people can't easily recognize one another anymore, communication breaks down, and any kind of 'hip culture' becomes impossible. :: I don't think the word 'hip' or any of the concepts associated with it will mean anything to my children's generation.

But what about popular music? Not enough is understood about how musical styles develop to predict what factors will be important in the next development, but that's no reason for me not to discuss some points which may be relevant.

To me, one of the most obvious things about pop music (though few pop music 'scholars' seem to be aware of it) is its close relation to dancing. People like to dance, and any form of music must be essentially danceable to attain wide popularity. This is especially true of black people, among whom in fact new dances

come first and the music springs up to meet the requirements of the dancers. I know next to nothing about the way dance styles change, but it seems to me that lots of forces are involved. There has been a steady progression in this century (and before too, I guess) from rigid, structured dancing to a looser, more expressive style. Certainly social forces are at work here, ideas of morality and so on, that have placed definite restrictions on the pace at which dance styles have been allowed to change.

The music itself has had no such restrictions; jazz was being played pretty much the same way 30 years before white people began dancing to it, and black people were playing and dancing to what is basically rock & roll in the late forties. So a case could be made that musical styles have become popular because they fit the way people wanted to dance at the time.

Another very obvious thing about pop music is the fact that it begins with black people, is picked up by hip whites, becomes popular among whites, loses its vitality, and degenerates while the blacks are meanwhile inventing something new. Black people seem to need their own in-group experiences that can't be shared with whites, especially in music, and this process has undoubtedly had a lot to do with the rich development of pop music in this century. :: So one approach would be to look to the blacks and see what they're doing. But there's a feedback process that needs to be examined first. The length of time it takes whites to pick up on black musical innovations has been growing progressively shorter until now it has practically reached the vanishing point. Black people were playing jazz 50 years ago and Dixieland for years before that. Whites picked up on it in the late thirties. They were playing R&B with electric guitars and all in the mid-forties. Whites got hip to it in the early-mid fifties. Blacks were playing pure rock & roll in the early fifties, and whites started doing it almost immediately, 2 or 3 years later, watching the new releases carefully and jumping on the good ones quickly with cover versions by the likes of Georgia Gibbs, the Crew Cuts, and Pat Boone, that sold in the millions.

For the past few years soul music has been the dominant force in black music. Yet while soul is popular among white kids, there's been no movement among white musicians to begin playing it. I think the mass-acceptance of soul music by the original black artists is responsible for this, because for the first time a black musical style doesn't need to be "cleaned up" and popularized by white musicians for white audiences that are afraid to listen to black music.

In the last year or two a lot of soul styles have been cropping up in white rock music. The syncopated, 'funky' beat ("Spinning Wheel", "Come Together"), the choppy guitar chording and short fast runs (Sons of Champlin, etc.) and, in part, the vocal styles of artists like Joe Cocker, Delaney & Bonnie, Dave Mason, et al.

But why has it taken so long for soul music to be assimilated into white music, when it's been the dominant form among blacks for almost ten years? During the sixties music went through two major and unexpected digressions. To begin with, The Beatles and their followers in 1963 turned up with a revival of the rock & roll of the mid-fifties mixed with some current soul songs. But they also had a third type of song, a purely white style of unprecedented vitality. I refer to songs like "She Loves You", "I Wanna Hold Your Hand", "Can't Buy Me Love", "All My Loving", "Hard Day's Night" and so on. Here again, as far as I can see, The Time Was Right, and suddenly any number of new groups were popping up, exciting and original music was being made. The time was right in the sense that the folk thing was pretty much played out and no clear alternative was being offered by the black musicians, for reasons that will be explored later. White, mid-sixties rock & roll flourished for a few years, then disappeared. Only a few diehards (like myself) still listen to or make such music.

The reason it disappeared is the second digression. "Psychedelic rock." LSD. Flower Children. All the rest. The San Francisco musicians were the first to express their drug experiences in their music, and it was good music. It was good because it wasn't about drugs ("I just dropped in to see what condition my condition was in"); it was music that couldn't have been made by people who hadn't experienced acid. The impact of drugs on the mainstream of musical development, though, occurred with the wide-scale popularization of drugs, in that much shallower people were having the drug experience and coming out of it with nothing profou but rather ideas like "Hey, I just had a heavy acid flash! Let's make a record about the windmills of the mind and the elusive butterfly of cosmic consciousness! Things weren't helped any by the fact that other shallow people bought up the records and thought it was all Very Significant.

1967 and part of '68 were the years of Psychedelic Rock. Some of it was good, most of it was worthless, but the significant fact here is that for the first and only time I know of an important trend in pop music arose without any cultural roots as a basis. That music didn't come from anybody's life; it came out of left field. It didn't reflect reality back to give people a better understanding of life as the best music does. All it related to was what went on in one individual's mind under the influence of a drug.

When the psychedelic thing died out after less than two years, it had already done its damage. It had effectively destroyed the development of white mid-sixties rock & roll. 1968 found everyone looking at his piles of pretentious psychedelic albums and feeling lost. Indeed, the pop music world was in limbo in 1968 and throughout much of 1969, and in this context it's easy to see why the "Rock & Roll Revival" happened. There was an instinctive grasping out for roots, for some music that was real, meaningful and satisfying. For this reason, also, the few groups that managed to keep their heads through it all and continued turning out honest music rose to unprecedented heights of popularity in the last 2 years of the sixties. The Stones' triumphant tour is the most obvious example, but more significant is the success of The Who and The Kinks, who both had their first large-scale hit albums in 1969.

So, let's put some of this together. What about black people? Soul music has shown no sign of change or development in 5 years or more. Everybody has been exposed to enough music by now so that it's hard to tell white from black sometimes, especially when both are copying from the same source. I think black people may be losing their position as innovators in pop music, partly because with increased afflence they're losing the unique experiences that spawned their music in the past. As far as dancing goes, the trend toward free and loose movement reached a peak in the LSD years with what was known in San Francisco as Freak Dancing. Shortly afterward the legions of youngsters doped up on marijuana began trooping in to the Fillmore to sit on the floors, and as long as marijuana is popular young whites will have no interest in dancing. That's just my opinion, of course, but there seems (as far as I can observe) to be a direct cause and effect pattern here, on a large scale (not to say that a particular individual can't enjoy dope and dancing both). Outside of the Fillmore, in the discotheques and clubs and at parties, the prevalent style of dancing seems to be the soul style, which is tight and rigid in a way never seen before. The pressures that drove the blacks to innovation in the past have plainly eased, and it doesn't look as if we can expect anything new from them in the foreseeable future, as far as music goes. So it doesn't look like dancing will be as large a factor as it once was.

Getting back to music, what comes next? Rock is still in a state of confusion, no doubt about that. All sorts of combinations of styles are being attempted in hopes of coming up with something that will become the next trend. We've seen soul rock (Joe Cocker), latin-soul-rock (Santana), jazz-soul-rock (BS&T), country-rock (one of the strongest movements, but lacking the necessary elements to give it world-wide appeal on any lasting basis) and, most promising of all, gospel-rock and gospel-soul-rock (Delaney & Bonnie, etc.) and a taste of "pure" gospel ("Oh Happy Day"). No one can deny that Gospel is an honest, rootsy music with great depth and power. It's also the only such form remaining that hasn't been bastardized and popularized into mediocrity, mainly due to black people's strong compnnctions against letting it out of the churches. They know what will happen.

But I don't think Gospel will be the next big thing. To return one final time to my "theright thing happens when the time is right" theory, I believe something will happen soon. I think the classical to jazz to pop to rock & roll to rock progression has ended. Each of those changes involved a fundamental change in the form and structure of music, as well as the instrumentation. I don't believe technology will be providing us with new instruments that will change the face of music. Moogs and such are gimmicks, and can be used to good effect as such, but electronic music will never achieve mass-popularity. All instruments, styles, structures, etc. are already possible in today's rock.

With communications as they are and the 'global community' predicted by McLuhan already taking shape among young people, music of universal appeal is needed, and to be universal it must be basic. People are becoming more and more concerned with things of truly basic importance, and any music that strikes a basic chord deep within its listeners will be popular. We're in the '70s now, and we have a need for our times to be reflected, and given form and meaning in the process, by our music. From time to time a musician or group of same will arise who are capable of doing so, using the styles and techniques available, with greater or lesser originality, and they will be the sensation of the moment. I personally believe that it's inevitable that a group will come along who will do for the seventies what the Beatles did for the sixties. And they needn't leave rock to do so, for rock has come to mean the music of our times, and as long as civilization continues on its present course, at least til the end of this century I'd say, rock will be with us.

Beyond that no one can say, but we can be sure that whatever life in the 21st century is like, the music that reflects the forces and pressures acting on people then in a form that provides meaning as well as emotional and spiritual catharsis will be the music that people listen to.

THE END, FOR NOW

R.I.A.W.O.L.
BY THE EDITOR

Good grief, not another rock magazine! Why, for Pete's sake? Surely there are enough already that everybody can read about his fave groups to his heart's content, and some would say that the market's even glutted. Well, I agree. The last thing in the world I'd do now is start another rock & roll magazine.

This thing you're reading, however, is something else again. Who Put the Bomp is rock & roll's first fanzine, by definition a thing produced and written by amateurs, for little or no profit, out of love for their hobby. The advantages of a fanzine are many: letters of comment, drawings, cartoons, and articles of any length can be published, with a wider range of subject matter than the professional magazines allow.

Hit Parader recently stated that it's the only rock magazine left that's not full of political crap. Well, they've got some competition now. Who Put the Bomp is devoted to the appreciation of music, and nothing else. Because so little really good rock & roll is being made nowadays, we'll be delving into the past frequently.

Some would criticize the Nostalgia Factor. Some say the music of the fifties was banal, others say we're evading the Important Social Issues of the day by remembering the high school record hops of our hazy childhoods. Nuts to them, we say. There were giants in those days, and their shadows still haunt the world of rock & roll. The issues were simpler then, perhaps: the kids wanted to rock, the grown-ups said 'no'. But then, I don't know about you, but I'd rather go down fighting for the right to rock than for the sake of closing an ROTC office.

I don't want to get into the habit of self-apology, so I'll set it out in front: I'm not omniscient; I'm not an "authority" on anything, even the music I love; and I'm not an especially gifted writer. I expect to make mistakes frequently, and I hope to be corrected. We can all learn from each other, if we want to.

For those who aren't familiar with the form, the essence of a fanzine is participation from the readers. Articles, reviews, drawings and such are submitted freely by the readers for publication. Readers are also expected to write letters of comment, giving their reactions to the magazine and their contribution to whatever discussions are going on. One incentive for doing this is the simple thrill of seeing your name in print; another is getting Free Issues.

There will be frequent reprints, mostly of stuff from old rock mags you're never likely to see, but sometimes (like in this issue) from current sources that you're not too likely to have seen either. This issue, with its preponderance of material about Sun Records, is a Theme Issue of sorts. I find it fitting in a way to begin this fanzine with a special issue on Sun, because in a sense white rock & roll as we've known it began with Sun Records.

I think it's a good idea to lump related material together in a single issue, and there will be future special issues whenever possible. Your suggestions would be appreciated. Any record collectors reading this are invited to write about their favorite old labels/artists, no matter how obscure. Also, any photos of rock artists dating from the fifties will be very gratefully used, and the utmost care will be taken to return them untarnished.

Please let me know how you liked this magazine, any ideas you have for improvements, whatever. Your interest will determine the amount of energy I put into it, the range of territory I try to cover, etc. I think the time is right for a rock & roll fanzine; I hope a lot of people agree.

* * *

Who Put the Bomp is distributed through REAP, the Rock Enthusiasts' Amateur Press (Assn.) as well as to the general public. REAP is a group of rock fans who also publish fanzines like this, though usually much smaller. The members send their fanzines to the Official Editor, who distributes bundles containing one copy of each zine received to each member. These mailings occur at six-week intervals. It's easy to publish your own fanzine; your local church, school, or community switchboard probably has a duplicator you can use. REAP currently has 16 members; the upper limit is 35. If you think you might be interested in joining, write for information to: Louis A. Morra, 14 Grove St., No. Attleboro, Mass. 02760.

DON'T BE SQUARE: SUBSCRIBE!

SQUARESVILLE COON TAIL DON'T KNOCK THE ROCK GET BENT SADDLE SHOES LAMPS
SILHOUETTES BUTCH WAX POST OFFICE THE MONOTONES BLUE BALLS PASSION PIT
 OUT TO LUNCH JAMES DEAN DUCKTAIL HOT LIPS WITH IT
FLAT TOP WHO WEARS SHORT SHORTS? M.M. WEENIE ROCK
SPIN THE BOTTLE THE LIVING END BOX CAR HOT TO TROT
SCREWY   B.B. 16 CANDLES
BILL HALEY SWITCHBLADE   JIMMY DODD
NIGGERLIPPING BAZOOMS   SOCK HOPS
B.M.O.C. FRANKIE AVAL   GOING IN BARE
BLOWING YOUR LUNCH   DIANA DORS MEA
PEGGED PANTS RUMBLES   ANNETTE PONYTAIL
J.D. BRANDO PLATTE   D.A. PECKER CH
AUL ANKA DOES SHE PUT   FRUIT BOOTS SO
BE THERE OR BE SQUARE   KNOCKERS HE
ATS AND KITTENS GANG BANG   RnR CRESTS
BEDROOM EYES THE 4-F CLUB RICKY   IT HAS A GOO
MERICAN BANDSTAND MAKE OUT ROCK AND ROLL   AN FREED
THE EDSELS GET A JOB COOL FABIAN   ZIP   VON DUTCH
LDIES BUT GOODIES PACHUCO STUD   SAL MINEO   WHEELS
CHICKEN FIVE POINTS FOR A PREGNANT NUN JUKE BOX JURY   SUCK G
EE YOU LATER, ALLIGATOR DION DE MUCCI TEEN ANGEL CRUISING WEDGIES
I'LL PLANT YOU AND DIG YOU LATER TEEN ANGEL POCKET POOL WHALE
OUL KISS KNOCKERS IS SHE A
FLYING SAUCER THE BIG BOPPER
LITTLE STAR TEENS AND QUEENS
WHO GOOSED THE MOOSE? CAPRIS
STRAIGHT ARRO   AT THE HOP
JUKE BOX JURY HEP CAT HANG
RRY LEE LEWIS RIP IT UP R&B
HALE'S TAILS SPINNERS PEEL

Speech bubble: "HI THERE, KATS AND KITTENS, TEENS AND QUEENS! WANT TO DIG THE DOINGS IN DISC-AND-DUNGAREE CIRCLES? SEE WHAT PLATTERS ALL THE HEPCATS ARE DIGGING? FIND OUT ALL THAT'S CLICKING WITH YOUR FAVE RAVE? THEN SUBSCRIBE TO WHO PUT THE BOMP, THE MAG THAT'S TOPS WHEN IT COMES TO KNOWING WHAT'S IN THE GROOVE WITH SOUND. YOU'RE A CUBE IF YOU DON'T DIG IT."

"I KIN DIG IT!"

Who Put the Bomp
64 Taylor Dr.
Fairfax, Calif. 94930

Hi there, fat cat. I don't want to be a square from Squaresville, so here's my
☐ $1 for 3 issues
☐ $2 for one year

NAME _____ ADDRESS _____
ZIP _____

METANOIA 5

MEET THE PRESS I had another first last week, when I visited the editorial offices of Rolling Stone. I went there to drop off some copies of my own rock and roll magazine, Who Put The Bomp, and hopefully to persuade someone there to give me a plug in their paper. Their offices are on the top floor of a 4-story brick building, but I didn't know what when I got there. Rolling Stone discourages visitors. The directory in the lobby contains no mention of Rolling Stone, and the stairs don't go anywhere, so after prowling about for a few minutes I was ready to give up. Finally I found the elevator. When the doors opened on the top floor I found myself in the middle of a large reception room. The secretary sits at a small desk heaped high with incoming subscription forms while a large switchboard blinks and buzzes constantly. Ignoring it, she talked to me for maybe 5 minutes about jewelry, magic, politics, and music before remembering that I'd asked to talk to a record reviewer. She ushered me through the impeccably furnished modern office to Ed Ward's little cubicle. Had a long talk with Ed; he's a fine person with excellent taste in music, a fact which had never impressed itself upon me from his writing. He dug WPTB, too, promising a nice plug in their next issue.

Before I left he took me back to say hello to Jann Wenner, the editor. Jann and I were old buddies from more than 3 years ago when he had been working for Ramparts, and I hadn't seen him in almost that long. It was a weird feeling, walking into his huge office, which looked like a spread out of Playboy. An enormous old carved wooden desk which covers half the wall dominates the room. In front of a full-length picture window Jann sat in a swivel chair talking to somebody. He was busy, so we just exchanged greetings. He was quite surprised to see me, and neither of us really knew what to say. A lot had happened in 3 years.

I talked to Ed a while longer, and we exchanged phone numbers, intending to get together some time and listen to records or something. As I was leaving, Pete Townshend walked in, just as if he were in the habit of visiting there every day.

"Hi Pete!" cried the receptionist.

I left, trying to convince myself I had plenty of interesting things to do.

Music editor of Rolling Stone Ed Ward and writer Ben Edmonds at the Fairfax cottage, ca. 1970.

HARRY WARNER I enjoyed the fourth issue of Karnis Bottle's Metanoia and felt particularly happy over the extreme faanishness of your editorial and the suggestion about keeping classics of fanzine writing in print. But I don't pretend to know how it could be done without an apparatus so elaborate that the project would collapse irrevocably over or rather under its own weight. Maybe the true solution will lie just a few years in the future. Office copiers are doing things more rapidly and less expensively than ever, if I may believe some publicity materials for the very latest and most expensive models. Wait a while longer and it's quite possible that everyone will have access to a machine that turns out copies in a couple of seconds for a penny or less per copy. Then a real system to keep fannish classics in print could be worked out quite easily. All you'd need would be someone who owns the classics and is willing to take ten minutes or so to fill orders via the high-speed, inexpensive duplicator down the block. Or look a few more years into the future, after almost everyone has his own video tape recorder. Even if the commercial interests make it impossible to do your own recording on it, fans will perhaps be ingenious enough to figure out a system, and then you can have hundreds of fanzines on a single reel of tape capable of being read through any television set with a stop-motion playback unit.

((How exciting! But for one thing, that's years off, and for another, the whole suggestion sounds rather fakefannish to me. A fanzine on videotape (or Xerox paper) just wouldn't seem fannish. Mimeo is quite cheap too, something like ½cent/page, and a person with a couple of hours spare time a day could handle the whole project easily and probably turn a small profit too.))

John Berry's correspondence wouldn't have been recognizable as such, if you'd just published this as a column by him. If I have attained any new accomplishments in recent years, it has been to snub ringing telephones when the circumstances warrant that treatment. Fortunately, mine has a volume control which when turned to its lowest position makes it inaudible from my bedroom with closed door.

Karnis Bottle's METANOIA No. 6

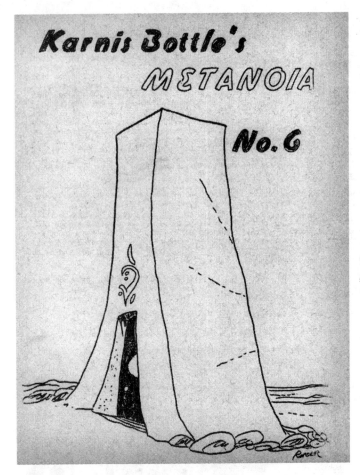

DANCING IN THE STREETS August sure has been an exciting month for us — just one thing after another. My Sense of Wonder got a real shot in the arm today from a totally unexpected direction, as I was running off some stencils in the heat of the afternoon. Suddenly the world was filled with music.

It was loud rock & roll music, and it "swung like mad", as Ralph Gleason sometimes says. It seemed to be coming from all around. Suzy thought it was a record, and I had to admit it sounded too good to be live, but no amplifier I could imagine would be capable of producing that kind of fidelity at that volume, so we set off to locate the band.

The music got louder as we approached downtown Fairfax (some 2 blocks from our house) and we saw that the parking lot in the center of town was beginning to fill up with people, some of them dancing. It wasn't until we were almost upon them that we realized the band was playing on the roof of Christiansen's Bakery. Besides the band, there were maybe 30 people up there, dancing and having a good time. As we got closer I became aware that they were playing a great arrangement of Dylan's "Highway 61".

The whole scene was somehow surrealistic. Suzy pointed out that of the 200 or more in the immediate area or drifting toward it, no one seemed older than 25 or so; most of the people around were teenagers. It was sort of like a scene from Only Lovers Left Alive, the simple exuberance of a hot summer day expressing itself through a spontaneous rooftop concert. No scowling oldsters were present, indeed no adults at all; no tac squads rushing to the scene in paddy wagons and self-righteous "the streets belong to the people!" posturing from the crowd, as the same event on Haight St. or Telegraph would've turned out. When the policeman drove past in his patrol car there were a few anxious looks, but he was smiling and flashing the "V" sign out the window.

We stayed through 3 or 4 songs; a drawn-out "Smokestack Lightning", a couple of originals, and some Kinks/Rolling Stones sort of rockers. The musicians, a nameless bunch of friends, were really outstanding, and the sound system was unbelievable. We dubbed the event "the Fairfax Non-Festival", in honor of the yearly Fairfax Festival, which had been cancelled this year due to some political ruckus with the conservative elements in the community.

Normally the Fairfax Festival attracts thousands over a 2-day weekend, with lots of music of different types, all the local artists and craftsmen displaying their wares, cotton candy and bicycle races, the whole thing, and all sorts of fun. This was no substitute for the Festival, but in a way it was even better, since apparently it hadn't been planned at all.

Wouldn't it be nice if things like that could happen everywhere, whenever people felt like getting together for a good time?

- - - - - - - - -

KARNIS BOTTLE'S mailbox

TED WHITE I'm curious about the whole recent Rolling Stone downer thing. I like RS a lot, although I think the record reviews are not only dreadfully uneven, but often just plain Wrong. But bad things seem to be happening lately. Advertising seems to be off quite a bit, the pages have been cut back to the 35¢-price-level (without cutting the price back), and I've been hearing all sorts of contradictory things about Wenner and the RS. Like, Independent News says RS is going to be the next One-Million-and-One Best Seller. But the advertisers have been going over to Crawdaddy. That seems foolish, unless they know something I don't know. And I've heard a lot of people are down on Wenner without knowing why about any of them. Compared with the other rock papers, I think Rolling Stone's prose is admirable. They seem to have at least some journalistic standards, while the rest of the papers allow such self-indulgent writing that it inevitably turns me off after a few paragraphs. But I know that a lot of people are down on RS for exactly this reason. I wonder why. Is readability really that objectionable to the Newly Hip? Oh well. I couldn't bring myself to read the Manson stuff. That this charlatan has become the new folk hero of the underground is a sad commentary on how easily the underground can be manipulated.

On the Crawdaddy front, things are bleak. The publishers seem to have been milking the till. All the most recent checks paid out -- to staff and contributors alike -- have bounced. (Mine was for $100, and it's the first time I've been burned professionally in nearly ten years.) The printer has been paid for none of the tabloid issues and is holding the 11th until he is paid. (Funny thing; I had a major piece in that issue. *Sigh*) The phones are off now, and I plan to raid the offices today for all I can carry away to hold in ransom for my money. And this at a time when advertising had doubled in the last two issues. Somebody just couldn't wait.

{{ Everyone seems to have different complaints about Rolling Stone, but it's pretty much agreed they're not doing the job they should be. John Wasserman, who replaced Ralph Gleason as the Chronicle's music columnist, ran a column last week explaining that RS had run out of money, three top editors had been laid off or resigned, and Greil Marcus (their best writer) had taken a leave of absence to work on his doctorate in Political Science. There was that item in Crawdaddy awhile back that they had hired some european designer to come up with a new format, which nobody around here can confirm, as well as all sorts of rumors floating around ("Wenner forced the whole staff to take a 10% pay cut so he could put paneling in his office") I think we can expect some big changes soon. As for Crawdaddy, no issue has been seen here since #7. I'm amazed their printer has trusted them for so long, but not that a crew of such inexperienced people has managed to grossly mismanage the magazine's financial affairs. Too bad, I hope they pull themselves out. }}

Greg, ca. 1969-70.

PAGE 58 — METANOIA #6 - AUGUST 1970 — BOMP! 2: BORN IN THE GARAGE

BY THE EDITOR

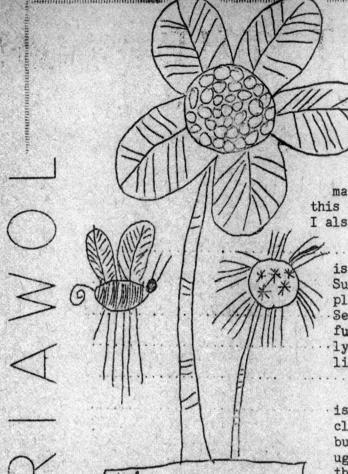

RIP AWOL

Well, here we are again—a month late perhaps, but here just the same. I'd like to keep to a regular schedule, but WPTB is published purely as a hobby, and the demands of making a living must take precedence. This issue was also hung up because I was awaiting an article that never materialized, which also accounts for this issue being so unbalanced, and for which I also apologize.

There were some omissions in the last issue, most notably in my review of the Sun reissue series, where I forgot completely to mention the "Golden Treasure Series", containing 67 reissued 45s. A full list of these will be sent absolutely free to anybody requesting it. The list includes the original release dates.

Since last issue the Sun album reissue series has gone up to 24 or so, including a couple of those anthology albums I was asking for. It looks as though Shelby Singleton plans on reissuing the entire catalogue eventually. Now ain't that good news!

THE AXE   Two hundred copies of the last issue were sent or given out, and the same goes for this one. For the most part they went to my mailing list of magazines and rock critics who have shown an interest in this type of music. Now, I don't see myself as an outsider trying to break into any "exclusive clique"—for one thing, I've had a good amount of experience in this scene and have known some of the top people in it on a personal basis for years—but, more importantly, that kind of snobbery doesn't interest me.

What I'm getting at is the reaction I've gotten to the last issue and some of my feelings about it. I publish WPTB for fun, and lose a fair amount of money on each issue. The only thing I'm interested in, aside from the pleasure of doing it, is knowing that others enjoy it.

I've gotten several fine letters of comment—which you'll find printed in this issue—and I wish to thank everyone who wrote for their consideration and encouragement. But 5 or 6 out of 200 isn't very good, you know, and I think that when I go to the trouble of seeking out your address and sending you a complimentary copy, the least you could do is drop me a postcard or something so I'll know if you liked it or what your opinion is.

Of course there's always the chance you didn't like it, which is the only way I can interpret non-response. Accordingly, all you freebies, this is the last complimentary copy you'll be getting unless I hear from you.

AND FURTHERMORE   This whole matter of friendliness and communication between rock fans is a subject I could go into at some length. Is it so hard to send a trade copy of your mag to another publisher? Apparently John Kreidl doesn't think so, and VIBRATIONS isn't exactly the most prosperous rock magazine. But what about the rest of you? I don't care about getting free copies--I already subscribe to most of the rock mags anyway--but it's the principle of the thing that matters to me. I'm interested in opening lines of communication between fans with common interests--to everyone's benefit--and I think that's a goal worth sacrificing a little ego for.

BUT SERIOUSLY, FOLKS... There are enough amateur rock publications now that we can begin developing some rules of social conduct which will promote the common good. To this end, I have some suggestions:

All of us publishers should begin accepting similar publications in trade. This not only increases communication among us, but encourages others to begin amateur magazines of their own. This doesn't represent any threat of competition--people who are interested in the type of thing we're doing will want to be getting all of the various publications--and besides, it's simply the decent thing to do.

We (and in this I include the large circulation magazines like ROLLING STONE, FUSION, etc.) should commence listing, if not regularly then occasionally, the other amateur publications, with information as to price and availability. This has the advantage of making the readers of any one magazine aware of all the others, and increasing the collective circulation of the field--as well as giving a boost to beginning publishers. A further development of this idea is to have reviews of the latest issues of these magazines, an area I'll be getting into soon.

The advantages to an increased degree of communication among rock fans are too obvious to be belabored. Authors of scholarly work or other amateur rock journalism will be able to select which publication suits their work best. Greater availability of information on the amateur press will bring in new writers and contributors. If we really have the interest in reading and writing about music that we pretend to, these must be acknowledged as worthy goals.

I'd like to point out in closing that enough special interest groups have been studied to establish common patterns of development. Science fiction fandom, some 40 years old, has the most advanced social order, but many other groups have followed similar paths. Jazz and folk music fandom in the fifties had incorporated all the developments suggested in this column and more, and provided highly successful and rewarding experiences for all the people involved. Rock & roll fandom is relatively young, but there's no reason we can't take advantage of existing knowledge to hasten its development into a living, healthy organism.

* * *

RECOMMENDED FANZINES:

STORMY WEATHER (Lenny Goldberg, 95 Moss Ave. Apt. 5, Oakland, CA 94611 6/$3) Oldies & newies, photos, interviews, reviews.

ROCK 'N' ROLL COLLECTOR (Roger 'Hot Rock' Ford, 27 Hartington Rd, Canning Town, London E16 3 NP.) For serious collectors only - heaps of obscure information

QUARTETTE (Dick Horlick, 1005 Market St. San Francisco, CA 94103 $1) devoted to black R&B vocal groups.

LENNY KAYE 418 Hobart Rd., No. Brunswick, N.J. 08902

Many thanks for WHO PUT THE BOMP, which I got in the mail a little while ago and found extremely interesting. To see something combining my two loves -- fanzines and rock 'n roll -- into a really finely done whole is nothing short of great, and anything I can do to help you will be done. I was particularly intrigued to read about REAP (probably since I'm about the only person alive to make it to the top - #1 - of the FAPA waiting list and not get in because I forgot to respond at the last minute... oh, well...).

It's nice to see such things happen, as it only means that new blood will be constantly shoveled into whatever the professional rock press happens to consist of, and on the other hand, the professional rock press people will have someplace to go to kind of relax and write about all the little esoteric things that interest them. Whatever, it can only bode for the good.

As to your first issue, I thought it was a really nice piece of work. The piece on Sun was excellent, well-deserving of reprinting in this country, and the reviews were all uniformly good. The layout and reproduction of the magazine was faultless, and the two-color mimeo worked well. In all, it's a fine job and only promises good ahead.

On another note, I've been throwing information into my column (on music, of course) for Cavalier on most of the amateur rock magazines, and in the...ummm..I think it's the December issue (which should be on sale around Nov. 1), I did a little thing on yours. I don't know how much effect it will have, since Cavalier's readership is not noticeably into much of anything, but I at least spelled your name right.

Again, thanks for the magazine and I hope to see a lot more of them.

{{Thanks, Lenny, for everything. You've accurately summarized my plans for WPTB, and if I can get it to the right people (and get a reasonable number of them to respond) it should be a success. Meanwhile, I hope you'll set an example by writing in about all those little esoteric things you've got on your mind... The chief problem with a zine like this is getting it to the people who'd be interested; I'm considering taking ads in the various trade papers, but I already lose 10¢ on each copy I sell, and I'm not sure that's the correct solution. I think the rock prozines should take a greater interest in the rock fan press (see Editorial). Now, if someone like yourself were to write an article on rock fandom for say, FUSION, it might put some interesting things in motion... }}

ooooooooooooooooooooooooooooooooooooooooooooooooooooooooooooooooooooooooooooooooo

Thanks to all who wrote. I'm really pleased with the response, though I'd like to see more, as I said in the editorial. A big part of the problem seems to be that most people simply aren't conditioned to writing letters in response to magazines. I'm thinking of someone who told me a great story a friend had told him, and suggested I send a copy of WPTB to the friend. I did, making reference to the story and suggesting it would make a good letter. He never wrote back, but I'm going to write the letter to show how it can be done:

"The article on Sun reminds me of a friend I used to have. This guy was a nut for Sun Records. He had, believe it or not, an alter in his living room that was dedicated to Jerry Lee Lewis. The fellow was an absolute freak for rockabilly records --whenever I'd run into him he'd collar me and lay on a rap about some new one he'd gotten, becoming very excited. One night we were listening to records and getting stoned, and about 2 am he started wondering what ever happened to Carl Mann. Finally he just had to know so bad he phoned Sam Phillips in Memphis, waking him.
  "You gotta tell me," he begged, "What happened to Carl Mann?"
  "Fuck off," said Sam Phillips, and slammed down the phone. "

METANOIA

Suzy models one of the necklaces made by Greg, holding the latest batch of leather goods turned out by her Snazzy Leather Company. 1969.

no. 7 - SEPT./OCT./NOV. '70

KARNIS BOTTLE'S METANOIA #7, Sept./ Oct./Nov. 1970, is a product of Greg and Suzy Shaw, of 64 Taylor Dr., Fairfax, CA. 94930 (453-9323) This monthly fanzine is available free on request to anyone who likes science fiction but doesn't have a compulsive need to talk about it, with a few exceptions. BRAIN TEASER: Find 3 errors in the above paragraph.

METANOIA, "THE REGULAR FANZINE" Well, here we are again, much later than ever, but not especially caring. These have been busy weeks for us, the busiest in recent memory. I'll try to give you an idea of what we've been up to lately in this issue, probably more than you care to know, but then this is supposed to be a "personalzine", isn't it?

To begin with, one of the biggest events of my life took place in September. After putting it off for years, and making up elaborate rationales for avoiding it, I've finally bought a car and learned to drive. Other long-cherished principles of mine have gone the way of my determination not to drive at the same time, including my vows against buying anything on time and borrowing money.

But let me start a little earlier. At the beginning of Sept. we found ourselves with a larger market for leather than we could keep up with, due to "back to school" buying. So we worked a couple of weeks' worth of 10-hour days, at the end of which we found ourselves with $700 in the bank. This alone was curious, because last Christmas we worked much harder for twice the time, had so much business we were forced to employ half our friends to help us out, had $500 checks coming in weekly or better -- and yet, at the end, we had practically nothing left over.

But as we sat around in mid-Sept. contemplating our $700, a brilliant and intricate plan took shape in our minds, dazzling in its logical simplicity and foolproof certainty. The months of Oct. and Nov. are very slow in the leather biz, you see. Ordinarily we'd spend these months goofing off, then work like maniacs to keep up with the demand in Dec. But what if we, instead, were to borrow some cash -- say $1500 -- and work 6-8 hours steadily for those two months? We'd have hundreds and hundreds of purses and vests on hand for the Christmas rush; we'd get rich!

Suzy's mother offered to borrow the bread for us, so we were all set. Except for one thing -- the one store we work through could never be expected to move $5000 worth of our merchandise in one month. The inescapable conclusion was that we had to have a car. A car was a rapidly-approaching necessity in any case, because Suzy is now afraid to hitch-hike and we are running out of friends willing to put up with taxiing her around.

Well, you can relax, because I'm not going to bore you with the details of what I had to go through before we got that car. It would fill the rest of this magazine. Bank loans were arranged, fell through, had to be arranged elsewhere. No insurance company wanted anything to do with me, because I was only 21 and hadn't driven before. Finally, after expending most of our $700 on insurance and going through a thousand other hassles, we found ourselves with a bright new slightly-used 1970 Toyota in our driveway.

Learning to drive it was another hassle, and though I speak in past-tense, I've only begun to learn at this writing. So cross your fingers for me, and have some forebearance if the next issue of METANOIA is a bit late. I look forward to almost three months of long days at the leather works combined with extensive amounts of long-distance driving. But if all works out, METANOIA might be coming to you next spring inscribed on tablets of solid gold.

"$1,000. That's not too much." **Frank Lunney, BAB-11

When Frank Lunney starts using Burbeeisms, you can be sure that something's in the air. In the air, everywhere! Even in Karnis Bottle's METANOIA. Yes, the fine and noble spirit of trufandom is moving again, and it is trying to move Bob Shaw from Ireland to Boston. And I see no reason why it shouldn't. After all, that's not too far.

I've decided to participate by dedicating an issue of METANOIA to the cause. The first issue of 1971, probably #9, will be a Special BoSh Issue. I don't know what the contents will be, but I promise you it will be as "stellar" an issue as I can make it. I wouldn't charge money for it if I didn't think it was worth something. Ah, yes -- money. The cost will be 50¢, all funds to be donated to the Fund. No one except contributors will get free copies. So send in your six bits now if you like, or later; but do it. It's the least you can do.

YES, IT'S
KARNIS BOTTLE'S
metanoia   NO. 8
(rhymes with "late")

The Beach Boys for President

THE EDITOR APOLOGIZES One of the hazards of publishing a monthly fanzine for awhile is that everyone assumes you've gafiated the first time three months go by without an issue. But I guess it's my fault for trying to fit a quarterly fanzine into a monthly schedule. To call #7 the "Sep/Oct/Nov" issue was barely permissible, but to follow it up with a "Dec/Jan/Feb/Mar" issue would be folly. So, METANOIA is now officially "irregular." I call this the February issue, though most of you won't get it until March, and I have hopes of getting #9 out in March as an *annish*, as well as the Bob Shaw Issue. By the way, all you sluggards who haven't sent in your 50¢ yet: better hurry. There won't be many more printed than I have advance orders for, so it's bound to become a collector's item. I have some terrific items lined up, and I expect that METANOIA 9 will be an even better issue than SCIENCE FICTION TIMES #437. How many of you can make that claim?

Last year's METANOIA was the product of my circumstances, and enough changes have occurred since then to make it impossible to continue in that way. When I began MET, life consisted of repititious leather work and boredom the rest of the time. I felt like recording my thoughts in a modest fanzine, and MET was the result. It was easy to put out monthly -- I could've done it weekly if I wanted -- and I had little reason to expect anything to change. But it did, and as METANOIA grew in size and reputation my extra-fannish life also grew, making for a tight squeeze.

My re-entry into rock & roll prodom has been chronicled in these pages, from my first attempts at record reviews to the ecstatic reports in #7 of my first sale. Since then I've sold more reviews and articles than I care to count, and the obligation to produce material for a paying market now occupies a large part of my mind.

Still another monkey is gibbering on my back in the form of WHO PUT THE BOMP. That fanzine was begun early last year at the request of Louis Morra, for his abortive rock apa, REAP. When REAP folded I felt like continuing to publish my thoughts on music, and to my surprise, the magazine has grown in six months to a position where the top pros in the rock field are telling me they think it is the most important publication currently coming out. I'm a sucker for that kind of talk, and to keep it coming in I've been devoting more time to editing WPTB, and producing some large issues.

I'm not making excuses for METANOIA's decline -- that would be dumb -- but simply trying to show you why I don't feel it's possible to continue it as a monthly.

What I will do is publish an issue whenever I find a spare week among my other activities. There's no telling how often that will be, but I'll be very surprised if four months ever go by without an issue. Unless some other big changes come along. Ya never know, ya know.

LIFE WITH DADDY-O Now that you've been filled in on my progress as a rock critic, it's time to catch up on local affairs. It's been so long that I've forgotten a lot of the goofy little stories I had about things that happen around here. A couple of the most interesting events have been written up more formally and will appear later on in this section. Aside from those, the biggest event was our taking in a houseguest. It was a girl named Marion whom we'd known casually. She's a bit of a nut, and one day she found herself on the fourth floor of a building and decided to jump. When she hit the ground her feet, legs and back were pulverized. They kept her in the hospital for two months and another two months in the mental ward, and by the time she was ready to be released Suzy and I had somehow agreed to let her stay here awhile, because her house has steep rickety steps and she would be wearing a body-cast and walking on crutches for a few months.

We thought she wanted to stay maybe a few days, but it turned out she intended staying a month. You would better comprehend the extent of our horrification at this news if you could but see our house, which contains only one large room with our bed in it, plus kitchen, bath, a roofed-over porch that serves as a workroom and a small closet-sized room across the kitchen that is normally piled high with junk. It was in the latter room that Marion slept, not 15 feet from our bed.

It was a hassle while she was here because she was constantly underfoot, asking silly questions, interrupting our work incessantly, and creating messes that Suzy was kept busy all day cleaning up. Plus, Marion seemed to attract people. Every day her boyfriend, whom we like, would visit with one ormore of his friends, whom we usually didn't. And since they usually stayed for supper, Suzy's work was further compounded. On top of that, it seemed that in some super-natural way Marion was responsible for all sorts of unlikely people coming to visit us. Acquaintances we hadn't seen in years were popping up every day or so. People from all corners of the country decided to spend the night while she was here. A surprise 2-day visit by James Wright, followed by a fun-filled overnight visit by Jonh Ingham were just two of the unexpected dividends of Marion's presence.

But she finally left after 3 weeks, and in retrospect I'm glad she stayed with us. Not only did Suzy and I both learn a lot about the limits of our tolerance, but through Marion we found a new friend. This is no light matter with us, for our standards for potential friends are very stringent. They must be cheerful, lovable, not pushy or judgmental, not users of drugs, and not into any weird political trips. Among other things. (We tried for awhile to exclude marijuana smokers, but found that we had no friends at all.) With these criteria, we now have 2 friends, or 3 including Poggi (pronounced Po'-zhi). Poggi came to visit Marion one day and we hit it off instantly. Though he was raised in San Francisco, he speaks with a strong Louisiana accent, and it's not an affectation. Hearing him speak is a delight. Where anyone else would say "Wow!" or "God!", Poggi says "dawg!" The greatest thing about him, though, is the way you can say any word or phrase and he'll come right back singing the first few lines of some old rock & roll or blues song that starts with it. We've made a game of it, saying things like "birdbath" and "shoehorn" but he always has a comeback. When nobody is saying anything he's likely to burst out spontaneously: "Hey little girl in the high school sweater..." Poggi collects blues records, and always brings a bunch for me to tape. We love him.

He's also the only person I've ever known who was heartsick. Ever since his true love left him for another guy, he mopes around singin' the blues. All his friends say she's no good, but he keeps wishin' and hopin' for her to come back. It's refreshing to see someone be so earnest about something as old-fashioned as love. There can't be many people like Peter Poggi left.

Sugarloaf modeling some of Suzy's Snazzy Leather wear on the cover of their otherwise very un-Bomp-like 1971 LP *Spaceship Earth*.

PAGE 64 — METANOIA #8 - FEBRUARY 1971 — BOMP! 2: BORN IN THE GARAGE

I mentioned to Jonh recently how at one time, drunk with power, I decided to make the rock & roll world over in the image of fandom. We had a good laugh over that one, but not for the reason you might think. The fact is that the people who write about rock are so anxious to become a fandom that their enthusiasm exceeds even mine in the matter. You should see the letters I got after the second issue of WHO PUT THE BOMP. Editors of rock magazines were writing to say they thought the fanzine concept was just what the field needed, writers declared in a chorus that it was about time there was a medium with no limitations on what can be written, and in short everybody thought the idea was just ducky. It appears likely now that the next year will bring a whole slew of imitators, and with them a whole new dimension of rock criticism.

At that Jonh and I got to talking about the advantage we possessed in having already learned at the feet of the masters, as it were, here in SF fandom. With the benefit of 30 years' collective experience in fanzine publishing, what seems to us a very routine matter of editing, appears to the other rock fans to be astonishing expertise. The apparent confidence our productions exude also attracts the best writers, helping still further to put us at the top of the field, ensuring that future fanzines will choose our example as a model.

So it looks like science fiction fandom, that degenerate old sot, is about to spawn still another bastard offspring.

Another surprising thing, to us, has been the response to Jonh's revival of the ill-fated REAP. Under Louis Morra REAP was a huge disappointment. Those fans who knew the most about rock didn't seem interested in joining, and what few did were soon discouraged by Morra's incompetence as an OE. Jonh changed the name to FRANK'S APA (get it? Get it??) and sent off a sheet explaining it to every rock critic he could think of, as well as fandom's leading rock fans. The response has been astonishing. Not somuch from the fans, but the critics, even "famous" ones like Jerry Hopkins, Lester Bangs and Lisa Robinson, have reacted with huge enthusiasm. The first deadline is April 1, so we'll see then just how viable the idea of a closed discussion apa for rock critics is. I have few doubts.

What it all ads up to, with the prozines re-evaluating their roles, looking for a wider audience and more diverse writing; with dissatisfied fans deserting the corrupt prozines (ROLLING STONE etc.) for the ones whose editors really care about rock & roll (only CREEM, at this point) and the fanzines like WHO PUT THE BOMP. The view that rock & roll is becoming like an underground cult to be kept alive in just such form as a fanzine has been making the rounds too, now that we appear to be several years from a rock & roll resurgence. The idea is to have the people who really care band together, contribute to each others publications (fan or pro -- there's not much distinction in this field) and discuss together the music they love. The reason a fan press becomes necessary is that, as the public becomes less interested in real rock & roll, the big prozines have to shift their interest accordingly to survive. People who've known how powerful rock can be in the hands of a Dylan, or a group like the Stones, Who or Yardbirds, aren't about to be satisfied reading about James Taylor. Hence an underground.

Do you see the parallels to fannish fandom yet, Terry?

AN OLD FAN AND TIRED, AT 22   I'm glad the discussion of fannishness has died down, because I don't think the issue has much validity any more. I think the signs of a revived fannish fandom were an illusion seized upon with varying degrees of desperation by a lot of people like myself who've been dissatisfied with what fandom's becoming. I read something recently that had a rather deep effect on me. It was an article written by Vernon McCain in 1952, talking about the prewar fandom that he'd just missed being a part of. He was waxing strongly nostalgic over an era of comaraderie and solidarity in fandom that he knew would never again be possible. This hit me because when I first came into fandom I had the same reaction when I discovered a large collection of fanzines from the early 50s and began to pick up some of the feeling that seems to have existed then among fans. It's clear now that those days are gone forever, and I have no choice but to conclude that the type of fanac that existed in the late fifties and early sixties is another relic of a bygone era, gone now having left no impression on the world but a wealth of fading memories in the minds of a couple ofhundred fans. None of it can ever return because the world has irrevocably changed. It seems to me that society is no longer producing the type of misfits who made the best fannish fans or the conditions that forced them to retreat into fandom, and while this may be good in ageneral sense it is unfortunate for fandom.

It pains me to see fandom coming to a place where it can be most properly defined as a group of fawning pro-worshippers, conveniently organized for more efficient exploitation by publishers and press agents. Sounds like a description of the Frankie Avalon Fan Club, doesn't it? Is that what we want to be? They used to say "It is a proud and lonely thing to be a fan." Looks quaint now, doesn't it? Another old truism rendered archaic by the advancements of the Space Age. Well, I feel too old to fight it. I also feel too old to fight any "Holy wars", but I seem to have one on my hands anyway, in the form of one of the young Turks of the ISFS.

EVERYONE'S FAVORITE FEATURE: And now kiddies, to round out the editorial section of this issue of METANOIA, we have my world-famous comments on the exciting world of rocknroll.

The most interesting thing happening in rock right now has nothing to do with music. I'm talking about the changes in the "rock press": nine different tabloid newspapers which provide American fans with their information on rock groups. What's happening is that the traditional folded-over tabloid format pioneered by ROLLING STONE is fast becoming obsolete, thanks in large part to the success of RAGS, which comes out as a saddle-stitched magazine, though still using newsprint. The magazine format provides a neater appearance, as well as better distribution and display opportunities. ROLLING STONE has no intention of changing, but the #2 and #3 papers do. The best rock magazine in the U.S. right now is CREEM, though it is only #4 at best in circulation. All the best writers are writing for CREEM now because of its editorial outlook (the difference between CREEM and RS is sort of like the difference between AMAZING and ANALOG). With the next issue CREEM goes to a RAGS-style format, in a drive to become the leading magazine. Meanwhile FUSION, which is #2 or #3 in circulation, plans the same thing for later this year.

Along with the changes in mechanical format, CREEM, FUSION, and RS too are trying to become more than mere "rock magazines." The emphasis now is on exploring all sorts of unlikely subjects which may throw some light on what's going on in the world. In 1970 several articles on comics and comic fandom (one of them titled "Fandom Is a Way of Life" !!) appeared in the rock press. This year science fiction fandom will come under the same treatment. Jonh Ingham has been commissioned by CREEM to do a confeport on the upcoming Westercon -- with them paying his airfare and lodging! They also want him to do an article on SF fanzines, and I've already done one on rock fanzines. Of course I don't mean to say that the rock magazines will only give coverage to fanzines. Several of them now have regular columns on politics, food, sports, films and books.

A new magazine is due to come out in San Francisco this month, edited by five former ROLLING STONE editors. It is to be called FLASH, and, if it succeeds, will go further than any other in reaching a broad-based readership. In addition to the usual book, film, record, concert etc. reviews, the first issue will have editorials on matters of importance to the "youth culture", columns on how to do various things, an article on wrestling during the years 1952-56 by Richard Meltzer (the most original writer in the English language since Tom Wolfe - only he's much better than Wolfe) with photos taken by the 8-year old Meltzer, and, finally, an interview with Groucho Marx. Oh yes, and Alexei Panshin will have an article dealing with films in the issue as well.

So anyway the next few months will see the first big change in the rock press since the field came into being 4 years ago. If it succeeds, we'll be reaching a much wider audience than ever before, and have a lot more financial success to pass around.

(continued on p.14 - 4 pages hence)

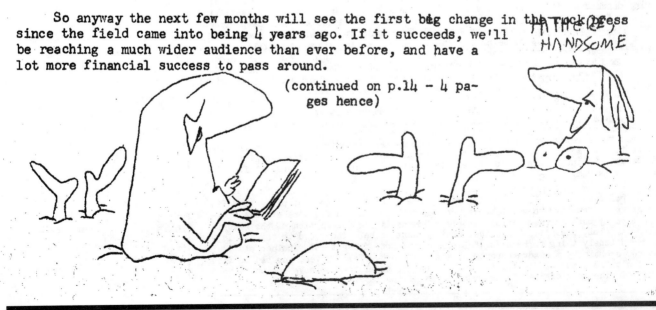

MUSICATORIAL, continued   Like I said, there's not an awful lot happening in the world of rock music. The deterioration of the established styles is proceeding, with no sign of anything that could be the start of a new period of growth. There is though, as there was during the similar dry period in the early 60s, a lot of good music coming out here and there; music that, though good, is only remarkable because of its defiance of the general downward trend. One sidelight that has interested me is the incidence of new groups whose repertoire consists of hard rock songs from the 50s. Always before, as with Sha Na Na, the music was only revived to be ridiculed. Now it is being taken seriously as the exciting form it is. In England the Wild Angels, eschewing long hair and psychedelic fashions, has built up a huge following playing old Elvis, Jerry Lee Lewis, Eddie Cochran songs with a freshness and vitality that has been absent too long from the music scene. The Wild Angels have spawned a dozen or so imitators in England, and here in the States a similar movement is underway, with groups like Brownsville Station, Frut, the Flamin Groovies, and Warren Phillips & the Rockets doing much the same thing, though with a good deal less polish.

One new record that has given me a lot of thrills is Bad Rice, by Ron Nagle. The lead cut, "61 Clay", has more power and excitement than anything I've heard since Let it Bleed. If you liked "Gimme Shelter", pick up this album. It should be released any day now.

My apologies to those who like to see more formal record reviews in these pages, but I'm afraid that's no longer feasible. If you like my reviews that much go subscribe to CREEM, where most of them are printed. Subscribe to it anyway if you dig rock, especially if you've wondered why a lot of people are calling ROLLING STONE "a load of rubbish" lately. There is an alternative... find out about it. (50¢ sample or $5 sub. to CREEM, 3729 Cass Ave., Detroit, Mich. 48201) Tell 'em Groucho sent ya.

The finishing touches are being put on this issue during the course of a madcap weekend during which I'm meeting Jonh Ingham at the airport, taking him along to Joh Berry's farewell party, introducing him later to the staff of FLASH, and sending him off to a wild party Atlantic Records is throwing for Aretha Franklin. Then, after tying up all my affairs here, I'll be driving to LA with Jonh to stay at his house for a week while I try to convince a plethora of record company officials it will be in their interest to take advertising in WHO PUT THE BOMP. I'll try to write up all these thrilling adventures for the next issue instead of the usual boring narratives. Wish me luck!

o o o o o o o o o o o o o o o o o o o o o o o
KARNIS BOTTLE'S METANOIA #8 is published irregularly as the official organ of the Society To Keep Greg Shaw in Fandom, a non-profit organization. It is free to all comers, but beware: not everyone can handle this heady brew. Editorial offices are at 64 Taylor Dr., Fairfax, CA. 94930, and if you care to speak to us the number is 453-9323. This issue will be finished on March 7, 1971.

FAME CAN BE A FLEETING THING   Our friend Peter Menkin, out of a job and broke, got the idea to do a story about Suzy's leather crafts for RAGS, the free-form underground "fashion" magazine. After phoning Baron Wolman to get authorization, he came over here to tell us the news. Suzy was very excited at the prospect of an article about her, especially since ROLLING STONE's story on me had just come out, so we invited Peter to come over the next day and do it. By coincidence, when he got here I was showing some of my old dance posters to a guy who was interested in buying them. They were arrayed all over the kitchen, and what with me dashing back and forth from my prospective customer to supervise the photography in the living room, I guess things seemed pretty hectic. We were expecting, though, that in writing his story Peter would draw on his knowledge of the way we live to do an honest portrayal of Suzy's talents. When he came over the next day with the finished story, it was so inappropriate that Suzy was deeply insulted and I informed Peter that if he allowed RAGS to print it, we'd sue. "You just don't understand, Peter!" I kept saying, "This story would fit beautifully in METANOIA, but we don't want half a million strangers to get the idea we're the couple of nitwits you portray us as!" "So print it in METANOIA!" he said.

So here it is, complete and unexpurgated.

SNAZZY LEATHER COMPANY

BY PETER MENKIN

Disaster struck the Snazzy Leather Company, Fairfax, California around three in the afternoon. Suzy and Greg Shaw (founders and owners of the well-known firm) dropped their various scissors, glue and leather thongs throwing up their hands in fear.

"But fear not," Greg said. "Though the television set may have failed us, the tube going on the blink, we shall persevere." Those weren't his exact words, but his exact actions were to pull from the closet, in which hang the various leather purses and vests produced by the Snazzy Leather Company, another television set. Their back-up equipment.

Plugging it in, while Suzy rushed to the phone calling a repair shop, the set came to life in sound only. "It's impossible," cried Suzy, according to highly unreliable sources. "Disaster can't strike twice in the same company, same house, same spot and same way."

Greg, again taking calm control, began to quiver when he realized he wouldn't get to see LET'S MAKE A DEAL. "It's my favorite show. I'm waiting for them to give away Rhode Island," he says.

As in all stress situations the human animal regresses and this case was no different. Suzy began cutting leather, cutting, cutting, cutting like mad as she does all day, every day. With her head down she couldn't see the set. She could hear it. Greg is the only one who cheats by looking up now and then when someone on THE DATING GAME or THE NEWLYWED GAME makes some fantastic remark.

It is a commonly known fact that the Shaws started Snazzy Leather for something to do while they watched television. "Two years ago," Suzy reports, "somebody gave me a bag in this very house. I said, 'Oh, my. I know what to do with this.'" And she and Greg have been doing. They are the only people mass producing leather handcrafted purses and vests on such a scale.

Their stuff now is sold in over 20 stores including places in San Francisco, the East Bay, Sonoma County, Sacramento, San Jose, Marin County and now the Greg, who is 21, has finally gotten his driver's license, they'll take a trip to LA. So far they have 300 purses and 2000 vests out. Pegasus is their biggest buyer.

It's a lot of handlacing and individual designing which makes "no two items alike," Greg says looking very mercantile. "Together we're able to turn out 10 purses a day. After Christmas, when we've got more cash together, we're going to get some people to help us.

Looking at the Snazzy Leather Company sales chart, which has some dramatic dips which drop so far it's frightening, Suzy gets up from the floor in front of the television and goes into Greg's room where the single sewing machine sits. Calling over the sound of the television she cries, "Gregory! I've got it. Let's rent a television."

Work stands still. The old posters of places like the Fillmore, Avalon Ballroom, the mimeograph machine which prints Greg's fanzine WHO PUT THE BOMP, the files filled with every rock paper ever published, stay right where they are as the two Shaws climb into their brand new demonstrator model white Toyota with automatic transmission and carrrreeeefullllly back out of the drive in search of a TV to rent.

--- Peter A. Menkin

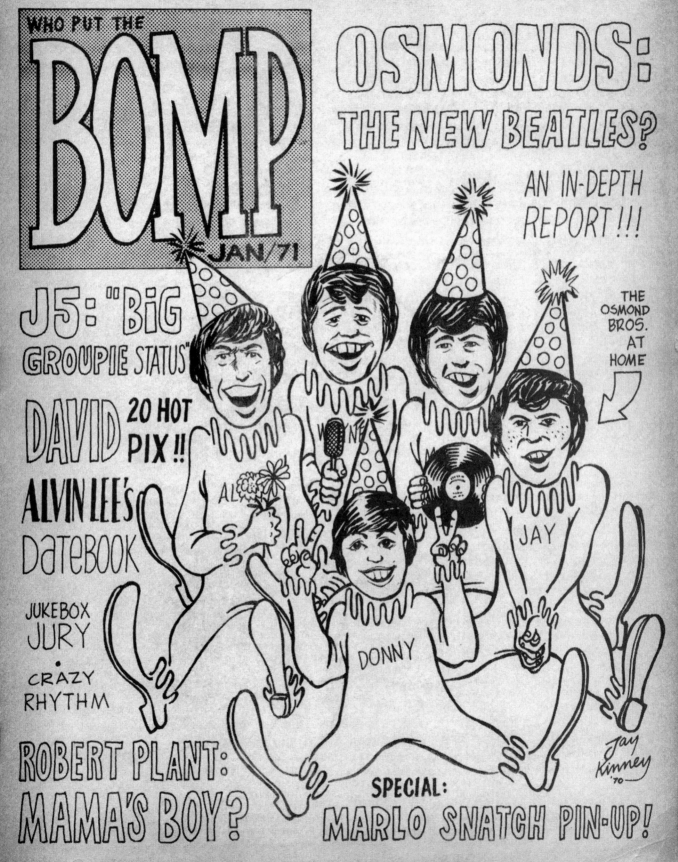

Welcome to the sixth issue of WHO PUT THE BOMP. I want to apologize first for the long delay between issues -- you know how it is. I hope to get several issues out this year. Currently I'm considering both a small, monthly WPTB and a fat, quarterly or so magazine. The advantage of the latter is that it allows me to run major features without eliminating any regular columns. The former plan has the advantage of keeping things moving. We'll have to just wait and see how it comes out, though. For the moment, we're "irregular".

Since the last issue I've been thinking about this magazine and what I want it to be. I've found out there are a lot more fanzines than I thought, and that the music of the 50s has been studied to a degree far beyond that of which I'm capable. That's cool with me anyway because the second cycle of rock & roll, which took place in the mid-sixties, is of much greater interest to me. My teenage years coincided with the 60s, and it's that music which made the strongest impression on me. This works out rather well because there's a lot to write about -- it's really an untouched field. For this reason I'm abandoning the plans I once had for special issues on Specialty, Imperial, Aladdin, companies like that, since others can do it so much better. (The music of the 50s will still be covered regularly in articles and reviews, but not exclusively.) Instead I'm putting my energy into planning 2 special issues covering the Surf/Hot Rod craze and the British Invasion. It's very important to me to put these 2 phenomena into perspective, and I need articles/discos for lesser artists in these 2 genres, articles or just comments on the social significance of these things, and in particular your theories on why the spirit of rock & roll chose to explode into life with the British thing and then die after burning so brightly for a few years. Can we assume it'll happen again in another 3 years as part of a regular cycle, or is it true that our negligence is responsible for its death, and if so what can we do toward seeing it reborn again?

The Surf issue will be sort of a lark; humor is the only way to approach the subject. Reminiscences of cruisin' in California, what it was like to be a surfer in Nebraska, how you scored with all the chicks after you had your front axle lowered, this is the sort of thing I want. The British Invasion issue will attempt to give an overall perspective on the thing, focusing on a few of the better second-string groups. The impact of the British groups was such that it'll take a long time to cover it all, and we'll be running feature articles on such groups as the Who, the Yardbirds and the Kinks all through this year.

You readers are requested to submit anything you think will fit in along these lines. Even a list of your favorite obscure records would be helpful. You'll find some further notes on this a few pages hence, to give you a better idea of my thoughts.

* * *

Maybe you've noticed the preponderant size of the lettercol -- about 25% of the magazine. This is unusual for a rock mag, but not so unusual for a fanzine. I'd like the lettercol to become a breeding ground for discussions; to me, it's one of the most important parts of WPTB. You're all encouraged to send in your comments on any of the matters raised in the letter section. STORMY WEATHER withholds the addresses of their correspondents, to protect their privacy. Since I have a much smaller circulation and WPTB is still sort of a family magazine, I've left the addresses in to allow readers to contact each other independently if they wish. Anyone desiring so can request to have his address withheld, however. We wouldn't want to cause any problems.

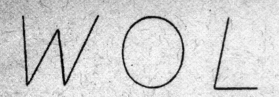

Well I assume most of you saw ROLLING STONE's treatment of the rock fan press. The article gave us fair coverage, though not as good as the longer one Ed Ward would have preferred them to use. I'd like to expand a bit on a couple of things in that article, though. First, I did not mean to say that I intended to organize a rock & roll collectors' convention if nobody else did. I was trying to say that I would <u>suggest</u> the <u>idea</u>, if it didn't come up soon elsewhere. I've never served on a con committee, though I've had close friends who did, but I know well enough the kind of work involved to know that it's not for me. For another thing, the idea is not as original as I once thought. A friend of mine named George Kistler recently returned from Europe and told me of having attended a blues collectors' convention there. The idea's in the air now, and that's enough for me. It'll happen soon enough.

Finally, I don't want to give other publishers the impression that their efforts have been characterized without their consent as "fanzines." I spent about 10 minutes trying to explain to Ed Ward that while science fiction fanzines arose to discuss the material in the sf "prozines", the rock fan press is, in asense, on an equal footing with the professional rock press, in that both concern themselves with creative effort in another field. While I'd like to see more discussion of the pro press in the amateur mags, the fact remains that the only essential difference here is one of circulation, profit margin, and perhaps a higher common interest level among our readers. Some of these "fanzines" appear in tabloid formats with circulations rivaling the smaller "prozines", and it would not be right to delimit their role with the former label.

Perhaps you're wondering what kind of response we got from the article. Well, about 25 people sent in 35¢ for a sample copy; only a few later subscribed. Interestingly enough, 30 or more subscribed sight-unseen. At any rate, we're glad to have had the exposure, and want to thank Ed Ward and Jann Wenner. I also wish to thank Lenny Goldberg, whose mention of us in ROCK brought in quite a few subscriptions as well. And, though we got no subs as a result, I'd like to thank Lenny Kaye for his kind review in CAVALIER. You're good people, one and all.

- -

THE DECLINE AND FALL OF EVERYTHING (A continuing story): A recent press release from Capitol Records reveals that Grand Funk played to standing-room-only crowds at Royal Albert Hall. Special boxes for the concert were reserved by such groups as Ten Years After, Black Sabbath, Humble Pie, the Rolling Stones and the Who. Twiggy was also in attendance.

- -

... Lenny Kaye writes that he and Richard Robinson are planning to put out a magazine called COSMIC FLASH--CRYSTAL SET. Material for the first issue includes R. Meltzer on bottle-cap collecting, an article on Laurie Records, and a regular feature called "Great Record Shops of the World" ... also from Lenny comes the news that Elektra is putting together a series of albums focusing on forgotten great singles of the mid-late sixties. This item replaces a paragraph I had written advocating a series of bootleg albums along these lines, so it's obvious that we're dealing here with an idea that's right for the time (take your hat off, Lester). The albums will each concentrate on a specific locale (So. Calif., Boston, NY, San Francisco, England etc.) and Lenny, who's coordinating things, is asking for suggestions. Send 'em to me, or directly to Lenny.

PRELUDE TO THE MORNING OF AN

1956-1956 was the Golden Age of rock & roll and it has been exhaustively researched, discographed and eulogized. 1963-66 was the Golden Age of Rock, and it has been almost totally ignored. This is partially because we are only now coming to realize how important the music of those years was, and also because it hasn't occurred to anyone to treat music so recent from a historical standpoint.

I hope to do something about that in WHO PUT THE BOMP, over the next couple of years if it takes that long. The emphasis will be on records, because that's the only evidence left, but personal recollections will be used when I can find them. There are whole categories of groups that can be dealt with. I'll try to give you some idea of what I mean in this article.

For the first time since the early 50s an indigenous music arose to meet the cultural needs of a teenage scene, and it was called Surf music. Based on a combination of old blues cliches and glossed-over Chuck Berry runs, it relied almost completely on rhythm and was essentially a very shallow music that never reached any kind of sophistication except through the Beach Boys. Yet it suited the times and groups sprang up everywhere to play it. Some of the big ones were Dick Dale & his Del-Tones, the Beach Boys, Jan & Dean, the Wailers, Ronny and the Daytonas, the Rip-Chords, the Chantays... It's my feeling that the music was much larger than surfing, because it was being played in various parts of the country before anyone ever heard of surfing. There was a big scene in the Pacific Northwest of groups playing instrumental rock. The Sonics, the Wailers, who had an early hit with "Tall Cool One", later went into surf without altering their sound much, and Paul Revere & the Raiders got a little slicker and went pop. But their line of development can be traced back to groups like the Ventures, Johnny & the Hurricanes, the Viscounts, the Royaltones, and Bill Justis. The same music was popular in other parts of the country too, and the "surf" label just provided a convenient catch-all term. There were probably hundreds of groups recording music in this vein, yet who remembers any of them now? Still, it was happening at the same time the Beatles were starting to get their sound together, and if they hadn't a whole new music might've developed here.

At the same time in England a new music was growing that was to provide rock & roll with a new structure and more vitality than it had seen in years. The first wave of hard rockers included the Beatles, the Stones, the Kinks, the Who, the Yardbirds, Them. The next generation was not long in coming and it gave us the Zombies, the Animals, the Pretty Things, the Tgoggs, the Dave Clark Five, the Hollies, the Small Faces, the Searchers, the Honeycombs, Manfred Mann, Gerry & the Pacemakers, Billy J. Kramer, the Nashville Teens, Herman's Hermits, Freddie & the Dreamers, and loads of others.

Americans were influenced by the British Invasion and soon groups were popping up here. The Remains, the Shadows of Knight, the Knickerbockers, the Young Rascals, the Outsiders, the Strangers, the Magicians, the Fugitives, the Vagrants, the Beau Brummels, Love, the Turtles, the Byrds... many more.

Then there were the San Jose groups, who had a hard rock sound based on the Who and the Yardbirds. Remember the Count Five, the Standells, the Syndicate of Sound, the Chocolate Watchband, the Golliwogs, the Harbinger Complex, Peter Wheat

INVENTORY OF THE 60'S

& the Breadmen, the New Breed, the Oxford Circle?

I have never seen a decent discography for any of the groups mentioned thus far. It looks to me like a worthy thing to do. I admit that most of this music was pretty bad compared to the rock & roll of the 50s, but a lot of it was good in its way and it deserves more attention than it's gotten so far.

The next issue of WPTB will carry a long article on the Kinks, which I'd originally planned to run this time but decided to devote more time to. It will concentrate on unreleased songs and un-collected singles, of which the Kinks have almost as many as some groups have on record. I believe I've tracked down all the little odds & ends, but there is one thing I need help with. To wit: what label were the Kinks originally on? Someone said Swan; can anyone confirm? I'd also like to know the numbers of the 2 singles they had on that label. After the Kinks I want to cover the Who. Anybody with information about unreleased Who material or obscure European EPs and such is urged to contact me. Does anyone know where "Barbara Ann" was released?

If things go as planned the issue after next will deal with the British Invasion. I still need articles on Peter & Gordon, the Nashville Teens, the Honeycombs, the Pretty Things, Ian Whitcomb. And if anyone knows about the Rockin' Berries, the Applejacks, the Johnny Howard Band, the Ivy League, Unit 4 + 2, or any other obscure English groups of the era, please tell me. Oh yes, and I need an article on the Troggs, the Merseybeats and Sounds, Incorporated.

That issue should come out in the summer. Then maybe later this year we'll get to the surf groups, and then next year perhaps we'll give some attention to some other corners of the 60s, like all those great chick vocal groups, Spector-produced and otherwise: The Shirelles, the Raindrops, the Exciters, the Marvelettes, the Orlons, the Chiffons, the Essex, the Dixie Cups, the Shangri-Las, the Blossoms, the Crystals, the Ronettes, Bob B. Soxx and the Blue Jeans...

If you feel as I do about this music, I need help with all of this stuff. Mike Saunders' article on Del Shannon is an excellent example of how a minor artist can be treated. I would prefer to have a complete singles discography for each artist, but if you have most of the records that's good enough. We can fill in the holes later. Let's get this done before the sands of time drift any deeper!

JUKE BOX JURY

HALL OF FAME   (little-known older records of note)

"Almost Grown"/"Lawdy Miss Clawdy" by Keith Dennis (Reprise 0390)

These sides, apparently dating from '64 or so, are good examples of how I think old songs can be successfully modernized. The atmosphere is relaxed, the performance clean and interesting. Jim Messina produced both sides, and the credit for their success belongs to him and the anonymous band. Keith Dennis has an adequate, but not distinctive voice, which is probably why he's still an unknown. But this is a good record, and I'd like to know about any more he did.

"Bald Headed Woman"/"Jug Band Music" by the Mugwumps (Sidewalk 900)

This record seems to be from the same period. It was produced by the infamous Mike Curb, who owned Sidewalk Records. These don't sound much like the Mugwumps who later became the Mamas and the Papas, but then again it might be. "Bald Headed Woman" is lifted directly from the B side of the Who's first single, "Can't Explain", and of course it's not up to their version. But it's interesting. "Jug Band Music" makes me think maybe this is those Mugwumps. They do an open, friendly rendition of the Lovin' Spoonful song.

"Angel Baby"/"Give Me Love" by Rosie and the Originals (Highland 1011)

Here's the record John Lennon was talking about as one of his all time favorites, and the direct inspiration for such songs as "Get Back" and "Ballad of John and Yoko". I just got it on the original label, and was quite surprised to find just how great the B side is. For one thing, it's definitely not Rosie or the Originals. It seems to be by some studio band who never got another chance to step out on their own. There's no drums at all, the bass carrying the beat, and some no-bullshit guitar player spitting out streams of brittle notes in all the right places. There's also a tasty sax solo, not to mention the vocal, which is pretty good itself. This is one of the best B-sides I know of -- check it out.

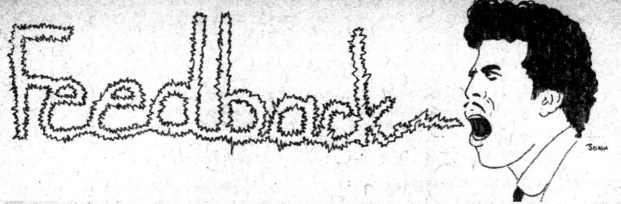

feedback

WALT TAYLOR: Amazing! The first true rock fanzine. I was into stf fandom myself a few years ago, but I gafiated very quickly, mainly because I found that I was less a trufan than a wide-eyed kid, mainly interested in the literature but not enuff to sustain more than a passing interest. With music, however, it is an entirely different story. I've been a professional singer for about five years, and a student and lover of rock and r&b for as long as I can remember.

Who is James Wright? His article about Reverend Jeter and the amazing Swan Silvertones was a very sensitive analysis of what may very well be the greatest black spiritual group in history. The new Specialty collection is a fine introduction to the group for anyone who has never been exposed to this music before. More by Wright!

All in all, I think that BOMP is a fine effort, and I hope that this so-called rock culture doesn't ignore the possibilities of such organizing. A Rock-Con, eh? It doesn't seem too far-fetched, but I would like to see how far this thing can go first. It's funny, but there are very few 'fans' anymore. Everybody who digs something with any degree of fervor is a 'freak'... film-freak, rock-freak, blues-freak etc. This makes BOMP the very first freakzine. That's nice...now we can be zine-freaks

/2014 Melrose Ave., Chester, PA. 19013/

{{ Heaven forbid! This is a fanzine and a fmz it'll stay! To me (with apologies to Liza Williams) the word "freak" conjures up images of yr typical stoned streetslob with a vocabulary of about 2 words: "far out" and "heavy". I guess it started with Zappa and his crew, but there certainly isn't anything "freaky" about today's freaks. I'd rather be a fan. :: James Wright comes to us from sf fandom, too. I'll try to get more out of him; he knows a lot about the Northwest punk-rock scene. }}

DAVE MARSH: I really think that WPTB is gonna be a really important medium because, as rock is ripped apart again, like in the late fifties, it's almost like keeping an underground cult alive. And really, we all know that they just don't understand, for the most part. I mean, do you see the pattern between the downfall of rock, as it became eaten up by the industry, in the fifties and then the rejuvenation and downfall of the sixties? And how it's really our failure because we were supposed to stop that cycle... you know, we were going to straighten things out. You dig? I feel apocalyptic as hell lately, look over my shoulder constantly, kind of thing. Sometimes I think that people who have a true aesthetic of raunch, a true love for high energy, gutlevel intensity in music are a cult on the order of the Rosicrucians...so anyway, we could run ads in crossword puzzle mags, write to SCRIBE GS/DMLB/LG/LK whatever and we'll turn ya on to the secret of sound. Something like that.

/3729 Case Ave., Detroit, Mich. 48201/

LESTER BANGS: I just got the first 2 issues of WPTB and I had to let you know how excited I was about your mag. It certainly does fill a real void, not only in being a magazine by & for fans, but in being chock full of some of the most interesting writing on the scene today.

Here's a story that might interest your readers, on the perils of being a rock-n-roll critic: One morning last year I was awakened at 7 AM by the mailman with an album by a group called Valhalla, sent special delivery from one Jim Foley (said group's manager) in New Jersey. With the album was a letter claiming that Greil Marcus, then reviews editor of ROLLING STONE, had been "very excited" by the record and recommended that Foley send it to me. Which I doubted, because it was pretty mediocre stuff: standard shrill amped-up noise.

Anyhoo, I had no intention of reviewing it but Foley kept pestering me, calling upwards of a dozen times and writing letters soliciting my opinions on a group whom I had nothing against but simply wanted to forget about, until finally just to get him off my back I wrote a 100-word review panning the album in RS—and writing it, I even felt kind of sorry for Foley thinking about him reading it after all his trouble, hype artist though he was. I was a goddam babe in the critical woods.

I needn't have worried, though, because the review was followed closely by a letter saying "thanks for the review, in a way you made many good points they didn't get a chance to truly show their stuff" etc. Also a personal Christmas card from the Jim Foley family and a free music book of all Valhalla's songs, most of which in musical interest lie about halfway between Grand Funk and Deep Purple.

It finally died out, though. I didn't hear from him for months, & the whole thing was forgotten until today, when I received this letter:

"Dear Lester,
"Your review of the new Stones album is, in my opinion, the finest piece of writing I've ever seen in ROLLING STONE.
"Each and every paragraph is incredible. And, aside from agreeing with virtually everything you state, I think you've come up with some phrasing classics, e.g. 'inane survey hit.'
"I'm delighted that it was your project to review this album, enabling this literary and critical treat to become a reality.
"This one gets lucited and goes on my wall. Yours sincerely, James Foley."

Never mind the fact that this review was hardly my most outstanding piece of writing, merely a competent piece of reportage that came nowhere near truly probing pieces on the Stones like Greil's Let It Bleed review. Or that the mind boggles at the vision of Jim Foley's office, walls entirely plastered with old record reviews sealed in lucite to cross the ages. What's truly sad is that he probably means every last word of it.
/463 N. First #D, El Cajon, CA. 92021/

alligator wine

I'm glad that so many people have responded to Jonh's circulars for FRANK'S APA. I think a group like this can serve a unique and invaluable function in the world of rock & roll. Hope so anyway.

Jonh will probably be describing the history of this group, how it was begun by comic and science fiction fan Louis Morra about a year ago, limped through four mailings and finally folded under the weight of Morra's incredible incompetence. But from the questions I was asked by a number of people Jonh asked to join this time around, I wonder if the whole concept of an apa, taken for granted by Jonh and me, is not a little alien to many of you. So, if I can, I'd like to delve briefly into the history of Amateur Press Associations.

The oldest and largest such organization is NAPA, the National Amateur Press Association. Membership is open to anyone who pays dues, and there are thousands of members. There are no activity requirements. The emphasis is on amateur printing techniques, and the contents of the magazines usually revolve around how they were printed. The apa format was adopted in 1938 by science fiction fans in forming FAPA, the Fantasy Amateur Press Assoc. Since message was more important to them than medium, they made a few changes. Membership was limited to 65 (and there is now a waiting list of about 50), activity was required at least once a year, in the form of original material. At the start members put through issues of their general-circulation magazines("genzines"), but after awhile it became the common practice to publish a small magazine especially for the apa ("apazines"), consisting mostly of comments on the previous mailing but with frequent insertions of more formal essays.

Since then there have been dozens of apas in fandom, many involving new twists on the basic concept. There have been apas with monthly, bimonthly, six-weekly, fortnightly, weekly and even daily mailings; apas for comic fans, monster fans, professional SF authors, SF fans under a certain age. TAPS and The Cult initiated a system of rotating publishing duties, so that as each mailing rolled around a different member would stencil letters from the other members and publish the whole thing himself. APA-L and APA-F grew out of club meetings in Los Angeles and New York respectively, and involved members bringing their pages to the weekly meetings to be collated, stapled together and distributed to attendees. The most recent development, the so-called "secret-apa" began with Lilapa and APEX in the mid-sixties, when a closed circle of friends decided to publish discussions among themselves on a frequent basis, limiting membership to a majority vote and invoking rules against showing the mailings to non-members. It is roughly on this model that FRANK'S APA has been based.

Jonh and I were struck with the volume of correspondence that seemed to take place among rock critics, indicating an unquenchable desire to talk with others of like mind about the music, or the publishing scene, or the mere gossip of the rock world. It seems a waste for much of the same information to make its way around through hundreds of similar letters when it can be written once, here, and read by all. Logical, eh? It is also hoped this group will spawn essays and discussions of the type not intended for the general public, but only for other critics and people in a position to put ideas into effect and make things happen.

Written and published for the first mailing of FRANK'S APA by Greg Shaw, 64 Taylor Drive, Fairfax, Calif. 415-453-9323. April, 1971. Contents copyrighted.
The Beach Boys For President

ALLIGATOR WINE   PAGE 2

So FRANK'S APA can function as a clearing house for rumors and information. It can also become a breeding ground for discussions, offering a huge improvement over the old system of saying something to one person in a letter, him mentioning the idea to someone else, the third person responding with his opinion which is then related to the first, and so on until the subject has been commented on by everyone, which might take months. Here, if someone says something like "Why not put out a bootleg Remains album?" by the time the next mailing comes out in a few weeks we will have the benefit of 20 people's advice on the matter.

These are just some of the things that can happen in a group of this nature. There are many more, and undoubtedly some that have yet to be discovered. I hope some of that discovery will take place in FRANK'S APA.

: :

In the last issue of WHO PUT THE BOMP I devoted much space to an appraisal of the rock press, taking each magazine as an entity and as part of a field. We are now coming into a period where things are changing so fast that my observations in that article may soon be outdated.

In the first place the whole concept of what makes a successful rock magazine is changing. The "rock magazine" itself is probably obsolete as a mass-culture item. (sub-culture, that is) The most innovative editors are now experimenting in search of a form that embodies the best in professional rock criticism with equally good coverage of other areas of pop culture. ROLLING STONE began this move last year by getting into politics and drugs, the other two hobbies of the Bill Graham generation. The attempt was a failure because they could not apply the expertise that was theirs in the music world, prompting comments of "stick to what you know, you guys!"

FUSION jumped in next, searching far afield for topics they felt would be of interest to the intellectual rock fan. Their first few months went badly also, partly because the editors lost sight of rock itself in their enthusiasm, and partly because their articles of "cultural significance" tended to be not so significant after all. The last few issues, however, have seen a slight upgrading on both counts, and FUSION still hasn't stopped experimenting. In April they plan to switch over to a saddle-stitched format.

RAGS was the pioneer with this format, gaining a large circulation in a relatively short time by abandoning the traditional, sloppy, folded tabloid format. RAGS has also been the model for other magazines in terms of its editorial innovations. The first rock magazine to pick up on the fact that tabloids are obsolescent was CREEM, whose first issue in the new style just came out. CREEM, by adopting this format and bringing in a much wider range of articles, hopes to carve out a new mass audience that could, theoretically, surpass ROLLING STONE's.

They won't have the track to themselves for long, though. The first issue of FLASH is out, staffed by some of the best editors and writers around, and dealing with every imaginable subject that would appeal to the enlightened reader. FLASH has a chance at some really big things, for its links to traditional rock writing are even weaker than CREEM's. The next few months will reveal how big a success CREEM and FLASH will reap, but I have few doubts that they will succeed. And then there will be imitators, of course. I've heard tell of a magazine called ZOOT starting in N.Y. along the lines of FLASH. Only time will tell, but you know what they say: two's competition; three's a field.

Looks like we've got a new field on our hands.

ALLIGATOR WINE   PAGE 5.
- -

PRETENTIOUS ESSAY OF THE MONTH - No. 1

I'm going to be very bold and offer some observations on where I think rock & roll is going. I do this, not because I feel you all to be a pack of benighted halfwits anxiously awaiting my enlightening pronouncements, but because I'm coming to doubt many of the commonly-accepted beliefs about the whole thing and would like to throw my doubts into the ring for your comment.

In the first place, I'm not at all convinced that the dominance of solo non-hardrock artists is nearly as complete as Jon Landau and all the other trend-watchers claim. In fact, I believe that right now we're in the midst of a rock & roll renaissance. The music of the last two years has driven many a dedicated fan to drink (hi, Lester!) but anyone can go crazy dwelling only on the bad.

Look, this period we're in now has been widely compared to its counterpart ten years ago, after the original rock & roll impulse had been bastardized to death by Dick Clark et al. Tin Pan Alley leapt joyfully into the breach and flooded the airwaves with so much shit that real music lovers abandoned the radio altogether and went looking for a substitute in jazz or folk music. It was that bad. Examine a list of the top 100 singles of 1961 or 1962, and try to find more than a dozen or so per year that were any good. And even those were by the likes of Del Shannon, Bobby Lewis, Ricky Nelson, the Dovells and U.S. Bonds, who wouldn't have merited two poops in 1956 when giants like Jerry Lee Lewis, Gene Vincent, Eddie Cochran, Fats Domino, Chuck Berry and Elvis walked the earth.

You could say the same thing today, that Southwind doesn't stack up very well against the Yardbirds, but you'd be missing the essential difference, which is that in 1961 those dozen or so singles were all there was. The formula for an album in those days was to surround a hit with 11 filler tracks, so unless you count obscure records that never made anybody's charts, it can truthfully be said that there weren't more than 50 good songs in the whole year!

When you consider that you've got to admit things don't look so bad now, accepting this as a similar interregnum period. Since the start of the year we've been supplied with so many good albums that I haven't had the chance to get tired of any of them yet before the next good one came. Here's a top-of-the-head listing of groups who are, in my estimation, doing something good with everything they release: Southwind, T. Rex, Flamin Groovies, Fleetwood Mac, Creedence, Beach Boys, Kinks, Dead, Capt. Beefheart, Van Morrison, Badfinger, Velvet Underground, Wild Angels, Siren, Savage Rose, J. Geils Band, Faces, Stooges, Alice Cooper.

And on the horizon we have Ron Nagle, Stoneground (who may turn out well, with good direction), Wilderness Road, Flash Cadillac, Christopher Milk, The Up (from all reports), and doubtless plenty I haven't heard of. Most of these artists will be putting out one or two albums a year, adding up to a respectable amount of good enjoyable rock & roll; a greater quantity, to be honest, than we've had in any previous year that I can think of.

Notice also that all the artists named are either groups or single artists with backing groups and a group sound. The "single artists are taking over" theory doesn't stand up to that evidence very well, does it? There may be a lot of Taylors, but certainly not that many! The solo artist trend has really been making inroads, not in the rock & roll mainstream, but among the fad-followers. And in a move of dubious wisdom, our old friend ROLLING STONE, that believer in the cosmic payoff, has thrown its full weight into this fad, supplying it with most of the credibility it enjoys among the young in general.

It's always been that way with ROLLING STONE, really. Not content to have the last word on what takes place in every back room of the music industry, Jann developed a desire early in the game to become a molder of public taste. Every writer knows that there are certain types of music to which you are not allowed to give a good review in RS, simply because Jann doesn't like it. I can easily imagine his train of thought: give bad reviews to English symphonic rock, good reviews to funky San Francisco dope bands. After awhile, sales among impressionable teenagers will reflect this bias, and gradually the groups Jann dislikes will decline in popularity.

His current campaign must represent more of the same. Somewhere he got the idea that acoustic troubadors would be the next "big thing", and decided to jump in on the side of the winners. Since that decision no group has appeared on the cover of ROLLING STONE. Even Nicholas Johnson and Joe Dallesandro have been featured, after the current crop of solo superstars was exhausted, rather than any of the excellent groups that have been studiously ignored. Interviews have followed the same predictable pattern, with Ben Fong-Torres squeezing out every last inane observation from the heads of David Crosby, Steve Stills, James Taylor and Leon Russell. Even the bacover album givaway features only solo artists now.

BOW DOWN BEFORE ME!

What I'm saying is that these artists have been built up in the public's (and our) minds as superstars by their constant appearances on the covers of ROLLING STONE, TIME, and all the other camp-followers. "Taylors - The First Family of the New Rock". That's subtle stuff, boy. Rather than call 'em "folksingers", which they plainly are, RS infers that they are leaders in the latest development of rock -- an easy step from there to the assumption that hard rock must be dead if these guys represent the mainstream.

Good rock & roll is all around; you just got to seek it out in magazines like CREEM, who have no (or different) axes to grind. What makes it easy to fall into the trap of believing the "rock is dead" talk, of course, is the absence of an overpowering rock & roll "movement", greater than the sum of all the music, that the public can have faith in, removing the need to worry about how any of the individual groups, which are after all only symptoms of the movement, are faring. We had it in 1956 when the Big Beat ruled the land and teenagers were, or should have been, awed with the social energy at their command. As things began falling apart in the late 50s, that "faith" I was talking about earlier came to the fore. Didn't you believe the Showmen when they said that "Rock and roll will stand!"? Didn't it send a thrill through you to realize you were a part of something so mighty nothing could crush it? It did me.

The fear then was that the old-line program directors would turn out to be right about R&R being only a fad, soon to be replaced with the "good music" of Perry Como and Tony Bennett. We didn't want it to happen; we really cared, strongly, for our music. At the risk of sounding like Paul Williams (may his rock & roll soul rest in peace) I have to point out that this was the first time in all history that a sub-category of music aroused such devotion among its listeners. I'm sure there are people who couldn't face the prospect of living without classical music, but you don't see any "Classical Music Will Stand Sonata In B-Flat"s. Of course the fear mentioned above and the frequent predictions of an imminent demise were never a part of classical music, but how about history's other persecuted musical styles? Try as you will, I don't think you'll find any "Dixieland Will Stand" rags or anything of that nature. Something different, some powerful zeitgeist, is involved in rock & roll.

That's how some a "more than human" Pop Spirit can arise, as it did in the mid-fifties and again in '64. The power is there all the time, if we can only tap it properly, and once we do it quickly grows beyond our control and starts looking like destiny, for awhile at least. For it can and does die if neglected.

I hope the above doesn't sound too mystical, but I really can't think of any other way to account for what things were like during those two peaks whose existence no one denies. Whether we can articulate it or not, or even recognize it, I think all of us are aware on some level of the "tone of the times" as far as rock & roll and pop culture goes. And that's why it's so easy to believe that rock & roll is dead; the zeitgeist is not with us at present.

There's no way to know how to get it back, unless Greil Marcus has some answers he's not talking about. It seems to take some incredibly charismatic, high-energy supergroup (or star) to act as a catalyst, but there must also be a lot of competent groups around ready to add their energy to the flow when things get moving. If the sign-readers are right and we're due for another resurgence of the spirit in two years or so, then it's the groups coming along now that will be the potential giants then. I say that because I think next time around the music will be so complex, conceptually if not technically, that wet-eared teenagers will not be able to set the standard, as has been traditional up to now.

Len Bailes, reading the first draft of this essay, had some comments that would not be out of place to insert here. He felt that the whole "zeitgeist" business could be rendered a hell of a lot less mystical by trying to define some of its elements or attributes. A large part of it, we decided, had to do with the popstar myth, the way figures like Elvis, Dylan, the Beatles, etc. were elevated to superhuman status and worshipped by their followers, adding a great deal of hysteria to the whole thing. There is some question as to whether anything like this could ever happen again. Or how necessary an element it is. We won't know until it happens (or fails to happen) I guess. Len also felt that Dylan's influence in the early-mid 60s was an essential factor in adding an element of maturity and intellect to rock. If he's right, will we need another figure to add still another dimension to rock (wisdom? spirituality?) next time around?

There are so many fantasies of what it will be like next time. Some think that freeform jazz, Captain Beefheart, Velvet Underground, Red Krayola and maybe Sam Samudio will come together (as influences) to make an abstract, mind-expanding "liberation" music. Others believe that bands like the Stooges and Alice Cooper, blazing trails in artist/audience relations and advanced systems of noise-modulation are the wave of the future. And there's strong support for the belief that vocal ability and group harmony will make a comeback. Len Bailes thinks the best hope lies in the groups being started by rock critics. (There's one to think about! And where does that leave Lou Reed?) But hell, you've probably got your own theory.

ALLIGATOR WINE PAGE 6

TAH-DUM!

I suspect that those things will all happen, and more that we can't conceive of now. The Phil Spector of bubble-gum music may be just around the corner, for all we know. I really can't imagine how a number of divergent forms can coexist in the midst of a zeitgeist explosion, because it never happened that way before, but my belief that it will happen is unwavering.

But, to return to the point that this rambling essay began with, the seeds of it all are among us now, if we can but appreciate them. Who, after all, paid any attention to the Rolling Stones, the Beatles, the Kinks or John Mayall in 1963? Things seem to be picking up steam, and if we can put our energy into those corners of the music world where The Spirit is stirring, it won't do any harm at all.

Might even help things along.

: :

And so we come to the close of the first issue of this apazine. Sorry to cut off in the middle of the page like this, but the deadline is breathing down my neck and there is no time to come up with something. Sorry also about the print-thru. Discovered at the last minute that I was out of good paper, and this pink stuff was all I had. The title "Alligator Wine", incidentally, is the title of an old rock 'n' roll record (can anyone identify it?), continuing the tradition of the first three issues of WHO PUT THE BOMP, which were subtitled, respectively, "Duke of Earl", "Da Doo Ron Ron" and "Whenever A Teenager Cries." I plan to use a different title each issue. So long until next time -- and don't forget those mailing comments.

Alligator wine: it takes two pints to make one cavort

You may not think the motel managing business is terribly exciting, and actually it's not, but it can be interesting at times. I guess most of you know that my mother owns a motel in Modesto, a large town in the middle of California's farm country, about 100 miles from here. Suzy and I went out there for Easter, and found to our surprise that a water bed had been installed in one of the rooms. We didn't get to sleep on it, as it is generally reserved for days in advance, but we went in and bounced on it. As a novelty it wasn't bad, though I doubt if we'll ever own one. This one had an advantage over all the others I've sampled in stores in that it was really filled with water, so much that the top of it was convex. That avoided the sloshiness one usually encounters in water beds. Mom told us that a couple of times a month groups of young kids ("hippies") take out the room, and that after they leave the place reeks of marijuana.

"How shocking!" commented Suzy.

"Oh, no," said my mother, "I say, 'let' 'em have a good time'. They're young, after all." I really began to wonder about my mom when I noticed a water pipe in her living room. I picked it up, examined it. It was a good water pipe, nicely balanced, esthetically designed. And it didn't seem to have been used yet. So I stepped casually into the kitchen with the thing in my hand and said,

"Uh, mom? Where'd you get this thing?"

Well, it turned out that she had bought it at an import place, not having the faintest idea what it was. She just liked the looks of it. I suggested she put it in the water bed room.

"You know," she added, "I never would have known what it was if some narcs that were staying here hadn't told me." Oh really? "Yes, we get them all the time. Once we had seven at once, staking out some big dealers. They all look like such nice boys, too. Long hair, regular hippie types. Wouldn't have known who they were if we didn't listen in on their phone conversations. Those Federal ones are sure tight-lipped. The State ones talked to us about their jobs, though, and told us what that thing was. Imagine that!"

Imagine that.

— —
              "That's Walter under the bridge."
— —

There comes a point in being a rock critic or publishing a rock & roll magazine where you can't go any further without meeting certain people in the industry. I had been sending letters crammed with lists of my published reviews to all the record companies, but the only ones who took note and put me on their mailing lists were those with whom I'd had some personal contact. This was getting frustrating so I decided, early in March, to make a trip to Los Angeles and stay there until I had been given my due at every company in town. In the back of my mind I was also hoping for some advertising. What the hell, I have a good magazine.

I drove down with Jonh Ingham, who had flown to SF to attend a press party and Aretha Franklin concert (courtesy of Atlantic Records), and stayed at his house. We got off to a good start Tuesday morning at Capitol, where Jonh already knew Liza Williams, the "promo man" there. "Who Put the Bomp" we told the secretary (Janet Planet) and soon Liza was running around the office yelling "the Bomp, the Bomp!" We were ushered into her office, given coffee, and treated like visiting potentates. Liza told us she would be leaving to start a new record company, and then promptly offered Jonh her old job. "It's not easy," she cautioned, "you have to fly all over the country meeting rock critics, promoting bands, etc. You have to stay at the finest hotels, eat at all the best restaurants on your expense account, and show up at a certain number of the parties, where you must at least pretend to have a good time. And you can't expect more than $850/month to start." But Jonh was willing anyway, so he made an appointment to talk to Liza's boss, and we left. (It later turned out that he didn't get the job, but only because of his age. But for awhile the excitement ran high.)

From there we went to Mercury (Records, that is) where we ran into Ron Oberman, the head promo man from Chicago, who had just written me a letter. He was glad to see us and extended every courtesy. We met Rodney Bingenheimer there too, a comic figure on the Hollywood scene, sometime sidekick to Kim Fowley, and former "Mayor of Sunset Strip." He gave me personal addresses and phone numbers for Del Shannon, Brian Wilson, and Rosie of the Originals. We went also to A&M, where we were treated coldly and asked for letters of recommendation (they told us that 35 people had come in already that week alone, claiming to write for the papers we represented. Gad!), and then back to Jonh's for dinner. That night was a press party for the Small Faces on an old Warner Bros. sound stage in Burbank, so we went over there to check it out. The party was in the middle of a huge grand ballroom set, circa 1790, that was sitting in a studio the size of a blimp hanger. All around the perimeter of the studio were old carriages, false fronts for Western sets, a 1910 Main St. along one wall, and in general all manner of fascinating props. The party itself was not so fascinating. A small crowd of Hollywood groupies, scenemakers, promotion men and writers like ourselves. (Nothing like the party Warners threw for the Faces in San Francisco, which went on all night with live music, a performance by the Cockettes, pranks by the Sexual Freedom League, and all sorts of madness) We did meet John Mendelsohn, who considers himself a superstar among critics and dresses accordingly, and the catered food (caviar thingies and other fancy stuff I can't describe) was delicious. But we left after an hour or so.

On Wednesday we went to RCA and met Grelun Landon, a fatherly type who runs his vast promotion dept. like a family. Mention the name of any musician, writer, whoever, and he smiles warmly and asks "Oh, and how is he? And his wife?" etc. He phoned Warner Bros. for us and set it up for us to go over there. When we arrived we were greeted with hugh enthusiasm, told that the latest Bomp had been passed around at last week's conference, that the Vice President wanted to meet us, and all manner of other wondrous things. We were invited to select albums of our choice from the catalogue, (we each checkmarked about 30) and then taken in to meet Pete Johnson, former critic himself who now ran the promotion dept. He cared not a whit for our credentials, but seemed to really enjoy our company, and proceeded to tell us his life story, of what a shy introverted person he was and how glad he was to be working at Warner Bros. where they didn't expect too much of him, etc. Then he took us out to lunch, at a Roy Rogers Roast Beef Sandwich place. I wanted to get some facts on unreleased Kinks songs from their vaults, but Jonh had an appointment at Capitol so we had to leave. We got to Hollywood with some time to spare so we visited Atlantic, Buddah and Columbia, all of which went very quickly. We were invited to select LPs from a list Atlantic was deleting, given a pile of stuff at Buddah by a guy who didn't seem to care as much about music as he did about charts, and treated to a half hour of off-color stories by Michael Ochs (Phil's Brother) at Columbia while he kept some businessman-types cooling their heels outside. I would rather have talked seriously about publishing and rock criticism, but Ochs was a Hollywood make-the-scene type, and there wasn't much we had in common. From there we went directly to Capitol where Jonh was interviewed for an hour while Liza gave me a tour of the building, which is shaped like a pile of platters.

That night we went to a concert at the Forum, for which we had been given front row tickets. The Faces, Savoy Brown and the Grease Band were playing. It was a good concert, the Faces a much more impressive act than I had expected, but the most interesting thing about it was the way the audience went insane, trying to rush the stage and being clubbed and carried off by a crew of ferocious-looking hippie guards. Anyone who so much as lifted a camera to shoot a picture was grabbed and hustled out the back door, begging and pleading. It was kind of sickening to see that kind of discipline required, but on the other hand the audience didn't deserve much better, from the way they stood and stomped their feet, screaming like spoiled brats for more after the Faces had turned in a brilliant set of over an hour and an encore to boot. (What's with audiences today, anyway? I've been to concerts where they still demanded more after _four_ encores.) We watched them hoot for ten minutes or so, then left.

On Thursday Jonh was down with the flu, so I went back to Warners alone. I was given free run of the vaults, promised all the advertising I wanted, and then offered something so fantastic I could hardly believe it. (That was the bit about the 8,000 copies of my next issue) Absolutely stunned, and loaded down with the albums and stuff they kept laying on me, I made my way out, uttering "thank you"s in every direction. From there I went to Anaheim to visit a guy named Art Turco who publishes a magazine devoted to artists like the Capris, the Harptones, and forgotten R&B singers in general. He is an unemployed aerospace engineer, and also collects science fiction, but, he told me, never felt the urge to get involved in fandom. Understandable, from the amount of energy he puts into his records. He has a whole room lined all around, floor to ceiling, with orderly shelves of 45s, filed by label. A high-powered stereo faces a reclining chair in the center of the room, in which I sat and was treated to some obscure vocal group sounds. The fanzine business as he knows it is very different from the way I see it. Turco is involved in a life-and-death struggle with R&B MAGAZINE, which also covers the same group of artists. Each feels that the other is plotting to get discographies and such into print first and steal away readers. It is a deadly and paranoid thing to be a rhythm & blues fan.

From there I went to Len Bailes' place where I was to meet this guy Alan who has an unbelievable collection of tapes and wants to put out some bootleg albums. He wasn't due to arrive for awhile so Len and I buzzed over to the LASFS meeting, as there was a certain fan I wanted to talk to. He was late arriving, but we talked with Don Fitch, the only person there who recognized us. The LASFS has been through a lot of changes, and many old time members no longer attend. It's now more of a meeting-place for repressed, intellectual teenagers recruited through local ads. Bruce Pelz, who now runs the club unopposed, doesn't seem to care what goes on there as long as money continues to flow into the Clubhouse Fund coffers. Back at Len's, Alan arrived and played us his tapes of Dylan live in England in 1965, the Beatles live at Hollywood Bowl (from an album Capitol had prepared but never issued), an album the Stones recorded in 1963, unreleased Who songs, and other goodies too numerous to go into. I was properly impressed, and promised to do what I could to put Alan in touch with a responsible bootlegger.

On Friday and Saturday I didn't do much. Finished up the record companies, visited a few people. On Sunday I went over to Len's and went with him to visit George Clayton Johnson, where we spent the afternoon rewriting his screenplay about Columbus sailing over the edge of the world and landing in the 20th century. We tried to do something about George's misconceptions of fandom, but to no avail. He is still determined to become a BNF, by hook or by crook. But he's a great person anyway.

The next day I came home; and that, teacher, is what I did on my vacation.

Rock, You Sinners!

Written and published for the second mailing of FRANK'S APA by Greg Shaw, 6 4 Taylor Drive, Fairfax, Calif. 94930 -- 415-453-9323. June, 1971 Contents copyrighted.
Last issue's title, "Alligator Wine", was taken from an old record by Screamin' Jay Hawkins. Since nobody took part in the grand identification contest, I may as well tell you that "Rock You Sinners" is a song by Art Baxter from a 1956 record.

Jay Kinney has been out here on the west coast for a couple of weeks, and he was good enough on his visit here to offer to do some drawings. Since I was just preparing to run off the first 6 pages of this, I offered him 2 stencils and began casting about for some topics to write on. I didn't have far to go because the June issue of CREEM with Greil Marcus' apocalyptic "Rock-A-Hula" piece is sitting here before me fairly crying out to be commented on.

It's a bit discouraging to devote as much time as I have (see ALLIGATOR WINE) to pondering the future of rock & roll and the forces at work on its development, only to have someone else come along like this with all the answers in a clearly ordered structure. And even more discouraging, when you plug the facts into the equation, to come up with Grand Funk as the missing ingredient. But logic cannot be denied, so we must come to terms with it.

I have never hated Grand Funk. I listened to their first 3 albums trying to hear what excites their fans so, made a lot of easy criticisms and snide remarks, and in general came away mystified. Then about the time Survival came out it all began to make sense, not just to me but to all the other writers who reviewed the album, and not just because of that album, which isn't much different than the previous ones. It fascinates me the way ideas like this tend to come along in simultaneous waves to everyone in this circle of people who think a lot about rock, but regardless of that it seems we've all been forced to admit the significance of that group, and the approach to music and life they represent.

This whole business of unification and exclusion is very important, and while Greil's perception in putting it all together is remarkable, I can't go along with his ultimate optimism for the rock. His arguments, to me, indicate that it's all over. We're divided now into taste groups dependent pretty much on our outlook toward life. In the 50s and early 60s we all shared the same outlook, and our music then was hopeful, open to new things, sensitive to beauty and subtlety, naive and brash. Among other things. Youth, as a social class, had never before tried to do anything on its own, and we all went into it the same, with rock as our marching song as it were. The years of failure and disillusionment and confusion, coinciding with the years of our lives in which our basic attitudes were being established, have left us scattered all over the philosophical landscape, based on our experiences. So you've got a lot of people who've met with nothing but frustration, and they just want to forget it all and listen to James Taylor or Melanie, you get people who've become hardened and go for 10 Years After and that stuff--you've got all kinds of groups, including us diehard rock&rollers'. But what about the Grand Funk generation? They're unified, sure. Through having grown up in terrible circumstances, taking reds since they were 12, thinking everything was hopeless and doomed from the moment they were old enough to think about such things, looking around at war and repression and seeing nothing to believe in--these kids were world-weary before they got into high school. Their formative years were not brightened by "Day Tripper" or "Like a Rolling Stone" and the closest they came to the delicacy of "Baby Blue" or "Lady Jane" was "Inna-Godda-Da-Vida". What more natural than that they should band together in despair (never even having had the chance to be "frustrated") and be reinforced by Grand Funk. But is this healthy? Are we excluded because they're on to something good we can't dig? NO! We can't dig it because our world outlook is different and we don't <u>need</u> shelter like they do. We still think there must be some way out of here.

This is not a healthy development of rock. It is a valid development, the music adapting itself to the needs of its followers, but it's never going to involve (nor should it) the over-18 rock audience, and I don't think it's going to leave behind any music that can be appreciated outside of the social circumstances that produced it. When the emotion of these years is past I don't think anyone will be able to explain the popularity of Grand Funk.

But if rock as we know and love it is going to rise again, it will have to be from the kids of the generation now in grammar school, and that's assuming society gives <u>them</u> something to be hopeful about by the time they're teenagers. Even so, however, too much time will have passed for them to have any ties with the tradition of rock & roll. Their major influences will in turn be Grand Funk and Bloodrock, and ...well, you can't get apples from a cactus.

- -
Where is Taco Pronto when we really need him?
- -

The life of a rock critic may be as exciting and glamorous as they say, but one thing's sure -- it's not the easiest way to get rich. Admittedly I'm in a difficult position, not being interested in most of the current music scene, not caring for interviews, basically just a record reviewer. I don't even go to many (well, all right, "any") concerts and only to rock clubs when someone special like Commander Cody is there (after all, I'm an old married man with a home and all, I can't go running around at night like I used to do when I was a kid) so my choice of things to write about is limited and my writing ability limits me even further, but EVEN SO there's got to be more markets than ROLLING STONE and FUSION, and I think it would be nifty if some of the more experienced writers reading this put in some suggestions. It would be nice if there were a Guild or something to insure that writers always get paid by these fly-by-night rock magazines, but I suspect that most of them would fold if they had to pay all their debts. How can these magazines be losing money with such large circulations and the generous ad rates paid by record companies? I hope I never find out first-hand.

> THE NEW MAILING OF THIS APA SEEMS TO HAVE ONLY 3 SHEETS OF PAPER!
>
> AH HA! ANOTHER WHOPPER, EH?

* * *

I'd like to ask all your help with some research I'm doing. I need facts on local teen bands of the mid 60s, esp. those who issued records. If you grew up in Cleveland or Denver or wherever, lemme know what the big teen clubs were, what groups played, what records they had, and any good stories you can recall.

RIAWOL*

You hold in your hands a very special issue of WHO PUT THE BOMP. From fewer than a thousand scattered readers you have become closer to 10,000, thanks to Warner/Reprise Records, whose mailing list of 8,000 will be receiving this issue free of charge. If you like it, and think we're doing a good thing, I hope you'll take the hint and subscribe.

If the regular readers will be patient, I'd like to say a few words about WPTB for the benefit of you newcomers. The Bomp is a magazine unlike any other, not an oldies magazine certainly, nor a journal of contemporary music (though we share elements of interest with both). We are devoted to music with that mystic scooby-doo, good rock and roll and nothing else. As a loyal Rockicrucian publication, we could do no better than to quote the words of Scribe Dave Marsh: "You know a Rockicrucian band when you hear it -- it's the one that's raucous and loud, the one people not only can but do dance to, the one where the excellence of the music always treads the fine edge of pure sound." Them's the ones we write about! (And others too...) We also tend to favor artists and aspects of rock & roll not generally written about elsewhere. The rock press only began in 1966, after all, leaving all the music from 1958 or so (where the oldie zines usually leave off) to then unevaluated. And through its own peculiar brand of tunnel-vision, that same rock press to this very day tends to ignore much of the contemporary music that we consider best. So, in a sense, WPTB is the most truly "underground" of underground magazines.

Except that we're not an underground magazine at all. We're a fanzine. "A fanzine", to quote from our first issue, "is by definition a thing produced and written by amateurs, for little or no profit, out of love for their hobby. For those who aren't familiar with the form, the essence of a fanzine is reader participation. Articles, reviews, drawings and such are submitted freely by the readers for publication. Readers are also expected to write letters of comment, giving their reactions to the magazine and their contribution to whatever discussions are going on." A published letter of comment is good for a free issue.

All our regular features are present in this issue, though severely edited and shortened to keep printing costs down. Past issues have been mimeographed, as will future issues until a few hundred more subscriptions come in. Mimeograph is nice in that it allows both writers and editor to stretch out -- a 60 page issue is not much more trouble than 40 pages. The letter column especially, usually 10 pages or more of discussions, has been pared unmercifully this time. We also review a lot more records ordinarily, especially 45s. But this issue will at least give you some idea of what we're into. The Kinks article is the first in a series dealing with important groups of the 60s who had a confused recording history. Future articles will cover the Who, the Stones, and the Yardbirds. And possibly Dylan.

The next issue, possibly the next two, will be concerned with the English Invasion. We hope to say a little something about all of the 50 or so groups involved as well as the managers and producers who were responsible for so much of it, examine the historical reasons for and the significance of this phase of rock & roll, and top it off with a huge discography. There will also be a light-hearted look at "Beatlemania", a collage of hilarious clippings from newspapers of the time, and reviews of some Invasion-era novelty records. If you have any records by English groups released in America before 1966 that you feel are obscure enough, please write and list them. We also still need articles on the Animals, the Nashville Teens, the Honeycombs, the Rockin' Berries, the Ivy League, Georgie Fame, Dave Berry, Billy Fury, the Applejacks, Alan Price, Shel Talmy, Andrew Loog Oldham, Brian Epstein and Mickey Most. And if we can find anybody to write about the early English blues scene, Alexis Korner, Long John Baldry, Graham Bond and the rest, we'll include that too.

Following that there will be equally special issues on surf music, instrumental rock, female vocal groups, and whatever else comes up. Interspersed with these will be ordinary issues, not unlike this one, full of serious articles, funny parodies, the best in rock cartooning, and all sorts of miscellaneous material by your favorite famous rock critics and our staff of absolute unknowns.

Our schedule is still uncertain at this point, hovering somewhere between "bimonthly" and "quarterly". Bigger, better issues naturally take longer to prepare when there's just one person doing all the work in his spare time, so the intervals will tend to vary with the size of the issues. But while

*Rock Is A Way Of Life

we may not be as regular as some professional magazines, we hope you'll agree WPTB is worth waiting for. And we intend to be publishing for a long time.

My deepest thanks and appreciation go out to all the wonderful people at Warner/Reprise and in particular, to Hal Halverstadt and Pete Johnson. Also to everyone who helped with this issue, especially Greil Marcus, Shel Kagan and Jonh Ingham.

Back issues of WPTB are very limited in supply. Number 6 can still be ordered for 50¢ and a few copies of #5 are left at $1 each.

+ + +

KSAN did a really magnificent thing one night a few weeks ago. At about seven o'clock they began a sort of spontaneous documentary on "cruising". I tuned in as they were talking, long distance, to a disc jockey in Bishop, Calif. Asking him about what kind of cruising was going on, they were told that it was too early for it to really start, but the kids generally went out "dragging the main", as he called it, from 9 to 2 or 3 in the morning. Then KSAN played 3 Jerry Lee Lewis records, "High School Confidential", "Breathless", and "Whole Lotta Shakin'", followed by a phone call to Fargo, N. Dakota (take note, Greil!). All the kids there were at a high school basketball game, but the jock was glad to describe how on most nights they got out on the main street and cruised from one side of town to the other. A little Chuck Berry "Maybelline", and "You Can't Catch Me" and we were listening to a disc jockey in South Carolina, speaking from a studio atop a drive-in movie, explain that everybody in his town loved to get loaded and bomb around the streets with their girlfriends. "What are the top records there?" asked KSAN. "Well, James Brown is big, and CCR, Pendulum..." "Aren't they one of those psychedelic hippy groups?" broke in KSAN. "Uh, un, I dunno. They say ignorance is bliss, and I been in Heaven a long time." "OK, thanks man," said the KSAN jock, Stefan Ponek, amid roars of laughter in his studio. Then they played "Under My Thumb" and some long rave-up from the first Savoy Brown album. In the middle of it, over the music, they got through to a station in Pekoe, Wis. where the practice of cruising is known as "shooting the loop and buzzing the gut", honest to God. In Alexandria, Louisiana, they all buzz down to the drive-in, located just past the new shopping center. The term there is "groovin'". They asked the guy to do an intro to KSAN's next commercial, which he did, a beautifully corny one. Some great Coasters songs, "Yakety Yak" and "Charlie Brown", and zap! we were in Toledo, Ohio, with WOHO. We heard some jock doing a rapid-fire Arnie Ginsberg routine, and then the connection was broken somehow. By this time people were calling in on the request line, requesting radio stations to be called. The guys in the studio were drunk with laughter, the whole thing was a beautifully bizarre situation. Then into Dylan's "Highway 61 Revisited" and I was pounding the table, swearing that I'd never heard a better hour in all my years of radio listening. It was like a trip into the past, hearing those moronic jocks talk about the local kids with their hot rods and bubble-headed girlfriends dragging down main street to the local drive-in. You could tell that Ponek too was flabbergasted at how easy it was to make contact with 1961, but I wonder what the guys on the other end thought about being interviewed by a bunch of hysterical people at a San Francisco radio station? At the end of the show, a few local listeners called in to say they thought "cruisin'" was exclusively a gay term; ah, these naive youngsters.

WHO PUT THE BOMP salutes you, Stefan Ponek, for originality and true rock and roll consciousness in broadcasting.

KINKS KOMPENDIUM

The Kinks stand out among the other rock groups of the 60s as having the most confused recording history of all. Not a year has gone by without some new material coming to light. In this article I hope to place the whole mess in some kind of order, and to comment on some of the unreleased sides on the chance that the public will never have the opportunity to hear them.

The accompanying lists are complete as far as American releases go (though it's remotely possible that "You Do Something To Me" was issued by Cameo), but the English listings represent only what I've been able to trace down. Obviously there's quite a bit missing for the years before '66, but as there was nothing in this period not also released in the U.S., it is of little import.

Their first release, "Long Tall Sally"/"I Took My Baby Home", is very interesting to hear. The resemblances to the Beatles, discernable at times throughout their first 5 albums, are blatant here. The sides stand as a study in Beatle-imitation. The constantly crashing cymbals, sloppy but enthusiastic playing all around, harmonica nearly overpowering the microphone; it all adds up to the reason this record failed, even though it was issued here twice.

"You Do Something To Me" and "You Still Want Me" were in the same style, and the record sold no more than 40 copies in England, according to their manager. I have no evidence that it was released here. If anybody has a tape of it....

The real anomalies, though, don't begin turning up until late '66, when "Sittin' On My Sofa" appeared on the flip of "Dedicated Follower." Of the next two Reprise singles, only one side ("Sunny Afternoon") ended up on an American album. That group of four songs is, however, available on the Sunny Afternoon LP, which every Kinks fan should rush right out and get. The songs include "Big Black Smoke", "Dead End Street" and "I'm Not Like Everybody Else", three of the very best obscure Kinks songs.

"I'm Not Like Everybody Else" is a powerful display of controlled energy and dynamic structure. It begins quietly but with ominour overtones. As the words of the title are repeatedly chanted, the energy level rises with Ray's voice to a screaming peak of self-assertion, Dave's guitar tearing like a whip into the spaces between the words.

"Big Black Smoke" opens with churchbells as a strong chunky beat comes in and carries us through a song about a girl who, sick and tired of country life, runs off to the big city to find ugliness and degradation. The bells return at the end to compete with the band in drowning the tiny falsetto voice that's wailing "Oh yea" somewhere in the middle of it all.

The theme of "Dead End Street" is similar to that of "Sunny Afternoon"; the narrator knows his fate and accepts it. The difference is that here he reveals a bitterness and cynicism that is missing from "Sunny Afternoon", reinforced by the tough instrumental backing. It's a hard decision which is the better song; they're both equally great in their own ways.

Things changed considerably for the Kinks after Face To Face. Sales on the album were very poor, and nobody was sure what would be best to put on the next one. Yet all the time Ray Davies, and his brother Dave now too, were writing more and more songs in the new, reflective style. Most of these were issued as singles in 1967, mainly to fulfill contractual obligations, but since their only album release that year was The Live Kinks, and the material was considered too dated by the time Something Else was being planned, those singles were not collected in LP form (though many of them had been minor hits in England).

Things got even more out of hand in 1968, following the dismal flop of Something Else, which was, ironically enough, possible the best album the Kinks have ever made. The loss in self-confidence must have been enormous, but they kept on writing songs and releasing singles. Nearly all the hard-to-get Kinks songs date from this period of 1967-8.

The first group consists of songs released on 45s. "Mr. Pleasant", "Autumn Almanac", "Wonderboy", "Polly", "Days", "She's Got Everything" and, in England, "Plastic Man" "King Kong" and "Act Nice and Gentle."

"Plastic Man" was probably thought too similar to "Well Respected Man" to go on an album. It's about this plastic guy, you see, who wears plastic clothes, eats plastic food, has no brains... but it's a nice rocking song, anyway.

"King Kong" is one of the most intense songs the Kinks have done. "I'm King Kong, got a hydrogen bomb, gonna blow up your houses, so you better beware..." The tension is chilling as Ray growls the lyrics through some kind of constricting distortion; then all relaxes as we are told, in the chorus, that "everybody wants power, everyone wants to be King Kong". Three verses of this, accompanied by a tingling organ and outstanding guitar work. A surprising song for anybody that thinks "Powerman" was a new development.

"Act Nice and Gentle" is a fine, lighthearted song that I often find myself humming as I stroll down the street. There's not much to it but a request to throw away your makeup and false eyelashes, and act nice and gentle to me, baby.

"Autumn Almanac" is a minor Kinks song, in that it doesn't say anything that hasn't been better expressed elsewhere. Mainly it's just Ray saying how much he likes living on his street, watching the leaves fall in the autumn.

"Wonderboy" is one of the most hopeful songs the Kinks have done. In it, Ray Davies exhorts a young man, "some mother's son", to go out and discover the wonders of the world "for it is at your feet." Notice that phrase "some mother's son", which later turned up as a song title on Arthur. You hear that sort of thing constantly throughout these discarded songs; key phrases, interesting licks, structural devices, inflectional experiments in the vocals... many of these songs were mined for effects Ray thought too good to remain obscure, in the writing of later songs.

"Polly wouldn't listen to her mama, Polly wouldn't listen to her papa; tried to make the swinging city scene..." but in the end she comes back as mama, or Ray, or everybody says, with finality, "I think that pretty Polly should've stayed at home." The loud, foreboding quality of the music doesn't fit well with the prosaic story being told, making this another minor, yet memorable, song.

"She's Got Everything" is a rocking song that sounds like something the Wailers might have done after some heavy listening to early Beatles albums. Built on a variant "Louie Louie" riff, its only lyrical content is "I've got a girl, oh so good, she's got everything", and a lot of "do, do do, do do do do"s in the background. The real meat of the song lies in Dave Davies' gritty guitar work and Nicky Hopkins' great honky tonk piano.

"Days" is one of their most accomplished songs from this period. It is beautiful, lyrically and harmonically. A simple love song really, "thank you for the days we spent together". The record is strengthened by an effective string section and carried along smoothly by Mick Avory's competent drumming. This would have fit perfectly onto the Village Green album (see later), and the English double album is almost worth buying for it alone.

That takes care of the songs that are available, one way or another, as singles. There is one other, "Susannah's Still Alive" which was issued on EP and 45 by Dave Davies, but that will be covered further on with the rest of Dave's releases. Meanwhile, you can get it on that double album.

There is some question as to whether or not "This Is Where I Belong" (from Four More Respected Gentlemen) was released. It may have been on an English or French 45. Anyone knowing for sure please write.

Next we move into the confusing realm of unreleased albums. Four More Respected Gentlemen was scheduled for release in 1968, even listed in the Schwann Catalog for awhile as Reprise 6309, and then scrapped. No one is sure exactly why, but several possible reasons come to mind. For one thing, Face to Face and Something Else had not sold well, so there was pressure from Pye and Reprise to follow them up with something commercial, or else. Undoubtedly a lot of soul-searching went on in an effort to understand why these fine albums had failed, and the only conclusion could be that America wasn't receptive to the kind of song the Kinks were then involved with, that being little vignettes of life in England. Since the songs on FMRG were even more in this vein, there was naturally some hesitancy about releasing them, considering the size of the American market.

Some of them were released as singles, which bombed, further reinforcing this theory. Perhaps the Kinks decided to wait and compose more songs, some of which might be more commercial. The next batch of songs was of the same sort though, and since the FMRG songs were so old by this time it was apparently decided to release the new ones as an LP. Eight new songs and two old ones were put together for an album that was never titled, though the number 6309 was carried forward by Reprise for it. There were misgivings about this one too, so more new songs were cut, more old ones thrown out, and the album finally came out as Village Green.

In England, two versions of this album seem to have been released. I have seen, in

English catalogs, title listings including the two extra songs listed in the discography. Later pressings contain the same songs as the American version, so the initial pressing must have been withdrawn.

But anyway, to return to the FMRG album, seven of its songs have never been released in any form. As an album it would probably have been a weak seller, for excepting "King Kong" the songs are quiet and subtle, lacking in "punch". They contain some brilliant lyrics though, and a lot of charming, melodic music.

"Till Death Do Us Part" is another of those songs like "Harry Rag" and "No Return" where the Kinks consciously work within some alien style just for the hell of it. The song seems to be based in large part on "The Poor People of Paris", an old pop hit of the mid-50s. There are some gems among the lyrics, like "If I were King, I'd tell my armies to change the world, and then I'd be like you want me to be."

"This Is Where I Belong" is a song of self-assurance, about knowing one's place in the world. Ray's tone of conviction makes it one of the strongest numbers in the lot.

"Lavender Hill" is unusual for its use of wah-wah guitar, one of the earliest appearances of this effect, and one of the few times (if not the only) that the Kinks used it. Like most of the songs on this album, it is concerned with security, settling down, and passing the years in pleasant surroundings. "If I could walk eternally into the land of make-believe, if I could live on sugar and honey... Lavender Hill is where I'd like to be."

"Rosemary Rose" is notable for the return of the "You Really Got Me" rhythm for a couple of bars, but otherwise it's a plain song about a simple girl. It's followed by "Easy Come, There You Went", a jaunty instrumental (their first since "Revenge") that highlights some lively piano playing. "Pictures In the Sand" is a cheerful ditty about passing time on the beach.

"Sing, Mr. Songbird, it helps me keep my troubles away" is the message of "Mr. Songbird", a light happy song with some pretty organ effects. And you may have heard "When I Turn Out the Living Room Light" on Warner Bros.' Big Ball sampler. It's a sparkling example of Ray Davies' sardonic wit. "And we don't feel as ugly as we really are, when we turn off the living room light."

"Where Did My Spring Go" is one of the frankest songs about old age that I've ever heard. It's downright depressing, Ray sounds so pathetic wondering what became of his energy, his hair, his skin, his muscles, his bones...

One song from FMRG was released by Reprise on their Kinks sampler, and by Pye as the flip of "Lola". It is called "Berkeley Mews", and it features a mandolin as part of a driving arrangement, not to mention the tongue-in-cheek Elvis ending.

From the untitled album, only one song never came out. "Misty Water" is an up-tempo number about nothing more than liking misty water, and something about Maria and her daughter also liking it. The song has some nice harmonies and generates plenty of good cheer.

Now we come to Dave Davies, who in 1967 began putting out a series of records under his own name, backed up by the Kinks. In July the first one came out, and it was released here in September. Both sides later appeared on Something Else. The second one was never released in America. The third single appeared, after SE, with "Funny Face" from that album and "Susannah's Still Alive", a new song. Then, almost a year later, a fourth came out in England only. "Hold My Hand" was one side, the other I don't know (can anyone help?). There was talk, for awhile, of putting Dave's songs out as an album, but in the end they only put 4 of the songs on an EP. Unfortunately, they were 4 that had appeared on albums, and the other 4 sides are now quite rare.

The only remaining oddity is the song "This Man He Weeps Tonight", which I haven't heard. Otherwise, unless someone can confirm a rumor in an old issue of MELODY MAKER that Ray Davies was to have issued an EP under his own name, with (according to my informant) unfamiliar titles, that is the end of the Kinks story.

AMERICAN SINGLES

[title, number, release date and position attained on BILLBOARD chart]

Title	Number	Date	Pos
LONG TALL SALLY/I TOOK MY BABY HOME	Cameo 308		
You Really Got Me/It's All Right	Reprise 306	9/64	7
LONG TALL SALLY/I TOOK MY BABY HOME	Cameo 345		
All Day And All of the Night/I Gotta Move	Reprise 334	1/65	7
Tired of Waiting For You/Come On Now	Reprise 347	3/65	6
Who'll Be the Next in Line/Ev'rybody's Gonna Be Happy	Reprise 366	6/65	34
Set Me Free/I Need You	Reprise 379	8/65	23
See My Friends/Never Met a Girl Like You Before	Reprise 409		
Well Respected Man/Such a Shame	Reprise 420	12/65	13
Till the End of the Day/Where Have All the Good Times Gone	Reprise 454	3/66	50
Dedicated Follower of Fashion/SITTING ON MY SOFA	Reprise 471	5/66	36
Sunny Afternoon/I'M NOT LIKE EVERYBODY ELSE	Reprise 497	8/66	14
DEAD END STREET/BIG BLACK SMOKE	Reprise 540	1/67	73
Harry Rag/MR. PLEASANT	Reprise 587	7/67	80
Waterloo Sunset/Two Sisters	Reprise 612		
David Watts/AUTUMN ALMANAC	Reprise 647		
WONDERBOY/POLLY	Reprise 691		
DAYS/SHE'S GOT EVERYTHING	Reprise 762		
Starstruck/Picture Book	Reprise 806		
Village Green Preservation Society/Walter	Reprise 847		
Victoria/Brainwashed	Reprise 863		
Lola/MINDLESS CHILD OF MOTHERHOOD	Reprise 930	9/70	1
Apeman/Rats	Reprise 979	12/70	

DAVE DAVIES:

Title	Number	Date	Pos
Death of a Clown/Love Me Till the Sun Shines	Reprise 614	9/67	
SUSANNAH'S STILL ALIVE/Funny Face	Reprise 660	2/68	

ENGLISH SINGLES

Title	Number	Date
LONG TALL SALLY/I TOOK MY BABY HOME		
YOU DO SOMETHING TO ME/YOU STILL WANT ME		
Till the End of the Day/Where Have All the Good Times Gone	Pye 7n 15981	
Waterloo Sunset/ACT NICE AND GENTLE	Pye 7n 17321	
Autumn Almanac/MR. PLEASANT	Pye 7n 17400	
Wonderboy/Polly	Pye 7n 17468	
Days/SHE'S GOT EVERYTHING	Pye 7n 17573	
PLASTIC MAN/KING KONG	Pye 7n 17724	3/69
Drivin'/MINDLESS CHILD OF MOTHERHOOD [by Dave Davies]	Pye 7n 17776	6/69
Shangri-La/THIS MAN HE WEEPS TONIGHT	Pye 7n 17812	9/69
Lola/BERKELEY MEWS	Pye 7n 17961	

DAVE DAVIES:

Title	Number	Date
Death of a Clown/Love Me Till the Sun Shines	Pye 7n 17356	7/67
LINCOLN COUNTY/THERE IS NO LIFE WITHOUT LOVE	Pye 7n 17514	
Susannah's Still Alive/Funny Face	Pye 7n 17429	
HOLD MY HAND/ ???	Pye 7n 17678	12/68

[Capitalized titles are not available on albums in their respective countries]

English LPs

The Kinks (Pye 18096, GGL 0357)
Kinda Kinks (Marble Arch 1100)
Kinks of Kontroversy (Pye 18131)
Sunny Afternoon (Marble Arch 716)
    Big Black Smoke, Sittin' On My Sofa,
    I'm Not Like Everybody Else, Dead End St.
Face To Face (Pye 18149)
Live At Kelvin Hall (Pye 18191)
The Kinks (Pye 18326) [2 records]
    Dead End St., Big Black Smoke, Autumn
    Almanac, Wonderboy, Susannah's Still
    Alive, Days
Something Else (Pye 18193)
Well Respected Kinks (Marble Arch 612)
Village Green Preservation Society
    (Pye 18233) Days, Mr. Songbird
Arthur (Pye 18317)
Lola Vs. Powerman and the Moneygoround, Pt. 1
Percy (Pye 18365)

American LPs

You Really Got Me (RS 6143)		9/64
Kinks-Size (RS 6158)		3/65
Kinda Kinks (RS 6173)		9/65
Kinks Kinkdom (RS 6184)		11/65
Kinks Kontroversy (RS 6197)		2/66
The Kinks' Greatest Hits (RS 6217)		8/66
Face To Face (RS 6228)		11/66
The Live Kinks (RS 6260)		9/67
Something Else (RS 6279)		1/68
Village Green Preservation Society (RS 6327)		1/69
The Kinks -- Then Now and Inbetween (Reprise -- PRO 328)		5/69
Days, Berkeley Mews		
Arthur (RS 6366)		7/69
Lola Vs. Powerman and the Moneygoround, Pt. 1 (RS 6423)		12/70

EPs

PYE nEP 24200 Louie Louie/I Gotta Go Now/I've Got That Feeling/Things Are Getting Better
PYE nEP 24203 You Really Got Me/It's All Right/All Day and All of the Night/I Gotta Move
PYE nEP 24221 Such a Shame/Well Respected Man/Don't You Fret/Wait Till Summer Comes Along
PYE nEP 24258 Dedicated Follower of Fashion/Till the End of the Day/See My Friends/Set Me Free
PYE nEP 24289 [DAVE DAVIES] Love Me Till the Sun Shines/Death of a Clown/Susannah's Still Alive/Funny Face
PYE nEP 24296 David Watts/Two Sisters/Lazy Old Sun/Situation Vacant

UNRELEASED LPs

Four More Respected Gentlemen (Reprise RS 6309)

Till Death Do Us Part
This Is Where I Belong
Lavender Hill
Plastic Man
King Kong
Berkeley Mews
Rosemary Rose
Easy Come, There You Went
Pictures In the Sand
Mr. Songbird
When I Turn Out the Living Room Light
Where Did My Spring Go

Untitled (RS 6309)

She's Got Everything
Monica
Mr. Songbird
Polly
Johnny Thunder
Days
Animal Farm
Phenominal Cat
Berkeley Mews
Misty Water

[Titles listed under "English LPs" do not appear on any American LP. Marble Arch is a budget reissue line; all English LPs except the first are still in print.]

Sam Swanson*

*Pseudonym for a well-known rock critic, used for obvious reasons.

his underlings on the other end. A conscientious pulp scribbler can even take the time to call or write those p.r. pricks and request tons of uncurrent classics from out of the catalogue (and of course he can always take a hike up to the office and find somebody with a key to the record cabinet and walk out with enough to give him a hernia).

When you get down to it anybody can call up those peckers and get results. It's not always so easy to get on a mailing list proper but it's easy as pie to just call up one of the secretaries and say you're doing an article on so-and-so and you need all the albums involved. They write down your address and in a few days you got 'em. Really easy. It's even easier if you get ahold of some letterheads from a mag (go to the office and take a look around and grab yourself a few), that way you don't even have to get nervous over a phone (and 6¢ postage is cheaper than a dime).

A Sam Goody's Discography

For some odd reason record companies still respect guys who write about the music. It must be to satisfy their own egos in regard to their product since radio play has to have more to do with insuring sales. And even a bad review is useful, it's good public relations to allow negative response and encourage critical analysis and controversy. So they send people free records. As if a review in Fusion or Changes could possibly yield more than 37 album purchases in either direct or indirect manner. A mere writer lucky enough to be on several mailing lists will receive literally hundreds of albums a week, at the very least 25 or so during any given six days of mail each week. Once in a great while if a review hack hasn't reviewed shit for a company in two years or so he'll get dumped off the list. But that's sort of with the assumption that he just might not care, like maybe he's not even listening to the stuff anymore. A simple phone call and he's back on in a minute with loads of apologies from the head of promotion or one of

Well anyway beyond whatever listening pleasure you might be after from the music contained in the grooves there's a wealth of wealth to be made from the albums as commercial commodities. You're not gonna wanna keep every album by the Putman Sisters, are you? Or even play all the cuts. So Sam Goody's in New York pays a buck for unopened review copies not stamped anywhere as promotional and not earmarked for dee-jays with suggested cuts. They gotta be clean and sealed. Once the plastic or cellophane or whatever it is has been broken the price goes down to

50¢. And if they're open they're also vulnerable to an inspection by the guy of the label inside. Like the wrapper might've been where the promo stamp was attached so they check inside on the record label itself. Promo copies identified as such are only a quarter. And there's a lot of stuff packaged in unlabeled plastic that still has some sort of giveaway on the inside label itself. Warner Brothers in particular is frequently guilty in this regard, they use a lot of white labels instead of the usual tan or olive green. Mercury sometimes too, white instead of red. So the record store guy knows as soon as he sees the color that you're only due 25¢. Capitol punches holes in the corner to fuck things up, you've gotta be a rare duck to get unmolested copies. Sometimes Paramount bangs an indentation into the back cover in so subtle a manner that even the reviewer's gonna miss it. But not the Goody's cretin, he always knows where to look.

There's this other store, Dayton's at Broadway and 12th Street (the only Goody's that buys stuff is the one at Broadway and 49th), that buys records but their prices are never predictable. Usually it's 50¢ per but occasionally it's as high as 65¢. Once in a while they pay less than 50¢ apiece but that's only when there isn't a single decent album in the pile. And they like to handle quantities of 50 or more, less than that and the prices are generally lower. So what it all amounts to is the opened stuff goes to Dayton's along with the deejay copies, and it's good business to occasionally throw in some genuine good ones to boost up the total value. So what that amounts to is there's gotta be lots of deciding as to whether or not a record is to be played at all. Like why jeopardize the chance of earning a full dollar, particularly with the meager prices paid for reviews and the odds against any random record being good anyway?

You can always _trade_ for known winners but the rate of exchange on that is piss poor, it's whatever the records you give them are worth versus list price, not even sales price for the store. So you might as well convert records directly into food-clothing-shelter-travel etc. money and buy the stuff you want cheaper somewhere else (but if you get on enough lists there's never a need to pay for anything). And, by the way, these places will only pay you the price of one record for multiple sets (I once got 50¢ at Dayton's for a 5-record Pablo Casals package from Columbia--unopened--it must've been around $35 list), so that sort of stuff is worth saving for better/worse times to come. Particularly since they weigh X times as much as a single album and weight is the all-important factor involved in the size of a stockpile to be liquidated (the heavier the pile the higher the necessity for a cab). Also, the earlier in the day (exclusive of lunch hours) the better, as the bank sometimes gets broken. One prominent Long Island rock writer brought in so many awesome heaps of vinyl (it must've been close to $300 in less than a week) just before Christmas last year that Goody's closed up shop for reviewers until February just to cool things.

Well this here's what I've sold Goody's in the last 2 weeks:

SWEET PAIN (United Artists UAS-6793)
LITTLE JOHN (Epic E-30414) (8 guys around the Golden Gate on the cover and they're not even the Beau Brummels, _you'd_ sell it too.)
BLACKSTONE (Epic E-30470)
MANDRILL (Polydor Stereo 24-4050)
PACHECO & ALEXANDER (Columbia C-30509) (John Hall's the producer:no Jay Lee, no listen)
THE SOUNDS OF SIMON, Joe Simon (Spring SPR 4701)
TOM PAXTON 6 (Elektra EKS-74066)
MORRISON HOTEL, The Doors (Elektra EKS-75007)
13, The Doors (Elektra EKS-74079) (Don't get me wrong, I love the Doors, these were just doubles, uh huh.)
ON THE WATERS, Bread (Elektra EKS-74076)
CLASSIC RUSH, Tom Rush (Elektra EKS-74062)
RAT ON!, Swamp Dogg (Elektra EKS-74089)
BREAD (Elektra EKS-74044)
SPACESHIP EARTH, Sugarloaf (Liberty LST-11010)
WAR (United Artists UAS-5508)
LOOK WHAT YOU'VE DONE TO THE MAN, Melba Moore (Mercury SR 61321)
JOE SPEAKS (Mercury SRM-1-607)
1+1+1=4, Sir Douglas Quintet (Phillips PHS-600-344)
LOOKS LIKE RAIN, Mickey Newbury (Mercury SR 61236)
LINDE MANOR, Denis Linde (Mercury IT 74004)
EXUMA #2 (Mercury SR 61314)
SALISBURY, Uriah Heep (Mercury SR 61319) (I sold three copies of this one, picked them up at the press party at Ungano's, press parties are another easy source of free food and records.)
THE SONG OF SINGING, Chick Corea (Blue Note BST-84353) (Now that Blue Note has abandoned its great old blue and white label what's so special about a Blue Note record?)
THIS IS MADNESS, The Last Poets (Douglas 7) (Good cover, it was a pity to see it go.)
WADSWORTH MANSION (Sussex SXBS 7008)
JUST AS I AM, Bill Withers (Sussex SXBS 7006)
HALF LIVE AT THE BITTER END, Biff Rose (Buddah BDS-5078)
COALITION, Elvin Jones (Blue Note BST-84361) (Elvin's great and all that, but the rest of the personnel is George Coleman on tenor, Frank Foster of Count Basie fame on tenor, alto and bass clarinet, and Candido on conga.)

BEAUTIFUL, Candido (Blue Note BST-84357)
WAYFARING STRANGER, Jeremy Steig (Blue Note BST-84354)
SACRIFICE, Black Widow (United Artists UAS-6786)
SOMETHING TO LISTEN TO, Jimmy McGriff (Blue Note BST-84364)
HARD AND HEAVY, Sam (the Sham) (Atlantic SD-8271)
BODY AND SOUL (National General NG 2002) (NG is no good in any language.)
SUGARLOAF (Liberty LST-7640)
BETTER TIMES ARE COMING, Rhinocerous (Elektra EKS-74075)
THE MARBLE INDEX, Nico (Elektra EKS-74029) (A color cover and I woulda saved it but it's black and white.)
LIVE CATFISH FEATURING BOB HODGE (Epic 30361)
LOVE REVISITED (Elektra EKS-74058) (I already got everything by Love, including the "Your Mind and We Belong Together" single)
THE AMERICAN REVOLUTION, David Peel & the Lower East Side (Elektra EKS-74069)
THANK CHRIST FOR THE BOMB, Groundhogs (Liberty LST-7644)
THE HUMBLEBUMS (Liberty LST-7636)
OPEN THE DOOR, The Humblebums (Liberty LST-7656)

That's Goody's and here's what I'm saving up for Dayton's:

THE BAND (Capitol STAO-132)
COUNTRY GOLD VOLUME II (Harmony H 30018) (Bargain labels are treated like shit promo copies.)
HALF BAKED, Jimmy Campbell (Vertigo Vel-1000) (Ditto.)
POSSUM (Capitol ST-648)
STREET CORNER PREACHER, Gene MacClellan (Capitol ST-660)
JERRY RIOPELLE (Capitol ST-732)
BLOODROCK 3 (Capitol ST-765)
THE CREDIBILITY GAP PRESENTS WOODSCHTICK AND MORE (Capitol ST-681)
SO THE SEEDS ARE GROWING, Joe South (Capitol ST-637)
DESPITE IT ALL, Brinsley Schwarz (Capitol ST 744)
A TRIBUTE TO THE BEST DAMN FIDDLE PLAYER IN THE WORLD, Merle Haggard (Capitol ST-638)
LORCA, Tim Buckley (Elektra EKS-74074)
SAME TRAIN, A DIFFERENT TIME, Merle Haggard (Capitol SWBB-223)
OKIE FROM MUSKOGEE, Merle Haggard (Capitol ST-384)
BRIDGE OVER TROUBLED WATER, Buck Owens (Capitol ST-685)
CLOSE-UP, The Beach Boys (Capitol SWBB-253) (All repeats or I'd never sell the Beach Boys.)
THE MUSIC LOVERS, Original Motion Picture Soundtrack (United Artists UAS-5217)
MAD DOGS & ENGLISHMEN, Joe Cocker (A&M SP 6002) (I saw the movie and, well, I never listen to an album more than once anyway)
BLOWS AGAINST THE EMPIRE, Paul Kantner (RCA LSP-4448)

And what albums have I kept? Well, I've kept only surefire winners such as these:

ONE KISS LEADS TO ANOTHER, Hackamore Brick (Kama Sutra KSBS 2025)
LOVE CALL, Ornette Coleman (Blue Note BST-84356)
TEENAGE HEAD, The Flamin Groovies (Kama Sutra KSBS 2031)
CONWAY TWITTY (MGM GAS-110)
THE DELFONICS (Philly Groove PG 1153)
TAKE IT TO THE STREETS, Elephant's Memory (Metromedia MD 1035) (Copy's too injured to be salable and anyway selling it would be an insult to Toby Mamis who gave me the copy and who's opening a community-owned record store that won't be paying for records but will instead be welcoming them as gifts.)
MOOGIE WOOGIE, The Zeet Band (Chess LPS-1545)
ODESSA, The Bee Gees (Atco SB 2-702)
BROWNSVILLE STATION (Warner Brothers WS 1888)
I NEED YOU, Elmore James (Sphere Sound LP 7008)
WHAT'S IN THIS LIFE FOR YOU?, Giant (Mercury SR-61285)

That's all I have and what more could a man need? In fact the very last one is a whole story unto itself and a case in point why records should never be wantonly opened right away. I have no idea what the platter sounds like nor could I care, yet I haven't sold it and never will. It's got a cover illustration of a large green dog with bloodshot eyes devouring a cutey whose clothes are ripped and shredded to bits. Good drool from the dog and good lipstick on the little honey. If the cellophane ever got broken anywhere the tension on the whole thing would be destroyed and the smooth, tight, shiny surface sent to kingdom come. The greatest cover in the world would lose all its gloss and gloss is at least half the show. I dust it off once a week.

[[NOTE: For some even odder reason, promo albums seem to command a much higher price on the west coast. Unopened ones can generally be traded across the boards for brand new LPs of your choice, even imports, or sold for $2 cash. Good promos go for $1, shitty ones for 50¢. Most reviewers trade 'em at used record stores so that for a given batch of 20 promos you can get 5 or more great out-of-print albums. I've gotten such gems as Fats Domino's first album, the Chantels, Johnny and the Hurricanes on Big Top, and Chuck Willis' King of the Stroll album in this manner. So if you're planning to become a rock critic, better move to California first.]]

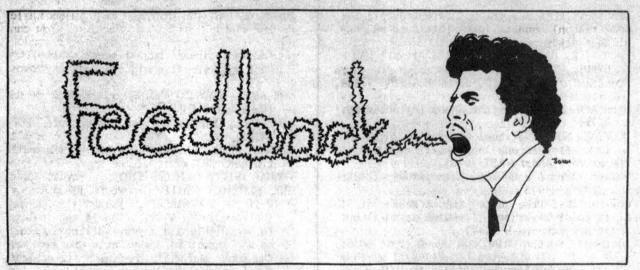

LENNY KAYE: WPTB, bless its little heart, has really come of age, I think, and your decision to leave the bulk of oldies writing to magazines like Record Exchanger and Rhythm & Blues Magazine is a wise one. In terms of material, there is a whole load of stuff from the sixties that fairly cries out to be written about; along with your ideas of surf and English issues, and that knock-down idea of the girl vocal groups (may I claim the Shangri-Las and the rest of Shadow Morton's family on Red Bird?)[[You got 'em!]], you could touch on that strange group of psychedelicized loonies on International Artist (like the Thirteenth Floor Elevators, and Mayo and the Red Krayola), the Night Owl people (Magicians, Strangers), Boston, etc. etc.

[[Yes, we'll get to all of that, plus lots of other goodies I'm not talking about yet--just stay tuned!]]

The poll was very gratifying, though I think you left out a category: namely that of Number One Fan Face, a perennial from Fanac days of yore. And my choice for that would be you, because there ain't anybody in that loose bounding called rock & roll fandom that does as much as you have. So, congratulations from me to you...

[[Thankee kindly.]]

LESTER BANGS: Man, it sure was great to get that latest issue of WPTB. I've been gettin' to like Rolling Stone a lot better lately, and putting my chips on Creem, but WPTB is such great reading like a breath of fresh air. Everything inside cooks except my letter, which sounds a bit snobbishly conceited and put-on of airs, but that'll teach me. What I'm not exactly sure, maybe not to write letters in the throes of beer no more but I'm doing that now so what shall it profit?

I'm listening to the new Archie Shepp album right now, the incredible sort of suite on side 2 called "Un Croque Monseiur (Poem For Losers)", which is some of the most fearsomely awesomely gorgeous music heard in moons and moons and more, so things can't be too bad. I got so sick of rock for awhile and all this pseudotortured folkhinged hackshit currently masquerading as sensitivity and poesy that about all I would listen to was jazz. Those phases occur every few months. Now I'm out of it and attention span geared back down to immediacy and thwack jivejoy so I hardly listen to any jazz at all, in fact this Shepp album is the first album that's brought me away from guitars and glottal loons and such for about a month so I guess it must be great. Followed by the new album on Mercury by this group from Britain called Jackson Heights who are also very good and who sound a bit like the great Crabby Appleton who by fishy coincidence I just happened to see when they opened at the Whiskey Valentine's weekend and visited and interviewed in lush Lawrel Canyon for tentative RS article which I'm struggling to edit down from a welter of snide sociological observations on LA press and Whiskey clientele (sullen defensiveness of a dumbfounded El Cajon rube actually) even now. Elektra paid to fly me and my girl up there for a hotcha weekend with a hotel room and everything. In fact we didn't specify it but the hotel was almost our favorite part. We were laying there watching Wagon Train Saturday afternoon when they called and said they were ready to take us to interview Crabby and we were actually pissed that we had to get up and go drink wine with popstars when we could lay there and finish our Western drama all in color. It was a great weekend tho. We really dug hobnobbin with the stars (not so many--I did meet two guys from Blues Image and drunkenly told them that I really dug "Ride Captain Ride" how good it sounded between CSN&Y's "Ohio" and LZ's "Whole Lotta Love" on Super Hits Vol. 5--meant seriously tho they took offence and stalked off for some reason) and LA journalists and hearing all the big rumors.

Lastly, I have just discovered a new taste treat: just take a 6-pak of Busch Bavarian, put it in the freezer until it's almost entirely frozen, so when you pop one about half to 2/3rds of it's like a beer popsicle inside, LEAVE IN THE CAN, then pour in as much good Jack Daniels Kentucky Sour Mash Sippin' Whiskey as your heart whims, for the whoopingest boilermaker of your life, Jack. Guaranteed to make you hop and holler and riccochet off the ceiling just like Uncle Scrooge (hero of lifetimes!) diving through his tides of coin. Send this paragraph to Richard Meltzer if you don't print it.

THE MAD PECK: I was gratified to win "The First Annual Who Put the Bomp Award" as best cartoonist. Nothing like being first in a field of one, I always say. Unfortunately it takes anywhere from three to ten times as long to do a cartoon review as a written one. Of all the magazines I have contacted, only Fusion is willing to pay enough to enable me to provide them (bless you Robert). One of the built-in difficulties of doing cartoon reviews is that the only way to do any truly objective criticism is to have one of the characters deliver a long-winded rant which slows down the cartoon. Also I find that the record companies assume that a cartoon about a record is a put-down. You'd think they would understand subjective criticism by now.

Actually I can only accept your award in the name of all the people who work for Mad Peck Studios. Several of them would like to put their two cents worth in.

THE MASKED MARVEL: Thanx, we needed that. Only last year we won "The Matchbook of the Year Award"--forty sacks of wood fiber compressed into an eight-by-twelve chevron shaped plaque with an inscribed piece of gold colored tin foil slapped on the front. But now this! No clumsy wall hanging crashing to the floor at odd hours or sloppy glue jobs peeling and cracking. Just a neatly typed announcement on newsprint. Onward and Upwards!

THE PHANTOM SPITTER: Did you ever feel like you were on the Dating Game via mail? Seriously, you guys and your mag are great! No waste of good space on your pages.

Besides shuffling around my 45s, making tapes is my favorite. At last we have direct control over each and every tune we hear in our parlors. No more sitting through a slow cut before we get to the tune we're crazy about. And what could be better than arranging tunes for a tape your friend plays while cruisin' around in his hot machine. You can put Elvis with Jerry Lee Lewis, Stevie Wonder with the Shirelles and Spencer Davis Group with Traffic. By the way, sweetie groups from the early and mid-sixties are my specialty--would love to send you something on them later.

[[Thanks for the offer! We probably won't get around to the girl groups until next year sometime, but you and anybody else with a fave bunch of honeys can sit down and write an article anytime at all, and I'll be happy to hold the manuscripts.]]

CURT EDDY: In a period when both music and music publications are on the same level as the economy, WPTB is a delight. This must come as no news to you though, for what other magazine or fanzine can boast of the reaction you have had from the more established rock critics. I only hope these people are putting their money where their heads are and spreading the word about Bomp. Simply seeing the re-appearance of Greil Marcus, Paul Williams, and Del Shannon in #6 was enough. The review of the rock magazines/fanzines was something I'd hoped for a long time. You did it in fine fashion.

[[Thanks for the kind words. We are finally starting to get known, mainly through the help of the established people you refer to. The only thing holding us back now is time and money--minor problems, ha ha!!]]

NICK TOSCHES: Your "American Rock Press" piece in the last issue was the most clearheaded, well-written, to-the-point article on the subject that I've ever read. Other publications that you didn't cover, but should be brought out in the open, I think, include: Living Blues ($2/four issues) a pro-format magazine from Chicago (917 W. Dakin St., Room 405; 60613) that flaunts some of the most imaginative essays, discologies and interviews related to contemporary blues around (great pix and record auctions, too); Hotcha! ($5/year) a weird German/English affair which, though largely obscure if you don't know German, always has fine new photos and cartoons and often discographies (Urban Gwerder, P.O. Box 304, CH-8025, Zurich, Switzerland); Record Research, ($3/12 issues), a tiny-type mag emanating from 65 Grand Ave., Brooklyn, NY 11205, which, though its direct relation to rock is often tangential, is tops in the pop/early jazz & R&B discography field, plus lots of historical ephemera and readership feedback (they also publish Blues Research but I haven't seen that one).

WALT TAYLOR: I am always interested in reviews by contemporary rock critics of early 1950's black R&B, because very rarely do they demonstrate any insight at all into the music. Your review of the "Black Harmony" album wasn't bad though, mainly because you didn't consciously treat the music in the LP condescendingly, as so many do. I despise the term "oldies" when used in reference to group vocal R&B due to the fact that the very transcendental nature of the moods, emotions, and techniques involved puts a sort of timelessness on the music, much the same as folk music and jazz. If something like "Sincerely" by the Moonglows, or going even deeper into the whole point of R&B, a song like "I'm Lost" by the MelloMoods is an "oldie but goodie" and nothing more, then isn't this true also of some of Charlie Parker's stuff, or early Miles, Diz, Lester Young, etc.? R&B has to be analyzed on its own terms and damn few know enough about what is involved here to comment on it honestly. Most people don't even know what to listen for.

[[Right on about "oldies". It would be nice to see this music get some artistic recognition too; not likely, though, with the records being as rare as they are.]]

GREIL MARCUS: Surf music--ahhech.
Did you know that Langdon Winner once led a San Luis Obispo surf group called the Revells, who had a small hit with "Six Pack" back in 1961? Oh, also. The B-side of "Angel Baby" was by the Originals. My brother met one of the cats at a summer camp in Marin and they talked about it. It was just one of those "left the tape running" things. More info--the Originals were together for ten years before they split, 1955-65.

[[Hmm, surf music in '61, eh? Was that the same group as The Revelles, on the Freeport label?]]

ED WARD: Gary von Tersch has a weird story about Zygote. Seems they found out that he was a Rolling Stone contributor, and sent him back all the manuscripts that he had pending with them, and a furious note to the effect of you lousy traitor, go peddle your trash elsewhere, we found out who you write for, and we're not going to return any of your correspondence with us. Bang. Gary sez they're a bunch of "idealistic kids" who publish only every so often--when their editor gets the bread from his dad. I always wondered how they could afford to put out ninety-something paged editions, in colors, without a page of paid advertising, and I just kinda assumed it was the Sicilian Businessmen's Administration that was stringing them along...

JOHN MENDELSOHN: Really, after all the quite contrived breast-beating (the obvious intention of which was to get record companies to give us more than a cursory examination) of my Rolling Stone piece, I still think that Christopher Milk is one day going to make some very beautiful music. We're by no means your classic instantly-identifiable Good Group--our harmonies tend to get a trifle dissonant live and we're never going to be that tight--but I know that we've got a lot of things that are currently fashionable to neglect down right: on record we want to be emotionally expressive and onstage we want to be thrilling. That's an oversimplification, obviously, but I really do think you know what I mean. It's getting better all the time too. Blind Surly Ralph doesn't write anything that doesn't have some very catchy melodic or harmonic bit in it somewhere. A lot of our stuff vividly displays the influence of early and mid-60s MAD Magazine, like our latest socko smash, "Second Hand Viola", was in fact directly inspired by this MAD film parody in which Bette Davis, as the domineering mama, tries in vain to make her son, played by George Chakiris, or somebody like that, become a professional concert ocarinist instead of a boxer. Our refrain: My only friend was a second hand viola comes by way of a group of mobsters led by Buddy Hackett coming into George's dressing room and announcing, We're gonna break your lips, kid, cos George didn't take a dive. The song is also about homosexual rape and humiliation, which my army phisical got me thinking about: see, I was trying to imagine what it would e like in prison. In our song the kid doesn't refuse conscription, but kills his mother's lover, "a famous gangland goon" with "a right hook just like Dempsey's that I didn't want to throw for fear they'd take my second hand viola." It's all very strange--what I hope is a distinctive blend of satire and pathos. One day I'll show you the MAD thing and play you the song and it will all become clear.

Sorry, I didn't mean to ramble like that. This, after all, isn't a C. Milk press release, but a letter of thanks and compliments.

[[Here followed a heap of praise for WPTB which I have blushingly edited out. And so ends the letter column; apologies to all whose letters we didn't have room for, some are being held over to next time. We Also Heard From Mike Saunders, Seth McEvoy, Marc Beard, Tom Hendricks, Jerry Kaufman, Glenn Crowell, Richard Meltzer, Keith Milton, Lisa Robinson, Melissa Mills, Waxie Maxie, Stuart Weiss, Vern Debes, Mike Willmore, Dave Marsh and probably many others that I've forgotten]]

[Last minit notes: Charlie Gillett is looking for "scurrilous anecdotes which indicate the nature of the men who stand between performers and audience" (managers, record co. execs, etc.). Write him at 11 Liston Rd, London SW4. And I'm looking for someone in Eng. or Europe to pick up used LPs for me in exchange for me doing the same for them here. Help, anyone?]

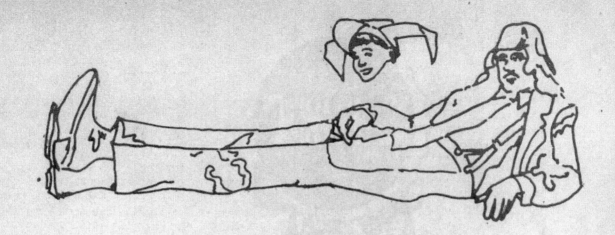

WHO PUT THE BOMP

PETE STAPLES   RONNIE BOND   CHRIS BRITTON   REG PRESLEY

ρρρρρρρρρρρρρρρρρρρρρρρρρρρρρρρρρρρρρ

    If any of you loyal readers have shared the indignant umbrage of the fellow on the opposite page, my only defence can be that we <u>have</u> stayed on schedule -- the "irregular" schedule announced 2 issues back. I'm pleased, actually, that so few have complained. In the old days when I was publishing MOJO-NAVIGATOR we used to get letters every day demanding to know where the new issue was. But you folks seem to realize that it takes time to prepare special projects. Now that you've got this issue, I hope you'll agree the wait was worth it.

    Last issue, small as it was, was a special project too. As you know, it was distributed by Warner Bros. in an attempt to gain us some new subscribers. And as you'll see from the length of the lettercol, we had a lot of response. That's great, and I wanna thank everybody who wrote, not to mention all the fine people at Warner/Reprise, from Pete Johnson, Hal Halverstadt and Judy Simms, all the way up to Stan "the man" Cornyn, for recognizing that fanzines are important, and for doing their best to help them prosper. In case you were wondering, we gained at least 50 subscriptions as a result, with about 15 borderline cases that may or may not have come to us thru the WB thing. And they're still trickling in at the rate of several per week, so it'll probably peak off at 100 or so. That's a pretty good response; not a great response, but a good one. It only proves there are at least 7,885 people who <u>don't</u> know a good thing when they see it -- welcome to the elite!

BITS AND PIECES

I have here a letter from R. Serge Denisoff, announcing a new magazine to be called The Journal of Popular Music and Society, "an interdisciplinary digest in the social sciences addressed to quantitative and qualitative research in the substantive area of popular music." Whew! He goes on to say, "The format of the journal will follow the standard organization found in nearly all professional and scholarly publications. The bulk of the journal will be devoted to scholarly articles followed by a review section on music books and a record review section. The record review section, unlike that in the music magazines such as ROLLING STONE and CREEM, will be patterned after The Journal of American Folklore model where an individual knowledgeable in a specific sub-genre will trace the impact of new releases upon the entire music scene. For example, one reviewer will cover all of the blues releases, while another examines the country and western sphere. These reviews will place releases into some kind of socio-historical context."

He plans to publish four times a year, and subs are $5, 4 for students, $12 for three years. The place to write is Bowling Green University, University Hall 101, Bowling Green, Ohio 43403. Best of luck, Serge.

As fanzine readers, you all have the unique opportunity to contribute information that we can use in preparing future articles. Right now we're doing research on a number of fronts that should result in a bunch of special issues next year, and we need your help. One area we're investigating is teenage instrumental rock (Johnny & the Hurricanes, Duane Eddy, the Royaltones, etc.). If you know of any records in this vein that were not national hits, and especially if you remember any bands in your region of the country playing this kind of music, please write to Tom Bingham, 126 Lincoln Ave, Dunkirk, NY. 14048. Secondly, if you have similar info on what I have chosen to call "punkrock" bands -- white teenage hard rock of '64-66 (Standells, Kingsmen, Shadows of Knight, etc.) get it to me as soon as possible. I need facts on the Guilloteens, Hombres, Wild Knights, Nightcrawlers, many more, plus all groups who had local records. Particular regions I need data on include Michigan, Memphis, Texas, New York-New Jersey, and Chicago.

There are also a number of records I need, which I'd appreciate all of you keeping an eye peeled for: ? & the Mysterians' 2nd album, Terry Knight & the Pack (Lucky Eleven 8000), the Inrhodes album, Battle of the Bands Vol. 1 (Panorama), Original Great Northwest Hits, Vol. 2 (Jerden), Top Teen Bands Vol. 1 (Bud-Jet), Thee Midniters (Chatahoochee 1000, Whittier 5000), Thirteenth Floor Elevators, all but their first album; Red Krayole, ditto; any LPs by the Sonics; Dave Allen Color Blind (all on International Artists), Surfin' Bird" by the Rivingtons (Liberty), "I've Had It" by Lonnie Mack (Fraternity), "Knee Poppin'" by the Dynamics (Seafair-Bolo), "When I Get Scared" by the Lovelites (Phi-Dan), "Quiet Guy" by Darlene Love/Crystals; "Crawling Kingsnake" by Buster Brown (Checker); "Feel Like I'm Falling in Love" by Jimmy Beaumont, "I Sit and Cry" by the Guilloteens.

I can use information on unusual/obscure girl group records, and on any non-Calif. surf bands. The Rivieras' album, if they had one. Memories of midwest surf bands, their lifestyle, etc. Credit will be given for all information used, and reasonable prices will be paid for any records you find for me. Get out there and dig. And if any of you have access to large numbers of old, cheap used/promo 45s, ask for my want list. I'm looking for a lot of things you might consider worthless.

MIKE SAUNDERS: I listened to the Who Sing My Generation LP the other day and really had my head shattered; it must have been at the right cosmic time or something. Who knows. Anyway, I heard the album like I haven't heard it in years, or maybe since 1966 perhaps. Actually I hadn't listened to it in a long time. The thing that struck me most is that I find their music on it almost frightening, in places, as Greil Marcus remarked about the first time he ever saw the old Who do "My Generation" live--it frightened him. On "My Generation" for example, it really almost feels as if the music is almost out of control. Entwhistle is practically the lead instrument on that song; he sort of holds it all together. But anyway, on "My Generation" and others Keith Moon is so prominent. His drumming is berserk, out of control, in the first place, and the sheer thought that he could be on top of the music is a bit scary musically. Anyway, I get a realsense of chaos from much ofthe album. There just doesn't seem to be a leader, a dominant musical personality, and the music at times seems almost precariously on the edge of exploding, just going up in a cloud of smoke & your speakers shattering. I really do think many of their things on the LP are incredibly violent and cold-edged, too. The thing is, the violence in their music seems to be very real--in the old days ((when a young man was a strong man...)) they used to fight on stage, and play against each other to see who would win the crowd. Keith Moon often did, which sort of fits in with the role he has on the album. At any rate, the violence seems very tangible: it's expressed at each other. Musically or otherwise. Just really a chaotic, teetering group, on the edge of who knows what. After that on out, Townshend took control of the group, and their albums seem like the Who singing his arty ditties, though Happy Jack is very good. It's not the same, though.

/ 242 Kingsrow Dr., Little Rock, Arkansas 72207/

RICHARD MELTZER: Hey, I just got the same ball for my IBM Selectric as you used on your last issue! Somebody told me it looked like a "grown-up's" typeface. Speaking of grown-ups it's nice to see that the serious metaphysical discussion of rock has gone back into private enclaves. From dust to dust. Greil's thing was real good and it's too bad there's no way you could possibly get Sandy Pearlman to write for you (he only writes once or twice a year and he's already fulfilled his personal quota for 1971) cause he did a real nice thing called "The History of Los Angeles" for Age of Rock 3. Pearlman's a weird guy, he was a classical and folk fan before the Byrds got him into rock and the link was Trini Lopez. He says he ran into you a few years ago with Paul Williams and he says there was too much dope in the air for his blood.

《If I'm not mistaken, that was the day we went over to KMPX and Paul said "fuck" right on the air. There was no dope there so Sandy must be thinking of later at Chester Anderson's place (rock press history buffs will be interested to know that I was responsible for introducing Paul to Chester, back in mid-'67). But anyway it's funny that he should associate me with the dope, since I never cared for the stuff & haven't used it in several years. :: Sandy can write for us if he wants, but I'm not making a deliberate effort to go Metaphysical. 》

Anyway, the English business. I remember when the Ivy League came out with that single that sounded just like the Beatles--at least as much as the Knickerbockers-- and there was a line in it "what you gonna do tonite, nobody to hold you tight, are you lonely." Well I used that in the original manuscript of what ended up as The Aesthetics of Rock (which wasn't my title, it was Something Else Press's, my title was even sillier, A Sequel: Tomorrow's Not Today) and somebody typed it up for me and it came out as "nobody to hold your thigh" and so when I was in New Haven and I saw their album in Cutler's Record Store I figured I'd buy it sooner or later. I think their only copy might still be there, I never bought it. Were the Newbeats English or were they from Nashville or Memphis or somewhere like that? 《 They were from Shreveport, LA, but recorded in Nashville 》 Oh yeah I remember when the early stuff was out like "Love Me Do" I heard this Charlie Parker cut called "Congo Blues", it was from a 1944 (46?) Red Norvo session with Dizzy Gillespie and Slam Stewart, there was this sequence of about three or four notes in it that were exactly what English stuff was beginning to get at. They never could have heard it (well maybe) but the point is I never heard anybody anywhere play that sequence of notes except Bird and some English people. Eric Dolphy almost came close to it a couple times but by then it was a near cliche that nobody was ever hitting exactly and he was playing it as a familiarly unfamiliar cliche. So I'd put it in an English discography except I don't remember anything about the label (altho it might've been rereleased on Charlie Parker Records-- in fact I'm sure I saw six takes of it on something on the Charlie Parker label, I think it was an MGM thing or something) or any of that for the original release. Speaking of that, you oughta see some of the guys who come in to talk archaeology at Village Oldies where Lenny Kaye works, guys who argue what number was on a record that the store can't verify. I hear Sam Swanson was refused a deal for all those Goody-bound throwaways, but Lenny brings his trash in there for trade-ins, Bleeker Bob runs the show and he's real mean and he has a meaner dog to back him up. Hey whaddayou know about some fanzine called Raps? I'm starting to get stuff like that in the mail and I always like those kind of fanzines because they enable me to get rid of my 8½x11 pieces of paper, do you know of any others I could dump stuff on? I don't remember what else I was gonna say except Fusion really stinks and deserves no credit at all, it doesn't even pay its writers anymore and I hope it folds real soon. Anybody know anything about the further adventures of Toni Fisher ("Big Hurt", "West of the Wall")?

《RAPS is one of the dumber of the new SF apas; I belonged for awhile, but only because some other people I knew did. There are hundreds if not thousands of fanzines published each year in the SF and rock worlds alone... ten Meltzers couldn't begin to get into them all. For the last 2 years AMAZING has had a fanzine review column -- get some back issues & read about some of the zines if you're really interested. 》

/c/o Peterson, 104 Perry St., N.Y., N.Y. 10014

RICH MANGELSDORFF: glad yr not entire an oldies mag, cuz i never loved rocknroll that much until '65. i was quite hip to what was happening & even played in some bands, but, basically it was jazz (konitz at age 9, mulligan-baker at 12, blakely jazz messengers & clifford brown at 14, horace silver, jackie mclean at 15-16, dig?) plus MAC and points north for BLUES,like,muddy & wolf & lowell fulson & lil jr parker, lil milton,bobby blue bland. impossible to get excited by buddy holly or gene vincentafter all that, ditto the everly bros.

((You snob! I personally, find it impossible to get into those screeching hom-players who drag a single solo into an interminably tedious hour, after hearing the tight, economical playing and well-controlled dynamic energy of Holly et al. for so many years. So there!))

English stuff and the genesis of the sixties rock scene fascinates me no end. also would like to see someone do research & an article on Huey Piano Smith & the Clowns, one of the few rock-type bands that had something more or less cool to offer. in fact, new orleans rock in general might not be a bad thing to explore, if you knew of anyone whos published research on it, hip me to where & how to get it.

((good idea, maybe some reader can help you. Haven't seen much on the subject myself. Would love to do it if I had the time. Maybe Charlie Gillet will tackle it.))

PHILIP HILDENBRAND: I am doing a research project on the way rock groups and solo artists influence people. Well anyway I'm taking a poll. I've only received a few replies from elsewhere so I would appreciate a lot of response. This isn't fake and I know what I'm doing, you might even get a personal response. Here 'tis. List:

a) your 5 favorite groups and give some reasons; go into some depth if possible.

b) your 5 favorite solo artists & the reasons

c) your favorite album

d) the group you dislike the most.

Thanks for your help and please write me at /2901 AltaVista Dr, Newport Beach, CA 92660/

((Wellsir. a) Stones, Kinks, early Who, Beach Boys, Flamin Groovies. Five ain't enough. What about Velvets, Standells, Yardbirds & Hep Stars? b) Dylan, Fats Domino, Jerry Lee Lewis, Van Morrison, Buddy Holly. Bet I missed some. c) silly question. Everyone's changes from week to week. Right now it's between <u>My Generation</u>, <u>Hep Stars On Stage</u> and <u>Dylan Live At Albert Hall</u>. d) Ars Nova. Or do you mean current groups? In that case it's BS&T. e) you didn't ask, but it's James Taylor f) the Stooges should be in there somewhere...))

ROB HOUGHTON: I wonder how many people out there realize just how great a seminal influence upon the state of rock & roll the group Love has been. They were somewhat like an American Kinks, a group whose influence spread far beyond the total sales of their albums. They spanned a period when people were just beginning to think of the music as ART, and hundreds of previously dispossessed folkies were planning to overrun the field with their technological innovations. Well, the folkies have just about ruined rock & roll, and have shown their true colors by the deluge of ledermusick with which they have inundated us. But it took courage and a slightly demented attitude to persist as a rock and roll band with no pretensions to anything greater.

Love was one of the first groups to surface in a period of freely available legal acid. There was something scatterbrained about them. The technique of calling out the instrumental breaks on the song "Gazing" where Arthur Lee yells "One time now" and "Johnny's turn now" harkens back to the Kingsmen's "Louie Louie" but still sounds like the early Byrds, though nothing so much like an open imitation, just the general L.A. feeling.

It is their first album which will be their classic. When I first bought it back in 1966, I felt like I had just bought a package of prophylactics. Arthur Lee's singing seemed to sound so mindless and stupid that my adolescent neo-intellectual tastes were embarrassed. But I bought it anyway, proof it had an attraction that I couldn't deny. I mean, it had songs on it that couldn't be matched by anyone else's first album. "My Little Red Book" starts out sounding twice as cloddish as Manfred Mann's version. And yet, who listen's to Mann's anymore? "Can't Explain", "A Message to Pretty", with its lyrics "I'll go slip-slip, you'll go slip-slip away". "Colored Balls Falling" is one of the first heroin laments to appear in the rock legerdemain, and the father to the Stones' anemic imitation "Sister Morphine".

Love went on to make several other albums since the first one, and many contain beautiful tracks. But it will be this first masterpiece that will be remembered. They were (and are) a hard luck group, never making the impact to assure a lucrative career. But then there's that first album to come back to again, and again, and again.

/1033 Greta St., El Cajon, CA. 92021/

((That's the sneakiest attempt I ever saw to get a record review past my watchful Editor's Eyes. I wouldn't have let you get away with it if you weren't from El Cajon and I didn't have a place in my heart for that album myself (tho I hated the later ones that Paul Williams was always gushing about.) But don't try it again, wise guy!))

((And that's all the letters I got so far. If any more turn up before thish goes to press, I'll stick 'em at the end. Meanwhile here's some that got crowded out last issue))

JERRY KAUFMAN: I don't like most of those groups from the fifties you and most of your readers like. I don't think it's "factionalism." I think it's the way I came up from childhood. John Kreidl comes close to my experience. I didn't know anyone who would say one good thing for rock until the Blues Project, the Mothers or Sergeant Pepper came out. And the Blues Project were my favorite group for awhile. Those people were the proto-hippies of Cleveland Heights. Until Freakout Sergeant Pepper and Live at Cafe Agogo, rock was dumb. The smart kids (middle — and low— class might have had something to do with it, but we always put it in terms of SAT scores, being very college conscious) were either classical or folk buffs.

I think I was worse about this than most, which is why I've never found it in me to like Elvis. I think you'll find most people with a background similar to mine dislike him or singers like him. (I used to be able to get a laugh just by saying Neil Sedaka, and I can still get groans from "rock buffs" by saying Beach Boys. (Maybe not your kind of buff.) And I think the reason why people don't appreciate the "real rock and roll" as you ask is tied up tight to this question. Most of us who call ourselves rock fans are mostly folk-with-drums fans. Thusly CSN&Y, etc. It took me a long time to appreciate Jerry Lee Lewis. Or the Stones. Yet they both have the Power. Maybe why I never liked them until the last two years, when I think I got closer to the power.

I've tried the Beach Boys again, and some of their stuff sounds good, if dumb, but Elvis sounds nothing more than dumb. I just can't get there. 《 You mean a guy has to be an intellectual before you can dig his music?? Sheesh... 》 Sha-na-na are tremendous live because they are aware of how out-of-place they are. Anyone serious would be laughed at just as hard, but with derision, not understanding. 《 Yer dead wrong--see my piece on this subject in arecent ROLLING STONE. 》 I do want to keep getting Metanoia, if it hasn't died yet. But I don't think Whomp is doing me much good, and there must be someone out there who's going to clomp onto it, onto my copy and say, "Yeah, Sam Phillips, yeah, I tried to call him, too." While I'm sitting here saying Sun Records? What'd they ever do?

/Apt. 63, 417 W. 118th St, NY, NY 10027/

《 You make some good points and I appreciate your honesty -- you gotta lotta insight too, for a folkie. Sorry, that was uncalled-for. If you can get as much fun outa CSNY as we can from the Flamin Groovies, more power to ya man! 》

(UNSIGNED): EDITOR BOMP: A WORD FOR OLD ROCK. SCOOBY-DOO. "PEPPERMINT BUBBLEGUM" ROCK SOUNDS REALLY NEAT (WPTB, JAN/71). HARD ROCK IS SO UN-ROMANTIC. IT'S A SLAMBANG SOCIETY, AND THERE'S CONFORMITY TO THE CURRENT THING. THE KID COOLS OUT BEHIND INNOCENT ROCK. THE KID DIGS ALL THOSE OLD NEIL SEDAKA RECORDS AND THE ONE HE DID WITH THE TOKENS. "I LOVE MY BABY". ANY 50s GROUPS. THE KID WANTS TO KNOW ALL ABOUT THE PARIS SISTERS. ANY CLUE WHERE I MIGHT GET PARIS SISTERS "LOOP-DE-LOOP" RECORD? OR THE CASTELLS RECORDING OF "SACRED", UNIQUES' "NOT TOO LONG AGO" AND FLEETWOODS' "BEFORE AND AFTER"? THE KID GIVES $2 PER COPY. BOMP IS A MAG I CAN BELIEVE IN AND IT'S NEEDED.

《 I'll sell you "Sacred", but who are you? 》

《 We get more goofy letters: 》

MR. GEORGE STEPHENS: My son left a copy of your magazine out in the kitchen yesterday when he went off to school for the day. I happened to pick it up out of curiosity, and I must wonder at how anyone could waste their time reading such trash. I am shocked at the subversive garbage contained in Who Put the Bomp, and I consider it an affront to all decency. Please have my son's subscription cancelled at once.

/3277 Oak Lane, Haywood, Kansas/

《 Hadn't you better talk it over with Leigh, first? 》

DON WEISER: It was cool of ya, man, to send me all the issues of your maggie. I agree 100% with your editorial about us Rock fans getting our balls together etc., but of course, you know that unfortunately such hot-stuff New-Left Aristocracy establishment tabloids as ROLLING STONE may not be too hip to your kinda plans.

..another thing that we resent is being called "oldies but goodies" freaks: well, shit, Rock aint old and aint goodie; "pop" music is much, much older than Rock and crap like the Carpenters, Bobby Sherman, Cat Stevens, Simon & Garfunkel, Frank Sinatra,etc. is much older than Rock; indeed, sexless whitewashed, sterilized, Tin Pan Alley, big city influenced "pop" music is very old. LITTLE RICHARD and CHUCK BERRY and ELVIS' music is young and fresh and crazy and sexy and emotional and fun and authentic American folk music from the rural South which makes the young (in age and spirit) wanna jump and shout and boogie and ball....which is more than any "pop" group like Jethro Tull could ever hope to do!

Why did KHJ and KRLA refuse to play "Freedom Blues"/"Dew Drop Inn" by Little Richard??? We made hundreds of requests to those racist-prejudiced pop stations!!!! But no luck!!!! Why does a cat, a miraculous genius like GENE VINCENT, not even have enough money to pay his telephone bill while pseudo-intellectual "underground" plastic fakers like Leon Russian, Joe CockSucker, Rod Screwart, Eric Crapton etc. are copying everything from GENE, RAY CHARLES, RICHARD, JERRY LEE and taking all the credit and money??????????? Why did they put such agreat American patriot and genius like CHUCK BERRY who wrote such pro-American songs as "Back in the U.S.A." and "Promised Land" in jail, while hate-preaching pseudo-revolutionaries like Jagger are putting down this country and having multi-million dollar ultra-exclusive Hi-Society marriages and getting all the publicity in the world!!!!

Fortunately, the "underground" establishment in this country seems to have jumped on the "Rock Revival" bandwagon and the same cats who were laughing in my face two years ago for listening to Little Richard are now extolling the virtues of Mr. Penniman!!!! Unfortunately, the record companies have only given us token support with the reissuing of some "oldies but goodies" collections, failing in most cases to promote the stuff!!!

They're also hyping us with Shanana, Flamin Groovies, Frut etc, some of whom are so talentless as to make the Monkees sound good!!! John Fogerty is about the only "new" Rocker with some concrete talent, but he lacks the stage act and emotionalism and earthiness of a Real Rocker!!!!

England has some excellent Rock bands: WILD ANGELS, SHAKIN STEVENS AND THE SUNSETS, HOUSESHAKERS who play 100% Rock, some classics, some new songs they wrote. But even these bands are exactly that: bands!!!!!!! Ther aint been yet a new SOLO singer plus back-up band, to come up with mostly new Rock songs (and some classics) and some old Rockers that few have ever heard (Down on the Farm, Let's Go Bopping Tonite, Hip Shakin Mama, Born To Rock, Blue Swingin' Mama and thousands of others) to come out of the backwoods and really rip it up!!!! No hype, no parody, no intellectualisms, no psychedelics, no fake "soul", but just pure, sincere, earthy, juicy, spontaneous, driving Southern Rock 'n' Roll with plenty of blues and hillbilly influences (no British influence!).

《《 Have you heard Commander Cody & His Lost Planet Airmen? 》》

The cats and chickies at my parties and dances go CRAZY-CraZy-CCCraZY, I mean, you shoulda seen them HOT PANTS (or shall I say SHORT SHORTS???) and them juicy boobs (no bras of course!!) barefeet hip-shaking mamas last Thursday nite at my place slippin'nslidin'n'boppin'n'rockin'n'sockin'n'rollin'n'reelin' on my desk and on my bed and all over the floor goin' absolutely bezerk, or berserk, whatever, doin' the Bop and the Boogie and the Chicken and the Boogaloo and the Ubangi Stomp and the Wang Dang Doodle and the Alabama Shake!!!!

Woweeeeeeeeee, we got that strobe light flashin' tuned to the beat of "Rockabilly Boogie" and "Good Golly Miss Molly" and big ole Elvis (well greased) poster and GENE Vincent poster in black leather and Eddie Cochran and Chuck Berry almost doing a guitar match, I mean, hell, we got that strobe going and Elvis seemed almost to come alive and grin down upon us from the wall condiscendingly and, I swear to God, Lawdy Miss Clawdy, evry time the strobe would flash, Eddie's guitar would like shine and Little Richard's teeth would like show in a big wide grin!!!!!!!!

When one babe took off her bra, that's when things started really goin' on!!! I mean, shit, what's all this bullshit about "oldies but goodies"???? Ain't no "oldies but goodies" lame brains around here!!! This is the breeding ground of the Rock'n'Roll Rebellion!!!!!!!!! This is the real "Underground"!!! It's the 1970's Rock'n'Roll Revolution ready to sweep the world again!!! Rockin'n'Ballin' it's all happening!!! The kids wanna have FUN-FUN-FUN-FUN!!!! That's why they're demanding Rock!

/1264 N. Hayworth Ave, Hollywood, CA 90046/

MELTZER ON THE TROGGS

Speaking of the Troggs and Miller beer I got two Troggs-and-beer stories for you. One is that was the summer my girlfriend ran off and married her math teacher and I was hard up so I went out on a blind date with my friend Gerber's woman's friend. They were both nurses and he eventually married his and he didn't like the way I was dressed at the wedding (I was wearing a stuffed bird on my shoulder) so he never talked to me again. Well anyway the nurse I got was the worser of the two and we doubled one night and went to some porn double feature in Hemptstead and every time I put my hand on her leg she took it off. We finally got to some bar that Gerber called Big Dick's cause the bartender was named Dick and they had Wild Thing on the juke box and I got real drunk and kept playing it and that was the only fun I had except for every time I went to take a piss from all the beer there was this cigarette filter in one of the urinals that I kept aiming for with my stream of piss. I kept trying to see if I could line it up a certain way, stand it on end or something. Next day we were all supposed to go surfing but I realized I couldn't stand her anymore so I told her I had a headache, surfing was still big then on the East Coast, Wild Thing and Wouldn't It Be Nice. And there's this other time when I was at the Gold Coast Too in St. James on the Island (Long) and it was the first discotheque in the whole area and they had a minimum and I was with Sandy Pearlman who didn't drink so I drank up all of his too and I put on Wild Thing and This Door Swings Both Ways but neither of them ever came on, the place closed before either one got on and I was real pissed off. Then there was this other time when there was supposed to be a party somewhere off-campus around Stony Brook that summer and I bought some Rupert dark beer (piss-poor) for it but it never came off. A couple months later school was in session and Tim Leary was lecturing there and Pearlman got to drive him back to the city (where they stopped in at the Village Gate to see the Byrds) and the beer somehow had gotten into Pearlman's refrigerator and it was rusty by then but Leary was thirsty and a real big drinker so it was plenty okay with him and he drank up about four cans of it and then he treated everybody in the car to the Byrds. I wasn't in the car, I wasn't even in New York State at the time and the only reason I mention it at all is that at almost exactly the same time I was buying the first Troggs album in New Haven. I bought it for With a Girl Like You cause I was sick of Wild Thing by then and the only incentive I needed to buy an album then (and now too I guess if I was still buying albums) was one good cut. There was another time too that beer and the Troggs intersected and that was when I was out in the Hamptons for an Allan Kaprow happening that same summer and I was with John Wiesenthal (who taught Jackson Browne how to play guitar when they were both high school surfers) and he ran into some girl and they were supposed to fix me up with one of her friends and it never came off and we (the three of us) went to some bar out there and I had to drive but I decided I was gonna get real drunk so he'd have to drive and once again Wild Thing was on the juke box and it would've been on the car radio too except that the car radio was broken (it got broken before Wild Thing was ever out so I never got to hear it on that car). The beer there was Budweiser, I'm sure of that.

ON THE STREET WHERE I LIVE: The history of this fanzine is the history of our (my adorable wife Suzy's and my) life on this street in Fairfax. "Neighbor Stories" has always been the most popular feature, a fact I attribute as much to the singularity of our neighbors as to my own writing ability. But besides providing me with an endless source of character studies, these folks have really taught me something about people, especially old people, and the way they choose to live.

Recently we were informed that we had passed some sort of probationary period and were now considered bona fide residents of Taylor Drive. Immediately the various neighbors began coming forward and confiding that they had thought us dirty creeps, probable dope peddlers and depreciators of property values, until they got to know us. We didn't say what we thought of them.

Now we are privy to all the neighborhood gossip, and we are coming to really know these people instead of regarding them as comic book characters. The funny thing is, everything we learn about them only reinforces the original impressions. I haven't run out of characters to portray--on the contrary, with the garbageman up the street who speaks only Portuguese and his attempts to talk to Suzy, and the drunken dwarf, and the ex-FBI agent with the flagpole who thinks I ought to want to be President, I'm not likely to run out for some time. But for this installment I want to bring you all up to date on what's been going on around here in the several months since the last issue of this fanzine appeared.

One reason that we may have been accepted as non-hippies is that so many real hippies have been infiltrating the neighborhood. Of course Fairfax and all of Marin county is crawling with them, but Taylor Dr. is in many ways a secluded backwater. Though only one block from the center of town, ours is the only street that wends its way up this particular little hill, and most of the residents have been here for many years, some of them 40 or more. New ones tend to come in only as old ones die. Sadly, there have been a lot of deaths lately, thus a lot of new neighbors. Up the street a bit is a house that has been growing progessively hippier over the years. When we first moved here we knew the people there, and though they had naked parties and played guitar and made leather belts, they weren't bad people. They they left for Europe or Canada or Mexico (one of those places hippies are always going to, anyway) and in moved some people with two huge painted buses which they parked along the narrow winding street without regard for others' garages, parking areas or passage. That was around the time of the Manson scare and we got a lot of people crossing the street when they saw us coming around then (even tho Suzy and I both dress straight and are well scrubbed). Not only that but they seemed to always have visitors who brought similar huge psychedelic buses, and we were glad when they moved out. Until, that is, we found they had been replaced by a guy with 2 huge dogs that rip up our flowers and garbage every night, walks around barechested wearing the same pair of tie-dyed multi-color deerskin pants and a feather in his hair, and has bongo parties about twice a week, where he'll sit up all night playing the same dumb rhythm on his drums and keeping everyone awake. Now a would-be rock band has moved in with him, and do they ever disturb the peace! And besides all that, he's a big time dope dealer.

Suzy and Greg with one of the Fairfax neighbors on the steps of their cottage.

Well all this gave Suzy ample food for gossip with the old ladies on the block, but nothing compared to the flurry of rumors that was stirred up by the arrival of a dope dealers' commune that moved in right across the street, two doors down, into a house that had been up for sale for many years. It has a high hedge and a fence with a large yard inside, but they always leave the fence open and no one could miss the dozens of pickup trucks, motorcycles, bicycles, sleeping bags, empty beer cans and wine bottles, and similar junk that litters the once-well-manicured lawn. And they have loud all-night parties every night--so loud we can't even hear the bongos any more. Not only that but they (or their friends) stand out on the sidewalk panhandling, loiter around the corner pay phone waiting for their connections to call, and who knows what else. In other words, they're everything they (the other neighbors) said WE were -- it's nice to be normal in comparison.

So you can see that the decline of Taylor Dr. is well underway. No longer can Mr. Celoni be seen sweeping the sidewalk in his bathrobe and straw hat, with his toy plastic broom. They took his wife away to the hospital and now he stays in bed all the time too. Some grandchildren take care of him. Johnny and Ethyl are still carrying on (and how!) across the street, and while they have no intention of writing a best-seller called "Sex in the 90s" they certainly could. But the ambulance comes to their house more and more often now. They won't be with us long. And our next door neighbor, Mrs. Heidemann, was taken away weeks ago, and isn't expected to last much longer. Soon her grandchildren will come and take away her beautiful old china and furniture, and rent her house to some, hopefully nice, new people. Duckmouth Doris, whose husband and she hate each other (they haven't slept together in 30 years) is finally getting a divorce. She found out about it when she got a letter from his lawyer. And was delighted. We asked why she hadn't asked for one years ago, and she said, "y'know, I never thought of it!" Doris isn't too bright.

Faithful readers will not yet have forgotten the story of how the man next door blew his brains out a few months back. His daughter the sleazy cocktail waitress lived there for awhile with her no-good unemployed hoodlum/bum boyfriend, but they couldn't meet the mortgage payments and ended up renting the place to a girl who has, thankfully, provided Suzy with some of the companionship she was lacking.

I don't know how it happens (such subtle mechanisms are far beyond the grasp of my dullmmind) but this particular part of the block has an infallible way of attracting only the most colorful characters. And our new neighbor Virginia is no exception. Though she is a very nice person (even if she's a food faddist who thinks Vitamin E will cure anything) she's not very attractive physically, as a result of a childhood bout with polio that left half her face paralyzed, so she's never been able to find a good man. But rather than settle for nothing, she goes after the real losers. Almost any hour of the day or night will find her in the local bar, or drunk at home. But she prefers the bar, for it is there that she picks up the old men (often in their 70s) that she brings home and carries on with. One was a tequila-guzzling Mexican, one a lecherous old Czechoslovakian, and her latest is a sotted bum in his 40s who insults her constantly and tries to put themake on Suzy.

When she's not bringing one of these characters home, she's doing something outrageous like jumping upon the table and dancing at a local restaurant (she was thrown out but the waiter brought her home--reminds me of the time she got a taxi ride here from San Francisco in exchange for screwing the driver) or going to the zoo and trying to get inside the gorilla8s cage ("he was a sexy gorilla!"). We're in for some interesting times with Virginia for a neighbor!

KARNIS BOTTLE'S MAILBOX

BOB SHAW: Many thanks for sending me the BoSh Fund/
annish of Metanoia -- and let me say right away that I both approve of and am grateful for the support of a fanzine "like MET". I had not intended to put down rock music in that Warhoon piece, or to attack any branch of pop as such. My target was all the nommercial, easy, uninspired, ordinary, money-motivated stuff to which we are subjected every day. Anything which comes into that category, I object to -- whether we are talking about music, art, furniture, machinery or science fiction. Compared to me, you are a world authority on rock music -- is there none of it of which you disapprove?

((Ha, that'll be the day! I'm glad you've clarified your intentions, though your Wrhn piece still seems unfair to me. But rather than start a dull debate over it I'll assume you erred out of ignorance, and happily drop the matter.))

Anyway, even if you loved all rock music unreservedly and I disliked all of it (which I don't) I would still appreciate MET because the great thing about fandom is that it is not like a political party in which one has to accept the entire manifesto or get out. Lots of my friends in fandom have views which I don't share on a whole range of topics, but it is precisely this which makes fandom so wonderful to me. How is it that a common interest in sf can weld together so many diverse individuals? I don't know, but I think there is some very important principle hidden there...

And speaking of long-haired young fans (as you did in the second part of your editorial), did you know I was one of the originators of that movement? Back in 1948, at a time when my relationship with my parents and employers was going through a bad patch, I decided not to conform in the matter of haircuts and I wore my hair very long. In those days a long-haired youth was really out on his own because adults went in for medium on top with short back and sides, and all with-it youngsters had crewcuts. But this suited me fine because by the simple expedient of not getting my hair cut for a year or so I really (I felt) staked out my claim to be an individual, and I soldiered adversity. The onset of dandruff eventually persuaded me to give it up, but by then I had made the comforting discovery that I would still be Bob Shaw even if I had no hair at all. Sounds trivial, but it was important to me at the time, and the legacy is that I know not to try to deduce anything about anybody from the length of his hair.

I much enjoy and approve of your Neighbour Stories, by the way. Nice reminders that when seen through the right eyes the whole world is a kind of fandom.

/ 6 Cheltenham Park, Belfast 6, N. Ireland 7

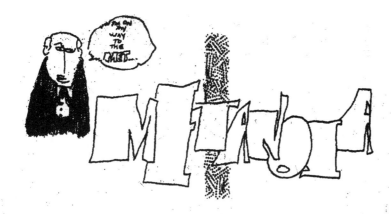

Yes, it's the 11th issue of KARNIS BOTTLE'S METANOIA already, written by Greg Shaw, 64 Taylor Dr, Fairfax, CA. 94930, and published by Len Bailes, currently of indeterminate address, for FAPA and the rest of the In Crowd. The only other way to get this magazine is to ask for it.
February, 1972

This issue's contest: identify the songs from which the linos are taken. (CLUE--I'm listening to 'em while I type this)

Yes, METANOIA's back again, composed this time on stencil, a first for this magazine. FAPA did it to me. Three months sounded like such a long time! What a joke. How was I to know that my opportunities for work and increased activity in the music press would increase so dramatically that I'd be left with less than a week-- 3 days to be exact--to put together the latest issue of one of fandom's leading zines. But that's the way it happened. I'll go on to detail some of those outside activities (at least I think I will--gee, composing on-stencil is kind of exciting; never know what might happen--) after I explain something else.

- -
"My dog Sam eats purple flowers"
- -

I want Bill Evans to note above the fact that Len Bailes is responsible for "Publishing" this issue. Yes he is, actually and literally. Len has been staying with us for a few days while looking for a job and a place to live in this area, and was in fact under the impression that his FAPA membership was a thing of the past, until I informed him that 8 pages plus dues would keep him in. I won't go into detail about where Len has been or what he's been doing the past few months that kept him from thinking about fandom (some of you already know), only ask you to believe that he has good and sufficient excuse for his inactivity, an excuse which also covers his disinclination to write 8 pages, as I at first suggested. We settled for saving his membership by letting him do the publishing chores of this issue, which coincidentally was just being prepared, and writing the column you'll find inside.

Okay, so just what is all this nonsense that's been keeping me from pursuing a sensible fannish career as publisher of a frequent fannish genzine? Well, for one thing, the rock music press is picking up. There are more magazines, more of them are paying (and paying more) and I've become part of a small circle of writers who pretty much dominate the scene, from San Francisco and New York, much the way an older fannish era was dominated (at least in spirit) by the same two cities, around 1959. That parallel comes to mind because the feeling is so similar. Few of us really write "music criticism" anymore. We either use the records as a takeoff point for wild and funny fantasies, or simply allow our imaginations to run rampant over the wider field of youth culture, commenting on whatever attracts our attention in a style of writing that many in the rock press are calling a "whole new thing". Basically, though, it's all stuff that's been done in fandom before, which is one reason I'm able to identify with it (I'm not one of the best writers in the field by any stretch of the imagination). It goes further than the style of writing, too; there is an air of faanishness currently pervading the field. Now, I was not a part of fandom in the late '50s or during any other fabulous fannish era, so my thoughts on the subject are largely a matter of speculation, but I always got the impression from the old fanzines that there was a sort of sustained, giddy group inspiration among the active fans of the period, wherein a great article would only spark other writers to even greater heights of brilliance. I now know that such a thing can be, for I have experienced it. To be a part of some large creative gestalt like that--there is no comparable experience. The new wave of fannishness centered around Brooklyn and Columbia, MO is starting to develop some of that feeling, and we may yet see fannishness again in fandom. At least now I'm able to recognize it, or its absence, rather than floundering about in theories and hopeful suppositions as I did in a number of earlier issues of METANOIA.

"I got a wing-wing, I'm gonna fly by"

OK, so I've been having a Fabulous Fannish Time in the rock press, and getting paid for it. What else? Well, when you're a guy who writes about records, the record companies are very interested in you. Not because your reviews have any effect on the volume of sales—everyone knows that's nonsense—but rather because you offer them a much needed excuse to spend money that might otherwise place them in a higher tax bracket. (One friend of ours told us that a recent album he produced made the company something like $3 million in clear profit. That same company put out close to 100 albums last year, of which maybe 5 did as well.)

The record companies host an endless round of press parties, in addition to sending out thousands of free copies of each new release. Beyond that, there are occasional whingdings that stagger the imagination of one unfortunate enough to be a non-rock critic. Already legendary is the junket to Texas sponsored by ABC in honor of Three Dog Night, in which several hundred press and media people were set loose in a first-class hotel, given unlimited use of room service, and a gala week of decadent activities. From all reports, room service privileges were abused with gleeful abandon. The various shops in the hotel were virtually looted--"put it on the bill" was the order of the day. Acquaintances of mine came away with new wristwatches, closetsful of clothes, gold cigarette lighters, all sorts of loot. One singleminded fellow found himself a whore who agreed to be billed through room service, and he wasn't often seen for the duration of the event.

I wasn't there, but in the last few months I've been a guest at several functions of a similar nature, a couple of which I've already written up for other fanzines (not that the quiet dreamers of FAPA would know the difference). There was the Impulse Records convention, with 3 days of room service champagne, the Grunt party with no room service but plenty of fancy catered food, and the special trip to LA (just Suzy and I got to go to this one) to meet the cast of "All in the Family" at a small, informal party. We were only in the hotel one day, but managed to go through $75 in filet mignon, eggs Benedict, baked Alaska, etc. Next week we're going back to LA for a five-day MCA Records convention, at which we'll be treated to a private banquet with live entertainment by Sonny & Cher, a trip to Disneyland, a trip to the Santa Anita race track, a tour of the Universal Studios, and lotsa other events. They're flying in 300 people, many of them writer friends of mine from other parts of the country. What usually happens is that the circle of 30 or so of us end up together in one room, ordering a continuous flow of the hotel's finest potables, with an occasional gourmet delight to ease our stomachs, talking late into the night. It's like if the book publishers gave all-expense paid trips to conventions to every fanzine book reviewer. I'm just lucky to be a rock fan as well as a SF fan (which I am, despite anything to the contrary you might read in this issue, like in Len's column. Just because he said he might write a story for me and I replied, "As long as it's not science fiction!").

And then there's my rock fanzine, which takes as much work as Dick Geis put into SFR, though admittedly the rewards are greater. I now get $115/page for advertising, and the temptation is to publish more often so as to get more of that filthy lucre. Unfortunately, the direction the magazine has been taking lately is toward 'theme' issues covering all aspects of a certain trend or style in popular music, which to do thoroughly means a lot of pages. The last issue was over 100 pages, the next will be around 60, the one after perhaps 120. That's publishing every three months or less.

Now do you begin to see why I only have 3 days for METANOIA?

who put the bomp

NEWS BULLETIN! WE HAVE JUST RECIEVED AN UNCONFIRMED REPORT THAT A PLANE CONTAINING BUDDY HOLLY, RICHIE VALENS AND THE "BIG BOPPER" IS MISSING...

GOSH!

RICKY... PLEASE... YOUR... ...HAND...

RIAWOL...

[Cartoon: Man with glasses saying "ACADEMICALLY SPEAKING, IT ISN'T A WAY OF LIFE UNTIL YOU'RE READY TO DIE FOR YOUR RECORDS!" Next to a radio/speaker blaring "NEWS FLASH! COLLECTOR DIES TRYING TO RESCUE ELVIS AUTOGRAPH FROM BLAZING CHEVY!!" Signed JONH]

By now you should've learned to expect the unexpected. I know I promised an English Invasion issue this time, but for a number of logistical reasons it turned out to be better to hold that for next time and use up some of the other material in my files. By chance I found myself with a lot of material in the same general subject area--rockabilly--so I pulled a few strings and came up with the selection of articles you hold in your hand, thus satisfying once again my preference for theme issues.

I remember stating once that the fifties had been so thoroughly mined and sifted through that I saw little point in concentrating our attention on them. Well, it turns out I was less than totally correct. I believe the material in this issue contains information not to be found elsewhere. And I hope you enjoy the photographs, many of which have never been published before.

Of course Rockabilly is too great a subject to be given our usual treatment. It would take a weighty tome to explore the details and the influence of this music. One day recently I was talking to Gene Sculatti, WPTB's expert on surf music and California teen culture. We were discussing whether it was possible to put an objective value on different styles of rock & roll. He startled me by saying that the more he listens to the rock of the '50s, the more he believes them to have been the music's most creative, exciting years. In all honesty, I have to agree. I remember very little before 1958 except the big hits, but as I go back and root out the records I find myself marvelling at their raw energy and honest emotion. When writing about the music of the 60s, which I also enjoy greatly but which satisfies me less deeply, I take it for granted that you readers are aware of the peaks whose valleys I'm exploring. If not, then please take this issue as a reminder to check out what you're missing.

Elvis levis
levis Elvis   -- Jeff Cloves, Ooooopbop sh'bam

ABOUT THE CONTENTS

Gene Vincent's death was a blow to me. I'm not really sure why--of the 30 or so songs of his I've heard, I am strongly impressed by only a handful. But much more impressive to me was Gene's simple presence in the world of rock--his appearance and style in the '50s, his tragic career and his association with so many other monumental rock tragedies, and the unavoidable reminder his latter days offered of the shameful way the music world ignores and defeats those who have passed their peaks. Ron Weiser's article, I believe, shows Vincent in the true light of what he was--one of rock & roll's great figures. Ron himself was very close to Gene for a couple of years before the end, and more of his reminiscences can be found in his own excellent rockabilly fanzine, ROLLIN' ROCK--see review in this issue.

Wanda Jackson may be a name familiar to you only as a country & western singer. That was the case with me until I found an old Capitol album, Rockin' With Wanda. Immediately recognizing it as a true classic, I scouted around for someone with more knowledge of her, and found my friend Rip Lay who was already in the process of arranging an interview with Wanda. His article sheds light on many of the rock & roll figures of the '50s, and contains much information never seen elsewhere. This was the only interview of its type she has ever given. Her country material is very fine and I recommend it without reservation, but even if you don't like country music you need only hear her early material to realize she was a great rocker in her own right. Check out Capitol's recent reissues on the Hilltop label and see if I'm not right.

There are only 3 known copies of Harmonica Frank's record on Sun, and Mike Willmore has one of them. His article on this obscure early country rocker is authoritative and interesting—and the first I've seen on the subject.

* * *

For those who haven't seen WPTB before, it isn't usually this oldies-oriented. The scope of our coverage includes everything from the earliest beginnings of rock & roll up to the present. Rock & roll—that's what everything you'll ever see in this magazine has in common. What we usually try to do is isolate some trend or style and analyze its place in the development of the music, using articles and reviews of specific artists as examples in a larger thesis which tries to cover the entire movement and place it all in perspective. In past issues this treatment has been given to English rock in the pre-Beatles years (#8) and in the future our gaze will turn to the English Invasion proper (#s 10 and 11). After that, we will be doing a surf/hot rod issue (probably next summer) and special issues are indefinitely planned for instrumental rock and the girl group sound. We are also open to suggestions. Between these special issues will be some not-so-special ones, dealing with various examples of American hard rock of the early-mid '60s. The emphasis here will be on obscure groups and labels, and local scenes. This is too broad a subject to be covered in one issue, but hopefully over the course of a couple of years we can get it all clarified. Other things I want to get around to are "psychedelic" studio rock, bubblegum music, folk rock, and chicano rock (Thee Midniters, etc.). I don't know if we'll ever get around to all these things or if my plans will change over the next two years, but that's the program as it stands now.

I also intend to start running label listings soon, as soon as I get any complete. And you can help! If you have any of the following, please send number, name of artist and both titles. INTERNATIONAL ARTISTS: 100,101,103,105-6,110-11,114-15, 118-9,123,127,129,131-2,134-5,137,140,143--; RED BIRD: 004,005,007,013,023,027,029, 034-5,039-41,044-47,049-52,054-57,059-65,067,069--; TOLLIE: 9002-4,6-7,9-14,16-18, 21-24,28,30,31-38,42,43,46,48,50--; ABNAK 100-107,109-113,115,117; ACTA: 800,812,816, 817,820,825-6,828,830,832-4,886--; TRIBE: 8300-7,9,11,13,15,18,20; PARROT: 40,000-8, 3000-8,300-11; PRESS: 5000-6,9; 9700-9800 series; LONDON 9600-9686; any oddities 9690-9830; 9767-9782,9784-89; 9803--; FONTANA 1800-1900 series. Also open to suggestion for other label listings.

Meanwhile thanks to everyone who has helped me find records. I'm putting together want lists, which have turned out to be extensive beyond my expectations. When it's finished I'll be running off copies, and if you're interested in getting one let me know. For now I'm most anxious to have anything by the Barbarians, and most anything on the following labels: Jerden, Etiquette, Seafair-Bolo (N. .); Hideout, A^2, Detroit Sound (Mich.); USA, Dunwich, (Chicago), Soma, Twin Town, Bear, Bangor, Witch, Turtle (Minneapolis); Tollie, Press, any of the stuff listed above for that matter. And any obscure oddities on local labels of punk rock, folk rock, girl group rock, English type rock, psychedelic rock, etc. Low prices only for most 45s, will also trade. Write first if possible.

Ahead of his Time:

With little doubt the most underrated Rock singer in the United States is Gene Vincent. Rarely, if ever, will you read in the press about his influence on today's music. The names of Elvis, Chuck Berry, Little Richard and Buddy Holly will pop up time after time, but not Gene's. Yet Gene has affected Rock music and the Rock Culture almost as much, in some ways even more, than the singers mentioned above.

It all started back in 1956 with "Be Bop a Lula." Capitol was searching for an answer to Elvis Presley and they came up with Gene; but Gene wasn't just another Elvis imitator: true, they both were hard Rockers, came from the South and had humble beginnings, but while Elvis' appeal was mainly to girls, Gene's tortured face, bony features, greasy hair and crippled leg didn't exactly make him fit the description of a "teen idol"! He was more of a "freak". The original freak. If I were a Zappa fan, I would say he was a Frank Zappa 13 years ahead of his time. Gene opened the doors to all those kids who were afraid to go into show business because of their less-than-desirable looks. At a time when the other artists were "pretty", Gene was ugly; he stood alone.

While today people like John Lennon may use the word "fuck" on records, in 1956 Gene had a song called "Woman Love" (for which he was sued by the State of Virginia and banned by U.S. deejays) where, between the various moans and groans, he slurs: "...a-fuggin' all the time..." Actually the adults may have had trouble comprehending the lyrics or could have interpreted the "fuggin'" for "huggin'", but when I asked

Gene Vincent's influence in Rock & Roll

Gene about this, he unequivocally replied that it was an "f". Then there was "Dance to the Bop" which went like this: "There's a lil juke-joint on the outskirts of town, where the cats pick 'em up and they lay them down..." or "Rollin Danny": "Lined six women up against the wall, and, I'm telling you, man, this cat he pulled them all..." Vincent paved the way for today's "heavier" lyrics.

But it wasn't only here that he was influential: seeing people like Jim Morrison and Joe Cocker wearing black leather on stage and doing those gyrations so familiar to all Vincent fans, I cannot help but think of him, especially considering that both Cocker and Morrison, by their own admission, are/were devoted Vincent fanatics. Jim Morrison considered Gene Vincent and Elvis Presley his two main influences. Like Gene, Jim was a "freak"; unlike Gene though, who spontaneously created an uncontrollable excitement on stage, Jim had to resort to fabricated gimmicks (see the Miami incident) in order to try to stir the same excitement. Was Morrison trying to surpass the wildness of his idol's stage act when he opened his fly in Miami? If you think this is far-fetched, you're wrong: about two months after the Miami incident, Morrison told Gene that one day he hoped to match the frenzy of a Gene Vincent concert. According to Gene's wife, Jackie Frisco, Jim was constantly saying how much he admired Gene and kept on repeating over and over: "Gene, you and I are so alike; we go together..." He and the other Doors came to Vincent's Elektra recording session

by ron weiser

and were raving how far-out the whole thing was.

When they talk about the Beatles and who had the most influence upon them, the names of the Everly Bros, Buddy Holly, Chuck Berry and Little Richard come up all the time. But what about Gene Vincent??? It seems here again his name is often forgotten by our "Rock" press. But you wouldn't forget it if you saw a copy of the photo I have of the Beatles all dressed in black leather suits (like their idol), signed and dedicated by each one of them to Gene Vincent, dated Hamburg 1962; at that time they were backing Gene up. And since I'm talking about the Beatles I won't omit that John Lennon is a raving Vincent follower and that "Woman Love" is one of his favorite songs (Rolling Stone, Nov. 23, 1968). Of all the stars present at the 1969 Toronto Rock Revival Show, Lennon spent all of his time with Vincent. I probably would be correct in stating that Gene was Lennon's main inspiration; so much that John listens to "Be Bop A Lula" every time, before going in the recording studio, to get inspired in the right mood.

Here's what some of today's other "stars" have to say about Gene. Roger McQuinn: "...that was "Baby Love", which was Gene Vincent; incidentally that was the first thing George Harrison learned how to play on the guitar..." Rolling Stone, Oct. 29, 1970. Mike Bloomfield: "...it was the sonority of those blues notes, I could hear them in Gene Vincent's guitar solos and Fats Domino's songs..." (that influenced him) Hit Parader, Feb. 1967. Skip Spence of Moby Grape: "...I learned from Gene Vincent's 'Be Bop A Lula'; we pantomimed that once in 7th grade. Smash!" Hit Parader, Feb. '68. And John Lennon again: "...and I'm still trying to reproduce 'Some Other Guy' sometimes or 'Be Bop A Lula'. But I'd like to make a record like 'Some Other Guy'. I haven't done one that satisfied me much as that satisfied me. Or 'Be Bop A Lula' or 'Heartbreak Hotel'..." Rolling Stone, Nov. 23, 1968.

Now since you're dusting off your back issues of Rolling Stone to check out what I said about Lennon, why doncha pull out that issue where Bob Dylan claims that Gene Vincent was one of the greatest influences in his career??? (I'd gladly give you the number if I could remember it). In any case it's not too hard to believe: when you play Dylan & Vincent records you can immediately spot the similarity in enunciation, even if their respective backing groups are quite different.

If you consider Dylan and Lennon superstars, then Elvis is certainly a super-superstar. Now some may claim that "Be Bop A Lula" sounded like "Heartbreak Hotel" and I agree that there is a resemblance, but then, one evening in 1968 you turn on the TV set and what do you see? You see the Elvis TV special: here is Elvis donning a black leather suit and you're trying to figure out where and when you saw such an outfit before!!!! Was it Jim Morrison? Maybe. But try to go back with your memory, if you can. Elvis had to borrow a Gene Vincent look to make his comeback as the King of Rock, after 8 years of lame, gutless and sugary Broadway-type movie songs!!!! Maybe without that black leather on your TV screen, Elvis wouldn't have had such an impact and his "comeback" might not have gotten off the ground as it did????? Speculation? Or is it?

It's no speculation though that Alice Cooper considered Vincent more of a "fellow freak" than anybody else, enough to dedicate a song to him on one of their albums. From black leather to blue denim: nowadays it is common to see artists come onstage wearing blue jeans; well, our man had a fixation with blue jeans of all colors, from "Blue Jean Bop" to "Red Blue Jeans and a Pony Tail" to green blue jeans (as in "Bop Street") to bell-bottom jeans, so popular now, which he was wearing back in 1956. The first time I walked into a "hippie-store" and saw those neck-chains with big medallions and pendants, I couldn't help but wonder if the person who launched this style hadn't somehow gotten the idea from a certain Gene Vincent who wore such a metal chain & medallion around his neck on stage 8 years earlier. Maybe Gene didn't influence him, maybe it would have come anyway; in that case Gene was still 8 years ahead of his time.

It is common knowledge that "Surfin' U.S.A." is nothing but Chuck Berry's "Sweet Little Sixteen" with new words, but how many of you know that Vincent's "Git It", recorded in 1957, already has the Beach Boys' surfing sound of the sixties??????? Now, didn't the Beach Boys record for Capitol as Gene? I wonder if that's the song (listen to it if you get a chance) that gave them their sound!!!!! It must be. I wouldn't be surprised since when Gene appeared at the Brass Ring in 1970, the Boys were there and so were the Faces with Rod Stewart and Kim Fowley and Del Shannon and Melanie and Delany & Bonnie and Ray Peterson and Flame and Joe Cocker and the list goes on and on. It was an irony that while few people off the street knew who Gene Vincent was to come and see him, yet the place was packed with....... celebrities!!!! Who else can claim to fill up a club with 90% celebrities and 10% common slobs like you and me?????

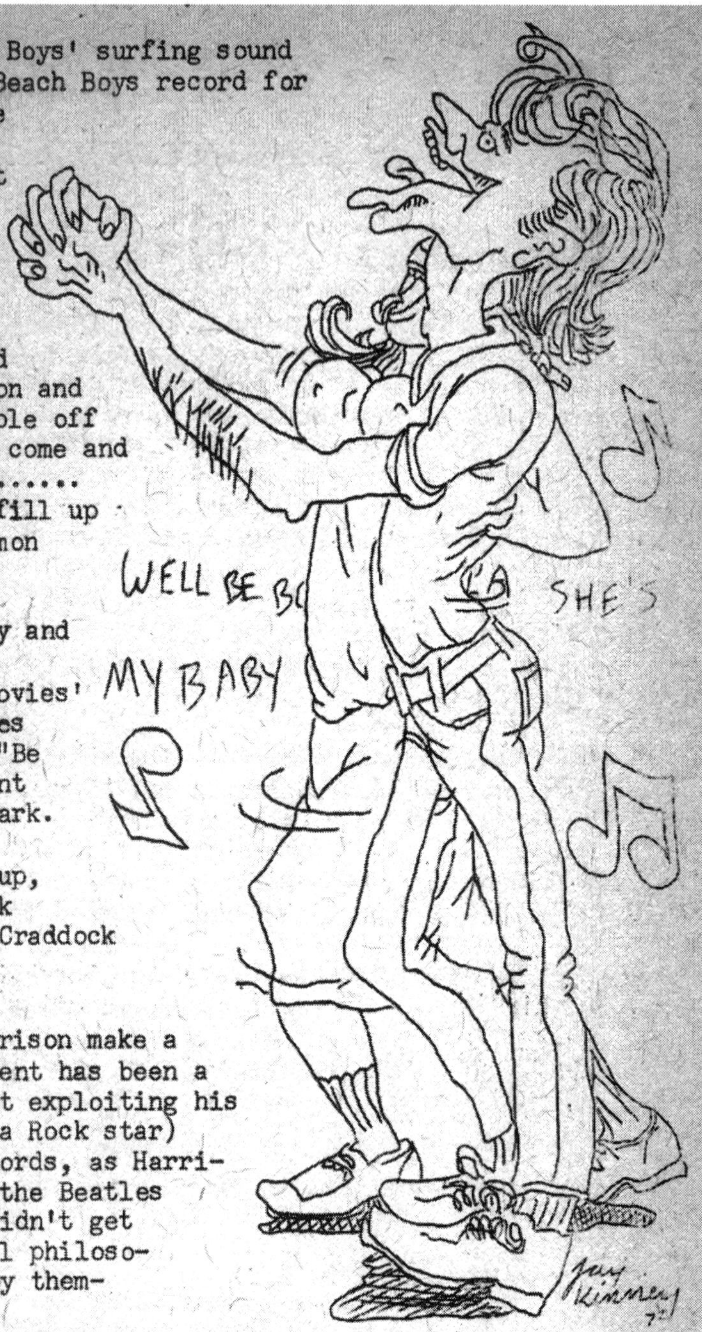

From Eddy Mitchell, Johnny Hallyday and black leathered Vince Taylor (France's greatest Rock stars) to the Flamin' Groovies' "Pistol Packin' Mama" to "...my baby does the Hanky Panky"--which is nothing but "Be Bop a Lula" revisited--Mr. Eugene Vincent Craddock's work has left an indelible mark. From Australia's own Vincent imitator Johnny O'Keefe to their biggest hit group, Daddy Cool, to England's hordes of black leather-clad Rockers, the ghost of Mr. Craddock carries on.

While today people like George Harrison make a big deal about Oriental religions, Vincent has been a convinced Buddhist for 10 years, without exploiting his somewhat unusual beliefs (at least for a Rock star) to get more publicity and sell more records, as Harrison has been doing. I wonder if, when the Beatles were living with Gene in Europe, they didn't get somewhat captured by Craddock's Oriental philosophies as to want to explore them more by themselves?

So far I haven't even mentioned Gene Vincent's backup band: the Blue Caps. Gene Vincent and the Blue Caps formed the first true hard Rock group in the world, thus setting the precedent for all who followed, from Buddy Holly and the Crickets to the Beatles to Creedence Clearwater Revival. I already talked about the Beatles; both Buddy Holly and John Fogerty witnessed the incredible Gene Vincent Stage Show of the late fifties; Holly even queued in line for an autograph.

The Blue Caps certainly contributed a lot to the animalistic and neurotic feel of the Vincent sound. Guitar was the thing with this group, in contrast to the piano-sax centered bands of Little Richard, Fats Domino, etc. There were two sets of Blue Caps: the first set consisted of Cliff Gallup on lead guitar, Wee Willie Williams on rhythm guitar, Jumpin' Jack Neal on standup bass and Dickie "Be Bop" Harrell on drums. This lineup is featured in the first two albums, Blue Jean Bop and Gene Vincent and The Blue Caps. Their sound is raw, savage and extremely aggressive: from the crashing-smoking drums, to the murderous ear-raping guitar solos of Gallup, to the screams and shouts which burst out at every instrumental break, it was a very violent sound, total madness. Revolution! The second set of Blue Caps consisted of Johnny Meeks taking lead, Bobby Jones on electric bass, Dickie Harrell still on drums and Paul Peek as a dancer-vocalist to complement Gene on the 2 hour long Gene Vincent Stage Show. (Paul Peek later recorded some real wild Rockers for the Atlanta label N.R.C., backed by Esquerita and his band; Esquerita is a wild madman who inspired Little Richard to play the piano; like Richard, he wears outrageous clothes and is a crazy screaming Rocker; he was introduced to Capitol Records by Gene and an album came out in 1958, which is no longer available. But, luckily, you can import from England the same album issued on the Ember label; his piano playing is really weird and unique, more aggressive and inventive than Richard's. If you dig savage rebellious Rock'n' Roll, you must get hold of this album).

If Cliff Gallup had a vehement extremely individualistic sound, Johnny Meeks incredibly enough had a style just as unique and imaginative. His technique consisted of trying to compete with Vincent's vocal workout, and just as Gene gives all of his emotions, feelings, mind, heart, soul and body to the song, in the same way Meeks squeezes every drop of blood out of those strings. His playing is not as bim-bam-boom as Gallup's, but is more insistent: if I may use this analogy, Gallup is like death through violent explosion, while Meeks is death by slow and painful torture!!!

If I'm using this spaced-out terminology, it's because the Gene Vincent sound instills something mysterious and sad. Even the happy songs have a certain neurotic feel, a certain melancholy in them, a melancholy that does reflect upon Vincent's troubled existence.

Perhaps the greatest credit to the uniqueness of Mr. Craddock's sound, is not the already numerous Super Stars he has already influenced, but the countless more who in the future will be fascinated and completely captured by it. You will see. If you want to refute this last statement (plus my own speculations throughout this article), fine; but, one thing that cannot be questioned are the actual factual statements of the above mentioned Super Stars concerning Gene Vincent's influence upon them.

(While Gene's records are available throughout the world, Capitol still refuses to release his product in America; anyone desiring to see this reversed, please write to me, asking Capitol to release all of Gene Vincent's recordings: GENE VINCENT MEMORIAL SOCIETY, c/o HOLLYWOOD ROCK'N'ROLL FAN CLUB, Ron Weiser, 1264 N. Hayworth Ave, Hollywood, Calif. 90046. Phone: (213) 874-0611 or 656-8892.)

feedback

<u>JAY KINNEY</u>: "James Taylor Marked For Death" is one of the best rock articles EVER. Who are these people who "may think it doesn't belong in this magazine"?? They're nuts if they're real. I mean, that Part Two was particularly GREAT--and I'm thankful that Lester's brain is pumping out this fine gaff for us to ruminate over. By now the Troggs piece has sort of melted into the Alice Cooper piece in Creem and together they're sort of my vote for "the Great American short Rock Novel of 1971" or something.

  《Most of those who wrote expressed similar feelings, but it seems to have rubbed a few the wrong way. Read on...》
  /215 Willoughby Ave #1212, Brooklyn, N.Y. 11205/

<u>DAVE ORTOLEVA</u>: Everything contained in this letter is my opinion. I do not pretend to speak for a majority of WPTB readers. Perhaps my views are those of the minority. Perhaps they are not. In any event, I felt it was necessary to bring them to your attention since I have a sincere interest in the welfare of your publication. After so many splendid issues, I don't want my favorite fanzine to deteriorate, which is exactly what <u>will</u> happen if you continue to publish articles like Lester Bangs' "James Taylor Marked For Death" that took up too much valuable space that could have been used for better purposes.

Bangs may be your choice (as well as Esquire's) for best rock writer of 1971, but in my book he gets the award for the Most Pretentious, Most Longwinded, Most Mind-Boggling, Most Contemptuous, and certainly the Most Over-rated Rock Writer, on the basis of that 24-page fiasco that he had the nerve to write, and that you had the misfortune to print.

Marty Arbunich, in the first letter in your "Feedback" column, shares my lament: "I don't buy (Rolling Stone) anymore because all those cats walk around with pencils up their asses." After reading Bangs' self-glorifying tales of pre and post-pubescent sexual bravado, I am convinced that he wrote his sickening tribute to the Troggs with a pencil tied to his penis.

I don't object to his praise of the Troggs (they were indeed a great group). I don't object to his indictment of James Taylor either. My complaint lies in the manner in which Bangs chose to write the article. I object to reading the muddled thoughts of a stoned person who revels in his capacity for using four-letter words, and flaunts his undeniable ability to use poly-syllabic words that require repeated references to a thick dictionary. Call these words "cosmic", "clever", "obscure", "arty", "erudite". Call them what you will. By writing all that verbose garbage, Bangs is just shouting to the world -- "Hey! Look how revolutionary and different I can be! Look everybody! I'm so intelligent--my fabulous vocabulary proves it! Now, with a talent like mine, it must mean that I know what I'm talking about, and that my life-style was and still is the best; that all you straights and pseudo-freaks out there should emulate me, sink into the mire with me--screw who you want, shoot or smoke who you want, use blasphemy especially when it's not necessary -- Show you're a decadent part of this screwed up generation. Be pretentious--outstanding--show your presence! Don't write a decent, informative, fanzine-type tribute to the Troggs! Instead, write an egocentric and glorious display of all your hang-ups, and occasionally mention the Troggs so the real fans will keep reading!"

It is articles like this that have caused Rolling Stone to lose many of its readers. Suggestion: stick wid de musik! Stick wid the detailed articles about performers, their histories, their discographies, their fan worship. Don't allow your writers to pour out their feelings ad nauseum. Facts, Greg, just facts, with some praise and criticism thrown in to maintain interest. I like WPTB too much and I won't stand by and watch it turn into just another rock magazine.

((While I really appreciate your honest concern, I think you've missed quite a few points here. WPTB is a rock & roll magazine, and anything to do with R&R is its proper concern. And that certainly includes adolescent sexuality. How we come to terms with our sexuality in our 'teens is inextricably bound up with our music--in the case of most of the people with a deep enough interest in the music to be reading this magazine, I'd guess that a lot of the energy of the libido was transferred to the music. Which is what Lester was trying to get at. His stories of teenage sexual fantasies being bound up in rock records should strike a chord in most members of our generation--they did in me, though my experiences were in no specific way similar. And if you don't think the macho energy of the Troggs had any effect on our high school sexo-emotional lives, you just plain don't understand rock & roll--or never experienced it in the fullest degree. Lester is longwinded, I'll grant you that, but I (and many others) find his use of words (how can you blame someone for having a large vocabulary? I guarantee he doesn't use a dictionary or thesaurus, as some writers--like Nick Tosches--do to excess without any complaint) and his literary imagination a delight to read. I can read for style as well as for content. I don't know Dave. While he does sometimes tread the boundaries of good taste, I find the article to be entirely to the point and pertinent. The only explanation I can find for your rather violent response is the possibility that his reminiscences reminded you of some unpleasant experience in your own adolescent years--I don't see anything in the article to inspire such a response. :: And by the way, Lester does not get "stoned" (he does drink a lot tho), doesn't consider himself a "revolutionary" (he hates hippies even more than I do!) and his "life style" is probably more akin to your father's than yours. I don't find his use of "blasphemy" gratuitous, and I will not censor my writers. But anyway, fear not: neither his, nor any other type of article will be allowed to dominate this magazine. I intend to always present a lively balance.))

KIM FOWLEY: Bob Arlen, lead guitar of "Poor Boy" Royaltones also lead guitar for "Hey Joe" the Leaves and for Robert Savage. ((Royaltones also back up Del Shannon on Amy--ed.)) Duane Eddy reportedly backed Louis Almodius last year. Lead singer of the Guilloteens' mother is a pro wrestler. Cliff Bennett became leader of Toe Fat. Andrew Loog Oldham used to sell ice cream at "all niters" at the Flamingo. The Spotnicks were from Sweden, big in Japan, South America. Cliff Richard & the Shadows recorded a South African EP while on tour there called "Live At the Colloseum." Why didn't Boyd Raeburn mention the films Cliff made with Billy Graham? It appears Cliff would be ideal for Mike Curb's MGM Records now.

Jet Harris & Tony Meehan had a hit instrumental in 1964 on British Decca called "Diamonds". Hank Marvin and Bruce Welch have a release (LP) on Capitol this year. I also believe Joe Meek produced the first tapes of Joe Cocker and Tom Jones. Billie Davis was Jet Harris' girlfriend. Alma Cogan, now dead, was married to Brian Morris, founder of the Ad Lib, London's first successful discotheque which catered to Beatles, Stones, etc. Alma was socially powerful on a "rock" Pearl Mesta level. She also recorded "Tennessee Waltz". One of the Four Pennies' wives appeared in the film "Alfi". Please let me write on P.J. Proby as I was his publicist-friend-M.C. and choreographer at the time (1964) when I lived in England. I also lived there in 1966.

Did you know that I wrote "Fluffy Turkeys", recorded by the Paris Sisters in 1968? It was never sold to a label and never released. I appeared on live TV in England with the Troggs. The shows were "Ready Steady Go" and "5 O'Clock Club". I sang "They're Coming to Take Me Away, Ha! Ha!" The Troggs sang "Wild Thing" and "With a Girl Like You". "Wild Thing" was originally recorded by Jordon Christopher on UA Records. He married Sybil Burton, Richard Burton's ex-wife. That's where Larry Page found the song.

/6000 Sunset Blvd. Hollywood, CA 90069/

((Sure, by all means write on Proby. I find the kind of details you provide endlessly fascinating. Thanks for writing.))

EDDIE FLOWERS: In the Ephemera thing in NHRP you mentioned a bootleg of the Stones called Battle. How can I get a copy of it? I find it very difficult getting ahold of early albums by the Who, Kinks and Stones. Has My Generation been deleted?

/Rt. 1, Box 22N, Jackson, Ala. 36545/

((My Generation is still in print but only in stereo. Battle is an east coast bootleg, it's never been on sale here. Also currently making the rounds in the east is a live Who bootleg that's excellent. I'm sure some of our eastern readers will be glad to help you out.))

PETE TOMLINSON: Tell Lester that the Troggs are still around, in some form. In a recent Melody Maker there was an ad for someplace where the Troggs were playing. Get this though--they were second-billed to a film--only a film!--of Emerson, Lake & Palmer wrenching their guts out! Where is there justice?

/27 Brookfall Rd, Edison, NJ 08817/

((Yeah, I saw that myself! That musta been some concert! The Troggs are still around, see the additions to the discography elsewhere thish. I was wrong about the release dates before, they had several records in 1971. But none issued in this country that I know of.))

JAMES F. McNABOE: Re the Troggs' liason with Miller beer: I assume you know by now that the commercial you heard sounded like the Troggs because it was the Troggs. If you don't have the record (Miller High Life GA 621) you can obtain a copy, which also contains versions of the commercial by Johnny Mack and Brook Benton, by writing to Miller Brewing Co. in Milwaukee as I did. The record was produced and sent by Miller's advertising agency, McCann-Erickson, but I cannot recall the exact address.

/175 Edison St., Clifton, NJ 07013/

((Incredible! I wrote as soon as I got your letter, about 2 weeks ago. Haven't had any reply yet. Thanks by the way for the 5 pages of comments on the NJ punk scene which I am saving to publish another day. Do you know anything about a group called Davy & the Badmen? (circa 1959...)))

BILL MALLEY: Regarding your Kinks Kompendium... in a very old issue of Tiger Beat magazine was an interview with Ray Davies. He told of his upcoming album (Face to Face) and mentioned that one of the tracks was to have been sung by Mick Avory. It was called "Violets and Daffodils". Last summer ('70) I was half-listening to a summer TV show with Dean Martin and a gang of girl singers called the Golddiggers. The GDs were singing a beautiful ballad and, as I listened, I remarked how much it sounded like a Ray Davies tune. Strangely enough, just as I said it, they sang the line "violets and daffodils remind me of you." I have no way to prove it, but I'm willing to bet that was the long-missing Mick Avery solo I heard.

MARK SHIPPER: I've got to tell you what happened last week. It was New Years day, actually, and I was driving down the hill to pick up my wife from work when the Real Don Steele (KHJ) blasted out the best news of the year—the Raiders were playing at Disneyland (that figures) that night! It was already 5 o'clock so we rushed back home, cancelled all plans, put on some fancy duds and took off as it's a long trip out to Anaheim from where we live. I really wanted to see them—you know, that whole Raider article ((in FLASH—see fmz reviews)) was based purely on memory. I hadn't seen them in four years & even then only on TV. I knew already that the Raider Stomp & the costumes were a thing of the past and recent singles of theirs have been uniformly lame. What we were driving to Anaheim for was the slight hope that a portion of the mid-sixties Raider excitement still existed.

Well, let me tell you the news: they were terrific. When that curtain went up and a ten-second guitar intro that we know & love so well ends, Lindsay darts on stage from out of nowhere, just GRABS hold of the mike and it's "WELL, HAVE YOU GOTCHORESELF A BRANEW BABY—DON'T TELLME MAYBE—IS IT SO, I GOT TA KNOW..." And I mean at full volume intensity with the band in back of him every step of the way. Whew! It was one of those cosmic moments when nothing, not sex, not dope, not even a million dollars falling out of the sky into your backyard, could touch it.

Well, excuse the excessiveness of the above, but Lindsay was great, really. The guy's got an unbelievable amount of stage presence to go along with a highpower voice and seeing it all just vindicated what I claimed in FLASH—there's not another lead singer in all of rock who could share a stage with the dude. Jagger can hop around up there like a Hollywood Blvd. butterfly, & Stewart can put his hands on his back & croak about Maggie May, & Cocker can walk around looking like he's spend the last eight hours rolling in a bed of fertilizer, but this guy Lindsay just winds up & socks and doesn't stop until the show's over. The fact is that if there's one band in the entire history of R&R that causes more snobbish crap to be thrown the way of anyone who digs 'em, I'd like to know about them (they'd probably be good, anyway).

Think about it. Tell somebody you dig Tommy James & the Shondells. You get it. Tell somebody you dig the Monkees. You get it. But you'll NEVER get it as hard as if you tell somebody you dig Paul Revere & the Raiders.

But I'd better stop this diatribe before I begin foaming at the mouth. One thing you might like to know—while researching an article on the Seeds I discovered the following priceless bit of info from TEEN SCREEN: It seems that Sky wrote "Pushin' Too Hard" in like ten minutes while his girl was shopping at the supermarket. He was sitting in his car in the parking lot & she'd been nagging at him all day, so he knocked out the whole thing right there in the parking lot.

Ten minutes! That's great. The first thing I'm gonna do when I become the Jann Wenner of rock n roll is make a rule not to review any album that contains a song that took longer than ten minutes to write. I love the part on the live Seeds album where Sky introduces "Pushin' Too Hard" — "...we wanna dedicate this song to society, it still has a message..." Yeah, sure, ya clown—you want your girl to get off yer back, what's all this "society" bullshit about? They were one of the all-time great punkers to ever climb on a stage, & I hope you guys do 'em up right.

/Box DH, Panorama City, CA 91404/

((Ever tried telling someone you like the Partridge Family?? Say, you sound like the kind of maniac this world could use a lot more of. Maybe you oughta collaborate with Lester on that Seeds article. Did you know that when I was a flower punk the Seeds were the only group of that type I liked? (I despised the Sonics. What an idiot!) All because they had long hair and songs about dope, of course. Actually in those days they were as far out as anything to be heard in San Francisco, except maybe the 13th Floor Elevators, who were acid-punk. I'll never forget my surprise on learning that the Seeds actually played teen clubs and were universally despised on the ultra-hip Pandora's Box circuit. I couldn't understand how anybody with hair that long could be such traitors to the psychedelic revolution.... Ah, innocence!))

KARNIS BOTTLE'S
METANOIA

METANOIA 12 comes from the same people who brought you #11, the harried but lovable Greg & Suzy Shaw of 64 Taylor Dr, Fairfax, CA. 94930. This issue is published in early May, 1972, for FAPA and sundry other deserving people. It's free for the asking, but you better be sure you know what you're asking for!

Well, gang, I'm still keeping busy in the rock & roll world--holding down 3 columns, one of which is syndicated in around 200 underground & college papers, getting ready to write my first book (I expect the contract to come thru any day now...), publishing a Greg-winning fanzine (I'm modestly anticipating the eventual creation of rock fan achievement awards...) and trying to keep up with the countless magazines that are now clamoring for my material. The time leftover for Metanoia keeps shrinking, in fact there was none this month; I had to put aside some pressing work so this issue could come out and Greg Benford's membership be saved. I just hope you're grateful, Benford. In fact I'm leaving a really excellent article by Richard Meltzer out of this issue because I fear I may not have time to run off & collate an extra 4 pages. How about that. But I like to think I'm still keeping up with fandom, even though I lack the time to give it the kind of work it deserves from a fan who gets as much gratuitous egoboo as I do...

I'm starting a business, too (yes, another one). Since I get people writing to me all the time wanting to know where they can get old records, I'm now selling rare rock records. I took a 2-week jaunt around the nether regions of the country (Memphis, Jackson, New Orleans, Houston, Dallas, El Paso, etc.) gathering old rarities, and now I have a pretty good stock. If only I had someplace to put it! My growing record collection has been forcing my books off shelves and into boxes which, since the closet is already jammed with old pulps, are being shoved under the sink, behind the water heater, etc. Everywhere I look, albums are piled to the rafters, boxes of records wait to be mailed or opened, and the place is a mess. I think it's about time we had more than a 1-room cottage!

But why should I worry when I've got Fate looking after my needs? Fate works in mysterious ways. This time she implanted our landlords' heads with the notion of selling this house. That's one way of getting us a bigger one! As I write this, the house has been on the market for 5 months, and every weekend has seen dozens of total strangers trooping through. Due to the fact that it's the lowest-priced house in the whole county, all the raunchiest customers come to us. The other day we came home to find a crowd of filthy bearded overnight dope-dealing successes stomping around in our living room. It occurred to me that somebody could run a great racket, representing himself as a prospective house buyer, being escorted through dozens of houses every day by the real estate people, then coming back with his gang to burglarize the likely-looking places.

As for why the landlady (her husband is her pawn...) thinks she wants to sell the place, she claims she just can't handle the mental strain of renting anymore--and I can well believe her. I think she's transferred her own fears of growing old to this house, for according to hear everything was brand new before we moved in, including the threadbare rugs, antique flowered wallpaper that's rotting off the walls, and foundation that contines (barely) to hold the house up without visible means of support. A termite man was here today, and he just shook his head and walked off mumbling...

We've always had to put up with her surprise inspections, usually at 8:30 on a Sunday morning, and with every one there's some ridiculous new complaint. Once we were blamed for the leaves falling off the trees in the fall. "It never did that when my mother lived here" she snarls. She's a nervous little rat-like woman who wears gaudy whore wigs and talks to herself. Her husband is just deaf enough to miss everything except loud conversation, conveniently enough for him. I remember one time, after we announced plans to plant a garden, she almost threw a fit. "If you loosen the soil, the whole house will slide down the hill!" she ranted. The house is on about a 5 degree incline. We planted the flowers anyway, against her better judgment, and now she blames us because the property next door is a few inches higher--even though it's been that way for at least 60 years, according to one veteran neighbor.

And of course we've driven her to distraction the way we're constantly ruining the interior. When we moved into this "furnished" house, we were expected to sleep in bunk beds on the enclosed porch, and find delight in a living room occupied by one worn rug, two stuffed chairs, 18 folding plastic chairs, one rickety card table and a piece of torn, transparent cloth stretched tight over the window. Well, we made curtains, put in a new rug on top of the old, and bought a bed, which we put in the living/bed room. The house has only one large room, plus a big kitchen and two enclosed porches which we use for work rooms. And a bathroom, which was painted black and orange. We changed that to yellow and orange, and painted the kitchen from red and green to red and brown. For that we still get complaints. Now that we're expected to move soon, we'll probably have to account (and pay) for all kinds of garbage that we apparently did something with.

Bed full of crazy hippies and probably a writer or two at the Fairfax cottage probably assembled/roped in for the latest collating party. June 1970.

But I didn't mean for this to become a diatribe against our landlady. We've since learned that she once spent some time in the state mental hospital, and it wouldn't do to make fun at the expense of a deranged mind.

When we learned that the house was up for sale, we feared an abrupt upheaval. We needn't have worried. Twenty or so real estate people have looked the place over and walked out shaking their heads. Occasionally one that hasn't inspected it first will bring over a client. I always let them in the front door smiling. As they enter the main room the agent always exclaims, "Oh, what a lovely big room." "Yeah," I chime in, "It's real nice. Of course, it's the only room..." When they get to the kitchen Suzy lets them know about the leaks in the roof, the decrepit shower, the defective wiring, and the total lack of a foundation. If the customer doesn't make a beeline for the door after that, the agent invariably takes a new hopeful tack. "Well, you could build a wall across this room and have a bedroom behind it, and maybe the owners would float a mortgage to have a foundation put in..." A few have fallen for this, but since the owners are out for some fast cash, they're not about to go for that.

So we're not worried. We'll have to move eventually, but we were sort of planning to anyway, around October. I want to spend a couple of years in Los Angeles, where in my business it's possible to make a lot of bread fast. Or so I hope. Anyway it looks like we'll be moving, though it's hard to conceive of actually moving this much junk. I must have 10,000 records, every rock magazine ever published, and about 5000 old SF magazines, as well as 8 file cabinets full of fanzines. But I'm sure I can't even begin to imagine the horrors of such a move, so I'll save the story for after the fact. Stay tuned.

Now that our life here faces a death sentence, I find all sorts of memories of the last four years rising unbidden from the recesses of my mind. For instance, I had nearly blotted out my almost two years as a proponent of Cosmic Consciousness. It's almost far enough back now that I can look at it and laugh, although not quite far enough that I don't feel twinges of embarrassment whenever I think of it.

I was a dupe, no doubt about that (although I can rationalize my behavior as that of someone willing to give every point of view a chance before passing judgment), but you should have seen some of the people I ran around with. Most of my involvement in the Spiritual Revolution was through one particular organization, Frontiers of Science, that I can dimly recall writing enthusiastically about in the pages of thankfully obscure fanzines back in 1969. The chief bigwig in this outfit was a fellow named Don Hamrick. Hamrick had been a respected physicist until he became interested in flying saucers, designed and built some electromagnetic transformer of supposedly cosmic capability, and sat within range of its effects until his mind became unhinged.

He had me believing that he had been to Mars, and received visits by his saucer friends all the time, out at his farm. He spoke a gibberish that I was convinced had to be Martian. Yet for all the strangeness of Hamrick, he was nothing compared to his cohorts. One of same, a middleaged follower of Subud, Alice Bailey, and every other crackpot religious cult, was a pleasantly batty lady named Pam. Pam's house was believed to be the center of some very high vibrational forces, and she was just full of stories of miraculous occurrences there.

One of the religions Pam subscribed to was a Japanese one called Johrei. A sort of healing cult, it specialized in passing out little emblems that had been blessed on some holy spot in Japan, and carried the power to transform the wearer into a healer. Hours on end they'd spend before their altar, pointing their palms at one another and spreading this sacred power.

On one such occasion, when according to Pam the room was filled with many thousands of astral beings, she confided in me the source of her house's power. It seems that there is a race of underground beings known as Titans (not to be confused with Deros) who, as I recall, are currently dedicated to building an undersea tunnel between China and the U.S. for reasons that, if ever I understood them, have escaped me. At any rate, these creatures had a control center carved out inside the mountain Pam's house was built on, and often in the bathroom she could hear them digging away. I went in there and heard nothing but the old pipes creaking. Pam knows the Titans are there, though, because she sees them all the time.

Even nuttier than Pam is Doug, a very warm and likeable retired architect who lives on a hill in Sausalito. Suzy and I used to go there all the time, just to listen to him describe the things he sees. His house is arun with little fairies, nymphs, and mythological creatures of every stripe. Once he reported with delight that he'd just been informed that his cat, who was recently deceased, had now been safely reincarnated in Egypt. Asked how he knew, he replied that the angel who lived up on the hillside had told him. Didn't we see her? Worse yet was his boarder, a proud old woman in her 90's who spent even more time talking to spirits than Doug did. It was disconcerting to listen to her real life reminiscences of her childhood life among the Indians, mixed up with stories of flying saucers and astral beings.

On the whole, I'm surprised I came out of that phase of my life with as much sanity as I've got.

R.I.A.W.O.L. (editorial)

What happened in England in the early '60s amounted to nothing less than the first rebirth of rock & roll. I have a rather elaborate notion of the meaning of rock & roll, involving complicated interrelationships of music with the teenage urge to rebellion and anarchy (among other things) and the ways that urge can be expressed and sometimes channeled through periodic outbreaks of fully developed youth culture.

But without boring you with that, I think it can be agreed that something died in 1958 and came back, in somewhat different form but with the same basic spirit, and flourished for awhile in 1963-7. Most of us would probably even agree that it died again after that and is only recently showing signs of a third incarnation. It is with the Second Rock & Roll Era, and its beginnings in England, that WPTB will hereafter be chiefly concerned.

It has been noted (see WPTB #8) that England was largely bypassed by the extreme rebelliousness of American rock & roll in the '50s. English kids, cowed by the weight of tradition and parental authority, were satisfied with the pale readymade rock stars they were offered, singers like Tommy Steele, Cliff Richard, Marty Wilde, Adam Faith, Billy Fury and so on that, wild as they may have started out, were quickly stripped of any qualities that appeared threatening to the adult status quo by the promise of big money on the "legitimate" cabaret circuit, where they all ended up.

Of course the American rockers had their following in England, and the Teddy Boys from all reports were every bit as murderous as their New York JD counterparts, but when the music died in the late '50s their culture faded away. Meanwhile in the rough seaport town of Liverpool the conditions were right for a teenage rebellion, and a lot of kids found themselves starting musical groups.

Skiffle music, with its easy washboard and gutbucket instrumentation, accounted for hundreds of teen groups around Liverpool as far back as 1955, and a good number of them, including the Beatles (then the Quarrymen) started playing rock when the skiffle fad died and American rock records started turning up around 1958. By 1959 instrumental music ala the Shadows was the big thing, but most groups did vocals as well, and as Bobby Rydell songs are not exactly suitable for rowdy dance halls, the classic rockers of Little Richard et al. lived on in these surroundings, at least in Liverpool and other provincial areas.

And so, following the thread of rock & roll, which has gotten pretty thin at times but never really disappeared except in terms of mass popularity, we take up our story in Liverpool....

LIVERPOOL

Liverpool rock as such dates back at least to 1959, when such groups as the Beatles, Rory Storm & the Hurricanes, Cass & the Cassanovas, Derry Wilkie & the Seniors, the Swinging Blue Jeans and Gerry & the Pacemakers had become the most popular local groups (with the Beatles, incidentally, bringing up the rear). There were a number of clubs around town, such as the Casbah (owned by Pete Best's mother), but things didn't really get underway until the Cavern, located in central Liverpool, switched over from jazz to rock and began attracting a regular and loyal clientele, sometime around 1960 or '61.

There were never enough jobs around Liverpool to support all the groups, and in 1959 many of the groups started accepting dates in Hamburg, a sort of sister city to Liverpool, across the English Channel. Hamburg was another dirty, violent city where hard core rock & roll was required to ease the frustrations of teenage life. Playing in Hamburg kept the early Liverpool groups raunchy while their counterparts in London and other parts were going progressively softer. (It was also in Hamburg, incidentally, that the Beatles got the idea for their famous haircuts.) Hamburg itself eventually developed a sizeable Liverpool-influenced rock scene.

By 1962 things were really happening. The Beatles were by now a local sensation, there were many other groups around including the Merseybeats, the Four Jays, the Undertakers, the Dennisons, Lee Curtis & the Allstars, the Remo Four, Gus Travis & the Midnighters, Billy J. Kramer, and the Big Three and more. There was a local pop newspaper, *Merseybeat*, that supported the Liverpool sound and gave the musical community a sense of solidarity. It was a scene very similar, in some ways, to that in San Francisco in 1966, before the rest of the world found out what was going on.

Around this time the nature of the music started changing, as well. The songs of Little Richard, Chuck Berry, Buddy Holly and the Coasters continued to be a mainstay of most groups' repertoires, but many of the musicians were also taking note of the renaissance of R&B that was going on in America, with the Phil Spector girl groups, and the revitalized R&B of New Orleans. This material was added to the classics of

the mid-fifties and somehow, when the Liverpool groups became proficient enough to write their own songs, they came out a curious blend of the two influences, mixed with a youthful, bouyant enthusiasm and an utterly confident way of bashing out songs that was different enough from the common fare to sound new, fresh, and very exciting. Thus was the Merseybeat born.

New standard songs emerged. Benny Spellman's "*Fortune Teller*" and Aaron Neville's "*A Certain Girl*", from New Orleans. Dionne Warwick's "*This Empty Place*", Johnny Kidd's "*Shakin' All Over*", Leiber & Stoller's "*Some Other Guy*," Plenty of songs from the Isley Bros. ("*Respectable*," "*Twist and Shout*,") and the Coasters ("*Searchin'*," "*Ain't That Just Like Me*," "*Poison Ivy*," "*Girls Girls Girls*," "*What About Us*," etc.). Girl group songs by the score. And, perhaps the definitive Mersey anthem, "*Hippy Hippy Shake*," from an obscure 1959 Del-Fi record by Chan Romero.

At this point we must deal with a point raised by Ian Maunder in his excellent Merseybeat retrospective in *Cream 17*. I take the liberty of quoting liberally from that article, because Ian expresses and illustrates his point so effectively:

"*We now come to a very obvious but pertinent question--if most of the groups used other people's songs, was there really a Liverpool sound at all? The answer is yes, there was a Liverpool sound, loud and raucous, but there was not a Liverpool style. This is a very important distinction. Style in pop music is that nebulous quality which enables an artist to inject his personality into any piece of music, thereby rendering that piece of music in a different way from previous interpretation... It was just this sense of style that 99 percent of the Mersey groups lacked.*

"*Unfortunately, the groups compounded the mistake of performing unoriginal material by the very nature of the material they chose to perform. Of all the many forms of American music they could have chosen to adopt, rhythm and blues and its cousin, soul music, are the most personal of all. They are dependant for their impact on the personal interpretation of the singer and also on the ability of the backing musicians. The essence of this music is improvisation, and an accomplished singer employs many little 'extras'. He or she may bend notes, stretch one note over several bars, whoop or holler as the spirit moves moves him and insert all sorts of vocal interjections ranging from Wilson Pickett's expressive grunt to the Cadets' 'Great googa mooga! Lemme outa here!' on their classic "Stranded in the Jungle." (These are the things which make such music, showing the singer to be involved in it. And this is where the copies fell down.*"

Ian goes on to detail the failings of the early Hollies, Searchers, Pacemakers, and Billy J. Kramer. Of "*Just One Look*," he says "*The effect that the Hollies had on this song is reminiscent of the effect the hordes of Attila had on the civilized world. They rampaged through in their usual brash, unsubtle way, with twanging guitars replacing the piano work.*"

His arguement is valid. Although one could debate his dismissal of the Searchers' "*Needles and Pins*," in general the Liverpool R&B cover versions were every bit as "dire" as he describes them. And yet, and yet...I *like* a lot of the records, and there must be some other explanation than bad taste. I

LIVERPOOL

think there is. Many of the Liverpool groups, like Rory Storm, the Del Renas, even the Undertakers and the much-touted Dennisons, leave me cold. In these groups I can't avoid the deficiency of lame English musicians trying to copy soulful R&B records, and falling flat. These groups were loud and racous, yes, but those two factors alone are not my definition of "The Liverpool Sound."

There is a definite Liverpool sound that I hear in the better Mersey groups, such as the Searchers, Swinging Blue

That's Brian Epstein himself, directly above, already looking bored moments after signing the hopeful Paddy, Klaus & Gibson, who (much to their lasting dismay) never generated the kind of hysterical response the girls at right are giving their Liverpudlian stablemates, the Beatles.

Jeans, Ian & the Zodiacs, Faron's Flamingos, and so on. I don't hear it so much in the Hollies, whose early cover versions of American R&B classics are admittedly lacking in grace. But the point is, there was more to Merseybeat than loud hackings of R&B songs.

It's very wrong to assume that they were only trying to copy the American records. They obviously liked the songs and the music, but I think they realized, in most cases, that they couldn't duplicate it. What the better groups did was adapt the songs to their own style--and there was, I believe, a Liverpool Style.

Let's face it, this process of adapting a more pure R&B source to some local style has been the basis of all white rock & roll. There's no such thing as purism in white rock, it can all be traced back to something originally stolen. So what? To deny what we are only brings about the abandonment of we are only brings about follies like the abandonment of surf music and folk-rock for "underground blues". The answer is not, as Maunder suggests, that the British groups should have sought out purely British sources for their music. That only produces groups like Fairport Convention, which are hardly rock & roll, or on the other hand records like "*Greensleeves*" by the Country Gentlemen, which are pure Merseybeat regardless of the subject matter. The answer, as I think people are beginning to realize, is to own up to the fact that we're white, blues and R&B have nothing to do with our culture, and while we must adapt that music in order to do anything interesting in a genre (rock & roll) so clearly descended from it, white rock & roll is only valid when it tries not to imitate its R&B sources but to express itself in styles that appeal to white teenagers. And that, I submit, is what the Mersey groups did and why they were so successful.

The Liverpool groups at their best had a style that only a deaf man could miss. That style was defined by close vocal harmonies, pounding drums, and above all a crashing, ringing torrent of chords from the rhythm guitar highlighted with cymbal taps from the drummer. Rhythm guitar was clearly the central instrument in Merseybeat. Nobody has ever pointed this out before to my knowledge, but if you sit down and listen to a lot of Mersey and Mersey-influenced records of this period, it's hard to refute. Any early Beatles hit will illustrate the point, "*All My Loving*" for instance. My favorite example is "*The Name Game*" by Dean Ford & the Gaylords (a group from Glasgow who later became Marmalade.) No attempt is made to duplicate the jaunty humor of Shirley Ellis' original--all is subjugated to that clanging beat.

This is in the grand tradition of white rock & roll--exaggerating the most superficially exciting element of a given style (as with blues and guitar solos, to cite one instance where it really got out of hand) to create music with no real depth but a very large immediate thrill, if done right.

This blend of harmonies and hard rhythm produced a distinctive style that can only be called Merseybeat. The rhythmic aspects were picked up by the early London R&B groups as well as all the beat groups around England. The very fact that it was called "Beat Music" indicates that the importance of the rhythm section was realized. Another interesting fact for students of rock history is that the term "Big Beat" came back into usage around this time. The Big Beat, as glorified by Fats Domino in his song of the same title, was originally used in the mid-fifties to describe the full, pounding sound of bands like Little Richard's. It referred to something different in the sixties, but the fact that it came back at all may indicate some awareness at the time that the Second Era of rock & roll was underway.

The music was designed and streamlined to create excitement in young white teens, and it had the desired effect as we're all aware. And yet, there was an odd sidelight to the worldwide success of the Liverpool sound, as pointed out by Ian Mauder. For some reason, the most popular Merseyside groups never seemed to make it on the national or international scene. Rory Storme, who was nearly always more popular in Liverpool than the Beatles, never even had a record out in the U.S. Huge local favorites like the Big Three, Kingsize Taylor & the Dominoes, the Dennisons and the Echoes are hardly remembered today, even though many of them are still around.

Once the Mersey boom was underway, it seems, being from Liverpool was no longer enough to guarantee national popularity. One needed an image with mass appeal, neither tied to nor entirely removed from one's provincial origin. And this is why, I think, the greatest successes from Liverpool were those in Brian Epstein's stable. Epstein was the manager of one of Liverpool's largest record stores when he discovered the Beatles (who were already local heroes). It was his record biz contacts that enabled him to secure EMI contracts for the Beatles and later his other acts. Before that it was unheard of for a non-London group to be signed, and though the companies came in force afterward to sign up just about every group in sight, it doesn't seem they really knew what to do with them. Epstein, a born entrepeneur, knew exactly what to do, and nearly all his acts (which included, besides the Beatles, Gerry & the Pacemakers, Billy J. Kramer, Cilla Black, The Fourmost, Cliff Bennett, Sounds Incorporated, and Tommy Quickly) were big successes.

Many contend that when Brian Epstein died, the Beatles began going down the drain. It was certainly the end for his other groups, who were all in decline anyway, and for the Liverpool scene, which had been left behind and forgotten, all the moreso when Underground rock hit England in 1967. Nowadays the Cavern is closed and condemned to be torn down, and the whole district a slum. But people still make pilgrimages from all over the world to pay tribute to the source of nearly all sixties rock. R.I.P., Liverpool.

----Greg Shaw

THE BEATLES

There's not much left to say about the Beatles. It's all been thoroughly documented, and there's no point in our rehashing it here. There are angles they haven't been analyzed from, however, and while I don't know if I'll uncover one or not, it is pertinent to this issue to mention a few things.

They were to the Second Rock & Roll Era what Elvis was to the First, and for about the same reason. People sometimes wonder why Elvis became the galvanizing symbol of it all when Memphis held other and (some say) greater singers from Carl Perkins to Charlie Feathers. We all know, of course. It was sex appeal, combined with a sense of style and flash, and an image that was precisely what the times demanded. Elvis became a symbol of defiance because he looked and acted the part, and a love idol for the same reason. And, not forgetting the prerequisite, his music was great.

The Beatles' music was great too, unquestionably better by 1963 than that of any other Liverpool group. With songs like "*She Loves You*" and others of that period, they had an unflagging energy and ceaseless enthusiasm that no one save Dave Clark could approach. These qualities were part of the tone of teen conciousness in the early mid-sixties, along with a nascent irreverence and sense of cultural adventure that the Beatles also exhibited from the start. They were models in that regard, and with their haircuts, intellectual leanings, flippancy, and neverending imagination, they helped guide youth culture in the direction the sixties had in store for it. It was that, perhaps more than their marvelous music and fine songs, that made the Beatles what they were.

There would have been an English rock renaissance in 1963-4 without the Beatles. But whether it would have ever been noticed in the States, against all precedent, is debatable. And whether there would have folk-rock and punk-rock to the extent they happened in the U.S. in 1965-6 as a result, is a question worth pondering indeed. Whether sixties pop would have exploded on any large scale at all without the Beatles can never be known, nor do we know if such a musical focal point is essential to a pop explosion, or if so to what extent. It's only happened twice, and each time someone was there. That fact has led to a widespread subconscious assumption that "a new Beatles" is inevitable. I am not entirely convinced. As signs of a new pop heyday increase daily, there is no sign of such an apocalyptic group or artist. I suspect that in looking for them so diligently, we take away any impact with which they might have sprung on us. For that and other reasons, I have my doubts. But in any case, there'll never again be anything quite like the Beatles.

—Greg Shaw

SWINGING BLUE JEANS

The Swinging Blue Jeans hit in March 1964 with "*Hippy Hippy Shake*," one of the all-time great oneshot rave records. It was a great record, but their followup, "*Good Golly Miss Molly*" only made #43 and that was about all America ever heard of the Swinging Blue Jeans.

They were one of the first Liverpool beat groups, formed in 1960 and soon abandoning trad for straight rock in a Little Richard vein. Of all the early Mersey groups whose records I've heard, only they along with Faron's Flamingos and precious few others came close to the fullness and raving energy of the Beatles. Their sound was the essence of what we've defined Merseybeat to be.

"*Hippy Hippy Shake*" is a fantastic song in any version, but theirs is hard to beat. "*Good Golly*" was another good example of how the Mersey beat could transform a seemingly overworked song into a discotheque treasure. After two releases, the Swinging Blue Jeans looked like real contenders in the English Invasion sweepstakes.

An album was released, an album I expected to hate after years of being told how lousy it was. But when I found it a year or so ago, I loved it right away. True, there are a few duds like "*Angie*," "*Think of Me*," and a poor cover of "*Save the Last Dance For Me*," but they are outnumbered by the two hits hits, a nice original called "*It's Too Late Now*," and three fantastic rockers in a row on side two: "*Shaking Feeling*", a wild upbeat original, a Merseyfied "*Shake Rattle & Roll*," and a good version of "*Shakin' All Over*." That's four "shakes" in a row if you count "*Hippy Hippy Shake*," and if they had gone gone on in this vein as the Kinks did with "K" titles, producing a whole array of "shake" records and culminating perhaps in a "Great Shakes" commercial, what a legacy we might have!

But somewhere things went wrong for the Swinging Blue Jeans. Their third single, Clint Ballard's "*You're No Good*" was slower, though still hard-edge. It was better than anything by Gerry & the Pacemakers, but it only barely scraped the American charts, although hitting #5 in England.

Perhaps it was a management problem—I can't help but feeling that under Brian Epstein they would have done a lot better. Certainly it wasn't their music at fault. Their next release, "*Tutti Frutti*" was a failure, along with all their subsequent releases, of which there were thankfully many. Another Clint Ballard song called "*It Isn't There*" sounds like a hit, but wasn't. As time went by, their music got more polished and subtle, more commercial (as witness a fine 1966 release, "*What Can I Do Today*"). On "*Rumors, Gossip, Words Untrue*" and its flip "*Now the Summer's Gone*" they sounded like an odd blend of Merseybeat and the Beach Boys, Brian Wilson harmonies and all, and on the following release "*Tremblin'*" (their last last in the U.S.) they sound unnervingly like the Hollies, possibly because of singer Terry Sylvester who had recently joined from the Escorts was about to leave them for the aforementioned Hollies.

The Swinging Blue Jeans had two more singles that I know of, followed by one as Ray Ennis & the Blue Jeans in mid '68 and one final release in early 1969, as the Blue Jeans, called "*Hey Mrs Housewife*." What Ray Ennis or any of the rest of them are doing now is anybody's guess, but of one thing there's no doubt: in the annals of rock history, the Swinging Blue Jeans have been given shamefully short shrift, and with their records now getting so hard to find, there's little chance of a bargain-bin revival like that the Troggs have lately received. Too bad.

—Greg Shaw

LIVERPOOL LEFT OVERS

In 1962 it was estimated that there were over 300 working groups in Liverpool. By 1964 it was probably closer to 1,000. There would be no point in trying to list them all; I've chosen to investigate only those who recorded, and of those only a fraction were any good anyway. Bill Harry (former editor of Mersey Beat) estimates (in his fine article on Liverpool, 10 years after, in Let It Rock, 11/72) that no more than 200 records were made by local groups, including those made in Germany, many of which were never released elsewhere.

In general, the best Liverpool groups were those grabbed by the big companies in the early days of the explosion. The leftovers were picked up by various minor labels, and although most of them came out in the States, such records are exceedingly hard to find nowadays. The exceptions are two "various artists" albums, recorded on location by Ember and Oriole respectively, the latter cut down to one LP for American release from a 2-LP English series. The Ember album captured Earl Preston's Realms, the Michael Allen Group, and the Richmond Group, recorded live at the Cavern with leading local DJ Bob Wooler as MC. The whole thing is pretty mediocre. It came out here on Capitol 2544, titled Where It All Began. A much better live Cavern recording, also MC'd by Wooler, came out only in England. At the Cavern (Decca LK 4597) included the Big Three, the Marauders, the Fortunes, Beryl Marsden, the Dennisons, Heinz, Dave Berry & the Cruisers, Lee Curtis & the Allstars, and Bern Elliott & the Fenmen.

The best Liverpool sampler of all, and one that can still be found through diligent searching, is The Exciting New Liverpool Sound (Columbia CL 2172), condensed from the British Oriole This Is The Mersey Beat albums. It opens with a 3-minute spoken introduction to the Mersey scene, then leads into "Let's Stomp" by Faron's Flamingoes, one of the wildest unsung Liverpool rockers. Sonny Webb & the Cascades, who described their music as "rockabilly," contribute three good songs in "You've Got Everything," "Border of the Blues" and the George Jones classic "Who Shot Sam." The Del Renas are represented by "Sigh, Cry, Almost Die" and "When Will I Be Loved." A resemblance to the Everly Brothers is not surprising. Mark Peters & the Silhouettes have a nice rocker called "Someday," and the album is rounded out by Earl Preston & the T.T.'s, sounding better than the Realms on Little Richard's "All Around the World," and Rory Storm & the Hurricanes butchering "I Can Tell." Storm couldn't sing at all, if this song is any indication, which leaves their longtime local popularity open to some speculation.

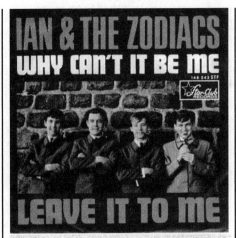

Also included on that album were two songs by Ian & the Zodiacs, who fortunately for us managed to get out an album (which, oddly enough, was issued only in the U.S. and Germany). A harmony-conscious group very close in sound to the Searchers, they formed rather late (1963) and got their start at the Star Club. They combined an interest in the Everly Bros. and Bacharach/David with a solid rhythm section and fine guitar playing to produce many excellent recordings. The album (Philips PHS 600-176, one of the few true stereo recordings of its time) is a classic, and one of my favorites. It includes an arrangement of "Good Morning Little Schoolgirl" that the Yardbirds shamelessly stole a year later, a fine "Rockin' Robin," a good rocker called "Jump Back," a nice version of "Hard Day's Night," an okay "Baby, I Need Your Lovin'" and their two almost-hit ballads "This Empty Place" and "The Crying Game" (also a hit for Dave Berry). There's also a solid beat number called "Clarabella" and an unbelievably good, pop hit-sounding Jagger-Richard song (also recorded by the Mighty Avengers) that is on a par with the best of the Searchers: "So Much In Love With You." An uncanny resemblance, really. Not only that; Ian & the Zodiacs also had singles that weren't on the album, like Jerry Lee Lewis' "Livin' Lovin' Wreck" (Philips 40244).

Another fine Mersey group was the Escorts, who had local hits before the Beatles. Their "Dizzy Miss Lizzy" is not the best version, but it rocks. They only had a few releases before Terry Sylvester left in early '66 to join the Swinging Blue Jeans, and later the Hollies (where he now resides), and they never had an album, but at least two singles came out here on Fontana and they're worth looking for. Also of note are the Cryin' Shames (not to be confused with the Cryan Shames, an American group from Chicago who had "Sugar and Spice" on the Destination label around the same time, 1966). Although they only made two singles, they are remembered still for the richly-textured, early Moodies sound of "Please Stay" (an old Drifters song), surely one of Joe Meek's alltime production achievements. The flip is a real surprise, too: a punk-rock song based on one of Dylan's tunes from Highway 61.

Of the biggest Mersey groups, not only did few succeed outside Liverpool, but few were any good in my judgement. The much-touted Big Three cut a local anthem in "Cavern Stomp" and had a minor hit on Decca with "Some Other Guy," but their records sound to me stiff and lifeless, and very badly sung. The group went through many personnel changes over the years and included at times many famous local musicians. Of the original group (who have just released a terrible reunion album on English Polydor), Adrian Barber went on to produce Vanilla Fudge, and Johnny Gustafson to join the Merseybeats.

The Merseybeats are another group that leaves me cold. They were together from at least '63 to '68, made one album that wasn't released in the U.S., and a lot of singles. Another one of those groups that was constantly changing personnel, they never made a single outstanding record. However, they did have the first English versions of "Mr. Moonlight" and "Fortune Teller," so give 'em credit for that.

The Fourmost did poor versions of Beatles and Coasters songs, and their records today have value far out of proportion to their intrinsic worth, because they were an Epstein group and recorded a couple of Lennon-McCartney songs that nobody else did. The vaunted Undertakers are still another example of the worst in Liverpool rock. Just because Jackie Lomax (who was lucky ever to have made a decent record) was in them, is hardly reason enough for the canonization that has taken place. They made three singles; loose, vaguely beat-like copies of Coasters, Barrett Strong and other American R&B hits. Barely worth listening to, when Liverpool also offered such groups as the Chants, who may've been black but had a good feel for pop and a Phil Spector sort of sound as evidenced on "She's Mine," along with a genuine knack for R&B.

The Mojos made one great record ("Everything's Alright") and scored hits with versions of "Seven Daffodils" and "They Say." The Mojos could be wild and raving as on "Everything's Alright" or as syrupy as they wanted, and most of their records were in fact ballads. But all were worth listening to in some way. Another important group was the Koobas. One of the first Cavern groups, they included none other than Tony Stratton-Smith. Although they were around for many years and had a minor hit with "The First Cut is the Deepest" (a Cat Stevens song also done by P.P.Arnold and, recently, Keith Hampshire) in '68, and an earlier one in '65 with "Take Me For a Little While" (which got them on a Beatles tour), they didn't have an album until '69, by which time they were far past their prime.

Many other Liverpool groups made records, of course, but none that had any lasting effect or that are likely to be found this side of the Mersey. In the end it was the freshness and enthusiasm of the Liverpool groups, as expressed through the superior music of the few really successful groups, that comprised that city's contribution to rock & roll.

--Greg Shaw

MANCHESTER and THE PROVINCES

After the success of the Liverpool sound, record companies began casting about for other Northern cities for whom a sound might be exploited--much in the way the American record industry tried to manufacture a "Boss-town Sound" in 1968. Most of the groups they found happened to be in areas surrounding London, but a few of the larger outlying cities produced small scenes of some note.

Newcastle gave us the Gamblers, the Quiet Five, Shorty & Them, and a few others. Birmingham was known as the home of the Moody Blues, the Rockin' Berries, Denny Laine & the Diplomats, the Uglys, Mike Sheridan & the Nightriders (who evolved into the Move), the Spencer Davis Group, the Cheetahs, the Redcaps, and a host of lesser groups who were collected on an album called Brum Beat (Decca LK 4598-E).

It was Manchester, however, that was picked to follow in Liverpool's path to glory. One of the nearest urban centers to the 'Pool, it also happened to be the home of some of the very finest British groups extant outside the latter city and London. In addition to the Hollies, Wayne Fontana & the Mindbenders, and Freddie & the Dreamers, there were many excellent, lesser-known groups.

The Country Gentlemen, led by Peter Cowap, made a classic upbeat version of the folk tune "Greensleeves" in 1963 that was a fairly large hit. Cowap later replaced Peter Noone in Herman's Hermits. The Toggery Five weren't great, but they did a fine, tense version of "Bye Bye Burd," probably lifted from the Moodies' repertoire, and a raunchy Them-style ballad called "I'm Gonna Jump."

If Mike Rabin & the Demons were from Manchesrer (nobody I've asked seems to know) their "Head Over Heels" can be added to the list of outstanding obscurities. The Four Just Men (sometimes known as Just Four Men) were a good, Liverpool-sounding group with one first-rate record titled "Things Will Never Be the Same" and several other singles. All the songs mentioned above, with the exception of "Greensleeves," are available on an out-of-print album "by" Freddie & the Dreamers (Tower 5003-A). Another Manchester group, the Hellions, had only one U.S. release, a single on Kapp called "Shades of Blue," written by Dave Mason and Jim Capaldi in 1965.

Manchester had no distinct sound that I can discern--the records I've heard are very Mersey-oriented, with solid rock backings and good arrangements. Perhaps not a "scene" in the sense of London or Liverpool, Manchester nonetheless produced some of the era's best recordings.

HOLLIES

There was a good appreciation article on the Hollies about a year ago in Fusion, which nevertheless, I feel, was slighting to their rocknroll efforts during the English Invasion. I hope I can amend what I feel are some injustices to their earlier efforts to succeed or fail basically on their merits as interpreters. Though in some instances unremarkable, a great number of their reworkings were, in fact, quite successful---and on occasion literally fantastic, the most outstanding example being their unbelievable cover version of Evie Sands' "I Can't Let Go" (Imperial 66158), which was a rather mediocre record in its original form. The following then, is basically a straight album-by-album evaluation of the early Hollies:

The Hollies' first American album Here I Go Again is mostly made up of rock and roll oldies, which are only partially successful. I like "Stay," because it's rocking and really speeded up from the original by Maurice Williams; "Do You Love Me" is good because it's so inanely done. "Rockin' Robin" is a great performance, helped a lot by terrific Elliott drumming. "You Better Move On" and "Talkin Bout You" are ok; "Lucille" and "Memphis" are not good. The most successful cuts on the album, not surprisingly, are the tunes veering more to commercial, pop rock and roll: "Here I Go Again" and "Just One Look" are rocking and excellent. The latter is particularit interesting, because they take Doris Troy's great huskily-sung quasi-R&B hit, speed it up, and turn it into flashy Hollies rocknroll. The one Hollies original, "Keep Off Of That Friend Of Mine," is also in the same melodic pop vein, and it's obvious how much better this type of material fits the Hollies' voices. Ahh Ahh....the closing cut of the album, Conway Twitty's "It's Only Make Believe", reminds one of the old lastdance ballads by teen bands at junior high school dances. Here I Go Again certainly is a weird album, though not too awfully successful.

A great deal of time separated the Hollies "Here I Go Again" LP and their second American album (took them a long time to get another hit over here), but the development of style, in the interim, is a knockout. The album, of course, is Hear! Hear!---and it's one of the best of the English Invasion. The pop rock rocknroll style hinted at on their first album is in full bloom here, and it works beautifully. "I'm Alive" "Put Yours(If In My Place," "Look Through Any Window", "When I Come Home To You," "So Lonely," "I've Been Wrong," and "Too Many People" are all in this style, and range from moderately good to great. This vein is samey, though, and a little bit tinny if used too much what makes the album work so well are the songs used to round up the LP. Just think, a great rocking version of the Impressions' "You Must Believe Me" from the Hollies! And then a terrific runthrough of "Lawdy Miss Clawdy", a passable "Down The Line," and that's it for the raunchy stuff on this album. Then there's

"*Very Last Day,*" sort of folk-rock, but it makes it. Lastly is a beautiful "*That's My Desire,*" perfect for the Hollies harmony---"Sherry I love you sp-woh-woh." *Hear! Hear!* is limited, a bit weird in places, and so trebley in its recording that some people might not even listen to it properly; but it's the best early Hollies album, capturing the whole lightweight rock-nroll aspect of their style quite well.

Beat Group, the next album, has a great Hollies hit in "*I Can't Let Go,*" but the album is mostly crap; aside from a couple good cuts on the first side, the whole album is pretty much a bomb. *Bus Stop*, though, is definitely a good album, even though quite scrambled from being thrown together from all the Hollies' English albums. The rock and roll cuts from their first English LP are surprisingly good: "*Whatcha Gonna Do 'Bout It,*" "*Candy Man,*" and "*Little Lover*". Then they do a good job on "*Sweet Little Sixteen,*" and "*Mickey's Monkey* is *amazing*, coming from the Hollies. Like their best interpretations, it's a distinctly different version from the original, mainly in being tighter and a lot more rocking. The very best cutso on *Bus Stop* are the later, more polished and melodic songs, which include "*Baby That's All,*" "*Don't Run And Hide,*" "*Oriental Sadness,*"and "*Bus Stop,*" a great onwardly-rocking hit. Like the title cut, the whole album rocks where it counts, and it adds up pretty well.

After *Bus Stop*, the Hollies started writing all their own material on *Stop Stop Stop*, an absolutely terrible album (partly due to their banjo fixation through the LP--remember the banjo on "*Stop! Stop! Stop!*"?) At any rate, the Hollies continued on into their second phase, quite downhill for a while (reaching a nadir of sorts with their horrendous *King Midas In Reverse* LP; sitars, ArtRock and all), but they somehow survived, lived on (markedly tightening up their vocals by replacing Graham Nash with Terry Sylvester), and blessed us in 1970 with *He Ain't Heavy*, a superb album.

The Hollies were an erratic band on record, somewhat impressive and somewhat not. Aside from their great vocals, their instrumental star was Bobby Elliott, one of the most underrated rock drummers of the English Invasion. Drum fans take note, as a great deal of his great rocking drumming is only heard on their early rock albums on Imperial. Elliott did quite a job in holding the Hollies' instrumental sound together on records; the guitars generally lacked punch, and the bass was usually insubstantial, but the drums were a solid rock. Most of all, of course, the Hollies' group singing was their start and end--when they finally got it polished, apparently sometime in 1965, it was just tremendous. To this day, they're one of the best-singing groups in rock history.

The Hollies had a tough time breaking through in America, and I remember when "*I'm Alive*"and "*Look Through Any Window*" were underground hits in 1965--the sort of singles that hid in Billboard's #100 to #130 "Bubbling Under" chart positions, and which you might hear once or twice on your radio. Nevertheless, "*Look Through Any Window*" eventually surfaced into a hit and nudged inside the Top 50; the Hollies subsequently appeared on *Hullabaloo* to play it, and it certainly was one of the exciting singles of its time. After another small hit with "*I Can't Let Go,*" the Hollies finally had a smash with "*Bus Stop*" and thereafter a string of hit singles in America. Unfortunately, "*Bus Stop*"'s breakthrough came near the end of the Hollies' first period, and it was their last real rock and roll effort. After that, the hard rock softened and their style changed. Nevertheless, had the Hollies had the chance to have umpteen hit singles in America in 1964-65, I bet they would have done quite well at it.

--*Mike Saunders*

ADDENDA TO HOLLIES ARTICLE

Some Background: Allan Clarke and Graham Nash sung together around Manchester as the Two Teens or Ricky & Dane as early as 1959. Eventually they got a group together with Don Rathbone on drums, and bassist Eric Haydock, called the Deltas. Shortly afterward they were able to lure local guitar hotshot Tony Hicks into the group and renamed themselves the Hollies, after the Christmas decoration. (Not Buddy Holly, as commonly believed). Rathbone left around the time of their first release in mid-1963, and was replaced by Bobby Elliott from Shane Fenton & His Fen-Tones. Haydock left in '66 in some bitterness, was supposed at one time to replace Pete Quaife in the Kinks, formed his own group which enjoyed no success, and vanished; he was replaced by Bernie Calvert from the Dolphins.

The Hollies' first single was a version of the Coasters' "*Ain't That Just Like Me*" (later a minor hit for the Searchers); to my ears it sounds shoddy, although undeniably enthusiastic. It missed the top 30, but the next release, another Coasters song, "*Searchin,*" hit #15 in the fall of '63 despite sounding even lamer. "*Stay*" made the top 10 in January '64 and inaugurated a spectacular two-year top-ten streak (including obscurer singles like "*We're Through,*" which appeared later on the *Bus Stop* LP, and the superb "*Yes I will,*" released only as a single here but later recorded by the Monkees under the title "*I'll Be True To You*"). The streak ended in late '65 when their controversial version of "*If I Needed Someone*" (George Harrison was immensely displeased with the group's performance and said so in print; on the other hand, pop papers like the *Music Echo* contended that the song was dismal and the Hollies had salvaged it as best as they could. On the whole, I think George was in the right - it's a curiously lifeless version; in any case Allan Clarke later admitted the group had made a mistake in recording it) barely made the top 20. "*I Can't Let Go*" then proceeded to hit #1 and the Hollies hit streak continued in Britian, with only one minor washout ("*King Midas In Reverse*" hit only #19) until early '72 when "*The Baby*" struggled to the edge of the top 20 and expired; their biggest U.S. hit, "*Long Cool Woman*" then failed to clear the British top 40, and the future there looks dubious.

The Hollies also recorded an entire album which was never released in the U.S. *In The Hollies Style* (later re-issued as a budget LP under the title *Vintage Hollies*). Appearing between the first album and *Hear Here*, it includes a spirited and garbled version of "*Too Much Monkey Business*," a tasteful rendition of Betty Everett's "*It's In Her Kiss*", a medley of "*Nitty Gritty*" and "*Something's Got A Hold On Me*"; plus seven original L. Ransford compositions, the best of which "*Time For Love*", although they're all pleasant. A nice album.

While I agree with Mike on the whole about the excellence of the Hollies' early material, I think he slights their more polished middle-period work most grievously. The *Stop Stop Stop* album seems quite pleasant to me, full of fine Hollies-style pop material like the hit "*Pay You Back With Interest,*" "*Suspicious Look In Your Eyes,*" and "*Peculiar Situation.*" And the next two albums, especially in their uncut British forms, represent a kind of pinnacle of eclectic British full-production '67 pop-rock (following in the wake of the Beatles, mainly), and would be extremely enjoyable for anyone save the most violently antipathetic towards E.B.F-P. '67 pop rock.

Evolution was the more conventional of the two, with any number of archetypal Hollies pop numbers ("*You Need Love,*" "*When Your Light's Turned On,*" "*Have You Ever Loved Somebody*"---previously a Hollies-written hit for the Searchers), and some fine examples of more ambitious material, both lyrically ("*Rain On The Window,*" "*Games We Play*") and musically (the brilliantly hard-rocking "*Then The Heartaches Begin*" and "*Lullaby To Tim*", which introduced the tremelo-vocal effect later utilized by Tommy James on "*Crimson & Clover*").

Butterfly (*King Midas/Dear Eloise* in the States) is a more wide-ranging, featuring various electronic effects on "*Try It,*" "*Elevated Observations*" and "*Postcard*" (British mix); Indian sounds on "*Maker*" and a hyperlush orchestral arrangement on the pretty "*Butterfly.*" It all works pretty well (if you discount some clumsy '67 style lyrics and a pair of trivially annoying numbers "*Away Away Away*" and "*Wish You A Wish*"),especially when combined with some great straight-pop rock numbers like "*Step Inside,*" "*Dear Eloise*", the lovely "*Pegasus*" and the big-production Spector/Walker Bros. type creation, "*Would You Believe*".

Several nice singles followed these two LP's, "*King Midas In Reverse,*" "*Jennifer Eccles,*"the U.S. only "*Do The Best You Can,*"and"*Listen To Me.*" Just before the last-named was released, Graham Nash left the group and was replaced by ex-Escort and Swinging Blue Jean Terry Sylvester. Their next album was the *Hollies Sing Dylan* project, which is highly enjoyable if you're not a Dylan purist (if there are any of those left). The group's first post-Nash single, the underpar "*Sorry Suzanne*", featured a delightful Clarke flip, "*Not That Way At All*" the next single. "*He Ain't Heavy He's My Brother*" restored the Hollies to American prominence. The subsequent album called *Hollies Sing Hollies* in Britian, had two songs chopped off in America (including one "*Soldier*", a twangy antiwar song, which has never been released here): it's a solid album, a return to a more conventional pop orientation but with continuing first-rate material for the most part (highlights: "*Why Didn't You Believe*", "*Dont Give Up Easily,*" "*Goodbye Tomorrow,*" and "*Marigold*"/"*Gloria Swansong*", which was eliminated from the U.S. LP but re-issued on the next one).

Subsequent singles including two of their best, the lovely ballad "*I Can't Tell The Bottom From The Top*" (April '70) and it's engaging flip, "*Mad Professor Blyth;*" and the rocking "*Hey Willy*" (May '71). In between there were the slightly substandard "*Gasoline Alley Bred*" and, in the U.S. only, "*Survival of The Fittest*", a track off their *Confessions of The Mind* LP (*Moving Finger* in the U.S.). This album was probably their worst yet, with some third-rate original material (two of the most mediocre were left off the American LP and "*Marigold*" was added, thereby raising the quality level, for once.) Still "*Survival*", "*Man Without A Heart,*" the sentimental, almost cloying "*Too Young To Be Married*,"and "*Frightened Lady*" were excellent, and it's a perfectly enjoyable LP.

Distant Light, was even weaker overall, with a sharp reduction of harmonies, but was redeemed by two strong American singles, the rocking "*Long Cool Woman*" and "*Long Dark Road,*" as well as "*Little Thing Like Love*" and "*To Do With Love*". Shortly after the album's release, lead vocalist Allan Clarke departed to go solo (later recording a generally disappointing LP), and Mikael Rickfors, from the Swedish group Bamboo, replaced him. With a big beefy voice, Rikfors changed the vocal blend of the group to an extent, demonstrated on the single "*The Baby,*" which is still quite nice, as is the more conventional-sounding flip "*Granny*". "*Long Cool Woman*" was pulled from *Distant Light* to become an American super-smash, the LP was released in this country, and a receptive audience was assured for the latest album, *Romany*, which except for a couple of dismally meandering balladic Rickfors showcases is quite good, mixing rockers (especially "*Won't We Feel Good*") and more melodic material (the title track) very tastefully indeed. "*Magic Woman Touch*" is doing fairly well as a single as this is written, and the Hollies seem prepared with fine records for years to come.

--*Ken Barnes*

WAYNE FONTANA & the MINDBENDERS

Chances are, all you remember of Wayne Fontana & The Mindbenders is "*Game of Love,*" if that. Through a clouded-up and murky memory, one might conjecture, "Yeah, a typical one-shot group..." But wrong! In 1965, Wayne Fontana and the Mindbenders released two singles and an album here in the U.S. that reveal them to be one of the most fascinating of any of the long-forgotten English rock groups.

First, a bit of necessary background. Running down the srarting lineup, it reads: Glyn Geoffrey Ellis, lead singer; Eric Stewart, lead guitar; Bob Lang, bass, and Ric Rothwell, drums. Ellis and his group the Jets were auditioning for Fontana records at Manchester in May 1963. Two of his group members

MINDBENDERS

didn't show up, so he had to call on two other musicians auditioning with other bands to help him--Eric Stewart and Ric Rothwell (Bob Lang was an original Jet). Miraculously, this motley pick-up group passed the audition and won a recording contract (after Ellis' name had been changed to Wayne Fontana, after the label, presumably). Just a step away from fame and fortune.

Their first release was Fats Domino's "*Hello Josephine*" in late '63, followed by a competent pop-rocker called "*Stop Look and Listen*," flipped by a rocking version of Bo Diddley's "*Road Runner*". Their first British chart hit was a lackluster rendition of Major Lance's "*Um Um Um Um Um*," in late '64/early '65; then "*Game Of Love*" became one of the most instantaneous #1 hits of the year. It was well worth the distinction, too, being a fine stupid-rock classic of sorts. Their follow-up single, "*It's Just A Little Bit Too Late*," was even better; it started out with a nice guitar riff over a neo-Twist beat, picked up from there and rocked like mad, and was really an infectious record. Even the B-side was good.

On their *Game Of Love* album, Wayne Fontana and the Mindbenders gave evidence of what their singles had hinted at: that they were an absolutely terrific singing group. The album opens with "*Game Of Love*," with its Coasters-basso licks by Bob Lang and some unearthly falsetto singing on the "*C'mon baby, the time is right*" bridges, Fontana and the Mindbenders quickly proceed to astonish by doing great things to Little Eva's "*Keep Your Hands Off My Baby*" from 1962. Then they're into "*Too Many Tears*," another great mouldy oldie, with some guy singing what sounds like at least two octaves above Fontana, in unison with the melody line. On these three songs and a couple of the other knockouts on the LP, "*You Don't Know Me*" and Ellie Greenwich's "*She's Got the Power*," Wayne Fontana and the Mindbenders are actually closer to the girl group rock of the early 60's than anything else, and they're great at it. Of their 50's rock numbers--"*Cops and Robbers*," "*Girl Can't Help It*," "*Git It*," "*I'm Gonna Be A Wheel Someday*," and "*Jaguar and Thunderbird*"--four of the five are passable; and the one failure, "*Girl Can't Help It*," is so spirited that it's enjoyable. Perhaps the best cut on the LP, "*A Certain Girl*" is a rocking lightweight version of the early 60's hit. Right after it, the album ends beautifully with a super-mouldy slow ballad, even complete with tinkling piano, "*One More Time*."

The whole style of the *Game of Love* album is quite unique for its time, because it's distinctly different from either the Mersey Sound or the heavies on the other side of the board (Stones, the Who, Yardbirds, Them). The recording itself is really lightweight and trebley, but it still doesn't ruin the LP, though the skintzey sound gives its results: the drums are the most prominent instrument, and the bass is hardly even audible half the time. Eric Stewart, the lead guitarist, is adequate though not very raunchy; the drumming, on the other hand, is really good. The virtues of this group and the reasons why I like them could be condensed very easily: Wayne Fontana and the Mindbenders really know how to *rock*, and their singing is great.

Wayne Fontana split from the group in early '66, a move which came to no good. Fontana as a solo artist became a wretched pop crooner, and the Mindbenders stayed together as a mediocre rock band, producing a crummy hit and a crummy album, subsequent cover versions of "*The Letter*" and the like. Eric Stewart later went on to Hotlegs and 10cc as well. Unfortunately, Wayne Fontana and the Mindbenders released but a fragment of their English output here in the States, and their second album has been out of print for several years. I'd like to hear it, because I can imagine what they did with "*He's A Rebel*" and "*Some Other Guy*," judging from the *Game of Love* LP and the Mindbenders' respectable version of "*One Fine Day*" on their *Groovy Kind of Love* album. Anyway, Wayne Fontana & The Mindbenders were a fine group, and their records are ripe for rediscovery.

--*Mike Saunders*

FREDDIE & the DREAMERS

If ever there was a blatantly manufactured British group, it seemed as if Freddie & The Dreamers were that band. Obviously, some British media-oriented smooth operators had unearthed this spindly Freddie Garrity character, rounded up four overaged bruisers from the probation rolls for a back-up band (a single glance at any of their album covers will confirm the higher truth of this supposition), created the "Freddie" dance, given the group some suitable simplistic musical material, and splashed them across the ever-incredulous U.S. of A. Of course--but it wasn't the case.

Freddie & The Dreamers, to the contrary, actually had a long and rather impressive career behind them in Britian; and in fact were one of the earliest successful top British groups--the first non-Epstein band to score a certified top-5 smash after the Beatles broke. (With a typically-inept-but-charming cover of James Ray's "*If You Gotta Make A Fool of Somebody*," which reached #2 in the summer of 1963). The group had formed in Manchester around the end of 1962 when Freddie decided to forsake his promising vocation as a milkman. He joined up with Derek Quinn, lead guitar and shades; Roy Crewdson, rhythm; Pete Birrell, bass; and Bernie Dwyer on drums. They played around locally did a gig at Hamburg's Top Ten Club, and cut a record for Columbia (U.K.), the aforementioned "*If You Gotta Make A Fool Of Somebody*".

"*I'm Telling You*," a bouncy number co-written by Freddie, also went to #2, in September '63; "*You Were Made For Me*," slightly more music-hall and less musical, hit #4 as the year ended; "*Over You*," with its modified "*Walk Don't Run*" intro, was #11 in April '64 and "*I Love You Baby*" reached #17 that summer. "*I Understand*," a change-of-pace ballad chestnut, regained a bit of lost ground by climbing to #6 at the tail end of 1964, which brings us up to the group's sudden (and inexplicably belated, considering they'd had British hits for over a year and a half) American conquest.

Dancing was still a crucial facet of pop music, and had indeed received a boost from the heavily televised fad of Go-Go dancing. So Freddie & The Dreamers' success was keyed to the "*Freddie*", a dance which basically defied formalization, and possessed the inestimable advantage of being instantly masterable by any reasonably energetic cretin. The origin of the Freddie is in doubt: the dance's namesake claimed that "while entertaining at local spas in England, the 'gyrations...were part of the act.'". But whatever its origin, Freddie's American introduction of the dance caused something of a sensation. Mercury Records had the rights to the most recent single, "*I Understand*," but its slushy qualities doomed it to second-class hit status behind Tower's release of the 19-month-old "*I'm Telling You Now*," which was perfectly suited to the "rhythmic structure" of the Freddie, and hit #1.

To follow up their #1 record, Tower put out a quickie album featuring the single, another pleasant track called "*What Have I Done To You*," and ten selections by other assorted British nonentities. Tower also revived "*You Were Made For Me*", which eventually hit #21 here, and released another LP with four selections each from Freddie, Tom Jones, and Johnny Rivers. Meanwhile, Mercury had beaten Tower to the punch by a couple weeks by rushing out a new single tailor-made for the dance craze, called "*Do The Freddie*." Although an obviously exploitative gimmick record, the single was quite catchy and remains attractive today, featuring gospelized back-up vocals four years ahead of Joe Cocker (sounding good for once, too--the back-up, not Cocker), fairly tasteful horns, and a rather strong lead guitar break (interspersed with absolutely hideous cackling from Freddie, to boot. "*A Little You*", a very pleasant, almost-rocking tune, was the follow-up in both Britain and the U.S., and hit #19 over there and a dissappoint-

FREDDIE

ROY

DEREK

ing #48 (compared to "Do The Freddie"'s #18) here; and that was about it as far as hit singles went.

Four legitimate albums were released in the States by Mercury (plus one soundtrack LP), and they're really not bad, if you take it with a lot of salt (or a Lot's wife). For instance, noted critic Mark Shipper's contention that the group's version of "Johnny B. Goode" is "unquestionably the most inept version ever put on vinyl" is a base canard and a grievous insult to Grateful Dead fans. Besides this stellar performance, Freddie and his somnambulistic cohorts render two Buddy Holly songs, "Kansas City," and "Money," all on one side of the first Mercury LP (Freddie & The Dreamers).

Do The Freddie is a more accomplished LP; the first side is mostly notable for the very polished title track and the pleasant British single "Over You." The second side, however, is virtually all mildly infectious British pop fare, highlighted by "A Little You", "A Love Like You,"and "Don't Do That To Me," which also appeared on the soundtrack LP to the movie Seaside Swingers.

This film was just one of the many multi-media projects Freddie & The Dreamers were involved in. One report in early '66 had them slated for a fall ABC-TV situation comedy/musical, with the network angling for Terry-Thomas to play Freddie's old man. But the courtship of Freddie's father fizzled out, and ABC apparently decided to let NBC blaze the trail with the Monkees. The Seaside Swingers flick did come out, however, with British popstars John Leyton and Mike Sarne; and a tour-de-force Dreamers track on the soundtrack LP "What's Cooking." Following on the heels of "Like A Rolling Stone," it's a 6-minute spectacular with a complex story line (involving Freddie's plight as an overworked master chef, described repeatedly as the "king of cheese souffle") and several intriguing shifts of musical direction (a mini-opera if you will) There are two surrealistic sequences surrounding the agonizing preparation of a culinary piece-de-resistance and during the (main) course of the song, the Dreamers are given a rare chance to show off their own vocal abilities, which they do in agreeably imbecilic fashion.

Freddie & The Dreamers' later career also included another movie, called "Cuckoo Patrol," which was later released in England. Freddie revealed in an exclusive Rona Barrett interview that the movie was based on the style of the Three Stooges (an early Manchester group who were also strong musical influences for British pop idol Ken Dodd); and Dreamer Derek Quinn added, more succinctly, "Being idiots, we decided to center the plot around five boy scouts, a master scout, and a cook. Since we all look marvelous in shorts, we play the boys." Tragically for American cinema buffs, the Boy Scouts of America threatened to raze all theaters which showed the films, and the timid distributors cancelled it.

Their fourth Mercury album, Frantic Freddie, is fairly strong as the group's albums went. Highlights are a chugging Anglicized version of "Short Shorts", carbon copies of "Zip-A-Dee-Doo-Dah" and Roy Orbison's "Crying" (falling of perfection only because of the thin, "gargly" nature of Freddie's voice and the group's lame back up vocals); and a provocative track entitled "Drink This Up, It'll Make You Sleep" featuring Freddie as your friendly neighborhood soper-market.

Fun Lovin' Freddie, their final U.S. album, is a general disappointment; its saving graces are the Merseybeats' "I Think Of You," a creditable remake of "I'll Never Dance Again," the pleasant pop ditty "Write Me A Letter," and "Don't Tell Me That," a nice beat number with an unidentified pianist (Nicky Hopkins? Ian Stewart? Freddie "Fingers" Lee?) raving in the background. On the other hand, selections like the incredible version of "Thou Shalt Not Steal" which sounds much more like "I Can't Stop Loving You" than Dick & DeeDee, bring the album down drastically. For completists only.

The group had several subsequent British releases after their American commercial demise. "Thou Shalt Not Steal" somehow hit #52 on the rather dubious Music Echo Top 100 of October '65, and later singles included "Playboy," "Turn Around", and a version of "Hello Hello." In addition, they were involved in an LP called Sing Along Party and then the no-doubt classic Freddie & The Dreamers In Disneyland; they concluded their LP career with a late '67 package called King Freddie & His Dreaming Knights, featuring versions of "59th Street Bridge Song," and "Juanita Banana". Several singles were released through the late '60's and early 70's, and the group played the coastal resort circuit (and, of course, the local spas), Freddie engaged in a bit of bantomine, and they have managed to straggle along. Currently they are one of the groups slated for the British Invasion tour package this year, along with Billy J. Kramer, the Searchers, and (rumor has it) the re-formed Three Stooges. Don't miss it.

---Ken Barnes

PETE

BERNIE

LONDON and the REST

DAVE CLARK FIVE

The Dave Clark Five were one of the biggest singles groups of the English invasion, and one of the best. It's important to understand them within this context; save for Weekend In London, their albums were as lousy as one might expect. But "Glad All Over," the first record to break the Beatles' stranglehold on the English charts, was a classic pop single, a masterpiece explosion of pure rocknroll—and besides, they had lots of other fine singles, enough to fill up two knockout Greatest Hits albums.

The DC5 had a distinct musical identity up through mid-1965, contrary to disparaging criticisms of them. First, they had an easily identifiable vocal sound, usually characterized by two-part vocals from Clark and organist Mike Smith; secondly, their records utilized some classic studio rock&roll production. Most noticable of all was the great studio job done on the drums (cymbals included); they always seemed to be super-echoed, clean, and forceful. The production work done on their raver singles perfectly matched the style of the group: crude, simplistic, and driving. With a vein like this, it's perfect to blend the instrumental backup into a wall of sound emphasizing the rhythm track: "Anyway You Want It" is a great example of this. They didn't call it the Big Beat for nothing!

Singer-songwriter-drummer-producer-manager. That's hot stuff---real credentials of multi-talent. Leon Russell or the Grateful Starship or Stevie Stills by any chance? Nope. Dave Clark. When the record books of rock history are sealed for the ages, down under the column for Who Did The Most All At The Same Time, it may still read just that: Dave Clark. This alone would make the DC5 a rather unique group, to say the least--and then there was the matter of that saxophone. The Dave Clark Five was the only English invasion group with a sax, regards going to Denny Payton. However, if you'll go back to "Locomotion" by Little Eva from 1962, on the part where she sings "Jump up! Jump back!" there's a sax raunching away over the three-chord changes. It's almost tempting to conjecture that the DC5 got their whole sound from this song, because it sounds almost exactly like their later style. The DC5 were probably the only English invasion group that would have even touched a sax; they didn't know that saxes were unhip in 1964 to most rock groups, they were completely beyond that sort of thing of hipness or unhipness. They just set out to do what they wanted to do, true artists, never straying an inch to the left or right. Dave Clark wanted to get rich. He did.

I suspect criticisms of the DC5 result largely from their being so pop-oriented, both in style and format, rather than one of the hard rock greats like the Stones, the Who, Yardbirds, Them et al. It's true, the differentiation is absolutely correct; I myself hear in the DC5 some influences that few other English groups appeared to have—early 60's pop rock 'n' roll like Dion and Neil Sedaka; and the Crystals, Ronettes, Chiffons, and other girl groups. Who else would've done a fitting version of Bobb B. Soxx's "Zip-A-Dee-Doo-Dah?" Of course Clark's group did their share of the obligatory 50's rock classics and R&B gear; but on their singles, the whole attitude of the former 60's pop rock 'n' roll style seemed to predominate, from ballads to rockers.

"Glad All Over," "Bits And Pieces," "Do You Love Me" (their first British hit, beaten handily on the charts by Brian Poole & the Tremeloes' version), "Can't You See That She's Mine," "Because," "Everybody Knows," "Anyway You Want It," "Come Home," "Reelin' & Rockin," "I Like It Like That," "Catch Us If You Can." These were some of the Dave Clark Five's hits from their golden period of popularity; and if you stop to figure it out, it comes out to almost twelve hits in one year's time--which is a hit a month! The whole point is, almost all were good singles, the whole pile of

DAVE CLARK FIVE
Epic Records

D.C. 5, contd.

them. After mid-1965 and "Catch Us If You Can," the DC5 became randomly imitative and went downhill from there, trying out one trend and then another. Even at that, though, they occasionally came out with a good single, like "I've Got To Have A Reason" or "Nineteen Days." On one occasion, they came up with a great one in "Try Too Hard."

They remained commercially successful long after most of their compatriots had fallen by the wayside; "Over And Over" was #1 here in late '65 and "You Got What It Takes" hit #7 in April '67, well after their supposed peak. They even made the British top 5 in late '67, after a lengthy absence (as soon as the DC5 hit in the U.S., they quite cold-bloodedly aimed their efforts at the American dollar almost exclusively, and as a result suffered a drastic drop in British popularity) with a ballad, their second hit under the title "Everybody Knows." A couple of spirited rock 'n' roll medleys (one basically a cover of Cat Mother's "Good Old Rock 'N' Roll) cashed in on the late 60's "rock revival" trend; and, although the Dave Clark Five as such broke up around late '69, an aggregation called Dave Clark & Friends (one being lead singer Mike Smith) continues to record, with some sprightly commercial singles (covers of Layng Martine's "Rub It In," Amen Corner's "Paradise") and an enjoyable '72 LP, with versions of such contemporary blockbusters as "Signs," "Southern Man," and "Draggin' The Line."

The Dave Clark Five weren't as important as the Beatles or Stones or Kinks-level groups; they were just as good in a different way, firstly and lastly as a consistent singles group. I think people have underrated the Dave Clark Five quite a bit--they were excellent producers of good, healthy, enjoyable schlock, consistently squeezed onto a 45 rpm record. For that, three cheers, a 95 at the least, and a reprise of the WHUMPADA THUMPADA CRASH drum intro to "Bits and Pieces."

---Mike Saunders

Ed Sullivan, champion of British music.

KINKS

They came from Muswell Hill, London, ranging in age from 17 to 20, and after two false starts they took off on a career whose longevity has been equaled only by the Stones and Hollies. The Kinks are well known for the Victorian fantasies of Ray Davies, commencing around the time of "Dedicated Follower Of Fashion," late 1966. Nobody talks much about their earlier stuff anymore, and nobody has ever considered it in the context of its time.

Their first two releases, "Long Tall Sally" and "You Still Want Me,"(1963) were in a very Liverpudlian, Searchers-like style that they claim was forced on them by the record company. Following their failure, the Kinks went ahead with their own style of music, based on Chuck Berry but totally distinct from the droves of Berry-influenced groups inhabiting London in those days. With the addition of Jimmy Page on second guitar (though not lead, as widely believed), the Kinks developed a sound that drew on the Mersey groups' emphasis of rhythm but exaggerated to the point that it became a trademark. They shared this exaggerated guitar sound with another early London mod group, the Who, with whom they coincidentally enough also shared their producer, Shel Talmy.

At the start, the Kinks were one of the most raw, crude, energetic groups around. Their first album (which contained, on the British pressing "I Took My Baby Home," which had been the flip side of "Long Tall Sally") included such ravers as "Beautiful Delilah," "So Mystifying," "Long Tall Shorty," "Cadillac," "I'm A Lover Not a Fighter," "Too Much Monkey Business,"and "Got Love If You Want It." In addition to this strong dose of Berry and Diddley, there were a couple of ballads (including the much-covered Searchers-like "Just Can't Go To Sleep"), "Bald-Headed Woman" and "I've Been Driving on Bald Mountain" (which the Who combined to make the B-side of "I Can't Explain") and, of course "You Really Got Me."

This, along with "Come On Now," "All Day and All of the Night," "Milk Cow Blues," Till the End of the Day," "It's Alright," "Who'll Be the Next in Line" and especially "Louie Louie", which they put on two albums, would be evidence enough to build a case that the Kinks were England's first punk-rock group. One could conjecture endlessly as to what was going through their minds on their first American tour when they appeared in Seattle with the Sonics, whose own version of "Louie Louie" was the ultimate in raunch, and whose original "He's Waiting" sounded like eight Jimmy Pages jamming on"You Really Got Me."

But it's not fair to compare English groups with American. In 1964, the Kinks were the ruling masters of British kineticism. Their songs bristled with energy and drive, except their ballads of course which were either adequate versions of Lazy Lester blues things or really effective melodic originals like "Something Better Beginning," "Tired of Waiting For You," or "It's Too Late."

Face to Face was the first album on which their artiness began to emerge, and although it was a transition that stretched over at least three albums and preceded an amazingly high-energy live album, it marked the end of the early Kinks.

Perhaps the most important thing about the early Kinks is the fact that they were the first group to write original rock & roll songs equal in power to the fifties material they started with. The Stones and Yardbirds didn't reach this stage until '65, and as for the Beatles--it's debatable. Their best songs were more pop than rock & roll, and by 1964 they were no longer trying to be raunchy. Compare the Kinks to a group like the Hollies, who tried to equal the impact of their favorite fifties songs and (despite what Mike Saunders thinks) generally fell short, and it's plain the Kinks had no peer in this regard. What an irony that the Kinks are at once one of most raunchy and also one of the most successfully effete groups England has ever produced.

--Greg Shaw

NASHVILLE TEENS

On the Nashville Teens' first album, the editor of Cash Box pontificated to the effect that it was "*a set that lends credence to the fact that the boys will not fall by the wayside of the 'one-shot' artists.*" The group promptly went on never to make another album, or another hit on the scale of "Tobacco Road"; however, they have managed to stay together in one form or another for ten years, the last seven firmly encamped by the "wayside", and are still making occasional records--good ones, too. The group got together in Weybridge, Surrey, around 1962; but things didn't start happening for them till early '64, when they got a new drummer, Barry Jenkins (from a group called Don Adams & The Original Rock 'N' Roll Trio, also featuring Albert Lee of Heads Hands & Feet and session fame); a new manager, Don Arden (now in charge of the Move/ELO/Wizzard conglomerate); and a new gig backing Jerry Lee Lewis on an English and Continental tour (in the process appearing on a live German album which is Lewis's best live recording ever).

Shortly afterward, they acquired a new producer, Mickie Most, and recorded a song by one of co-lead vocalist Arthur Sharp's favorite composers, John D. Loudermilk's "Tobacco Road" (previously cut by Billy Lee Riley). The song, with its ferocious beat and pulsing piano pyrotechnics, was a British invasion classic and quickly achieved top 10 status on both sides of the Atlantic. The Teens made a fast dash to the States, playing on one of Murray the K's Brooklyn Fox extravaganzas, and also cut an LP. It was a solid period album, with energetic piano-dominated workouts on R&B staples like "Mona," "Parchment Farm," "I Like It Like That"; plus their follow-up single ; "Google Eye" (also written by Loudermilk). This record, the saga of a legendary trout (heroic subject matter), was hampered by a low-keyed, unexciting first half, and bombed badly in the States (although reaching British top 20). The next single, a wild stomper called "Find My Way Back Home," also failed; and a last-ditch effort, a fairly anemic cover of Marianne Faithfull's "This Little Bird" (composed by one J.D. Loudermilk), produced by Andrew Loog Oldham (perhaps trying to steal the sales thunder from his former protegee's version), merely

The Nashville Teens continued to release singles from 1965 through 1972, the most successful of which was a nice, late '65 pop-rocker called "I Know How It Feels To Be Loved." In 1968 they recorded a version of "All Along The Watchtower," and a year later covered Don Fardon's "Indian Reservation" (yet another Loudermilk song). 1972 brought an excellent comeback attempt with a Roy Wood-produced rendition of "Ella James" which some prefer to the Move's performance (the flip, "Tennessee Woman," was also a fine hard rocker); it went by virtually unnoticed, however. Many of the original group members had departed long ago--Jenkins joined the Animals in '66, pianist John Hawken went to Keith Relf's Renaissance, and onetime Teen Dick Horner is now part of Uncle Dog; but the Nashville Teens continue to slog onward, playing occasional British dates and still waiting for that elusive second shot--which unless the time is right for a revival of Loudermilk's 1961 chartbuster, "The Language of Love," looks more unlikely all the time.

--Ken Barnes

BRITISH R&B

"Keith Richard is the mainspring of rhythm & blues" --Fab Magazine, 1964

As the Liverpool groups dominated English rock in 1963, their success made record companies more open to rock groups in general, and by 1964 enough groups from around London had been signed up to make that city the next center of activity and provide the extra push needed to carry the fading Merseybeat explosion through another two years. To us in America, all the English group records sounded pretty similar (certainly the distinction between, say, Manchester and Birmingham groups was lost on us), but the difference between the Liverpool and London scenes is very important and worth investigating.

Although London produced its share of Mersey-sound groups (Dave Clark Five, Migil Five, Brian Poole & the Tremeloes), the city's real contribution grew out of the R&B revival started in the mid '50s by Chris Barber, Alexis Korner, Cyril Davies and their crowd. The growth of British R&B can be traced to March 1962, when Davies and Korner opened the Ealing Rhythm and Blues Club, because of pressure from trad jazz fans and blues purists when amplified blues was introduced in sets by Korner's popular group Blues Incorporated, at the jazz clubs where they'd been playing.

Their following grew, especially among the younger fans, and by summer the group (which then included Jack Bruce, Ginger Baker and Dick Heckstall-Smith, and on occasion Mick Jagger, Paul Jones and Brian Jones) was given a residency at the top jazz club, Chris Barber's Marquee Club. A lot of young musicians began hanging around, and forming groups of their own. And as this happened, the fairly traditional arrangements of 1962 gave way in 1963 to a more commercial Mersey-influenced style.

The groups around then were few. The Stones got together during the summer of '62, with Charlie Watts and Mick Jagger from Korner's group, and Brian Jones from a group called the Roosters (which had also included Eric Clapton, Paul Jones and Tom McGuiness) With Dick Taylor, original Stones guitarist and reputedly the style-setter of the era, these people and the groups they came from were the source of London R&B.

Other groups active at the time included Brian Knight's Blues-By-Six (who according to one story topped the bill at the Stones' first Marquee appearance), Graham Bond's Organisation, and Georgie Fame's Blue Flames, who held down a residence at the Flamingo Club, about which more later.

From strict Chicago blues, the Stones took the whole scene to a new level by introducing Chuck Berry, Buddy Holly, Marvin Gaye, etc. into their repertoire. The Liverpool groups used this same material of course, but usually Merseified it beyond recognition; the Stones were fanatically true to the original spirit of the music. Despite this, their controversial reputation in those days was due as much to their lack of musical "purism" as anything else, but the reaction of the older purists didn't matter as much as that of the younger fans who were inspired by them. By the end of 1963 they had been joined by such groups as the Cheynes, Alex Harvey's Soul Band, Ray Anton & the Peppermint Men, the Zephyrs, and others less famous. With the exception of Harvey, they were all strongly Stones-influenced.

As the formative year of English R&B, 1963 produced a lot of good music. All the above groups made great records, far superior to most of what went down in '64. They took the heavy Mersey rhythm (rhythm guitar was still the dominant instrument in English rock) and applied it to some of the same R&B/rock & roll standards that had been done by the Liverpool groups, but with a difference. In contrast, they seemed more fascinated by the music itself than the mere fact that they were playing it. There was no artificial excitement, it all rose directly from the music. The early Stones-influenced groups seemed to prefer fast songs, and usually speeded them up even more, but somehow they always sounded tighter and more in control. There was great tension in records of this period, and Keith Richard's early staccato guitar style was widely and effectively imitated.

The best records of the year, for me, were "Respectable" by the Cheynes (easily the best version I've heard), "You Can't Judge a Book" by Ray Anton & the Peppermint Men, and "Country Line Special" by Cyril Davies' Allstars. Davies had broken off from Korner's

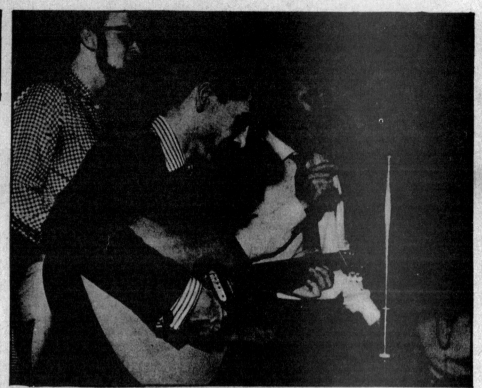

At the Marquee Club in 1961. We see above, from left to right: Dick Heckstall-Smith, Alexis Korner, and the late Cyril Davies.

band in early '63 and started his own group, including Long John Baldry, another Korner expatriate. Blues Incorporated lost a lot of members that year, as they left to form groups of their own, and Korner himself eventually went solo. "Country Line Special" is the definitive 1963 English R&B jam, with a stunning guitar break by someone who had Keith Richard's style down cold, and featuring Nicky Hopkins on piano, in what is said to have been his first recording.

1964 was the year it all broke loose. While the best Liverpool records came out that year, they were by groups like the Searchers, Merseybeats, Cilla Black, and the Beatles, who were known internationally, on tour constantly, and not really part of any localized scene. That doesn't make their records any less great, but it does indicate that the seeds of creativity and experimentation had drifted elsewhere--to London.

The London R&B scene had its full flowering in 1964. The Stones, having already outgrown the Marquee, passed on their Crawdaddy Club residency to the Yardbirds. The Spencer Davis Group, Gary Farr & the T-Bones, Manfred Mann, the Bo Street Runners, and the Authentics (all excellent groups) also began playing the Marquee, Flamingo and Crawdaddy clubs, with other clubs such as the 100 Club, the Studio 51 Club, Eel Pie Island, and Klook's Kleek joining in. All these clubs were located within a fairly close distance of one another, and it made for a real jumping scene.

The 100 Club boasted the Pretty Things, Dick Taylor's new group and pioneers of the crude, exaggeratedly raw sound that was much copied in later years, particularly by American "punk rock" groups. The Artwoods (including Jon Lord and Keef Hartley), Graham Bond's Organisation, the Fairies (great group in-

BRITISH R&B, cont.

cluding Steve Howe, now of Yes, and Twink), the Tridents (with Jeff Beck) and the Soul Agents also played there.

Also on the scene were Eric Clapton's Powerhouse (briefly) featuring Jack Bruce, Stevie Winwood, Paul Jones, Ben Palmer and Pete York, and, one of the most popular groups, Long John Baldry's Hoochie Coochie Men. Baldry had left Korner's band along with Davies to start the Allstars, and after Davies' untimely death in early '64, the name was changed to Long John Baldry's Allstars with the addition of Rod Stewart, and then to the Hoochie Coochie Men (and later to Steampacket).

The Marquee, Crawdaddy, Ealing, Studio 51 and 100 Clubs pretty much specialized in the guitar-heavy, raunchy Chuck Berry groups typified by the Stones and Pretty Things. Some of them were good, many of them terrible, and others like the Downliner Downliners Sect, so exaggerated that their records, while admittedly bad, are fascinating. They were like the American punk bands of a year or two later--all form and no subtlety.

But the best punk R&B came from the Stones, Yardbirds, Pretty Things, Cheynes, T-Bones, and the groups that evolved from this scene in '65 and '66--the Who, Creation, Troggs, Eyes, etc. These groups were as close to the wildness of classic American rock & roll as anybody from England has ever come.

At the same time all this was going on, another R&B scene was taking place in London, including John Mayall and his frequent venue Klook's Kleek, but centered around the Flamingo Club. The Flamingo was one of the first clubs to go R&B, in mid '62, but unlike the Marquee it catered to a predominantly black audience, both West Indian and GI's. The original house band was the Blue Flames, featuring Georgie Fame. Formerly Billy Fury's backing group, they became very popular with a brand of R&B based on Ray Charles, Bobby Bland, James Brown, etc. In other words, big band jazzy R&B with horns. Groups who worked in this style included Chris Farlowe & the Thunderbirds, Zoot Money's Big Roll Band, the Graham Bond Organisation, Tony Knight's Chessmen, John Lee's Groundhogs (later the Groundhogs), Brian Auger & the Trinity, John Mayall's Bluesbreakers, the Gass, Hogsnort Rupert's Good Good Band, and on occasion, the Animals and the Moody Blues.

There seems to have been a sort of friendly rivalry between adherants of the two schools, with the guitar bands being looked down upon somewhat by the admittedly more sophisticated jazz-oriented fans. The recorded evidence probably doesn't capture either style at its best, but it's easy to imagine that Farlowe, Fame, Bond, etc. were just as great in their way as the Stones and the other Marquee groups whose sound we know so well. They too played a lot of loud, fast, rough songs, but with saxophones and all the sound must have been much fuller. See Richard Williams' letter in this issue for further amplification on the subject.

A large faction of the Flamingo crowd was composed of West Indians, who were just beginning to emerge as a coherent social force in England. Their music was soul, and so they gravitated to hear Fame, Money, etc. There were also Jamaican singers and groups, such as Jimmy James & the Vagabonds, and later Jimmy Cliff, but the most popular act of all with the Jamaicans was Geno Washington, an expatriated American who had a minor hit here with "Geno's a Coward" and doesn't seem too well regarded among the white R&B enthusiasts.

By 1965 R&B was about at its end as the dominant style around London. The Mods who had grown up on R&B were beginning to create their own music, American trends like folk-rock were being felt, and also the leading groups had once again graduated to international stature. Good R&B continued to come out, as did Merseybeat records for that matter, but the focus of creativity was clearly shifting again.

Many of the R&B people retreated into purism, and British Blues (as documented in the Immediate/RCA "Anthology of British Blues" series and many other recent packages) was born; a very self-conscious style divorced from pop. And yet, ironically, although many of these blues musicians were forced off the scene by pop music, it was their blues purism that resulted in 1968's outbreak of boogie bands such as Savoy Brown and Ten Years After, which following the reign of Underground Rock managed to forestall the return of pop music by another five years.

---Greg Shaw

(For further information on the early R&B club scene, check out John Pidgeon's excellent article in the 2/73 issue of Let It Rock. John, we understand, is preparing a book on the subject of English R&B.)

PRETTY THINGS

The Pretty Things were basically a fringe group, in terms of mass popularity, record hits, lasting success, etc. But their image and sound were removed from the mainstream as well, and their exalted reputation among British Invasion devotees is an example of a group which was treasured for its extremes. No one looked quite as scruffy or disreputable as the Things ("as all their fans call them"--first LP), no one else cavorted onstage so manically ("...bangs about the stage like some maimed gorilla"--Nik Cohn describing lead singer Phil May)--even their name was outrageous.

More importantly, though, no one else carried the standard R&B/blues/rock & roll repertoire of the times to such extremes. The Rolling Stones, most significantly, and many other groups to a lesser extent were instrumental in rendering the purist approach to the music obsolete and steering the trend to a rawer, harder, faster, more exciting British sound; but the Pretty Things were even wilder. Their slow blues were a chaotic jumble of shrieking harp and frantic clusters of guitar notes, while the upbeat material was revved way up, coarse, sloppy and primitive, with May lurching and slobbering and squealing the vocals, on the crudest, most unpolished level imaginable. Naturally, it was exciting as hell, and on their best records ("Midnight to Six Man," "Rosalyn," "Come See Me") the Pretties approached the loftiest punk-rock pinnacles.

The group got together in London in '63, with the crucial band members being Phil May and lead guitarist Dick Taylor, formerly Rolling Stones bassist and apparently a seminal figure in the London R&B boom, a trendsetter in music, fashion, and pop affairs in general. Their first record was a Bo Diddley-based tune called "Rosalyn"; it wasn't a hit but it was one of their all-time best, a relentless rocker with a great "Fortune Teller"-type intro. Next came "Don't Bring Me Down" and "Honey I Need,"; archetypal Pretty Things rockers, with trademarked snarling May vocals; both of these were substantial hits and an album followed.

The LP was a fine showcase of the Pretty Things' musical range--slow blues, uptempo blues, and lively R&B/Berry/rock & roll tunes. Not a particularly wide range, but one the group had mastered, in that they employed the same raving sledgehammer approach to each style (so that "Unknown Blues," for example, is so cluttered as to constitute a hilarious parody of the ultra-solemn slow blues atrocities which were later to develop in Britain). Best tracks, beside "Honey I Need", were probably the three Bo Diddley numbers, "Pretty Thing," "Road Runner" (a driving version which doubtless influenced the Gants, etc.), and the more obscure "Mama Keep Your Big Mouth Shut." Also worthy of comment were Berry's "Oh Baby Doll" and "13 Chester St." (actually Slim Harpo's "Got Love If You Want It" in very thin disguise).

The American version of the album dropped "Oh Baby Doll" and "Mama Keep..." plus two lesser numbers, replacing them with the strong singles "Rosalyn" and "Don't Bring Me Down," plus two flip sides, one a boring slow blues, the other a fine original rocker, "I Can Never Say," which is almost melodic. Neither the LP nor any of the group's singles were ever hits in America, and a significant portion of their early work was, unfortunately, never released here.

Their next single was the old Betty Harris hit "Cry to Me," also covered by the Stones, but the Things' version was very odd, strangely uptempo and with a pronounced beat, none of which really seemed to fit--and the disc was only a minor hit. A British EP featuring a fine beat group performance of Harpo's "Rainin' In My Heart" as lead track also contained an unusually melodic and attractive cut called "Sittin' All Alone."

Then in late '65 the group's second album, Get the Picture, was released (in England only). It opened with a jolt, a burst of pure Sonny Bono-style folk rock guitar, leading into a fine song called "You Don't Believe Me" which was markedly different from anything previously attempted, and successful at that. The entire first side was quite entrancing, with the tough, punk-like "Get the Picture," "Rainin' In My Heart," and the rather scary "Can't Stand the Pain," with its tormented tremeloed guitar lines standing out. Also notable were "We'll Play House," for sounding extremely similar to "13 Chester St." and "Buzz the Jerk" for its demonstration of the Pretty Things approach to funky soul numbers--crashing through them just like anything else they did. Side two has some pretty pedestrian material, notably a confused and unsuccessful electric folk experiment, "London Town"; but "Gonna Find Me a Substitute" is enjoyable in its resemblance to "Walking the Dog," and "I Want Your Love" is a great commercial rocker, with the immortal exclamation, "Saints preserve me, I just gotta love ya!"

Following the album came their two finest singles, "Midnight to Six Man" with its terrific opening punk riffs (it was subsequently covered by a few American bands, in fact) and "Come See Me," a raw sonic assault vaguely based on a "What'cha Gonna Do About It" chord progression which was designed to plaster any listener against the wall in the first few seconds. The first-named record was a minor chart item, the second missed entirely, and any commercial stature, however slight, that the Pretty Things had achieved was now dissipated. The next single was a fairly lackluster cover of the Kinks' "*House in the Country,*" followed by "*Progress,*" a rather enjoyable beat number marred by clumsy horns.

Their third album, *Emotions*, in early '67, was a radical change, featuring such alien impedimenta as acoustic guitar, strings, harmonies, raga-like scales and (worst of all), incredibly imbecilic and intrusive horn arrangements on about half the tracks, sometimes so obnoxious as to presage latter-day cacaphonies by Chicago or BS&T. A few of the tracks were pleasantly melodic or at least slightly reminiscent of the old snarling style ("*One Long Glance*"), and a cut called "*Tripping*" was a rather amusing example of the British psychedelia blues; but as a whole the LP is eminently forgettable, even disastrous.

Dick Taylor left the group shortly afterward (as did drummer Viv Prince, apparently quite a character in his own right); John Adler (Twink), formerly of the Fairies, joined up from Tomorrow, and the group entered a new phase which is more the province of fanatic art-rock camp followers and much less interesting to my way of thinking. This phase would include their pre-*Tommy* quasi pop-opera *S.F. Sorrow*, some of which is marginally enjoyable; their dreadful follow-up LP in the same vein, *Parachute* (both issued by Rare Earth in the States); an odd 1970 single, "*October 26*"/"*Cold Stone*" (the latter a tolerable heavy rocker) and the group's '72 vintage LP, *Freeway Madness*, which seems so generally slow-paced as to be little better than an instant nod-out. Phil May is the only original thing left by now, but they still play frequent British gigs, and even reportedly include a sprinkling of 1964-5 numbers. That's just fine, for it will be for those demented early ravers that the Pretty Things will most and longest be cherished.

---Ken Barnes

DOWNLINERS SECT

To many people in England, the Downliners Sect were a joke, at best a gross caricature of all that was bad about British R&B. And maybe they were. But anybody who's disliked that much is certainly worthy of investigation. In actual fact, as implied elsewhere, the Downliners may well have been one of the first and few genuine English punk-rock bands, although letting in any Limeys at all calls for liberal stretching of the definitions.

But anyway, I must admit I like some of their stuff. Their music was an exaggerated version of the early Pretty Things sound--R&B classics transformed into coarse, raving attacks, all subtlety crushed under those relentless rhythm chords and tasteless vocals. Their idols were Chuck Berry and Bo Diddley, and they are best remembered for anthems like "*Sect Appeal*" and "*Be a Sect Maniac*" which took Bo's already simple beat to new plateaus of simplicity. Abysmal records, admittedly, although Lester Bangs has been known to foam at the mouth on hearing them.

But the Downliners didn't restrict themselves to that. In fact, they jumped on every trend they could find. Their second album, *The Country Sect*, anticipated country-rock by several years, although their next, *The Rock Sect's In!* was equally late in acknowledging the arrival of rock & roll. A pretty lame album too, with shitty versions of "*Hang On Sloopy,*" "*Fortune Teller*" and (!) "*May the Bird of Paradise Fly Up Your Nose.*" Rather good version of Fats Domino's "*Don't Lie to Me,*" although they perpetuated Chuck Berry's theft of the song by giving him credit. But that's okay; the fact that they learned all they knew about R&B from two or three Marble Arch reissue albums and the Rolling Stones is half the charm of these English R&B groups. That country album, incidentally, is quite strange. It goes from "*Wolverton Mountain*" to strictly Nashville country to hootenanny stuff to actual country-rock.

But all gimmicks aside (and not forgetting their classic "*Sick Songs*" EP), the Downliners Sect actually had a few excellent songs, mostly on their first album. Besides the steamroller treatments of Chuck Berry and Jimmy Reed, the album includes one of the alltime great stops-out raveups, "*Bloodhound,*" and an equally wild number called "*One Ugly Child,*" on which they were joined by Nicky Hopkins, playing superb piano. Good lyrics too, like "*you belong in a cage, who turned you loose on me?*"

No, the Downliners weren't all bad. Two of their singles are also worth searching for. "*Glendora*"/"*I'll Find Out*" is a wild raving rocker, and "*The Cost of Living*" is a less crude, professionally arranged pop-rock single with some nice piano, and as it was the last thing they recorded it shows there might have been promise for the Downliners Sect after all. But, all told, I think I'd still rather hear them any time than John Baldry, Dave Berry, or some of the other people the blues purists favored. Tasteless to the end, I guess.

---Greg Shaw

YARDBIRDS

The Yardbirds always get plenty of lip service. They're the ones even those snobs who never listened to rock before *Sgt. Pepper* always admit were "*ahead of their time.*" Of course, they're usually referring to the Jeff Beck Yardbirds, of "*Shapes of Things*" and "*Happenings Ten Years Time Ago*" fame, and while those 1966 records are unquestionably fantastic, the 1963-5 Yardbirds are of more pertinence to our story.

They started in '63 as the Metropolitan Blues Quartet, consisting of Keith Relf, Chris Dreja, Paul Samwell-Smith, Jim McCarty and Tony Topman. After losing Topman and replacing him with a clean-cut looking youngster named Eric Clapton, they changed their name to the Yardbirds (after something they

The Downliners Sect, with their idol Jimmy Reed

read on an old blues album, natch) and soon became so popular among London's early R&B fans that, when the Stones moved out of their Crawdaddy Club residency, the Yardbirds were ready to take it over.

Their first recordings stem from a date they were fortunate enough to have gotten, as Sonny Boy Williamson's backup band. An album came out three years later, and it tells us little about the Yardbirds except that they were a competent blues band; they didn't once try to steal the spotlight from Sonny Boy. Their real debut came in 1964 with an album, *Five Live Yardbirds* (English only) that clearly demonstrated one thing: whatever the Yardbirds were doing, they were doing it better than anybody.

With songs like "*Smokestack Lightning,*" "*Good Morning Little Schoolgirl,*" "*Too Much Monkey Business*" and "*Respectable,*" they were fully in the thick of the London R&B style described earlier. Instrumentally they had no equal except the Stones, and in fact they had a much fuller sound than the Stones' early records. Vocally, Keith Relf wasn't in the same league as Jagger--his voice was more of a Pretty Things/ Downliners Sect rasp--but for the kind of music they were playing, it only added to the effect.

If rhythm guitar did indeed play the central role we have ascribed to it in pre-1965 English rock, then on that score alone the Yardbirds may have been in contention with the Kinks for the most representative rave-up group of that era. And taking into account their imaginative yet single-minded dedication to their sound, the Yardbirds may well emerge the victors. For they were, above all, a guitar band. The lineup was bass, drums and two guitars, with Relf playing a bit of harmonica. No Nicky Hopkins sessions for them. And with Clapton in the group, it was like having two rhythm guitars plus lead. Nobody else except Jimmy Page understood the dynamics of power rhythm chording like Clapton, and Page at that time wasn't a regular member of any group. He also wasn't, in those days, as accomplished a guitarist as Clapton. He could match him in power, but Clapton had a subtlety, a way of inventing riffs off the top of his head to fill each little nook and cranny of a song with deft precision. His records with the Yardbirds are showpieces of English R&B guitar technique.

Although their early repertoire included many blues and R&B classics, there was never any pretense of trying to "popularize the blues" or any of that foolishness that even the Stones were prone to.

Whether they realized it or not, the Yardbirds were doing something far more important in searching for the new energy levels that could be reached by adapting blues material to the English R&B form.

Their first American album, *For Your Love*, is the best example of this. Songs like "*I Wish You Would,*" "*I'm Not Talking,*" "*Good Morning Little Schoolgirl,*" "*A Certain Girl*" and "*My Girl Sloopy*" were stripped of whatever bluesy, relaxed humor they had in the original versions, and streamlined into powerhouse, mind-destruction assaults that have lost none of their power after eight years. Perhaps my favorite Yardbirds song is a Relf original that sounds like an adapted R&B number but isn't--"*I Ain't Done Wrong.*" The dynamics in this song are just incredible; listening to it never fails to be a sense-numbing, spine-tingling experience. It was Eric Clapton's amazing speed and rhythmic sense that made the early Yardbirds as great as they were.

Clapton, though, had no idea how important what he was doing was. He was feeling the itch to go off and copy Freddy King records, and when the rest of the group wanted to become more pop-oriented, he walked out. Perhaps in spite, there is no mention of him on any American Yardbirds album (except the re-issues). Jeff Beck is given all the credit on the first album, where he only played on a few of the less interesting songs like "*My Girl Sloopy.*" It's easy to tell who is who, because in contrast to Clapton, Beck had a very fluid lead style and no feeling for rhythm dynamics at all.

On the second American album, *Rave Up*, Clapton appears throughout side two (taken from the English live album), and if Beck is indeed responsible for the guitar work on side one (there is still some conjecture) then he did a fine job of imitating Clapton's style on "*You're a Better Man Than I,*" "*Heart Full of Soul*" and "*The Train Kept A-Rollin'.*" On close inspection, though, the depth and fullness are noticeably lacking. The Yardbirds remained a great R&B-based pop group for another couple of years, but who knows, if Eric Clapton had stayed on, what wonders might have resulted? At the very least, the entire course of heavy metal music would have been changed, and Mike Saunders might have been a happier man today.

---Greg Shaw

like the Sweet in 1973, the arrival of Underground Rock in 1967 relegated pop to a ghetto of non-respect from which it is only just now emerging.

SHEL TALMY and POP ART ROCK

THE PARAMOUNTS:

The Paramounts represented a very similar case, although with them the point is even better taken since they were active so much earlier. Their second record came out in early '64, following a poor version of "Poison Ivy," a double oldie of "Little Bitty Pretty One" and "A Certain Girl." "Pretty One" is a great upbeat adaptation, while the other deck is a pretty straight copy of Aaron Neville's original. The Paramounts' virtues were evident from the start: powerful keyboard and vocals, fine drumming, and a real sense of group cohesion. The roots of Procol Harum can clearly be heard in these early recordings, especially on the Brooker-Trower originals like "It Won't Be Long." Along with "Poison Ivy," the Paramounts recorded some rather odd songs in their two year reign, including P.F.Sloan's "Lolipop Train" (as "You Never Had It So Good") and, for their only U.S. release, a song called "The Girls With Black Boots." Their records today are highly sought-after because of the fact that they became Procol Harum, but they are quite worth getting for their musical value alone.

GARY FARR & THE T-BONES:

No, they didn't record "No Matter What Shape." I remembered the T-Bones for years after they appeared on Shindig's "Richmond Jazz Festival" special, and have since acquired a tape which proves that their one number was one of the hardest rockers of that show. However, of the three records they made in 1965-66, I've heard one ("Give All She's Got") and it's pretty lame.

The group included Keith Emerson and Lee Jackson. Gary's father was world-famed boxer Tommy Farr and his brother was Ricky Farr, the Isle of Wight festival promoter. They were managed by Giorgio Gomelski, owner of the Crawdaddy Club. In late '65 they broke apart, with the T-Bones backing P.P.Arnold awhile, and Farr pursuing a solo career that took him from Columbia to Dandelion to Marmalade back to CBS. He had a solo LP in '71, but never a real hit.

While the singles are pretty scarce, the T-Bones can also be heard on Vol. 8 of Gomelski's "Rock Generation" import series.

---Greg Shaw

THE MODS

When the London R&B scene diverged into blues purism on the one hand and rock & roll stardom on the other, the city was left with a fantastic, swinging club scene that was far from ended, and a vast number of groups who had been influenced by the excitement of the R&B groups but a generation removed from their roots. They were not staunch blues fans for the most part, but rather part of 1965's blossoming Mod scene and its more pop-oriented contemporary trends, and they were interested more in the superficial glamor and excitement attached to being in a band than in popularizing Muddy Waters.

Influenced heavily by the Liverpool sound, the Mod groups and especially the post-Mod pop groups of 1966 were the last vestige of the Merseybeat revolution. While groups of this type have never left the scene, as witness groups

"Pop Art Rock" was a phrase I always liked. It seemed to capture the spirit of the post-R&B London scene in '65 and early '66, or at least the way I think of the scene as having been. The phrase seems to have been popularized by Pete Townshend, who in early interviews spoke often of his recent days at art school and his fascination with Gustav Metzger, an artist of the auto-destructive school. The press took it up and used it to describe the music of the Who and any other group that shared certain qualities with them. It was often used derisively, as if the writers considered the idiom limited and rather uninteresting.

This was to be expected, since most of the pop writers then were carryovers from the British pop scene of the '50's. As noted in WPTB #8, British rock in the '50s was recorded, engineered and often played by session men in their 30s and 40s. Consequently the records were very clean sounding, almost sterile, lacking in real teenage depth and gut energy. So naturally critics with this as a standard looked down on "pop art rock," which they took to be anything loud, with distortion, feedback, or lyrics that commented on youth culture (even obliquely, as with Daltry's pill induced stuttering in "My Generation").

It was, for awhile, a real genre--just as real as the short-lived Mod culture of which it was an outgrowth.* The first Mod group was the Who, but they were soon joined by a host of imitators. Because it was a limited idiom, limited by the lifestyle of its audience, and because the Who had caught that style so well in their music, the other groups were content to shamelessly lift riffs and themes from Who songs to form the basis of their own material. And yet, much of it was excellent.

If you can get over the self-consciousness of it all, there is some fascinating social commentary in songs like "March of the Mods" and "Return of the Mods" by the Executives, or "I'm Rowed Out" "The Immediate Pleasure" and "My Degeneration" by the Eyes, the last a Who-parody. "Look At These Faces," said their first EP, "faces" being the Mod term for personages. There they stood, wearing striped shirts which featured a big eye in the center with a picture of the respective Face inside it. Great! Another outstanding pop-art record is "Smashed! Blocked!," produced for John's Children by the ubiquitous Simon Napier-Bell, an amazing pre-psychedelic representation of the pill-blocked Mod mind.

* For a good in-depth discussion of the Mod phenomenon, see Gary Herman's book *The Who*.

But for my money, the best pop art group of them all, next to the Who and the Small Faces, was the Creation. The Creation included Kenny Pickett, Eddie Phillips, Jack Jones, and ex-Birds Ron Wood and Kim Gardner. They had Townshend's sound down so well that the opening of "*Biff Bang Pow*" is virtually indistinguishable from that of "*My Generation*," but they weren't just copyists. Every one of their sides that I've heard has been able to stand on its own—good hook, throbbing beat, beautifully poised dynamic tension, and always interesting experimental guitar sounds. They were the first, for instance, to use a violin-bow on a guitar, an effect that didn't go unnoticed by Jimmy Page.

Their songs themselves were also pop art on another level, one never reached by the Who. The Creation wrote songs *about* the Mod culture symbols, which may've been an easy copout in 1965 but from our distant remove their songs are priceless. "*Painter Man*" concerns the travails of a frustrated, mildly talented art school student who desperately wishes to be *happening*. "*Can I Join Your Band*" might almost be a sequel, "*Biff Bang Pow*" takes off on the Batman craze, and "*Nightmares*" and "*The Girls Are Naked*" also make statements about current events. Many of the Creation's other records were in the same mold, and equally good. Perhaps one reason they were able to achieve the Who's visceral impact where others failed was the fact that they were produced by Shel Talmy.

Of all the English rock & roll producers, I think Talmy was the best. He was not a slick producer like George Martin; he understood the need for sloppiness and a rough edge, and knew how to translate those qualities into excitement on record. Compare Joe Meek, whose records also sounded rough but only impress one as being poorly recorded. Miki Dallon, who produced good records in this period by the Sorrows and the Boys Blue as well as himself, came close to the sound, but lacked the immediacy of Talmy's records. Larry Page's groups such as the Clique and later the Troggs, had the same rawness, but in his hands always come out sounding too controlled, too deliberate. Good, but like bubblegum music, in a different way. I can't take Mickie Most seriously, and no other English producer was even in the running.

Shel Talmy's history is not very well known. He grew up in Los Angeles, and went to England in 1963 with a letter of introduction from Nik Venet stating that he had produced all manner of records, including the Beach Boys. Of course he hadn't, but he did have some engineering experience, so after he talked his way into a position at Decca he knew what to do. His first big assignment was the Bachelors, who started out as a country group but grew, with Talmy, into one of England's top pop groups. Talmy had a name then, and groups like the Kinks and the Who came to him when they needed a producer. The sound he achieved with them, with its deftly modulated frenzy, was the best thing happening next to the Beatles and the Stones, and arguably equal.

Most of the big producers in those days became almost popstars in their own right, and sought to capitalize on the fact. Meek, George Martin, Oldham, Page, Mike Leander and others named orchestras after themselves and released instrumental versions of their groups' hits. Larry Page started his own label Page One in '66, following the lead of two other producers who had opened record companies in '65—Andrew Oldham and Shel Talmy.

Oldham's Immediate Records was a big success, Page One fairly successful, but for some reason Shel Talmy's Planet Records went nowhere, despite constant hyping in the gossip and review columns of all the pop weeklies. I haven't heard all his releases—only those that were issued in the U.S., actually—but the ones I have heard were in the same sort of consciously pop-art style as the Creation, who were also on Planet and gave the label its largest hit.

Both "*Painter Man*" and "*Making Time*" by the Creation made the charts, as did "*It's Not True*," a rather lame version of the Who song by the Untamed. The Creation records came toward the end of the label's run, and it may have been the success of "*Making Time*" that prompted Talmy to seek U.S. distribution. He signed an agreement with Jay-Gee, who at that time were distributing a plethora of minor labels. Not too surprisingly, none of the records went anywhere. But then, even the Who had a rough time hitting the American charts before 1967.

Of his first 15 records, why Talmy chose to issue only "*It's Not True*" and John Lee's Groundhogs in the States I can't imagine. The National Pinion Pole did pretty well in England. And what about the Orlons' first British recording? Probably the fact that Planet was failing by the time U.S. distribution got underway had something to do with it. While a brilliant producer, Talmy was new to the business end, and ran into problems with distribution as well as those arising from the fact that he was signing far too many acts.

At any rate, Planet folded in early '67 and Talmy continued to produce the Creation on Polydor. For some reason they were very popular in Germany and had one or two albums issued there and nowhere else, plus singles. For the last five years Talmy has been out of the production spotlight, (except for Pentagle, a far cry from earlier efforts) meanwhile keeping busy with films and book publishing. He has returned recently with an album by Seanor & Koss (of Savage

Grace) on Warner Bros. and String Driven Thing on Charisma. Shel Talmy may still be around, but although he talks of getting the Creation back together for Pickett and Phillips, anyway), I'm sure he'd be the first to agree that pop-art rock was irretrievably tied to the era of British pop that died in 1967 with the advent of psychedelia. *Sic transit gloria.*

---Greg Shaw

PLANET DISCOGRAPHY

England
101 DAVE HELLING--Christine/Bells
102 TONY LORD--World's Champion/It Makes Me Sad
103 THE UNTAMED--It's Not True/Gimme Gimme Some Shade
104 JOHN LEE'S GROUNDHOGS--I'll Never Fall In Love Again/Over You Baby
105 THE TREKKAS--Please Go/I Put A Spell On You
106 DANI SHERIDAN--Guess I'm Dumb/Songs Of Love
107 STEVIE HOLLY--Strange World/Little Man
108 THE TRIBE--The Gamma Goochie/I'm Leaving
109 LEAGUE OF GENTLEMEN--How Can You Tell/How Do They Know
110 PERPETUAL LANGLEY--We Wanna Stay Home/So Sad
111 NATIONAL PINION POLE--Make Your Mark Little Man/I Was The One You Came In With

112 EUGENE FERRIS--There Was A Smile In Your Eyes/Soft Moonlight
113 LINDSAY MUIR'S UNTAMED--Daddy Long Legs/Trust Yourself A Little Bit
114 JOHN LEE HOOKER--Mai Lee/Don't Be Messing With My Bread
115 PERPETUAL LANGLEY--Surrender/Two By Two
116 CREATION--Making Time/Try And Stop Me
117 ORLONS--Spinnin' Top/Anyone Who Had A Heart
118 THE THOUGHTS--All Night Stand/Memory Of Your Love
119 CREATION--Painter Man/Biff Bang Pow
120 A WILD UNCERTAINTY--Man With Money/Broken Truth
121 GNOMES OF ZURICH--Please Mr. Sun/I'm Coming Down With The Blues
122 THE CORDUROYS--Tick Tock/Too Much Of A Woman

U.S.
104 JOHN LEE'S GROUNDHOGS--I'll Never Fall In Love Again/Over You Baby
116 CREATION--Making Time/Try And Stop Me
117 UNTAMED--It's Not True/Gimme Gimme Some Shade
118 THOUGHTS--All Night Stand/Memory Of Your Love
119 CREATION--Painter Man/Biff Bang Pow
120 A WILD UNCERTAINTY--Man With Money/Broken Truth

SORROWS, DON FARDON & MIKI DALLON

"Miki Dallon is the logical successor to Elvis"
-Steve Sholes

One of the most remarkable sounds of 1965 was a record called "*Take A Heart*" by the Sorrows. Dominated by a loud, rough bass pulse, it featured a melody that sounded like a guitar solo and a savage guitar part right out of the early Yardbirds. A sensational record, and it was followed by the equally sensational "*Let The Live Live*" and "*You Got What I Want*," which sounded like a supersession between the Yardbirds, Small Faces and Standells. There were a bunch of other singles, none in the same class, and an album, before the lead singer broke away to begin a solo career.

The Sorrows were Pip Whitcher (lead guitar), Philip Packham (bass), Bruce Finley (drums), Wez Price (rhythm) and Don Maughn (vocals). All their good songs, including another called "*She's Got The Action*," were written by a young man named Miki Dallon, soon to become one of England's best producers. On their album, the Sorrows also recorded the Strangeloves' "*Cara-Lin*" and an odd put-down of the Dylan/Donovan folkies titled "*Don't Sing No Sad Songs For Me*." Of all their output, only the "*Take A Heart*" single was released in the States.

In 1967 Maughn left the Sorrows, calling himself Don Fardon and recording under Dallon. He eventually became the first artist on Dallon's record label, Young Blood, formed in 1969. Fardon scored an immediate hit on the Continent with a cover of the Box Tops' "*The Letter*," and even dented the American charts with a remake of "*Take a Heart*." Then, of course, there was his international hit "*Indian Reservation*." It was Dallon who had the idea of applying a hard beat to this John D. Laudermilk song, and the sound was strangely reminiscent of the throbbing "*Take A Heart*" beat. Fardon had an album here on GNP Crescendo with "*Indian Reservation*" and various Dallon songs and cover versions of hits.

This was followed by an album on Decca with a few cover bubblegum songs and a remake of "*Let The Live Live*." They can't seem to keep away from those early Sorrows hits, although the originals can't be touched. Dallon himself cut "*Take A Heart*" backed with "*You Got What I Want*" with a group called the Boys Blue (released here on ABC) and even had a brief recording career himself, producing at least two singles, one a great raver titled "*I'll Give You Love*" (issued here on RCA). Fardon and Dallon are still together, and Young Blood Records a thriving concern, although it's been some time since Fardon's last hit. How about a remake of "*You Got What I Want*"?

--Greg Shaw

SMALL FACES

"How did the Small Faces get their name?" queried publicist Tony Brainsby on the back of the group's first album. He proceeded to answer his own question with consumate inanity: "Just one look at them is sufficient to see that they do indeed have small faces." Nice try, Tony, but--the "Small" portion does derive from the group's stature (no one over 5'4), while "Face" was a Mod term denoting a personage of importance (viz. the High Numbers' "I'm The Face"). The Small Faces inherited much of the fanatic Mod adulation enjoyed by the High Numbers, representing as they did in appearance and spirit the quintessential Mod band; and they scored a smash hit a scant few months after their formation in London, around mid-65. The group originally comprised drummer Kenny Jones, Ronnie "Plonk" Lane on bass, organist Jimmy Winston, and on vocals and guitar, Stevie Marriott, a former teenage actor who had also previously recorded with a group called the Frantics.

The Small Faces' first single, "What'Cha Gonna Do About It" (written and produced by ex-Shadow Ian Samwell), broke into the top 20 in the fall of '65. It was an exciting if derivative record, incorporating barely-controlled Who-like feedback leads over a chord structure lifted from the Stones' version of "Everybody Needs Somebody To Love" (a riff later utilized by such ravers as the Pretty Things' "Come See Me" and the Montanas' "That's When Happiness Began"). The flip was a passionate rendition of Timi Yuro's "What's A Matter Baby" which provided a showcase for Marriott's leather-lunged, soul-styled vocals, one of the group's major strengths.

The follow-up single, a moody, powerful tune called "I've Got Mine," was a relative stiff, but the third record, "Sha La La La Lee," was the group's real breakthrough. An irresistibly bouncy ditty, it hit the top 5 and paved the way for their first album, entitled simply Small Faces. Just before the LP's release, Jimmy Winston had been replaced by Ian MacLagan, although Winston did play on the album (he subsequently cut a version of "Sorry She's Mine," a track from the LP.) The album itself is a wild, raw assemblage of Anglicised R&B--the Small Faces incorporated their strong R&B influences more prominently than most of their contemporaries, as evidenced chiefly by

Marriott's soul-belting style and gospel-derived vocal interjections. "Whatcha Gonna Do About It" and "Sha La La La Lee" highlight the set, along with several energetic originals and a couple songs written by Kenny Lynch (co-writer of "Sha La La La Lee" and a former (63-4)solo star in his own right. Included among the originals was a number called "You Need Loving" which, as is well known, was nicked by Led Zeppelin in near-entirety for their "Whole Lotta Love," down to the very vocal intonations.

Once established, the Small Faces continued to churn out hits -- the infectious "Hey Girl," "All Or Nothing," and "My Mind's Eye," (a more muted, experimental effort) all scaled chart heights. "All Or Nothing," an explosive number, was perhaps the best of the three (with a hypnotic flip called "Understanding" to boot), although "My Mind's Eye" choral innovations were quite intriguing, especially on the more polished LP version (its flip, "I Can't Dance With You," is one of the group's most obscure tracks but unfortunately also one of their least distinguished). The group's first recording of 1967, however, a tune called "I Can't Make It," was a failure, missing the top 20; and understandably so, as it was a rather featureless if pleasantly rousing rocker, much inferior to their previous six singles. The B-side, "Just Passing," was an amusing Lane-sung sound effect novelty lasting all of 66 seconds, very quirky indeed (and co-written by someone named O'Sullivan--but it couldn't be....).

In mid-'67 the group switched labels from Decca to Immediate. Decca retaliated by dredging up a track called "Patterns," a substandard though enjoyable "Gloria"-variation, for an unsuccessful single; and by releasing another album, From The Beginning. This LP is a combination of five singles (up to "My Mind's Eye" but omitting I've Got Mine), two tracks which later appeared on the group's first Immediate LP ("Tell Me Have You Ever Seen Me") and the powerful "My Way Of Giving," later a hit for Chris Farlowes and re-recorded by Rod Stewart); and seven other cuts, consisting of two enthralling originals ("That Man" and "Yesterday Today And Tomorrow"), one feedbacked instrumental, and four covers of American material.

These last are perhaps the most interesting, including as they do the best ever rock 'n' roll rendition of Marvin Gaye's "Baby Don't Do It" (eclipsing the Who's and the Band's versions, and even the Wailers'), a lurching performance of Del Shannon's "Runaway" with a strange neo-operatic prelude, and churning versions of the Miracles' "You Really Got A Hold On Me" and Don Covay's "Come Back and Take This Hurt Off Me." All in all, the album stands as one of the premier British rock R&B classics of the era.

It was followed in short order by the first Immediate releases, "Here Come The Nice," a paean to the joys of speed and a smash hit; and "Itchycoo Park," a quaintly-titled flower-era ditty which was also hugely enjoyable, re-introduced the phasing effect first heard on Toni Fisher's "The Big Hurt," and was even bigger than "Nice".

An album followed

An album followed shortly, called Small Faces (again), with the two fine tracks from From The Beginning and an inconsistent group of new originals, ranging from dire cute stuff ("Happy Boys Happy," "Eddie's Dreaming") to piquantly attractive material "Feeling Lonely," and the wistful "Show Me The Way"). As a whole, the album suffered from a dearth of the raw rocking spirit which infused their first two LP's, although the new polished sound was enjoyable in its way.

Meanwhile, something entirely unexpected had transpired--"Itchycoo Park" had become a hit in the

United States. None of the group's previous British chartbusters (released variously on Press, RCA, and Immediate/UA, if at all) had made the least impact on the American record-buyer, but "Itchycoo" had caught on among the secondary radio markets and slowly built to a sizable (#16) hit. An American album was thus called for, and Immediate (now affiliated with CBS) proceeded to take "Here Comes The Nice," "Itchycoo Park," and the new British single, "Tin Soldier," along with their flip sides, plus six tracks from the English album; and whether from blind luck or design, compiled a package which holds up better than its British counterpart. This surprising circumstance is partly owing to the strength of the single sides, of course, particularly "Tin Soldier," which is perhaps the group's premier rave-up rocker (its flip side, "I Feel Much Better," is another attractive rock tune which also features a children's chorus à la Keith West's "Excerpt From A Teenage Opera" and Traffic's "Hole In My Shoe"-- the Small Faces were right on top of every trend, as soon as it surfaced). But also the tracks selected from the British LP were among the strongest ("Show Me The Way," "My Way Of Giving"), with none of that album's annoying piffle.

"Tin Soldier," despite (or because of) its brilliance, was a meagre hit in both Britian and the U.S. The next single, "Lazy Sunday," was entirely different stylistically, a happy-go-lucky rollicking tune complete with exaggerated accents and an overall vaudevillainous spirits. A large-sized hit in England, it went nowhere in the U.S. Meanwhile, the group was readying their next album, which when it appeared boggled observers everywhere. The package was circular

in shape, with a tobacco-tin cover (entitled Ogden's Nut Gone Flake), with a vast array of colorful pictures inside the complicated folds of the jacket, and a rather unusual group of songs as well. Side one was a relatively straight set of six songs, including "Lazy Sunday," and chiefly notable for a pair of power-packed rockers, "Song Of A Baker" and "Afterglow" the latter featuring a decent Dean Martin imitation at the beginning). The other side, however, was a conceptually-linked six-pack tied together by a dialectically incomprehensible narration by British comedian Stanley Unwin, all purporting to tell the tale of a fellow named "Happiness Stan," of his travels and travails in search of the missing half of the moon, in the company of a voluble super-fly and an old hermit. The whole assemblage is enchanting, and the music itself is fine as well, especially "Mad John" (later an obscure American single).

After Ogden's (a #1 album in England and an American chart-maker as well, even without a hit single), the group became frustrated. Tired of slogging around Britan eternally, even with their newly-added traveling-horn section, and seemingly unable to make an American trip, the Small Faces finally packed it in around the latter part of 1968. They had released one more single that summer, a bizarre good-time number called "The Universal" (with an equally bizarre flip, "Donkey Rides A Penny A Glass"), a middling British hit and American failure; and Immediate posthumously released a single of "Afterglow" and "Wham Bam Thank You Mam'" a heavy rocker more in the style of Humble Pie, the group formed by Marriott and ex-Herd idol Peter Frampton upon upon the Small Faces' dissolution. And that was almost all for the Small Faces, until their early 1970 resurrection with Rod Stewart and Ron Wood and subsequent smashing success, all of which is well-known.

Immediate released a double LP memorial called The Autumn Stone, a tremendous record including most all their singles (with the exception of "I've Got Mine" and "Patterns"), semi-obscure flip sides ("Just Passing" and "Wham Bam"), three live tracks ("Rollin' Over" from Ogden's, a ponderous but powerful version of "If I Were A Carpenter," and a slightly overblown soul extravaganza with Brenda Holloway's "Every Little Bit Hurts", on which, along with "Rollin' Over," the listener is finally able to hear the group's vaunted traveling horn section), and five hitherto-unreleased studio tracks. Two of these, "Collibosher" and "Wide Eyed Girl On The Wall," are sketchy instrumentals possibly intended for later vocal tracking, but the other three are excellent--"Red Balloon" is another rocked-up Tim Hardin tune, "Call It Something Nice" is a pretty harpsichord-styled number (although incorporating certain "Mad John" riffs in toto), and "The Autumn Stone," with its brooding flute accompaniment, shows off a different, and impressive, side of the group. The album plays brilliantly, and hopefully much of the material from it might be released someday here (as Ogden's has been by Abkco, who own the Immediate material). Meanwhile, MGM here somehow managed to acquire the Small Faces' Decca output, and have released two LP's (Early Faces in mid-'72 and History of Small Faces in February '73) in embarrassing

SMALL FACES, contd.

ly haphazard and shoddy fashion (History repeats five out of a meager ten cuts from Early Faces, with so much more languishing in the vaults). Still these LP's mark the first American appearances of such songs as "Runaway," "Shake," and "Sorry She's Mine," as well as the first LP appearances of "I've Got Mine" and "Understanding." There's also a song on Early Faces labelled as "What's A Matter Baby" which is nothing of the sort, instead being a song presumably titled "Little Pictures" which might be the Small Faces (although it never appeared anywhere else before), or might even be a September '65 vintage tune by that title done by Adam, Mike &Tim, or might be something else entirely (any aid in clearing up this mystery would be appreciated). It is nice to have "Sha La La La Lee", "What'cha Gonna Do About It," "Hey Girl," and "My Mind's Eye" back in American circulation (although "All Or Nothing" is inexplicably absent), along with the aforementioned tracks, but it's still advisable to skip the MGM packages and their reprocessed stereo and seek out the original British Decca albums.

---Ken Barnes

THE WHO

Above, the Who in London, 1965. Note their fashion-conscious attire. At right, trade ad for their second single as it appeared in Billboard.

MEMORIES OF MY YOUTH
By Mike Saunders

I was born on May 1, 1952. Very little of importance happened during the first twelve years, but after that events really began to pile up. One was the first record I ever bought: "Heart Of Stone" by the Rolling Stones. The first album I ever bought, The Rolling Stones, Now!---buying an album was quite a special occasion on an allowance of $1.50 a week. Most of all, I remember The Who. They made the biggest impression of anyone on me; more than any other group, they focused the whole incredible excitement of discovering something as thrilling as English Invasion rock, fantastically exciting music played by nifty looking rock stars. So while I had missed the Beatles' invasion by a sheer age factor, I was lucky enough to catch the whole feeling the second time around with the Who - when you played "I Can't Explain," it was like whop, bam, boom! "The first Pop Art record," Pete Townshend called it. One can hardly disagree.

I had rather schizophrenic taste in those days-- not bad, just irrational. While on one hand I instinctively loved tons of great rock records, I also would refuse to listen to anything that had horns in it. When you're a kid, you're influenced a lot by superficials and pure style, you know; I disliked the Beatles because I thought they were a bopper group. The Stones were the ones I identified with, scruffy and rebellious. But after the Stones cut "As Tears Go By," I denounced them as well. Good god, strings and horns and crap! They were betraying rock and roll, obviously, to my eyes---so from then on the Who, as well as remaining my heroes, commanded all of my devotion.

Part of the early Who legend includes their three 1965 appearances on Shindig. On the first one (in March, I think) they played their debut single, "I Can't Explain," which was merely enough to shock you into the next room from sheer excitement. It sounded a bit less revelatory on my record player in the safety of my room, but nonetheless pretty heady stuff for my 12-year old ears. I can't even explain what rock seemed like to me at my age and situation, as I had been exposed to absolutely nothing resembling youth or peer-culture in my whole life---when I bought my first rock and roll records, I hid them from my parents & took them downstairs and played them loud when no one was home. I was naive and innocent, I guess, perfect fodder for the addictive mania of rock&roll.

The Who's second Shindig appearance consisted of playing "Daddy Rolling Stone," a wild James Brown number on the English B-side of "Anyway Anyhow Anywhere." Then was the crusher, their third and final appearance: It consisted of the Who live, at a fete called something like "The Richmond Jazz Festival"---great balls of fire! Jesus! Appearing alongside the Animals, the Yardbirds, and Manfred Mann, the Who made the former three all seem positively limp (what with the Animals routinely running through "We Gotta Get Out Of This Place," Manfred Mann being censored but all through their "If You Gotta Go, Go Now," bleebs and pops gurgling all over the place, and the Yardbirds doing an absolutely horrendous long version of "My Girl Sloopy"). First the Who gave a live rendition of "Shout," and then they literally smashed their way through "Anyway Anyhow Anywhere." Toward the end, and it was quite long, Townshend took off his Rickenbacker, took a few swings at his amp, and then heaved his guitar over the equipment in the first act of rock auto-destruction ever to appear on TV---I swear my eyes were bulging-- immediately followed by nothing less than a manic Keith Moon drum solo, in an age when most rock drummers were limited to simple fills and Ringo-ish thunk-a-thud- thud paradoodles, or whatever you call 'em. He knocked his drums over too, in case you're wondering. You can bet your surfboards it was an eventful day for me when my order for "Anyway Anyhow Anywhere" came in at the record store.

I still remember hearing "My Generation" for the first time. It was in December 1965, and I was at my grandmother's house for the evening, whiling away the time listening to the radio. Then all of a sudden this incredible noise came blasting out over the radio. Great God, was this the Apocalypse? A new record--by my heroes, the Who!--and it was also stone great. Though it only rose to #74 nationally, "My Generation" hit the Top 10 in Little Rock, an event that was enough to send me into incessant raving to friends and standers-by about my idols. I'd grab a KAAY Top-40 survey, point to the #10 slot and shriek deliriously, "LOOK, LOOK, IT'S RIGHT THERE!! IN THE TOP TEN!!!" When The Who Sings My Generation was released in early 1966, I spent the whole next year trying to emulate Keith Moon's drumming on my $180 Japanese drumset, never did, you understand, but it was fun; though I might not have been able to reproduce them, I'm sure I had Mr. Moon's every lick and inflection memorized into my mind a thousand times. The album itself was inspirational--actually it was like one big single. Play one side, flip it over, and so on into the night.

I also remember our 12 year-old neighbor and I riding up to the shopping center on our bikes, proudly wearing our hand-drawn Keith Moon bullseye T-shirts. Our junior high classmates thought we were out of our skulls. But, all the same, I even made myself one with a blue circle and two red arrows, just like I had seen Roger Daltry wearing in a picture of the Who in Flip Magazine.

True to form, the Who's followup to "My Generation" didn't come out for months and months: "Substitute." That was during late spring, so I spent whole evenings calling up KALO and requesting it during their new releases show. Eventually it got onto the show's top five for the week, and hence, onto the playlist, and hence, stocked in a couple of the local record stores, all apparently due to my unflagging fanaticism. Even if it never made the charts and nobody bought it! There never was a followup to "Substitute," as Decca released various My Generation tracks here and in England; not until "I'm A Boy" did the Who come out with a new single. Inbetween, I played The Who Sings My Generation eternally and wondered what was coming off.

A common belief is that the Who's failure to crack America in 1965 and 1966 was the fault of lack of publicity by uncaring record companies. Mmm, it's hard to say. But anyway, here's something that ought to be of interest: there're full-page ads in Billboard for the Who's first four singles! Look them up at the library sometime, if they happen to keep a Billboard file (which sadly, is rare); the "Anyway Anyhow Anywhere" ad is especially fascinating, because the Who looks definitely short-haired and scruffy Sheperds' Bushmodish, which is to say, dated by 1973 standards. Do looks make the band? Obviously, no.

* "I Can't Explain" ad, 2/13/65, p.11; (4/3/65)#93
"Anyway Anyhow Anywhere" ad, 6/5/65, p.7; -
"My Generation" ad, 11/20/65; p.18;(2/12/66)#74
"Substitute" ad, 4/2/66,p.19;--

TROGGS

It may seem redundant to speak of the Troggs, when two issues back Lester Bangs spewed forth a good 25,000 words on the subject. However...as great an article as it was, it didn't begin to cover the Troggs' music or their place in a purely English context. We can't do that completely here, but there are a few things worth mentioning.

They came late in the English Invasion--1966, the transitional year. The Underground was beginning to stir, Cream was already together, Hendrix was around, but English pop was dominated by groups who had evolved directly out of Merseybeat and owed much of their sound to it. Groups like Dave Dee, the Small Faces, the Move, the Who, Jonathan King's various productions, and the Troggs (not counting, of course, the Beatles, Stones, Kinks, etc. who were still around, but were evolving by then in their own directions, no longer part of any particular local style or scene).

The groups of this period had, in general, a less spontaneous sound than their predecessors--in many cases it was a calculatedly manufactured style, the roots of what pop was to become after its impending schism with the Underground faction, and what it remains today despite the recent reunion. In discussing this type of pop, whether it be the Partridge Family or the Electric Light Orchestra, the criteria are different from what's usually applied to rock. The mere fact that a record is *manufactured* should not be held against it--we should only consider how *well* constructed it is, for that's where its virtues are to be found.

The Troggs were in at the ground floor of bubble-rock, and like their early American counterparts such as the Ohio Express, they had strong roots in punk-rock which gave their music a vitality later bubblepop groups couldn't match. They were managed and manipulated by Larry Page, who had been around awhile producing various R&B and pop groups, and it was the early success of the Troggs that enabled Page to start his own label, Page One, later one of England's most prolific singles labels.

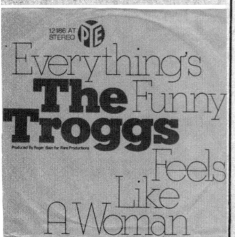

The Troggs built their sound on heavy beat, loud bass, constant fuzztone, raunchy vocals, and suggestive lyrics. They never lost this orientation (their 1972 release, "*Feels Like a Woman*" is, if anything, their most punkish yet), and while they could sound like the Archies, they were just as likely to sound like the Standells on the next cut. Their early recordings included Chuck Berry songs like "*Jaguar and the Thunderbird*" and "*Little Queenie*," Bo Diddley's "*Mona*" and, to prove they knew what they were about, "*Louie Louie*." They did the original versions of "*Anyway That You Want Me*" (a hit for Evie Sands) and "*Evil Woman*" (Spooky Tooth). They had some bombs, yes, but on the whole the Troggs were far better and more creative than they are generally given credit for, even by the "punk-rock" brigade.

They also had an inordinate amount of material that never came out in the U.S. An entire album's worth of softer songs, *Cellophane*, remains unissued except for one song, "*Love is All Around*." It includes two classics, "*All of the Time*" and a standout rocker called "*Seventeeen*." Most of the songs on *Trogglodynamite* are similarly foreign to American ears. Then, besides two volumes of greatest hits, there was another English album which collected most of the late singles that, while they did come out in America, are and were almost impossible to find. Great ballads like "*You Can Cry if You Want To*," the maniacal "*The Raver*," the insistent "*Lover*," and, possibly their best, "*Surprise Surprise*," featuring a real Marquee-Club-like raveup at the end, with Nicky Hopkins on piano.

Of the singles that didn't come out here, "*Maybe the Madman*" from 1968 is the most sought-after. It captures a rare psychedelic moment for the Troggs, a real product of its times and yet a bit of a spoof as well, like Episode Six's "*Mr. Universe*." A weird record, too. Equally weird is a song that, as far as I know, is available only on a German album titled *Hip Hip Hooray*, which may be similar to the almost unknown British album *Mixed Bag*.

The song is "*Purple Shades*," and bizarre is the only word for it. It's their "*Lucy in the Sky With Diamonds*". The lyrics include lines like "*bamboo butterflies, twice their normal size, floating around in my mind.*" The musical backing is straight Troggs, unlike "*Maybe the Madman*"'s freakiness, but somehow that only adds to the weirdness.

This album also includes "*Marbles and Some Gum*," never out in the U.S., and one other mystifying cut. It's called "*Off the Record*," and like the Beach Boys' "*Our Favorite Recording Sessions*" it's an in-studio talk, joke and insult session. I don't know where you can get this album, so eat your hearts out Troggs fans.

Even that isn't the end of Troggs ephemera. I have listings for an album called *Mixed Bag*, a solo album by Chris Britton, and solo singles by Ronnie Bond and Reg Presley--none of which anybody seems to have seen. This is the kind of group collectors love, but the Troggs are also a group every rock fan should be supporting. They're still around, had a hit last year in South Africa with "*Everything's Funny*"(the ballad their record company insisted on pushing as the A-side of "*Feels Like a Woman*") and according to interviews, they're determined that their fuzztone raunch style will live again. Personally, I think their time will come very soon. They were just six years ahead of it, that's all. As the liner notes of *Cellophane* pointed out, in 1967:

"*The Troggs are really pop in perspective. There have been too many cynics who have regarded them as a bit of a joke. Through the past few months of psychedelia and electrola they have been quietly providing uninhibited rock and roll with gentle ballads. No message--no instructions on how to live a happier, fuller life--just the simple suggestion that it might be a good idea to have fun, dance and enjoy yourselves. And that is why the Troggs, having Trogged--Troggle on!*"

I couldn't have put it better myself.

--Greg Shaw

NON-ENGLISH BEAT GROUPS

The beat sound was, of course, not confined to the British Isles. Some of the best records in the style (such as "She's the One" by the Chartbusters, "Roses Are Red" by the You Know Who Group, "It's Cold Outside" by the Choir, and hundreds more) were made by American groups. Those, however, will have to wait for future issues. But many other countries boasted English-inspired rock groups as well. Australia had a great many, although with the exception of one they were never heard of in our hemisphere. That exception, however, was one of the finest groups of its era: The Easybeats.

EASYBEATS

Although native Britons, the Easybeats were originally based in Australia, and by the end of 1965 were the reigning local group, provoking dramatic outbursts of "Easyfever" wherever they played. In early '66, the group ("Little Stevie" Wright, lead vocals; George Young, rhythm guitar--and brother of Grapefruit's George Alexander, though how there came to be two Georges in one family is still a mystery; Harry Vanda, lead guitar and songwriter, with George; Snowy Fleet, drums; and Dick Diamonde, bass) travelled to London, arranged a worldwide recording deal with United Artists, and hooked up with famed producer Shel Talmy.

In March '66 they had a massive Australian hit with a mildly funky, slightly Beatle-like original called "Make You Feel Alright (Women)"; it was released in the States with a delightful picture cover graphically illustrating the Easyfever phenomenon, and a flip, "In My Book," an affecting early '60s type ballad, which was never released on a subsequent album. It was not successful outside their home base, but another single, "Come and See Her," and an "Easyfever" EP stayed in the Australian top 10 for weeks on end.

Ultimately they were all eclipsed by the next single, "Friday On My Mind," which shortly thereafter took off in Britain as well, and finally became a large-sized American hit. With good reason, too--the song was completely irresistible, with a distinctive pulsing beat stemming from the unusual rhythm guitar, and infectious Morse code harmonies--and it was a classic teenage weekend song in the Eddie Cochran tradition, to boot.

An album followed in early '67, and it was a superb pop-rock showcase--the group seemed somewhat similar to the Who in vocal inflections, bass lines, and teenage lyrical themes, but the music was basically very distinctive, complex, intriguing material, with unexpected instrumental breaks, fine harmonies, and vast overall exuberance. Some of the best cuts were "Do You Have a Soul," with its dizzying changes, "Saturday Night," "You Me We Love" (potentially a great Reg Presley vehicle), the title cut (of course), and a version of "River Deep Mountain High" which suffered production-wise but was probably the best beat group rendition ever (vanquishing Deep Purple, the Animals, the Badd Boys, etc.). With only one poor track ("See Line Woman"), the LP was a triumph then and sounds perhaps even better today.

The Easybeats' next single, "Heaven and Hell," suffered from a tardy release date (August '67, some 9 months after "Friday" was first issued), a taboo-violating title, and possibly a touch of overcomplexity; but despite its widespread commercial failure, it was one of the finest singles of its time. Admirably produced by Glyn Johns, it featured electrifying guitar figures, great dynamics, and a stunning middle section with absolutely celestial harmonies. Their next single, "Falling Off the Edge of the World," was almost as good, an emotion-fraught massive production pop number about marital infidelity. In both its relative lack of rock & roll foundations and its more adult subject matter, the record marked a significant directional change away from teenage concerns; but the song itself was so well-executed that it ranks with the very best records the Easybeats made--it was another chart absentee, however.

"The Music Goes Round My Head," in early '68, was even less commercial and rock-oriented, an odd melodic structure featuring frequent and disconcerting clarinet fills--strangely compelling but hardly a galvanizing hit. Then their worst single to date, a melodramatic pop showstopper ballad called "Hello How Are You," became a surprise top 10 hit in Britain, and another album followed (released in the U.S. in late '68). The last three singles were included, plus nine other cuts of dramatically varying quality. Versions of "Can't Take My Eyes Off You" and "Hit the Road Jack" detracted considerably, but pleasant originals like "Land of Make Believe" and "Fancy Seeing You Here" compensated nicely.

And the LP opened in ferocious fashion with the group's next American single, "Gonna Have a Good Time," a British punk classic about a fabulous dance featuring everyone's favorite femmes fatale (sic), Bony Maronie, Long Tall Sally, and Short Fat Fanny. It would have been cheering to learn of their presence on the radio in early '69, but the single unfortunately failed to hit once again, and the Easybeats subsequently departed UA.

In November '69 they reappeared with a new vocalist, a chap known as Russell; a new label, Rare Earth; and a single called "St. Louis." An energetic straightforward rocker, it managed to crash the American charts (for the first time since "Friday"), but Rare Earth did not issue a follow-up album (although it was listed briefly in some catalogs). One did appear in England, called Friends, (on Polydor) and it was rather disappointing. The main problem was the lack of Vanda-Young songs (previously prolific, they were represented by only two of 11 songs). Russell contributed a couple of fairly catchy cuts, but more often was responsible for overblown pop drivel or mediocre funk numbers, also singing the former in one of those typically beefy Rare Earth-label /group voices. Periodic horn intrusions didn't help either, and the album remains deservedly obscure.

One more single from the LP was issued in the U.S. in June '70, an unimpressive track called "Who Are My Friends," but the Easybeats as such were through, and broke up shortly afterward. Vanda and Young, always the key members, did continue, however, surfacing on British Deram under the name Haffy's Whiskey Sour with a fine single, "Shot in the Head"/"Bye Bye Bluebird." The latter was an excellent rocker with a riff similar to "Natural Man" (see below), while "Shot" was a solid blues-rocker later covered by Savoy Brown (the Vanda-Young team was covered often--in '67 they penned Los Bravos' comeback hit "Bring a Little Lovin'", "Come In You'll Get Pneumonia" was covered by Gary Walker's group Rain, among others, and "Gonna Have a Good Time" was recorded many times--the Clinger Sisters, Jamie Lyons (of the Music Explosion), the British group Black Claw, to name but a few).

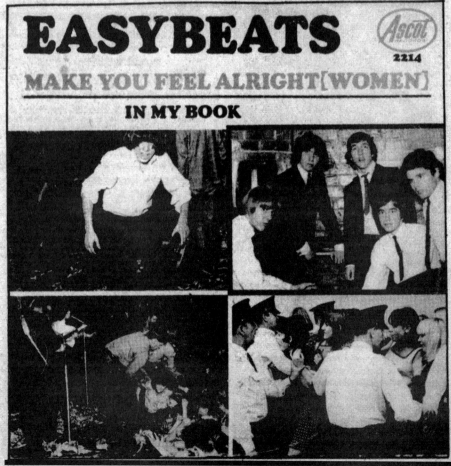

Finally in late '72, under the name Marcus Hook Roll Band, Vanda and Young unleashed a monumental blockbuster of a single called "Natural Man." Lyrically a fascinating socio-cultural survey of the early '70s from a confused teenage viewpoint, it was overflowing with terrific musical hooks and riffs, building to a tension-filled frenzied climax. The flip, an energetic dance number called "Boogalooing Is For Wooing," was excellent as well, and all in all the single easily ranked as one of the most criminally overlooked commercial failures of 1972, a year replete with such injustices. Another, inferior single ("Louisiana Lady") followed, and then a squib in Billboard reported that Vanda and Young were returning to Australia in a local production capacity. It was a depressing end to a seven-year hit-and-miss (chiefly the latter) affair with pop stardom, but during its course the Easybeats in their various incarnations did make some of the finest high-spirited rock & roll around, and should be suitably commemorated.

---KEN BARNES

Rockin' Around the World

Probably the largest beat cult outside England and America existed in Germany. Before Liverpool groups started playing there, German rock consisted at its best of close imitations of American rockers like Elvis, Gene Vincent, etc. Rock & roll is essentially a product of American culture, and while Britishers can get close to it via shared language and some cultural similarities, no non-English speaking country prior to around 1969 managed to produce any rock that wasn't totally derivative.

But the Germans were, of course, turned on by all the excitement taking place across the Channel, and soon there were German beat groups making the trek to Liverpool, where for some reason they were as popular as the Liverpool groups were in Hamburg. There's no telling how many such groups there were, as only a few left any recorded heritage, but the evidence left by those few speaks well for Germany's contribution to the Big Beat.

One such group was the Rats, who I'm told included Mick Ronson (currently David Bowie's guitarist). Of their three releases I know of, most were blues songs like "Spoonful," "Parchman Farm" and "Everyday I Have the Blues." I have "Spoonful" on an American single, and can attest to its excellence. The sound is solid Mersey, especially the flip which is a typically Liverpool upbeat ballad.

Of all the German groups, only one had any impact in England or America. That was the Rattles. Perhaps it was the mystique of coming from the Star Club, where the Beatles first began to take off, but whatever the cause the Rattles became very popular in Liverpool. They had shared a lot of bills back in Hamburg with the Searchers, whose first recordings were done there, and eventually an album of the two groups was issued, on which the Rattles material generally outshone that of the Searchers.

One of the oddest inequities of the English Invasion is the fact that, although they had to my knowledge no singles released here, there was in addition to that Searchers album, an entire LP of The Rattles' Greatest Hits which wasn't, I believe, even released in England! Anyway, we should count our blessings, because it's one of the era's best albums. The Rattles were better than most of the Liverpool groups. They sounded completely relaxed and natural with the material, had a fine sense of rave, a fantastic beat, sounded at times like the DC5 and early Manfred Mann, and could always be counted on to do enough Chuck Berry and Buddy Holly songs to keep things rocking. They recorded "Hippy Hippy Shake," "Sha La La La La," "Roll Over Beethoven," "Bye Bye Johnny," "Shame Shame Shame," "Zip-A-Dee-Doo-Dah" and a great song called "Las Vegas." Their choice of songs was generally pretty sound as far as their style was concerned, and somewhat more imaginative than many of the groups who never seemed to run out of Coasters and Isley Bros. material.

What many don't realize is that the Rattles never broke up. They released a wild scorcher called "The Witch" in 1969, sounding somewhat like Deep Purple, were back in '71 with a similar number "Devil's On the Loose," and have a new one, "Devil's Son," just out. Undoubtedly they've been recording continuously in Germany through the years, and there must be dozens of records unknown to us. Any reader having knowledge of same is urged to get in touch--this is one group whose greatness has survived the years, even if they are virtually forgotten.

There's one other group that needs to be mentioned in the context of German beat music, and that's the Lords. I don't think any of their records came out in England or America, but they had such a good feeling for the music that they deserve some recognition. The Lords specialized in cover versions of English minor hits, and they picked some strange ones. For instance, they took the Country Gentlemen's arrangement of "Greensleeves," and also did versions of "Shakin' All Over," "Que Sera Sera" and "Seven Daffodils," based on English records that had never made the top 20.

Unfortunately I don't have either of the two albums released by the Lords during their beat phase, but if the three singles I have are any indication, they must have been great. They weren't especially creative, but they had the tone and every nuance of Liverpool rock down to a science. Their English, however, left a lot to be desired: "quivers down ze backhbone, I got sie shivers in ze kneebone, veil ze krammers zit da schpinebone..." Great fun, tho.

Like the Rattles, the Lords are still active. I have three albums by them released in recent years. One, Ulleogamaxbe, was made during their psychedelic phase. Where originally they looked a bit like the Pretty Things, by 1969 they were wearing robes and exuding flowers. On Shakin' All Over '70 (which incidentally leads one to wonder whether they were aware of Johnny Kidd's exceedingly obscure "Shakin' All Over '65") however, they were into a nice late-sixties English pop sound, and nowadays they're probably into either heavy metal or space rock. If anyone knows more about them, I'd appreciate hearing.

Oh, I almost forgot Drafi. Drafi was and is a German pop singer on the order of Engelbert Humperdinck, and I wouldn't mention him except for the fact that he made some excellent beat-style records in '65 and '66. "Come On Let's Go" (not the Ritchie Valens song) combines German and English lyrics with a great beat and some frantic raw singing. It was his first record, as "Drafi Deutscher & His Magics." The flip, "Shake Hands" is pretty wild too. It was one of three singles he had out here on London. But his first real hit was the ballad "Amanda," without the group, and that set the direction he was to follow. And disqualified him, alas, for a longer article in these pages.

Scandinavia was the source of a few good beat groups. Sweden had been known in the early '60s as the home of the Spotnicks, an instrumental group who put out around 20 albums before they were done. In 1965 an English group called the Renegades migrated to Finland and announced that they were going to become the Beatles of that country. And it worked! "Cadillac" became a huge hit, there and in England, and was covered everywhere; in Denmark by Sir Henry & the Butlers, and in Sweden by a group called the Hep Stars.

The Hep Stars had no originality, but they had an amazing affinity for beat music, a taste for oldies, and a compelling sound featuring heavy rhythm guitar and lead organ. They left behind as their testament one incredible live album, containing versions of "Cadillac," "What'd I Say," "So Mystifying," "Only You," "Wear My Ring Around Your Neck," "Surfin' Bird," "Talahassee Lassie," "If You Need Me," "Farmer John," "Bald Headed Woman" and "Whole Lotta Shakin'." The album has powerful kinetic force, one of the all-time great live albums. Unfortunately their studio versions of the same songs are as lacking in excitement as the album was replete with it, and are on the whole a disappointment. A cover of Mike Berry's "Buddy Holly Tribute" is about the best of the lot. They stayed together until about 1972, changing with the times, going through Psychedelic and ending up with Neil Young imitations. Too bad.

As for the rest of Europe, well, France must've had a small scene, but all I know of is Johnny Hallyday, who did cover versions of English hits just as he's covered everything else through the years. Italy must have had something too, since the Stones and Yardbirds recorded material in Italian specifically for that market, and the Beatles had a live album mistakenly issued there by EMI. There were probably local groups doing Mersey stuff in South Africa too, but I have no source for information except that Mickie Most had a successful recording career there before moving to England, the Troggs have always been popular there, and rock always seems to be in demand. Merseybeat was a worldwide phenomenon, and wherever there were recording facilities and a leisure class, kids were undoubtedly copying the music on record.

One of the larger such scenes, and one I do have some knowledge of, existed in Mexico. When I was living in San Francisco, I once found a store in the Mexican district that had a whole bin full of different albums with Mexican versions of English songs by the Stones, Yardbirds, Zombies, Kinks, etc. The groups looked pretty sharp, and I would've loved to buy 'em all, but not at $6.98 a shot. I did however pick up one used album that was probably somewhat representative.

Meet the Fabulous Thunderbirds isn't strictly Mexican. The Thunderbirds were American Indians from the Pueblo village of Isleta, near the Mexican border, and the album was on an Albuquerque label called Red Feather. But it's close enough. The songs include "Route 66," "Chains," "Twist & Shout," "Hot Pastromi," "Let's Dance," "Glad All Over," "Roll Over Beethoven" and "Reelin' & Rockin'" (not the C. Berry song). Then there was Berry's "Everybody Rock" and the obscure Carl Dobkins oldie "If You Don't Want My Lovin'" as well as a Rod Bernard song! Performances vary from excellent to poor, but what's interesting is the way beat music infiltrated into the most remote cultures and excited teenage imaginations across the board--and also, of course, the way in which local influences changed the music. On this record, amusingly enough, the Thunderbirds picked up Mick Jagger's garbled enunciation of the place names in "Route 66," and garbled them further till they came out gibberish, despite the fact that the cities named, such as Flagstaff, Kingman and Barstow, were in the group's own vicinity. Talk about rock & roll's power to override conditioning!

NOVELTIES

One guage of the impact of the Beatles and the English Invasion is the number of records that were made by Americans, about them. Fans of novelty records know that there are three distinct sub-genres that make up the majority of such records, within the field of rock: flying saucer records, Elvis records, and Beatle records. And there were more Beatle novelties than the other two categories put together.

I know of nearly 60, and I don't claim to know about them all. Most of them involved some play on the idea of hair, or bugs, and most were centered on Ringo. Some were by girl groups, and were on the order of "I Want a Beatle For Christmas." Some of the better Beatle novelties were "I'm Better Than the Beatles" by Brad Berwick & the Bugs, "My Boyfriend Got a Beatle Haircut" by Donna Lynn, "The Beatle Flying Saucer" by Ed Solomon, "Frankenstein Meets the Beatles" by Jeckyl & Hyde, "The Beatles' Barber" by Scott Douglas, "Letter From Elaina" by Casey Kasem, and "The Guy With the Long Liverpool Hair" by the Outsiders, a punk-rocker in which a guy tries to explain to his girl that he hadn't been seen out with another chick, it was only a pal from work with the new Beatle haircut...

A lot of famous people made Beatle novelty records. Cher did "I Love You Ringo," as Bonnie Jo Mason, produced by Phil Spector. Allen Sherman recorded "I Hate the Beatles." Johnny & the Hurricanes did "Saga of the Beatles," an unbelievably bad vocal. British pop columnist Penny Valentine had "I Want to Kiss Ringo Goodbye." Ella Fitzgerald did "Beatle Beat." Gene Cornish & the Unbeetables (the Rascals) did a whole album, featuring "I Wanna Be a Beatle." Sonny Curtis cut "A Beatle I Want to Be."

My favorite novelty is Buchanan & Greenfield's "The Invasion," because it catches perfectly the whole initial sense of American record biz paranoia that greeted the Beatles' blitz of the charts, and the thinly-veiled contempt for their hair and music, that I detect in most of the non-girl Beatle novelties. It's also a very hot, exciting record; perhaps the beat Buchanan ever made.

Then there were the albums. The bootlegs, the phony Ed Rudy interview albums with the Beatles, Stones, DC5. One strange one called Beatles Blast in Stadium that consists of interviews with screaming girls at a Beatles concert. There was an album of Beatle songs by the Chipmunks, and a comedy album on Swan called It's a Beatle World!!

Especially interesting were the ones designed to fool parents into thinking they were buying their tots Beatle albums. An LP of Beatle songs by the Haircuts. The Hit Sounds From England by the Liverpools. The Beatle Beat, by the Buggs. Beatlemania by the Bearcuts, and Beat-A-Mania, by artists unnamed, both "recorded in England," the latter "live," and full of Beatle songs. These are especially frustrating, because they all contain a few original songs that are quite good, and one wonders what English group, perhaps an obscure favorite, provided the tracks. Many like to believe that the Buggs were the Hollies, because their album included "Just One Look." One of my favorite frauds is an album by B. Brock & the Sultans, on Crown. All the songs have "Beetle" in the title, except "The Saints" and "My Bonnie," evidently included to fool those hip enough to recognize the titles of the Beatles' rare Atco single. The other songs are all surf instrumentals.

One I'm particularly fond of is Monster Melodies by Frankie Stein & His Ghouls, which I bought because of my interest in monster music, then discovered to my astonishment that it consisted of crude jazzy sax solos overdubbed onto Beatle and Kinks instrumental tracks!

Counting album tracks and singles I have yet to discover, there were likely over a hundred novelty songs about the Beatles, although I know of only a handful that were released in England. But when that many people are talking about something on record, you can be sure some pretty big phenomenon is underway. As if we needed to be told! These novelty records, by the way, are nowadays among the rarest of '60s recordings. If you've got any, hang onto 'em.

The SCENE

There was more to the English Invasion than just the music, y'know. I mean, that's the whole point of all this. Rock & roll can be an integral part of teenage culture, or it can lose touch and move into the background. Most of the time it alternates between the extreme limits of each condition. As we emerge from the second great rock recession, and observe the first such transition since the awakening of rock fandom's critical process, a lot of things become clear.

There are more reasons why we can refer to the years 1955-59 and 1963-67 as definite "rock & roll eras" aside from the fact that the percentage of good music took a sharp rise at their start and an equally abrupt decline at their close. In sheer quantity, there was probably more good rock out in 1971 than in '63 or '58, but it didn't matter because it all added up to a bunch of disconnected flukes and one of the worst years rock's ever had.

The crucial difference is one of context. An album like Teenage Head by the Flamin' Groovies was buried in 1970 because of the sheer weight of garbage it had to push its way out from under to even be heard. Today, the same album would be hailed as a masterpiece. Two years ago, rock & roll had no context. Even the best stuff lost a lot of sparkle because the battle seemed so hopeless. The situation in 1962 is quite analogous, and as rock begins taking on context once again in 1973, it's useful to look back on what happened the last time.

The first rock & roll era was important, not so much for its music, nor for the ephemera of youth culture that surrounded it (leather jackets, pony tails, hotrods, record hops, slang, etc.), but rather for the special magic that resulted from the interworking of the two, in other words the sense it gave kids of belonging to a real youth culture, with symbols and standards and all, that was theirs and theirs alone. That's why there's such a growing "oldies" movement. I went into this at some length for an article in Crawdaddy a couple of years ago, and what I said then still goes.

It's the cultural feedback that pushes rock & roll to its real heights, and what makes the Merseybeat years so important is the youth/rock culture that thrived then. One of the first signs of a revival in youth culture is a special interest in fashion. English pop fashion had its roots in the '50s, with Mary Quant and the beginnings of Carnaby Street.* In 1961 the Beatles hooked up with some German intellectuals who introduced the haircuts and collarless jackets that sparked rock fashion in Britain.

With new trends in fashion and music going on, there inevitably arises a creature known as the Dedicated Follower of Fashion. These types are shallow, superficial and phony. They exist to be clothes-horses and bearers of the latest music gossip. And yet, as the Kinks seem to have recognized, they are necessary to the whole process. They are the pollinators of style, and together they make up a Scene.

The Scene is the essential setting for everything that takes place in pop culture. It consists of a few central figures, culture heros, surrounded by parasites and would-be scenemakers, themselves surrounded by the masses of teenagers, anxious to get as close to the source as they can, which is limited on the mass scale to records and pop magazines.

The pop journals are a good reflector of pop culture. They point up the fact that it's not always the musicians who are the central figures in a pop scene. There are always certain gadflies who exhibit such a sense of style that their doings become news as much as those of the rock stars. Girlfriends of the stars and their sisters become similarly enshrined. Then there are the musicians themselves, and the producers, the disc jockeys, etc. Not all of them, just the ones with a flair for style and social exhibitionism.

England's pop papers of the period are full of pictures and stories on these types, all of them, and they helped create an image of glamorous excitement that was known throughout England and the world as Swinging London. The clubs, the parties, the fashions, the Shrimptons and the Ashers, the Cathy McGowans and the Jimmy Savilles, the Andrew Oldhams and the Jonathan Kings, the Micks and the Brians and all the rest--these were the personalities at the center of it all, they gave the scene its flavor, and the excitement of their lifestyles provided the inspiration for repressed teenagers everywhere.

Maybe it was in large part a phony, drummed-up excitement, but it always had the strength and exuberance of the music to fall back on, and the music itself was pushed to new extremes by the energy of the scene, and the need to be competitive within it. This scene, this social context in which the music existed, was bolstered and propagated by all the media--films, press, radio, TV, graphics, fashion, and so on. Melly's book gives the definitive rundown on all this. Right now we just want to examine a few aspects of some of these media.

PRINT: The established music weeklies were quick to pick up on Merseybeat, but the publications that sprang up after that are of special interest. Mersey Beat chronicled the early Liverpool scene, and helped focus local solidarity. (Brian Epstein was a columnist before he ever met the Beatles!) Later, it became Music Echo, which prior to merging with Disc in early '66 had an entire page of Liverpool news and trivia each issue, and was on the whole the most pop-oriented of all the papers. Andrew Oldham was a staff columnist, and his successor was Jonathan King.

Really, though, the best publications were those issued by the fan clubs. Beatles Monthly, Stones Monthly, and all the various newsletters dedicated to the Yardbirds, Who, Kinks, Zombies, and the obscure groups too, had a lot to do with spreading pop mania. They supplied their members with cards, buttons, special records, autographed photos, and all kinds of gossip, which kept the ephemera spreading at a fantastic rate. It's interesting to note that in the past year or so we have seen the beginnings of some new, dedicated and hyperactive fan clubs, for groups like the Move, the Kinks, David Bowie, and... the Beatles!

In America, Hit Parader provided intelligent commentary on the music together with plenty of photos and mania-inducing gossip--3 separate, info-packed gossip columns and a special section of news from England. In those days, HP was the perfect rock publication. They wrote about blues and jazz, were aware

---

*Incidentally, this whole aspect of the relationship between rock and culture is discussed brilliantly, in great detail, in George Melly's remarkable book, Revolt Into Style (Anchor).

of esoterica, and had peerless editorial perspective and even some thoughtful writing, yet they also played up the excitement of it all, which the "underground" rock press helped kill off the music by not doing.

Anyway, Hit Parader was soon joined by countless other publications that played up the excitement to an even greater extent, leaving out the intelligence altogether. Papers with names like Record Beat, National Blast Weekly, Vox Teen Beat, World Countdown, Teenset, Hullabaloo, Weekly Beat, and Wild Wild Groups appeared. National Record News headlined, "BEATLEMANIA SWEEPS U.S." Blast devoted its cover in Nov. '65 to banner headlines reading: "MICK LEAVING STONES".'

The real proliferation of these papers occurred on the local level, with radio stations putting out or sponsoring tabloids full of news and pix and contests and letter columns and excitement. The KFWB/KEWB Hitliners and the KRLA/KYA Beats were the best on the west coast, but others are valuable for their reportage of local bands, who were of course all trying to look and sound English.

Few of these publications lasted more than a few issues, but as with the groups it was a great time to cash in, and there was room for all of it.

RADIO: Because of the BBC's policy of playing only a portion of each record, some alternative was needed if the kids were to hear the new beat sounds. The pirate stations came along to meet that need. For a report on that, we turn to Terry Waghorne in England.....

Three of the original Radio Caroline disc jockeys: Chris Moore, Carl Conway, and Simon Dee

PIRATE RADIO IN THE U.K.

In the mid-sixties, British radio broadcasting was revolutionised by the advent of offshore commercial radio, or the pop pirates as the establishment referred to them, and as they are now best known. It all began during the Easter of 1964...the end came just over four years later. The pirates' absence has always been conspicuous. The manner of their demise, a broadside of government legislation, still rankles, for it was their very existence which underlined the immense need for a commercial radio setup in Britain.

When the vessel M.V. Caroline began broadcasting on 199 metres medium wave, the BBC's vast listening audience, tempted by the sheer novelty of non-stop pop music, tuned in in their thousands. In a matter of days Caroline, anchored off Felixstow on the coast of southern England, became a household name. Its first disc jockeys, Simon Dee, Chris Moore, Carl Conway and Tom Lodge, were as well known as many of the BBC's long-serving stalwarts.

Looking back, it's hardly surprising that Caroline gobbled up so much of the BBC's listening audience in so short a time. The Beeb's amount of 'needle time' was woefully limited, and it wasn't possible to advertise with them. Caroline's very existence meant exciting possibilities for businesses both large and small, especially for teen and pop oriented products. At first only small traders from the south paid for plugs, but a few months later, Radio Atlanta began test transmissions employing budget line 45s.

Its top DJ was Australian Tony Withers, who later changed his surname to Windsor. Atlanta, however, didn't last very long. Caroline's boss, Ronan O'Rahilly, moved fast--a white paper entitled "News Release-Commercial Radio Merger" was issued. Its text read: "The Directors of Project Atlanta and Planet Productions Limited today issued a joint statement announcing a merger between Radio Atlanta and Radio Caroline. The companies are responsible for the advertising and selling of time on the two off-shore commercial radio stations. Mr. Allan Crawford, Managing Director of Project Atlanta, and Mr. Ronan O'Rahilly, Managing Director of Planet Productions, will become joint managing directors of the new operation."

The ship Caroline, it was announced, would sail to the Isle of Man to a position five miles from Ramsey, continuing to broadcast en route and remaining on 199 metres. The ship Atlanta would continue broadcasting from its position, to the Greater London area and southeast England under the national call sign, Radio Caroline. In their joint statement, Crawford and O'Rahilly said:

"The decision to merge was taken in view of the enormous interest from the public and advertisers in other parts of England outside the original broadcasting area. This network will cover the most populous areas of Great Britain. All departments will merge from one office. The Caroline Club and other land-based operations will continue and be extended to cover the new broadcasting area."

This was really telling it to the people. Caroline Club figures swelled, 199 car stickers were handed out by the wadful, and big but big advertising came Caroline's way-- the giant Nabisco Foods Ltd, Pepsi, Bullova Watches and many others, all poured money into the kitty, thus ensuring that Caroline was no 9-day wonder. This meant a throbbing headache for the BBC, they had no readymade answer, and the arrival of Radio London, a slick, highly professional, mid-Atlantic styled enterprise, drove more nails into the BBC's coffin. And it didn't end there. Pop singer Screaming Lord Sutch, a zany genius for creating his own publicity, launched Radio Sutch off the Kent coast, or rather he commandeered an old sea fort. Later he sold it to his manager at the time, Reg Calvert, who renamed it Radio City. There was more than one battered old sea fort--suddenly radio's 309 and King existed. And finally, along came Radio's Britain and England!!

The pop pirates' influence in the record business cannot be overlooked. They played more or less what they wanted to and when. Mass airplay by Caroline took Dionne Warwick's "Walk On By" into the charts; the Righteous Bros. recording of "You've Lost That Lovin' Feeling" lay around unnoticed as Cilla Black's cover version shot towards the top of the charts. But Caroline switched to the American recording, mass plugging for it resulted in a #1 hit two weeks later. Later on, many of the pirates brought different styles of music into the average British household.

Later on, many of the pirates brought different styles of music into the average British household. Mike Raven on Radio 309 converted many listeners to the blues. Johnny Walker on Caroline boosted soul music in Britain. On the same station West Indian Blue Beat and later, its variations Ska and Rock Steady won generous airtime. The Beatles and the Rolling Stones were high on the pirates' list of most played artists. Radio City in particular spotlighted these two groups.

Radio London made up its own chart. It changed rapidly, many new releases by unknown artists were featured. London, like Caroline, also helped bring Jim Reeves to the fore as a hit parade name, and like the other pirates they spun records by deceased artists, something the BBC seemed loathe to do.

Eddie Cochran for instance was rarely heard on their popular music waveband, the Light Programme, after his death, and other dead stars weren't featured at all.

One record company, Major Minor (now defunct) bought air time to familiarise record fans with such names as the Coloured Raisins, the Equals, David McWilliams, Sugar & Dandy and the Dubliners. But other companies and some artists had a cooler attitude toward the pirates. Disc sales were falling drastically at the time of the pirates' peak in popularity. Whether this fact was taken into consideration when the government drew up its legislation, I don't know, but there was great pressure from various quarters for government action. The additional fact that the establishment wasn't receiving any revenue from the pirates was another thorn in the flesh.

And so, at the height of its popularity, commercial radio was duly torpedoed. All except Caroline threw in the towel without a fight--from a financial point of view, a good policy as it was an offence to work for and advertise with the pirates. Caroline North & South battled on for several months before both ships were towed to Holland for, as one spokesman said, "refitting." Neither has ever broadcast since.

Later that year, 1967, the BBC launched Radio 1, staffed by many pirate DJs! However, Caroline and London aren't forgotten, probably because 70% of Radio 1's needle time is woefully misused.

Commercial radio is scheduled to return sometime in 1973, some 60 land-based stations are planned. Now legalized, perhaps the story will after all have a happy ending. Whether or not Ronan O'Rahilly and the other much maligned pioneers will find a slot in the new setup remains to be seen. Their reward for revitalising radio broadcasting was, in the end, meagre. Britain's "Swinging Sixties" owed much to these men. It was an era in which the younger generation's needs were, as entertainment was concerned, fully met. The pop pirates can rightfully claim much of the credit for this. Ironic then that they should be outlawed and killed off, but indeed the lot of a pioneer is not always a happy one.

---TERRY WAGHORNE

TELEVISION: England has always had plenty of rock on TV, thanks chiefly to Jack Good. Throughout the sixties there were usually at least three or four weekly rock shows. The content of most of these was roughly equivalent to that of Bandstand and its imitators, admittedly, but in Jack Good's productions at least there was usually a greater sensitivity to the actual tastes of the audience, and some truly exciting stuff was often worked in. But America didn't have its taste of high-energy pop TV until Good came over, on a hunch, to see what was happening, and ended up producing the greatest rock show of all time--Shindig.

ROCK & ROLL TV IN AMERICA

Here is is, 1973, and rock history is repeating itself once again. The networks of NBC and ABC have once more started showing rock TV shows for our consumption and exploitation. Though In Concert and Midnight Special have only been on for a few months, it's pretty obvious that, although both shows suck, In Concert is a lot better than Midnight Special. ABC has always had a slight edge in taste when it came to presentation of rock groups. In Concert has no MC and showcases just a few bands in its hour and a half time period. Sure, there are gobs of commercials, but that's what TV's all about to begin with, and commercials have been the most interesting things on the video for the last few years anyway. Nothing beat the thrill I got when I saw the newest For Brunettes Only commercial. After our dazzling brunette comes out of the phone booth a new woman, she sells some deodorant on top of it. Really too much.

Midnight Special, on the other hand, is just plain awful. It's bad enough that Mac Davis is allowed to breathe. Would you want him to host your rock show? There's plenty of performers on Midnight Special, but nobody gets to do more than two songs, and they better be hits. The audience is small and sits around the stage area (real informal like, y'see) and nods out 'cause there's nothing to get excited about. At least In Concert changes locales and has a somewhat derelict band of freaks in the audience to look at.

These new shows bring to mind the real golden age of TV as far as rock & roll is concerned: the mid '60s, when both nationally televised and local shows ran amuck on the tube without the slightest inclination towards meaning or purpose. It was paradise for those of us who were teens then. We'd have our radios tuned to our favorite station all day and night, maybe buy a few singles or maybe even an album. There weren't many concerts to go to, and so your main audio/visual contact with the stars was the box, and you certainly weren't let down too often. There was no way to miss the groups, since they all did the TV circuit, from the king, Ed Sullivan, to Shindig, Hullabaloo, Hollywood Palace and generally any variety show that wanted to stay high in the rating wars. Local disc jockey heroes usually had a rock dance show of some sort, like Lloyd Thaxton and Sam Riddle in the West and Jerry Blavat and Clay Cole in the East.

Shindig and Hullabaloo, appearing at prime time, were by far the most popular. Shindig was the brainchild of British entrepeneur Jack Good (who had pioneered rock TV in

Jack Good, father of rock & roll TV

England in the '50s). He pulled some teeth with the ABC brass and sold them on the idea of a live rock & roll show to be filmed before a live audience. Jimmy O'Neill, the pompadoured west coast DJ, was selected to be the host, and he was neat and wholesome and adequately charming. O'Neill was capable of doing many things, especially asking teenagers their name and age almost as well as Dick Clark.

Who can forget the Stridex Medicated Pad commercials on Shindig? Here's this sink in the middle of a studio, with a mirror and a towel. "Okay Eddie, go wash your face with plenty of soap and water." While Eddie scrubs his zit-covered face, O'Neill tells us of the immeasurable qualities embodied in the Stridex pad. "Is your face really clean?" "I think so." "Okay Eddie, rub the pad across your face." Voila, dirt. Living proof that Stridex medicated pads clean dirt and grime from your face better than soap and water. Did'ja ever notice that the dirt always seemed to come from O'Neill's fingertips when he grabbed the pad back from Eddie?

Shindig had a bunch of regulars that were on almost every show, and you could pick your fave from all walks of popdom. Bobby Sherman rivalled O'Neill for DA honors, and, better than that, Sal Mineo discovered him and got him on the show. Glen Campbell was the resident folk singer, with a long pony tail hanging down his back. His forte was the protest song and I remember hearing his single of "Universal Soldier" once on the radio. Glen was into his twelve string then, and never even did any fancy picking, intent as he was on making it as a folkie. Donna Loren, what a fox! Dark haired little devil she was, with a great low voice that didn't fit her looks. More peole knew her from her Dr. Pepper commercials than from Shindig, but more still will remember her from her beach movies with Annette the F. and Frankie the A. Donna once told Elvis where to get off and got kicked off a movie she was to co-star with him in. Real class.

Sonny and Cher were on so much that they could be considered regulars. Recalls Cher: "Sonny and I used to go by the Shindig studio and literally beg Jack Good to listen to us. We would leave our record ("Baby Don't Go") write letters--signing fans' names--and make hundreds of phone calls requesting Sonny & Cher, but to no avail. One day we got into his office, and when Jack walked in we jump-

ROCK & ROLL TV IN AMERICA, contd.

ed up and started singing and dancing. All Jack did was look at me, then at Sonny, and say, 'Cher is very pretty.'" He finally let them go on, for twelve seconds. But the sheepskin vests and Cher's bellbottoms brought them back many more times. Each time they'd finish a tune, Sonny would rest his head on Cher's shoulder. True love!

The Righteous Brothers and the Blossoms were the best of the regular cast. Bill Medley and Bobby Hatfield worked super hard on Shindig, and it finally paid off when Uncle Phil grabbed them and made them stars. The great thing was that ever teen who watched Shindig could feel that he or she was a part of their success story. Ah, America, land of opportunity. The Blossoms were led by the great Darlene Love, with her overlapping front teeth. Strange how they were always

Jimmy O'Neill

dressed so out of synch with everyone else. They seemed like a bit of nostalgia even then. But Darlene and the girls found in Shindig a new life, making it to an Elvis tour and tons of session backup vocal work with the best of 'em.

And the Shindogs! They hardly did anything on the show, but what a band! James Burton was the original guitarist, but he left to do more session work after awhile, so Don Preston replaced him. Joey Cooper on rhythm guitar, a nonfat Delaney Bramlett on bass and lead vocals, Chuck Blackwell on drums and Glen Hardin on organ. I remember never hearing anything they did cause the girls were screaming so much, and if you didn't recognize a song within the first four bars, that was it, cause that's all you could hear before hysteria set in.

The Shindigger dance troupe was pretty nondescript. They never knew what they were supposed to be doing, and they usually collected in the back of the stage and made believe they did, which only made it look worse. Carol Shelyne, the blonde with the big round lensless glasses, was the only one worth remembering, if only because how many of us knew someone with round lenseless glasses?

The Stones were on a few times, doing mainly tunes from their first three albums. They'd start with "Around and Around," just to shake everybody loose. Then a slow one like "Off the Hook" or "Pain in My Heart." Back to a rocker like "It's All Over Now" or "The Last Time." Keith never played the same solo twice on the speaking part of "Time Is On My Side," and Mick would always walk into a different edge of the stage.

The Who usually did "I Can't Explain." Sometimes they'd score with "Anyway, Anyhow, Anywhere," complete with drum solo, and once they even did "Daddy Rolling Stone." Those were the days when Keith Moon wore his bullseye T-shirt and he played with his sticks dangling from bent wrists. Ray Davies even let Dave sing "I'm a Lover, Not a Fighter," probably so he wouldn't feel bad about not being able to take much of any kind of solo, cause he didn't know how yet. Eric Burdon's pimples never seemed to get suppressed, no matter how much makeup they smeared on, and it was hard to believe that the Beau Brummels weren't from England.

Shindig's format was haphazard, but in a strange way, very innocent and delightful. They just sort of stuck people on, with no real continuity or reason. Kind of like the way you put on records. On a given night anyone could be on, from the Stones to Patty Duke to Donovan. Sets were minimal, just some props against a blank backdrop. Neil Sedaka would climb a set of stairs for "Stairway to Heaven," the dancers would be lollipops for Millie Small, etc. When the big names were on, the stage would be bare, and the camera was just like our virgin eyes, scanning the stage, focusing on each member of the band for a few seconds. Complete frenzy. Ray Davies wobbling a forefinger at us. A Mick Jagger handclap or maraca. Keith Richard's big ears. Dave Clark's pasted-on smile. A Mike Love squint.

The bands really played it up for the camera, and they also seemed to control the whole environment. When the Stones brought Howlin' Wolf with them to sing "Little Red Rooster," O'Neill tried to do a voice over introduction of the Stones, and Mick grabbed the mike and told Jimmy to shut his trap. At least someone was aware that cultural education was in process each time the cameras rolled.

Hullabaloo was guided by pipe smoking exec Gary Smith of NBC, and its main goal was cashing in on the action Shindig was getting. It took over the 7:30 Monday night slot in mid season, hoping to outdo Shindig on every level. The early time slot (Shindig was on Wednesdays at 8:30) was utilized pretty well. A more family oriented show, Hullabaloo stank of commercial flash. There were different guest hosts each week. Noel Harrison, George Hamilton, Brenda Lee, Michael Landon. It got worse as each week progressed, but we needed it and bleeded it, so we sat there staring anyway.

Hullabaloo was sponsored by Yardley cosmetics, and a Yardley commercial could save any dying show. You got a scene in London with fluffy dogs and extraordinary blondes that fluttered their false eyelashes and had seven feet of legs. Any young punk that didn't run to the john afterwards to get his rocks off just didn't know how to live.

Hullabaloo had regular features, like Brian Epstein's taped spots and the unforgettable "Hullabaloo Discotheque." The Discotheque looked like it was conceived by Russ Meyer. There were flashing neon lights, the stage was high off the ground, and there were go go girls in plastic cube booths on all sides. Whenever Lada Edmunds Jr. was one of the go go girls, you could bet that your old man would be at your side drooling. The red headed "avant garde" dancer could shake her tits underneath those Hullabaloo sweatshirts better than anybody else on the scene in '65 and '66. Sometimes they'd give her a solo spot, or she'd join Joey Heatherton, a frequent guest, for some pulsating number.

Brian Epstein's spots were boring cause he was, but at least the Beatles were on once, doing "Day Tripper" on a fake train and "We Can Work it Out" with John on organ and George on acoustic. They lip synched, something Hullabaloo was notorious for making their guests do, and I remember John sneering and missing a finger move on purpose. (They played live on Shindig, doing "Kansas City,"

"I'm a Loser" and "Boys.") Brian brought a lot of women on, though, and that was nice, especially when it was Marianne Faithfull, Dusty Springfield or Sandie Shaw, who was rumored to go barefoot a lot while performing.

Hullabaloo did give us our first glimpses of the Hollies, Wayne Fontana & the Mindbenders, the Lovin' Spoonful and the Rascals. The Rascals were in an alley, dressed in knickers, hiding behind garbage cans. Creative art department, huh? The Hollies did "Look Through Any Window" when they were on, and they did an instant replay of Tony Hicks' guitar break when the song ended. The Byrds were introduced on Hullabaloo, and they sang "Mr. Tambourine Man." Were they a sight! Crosby was wearing his cape to hide his spreading middle, causing him to sweat like hell under the hot lights. McGuinn had his grannies cocked at perfect camera angle, and Gene Clark had not one, but two tambourines. And Herman's Hermits and Billy J. Kramer were always good for a laugh.

The competition was hot and heavy between the two shows and Jack Good came up with the idea of two half hour Shindigs, just like Peyton Place. Tuesday and Thursday were the new days, and though it seemed like a good move, it backfired. Shindig began slipping and ABC got worried. Hullabaloo had its set spots, so they didn't have to worry that much about programming, especially after the Hullabaloos got started and were on every other week. But Shindig's disjointed format didn't make it in a half hour spot. It started and it was over. No longer could the Animals or the Beach Boys do five or six tunes. Things got cramped, and even though Sonny & Cher and the Righteous Brothers had hits on the radio, the ratings started to slip.

ABC made up its mind in the middle of the season, and by June '66, Shindig was dead. Instead of grabbing the whole audience, Hullabaloo started slipping too and it got axed also. Just how all this happened is pretty much a mystery to everyone. An important thing to remember is that punk rock was in full swing by '66, and whereas the high school prom had once been unable to provide good entertainment a short two years before, now every city had their own dynamite band. The British bands had played themselves out to a large extent, and if you lived in Minneapolis, the Trashmen were all you needed for a good time. Bands practiced in pop's basement and garage. No time to watch those farts on the tube anymore; everybody was a star now.

SHINDIG

Local rock shows that were syndicated did a little better since they could be aired at relatively calm times like Saturday afternoons or early Sunday night. If you were into the Strangeloves, Sam Riddle had them on at least twice a month. Lloyd Thaxton was good for a big band or two now and then. Even Soupy Sales in New York had rock acts on his Saturday show. It might have been the only place that Jerry Lee Lewis got work for a year or two. The Shangri-Las, the Shirelles and the Detergents were on a few times, and, of course, Tony and the Tigers, featuring Tony and Hunt Sales.

The true punk haven was Upbeat, filmed in a garage in Cleveland. A real hotbed of activity, Cleveland brought together a lot of the midwestern bands. Upbeat had 'em all. Cheesy Don Webster was the host, Bonnie Bel's Lotion was the sponsor. Jeff Kutash was the fag that led and performed with the Upbeat dancers, and the GTO's were the house band. ? & the Mysterians, the McCoys, the Shadows of Knight, Bob Seger, the Blues Magoos. I saw all of them on Upbeat. And, oh yeah, what's his name--Terry Knight & the Pack-- they were the house favorites, expecially when Terry got on his knees to sing "I Who Have

That's Jack Good up above, surrounded by a bevy of bouncy Shindig dancers.

Nothing." Blue Cheer and Steppenwolf appeared regularly, but by that time people were going to concerts so it all didn't matter anymore.

I guess it was that feeling of being right up front that made Shindig and Hullabaloo so appealing. More fun than a record, less hassles and less expensive than a live show.

The Shindogs (left) included James Burton, Don Preston, Delaney Bramlett and other renowned musicians, but were no less important to Shindig than Jack Good and those wild young female dancers (above).

It was a more than comfortable middle ground to be in, and you really felt that the bands were playing for you and you alone. I have tons of memories and tapes that will never leave me, thank God. So pick up a pen and write ABC today! If they can rerun McHale's Navy and The Untouchables forever, they can show old Shindig shows too. Oh, well. Back to my crusty, moldy Flips for more sweet release.....

---BILLY ALTMAN

SUMMARY

Fittingly enough, as I pen these closing words, Richard Nader's "English Invasion Revival" show is being screened on "Midnight Special". Having spent nearly two years researching and putting together this issue, seeing this show naturally gives rise to many thoughts. When we began work on this issue, there was no hint of anything resembling a "sixties revival". Now it is evidently upon us.

The fifties revival (which, incidentally, is still going strong and getting bigger all the time) taught us one important lesson: that "oldies" can be broken down fairly readily into those which nowadays sound dated, and those that don't, and also that there are two types of oldies fans--those who can differentiate and (in the vast majority) those who can't. From the way 50's rock was aesthetically butchered by the latter group of nostalgists (remember Sha Na Na?), those who really care about the music for its own sake should have been alerted to the necessity of preventing the music of the sixties from suffering a similar fate when its turn inevitably came up.

Regardless of what they say, the Richard Naders of the world will always choose to milk nostalgia over supporting music, because that's where the money lies. That's why he booked a tour with Herman's Hermits, Billy J. Kramer and Wayne Fontana instead of the Dave Clark Five, the Troggs, the Zombies, the Nashville Teens or the Swinging Blue Jeans. Maybe the fact that the tour bombed can be taken as some indication that audiences are a little wiser and more critical when it comes to the music of the sixties. Certainly we've seen a reluctance to segregate the best 60's rock as "oldies" in the cavalier fashion that 50's music was long ago written off. Hip FM stations don't feel the need to program weekly shows hosted by people with names like "Doctor Oldies" to play Dylan, Hendrix, Byrds, Stones, Beatles, etc. That stuff is treated with as much respect as the very latest Captain Beyond release, with the implicit recognition that good music simply doesn't age.

Getting back to the English Invasion and this magazine, what we've tried to do is lay out the basic foundations for an educated understanding of the roots and beginnings of sixties rock--or rather, the Second Rock & Roll Era, as we've defined it. I think the only way to halt the advancement of oldies consciousness is to decide for ourselves what constitutes an "oldie" as opposed to music that means something and deserves to be taken seriously. It isn't enough that the Beatles have acceptance--you can hear 'em on the oldies stations now too, for that matter. If the work of the early Beatles and Stones is acknowledged, why not that of the Searchers, Troggs, Pretty Things, Walker Bros., etc.? If one of Ian & the Zodiacs had gone on to join Crosby, Stills & Young, then we'd be hearing their stuff on the radio too. But it should be the *music* that's considered on its own terms, and that's what we'd like to see happen.

Accordingly, this special double issue of *Who Put The Bomp* has been rather heavily analytical, as we've attempted to chart the development of a sound and style that had a direct influence on just about everything that subsequently took place in rock & roll. The groups have been examined and evaluated on the basis of what they contributed to the music of their era and to the lasting body of rock culture, and whenever possible, patterns of influence and development have been pointed out. We don't pretend that this has been a comprehensive survey. Some groups, such as the Stones, were left out because there wasn't much new to be said about them. Others, like Cilla Black or Chad & Jeremy, because musically they were too peripheral to the subject matter, even though they were among the biggest in sales and will probably be in some future Nader package. And others, among them Chris Farlowe and Sandie Shaw, because there just wasn't room or need for a full treatment.

But I believe we have made a good start toward understanding what the English Invasion was all about. There are many important ramifications that we haven't even touched on, of course. One of the most significant aspects of Merseybeat, as the keynote of the Second R&R Era, is the manner in which its guitar and vocal sound crept into all varieties of music during its era, and also the way the British approach to song structure was taken up by everybody to give the era a sort of diverse homogeneity of sound. Beyond even the Beatle imitators, another entire subject that we'll be tackling in future issues, it's amazing how you can date records by the likes of Brenda Lee, the Four Seasons, the Everly Bros., Bobby Vee, Gene Pitney and many others, by their obvious Mersey influence. So much music of the mid-sixties is worthy of more respect than it's gotten, and we'll get to it all eventually, but for now at least we've pinned down the source.

The Liverpool groups were, of course, not the real source of sixties rock. Two big styles came before and played an even more basic role: surf music, which (with Merseybeat as a later catalyst) spawned the whole West Coast sound, and (more important yet) the girl group/Brill Bldg. style, which was one of the prime influences on the early British groups. We'll be getting to those subjects in future issues as well, along with a region-by-region tracing of the 1964-7 "punk rock" boom in America, folk rock, some early psychedelia, and all the other little unclassifiable trivia that made up the Second Rock & Roll Era.

Let's return to that term a little bit, because I think it's a vital part of the new approach to rock history we're trying to build. I'm very much opposed to the idea of classifying music according to its date of release; I favor a stylistic aesthetic that compares a record with others of its type. What kind of sense can you make of a year in which some of the best records have been made by Dave Edmunds, the Raspberries, and Slade? The only sane way to discuss Edmunds and the Raspberries is in terms of, respectively, Phil Spector and the Beatles, while bands like Slade, the Sweet, Mott The Hoople, and ELO clearly belong in the 70's and the newly-emerging Third Era.

Taking into account such throwbacks as the Raspberries, and the others that are bound to follow (and incidentally the fact that these bands are working with styles created in the sixties should have no bearing on their commerciality in today's market), there was such a clear-cut hiatus of rock & roll/pop music between 1967 and 1972 that we should have no trouble accepting the sixties (1961-7) as a discrete musical epoch (we could do the same for 1967-72, with its psychedelia, boogie-blues and singer-songwriters, but it would be too depressing even to contemplate).

Anyway, there's sure to be plenty of discussion on this issue in the lettercol next time, so let's hold it for now. The point is that with this definition in mind, and the English invasion as a reference point, *Who Put The Bomp* will be dedicated to investigating the Second Era of Rock & Roll, for the forseeable future. This doesn't preclude the possibility of articles on artists of the 50's or 70's, however, because the lines of influence stretch tightly in both directions and we mustn't forget the larger picture.

LAST WORDS

It took us much longer than should have been necessary to get this issue together, and while we have plenty of great excuses, I still feel an apology is due all our patient subscribers. Things should go more smoothly from here out, now that we're settled in Los Angeles, established in our new format, and blessed with a sorely needed helping hand. With this issue, former contributing editor Ken Barnes joins our staff as co-editor, so in the future *WPTB* should be better written, better researched, and more frequent. In addition to his fine contributions in this issue, Ken has done more than his share of the tedious research that went into the project, undoubtedly avoiding still more months of delay.

One project in particular on which Ken's help has been indispensable is discographical research. You may have noticed the singular lack of discographies in this issue; when I started out to compile listings of every record issued by every English rock/pop artist during the years 1962-7, I didn't quite realize how extensive it would turn out to be. The listings are now as complete as we can get them, including hundreds of groups, and packed with astonishing information. It's more an encyclopedia of English rock than a mere set of discographies, as there are also facts about each artist, personnel of groups, where they came from and where they went, what the records sounded like, and a brief rundown of each act's career. Plus, of course, all releases are listed with both U.S. and U.K. numbers, as well as appearances on V.A. albums, dates, and other odd facts. The whole thing will be published in the near future as a separate book, with the addition of lotsa photos, original art work, and some other goodies. It's an item no serious student of rock & roll will want to miss. *Bomp* subscribers will receive the book in lieu of one of their issues (unless they request otherwise); all others can get it for $1.00, and I'm taking advance orders now. And by the way, this project does not conflict with Alan Betrock's *Book Of U.K. Discographies*, which we highly recommend, since the latter volume covers mostly late sixties groups and there is very little overlap. For a copy, send $3 to Alan at Box 253, Elmhurst-A NY 11373.

Starting next issue, *Who Put The Bomp* will include a couple of new features. We're adding an "addenda" column, in which we'll print all the corrections and omissions you readers are sure to catch. Please don't tell us about groups we "missed" until you see the discographies, but there are bound to be hundreds of loose ends arising from that, and we'll appreciate your help in tying them up. Plus, bowing to popular demand, we're beginning a swap column where readers can buy, sell and trade records, tapes, ephemera, whatever. The cost for ads will be 25c per word.

And that's it for next issue. Hope you enjoyed it, sorry again for the delay. From here on out things will really be happening, so make sure your subscriptions are up to date. *And don't forget to keep on shakin'!!*

--Greg Shaw

FEEDBACKKKKKKKKKKKK
SUNN
letters
Kinney

Dear Greg,

WPTB's numbers 7,8,and 9 just arrived-many thanks. No. 8 is very impressive, but I have a few quibbles.

1. Music hall in England was a native form of pop music and was not an outgrowth of Vaudeville. It related to traditional, rural folk music as urban blues related to country blues if you can buy that. When people began gathering in cities in the early 19th century (industrial revolution etc.) they sought their leisure in beer houses/gin palaces/pubs; singers and songs got louder, cruder and began to mix with politics, speeches, comics etc. it was an entertainment created by common people out of their own experience. In the hey day of music hall(the 1890's) the scene was quite like black culture-thousands of local pubs and halls, in the big cities, huge halls with endless bills, good and bad (like the Apollo.) It was then that people realized that there was a mass market which could be tapped by professionals-the 1900's saw the development of tin pan alley (the music publishing business, pushing your ballads and clever lyrics), 'star' performers, package tours (including from America, Buffalo Bill, vaudeville, and the first introduction into England of 'coon' acts, minstrels, dances.)

The essence of music hall was the message rather than the medium, and the message-- working class solidarity, humour, political comment, warmth -- has survived, just about. The best rock account is the Stones' ambiguous "Salt of the Earth." By the 1920s the mass medium, pop music as such, was show-biz, itself heavily Americanized -- we did get the jazz and blues influences and like you had a huge swing/big band craze. I read someone's memories of being a teenager in Salford (Lancashire) in the 1920s -- he used to dress sharp, hang around street corners in a gang, go to dance halls and learn all the newest American dances -- sounds familiar! The roots of the '40s jazz revivalism were the kids who grew up in the thirties and found fellow jazz purists in the army during the war. England wasn't as dead as you suggest -- the best account of the scene during this period is in Francis Newton's The Jazz Scene (a Penguin in England.)

2. I'm sure the reason why recorded rock (except the Shadows) was so pathetic was because the structure of the music industry hadn't changed since its creation in the 1920's -- no local markets, no independent record companies/producers/studios, no way to handle teenagers -- it was dominated by music publishers (the machinations of men like Dick James are significant for English rock to this day.) We were as good fans of rock 'n' roll as anyone but performers couldn't get off the ground because of the Norrie Paramours and Larry Parnes who were hung round their necks -- this affected the songs they had to sing them in, etc.. Charlie's book (The Sound of the City by Charlie Gillett) confirms this effect of the English music business, so do two other good descriptions of the 1950's: George Melly's Owning Up (an English Penguin) (he was in a trad band at the time) and Eddie Rogers' Tin Pan Alley (I don't know the publisher) -- an implicit account by one of its stalwarts of why the industry was threatened by rock 'n' roll.

Nambie pambies yeah -- but you never went to the pubs and halls where most of the native (unrecorded) rockers played. I was too young but I heard about the blood and the raunch -- the music can't have been all soft (it's time someone remembered those days first-hand.) Lack of commitment and conviction? Well, it took time to become an ingrained rocker and, fuck it, those groups hadn't been doing nothing between hearing Bill Haley and exploding into the Mersey Sound. You should get something written on the German Club scene and how it kept the lads going until they were tough enough to ignore English show-biz. That's the big thing they did -- Beatles, Alexis Korner and the mates, pirates -- and the details of that story (not just a musical one) have still to be written. (Meanwhile show biz is fighting back. England's too bloody small. Robert Stigwood etc. are too bloody powerful.)

3. Jet Harris was about the first bad boy of English pop (Terry Dene was the very first.) When he got done for dope I fell in love with Billie Davis as she promised, through her tears: "I will stand by him forever." She didn't. She did make a great record -- "Tell Him," a cover of the American hit by the Exciters (who also did the original "Doo Wah Diddy Diddy".) She had been the voice for Mike Sarne (on "Will I What " or "Come Outside" or both) who went on to Myra Breckenridge. She's still about and I read somewhere that she's going 'heavy' (i.e. on to the college circuit)--she's a good singer but her material is usually lousy. There's another (brief) story for you -- England's female rock history.

4. The Troggs made "Lost Girl"/"Yellow in Me" for CBS before "Wild Thing." Nobody bought it so CBS turned "Wild Thing" down. Larry Page was the Kinks' first manager and also handled the Riot Squad (Mitch Mitchell on drums I think.) He found "Wild Thing" in a pile of demos (Made by Chip Taylor himself according to Reg Presley) together with "Did You Ever Have to Make Up Your Mind," which the Troggs also prepared -- imagine if they'd released that instead!! As it was they were beaten to release by the Hedgehoppers Anonymous, who had had a hit with Jonathan King's "Good News Week" and followed up with a close harmony version of "Wild Thing"!!

SIMON FRITH
London

.....Received Bomps coupla day ago and can't hardly wait to write to you with grateful thanks and admiration for both issues. After all the rubbish and self-indulgent one-upmanship of Creem and Creem, (do you see U.K. Cream and Zigzag?) they are a joy -- read 'em both from cover to cover with almost total enjoyment. The weakest stuff, to my taste, comes from the professionals amongst your contributors -- like at least one of your correspondents I find Lester Bangs a bit much--praps it's a Transatlantic thing but I find it difficult to follow what he's on about. But that's a petty gripe--they really are magnificent --graphics and all. What I really like is the stuff like the Wanda Jackson piece--really loving felt writing. I've never heard Wanda to my knowledge, but that bloke has convinced me that she's the greatest white she-rocker ever without me listening to a note.

One or two bits of trivia in relation to 8 and 9 which may interest you. Zoot Money now playing in Grimms Roadshow--an amalgam of poets and musicians comprising Scaffold, Neil Innes (of Bonzos), Adrian Henri and Brian Patten (poets) and bass and drummer.

Alan Caddy was co-producer (with Steve Rowland) of an LP called THE BROTHERHOOD (1966) of two London street musicians -- or buskers -- Don Partridge and Pat Keane. Don Partridge went on to have a couple of hit singles and just recently I saw a film with Tom Courtney called Otley (about 1969) which Partridge did music for.

Adam Faith, now very successful TV actor in Cockney Sparrow series called "Budgie" -- no singing, he's grown his hair long and the boutiques are selling Budgie posters and Budgie jackets -- it's an amazing comeback and he really is good in the part -- he may well end up as the most successful survivor from that era.

Just after Trems and Poole split I met Poole at a party -- very sad. Trems' first single had just make Number One but Poole insisted it was a flash in the pan and they couldn't make it without him. In fact he's done nothing but is still working the clubs.

Terry Dene was singer from Steele era -- closest English singer to Elvis -- they even made the movie, The Terry Dene Story -- very erratic, nervous breakdowns, drink, broken marriage to English girl singer Edna Savage. Rather like Jet Harris. Now does evangelical work, "How the Lord rescued me from the evils of show business."

Rumors of Jet Harris gigging around again. Hope it's true.

Some People first English film about pop ever to get it right (even if only in some respects.) Good scenes of rock bands getting together and learning to play. Ray Brooks, actor who played leader of group, now making records himself and just brought out LP. "Eagles" sounded OK in film to me but records were poor. I regard it as an important pop film tho, for all its faults.

I think most kids interested in rock in late fifties here were so interested that they really dug out information and although they wouldn't have chance of seeing performers as often as their American counterparts they probably knew as much about music-it's probably safe to say that early English rock performers consciously knew a great deal about their influences and sources

Anyway, Greg, rest assured that rock lives in U.K. -- radio is a joy at the moment with everybody, yes everybody, playing old rock and reissues falling like rain.

JEFF CLOVES

I enjoy reading good or bad articles on Buddy Holly -- I personally think that Greil Marcus is not a fan of Buddy Holly & the Crickets. First, it was not the same Crickets who made the LP ROCKING 50's R&R as the musicians who accompanied Buddy Holly on his last trip, who included Waylon Jennings, Earl Senk and Tommy Allsup. (By the way, it was W. Jennings who gave his seat at the last minute to the Big Bopper -- so at least a Cricket was big enought to be invited.)

JEAN-PIERRE CHAPADOS

I never thought of rock & roll's popularity attracting so many young musicians before, but it makes a lot of sense. The majority of both classical and jazz musicians were introduced to their instruments because their parents forced them to take lessons. But rock players picked up guitars and drums because they wanted to, not because they were under pressure to do so. There was no parental compulsion; discouragement, if anything. And of course, early rock did not require vast amounts of technique (which is not to say that certain musicians did not possess this technique,) so a player could pick up a few bucks and a few girls without years of patient study and boring chord lessons and the like. But lack of formal study had its benefits; there were no standards that had to be met in that you did not have to play in one certain "legitimate" way as classical musicians are forced to do (though less so now.) so depending on amount of training and what sounded good to the player, he was able to develop his own style quite easily, even unconsciously. There was also no pressure to stick to tried-and-true constructions, so deviants were not frowned upon, unless they were a little too blatant. Does that make any sense?

As for the record people who should be written about, how about Major Bill Smith, Bob Crewe (with and without Frank Slay), Joe Cuoghi, Jim Monsour, Rene Hall, Nik Venet, Sam Charters, Shel Talmy, Jesse Stone, Sill/Hazlewood, Harry Carlson, Norman Petty, Carl Davis, Hutch Davie, Archie Bleyer, Dave Appell, Bernie Love, Dave Burgess, Jerry Blaine, George Paxton, Bob Residorf, Art Rupe, Ewart Abner, Harvey Fuqua, well the list is endless -- writers, producers, arrangers, studio musicians, maybe even a few engineers.

I haven't heard much English '50's rock, but judging from the little I have heard, it is pretty poor. Too poppish, as if they didn't really understand what it was all about, so they let their regular pop musicians and arrangers run the scene. This past week I saw a 1958 movie called The 6-5 Special, which besides some well-known people like Pet Clark, Lonnie Donegan, Johnny Dankworth, and Russ Hamilton, mixed up such blatantly pop artists as Desmond Lane and Joan Regan, and a few others with supposedly rocknrollers like the John Barry Seven and the King Brothers, and showed just how little difference there was in approach between British pop and rocknroll; except for instrumentation up front and rhythmic factors, both musics were displayed as equal forms of popular entertainment, much like some of the highly commercialized teenage pop that American producers tried to pass off as rocknroll (and succeeded) in the late '50's, stuff like Anka, Avalon, Fabian, etc. Teenage pop, not rock. There were two acts (and that's the right word for this stuff, acts, not artists) that were quite enjoyable to a rocker. Jim Dale (I think that's his name) did a very good version of "The Train Kept A-Rollin'" marred only by the overly-pop arrangement. And there was a trombone-playing (!) Haley type named Don Lang who, if you accept him as an imitator, was quite good.

One thing I was very surprised to learn (and there was no evidence of this in the film, so it may have been a later development, or a highly localized phenomenon)was that England had their own doo-woppers. Screamin' Steve told me such groups as the Escorts, Drifters, Swallows, and Bopniks have quite a following, but I've never heard anything about any of them. What do you know about this?

I remember seeing Wanda Jackson at the Chautaqua County Fair many years ago with Red Foley. I remeber her doing "Let's Have A Party" and I'm sure it was before it became a hit. It was probably about 1959, maybe even '58 (I know it was September). This was at the age when we still didn't like girls, but all the little rockers fell madly in love with her. Does that fit in with your answer to Dave Ortoleva?

"Right Or Wrong" was the perfect record of the day. Notice that the melody tends to sound silly when sung choppily. Then listen to Wanda. If she did nothing else, the vocal on "Right Or Wrong" would ensure her of her place in C&W history. She always was best on slow stuff. When someone like Connie Francis sang a ballad, she sounded as if she were wallowing in passionate tears. Wanda's twinge had that touch of remorse, but she was always in complete control of her emotions. And that's great singing. I sorta lost track of her a couple years after that, though "Tears Will Be the Chaser for Your Wine" was a decent enough record. Too much of her recent stuff is over-arranged. You know what I think of "modern" country music. The big production jobs prevent me from getting close to the singer or to the song. Maybe I should listen to recent Wanda again, blotting out the arrangement if possible.

Hound Dog George Lorenz, died on Memorial Day. I don't know how history will treat him, and already his national status as a rocknroll radio pioneer is not high, but there is no question that he influenced a lot of people in this area, myself no less than any other, and he was one of the very first to play race music on a lily-white station anywhere, so I'm sure at least a few people will regard him kindly. Someone once said that he invented the oldie-but-goodie concept on WKBW, but I knew he was doing oldies on WJJL in Niagara Falls even before his KBW days. Are there any other challengers for the OBG-inventor-crown anywhere?

TOM BINGHAM

.....Years ago, in '64 and then '65, I traveled around 10,000 miles by bus seeing the Rolling Stones when they toured... I'm not too shy but I'm a nervous type, and for a nervous type I had a grand time. Wrote a seven page story about my first trip in '64 to the Chicago Tribune and they printed it in their Sunday Magazine section; missed a concert; missed buses; met the Stones; got backstage a number of times; got interviewed over the radio in Louisville in the middle of the night when I was dead tired (I wish I could hear it now, I bet it was funny); saw shows in Chicago, Detroit, Milwaukee, San Bernardino, Sacramento, Long Beach, Dallas, Ft. Worth, and a fe other places; stayed at the same hotel as the Stones for several days, and on the same floor, with Andrew Oldham and Terry Knight across the hall from my room and the Stones down at the end of the hall; had an article in Hit Parader about the second time I traveled to see them. So, a little shy maybe even nervous, but I do have a sense of adventure.

But Kim Fowley, I like him more than I liked the Stones! And I'd rather know him than have ever met them.

I once went to a Ku Klux Klan rally, it was an open rally, at night, in a cow pasture, had someone drop me off and I told them to pick me up at a certain time, so I was all by myself, when I was 18 or so, all because I wanted to take pictures. But I didn't have a good camera so only got a few and they weren't good, well, one was, but the negative got lost sad to say. One Klansman with a handgun and a shotgun kept telling me to move back every time I tried to get closer to the speaker so I could get pictures. Brian Jones liked the pictures and he wanted a Klansman robe, so when I got back from Detroit, I got the names of some local members and merrily proceeded to call them and ask if they knew where I could get one. Of course no one even admitted that they knew what I was talking about but I tried. I even wrote the Imperial Wizzard.

Yet, to go up to Kim and tell him I want to hear his records, I just can't! Maybe eventually, but for now, no hope.

Oh, that Kim Fowley. Maybe, when I go to pieces trying to hear his records, gather up pictures and articles, maybe when "they" put me in a home, someone will tell Kim and he will send a card.

JERI HOLLOWAY

(- Kim or any of his other fans can write to Jeri c/o WPTB... -- What was Terry Knight doing there with Oldham? This whole Knight-as-Sixth-Rolling-Stone legend needs to be cleared up. Ed)

.....Like Lester Bangs says, the party hasn't been around for a while. I sold my amp and bass a month ago for a lot of reasons, but the main one was that it wasn't fun anymore. I mean here I was, bored by the music I was playing at about the same time I began to acquire some proficiency on the instrument. It's always been more of a rush to play for the dance, rather than dance, but the same thing happens on both sides of the lights -- eventually things aren't as exciting as they used to be. You can try all you like, you can play rock 'n' roll all night long, and maybe one or two kids in the audience like it, if you're lucky. Lots of people requesting Led Zep songs, lots of people too stoned to move, and we've all heard it before anyway. The boredom threshold is low in our generation, and the auditory reaction has set in.

Maybe literacy and writing about rock did it in. If McLuhan is right, and if the Party is a tribal affair, literacy should do the same thing to that tribal culture that it did to all the others: kill. Or at least hypnotize. The end result of this is a change in values, in orientation, to the more easily acquired characteristics of the civilization that post-industrial man (that's us) were supposedly evolving beyond. Thus, articles as beautiful as Bang's require the loss of the tribal thing. While I can dig it, what happend to the resurgence. Can Lester and Greil and you refrain from commenting on it, nourishing it with publicity and newsprint, and ultimately killing it with literacy? If you can, what about the upandcoming kids who are cursed with the literate style? Will they have the wisdom to keep from fucking up the thing they love? It's a lousy situation, all the way around.

GREG BURTON

(-Yeah, I think you're right, but the rock press ain't gonna go away just because it would be a good idea. Anyway, rock 'n' roll has proved resilient enough to get around it. It's coming back again, minus the spontaineity, but having made a virtue of the self-conscious contrivance made necessary by the critical process. So what's to complain about...Ed.)

.....One of the things that really makes the BOMP a pleasure is the thematic concept of each issue. And if there is a BOMP poll about this sort of thing, I'd vote that you should sort of "roll with it" and if you get an issue's worth of good stuff that you'd like to put out, put it out. Anyway, the flexibility (like latitude for the Troggs piece) is a big part of the fun of fanzines and BOMP's quality is always so high that I don't think most readers will mind the temporary sidetracks.

The complaints about Lester Bangs' Troggs article were all my reason for liking it. So thanks for running a dandy article that couldn't have appeared anywhere but in a fanzine (unless Mel Lyman had played bass for the Troggs and Bangs had concluded with positive proof that Reg Presley was a Nark.)

MIKE CULLEN

.....The Journal of Popular Music and Society plans to print a symposium on rock reviewing. All reviewers are welcome to write a piece (gratis -- we have no money) on their craft and how they feel about the numbers of records they get, how they choose what to review, etc. We especially want Rolling Stone, Creem, Rock, Phonograph Record Magazine, and WPTB people. Papers should be sent to R. Serge Denisoff, Popular Music and Society, Bowling Green State University, Bowling Green, Ohio 43403.

R. SERGE DENISOFF

.....I agree with you that among the BOMP's readers can be found the answers to almost all questions relating to rock 'n' roll, so there is no need for an oldie answer men, as David Sharp suggested. As an alternate, I put forth the following: Allow any of the readers to characterize themselves as experts in a given field, list their names and addresses ina regular column, and allow readers to send in their questions with a stamped reply envelope, for a response somewhat quicker than it would appear in BOMP, due to your "regularly irregular" publishing schedule. I for one, would be happy to volunteer to answer queries concerning 50's and 60's vocal groups. Although I would be the first to admit that my knowledge doesn't equal that of the regular contributors to RECORD EXCHANGER, BIM BAM BOOM, BIG TOWN REVIEW, etc., I think I might do well with the average BOMP reader's requests since you don't have a specialized audience.

I've already written to Russ Pomeroy (see suggestion above) to inform him the identity of the "bop-a-cow" record excerpted on Buchanan and Goodman's "On Trial," but I thought other readers would like the answer as well; since they saw the question. The song is "I Promise to Remember" by Frankie Lymon & the Teenagers on Gee GG-1018. The flip, by the way, is "Who Can Explain?" which begins "Um-a-num-a-num-a-num-a-num." How about a feature on guttural rock? ("Mope-itty Mope", "Ala-Men-Sy", etc.)

JIM McNABOE

(-Believe it or not, we've got one in the work -- don't we, Walt?.Ed)

.....Wanna hear what Lester Bangs wrote me?

"...It ain't even rock and roll at this point, it's just a spirit, a feeling that can't quite be described (maybe total tastelessness?), like I was glad when you said in TWG that it's also about TV, sports and everything. I think TV is at least as important as rock 'n' roll, and so's booze, and most of all so's getting laid, so what's all this rock 'n' roll dialectical bullshit running off at the mouth all over the place? A moribund institution that ain't even been around long enough to be a fuckin' institution, that's what."

I think that was great. He really grasped the concept of what I think rock and roll is all about. It reminded me of one of my favorite rock and roll lines. From "Do You Believe In Magic" -- "It's like trying to tell a stranger about rock and roll." Any scholarly disseration on rock is hypocritical of its subject. Rock and roll is great because it is bad. I actually buy albums because they're mediocre. And when somebody asks me what type of music I like I always say "Loud, obnoxious rock and roll." Rock and roll goes beyond good or bad. After all, what is good rock, the Stooges or Chicago? Rock even transcends music. As Lester said, it's a spirit, and I can feel that rock and roll spirit whenever I watch TV, play basketball, fuck, get drunk, or eat greasy hamburgers with lots of fried onions. Try to explain that to a stranger.

ADNY SHERNOFF

.....Can anyone explain the album THE ORIGINAL GREATEST HITS - Greatest Records GRC 1001-1964? This album contains 12 Beatles' songs. All of them sound exactly like the V.J. and Capitol recordings to my ears except "Love Me Do" which has an obviously different vocal. The Beatles aren't pictured or named anywhere on the cover. I can't believe this wasn't recorded by the Beatles. If another band did it they should go on tour.

MIKE WELDON

.....I was very interested in Mike Willmore's stuff on Fame and Money, mostly because it was about a period to which I was very heavily committed (as a listener.) Perhaps I might add a few points which could be helpful to you and your readers.

Fame and Money represented something which might be called the Flamingo Era, because the Flamingo Club in Wardour Street, London was where the whole thing happened. It started, I guess, around 1963, and was rooted in the West Indian immigrant population of Britain. Blue Beat (now metamorphosed into Reggae) had already started, and the West Indians became a strong influence on certain young British musicians who were into R&B. This wasn't the R&B of the Yardbirds and the Stones -- it was a more sophisticated kind of music, descended from the jazz-slanted approach of Ray Charles, Fats Domino and, later, Bobby Bland, and the crucial point was the use of horns and Hammond organ. I remember that we didn't even have a name for the kind of music it was, but I like to think of it as a kind of early jazz/rock, for reasons I'll go into later.

Fame's Blue Flames were always just about the best band: everybody loved his stoned, slurry voice and the way he sang King Pleasure's "Moody's Mood for Love" and "Parker's Mood.", Georgie was always very fond of Pleasure and Mose Allison -- probably his two biggest influences. He also had a knack of digging up obscure R&B songs: "Pink Champagne," "Monkeyin' Around," etc. His regular musicians in the early days included Eddie Thornton (a West Indian) on trumpet, Mick Eve on tenor, Johnny Marshall on tenor and baritone, Boots Slade on bass, and Red Reece on drums. All solid musicians, more concerned with swinging in the jazz sense than with rock 'n' roll.

Thornton stayed with him throughout most of the Blue Flames' life, but others who were important were Peter Coe (tenor, alto), Glenn Hughes (baritone -- a terrific musician who was in a trio with John McLaughlin and Rick Laird, but died a few years ago when his apartment caught fire,) the great Cliff Barton (ex-Hoochie Coochie Men) on bass (also dead -- he got the best bass-guitar sound I ever heard, by sticking a piece of sponge under the strings of his Epiphone, behind the bridge I think) and Bill Eyden (ex-jazzer) on drums. Eyden was replaced by Mitch Mitchell who'd jammed with the band a few times. Mitch was only about 18 at time, but I remember thinking what fantastic chops he had even then, although he wasn't as relaxed as Eyden and Reece. Another important cat was Speedy Acquaye, a black conga player of some virtuosity who was in and out of the band at various times (later also an occasional member of Air Force with Ginger Baker.)

None of Georgie's albums match what the band was like live. I saw them many times, and they used to lift the roof off -- the kids even applauded the solos, like a jazz audience. It's difficult to describe the sound they made, except to say that it was fat and satisfying, with a solid base (Fame playing simple chords on the Hammond) and simple but neatly-voiced horn charts. The rhythm section always cooked.

There was another band that I liked nearly as well: Herbie Goins and the Nightimers. Herbie was an ex-G.I., tall and skinny, who sang quite like Bobby Bland. In fact, the highlight of his act was usually the Bland songs: "Turn On Your Lovelight," or "36-22-36." But his band was outasite. Mick Eve and Speedy Acquaye were there, as was organist Mike Carr, but the highlight was a genius from Barbados called Harold Beckett, who played trumpet and flugelhorn. Beckett played with Mingus in the early Sixties, when Mingus came to Britain to make the movie All Night Long, and now, finally, he's accepted as one of the two or three best trumpeters in Britain. Harry didn't enjoy the Nightimers too much, but he used to get them featured on good treatments of "The Sidewinder" and "Comin' Home Baby" which they played before Herbie came on. Kids who'd never consciously listened to a note of jazz in their lives used to clap Harry's fine solos in a very honest way.

Zoot Money never turned me on too much -- perhaps because he spent too much time droppin his trousers and not enough singing. But "Back Door Man," off his first album, is a minor classic, and his guitarist, Andy Somers, was an unsung original with a lithe, flowing style (Zoot's band turned into Dantalion's Chariot in 1967, in deference to the power of flowers, but broke up in America. I believe Somers is now teaching guitar in California.)

One thing Willmore didn't mention was that Zoot's alumni went on to greater things: Paul Williams to Juicy Lucy, Johnny Almond to Mayall and Mark Almond, and Colin Allan to Stone the Crows if you call those greater things. I don't. Let's see, who else... Ronnie Jones (another ex-G.I.) and the Blue Jays were pretty good, although Jones' voice edged on pluminess; Chris Farlowe & the Thunderbirds were a gas (Dave Greenslade -- ex-Colosseum -- on organ, and Albert Lee -- now Head Hands and Feet-- on excellent guitar) but the only record which represents Farlowe at his best was a two-part single of "Stormy Monday Blues," which he put out under the name of Little Joe Cook.. I was among the many who thought that L. J. C. must be some great, undiscovered black bluesman! The original label of this was Sue, but it later came out on a cheap E.M.I. label, on an album of early Farlowe material. (By the way: Herbie Goins had an album on Columbia called NO. I IN YOUR HEART.) There was also the Graham Bond Organisation, but they were rougher and raunchier, not quite part of the same musical scene.

Anyway, like I said, this music probably couldn't have happend without the West Indian influence. The immigrants provided Britain's first really organised dope scene, by opening small illegal clubs called "shebeens" in private houses, where all the sundry could smoke the best Jamaican dope and buy canned Long Life beer at suitably inflated prices. For a time, they provided the biggest audience for this music -- and you can hear them in the "Rhythm and Blues at the Flamingo" audience. Then it was taken over by the white kids, who elevated Geno Washington and the Ram Jam Band to the top position in the club scene (these were all, it goes without saying, club bands -- small, smokey clubs with low, sweaty ceilings.) Washington, another American, was rubbish, actually, and his band wasn't much better. They took the worst elements of Fame's music, added a patina of Reddingesque hysteria, and bored the pants off everyone who was into listening to the music. But they broke just about every box office record in the whole country. I guess the whole scene only lasted from '64 to '66, but it was great while it happened, and I've never seen happier audiences, with a more genuine involvement.

Fame, Goins, Money, Jones, Farlowe, and their musicians were the reason why BS&T came as no surprise to some people, who thought that the aforementioned bands had a whole lot more guts and drive, and were fun too. (oh, I also forgot to say that the Markays were a heavy influence on everybody I've mentioned.

That's the difference between the Stones/Yardbirds/Marquee R&B bands and the Fame/Money/Flamingo R&B bands: the former were lousy musicians but enjoyed themselves and pulled the chicks, while the latter were great blowers who were sometimes doing it for the bread between jazz gigs and had minimal sex appeal. Naturally, it was the former who lasted longest and were more influential.

RICHARD WILLIAMS

Dear Sweet Jane and Lonesome Cowboy Bill,

I found a reason to write you: I've been set free! It's early Sunday morning -- I'm beginning to see the light (but who loves the sun?) (I do) while listening to some rock and roll music on the stereo and waiting for the man. Femme fatale, head held high, long blonde hair streaming, pale blue eyes gleaming is trying to lay some kinda love on me but I haven't got the time --time now.

Candy says Jesus knows what goes on and that we should cool it down even though it's the new age. Well here she comes now and there she goes again.

Meanwhile, I'm taking the train around the band to meet European Son who is bringing us a gift of heroin plus some bread for Lady Godiva's operation. (Speaking of her, I heard her call my name last night) When I went to her room she told me she though she heard the black angels death song. I told her not to worry because Billy, Sally, Waldo, Marsha, Sheila et al will run, run, run, like white light white heat down Fifth

The Velvet Underground, ca. 1966

Avenue to keep her company after the operation. Candy said "I'll be your mirror if you like." Lady Godiva said that she'd feel so much better when it was over and done with. Then she could put on her boots of shiny leather and be Venus in furs once again. She'd sleep for a million years and then a sweet nothin' would be better than enjoying all tomorrow parties.

Well, that's the story of my life up to now, let's hear from you.

Love,
SISTER RAY

PS.S They never did solve that after-hours mystery which I was sent up for.

.....Lester Bangs' article on the Troggs excited the hell out of me. It's just fantastic to read someone's views that are as pointedly right on as his. I Had told myself long ago that no one shared my views so I might as well learn to live with it, well, Lester knows! I am sick of all the groups these days. Bands with no class, no pull, no charisma to speak of, and no sex. There are a few exceptions, but for the most part every band just doesn't have it. I'd give twenty years of my life to go back and spend from 1960-1968 in England. Well, perhaps only ten years. I have hopes for the future. Another band is going to come along and knock everybody on their ass. They may start slow and take a while but they'll grow into something that will really do everybody in. They won't be today's musicians, but real freaks, throwbacks to when music had principles and class when even kids learning to play were after something that completely eludes the G.F. Railroads and the Emerson Lake and Palmers. Throwbacks with enough looniness hyped up by the excitement of creating something fresh to go and do it. And I betcha their name starts with a "The."

WARREN CANN
1150 E. 29th St.
Vancouver 10 B.C.
Canada

.....Python Lee Jackson, the band backing Rod the Mod on "In a Broken Dream" may well be the same bunch who left Sydney, Australia in 1965 or 1966 after dominating the R&B scene there for a good two years. They were called Python Lee Jackson and they went to London without their singer, a blind cripple named Jeff St. John, who had an untouchable "outsider" image, dancing without the use of legs on a stool in front of the band. His voice, not unlike Steve Winwood's, had a fantastic range and the band could cut any crowd up with, as I recall, nothing bigger than 30 watt equipment.

Python Lee Jackson were badly missed in Sydney until the burgeoning R&B scene they spawned produced a replacement, Phil Jones and the Unknown Blues who dominated the scene for the same period as PLJ. This band also split and its lead singer learned piano and ended up with London devotional rockers Quintessence after changing his name to Shiva. I understand he has now left the band, taking one other member with him.

In the mid and early 60's these bands didn't play large gigs or clubs or anything, there were "underground" gigs at private parties, that would charge admission to pay for the band, or student balls. I first saw PLJ at a "demolition" party in an old building in downtown Sydney where they were lucky to escape with their gear unscathed as the buildings' wreckable-by-hand appendages were torn assunder in a beery bevy of student action. The bands recorded little, if at all. When they did it necessitated a dilution of their sound to produce what the fiftyish old men who ran the records companies regarded as a "hit", which they invariably weren't.

The other memorable figure from that period in Sydney was/is Billy Thorpe who has led a band of changing personnel, the Aztecs, since 1963 or 64, Vince Melouney was lead guitarist before he went to the Bee Gees. Thorpe is currently king in Australia if you ignore Daddy Cool. He is definately worth a listen, as I recall has always had difficulty getting his sound down. It would mean a visit to Australia because he has refused to leave even after an offer to live in England from Robert Stigwood, himself an Australian.

There were a lot of bands that period with world-wide potential, one, The Loved Ones, received an offer of management from Chas. Chandler who had come to Australia looking for bands in 1966 or 67. The band couldn't get a release from its existing management and Chandler flew out to sign up Hendrix, this band had a few singles and one or two albums out.

In Sydney the Starving Wild Dogs and Dr. Kandys Third Eye were also memorable. The Dogs' bass player Terry Wilkins joined up with a country rock group, The Flying Circus, who after considerable commercial success in Australia, came to Canada two years ago and after putting a northern ice-hard

more FEEDBACK

edge to their sound (more rock and less country, sort of early Crazy Horse evolved) are currently recording.

DREW METCALF

.....I thought the pieces on Georgie Fame, Zoot Money, Graham Bonds, etc. a little out ofplace in your "pre-invasion" English issue, since they were all post-Mersey beat -- roughly contemporary with the Yardbirds, etc. Some stuff on Jack Good's T.V. shows; Adam Faith (the biggest solo name of the time, after Cliff-- he was the soft-sounding one-- Britain's Buddy Holly); Billy Fury; the John Barry Seven (did you know that Barry led an incredible instrumental rock group for half a decade before becoming a composer of movie scores?); Lonnie Donegan; etc. would have gone down well. If you ever have another English archives WPTB, I'll do the lot for you, or sort out some people who can. (Sorry -- on checking, I've just realized that you did mention Adam Faith, but he was much, much bigger than you indicate.) There were, when I think back on it, an incredible number of people who managed consistent success for long periods -- 2 to 3 years in some cases -- before being drowned under the Mersey wave. How do names like Emile Ford, Shane Fenton & the Fentones, Vince Taylor (U.K. expatriot who became a rock star in France) Craig Douglas (he was more like Pat Boone than was Adam Faith), Tommy Steele and Tony Newley (poprockers both, long before their Broadway days), Bert Weedon and the Brook Brothers grab you? They all made at least a couple of good discs. The Four Pennies, whom you do mention, were also placed a bit early. Although musically they appear pretty 1962-ish, their first major hit was "Juliet" in the spring of 1964, at the height of Merseybeat.

BARRY LAZELL

Dear Greg...,

Something I think would interest you -- in the South there is a music cult built around 50's and 60's R&B called "Beach Music" (no relationship in the least to Surfing music). Its popularity ranges from Virginia to Florida and centers in the Myrtle Beach-Ocean Drive, South Caroline area. Atlantic released on album, #8140 titled BEACH BEAT, including "One Mint Julep," "Zing Went the Strings of My Heart," "Thank You John" (Willie Tee) and "Drinkin' Wine." These are some of the most popular songs. "60 Minute Man" has been on the jukebox at Ocean Drive Pavilion for over 20 years, first as a 78 and then reissued as a 45. "Shag" dance contests are popular in this area. This isn't a faddish cult based on recent white imitators. I've remembered this type of music being extremely popular since it was first issued. I believe this is peculiar to our part of the country.

NELSON LEMMOND
416 W. Park St.
Carry, N.C.
27511

(-There was also Atlantic 8191, BEACH BEAT VOL. 2-- Ed.)

.....I don't agree at all with your lumping together Kinks, Troggs, Beatles, Stones, etc. with fifties rock 'n' roll. What makes one kind of music different from another is not just the style but mood and the mood of the sixties was very different from the mood of the fifties.

I feel I'm qualified to discuss this as I'm 32 years old and have lived through fifties rock 'n' roll, late fifties pop, group stuff (Beatles, Stones, etc.) Soul, Tamla, Folk Rock, Heavy/Acid rock, etc. I don't just like fifties rock 'n' roll but can honestly appreciate any kind of popular music except post-1968 heavy rock.

I remember with pleasure the impact of the Beatles in Liverpool and then nationally. In 1960 (approx.) I was in a dim club in Liverpool when a small leather-jacketed figure in dark glasses approached me and introduced himself as Stuart Sutcliffe. (We went to the same school.) I asked what he did for a living and he replied: "I'm playing in a group. We've just come back from Hamburg." "What's the name of the group?" I asked. "The Beatles," he replied.

I had to stifle a laugh. At that time I thought it was spelled "Beetles." They'll never get anywhere with a name like that, I thought. Not long afterwards I heard he'd died of a brain hemmorhage. What's often forgotten about these Mersey groups (& others) is that in the beginning they all played rock 'n' roll and very good rock 'n' roll too. Better, in my opinion, than any of the "revival" groups of today, the British ones anyway.

NEIL FOSTER
VINTAGE ROCK 'N' ROLL
APPRECIATION SOCIETY
16 Coniston Ave.
Prescot, Lancs.
England

.....How about a second rockabilly issue sometime? There's a lot of people left to do one on. Buddy Knox, Carl Perkins, Charlie Gracie, and my all time favorite Ronnie Hawkins to name a couple. Anyway #9 was outasite, I sat down and read it cover to cover all at once, and I've never done that with any rock magazine.

BOB WESTFALL

.....Allow me to answer a couple of minor questions raised by readers last issue. (A) "Coming of the Roads" (Russ Pomeroy) is by Judy Collins and is one her fifth album (also on the Elektra sampler GARDEN OF DELIGHTS. (B) "Stagger Lee" (David Holcomb Sharp.) One version cimilar to the one he describes is by Julius Lester and is on one of his two Vanguard albums. He's right, it's great. The definitve black "Stagger Lee." Lester is a black writer of note (a Guardian column and several books including Look Out Whitey.)

JOHN SIMMONS

(-But was it played on the radio? I think the version David heard is more likely to be something from the fifties, like Archibald's "Stack-O-Lee," out of print on Imperial's HITSVILLE VOL, 2 album.)

.....I really enjoyed issue No 8 and can hardly wait for No. 9. The articles on The Troggs and Zoot Money were great. Anyone who has heard Peter Green's THE END OF THE GAME might be glad to know that Zoot played piano on it. Yet the album is not nearly as good as the stuff he put out several years ago.

Mike Willmore indicated in his discography of Georgie Fame that he had no idea why Fame's last album released in the U.S. was titled SHORTY. It was called this because Shorty was the name of a group of studio musicians who played with Fame on that particular LP. It was make up of Colin Green (guitar) and Brian Odgers (bass) who both played with Fame as members of the Blue Flames when they backed Billy Fury.. Shorty also included Alan Skidmore (drums) toured the U.S. with Jeff Beck before joining Georgie. I hope this will clear that up.

BERNARD WATTS

.....Do you have any ideas where I could get copies of the Troggs 45s "Easy Loving" and "The Raver"? And I know the Seeds have had two 45s in the last year on MGM, do you know what they are and if the group is still recording?

ARCHIE PATTERSON
2326 E. Thomas, Apt. E
Fresno, CA 93701

(.-Maybe some reader can supply the Troggs discs you want. The Seeds are no longer recording; the two MGM records were "Bad Part of Town"/"Wish Me Up" (14163) and "Did He Die"/"Love in a Summer Basket" (14190). I don't know where you can get them.-- Ed.)

.....In a never-ending effort to link rocknroll with revolutionary consciousness, no matter how contrived the connection, I'd like to point out an historical addition to Greil Marcus' piece on the Crickets, the Death of Buddy Holly, and laundromats in #7. One of the national -- or was it regional -- SDS meetings in the mid-sixties was held in a town in northwest Iowa. I forget the year -- it was sometime after Johnny Stomapanto got offed by Lana Turner's daughter and before Ed Sanders wounded Charlie Manson-- anyway, it was before any pretense of merging culture and politics came about, and the SDS meetings in those days were a drag for the most part. A few people got tired of the sessions, they went by parliamentary procedure or Robert's Rules of Order or something back then, and decided to go out cruising the Iowa countryside for a nice place to do some acid, and suddenly a roadside sign to The Town where the Valens/Bopper/Holly crash took place appeared. So the car roared off in that direction immediately, and upon reaching said destination the occupants consumed LSD. Indeed, there are very few events in recent social history which can match the spectre of a bunch of acid-infested SDS folk singing fifties rocknroll at the site of The Crash. Put that in your waterbed and roll around. (J. P. Richardson was The Big Bopper's real name; what was the pilot's real name?)

— Speaking of class consciousness songs (and who isn't these days), the singers of the two finest examples of this are both releasing albums soon, and it will be interesting to see how the lumpenhippy class reacts. I'm speaking, of course, of Billy Joe "Down in the Boondocks" Royal and Dickie Lee, who did "Patches." Billy Joe is the supporting act under Fats Domino at the Flamingo in Las Vegas, and resembles a cross between Tom Jones and the guy who models hip wigs in the LA Free Press ads. Incidentally, it's too bad one-hit singers like Royal and Lee have to be identified by their hits as part of their name. Of course, BJR has a three-part name and a four-word hit title, so maybe it could be broken down to Billy "Down in" Joe "The Boondocks" Royal. When country singer Tom T. Hall was introduced at Nashville West in Tucson a while back, the emcee said "And Now! Let's hear it for Tom T. tell-it-like-it-is Hall! And the funny thing is Hall never had a hit by that name, although he often does follow those words.

Billy Joe "Down-in-the-Boondocks" Royal

Why stop at flash-in-the-pan artists? Why not identify consistent singers with songs too-Bob "Subterranean Homesick Blues" Dylan, John, Paul "Magical Mystery Tour" George and Ringo, Elvis "Love Me Tender" Presley, Carole "Tonight's the Night" King, Harry "Banana Boat" Belafonte, Michael "You Sent For Me Sir?" Anthony, Perry "don't call me chief!" White, John F. "ask-not-what-your-country-can-do-for-you-ask-what-you-can-do-for-your-country" Kennedy, and on and on.

TOM MILLER

.....Do you know of anyone who has a tape of the Roy Buchanan NET TV broadcast, preferably on reel? You should have a special column in your magazine for tape collectors like myself who collect rock TV shows, Shindig, etc.

TONY CABANELLAS
806 E. Main
Belleville, Ill.
62221

(-For now, the lettercol will have to do. I'm looking for the two live Flamin' Groovies broadcasts from San Francisco, myself. I've been collecting information towards starting some kind of tape collectors' society, which I'd gladly turn over to some qualified person with enough time to do it. I have a lot of tapes myself which will be offered for trade or sale soon. In the meantime check out Alan Betrock's rock ephemera adzine (37-06 89th St., Jackson Hts, NY 11372) -- Ed.)

TO TOM HENDRICK:

Well, I don't know you guys.. I was around in the British music scene at the time you mentioned. I didn't buy any English records pre-Cliff Richard because all material was "Housewives' Choice" stuff; of course, there was Tommy Steele, covering "Tallahassee Lassie" and doing quite well, and there was this manager Larry Parnes with his stable of rockers tearing them down in the local concert halls -- i.e. Marty Wilde, Billy Fury, Adam Faith (yes, even he could whoop and holler on stage) Vincent Eager and the inimitable Wee Willie Harris who on one occasion dyed his hair green -- Harris was nothing to do with Larry Parnes, he got his trip together at a Soho Nitery (as they say) called "The Two I's" where Tommy Steele got his big break. I seem to remember some talk show on English TV got all these guys together and they did this fantastic rap on the good old days of rock 'n' roll with some stories about how Vince Eager (I think) did this leap into the orchestra pit as part of his act and broke his arm and scrambled back up and kept on chooglin'. Of course, you had your line of musical difference between the north of England and the South for a peculiar reason. In the South the only source of material came from those records released by American labels as sales items to the public. In the North of England there is a great concentration of seaports and merchant seamen. These guys got themselves into America and they picked up the black records and they brought 'em back and they played them for their friends and all their friends -- like in Liverpool for instance where the churches were trying to get the lads off the streets and into Youth Clubs -- well, they were getting bands together and playing guitars instead of stalking the streets with bicycle chains and they liked the records and they played them on stage and they played them in Germany. A few tunes on the PLEASE PLEASE ME album were versions of tunes that were not available to the English public except on special request and you never got to hear them except on Radio Luxembourg from 7:00 p.m. onwards and in the South pretty bad reception was the rule. Of course, I was lucky as the manager of one of our local record stores was Arthur Sharp of the Nashville Teens who was picking up on the trends as fast as they came down -- and for the record I would like to say that at the time the Nashville Teens were operating they were a far finer band than the Beatles -- but maybe I'm prejudiced. Billy Fury had some hits with original material ("Collette" on Decca and I still have my copy and it's still great) but he was from Liverpool and there was this mucky muck prejudice going down in the radio world (such as it was) about playing records by unknown artists and there were few jocks in those days who were prepared to take a risk. There is still a jock in England called Jack Jackson who has never played a record by the Beatles because he doesn't like them and it doesn't seem to have hurt his ratings one bit, with the housewives) David Jacobs ran a show on Saturdays on BBC TV called Juke Box Jury and was doing his darndest to give people a break but he could only program a few at a time. I wonder if Kim Fowley remembers a show called "6.5 Special" which was originally skiffle artists and then nibbled at rock and got cancelled. There was an even earlier show with Kent Walton called "Cool for Cats" which consisted of taped records and people dancing in rather contrived sets. He had some American product happening but the show was on really late at night-- it might even have been the last show of the evening and not too many kids could sit up past 9:00 at night in those days; I had my mother compromised into letting me watch it and heard Paul Anka for the first time (and didn't like it, may I add) but someone sneaked a record called "When" by the Kalin Twins onto BBC radio and that was it -- I went searching for all the obscure American records I could find, but it was really tough. I was working in a record store one time and ordered 7 copies of "I'm Into Something Good" by Earl-Jean (of the Cookies) and got fired because he wanted Herman's Hermits version and that's the way it was. And by the way, Cliff Richard could sing great rock 'n' roll. If you liked "Move It" try getting hold of a version of "It'll Be Me" -- dynamite. Also, try getting hold of Tommy Steele singing "TallaHassee Lassie" -- it has more energy than Freddy Cannon's version.

I just took a look at Doug Hinman's thing on Davies, Baldrey and Alexis K. Wow, the more I th about it there was a hell of a lo happening at home. This trend wa kind of exclusive to the South. Rolling Stones used to be a local band playing club-circuit called the Ricky-Tick Club which was owned by Rik Gunnell. Rik is now in LA doing some stuff with Rober Stigwood, God bless him. He brought music to the kids in the South-East (and good music -- we had all the black Southern American greats; the Yardbirds, the Stones, John Mayall, Cyril, Chris Farlowe and the Thunderbird John Lee Hooker, Howlin' Wolf, Lightnin' Hopkins) the guess on Keith Richards being on "Country Line Special" is probably accurat tho' I have no way of proving it- I know that Cyril gave all the Stones opportunities to get up an play with him whenever both parti were inclined and definately help them get their shit together by turning them on to whatever records he managed to get his hands on that no one else could get. This is also true of Alexis Korner, of course; but many acknowledgements have been made t Alexis in his time. These guys were a tight clique, just like th Beatles had their clique up North and were getting it all together. But the South was blues-oriented for sure and no sales resulted bu we did have a good time on Friday nights. Funny you should mention Zoot Money. Zoot is in LA and was last seen in the company of Eric Burdon. What he' up to now is anyone's guess but I'm sure it's musical and I'm sur it's cool. I was at the last gig they ever played as the Big Roll Band at Manor House in the Seven Sisters Road and it was as sad a occasion as you could wish with the booze and tears flowing . Present was one Johnny Almond and we all know how well he came alon mind you he was only seventeen when he was blowing horn for Zoot but that was a pretty tasty brass line he had going, old Zoot. Also Colin Green was his drummer -- no a lead player. Brian Odgers bass work can be heard on the first Shawn Phillips album, by the way. Sounds to me like Boyd Raeburn go his information on the Shadows/Drifters from a little paperback called "Me and My Shadows" purportedly written by Cliff Rich so English Ghost Writer Speak Wit Forked Tongue -- and mindrotting trivia would have been a good critique for the book, by the way

There is a fine single by Georgie Fame called "Do Re Mi" ar another called "Do the Dog" -- Georgie used to play a club calle the Roaring Twenties on Carnaby Street that was almost exclusivel Jamaican and those guys dug the shit out of Fame and did their be at trying to keep him exclusive because of his "black sound"; you know, West Indian. He was pretty crazy and used to wear a blue-bea hat and had colored conga players which was unusual for the early sixties.

Zoot Money formed a band cal Dantalians Chariot (from the guy the Bible who had the chariot with all the brass on it that dazzled his enemies) and they made a reco called "Madman" and played a few gigs, the most memorable of which was the ones they played in Cornwa during a slump in the season and took strobe lights along (just ab the first band to ever use them) which was most hysterical and cou be the subject of an article in itself.

I've gotta stop; if there ar any more specifics maybe I can he -- I just realized that I'm a potential mine of information!

SALLY STEVE

(-Thanks Sally; I'll be anxious t hear your remarks on this issue!

WE ALSO HEARD FROM: Ed Hunter, Mike Simmons, Steve Jamieson, Richard Reed, R. Serge Denisoff, Bob Tremain, William Schurk, John Benda, Mike Ward, Terry Hughes, Pete Tomlinson, Cary Baker, John Tiglias, Scott Fisher, Larry Bianca, Ken Barnes, Paul Secor, Robert Pruter, Steve Cochrane, Greg Matheson, Fred Masotti, Kim Fowley, Russ Pomeroy, Phil Fox, Frank Brandon, Eddie Flowers, Barry Margolis, John F. Mehno, Jim Roup, Michael Paull.

THE BEAT
Editorial by Greg Shaw

We saw in the last issue how the influence of '50s rock, applied to the local vitality of a city like Liverpool, was able to create an incredible impact. The same process has been observed in other places, other times. Memphis in 1956, San Francisco in 1966, and going back beyond rock to Chicago in the '40s, St. Louis and Kansas City in the '30s, New Orleans in the '20s etc etc.

What we're talking about seems to be a process whereby the great untapped potential of music to affect people on a major scale has been tapped from time to time, refined through a particular stylistic or aesthetic approach, and focused through a given city or region where some combination of factors has produced the proper chemistry.

In rock, more than in other musical genres, it has worked this way because of the rapid turnover of styles, fads and fashions--or more precisely, of generations. Regardless of what some would have you believe, rock & roll is essentially teenage music; as each generation grows older, its tastes require something more complex, and the big problem in recent years is that a lot of people have been unable to accept the fact that most of what we call rock is not rock & roll.

But that's another tangent. The point is, rock & roll is not 1955-58; it's 12-17. Each generation is influenced by what it hears, up to about the age of 12-13 when many kids get instruments of their own and begin trying to duplicate it. Kids of this age go for simple music, which fortunately is about all they're able to play themselves, so after a couple of years they form bands and copy records, eventually breaking up when they go off to college, or maybe continuing awhile longer, sometimes even becoming local or national stars if indeed there was any talent present. But those teenage years, that's when rock & roll is most important to them.

This is where regional music scenes become important. One group in an area finds a successful sound, others imitate it, the whole thing is refined, and then, sometimes, it breaks out. Granted, most of it is totally derivative, imitative and ultimately worthless. But then again, when you pick up some of these local records cut by high school kids, it's amazing what some of them manage to some up with. With no idea what they're doing, they break all the rules, and occasionally the product is sheer brilliance.

It's this freedom to experiment, combined with regional influences that tend to have more genuine vitality than any homogenized international musical style, that enables major breakthroughs in pop music to emerge from the most out-of-the-way, unexpected places. I mean, Liverpool! Who would have thought?

Most of the Liverpool musicians were around 16-20 when things started popping in 1962. They were old enough to have played in skiffle bands (the British mid 50s equivalent of simplistic rock & roll) and they also remembered and knew the most primal American rockers of the era--Presley, Lewis, Perkins, Penniman, Domino, etc. So there was no question about what music they'd play, and the regional influences provided the rest.

In America, it happened somewhat differently. The generation who grew up imitating Elvis was cut short in 1959 when lone Southern rockabilly singers were forced out of the marketplace by teen idols backed by high-powered moguls out of Philadelphia and New York. The same thing was happening in England of course, and there was a period from around 1959-62 when the two countries followed a parallel course, with local bands playing mostly instrumental music, based on the Ventures and the Shadows, respectively.

Where it branched off was 1962, when the Liverpool influence (an unexpected fluke breakthrough) got all the instrumental groups in England into vocals and '50s classics. America meanwhile was coming off two years of Twist-mania and other dance crazes, which had the effect of bringing an R&B influence into American instrumental music, as well as giving a boost to R&B itself.

By 1963 R&B in America was booming, with the aforementioned dance bands and dance craze records, the Phil Spector style girl groups, the growth of Motown etc. England had no comparable counter-force to its white musical style of Liverpool, which was certainly based in early 60's American R&B, but only at second hand.

For all of these reasons, American teenage music didn't take a new direction until surf music, which had its national impact in 1963-4. Surf music changed everything, just like Merseybeat did in England, and between the two styles they had kids all across the country coming up with local variants.

Previously, local bands were dance bands and nothing else. There were scenes of a sort--the Northwest with the Wailers, Kingsmen, Raiders etc., and other areas with similar bands but without local record labels that lasted long enough to make any impact. But the really prolific local scenes of the mid 60's began developing only when the mixture of dance R&B and Merseybeat was catalyzed by surf music, a style easily adaptable by instrumental bands.

The Astronauts, the first really big rock group to emerge from Colorado, were the inspiration for hundreds of others who followed in their path to create the short-lived but prolific Colorado music scene--ten years before John Denver!

The Astronauts sprang up in Denver, and were soon copied by a hundred local groups. The Wailers in Seattle began promoting themselves as a surf band. The Trashmen in Minneapolis, as well as a plethora of other bands, began unleashing a torrent of exciting new sounds. And so it was across the country. Surf/hotrod music, combined with Merseybeat, produced a hard, fast, simplistic form of music, while the R&B background of the musicians and other factors like the availability of more modern guitars and amplifiers, not to mention the introduction of the fuzzbox, and the added stimulus of Dylan, folk and folk-rock, sparked an amazing era in the history of American rock.

It was an era in which local bands with a locally inspired approach to combining these influences, were able to reach national stardom--a stardom that didn't last long, perhaps, but long enough to get out a couple of albums and a few hit singles, leaving behind the short-lived style known as 'punk-rock' and evolving directly into acid-rock and the 'progressive' music of today.

For a very large generation, larger than that which regards the 50s so nostalgically today, this was the Golden Age of Rock & Roll. These were their teenage years, before they outgrew the simple joys of plain old 3-chord progressions. If you're in your 20's now, they were part of your teenage years.

As promised in issues past, we're going to be examining these local scenes one at a time, along with other peripheral aspects of the same era. Let this issue serve as an introduction, setting the premise for what's to come. The groups covered here-The Standells, Leaves, Seeds, Knickerbockers, Beau Brummels, etc.--each have their own story. Each was part of one or another local scene, and each outgrew it to a more lasting extent than most of their contemporaries. And that's about all they have in common, except that they were all punks, they were all great, and they've all been long overdue for more recognition.

The most interesting thing about these groups may well be the fact that they were so atypical of the punk-rock genre. In my review of Nuggets that appeared in Rolling Stone, I tried to draw an analogy between punk and rockabilly, a connection I think could use some expansion.

Rockabilly artists fall readily into two categories: the handful who had hits (Presley, Lewis, Perkins, Orbison, Cochran, Vincent, Holly, and that's about all) and the hundreds that were totally unknown, regardless of what may have been equal ability (Feathers, Mac Curtis, Johnny Carroll, etc). The odds against the rockabilly artist were much greater than those confronting practicioners of other styles, partly because the music itself was too raw for the masses, and partly because the genre itself was a short-lived transitional reaction to a collision of larger forces that was taking place in pop music.

In 1955, popular music, dominated for decades by crooners and big bands, was being assaulted by country & western, rhythm & blues, and the sudden appearance of a vast generation of teenage music consumers. It was chaos, and when the smoke cleared rock & roll would be left as a strong, fairly unified force. But rockabilly was a limited, intense style that was around for three years as best and at its peak for only a year or so, at the jagged edge where country and R&B first met. As such, it holds a strange fascination to this day, and remains one of the most powerful genres in the rock & roll idiom.

With punk rock, you can apply the above equation almost exactly. Out of thousands of punk records released on weird local labels from the backwaters of the country, only a very few made the national charts at all, the rest were lucky to get local play, great as they were. The punk style was just too hard, too offensive, too insulting to all musical and social standards. The music itself was a reaction to the input of Merseybeat and Dylan on the traditional rock/R&B/dance band style, coinciding with another large-scale outburst of teenage energy. Its evolution can be traced from 1964, but 1965 and 1966 were its main years, after which protest became more sophisticated and most of the punk musicians dropped out or went into acid rock.

The parallel holds up, on these and other points as well. Which is, I suppose, of no more than passing interest except to those looking for more evidence in support of the "Ten Year Cycle" theory. Viewing the '70s in accordance with that theory, we see ourselves now involved in a scene similar to that of 1962-3, with plenty of holdovers from the previous decade still knocking around, and new trends (glitter, production pop, the mod revival) slowly gaining more acceptance but still awaiting a catalyst.

Whether there will be a 70's equivalent to punk-rock and rockabilly remains to be seen. There would need to be a much higher level of teen mania, and at least a couple of overwhelming new musical influences. Obviously, anything like that would have to be a couple of years off at this point. When it arrives, if it arrives, then we'll truly be able to say the '70s have a style of their own. For punk rock, and rockabilly, were to my mind the purest crystalization of the attitudes, stances, and musical essences of their respective decades.

If any of you readers have any comments to add to this discussion, I'd appreciate hearing them. It will probably become a lot more clear as we get deeper into discussing all the individual groups and regions that made up the punk era, and I think the end result will be the most accurate basis for understanding rock in the '60s that has yet been devised.

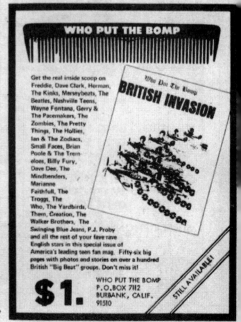

WHO PUT THE BOMP

Get the real inside scoop on Freddie, Dave Clark, Herman, The Kinks, Merseybeats, The Beatles, Nashville Teens, Wayne Fontana, Gerry & The Pacemakers, The Zombies, The Pretty Things, The Hollies, Ian & The Zodiacs, Small Faces, Brian Poole & The Tremeloes, Billy Fury, Dave Dee, The Mindbenders, Marianne Faithfull, The Troggs, The Who, The Yardbirds, Them, Creation, The Walker Brothers, The Swinging Blue Jeans, P.J. Proby and all the rest of your fave rave English stars in this special issue of America's leading teen fan mag. Fifty-six big pages with photos and stories on over a hundred British "Big Beat" groups. Don't miss it!

$1.

WHO PUT THE BOMP
P.O. BOX 7112
BURBANK, CALIF.
91510

STILL AVAILABLE!

In case you haven't noticed, Who Put The Bomp has been a jointly-administered affair since the British Invasion issue. This first installment of what threatens to become a regular column is designed to emphasize that circumstance, as well as to comment on oddball records and facts/rumors/legends which don't fit in anywhere else, to tie up other assorted loose ends, and to allow me to shoot off my typewriter in general. Reverberation actually should have appeared last issue, but we were a bit rushed, having only 18 months to slap it together.

Since the British Invasion issue was assembled with such blinding speed, naturally numerous errors (some of which were cringingly cretinous) and oversights slipped past our crack proofreading team (who can normally spot the alcoholic percentage on a bottle of rum two miles away). We got a lot of helpful corrective correspondence, for which we're extremely grateful. Most of the information can be found in the Feedback section, and the rest will be recorded in the hopelessly bulging Merseybeat Discography Project files (nearing completion but still full of holes, and tentatively scheduled for early 1982 publication--just kidding, I hope). Anyway, we're still in avaricious need of further info, so any tidings you have can be sent either to Greg at his well-known box number or alternatively to me at P.O. Box 7195, Burbank, CA 91510 (fanzine publishers, also take note). All minutiae are welcomed.

Speaking of fanzines, which we sometimes do, I haven't seen too many lately and Greg has a pretty comprehensive rundown (in a non-pejorative sense) elsewhere in these pages; but I would like to register my own adulatory plug for Alan's TRM, which has become frighteningly authoritative and always entertaining as well. And I'll add an advance plug for a one-shot called Brain Damage, which was supposed to be ready last December and, if the publishers get their way, may never come out. Seriously, it is almost finished, and should emerge around the same time as this Bomp does (and there's a helpful prediction). Said publishers/editors are three of rock fandom's most luminous lights--Gene Sculatti, Mike Saunders, and Mark Shipper. I wouldn't want to give the contents away (I sure wouldn't want to sell them, either), but parodies run rampant, and it should be hilarious. It better be, after all this gratuitous hype.

Hype should also be forthcoming for the Rollin' Rock Rebels. I don't plan to use this column to plug bands in general, and I'm not widely known as a bopping rockabilly fanatic either, but this aggregation (assembled by, as you might've guessed, Ron "Satyr Bud" Weiser) deserves all the raves they can get. Comprised of young local rockers, plus that Eager Boy himself, Texas rockabilly legend Ray Campi, and the pride of Boston, Tony Conn, the Rebels mix obscure and well-known classics and rock the hell out of them. Superb playing and singing and infinite enthusiasm make the Rebels an unforgettable attraction in my book--not to mention the mind-boggling spectacle of Conn rolling on the floor savagely attacking his Fender bass (just like he did it in '56 for Life Magazine's photogs). Not to be missed!

CULT 45's: Wherein we examine recorded curiosities which deserve a solo spotlight in the mag. This will hopefully be a continuing feature of this column, and ideas, suggestions, and worthy records are welcomed....

MOMENTS--You Really Got Me/Money Money (World Artists 1032)

I was playing a few new records I'd recently unearthed, and happened to spin this one just as I was reading a letter to the Bomp from Don Hughes. He mentioned an interim association of Steve Marriott's between the Frantics (and his bouncy solo outing "Give Her My Regards") and the Small Faces, called the Moments, wondered if they had a record out; and suddenly (not a moment too soon) it clicked. The B-side is more identifiably Marriott, a rollicking lazily-paced song more like some of the more lethargic Humble Pie tracks or something like "The Universal" rather than the hard-rocking early Small Faces sound. It was written, incidentally, by Alan Caddy of the Tornados and Don Charles, a stock balladeer who did have one interesting Merseyish rocker, "She's Mine", on the World Artists issue just before this one. "You Really Got Me" is an oddly jerky cover, quite interesting. Coming out after the Kinks had already bottled up the hit, it was doomed to instant obscurity, and I don't know if it ever came out in England at all.

JEFFERSON HANDKERCHIEF--I'm Allergic To Flowers (Challenge 59371)

A priceless artifact of 67's floral era by title alone, but a neat record in itself. A sinuous, pseudo-oriental arrangement sets the scene as the protagonist delineates his girl's charms ("she wears a button on her shoulder saying "I'm a Flower Child"). But when she hands him a rose, he's racked with sneezes and wails the title phrase--most heartrending. It was conceived by Dave Burgess (of "Tequila"/Champs fame) and Challenge staffer Keith Colley (who wrote some Knickerbockers singles and had Spanish language hits on his own, plus one quasi-apocryphal disc called "Chocolate Record", featuring the punch line: "If you don't like it, you can eat it!" Any info on that one will be vastly depreciated).

STATE OF MICKY & TOMMY--With Love From 1:00 to 5:00 (Mercury 72712)

This came out in summer '67, with a delightful light melody combined with crashing (though undermixed) Who/Creation instrumental work (drumming especially), plus orchestration again not far removed from the Creation style. It's a mesmerizing record, but seems hopelessly anonymous. Micky and Tommy are surnamed Jones and Brown, presumably. Another record, "Frisco Bay" (72758, somewhat inferior) is produced by Lou Reizner and arranged by Jim Sullivan (perhaps the Big Jim Sullivan of Tom Jones fame?), so maybe they're English (maybe it's even Micky Jones of Man, for all I know). Anyway, a terrific record.

THE CRAIG--I Must Be Mad (Fontana 1579)

Some theorists hold that the best rock & roll is made by artists constantly working on "the edge" (of psychotic crack-up, total breakdown, etc.). I'm sure this demented record isn't what such theorists had in mind (they're talking about lyrical speed demons like mid-sixties Dylan and Lou Reed, more likely), but it's right there overhanging that mystical chasm. It opens with breakneck guitar leading into a pulsing riff punctuated by savage slashing chords and machine-gun drumming faster than anything since Love's "Seven & Seven Is" (an edge classic in its own right), and even wilder. There's a piercing, frantic lead break, and the record is constantly teetering on the brink of uncontrollable frenzy. The most manic record I've ever heard. Produced by Larry Page in early 1967.

GRAPES OF WRATH--Cause It Was Her/For Every Year (Vita 006)

A wild number set to a pulsing two-chord riff, the record sounds like a cross between "Gloria" and "Pushing Too Hard" (musically more like the former, vocally like the latter) with more Seeds influence in the "Girl I Want You" organ. The flip's kind of interesting, too--the instrumentation and the "Turn Turn Turn" type lyrics are obviously Byrds-inspired, but the vocals sound like the Brothers Four or one of those MOR/folk smoothie quartets. Label's from San Pedro, if that helps.

MASS CONFUSION ROCK BAND--The War Rages On/Mass Confusion (Malibu 101)

The A-side is a rather dirge-like protest song, musically/vocally not unlike some of the slow numbers on Love's first album. The lyrics are great, though--"orders come from high above/Are you a hawk or a dove?" --and near the end of the song switches targets bewilderingly:

"People who say they care
Walk with flowers in their hair
They say love is all we need
Yet there's no substitute for speed..."

But the flip is even stranger, an ominous tune punctuated by occasional rock flurries which manages to drag virtually the complete scope of modern sociocultural phenomena into its remarkably murky world-view. Lyric samples follow:

"I walk through bowers of flowers and bomb shelters
Looking for symbols and puppy dog tails"

"Should I smoke menthol or charcoal or mary
Ask Maharishi if God isn't dead?"

"I walk through bowers of flowers and bomb shelters (4th repetition of an apparently cherished bit of deft phrasing)
Wondering if someone is waiting for me
Take out the trash, that's the fifth time I've told you
I'll take my surfboard and head for the sea"

The chorus sums it up, I guess:

"Listen to the sound of our mass confusion
Maya Maya Maya it's all illusion"

D-MEN--Don't You Know/No Hope For Me (Veep 1206)
Don't You Care/Mousin' Around (Veep 1209)

An East Coast band of general obscurity, the D-Men's output on Veep (a UA subsidiary not known for anything but R&B in general) is quite impressive. "Don't You Know" has a calliope-style organ and is otherwise an excellent ersatz Merseybeat tune, while "No Hope For Me" has a modified "Be My Baby" beat (substituting a guitar chord for the emphasized drum shot), organ similar to the A-side (sounding almost like Del Shannon's stuff here) and a fine folk-rock sound. "Mousin' Around" is a forgettable instrumental, but "Don't You Care" is a raucous pop-rocker, not as good as the first single, but notable for an energetic guitar break extremely similar to the Stones' in "It's All Over Now." The group may well be faceless pawns of the Wadhams/Askew team, later responsible for the Fifth Estate and the Blades of Grass--they get the writing credits. Anybody have more information?

This could go on for days (and probably will below), but I'd better hold up for a minute. I'll tack a batch of adderda and other semi-factual oddities to the end, and wind up by once again inviting correspondence, advice, and slander. Also, for informational purposes (not to mention the aggrandizement of my personal record collection), I'm looking for interested readers who'd like to sell/swap records--particularly from Britain and Europe and Australia, but also here in the States. Also surveys (and by the way, did any of the pirates in Britain ever issue printed surveys?). Old copies, xerox/facsimiles, anything along those lines from '56 through '68 (after that they become pretty well homogenized). I can trade xeroxes of '65-67 L.A. surveys and suchlike minor inducements if anybody's interested, but in any case all tunedexes are eagerly solicited.

ODD ZEN ENDS

A few stray corrections/additions regarding last issue.... Gerry & the Pacemakers' "Don't Let The Sun Catch You Crying" was an original song, not to be confused (except by me) with the Ray Charles single of the same title...Dick Taylor remained with the Pretty Things through S.F. Sorrow, as was not reported in the original article...The John Stewart teamed with Scott Engel on the exploitative Tower "Walker Bros." recordings turns out not to be John Maus as I erroneously assumed. This duo also recorded as the Madmen on Cloister 6303, a spectral monster instrumental called "Haunted". Live that down, Scott ...On the Planet label, the Corduroys' "Tick Tock" (122) did come out in the U.S., which probably means 121 (Gnomes of Zurich) did too....

When "To Sir With Love" hit, both Pickwick and Parrot rushed out slapdash LPs containing a good portion of Lulu's Decca material, with and without the Luvers. The Pickwick budget item (Lulu!) has a lot of orchestral/pop tracks from her second British LP, but also includes "He's Sure The Boy I Love" and a couple of raspy rockers (check out Darin's "Dream Lover"). From Lulu With Love is also plagued with slush like Chris Montez's "Call Me" (a British single for her), but has the essential rockers--"Shout", the Stones' "Surprise Surprise", and the sublime "I'll Come Running"; plus "Here Comes The Night" and (surprise, surprise) "Lies" by the Knickerbockers. Everything but "Just One Look", in fact...And yes, Jimmy Page was definitely one of Neil Christian's Crusaders....

Both the Overlanders and Unit 4+2 were rather cavalierly dismissed as "folk groups" last issue. They were that, basically, but both made a few really excellent records. The Unit 4+2's later, less successful releases were often fascinating (particularly "I Was Only Playing Games" (London 1009), displaying Beach Boys-like complexity). The Overlanders cut an interesting folky treatment of Johnny Preston's "Cradle Of Love" (Hickory 1362), but their crowning achievement was "Don't It Make You Feel Good" (Hickory 1275), a stirring beat number with chord changes straight out of Bruce & Terry or the Fantastic Baggies. The song was written by the Shadows (their slightly less sparkling version is on The Shadows Know LP, Atlantic 8097); and it's interesting in light of Hank and the boys' influence on all the American instrumental surf bands that they could also write one of the few British songs that qualify for the vocal surf genre. In passing, all the Shadows' vocal numbers I've heard sound quite strong (including the two Marvin Welch & Farrar albums, good Marmalade-like harmony material)....

Another highly recommended single of the era is Ian & the Zodiacs' "No Money No Honey"/"Where Were You" (Philips 40369), one side a raving rocker, the other a lovely, ethereal, harpsichord/tympani-dominated tune. Recorded in Germany, it was arranged by Klaus Doldinger, a big name in Teutonic cosmic-rock circles these days....

Touring the Midwest of late: the Ohio Express and 1910 Fruitgum Company. Bring back bubblegum...and on that note, it turns out the original version of "Little Bit Of Soul" (a Carter-Lewis tune) was cut in 1965 by a British group called the Little Darlings (UK Fontana 539)...And finally, do your best to get hold of the Creation reissue (UK Charisma CS 8); a truly fabulous album.

LOVE THAT DIRTY WATER

THE STANDELLS

BY GREG SHAW

It goes without saying that the Standells are one of the most important groups of all time. No pre-'66 group from LA could even compare to them except the Seeds, and there were few anywhere who could approach their faultless distillation of all that made up the "punk" style--Stones riffs, taunting vocals, vicious lyrics, burning fuzztone, everything right down to the black turtlenecks was absolutely archtypal. They were one of the first punk groups, along with the Kingsmen and Raiders, and one of the longest-lived as well.

Although they recorded extensively before really making it, it was the entrance of producer/songwriter Ed Cobb that was their turning point. Cobb, a former member of the Four Preps, 'was a punk pioneer, single-handedly exploiting the rich San Jose scene (Chocolate Watchband, E-Types, etc.) and being closely involved in the great Tower/Sidewalk group of labels. It was Cobb who wrote and produced what was to become the Standells' anthem, "Dirty Water."

"Dirty Water" was one of those perfect records, almost in a class with "Louie Louie." Built on a simple yet unforgettable six-note riff, it featured a rasping, sneered vocal and an early Stones harp solo. It was a huge national hit, far bigger than most other classic punkers. The album that followed, their first with Cobb, was a masterpiece. There they stood on the cover, looking like Terry Knight & the Pack, dressed in mod clothes from Macy's "Tiger Shop," looking cool and curling their lips slightly. Inside was one of the best albums of rock's best year. It opened with "Medication," an absolute classic of droning fuzztone/reverberation spiff. And the lyrics! "She does to me what other girls don't do; she blows my mind when she starts to shake." This paean to the fabled Girl Who Does It is followed by an equally classic mockery of the equally fabled Girl Who Holds Out, a contemptuous number called "Little Sally Tease" (also cut by the Kingsmen, Don & the Goodtimes, and others).

Still on side one, we go through a slow filler called "There's a Storm Comin'," and into "19th Nervous Breakdown." Sneers and contempt are again the order of the day, as the Standells pay tribute to the acknowledged masters of scorn. They put on a good show, matching the taut electric fullness of the Stones' sound almost exactly, from a simpler, more earthy angle. And this is followed by "Dirty Water," closing out one of the finest LP sides in all rock & roll.

The other side is weaker, but still adheres to the rock-bottom essence of punk structure. The chords change from E to A and go through all the other time-hallowed progressions with the assurance of Guy Lombardo playing "Auld Lang Syne." It includes "Hey Joe," the unfailing clue that you hold a 1966 album in your hands. Side two also contains "Rari," the haunting flip of "Dirty Water," with great echo-chamber harmony, a driving, yearning plea for a girl to dance, and the best four-bar freakout instrumental break this side of the Yardbirds. But the honors for side two must go to Ed Cobb, who delivered another immortal statement in "Sometimes Good Guys Don't Wear White." In those days we were all eager to be impressed by this kind of high school philosophy (witness the earnest attention given songs like "Universal Soldier" and "Mister You're a Better Man Than I"). But the Standells, while delving into the genre, lay waste to these Ivory tower musings with smug ass-kicking righteousness as they taunt: "If you think those guys in the white collars are better than I am baby, flake off! You don't dig this long hair, get yourself a crewcut!!"

The Standells were well established two or three years before Cobb met them and produced "Dirty Water." Larry Tamblyn (who'd recorded and produced records on Faro, an East LA label) teamed up with Tony Valentino in 1962, and in '63 picked up Gary Lane and Dick Dodd, a former Mouseketeer. In 1964 they appeared in Get Yourself a College Girl, a strange movie featuring the DC5, the Animals, Stan Getz and Jimmy Smith. In it, they performed two songs: "The Swim" and "Bony Moronie." The cover photo shows them in high-styled pompadours, matching tuxedos and ties. In those days they were the classic proto-punk band, their repertoire consisting of work-em-up standards like "Shake," "Ooh Poo Pah Doo," "Money " and the inevitable "Louie Louie." This period is well-documented in their Liberty album, In Person at P.J.'s, recorded live.

It features the above songs in addition to "I'll Go Crazy," "Linda Lou," "So Fine," "Help Yourself" and "Peppermint Beatle." The seeds of later greatness are clearly present, the major differences being the dominance of the organ, the relatively passive role of the guitar, and the reliance on established, over-worked material. But their nascent ability is as obvious as it must've been to Ed Cobb.

Other early credits for the Standells include music for the films, Zebra in the Kitchen and When the Boys Meet the Girls, appearances on "Shindig," "Ben Casey," "The Bing Crosby Show," "The Munsters," "American Bandstand," "The Lloyd Thaxton Show," "Shebang," "Shivaree," "Hollywood A Go Go" and "Hollywood Discotheque." Also under their belts were tours of Japan and Central America. In short, they had paid their dues by the time success found them.

Getting back to 1966, "Sometimes Good Guys Don't Wear White" was put out as a single from the first Tower album, became a minor hit, and was featured on their next LP as well. That album led off with "Why Pick On Me," notable for its near-Eastern ragarock overtones. Its message was the usual one of outraged pride. The source of the Eastern influences become clear with the next song, "Paint It Black." Yes, it's back to the Stones, whose own version of the song was one of the most powerful things on the air at the time. This is less successful than "19th Nervous Breakdown," as the crucial drum part is beyond the abilities of Dick Dodd. Much better is "Black Hearted Woman", a cry of rage underscored with mysterioso organ and pinging guitar notes. The album also includes a version of "My Little Red Book", that's better than Manfred Mann's but not as good as Love's, a kinda right-on song called "Mr. Nobody", and a great Cobb number, "Have You Ever Spent The Night In Jail". They knew their audience, these guys did, and they weren't talking about any dumb drug bust either. When they sing "have you ever spent the night in jail? Well I have..." you know they were there for something basic and teenage, like swiping hubcaps, or cruising around with open bottles of Colt 45 in the car, or crashing a frat party, or maybe even trying to run some old codger off the road. The kind of stuff any kid could identify with.

Though they had replaced bassist Gary Lane with Dave Burke, probably because of Lane's adamant refusal to comb his hair down over his forehead, this second album was a marked comedown from the first. But the third was worse yet, being little more than a shameless sellout. The Hot Ones presents their versions of eight current hits, plus reruns of "19th Nervous Breakdown" and "Dirty Water." Their limp arrangements of "Sunny Afternoon" and "Sunshine Superman" are somewhat mitigated by "Last Train to Clarksville," and they almost pull off "Lil' Red Riding Hood" and "Black is Black," but "Eleanor Rigby" is a real stinkeroo and they should've known better than to pit their talents against "Wild Thing."

Of course, we must appreciate their position. It was now the early part of 1967, and nobody wanted to hear about dirty water; if you were hip, the place to be was San Francisco, blowing your mind with the Grateful Dead. The Standells were lucky enough to even be allowed to record at this point...it's a wonder they were able to make one last album--and that it turned out so well.

Between The Hot Ones and Try It, the Standells were involved in an extraordinary film called Riot on Sunset Strip, based on the Strip riots of summer '66, and released in 1967. I don't know how much publicity those riots got outside of California, but here they were big stuff. The Sunset Strip--actually a mile or so stretch of it just west of Crescent Hts., was THE hangout for kids during the period equivalent to the beginning of the Haight/Ashbury in San Francisco. The teenagers felt the same desire to gather and make the scene communally, but in the absence of a bohemian community to do it in they were left to mill on the sidewalks that connected the various teen clubs and hotdog stands that passed for meeting places. The Whiskey, Pandora's Box, The Trip, It's Boss, Ciro's...the legendary names, now mostly gone, were the focal points of a scene dominated by Sonny & Cher, Love, the Mamas and Papas, the Turtles, P.F. Sloan, Rodney Bingenheimer, Kim Fowley and the Byrds--stars who, in those days, still walked among the people and made the Strip scene themselves, much as the Dead and the Jefferson Airplane were part of the street scene up north.

It was a scene of teenyboppers in bellbottoms with go-go boots, polka dot shirts and Jim McGuinn granny glasses, desperate to escape their drab impersonal surroundings, and finding their only haven in these small clubs that dotted the cold, wide expanse of Sunset Blvd. Rock music drew them there, but those who couldn't afford to get into the clubs, or had just left, or simply liked the street scene better, gathered until the sidewalks were jammed for blocks and the big hotels and restaurants

"Did Pink Floyd belong to the Standells' fan club?"

in the area began complaining that business was being scared away. The cops moved in, made mass arrests, busted heads, and provoked the riots. And that was the end of the Strip scene.

But not without a lot protests, on the street and on record. The Riot on Sunset Strip film, pure exploitation though it was, ("...the mod, mad world of the Hippies, Teenyboppers and Pot-Partygoers...out for a new thrill or a new kick! The most shocking film of our generation!") was the source of a great collection of songs that came out as the soundtrack. Along with a few losers, there was "Sunset Sally," a rare Mugwumps track, "Like My Baby" by Drew, which was Dylan's "Spanish Harlem Incident" via the Byrds with the lyrics changed to: "See the girl, she wears dark glasses...", "Sunset Theme" by the Sidewalk Sounds, and "Children of the Night" by Mom's Boys, a teenybop protest song in the same mold as Sonny's "Laugh at Me." But moving past even these, we come to four real monsters.

Two belong to the Chocolate Watchband, and if the stuff in their albums was like this, they might not have been forgotten so fast. Perched atop the absolute pinnacle of starry-eyed British Invasion vainglory, they scream out a killer song called "Sitting There Standing," a Yardbirds "Nazz are Blue" ripoff just bursting with Jeff Beck power chords and Chicago blues runs, the bass surging along past the point of distortion, and the vocalist ranging from hoarse snarls to high-pitched wails. It's fantastic, surpassed only by their other number, "Don't Need Your Lovin'," which gives the same treatment to the Kinks' "Milk Cow Blues," bringing in tambourines and maraccas to carry the whole production to the ultimate level of greasepunk thunder.

Impressive, indeed, but nonetheless totally outclassed by the appearance of the Standells, with a song so supernally magnificent on a grungy California punk level that it puts those two shining Watchband monuments and all their own previous work in the proverbial shade. I refer to the title song, "Riot on Sunset Strip," which is the quintessence of LA punk and one of those rare songs whose lyrics bear quoting in full:

I'm goin' down to the Strip tonight
I'm not gonna stay home and trip tonight
Long hair seems to be the main attraction
But the heat is causing all the action
  Bright lights everywhere
  Pretty girls with long blond hair
  Whatsa matter people? They don't care!
(chorus)
Just doesn't seem fair
To bug you cause ya got long hair
Even the parents are beginning to stare
Because of the sirens, on our street
It used to be neat, now it's just a place
For black and white cars to race.
  It's causin' a riot. It's causin' a riot, yeah!

The music is matched perfectly to the spirit of the lyrics, featuring an unforgettable guitar riff, every bit as inevitable as Keith Richards' on "Satisfaction," and actually more effective in the context of the song. Frustration and defiance color each word and note. It's also among the most powerful calls to violence rock has produced, capturing the potent thrill of rebellion in a way no one else has surpassed. The only record to approach this glorification of insurrection is the Beach Boys' overwhelming "Student Demonstration Time." Like the latter song, "Riot" features the sound of police sirens spliced in at the proper moments and succeeds totally in evoking the excitement of self-righteous confrontation. If it had come out during the riots, instead of a year later, who knows what might have happened?

Perhaps it was this film appearance that persuaded the moguls at Tower to give the boys one more chance, but they were hedging their bets just the same. Not only was "Riot on Sunset Strip" included, but both sides of the cover were taken up by the most outrageously crude hype since those old "party records" that promised naughty delights untold and delivered only a disappointing collection of tired dirty jokes. "Banned!" It screamed. "The most talked-about record of the year -- the most controversial record of the year -- the most exciting record of the year!" The record referred to was "Try It." Never heard of it? Not surprising; the whole controversy was the product of Tower Records' merchandising division, with perhaps a puny core of truth where some local radio station refused to play it because the group hadn't had a hit in two years.

Certainly there was nothing about the song that lent itself to controversy or censure--as the Ohio Express proved shortly after when they released it as their second single. Whereas a group like the Troggs, whose "Gonna Make You," "Give It to Me" and several others actually were banned, could justly have made such claims, "Try It" was surprisingly tame. "Baby, I can tell you want some action; well action is my middle name. C'mon and try it..." What's the big deal? But if you can forget your outrage at not being titillated, "Try It" is a fine song, in a class with the material on their first album. Another which deserves equal acclaim is "Barracuda," though it suffers from the excessive echo that ruins "Ninety-Nine and a Half," as if a return to Wilson Pickett didn't in itself herald the imminent demise of the group. Worse yet, they were penning imitation Pickett songs like "Can't Help But Love You" and padding things out with old standards like "St. James Infirmary."

But on the plus side, besides the three songs mentioned, we have "All Fall Down," which is truly remarkable for its resemblance to Pink Floyd's "Set the Controls For the Heart of the Sun"--the same basic riff, same organ sound and all, which

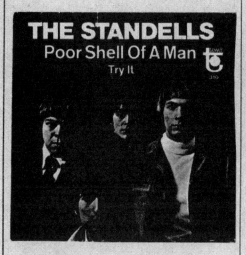

leads to interesting speculations. Were Pink Floyd members of the Standells Fan Club? Not as outlandish a notion as you might think; the song ends in a welter of electronically-produced psychedelia and must've been released about the same time they were looking for a followup to their first album, also on the Tower label. Who knows, if the Standells had taken a hint from their pals the Chocolate Watchband and set their controls for outer space, we might have today a space-rock group that could put Hawkwind, Amon Duul and yes, even Pink Floyd themselves to shame. Can you imagine, "Riot on Deneb XII?" The world will never know what is missed...

But the Standells, alas, were too deeply steeped in punk tradition to venture far from those first ten chords, and they were getting along well enough as a nightclub act to have some vested interest in maintaining their image. So, like a thousand other groups that future generations will surely vilify us for not recognizing in their time, the Standells put out a few hopeful singles and petered off through the land of Las Vegas dates and declining bookings right into the inevitable oblivion which has claimed some of the greatest talents of our time. There they stand, arm in arm with the Trashmen, the Wailers and the Thirteenth Floor Elevators, hustled by an insensitive public into a tragic obscurity. I mean, when even a single like "Animal Girl" doesn't make it, you know Fate has turned its back on a group. So the Standells, when you come right down to it, never had a chance.

All the same, they're still around. After Dick Dodd left and put out a solo album with Ed Cobb, the others found a replacement and kept playing whenever they could, holding down day jobs on the side. I last saw them in late 1972, in a small Van Nuys club, playing the hits ("Honky Tonk Women," "Maggie May") and an occasional oldie for the faithful. They sounded great, although the eight other people in the club seemed more interested in their drinks and their dates. But that's the kind of place the Standells started from, so you could say they're back where they belong.

STANDELLS DISCOGRAPHY

LARRY TAMBLYN
Patty Ann/? - Faro 601
The Lie/My Bride To Be - Faro 603
Destiny/This Is the Night - Faro 612

LARRY TAMBLYN & THE STANDELS (sic)
You'll Be Mine Someday/The Girl in My Heart - Linda 112

THE STANDELLS
Zebra in the Kitchen/Someday You'll Cry - MGM 13350
Peppermint Beatle/The Shake - Liberty 55680
Help Yourself/I'll Go Crazy - Liberty 55722
Linda Lu/So Fine - Liberty 55743
The Boy Next Door/B. J. Quetzal - Vee Jay 643
Don't Say Goodbye/Big Boss Man - Vee Jay 679
Dirty Water/Rari - Tower 185
Sometimes Good Guys Don't Wear White/Why Did You Hurt Me - Tower 257
Why Pick On Me/Mr. Nobody - Tower 282
Try It/Poor Shell of a Man - Tower 310
Riot on Sunset Strip/Black Hearted Woman - Tower 314
Ninety-Nine and a Half/Can't Help But Love You - Tower 348
Animal Girl/Soul Drippin' - Tower 398

DICK DODD
Little Sister/   -Tower 447
Guilty/Requiem: 820 Latham - Attarack 102

ALBUMS
Get Yourself a College Girl - MGM E/SE-4273
Bony Moronie; The Swim

The Standells In Person At P.J.'s - Liberty LST-7384
Help Yourself; So Fine; You Can't Do That; What Have I Got of My Own; Money; I'll Go Crazy; Bony Moronie; Ooh Poo Pah Doo; Linda-Lu; Louie Louie

Live And Out of Sight - Sunset SUM-1136
Louie Louie; Ooh Poo Pah Doo; Bony Moronie; I'll Go Crazy; Linda Lu; Shake; Peppermint Beatle; So Fine; Help Yourself; Money

Dirty Water - Tower ST 5027
Medication; Little Sally Tease; There Is a Storm Comin'; 19th Nervous Breakdown; Dirty Water; Pride & Devotion; Sometimes Good Guys Don't Wear White; Hey Joe; Why Did You Hurt Me; Rari

Why Pick On Me - Tower ST 5044
Why Pick On Me; Paint It Black; Mi Hai Fatto Innamorare; Black Hearted Woman; Sometimes Good Guys Don't Wear White; The Girl and the Moon; Mr. Nobody; My Little Red Book; Mainline; Have You Ever Spent the Night in Jail

The Hot Ones! - Tower ST 5049
Last Train to Clarksville; Wild Thing; Sunshine Superman; Sunny Afternoon; Lil' Red Riding Hood; Eleanor Rigby; Black is Black; Summer in the City; 19th Nervous Breakdown; Dirty Water

Riot On Sunset Strip (Soundtrack) - Tower ST 5065
Riot On Sunset Strip; Get Away From Here

Try It - Tower ST 5098
Can't Help But Love You; Ninety-Nine and a Half; Trip to Paradise; St. James Infirmary; Try It; Barracuda; Did You Ever Have That Feeling; All Fall Down; Poor Shell of a Man; Riot On Sunset Strip

First Evolution of Dick Dodd - Tower ST 5142
Lonely Weekends; Tell the Truth; Stone Blues Man; You Lied to Your Daddy; Under Construction; Twenty-Four Hours of Loneliness; Little Sister; Mary, Mary, Row Your Boat; Here We Go Again

The Strange Fate of Sky Saxon & The Seeds

By Ken Barnes

At one point in the legendary T-N-T Show, filmed at Hollywood's Hullabaloo Club, Petula Clark is belting out one of her big beat ballad while strolling down the aisle through the audience. The camera pans across hundreds of ecstatic girls and enthusiastic, clean-cut boys; but then, as Pet approaches the front, you see this tall fellow in the aisle seat with a big grin and unbelievably long hair, down to his shoulders. He's leaning out into the aisle, and as Miss Clark passes by, she smiles gamely and clasps his outstretched hand, and he looks tickled half to death. The show goes on, but movie audiences across the land must have wondered fleetingly just who the hell that long-haired geezer was....

Turned out he had his own band, then playing the airport lounge circuit and other small clubs around L.A., hyping themselves to deejays, and even cutting a few records, none of which went anywhere. A few months later, however, the guy with the long hair and his band were to capture the hearts of the entire Sunset Strip and beyond, and establish a legend that lives on (tenuously enough) to this day. His name: Sky Saxon (Richard Marsh, originally), and his band was the Seeds.

The Seed's first record, "Can't Seem to Make You Mine," was released around July '65, on the local GNP Crescendo label. It was a completely boggling record, spotlighting an almost ethereal piano (fairly unheard of at the time) and any number of indescribably anguished howls by Saxon at the end of every line. Further propelled by an instantly catchy tune, it was a unique sound, but the record was played about twice and then disappeared. They followed it up a few months later with a pulsing rocker called "You're Pushing Too Hard," and then with a lighter, fast-paced number, "Try to Understand," but both of these failed to score either, garnering even less airplay.

Two fo the early flip sides deserve mention before moving on -- "The Other Place," on the back of "Try to Understand," was a gritty ditty vaguely reminiscent on the Stones' version of "Downhome Girl," with a truly raunchy sax break (a first-and-only appearance in the Seeds' repertoire) and a great spoken ending, comparable to the Standells' immortal achievements in this area. And "Daisy Mae," the first single's B-side, is a Seeds' classic, a hyperadrenal tribute to Little Richard, performed in riproaring rock 'n' roll style with fairly spiffy piano and guitar breaks, while Sky managed to mention all the right girls -- Long Tall Sally, Miss Molly, Short Fat Fanny, Bony Moronie, that crowd -- along with that poshest of thrill spots, Blueberry Hill, in the course of his paean to Daisy Mae (unaccountably pronounced as if she had stolen her first name from a prominent Cuban bandleader). The Penniman-style whoops alone are worth the price of admission (which was originally $1.00, but may well be higher now in collectors' circles).

Meanwhile, the local group Love had scored an astonishing success by releasing an album in advance of their single ("My Little Red Book"), selling thousands of LP's around the area. The Seeds and GNP decided to corner a piece of this new action, and so in the late spring of '66 their first album (The Seeds) suddenly appeared in local stores. A combination of an arresting cover photo and a lot of word of mouth got the Love album off the ground, and the same factors operated with the Seeds -- although their cover wasn't particularly attention-grabbing in itself, the group sure was. Four sullen toughs with the longest hair anybody had seen; Sky hyper-cool in a pair of weird insect-orb shades, guitarist Jan Savage (the Indian of the group) with a couple of feathers in his headband, and Daryl Hooper (keyboards) and Rick Andridge (drums) looking equally surly. I'm sure hundreds of albums were purchased (like mine) out of pure curiosity, and the word quickly spread among Strip habitues and high school cognoscenti. Rumors were soon buzzing about a seven-minute track slated for their next album called "Acid" (!) and the first LP became a prototypical underground sensation.

With good reason, too -- it's a great album, probably their best. The top track is generally held to be "Pushin' Too Hard," their most famous song and the archetypal Seeds tune -- a relentless two-chord riff propelled by the distinctive electric piano and a super-simplistic but entirely appropriate guitar break. The words were supposedly composed in a frustrated ten minutes in a supermarket parking lot (according to Mark Shipper's bulging Teen Screen files), thus qualifying as rock 'n' roll lyrical art of the highest echelon; and Sky's punkish snarl was never more vicious as he spat out the spiteful message. "Pushin' Too Hard" was so good, in fact, that the Seeds used the riff over and over again during their career, especially on this album, where "No Escape" (except for one chord change) sounds exactly like it (on the live album the audience went wild over the intro, under the impression that it was "Pushin'"), and "You Can't Br Trusted" isn't far removed either.

But no matter, the Seeds were true Occult Masters of Plagiarism, stealing from themselves and others with superb taste; and the whole album was laced with outrageous melodic ripoffs, such as "Nobody Spoil My Fun" (another "Downhome Girl" cop) and "Lose Your Mind," straight from the Stones' "Not Fade Away" (the shameless Saxon even sang "gotta love won't fade away" at one point). In addition, "Can't Seem to Make You Mine" and "Try to Understand" are on the Lp; and there's also the frenzied white-noise ending of "Girl I Want You," the mesmerizing pre-Dr. John voodoo incantation "Evil Hoodoo," and the hilarious call-and-response opening of "It's a Hard Life," among many other highlights.

The record company had re-released "Pushin' Too Hard" as a single, and it was once again going nowhere, when suddenly a late-night deejay character with the agreeably cuddly moniker of "Huggie Boy" (an East L.A. legend in his own right), on a basically middle-of-the-road L.A. station, KRKD, started playing the hell out of it (as well as "Psychotic Reaction," both of which he eventually caused to break nationwide, a feat for which he deserves a prominent bust -- for cocaine, at least -- in the Punk-Rock Hole of Fame). Other L.A. stations jumped on the disk, it became a huge smash, and the Seeds began fomenting widespread teen hysteria in the Greater Southern California region. Playing at U.C. Santa Barbara in the fall of '66, they shut down the headlining Jefferson Airplane; and a few months later an appearance at the nearby Earl Warren Showgrounds sparked near-mob scenes and repeated stageward assaults -- even screams. Daryl Hooper seemed, to the impressionable teenaged Seeds fanatic viewing the show, to be the most phenomenal keyboard artist extant, and his feat (seldom seen in that pre-Doors era) of simultaneously playing organ bass and electronic piano was truly awesome. Jan Savage appeared a consummate guitar technician (which he was; no one ever topped him in the realm of one-note guitar solos), and Sky's magnetism was all-encompassing -- the American Jagger, without doubt.

The Seeds were flowering before the days when Dylan made year-or-more gaps between albums fashionable, so their second album, A Web of Sound, came out in late September '66, just as "Pushin' Too Hard" from the first album was starting to hit locally. The cover shot revealed Sky's prompt adjustment of his lank locks to a more conventional mod British popstar length, and the group in general looked less forbidding. The album itself was a bit more polished, too, but was once again excellent (dig the Oldhamesque liner notes by producer Marcus Tybalt, also). Aftermath had just come out and "Goin' Home" had dazzled everyone's imaginations; so the Seeds jumped on the long-band wagon with a 14 1/2 minutes (longest ever at the time) cut called "Up In Her Room," a crypto-psychedelic sextravaganze (perhaps a mutation of that rumored "Acid" track, which never did materialize). There were some electrifying sequences (especially the rave-up ending with "Sha La La"'s lifted from "Goin' Home"), and while its novelty was fresh it seemed quite impressive; but now (thanks to scores of subsequent seventeen-minute stultifiers) it tends to drag and, in combination with a slightly subpar cut called "Just Let Go" which precedes it, renders that side of Web of Sound one of the group's low points.

The other side is dynamite, though, featuring the follow-up to "Pushin' Too Hard", "Mr. Farmer," and five other delights. "Mr. Farmer" was the Seeds' first venture into sociocultural regions and, with all the growing-seeds imagery and suchlike, is a precursor of their subsequent plunge into the flower power milieu; however, pretension is minimal in this number, with lines like "He's always wearing seedy clothes" and "he looks like something from a very bad dream" keeping the tone light. Musically, it's more organ-dominated (as is the LP as a whole); commercially it was a top ten hit in L.A. but had only marginal national success. Otherwise, "I Tell Myself" and especially "Faded Picture" marked a more reflective and melodic approach for the Seeds, the former being very catchy (note the inexplicable overdubbed nasalities at the end, too) and the latter being quite poignant, what with Sky's passionate yearning to return to his innocent childhood and all that. "Rollin' Machine" and "Pictures and Designs" are rockers; while "Tripmaker" is a bona-fide stunner, riffs capped from Kinks' "Revenge" (possibly by way of Jimmy Page's "She Just Satisfies," if Sky ever heard it), and fascinating lyrics (especially at the time, when people could derive immense gratification from recognizing Donovan's "sugar cube" references in "Hey Gyp") about the subterranean tripmaker with his "orange, green and white crystallized powders," not to mention a Dylanesque police whistle, to boot.

After "Mr. Farmer"'s local success in early '67, the Seeds were in solid shape. The Byrds were starting to fade, Love were becoming increasingly erratic, and Beach Boys were inactive, Buffalo Springfield were just becoming popular; so if you were "too old" for the Monkees, the Seeds were tops in L.A. (unless you were an ultrahip snob who liked San Francisco groups). "Can't Seem to Make You Mine" was re-released and hit #2 in L.A., and the group became so big that fans began to pressure the leading pop paper of the era, the KRLA Beat to run some articles on the boys, which were duly published and make fascinating reading, thanks to the hyperbolic efforts of the fabulous Lord Tim.

"Lord" Timothy Hudson was an English hustler type, an erstwhile KFWB deejay who was later involved with such stellar aggregations as the Lollipop Shoppe, but his big triumph was the Seeds. He apparently hooked up with the band around early '67, and began barraging what media there were with orotun pronunciamentos like "The Generation of Seeds will overcome the Age of the Stones in six months" (June '67), and writing bios wherein Daryl Hooper gave his official age as "200 or more", playing himself up as a reincarnation of the great classical pianists; he reputedly got his start as a "stand-in for Beethoven" (a lovely hype, considering Hooper's apparent actual level of keyboard virtuosity). Tim was also responsible for the "Flower Power" tag which adhered albatrass-like to the group for the rest of their career; he had Sky saying things like "The farmer lives by the elements alone, the sun, the rain, and the earth, but the earth needs its seeds to sow the flower generation of the leaf and crying there on the earth below" or, more coherently, "Our sound is definitely not rock 'n' roll. Rock 'n' roll was started by Alan Freed. It's all about baggy pants, short hair, and dull colors. The sound has changed. Our music is blossoming forth with power and color. So we've given it a new name, one that fits the sound: flower music."

The first example of flower music was the Seeds' third album, Future, and the whole trip was set down for posterity. From the florid jigsaw-puzzle cover painting to the incredible hyperspaced liner notes (by Lord Tim and Marcus Tybalt) to the even more videtly florid interior, it's flower power in its supreme ascendence. The lyrics were printed for the first time (previous avoidances perhaps being influenced by mildly embarrassing stylistic quirks such as Sky's obsessional use of the phrase "night and day,' on the first album, in at least ten separate instances on seven different songs); on a profusion of parti-colored petals. Both the archtypal punk raunch of the first album's verbal content and the incipiently psychedelic punk raunch of the second gave way for the most part to beatific visions ("March of the Flower Children," "Travel With Your Mind"), ominous nightmares ("Falling," "Six Dreams," "A Thousand Shadows"), and garbled social commentary ("Where Is the Entranceway to Play," "Two Fingers Pointing on You"). The basic keyboard/guitar/bass/drums sound was augmented (generally pointlessly) by tubas, cellos, stringed harps, sitars, tablas, and flugalhorns; but with all that it's still a fine album, ridiculous and sublime and suited for both terpsichorean and navel maneuvers. The genius of Sky Saxon and the Seeds was to all-pervasiveas to overcome any formal or conceptual roadblocks (well, almost any; cf. the blues album, below).

Hollywood, California
481 - 3705   THE AMOEBA   Recording Artists Gold Chip Records

An obscure, early lineup of The Seeds. No known recordings. Photo courtesy Mark Shipper.

Weaknesses were rife on Future, and the general quality of the songs had deteriorated to an extent. The lurching tubas of "Two Fingers" and "March of the Flower Children," and the inept crypto-raga arrangement of "Travel with Your Mind" were rather irksome; and "Falling," a seven-minute bad-trip nightmare, can be a profound downer in certain moods, such as the one brought on by listening to all five Seeds albums chronologically in one afternoon in preparation for an article. On the other hand, it can be quite effectively hypnotic, and songs like the one-chord wonder "Now a Man" or the obscurantistically mysterioso "Six Dreams" were undeniably impressive. "Where is the Entranceway to Play" contained the immortal lines of poesy, "Like a pheasant under glass you're wilting away," and the album's spoken intro was likewise classic. "Painted Doll" tried too hard for poignancy, and was not materially aided in this pursuit by the odd strangled croon essayed by Sky therein, but it's ultimately sort of touching and amusing at the same time; and "Flower Lady and Her Assistant" made a solid sequel to "Mr. Farmer." "A Thousand Shadows" and "Out of the Question" sounded quite anachronistic, the former because it was another complete self-plagiarization of "Pushin' Too Hard" (with an added gratuitous spoken intro, Sky mumbling something about "I did it all for you, my flower child"), and the latter because it actually dated from late '65 as the flip side of their second single; it's a relentless rocker which is one of my all-time Seeds faves, and top cut on the LP.

Future, even without a big hit single ("A Thousand Shadows" midcharted locally), made the LP charts in the 120's; but then the Seeds ran into commercial trouble. Personal appearances continued to go over well, but a late '67 single, "The Wind Blows Her Hair," was a dismal failure (it was a very pleasant sentimental love tune, pretty but overly repetitious even by Seeds' standards, and not very commercial). As intimated above, they'd started to lose the hippies when "Pushin' Too Hard" became an AM hit, and when they lost the radio boppers deserted the fold as well. And then, to seal their fate, they released an LP called A Full Spoon of Seedy Blues (mysteriously credited -- from a commercial standpoint -- to the Sky Saxon Blues Band, despite the suggestive album title, pictures of the first three Seeds albums on the back cover, and a recognizable front cover shot of the group. Credit Sky with prescience for anticipating the subsequent '68 blues boom, but otherwise a worse move couldn't have been made.

Aside from possible identity crises among unaware consumers, the album was comprised of incredibly inept and wretchedly lame blues renditions, enough to instantly turn off all but the most devoted fans (many of whom passed up this LP and wrote the group off). Today, in small doses, the album is a hilarious unconscious parody of the most dandy species of white blues bands, but at the time outrage was more likely reaction; and the LP certainly had a drastic effect on the group's career. What highlights there were on the record consisted mostly of Sky's low, down-and-dirty blues grunts and insinuating vocal growls, but such transient amusements are overshadowed by the stunning liner notes. First, Muddy Waters deposes:

"I sincerely believe that at last America has produced a group to be another Rolling Stones...When you hear this new blues album, you, the listener, will under-

stand why I am so strong in my belief in the future success of these artists. Enthusiasm, desire, understanding, and above all ability made this session for me one of the greatest ever...Blues belongs to the soul, and they've got it!"

Then a Variety staffer appends an even more ludicrously laudatory LP review, opining that "With this ebulient [sic] bow blues offering, Saxon puts himself in the same league with such heavyweight blues belters as Joe Turner, Muddy Waters, and Joe Williams."

Anyway, Seedy Blues died the death (leaving the unanswered question of what ever possessed Saxon to record a blues album in the first place), and the Seeds' following began to diminish. They took to playing smaller venues, and still managed to attract a sufficiency of fanatic femme fans, but they were on the

downhill slide for certain now. Sky took to affecting a sleekly-styled mod haircut fresh from a Hollywood barber shop, and, rather inexplicably, a white burnoose (fresh from a Hollywood Berber shop, no doubt); and this Desert Chic image must have made a substantial impression (one way or another). But as the group continued to slide, they paradoxically produced a stellar recording effort, Raw and Alive—The Seeds in Concert (at Merlin's Music Box in Orange County; one of the small dives they had taken to frequenting). Humble Harve, a notable L.A. deejay did a solid Brother Jesse Crawford number (a year ahead of the MC5, too) to get things rolling, and the excitement seldom lagged. The LP contained solid versions of "Mr. Farmer," "No Escape," "Can't Seem to Make You Mine," and a more listenable 10-minute "Up In Her Room" (with a few new lyrics); plus six new songs, all good. Most of them shared a strange recurrent gypsy motif especially "Forest Outside Your Door" and (naturally) "Gypsy Plays His Drums," but in any case, all the

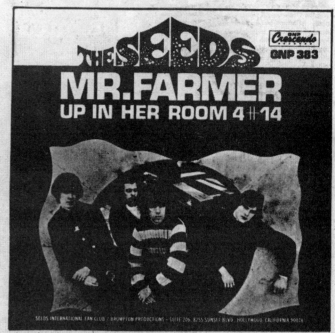

A couple of the Seeds' more unusual picture sleeves. The one on the left was printed full color on an oversize transparent polyethelene bag with a "love & peace to the world" illustration on the back, and is the rarest Seeds sleeve of all.

new cuts are enjoyable ("Night Time Girl," "Mumble and Bumble," and "900 Million People Daily All Making Love" being the stellar novelties). Then there's "Satisfy You," a brand new Seeds classic with killer chords and lyrics from the first album mold, combining sex and radios and TV's in quintessential teenage fashion. The LP closed with, appropriately, "Pushin' Too Hard," with Sky dedicating it to "Society, 'cause it still has a message."

Raw and Alive was the last Seeds album. They continued to decline, playing prestige gigs like the Monrovia (Ca.) Teen Club (in the basement of a suburban church), and turning down other dates because Sky didn't want to "reduce his fee," (according to that eminent observer Lord David Sutch, writing in World Countdown, summer '69). There was a final concert at the Santa Monica Civic which reportedly went quite well, with Neil Young leaping up to shout a request for "Pushin' Too Hard;" and there was a final mid-'69 GNP single, a double-sided attempt composed by the legendary Kim Fowley and current Phonograph Record publisher (then World Countdown editor) Marty Cerf. Covering all the bases, one side ("Falling Off the Edge of My Mind") was a kind of bouncy acid country ditty, with some histrionic grunts by Sky; while the other ("Wild Blood") was a mildly heavy blues/rocker, half of which was blatantly copped from the Troggs' "I Can't Control Myself." Naturally, an ace record, but again a commercial failure.

Nothing was heard from the Seeds or Sky Saxon for two years, but then they suddenly reappeared, on the MGM label (after the dope purge, too), with a single called "Bad Part of Town." Result, instant classic, albeit more scrambled than usual. It seems that Sky had been in the habit of issuing vainglorious proclomations about being the best band in the world during the Seed's ascendancy, and had developed a strong psychedelically-induced messianic complex. Meanwhile, associates and hangers-on were robbing him blind, reducing him to a state of delusional destitution in Topanga Canyon. The MGM association was somehow realized during this period; and "Bad Part of Town" has a decidedly screwloose aura, in the playing, Saxon's phrasing (much last-minute syllable-stretching to fill lines), and the muddled lyrics ("Working in the coal mines of Pittsburgh and Philly, P-A"). It was a great song, though, with a captivating fuzz riff and much throwback charm. The flip, "Wish Me Up," was an oddly diffuse but pretty slow tune.

MGM resolutely released a second Seeds single in '71, topside being a simple-minded flower song called "Love in a Summer Basket," with an extraordinarily ill-fitting rock-out break. Rather dismal, but the B-side, "Did He Die," was quite fascinatingly demented, full of disjointed tempo changes and a degenerated Doors-like monologue about some enigmatic Western killer figure. The record was cut off in mid-scream, and sounded definitely headed 'round the bend.

* * *

As of now, the other Seeds have long since scattered to destinies unknown (likewise unknown is the actual personnel on the MGM singles; the last GNP sessions were quite short on original group members). Sky (now calling himself "Sunstar") has become increasingly shabbier and other-worldly, at one point offering the rights to his compositions for $200 while claiming his new music would sell "100 million" if only some company would see the light.

In the spring of 1973, famed impresario Mark Shipper became interested in cutting a single on Sky, backed by L.A.'s latter-day punk-rockers, the Droogs, to whom Saxon and the Seeds were legendary heroes. There accordingly transpired a luncheon meeting attended by Mark, myself and (briefly) Greg Shaw; Sky was accompanied by a diffuse individual known as "Rainbow," apparently a guitarist. Saxon, sporting a lank full beard and drooping mustaches, boasted endlessly about his musical prowess, relating how the Rolling Stones were afraid to play on the same bill for fear of being "wiped off the stage," how his new music could outsell the Beatles, how he'd been to see God and come down again to tell the world, with constant effusions regarding Rainbow's guitar genius as well. All the while he stirred massive dollops of strawberry syrup into a cup of cold, muddy coffee, sipping at it as if to obtain some form of vital sustenance, but contriving to allow most of the viscous liquid to drip slowly from his mustache ends. He was eager to work with the Droogs, but logistical reasons prevented it; however, we did hear a tape of his latest musical creations. And through all the rambling hellfire monologues and inept playing (particularly Rainbow's), the old Sky Saxon magic was still there, voice as distinctively nasal and cutting as ever, with some potentially (if edited severly) excellent songs.

When last heard from, Saxon had lost his gig as dishwasher at a Sunset Strip health food joint and would talk of nothing but the Seeds' TV appearance on "The Mothers-In-Law" some seven years ago. His post-Seeds travails qualify him as one of the most drastic casualties of the "psychedelic era," but his music, his stance, and his image will endure as classic for the genre and the period. Whether as a warning against the perils of megalomania (Saxon's Stones boast was apparently broadcast from '67 on), a saga of the seamy underside of the rock and roll business (he was easy prey for all manner of financial/spiritual ripoffs), or (preferably) a celebration of some of the Sixties' rawest, rockingest music, the Sky Saxon & the Seeds story is one to remember.

* * *

SEEDS Discography

SKY SAXON

They Say/Go Ahead and Cry - Conquest 777

THE SEEDS

Can't Seem to Make You Mine/Daisy Mae - Crescendo 354
You're Pushing Too Hard/Out of the Question - Crescendo 364
The Other Place/Try to Understand - Crescendo 370
Pushin' Too Hard/Try to Understand - Crescendo 372
Mr. Farmer/No Escape - Crescendo 383
Mr. Farmer/Up In Her Room - Crescendo 383
Can't Seem to Make You Mine/I Tell Myself - Crescendo 354
March of the Flower Children/A Thousand Shadows - Crescendo 394
The Wind Blows Your Hair/Six Dreams - Crescendo 398
Satisfy You/900 Million People Daily - Crescendo 408
Wild Blood/Fallin' Off the Edge of My Mind - Crescendo 422

Shuckin' and Jiving/You Took Me By Surprise - Productions Unlimited AJ 22
Bad Part of Town/Wish Me Up - MGM 14163
Love in a Summer Basket/Did He Die - MGM 14190

ALBUMS

The Seeds - Crescendo 2023
Can't Seem to Make You Mine; No Escape; Lose Your Mind; Evil Hoodoo; Girl I Want You; Pushin' Too Hard; Try to Understand; Nobody Spoil My Fun; It's a Hard Life; You Can't Be Trusted; Excuse, Excuse; Fallin' In Love

A Web of Sound - Crescendo 2033
Mr. Farmer; Pictures and Designs; Tripmaker; I Tell Myself; A Faded Picture; Rollin' Machine; Just Let Go; Up in Her Room

Future - Crescendo 2038
A Thousand Shadows; March of the Flower Children; Travel With Your Mind; Painted Doll; Flower Lady; Six Dreams; Out of the Question; Where Is the Entrance Way to Play; Now a Man; Two Fingers; Fallin'

A Full Spoon of Seedy Blues - Crescendo 2040
Pretty Girl; Moth and the Flame; I'll Help You; Cry Wolf; Plain Spoken; The Gardener; One More Time Blues; Creepin' About Bussin' Around

Raw & Alive - The Seeds In Concert - Crescendo 2043
Mr. Farmer; No Escape; Satisfy You; Night Time Girl; Up In Her Room; Gypsy Plays His Drums; Cant Seem to Make You Mine; Mumble and Bumble; Forest Outside Your Door; 900 Million People Daily All Making Love; Pushin' Too Hard

THE GNP CRESCENDO STORY
by Greg Shaw

Gene Norman

The Seeds' label, GNP-Crescendo, has an amazingly varied history for one so small, and is long overdue for some retrospective investigation. Gene Norman (the GNP in the name stands for Gene Norman Presents), who has operated the label in various forms for some twenty years, has much in common with the men who founded Atlantic in the late '40s. A jazz fan and collector himself, he started his own label as a means of being more closely involved with the music, and gradually broadened his roster to include rhythm & blues groups, among them the Robins, who later went to Atlantic as the Coasters.

This was on the Whippet label, an early subsidiary of GNP, which Norman might have been able to build into a large west coast R&B label on the order of Imperial or Modern. But Gene Norman never put as much effort into developing his record business as Wexler and Ertegun put into theirs, primarily because the record business was only a sideline for him. His real income came from the restaurants and night clubs he owned, with the record label as a vehicle for recording some of the acts that performed in his clubs. So after the Robins, whose "Cherry Lips" was a sizeable hit for Norman, his label was little heard of until he began signing a few of the groups that, as surf music fever struck California in 1963, were making the rounds of record companies, big and small.

Crescendo issued a few surf albums, with groups like Dave Myers & the Surftones (one of the best), the Renegades, and the Good Guys (with their Skateboard Music), and as 1964 rolled in GNP began putting out more and more material of interest. Beatle novelties like "I'll Let You Hold My Hand" by the Bootles, girl group records by the Fashionettes and the Popsicles, and foreign groups like Billy Thorpe & the Aztecs (Australian) as well as recording local jerk bands like Jay Bentley & the Jet Set, Sonny Bono oneshot deals like "The Addams Family Theme" by the Fiends, and local would-be teen idols like Delaney Bramlett.

But none of this really sold, and until the Seeds broke with "Pushin' Too Hard", GNP's bread and butter came from the myriad Billy Strange and Joe & Eddie records issued by the company. As the Seeds proved new teen sounds could be successful, Norman inked more and more local groups, and while none of them went very far, there were some very fine sounds indeed put out by the likes of Mark & the Escorts, the Bows & Arrows, (with an obscure folk-rock Dylan cover) the Lyrics (a first-rate punk band), the Other Half (whose "I Need You" was a fairly large local hit, and a fine punker), the Foremost Authority, the Trippers, the Fire Escape (with a great album including "Psychotic Reaction", "Talk Talk", "96 Tears" and Kim Fowley's classic "The Trip") and so on.

By 1968 both the Seeds and the LA teen scene were pretty much washed up, but GNP continued issuing records of note, primarily foreign acquisitions such as Ola & the Janglers' "California Sun" and "Let's Dance" and Don Fardon's "Indian Reservation" (the original version, and a hit, reaching #20 nationally in late '68). Around that time Norman also put out good records by the Paris Sisters and the Chantelles, and also picked up the Rumbles, Ltd, an excellent teen vocal group (sometimes reminiscent of the Four Seasons) from Omaha, who had recorded on Mercury, Capitol and Sire, as well as local labels.

If he'd had the resources, Norman could have built a group like the Rumbles into a nationally known act; he could have followed up Don Fardon's success; he could have broken Ola & the Janglers, who are huge in Europe. But it just wasn't possible. So GNP Crescendo is still there, in a tiny little office at the very end of the Sunset Strip. Every now and then they get a freak hit, like Python Lee Jackson's "In a Broken Dream" (another record that should, by all logic, have been much bigger) but the bills are still paid by Billy Strange and the other MOR product (the Mom & Dads, Mayf Nutter, Bobby Nelson, the Manzanilla Voices).

GNP Crescendo is one of the last of a nearly extinct breed of small, old-time independent record companies, and it's the kind of company we could use more of today. Even now, a group could walk in with a reasonably good record and get signed, after all the big companies have said no. Just recently, Norman's son Neil cut his first record, a weird psychedelic space-rock freakout number called "Phaser-Laser". If GNP were no longer in business, I wouldn't have ever heard that record, which is reason enough for hoping they stay around. Someday, I have a feeling, the next Seeds will walk through the door, and once again GNP-Crescendo will be a label to reckon with.

* * *

ABOVE--The Rumbles, Ltd, Omaha's greatest contribution to rock & roll, along with the Coachmen ("Mr. Moon"), later known as Professor Morrison's Lollipop. With their Four Seasons harmonies and solid pop potential, the Rumbles were one of GNP's latest (1969) bids for success. The Bootles, below, were one of the first, with their 1964 release, "I'll Let You Hold My Hand". But what they were offering, on record at least, nobody was buying....

DISCOGRAPHY

What follows is a selected label listing for GNP, eliminating all MOR, jazz and other irrelevant releases. This listing is taken from the company archives, so you may assume that every GNP release of interest is included here.

311 The Bootles - I'll Let You Hold My Hand/Never Till Now
318 Oliver Morgan - Who Shot the Lala/Hold Your Dog
322 Fashionettes - Daydreamin' of You/Only Love
325 Berna-Dean - This is the City/What's That You Got
326 Good Guys - Asphalt Wipe-Out/Scratch
328 Delaney Bramlett - Heartbreak Hotel/You Never Looked Sweeter
329 Ambertones - Charlena/Bandido
331 Mr. Lee - Lucille,Lucille/It's a Sin to Tell a Lie
332 Jay Bentley & the Jet Set - Watusi 64/I'll Get You
335 The Fiends - Theme From 'The Addams Family'/Quetzal Quake
336 Popsicles - I Don't Want to Be Your Baby Anymore/Baby I Miss You
339 Delaney Bramlett - Liverpool Lou/You Have No Choice
340 Billy Thorpe - Over the Rainbow/That I Love
345 Gene & the Esquires - Space Race/Rave On
346 Aztecs - Summertime Blues/Whatcha Gonna Do 'Bout It
347 Jay Bentley & Jet Set - Come On-On/Everybody's Got a Dancing Partner
348 Steve Wilson - Pretty Little Angel/When Will I Learn Not To Cry
350 Mark & the Escorts - Get Your Baby/Tuff Stuff
354 Seeds - Can't Seem to Make You Mine/Daisy Mae
356 Bows & Arrows - I Don't Believe You/You Know What You Can Do
357 Ray Brown & the Whispers - Fool Fool Fool/Pride
358 Mark & the Escorts - Dance With Me/Silly Putty
359 Billy Thorpe & Aztecs - Twilight Time/My Girl Josephine
361 Gene Norman Group - Masters of War/Don't Think Twice
362 Challengers - Man From UNCLE/The Streets of London
363 Delaney Bramlett - Better Man Than Me/Without Your Love
364 Seeds - You're Pushing Too Hard/Out of the Question
368 Challengers - Walk With Me/ How Could I?
370 Seeds - The Other Place/Try to Understand
371 Billy Lee Riley - Gonna Find a Cave/That's the Bag I'm In
372 Seeds - Pushin' Too Hard/Try to Understand
376 Challengers - Wipeout/North Beach
377 Billy Lee Riley - Way I Feel/St. James Infirmary
378 Other Half - I've Come So Far/Mr. Pharmacist
381 Lyrics - My Son/So Glad
383 Seeds - Mr. Farmer/No Escape
384 Fire Escape - Love Special Delivery/Blood Beat
385 Delicatessen - The Red Baron's Revenge/The Dog Fight
386 Fourmost Authority - Dance, Dance/Left Hand Lawyer
387 Trippers - Taking Care of Business/Charlena
393 Lyrics - Wait/Mr. Man
394 Seeds - March of the Flower Children/A Thousand Shadows
396 Challengers - The Water Country/Everything to Me
398 Seeds - The Wind Blows Your Hair/Six Dreams
400 Challengers - Before You/Color Me In
403 Foremost Authority - Childhood Friends/Woe Is Me
404 Graduates - Listen to the Music/(The Shape of) Things to Come
405 Don Fardon - Indian Reservation/Dreaming Room
406 Tony Ritchie - Comin' On Strong/Could You Really Live Without Her
407 Renaissance - Goomboy/The Hi-Way Song
408 Seeds - Satisfy You/900 Million People Daily
410 Paris Sisters - Stand Naked Clown/Ugliest Girl in Town
412 Challengers - Chitty Chitty Bang Bang/Lonely Little Girl
414 Tony Ritchie - Has Anyone at the Party Seen Jenny?/You Can't Win
415 Chantelles - Out of My Mind/More to Come
416 Fourmost Authority - Go For What You Know/I Can't Get By
418 Don Fardon - Take a Heart/How Do You Break a Broken Heart?
421 Don Fardon - Sally Goes Round the Moon/How Do You Break a Broken Heart?
422 Seeds - Wild Blood/Fallin' Off the Edge of My Mind
423 Ola & Janglers - Let's Dance/Strolling Along
424 Don Fardon - Running Bear/Ruby's Picture
426 Flying Circus - Hayride/Early Morning
427 Ola & Janglers - What a Way to Die/That's Why I Cry
429 Johnny Apollo - I Don't Need No Doctor/Good, Good Woman
430 Rumbles, Ltd. - Try a Little Harder/California My Way
432 Ola & Janglers - California Sun/Baby, Baby, Baby
449 Python Lee Jackson - In a Broken Dream/Doin' Fine
462 Rod Stewart - Cloud Nine/Rod's Blues
473 Neil Norman - Phaser-Laser
475 Bill Haley - I'm Walkin'/Crazy Man Crazy

THE LEAVES
by Ken Barnes

The Byrds' effect on the midsixties rock scene is incalculable (and prime fodder for in-depth analysis someday), but Los Angeles was most thoroughly galvanized. Folk-rocking Dylan-adaptors sprung up like weeds, and it's surprising no group called itself the Weeds, considering the prevalent naturalistic vogue in pop nomenclature. After all, in just a few months in 1965, there were the Seeds, the Grass Roots, and the Leaves, all with shallow roots stemming from the Byrds, Beatles and Stones, unfolding brash new protest statements and flourishing all over the local landscape.

The Leaves dropped into this febrile folk-rock ferment from suburban Northridge's San Fernando Valley State campus, where Bill Rinehart and Jim Pons had a band. After reshuffling their personnel to include vocalist/guitarist John Beck, guitarist Robert Lee Reiner and drummer Tom "Ambrose" Roy, they landed a gig at the then-thriving Ciro's bistro (where the Byrds were first propelled toward stardom). Attention was drawn, and they were signed to Penthouse Productions (run by Norm Ratner and controlled, I think, by Pat Boone, whom a few of the Leaves backed up on his folky Departures LP on Tetragrammaton some years later) and Mira Records, helmed by Randy Wood of Dot and Ranwood fame.

Mira and its more R&B-oriented counterpart label Mirwood were fascinating enterprises. Among their artists were the Olympics; famed car-song composer and ex-Teddy Bear Carol Connors; the Family Tree (who evolved into Roxy and thence the Wackers); the Gas Company, whose 'Blow Your Mind' was one of the most shrilly self-righteous generation gap tunes on record; the fabulous Bees, worthy of (and slated for) a short article of their own; and Teddy & Darrel, "Two Sweet Guys??" (as the record label expressed it), whose limp version of "Wild Thing" was one of the first instances of gay-rock emerging from the closet (which is where Teddy & Darrel presumably returned, promptly). Aside from the Forum's "The River Is Wide" (later a Grass Roots hit), and Jackie Lee (previously and concurrently half of the Bob & Earl duo) with "The Duck", the Leaves were the labels' premier hitmakers.

They kicked off their recording career in fine folk-rock fashion in late summer '65 with the self-composed "Too Many People". Wailing off-key harmonica and a clumsy but catchy beat propelled diatribes courageously assaulting the ethic of "Work from 9 to 5 just to keep myself alive; wear a suit and tie when I'd rather sit and die" and so forth. The flip was naturally a Dylan song, "Love Minus Zero", given an attractive Byrds/Turtles treatment. There was some L.A. airplay, but no hit.

The next Leaves release was a tune acquired from Frank Werber's (of Kingston Trio and We Five repute) publishing interests, written by a Bay Area folk artist named Billy Roberts but mistakenly credited by Werber to another of his contracted songwriters, Dino Valenti (alias Chester Powers, who, legend has it, turned over to Werber all rights to his composition "Let's Get Together" in return for being bailed out on a dope bust). The Leaves' "Hey Joe Where You Gonna Go" originally released around November 1965, was the first rock version of the song, claims by Love (whose LP rendition emerged before the Leaves' eventual hit recording) notwithstanding. This was a crude, frantic performance, sounding as if it had been recorded in one take. It was sloppier, speedier, perhaps a bit more exuberant than the hit version, but patently less effective (and again, not a hit). The flip, a Rinehart/Pons original called "Be With You" was interesting as well, a highly likable Byrds/Beatles-type number.

The Leaves subsequently re-recorded "Hey Joe", slowing it down a bit, adding some power fuzz licks, more distinct guitar work, and a strong-impact instrumental bridge. With these changes and the already-present relentless rapid-fire riffing and desperate vocals, the song had all the ingredients for a hit and a future folk-punk monument. In April '66 it began to take off locally, becoming a colossal LA hit and all-time (with "Gloria") garage-band standard. Nationally the record was not as all-encompassing, failing to dent the Top 30. But it was successful enough to justify an album, likewise entitled Hey Joe.

Somewhere shortly before the album's June release, Bill Rinehart deported the band he'd co-founded (he went on to the abortive Gene Clark group, thence to the Merry-Go-Round, where for some reason he never wrote anything, and lastly to a 1973 solo single on the Mums label, an undistinctive version of Del Shannon's "Runaway"). His replacement was Bobby Arlin, who'd played around with various East L.A. aggregations.

The album was one of those delightfully derivative period collections, the chief influences being the contemporary holy trinity of Beatles, Stones, and most of all the Byrds (with a bit of Searchers as well). Leadoff track and standout cut was "Dr. Stone," an early marijuana double entendre song with a wild maracca-abetted Bo Diddley/Stones beat. "Back on the Avenue" was a spirited instrumental with an exceedingly strong resemblance (no doubt coincidental) to the Stones' "2120 S. Michigan Ave.". "Just a Memory" and "Girl from the East" were appealing, slow, slightly Mersey-ish tunes (the latter composed by the notorious Bobby Jameson); and there was a straightforwardly tedious treatment of Lee Dorsey's "Get Out of My Life Woman."

The Leaves paid Byrds-homage by cutting "He Was a Friend of Mine," retaining the Byrds' folk-rock instrumental treatment (with some "When You Walk in the Room" riffs to boot) but employing the old folkie lyrics. And Arlin's "War of Distortion," an early psychedelic novelty about "Things that make it, things that dangle; distorted sounds from every angle," full of swooping slide whistles and primitive alternating-speaker stereo effects, also featured the most uncanny McGuinn-vocal parody ever waxed. They also included the Searchers' "Goodbye My Lover," again very Byrds-like, and threw in a perfunctory "Tobacco Road" for added Anglo attraction. Another standout was Boyce/Hart's "Words," later of course a Monkees smash but even then a popular number (also recorded by the Boston Tea Party and Penthouse's Regents, the latter a minor local hit); the Leaves' version is probably the best. The hit version of "Hey Joe" was included, and in addition a more polished version of "Too Many People," with a standout guitar break. Hey Joe was by no means a landmark album, like the debuts of the Byrds and Love, but it was delightfully typical somehow, and highly enjoyable.

Mira could not, unfortunately, follow-up the hit. The immediate attempt was (again) "Too Many People," in what sounds like a third version (differing slightly from the LP rendition), which went nowhere at all. Various other permutations of "Girl from the East" and "Get Out of My Life Woman" were essayed, seemingly everything but the obvious hit choices, "Words" and "Dr. Stone;" but the Leaves never again had anything remotely resembling a hit.

However, they managed to obtain a contract with Capitol in early 1967, initially releasing a single, "Lemmon Princess"/

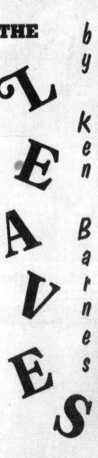

"Twilight Sanctuary," one of the stranger records of an era not exactly deficient in strange records. "Twilight" was one of the earliest L.A. country-rock fusions, full of superfluous whoops and such, but a likable record with attractive folk-rock vestiges. But "Lemmon Princess" was a bizarre waltz-time exercise in diabolical possession, way ahead of its time, with the usual complement of freaky effects and irresistibly dumb lyrics. It was indicative of a zany "War Of Distortion"-inspired direction which dominated much of their Capitol LP, All the Good That's Happening (Flashback).

This album came out despite "Lemmon Princess"'s decisive lack of success; and, while definitely not up to their first, had much interesting material. There were four covers, the most unusual being Manfred Mann's jokingly-autobiographical "One in the Middle," which was suitably Americanized to feature lines like "Jim Pons plays the bass," etc.. Donovan's "To Try for the Sun" is on the surface a straight folky version, but the vocals were so relentlessly deadpan-dumb that I've never been quite sure whether some sort of send-up wasn't being perpetuated. "Let's Get Together" (the Jimmy Reed song) established the useful transition between 12-bar and 12-string blues, and is entertainingly shoddy; while Buffy Ste. Marie's "Codine," in an agonized McGuinn vocal style performance, compared quite favorably with version by Quicksilver Messenger Service or (more obscurely) Sean & the Brandywines' early '66 treatment on Decca, and Matthew Moore Plus Four's original rock rendition in 1965 (White Whale).

Much of the remaining material was quite trivial, notably the 4 1/2 minute one-chord mostly-instrumental "Flashback (The Rhythm Thing)" and the 35-second "Introduction to a Cartoon Show." "On the Plane" was a pleasant slow tune with an astonishing vacuity of lyrical content; and "The Quieting of Oliver Tweak (The Stone Freak)" (by one Michael P. Whalen, who had an album on the Pete label later, an impressive pinnacle of achievement) is an atrocious megaphonic bit of vaudevillian drivel. Two originals, however, "Officer Shayne" and "With None Shoes," feature fairly demented lyrics and catchy tunes (the latter's sounding quite similar to the Robb's "Race with the Wind"), and the overall impact of the LP is enjoyably positive.

But that was the end for the Leaves as far as recording was concerned. They gigged obscurely for a while afterward, and there were persistent rumors of their reforming and recording again through 1968 and 1969, but nothing ever came of it. Jim Pons left the group in '67 and joined the Turtles, moving on subsequently with Howard Kaylan and Mark Volman to the Mothers and the Flo & Eddie band. John Beck co-produced "Lady-O" for the Turtles in late 1969; otherwise his post-Leaves career is unknown to me. And Bobby Arlin formed the Hook (with Buddy Sklar), a most horrendous power trio who had two albums on Uni of minimal merit and were at least three times as bad live (on the second album, the original three were joined by organist Denny Provisor, a long-time L.A. figure who'd made a brilliant folk-rock record on Valiant, "It Really Tears Me Up," and later became a Grass Root). Recently Arlin produced and masterminded a new version of "Hey Joe" by a group called Wonderlick on MGM; the record is quite decent, though the group was rather dismal live.

The Leaves were in no way crucial to the development of rock and roll, and weren't exactly major innovators either. But their one undeniable classic entitles them to a niche in the midsixties rock saga, and their records are well worth the attention of anyone whose interest lies in that direction. To place in the sadly-appropriate past tense the declaration on the back of their first album, the Leaves were part of what was happening.

LEAVES DISCOGRAPHY

Mira 202 Too Many People/Love Minus Zero
207 Hey Joe, Where You Gonna Go?/Be With You
213 You Better Move On/A Different Story
222 Hey Joe/Funny Little World
222 Hey Joe/Girl From the East
227 Too Many People/Girl From the East
231 Girl From the East/Get Out of My Life Woman
234 You Better Move On/Be With You
Capitol 5799 Lemmon Princess/Twilight Sanctuary

Mira LP 3005 Hey Joe
Capitol LP 2638 All the Good That's Happening/Flashback

THE KNICKERBOCKERS

by Bill Small

with additional material by Ken Barnes

The Knickerbockers were formed in mid-1964 during the height of the Beatles craze, as a sort of Junior Four Seasons with guitars. They played at local high schools and colleges in the upstate New York area and featured entertaining stage patter as well as polished imitations of other bands, always an important part of their act. The band consisted of Buddy Randell, lead vocalist and sax (he played with the Royal Teens and co-wrote "Short Shorts"); Jimmy Walker on drums; and brothers John and Beau Charles on bass and guitar.

Their big "Break" came in early 1965 when they performed with Jerry Fuller, a small-time solo act ("Shy Away," etc.) signed with Challenge Records in Hollywood. Fuller liked their commercial style, their straight appearance (the Knicks wore matching charcoal suits with hair styles reminiscent of the previous decade) and their professional manner, so he signed them to Challenge.

The Knickerbockers' first single effort was penned by Fuller, titled "All I Need is You." With great four-part harmony and a gentle bleating sax, Jimmy plaintively declared, "I don't need a bright moon, I don't need the month of June; They say you need these things for true love to bloom, but all I need is you.. you..." ; hardly competition for the Beatles in late 1964 (the flip, "Bite Bite Barracudo," was a particularly lame car tune, written around a strikingly ill-conceived ferocious-fish metaphor).

An unusual and highly obscure first album followed shortly afterward, *Sing and Sync-Along with Lloyd/Lloyd Thaxton presents The Knickerbockers* (with guest vocalist Phyllis Brown on three tracks). The album was made up of stock cover versions ("It's Not Unusual," "King of the Road," and Challenge's own "In the Misty Moonlight"), but with a couple of odd touches. For one, after the songs ended, there was another minute's instrumental run-through allowing the listener to sing along, a la the Beach Boys' Stack-O-Tracks, etc.. And the record featured an amusing gimmick called here "Trick-Track," otherwise known as the "Magic Record," wherein the grooves were set up so that any time you placed your needle down you could get any one of the five tracks on the side, quite unpredictably--very entertaining, a real mind-boggler for all your friends, but a royal pain if you had a passion for Phyllis Brown's version of "Girl from Ipanema" and got the Knicks' "Hully Gully" six times in a row instead. At any rate, as the liner notes said, "It's almost as good as having Lloyd host your next party!" and there was an excellent cover of "I Want to Hold Your Hand" buried within, a sign of things to come.

A second album came out in early 1965, *Jerk and Twine Time*, again all covers except for a single, "Jerktown;" they opened up with "You Really Got Me" and "All Day and All of the Night" (inspired programming), closed with "She's Not There" and filled in the middle with dance numbers.

The third single hit the jackpot, however. "Lies" was an unabashed Beatle imitation, sounding more like the Beatles often did in late '65; in fact, when the record broke in Los Angeles many high school kids were firmly convinced it was the Beatles masquerading. At any rate it became a huge seller for Challenge (inspiring a large-scale label move into the teen field which produced great, --or at least interesting--records by the Brogues, an important early Bay area band, Christopher & the Togas, Don Grady, Finders Keepers, Peter Pan & the Good Fairies, We the People, and "I'm Allergic to Flowers" by the Jefferson Handkerchief. The Brogues and three We the People singles are especially notable for savage hard-edged punk performances).

The Knicks' follow-up album featured accolades from the stars[Brian Wilson: "These guys have class"; Ian Whitcomb: "I think they're tickety-boo (American translation--out of sight)"] and a pretty good batch of songs. Side One was Beatle-flavored material in the style of the hit, notably Glen Campbell's excellent "Can't You See I'm Tryin'" (later a Fireballs flip side) and Seals & Crofts' "I Can Do It Better" (both members of the devotive duo had been members of Challenge's mainstay instrumental group, the Champs, and Jimmy Seals had two singles on his own on Challenge in 1964-5 -- not bad, either). Side two featured a Righteous-Brother-like "You'll Never Walk Alone" and "Harlem Nocturne;" and all in all it was an excellent album effort (arranged by Leon Russell, too, for those keeping score).

On the strength of their hit and their talents of mimicry, the Knickerbockers became regulars on "Where the Action Is," where the decidedly porcine contours of Buddy Randell's face distracted many viewers to a considerable extent and obscured the fact that they were doing some fine cover material. "Lies" proved to be a one-shot, unfortunately; the follow-up "One Track Mind," a similar-styled number, had only moderate success and nothing else really made it. Nonetheless, "High on Love" and "Love is a Bird" were terrific harmony rockers. On the other hand, "Chapel in the Fields" was a fairly dire slow tune, and "Can You Help Me" was dismal funk (its flip, "Please Don't Love Him," was an excellent Four Seasons-style record, though). Near the end, Challenge resurrected "Wishful Thinking" and "I Can Do It Better" from the LP as singles, but they fared no better; the Knickerbockers never re-captured the hit-record elixir.

Later on there were Jimmy Walker solo singles (Challenge and Columbia) and likewise for Buddy Randell (Uni); and Walker "replaced" Bill Medley in the Righteous Brothers for an unsuccessful spell. The Knickerbockers, despite great musical strengths (vocals especially) hit with the imitation gimmick, and never really came up with anything startlingly out of the ordinary again. Mimic-oriented groups, while quite successful in live performances, often enough, have problems translating that aspect to record (and at least the Knickerbockers did far better than their Los Angeles impressionistic successors, the Knack). The Knickerbockers merely made excellent records, but without real distinctiveness. Brian Wilson notwithstanding, it wasn't enough just to "have class."

KNICKERBOCKERS DISCOGRAPHY

Challenge
- 59268 All I Need is You/Bite Bite Barracuda
- 59293 Jerktown/Room For One More
- 59321 Lies/The Coming Generation
- 59326 One Track Mind/I Must Be Doing Something Right
- 59332 High On Love/Stick With Me
- 59335 Chapel in the Fields/Just One Girl
- 59341 Love is a Bird/Rumors, Gossip, Words Untrue
- 59348 Please Don't Love Him/Can You Help Me
- 59359 What Does That Make You/Sweet Green Fields
- 59366 Come and Get It/Wishful Thinking
- 59380 I Can Do It Better/You'll Never Walk Alone
- 59384 As a Matter of Fact/They Ran For Their Lives

- LP   Sing & Sync Along With Lloyd/Lloyd Thaxton Presents The Knickerbockers
- LP 621 Jerk and Twine Time
- LP 622 Lies

BUDDY RANDELL
- Uni 55209 Be My Baby/Randi, Randi

JIMMY WALKER
- Challenge 59392 Always Leaving Always Gone/Drown In My Broken Dreams
- Columbia 44742 Dawn (Go Away)/The Greatest Love
- Columbia 44884 I Got the Best of You/Your Past is Beginning to Show

Last minute addition: Buddy Randell sang lead on a late '71 Paramount single (0126) by a group called Blowtorch. Titles were "I Want Sugar All The Time"/"C'mon And Get It", and sadly it's really nothing special.

THE BEAU BRUMMELS
BY BILL SMALL

Left to Right: Sal Valentino, John Peterson, Ron Elliot, Ron Meagher.

(The Beau Brummels were largely responsible for setting the stage for the American counterattack against the British Invasion. Ahead of their time in many ways, their rich vocals and electric 12-string presaged (along with the Searchers in England) the Byrds and folk-rock. They were the first new American group to score a major hit with a novel sound during the Britain-dominated year of 1964, and they also helped focus attention on San Francisco as a musical center, for good or ill. Interestingly, February '74 brought tidings of the group's reformation (with the original musicians), rendering the following chronicle even more appropriate... Ed.)

The Beau Brummels were formed early in 1964 by lead singer Sal Valentino, and originally were five in number—also including Ron Elliott on lead guitar; Ron Meagher, bass; Declan Mulligan, rhythm guitar; and John Peterson, drums. By summer of that year they were playing all over the Bay Area in clubs and bars, and it was in one of these dives that they were "discovered" by Tom Donahue, well-known disc-jockey at KYA-San Francisco, who was looking for talent to sign for his new label, Autumn. Donahue liked the group's sound and was impressed by Elliott's composing skills. The group auditioned and cut their first release, "Laugh Laugh," the same day. It was a smash.

A lot of credit can be given to Donahue and producer Sylvester (Sly) Stewart here. From the very first all the Brummels' recordings were cut in true stereo and the production was excellent, especially by standards of the time. Introducing: The Beau Brummels, the group's first LP, was released in late 1964 and in many ways was one of the best albums of that year. Unlike most American bands, the Brummels had a definite style. They didn't try to imitate anybody in particular, though the British influence is obvious on several cuts, particularly "Not Too Long Ago" and "They'll Make You Cry." The album has its share of solid rockers (notably the often-covered "Still in Love With You Baby" -- cut by the Kitchen Cinq, Boenzee Cryque, Planned Obsolescence, and many others) as well as some softer ballads. It even contains a standout version of "Oh Lonesome Me" which predates Neil Young's version by a good five years. In all the LP is admirably well-done; the styles are fully developed and highly enjoyable.

Though it's not very well remembered, the follow-up single, "Just a Little" was a big hit as well. The Rascals thought it good enough to record for their first LP, and the single did make Billboard's Top Ten. Later releases "You Tell Me Why" (the "You" added so as not to confuse it with the Beatles number) and "Don't Talk to Strangers," both superb records, didn't go too far sales-wise.

With many mid-sixties bands turning out three, four, or five LP's a year, the Brummels took their time in recording and it wasn't until late 1965 that Beau Brummels Volume Two came out. By this time they had lost rhythm guitarist Mulligan, but they seemed to get by without him quite adequately. There wasn't much overdubbing going on on the second LP either. It's really quite advanced for its time with some surprising experimentation taking place, odd progressions and chording, yet still pretty much good old rock and roll. Sal had begun helping out with the writing chores, and his one independent original song, "That's Alright," is one of the album's best. The group tries some harmony but it doesn't quite come off except on "Sad Little Girl," a slow number with a long effective buildup. It's a good LP, though one gets the idea that the band was trying some new ideas that hadn't quite jelled at the time.

Late in 1965, the group released its fifth Autumn single, a John Sebastian tune, "Good Time Music." This was quite an unexpected turn from their past attempts; rather than Sal up front singing, the whole band tried to work together in three-part harmony. It didn't work, despite the rocking beat and catchy chorus. About this time Autumn was undergoing financial difficulties, and their entire stock of artists was bought by Warner Brothers. At the time this included, besides the Brummels, the Mojo Men, the Tikis (later Harpers Bizarre) and the Vejtables (who ended up instead on the Uptown label). None of these acts really made it, yet their combined presence and direction has been cited as a major force in shaping Warners' attitudes and history. At the time, the Beau Brummels appeared to be the most commercially promising of the Autumn groups (although as it turned out the Mojo Men and Harpers Bizarre had the hits).

It was decided that the Brummels should update a Dylan tune in early 1966. "One Too Many Mornings" was chosen and the recording is an alltime low. Not even Sal's voice can bring this one across; the lyric is at complete odds with the souped-up rock tempo. A bomb and deservedly so. The group's next effort was a Valentino tune, "Here We Are Again," a nice sort of song with nothing especially outstanding about it. The B-side, "Fine with Me," is an Elliott original and quite good. Recording in the big time now, the group used overdubbed voices in excellent harmony and created a chirping, squawking rock masterpiece which always puts the listener in a good mood (It was subsequently a single by Sacramento's New Breed, later Redwing).

Along about this time Warners decided to release an LP by the Beau Brummels. This was summer 1966 and the band was still remembered. Although they hadn't had a hit single, an LP was planned to consist of other people's hits. Beau Brummels '66 featured such memorable ditties as "Louie Louie," "Mrs. Brown," and "Play with Fire," and the less said about it the better. Valentino does justice to "Monday Monday," but in the background some idiot is whispering "Cass...Cass...," wrecking the one decent number in the whole batch. It's thoroughly disappointing and completely worthless in evaluating the group's developing musical progression.

In late '66, the release of Tim Hardin's "Don't Make Promises" transpired. The group performs admirably and the song is perfectly suited to Sal's voice, which by now had developed a depth and resonant maturity which was quite striking. The other side of the single, Elliott's "Two Days Till Tomorrow" is an orchestral number complete with violins. It's a little gushy but enjoyable enough, and perhaps indicative of the group's direction.

Another single, "Lower Level," was interesting and somewhat innovative for the period, but the B-side, the beautiful "Magic Hollow," was a milestone. Singing of magic and mystery, Sal's voice had never sounded better, and the group had suddenly acquired a harpsichordist (who later proved to be Van Dyke Parks lending a hand). In a lilting and wistful fog-echo Sal sings of faraway and "Magic...magic..."

The album Triangle could easily be one of the greatest albums to come from the mid-'67 era. By this time the Beau Brummels had dwindled to three: Valentino singing, Elliott writing and playing vibrant guitar, and Meagher still laying down his subtle bass lines. The Beau Brummels were strictly studio by this time but that didn't matter. Triangle is beyond adequate discription in words; one has to hear it to understand and fully appreciate its merits and implications. Yet for all its beauty the LP was largely ignored.

Sometime early in 1968, "Are You Happy," one of the better Triangle tunes found its way onto 45 rpm, the flip side being a new tune, "Lift Me," which proved to be an indicator as to the group's next direction. Another single, "Long Walking Down to Misery," seemed to further establish this direction. Both songs have country overtones — the guitar riffs and general pace of the band lean that way, though not to a great extent. I'm not much of a country enthusiast, but I do like these singles.

Late in '68 Warners finally released what was to be the Beau Brummels' last album; Bradley's Barn, named after the studio in Nashville where it was recorded, is a good solid, slightly countrified rock album. At last the promise vaguely hinted at in "Oh Lonesome Me" was realized. From the notes we learned that the Brummels were now down to two members (Sal and Ron), but some very able session men, including Jerry Reed, lent a hand and came up with some really fine countrified easy-going rock. Tracks like "Jessica" and "Love Can Fall a Long Way Down" are pleasant, easy to listen to, and all-round good music. Another single, "Cherokee Girl," was pulled from the album, but went nowhere; and for the Beau Brummels, that was it.

I'll never understand why the subsequent singles were termed solo efforts on the part of Sal Valentino, because Elliott is there and there's not much change from the style of the last album. "Alligator Man" is a golden oldie penned by Floyd Chance, and

BRUMMELS SUED FOR ONE MILLION DOLLARS

The Beau Brummels along with their former managers, Tom Donahue and Robert Mitchell, and their present manager Carl Scott are being sued by Declan Mulligan, former member of the group. Mulligan is seeking damages totaling $1,250,000 from his former partners.

Mulligan, if you remember, was one of the original Brummels who left the group about a year ago.

Several months after his split the other Brummels told *The BEAT* Mulligan had left for several reasons, one of which was his desire to go back to his native Ireland.

At that time, Sal Valentino stated that he felt the group had not suffered a tremendous loss when Mulligan made his exit but Ron Elliott disagreed saying that they had lost because they were minus one guitar—thus, changing their sound to a certain extent.

Mulligan now declares that he was the founder and leader of the group and charged in a San Francisco Superior Court that his four fellow Brummels had frozen him out of the business a year ago and have excluded him from their profits ever since.

The attorney for Mulligan said the Brummels have had two hit singles and two hit albums, grossing sales in excess of one million dollars since they began recording in 1964.

Their biggest hit, "Laugh, Laugh," sold more than 500,000 copies and was one of the biggest American-made records sold in England.

Mulligan is, therefore, seeking $250,000 in general damages and one million dollars in punitive damages plus the dissolution of his oral partnership with the other Brummels and a settlement of what they allegedly owe him.

At the time of this printing, the Brummels were filling concert dates on the East Coast and their manager was unavailable for comment.

OLD TIME BEAU BRUMMELS, way back when Declan Mulligan (left) was a member of the group. Mulligan is now suing the Brummels and their managers for over one million dollars in general and punitive damages.

I've always liked it quite a bit. It sounds countryish again, though not overly so; I'd compare it to "When You're Hot You're Hot" or something in that vein. Nonsensical but fun. "Friends and Lovers" is Sal's bid for the easy listening market, very uninspired. The last effort, "Silkie," even rated a review in Rolling Stone. Again, it is countryish but only on the surface, there being folky roots and some real tight musicianship involved.

After this, Sal became involved in Stoneground and of late Elliott has been involved in production work (as he had been since '66 or so; his tune "Puppetmaster," which he produced for a Bay Area gang called (Butch Engel &) the Styx, was a great record). Elliott also released an LP, The Candlestickmaker, late in 1969 which was generally ignored; countrified folky stuff that goes down fairly well. There's some excellent guitar work (and Sal was there to help out too), and in all the LP is really OK. Elliott's voice is a little rough and certainly a far cry from Valentino's but it does suit his songs and is pleasant enough. He also was part of a forgettable group called Pan (one album on Columbia in 1973).

In '68 Vault Records issued a couple albums, combining unreleased tracks with old Autumn releases. The Best of the Beau Brummels is really a must for any rock collector interested in this period, as it contains the very best tunes from the Autumn days. Volume 44 is interesting for its alternate versions of several excellent tunes and a few unreleased cuts, but is of no real interest to non-Brummel enthusiasts.

In all the Beau Brummels produced about six albums worth of excellent, listenable music, ranging from folk to country to downright rock and roll. It's good clean stuff and still stands up very well today. Pick up on them and enjoy some roots; they were a memorable and always interesting group.

BEAU BRUMMELS DISCOGRAPHY

Autumn 8 Laugh Laugh/Still In Love With You Baby
10 Just a Little/They'll Make You Cry
16 You Tell Me Why/I Want You
20 Don't Talk to Strangers/In Good Time
24 Good Time Music/Sad Little Girl
WB 5813 One Too Many Mornings/She Reigns
5848 Here We Are Again/Fine With Me
7014 Don't Make Promises/Two Days Till Tomorrow
7079 Magic Hollow/Lower Level
7204 Lift Me/Are You Happy
7218 Long Walking Down to Misery/I'm a Sleeper
7260 Cherokee Girl/Deep Water
(Sal Valentino)
7268 Alligator Man/An Added Attraction
7289 Alligator Man/Friends and Lovers
7368 Silkie/Song For Rochelle

ALBUMS

12-64 Autumn SLP 103 Introducing the Beau Brummels
10-65 Autumn SLP 104 Beau Brummels, Volume Two
8-66 WB WS 1644 Beau Brummels '66
8-67 WB WS 1692 Triangle
10-68 WB WS 1760 Bradley's Barn
4-68 Vault LPS 114 Best of the Beau Brummels
9-68 Vault LPS 121 Volume 44
(Gentle Wanderin' Ways; Fine With Me; Dream On; I Want More Lovin'; I've Never Known; Oh Lonesome Me; When It Comes to Your Love; Doesn't Matter; More Than Happy; That's All Right; Can It Be; Louie Louie)

RON ELLIOT

10-69 WB WS 1833 Candlestick Maker

UNRELEASED AUTUMN TRACKS

Autumn recorded far more material with the Beau Brummels than was ever issued. The album which came out as Vault 121 was recorded in mid-'65, during the same period Volume Two was cut, and was originally intended as the third Autumn LP. "Fine With Me" and "Gentle Wanderin' Ways" were also mixed down to be the final Autumn single, but never issued. Excluding the tracks which surfaced later on Vault, these are the remaining unissued songs:

That's All That Matters; Peepin' and Hidin'; Sweet Georgia Brown; Here I Am In Love Again; My Lovin'; I Will Go; I'll Tell You; I Grow Old; She Loves Me; Lonely Man; She's My Girl; It's So Nice; You Don't Want My Love; News; Pity the Cool (could be typo for I Pity the Fool); Love is Just a Game; Talk to Me; It Sounds Like Rain; Low Down; How Many Times; Brown Eyes; Don't Do This to Me; I'm Alone Again; I Will Love You Still; Hey-Love; Tomorrow is Another Day; Some Day; Dec's Song; I'll Never Fall in Love Again (w/Bobby Freeman); Pete's Tune; The Jerk (w/Sly Stewart);

Some of these may have been issued under other titles, but the remainder still languish in the can, despite the fact they have been bought and sold twice already. Vault Records, which purchased the Autumn tapes at the same time Warner Bros. purchased the artist roster, sold Autumn to United Artists in 1973, in whose hands the possibility of a 'Great Lost Beau Brummels Album' still resides....

BEAU BRUMMELS — NAMED BEST NEW GROUP — DOING BYRDS' BIG HIT, "MR. TAMBOURINE MAN."
BEAT Photo: Robert Custer

AUTUMN RECORDS
by GREG SHAW

Autumn was begun in the early part of 1964 by Tom "Big Daddy" Donahue and Bob Mitchell, leading DJs on San Francisco's top-rated KYA who were expanding into the music biz by promoting star-studded shows at the Cow Palace and getting involved with local musicians on the North Beach (go go club) scene. Later in '65, Donahue and Mitchell opened a club called Mothers in North Beach, bringing in the Lovin' Spoonful and the Byrds and helping ignite the San Francisco Sound.

But in 1964 they were still mainly jocks. Bobby Freeman, a San Francisco musician who'd had a few hits in the '50s, was in residence at a North Beach disco, and using the studio downstairs at KYA, Donahue began cutting a few songs with him, as well as others including Dino Valenti, Gloria Scott (perhaps the first he recorded, in late '63), Jim Alaimo, the Vejtables, the Carousels, the Spearmints, Tyrone Spencer, Jim Washburn (another KYA jock) and Sly Stewart. Although all the above cut at least a few songs before mid-64, it was Freeman who had the first release on Autumn.

"Let's Surf Again" didn't do much, but "C'mon and Swim" which hit at the height of the Carol Doda controversy, was a runaway smash, and Autumn was in business—although both partners remained at KYA, Mitchell until his death in '66 and Donahue until '68 when he went over to KMPX-FM. Sylvester Stewart, who'd been in various soul bands and was a jock on KDIA, joined Autumn as staff producer & arranger. He also cut a lot of songs himself, hardly any of which were released. In addition to his solo stuff, and an unreleased live album On Stage With Sly (7-64) he recorded with many of the Autumn artists, including Bobby Freeman, Little "E", and the Mojo Men, doing songs including "Beatle Haircut" and appearing on stage with them for a long period of time.

Autumn was as selective as Philles in releasing singles, a policy which did not, however, bring them an equal share of hits. Many groups were recorded extensively but never released at all. Dino Valenti cut eight songs in early '64, Gloria Scott & the Tonettes did several, as did Ramona King. The Tikis recorded almost enough for an album. The Charlatans put down four tracks, their earliest recordings. Looking over the master tape catalog, there are also several baffling instances where a group cut just two songs in 3-track stereo, on which a mono master was later made, but no single issued. Gear One, with "I Should Be Glad"/"Hello Little Girl" (5-65) might've been interesting, same for The Us, with "Just Me"/"How Can I Tell Her". Little "E" (Emile O'Connor, a legendary '50s Bay Area doo-wop king) cut three or 4 tracks that would surely be worth a listen. Not to mention The Girls, and The Bundles, probably a punk band, with "Mark My Words" and "Watch Me Girl" in 8-65. Autumn 4, a semi-surf sound, came out as The Upsetters, though the group was called first The Dreamers then The Impax on early takes of the song.

The demise of Autumn came about for fairly obvious reasons; while "Don't Talk to Strangers" and "I Still Love You" were pretty big around SF, Autumn had no national hits after #10. They were just a little ahead of their times, that's all; one of their last signings was the Great Society, whose "Someone to Love" (the original version) received strong initial airplay in the fall of '66. If they could have broken that record, and stayed in business long enough to sign up some of the other local groups like Big Brother & the Holding Company, the Charlatans, etc...or even kept the Great Society together and built Grace Slick into a star...Autumn could've been the hometown label San Francisco never had, and gone on to even greater things. Hell, if they'd just hung onto Sly for a couple of years... but then nobody in San Francisco ever did know how to run a record company.....

AUTUMN DISCOGRAPHY

1 Bobby Freeman - Let's Surf Again/Come to Me
2 Bobby Freeman - C'mon and Swim, pts 1 & 2
3 Sly Stewart - Scat Swim/I Just Learned How to Swim
4 Upsetters - Draggin' the Main/Autumn's Here
5 Bobby Freeman - S-W-I-M/That Little Old Heartbreaker Me
6 Rico & the Ravens - Don't You Know/In My Heart
7 The Spearmints - Jo-Ann/Little One
8 Beau Brummels - Laugh, Laugh/Still in Love With You Baby
9 Bobby Freeman - I'll Never Fall in Love Again/Friends
10 Beau Brummels - Just a Little/They'll Make You Cry
11 Mojo Men - Off the Hook/Mama's Little Baby
12 Dixies - Geisha Girl/He's Got You
13 Carousels - Beneath the Willow/Sail Away
14 Sly - Buttermilk, pts 1 & 2
15 Vejtables - I Still Love You/Anything
16 Beau Brummels - You Tell Me Why/I Want You
17 Chosen Few - I Think It's Time/Nobody But Me
18 Tikis - If I've Been Dreaming/Pay Attention to Me
19 Mojo Men - Dance With Me/Loneliest Boy In Town
20 Beau Brummels - Don't Talk to Strangers/In Good Time
21 Casualias - Just For You/This is a Mean World
22 Charity Shayne - Ain't It? Babe/Then You Try
23 Vejtables - The Last Thing On My Mind/Mansion of Tears
24 Beau Brummels - Good Time Music/Sad Little Girl
25 Bobby Freeman - The Duck/Cross My Heart
26 —
27 Mojo Men - She's My Baby/Fire in My Heart
28 The Other Tikis - Bye Bye Bye/Lost My Love Today

NORTH BEACH (Autumn subsidiary)

1001 Great Society - Someone to Love/Free Advice
1002 Little Juarez - The Corner Bullfight/El Jefe (The Chief)
1003 Chosen Few - I Think It's Time/Nobody But Me
JEST (Autumn subsidiary)
1 Au Go Gos - All Over Town/Waited For You

SPECIAL SUPPLEMENT!!

This is the first installment of our long-promised series of reports on local American rock scenes of the mid-Sixties. Future installments will include Ohio, Texas, Colorado, the Pacific Northwest, and Chicago. If you have information you feel would be useful in these areas, please write.

SOUNDS OF THE SIXTIES

PART ONE: THE BAY AREA

BY GREG SHAW

SAN FRANCISCO

San Francisco had perhaps the most unusual local music scene of any major American city in the Sixties. The closest parallel is with New York, which also had no punk bands to speak of, although the suburbs were crawling with them. San Francisco has many large residential districts that must surely have produced groups, but for some reason none, or hardly any, of them left any recorded trace. It can't be for any lack of recording facilities, for San Francisco had a lot more to offer than San Jose, chiefly the Golden State Recording Studio, where a group could cut demos and even release them on the studio's own label.

Oddly enough, the rare local records that do occasionally turn up are by groups that I, as a kid growing up in the area, never heard of, and always on a one-shot label. "Don't Walk Out On Me" by the Mark of Kings on Flip Top 2192. "Plastic People" by Wildwood on Magnum 420. "The Fire I Feel" by the Karpetbaggers on Trig 202. Nobody ever heard of these records, but the labels all bear San Francisco addresses.

The problem with San Francisco was (1) there were no real clubs or places for local bands to play in '64 and '65 and (2) the psychedelic thing, which was influencing all the local kids by '65, just as the punk trend was catching on nationwide. And by 1966, the peak year for punk, San Francisco punks were all in acid bands.

We'll explore this relationship between punk rock and the roots of psychedelic music in some future issue, because I think it's an important and overlooked transition phase, but for now I'd like to stick with the Bay Area punk scene, such as it was.

Actually there was an active, healthy and quite prolific punk scene on the suburban fringes of San Francisco, to a small extent in Marin County, a heavy concentration in the East Bay (Oakland, Alameda, Walnut Creek, San Leandro, extending out to Stockton and the Altamont area) and a loosely connected, extremely hot scene in San Jose (about 50 miles South of SF), which extended out to Santa Cruz and up the peninsula almost to San Francisco itself. Then there was a scene in Sacramento, some 200 miles away, that was also somewhat connected.

Most of the "San Francisco Sound" musicians came from folk, jug band or jazz backgrounds, but a few paid their dues on this punk circuit. Two of the members of Quicksilver had a band called the Brogues that issued 3 singles. The drummer of Blue Cheer came from a Sacramento group called the Oxford Circle. And the Wackers evolved out of the Family Tree, which appeared frequently in '66 doing mostly Beatles songs. Bob Segarini of that group has told me many stories of the Northern California teen group scene, most of which are too involved to repeat and should be the subject of an interview with Bob one of these days. There were a lot of groups, though, and a lot of teen clubs and dances, and quite a few of the musicians from that scene are still active in California-based groups.

SACRAMENTO

Sacramento is a city whose teen demographics merit more study than they've been given. The Beach Boys chose Sacramento because it was one of their most loyal markets. Completely landlocked, it always had plenty of local surf bands and surfer stomps. And, lest we forget, Gary Usher dedicated a song to the city.

Sacramento had three labels that I know of active in the punk era. The most prolific was Diplomacy, which started with Jim Doval & the Gauchos, a disco dance type band that I believe appeared on Shindig a few times. They had one album issued, The Gauchos (ABC-Paramount 506) recorded live in Fresno, Calif. The label was basically soul-oriented, but they had one excellent punk-pop band that appeared a couple of times at the Fillmore and later went on to become known as Redwing. That group of course is the New Breed, who also recorded at the time for World United and Mercury.

I know of only 3 releases on World United, two by the New Breed and one by the Oxford Circle (a wild screamer). The WU records had a better recording quality and were better musically than any of the other local releases, but only "Want Ad Reader" became a hit locally. The follow-up, "Sound of the Music" was an even better record, well produced with nice harmonies. On the flip was a Beau Brummels song. The group's only Mercury release is a fine version of the Zombies' "Leave Me Be." Much later, the New Breed was brought to Fantasy Records by Creedence Clearwater, who remembered them from the punk days and knew how good they were.

THE EAST BAY

The East Bay is one of the tougher parts of the Bay Area. Most of the greasers in Northern California live there, and preserve the punk lifestyle amid the grimy factories and shabby tract houses that make up the area. From the point

The New Breed made a lot of noise on the West Coast with their first single, Green Eyed Woman. Hope we'll be hearing more from them.

where Berkeley and Oakland meet, all the way down the east side of the Bay to the bottom tip and up to San Jose this environment stretches, completely foreign to the cultured reality of San Francisco or the intellectual mentality of Berkeley.

There has always been local rock & roll in the east bay. In the '50s there were rockabilly singers and R&B groups ("WPLJ" by the Four Deuces came out of Oakland, as have many fine blues recordings). In the early '60s there were

SACRAMENTO LABELS

WORLD UNITED RECORDS

001 New Breed - Want Ad Reader/One More For The Good Guys
002 Oxford Circle - Foolish Woman/Mind Destruction
003 New Breed - The Sound of the Music/Fine With Me

IKON RECORDS

169 R.C. & the Tambourines - Quirk/Tambourine
517 Yo-Yoz - Leave Me Alone/Stay With Me
-- Fabulous Futuras - La Do Da Da/When You Ask About Love

Ikon was an interesting label with an indecipherable numbering system. There's no number at all on the Fabulous Futuras record, a fine cover of the Dale Hawkins song, and the Yo-Yoz record is a quite charming minor-key ballad. The label's main problem is that all their releases sound like they were recorded on defective cassette machines, which may be why they never got far.

DIPLOMACY RECORDS

1000	Jimmy Sandoval & Gauchos - Love Me One More Time
1	--
2	--
3	--
4	Just Taylor & Dippers - Over & Over/Goin Ape
5	Jim Doval - Stranded in the Pool/Right Now
6	Jim Doval - Beattle Rule/Pink Elephanta
7	Jim Doval - Boney Maroni/She's a Very Nice Girl
8	--
9	Sis Watkin's - Here I Stand/Only You Can Give
10	--
11	--
12	--
13	--
14	--
15	--
16	--
17	Jim Doval - Maka Keep Yo! Big Mouth Shut/She's So Fine
18	--
19	Sandy Borden - Stand By Me/Deeper
20	Jimmy Holiday - The New Breed/Love Me One More Time
21	--
22	New Breed - I'm in Love/Green Eye'd Woman
23	Jimmy Holiday - I've Been Done Wrong/I Can't Stand It
24	Diplomettes - My Intuition/Sit Yourself Down

many dance bands, among them Tommy Fogerty & the Blue Velvets, and teen bands from Merced and Stockton (40 miles east, real "American Graffiti" country) used to come to Oakland to record. The Merced Blue Notes released records on Galaxy, the Fantasy subsidiary, as well as the local Frantic label that had other proto-punk stuff.

Fantasy was the Bay Area's only real record label in the early '60s, having national hits with Vince Guaraldi and selling lots of jazz and Lenny Bruce albums. In 1964 they signed Tommy Fogerty & the Blue Velvets, and the company's owner changed their name to the Golliwogs.

The Golliwogs did mostly British-derived rock, which set them apart from the majority of East Bay groups who did R&B at that time. But by 1965 they were joined by others, such as the Harbinger Complex, who did all Stones & Yardbirds (and played at my high school senior dance with yours truly providing a gen-yew-ine San Francisco-style light show with the AV dept's opaque projector...) and William Penn & His Pals, who did a lot of Raiders material. These and many other bands fought it out regularly at the many teen clubs and "Battles of the Bands" that characterized the era.

There were two main promoters who sponsored punk dances in those days. Al Manning of Action USA used Longshoremen's Hall in San Francisco (on weekends when there wasn't a Trips Festival taking place there) to bring in acts like the Wailers, Hondells, Leaves, Turtles, and many of the East Bay groups. Then there was Pete Paulsen and Bill Quarry of 'Teens & Twenties' who managed several groups out of San Leandro and sponsored dances at various armories and gymnasiums around the East Bay. Their biggest groups were Tom Thumb & the Hitchhikers, Stanley & the Four Fendermen, and the Harbinger Complex. A number of other groups on this circuit were managed by Barry Carlos of Go-Teens Productions, including Peter Wheat & the Breadmen, the Canadian Fuzz, the Immediate Family, and the Nightcaps.

Some of the clubs where these groups would appear, teen clubs that advertised on the Top 40 radio stations and drew the high school crowd on weekends, included the Bold Knight in Sunnyvale, the Cinnamon Tree in San Carlos, Boss-a-Go-Go in Oakland, the Continental in Santa Clara, the Wildcat A-Go-Go and the Casino on Catalina Island (a popular resort, immortalized by the Four Preps in "26 Miles"--see later for an interesting parallel) the Rat-Fink a-Go-Go, Vets Hall in Oakland, the Rollarena in San Leandro, the American Legion Hall in Redwood City, Wayne Manor in San Mateo, Winchester Cathedral in Redwood City, the Big Beat A-Go-Go, Foresters Hall in Livermore, Tracy Ballroom in Tracy, and of course all the local high schools, universities, junior colleges, and frequent events sponsored by private groups.

It was a happening scene, all right. There was even a teen club, the Tiger-A-Go-Go, at San Francisco International Airport--in San Bruno (on the Peninsula, 12 miles south of SF) where I lived, as did the original Grass Roots, led by Bob Fulton, who if memory serves were also responsible for "My Lovin' Baby" by the Beauchemins (Mustang 3015). The only reason I bring up the Tiger-A-Go-Go is that it was the subject of a musical tribute by Buzz & Bucky (Cason & Wilkin, also known as Ronny & the Daytonas, whose "GTO" had just hit the charts)

Tiger-A-Go-Go/Bay City - Amy 924
A cool, semi-surfing sound record with great

Tom Thumb & the Hitchhikers: Dennis Dixon, Richard Alves, Paul Herrera, Ken Hampton, Steve Hoffi

lyrics: "We hit the Golden Gate city on a Saturday night now, we met a California hippie said come along with me, I'll get you to the Tiger on time..." This was 1964, before anybody in California had even heard the word 'hippie', and the guys who made the record were from Nashville to boot! A real oddity.

There were a few groups on the Peninsula, but I don't think any of them recorded except of course the Grass Roots, who later played a few gigs at the Fillmore under another name after Sloan & Barri appropriated theirs for the "Let's Live For Today" group. I remember the Flamin' Groovies, who were then called the Chosen Few, being around a lot, but for the most part it was the San Jose groups that were most frequently featured at Peninsula clubs, of which Wayne Manor in San Mateo was the most popular among the kids at my school.

SAN JOSE

Without a doubt, San Jose was the hub of it all. San Jose is a lot more than most people realize; it's the fastest-growing city in California, maybe in the US, a miniature Los Angeles, creeping out in all directions from what was, 20 years ago, a sleepy little South Bay town. In the '50s industry discovered the cheap land, favorable zoning and available labor (mostly Mexican) and soon San Jose was the biggest bedroom community in Northern California. In the '60s, there were a lot of teenagers loose in the area, and the teenage community covered much of Santa Clara county and extended out to Santa Cruz, the nearest beach, where kids from the Bay Area and LA alike would spend summers surfing and partying.

EAST BAY LABELS

A few local punk groups besides the Golliwogs released singles on Fantasy (the Shillings, the Coachmen, the Chessmen, Tommy & the Hustlers) before the company decided to start a new subsidiary for their teenage releases: Scorpio.

SCORPIO RECORDS

401 --
402 Group 'B' - Stop Calling Me/She's Gone
403 Tokays - Now/Ask Me No Questions (10-65)
404 Golliwogs - Brown-Eyed Girl/You Better Be Careful
405 Golliwogs - Fight Fire/Fragile Child
406 Group 'B' - I Know Your Name Girl/
407 Fantastics - Malaguena/Dance For An Unnamed Gypsy Queen
408 Golliwogs - Walking On the Water/You Better Get It Before It Gets You
409 Tears - Weatherman/Read All About It
410 --
411 --
412 Creedence Clearwater Revival - Porterville/Call It Pretending

AMBER RECORDS

3537 Barry Carlos & Night-Caps - Are You Running Away/Don't You Know   (4-65)
6657 Peter Wheat & the Breadmen - All the Time/Baby What's New
4086 Ray Ghiggs - The Monkey's Disgrace/The Persian Cat
101 What-Nots - Nobody Else But You/Look Down

Amber Records was probably owned by Barry Carlos, and there were probably other releases, though it's impossible to tell from the numbering system. The last one listed, #101, has a different color label and may not be the same company.

Stanley & the Four Fendermen: Bob Manning (drm) Stan Weisenberger (voc.) Dana Scholtz (gtr) Gary Lucas (bass) Ron Stearns (organ)--they won the Hayward Recreation District's "Battle of the Bands"

SPECIAL PUNK SUPPLEMENT, cont.

The earliest known San Jose label is Hush, started by Gary Thompson in 1958. Joe Simon made his earliest recordings for Hush (actually based in Mountain View, a suburb of Palo Alto) with his group the Goldentones, and had a couple of minor hits. When Vee-Jay bought out Simon's contract, Hush became inactive until 1966 when they signed the Syndicate of Sound after hearing a demo of "Little Girl" cut at Golden State in San Francisco.

Actually, it had been active before that, with several surf records coming out on the Twilight label, some of which were local hits. "Surf-a-Nova" by the Tri-Tones has the distinction of being a surf/girl group record, and a good one. In 1966, Twilight was joined by Hush and another subsidiary, Duane, in releasing local punk product. The Brogues (early Quicksilver) record was a minor seller, along with the Wm. Penn, and of course "Little Girl" was a national smash on Bell, bringing Hush its only gold record.

HUSH · TWILIGHT · DUANE

HUSH
- 1000 Ben Joe Zeppa - Young Heartaches/Ridin' Herd
- 100 Ben Joe Zeppa & Hot Notes - Louise/Doctor Doctor
- 101 Goldentones - Little Island Girl/Doreetha
- 102 Goldentones - You Left Me Here to Cry Alone/Ocean of Tears
- 103 Joe Simon - It's a Miracle/Land of Love
- 104 Joe Simon - Everybody Needs Somebody/Call My Name
- 105 Misfits - My Mother in Law/Give Me Your Heart
- 106 Joe Simon - Pledge of Love/It's All Over
- 107 Joe Simon - Troubles/I See Your Face
- 108 Joe Simon - I Keep Remembering/
- 228 Syndicate of Sound - Little Girl/You (originally released on Scarlet 503)
- 229 Gerry & Leslie - I Like That Girl/Me Love Am Gone
- 230 Wm. Penn & Quakers - Little Girl/Somebody's Dum Dum
- 231 Diminished 5th - Doctor Dear/Do You Hear

DUANE
- 100 --
- 101 --
- 102 --
- 103 --
- 104 Wm. Penn & Quakers - Coming Up My Way/Care Free

TWILIGHT
- 360 Timbre Cling - Lovin' Care/Danny Boy
- 401 --
- 402 --
- 403 --
- 404 --
- 405 Parallels - Surf-a-Nova/Da Dipty
- 406 Tri-Tones - Surf-a-Nova/Kiss and Run
- 407 --
- 408 Brogues - But Now I Find/Someday
- 409 --
- 410 Wm. Penn & Quakers - Ghost of the Monks/Goodbye My Love

NOTE: Wm. Penn & the Quakers was the same as William Penn & His Pals, a San Carlos (near Redwood City, 15 mi. from San Jose) group that did DC5, Raiders, Animals material, toured widely all over California, and featured Gregg Rolie (later of Santana) on organ.

The Mourning Reign, one of San Jose's biggest.

In 1966, the biggest San Jose groups were Count Five, the Chocolate Watchband, the Jaguars, the E-Types, the Mourning Reign, and the Baytovens. All these groups had local hits, but no national attention was focused on San Jose until May of that year, when Count Five broke nationally with "Psychotic Reaction", featuring their amphetamine Yardbirds imitation. The group released many other records, but never had another hit; they're still around, working in local factories and body shops. The next hit out of SJ was "Little Girl" by the Syndicate of Sound, which many people consider the best San Jose records. It had all the elements of a great punk song--taunting, insulting vocals, simple, grungy guitar chords, even a fuzzy tambouring. The SofS went on to record for several labels, without success, altho their 1969 Capitol single was a good try, with a fine Kinks cover on one side and a great psychedelic Animals arrangement on the other.

After the success of these records, a producer/songwriter/entrepeneur from LA named Ed Cobb (formerly a member of the Four Preps, and author of Brenda Holloway's "Every Little Bit Hurts") moved in to sign up the best of the remaining groups for his Greengrass Productions, which had a contract to supply masters to Capitol for their Tower and Uptown subsidiaries. Already successful with the Standells, for whom he wrote "Dirty Water", Cobb signed two of San Jose's best groups, the E-Types and the Chocolate Watchband, and took them to LA to record.

The E-Types had already issued one record locally, on the Link label, which was picked up nationally by Dot. Cobb recorded them on Uptown, Tower, and his own Sunburst label, but couldn't get a hit outside San Jose, although the group itself was potentially the city's best; their first record was a finely-produced, polished, Beatle-like rocker, the Sunburst record was probably the best version of Lennon-McCartney's "Love of the Loved", "Big City" was also excellent, and "Put the Clock" was a commercial Bonner & Gordon (who wrote many Turtles hits) song.

The Chocolate Watchband could have been the raunchiest punk group to emerge from San Jose, as evidenced by the two songs Cobb put on his "Riot On Sunset Strip" soundtrack, and "Let's Talk About Girls", immortalized on Nuggets. Their 3 albums all had a modicum of punk material--"I'm Not Like Everybody Else", "Medication", "Midnight Hour" and the great "Are You Gonna Be There (at the Love-In)" but the covers were full of pyramids, gods-eyes etc. and the psychedelic songs like "Inner Mystique" tended to dominate. The Chocolate Watchband were the first major punk group to succumb to the San Francisco syndrome; by 1967 most of the San Jose groups were trying to sound like the Grateful Dead and the city boasted light shows, love ins and all the rest. A sad ending.

But we're not at the end yet. The Watchband had a local Bay Area hit with "No Way Out", which even got on KYA. On the whole, however, Ed Cobb's attempt to bring San Jose to the world was a failure. An interesting sidelight is the existence of a record on Uptown 745 by a William Penn. Cobb had nothing to do with it, and it's known that there were Wm. Penn groups in other parts of the country, but who knows?

Which brings me to another mystery. One of the greatest psychedelic punk records of all time is "Blow My Mind"/"Swami" by the William Penn Fyve on Thunderbird 502. From the names, it's the same group as on Hush/Twilight, but the record is distributed thru a company in Buffalo, NY and must have come out much later, during the Maharish era. It's full of raw fuzz guitar and great, dumb mystic lyrics. "Blow My Mind" is a classic 2-chord punk rocker.

There were two other labels of some local importance, Jaguar and South Bay. Jaguar had the Jaguars, an extremely popular R&B band, and they also had Gropus Cackus, a group from somewhere in the East Bay that is still together (they had a single on Bell a couple of years ago).

South Bay was a strange label. Its first release was by the Preps, who'd had a single out 2 years previously on the Warped label. They changed their name to the New Arrivals, and according to their bio they were 'clean-cut, collegiate, preferred tuxedos'. They sounded sort of like Dino, Desi &Billy--as did the Odds & Ends, who may've been the same people. Starting with #104, they were a "Macy's/7-Up Production"--the two companies had a promotion going where they had groups playing at Macy's 'Tiger Shops' and kids would come to hear them, buy clothes, and enter contests & stuff. Macy's/7-Up had 2 other records, "It's Like Now, Baby" by the Vandals and an EP by Holly Penfield & the Fifth St. Exit,

songs composed by members of the New Arrivals. There was also a San Jose group called the 4th St. Exit, who had one excellent punk record, and there could be a connection.

A few of the better odd records from San Jose included "Waiting For You" by the Baytovens with a strong Liverpool sound, "I'm Not There" by the Lil' Boys Blue, which sounds like "Liar, Liar" by the Castaways, "It Couldn"t Be True" by the Twilights, aged 10-12 (the record came with an annotated picture sleeve), "Suzy Creamcheese" by Teddy & His Patches, a psychedelic raveup masterpiece, "Since I Met You" by the Marauders, and "Evil Hearted You" by the Mourning Reign. Another to look for is "I Think I'm Down" by the Harbinger Complex on Brent 7056.

The San Jose scene had a minor rebirth in 1968 when People hit #14 nationally with a cover of the Zombies' "I Love You" and went on to record 3 albums. That year also produced Orphan Egg, with an album on GNP, and Stained Glass, who came a little earlier (1967 was their big year) with one good single, Mann-Weil's "We Got a Long Way to Go" and 2 LPs. From then on, it's been strictly downhill. The Doobie Brothers have been the only thing to come out of San Jose since. But it was a great scene while it lasted.

William Penn & His Pals: Mic Leidenthal (bass), Mike Shapiro (lead gtr), Ron Cox (drums, grp leader), Neil Haltmann (vocals), Gregg Rolie (organ), Jack Shelton (rhythm gtr).

SAN JOSE GROUPS

CHOCOLATE WATCH BAND

Uptown 740 - Sweet Young Thing/Baby Blue Trap
Uptown 749 - Misty Lane/She Weaves a Tender
Tower 373 - No Way Out/Are You Gonna Be There
Tower LP 5096 - No Way Out
Tower LP 5106 - The Inner Mystique
Tower LP 5153 - One Step Beyond
Tower LP 5065 - Riot On Sunset Strip: Sitting There Standing; Dont Need Your Loving

E-TYPES

Link E-1 - I Can't Do It/Long Before
Dot 16864 - I Can't Do It/Long Before
Uptown 754 - Big City/Back to Me
Tower 325 - Put the Clock Back On the Wall/4th Street
Sunburst 001 - The Love of the Love/She Moves Me

COUNT FIVE

Double Shot
104   Psychotic Reaction/They're Gonna Get You
106   Peace of Mind/The Morning After
110   You Must Believe Me/Teeny Bopper, Teeny Bopper
115   Merry-Go-Round/Contrast
125   Declaration of Independence/Revelation in Slow Motion
141   Mailman/Pretty Big Mouth

DSM-1001 - Psychotic Reaction

SYNDICATE OF SOUND

Scarlet 503   Prepare For Love/Tell the World
Del-Fi 4304   Prepare For Love/Tell the World
Hush 228   Little Girl/You
Bell 640   Little Girl/You
Bell 646   Rumors/The Upper Hand
Bell 655   Good Time Music/Keep it Up
Bell 666   That Kind of Man/Mary
Buddah 183   Mexico/First to Love You
Capitol 2426 You're Looking Fine/Change the World
Buddah 156   Brown Paper Bag/Reverb Beat
Buddah 183   Mexico/First to Love You

Bell LP 6001 Little Girl

STAINED GLASS

RCA 8889 - How Do You Expect Me/If I Needed Someone
RCA 8952 - My Buddy Sin/Vanity Fair
RCA 9166 - We Got a Long Way to Go/Corduroy Joy
RCA 9354 - Mediocre Me/A Scene In Between
Capitol 2372 - Farenheit/Twiddle My Thumbs
Capitol 2521 - Gettin' On's Gettin' Rough/ The Necromancer

Capitol LP 154 - Crazy Horse Roads
Capitol LP 242 - Aurora

PEOPLE

Capitol 2078 - I Love You/Somebody Tell Me My Name
Capitol 2251 - Apple Cider/
Capitol 2499 - Ulla/Turnin' Me On
Paramount 0005 - Livin It Up/Love Will Take Us Higher and Higher
Paramount 0011 - Sunshine Lady/Crosstown Bus
Paramount 0019 - For What It's Worth/Maple St.
Paramount 0028 - One Chain Don't Make No Prison/Keep it Alive

Capitol LP 2924 - I Love You
Capitol LP 151 - Both Sides of People
Paramount LP 5013 - There Are People

THE SAN JOSE LABELS

JAGUAR RECORDS

101 Jaguars - You'll Turn Away/The Gorilla
102 Jaguars - Another Lonely Night/Nite People Make It
103 Venus Flytrap - Have You Ever/The Note
104 Jaguars - St. James Infirmary/Good Time
105 ---
106 Gropus Cackus - Gimme Some Lovin'/Music Maker

SOUTHBAY RECORDS

001 Preps - It Ain't Green Cheese On the Moon Baby! (it's Mozarella/The Moonracers
102 Odds & Ends - You Dont Love Me/Be Happy Baby
102 New Arrivals - Take Me For What I Am/ You Know You're Gonna Be Mine
103 New Arrivals - Scratch Your Name/Just Outside My Window
104 New Arrivals - Just Outside My Window/ Let's Get With It

MISCELLANEOUS SAN JOSE RECORDS

Golden Gate 0011 - Vandals - It's Like Now, Baby/Wet & Wild/Mustang George
Mach's 7-Up 101 - Fifth St. Exit - It's a Goin' Thing/The Uncola Song/The Days and the Hours/Blue Bridge
Rowena 792 - 4th St. Exit - A Love Like This/ Strange One
Chance 101 - Teddy & His Patches - Suzy Cream-Cheese/From Day to Day
Skyview 001 - Marauders - Since I Met You/I Don't Know How
Twilight - Twilights - It Couldn't Be True/ Sum'pin Else
Bat Wing 2003 - Lil' Boys Blue - I'm Not There/ Take You Away
Belfast 1001 - Baytovens - Such a Fool/Waiting For You
Warped 5000 - Preps - Night Theme/What?
Contour 601 - Mourning Reign - Evil Hearted You/ Get Out of My Life Woman

JUKE BOX JURY JUNIOR

BY GREG SHAW

I always enjoy discovering new singles of merit, which is the main reason I haven't gotten bored with my "Juke Box Jury" column (currently in Phonograph Record Magazine) even tho I've been doing it for almost four years. But I really prefer finding great, old singles I'd never heard before; they can shed so much light on the development of artists, producers, writers, labels, regions, etc. Compared to that, all a new single can do is sound good. As it's shaping up now, the 60s will probably turn out to have produced 100 times as many good, obscure records than the 50s did, and we're only beginning to discover how many that really is. This column will be devoted to discussing some of my more intriguing discoveries, and discussing questions raised by them. Naturally, if you have anything to add, your comments will be appreciated.

The Edge - Seen Through the Eyes/Something New - Enith 1011

There's gotta be some kind of story behind this record. Altho on a small, ephemeral LA label (more on that later...) it has a tremendously powerful production sound, full orchestration, and an overall quality you wouldn't expect. The group also must have made other records, they couldn't have been this great and just vanished. The names of the writers are J.W. Keith and R. Barcellona. They sound something like the Left Banke, even more like Stories while Michael Brown was a member--that kind of moody, Zombies-inspired, heavily produced pop. The A side is far better than anything done by the Left Banke; I'd rank it with something like "Love is in Motion." The label started out as Zenith, until they found out the electronics co. had already used the name on records. So they dropped the Z. They had at least 3 numbering series and obviously several more releases than those I'm about to list. Further info is definitely wanted!
ENITH T-5 Nick Venet - Lost and Found/My Dream
   712 Dell-Coeds - Love in Return/Hey Mr. Banjo
   719 Stan Worth - Wiggle Wobble Walkers/Roman Holiday
   722 Ex-Cel Five - Dancing Girl/Talk is Cheap

Fresh Windows - Fashion Conscious/Summer Sun Shines - Fontana TF 839 (E)

This is exactly the sort of record somebody ought to make today; I went nuts the first time I heard it and it still arouses me every time. It's kinda like "Dedicated Follower of Fashion" only it's about a girl, and it's not the least bit snide; what it really is is a glorification of those hip, mod girls you see doing the Frug in all those old beat flicks. The chorus is "Cuz she's a short-skirted, fashion-conscious long-haired girl" (can't you just see her?) drawled out in a heavy British accent over a pounding Troggs beat, while the verses mention all kinds of trendy Carnaby styles. Unfortunately it never came out here, and is obscure in England, but this is one well worth searching out.

The Tornados - Granada/Ragunbonemon - Columbia 7455 (E)
The Peeps - Now is the Time/Got Plenty of Love - Philips 40315 (A)

Here are two equally great, unknown British B-sides. The Tornados of course had "Telstar" and many other somewhat less thrilling instrumentals, of which "Granada" is one. But the flip is one of their rare vocals, and it's the kind of song that can easily insinuate itself into one's skull. The vocals are excellent, in a sort of Buddy Holly/Del Shannon vein, with the one pre-dominating in a vaguely folk-rock style, while the song, melody and lyrics are strong and the production...well, Joe Meek must have been on something when he did this.

The Peeps were also British, this is their only release I know of (9-65), and the A-side is a nice, Kinks/Searchers thing with full harmonies over a choppy rhythm and decent hard rock beat track. Turn it over, tho, and discover an absolute stone-killer upbeat ballad in an amazingly pure Searchers/Ian & Zodiacs vein. On the chorus it picks up speed and sounds almost Beatlish. Can't imagine why it wasn't a monster hit....

Jeremiah - Goin' Lovin' With You/No Sense Nonsense - Philips 40321

You'll notice a few Philips records in this column; I've been getting into that label lately, they had some great undiscovered things. This one was masterminded by Kornfield & Duboff, who recorded "Goin Lovin" on their own as the Changin' Times (followup to their hit "Pied Piper", the original), also on Philips. Dunno who Jeremiah could be, he's got a punk rasp Sonny Bono voice and a good raw production sound. A side is a pleasant bubblegummy ballad (a Koppelman-Rubin product) but the flip is a really diverting protest ditty, with Dylan-parody harmonica and classic dumb lyrics like "they say my shirts should be white collar--who needs 'em anyway?" Among other things, Jeremiah protests kids who dress sloppy. I like a punk who stands up for what he believes in.

Chris Sandford - I Wish They Wouldn't Always Say I Sound Like The Guy From the USA Blues/Little Man--Nobody Cares - Fontana 1534 (A)

That last one reminded me of this. It opens with a few wheezy gasps on the harp while Chris drawls out the title in a real ringer of a Dylan takeoff (and there were enough of those for a meaty article, I'm sure...) then goes into a tale of how the singer was pegged by a record exec to be a teen star, made to wear denim jeans and sing funny...on obvious parody of Donovan's career. Sandford made several records in England, this is his only known release here.

The Others - Oh Yeah!/I'm Taking Her Home - Fontana 1944 (A)
The Fairies - Get Yourself Home/I'll Dance - HMV 1404 (E)

English readers mention both these groups in our lettercol this time. I've had the Others disc for quite awhile, it's one of my longtime faves, one of the most genuinely raunchy records to come out of England. The Fairies I just got, and I play it constantly. It's from '64, and not only is it the most authentic punk rock record I've heard from England, it anticipates American punk rock by two years. Considering Twink was a member of the Fairies at this time, and later joined the Pretty Things when both of them were in their spacy phases, it's interesting how similar to the Pretties this sounds. Similar, but rawer, cruder than the latter group ever was. Heavy, pounding garage echo drums. Blistering grunge guitar. And a vocalist with an uncanny resemblance to Sean Bonniwell. Truly fantastic. Both sides, too.

The Trems - You Can't Touch Sue/Story for the Boys - Epic EPC s 1972a (German)

It's the Tremeloes, but you'd never recognize 'em. This record, which comes with a great flashy pic sleeve, came out only in Germany, unlike the previous two Trems releases in England. It sounds like the Sweet, a perfect Rodney's disco record. Worth whatever it takes to get it, glam fans.

The Whyte Boots - Nightmare/Let No One Come Between Us - Philips 40422

Well I've saved the killer for last...records like this make me wish we could offer an audio supplement with each issue... Imagine if you can the Shangri-Las at the ultimate they never reached. That same voice, but more sultry, with a pout you can really get your teeth into, opens the record with this line, over dramatic castanets: "Yeah...no boy's worth the trouble I'm in!"

But there are other twists ahead as the scenario unfolds. Here she is, standing with her friends, as the other girl, the one who took her Bobby away (showin' off in class, wearin' his ring) walks by. They urge her on--go on, you can beat her, wipe that grin off her face! She didn't want to fight, but they were all pushing her forward...then, screams, chaos, scratching kicking, bloodlust; a little whimper, a dead thud. What happened? Police sirens draw closer as she sobs, I didn't mean to hurt her, I didn't wanna fight, honest...

Great plot, right? But that's only half of it. These girls are absolutely amazing singers, and whoever produced this record (P.Sawyer & L. Burton) could teach everybody a few lessons. It's tight, dynamic, with two distinct melody hooks each powerful enough to sustain a top-notch hit. You gotta hear this song, the way it builds, the way the girls are always in there, up front, projecting an image as street-tough and trashy as, well, the Dolls, for lack of a comparable girl group. This is without a doubt one of the top five girl group records of all time. And amazingly, no one seems to know about it. Let's hope more copies turn up soon so more people can hear this classic.

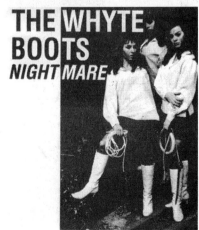

EDITED BY KEN BARNES

WHISTLING JACK SMITH UNMASKED

.....A while ago I read your British Invasion issue of WPTB. I thought I'd write to you about a few points in that issue.

Firstly, Pinkerton's "Assorted" Colours. This group became the Flying Machine while they were making a series for Yorkshire TV...Apparently the Flying Machine were a big deal in America but did nothing here. The Flying Machine still exist playing in north country clubs but they don't have a record contract. A mate of mine remembers that Pinkerton's records were given away as prizes in kids' comics.

Freddy Garrity and his motley crew are still in existence--they do kids' TV programmes, they're a bit dated now.

The Pretty Things come from the same art college in Southeas London as David Bowie (see the connection)....

Has Sister Ray read Nigel Trevana's excellent 40-page book/ mag. on Lou Reed and the Velvets? If not I can highly recommend it. It's obtainable for 40p or equivalent + postage from White Light, Manderley, Alexandra Road, 1 Hogan, Redruth, Cornwall, U.K. --a long address.

England has another great new magazine following in the footsteps of Zigzag, Fat Angel and Supersnazz. It's called Omaha Rainbow (after the John Stewart song) and you can get it for 10p + postage from Peter O'Brien at 10 Lesley Court, Harcourt Road, Wallington, Surrey, U.K. The latest issue contains a Country Joe & the Fish chart by me as well as things about Dylan and other goodies.

Kerry Scott who wrote "International Heroes" is an English folk singer. I also have a single of Fowley's on the Action label called "Born To Make You Cry"--now that is weird, does anyone know anything about it?

Zoot Money of Dantalion's Chariot is now in Grimm's--a comedy band formed from the Scaffold, the Liverpool Scene and the Bonzo Dog Doo Dah Band. Also in Grimm's is Neil Innes, who is always seen wearing a yellow plastic duck on his head (I once saw him playing in a football match against Monty Python's Flying Circus).

A band similar to the Creation that you missed out is the Smoke. They made a weird single called I think "Jack Eats Sugarlumps" (--"My Friend Jack", Columbia 8115--Ed.).

Peter Frampton of the Herd confessed that they never played on their records, tut, tut (wasn't "From The Underworld" great though?).

I have been listening to a lot of Kim Fowley of late. His Love Is Alive And Well album is excellent--10 minutes each side. "International Heroes" and "ESP Reader" are weird.

Tommy Moeller (of Unit 4+2) had a brother who was Whistling Jack Smith who recorded "I Was Kaiser Bill's Batman"....

—DAVID HAMILTON

(--"Born To Make You Cry" came out here on Original Sound 98, and was Fowley's last record before the Capitol stuff in '72. And Zoot Money has recently reformed his Big Roll Band, with Andy Somers and Paul Williams; they're gigging about currently.--Ed.)

IN DEFENSE OF BECK

...As good as the issue is you messed up a few things in your Yardbird piece. You slighted Beck when you gave credit to Clapton on "I Ain't Done Wrong" and questioned Side 1 of Rave Up. Eric left the group in mid-December '64 and "Wrong" was recorded 5 months later with Jeff at Advision Studios--London, May 1965. Clapton stormed out of Olympic Studios in the middle of recording sessions when he found out "For Your Love", that "pop rubbish" (his quote) was to be recorded. His last effort with the group was "Got To Hurry" from those Olympic sessions. Incidentally, Jeff replaced Eric in a matter of days (due to a tip from Jimmy Page to Keith Relf) and Jeff played harpsichord not guitar on "For Your Love" I.B.C. Studios, Dec. '64. Because of Clapton's antics in refusing to record that crucial third single he is not credited on either For Your Love or Rave Up. Also, all of the first side of Rave Up is Beck. The earliest recorded track on it is "Heart Full Of Soul", Advision Studio--Feb. '65, a few months after Clapton's departure....

—BEN RICHARDSON

COME AGAIN PLEASE?

...I was absolutely nutted by the Shel Talmy and Pop Art Rock stuff...Someone would call my name. No answer. So I've been marked down as absent. Shit when you're alive who wants to get serious. Not me. Never. I've had a lot of trouble over that.

The Creation went completely unnoticed here and I'll never understand it. From the first, '64, the English thing seemed to mean more to me than most American sides. Except of course those American punkoids that threw out the same raw wildness right into our own backyards. You know who they are. The sound was simple. A bit raw. Oh hell I just loved it. And so when the first little energy happened around the Creation I

heard about it and made sure others could too. And the violin thing Page grabbed up. Page should really own up. Ah maybe not that so much as having the chance to rave about struggling bands. Very special bands. He didn't. He just didn't do it. Probably one of the biggest reasons I cared about Brian Jones as much as I did (and still do) even more than his Stones focus--which did burn down sooner than anyone at that time knew--was that he always pushed names--ideas--curiosities--at the media. So some little teen tramp like myself could finally go out and find some new excitement. Somewhere.

Anyway another personal favorite was the Easybeats piece. When I first heard FRIDAY ON MY MIND I was absolutely miserable. School made me puke. Literally. I was so bored so low-looking that the only thing I could do was puke. I did all over my Geometry teacher's book. He hated me. My girlfriend's (at that time) parents forbid me to ravage their daughter until my ears again made an appearance. And I was fixing a ham sandwich in the afternoon, AM radio blasting boogaloo when this amazing guitar came out. I ran for that knob so fast that sandwich was still in the air and back in my hand before it could move. And that line "Even my old man looks good". Well I went in and aimed my peepers at 'em. Yeah my old man. Looked right at 'emand he still looked lousy. Oh well. Absolutely irresistible tune....

Just like Mike "Kernel" Saunders' fanatic finger work for the Who's "Subsitute" I personally got the Move's "Fire Brigade" played 12 more times than it would have been played. Which was 12 times. Much like Mike I couldn't tell you (maybe I could--yeah I could) what this stuff did to me. When I first heard "Fire Brigade" I called KOL and screaming and straining demanded they play it again. Well very politely (condescendingly is hell actually) they said "maybe next hour". Next hour no sirens. Nothing. Bastards. So when request time came I blitzed the station with a variety of visual and oral entertainments rarely registered in human moves. Those magic moves people babble about. Had them baffled alright. They told me one more dumb accent and I'd never hear it again. Hiss hiss....

And the first American appearance of Jeff Beck in the Yardbirds on Shindig. They went into "Heart Full Of Soul". And then came the solo and he BLEW IT!!! Completely messed it up. Missed it. Missed it bad. I thought he stunk. That hasn't changed much. No--I do like Becky. He's not predictable. A surprise or two is still in him.

Before I say--see ya-- I'd like to tell you something about that Sonics thing in the back of WPTB. They were big here, monsters even. But not at the Lake Hills Arena in Tacoma but at the Lake Hills Roller Rink in Lake Hills, a suburb of Bellevue. Where I'm from. Rich. Fat. Exclusive. Bellevue. High tone white light time. Tension in every direction. Mean minds. Not quite sane as sure--twisted chemical meanness. A weird suburb stomping scene. Elliot Murphy has a little of that on record. Suburb steaminess. Perfect conditions for classic rock & roll riot. Gee. Anyway Lake Hills Roller Rink is seedy and grimy also cramped and cracked and if I can remember it right scary in a way 13 year olds get when they're unsure of themselves but everybody's screening a crisp coolness and you're stuck on a dance floor groping about to "the Witch" or "Psycho" or "Strychnine". All No. 1 smash boni-ma-roni-runaway mad classics. The guys are all busted up and blown away in different places now. I do know that the ex-lead guitarist is working in a music store in town and if there's anything you want to know I can get a personal exclusive interview on the Sonics "Story". Wow.

Send me a postcard drop me a line
Stating point of view.
Indicate precisely what you mean to say
Yours sincerely, wasting away,

— MR. MOONLIGHT

...About the Troggs. I own the Mixed Bag LP which does seem hard to come by considering mine has no LP cover to it! "Purple Shades" is on the LP. If you'd like any further information on the album let me know, OK? Is there any truth to the rumor that David Bowie was in the Riot Squad?

About the Episode Six. I once met Roger Glover and had a good talk with him about the Episode Six. He told me they released 13 singles in their lifespan....

The Rats were English (as far as I know). They evolved later into Ronno who also included Trevor Bolder and Woody Woodmansey. I know of two 45's, "Spoonful" and "Sack O' Woe". Their both on Columbia, I believe. If you know any more I'd appreciate any info.

About the Rattles. I have on tape one other A-side called "Can't Have Sunshine Everyday" released in '71 or '70. They still exist because on the back of a German magazine, Bravo from Sept. '73 there's a color pin-up of the band. It also states that their newest LP is called Tonight The Rattles Starring Edna. I hope this little bit of information helps!

DANNY

(--I'm sure many readers--including myself--would appreciate a track listing for Mixed Bag. OK?--Ed.)

MORE FAB FAX ON BRITAIN'S BIG BEAT

...I've noted down some points brought up by some of the features which (I hope) may be of some interest to you.

The Dakotas followed up "The Cruel Sea" with another instrumental but I can't really be sure of the title. The one which springs to mind is "Magic Carpet". Anyway the two singles (A and B sides) were subsequently released as an EP.

more FEEDBACK

I had forgotten all about Faron's Flamingos. They were on a television programme which basically was "What The Beatles Left Behind" along with Rory Storm and the Hurricanes and I think Ian & the Zodiacs. Faron was a real extrovert character and the group recorded by far the best British version of "Do You Love Me" which came out about 2 months before either Brian Poole or the Dave Clark 5. And the Escorts. I always thought the reason "Dizzie Miss Lizzie" failed was because it was so stylistically similar to the Swinging Blue Jeans' "Hippy Hippy Shake" both released about the same time. Their next single was "I Don't Want To Go On Without You" which came out a week before the Moody Blues'. It was the centre of a minor fuss, one week the Escorts said they were upset at the Moodies recording it just after they had, the next week Mike Pinder slated the Escorts, saying they took it from the Drifters' original and not from the Escorts and did not really care about lesser groups or something along those lines. I must disagree with your attack on the Merseybeats. Although far from world shattering, they did make some good singles in "Don't Turn Around", "Last Night", and (especially) "I Stand Accused". When they became the Merseys, they made a good stab at "Sorrow" (not as good as the McCoys) and followed it with Pete Townshend's "So Sad About Us".

The Poets and the Beatstalkers headed a small but lively Glasgow scene. Live the Poets were amazingly good mixing original numbers and Tamla. They did superb versions of Smokey's "I Second That Emotion" and "Tracks Of My Tears". The Stoics played similar material but relied more strongly on instrumentalisation. Unfortunately they recorded late (as the Dream Police) and were produced by Junior Campbell (then still with Marmalade) relying on his influence to a great extent. The Pathfinders were something else, very tight with an excellent lead vocalist in Ian Clews. Success did not come in the provinces, they moved to London and signed to Apple as White Trash (or Trash). Despite 2 fabulous singles ("Road To Nowhere" and "Golden Slumbers-Carry That Weight") and much publicity the group failed eventually leaving Apple in favour of Polydor. They changed their names again, this time to Jody, recording a couple of very commercial (and not so hot) singles before disappearing. However, Timi Donald has reappeared in Blue with ex-Poet and Marmalader Hugh Nicholson (the other Blueite Ian MacDonald fits in somewhere but I can't remember where). It's a shame the Pathfinders did not do better, even on the basis of their live act alone they deserved some means of success.

I had forgotten all about the Fairies as well. I saw them on TV singing "Come Get Yourself Home" sounding remarkably like the Pretty Things. They really were good, eventually becoming Tomorrow)with Keith West) and producing some fine "Flower power/Mod" singles such as "Revolution" and "My White Bicycle". I alsays associate them and John's Children together although I do prefer the Children. A friend of mine met the Pretty Things in a chip shop around the time of "Honey I Need". Even then they were not on speaking terms with Viv Prince! The Pretty Things released two singles between "Emotions" and S.F. Sorrow, "Deflecting Grey" and "Talking About The Good Times", both of which were exceptionally fine (heavily influenced by "Strawberry Fields"). "Deflecting Grey" had about 4 different tunes crammed into it. Nevertheless they were excellent despite the lack of identity which their early work had.

The Creation have an album released now on Charisma with both Planet and Polydor stuff. Ready Steady Go had them on the day "Making Time" was issued and it really sticks in my mind, especially the bowed guitar. Pye have been doing their usual reissue raking lately, having come up with the Golden Hour of the Kinks and likewise of the Searchers. Volumes One of each are fairly predictable but Volumes Two consist mainly of B sides and each boast all the cuts from celebrated EP's (Kinks: Kwyet Kinks and the Searchers' Ain't Gonna Kiss Ya). Both the albums have got 25 songs on them.

Another TV contemporary of RSG was Discs A Go Go which was a rather lame programme (compered by a guy who did and still does the wrestling on the TV every Saturday). However it did feature lesser groups. The Toggery Five were on one week with a single "I'd Rather Go Out With The Boys (Than Out With You)" which I still remember the tune of despite only hearing it that once. The Yardbirds were on too (while Keith Relf was in hospital) and Eric Clapton was doing lead vocal chores ("Good Morning Little Schoolgirl"). It must be about the only film footage of the Yardbirds with Clapton.

--BRIAN HOGG

BEAT MANIA

...Did you ever hear an LP called Beats by the Beats? I've played this one even more times than any Move record. It sounds like the Beatles but with Vivian Stanshall on some vocals and Bev Bevan playing the drums. A lot of originals on this one too. It's on Design Records and makes the Buggs look sick by comparison....

--ED PINIGIS

...A few corrections that may or may not be pertinent...and some points I feel shouldn't have been overlooked:

Gerry & Pacemakers: mention of his "Girl On A Swing" single, but no mention of album of same name which included that all-time "rock classic", "Strangers In The Night" (!). Also, Gerry did have some great album cuts ("Strangers" not one of them!) tho the opposite was indicated most everywhere in your magazine. Examples: "A Shot Of Rhythm And Blues" from 2nd Album, a terrific version of the song, infectious, melodic, exciting!

Dave Clark Five: My own personal favorite 60's British group. I must disagree with Mike Saunders' comment that "Having A Wild Weekend" was a "terrible" movie. It was acclaimed in most reviews I read, including a long one in Time magazine. It was overlooked by most young people because of its title, I believe (and sparse publicity). Had it retained its English title (Catch Us If You Can") I feel fans would have related it to the current hit, and would have gone to view it. There was also no mention of Dave's influence on up-and-coming drummers. A whole article could be written on the subject, but capsulizing: Dave's group was the first to bring any kind of focus on the drummer as anything more than a timekeeper. He had flash and style, and most of all prominence. (Who can forget that astonishing intro to "Bits And Pieces" and the bomp-bomp in "Glad All Over", or the machine gun intro to "Do You Love Me"?--all of which used to be banged out on lockers by beginning drummers back in Jr. High).

No mention was made of their bizarre experiments, or of their parodies of other pop groups and people (Dylan, Walker Bros., etc.) No mention of their "Hey Jude"-ish version of "Get Together" from their If Somebody Loves You English EP.

Walker Bros.: Just a personal taste point: I do not find the Scott Walker/Engel Brel stuff "dismaying"--melodramatic, yes, but that is its appeal. Brel's lyrics lend themselves to melodramatic interpretation. With each Scott LP the two things I look forward to most are the Brel interpretations and Scott's poetic compositions.

Easybeats: Part of the excitement credits for the all-time Easybeat song "Gonna Have A Good Time" must go to Steve Marriott, who sang back-up vocals.

Small Faces: Trivia note--both Marriott and future Pieman Peter Frampton were child stars; Frampton could be seen recently on L.A. TV in a movie called "Davy", from when little Pete was about 8 years old.

Shindig: One of my favorite memories was the jam between the Dave Clark 5 and the Beach Boys with Clark and Wilson (Dennis) doing double-drum chores and Lenny Davidson cutting loose with some blistering guitar. 'Twas on a Christmas show.

---WILLIAM STOUT

...This magazine is a true mine of information. What a lot of work you have done. And I know what I'm talking about: for the last two years I have been co-written on a Danish edition of a "Who's Who In Rock 'n' Roll". And that kind of work does take a long time!

Of course I have not been through the hole magazine yet. And certainly not with the magnifying glass! Nevertheless I have found a few places where I maybe can give a few supplying informations. Only maybe 'cause I don't think I can tell you anything new. Just two pieces of informations (certainly unusefull) on groups that have had my interest:

The T-Bones (Gary Farr, Keith Emerson, Alan Turner, Keith Jackson and David Langston) are vocal-backing on a CBS-single with Chris Barber and Kenneth Washington called "If I Had A Ticket". It's only the A-side (CBS 202394)--and it's recorded on April 26 or 28 1966.

To the Riot Squad I can tell you that David Bowie once was a member too--as a saxophone player--and as far as I know he's the sax-player on the Riot Squad single "Anytime" b/w "Jump" on Pye 15752. I don't know when that single was released. It seems to have been sometime in '65....

---JAN SNEUM

...Congratulations on the British Invasion issue--I was glad to see "You're No Good" by the Swinging Bluejeans mentioned--except for a few Dave Clark 5 songs it was the only British invasion single I bought at the time and it's still one of my favorites. When the Beatles first hit I dismissed them as being for girls. At school (6th grade) I took a poll of the Beatles vs. the Trashmen as best group--the Beatles won of course and I soon admitted I liked them but briefly had a Dave Clark 5 fan club and wore a button with Mike Smith on it. One girl joined and I soon after started the Royal Order of Ghoulardi Fans (R.O.G.F.) which boasted about 10 members and lasted almost a year. (Ghoulardi is known for once having the Rivingtons on his show singing "Papa-Oom-Mow-Mow" afterwhich he pulled on the bassman's lower lip and said "Liver." He also had a local band who wore their hair longer than Blue Cheer but were exposed as fakes when he pulled one of their wigs off).

I play drums in Mirrors, formed by two long time Velvet Underground freaks, which recently was joined by Jim Jones on bass who you have corresponded with and has the largest rock collection I've ever seen (not to mention a tape of "Little Shop of Horrors") --We do great versions of the Troggs' "Feels Like a Woman" and the Velvets' "Ferryboat Bill."

--MICHAEL WELDON

...Not wanting to discredit anything in your Who Put The Bomp British Invasion issue, you left out many Swinging Blue Jeans records--from the post-Ralph Ellis period:

1. Sandy/I'm Gonna Have You--Terry Sylvester's first record with the group--he sang lead on "Sandy".
2. Rumours Gossip Words Untrue/Now The Summer's Gone
3. Tremblin'/Something's Coming Along (B-side featured in the film "Poor Cow") at this point ex-Escort Mike Gregory joined the group on bass guitar--Les Braid moved to keyboards.
4. Don't Go Out Into The Rain/One Woman Man

Ray Ennis & the Blue Jeans:

5. What Have They Done To Hazel/Now That You've Got Me --last record with Terry Sylvester.
6. Hey Mrs. Housewife/Sandfly--lineup: Ray Ennis, Les Braid, Norman Kuhlke, Mike Gregory, Tommy Murray.

Music Motor:

7. Happy/Where Am I Going--lineup: Ray Ennis, Les Braid, Tommy Murray, Mike Gregory, Kenny Goodlass (Mike Gregory sang lead on "Happy"--Kenny Goodlass formerly with the Escorts, replacing Pete Clark for 3 records).

Swinging Blue Jeans:

8. Rainbow Morning/

I don't know if these were left out because of space or what, but I thought you'd like to know.

...Escorts trivia you might not know: Escorts wanted their first single to be "Fortune Teller"--not "Dizzy Miss Lizzy". "DML" went to #1 in Texas--reason: Pete Clarke's brother a DJ there. Lineup: Terry Sylvester (vocals/guitar), Mike Gregory (vocals/bass), John Kincade (guitar), Pete Clarke (drums). "I Don't Want To Go On Without You" drummer change, enter Kenny Goodlass. Single would have broken but Moody Blues issued it same week.

"The One To Cry", "C'mon Home Baby" (same lineup). "Let It Be Me": lineup change (Pete Clarke rejoins, he produces and arranges record). Terry Sylvester leaves....

"From Head To Toe"/"Night Time": lineup: Mike Gregory, John Kinrade, Frank Townshend (drums), and Paddy Chambers (vocals/guitar). B-side was written by Chambers with Paul McCartney and produced by McCartney.

--JANIS SCHACHT

...Two Things. You seem not to realize that Megan Davies of the Applejacks is Ray Davies' sister. At least you should've mentioned it. Second, Dave Berry did have another hit in England called "Mama".

And "Mozart Versus The Rest" by Episode Six sounds like Love Sculpture's "Sabre Dance" and I have it on tape. Looking forward to the next issue....

--IMANTS KRUMINS

...One mistake I must correct (I'll stand being corrected if I'm wrong, in fact if I am I deserve to be kicked in the head). The Hellions were from Worcestershire. Dave Mason was the lead guitarist, Jim Capaldi the drummer, and I think Luther Grosvenor (late of Spooky Tooth, Stealers Wheel, a solo stretch and now known as Aerial Bender with Mott the Hoople) on guitar. They made maybe 4 or five singles over here mainly on Piccadilly (subsidiary of Pye). They eventually broke up. Dave Mason became Spencer Davis's roadie, and Capaldi and I think Luther G formed Deep Feeling who played around Brum just before/same time as the Move were formed. They eventually went to London, backing Annie Ross, playing jazz clubs. Then they returned to Brum (mainly Elbow Room) and from that Traffic were born (I think Dave Mason played with D.F. for a time after his stint as roadie to S.D.)....

Have you ever heard of the Front Line? I'm not sure if they are English or American. They recorded on Atlantic, 1965, Atlantic 4057--I Don't Care/Got Love--songs by Larrigan, Philippet. A g0od single, aggressive-punk sound....

--ROGER CARELESS

(--The Front Line is definitely a fine record. I'm sure it's a California group; it came out here in '66 on York 9000, Charlie Greene/Brian Stone's short-lived label then distributed by Atlantic (later Bell)--Ed.(KB))

(According to a letter that appeared recently in TRM, the Front Line were a Bay Area group, originally called the Turtles until the Crossfires took that name, and including Gary Philipit, later of Copperhead fame. All this was new to me, altho I knew the original Grass Roots in San Francisco before their name was given to an LA studio group. Maybe Walsh's informant got the two stories mixed up, although how the Front Line entered in I dunno. Anyway it's worth checking out...which reminds me, we're looking for copies & information re any records on Greene & Stone's PALA label--Ed.(GS))

PRETTY THINGS IN NEW ZEALAND

...I didn't immediately leap into WPTB coz I get the feeling that New Zealand is even better off than America for all the stuff you covered--and as someone who has reread his Record Mirrors (the best English magazine for the WPTB period I think) about twelve times and GROWN UP with the Pretty Things and the Who and the Small Faces and all that, well...I thought WPTB was more for Americans who missed out on it all. Anyway I finally did get around to reading it and was suitably impressed--really! It reminded me that I love reading about those bands over and over and over. And little bits like the comment on the Things' "Midnight To Six Man" being one of their best singles, etc. etc., confirmed that all this was being written by people who know. Incidentally "Midnight To Six Man" didn't come out in New Zealand coz when the Things toured here they outraged us so much by drinking whiskey on stage and lighting the stage curtains and staggering drunkenly onto the stage during Sandie Shaw's act and carrying dead crayfish onto our national airways etc etc etc (most of that was drummer Viv Prince who was the archetypal raver plus a brilliant drummer--"Roadrunner"--and who made a superb single called "The Light Of The Charge Brigade" on Columbia which was actually a middle of the road instrumental out of the famed Carter-Lewis stable) and anyway after the Things had completely destroyed our country they were forbade ever to return and their records mysteriously stopped coming out here. About two years later the abysmal Emotions made it here but meantime their "Midnight To Six Man" was changing hands for $20 a copy to people with tombstones in their eyes.

So anyway as I read thru WPTB I think of about a hundred things to say as I read each page which I promptly forget as I move onto the next page--but in the Small Faces article for example it could perhaps have been mentioned that "Afterglow Of Your Love" was a magnificent single (some of us say their best) and that the single version was faster than the album version (hence even better) and that "Wham Bam Thank You Mam" was actually the A-side (in NZ anyway and I think England too). And the fact that Marriott shouts "piss off baby" before one of the choruses could have been mentioned too seeing as it was such a daring thing to be done for those days. And it could also be mentioned that Ogden's Nut Gone Flake originally had their version of P.P. Arnold's stupendous "If You Think You're Groovy" at the end of the first side only they put the single on instead at the last minute. Most Faces freaks really wanted to hear them do that one.

The La De Da's: Maori Phil Key, Bruce Howard, Brett Neilson, Trevor Wilson, Kevin Borich (1966 photo)

And that leads onto the La De Das from New Zealand, surely even better a white R&B covers album than that done by the Small Faces? Even better than Spencer Davis? It also has "How Is The Air Up There" and "Pied Piper" and "On Top Of The World" which was their first number one, tho I really never LOVED their R&B things seeing as I preferred pop-rock things. Didn't America get the Parlophone album of Easybeats biggies? 14 tracks up to "Friday On My Mind". The Easybeats were miles better before that single than after and this album is absolutely essential. All the biggies are on this one ("Women"/"Wedding Ring"/"She's So Fine" etc.). The EP was magnificent too ("Easyfever", etc etc.).

--ROY M. COLBERT

(--Also slated at one time for the Ogdens slot occupied by "Lazy Sunday" was an impromptu recording of the Ronettes' "Be My Baby". Would've loved to hear that, too...In an earlier letter Roy turned us on to some more fabulous Australia/New Zealand records, two of which deserve special mention because they were released in the U.S. The Groop (Australian band led by Brian Cadd, who has an undistinguished album out here on Chelsea): "Woman You're Breaking Me" is a brilliant pop-rocker with great neoclassical riffs, truly delightful. Came out here on Jamie 1349, and there's a lesser follow-up on Jamie 1371, a version of the Band's "We Can Talk". There's also two records on Bell here by a group of the same spelling, but the sound, writing, and production credits are all different so I don't know. The other knockout was by the Fourmyula from New Zealand, who had at least 8 local Top Tenners. This one's called "Nature" (Bell 879), and it's an absolutely stunning pop harmony record, totally irresistible and an instant favorite of everyone who hears it. Flip's another Top Ten item called "Home". Look out for 'em--Ed.)

WALKER BROS., IVY LEAGUE

...I was especially pleased to see an article on the Walker Brothers.. Did you know that Scott Engel stayed in a monastery on the Isle of Wight for a time? He left after fans found out he was there.

According to Mike Vernon's liner notes in the History Of British Blues on Sire, Keith Scott might have played piano on "Country Line Special", not Nicky Hopkins. He also lists Bernie Watson as probable guitarist...Vernon also says in the liner notes that he sometimes sang with the Yardbirds when Relf was ill.

Neil Landon must have joined Fat Mattress after the Flowerpot Men because he is the lead vocalist on both of their LPs. Ken Lewis and John Carter can be found singing background vocals on Marc Wirtz's Balloon. I recently sawon an import list that Pye has released a Golden Hour LP of the Ivy League. Should be worth getting, there might be over 20 songs on it....

--BERNARD WATTS

(--Golden Hour Of The Ivy League (GH 542) has 25 selections--all their singles, most B-sides, and odd LP tracks and whatnot. Included is their original version of "My World Fell Down", later gimmicked up with--so legend has it--Beach Boys Smile tracks by Gary Usher with his group Sagittarius. It's a fine collection--Ed.)

COUNT FIVE AWESOME; YARDBIRDS BORING

...The mag looks excellent. I've only glanced so far but I did read the letters page, both Simon's and Richard's letters were very valid in their own way. I've been playing through a lot of these records and although many of them consolidate my low opinion of sixties English rock, the amount of really exciting competently performed stuff is amazing. There was a lot of stuff I obviously missed in the sixties. I fell into the category that Richard describes, only a handful of British bands including Fame and particularly Goins, Mayall, Yardbirds and Bond were allowed to cover R&B stuff and be appreciated. We were all very proud of the fact that it took English bands to show U.S. kids how important Chicago and all Blues in fact were. The old term familiarity breeds contempt is never better utilised when describing localised or indigenous rock. Although I hold the Standells' "Dirty Water"/the Kingsmen's "Louie Louie"/Count Five's "Psychotic Reaction" and many others in awe as great records I would no doubt have treated them with the same disdain the Yardbirds received when performing at Leicester's premier rockspot of the sixties the Il Rondo when (can you believe anyone doing THIS to Cream a few years later?) I left the auditorium in the middle of Clapton's "Spoonful" solo, crossed the alley out back and drank a couple of pints of beer in the adjacent pub whilst still able to hear the music and get back to the stage before he ended. And you thought he played long solos with Cream. They didn't call him "Slowhand" for nothing. Leicester used to move like mad once (after all Family are all local lads) and I could reel off loads of old tales like when the Beatles closed the first half of a headline show by Del Shannon. In fact when I get through all I'm working on at the moment...I'll try and do it for you. Why not try and get a similar survey from others in biggish UK cities--Manchester, Newcastle, Birmingham, Glasgow, etc. Could be very interesting for U.S. readers in the same way as Blues and Rockabilly etc. regional breakdowns are at the moment...

--BOB FISHER

ROCK ON CANADIAN TV

...At the moment I'm not going to comment at length but just mention a few anecdotes and stuff which are running through my mind at present.

I was truly pleased with, and read with a proud smile, the articles on the Walker Bros. and P.J. Proby. Proby particularly had a great influence I'm sure--not only was he a fantastic singer with his power, wide range, great phrasing and diction but he had such a fine sense of style and fashion and entertaining. He was a primary influence on the almost-as-pompous and imposing Carl Wayne (for reference see article in NME Feb. '68 in which Wayne lauds Eddie Cochran, Proby, and Shirley Bassey). Nik Cohn really captured Proby's mentality and graces with his anecdote on Jim's drunken "life story" narrative. Proby's a minor legend now and he was indicative of the vitality and frantic energy of the era.

Also, the article on Rock & Roll TV in America was a most necessary inclusion, since as we well know, its doubtful that the Beatles might not have broken without the massive exposure on the Sullivan show--where their charisma counted as much as the music.

My first visual exposure to the Beatles was not on Sullivan but some months previously on the Jack Paar show via a film clip of a live gig in (I think) Birmingham. At the impressionable age of 12 I was floored by their powerful sound ("She Loves You") and by the hysteria they instigated.

The idea of presenting rock and roll in snatches on variety shows has always intrigued me. A three-minute stint in the midst of all that MOR schlock and mindless comedy was a perfect vehicle to spotlight the guttural power of r&r. Presley on Sullivan and Dorseys (I saw it when I was 5 or 6 years old the memory is very, very vivid), Beatles and Stones on Ed's biggie.

One of my favourite shows was Red Skelton which I watched without fail for two years solid. I saw the Manfreds, Hollies, Rockin' Berries (a rarity) and the Stones in a film clip doing "Carol" and "Tell Me" on the steps of the London Palladium with a Cliff Richard poster in the background--ironic, huh? One of my favourite memories from the Skelton show was the night the Kinks were featured. The chorus did their usual bit, singing the announcements, "and our guest stars--the Kinks"--and there they were, Ray grinning cynically, the debut of those now famous gapping choppers--but they didn't appear and I was so angry I almost wept.

However the two TV gigs I've cherished most in all likelihood haven't been aired in the States. They are:

1) The Who on film in a Canadian Broadcasting show called Take Thirty, filmed in London. It was a live gig, a London concert, and the Who ripped thru "Jenny Take A Ride" (incredible, the chords) and "My Generation", during which Townshend smashed the guitar to pieces. The camera zoomed in on his face and he looked terrifying. The show was aired Oct. 3, 1966, and I ordered it 2 years ago to show for a history class but they sent the wrong show. I do intend to get a hold of it and video tape it sometime in the near future.

2) The other show appeared (I think) in late June or early July '66 as part of a series of odd films called "20/20" on the above-mentioned CBC. It was called "Pretty Things" and yep, it was that band alright doing "Midnight To Six Man", "LSD", etc. (I believe) at the Marquee. A truly incredible film which captures the Pretties raunch animalism. It's probably why I sort of worship them.

Also I should mention I picked up a single last week on Much called "Satori"/"Ayala Red" by a group called the Mighty--both decks written by Pagliaro and produced by M. Pagliaro and G. Lagios. Both are instrumentals, one with a voice akin to Page yelping in the background. An oddity but not of much interest. Now if he could only come up with another "Lovin' You Ain't Easy" or "Some Sing Some Dance"....

--BOB LAWRENCE

FREDDIE & THE SCAPEGOATS

...Got the Bomp the other day. It's a fine job, albeit a little hard to read--I liked the old format better, I think I've said that before--but I miss the humor and general irreverence that was present in this issue only in the letter column. I also think there's a problem when you do one of these (essential) issues that covers a subject systematically by groups--there's been a rock writer's syndrome for some time where everyone looks around for some singer or group that no one else cares about and over-praises them in order to make his point--or his reputation. A lot of the pieces in this last issue grievously overrate the groups--I mean what's wrong with saying Freddie & the Dreamers were unadulterated shit? Or maybe it's just a problem in differentiating between enthusiasms. "Good" slides so easily into "genius"....

--GREIL MARCUS

(--Once more we're forced to take up the cudgels for the beleagured Freddie & the Dreamers--(A) the piece on the Manchester madcaps was quite obviously tongue-in-cheek, a device presumed by its author to be rather more appropriate than saying they were unadulterated shit, and (B) quite often Freddie's music was at least fairly adulterated; "A Little You" and a number of LP tracks are thoroughly competent lightweight Merseybeat, though the music was of secondary importance to the comedy.

With that fiery defense out of the way, allow me to tender fervent compliments on your Bobby Vee liner notes, a definitively evocative piece.

(I dread to conceive of the reaction had the original MS of the Freddie article run last issue--it was nearly twice as long, with about five times as many excruciatingly coy witticisms, and may well have cost WPTB half its subscribers)--Ed.)

more FEEDBACK

OUR KIND OF GIRL!

...I used to watch Shindig & Hullabaloo faithfully. Wore the grooves out on the first Stones LP. Used to be able to do a god Jagger imitation. Brian was my fave Stone. Was in love with Ray Davies until I read where he was married. My little sister cried the first time she saw Geoge Harrison on TV. My other sister could do the Freddie. I thought Dusty Springfield was great and I wanted to look that way too. Sandie Shaw's "Girl Don't Come" and "There's Always Something There To Remind Me" are still two of my all time fave songs. I used to stay up late with the radio turned down low just to hear "All Day And All Of The Night" one more time. I loved the Yardley adverts on TV. Lennon was my fave Beatle and I tried in vain to get one of those black leather caps he used to wear. The Hullabaloos were uglier than the Stones and I liked it. Used to be turned on by P.J. Proby and got my first inklings of what sex was all about when I saw him on "Piccadilly Palace". Saw "Hard Days' Night" 6 times in one day. My Mom liked "Hippy Hippy Shake"! I used to bum money off people to buy 16 and Flip. Slept with John's first book--In His Own Write--under my pillow. I'm still in love with Colin Blunstone. Never got to see the Beatles live. "Tell Me" was my fave early Stones song. I almost cried the first time the Beatles left to go back to England. And someday, I used to tell myself, I'll get to go too...

Those are just a few of the things reading the British Invasion brought back. Many many thanks for taking the time to write it. It was well worth the wait....

--BILLIE SANDERS

MOD MEMORIES

...When I last wrote I stated that Steve Marriott made a record with his backing group the Moments...around late'64 and early '65. He played regularly at my local "beat club" of the time, in Hounslow. The Attic Club....

If you would like me to, I'll take some photostats from old record papers and the pop music press that would be of interest...e.g, a feature on the High Numbers, Rod Stewart, and West London Club Guide with all the groups featured each night....

Throughout the copy of WPTB, I saw various mentions to books that seem to be available in the States, not to mention the Richmond Jazz Festival TV film. I went to that festival (August 1965) where in one night I saw the Who, Moody Blues and Yardbirds. Those were the days! I give anything to see that film. Yeah, honest you've no idea how great it was living round here around '64 to '66. It sounds unbelievable today when you tell younger kids that you could see stars like Pete Townshend, Mick Jagger and the Small Faces walking down Richmond High Street! I and a few friends had a long talk in Hounslow Bowling Alley of all places with none other than Steve Marriott. He asked me where I got my shoes from! You've no idea how great I felt....

You say also that the subcultures of R&R interest you, e.g., Teds, Hippies, Mods, etc. Well if you want the closest definition I've ever seen to a "working-class West London 16-18 year-old Mod" in 1965, Look at, study and listen to Quadrophenia, the latest Who LP. Nostalgia trips all the way! Well for me anyway.

Well, that's about it, I think, just wanna give a mention to two great R&B discs that were never mentioned in the B. Invasion issue. "Oh Yeah"--the Others, "Parchman Farm"--the Rats. The Others were group of schoolboys that went to the local grammar school, 10 mins. walk from my house....

--DON HUGHES

LOCAL CORRESPONDENTS WANTED

...I was overwhelmed by the new Bomp, though a little disturbed on the side to see the proclamation, "Not a fanzine", and a definite shortage of fandom bliitherings. That stuff did a lot in previous Bomps to break up and make palatable the mass of data, even give it meaning and put it in perspective. Please give a little more attention to all of this if this turns out to be the popular complaint.

I'm salivating for a Chicago-punk section in Bomp (and would be more than happy to lend myself for the purpose of doing research for it). That stuff will be the bargain bin fodder in a few years. And lest we forget the Shadows of Knight, T.S. Harry Webb & the Flock, the Mauds, Buckinghams, New Colony 6, the Ravin' Kind, Illinois Speed Press, etc. etc. Anytime you're ready....

(from a later letter...)

Here's a suggestion for WPTB, which you may either choose to look into or discard; however, please consider publishing this letter as some other zine, fan or pro, might be interested.

What I propose is a section devoted to regional correspondence. Certainly there are emerging third-generation rock scenes in cities like L.A., Austin, Atlanta, New York and Chicago. Bands like the Hollywood Stars, the Dynomiters, Hydra and Pentwater will soon be spreading their music nationwide. If you were to choose someone from each of these cities to document the local scenes, however at-the-time esoteric, this could prove invaluable when in later years we attempt to write the history of 70's rocknroll.

Consider: If some 1967 rock publication had thought of having local correspondents, we'd know a lot about Cyrus Erie, Eric Carmen, and what has now become the Raspberries, thru gossip received from the Cleveland correspondent. Imagine if there had been a Chicago correspondent to tell us about T.S. Henry Webb's participation in such bands as the Flock and Dick Caine & the Exploders! Webb is soon to sign to Epic, and is one of the most lauded uppin'-comers around. Ditto with the Dunwich scene, the Mauds, Buckinghams, USA label, Perry Johnson when he had the Royal Blue/Venue labels (he's with Dharma now), etc. A Miami correspondent could cover the Henry Stone scene; one from Austin, the armadillo world; the possibilities are endless. And think of what an important reference such gossip would become once fully fermented. Think about it.

--GARY BAKER

(--Readers who would like to send us short pieces on local acts of interest (w/photo if possible) are welcome. And a Cleveland columnist would be terrific....--Ed.)

Chicago punk, coming up...

HOW TO REPACKAGE A CHEESY ANIMAL

...The Animals album bothered me pretty much when it first appeared, especially as I had written to Mike Ochs some months earlier to volunteer my interest in helping to compile an Animals repackage. I proposed two albums, Bigots, Big Heads, And Bad Service In Restaurants (a 2-record set of the 1963-66 Animals) and Psychedelic Schlemiel (a single LP of the 1967-8 Eric Burdon & the Animals). Of course I knew that was mostly fantasy, as was certain that MGM would never buy those arrangements and titles (they'd call it The Very Best Of Eric Burdon & The Animals, Vol. XVII), but I still wasn't prepared for the absolute awfulness of the actual Abkco reissue. I was plenty pissed, and I wrote a nasty review for PRM.

After I read Greg's review, I began to mellow a lot about the Animals reissue--like he said, the music is great, and transcends the tawdriness of the packaging. If people want intelligent commentary on the songs, they can follow along with my WPTB article as a concordance. Billy Altman came to much the same conclusions as Greg in his Creem review of the Animals album, only he also warmed my heart for ever and ever by admitting that "the Animals and Eric Burdon were, at their prime, filthier and less socially redeeming than the Rolling Stones"--I've been trying to hammer that idea into people's thick heads for ten years come this August. All the dudes who are having nervous breakdowns over the Stones' current decline could have gotten that trauma over with clear back in 1966 if they'd cast their lot with me--doing that shit at 19 sure toughened me up for the "death of rock" and all the hassles that've come since.

Which is partly why I'm not losing too much sleep over the Abkco Animals set--as Greg wrote, the time to do it right probably hasn't come yet, and the Abcko album can help keep the Animals' recordings available until then. I don't know how to explain my aversion to "scholarly" repackages to you--I'm thinking of my Eddie Cochran Legendary Masters album. It's just perfect at getting the reissue job done--song selections, Lenny Kaye's notes, everything--yet I don't play it often, and I think that's because the package seems so bland and out-of-context in comparison to the music--it's not what the fifties looked like. I don't mind cheesiness per se, I just don't like the non-Animals-representative cheesiness Abkco used. If I got to do Psychedelic Schlemiel my way, I'd use that photo (appeared in Rolling Stone ca. 1969) of Burdon lying between Jimi Hendrix's legs, staring worshipfully up at his balls. What a consummate portrait of the Eric ethic!

--RICHARD RIEGEL

(--I don't mind cheesiness per se either, but shoddy reissues--in regard to the music--piss me off. When I play the Eddie Cochran package, I get 30 well-programmed songs, close to the best 30 that could have been selected. When I play the Animals album--which I don't, generally--I get a miserable 20 randomly-programmed, randomly-selected songs, complete with glaring omissions and pointless juxtapositions. I can live with a crappy package (or an overly-sterile one), but a dismal job on the music deserves to be slagged. Anyway, hope you have better luck when the time comes for the definitive Lou Christie repackage--come to think of it, wouldn't mind getting involved with that one myself--Ed.)

GET OUT THOSE WANT LISTS

...A few...interesting recent finds: "The Rains Came" (Sir Doug) by Big Sam and the House Wreckers on Eric; "Boy Wonder" I Love You" by Burt Ward on MGM written by Zappa; a James Gang record on Ascot (can't stand the group or the record but it sure seems like it oughta be a rare early record; an EP from Poland by George and the Beatovens with pic jacket and liner notes and songs all in Polish; another Wylde Heard record (I have one on a local label) this time on Philips with pic sleeve and bio on the back containing the great phrase "Bill, the bass guitarist and lead singer, who can play the bass as easily with one finger as he can with four..." A guy like that should be famous. Probably the record I'm most proud of having garnered recently is "Save"/"The Syracuse" by Felix & the Escorts on JAG records. Since I was a student at Syracuse Univ. this record is of particular interest to me. A friend of mine is on it--later with the All Night Workers on Round Sound, Cameo, Mercury--and he once offered me $50 for this record if I could find it. He said the group recorded, walked out of the studio, turned around, and the studio had vanished, etc. He didn't have a copy himself and didn't even know if it was really ever released. Anyway, the other members of the group were Felix Cavaliere, later of the Rascals; Mike Esposito, later of the Blues Magoos; with technical advice from Lou Reed who was also at school in Syracuse at the same time. The same cuts have appeared on a Design album featuring the Young Rascals and the Isley Brothers....

I have an instrumental on Capitol by Arthur Lee and the L.A.G.'s. Is this in any way possibly connected with Love?

At some point Bomp should do something about those groups that implied they were British, i.e. Great Scotts, Scotland Yardleys, Playboys of Edinburgh, etc....

Anyone really interested in the Pirate Radio scene in England in the sixties ought to pick up (or try to) When Pirates Ruled The Waves by Paul Harris, 1968, Impulse Publications, Ltd. As far as I know it was only printed in England so someone from over there should be assigned the task of checking out additional copies. As long as I'm plugging books let me make slight mention of my friend Arnie Passman's book The Deejays on Macmillian.

The Bomp mentioned the vagueness of the Dakotas backing Billy J. Kramer. From the English album Listen: Mike Maxfield, lead guitar; Ray Jones, bass guitar; Robin Macdonald, rhythm guitar; and Tony Mansfield, drums. Liner notes point out that his first group was the Phantoms and then a name change to the Coasters who decided to be semi-pro while he went pro and joined up with "Manchester's top instrumental unit, the Dakotas"....

--FRANK BRANDON

BLUE JEANS BOP

...Thanks for WPTB No. 10-11. Tho I'm a 50's rock'n'roll maniac, I really enjoyed your British Invasion issue. Just a few comments about the Swinging Blue Jeans. They certainly DO enjoy a revival nowadays. A reissue of "Hippy Hippy Shake" was a smash hit in Germany in the summer of 1973, and they've been touring a lot here in Scandanavia. They are as busy as they were in the old days, and they even released an album called Hippy Hippy Shake, recorded in Sweden April 16-17th, 1973, and the tunes are: "Hippy Hippy Shake", "Bad Moon Rising", If I Were A Carpenter", "Good Golly Miss Molly", "Radancer", "Blowin' In The Wind", "Long Tall Sally", "Cottonfields", "Lawdy Miss Clawdy", "Bony Maronie", "You're No Good" and "Summertime Blues". They're not in any respect as wild and exciting as they used to be, I'm sorry to say.

I am really looking forward to a SURF/HOT ROD ish of WTPB. Now THAT should really be something!!!!!!! What about a general issue on the early 60's pop scene???!!

Shake & Boogie
RUNE HALLAND
Whole Lotta Rockin'

WE ALSO HEARD FROM: Greg Chiappuzzo, John McCarthy, Tom Small, Doug Hinman, John Koenig, Dave Cochrane, Sue Fredericks, Jay Kinney, Andrew Lauder, Ellen Sander, Chris Hanley, Allen Hertscher, Art Schook, Jonathan Kuntz and many many many more. Thanks one & all, and keep those letters coming.....

With this issue, you'll notice quite a few changes. Ken Barnes' "Reverberation" column and my own "Juke Box Jury Jr." will appear henceforth in every issue, full of info on obscure classics. The "Fanzines" column this time is a hopefully complete guide to all rock fanzines currently publishing. In future columns I will try to limit it to more detailed reviews of whatever new zines are received. If you put out or are thinking of starting a fanzine, be sure and put me on your mailing list so I can review your zine.

You'll also notice in this issue a general improvement in layouts and photos. There'll be further improvements in the appearance of the magazine, the first priority being larger type. We're really sorry about this, but at least the type is bolder than last issue and you should be able to make all of it out.

Also starting this issue, we'll be running a series of label profiles and listings. In general, we'll try to include all or most of the labels relating to the artists covered in a given issue, and also covering many small labels that had a good percentage of English, punk, and other interesting releases. If there are any you'd like to see (and please, don't ask for Phillies! Let's see some imagination...) let us know.

For now, we could use help with these labels: Lawn, RSVP, Valiant (both 6000 and 700 series), Amcan (403,405,407--) Karate, World Artists (any before 1018; 1020,1026,1028,1035, 1037,1039,1040,1042-44,1047,1050,1054,1059-61,1063--), American Arts, We Make Rock N' Roll Records, Boom (001-5, 008-11, 013,015-21, 023--)Super-K (1,2,3,5,6,7,9,11,12,13, 16--; 104--) Attack (1402,1403,1405--), GAR, Prism, Counterpoint, Claridge (302,305,307, 310, 311,313, 314,315,316, 318--) Southern Sound (101,102,103,105,106,107,108,109,111, 112,113,115-19,121--; 201,203,205--). We need name of artist, both titles, and any interesting info regarding producers etc.

* * *

We've received many inquiries regarding the forthcoming book of UK discographies/Encyclopedia of British pop. We're still working on it, folks. It won't be published until we've exhausted all sources of making sure it's as complete as possible, which means another couple of months at least, maybe more. But bear with us, please; it'll be worth it.

* * *

Anyone who has any unusual tapes, whether of live concerts, broadcasts or unreleased studio material by any rock act, should contact Charles Mayette, 28 Driftwood Ave, Novato, CA 94947. Charles has probably the most comprehensive library of rare tapes in the country, and if you have something of interest he can trade you tapes of just about anybody you want. When writing, enclose $1 and ask him to send you his mind-boggling catalog of tapes.

Greg's Errata & Addenda

This column is reserved for new information relating to articles, reviews, discographies, etc. published in previous issues. No significant addenda were received on #11, except for the disclosure that the Corduroys record (Planet 122) came out here...but Ken's already covered that in Reverberation. But please, if you have any facts relevant to material in this issue, send it c/o this column...

This is one of the real mystery labels of the '60s. Their 3 known releases were all British semi-hits of 1964, and none from Liverpool. The Paramounts of course were an early version of Procol Harum, and this was their only US release.

902 is Roy Wood's old group doing an excellent Beatle rave-up, and both are quite rare and worth having. Leyton was an early-60s British crooner and this record is not especially interesting.................Greg Shaw

901	John Leyton	I Guess You Are Always On My Mind/ Beautiful Dreamer
902	Mike Sheridan & the Nightriders	Please Mr. Postman/ In Love
903	Paramounts	Poison Ivy/I Feel Good All Over

The Mike label was "a product of Andover Record Corp." and if there was an Andover label I'd like to see some listings for it... Mike didn't have many releases, but they did have three by Randy & the Rainbows, an excellent & underrated harmony group. Mike's other known releases include a cover of Bob Lind's "Mr. Zero" which we all know from the Keith Relf version, and the American release of Graham Bonney's big British hit, "Baby's Gone". 4003 is a nice folk-rock/pop production. Info is needed on all missing numbers, and I could use copies of the Randy & Rainbows discs.........Greg Shaw

4200	London Knights	Go to Him/Dum Diddiee Dee
4001	Randy & the Rainbows	Lovely Lies/I'll Forget Her
4002	Linda Rae	Look for the Rainbow/Tweenager? Tomorrow
4003	Attic Sounds	Pitter Patter/Where Are You
4004	Randy & the Rainbows	He's a Fugitive/Quarter to Three
4005	Half a Sixpence	Mr. Zero/Can It Be
4006	--	
4007		
4008	Randy & the Rainbows	Bonnie's Part of Town/Can It Be
4009	Graham Bonney	Baby's Gone/Later Tonight (1966)

The Independence label was formed in 1967 by Phil Skaff. Skaff was an Executive Vice-President at Liberty Records who had the ambition to form his own intentionally small label. He lined up independent distribution and most of the records released were master purchases, from Pye and EMI in Britain or local American labels.

The one exception was Skaff's signing of Delaney Bramlett, late of the Shindogs (whose Joey Cooper also released a record on Independence). Skaff was advised on the Bramlett signing by Leon Russell, the former Liberty staff producer; and the Bramlett record, and especially the Delaney & Bonnie single, seem to be the records Skaff took most pride in.

The one he was least proud of was a master purchase of a disk by a Pekin, Ill. band called the Third Booth. A slashing hard-edged rocker, "I Need Love" is easily Independence's best from a Bomp standpoint, along with the Montanas' "Difference of Opinion."

The Montanas, basically a smooth British pop group masterminded by Tony Hatch of Pet Clark/Jackie Trent fame, were the most successful Independence act, reaching the Top 50 in early '68 with "You've Got to Be Loved," "Difference of Opinion", a jagged pseudo-psychedelic rocker, was the flip. The Montanas recorded for Pye in England, had a couple of releases on Warners in the States (including a dynamic Addrisi Bros. pop-rock ditty called "That's When Happiness Began") and were signed by Skaff after hearing a demo of "Take My Hand". They issued five singles on the label, but only #83 made the charts.

In fact, it was Independence's only chart single. However the label's records sold well enough in local areas to endure thru mid-1969, a two-year run. Independence was not crucial to pop history or even an overwhelming success, but its operating philosophy of assorted master purchases did produce an interesting blend of releases................Ken Barnes

76	Delaney Bramlett	Guess I Must Be Dreamin/Don't Let It
77	Joey Cooper	Raspberry Rug/Just Like You
78	Delaney & Bonnie Bramlett	You've Lost That Lovin' Feelin'/? (their first record together)
79	Montanas	Take My Hand/Top Hat
80	Delaney & Bonnie Bramlett	Goodbye My Lover Goodbye/ (unreleased) Searchers' song
81	unreleased	
82	Clouds	Visions/Migada Bus (LA group, originally released under group name Looking Glasses, on Media Records)
83	Montanas	You've Got to Be Loved/Difference of Opinion
84	Barry Lee Show	I Don't Want to Love You/Over and Over (British act which also recorded for Ascot)
85	Puppet Children	Puppet Children/Save Yourself For Me (American act produced by Wilder Bros, onetime Dick & Deedee producers)
86	Third Booth	I Need Love/Mysteries
87	Montanas	I'm Gonna Change/A Step in the Right Direction
88	Chevrons	Love, I Love You/Dreams (Omaha group)
89	Montanas	Run to Me/You're Making a Big Mistake
90	Roger James Cooke	Skyline Pigeon/I'm Burning (the Roger Cook of the Cook-Greenaway/David & Jonathan team)
91	Marlene Dietrich	Where Have All the Flowers Gone/some, In German (unreleased. Previously issued on Liberty in mid-60s during Skaff's tenure)
92	Roger James Cooke	Not That It Matters Anymore/Paper Chase
93	Montanas	Heaven Help You/Round About
94	Chevrons	Mine Forever More/In the Depths of My Soul

WHO PUT THE BOMP!

$1.00 / SPRING 1975

"THE MAGAZINE FOR ROCK 'N' ROLL FANS"

The Flamin' Groovies
Will '75 Be Their Year?

The History of Michigan Rock
Bob Seger, MC5, Mitch Ryder, SRC, Rationals, Suzi Quatro, ? and the Mysterians, Terry Knight

Beatle Novelties
A Complete Listing

The Rockabilly Revival
It Must Be Goin' Round

The Rise & Fall of the Hollywood Stars

PLUS: Discographies, LP & Singles Reviews, Columns & Features...
....and much more!

Back again with the second column-as-we-see 'em--more obscure classics, oddments, name-dropping and shameless solicitations for rare records. By the way, if any of my fanatic followers out there (you know who you are--wish I did) are wondering why my byline in this issue is restricted to this column and the Beatle novelties--well, "space limitations" prevented the inclusion of my meticulously-researched survey of the Santa Barbara-Ventura-Oxnard rock scene and a definitive, scholarly Swingin' Medallions overview. At this rate I'll have to start my own fanzine...

WE GOT A THING, IT'S CALLED RAIDER LOVE

One of the distinct advantages of living in Southern California is the opportunity to catch Paul Revere & the Raiders' semi-annual stint at Knott's Berry Farm. Figuring it was about time for a Raiders update, Terry and I, along with Mark and DeeDee Shipper (Mark, as you'll recall, was singlehandedly responsible for the Raiders Revival of '72--in fanzine circles, at any rate), made the run.

What a show! First thing you ought to know is the boys are back in uniform--three corner hats and everything! Sometimes they do steps, too. Second point is that Mark Lindsay doesn't come on till halfway through (attired in a smart jumpsuit--brilliant, in fact). Revere dominated the Lindsay-less segments with an irritatingly hokey accent, cornfed comedy (abetted by Keith Allison, the stiffest straight man I've ever heard), and his cheesy Edsel-grille piano (the ultimate in grille cheesiness) with actual headlights.

In their first set they launched into a series of earlyLP cuts ("Do You Love Me", "Ooh Poo Pah Doo") and proceeded to perform over 20 songs in two sets, including a dozen of their hits from "Louie Louie" to "Indian Reservation" ("Steppin' Out", "Just Like Me", "Him Or Me", "Mr. Sun, Mr.Moon" and a great "Hungry" among them). Lindsay was below par at first (contributing the lamest version imaginable of "The Bitch is Back"), but caught fire in the second half, when the group pounded out a ferocious "Taking Care of Business" that topped BTO and sounded a lot like vintage Slade. Although a rather jaded attitude seemed quite apparent at times, the Raiders still put on a peerless performance. Hope they keep plugging (and make another record, damn it).

CULT 45's

Seems to be Shipper's month--his former clients, the Droogs, have a new record out and it's easily their best yet. "Ahead of Love" (Plug & Socket PNS 003, for those who're counting) has a great chorus, a vastly compelling guitar hook and a wild multitracked break (or so it sounds). "Get Away", the flip, is even better, a vicious rocker with a slight Seeds flavor, but more adventurous than anything Sky Saxon ever sang--inspired stuff. If psychedelia and progressive rock had never happened, this is how '66 rock might have evolved by '74. Though he and the Droogs have come to a parting of the ways, you can still get the record through Mark at Box DH, Panorama City, CA 91402 ($1.75 ought to cover it).

DRUIDS - "Cool Calm & Collected"/"Sorry's Not Enough" (MNO 101)

This was right next to the Droogs on the shelf, and turned out to be much more brilliant than I'd remembered. A-side has a hypnbotic two-chord folk-rock riff and is an excellent American adaptation of the Merseybeat and Byrds' innovations. The flip eclipses it, though; perhaps the best Merseybyrds combination I've heard. Great bridge, great chorus, great surf/folk-rock guitar riff, tremendous record. With a little luck they could be even bigger than the Grodes.

FAINE JADE - "It Ain't True" (Providence 420)

Heard this at Greg's two years ago, finally found it. This mysterious disk sounds like it's threatening a psychotic crack-up (like the Craig, last column) but never quite gets there. It's got a simpleminded two-chord tune & a fruity vocal, but there's a vicious recurrent moronic fuzz riff and the nastiest one-chord fuzz drone break ever conceived--really grungy. Amateurish, inept, crazed, and near-brilliant. It's the flip of a perfectly innocuous, trivial pop ditty. (Collectors note: Faine Jade also made a forgettable LP on the RSVP label that turns up occasionally in cutout bins.)

KEITH EVERETT - "Don't You Know"/"Conscientious Objector (TMP-Ting 118)

First called to my attention by Mike Saunders, but he underrated the A-side (a hit in Chicago in '65 or '66). It's one of the best minor-chord Zombies variations around, with a bizarre break which sounds like Everett trying to imitate a lead guitar with his voice, as if they couldn't afford the extra instrument on the session. The flip is a reactionary folk-rock expose (sample: "They hide under the name of conscientious objectors/They might as well be defectors"), enjoyable stuff. Somebody ought to explore the realm of right-wing rock (Spokesmen, Jan Berry's "Universal Coward" and numerous records on Anthony J.Hilder's Impact label, which bear charming inscriptions like "Our CountryCan Never Go Right By Going Left"--even on surf instrumentals).

*Faine Jade: at the brink of psychosis.

TRACEY DEY - "I Won't Tell" (Amy 912)

Very probably Bob Crewe's greatest girl-group production, something like the Four Seasons meet the Ronettes. Full-to-bursting production job, with a monster chorus and great singing by Tracey, whose other records are good enough but nowhere near this one. Some odd effects, too--a Jewel Akens-style lead (three months before "The Birds & the Bees" came out), a false ending, and a very strange massed-strings maneuver that sounds like a mellotron.

KNICK-KNACKS - "Without You" (Columbia 43600)

A light, delicate record with infinite appeal. The lead singer's voice sounds like the leaders of the Shangri-Las or the Angels, but more vulnerable; and the spoken parts and chorus add up to a perfectly charming single.

NEW GENERATION - "Smokey Blue's Away"/"She's a Soldier Boy" (Imperial 66317)
U.K.BABY - "Heartbreaker" (Imperial 66409)

These are early Sutherland Brothers relics, and quite impressive. "Smokey" is a lachrymose lament in a string-laden folky pop arrangement, pleasant enough. But the flip is superb, neat harmonies a la the Sutherlands of today, a great hook bridge, and powered throughout by that archetypical hyperactive late '60s British bass style (pioneered by John Entwhistle earlier and heard on records like "Love Grows" and "Nothing But a Heartache", among many others). Fine effete stuff, right up Alan Betrock's alley.

"Heartbreaker" (written by Iain Sutherland and probably sung by him) is a straightforward rocker with nice melodic touches and a break straight out of "It's All Too Much" by the Beatles, very commercial-sounding. And from the same period (Imperial 66390) and producer (Barry Kingston) comes a record by the Eggy (clever name), "You're Still Mine". It's a raucous pop-psychedelic showcase, a fine synthetic pop tune interrupted by disembowelled guitar sounds (much like Jeff Beck's "Hi Ho Silver Lining"). "Hookey", the flip, is slightly more normal, a heavy rocker with a stomping chorus sounding like the Equals--an underrated group in their own right.

Finally, I tracked down the Searchers' 1972 album *Needles and Pins* (British RCA 1480), wherein they re-cut several of their hits, and it turns out to be first-rate. Most of the tracks (especially "Take Me For What I'm Worth", "Needles and Pins" and "When You Walk in the Room") retain the economy and sparkle of the original versions but are just different enough to make the album sound fresh and exciting. An infinitely playable LP.

OTHER PICKS TO CLIQUE: Apple's "Buffalo Billycan" (Page One 21,012) sounds uncannily like Syd Barrett... Nazareth's "Love Hurts" (Mooncrest 37--UK) is an impassioned rock rendition of the Everlys/Orbison classic... "Rainbow Ride" (Steed 711), Andy Kim's greatest, and the Ides of March's "Girls Don't Grow on Trees" (Parrot 326), both terrific "Last Train to Clarksville" ripoffs... "Ahh..." by Amnesia is a fine heavy riff-rocker; it's new and available from 10107 Arden Ave, Tampa, FLA. 33612... "There's Not One Thing" by Manchester's Just Four Men (Tower 163, on the flip of Freddie & the Dreamers' "Send a Letter to Me") is an excellent Searchers-style tune; even better in the same vein is the Outlaws' "Don't Cry" (Smash 2025)... And many more, but time prevents....

Remember, you too can win fame and glory by nominating your own Picks to Clique--just send deserving records to me, care of this column, P.O. Box 7195, Burbank, CA 91510. Decision of the judge (me) is final (cute way to score records, eh?). Seriously, any kind of feedback is welcomed.

Winding up, the Rollin' Rock Rebels (heavily plugged last issue) broke up within a week of publication--power of the press. Turns out the State of Mickey & Tommy, spotlighted last issue, were a French duo who also wrote songs and arranged for Johnny Hallyday, the chameleonic Gallic pop idol, during his flower-power phase. Finally, my compliments to Jay Kinney for his disturbingly accurate caricature within the *Reverberation* logo above. I don't normally swing baseball bats at garbage cans, though--except in the most figurative sense!

THE RETURN OF THE FLAMIN' GROOVIES
AMERICA'S COOLEST TEENAGE BAND IS MORE ALIVE THAN EVER!

BY GREG SHAW

"I reckon that in 1980 or so, those of us who survive will look back and view 1968-72 as the years of sterility, mediocrity and excess. And among those who are smashing into the apathy and prolonging the myth of excitement through these dead years of rock are the Flamin' Groovies." -- Pete Frame, ZIGZAG 25

In the last two years we've seen revivals of everything from Beatlemania to bubblegum and surf music, but the one thing that's been missing since about 1967 and most blatantly absent from today's music scene is the good old teenage rock & roll band, the kind there used to be thousands of, the kind from which every major innovation in rock has sprung.

Things are changing. Rock & roll bands (as opposed to supergroups, concept groups, and groups dedicated to maintaining an aesthetic distance from their audience) are once again appearing. Local bands are popping up around the country playing good, simple '50s and '60s derived rock & roll, and soon they'll be everywhere. In that light, it's interesting to look around and see what became of their counterparts in the '60s.

The ones that made it (Stones, Who, Beach Boys, etc) big enough at the time have stayed around, fighting a losing battle against the onset of age. But those who hadn't made it when the style went out of fashion in 1968 were decimated almost totally.

What happened to the Standells, Seeds, Shadows of Knight, Knickerbockers, 13th Floor Elevators, Clefs of Lavendar Hill, Sonics, Outsiders, Astronauts, etc. etc. ad infinitum? Did these bands stick it out, struggling to keep the music they'd created alive?

No, they didn't. When things began to change they either gave up and left music completely, or sold out to what they hoped would be commercially acceptable, whether it be psychedelic grunge, jazz rock, country rock, or a local production of "Hair", just as most of the '50s rockers had jumped into country or bland pop mediocrity at the first opportunity.

Only a handful had the dedication, the commitment, the strength of purpose to stay with what they believed in, even if it meant years of working in small clubs

Photo by Richard Robinson

The '75 Groovies: Chris, David, James, Cyril and George--watched over by St. Brian

with little compensation or recognition. And in 1974, these hardy survivors began at last to reap some of their overdue rewards.

The Raspberries (who've been unwavering Mods since '65) have finally been accepted on their own terms, and should be stars from here onward. Earth Quake (who also started in '65 with Kinks and Yardbirds material) are building a national following through singles on their own Beserkley label (after being screwed around by a record company that didn't understand or believe in them) and the Wackers (who I first saw in '66 doing all Beatle songs) have changed personnel and returned as the Dudes, currently one of the most popular bands in Canada and ready for an American breakthrough.

It hasn't been easy for any of these bands, but having stuck it out they're now prepared to take on the '70s with a hard-won sense of unity and sheer experience that no come-lately group could stand up against.

The Flamin' Groovies have endured perhaps more hardships and disappointment than any of their fellow survivors, been screwed so many times by managers and record companies that it became a way of life, and been without a recording contract for so long that some of their best friends aren't even sure if they're still together. But they are, and all the hard times have only intensified their dedication. Strange as it seems, they are infinitely better today than ever before, and even though they haven't played together publicly since leaving England in '72, their music has continued to grow and evolve. When the Flamin' Groovies finally emerge, I can't think of any band in the world with greater potential to create real mania and show the world what a rock & roll band should be.

1975 will be the Flamin' Groovies' tenth year in the arena. In 1965, as the Chosen Few, they were one of the many garage bands around San Francisco (and as an interesting sidelight, both Earth Quake and the Wackers are also Bay Area bands, which puts 3 of the 4 survivors I can think of in an area that's rarely thought of these days as the home of anything teenage).

Cyril Jordan (guitar), Roy Loney (vocals), George Alexander (bass) and Tim Lynch (rhythm) were in school together and had this band which played school dances and social affairs. Roy and Cyril were collectors and fans of '50s rock, as well as being heavily into the Stones, Lovin' Spoonful, Kinks, Byrds, DC5, Raiders, and of course the Beatles. This group jammed a lot, but did no professional gigs. They also bore no relation to the Chosen Few who recorded on Autumn, nor any of the other Chosen Fews you might be familiar with.

In 1966 they changed their name to the Lost and Found with the addition of Ron Greco on drums. This band also did little of note, and in the summer they broke up. Cyril and Tim went to Europe for the summer, while George joined a group called the Whistling Shrimp. That fall, they all got back together as the Flamin' Groovies.

The Lost & Found at a 1966 Battle of the Bands. L-R: Roy, Tim, Cyril, George & Ron Greco. Off to the left, the Mystery Trend were setting up. Butch Engle & the Styx eventually won

A rare shot of the Chosen Few, outside the gym where they first played "Louie Louie".

The San Francisco scene was in full swing by then, with plenty of jobs for local bands (this was a few months before the armies of out-of-town musicians moved in) so the band began getting more serious. Danny Mihm was brought in as drummer (he'd been in the Whistling Shrimp with George, and subsequently with Andrew Staples, who changed their name to Group B and issued 2 singles on Scorpio--see WPTB #12). Another '50s collector (as well as a former juvenile delinquent), Mihm became an integral part of the group, and thus their music took on an unusual blend of Chuck Berry, Elvis and the '50s rockers, combined with a good-timey Spoonful sound and a Beatles verve.

Unfortunately none of this was what the folk/psychedelic/freakout oriented San Francisco scenemakers were interested in, so the Groovies were never accepted by the older "hip" community that ruled the S.F. rock scene. They had a few gigs at the Fillmore and Avalon ballrooms, but played mainly the smaller clubs, along with a lot of out-of-town gigs.

In 1968 they joined several other local bands (Country Joe, Mad River, Frumious Bandersnatch) who had put out EPs of their own music. Independently, they recorded and pressed 2,000 copies of a 10" LP with seven songs called Sneakers, which is now one of the most sought-after collectors' items of its era.

Sneakers caught the Groovies at their earliest stage of development, and it reveals their orientation quite well. There aren't any overt oldies included, the songs are all originals, with a good-humored buoyancy and sense of simple fun combined with an overall rock & roll sensibility. There was nothing like it in San Francisco at the time except for the Charlatans, who were already fading in popularity as the scene began taking itself too seriously.

Following this, the Groovies were at the peak of their local popularity, playing frequently at the Straight Theatre (an old movie house in the heart of Haight St. whose expensive renovation, financed by a group of LA music biz investors, was finished just as the Haight scene began fading away....) where they put on shows with the Charlatans.

With the success of Sneakers, and since they were about the only San Francisco group still unsigned, their manager Alfred Kramer (formerly an assistant to Bill Graham) was able to get them a deal with Epic Records. Thus began the first of the Flamin' Groovies' recording fiascos. They went to L.A. to cut an album, and a guy named Steve Goldman was brought in as producer. According to the group, he had no idea what he was doing, spent hours every day just setting levels, and managed to stretch the sessions out to 2 1/2 months, at a cost of $80,000.

The group meanwhile was playing constantly around LA and San Diego, where they worked up a version of "Rockin Pneumonia" that was to become their first single. Initial response was strong; it got airplay in New York and San Francisco, making the Top 30 at KFRC, with one of the country's tightest playlists. Epic was caught by surprise, having no backup copies for the stores, and no coordinated promotion effort planned. The stations that were playing it stopped when they got no sales reports, and the record died. The album, pressed in very small quantities, had an overall fun-and-good times sort of flavor and included several strongly commercial tunes. When nothing happened with it, the Flamin' Groovies left the label dissatisfied.

At this time, they were touring and performing heavily. They were enormously popular in Detroit and the midwest. One tour took them through Omaha, Salt Lake City, Cleveland, Philadelphia, and Cincinnati (where they appeared at Ludlow's Garage on a bill with the Stooges and Golden Earrings--what a show that must've been!).

Meanwhile, they had started getting involved in the San Francisco scene. Bill Graham had just moved out of the old Fillmore Auditorium and relocated at the Carousel Ballroom downtown, so the Groovies rented the old Fillmore in the spring of 1970, as a rehearsal hall which

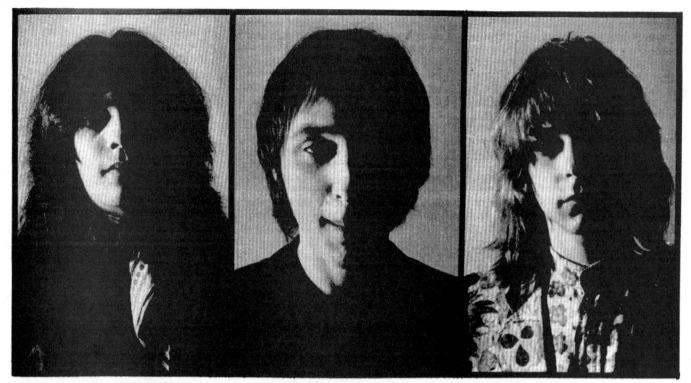
●In all honesty, girls, how long's it been since you cast your orbs on three such obvious teenage dreamboats?

they used themselves and rented out to other local groups. Soon they were promoting dances there. They booked acts ranging from the Grateful Dead and Hot Tuna to Pink Floyd, with themselves as the house band. Sez Jordan: "when we got back to San Francisco we had really changed, mainly from seeing the MC5. We had a new sense of energy and stage movement, and we were really getting hot."

The old Fillmore was getting hot too, as more and more of San Francisco's original rockers (who had given up the scene in disgust when Graham began to monopolize everything) began coming out of the woodwork for the Groovies' weekly dances. The culmination of it all was one show which starred the Stooges, Alice Cooper, and the MC5. It went on all night, and people were talking about it for weeks.

Unfortunately it all ended when the Groovies' business manager ran out with all their money. They went back on the road to try and get things moving again, and ended up in New York with no money in their pockets and sad prospects. This was when local hustler Richard Robinson found them and promised he could get them signed to Kama Sutra with a $16,000 advance. This sounded good to them, and so they made the deal. An album called Flamingo was cut at Pacific High Studios in San Francisco, with Robinson as producer, Richard Olsen from the Charlatans as engineer, and Commander Cody as guest pianist.

It was an excellent album, with a heavier, more Stones-like feel than Supersnazz, which had been more in the group's original Charlatans/Spoonful mold. It got impressive reviews (Ed Ward: "One of the year's ten best. In their own natural way, these guys are doing what the Stones have to try harder and harder to do." Lenny Kaye: "One of the finest rock albums to be released this year.") and it looked like the band was on its way to success and stardom at last.

In early 1971 they returned to New York to cut a second album for Kama Sutra at Bell Studios. Word quickly spread around town that the sessions were the in-crowd happening, and the studio became a real scene, with all the rock writers in New York and quite a few assorted musicians adding their presence and (in some cases) talents. Guest musicians included Jim Ibbotsen, Jeff Hanna and Jimmy Fadden of the Nitty Gritty Dirt Band, Jim Dickinson, and even Richard Meltzer.

On its release, Teenage Head was immediately acclaimed as a classic. Coinciding with the release of the Stones' Sticky Fingers, the album forced many reviewers to the conclusion that the Groovies held the edge as '70s rock & roll punks. But there were still problems. Neither Kama Sutra album was selling, and the company didn't seem interested in doing much promotion or advertising.

During the Teenage Head sessions, Tim Lynch was arrested for draft evasion, and replaced by James Farrell, whom they'd known through Mike Wilhelm of the Charlatans (who was then fronting a band called Loose Gravel). Chris Wilson, the Groovies' current lead singer, was another Loose Gravel alumnus.

"Roy was starting to get weird," recalls Jordan. Although Loney had up to then written most of the group's songs, now it seemed "he was trying to get us to do different material, songs so lame even James Taylor wouldn't sing them. We did a short tour at that time, out through Detroit and Ohio, where we got screwed bad by a promoter. When we got back, Bill Graham wanted us to play the Fillmore, but we had to do two sets and we didn't have enough songs worked up, so I told him we couldn't make it. Roy and I had a big argument about that, he thought we should go on anyway. After that, he left the group."

The Flamin' Groovies did eventually play the Fillmore, as part of the special "Closing Week" series of concerts at Fillmore West, which were broadcast in full over KSAN-FM in June, 1971. The Groovies did a dynamite set which included "I Can't Explain", "Sweet Little Rock & Roller", "Have You Seen My Baby", "Road House", "Doctor Boogie", "Slow Death", "Shakin' All Over", "Teenage Head", "Louie Louie" and "Walking the Dog".

Following that, they did a series of gigs at local clubs like Keystone Korner, the New Orleans House, and the Longbranch Saloon in Berkeley, where I saw them a few times in late '71. The Longbranch has been the home of Earth Quake and Asleep at the Wheel. It's a rough little room on the bad side of town, with sawdust on the floor and lots of cheap beer. It was perfect for the Groovies, who commanded the stage like true rock & rollers, giving me a weird kind of deja-vu feeling that this was what it must've been like back in England in the first days of the Yardbirds and Stones. They were electrifying, Cyril with legs apart, bending into his guitar; Chris leaping about the small stage, pointing his finger and shaking his hair. This is the last of the true Mod bands, I thought, though the hippies and bikers in the club didn't seem to be aware of it. They just danced.

But things were at a standstill for the group, however great they were becoming. They still had trouble pulling more than 50 or so to their gigs, and eventually they decided it just wasn't happening. Cyril considered starting a new group with Mike Wilhelm, but finally they agreed to give it another go. After a short-lived tenure as the Dogs (they thought a new name might help, but soon realized they were better off with one people were at least familiar with) they decided on one last-ditch effort.

They wrote a letter to Andrew Lauder, head of A&R at UA Records in England. They'd known Andrew through Robinson, and knew he was a fan of theirs. Maybe, they thought, if they could go to England, they could get a fresh start. Lauder liked the idea, and sent Cyril some money to come to London and discuss it. UA agreed to bring the group over, and when they arrived it seemed that UA was committed to building them into the next pop sensation.

All decked out in flash velvet duds, and equipped with the latest gear, they blitzed England, playing something like 250 dates, all across the country. Everywhere they appeared, the audiences went crazy. Mania scenes were the order of the day. At one show, they even observed the kids in the audience spontaneously locking arms and swaying back and forth to the music. It was like nothing the Groovies had ever seen. They played the Cavern Club too, where people told them the walls had heard nothing like it since 1964.

The original plan was to cut five singles, building the group as a phenomenon along the lines of Slade and Sweet. Cyril looked up his longtime idol Dave Edmunds, who agreed to produce them. Eight songs were cut at Rockfield Studios. The first single was "Slow Death", a four-minute anti-drug song that was issued against the group's judgment. They feared it would be banned by the BBC, and they were right. It got to #1 in Switzerland however, and was popular all over the Continent, particularly in France.

After one of their shows, a critic from Melody Maker named Roy Hollingworth wrote a scathing review, the basis for which seemed to be that he had been kept from going backstage or something equally petty. UA was shaken, however, and seemed to lose interest from that point. The Groovies went off to France, where they toured widely and were received like superstars. It raised their spirits, but when they got back to England and found that their second single (an old Frankie Lee Sims song called "Married Woman") had been pressed in quantities of less than 400, they realized something was wrong.

The song they'd wanted out was "You Tore Me Down", an electrifying Beatle-inspired track on which Edmunds had lavished the full Spector production. Martin Davis (President of English UA), who evidently had them type-cast as a '50s group, turned thumbs down. It was an impasse, and the group decided to return to America where, it was implied, they would relax for awhile and then be brought back to England to resume their quest for stardom. And that was the last they heard from UA.

Fortunately, they'd signed no contracts with UA, so they were free to pursue an American deal. Unfortunately, nothing came through. Danny Mihm left the group, replaced briefly by Terry Rae (who left to join the Hollywood Stars) and eventually by David Wright, who'd played in local bands in Nebraska along with Jeff Richardson, the Groovies' new manager. They got close to deals with several companies, including Mercury and Capitol, and even cut some demo tapes for the latter (including an incredible pop masterpiece called "Shake Some Action"), but something always went wrong.

And that brings us up to late 1974. Towards the end of the year, noting the success of Earth Quake, the Groovies decided it wouldn't be a bad idea to put out their own records again. If the big companies weren't interested, at least they knew the fans still were. An arrangement was made with Who Put the Bomp to press and distribute "You Tore Me Down" (the tapes of which they owned) and cut a B-side. The song recorded was the Raiders' "Him Or Me (What's It Gonna Be?)", which was taken at a faster tempo, with three guitars and and a 12-string overdub, giving it a slight folk-rock flavor. It's a powerful recording, and coupled with the tremendous Edmunds-produced A-side, this new single is without a doubt the high point of the Flamin Groovies' career.

"It's like after all these years, we've finally found our own sound," says Jordan. "Before, we were trying to go in too many directions. But the group is together now like never before, we've written some new songs you wouldn't believe, and we're ready for action."

•Early 1973, just back from England and ready to kick out some jams. As it turned out, however, all that got kicked out was the drummer

Among their plans are recording with Brian Wilson and Spring ("We got to be tight with them over in Holland; we were gonna do a version of "Keep Your Hands Off My Baby") and more work with Edmunds, whose ideas are amazingly parallel to their own. ("In fact, there was even talk of him joining the group. We'd like to have him tour the U.S. with us.")

It took time for the cycle to come around again, but 1975 will be the year of teenage rock & roll, and nobody is as good or as experienced or as real as the Flamin' Groovies. They're gonna make it this time.

(See following page for complete Flamin' Groovies discography and special record offer.)

THE FLAMIN' GROOVIES
DISCOGRAPHY

SINGLES:

11-69	Rockin' Pneumonia and the Boogie Woogie Flu/The First One's Free		Epic 5-10507
2-70	Somethin' Else/Laurie Did It		Epic 5-10564
71	Have You Seen My Baby?/Yesterday's Numbers		Kama Sutra 527
72	Slow Death/Tallahassie Lassie		UA UP 35392 (E)
72	Married Woman/Get a Shot of Rhythm and Blues		UA UP 35464 (E)
74	Jumpin' Jack Flash/Blues From Phyllys		Skydog FGG 002*
-75	You Tore Me Down/Him Or Me (What's It Gonna Be?)		Bomp 101

EPs:

- 68 Sneakers: I'm Drowning/Babes in the Sky/Love Time/My Yada/Golden Clouds/The Slide/Prelude in A Flat to Afternoon of a Pud — Snazz B-2371
- 74 Grease: Let Me Rock/Dog Meat/Sweet Little Rock 'N Roller/Slow Death — Skydog FGG 001*

ALBUMS:

- 69 Supersnazz (Epic BN 26487) Love Have Mercy/The Girl Can't Help It/Laurie Did It/A Part From That/Rockin' Pneumonia and the Boogie Woogie Flu/The First One' Free/Pagan Rachel/Somethin' Else/Pistol Packin' Mama/Brushfire/Bam Balam/Around the Corner
- 70 Flamingo (Kama Sutra KSBS 2021) Gonna Rock Tonite/Comin After Me/Headin For the Texas Border/Sweet Roll Me On Down/Keep a Knockin'/Second Cousin/Childhood's End/Jailbait/She's Falling Apart/Road House
- 71 Teenage Head (Kama Sutra KSBS 2031) High Flyin' Baby/City Lights/Have You Seen My Baby?/Yesterday's Numbers/Teenage Head/32-30/Evil Hearted Ada/Doctor Boogie/Whiskey Woman

*NOTE: These Skydog records were issued by the Flamin' Groovies fan club in France. They were made from live tapes recorded in the Groovies' San Francisco garage. "Jumpin Jack Flash" comes with a great picture sleeve adapted from the Stones' "Got Live If You Want It" EP jacket. The EP also comes with a deluxe cover and jacket.

SKYDOG RECORDS

Grease: A four-song EP, 33 1/3 rpm, recorded live in San Francisco by the Flamin' Groovies. The sound is raw, crude, basic and tough. The material is pure, energetic rock & roll. "Let Me Rock" has a solid Stones/Mott guitar riff crashing through it. "Dog Meat" is like the Easybeats doing Eddie Cochran. Kineticism abounds. "Sweet Little Rock & Roller" is the kind of rocker the Groovies have always been renowned for, and "Slow Death" is an early arrangement of the song that later came out on British UA.

Alive Forever! (more grease): An extended-play 45 (each side over 5 minutes) of the Flamin' Groovies, also recorded in San Francisco, 1971. "Jumpin Jack Flash" needs no introduction; "Blues From Phillys" is a great, noisy rocker with roots in "Under My Thumb". Fantastic heavy-gloss picture sleeve.

Skydog Records are put out in France and Holland by a group of fans dedicated to the Flamin' Groovies, the MC5, the Velvet Underground, Blue Oyster Cult, Kim Fowley and other cult-appeal artists. Although the tapes are of course home-made, the quality of the packaging and pressing on these records is the highest. Skydog Records are available in the United States exclusively through Who Put the Bomp.
PRICES: Grease EP, $6 -- Alive Forever! 45, $4 -- Also available, Skydog LP 401, Rock 'n' Roll Animal by Lou Reed, a live bootleg of fair quality including "Heroin", "Waiting For the Man", "White Light White Heat" and 5 other cuts -- $8.

SPECIAL OFFER TO BOMP READERS

The new Flamin' Groovies single "You Tore Me Down"/"Him Or Me" is now available on Bomp Records. This first pressing is limited, and there may never be a second pressing on this label. Furthermore, a small number of picture sleeves have been made. These will not be available on store copies, they're intended for promotional use and for Bomp readers who order the record by mail. The supply is limited and when they're gone, there won't be any more. These are sure to be collectors items before long, so you'll want to get yours now.

Price: $1.50 per copy, postpaid
$2.00 with picture sleeve

Who Put the Bomp, Box 7112, Burbank, CA

One of the hardest-to-find collectors' items of the '60s is the Flamin' Groovies' Sneakers LP, put out by the group in 1968 and never available outside the San Francisco area. It contains seven full original songs of surprisingly good quality. Copies of Sneakers have gone for around $25 each in our auctions, when we could get them, and there's never been enough to fill the demand for this sought-after album.

However, we've located a small quantity of mint, sealed copies, which are being offered to Bomp readers only (no dealers please) for the ridiculously low price of $15. Yes, for hardly more than the price of a tank of gas, you can have a genuine rock classic. And, at the same time, help out everyone's favorite underdog band. Because the profits from the sale of these albums will go toward helping the Groovies buy some of the equipment they need to go on the road again.

Needless to say, the supply is limited, so be sure to get your order in soon. As a special bonus, for those who request it, you can have your copy autographed by one or more members of the Flamin' Groovies, at no extra cost.

The weird world of BEATLE NOVELTIES

BY KEN BARNES

Beatles nostalgia, the sole portion of the touted '60s nostalgia boom to really take off, is still raging out of control. Although a bit mystifying, this mania gives us a convenient excuse for delving into the fascinating netherworld of Beatle novelties--records (mostly from '64-65) attempting to exploit Beatlemania for commercial gain (usually in the crassest manner imaginable).

Interestingly, their success rate was perfectly dismal. Only four Beatle novelties made the *Billboard* charts; only one ("We Love You Beatles" by the Carefrees) ascended higher than the 80's. But that didn't stop the record nabobs (153 attempts by our count, doubtless quite a few more as yet uncollected). Being in a wide-open commercial market suddenly hit by an inexplicable but overwhelmingly commercial phenomenon, they responded with a wild and wondrous welter of novelty items, on a profusion of labels.

It's startling to note the number of well-known musicbiz personalities involved. Besides your anonymous groups and local DJs (Casey Kasem, Tom Clay, Arlen Sanders), there were old-liners from the middle of the road (Ella Fitzgerald, the Four Preps, and Allan Sherman) and faded hitmakers of the past hoping for a last free ride on Beatle coattails (Johnny & the Hurricanes, Larry Finnegan, the sublime Ernie Maresca, and even the recently-hot Angels, who began their downward slide with "Little Beatle Boy").

One-shot novelty artists figured the Beatles were a surefire gimmick for repeat success (Rolf Harris, Murray Kellum, Bill Buchanan of "Flying Saucer" fame). Larry Williams and Johnny 'Guitar' Watson cut a Beatle novelty; so did Booker T. & the MG's. And a few Beatle novelty artists went on to become rather well-known in their own rights-- Penny Valentine (later a top pop journalist for *Disc & Music Echo* and *Sounds*), the Bon Bons (later the Shangri-Las) and one Bonnie Jo Mason (now re-united with the producer of her "Ringo I Love You", Phil Spector, and better known as Cher).

The records themselves break down into a number of categories. Most easily dispensable are the stock instrumentals dressed up in Beatle titles (Benny & the Bedbugs' "Beatle Beat", the Buddies' "The Beatle" etc). Then there are the non-rock novelties--hostile ("I Hate the Beatles" by Allan Sherman, "Letter to the Beatles" by the Four Preps); slushy ("Letter From Elaina", Casey Kasem; "Letter to Paul", Arlen Sanders); or satirical break-in records (Buchanan & Greenfield's "The Invasion" is, as you might expect, pretty funny; Ed Solomon's "Beatle Flying Saucer" is not).

Often the name alone was the thing. Novelties were cut by the Beatlettes, the Female Beatles, the Canadian Beadles, the American Beatles, the U.S. Beatle Wiggs, the Buggs, the Bug Collectors, the Insects, the Baby Bugs, etc. A few of these had nothing else to do with the Beatles. Others, like the Buggs' "Buggs vs. Beatles" and the Bug Men's "Beatle You Bug Me" carried American resentment/envy/hostility to the rock front.

There were a few generalized comments (Vito & the Salutations' "Liverpool Bound") or takeoffs on other British hits ("Mrs.Brown You've Got a Lovely Daughter" inspired several) but the majority by far were unabashed Beatle tributes, mostly sung by apparently lovelorn females. Most were aimed at the Beatles in toto, but of the individualized paeans, Ringo scored a stunning sweep. John and Paul got theirs later on, after John became controversial and Paul "dead", but in 1964-65 Ringo had the market virtually all locked up. To date, there are no known George novelties.

Beatle novelties had run their natural course by early 1965 (Angie & the Chiclettes' "Treat Him Tender Maureen", directed to Ringo's newlywed wife, was one of the last of the breed in the spring of that year). Aside from the aforementioned John and Paul topical numbers, a few song-title tributes (see below) trickled out. But the initial Beatlemaniacal fervor obviously could never again be matched. Nor have any other acts been eulogized in anywhere near that profusion. There might have been a few for Buddy Holly, Johnny Ace and other '50s casualties, and Elvis generated a dozen or so. In the '60s, there were death records for Janis, Otis and others, and marginal efforts like Kristofferson's "Blame It On the Stones" or Blossom Dearie's "Sweet Georgie Fame". Recently the Osmonds inspired a few British-made bouquets (amusingly enough, the tune of "My Bonnie", used by Bonnie Brooks and others for "Bring My Beatles Back to Me" was also employed for a ditty called "My Donny Lies Over the Ocean"). But "a few" doesn't quite match 150--the whole Beatle novelty boomlet, then, stands as yet another tribute to the unparalleled impact of the Beatles.

A FEW HIGHLIGHTS

The Beatles naturally aroused considerable envy in American males, who watched mystified as four scrawny mop-tops won the hearts of almost all American females. Fortunately, there were American rock artists to give voice to these inchoate emotions. Sonny Curtis (the ex-Cricket and singer/composer of the *Mary Tyler Moore Show* theme) put it simply: "A Beatle I Want to Be" he proclaimed through a Lou Adler production featuring some tasty Merseybeat facsimile sounds. Gene Cornish & the Unbeetables (yes, *that* Gene Cornish rascal) nursed a covert desire for tonsorial liberation--"I want to be a Beatle and never comb my hair." A good record.

For Ray Ruff & the Checkmates down in Texas, the situation was a bit aggravating. "She told me 'you're square' cause I didn't have shaggy hair", Ray sings, to a tough Buddy Holly-ish track. But in Minnesota, it was a state of outright war. The Buggs (not related to the Beatle-imitating album group), to the tune of "I Want to Hold Your Hand", laid down a pugnacious challenge: "We'll have to rumble, Beatles vs. Buggs" and even threaten to unleash, if necessary, the ultimate weapon--Raid.

The B.R.A.T.T.S. (Brotherhood for the Re-establishment of American Top Ten Supremacy), as their name implies, were visibly upset about the British taking over, armed with a "Secret Weapon"--an unnamed Liverpool band. No alternative is proposed, however, during the course of this Coasters-style novelty. Brad Berwick's frustrations can't be contained, though: "I'm Better Than the Beatles" he proclaims, elaborating in the flattest of tones: "Once the Beatles hear my song, they're gonna pack their things and go." Furthermore, they'll try to buy up all of Brad's records in the stores, and when that fails, they'll dissolve helplessly, relegated thenceforth to menial servitude ("Paul and John will mow my lawn"). The author of these gloating sentiments, we learn from Jayne Mansfield's picture sleeve notes (honest!) was Robert Young's co-star in the short-lived pre-Welby series *Window on Main Street*. Brad later moved into patriotic answer records, tackling Barry McGuire and other nabobs of negativity head on.

Murray Kellum, once a Long Tall Texan, dreamed he was a Beatle, onstage with the other 4 while "37 acres of twisting little shakers were screaming all over the place." It seemed idyllic to Murray. Meanwhile, Neil Sheppard (a recurring name on early '60s records) has got it all figured out. The title says it all: "You Can't Go Far Without a Guitar (Unless You're Ringo Starr)". He proceeds to sum up rock & roll history, detailing the rise of Elvis, the Beach Boys, the Rolling Stones, and the Beatles to a pronounced "Peggy Sue"/"Sheila" beat.

On the distaff side (as they used to say), adoration is the reigning emotion. The Patty Cakes (brought to you by those bizarre types responsible for the wondrous Jaynetts) delve into early generation gap outbreaks, declaring that despite their parents' decided disapproval they understand "them" (the Beatles, natch). Charmingly inept lead vocals add to the appeal of this pretty number.

The fabled Bonnie Jo Mason record, produced and co-written by Spector and starring Cherilyn LaPier, one of his background vocalists, is far from a patented Spectorian blockbuster. It's based pretty closely on (as usual) "I Want to Hold Your Hand", and is a well-wrought imitation. The incidental circumstance of the record's non-greatness does not in the least detract, of course, from its status as perhaps the most coveted Beatle novelty single extant.

Angie & the Chicklettes (the same Feldman-Goldstein-Gottehrer group who cut the amazing "I Want You to Be My Boyfriend" on Josie earlier) display admirable restraint and good will towards Maureen Starkey, who had just stolen Ringo away from 10 million American competitors. "Treat Him Tender, Maureen" they sing wistfully, evidencing

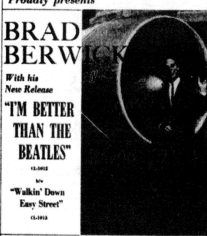

every confidence in her ability to do so, but with a faint undertone of warning present too.

Best of the gratuitously-titled novelties (a sorry lot in general) is probably the Standells' "Peppermint Beatle", a lively dance rocker born of "Little Latin Lupe Lu." Other male tributes are more topical. Arlen Sanders, an LA dee-jay perhaps inspired by Casey Kasem's ultra-lush Beatle sob story "Letter From Elaina" (a good-sized Calif. hit), reads a girl's melodramatic "Letter to Paul", made up of various amatory Beatle song titles. The record is more noteworthy for its flip, an amusing, plagiarized update of "Hotrod Lincoln" called "Hopped Up Mustang", with a raging surf instrumental backup.

Harry Nilsson co-wrote the Foto-Fi Four's "Stand Up and Holler". The label orders "Play this side with film", and the record indeed seems designed to stimulate organized cheering when the Beatles appear on screen.

For some, the advent of the Beatles created troubling new dilemmas in their everyday lives. The Newbeats-styled lead singer of the Manchesters (written/arranged by David Gates) feels constrained to declare "I Don't Come From England" and the remainder of the song concerns his ongoing rivalry with a Johnny Cymbal-like bass singer, who thinks the lead vocalist sings like a girl (the Barbarians were still making similar implications in the fall of 1965).

In Donna Lynn's case, her boyfriend's new "Beatle haircut" had rendered him irresistible to all the girls in the neighborhood. Donna, who'd earlier jumped aboard the novelty bandwagon with "I'm in Love With George Maharis", had a clever solution, though--she got a Beatle haircut too. The Outsiders (almost certainly not an earlier version of the "Time Won't Let Me" group) had no such luck, though. Their girl thought she spotted them with another girl, but it was actually a guy sporting that long Liverpool hair. But when they take the girl to meet him, he's just returned from the barber shop, so they're still in hot water.

POST-MANIA NOVELTIES

After 1965, as mentioned previously, only the most significant Beatle events provoked recorded reactions. In 1969, a plaintive lass named Rainbo made a melancholy profession of her undying love for John Lennon--"The trip we took with Lucy was a trip I won't forget", even though "putting down your guru brought confusion and regret." Finally she admits, "I loved the things you showed me up till now John/But ever since that picture I don't think my love will be the same"--that nude photo on *Two Virgins* was just too much for the poor girl.

The McCartney death hoax motivated a group called the Mystery Tour to record an elegiac

Artist - Title	Label
AMERICAN BEATLES - She's Mine/Theme of the American Beatles	BYP 1001
AMERICAN BEATLES - It's My Last Night in Town/You're Getting to Me	BYP 101
AMERICAN BEATLES - Don't Be Unkind/You Did It To Me	Roulette 4550
AMERICAN BEATLES - School Days/	Roulette 4559
ANGELS - Little Beatle Boy/Java	Smash 1885
ANGIE & CHICKLETTES - Treat Him Tender Maureen/Tommy	Apt 25080
ANNIE & ORPHANS - My Girl's Been Bitten by the Beatle Bug/	Capitol 5144
BABY BUGS - Bingo/Bingo's Bongo Bingo Party	Vee Jay 594
BAGELS - I Wanna Hold Your Hair/Yeah Yeah YeahYeah	Warner Bros 5420
PENNY BAKER & PILLOWS - Bring Back the Beatles/Gonna Win Him	Witch 123
BEATLETTES - Yes, You Can Hold My Hand/	Assault 1893
BEATLETTES - Only Seventeen/Now We're Together	Jubilee 5472
BECKY LEE BECK - I Want a Beatle for Christmas/Puppy Dog	Challenge 9372
BEDBUGS - Yeah Yeah/Lucy Lucy	Liberty 55679
BEEHIVES (European) - I Want to Hold Your Hand/She Loves You	King 5881
BENNY & BEDBUGS - Roll Over Beethoven/The Beatle Beat	DCP 1008
BRAD BERWICK - I'm Better Than the Beatles/Walkin' On Easy Street	Clinton 1012
SHARON BLACK - Mother Dear You've Got a Silly Daughter/	Philips 40290
BON BONS - What's Wrong With Ringo/Come On Baby	Coral 62402
BONNIE & BUTTERFLYS - I Saw Him Standing There/	Smash 1878
BOOTLES - I'll Let You Hold My Hand/Never Till Now	GNP 311
BO-WEEVILS - The Beatles Will Getcha/	United States 1934
B.R.A.T.T.S. - Secret Weapon (The British Are Coming)/	Tollie 9024
BRET & TERRY - Beatle Fever/The Beatle	Prestige 313
B. BROCK & SULTANS - Do the Beetle/	Crown 5399
BONNIE BROOKS - Bring Back My Beatles to Me/A Letter From My Love	UA 708
DORA BRYAN - All I Want for Christmas is a Beatle/	Fontana 427 (E)
BUCHANAN & GREENFIELD - The Invasion/What a Lovely Party	Novel 711
BUDDIES - The Beatle/Pulsebeat	Swan 4170
BUG COLLECTORS - Beatle Bug/Thief in the Night	Catch 103
BUG MEN - Beatle You Bug Me/	Dot 16592
BUGGS - Buggs vs. Beatles/She Loves Me	Soma 1413
BULLDOGS - John Paul George & Ringo/	Mercury 72262
DAWS BUTLER - Ringo Ringol/Clementine	Merri 6011
CANADIAN BEADLES - Love Walk Away/I'm Coming Home	Tide 2006
PETE CANDOLI - Beatle Bug Jump/	Nan 3004
CAREFREES - We Love You Beatles/Hot Blooded Lover (#39)	London Int. 10614
CATERPILLARS - The Caterpillar Song/Hello Happy Happy Goodbye	Port 70038
CHUG & DOUG - Ringo Comes to Town/	Charger 101
TOM CLAY - Official IBBB Interview: Remember We Don't Like Them We Love Them	ZTSC 9743
BILL CLIFTON - Beatle Crazy/Little Girl Dressed in Blue	London 9638
BOBBY COMSTOCK & COUNTS - The Beatle Bounce/	Lawn 229
GENE CORNISH & UNBEETABLES - I Wanna Be a Beatle/Oh Misery	Dawn 557
CAROL CRANE (Mrs. Brown's Lovely Daughter Carol) - Frightful Situation/What Else Do You Do For Kicks	Challenge 59292
SONNY CURTIS - A Beatle I Want to Be/So Used to Loving You	Dimension 1024
LINK DAVIS - Beatle Bug/I Keep Wanting You More	Kook 1026
RONNY DAVIS - Let's Beetle in the Rocket	Sheridan 573
DEL RICOS - Beatle Crawl/Beatle Hootenanny	Roulette 4616
DETERGENTS - Mrs. Jones (How 'Bout It)/Tea & Crumpets	McSherry 1285
DETOURS - Bring Back My Beatles to Me	Apogee 105
SCOTT DOUGLAS - The Beatles' Barber/The Wall Paper Song	Diplomacy X5
JIM DOVAL - Stranded in the 'Pool/Right Now	Golden West
EXTERMINATORS - Beatle Stomp/	Chancellor 1143
EXTERMINATORS - The Beetle Bomb/Stomp 'em Out!	Express 801
CARLO FAIR - Beetle Bounce/	Dot 16688
FANS - I Want a Beatle fo Christmas/How Far Should My Heart Go	20th Century 531
FEMALE BEATLES - I Want You/I Don't Want to Cry	Limelight 3022
TINA FERRA - R (Is For Ringo)/Modern Youth	Academy 112
GARRY FERRIER - Ringo-Deer/Just My Luck	Ric 146
LARRY FINNEGAN - A Tribute to Ringo Starr (The Other Ringo)/	Verve 10340
ELLA FITZGERALD - Ringo Beat/I'm Falling in Love	Arhoolie 507
FONDETTES - The Beatles Are in Town/	Foti-Fi 107
FOTO-FI FOUR - Stand Up and Holler/same	Capitol 5143
FOUR PREPS - A Letter To the Beatles/College Cannonball (#85)	Temple 2081
FRENCHY & CHESSMEN - Beetle Bebop/	Mutual 510
ROBIN GARRETT - Ringo's Revenge/You Run Around	Parkway 899
HAIRCUTS - She Loves You/Love Me Do	Parkway 903
LARRY HALLOWAY - Beatle Teen Beat/	Fortune 861
DAVE HAMILTON - Beatle Walk/	Rose 003
JOHNNY HAMPTON - Beatle Dance/	Epic 9721
ROLF HARRIS - Ringo For President/Click Go the Shears	Capitol 5447
CONNIE HOLIDAY - Mrs. James I'm Mrs. Brown's Daughter/Old Friend	Merri 6011
HUCKLEBERRY HOUND - Bingo Ringo/	Gaye 004
GEORGE HUGHLEY - Do the Beatle	Applause 1002
INSECTS - Let's Bug the Beatles/	USA 791
JACKIE & JILL - I Want the Beatles For Christmas/Jingle Bells	DCP 1126
JECKYL & HYDE - Frankenstein Meets the Beatles/Dracula Drag	Jeff 211
JOHNNY & HURRICANES - Saga of the Beatles/Rene	Sabra 555
JONES BOYS - Beatlemania/Honky	Ware 6000
JUDY & DUETS - Christmas With the Beatles/The Blind Boy	New Design 1008
JUSTICE DEPARTMENT - Let John & Yoko Stay in the USA/	

"Ballad of Paul." They lead you through a thorough discussion of the clues, sort of a solve-it-yourself puzzle with an ambiguous ending apparently blaming it all on John. On the flip, they reverse the tape. Cute.

Terry Knight, never a slow reactor, came out with "St. Paul," a melange of mystical mumbo-jumbo with strange religious implications, some dumb lines about Sir Isaac Newton, and a lot of general lyrical and musical dolefulness.

Finally, the break-up of the Beatles in 1970 reached a Canadian group called Moran in early 1973 (that is, the implications of their irrevocable split penetrated their awareness.). Result: a catchy little number called "The Beatle Thing," bemoaning their collective passing. Interspersed through the lyrics were a few Beatle song titles, harking back to a venerable tradition.

That tradition was reinvoked in 1967 by Nilsson on his first RCA single, consisting of intricately-woven excerpts of Beatle songs built around a "You Can't Do That" framework. Just as good is a mysterious 1973 release by a pre-adolescent named Peter Ryan, masterminded by Bobby Flax and Lanny Lambert (writers of Bullet's "White Lies Blue Eyes" and Stories' recent "Another Love") on a tune called "If We Try". This is an astounding concatenation of Beatle titles, integrated into a fairly consistent lovelorn theme and an irresistible original tune. Counting casually, I came up with approximately 30 titles, not counting repeats, and it's all in all a rather staggering record (I'm afraid, however, that its issuance on the short-lived Aardvark label may hinder its general accessibility. It's worth digging up, though).

Those are some of my favorites, though I'm sure there are many more worthy of immortalization that I haven't heard yet. We welcome your additions to the accompanying list, compiled by Greg Shaw, Alan Betrock (many thanks) and myself.

Artist - Title	Label
CASEY KASEM - Letter From Elaina/Theme for Elaina	Warner Bros 5474
MURRAY KELLUM - I dreamed I Was a Beatle/Oh How Sweet it Could Be	MOC 658
DAVE KING - The Beatle Walk/	Teia 1004
LENORE KING & TOMMY ANDERSON - Beatles is Back Yea Yea Yea	Her Majesty 101
TERRY KNIGHT - Saint Paul/Legend of William & Mary	Capitol 2506
LADY BUGS - How Do You Do It/Liverpool	Chattahoochee 637
PAULA LAMONT - Beatle Meets a Lady Bug	Loadstone 1605
LARRY & JOHNNY - Beatle Time pts. 1 & 2	Jola 1000
VERONICA LEE & MONIQUES - Ringo Did It/Foreign Boy	Centaur 106
LIL WALLY & VENTURAS - Welcome Beatles/	Drum Boy 108
LITTLE CHERYL - Yeh Yeh We Love 'Em All/Nick & Joe	Cameo 307
LITTLE LADY BEATLES - Dear Beatles/	Applause 1002
LIVERS - Beatle Time/	Constellation 1605
DICK LORD - Like Ringo/The Name On the Wall	Atco 6331
DONNA LYNN - My Boyfriend Got a Beatle Haircut/ (#83)	Capitol 5127
LYNN & THE MERSEY MAIDS - Mrs. Jones Your Son Gives Up Too Easy/	Ric 161
MAD ENGLISHMEN & FURYS - Beetle Mania	Vee Six 1023
MANCHESTERS - I Don't Come From England/Dragonfly	Vee Jay 700
ERNIE MARESCA - The Beetle Dance/	Rust 5076
MARTY & MONKS - Mrs. Schwartz You've Got an Ugly Daughter	Assoc. Artists 3065
BONNIE JO MASON - Ringo I Love You/Beatle Blues	Annette 1001
MR. MILLER & BLUE NOTES - Mrs. Brown You've Got a Lovely Daughter/ I'm Henry VIII, I Am	Swan 4256
HARV MOORE - Interview of the Fab Four	American Arts 20
MORAN - The Beatles Thing/Lady Loves Me	Epic 10987
GENE MOSS - I Want to Bite Your Hand/	RCA 8438
MOTIONS - Beatle Drums/	Mercury 72297
MYSTERY TOUR - Ballad of Paul/same (reversed)	MGM 14097
NAN & JAN - Beatle Bop/Believe it or Not	Debby 069
NILSSON - You Can't Do That/Ten Little Indians	RCA 9298
OUTSIDERS - The Guy With the Long Liverpool Hair/The Outsider	Karate 505
GIGI PARKER & LOVELIES - Beatles Please Come Back/In This Room	MGM 13225
PATTY CAKES - I Understand Them/same (instr.)	Tuff 378
DORI PEYTON - Ringo Boy/In the Spring of the Year	Ottie 101
PHAETONS - Beatle Walk/	Shara 103
VIV PRINCE - Light of the Charge Brigade/Minuet for Ringo	Columbia 7960 (E)
DONNY RAE & DEFIANTS - Beatle Mania/	Arlen 521
RAINBO - John You Went Too Far This Time/C'mon Teach Me to Live	Roulette 7030
RAINBOWS - My Ringo/He's Hooked on J's	Dot 16612
RAJAHS - Tribute to the Beatles EP (Australian)	Sunday Mirror 002
DELL RANDLE - Introducing the Beatles to Monkey Land/The Monkey & The Beatles	Shakari 101
CINDY RELLA - Bring Me a Beatle for Xmas	Drum Boy 112
RON RINGO - Ringo's Jerk/Queen of the Jerk	Juggy 701
ROACHES - Beatle Mania Blues/Angel of Angels	Crossway 447
BOBBY ROBERTS - The Beatles for Xmas/	
RAY RUFF & CHECKMATES - Beatle Maniacs/Took a Liking to You	Lin 5034
PETER RYAN - If We Try/I Can Hear the Music	Aardvark 101
ARLEN SANDERS - Letter to Paul/Hopped Up Mustang	Faro 616
GARY SANDERS - Ain't No Beatle/Ain't I Good to You	Warner Bros 5676
MIKE SARNE - An Englishman Sings "America Swings"/Can't Wait	Ascot 2213
SAXONS - Tribute to the Beatles EP	Mardan 16084
SAXTONS - The Beatle Dance/Sittin' On Top of the World	Regina 305
SCRAMBLERS - The Beatle Walk/The Beatle Blues	Del-Fi 4237
NEIL SHEPPARD - You Can't Go Far Without a Guitar (Unless You're Ringo Starr)/Betty is the Girl For You	Almont 314
ALLEN SHERMAN - I Hate the Beatles/	Warner Bros. 5490
ED SOLOMON - The Beatle Flying Saucer/Whistling Drifter	Diamond 160
SONNY - Beatle Squash/	Bee
STANDELLS - Peppermint Beatle/The Shake	Liberty 55680
STARLETTES - Ringo/All Dressed Up	Siana 717
SWANS - The Boy With the Beatle Hair/Please Hurry Home	Cameo 302
TEEN BUGS - Yes You Can Hold My Hand/	Blue River 208
DARLENE TERRI - Ringo Ringo/A Real Live Boy	Columbia 43042
THREE BLONDE MICE - Ringo Bells/The Twelve Days of Christmas	Atco 6342
TRIBUTES - Ringo Dingo/Here Comes Ringo	Donna 1391
TWILITERS - My Beatle Haircut/Sweet Lips	Roulette 4546
JEANNE TURNBOW - Beattle Bug1summertime	Ben-Ron 1393
UPFRONTS - Do the Beatle/	Lummtone 114
U.S. BEATLE WIGS - She's So Innocent (Oh Yeah!)/Finger Poppin Girl	Orbit 531
GARY USHER - The Beetle/	Capitol 5128
PENNY VALENTINE - I Want to Kiss Ringo Goodbye/	Liberty 55774
VERNONS GIRLS - We Love the Beatles/Hey Lover Boy	Challenge 59234
VICE ROYS - Liverpool/	USA 761
VITO & SALUTATIONS - Liverpool Bound/Can I Depend on You	Wells 1008
VULCANES - Liverpool/	Capitol 5285
WEEKENDS - Ringo/I Want You	Le-Mans 001
WHIPPETS - Go Go Go With Ringo/I Want to Talk With You	Josie 921
BOBBY WILDING - I Want to Be a Beatle/Since I've Been Wearing My Hair Like a Beatle	DCP 1009
PAT WYNTER - Ringo I Want to Know Your Secret/	Take Five 631
KENNETH YOUNG & ENGLISH MUFFINS - Mrs. Green's Ugly Daughter	Diamond 183
LEON YOUNG STRING CHORALE - John Paul George & Ringo/	Atco 6301
YOUNG WORLD SINGERS - Ringo For President/A Boy Like That	Decca 31660

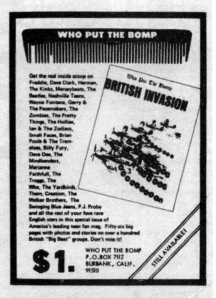

WHO PUT THE BOMP

Get the real inside scoop on Freddie, Dave Clark, Herman, The Kinks, Merseybeats, The Beatles, Nashville Teens, Wayne Fontana, Gerry & The Pacemakers, The Zombies, The Pretty Things, The Hollies, Ian & The Zodiacs, Small Faces, Brian Poole & The Tremeloes, Billy Fury, Dave Dee, The Mindbenders, Marianne Faithfull, The Troggs, The Who, The Yardbirds, Them, Creation, The Walker Brothers, The Swinging Blue Jeans, P.J. Proby and all the rest of your fave rave English stars in this special issue of America's leading teen fan mag. Fifty-six big pages with photos and stories on over a hundred British "Big Beat" groups. Don't miss it!

$1. WHO PUT THE BOMP P.O. BOX 7112 BURBANK, CALIF. 91510

STILL AVAILABLE!

ALSO AVAILABLE: #12, with the Seeds, Standells, Leaves, Beau Brummels, Knickerbockers, listings for Autumn, GNP Crescendo, Tollie, Interphon & more, plus the history of punk rock in Northern California. Still only $1, while they last.

If you like Bomp, don't forget The Rock Marketplace. The ultimate source for '60s and '70s collecting info, great articles & discographies. Sample only $1 from Alan Betrock, Box 253, Elmhurst-A, NY

JUKE BOX JURY JUNIOR

BY GREG SHAW

Capt. Groovy - "Captain Groovy and His Bubblegum Army" - *Super-K SK 4*

Bubblegum music is an aquired taste so I don't expect everyone to share my affection for the Archies, Lancelot Link, etc., but this is one record no reader of this magazine could fail to love. Perhaps the ultimate accomplishment of the Katz-Kasenetz team, this side takes early bubble at its punkiest (as Ohio Express' "Try It") and elevates it to heavy metal, throwing on a heavy dose of British psychedelic pop. Even Jimi Hendrix would've loved this record. Where bubblegum is almost by definition totally controlled and predictible, this one threatens to break through into sheer mania.

Vamp - "Floatin' " - *Atlantic 584213* (E) '68

Here's a record that deserves to be better known. The first time I heard it, I thought I was hearing the best record Bowie ever made before 1972. It turned out to be not Bowie at all but Viv Prince--sure sounds like him tho. The song is a lazy, thickly-textured ballad with some gorgous, English-accented melodies and fantastic drumming

McKinleys - "Someone Cares For Me" - *Swan 4185* (A) 4-64

The McKinleys were a British girl group who made several other records, but this is their classic. Written by Carter & Lewis at their best, it could've been meant for the Crystals, and whoever produced it obviously had that in mind. You never heard so many castanets on an English record!

The Group - "Baby, Baby It's You" - *Warner Bros. 5840* (A) 7-66

This Gary Zekley production sounds like Brian Wilson and Curt Boettcher interpreting "Be My Baby." The melody and lyrics are a little too obviously derivative, but considering what it's derived from, it's a strong tune with exceptional production. Watch out for it.

Walkers - "Sha-la-la-la-la" - *Sunburst 522* (A)

This excellent record is the only known American release by one of the top Danish groups circa 1968. The tune is fairly straight, catchy bubble-pop, but the singing and production are so strongly English that it's disconcerting. And the flip, "High School Queen", sounds like Dave Edmunds doing a Paul Simon arrangement of "Beach Baby". A real oddity.

King Uszniewicz & His Uszniewicz-Tones - "Surfin' School"/"Cry on my Shoulder" *1-Shot 175* (A)

Talk about your mystery records. The only thing I know for sure about it is that Al Nalli (who manages Brownsville Station) put it out. It could well be Brownsville. Quite simply, it's the crudest garage record I've ever heard. No group, no matter how bad, could have seriously made this record--whoever did it had to work at making it sound this way. I mean, in the first 8 bars they blow an E-to-A change. And the lyrics: "Surf surf baby, gonna surf all the way to school..." The singer then yells "Do the surfer stomp!" and in comes a kazoo doing a parody Steve Douglas sax solo. The drummer meanwhile is stumbling all over in search of the beat. This is better than the Bonzos--one of the most amazing rock satires of all time.

Junco Partners - "Take This Hammer" - *Columbia DB 7665* (E) '65

Talk about dynamics--this is one of the most kinetic records ever, on a par with the Yardbirds and early Kinks. The song is an old skiffle standard done in British R&B style, dominated by rhythm guitar, harp, and a raw vocal. There are no guitar solos, no flashy effects, just a solid rhythm that doesn't let up for a second, a guitar lick thrown in here and there. Extremely understated, but that only adds to its power. They start to get down toward the end with a harp solo that cuts Cyril Davies (in fact this is the only English R&B disc I've heard that tops "Country Line Special") and then it's over. Hear it if you can; it's a classic.

Leon Russell - "Everybody's Talking 'Bout the Young" - *Dot 16771* '65

This is a classic too, of a different sort. Haven't you always wanted to hear Leon sing a corny Sonny Bono protest song? This hard-to-find disc, the rarest of Leon's solo releases from his mid 60s session days, is the answer to your dreams. Co-written by J.J.Cale, it hits all the bases Barry McGuire missed--Cuba, the Congo, middle-aged adults, the Klan, and of course China, Vietnam and the atom bomb. And for a surprise twist, Leon puts down the protesters and defends our fighting boys. This must've been one of the first anti-protest protest records.

The Thyme - "Love to Love" - *Bang 546* (A) '66

This record, produced by A-Square but leased to Bang, is probably the best-produced pop single made in Detroit in the mid-60s. It's a Neil Diamond song, which helps, but instead of Diamond's usual formula, this tune sounds like something from the Zombies, with an unforgettable minor key melody and a tasty guitar/electric piano solo. Hard to believe this wasn't a big hit, but it will be around your house the minute it hits your turntable. (For more on the Thyme, see page 40)

Apple - "The Otherside" - *Page One POF 110* (E) '68

Apple had a couple other singles on Page One and a cover of Scaffold's "Thank U Very Much" (Smash 2143) released here, but this one stands out as an undiscovered classic. It combines early English pop psychedelia (like the first stuff by Pink Floyd, Soft Machine, etc., when they were making pop singles) with a Mod sort of mentality reminiscent of the Sell Out Who. Pounding electric pianos and soaring guitars make this a truly atmospheric record. Oddly enough, it was the B-side of a boring number called "Doctor Rock".

AC/DC - "Can I Sit Next to You Girl"/"Rockin' in the Parlor" - *Albert Productions AP-10551* (Australian '74

Vanda & Young have been back in Australia for 2 years now, and produced a few things, including a new album by Stevie Wright, their former vocalist with the Easybeats. But this record tops them all.

AC/DC is most likely just V&Y with some studio guys; if it is a real group, their similarity to the early Easybeats is startling. The Easies, of course, were known for their overpowering dynamics and taut kineticism. And this record is a modern evolution of that classic sound, with heavy '70s riffs and themes—as if the Sweet had listened nonstop to "Friday On My Mind" and "Sorry" and "Easy As Can Be" for a week and then gone out to try and outdo it.

"Rockin' in the Parlor" is a good, 50s-ish tune, not unlike recent Mud singles. But "Can I Sit Next to You Girl", a real teenage stomper in the Chinnichap tradition, is the real triumph. It starts off like "Rubber Bullets", builds right into a power chord structure just bristling with energy, and includes some incredible dynamic effects—like pure fuzz noise echoing from channel to channel, then fading out as a machine-gun rhythm guitar fades in, rising to a powerful blast as they scream out the title over and over. Overall, a stunning record.

The Pebbles - "No Time at All" - *UA 4C-006-95088* (Dutch) '74

Not only Zombies, but a bit of Searchers and early Colin Blunstone go into this mesmerizing record. The crisp, precise perfection of '65 English pop is resurrected brilliantly here, with soft breathy vocals and a terrific guitar break. The Pebbles have a couple of other singles out in Holland, plus an album in England that unfortunately doesn't include this song and is not really remarkable. On the basis of this song, though, the Pebbles could turn out to be a very important group.

Rainbow Stardust - "Two Shy"/"Juicy Groove" - *Lovestar Records* '74

This is the closest thing to a new Seeds record there's ever likely to be. Rainbow has been the guitarist in Sunstar's (nee Sky Saxon) band for a couple years now, and this debut disc shows him to be every bit as great a singer as he is a guitarist. Sky claims he's the world's greatest guitar player. If you think the Seeds were better than the Stones, you'll probably agree with him.

Actually, this is not a bad garage punk record. With decent production it could be okay. The subject matter is fine, "want to need you, but I'm too shy..." Teenage as could be. Don't know where you can get it though—maybe if Rainbow reads this, he'll let us know...

GREMMIE'S GOSSIP: Dave Edmunds plans to put out an album soon containing "Baby I Love You" and some of his other masterpieces....Brinsley Schwarz have a new 45 in England, a high-energy remake of Tommy Roe's "Everybody"...also new from the UK is "Tell Me Why"/"I Should'veKnown Better", a 2-side Beatle remake by Limelight (UA 35779)...Blue Cheer have reformed & cut a demo of a Kim Fowley song called "Fighting Star"...Vanda & Young recently produced "My Little Angel" by William Shakespeare, followup to his #1 Aussie hit "Cant Stop Myself From Loving You".

SOUNDS of the SIXTIES

Part Two: MICHIGAN

BY DICK ROSEMONT

Michigan, and Detroit in particular, spawned one of the most prolific and influential music scenes of the '60s. Motown of course paved the way for the soul music explosion, and produced some of its most enduring stars. But beyond that, Michigan as a rock & roll center has a rich history that's never been fully acknowledged, let alone documented.

As established elsewhere, soul and grit were integral elements of every Detroit musician's style, from Grand Funk to Suzi Quatro, they all name Motown as their prime influence. Because of this, Michigan rock has always embodied an extra special quality of earthiness and strength.

The punk era sparked an awesome amount of local recording in Michigan, and unfortunately for us, these records are among the rarest of their period, compared to local records from other regions which can still be fairly easily obtained. The nationally-released Michigan records, however (particularly those of Mitch Ryder, Question Mark & the Mysterians, SRC, Bob Seger, the MC5 and the Woolies) provide ample evidence of the region's identity and value as a punk center, even before the underground era of the Grande Ballroom, Stooges, Brownsville, Frost, Amboy Dukes and others whose work is better known to today's audience.

Dick Rosemont, our Michigan correspondent, has done an amazing job of researching and rounding up details of the early days of Michigan rock. Except for Dan Bourgoise's introductory history of pre-1964 Detroit, Dick is responsible for the entire bulk of the articles and discographies included here, and without his contribution, this survey could never have been possible.

THE EARLY YEARS

BY DAN BOURGOISE

Rock & roll was delivered to Detroit in the mid-Fifties by radio personalities like Micky Shorr, Casey Kasem, Jack the Bellboy, Robin Seymour and Tom Clay. The Motor City certainly had its share of 'race records' and hillbilly music, but both elements were far too polarized to bed down and spawn a new strain. That marriage would have to be consummated elsewhere. However, as rock began to dominate the airwaves, only a few locals (LaVerne Baker, Jackie Wilson) ever dented the national charts.

By the end of the '50s and in the early '60s, a rock culture was beginning to form. Jack Scott had a string of hits and his local club was the hottest and most influential music spot of its time. Dances were held every weekend at the Walled Lake Casino, hosted by DJ Lee Alan, featuring out-of-town artists who lip synched their hits and scores of local bands who always played for free.

Appearances by area favorites such as the Royaltones, Johnny & the Hurricanes, Steve Monahan & the Tremelos, Paul London, the Young Sisters, Little Stevie Wonder, and a 16-year-old Diana Ross & the Supremes were common at 4 or 5 different hops in one night. In 1961, Del Shannon became a local phenomenon when "Runaway" sold 4 million copies worldwide. Shannon's continued hit streak, coupled with the early success of Motown Records, gave young Detroit musicians the feeling that they might now indeed be in a position to shape and influence the sound of rock & roll.

The opportunities for a career in music were very limited to Detroiters in the early '60s. Other than Motown, the city had very little to offer. There was Fortune Records, a seedy little operation on 3rd St. that scored with Nathaniel Mayer and Nolan Strong. Probably the most successful independent company was run by Harry Balk & Irving Michanik. Their success with white acts like Johnny & the Hurricanes and Del Shannon made them unique in the city. However, their business tactics were devious; as was common in those days, when they signed an artist he became their property. They produced all recordings under the banner of Embee Productions (most of which were released by the NY-based Big Top label) and their publishing arm allowed them to gobble up the songs of any promising young writers who came to them in hopes of hitting the big time. Under the pseudonyms of T.King and I. Mack their names went on every record as writers and they took most of the royalties.

The only artist who fought back against this was Del Shannon, who finally got free in 1965, though lawsuits are still going on to this date and all royalties from his many hits have remained in escrow pending settlement.

When rock was grown up enough to enter the bars, musicians could realize the dream of earning a living and having fun at the same time. The local Detroit bands sustained and prospered as the English Invasion increased the respectability of rock groups. All musical forms were neatly incorporated into the show, and played with a vigor that would later become the Motor City trademark. Among the best bands of this era were Billy Lee & the Rivieras, Doug Brown & the Omens, and Jamie Coe & the Gigolos.

Jamie Coe & the Gigolos were Detroit's most popular bar band. His "How Low is Low" was a huge local hit and did well nationally. He also scored with "The Fool" on Big Top. Coe was another of Balk & Michanik's artists and, while being important locally for many years, he never achieved any real national importance.

Constantly challenging Coe for best band was the younger Doug Brown & the Omens, from nearby Ann

Del Shannon, Detroit's first rocker.

Arbor. Brown attracted a huge following and his bands were always among the tightest and played the best rock & roll. Brown's stage presence and leadership were legendary.

The band was rarely recorded, but a solo Doug Brown single was released on Checker in 1962--I believe it was called something like "Susie Baby". Brown always stayed on top of all musical trends and had a keen ear and awareness. In 1964, he began working with a 17-year-old protege named Bob Seger, and the two wrote many songs together. Brown & Seger went into the studio with the Omens and Steve Monahan and recorded demos of all their original material, paid for by Del Shannon, who became their publisher. Later, after Shannon moved to California, Seger joined the Omens and with organist Al Collini and drummer Bob Evans (later with Smith) this was one of Doug's most powerful bands.

Dan Bourgoise grew up in Detroit, managed a record store there in the early '60s, and was the first to record Bob Seger and Doug Brown. He's worked with Del Shannon for many years, and co-authored several of his songs.

MICHIGAN PUNK-ROCK

SUBURBAN DETROIT

Detroit proper never had much of a local scene (other than Motown, of course). Everything came from the suburbs, but it was called Detroit. The suburbs are Detroit--to some, Ann Arbor is Detroit. To the rest of the country, Detroit was Motown Records. But out beyond the inner city lay a punk scene that was to emerge as one of the most vital, creative, and musically unique of all regional scenes of the Sixties.

Before 1964, the area had its handful of high school bands, playing the usual teen hops and annual State Fair "Battle of the Bands" competitions. If you were lucky, you got to accompany a local DJ at the Walled Lake Casino or Motor City Roller Rink. These spots were greasy all the way; always full of the rebellious youth that characterized the era--Michigan had its American graffiti too.

The rise of a tangible local scene paralleled the development of the Hideout teen clubs and record company. Dave Leone and Ed "Punch" Andrews recognized the potential for a regular club featuring live bands. They had been impressed with a group called the Fugitives, out of Birmingham, and set them up at a rented hall in Harper Woods. Opening night of the Hideout ("It sounded like a good name...") in May of '64 brought 87 people and two fights. But here was this band playing songs like "Louie Louie" and doing things people had never heard before on stage. The word spread; two weeks later, 337 teenagers showed up.

Suddenly there was an organized spot for kids to go on Friday nights. The Hideout thrived; and in addition to growing audiences, there were growing numbers of local bands. The Hideout spurred this growth, although with the onset of the British Invasion and rampant teen mania, the timing was right. One of the first regular Hideout bands was the Pleasure Seekers, formed by a former Hideout concession stand cashier--Suzi Quatro.

The Fugitives went on to become the name band in the area. Originally called the Tremelos, they were 5 innovative high school students, who you'd see in class Monday despite the fact you'd seen them on stage as stars Friday night. The core of the band (Gary Quackenbush, Glen Quackenbush and Elmer Clawson) later evolved into the Scot Richard Case (with of course Scott Richardson). They were into the Pretty Things and Cream before anyone had heard of them. When *Fresh Cream* became popular, people still associated "I'm So Glad" with the Case due to their previous cover version.

THE BOOM BEGINS

By 1965 there were countless punk bands popping up, particularly in the richer suburbs of Grosse Point, Birmingham, and Bloomfield Hills, where parents could shell out $1000 for equipment and not miss it. High school sock hops were passing up DJs as attractions and offering "Live Bands!" Other clubs were started--the Hullabaloos, the Crows Nest, the Pumpkin, the Birmingham-Bloomfield Teen Center. A second Hideout opened in Southfield, drawing over 600 the first night. It seemed as though everyone and his brother was in a group.

Most bands at this time built their reputations through live appearances as opposed to radio exposure. Motown was the only major label and they were all-black

at the time. Local labels soon came into being, however—although more for the purpose of promoting the groups than to seek hit records.

Dave Leone started Hideout Records right after the club hit. Previously he had produced the Fugitives on D-Town (a small R&B label) but the records had no distribution. The few copies pressed were passed around town to promote the band and are virtually impossible to find today. The first Hideout release was an album titled *The Fugitives at Dave's Hideout*. The record itself was technically awful—a basement recording fed through a PA at the Hideout and re-recorded with enthusiastic crowd reactions. The material ranged from "Love Potion #9" and "Louie Louie" to originals like "Friday at the Hideout". 500 copies were sold for $3 each at the hall.

The first Hideout single also has an interesting history. The Underdogs, a Grosse Pointe band, had become popular at the Hideout and Leone wanted more exposure for them. A friend supplied an "original" poem that was set to music and recorded. "Man in the Glass" was then subjected to a massive promotional campaign. It started to get airplay and was even picked up by Reprise Records. Then Leone discovered the lyrics were cribbed verbatim from a poem used at Alcoholics Anonymous meetings! He was forced to let the record die.

The Underdogs later became one of the first white acts signed to Motown. "Love's Gone Bad" on their VIP subsidiary was quite popular and a fine cover of the Chris Clark song.

As the demand for bands grew, disc jockeys started getting involved. For his part in helping get a record played, a DJ would ask the group to appear with him at one of his self-promoted hops. A number of acts got their songs played this way, such as Tim Tam & the Turn-Ons (whose Four Seasons-like "Wait a Minute" became a large regional hit) and the Shy Guys. The Shy Guys even re-cut their hit "We Gotta Go" with new lyrics about WKNR jock Scott Ragan ("The Burger Song").

The Reflections, like Tim Tam & the Turn-Ons, were a singing group who appeared with other bands who provided instrumental backup. Their original hit version of "Just Like Romeo and Juliet" reached the Top 10 nationally in 1964. They put out many follow-ups on Golden World and later ABC, but never scored again.

Golden World, their original label, was the product of Ed Wingate, who also headed Wingate, Ric Tic and other minor labels. The labels' releases were mostly soul (Gino Washington, Edwin Starr, Detroit Emeralds) with a bit of jazz and rock.

1965-67 brought a steady stream of popular groups and hit records. The Tidal Waves and the Wanted scored with covers of "Farmer John" and "Midnight Hour" respectively, after being picked up by national labels. A punk band called the Unrelated Segments had a couple of fine hits, "Story of My Life" and a strange follow-up, "Where You Gonna Go." One of the few songs reflecting the British sound was the Human Beings' (not to be confused with the Human Beinz, from Ohio) "Because I Love Her", complete with 12-string and fake accents. This was probably the best produced local record which never made it, despite being released nationally by Warner Brothers.

There were many other notable records that never got exposure. The groups that opened Hideout #2 both laid down fine original material, the Yorkshires' "Tossed Salad" displayed strong vocal ability, while the Oxford Five's "The World I've Planned" was smoothly catchy.

Regarding the Yorkshires, I'm convinced they initiated the popularity of Them's "Gloria". After receiving the British single and working up the tune, they drunkenly got into an extended, "risque" rendition, and from then on the song was notorious. Groups were even forbidden to play it at certain Catholic high schools! Unfortunately, the Yorkshires never recorded the song, and it took the word spreading to Chicago for the Shadows of Knight to cash in.

For fans of early Suzi and Patti Quatro, there's the Pleasure Seekers' "Never Thought You'd Leave Me" and their later single on Mercury—two of the rarest Michigan records. Another Hideout release not to be overlooked was "Such a Lonely Child" (written by Bob Seger) by the Mushrooms, containing future Eagles member Glenn Frey. It was another pseudo-English production, this time reflecting the Kinks.

MITCH RYDER

More than anyone else, it was Mitch Ryder who catalyzed the teen rock revolution in Michigan. He was the first since Del Shannon to make it nationally as a white teen star, and he was the first to present the Detroit version of blue-eyed soul that was to form the basis of the local sound. His band was the model on which hundreds of kids fashioned their groups.

• Mitch with Smokey Robinson at the Twenty Grand, '64

He entered music with a high school band called the Tempest, which didn't last long. After that he spent a couple of years hanging out with black musicians at jazz clubs like the Village and the Tantrum, eventually forming an all-black group called the Peps, doing Smokey Robinson material. After an audition with Thelma Gordy, the Peps were signed to Tamla, but Mitch left the group because of money disputes, returning to the Village where he was soon headlining under the name Billy Lee. Billy Lee & the Rivieras became the hottest of the greaser bands in 1963, and cut their first record for Reverend James Hendricks' *Carrie* label. The Rivieras consisted of Jim McCarty on guitar, drummer John Badanjek, bass player Earl Elliott and Joe Kubert (who'd been with Mitch since the Tempest) on rhythm. After another local record, which received slight airplay on WXYZ, Billy Lee & the Rivieras became the house band at the Walled Lake Casino, which was *the* place to go in those days. They were drawing as many as 3,000 a night when Bob Crewe, a young New York producer, heard a demo tape and signed them.

They spent six months in New York, practicing in a hotel room until Crewe thought they were ready to record. Then they cut a 4-track stereo tape of all the songs they'd been doing live, and from that Crewe selected "Jenny Take a Ride" for the first single. The song went Top 10 in December '65, and introduced the 2-song medley form that Ryder carried through several other smash hits, the biggest of which, "Devil With a Blue Dress/Good Golly Miss Molly" reached #4 in Oct. '66. The name Mitch Ryder was chosen from a phone book because Crewe thought Billy Lee & the Rivieras sounded too dated. Overnight, Billy Lee was forgotten and Mitch Ryder was a star.

Crewe, however, wasn't satisfied with that. His machinations with the group constitute one of the all-time legendary stories of rock manipulation. Thinking Ryder would make a great Vegas-type superstar, he worked to split up the band, finally succeeding during the recording sessions that produced "Devil With a Blue Dress" and the rest of Mitch's subsequent hits prior to

And the Motor City Five (MC5) were even kicking around the studio in their early days. "One of the Guys"/"I Can Only Give You Everything" (the Them/Troggs tune) hinted at their transition from a soul group to a kick-ass rock & roll band. Their ultimate in high energy display has to be the early recordings of "Borderline" and "Looking at You" on A-Square (tho actually put out by John Sinclair), both of which showed up in weaker versions on albums.

"What Now My Love." By then, he had Mitch wearing $10,000 costumes, touring with a 40-piece band, and paying for it all out his royalties to the extent that at one time he was in debt to Crewe for over $100,000. Ryder later claimed to have received nothing more than a $15,000 advance during the course of all his million-sellers. Finally, after several years of legal hassles and financial disasters, all of which struck at a time when Ryder should have been taking advantage of his string of hits to build a solid career foundation, he was able to get free of Crewe. But by then his name had faded, his band was gone, and despite a new label (Dot) who made a good move in sending him to Memphis to record at Stax, his career seemed finished. Another couple of years elapsed before Ryder announced a new group called Detroit, whose superb debut album on Paramount drew rave reviews and a bit of airplay. Mysteriously, then, that band also disappeared, and to this date there has been no news of Ryder or his activities. It's too bad, because what he represented in '65 is still valid (and much needed) today: rock & roll as tough, gritty and real as it comes. Mitch Ryder, wherever he is, is still the spirit of Detroit. Let's hope he shows up again soon.

—Greg Shaw

MITCH RYDER DISCOGRAPHY

(Billy Lee & Rivieras)
Carrie ? Fool For You/? ('63)
Hiland ? Do You Wanna Dance/? ('64)

(Mitch Ryder & Detroit Wheels)
New Voice
801 I Need Help/I Hope
806 Jenny Take a Ride/Baby Jane
808 Little Latin Lupe Lu/I Hope
811 Break Out/I Need Help
814 Takin' All I Can Get/You Get Your Kicks
817 Devil with a Blue Dress/I Had it Made
820 Sock it to Me Baby/I Never Had it Better
822 Too Many Fish in the Sea/One Grain of Sand
824 Joy/I'd Rather Go to Jail
826 You Are My Sunshine/Wild Child
828 Come See About Me/Face in the Crowd

Dynovoice
901 What Now My Love/Blessing in Disguise
905 Personality & Chantilly Lace/I Make a Fool of Myself
916 The Lights of Night/?
934 Ring Your Bell/Baby I Need Your Loving & Theme For Mitch (also Dynovoice 305)

Avco
4550 Jenny Take a Ride/I Never Had it Better

Dot
17290 Sugar Bee/I Believe
17325 Direct Me/?

(Detroit)
Paramount
0051 I Can't See Nobody/?
0094 It Ain't Easy/Long Neck Goose
0133 Rock & Roll/?
0158 Gimme Shelter/Oo La La Dee Da Doo

LPs
Take a Ride - New Voice 2000
Breakout - New Voice 2002
Sock it to Me - New Voice 2003
All Mitch Ryder's Hits - New Voice 2004
Sings the Hits - New Voice 2005
What Now My Love - Dynovoice 31901
All the Heavy Hits - Crewe 1335
Detroit/Memphis Experiment - Dot 25963
Detroit - Paramount 6010

FROM THE SUBURBS TO THE STREETS

1967 was the transition year, bringing the rise of ballrooms and flower children. Dave Leone, returning from National Guard active duty, found the Hideouts nothing like the way he'd left them, and was forced to sell out to Punch. Local groups split up as members graduated from high school. Clubs in rented halls faced mounting neighbor complaints...larger facilities were needed for growing crowds. National acts were becoming realistic attractions.

Nearly overnight, the Detroit scene focused on the Grande Ballroom, opened by a foresighted Dearborn schoolteacher-turned-entrepeneur: "Uncle" Russ Gibb. Many bands continued intact (Rationals, Woolies, MC5) while others modified (Fugitives to SRC, Frost to Bossmen, Scarlet Letter to Savage Grace). At the same time, a second wave of local groups blossomed. Bands like Brownsville Station, Amboy Dukes, Psychedelic Stooges, Sky, 3rd Power, Frijid Pink, Frut, Teagarden & Van Winkle, and the Up were born out of the ballroom days.

Theories abound as to why more Detroit acts weren't successful nationally, from "the management never matched the talent" to "the talent was just a lot of energy." A number of national labels--Cameo, Warner Bros., Capitol--made serious efforts to develop something out of the scene, but never came up with anything more than one-shot hits. All the same, everyone seems to agree that the times were fun--and that, more than hit records, is what the Punk Era was all about.

ANN ARBOR

It's difficult to separate Ann Arbor from Detroit, even though some 20 miles of desolate marsh lies between them. Ann Arbor is primarily a college town, with the student populace and energy level that implies, as well as the diversity of backgrounds. Many of what became known as Ann Arbor bands had actually originated elsewhere.

Most everything in Ann Arbor had some connection with A-Square Productions, headed by Hugh "Jeep" Holland. Holland managed bands, ran A-Square Records, and later booked Detroit's Grande Ballroom.

The Rationals were the first group to come under Jeep's wing. With experience (and unchanged personnel) dating back to '62, the Rats were led by vocalist Scott Morgan. Their first recording was A-Square's initial release, a soulful rocker called "Look What You're Doing to Me Baby". It was crude but hinted at things to come, especially from Morgan. "Feelin' Lost", a distinct blend of the Kinks and *Beatles VI*, was a better record but still brought them little exposure. As the Rationals' popularity grew, Jeep was determined that they make the local charts. Their third release was a fantastic version of Eddie Holland's "Leavin' Here" backed with an equally exciting cover of "Respect"--considerably pre-dating Aretha's.

As "Respect" showed signs of becoming a hit, Holland substituted "Feelin' Lost" (an original) for "Leavin' Here". This coupling was sold to Cameo, where it broke nationally, then fell off as Cameo's financial troubles began (more on that later).

While with Cameo, the Rationals cut an inferior version of "Leavin' Here" and a competent rendition of Barry/Greenwich's "Hold On Baby." The band was entrenched in an R&B vein, and Scott Morgan became "The Legendary White Boy of Soul", rivaling even Mitch Ryder. Breaking off from Cameo, the Rats recorded the finest ballad ever done in Michigan, the Goffin-King tune "I Need You." It was amazing to see everyone stop and listen to it at the "high-energy" Grande.

In 1968, the Rationals split with Jeep and set up their own label, Genesis, with eternal DJ Robin Seymour. Its only release, "Guitar Army" just didn't make it. The group then signed with Bob Crewe (who may have been hoping to find another Mitch Ryder) and issued their only LP. Its highlight was "Handbags & Gladrags", a version that supposedly inspired Rod Stewart to tackle the song.

Scott Morgan is still hanging around Ann Arbor today, but many feel he's not what he used to be. He'll always be a local boy it seems, and maybe that's why he turned down an offer to join Blood, Sweat & Tears after Al Kooper left.

THE SRC

Jeep Holland was the man responsible for uniting Fugitives members with Scott Richardson (late of the Chosen Few) to form the Scot Richard Case (later shortened to SRC). In addition to their relatively lame recording of "I'm So Glad", Holland released "Get the Picture" (a Pretty Things song) after the band left him. They were billed, somewhat bitterly, as "The Old Exciting Scot Richard Case." I've never heard the record, but I suspect it's worthwhile, especially considering the Rationals were on the flip.

SRC was one of the most persistent bands around. After signing with Capitol, they built a studio (Morgan Sound Theatre) to facilitate their recording, as well as a service to other locals. Of their 3 LPs, *Milestones* remains the standout. Self-produced, it ranged from the ultra-tight "Up All Night" to a fine arrangement of "In the Hall of the Mountain King" (always a favorite of the Grande crowd). And for not being much of a singer, Scott Richardson managed to sound amazingly like Colin Blunstone on the epic "Angel Song".

In an attempt to "start clean and have a hit record", SRC became Blue Scepter around 1970. Blue Scepter's only release was a dreadful Motown arrangement of the Pretty Things' "Out in the Night." Back to SRC, their last record was a commercially oriented "Born to Love" on the group's own label, Big Casino.

A-SQUARE RECORDS

101 Rationals - Look What You're Doing to me Baby/Gave My Love
102 Rationals - unreleased
103 Rationals - Feelin' Lost/Little Girls Cry
104 Rationals - Leavin' Here/Respect
105 Rationals - Hold On Baby/Sing†
106 Rationals - Leavin' Here/Not Like It Is†
107 Rationals - I Need You/Out in the Streets (Sing!)
201 Thyme - Somehow/Shame, Shame
202 Thyme - Time of the Season/I Found a Love
301 Scot Richard Case - I'm so Glad/Who is that girl?
333 MC5 - Looking at You/Borderline
401 Apostles - Stranded in the Jungle/Tired of Waiting
402 Old Exciting Scot Richard Case - Get the Picture/Rationals - I Need You (Kinks song; diff.from 107)

†Numbers assigned, but records issued on Capitol only

(The reason for the confusing number system is that each group was originally assigned its own prefix. The MC5 record was produced independently by the group without Jeep Holland's knowledge; thus the odd #)

HIDEOUT RECORDS

1001 Underdogs - Man in the Glass/Friday at the Hideout (Judy Be Mine)
1002
1003 Four of Us - You're Gonna Be Mine/FreeFall
1003 Four of Us - You're Gonna Be Mine/Batman
 (Both B-sides on 1003 are the same; title might've been changed to cash in on Batman craze. The Fugitives also did this song, as "Fugitive".)
1004 Underdogs - Little Girl/Don't Pretend (also on Reprise 0446)
1005 T.R.& the Yardsmen - I Tried/Movin' Up
1006 Pleasure Seekers - Never Thought You'd Leave Me/What a Way to Die
1007 (Punch Records) Torquays - Shake a Tail Feather/Temptation
1008 (Punch Records) Doug Brown - T.G.I.F./The First Girl
1009 (Punch Records) Henchmen - Please Tell Me/Livin'
1010 (Are You Kidding Me? Records) Beach Bums - Ballad of the Yellow Beret/Florida Time
1011 Underdogs - Surprise Surprise/Get Down on Your Knees
1012 Four of Us - I Feel a Whole Lot Better/I Can't Live Without Your Love
1013 Bob Seger & Last Heard - East Side Story/East Side Sound
1014 Bob Seger & the Last Heard - Persecution Smith/Chain Smokin'
1121 Mushrooms - Such a Lovely Child/Burned
1221 Talismen - Vintage N.S.U./Taxman
1225 Mama Cats - Miss You/My Boy
1232 H.P.Movement - Heavy Music/Heavy Music Live
1070 Sunday Funnies - Heavy Music/Path of Freedom
1957 Brownsville Station - Rock & Roll Holiday/Jailhouse Rock (also issued on Polydor)
1080 Phantom - Calm Before the Storm/Black Magic, White Magic (also released on Capitol)
1236 Bottle Co. - Barkley Square/Lives for No One

LP 1001 - Fugitives - *At Dave's Hideout*
LP 1002 - *Best of the Hideouts* (Underdogs: Man in the Glass, Friday at the Hideout, Surprise Surprise; Four of Us: Feel a Whole Lot Better, I Can't Live Without Your Love, Baby Blue; Pleasure Seekers: Never Thought You'd Leave Me; Yorkshires: I Go Crazy, Hey, Hey, Henchmen: Please Tell Me; Doug Brown: First Girl)
LP 1003 Ron Coden - *At the Raven Gallery*
LP 1003 Pep Perrine - *Live and In Person*
 (Coden's was first assigned the number and was so obscure it was overlooked when Perrine's album came out years later.)

NOTE: After the first 14 releases, the numbering system went random, so it's hard to be certain what was released. Any additions will be welcomed.

BOB SEGER

One of the foremost talents to emerge out of Ann Arbor was Bob Seger. From the early '60s on there was always a Bob Seger & the "This" or "That." By '65 he had joined Doug Brown & the Omens as organist. The Omens were one of the few area groups not connected with A-Square, as they played Detroit a lot and fell in with the Hideout crowd.

Seger's first recording experience (after his Del Shannon demos) came doing backing vocals on "T.G.I.F."--a truly awful record. Then, as Dave Leone says, "Doug Brown had the respect to admit   Bob was also a writer and a singer." What resulted was one of the oddest records ever: "The Ballad of the Yellow Beret" by the Beach Bums, on Are You Kidding Me? Records (actually Hideout, though they didn't quite want to admit it). An obvious take-off on the Barry Sadler hit, it was the first of many socially relevant songs by Bob, but also one of the first anti-protest records (Seger & Co. were apparently quite serious in this vicious attack on draft evaders) and rather odd for one who was soon after making radical statements.

"Yellow Beret" caught on in some smaller outstate markets, and college students loved it on a camp level. Then came a telegram from Barry Sadler threatening a lawsuit. Dave Leone had to let another record die.

"East Side Story" was Seger's first record under his own name, despite the fact it was Doug Brown, Seger, and leftover Omens performing. After the session they came up with the name Bob Seger & the Last Heard (Leone never liked the name as it inevitably came out sounding like Last Turd!).

"East Side Story" shot up the local charts. Neil Bogart of Cameo Records picked up the song in his sweep of Michigan music, as well as the follow-up "Persecution Smith." "Vagrant Winter" and "Sock it to Me Santa" followed as Cameo-only releases, and had little success, although "Santa" is a classic (including the great lyric: "Santa's got a brand new bag!") as is the flip, "Florida Time", the only known song to glorify Florida's surfing scene.

Then came the big one--"Heavy Music", a Seger/Brown masterpiece that would be right at home on today's charts. For those not fortunate enough to have the single, get hold of *Smokin' O.P.'s* (Reprise 2901) where it's reproduced. The 45 is worth finding, tho, for the alternate take on side 2, where Seger proclaims "N.S.U., SRC, Stevie Winwood got nothin' on me!".

With "Heavy Music", Bob Seger firmly established himself as a singer-songwriter-performer. Doug Brown went his own way (becoming Fontaine Brown in Southwind) and Seger accepted Punch Andrews as his manager (a factor contributing to the split of Punch and Dave Leone).

"Heavy Music" was a Midwest monster and if it hadn't been for Allen Klein's shady business practices, the song might've gotten the national recognition it deserved. Klein was suspected of illegally manipulating Cameo's stock and the government stepped in, freezing the company, and virtually causing the label to disappear.

Seger then moved to a "legitimate" company, Capitol (as did many ex-Cameo acts) and had his biggest hit with "Ramblin' Gamblin' Man" (#17 in '*Billboard*'). It was followed by "2+2=?", another war statement. After numerous singles ("Lookin' Back" probably the best) and five albums for Capitol, and countless personnel changes, Seger and Punch turned independent, forming Palladium Records (as an extension of Hideout Records, which still exists on paper), with distribution through Reprise. Palladium has produced a number of successful artists, including Brownsville Station, but Bob Seger is still looking for that gigantic nationwide hit that's always eluded him.

BOB SEGER DISCOGRAPHY

(As the Beach Bums)
Are You Kidding Me? (Hideout) 1010 Ballad of the Yellow Beret/Florida Time
Hideout 1013 (also Cameo 438) East Side Story/East Side Sound
Hideout 1014 (also Cameo 465) Persecution Smith/Chain Smokin'
Cameo 444 Sock it to Me Santa/Florida Time (same)
Cameo 473 Vagrant Winter/Very Few
Cameo 494 Heavy Music, 1&2
Capitol 2143 2+2=?/Death Row
Capitol 2297 Ramblin' Gamblin' Man/Tale of Lucy Blue
Capitol 2480 Ivory/The Last Song
Capitol 2576 Noah/Lennie Johnson
Capitol 2640 Innervenus Eyes/Lonely Man
Capitol 2748 Lucifer/Big River
Capitol 3187 Lookin' Back/Highway Child
Capitol LP 172 - *Ramblin' Gamblin' Man*
Capitol LP 236 - *Noah*
Capitol LP 499 - *Mongrel*
Capitol LP 731 - *Brand New Morning*
(additional material on Palladium/Reprise, all from LPs)

WESTCHESTER RECORDS

1000 Yorkshires - And You're Mine/Tossed Aside
1001
1002 Fugitives - You Can't Make Me Lonely/I Don't Wanna Talk
1003
1004
1005 (LP) *Friday at the Cage a Go Go* (retitled *Long Hot Summer*) Oxford 5: Gloria, All I Really Want to Do, The World I've Planned; Lourds: Shake a Tail Feather, Out of Sight, Good Lovin'; Individuals: That's How Strong My Love Is; Fugitives: Said Goodbye, You Can't Make Me Lonely, I Don't Wanna Talk
(Note: The Lourds included first Amboy Dukes singer John Drake, and possibly Ted Nugent.)

THE FUGITIVES/SRC

FUGITIVES
D-Town 1034 A Fugitive (vocal)/A Fugitive (instr)
D-Town 1044 On Trial/Let's Get On With It
Hideout LP 1001 *Fugitives at Dave's Hideout*
Westchester 1002 You Can't Make Me Lonely/I Don't Wanna Talk
Westchester LP 1005: Said Goodbye

SCOT RICHARD CASE (SRC)
A-Square 301 I'm So Glad/Who is that Girl?
A-Square 402 Get the Picture/The Rationals-I Need You
Capitol 2327 Black Sheep/Morning Mood
Capitol 2726 My Fortune's Coming True/Never Before Now
Capitol 2457 Up All Night/Turn into Love
Big Casino 1001 Born to Love/Badaz Shuffle
Capitol LP 2991
Capitol LP 123 - *Milestone*
Capitol LP 273 - *Traveller's Tale*

(as Blue Scepter)
Rare Earth 5040 Out in the Night/Gypsy Eyes

THE SHY GUYS

Panik 511 We Gotta Go/Lay it on the Line (also on Palmer 5005)
Burger 5004 The Burger Song/
Palmer 5008 Where You Belong/A Love So True
Canusa 503 Feel a Whole Lot Better/Without You
UNI 55033 Rockin' Pneumonia & the Booga Loo Flu/Are You My Sunshine (same group?)

Hideout 1004 Little Girl/Don't Pretend (also Reprise 446)

THE RATIONALS

Danby's Men's Shops (no #) - Turn On/Irrational
A-Square 101 Look What You're Doin'/Gave My Love
A-Square 103 Feelin' Lost/Little Girls Cry
A-Square 104 Leavin' Here/Respect
A-Square 104/103 (also Cameo 437) Respect/Feelin Lost
Cameo 455 Hold On Baby/Sing
Cameo 481 Leavin' Here/Not Like it Is
A-Square 107 (also Capitol 2124) I Need You/Out in the Streets (Sing!)
A-Square 402 I Need You/Scot Richard Case - Get the Picture
Genesis 1 Guitar Army/Sunset
Crewe 340 Handbags & Gladrags/?
Crewe LP 1334 - *The Rationals*
(Related Material)
Rainbow 2 Lightnin' - Hijackin' Love/First Time I Saw You Baby
Detroit 1000 Scott Morgan - Take a Look/Soul Mover

THE UNDERDOGS

Hideout 1001 (Also Reprise 0422) The Man in the Glass/Judy Be Mine (Friday at the Hideout)
Hideout 1004 Little Girl/Don't Pretend
Hideout 1011 Surprise, Surprise/Get Down on Your Knees
VIP 25040 Love's Gone Bad/Mo Jo Hanna
Hideout LP 1002: Man in the Glass; Friday at the Hideout, Get Down on Your Knees, Surprise, Surprise

SVR RECORDS

1001 Boys - I Wanna Know/Angel of Mine
1002 Boys - It's Hopeless/How do you do with Me
1005 Perfections - Am I Gonna Lose You/I Love You, My Love
1007 Tidal Waves - Farmer John/She Left Me All Alone (also released on HBR 482)
1008 (unknown) - Shake a Tail Feather/Night Walkin' (SVR Productions)
HBR 501 Tidal Waves - I Don't Need Love/Big Boy Pete
HBR 509 Four Gents - Soul Sister/I've Been Trying
HBR 514 Unrelated Segments -Story of my LIFE/It's Unfair
HBR 515 Tidal Waves - Action!/Hot Stuff!
Liberty 55992 Unrelated Segments - Where You Gonna Go/It's Gonna Rain
Liberty 56062 Unrelated Segments - Cry Cry Cry/It's Not Fair

(SVR was run by John Chekaway and Dick Cioffari. It was originally intended to be a classical label (their first and only LP was) as the initials SVR stood for Sergei Vassilievitch Rachmaninoff. The company was based in Lathrup Village.)

PALMER RECORDS

5001 Girls From Syracuse - Love is Happening to Me Now/We Could Have Danced
5002 Tim Tam & Turn-Ons - Wait a Minute/Openia
5003 Shy Guys - We Gotta Go/Lay it On the Line (orig. released on Panik)
5006 Tim Tam & Turn-Ons - Kimberly/I Leave You in Tears
5008 Shy Guys -Where You Belong/A Love so True
5009 People's Choice - Hot Wire/Ease the Pain
5014 Tim Tam & Turn-Ons - Don't Say Hi/
5015 Tommy Frontera - Street of Shame/Merry-Go-Round
5018 Trademarks - I Need You/If I Was Gone

WHEELSVILLE RECORDS

101 Jimmy Gilford - I Wanna Be Your Baby/Misery St.
109 Fabulous Peps - With These Eyes/Love of My Life

IMPACT RECORDS

1003 Boss Five - Please Mr. President/You Cheat too
1004 Jock Mitchell - Work With Me Annie/Much You May Lose the One You Love
1007 Shades of Blue - Oh How Happy/Little Orphan Boy
1014 Shades of Blue - Lonely Summer/With This Ring
1015 Shades of Blue - Happiness/The Night
1017 Volumes - The Trouble I've Seen/
1019 Inner Circle - Sally Go Round the Roses/
1022 Human Beings - I Can't Tell/Yessir, That's my Baby
1024 John Rhys - Boy Watchers Theme/Nothing but Love
1025 Sixpence - You're the Love/What to Do
1026 Shades of Blue - How Do You Save a Dying Love/?
1028 Shades of Blue - Penny Arcade/?
1029 Wheels - Dancing in the Street/A Taste of Money
LP 101 - Happiness is the Shades of Blue

JAMIE COE & GIGOLOS

Addison 15003 School Day Blues/I'll Go On Loving You
Big Top 3107 But Yesterday/Cleopatra
Big Top 3139 The Fool/Got that Feeling
ABC-Paramount 10203 I'm Getting Married/2 Dozen & a Half
ABC-Paramount 10267 How Low is Low/Little Dear, Little Darling
Enterprise 5005 The Dealer/Close Your Eyes (also released on Reprise 295)
Enterprise 5055 I Was the One/Good Enough for You
Enterprise 5080 Green Back Dollar/But Yesterday (also released on Cameo 424)

• The original MC5 in action; their best song, "Black to Comm". was never recorded.

SEASON OF THE THYME

Ann Arbor bands should be remembered for their vocal power--save for Scott Richardson. The Thyme relied on harmonies more than a single voice, and were exceptionally good at Byrds numbers. An early recording of theirs came out on Bang, called "Love to Love." Written by Bang star Neil Diamond, the song had potential but lacked production. After minor personnel changes, the Thyme recorded on A-Square--a haunting psychedelic ballad "Somehow" complete with fuzz guitar, and an exceptional cover of the Zombies' "Time of the Season". Their version got initial airplay but was left behind as the original took off. Surprisingly, the Thyme's was an extremely full-sounding record despite the lack of keyboards. Ralph Cole's 12-string work was perfect. Cole (who later started Lighthouse with Skip Prokop) always performed with his trusty double-neck Gibson. After Thyme's breakup, bass player Al Wilmot joined SRC.

THYME DISCOGRAPHY

Bang 546 Love to Love/Very Last Day
A-Square 201 Somehow/Shame, Shame
A-Square 202 Time of the Season/I Found a Love

LANSING/E. LANSING

East Lansing is only 70 miles from Detroit, yet its music scene was completely detached. Most groups were Michigan State students who had graduated from the Motor City. Francis X & the Bushmen, longtime favorites at frat parties and dorm mixers, were transplanted Detroiters. Of course there were high school groups--Paris Bakery, Chancellors, Mission Frost--but nothing you wouldn't expect from any mid-size US city.

One of the exceptions was the Plain Brown Wrapper, composed of serious professional musicians. As a versatile 5-man group, they could reproduce side 2 of Sgt. Pepper perfectly. Unfortunately their recording career never matched their talent. Their only record worth anything was a cover of Steve Miller's "Junior Saw it Happen."

Another in the wave of futuristic songs (ala "2525") was "200 Years" by a group called Maxx. They were a popular "heavy" band, noted for their over-extended performance of "Inna-Gadda-Da-Vida."

THE WOOLIES

The Woolies are undoubtedly the best-known group out of Lansing, through their version of "Who Do You Love". The band (still active) was organized in East Lansing, although its members came from Dearborn. Led by Bob Baldori, the Woolies headed to Chicago in '65, where they cut "Black Crow Blues" for an outfit called Triangle Productions. The record went nowhere but the group gained a following at MSU.

In the summer of '66, the Woolies entered the Vox Band-of-the-Land competition at the Michigan State Fair. They won, but failed to see any of the promised trip to Hollywood, recording contract, or Vox equipment. After threatening lawsuits, the Woolies squeezed a flight to LA out of the contest agency. Carrying demo tapes, Baldori made the proverbial rounds of record companies and hit it off with Lou Adler, at that time with ABC/Dunhill. The band landed a contract and cut some tracks, including "Who Do You Love."

The record started to take off, but Dunhill it turned out was promoting the B-side, and in the confusion the record died, having reached #95 nationally. Meanwhile Adler had left Dunhill and the Woolies were stuck with a contract they no longer wanted.

• The Woolies, still playing bars after 8 years...

Back in East Lansing, Baldori realized the Woolies would be better off with their own label, "to do it right." Spirit Records was formed, but its early releases were non-Woolies, as the band was still tied to Dunhill. Spirit 1001, "You Haven't Seen My Love" by the Ones, remains one of the best songs on the label. (The Ones went on to sign with Motown).

Stormy Rice, who sang the lead on "Who Do You Love", felt East Lansing wasn't the place to make it. He packed up again for LA and subsequently recorded for Lou Adler's newly-formed Ode Records. Among the releases was the Moody Blues' "Go Now" as Stormy & Gabriel.

In the time since "Who Do You Love" the Woolies have been hanging out in East Lansing, playing bars, backing up Chuck Berry whenever he comes to Michigan, and releasing records...still waiting for that Big One to happen. Most have been weak blues recordings receiving sporadic local airplay.

SPIRIT/MONSTER RECORDS

SPIRIT
- 0001 Ones - You Haven't Seen My Love/Happy Day (originally released on Fenton 2514)
- 0002 Moppets - Cry Just a Little/Come See About Me
- 0003 Woolies - Bring it With You When You Come/We Love You B.B. King
- 0004 Next Exit - Soulful Child/I Know
- 0005 Coffee House Blues - Getting Over You/Goodbye Baby
- 0006 Woolies - 2-Way Wishen/Chucks Chunk
- 0007 Woolies - Vandegraf's Blues/Vandegraf's Blahs
- 0008 Woolies - Super Ball/Back for More
- 0009 Woolies - Ride Ride Ride/We Love You JB Lenoir
- 0010 Plain Brown Wrapper - Stretch out yourHand, 1 & 2
- 0011 (Ozone Records) Due East--Greek House/Knoxville High
- 0012 (Bomb Records) Otis - Everyday Grind/Livin' With My Cousin
- 0013 Woolies - Who do you Love/Feelin' Good
- 0014 Woolies - The Hootchie Cootchie Man is Back/Can't Get that Stuff

(LPs)
- 2001 Woolies - *Basic Rock*
- 2002 Bob McAllen - *McAllen*
- 2003 Ones - *Back Home at the Brewery*
- 2004 Earl Nelson Singers - *Lift Every Voice*
- 2005 Woolies - *Live at Lizard's*

MONSTER
- 0001 Magic - I Think I Love You/That's How Strong my Love Is
- 0002 Plain Brown Wrapper - Junior Saw it Happen/Real Person
- 0003 Bhang - Black Eyed Peas/Mellow Day

(Both labels were run by Bob Baldori. Spirit is still active.)

FLINT/SAGINAW

Flint-Saginaw, the upper wastes of Northern Michigan, may seem an unlikely hotbed for musical activity, but 3 important acts came out of the area--Terry Knight & the Pack, Dick Wagner's Frost, and Question Mark & the Mysterians.

Terry Knapp *cum* Terry Knight had been a disc jockey at CKLW (Windsor/Detroit) in the early '60s. By '65 he was ready for a taste from the other side, and assembling the Pack, scored locally with a decent "Better Man Than I." The record was on a Flint label, Lucky-11, and when the omni-present Cameo stepped in this time, they picked up the whole company. Thus it became Lucky Eleven Records, distributed by Cameo-Parkway.

After a couple of weak follow-ups, Knight & Co. hit again with "A Change is on the Way", an original in the "Shape of Things to Come" vein. Then came the dramatic "I Who Have Nothing" which hit the Top 50 nationally.

Eventually Knight split to make solo records, with the group continuing as the Fabulous Pack. A "Harlem Shuffle" remake from the Pack stirred interest locally while Terry's efforts were dismal ("Lizbeth Peach" with its pseudo-sophistication). Their "Widetrackin' " (referring to Widetrack Drive in Pontiac) was a reasonable rocker, with harmonies foreshadowing Grand Funk. Following Cameo's legal collapse, Lucky-Eleven went independent again at this time.

When Capitol Records picked up the pieces after Cameo--signing the Rationals, Bob Seger, Question Mark & the Mysterians and Terry Knight--the Pack weren't far behind. After a fair recording of "Next to Your Fire", Pack members Mark Farner (formerly of the Bossmen) and Don Brewer came together with ex-Mysterian Mel Schacher as Grand Funk Railroad.

Dick Wagner was one of the most musically active people in the state--at various times being a writer, producer, singer, guitarist and performer. Wagner's group, the Bossmen, was quite popular at all the area high school hops and Saginaw's weekend hotspot, Daniel's Den. The Bossmen did have some interesting records, like "Here's Congratulations" with its Searchers flavor and strange 12-string/piano break, and "Help Me Baby" sounding like the Beatles' "Bad Boy." ("Help Me Baby" showed up later on the second Frost album).

LA CAVE
Cleveland's House of Folk Music
10615 Euclid Avenue
presents
TERRY KNIGHT AND THE PACK
"I WHO HAVE NOTHING"
"BETTER MAN THAN I"
"A CHANGE ON THE WAY"

Three Days Only
Thurs., Fri. & Sat. Nov. 24-25-26
Reservations 231-9405 OR 432-2990

When the Bossmen became the Frost (the first records billed them as Dick Wagner & the Frosts) their popularity spread to Detroit. The Frost then became part of the second wave of Michigan bands in the late '60s/early '70s. Of the group's three Vanguard albums, the first (*Frost Music*) was excellent. Dick Wagner has continued in music, mostly as a guitarist, and among other things was part of Lou Reed's band on his live album.

QUESTION MARK

Question Mark & the Mysterians fulfilled the dream of every punk band--a national #1 hit (#2 in total sales for the year)--and with a home recording at that! On paper, "96 Tears" is nothing; songs don't come any simpler. But the performance was perfect, and the record became an instant classic.

Question Mark (Rudy Martinez) and his Mysterians were Texas Mexicans relocated in Michigan. They were just like 1000 other bands in the land, their gimmick being an "anonymous", mysterious singer. But Martinez wasn't afraid to write and sing. Even if the songs were simple, they were usually catchy. "96 Tears" was totally infectious. Taken (according to legend) from a record called "Tears" by an Ohio group known as Patti & the Playboys, "96 Tears" was originally released on Pa-Go-Go Records out of McAllen, Texas. Interestingly, a Flint group called Count & the Colony also recorded on Pa-Go-Go, a Dick Wagner song published by Mysterians Music! Cameo picked up "96 Tears" almost immediately--Bogart's ear for bubblegum was never more sure. was never more sure.

Of course it was all downhill after that. "I Need Somebody" was okay, but nobody would've paid it any attention if Question Mark hadn't made his name. After two other quick chart records, the Mysterians were back where they started--nowhere. Their two Cameo LPs had all the qualities of supermarket records. But the group stayed alive, label hopping and releasing songs that made them appear stuck in a 1966 time warp. Last word was that Rudy is still gonna "make it" again.

OUR MEN IN FLINT

Another label out of Flint (actually Mt. Morris) was Coconut Groove. Run by local booking agent Paul Potts, I know of only 2 releases on the label (though I'm sure there were many). The Lime Frost's "Post Bellum Blues" (2036) and "So Many Times Ago" by the Dynasty (2038) were both psychedelic numbers. "Post Bellum Blues", a drug oriented drone, was probably inspired by the Velvet Underground's "Heroin."

Credit for a number of popular Michigan records should go to WTAC radio in Flint. Being in a sub-secondary market, they were free to play local and unproven records. In addition to "96 Tears", WTAC is generally acknowledged to have broken the Who in this country.

OUTSTATE BANDS

From the number of Michigan records I've seen that can't be tied to any of the areas covered, it seems an awful lot of outstate bands recorded in Michigan. With all the small offbeat labels, it must have been easier for

LUCKY ELEVEN RECORDS

- 225 Terry Knight & Pack - I've Been Told/How Much More
- 226 Terry Knight & Pack - Better Man than I/Got Love
- 227
- 228 Terry Knight & Pack - Lady Jane/Lovin' Kind
- 229 Terry Knight & Pack - A Change on the Way/What's On Your Mind
- 230 Terry Knight & Pack - I (Who Have Nothing)/Numbers
- 231 Bossmen - Baby Boy/You and I
- 232 Jayhawkers - A Certain Girl/Come On
- 233 Kay Tolliver - Heartache is my Middle Name/My Heart's Not Expected to Live
- 234
- 235 Terry Knight & Pack - Love Love Love Love Love/This Precious Time
- 236 Terry Knight & Pack - The Train/One Monkey Don't Stop No Show
- 237 Debutantes - Love is Strange/A New Love Today

- 001 Bossmen - Tina Maria/On the Road
- 002 Chuck Slaughter - Get the Best of Livin'/Woman, a Pretty Woman
- 003 Fabulous Pack - Harlem SHUFFLE/I've Got News For You
- 005 Roxy Williams - Let the Horses Run/You're the One
- 007 Fabulous Pack - Widetrackin'/Does it Matter to you Girl
- 009 Anglo Saxton - Ruby/You Better Leave Me Aloe (also released on Tower 401)

- 351 Sylvia Jo - Come Hell or High Water/I'm Living
- 352 Mark Farner - I Got News for You/Down in the Valley
- 360 Janett Howell - A Man Like You/I Live for You
- 366 Mark Farner & Don Brewer - Does it Matter to you Girl/We Gotta Have Love
- 367 Sherri Jerrico - A Smile Never Hurt Anybody/If You Are There ('75 release; label relocated in Nashville)

TERRY KNIGHT

- Cameo 482 Lizbeth Peach/Forever and a Day
- Cameo 495 Come Home Baby/Dirty Lady '67
- Capitol 2409 Lullaby/Such a Lonely Life '68
- Capitol 2506 Saint Paul/William and Mary '69
- Capitol 2737 Lullaby/I'll Keep Waiting Patiently '70

QUESTION MARK

- Pa-Go-Go 102 96 Tears/Midnight Hour (a shortened version appeared on Cameo 428)
- Cameo 441 I Need Someboey/"8" Teen
- Cameo 467 - Can't Get Enough of You Baby/Smokes
- Cameo 479 Girl (You Captivate Me)/Got To
- Cameo 496 Do Something to Me/Love Me Baby
- Super-K 102 Hang In/Sha La La
- Tangering 989 Ain't it a Shame/Turn Around Baby
- Cameo LP 2004 - *96 Tears*
- Cameo LP 2006 - *Action*

THE BOSSMEN

- Dicto 1001 Here's Congratulations/Bad Girl
- M&L 1809 Help Me Baby/Thanks to You
- Soft 121 Take a Look/It's a Shame
- Lucky Eleven 001 Tina Maria/On the Road
- Lucky Eleven 231 Baby Boy/You and I
- Dicto 1002 Wait & See/You're the Girl For Me

(as Dick Wagner & the Frosts)
- Date 1577 Bad Girl/A Rainy Day
- Date 1596 Little Girl/Sunshine
- (3 LPs and various 45s by Frost on Vanguard)

THE WANTED

- Detroit Sound 222 (also A&M 844) In the Midnight Hour/Heia to Stay
- Detroit Sound 230 Knock on Wood/Lots More Where They Came From
- A&M 856 Don't Worry Baby/Big Town Girl

these groups to get on vinyl than some of the big city bands. Since there was more chance for airplay, outstate bands quite likely were more inclined to invest in recording.

Fenton Records (from Fenton, Mich.) is the one label that pops up everywhere. The ones I've come across differ so in numbering, it's hard to determine how many were released. Some of the odder ones are the Quests' "Scream Loud" with its falsetto harmonies, backed with an eerie reverberated instrumental called "Psychic", and "Faith 7" from Dave & the Shadows--a sort of "Telstar" from the backlands.

One characteristic that typified a lot of the outstate records was a strong English influence. The Rainmakers, out of Traverse City (home of the infamous Tanx Haus) did an original "Tell Her No" (Phalanx) that could easily be mistaken for Billy J. Kramer. Another Phalanx release, "She's Gone" by the Tornados, was interesting for its echo mix on the vocals. A fine record on Enterprise (possibly a Detroit label) was "I'm a Clown" by the Lazy Eggs, combining the sound of the Searchers and the Kinks. "Nightlife" by the Del-Tinos (Sonic 1451) was a direct take-off on the Stones' "Time is On My Side."

DICTO RECORDS

1001 Bossmen - Here's Congratulations/Bad Girl
1002 Bossmen - Wait & See/You're the Girl For Me For Me
1003 Bells of Rhymney - The Wicked Old Witch/She'll Be Back
1004 Sand - Sleep/Desperately

Dicto Records was headed up by Dirk Wagner, who acted as producer on all the above releases.

PROPHONICS RECORDS

Prophonics Records and studios were run by promoter Paul Potts out of Mt. Morris (Flint). Most Prophonics releases were country, but he had other labels for groups who recorded at the studio including Coconut Groove and Washington Square.

NOTABLE PROPHONICS RELEASES
2026 James T. & the Workers - Let Me See You Crying/I Can't Stop
2027 7th Court - One Eyed Witch/Shake
2028 Incredible Invaders - This Time/Boy is Gone (different take from Fenton 2040)
2029 Cecil Washington - I Don't Like to Lose/The Light Of Day
Washington Square 2023 Warlocks - Girl/Hey Jo
Washington Square 2025 Dimensions - Treat Me Right/We're Doing Fine

COCONUT GROOVE
2031 Soul Incorporated - My Proposal/Message to Michael
2032 Cherry Slush - I Cannot Stop You (written by Dick Wagner)/Don't Walk Away (also on USA 895)
2033 Flower Company - Did you Love me from the Start/Hey Joe
2035 Elation Fields - Light Side Table/Heat Wave
2036 Lime Frost - Post Bellum Blues/Pi O Ti
2038 Dynasty - So Many Times Ago/I Need You
2039 Nocturnal Day Dream - Had a Dream Last Night/Dark Dreary Night
2040 (mislabeled 4020) - Corrupters - I'll Go Crazy/I Feel Good

USA 899 New Breed - I'm Comin' To Ya/?

FENTON RECORDS

942 Dave & Shadows - Faith 7/Playboy
2032 Quests - Scream Loud/Psychic
2040 Lyn & Invaders - Secretly/Boy is Gone
2066 Chancellors - Once in a Million/Journey
2070 Plagues - I've Been Through it Before/Tears From My Eyes
2072 Chancellors - Dear John/5 Minus 3
2088 Tribe - Fickle Little Girl/Try Try
2216 The Mussies - Louie Go Home/12 O'Clock July
2508 Black Watch - Left Behind/I Wish I Had the Nerve
2514 Ones - You Haven't Seen My Love/Happy Day
2518 Headhunters - Times We Share/Think What You've Done

THE REFLECTIONS

Golden World 9 (Just Like) Romeo & Juliet/Can't You Tell by the Look in My Eyes
Golden World 12 Like Columbus Did/?
Golden World 15 Oowee Now/Talkin bout my Girl
Golden World 16 A Henpecked Guy/Don't Do That to Me
Golden World 19 Shabby Little Hut/You're My Baby
Golden World 20 Poor Man's Son/Comin' at You
Golden World 22 Wheelin Dealin/?
Golden World 24 Out of the Picture/June Bride
Golden World 29 Girl in the Candy Store/?

LP 301 - Just Like Romeo & Juliet

ABC 10794 Just Like Adam & Eve/Vito's House
ABC 10822 Long Cigarette/?

LABELS NOT LISTED

Wingate, Drew, Sidra, Dearborn, Golden World, Enterprise (all had some teen-oriented releases, but were primarily soul labels--as were of course dozens of other Detroit labels whose output does not fall within the scope of this survey...)

MISCELLANEOUS MICHIGAN RECORDS

BED OF ROSES - I Don't Believe You/Hate - Deltron 813 (Saginaw) '66
BLUES COMPANY - You're Dead My Friend/I'm Comin' - Pear
BLUES COMPANY - Experiment in Color/She's Gone
DOUG BROWN - Susie Baby/? - Checker '64
CAMEL DRIVERS - The Grass Looks Greener/It's Gonna Rain - Top Dog 200
CAMEL DRIVERS - Sunday Morning 6 O'Clock/Give it a Try - Top Dog 103 (also Buddah 61)
CAMEL DRIVERS - Everybody's Got to Do His Own Thing/Don't Throw Stones at My Window - Buddah 85
CAPREEZ - Rosanna/Over You - Sound 126
CAPREEZ - It's Good to Be Home Again/How to Make a Sad Man Glad - Sound 149
CAPREEZ - Soulsation/Time - Sound 171
CARNIVAL OF SOUND - I Can't Remember/Don't Come Around - USA (prod. D. Wagner)
CHRIS CARPENTER - Waterfalls/This World - UA 50266 (orig. on Sidra)
COUNT. & COLONY - Can't You See/That's the Way - Pa-Go-Go 121   (Flint)
DEL-TINOS - Nightlife/Pa Pa Ooh Mau Mau - Conic 1451
JIMMY DENSON - Since I Lost You/Easy Steps - Chestnut 1
MICKEY DENTON - Dance With Me Mary/The Other Side of Betty - Bigtop 3142 (many other releases)
DETROIT WHEELS - Linda Sue Dixon/Tally Ho - Inferno 5002
DETROIT WHEELS - Think/? - Inferno
DETROIT WHEELS (as WHEELS) - Dancing in the Street/A Taste of Money - Impact 1029
FABULOUS PACK - Tears Come Rolling/The Color of Our Love - Wingate
FERIS WHEEL - Best Part of Breaking Up/Woman - Magenda 5653 (Saginaw)
FRUT OF THE LOOM - one Hand in Darkness/A Little Bit of Bach - Loom 101 (later FRUT)
JOHNNY GIBSON - After Midnight/Walking On Down - Bigtop 3118
JOHNNY GIBSON TRIO - Beachcomber/Swanky - Twirl 2012
GRIFS - Catch a Ride/In My Life - AMG 1002 (also on 5D)
H.P. & THE GRASS ROUTE MOVEMENT - You Don't Know Like I Know/On the Road - BBTC 3021 (written by Dick Wagner)
NICK HARRIS & SOUNDBARRIERS - Music, Music/Big Nick - Northwest Sound 10
HITCH-HIKERS - Someday Baby/Make Me Feel Good - Phalanx (pre-Thyme)
HITCH-HIKERS - You're the One/Whispering Waves
HUMAN BEINGS - An Outside Look/I Can't Tell - Impact 1022
HUMAN BEINGS - Because I Love Her/Ain't That Lovin' You Baby - WB 5622
TOM LAZAROS - All Your Little Games/Just Walk Away - Sound Patterns 9010
LAZY EGGS - I'm Gonna Love You/As Long as I Have You - Enterprise 5060
LAZY EGGS - I'm a Clown/Poor Boys Always Weep - Enterprise 5085
LITTLE SISTERS - First You Break My Heart/Just a Boy - Detroit Sound
TED LUCAS - Head in California/My Dog - Zonk
MAXIMILIAN - The Wanderer/The Snake - Bigtop 3069 (Max Crook, Del Shannon's keyboard player)
MAXX - 200 Years/Castles - Mainstream 714 (orig. on Signal Records)
MC5 - I Can Only Give You Everything/I Just Don't Know Why - AMG 1000
MC5 - I Can Only Give You Everything (remix)/One of the Guys - AMG 1001
ME & DEM GUYS - Mercy/Wail It - Dearborn 511
ME & DEM GUYS - Love Me/Yep - Dearborn 513
ME & DEM GUYS - Smiling Phases/Mercy, Mercy - Pyrennes 2
ME & DEM GUYS - Black Cloud/Come On Little Sweetheart - Coral Gables 2082
MISTY WIZARDS - It's Love/Blue Law Sunday - Reprise 0616
MOTOR CITY BONNEVILLES - High School Sally/Wrong Side - Red Rooster 310
ONES - You Haven't Seen My Love/Hapy Day - Fenton 2514
ONES - Don't Let Me Lose This Dream/I've Been Good to You - Motown 1130
PACK - Next to Your Fire/Without a Woman - Capitol 2174 (others as FABULOUS PACK)
PLAGUES - That'll Never Do/Badlands - Quarantined 41369
PLAIN BROWN WRAPPER - And Now You Dream/You'll Pay - This is Music 2114
PLEASURE SEEKERS - Light of Love/Shme - Mercury 42542 (also see Hideout discog..)
POPCORN BLIZZARD - Once Upon a Time/Hello - Magenda (Saginaw)
PRECISIONS - Instant Heartbreak/Dream Girl - Drew 1004
PRECISIONS - If This is Love/You'll Soon be Gone - Drew 1003
PUPPETS - Love is a Beautiful Thing/I Ain't Gonna Eat Out My Heart - Red Rooster 311
LINDA RAE - Earthquake/Winter Time - Meadowbrook 1002
RAINMAKERS - Don't Be Afraid/I Won't Turn Away Now - Discotheque 875
RAINMAKERS - Tell Her No/You're Not the Only One - Phalanx 1029
RAINMAKERS - House of the Rising Sun/Do You Feel It - Lee 9178
SCARLET LETTER - Macaroni Mountain/Outside Woman Blues - Mainstream 691 (pre-Savage Grace)
SCARLET LETTER - Mary Maiden/? - Mainstream 696
SIXPENCE - You're the Love/What to Do - Impact 1025
SOUTHBOUND FREEWAY - Psychedelic Used Car Lot Blues/Southbound Freeway - Terra Shirma 67001 (also Roulette 4739)
SOUTHBOUND FREEWAY - Crazy Shadows/Revelations - Swan 4272
SPIKE DRIVERS - High Time/Often I Wonder - Om
SPIKE DRIVERS - High Time/Baby Won't You Let Me Tell You How I Lost My Mind - Reprise 0635
SPIKE DRIVERS - Strange Mysterious Sounds/Break Out the Wine - Reprise 0558
SUNLINERS - The Swingin' Kind/All Alone - Golden World (pre-Rare Earth)
THEO-COFF INVASION - Noctgurnal Flower/Lucky Day - Dearborn 525 (Dennis Coffee's first, '68)
THIRD POWER - We, You, I/Snow - Baron 626
THREE REASONS - Cruel Cruel Cruel/Beachtime - Wheel-City 0041 (D-Town sub.) 8-65
TINO & REVLONS - Little Girl, Little Girl/Rave On - Dearborn 525
TINO & RENIGADES - Lazy Mary Memphis/I'm Coming Home - Dearborn 530
TONTO & RENIGADES - I Knew This Thing Would Happen/Little Boy Blue - Sound of the Screem 2212
TORONADOS - She's Gone/Rainy Day Fairy Tales - Phalanx 1014
UNDECIDED? - Make Her Cry/I Never Forgot Her - Dearborn 542
ROBERT WALKER & NIGHT RIDERS - Keep on Runnin'/Everything's Alright - Detroit Sound 224
TIMMY WILLIS - Don't Let Temptation/Gotta Get Back to Georgia - Veep 1288, Sidra
WOOLIES - Black Crow Blues/Morning Dew - TTP 156 (first release)
WOOLIES - Who Do You Love/Hey Girl - Dunhill 4052
WOOLIES - Love Words/Duncan & Brady - Dunhill 4088
YOUNG MEN - A Young Man's Problem/Angel Baby - Maltese 105 (protest song)
YOUNG SISTERS - Casanova Brown/My Guy - Twirl 2001
YOUNG SISTERS - Jerry Boy/She Took His Love Away - Mala 467   '64

KIM FOWLEY: The Leaves at one time had an import copy of "Nowhere Man" before it came out here and were doing the song live. People were saying they'd finally gotten better, until the Beatles version came out and they realized it wasn't an original. They used to do "Hey Joe" live long before they recorded it. I was sitting at a table once with Jerry Dennon of Jerden Records, and when I heard them do "Hey Joe" I said to him, "that's the next 'Louie Louie'". Dennon said, "no way." I also had a record on Mira, "American Dream" /"The Statue". The B-side was produced by Danny Hutton and featured Sonny & Cher's band. It was covered by Tommy Sands on Liberty. Incidentally, the Randy Wood who owned Mira/Mirwood was a black guy, a different person from the Randy Wood of Dot/Ranwood fame.

Marcus Tybolt was Sky Saxon, don't think you mentioned that. Jerry Williams was Swedish, not German. He cut "Garden of Imagination" which I co-wrote with Jan & Bernie Zackery, who also wrote "River of Salt" which Bryan Ferry did on his first album. The only other thing they did was a song called "World's Champion" which I also co-wrote. We sent it to Shel Talmy and it was cut by Tony Lord as the second release on Planet.

I wrote "Sea of Faces" which Unit 4+2 recorded but never issued. Another English group called Ways & Means did it on Pye. When I was in England I lived with P.J. Proby and Viv Prince. Proby wrote "Ain't Gonna Kiss Ya" for the Ribbons, covered by the Searchers. I produced that Hellions record with Jim Capaldi, etc. Luther Grosvenor was not in the group at that time. I also had European rights to the Sonics material, but couldn't get anybody to put it out.

As for the Standells, "Try It" was #1 on KRLA, not a flop as you said. It was another record that Huggie Boy broke. Gary Leeds of the Walker Bros. was once a Standell, in their Vee Jay days. He now works in a take-out food place in Sun Valley.
Hollywood, CA.

RALPH BUONAGURA: Thank God for WPTB. The folks here in Brooklyn are definitely not as conscious of the importance of 60s music as they should be.

Enjoyed your piece on the Seeds, Since then there was a mention in Melody Maker that Sky Saxon had finished recording an album and was raving on about its excellence in his usual fashion.

The only local scene around here revolves around copy bands who do nothing but music by the heavies (Led Zep, TYA, Chicago, etc); but in 1967 there was one band that was worthy of exposure. They were called the Unplastic Revolution (really) and they combined elements of the Stooges and the Who. If they had got out of Brooklyn they might have been monsters.
Brooklyn, NY

(-Don't get yer hopes up, Seeds fans. There's a lot of 'new' Sky Saxon material recorded, but only garage demos, and none are likely to be sold in the near future. However, it is interesting to note that Sky, Sean Bonniwell and Lord Tim are all currently being managed by a guy who used to run Bido Lido's. The punk-rock revival does seem to be gathering steam... -GS -).

FRED MASOTTI: Enjoyed the latest issue. Great stories, and Ken Barnes' "Reverberations" column and the best fanzine review section yet. Also the "Sounds of the 60s" is another great idea. Publish the Pacific Northwest area next, okay? (- Coming soon -GS -).

About a record in Ken's column by the D-Men on Veep. I remember seeing them on Hullabaloo and they were an Eastern group whose first names all started with the letter D.
Hamilton, Ontario

(- Another mystery solved.... -)

PAUL LOVELL: I saw your mention of the Gauchos. They were indeed on Shindig as speculated, and also on an album entitled ABC-TV Shindig (Paramount 504). The album also has the Shindiggers (four numbers), Tommy Roe, the Tams, the Impressions, Steve Alaimo, Fats Domino, the Sapphires (great song called "Why Don't You Let Yourself Go") and the Spats.
West Roxbury, Mass.

(-Yeah the Sapphires were great. This was the same group that had a hit with "Who Do You Love" on Swan. Watch out for their "Slow Fizz" single on ABC.-GS)

BRIAN HOGG: Thanks for printing my letter in #12. A really fine issue it was too. A coupla points about Chris Sandford. We have a TV series called "Coronation Street". It's supposedly a typical north of England terraced street and is on twice a week. Well, Chris Sandford played a character in the series around the time of his first release. He'd been on the programme regularly for a short time before as the mate of the local spiv Jed Stone. Well Jed decided to groom the lad for stardom. I can't remember the name of the character Chris played, but his records were released on the programme under the name of Brett Falcon. When they were released for real, they came out under the name of Chris Sandford. At the time, "Coronation Street" had the highest viewing figures of any TV programme so it was some way to break a record.

I like the idea of listing the fanzines. Did you get a copy of ours (Hot Wacks)? I'm starting up my own sometime in the new year, hopefully. It's gonna be called Bam Balam and will be solely on sixties U.S. groups. Issue one should have Paul Revere, the Flamin' Groovies, and the Cryan Shames...
Flat 1, Castellau House
Dunbar, E. Lothian
Scotland

I. KRUMINS: The State of Mickey & Tommy were French and very popular in France in the mid-late sixties. They had lots of good rock stuff over there. Ray Phillips is the only member of the original Nashville Teens left, but recently I heard someone called Ray Phillips (dunno if it's the same one) was forming a band called Woman.
Hamilton, Ontario

BILL JENTZ: Peter & Gordon may have broken up in '68, but in the summer of '69 they had a minor hit in Washington, DC called "I Can Remember (Not So Long Ago)". I've been trying to get it for 5 years--can anyone help?
23 Navajo Ave.
Lk. Hiawatha, N.J.
07034

more FEEDBACK

JOHN JOHNSON: "Baby Let Me Take You Home" was first done by Hoagy Lands (Atlantic 2217), released 3-64. Produced by Bert Berns.
Pullman, Wash.

(-Can anyone verify whether this pre-dates the Mustangs version on Keetch 6002, an Atlantic-distributed label owned, I believe, by Bert Berns? -GS -)

DANNY BENAIR: A couple of notes on your letter column. The harpsichord on "For Your Love" is played by Brian Auger, not Jeff Beck. Brian Auger told me this himself. David Bowie never recorded with the Riot Squad. A friend of mine asked him. And Mick Ronson is not on "Sack O' Woe" by the Rats. It came out before he joined. He is on "Spoonful" tho, and "New Orleans" I believe.
Panorama City, CA

(- While musicians are notoriously unreliable sources of information, we tend to agree that Bowie never recorded with the Riot Squad. The bit about Auger is a new one on us, tho. Anyone got further evidence? - GS -).

FRED PATTERSON: Why didn't you guys give the Chocolate Watchband a bigger write-up? Your brief article left some questions unanswered. For example: Who was in the band? None of their albums give any names. Also, I have a single by a group called the Hogs (HBR 511). One side is "Blue's Theme", produced by Ed Cobb. The other is called "Loose Lip Sync Ship" and was written by Dave Aguilar and Mark Loomis (both of whom wrote songs for the Chocolate Watchband at one time or another) and produced by the Phantom. This tune is in 4 parts, the first of which is a note-for-note reproduction of "Gossamer Wings" from the No Way Out LP. The next part is a 50s-ish riff and talk sequence: "Oh baby, please come back to me, without you baby my whole complexion is a mess." The voice sounds exactly like Frank Zappa! Part 3 only adds to the mystery by being a Cecil Taylor type piano solo with mumblings in the background, sounding something like "Help I'm a Rock." This monstrosity climaxes with a church organ and a congregational singing of "Row Row Row Your Boat". And all in 3:02! What's the story?

(- I've wondered about that record for years. I'm convinced it was done by Zappa. The Watchband track could've come from Cobb or Aguilar, both of whom were active on the LA scene at the time. Can anyone clarify further? Kim? -GS-)

Also, regarding the album Have You Reached Yet by Clap. These guys grew up in my neighborhood and are THE band of the local scene, although there are others that are noteworthy--like R. Mutt (whose songs include "Pushin Too Hard", "You're Gonna Miss Me", "TV Eye" and "Horse Latitudes") and the Imperial Dogs (who look like Nazis in drag & use whips and flags with a picture of a dagger piercing a rose. They played at Rodney's recently, and freaked everybody out when the lead singer assaulted a guy in a wheelchair in the audience.

But the Clap is good. I saw them one time and they gave two guys a six-pack to take their clothes off on stage, which they did. Another time the lead singer wore a Nehru jacket and looked just like Sky Saxon. The album came out in '73, not '71.

In your Beau Brummels article you failed to mention the group called Pan that claims Ron Elliot and put out an album on Columbia (KC 32062). Elliot also played on the latest Randy Newman LP.
Torrance, Calif.

TIM DOHERTY: Fine job on #12. The Seeds & Standells articles brought back vivid memories. I remember a TV show hosted by Art Linkletter that had the Standells vs. some preacher in a 'debate' on censorship. The bone of contention was "Try It". The preacher said it was obscene. The Standells, looking like 5 Italian waiters in their suits and slicked hair, just kept cracking up. The preacher knew he was being grossed out, but went along with it. Valentino kept shouting "you got a dirty mind!" at him. The audience loved it.

And the Seeds... KHJ Appreciation Concert, all seats 93¢ at the Hollywood Bowl, April '67. Supremes, Johnny Rivers, Seeds, 5th Dimension, Brenda Holloway The Seeds stole the show. Saxon danced all over the grass. They and Love played Bido Lido's for years. I hope you do a whole issue on LA '65-66 sometime...
Pacific Palisades, CA.

(- We're planning a Protest Issue that just might fill the bill. There was too much music to definitively cover in one issue, but it would be fun to try and isolate the spirit of the old Sunset Strip era. -GS -).

S. MEYER: I like yer idea of doing regional rock scenes. The best recording groups here were the Wildweeds with Al Anderson (now of NRBQ), Shags & Bluebeats. If you can find info on last 2 groups, let me know. Bluebeats had a GREAT 45, "Extra Girl." Some other bands that may have recorded were Damn Yankees, Quiet Ones (who were the house band at Bushnell Pk.(Hartford) "free things" for 4 summers. They broke up into Ghost Dance and Poison Foot, and I think they recorded as Syncron on Poison Ring Records). Also on Poison Ring were a band I went to college with--Fancy, with an LP called Fancy Meeting You Here.
Brockport, Connecticut

(- Good to know the origin of that Fancy LP. That should settle those persistent rumors that the "Wild Thing" group had something to do with it. I have a record by the Shag--"You're a Loser"/Crying" on Jo-Jo 101. Is this your Shags? There's also "Mean Woman Blues" by a Shags on Capitol 2511. Probably same group, with an Orbison song on each record. Incidentally, I could use that Fancy LP and the Bluebeats 45. - GS -).

SUE FREDERICK: You requested info on certain labels. Concerning Prism, while it's feasible others may have used it, Buddy Holly was forming his own label to be called Prism, at the time of his death. He wanted to establish a regional recording center at Norman Petty's Nor Va Jak studios in Clovis, NM. Buddy wanted to aid and produce struggling young, unknown artists and also produce his own recordings to be issued on the Prism label (planned and unrealized projects included an album of spirituals and one of Ray Charles songs). Among the artists he was helping were Lou Gardino and Waylon Jennings. Gardino recorded Holly's composition "Stay Close to Me" and Buddy produced and played guitar on Jennings' first record (King Curtis played sax on this and at least two other Holly tracks) "Jole Blon"/ "When Sin Stops" (Brunswick). Some business cards and record labels were printed but no records were ever released, as far as I know. Executives were to be: Pres.- Buddy Holly; Promo - Ray Rush; Sales - Norman Petty. None of the plans for Prism were realized, of course, due to Buddy's tragic death.

You missed two fanzines. "Hit-Memories" started in Jan '74. Written in Dutch, it lists birthdays of stars for that month and hits for that month from 55-73 in US, UK and Holland. Editor is Gaatse Zoodsma, Eewal 29, Birdaard, Friesland, Holland. Also "Big Beat of the Fifties", organ of the Aussie Rock and Roll Appreciation Society. Editor, Paul Simons, 22 Girloch Dr, Frankston, Victoria, Australia 3199.

How about articles on Del-Fi, Doors, Bobby Fuller, Buddy Holly, and 13th Floor Elevators?
Richmond, CA.

(- Del-Fi/Donna/Mustang and Bobby Fuller will be coming up in time. We're trying currently to track down info on some of the dozens of recordings Bobby made back in Texas. As for Prism, the label we need info on was based in Dayton, Ohio, and issued many records by local groups ca. 64-67. Your info on Holly's label, however, is fascinating and much appreciated. -GS -).

KEVIN WALSH: Great issue, esp. your survey of Bay Area

more FEEDBACK

punk. But what of the North Bay sound? The Front Line, the Pullice, the Electric Train? I talked to Gary Philippet today (he was in all 3), he was in the Train at the time the ID Band Book came out, tho he wasn't in the picture.

As for the Front Line, and my letter in TRM, the story about them being the original Turtles is true. Gary was in the group, they signed with Frank Werber to cut some demos, altho nothing came of the sessions. A promo man for Werber went to LA, and met the Crossfires or their manager. He gave them the Turtles name, and changed that of the Turtles to the Front Line.
San Rafael, CA

(- Okay, Mark and Howard--whaddaya got to say about that? -).

TONY MARTIN: A few years back, while I was living in Manchester, I had the Paramounts staying at my place for a couple of nights whilst rehearsing for their appearance backing Sandie Shaw at a nightclub, Mr. Smith's. The gig was notable for Sandie splitting after the first night, claiming some fake illness. Much more entertaining were JimmyPowell and his Dimensions. They were a gas, more concerned with laughs than anything else. Mind you, Jimmy could sing! He was screwed outta thousands on "Sugar Baby Pts.1&2." I also spent some time with the St. Louis Union, another fine bunch of guys. They were highly placed in a Melody Maker competition, made a few records--"Girl" etc--then faded. Like most groups of the time, the great appeal was American r&b/soul. I remember Union going to lengths to acquire a copy of "Ain't Love Good Ain't Love Proud" by Tony Clarke, then rehearsing it intently to wow the fans at the Twisted Wheel.
Croydon, Surrey, UK

NOEL De COURCY: Johnny Chester & the Chessmen and April Byron (Interphon discography, WPTB #12) were part of the Melbourne rock/pop scene during the early '60s. April Byron was on the scene during '65 and early '66, she made about three records for the Astor label. "He's My Bobby" struggled into the lower half of the Melbourne charts in late '65. Johnny Chester & the Chessmen were a very popular Melbourne band, formed in 1959. They were often in the Top 40 charts with records like "Hokey Pokey", "California Sun", "Teeny", "Shakin' All Over", "Bye Bye Johnny" and "Summertime Blues." They were also a supporting act to quite a few US rock acts that toured Australia, like the Beach Boys, Roy Orbison, Del Shannon, Chubby Checker, Bobby Rydell. They disbanded in mid '65.
Melbourne, Australia

BERNARD KUGEL: Bomp #12 was a really great American followup to the British issue. First off, your Standells piece was fine. But I think you should have mentioned in more detail their very memorable appearance on "The Munsters" when they played an outasight version of "I Want to Hold Your Hand" and a fantabulous original, "Do the Ringo", with some really neat organ work.

We now come to my favorite page of the whole magazine: page 17. Why is it my favorite page? Well, partly cause of those four lovely ladies on the opposite page, but mostly cause of those dynamite records mentioned under the Hard Up Heroes album cover. Lately I've been listening to lots of early '60s British stuff, especially the great Searchers, DC5, and the terrific Cliff Bennett and the Rebel Rousers. Cliff and his gang are on an out of sight German album called Liverpool '65 which also features the Naturals, the Swingin Blue Jeans, and the Zephyrs, among others.
Brooklyn, NY

(- I'd like to get hold of that album, if anyone happens to spot one somewhere...
...GS-)

DON HUGHES: Your editorial was fantastic. It's everything that I've been thinking but couldn't put into words. I really wish you & your readers lived here, there's no one here into '60s rock. It's terrible, all this bloody imitation '50s R&R.

I recently got my stepfather's friend chattering about the old days, when he was none other than the proprietor of the Attic Club in Hounslow, where Steve Marriott & the Moments were a regular attraction. He claimed he had a tape of the group doing well known Beatles and Stones songs--how about that! Time slipped by and Marriott hit the big time, and when Bill Channel (his name) went to look for that tape and hopefully cash in, he found that some bastard had slipped in and pinched it!

On to another subject--The Others. I told you they were a local group to me. Well they did only make one record, then they had to cut their hair to go back to school! But they didn't sink without leaving a trace, because some smart-ass publicity boy from Phillips must have rung up the People (a Sunday newspaper) and told them the story. Naturally the People ran anear full page article on the group--which I'm trying to locate. If I do, I'll send you a copy.
Middlesex, U.K.

HEY KIDS!!

Dean Torrence (of Jan & Dean) has put together a special Summer Fun Kit—just for BOMP readers!

YOU GET:

- *Save For a Rainy Day* LP (worth over $15!)

- Jan & Dean program book -- 14 pages of photos, ads, fan club stuff, and a photo album of Dunhill artists! Designed by Dean in 1965.

- Chad & Jeremy pictorial book -- designed by Dean, lavish 11x11 book, packed with pictures, drawings, & other goodies

- 1968 concert flyer featuring BLUE CHEER, ERIC BURDON & ANIMALS, and the COLLECTORS. Designed by Dean.

ALL MINT, ALL ORIGINAL
LIMITED QUANTITY!

Send $10 to WHO PUT THE BOMP
Dept. J&D, Box 7112, Burbank, CA 91510

YOUR AD IN THIS SPACE

REACHES MORE THAN 15,000

(more like 30-40,000, with minimum established pass-around ratio)

confirmed, hard-core record collectors and rock fanatics. It's the most select readership of any rock magazine today.

Whatever you have to sell—old records, new records, imports, magazines, books, stereo accessories & equipment, 45 spindle adaptors, T-shirts—whatever it is, you won't get a better response anywhere else.

SHOULDN'T YOUR AD BE HERE??

Send for rate card today.

And so another issue comes to a close. As you can see, we've made a few improvements, and as always we welcome your suggestions. Our most popular request has been for larger type (although Crescenzo Capece says he likes the microtype) and we've fulfilled that one at last. Next issue we hope to add more pages, more features, and maybe a little color.

Still need listings on certain labels. Can anyone help with Fontana (18-1900 series), Boom (003,4,8,10,11,18,19,20), Claridge (302,5,7,10,11,13-16) Southern Sound (103,5,7,8,9,11,12,13,16,17,19,21,22) Lawn (204,7,8,9,11,12,14,15,16,17,21,22,23,26,28,31,33,37-43,47) Valiant (704-10,13,17,22,38,40,46,49,52,53,57,59,62--) Amcan (403,405) Super-K (1,2,3,5,6,13,16--) Corby (any but 202,3,4,6,8,11,16,17) American Arts (1,3,5,7,9,11-13,15-19,21) and International Artists (101,3,5,10,14-15,18,32,34-5,37,40,43--)

Latest report on the Encyclopedia of British Rock: not finished yet. Also, since the volume of material has grown so vast, we're looking for an outside publisher. (Any leads would be appreciated). Meanwhile, anybody who sent in $1 to reserve a copy can have it back if he likes....

A couple of publications I want to give a last-minute mention to. Michael Lydon (one of Rolling Stone's founding editors and a fine writer) has written a book with Ellen Mandel called Boogie Lightning. It's published by Dial Press, and is worth seeking out. Also worthwhile is a fanzine called Reviewsit (Tom Luba, 614 1/2 N. Oneida, Appleton, Wis. 54911) dedicated to overlooked new albums. New issue is 8 pages and quite nice.

Finally, I'd like to urge everyone to call your local radio stations and demand that the new Flamin' Groovies record be played. If they don't have it, send me the name of the program director and I'll make sure they get one. I'm also looking for people to distribute the record & Bomp in various cities. Please write if you're interested................Greg Shaw

LABEL LISTING ADDITIONS

Mike 4006 - Tock N. Tock - Daydream/Mike's Nickelodeon

Diplomacy 3 - Jim Doval - Donna/Scrub

Tollie 9006 - Big Three - Winken, Blinken & Nod/The Banjo Song (4-64)

Interphon 7709 - Takers - Think/If You Don't Come Back

Takers formerly the Undertakers (Liverpool). Diplomacy label apparently not from Sacramento, although it issued a lot of masters from there. Big Three on Tollie possibly the Mama Cass group. Liverpool Sound Records was formed 2-64 by Lee Hartstone's Independent Producers Group (IPG) in New York. Folded after first 3 releases (all Birmingham groups) bombed. Enith label still in business in LA. Jack Hoffman & Norman Malkin produced most records on the label, also a Doug Dillard album (Douglas Flint Dillard, 20th Century T-426) as an Enith Production. Additional Enith listings:

712 - Dell-Coeds - Love in Return/Hey Mr. Banjo

715 - Danny Welton - Sure Dreamin/Hootchee Kootchee Mana

720 - Rubies - Sugar Cane/Is a Man Really Worth It?

SEEDS

Ken Barnes recently uncovered what must be Sky Saxon's first solo record, ca. 1962, under his real name, Richard Marsh:

Shepherd 2203 - They Say/Darling, I Swear That It's True

STANDELLS

Ooh Poo Pah Doo/Help Yourself - Sunset 61000

(as The Sllednats)

Don't Tell Me What to Do/When I Was a Cowboy - Tower 312 (5-67)

LEAVES

Mira 220 - Be With You/Funny Little World

Leaves album on Mira also reissued on Sutton, Mira's budget line.

BAY AREA

As expected, in covering such a large region, our listings turned out to be far from complete. There are probably a few dozen more Bay Area records yet to be discovered, but here are a few important additions:

Butch Engel & the Styx - I Like Her/Going Home - Loma 2065 (San Jose)

Harbinger Complex - I Think I'm Down/My Dear and Kind Sir - Brent 7056

Roy Montague - What's Holding/Revenue Man - Duane 103

Kaynines - Angel Eyes/That Ain't Right - Amber 3352 (East Bay)

Parrish & Wilde - Don't Fight It/Don't Take This Love Away - Invader 407

Merced Blue Notes - Mama Rufus/Bad, Bad Whiskey - Galaxy 744

Merced Blue Notes - Thompin'/ - Galaxy 748

Little Ronnie & Chromatics - I Was Wrong/pt. 2 - Galaxy 751

Fabulous Ballads - God Bless Our Love/pt. 2 - Bayview 11426 (' 67) (Also LP: Here We Are - Bayview 1967)

Gloria Scott & Tonettes - I Taught Him/ - WB 5413

A better shot of the New Breed, ca. 1966

Gloria Scott & the Tonettes recorded extensively for Autumn Records, although nothing was issued. This one, which dates from early '64, was apparently leased to Warner Bros. Anybody know of any others?

The Merced Blue Notes were from an area about 50 miles east of the Bay Area, (where American Graffiti was set) and were the most popular band around in the early

THE PULLICE One of Marin's finest.

'60s; they played all the major dances and hops in Merced, Modesto, Stockton, Manteka and the surrounding region. They must have recorded more records for Galaxy (a Fantasy subsidiary).

Kevin Walsh of San Rafael asked why I didn't devote more space to Marin County. Mainly because so few recordings

The Danes, from Santa Rosa

were made by Marin bands. The Sons of Champlin were probably the first to record, and by then the punk era was long gone. I read in World Countdown that the Newman Center of Marin issued an anthology LP of local bands, but nobody seems to know about it.

I remember a lot of the Marin bands though. The Freedom Highway, who did Travis Wammack songs like "Scratchy" and Dylan songs nobody else ever touched, like "Oxford Town". The Electric Train were good, and survived well into '67 playing the Avalon occasionally. And there was J.C. & the Disciples, who all looked about 14. The Pullice were one of Marin's biggest bands. I knew those guys, they were in and out of all kinds of Marin groups over the years. Gary Philippet (now in Earth Quake) was in this group.

A lot of the Marin bands played the Armory dances in San Rafael, or the Vets Hall dances in Santa Rosa, a couple hours north toward Sacramento. There were bands in Santa Rosa too as I recall, though again none seem to have recorded anything.

CLASSIFIED ADS 25 CENTS PER WORD (see p.3)

OLDIES! Auction, set price listings: '50s & '60s. John Jackson, 14 Stiles Dr, Melville, NY 11746.

FOR SALE: Thousands of '60s/early '60s R&R, rockabilly, R&B, Hillbilly records SANE PRICES. please write for my latest list. Craig Moerer, Box 13247, Portland, Oregon, 97213. Send want lists.

SIXTIES set sale plus giant Beatle auction. Dan Charny, Box 7785, Pittsburg, PA 15215

WANTED: Issues 1,2,3 *Who Put the Bomp*, issues 3,5 *Bim Bam Boom*. Top prices paid, state condition and price. R. Shannon, 1839 Fernwood Rd, S. Belmar, NJ 07719

"*The Buddy Holly Story*", 1974 book with full story on Cochran, Holly, Valens, Big Bopper, Crickets & more. Many new facts. $12. Also, *We Still Remember* LP with rare Cochran & Holly cuts, Norman Petty talking about the plane crash, message from Mr. & Mrs. Holley, tracks by Bopper, Valens, plus photos & sleeve notes. $6. Order from Bob Clarke, 7/53 Somerset St, Richmond, Victoria, Australia 3121. Postpaid.

SALE/TRADE--Punk, English rock. Joe Sicurella, 26 Wood St, Rutherford, NJ 07070.

SPECIALTY LABEL LISTING BOOKLET R&R, R&B, Popular singles series 1946-1964, plus complete history of the label. Compiled by Mike Leadbitter, Hugh McCallum and Tez Courtney (*Bomp* recommended!). Send one US dollar bill or 10 IRCs to T. Courtney, The Green, Dodford, Nr. Weedon, Northants, U.K.

FOR SALE: Over 400 45's. Send for auction list. Alan G. Thompson, Box 503, Geneva, Ill. 60134.

AUCTION/TRADE, giant list coming soon. Write to Michael Ochs, c/o ABC Records, 8255 Beverly Blvd, Los Angeles, CA 90048.

COMING NEXT ISSUE: Flo & Eddie answer your questions. That's right, the two nabobs of nuttiness have volunteered to give *Bomp* readers the inside scoop on the Turtles, T.Rex, Dino Desi & Billy, or any of the other famed superstars they've known and worked with over the years. They'll also tell you inside fax about what it's like being rock stars, how *you* can learn to play "Miserlou" in only two months, and just about anything else you'd care to know. So get your questions in--the wilder the better--and watch for the answers next issue.

HELLO! ILLYA HERE, TO TELL YOU ABOUT THE EXCITING WORLD OF BOMP!

Да! LET'S FACE IT! THINGS HAVE NEVER BEEN THE SAME SINCE THEY CANCELLED 'MAN FROM U.N.C.L.E.'! VELL, AT LEAST I GOT TO MAKE A GREAT RECORD ALBUM BACK THEN AND IT'S A RARE, RARE ITEM THESE DAYS. PERHAPS YOU'RE WONDERING ABOUT JUST SUCH **ROCK HITS** AS MY ALBUM, OR, SAY, "I'M A NUT" BY LEROY PULLINS? NYET? Да! THEN, **WHO PUT THE BOMP** IS JUST THE MAGAZINE FOR YOU!

THE ZINE THAT BROUGHT YOU SUCH EXCLUSIVE FEATURES AS:
- THE INSIDE SCOOP ON WAYNE FONTANA'S SHOCKING COOTIE INFESTATION...
- FOTOS FROM TIMMI YURO AND LOU CHRISTIE'S WEDDING...
- AN IN-DEPTH ARTICLE ON THE FAMOUS MANN-WEIL VS. GOFFIN-KING TAG-TEAM WRESTLING MATCHES
- and GOD (CLAPTON) ONLY KNOWS WHAT ELSE...

ANYWAY, TO GET TO THE POINT OF ALL THIS NONSENSE... YOU CAN STILL SUBSCRIBE TO BOMP AT THE PRE-INFLATION PRICE OF JUST $8 FOR 12 ISSUES, OR $9 FOR 12 ISSUES-OVERSEAS SURFACE MAIL, OR $1.50 @ AIR-OVERSEAS MAIL. (CHECKS OR MONEY ORDERS ONLY..)

JUST MAIL IN THE MOOLA AND THE COUPON BELOW OR A REASONABLE FACSIMILE...YOU'LL BE GLAD YOU DID!

WHO PUT THE BOMP!

Fall 1975 $1.00 /40p (UK)

CALIFORNIA SURF ROOTS
A Bomp Beach Bonanza!

Plus: Paul Revere & the Raiders; 13th Floor Elevators; Shocking Blue & Dutch rock; Merseybeat; & much more!

The BEAT Editorial by Greg Shaw

You can all breath a sigh of relief, because for once this column will not consist of a weighty discourse on the state of the world and the future of rock & roll. Instead, I'd like to talk a little about the magazine itself.

To begin with, as I'm sure you've notice, *Bomp* has become something more than just a rock fanzine or an oldies magazine. Although we strive to maintain the fannish spirit and amateurish (in the best sense of that word) approach, evidence is beginning to mount that the audience for a magazine of this type is much larger than any of us originally thought. *Bomp* is now sold in record stores and other locations all over America and in 8 countries around the world, and it seems that wherever we put it out, it sells. Not merely to "record collectors", but to a broad spectrum of music fans. What that means is that the old stereotype of the collector or serious fan as an insignificant minority whose tastes can be blithely written off by the record industry, is simply wrong. It may have been correct at one time, but in 1975 it appears that the average record buyer is determined to learn as much as he or she can about the entire history of the music, not to mention the incredible diversity of artists and product available today.

This is where magazines like *Bomp* who help the reader educate himself, rather than pandering to the superficial interest of the lowest common denominator, seem to fill a void. The success of oldies-format radio, the various repackage albums, and the actual comebacks of artists once considered irretrievably linked to the past, all indicate the same process at work.

To me, this is a very exciting prospect. A more enlightened mass audience makes things easier for those struggling to preserve the details of rock history, which is of course good. It's also good that today's rock audience is more willing than that of a few years ago to allow (and even encourage) influences from past styles to be injected into contemporary music, a crucial process in rock's cyclic rejuvenation process, and one that was shut off for many years. Most important, though, is that people are aware of the continuity of rock as an ongoing popular art form. Unlike the traditional oldies magazines, *Bomp* has always tried to relate the past to the present, and vice versa—for the parallels are endless, and profoundly relevant to any understanding of how and why music is made as it is.

If I could predict a direction for *Bomp*, I think it would be to make a real effort to determine the extent of that portion of the rock audience that considers itself more than just casual consumers, but serious fans or even collectors on some level. I'm convinced that, far from the vocal minority we've been typecast as, we may just turn out to be the silent majority as well.

This column is turning out to be a lot of fun to write—which, to put it mildly, is not always the case with other projects. But sitting around listening to the records covered below puts me in a great mood, and reminds of of why I got involved in all this in the first place — to hear exciting music. You'd be amazed how easy it is to forget, sometimes. Well, enough platitudinizing.

ROKY & HIS FRIENDS

The above head celebrates the highlight of the current LA concert season—an unscheduled and improbably electrifying appearance by Roky Erickson, legendary former lead singer with the 13th Floor Elevators, at the unlikely venue of the Palomino, the top local country nightclub, with Doug Sahm and band. Roky had it totally together for four songs, three new ones and "You're Gonna Miss Me," the intro of which was one of the most thrilling moments experienced live in recent years. The new stuff was very strong—"Shake Me Lucifer," a fast, fierce blues-rocker; "Starry Eyes", a pretty, early '60s type tune (echoes of Buddy Holly and Ral Donner); and the heavy metal (riff lifted from Hawkwind's "Master of the Universe") neoclassic "Two-Headed Dog". For further details on Roky's recent doings, see the full-length report elsewhere in this issue.

• Roky Erickson, as he appeared recently in LA at the Palomino (see above). If you missed him....... well, he *did* predict it........

Other live highlights lately have included the Hollies (first time in LA with Allan Clarke since 1967, and a joy to see) and the Beau Brummels. The Brummels surprised me; I liked their LP a lot but it's on the low-key side. In person their vocals were top-notch but the sound was dominated by ringing dual guitar work from Dan Levitt and Ron Elliott. The sound was a pristine survival from the '65 folk-rock era with consummate interwoven intricacies.

Not a highlight, though, were the Stones—ragged, over-extended, and almost totally devoid of the power once almost exclusively theirs. If that was the world's greatest rock band (as the media slavishly and unceasingly reminded us) I may have to convert to MOR. In many ways I liked the Grass Roots (who played Knotts Berry Farm in a comeback bid the next week) better—no nonsense (not much, anyway, except from my former hero Denny Provisor, whose "It Really Tears Me Up" (Valiant 728) is still a folk-rock classic, but who jacked around to excess) and all the hits.

I do find myself, however, listening to *Metamorphosis* more than almost anything. Hearing the Stones do those fey Oldham production extravaganzas like "Each and Every Day" and "I'd Much Rather Be With the Boys" ("faggy pop," Gene Sculatti capsulized it) is delightful and makes for an amusing ironic counterpart to their hard-core R&B image of the time. (*Ed. note:* Has anybody heard the Toggery Five's version of "I'd Much Rather Be With the Boys"?) It's also great, of course, to have the Troggs back on LP—a few too many standards but that same ineffable spirit. Reg Presley endures.

CULT 45's, Part III

POETS - "Call Again"/"Some Things I Can't Forget" - Immediate 006 (E) 10-65
TONY JACKSON GROUP - "You're My Number One" - CBS 202039 (E)

Two British delights. The more I hear by the Poets (actually from Scotland and tied in vaguely with the Marmalade/Blue/Trash—whose "Road to Nowhere" is positively staggering—family tree), the more I like them. Their hit "Now We're Thru" and its flip are

---

Are You Getting It Regularly?

Who Put the Bomp can now be delivered to your home for three years at a price *25% off* the regular rate! That's right, no more wondering if you've already sent your dollar, no more pestering your local record store to see if they've got it in yet. As a subscriber, you get it faster, cheaper, and more reliably. And what's more, our rates haven't gone up in 3 years, so if they should, you'll still receive your full subscription at the old rate! You can't hardly beat that!!

As a subscriber, you'll also receive, absolutely free, our regular auction & sale lists for rare records, plus other special mailings and offers from time to time. You can also receive our auction lists without subscribing, by checking the appropriate box below, but of course our subscribers always get priority treatment.

BOMP RECORDS

And don't forget Bomp Records. If you like any of the stuff we write about, you'll love our first three single releases:
- The Flamin' Groovies - "You Tore Me Down"/"Him Or Me" - $1.50, $2 w/pic cov.
- The Poppees - "If She Cries"/"Love of the Loved" - $2
- The Wackers - "Captain Nemo"/"Tonite" - $2

Buy all 3 for $5, or the Poppees & Wackers for $3.50

BACK ISSUES

We also have these back issues available:
- No. 11 - British Invasion (special double issue) only $1
- No. 12 - Seeds, Standells, Leaves, Beau Brummels, punk rock - $1
- No. 13 - Flamin' Groovies, Michigan rock, Beatle novelties, Hollywood Stars, Cameo Records, Rockabilly - $1

Who Put the Bomp, Box 7112, Burbank CA 91510.

Dear Bompers:
I like your offer & have checked the appropriate box below:

☐ 12-issue subscription - $8 ($10 Canada & overseas)
☐ Send regular record auctions. I'll subscribe later.
☐ Send the back issues I've circled, at $1 each: 11 12 13
☐ Send Poppees & Wackers 45s, both for $3.50. ☐ Send Groovies

Name _____ Age _____
Address _____ Amt. enclosed _____
City _____ State _____ Zip _____

Reverberations By Ken Barnes

excellent Zombies-style records, and "I Am So Blue" is even better, but this one's the topper (so far). The A-side is a perfectly lovely minor-chord gem, with a vocal that reminds me somehow of the Baroques (a Canadian group of whom I'm quite fond; one album on Cadet Concept). The flip is more upbeat, with a strong Andrew Oldham production, but with the same minor-chord charm.

Tony Jackson (the ex-Searchers singer/guitarist) came up with a beauty here. It has one of the best UK folk-rock riffs ever concocted, great production sound; a erfectly mesmerizing record. Peter Cowap (well-known Manchester figure) wrote it, and it should have been a smash—if Herman's Hermits (whom I'm vaguely reminded of by the song and who were known to record Cowap numbers) had cut it, it would have been.

PAT POWDRILL - "Happy Anniversary" - Reprise 20,204 - 1963

I have no idea who she is, but she mystifies me. Her first record is an average girl-group style performance of P.J. Proby's "I Only Came to Dance With You" (also an early Walker Bros. cut), arranged by Jack Nitzsche (Reprise 20,166). But "Anniversary" is an uncanny Chiffons soundalike, written by Ellie Greenwich and Tony Powers, an enchanting record with no resemblance to the first vocally. Two years later, in '65, she crops up on Downey 139 (home of the Chantays) with Goffin-King's "I Can't Hear You" (cut by Dusty and Lulu in England). It's a Motownish rocker, good but with no trace of Chiffons in the vocal. Baffling, but worth investigating.

BETHLEHEM EXIT - "Walk Me Out"/"Blues Concerning My Girl" - Jabberwock 110 - 1966
ODDS & ENDS - "Cause You Don't Lve Me" - South Bay 102 - 1966

Two from the Bay Area. "Walk Me Out" is a fast folk-rock version of "Morning Dew", easily the best I've heard. The flip is a super-speedy blues, Yardbirds-like, frantic and exciting. The record's juxtaposition of folk- and hard-rock approaches the former pinnacle in the field, the Becket Quintet's "Baby Blue"/"No Correspondence" (Gemcor 5003/A&M 782). The Odds & Ends was listed in the San Jose/Bay Area roundup a while back here, but is a dynamite stomping folk-rocker with an ethereal chorus, very intriguing structure and fast becoming a favorite.

WARNER BROTHERS - "I Won't Be the Same Without Her" - Dunwich 131 - 1967
TWILIGHTS - same - Capitol 5796 - 1-67

Goffin-King department. The Warner Brothers handle this generally-unknown G-K gem in heavy folk-rock fashion, with odd chanting and feedbacked guitar—all in all one of Dunwich's best, and that's a tall order. The Twilights, one of Australia's biggest and best bands, apply more polish and Mersey flavor, and a little less raw edge, but overall it's a tossup. Terrific song.

• Robb Storme: an unexpected gem.

ROBB STORME GROUP - "Here Today"/"But Cry" - Columbia 7993 (E) 1966
GIANT JELLYBEAN COPOUT - "Awake In a Dream" - Poppy 504 - 1968

Beach Boys cops here. The Robb Storme benefits from a crashing production, with tight harmonies, and is a bravura performance (the B-side is a catchy, delightful melody that approaches proto-bubblegum, quite wonderful). The Copout, produced by James Ryan (of the Critters?), is a post-"Heroes & Villains" affair, similar to Flowerpot Men/10cc stylings in that vein, and quite striking. It got some regional play in '68.

NINO TEMPO & APRIL STEVENS - "I Love How You Love Me" - Atco 6375 - 1965
PAUL & BARRY RYAN - same - Decca 12445 (E)

Nino Tempo has made a lot of good records—forget "Stardust" and those, but don't forget "All Strung Out" on White Whale, a fine neo-Spector production. This is Nino & April's best, though, backed by the famed Guilloteens. Folk-rock all the way, fuzz guitars, big production, good vocals, in a smashing uptempo transformation of the Paris Sisters goldie—and, just to spice it up, bagpipes skirling away (learned specifically for this session by the enterprising Nino, or so they said).

Imagine my surprise, then, upon receiving (after years on my want list) Paul & Barry Ryan's 8-months-later version, produced by ex-searcher Chris Curtis. It's a total cop, right down to the bagpipes, but it lacks that distinctive Guilloteens/Nino Tempo sparkle. Quite a curious development, in any case.

HEARD - "Laugh With the Wind"/"Stop it Baby" Audition 6107
HYSTERICS - "That's All She Wrote"/"Won't Get Far" - Tottenham 500

I put these together because the records look alike (lettering and label design) and because they're totally unknown (to me) but fabulous records. The Heard's top deck has a stunning hard-rock intro that shifts into light, harmonic folk-rock with one of the dumbest, most prosaic 12-string leads imaginable—great record. The flip is equally strong, a great hard-rock "I Gotta Move" (Kinks) cop.

The Hysterics' A-side is an appealingly crude crypto-Mersey folk-rocker, but the B-side has Seeds-style electric piano and a delightfully awful harsh, snarled vocal—tremendous Seeds imitation.

BOYS NEXT DOOR - "There is No Greater Sin"/"I Could See Me Dancin With You" - Cameo 394

Another testimonial to the versatile genius of the Tokens, who produced. Big kitchen-sink folk-rock-turned-pop production on top (an Al Kooper song, too), reminds me of the Myddle Class somehow. The B-side (later a Tokens flip on Buddah 174) is a falsetto surf-style beauty, equally killer. The Boys Next Door have at least two other fab folk-rockers on Atco.

PERPETUAL MOTION WORKSHOP - "Infiltrate Your Mind" - Rally 66506

Written and co-produced by the enigmatic Simon Stokes, this LA record features incredibly vicious guitar raveups, like the Music Machine's great "Eagle Never Hunts the Fly" trebled in intensity.

ONE-HIT WONDERS - "Hey Hey Jump Now" - CBS 7760 (E) 1965

Actually Mike Berry (the early-'60s British hitmaker) in all probability. The opening is amazing, a cross between "Everybody Needs Somebody to Love" (someday I must explore the genesis of that riff, one of the all-time greats) and the Syndicate of Sound's "Little Girl." It doesn't quite live up to the intro, but deserves mention for that and for their delightfully candid name.

JOOK - "Crazy Kids" - RCA 5024 (E) 1974

Alan Betrock's already rhapsodized about this 1974 disk, but I've got to add my bit. With its frantic pace, elegant-but-noisy guitar lines, and typically British-moderne teenage-condition lyrics, this record is everything the Sweet could and should have become and never have. Brilliant.

TRASHMEN - "Same Lines" - Tribe 8315 1-66

And finally....I'm assured this is the same Minnesota group that did "Surfin Bird", though how they got hooked up with Huey P. Meaux in Texas is beyond me. Anyway, this sounds like Bob Dylan singing the Stones' "Empty Heart", which is great in itself. But they've got their Dylanesque whiner vocalizing the stupidest, most trivialized lyrics imaginable, stretching syllables lamely in a vain attempt to fit the meter—just too much irony for one song.

ODD ZEN ENDS

Knickerbockers update—their last record, "As a Matter of Fact"/"They Ran For Their Lives" (from the movie of the same name??) might be their best—compelling material and vocal by Jimmy Walker on the A-side (great fuzz riffs too), and fast folk-rock on the back..... Finally got hold, after endless curiosity, of the Rockin' Vicars' Pete Townshend-written "It's Alright" which turns out to be a cop from "Kids Are Alright" for the most part. Neat though....

New local stuff: *Bomp*'s always supported Mogan David & the Winos through their travails, and it pleases me to report that their latest 45, "All the Wrong Girls Like Me" (by the Winos, solely) is a seductive ditty backed by a first-rate (Dakotas-influenced) surf instrumental, "The Savage Surf." Available for $1.25 from Rhino Records, 1716 Westwood Blvd, LA 90024; and why not order "Go to Rhino Records", a shameless plug for the parent record store and the first recording in years by Wildman Fischer (Winos on the flip too). Same price and a bargain..... And apropos of Roky Erickson, Greg Turner has pressed a single of his first known recordings with the Spades (pre-Elevators), fascinating versions of "You're Gonna Miss Me" and "We Got Soul" (basically the same as "Don't Fall Down" from the first LP. Order from International Artists Fan Club, 4857 Beeman Ave, N. Hollywood, CA 91607. $2.75 including postage.....

Lou Reed discovery (gotta have one of those every once in awhile): the first cut on the second side of the Downliners Sect's *Rock Sect's In* LP is co-written by a Reed-Cale combination, which is either a long tall coincidence or another relic from Reed's closet..... For all you Phil & the Frantics fans, the legendary Phoenix aggregation's first record (presumably) has been unearthed—"She's My Gal"/"Koko Joe" (La Mar 100) Okay rockers but no Zombies overtones; still an invaluable addition to the archives.

Remember, any communications or record offers (plus Dutch information/records; see article) should be directed to Box 7195, Burbank, CA 91510. Can't promise a prompt reply all the time (as several correspondents can attest), but I appreciate any word and will do my best to respond in the usual sprightly fashion.

THE BIRTH OF SURF

by Greg Shaw

It's an accepted fact of life now that, with the coming of summer, each year brings a new Surf Music Revival. The growth of this surf music renaissance over the past three years has been well chronicled here and in *Phonograph Record Magazine*, as have the latest activities of its leading lights, the Beach Boys, Jan & Dean, and Bruce Johnston. The Beach Boys seem finally to have been accepted at large as the true national resource they are, as surf music itself gains grudging acceptance and respect from those who once scorned it.

All of which gladdens us immensely, here at *WPTB*. At times it seems to me that the overcoming of "oldies" prejudice (that word, shamefully condescending even when used by fans, is finally beginning to disappear), which just a few short years ago kept a lot of fine music (including surf) from being taken seriously, has been the greatest accomplishment of the rock press in recent years. It's a good sign, indicating a growing awareness and sophistication among rock fans as a whole.

And yet, despite all the critical and historical evaluation that has been lavished on surf music, the emphasis has been almost entirely on the vocal forms of the music, introduced by the Beach Boys in 1961 and popularized by many during 1963-65. This period, while admittedly more interesting in its cultural ramifications and more easily accessible to today's musical standards, represents only the second half of the surf music story. Rather than go over this well-travelled ground, we thought it might be interesting to go back and take a look at where surf music came from—for it most certainly did not spring full-blown from Brian Wilson's brow one fateful day in the sand at Huntington Beach.

The term "surf music" originally referred to a style of instrumental rock introduced by Dick Dale (whose germinal role is examined in a separate article......) and popularized by a great many local bands, chiefly in Southern California and the San Joaquin Valley of Central California, but found elsewhere around the country, particularly (and most surprisingly) in the landlocked Midwest. The Astronauts from Colorado were among the most successful early surf music bands.

Dick Dale clains to have invented his intense, staccato style of guitar picking to simulate the sensation of riding the waves—which his music certainly did. Equally important was his use of tremolo and reverb to achieve a characteristic sound that distinguished surf music from previous forms of instrumental rock, which it otherwise closely resembled.

Instrumental rock, another important sub-genre long overdue for recognition, was in a sense the missing link between '50s rockabilly and '60s garage bands. At a time when the trend was toward studio-manufactured singing idols taking over the charts, local dance bands kept the grass-roots foundation of rock & roll alive.

In 1959, instrumental rock was the most widespread new trend. The first instrumental hits were considered novelties, like Duane Eddy's "Rebel Rouser" or the Tune Rockers' "Green Mosquito", but by 1959 the raw vitality of this sound had inspired hundreds of local bands who had been playing rockabilly-derived music but, since the demise of that genre, gaining no commercial acceptance. The link between rockabilly and instrumental rock (which I don't think has been suggested before......) can be seen in groups such as the Fendermen and the Rock-A-Teens, who had rockabilly and instrumental hits respectively, and both of whose albums contained an equal portion of each style. Most of the instrumental groups, however, were strictly that, and the strength of the style was its perpetuation of hard-rock values in a time when everything was going soft. The best records of Johnny & the Hurricanes, Link Wray, and the Royaltones (to name but a few) were every bit as savage and unremittingly tough as any vocal rocker you could care to name.

The other virtue of instrumental rock was its adaptability. For material, many groups chose standard or classic melodies, which they "rocked up" (cf "Red River Rock", "Beatnik Fly"). Thus, groups with no songwriting ability could still come up with 'original' tunes. Also, it was easier to merely play than to sing and play at the same time, another factor which encouraged many thousands of kids to start instrumental combos around the country. And of course, anything that brings more people into rock & roll at the basic grass-roots level, encouraging local scenes and styles, can only be beneficial to the music's development. And as for adaptability, it was a simple matter for these same bands to switch over to Twist and other R&B-influenced styles in 1960-61, when the dance fad era came in.

It was this preliminary period of 1959-61 that set the stage for surf music. The local dance bands that evolved from the local instrumental bands set a model for the surf bands that followed, exposed them to the influences and basic styles of rocked-up classics, adapted R&B styles, and above all the Texas shuffle/blues styles of Freddie King, Bill Doggett and others that were adapted by these white bands, that laid the structural groundwork for so much of surf music.

1961 was the key transitional year, during which a number of oddly undefinable records made the charts, such as "LSD 25"/"Moon Dawg" by the Gamblers (a record ahead of its time in more ways than one, this was also the first version of "Moon Dawg," later done by the Surfaris and the Challengers. "Stick Shift" by the Duals (even more ahead of its time, as an instrumental hot rod record) and "Mr. Moto" by the Bel-Airs featuring Richard Delvy (never a national hit, but big regionally). These records, and a few others, were much too late to be part of the instrumental era, yet much too early to be considered surf records, though stylistically they were clear precursors of that style.

These groups, along with Dick Dale, were busy during 1961-62 evolving an instrumental style derived from the previous era but geared specifically to the local Southern California audience whose eagerness to embrace a musical style to reflect the new summer/sun/beach/affluence/mobility lifestyle that was emerging in the early '60s, particularly in Southern California, can be seen in the hero-worship accorded Dick Dale and the Beach Boys.

Because of the conditions peculiar to Southern California--the overnight sprawl of suburban and exurban developments, the emergence of a newly-affluent generation of post-war offspring from millions of first-generation Los Angelinos, coupled with the natural climate and topology of the region, Southern California was the inevitable home of surfing music, and really the only part of the country that could boast more than one or two surf bands. For a time, there were scores of them, and an output of records (mostly on ephemeral local labels) that will never be fully catalogued. By 1963 there were several national hits from this scene—"Pipeline" by the Chantays, "Wipe Out"/"Surfer Joe" by the Surfaris, "Penetration" by the Pyramids, etc. These records, originally local then picked up by larger labels for national distribution, represented the final flowering of surfing's original instrumental sound. Despite many fine subsequent efforts, by the Superstocks and many others, after 1964 it was almost strictly a vocal sound, at least as far as the national audience was concerned. The local audience as well, I think, tended to prefer the more literally identifiable-with Beach Boys, if only because the surfing fad had brought in a lot of people who didn't really surf but liked to make the scene. The remaining instrumental bands recorded extensively for Del-Fi, which issued an awesome number of surf-related albums, but these were purely a local phenomenon that sold only to a limited hard core of fans.

The task of compiling complete lists of surf record releases is, as I've said, practically impossible. Though it only flourished a short time, the surf trend inspired countless groups to issue their own records for the benefit of their local followings. We're going to list as many as we can, and welcome all additions, but it's unlikely the true extent of instrumental surf recordings will ever be known.

DICK DALE: the man who invented surf music

By JOHN BLAIR

*"Real surfing music is instrumental.....
characterized by heavy staccato picking
on a Fender Stratocaster guitar,
and it has to be a Stratocaster."* — Dick Dale

On a warm Saturday afternoon last May, I spoke with Dick Dale at his home in Huntington Beach, reminiscing about the early days of surf music and the memories of his involvement in the youth scene of Southern California at the time.

Dick Dale's importance as the originator of surf music, as a man who was (and is) very sensitive to his music, and as a performer and trend-setter, is not to be underestimated. In reference to his immense popularity at a time before his records were played on the radio, he said: "We started at the Rendezvous Ballroom in Balboa, which was way down at the end of the peninsula, and they said nobody would come to my dances because the Ballroom was too far away and no one will want to drive that distance. We played there for nearly three years and had about 4000 kids every night we were there. The line of cars stretched all the way from Newport Beach out to the Coast Highway. They wanted to close down Balboa because the line of cars was creating a hazard.

"When we went into the Pasadena Civic, they only let me stay there a month because they started having 3000 kids show up for the dances and they'd never had that many people coming there before.

"It's true I had no records. In fact, I told the kids I had no money to go out and cut records. It was more or less a personal thing. We became very close. Many of them would come to my home, we would surf together and I would go on outings with them."

For Dick, surf music came out of a desire to create a sound on his guitar that matched the feeling he had while riding the waves on his surfboard. "There was a tremendous amount of power that I felt while surfing and that feeling of power was simply transferred from myself into my guitar when I was playing surf music. I couldn't get that feeling by singing, so the music took on an instrumental form."

I asked him if this instrumental vehicle for surfing music had been influenced by any particular artists or styles. "No, it just came out of me. One day I just started picking faster and faster like a locomotive. I wanted to make it sound hard and powerful. There wasn't anybody who influenced it actually. I mean, there's nothing to influence you once you create a new style and stick to that style."

Back when he first picked up a guitar and began learning to play, Dale's influences were mainly country & western. "The first instrument I picked up was a ukelele. Since I'm left handed, it was difficult to form chords that way and nobody was willing to teach me because of that fact. I certainly didn't want to learn how to play right handed because all my power and rhythm was in my left hand.

"After I got my first guitar, people would say to just form ukelele chords on it and muffle the fifth and sixth strings. So that's what I did. The first song I remember learning was 'The Wild Side of Life.' Then I learned 'The Tennessee Waltz' and I listened to Hank Williams and Hank Snow and started singing country songs.

"It wasn't until after I came to Southern California that I learned to form a full 6-string chord. Up to that time, I was always using only four strings."

Regarding some of his early idols, Dick said: "Back in the Fifties I thought Eddie Cochran was good. Ritchie Valens was another one that I felt was truly great. As a matter of fact, we had the same manager for awhile. I remember at his first major stage appearance in Long Beach with me, he only had two songs prepared to do on state, 'La Bamba' and 'Donna.' Well, the audience gave him a standing ovation and wanted him back for more. Ritchie was backstage wondering what to do and I told him to just go back out there and do 'La Bamba' again. He did that song three times and every time I said go back out and do it again.

"There were people we worked with back then at places like Long Beach and the El Monte Legion Stadium that I felt were really great. There was Sonny Knight, Joe Houston, Little Julian Herrera, Johnny Otis and Mike Dacey, who's one of the finest guitarists you'll ever hear."

•Dick Dale at home, 1975. Above, Dick and an early group of Deltones, ca. 1965. L-R: Bill Barber, Rick Rillera, Nick O'Malley, Jerry Stevens, Dick, Frank Armando, Barry Rillera.

It was chiefly because of Dick's great popularity in Southern California that scores of garage bands sprung up practically overnight to play this new style called surfing music. The majority of these groups never saw a recording studio, but there were a few who did record and even fewer who enjoyed successful hit records. Some of these bands were formed as a direct result of personal contact with Dick.

"I have a little music store down at the beach at one time and a lot of kids would come to me for guitar lessons. It's funny because I didn't know a lot about music and I didn't believe in a lot of music theory anyway, unless you wanted to become a studio musician. So I would guarantee them that I could teach them how to play a song in one day so they could learn chords and the whole song without a lot of theory. Well, so many kids came down to me that I had to raise my prices from something like $2.00 an hour to $25.00 an hour just to get them out of there, but they would pay the higher price anyway.

"So some of these kids eventually went out and formed their own groups and I felt good when I'd see some of my students playing with their own bands. There were guys like Dave Myers, who formed the Surftones and then later changed it to the Prophets because everybody teased him about the similarity between Surftones and Deltones and the fact that he would change the color of his guitar every time I changed mine.

"I can't remember the man's name now, but there was another guy who wanted me to help him form a group when I was just starting out here. He later formed his own band, called the Rhythm Rockers, and went on to become the manager of the Righteous Brothers.

"There was actually very little happening during the first two years I started playing surf music. After about two and a half years, surf bands started to spring up. I remember the Surfaris and the Pyramids and it was about this time that I started to actually meet certain people at my dances like Jan & Dean, the Beach Boys and Jimi Hendrix, who said that he patterned his guitar style after me.

"There was another band, Eddie & the Showmen, who I had heard were exact duplicates of my band and my sound. In fact, a girl came up to me once and asked me why I imitated Eddie & the Showmen."

I asked Dick to characterize the surfing scene in Southern California during the early '60s. "Lots of people wore Pendleton shirts, of course, and there were the big decorated surfboards with the stringers and just about everybody drove around in woodies. Dana Point and Huntington Beach were the popular surfing spots. You saw a lot of baggies and catins, a type of canvas trunk. There were a lot of bikes, the bike scene was fairly popular, and of course the guys didn't wear long hair.

"Surf music gradually started making the beaches a popular place for people who weren't surfers. These were the hodads and the greasers in their lowered Chevys who came from LA or Long Beach, for instance, just to cruise the beach to see what was happening. You could always tell someone who wasn't a surfer on the beach from his cut-off Levis. Surfers just didn't wear cut-off Levis.

"Then there were the gremmies, the little kids too small to surf, who were always spitting on the beach and breaking bottles. They were a real pain in the neck."

Since the music that Dick was playing at all of his dances was chiefly instrumental, I wanted to find out what some of his favorite instrumental music has been over the years. "Well, you know Mason Williams used to come over to my house a lot and when 'Classical Gas' came out, I though it was tremendous, but I didn't know he was the one doing it at first. I loved 'Honky Tonk', 'Raunchy', 'Caterpillar Crawl', a lot of Joe Houston's material and some of the background music used by Bill Haley on his vocals.

"'Rumble', 'Memphis' and 'The Lonely Bull' by the Tijuana Brass are favorites of mine also. I still enjoy 'The Theme From Exodus' and it still sends goosebumps up my back."

One side of Dick Dale is that of the talented musician who commanded a huge following in the early '60s and who started the whole surf music phenomenon. Another side of Dick Dale, though, is that of a sensitive, emotional man who cares about other people, which is probably a major clue to the success he established for himself locally and the self-imposed lack of success he attained nationally. His humanitarian aspect came out when we talked about the high points of his career and what he would change if he could do it all again.

"One of the greatest feelings I've ever had in performing was at one of my dances. There was a paraplegic kid in a wheelchair who couldn't move at all. He never missed one of my dances and as time went by, he started getting more and more involved in the music. One night he started moving an arm that he'd never moved before to the beat of the music and, pretty soon, he'd start moving a leg. After awhile, he could speak my name and we could carry on short conversations together. That was a really beautiful thing.

"I guess if I had the chance to do it all over, I'd probably do it a little bit differently. If I knew what was in store for me, I would handle it differently financially. I'd become very business-like in the matter and not believe in so many people and in so many promises."

(Editor's Note: A detailed Dick Dale biography and discography can be found in Rock Marketplace #9, $1.60 from Box 253, Elmhurst-A, NY 11380.)

SURFIN' IN THE SAN JOAQUIN

By BILL SMART & JOHN BLAIR

Although Fresno, California is certainly not the legendary "Surf City", its unique location, cultural composition and musical heritage make it most worthy of investigation. Fresno and that portion of the San Joaquin Valley which it dominates has traditionally, because of its novel equidistant location, been influenced by both the Los Angeles and San Francisco scenes. The Spanish culture is also an important factor in analyzing the musical scene in the area, regardless of the time period in question. While instrumental music may have had its supporters across the country during the turn of the decade (1959-61), it was never more popular anywhere than it was in the San Joaquin Valley.

All these factors combined to produce a veritable hotbed of instrumental activity by the time surf music came into existence. Despite the fact that there were no local labels or recording studios to speak of, and the nearest major facilities 300 miles in either direction, many noteworthy sides were waxed, and there were enough local promoters and halls to keep the groups active.

The Revels, from Bakersfield, had come and gone for a two year series of road tours and returned again by the time garage group fever had infected the area. Their solitary hit, "Church Key" was a *sine qua non* among all local bands. I remember them as the "Bakersfield Revels" which I interpreted as local pride, but which was probably to distinguish them from the R&B group of the same name. At any rate, the strength of their local popularity kept them employed far past their prime (if, indeed, they ever had one) and well into the surf era.

In addition to a number of singles on Impact and one on the Swingin' label, they released one LP on Impact. The album features twelve classic instrumentals, typical Tony Hilder liner notes, and a cover which depicts the elusive Troyce Key posing as a Revel.

Similarly, the flexible Charades from Tulare had also become associated with the surf scene. Formed as the Latin Knights in the late '50s, the Charades were a mixed R&B vocal group who were popular at teen dances and battles of the bands in the Valley as well as in the Santa Maria/San Luis Obispo area.

Several singles and cuts on sampler LPs were released from 1962-64, the most noteworthy of which featured the backup band. "Sophia"/"Christina" by the Charades Band on Impact 32 blends the best Valley traditions into a double-barreled instrumental Latin-surf classic.

One guitarist for the Charades was talented enough to branch out on his own. A young Tommy Johnson recorded "Give Me Justice" on the obscure Atoll label in 1964. Ray Baradat and his Charades were befriended, written for, and often accompanied by a Delano group known alternately as the Soul Kings and the Rhythm Kings, who also possessed that greasy surf sound.

Al Garcia's groups, regardless of which name they used (including The Link Eddy Combo and perhaps Al Anthony), were responsible for an untold number of singles and album cuts on various and sundry labels in addition to performing as backup on scores of Hilder-produced tracks. They also toured as the Piltdown Men road group. The Link Eddy Combo, incidentally, was named after Lincoln Mayorga, the prolific LA studio musician, and Ed Cobb, of Four Preps and Standells fame.

Both Al Garcia and Ray Baradat employed the talents of many local Chicano musicians in their various groups. The influence of Spanish music is undeniable in any analysis of instrumental surf from Dick Dale to the Surfaris, but neither Ray nor Al would have admitted to playing "surf" music at the time!

The Latino musician was encouraged and supported by his family in guitar playing when few others were. It was considered a proper masculine pastime and, melting-pot myths aside, the Chicano musician often did play in mixed Anglo-Chicano groups. Artists like Santo & Johnny, the Fireballs, the Champs and Freddie King influenced these budding musicians as well as Mexican performers. They had the jump on us! The result was a host of fine instrumentals which were Anglicized enough for consumption by the masses.

"Latinia" was written by a Chicano who admits Santo & Johnny's influence ("Slave Girl" on the first Santo & Johnny album is "Latinia", nearly note for note) and who played in a mixed group, the Sentinals. "Torchula" is similar, but with the Champs as the inspiration. Including a Chicano musician in groups was not a result of fair employment legislation, but a natural consequence of having so damn many talented Latins around.

Pat and Lolly Vegas, who have since gone on to fame as Redbone, are native Fresno *mestizos* who hit the surf circuit for a short jaunt as the Avantis after "Wax 'Em Down" was released as a single on the Chancellor label.

Since Pismo Beach and the central coast area was the closest "surf" to Fresno, the music of this coastal area and that of the central Valley shared many traits. The most popular radio station in the San Luis Obispo area was KAFY, Bakersfield's rebel independent station. Many notable groups originated in these coastal regions within earshot of KAFY, over a hundred miles away; groups like the Counts, the Roulettes, the Biscaynes, the Impacts and the matchless Sentinals. Most of these acts displayed an awareness of as much James Brown and Marvin Gaye as Ventures and Dick Dale, like many of their inland counterparts.

Another Fresno act, Jim Waller & the Deltas, were responsible for a number of surf tracks. They were an accomplished top-forty vocal/instrumental group with an enormous local following. The Deltas were the house band at the Marigold Ballroom and backed artists like Little Eva and Gene Pitney when they appeared there. Tony Hilder produced at least 16 surf tunes with them which appear, in typical Hilder fashion, scattered over a minimum of five albums, five labels, and one single release. There were other non-surf (and non-Hilder) recordings, but nothing to match the instrumentals on their Arvee album. Jim Waller, along with the other Fresno favorites, inspired a vigorous generation of local punkers for years to come. But that, as they say, is another story.

The Tony Hilder Story

By JOHN BLAIR & BILL SMART

Any attempt at a comprehensive survey of the surf music scene without mentioning Tony Hilder would be flagrantly incomplete. He was responsible for more local surf music being recorded and released than any one individual. Hilder remains, however, a man shrouded in mystery.

Anthony John Hilder's name, whether as writer, producer or publisher, can be found on countless albums and 45s. Were it not for the poor credits on many of the LPs, which include some "budget" products, his name would appear even more often.

"Church Key", "Latinia", "Please Be My Love Tonight", and "Surfin' Tragedy" were a few relatively less obscure waxings brought to us by the same man who enlightened politically aware music fans with right-wing slogans printed right on the labels. "Our

Country Can Never Go Right by Going Left", "God Bless America", "Au-H20-1964" were actually printed on Hilder's Impact labels, a phenomenon that may have strongly antagonized program directors of opposing persuasions!

In recent times, Hilder has proved unwilling to discuss past experiences and refused to divulge even the year of his birth. He allegedly initiated his involvement in the record industry in the late '50s as an A&R man for the Kent/Modern organization, working with such LA artists as Jesse Belvin and Charles Wright.

Belvin and Wright, Hilder maintains, were singers on the recorded version of "You Cheated" by the Shields.

It was during this period (1956-59) that Hilder developed professional contacts which would later prove invaluable to him. Bruce Morgan, who together with his parents owned and operated a mastering and recording studio, was one such individual. The Morgans assisted the early Beach Boys before their bond with Capitol (and issued their first record, as Kenny & the Cadets) and Dorinda Morgan wrote "Confidential" for Sonny Knight. Another association which endured was with Robert Hafner. From the early years until the middle '60s, Hafner wrote, performed and produced for Hilder, becoming his closest co-worker.

In 1959, Hilder left Kent/Modern to pursue independent ventures. He formed his first label, CT, and released two singles. Other releases on Challenge and Jaguar from this period also bear Hilder's name, either as publisher, writer or orchestra leader.

A second independent label, Impact, was formed as an outlet for those masters which Hilder could neither lease nor sell outright to others. Impact's first release was "Church Key" by the Revels, which featured Barbara Adkins laughing her way to fame and fortune as Mrs. Tony Hilder. The label featured, though not exclusively, local groups doing original material, and of course those absurd political slogans. The search for marketable talent sent Hilder into the grass roots to locate such unforgettables as Bob Kuhn, Eddie Snell, Sandra Teen and Bob (Linkletter) Preston.

Although many of Hilder's efforts were farmed out to other labels, he did manage to release at least 33 Impact singles and two LPs. Typically, the results of assorted sessions in the studio would be compiled into samplers and peddled to the highest bidder. This musical malpractice did not exclude selling the same masters to different companies.

That Tony Hilder was operating on the proverbial shoestring may not at first be obvious, but he sold the master of "Hanging Twenty" by Dave Myers & the Surftones to Bob Keene at Del-Fi for $100. The sessions that produced the tape cost him $50 and the group got nothing. Bob Hafner, Hilder's "arranger", continued to pump gas for a living. "Surf" album masters were purchased by Del-Fi ("The originators of surf music"), GNP, GSP, Northridge, Arvee, Sutton, Shepherd, Guest Star and perhaps many others.

Singles were scattered about on labels in much the same way, and Bamboo, Arvee, Faro, Challenge, Northridge, Reprise, Sharon, Liberty, Tollie, Ava, Original Sound and Era all released Hilder products.

Political activity prior to the national 1964 elections prompted Hilder to express his convictions on his Impact label as mentioned previously. Several singles were blatant rightist manifestos. "John Birch American" by the New Breed, "Voice of Liberty" by Bob Preston and "Our Opinion of Barry Goldwater, the Next President" featuring Efrem Zimbalist, Dr. William McBirnie, Walter Brennan, Ronald Reagan, Joe Snell and Robert Stack, backed with "Discrimination—Think of How You Can End It" were all actual Impact releases.

Tori Ltd. is yet another label which Hilder piloted, but no releases are known.

The defeat of Barry Goldwater and the demise of surf music marked the end of Tony Hilder's active involvement in the music industry. He is now employed as a salesman of freeze-dried food products in Southern California, writing reactionary declarations in his spare time.

TONY HILDER DISCOGRAPHY

IMPACT ALBUMS
1. The Revels - *The Revels On a Rampage*
2. V.A. - *Shake, Shout and Soul* (Little Ray, Surfaris, Steve Korey, Dave Myers & the Surftones, the Virtue Four and the New Dimensions)

IMPACT SINGLES
- AV-1 V.A. - Our Opinion of Barry Goldwater—The Next President/Discrimination
- 1 Revels - Church Key/Vesuvius
- 2
- 3 Revels - Tequila/Intoxica
- 4 Sandra Teen - Stranger in Love/Angel Baby
- 5 Spektrums - The Santa Maria/Sundown
- 6
- 7 Revels - Commanche/Rampage
- 8 Bob Kuhn - Rendezvous/A Serenade to Julie
- 9 Eddie Snell - I Feel Like Crying/Unless Things Go Your Way
- 10 Ramblers - Funny Papers/Yaba Dab Ah Doo
- 11
- 12 Guiseppi Apollo & Revels - Bright Star/All Because of You
- 13 Revels - Party Time/Soft Top
- 14 Breakers - Surfin' Tragedy/Surf Bird (Stowaways, Udy Sisters, Jim Waller & Deltas)
- 15 Don Mikkelson - I Cant Get Over the Blues/Now You're Gone
- 16 Dannie Toliver - Little Boy Blue/Take a Chance
- 17 Shorty Bacon - Ten Times the World/What's Wrong With You
- 18 Hollywood Rebels - Thriller/Rebel Stomp
- 19
- 20
- 21
- 22 Revels - The Monkey Bird/Revellion
- 22 Revels - Revellion/Conga Twist
- 23 Jesse Belvin - Looking for Love/Tonight My Love (released posthumously)
- 24 Bob Vaught & Renegaids - Bo' Gater/Church Key Twist (also released on Bamboo 520)
- 25 Evan & Emperors - LA Freeze/Emperor's Twist
- 26 Lil' Ray & Premiers - Shake, Shout & Soul/Soul & Stomp
- 27 Dave Myers & Surftones - Church Key/Passion
- 28 Materlyn & Cupons - I'll Be Your Love Tonight/Turn Her Down (answer record to the Charades release on Ava sung by Hilder's sister-in-law)
- 29 New Breed - John Birch American/Lexington Green
- 30 Lil' Ray & Midnighters - Loretta/My Girl
- 31
- 32 Charades Band - Christina/Sophia
- 33 Bob Preston - The Letter/Voice of Liberty

CT LABEL
- CT 1 Vi Hall - It's Graduation Time/Endless
- CT 2 Marc Wayne - Let it Rain/Miracle of Love

JAGUAR LABEL
- 3029 Carousels - Rendezvous/Drive-In Movie

SHARON LABEL
- 102 Al Anthony - The Soul/Angie

REPRISE LABEL
- 20002 Link-Eddy Combo - Big Mr. C/Man with the Golden Arm
- 20180 Biscaynes-Church Key/Biscaynes-Moment of Truth

NORTHRIDGE LABEL
- LP 101 - V.A. - *Surf's Up at Banzai—Pipeline* (Soul Kings, Dave Myers & Surftones, Surfaris, Neal Nissenson, Jim Waller & Deltas, Doug Hume, Biscaynes, Bob Vaught & Renegaids, Bob Hafner)
- 1001 Biscaynes - Church Key/Surfaris - Moment of Truth
- 1002 Charades - For You/Surf 'n Stomp

ORIGINAL SOUND LABEL
- 47 Charades - Take a Chance/Close to Me

AVA LABEL
- 154 Charades - Turn Him Down/Please Be My Love Tonight

ARVEE LABEL
- 5072 Jim Waller & Deltas - Church Key/Surfin Wild
- LP 432 - Jim Waller & Deltas - *Surfin' Wild*

ERA LABEL
- 3082 Sentinals - Latinia/Torchula
- 3117 Sentinal Six - Infinity/?
- ???? Sentinals - Latin Soul/?
- ???? Sentinals - Christmas Eve/?

FARO LABEL
- 617 Little Ray - Karen/Come Swing With Me

VELPA LABEL
- 100 Al Garcia & Rhythm Kings - Simply Jane/Velpa

TOLLIE LABEL
- 9014 Rhythm Kings - Latin Ska/Burleska (old Hilder tracks with new overdubbed vocals)

LIBERTY LABEL
- 59491 Emmett Lord - Women/Turn Him Down

SUTTON LABEL
- LP 338 Sentinals - *Vegas Go Go*

CHALLENGE LABEL
- 59056 Billy Watkins - Unforgettable/Rendezvous
- 59077 Carl Cotner - Bright Star/Do You Know Why
- 59078 Billy Watkins - Go Billy Go/The Good Times
- 9178 Rhythm Kings - The Soul/Border Town

DEL-FI LABEL
- LP 1232 - Sentinals - *Big Surf*
- LP 1241 - Sentinals - *Surfer Girl*
- LP 1234 - Impacts - *Wipe Out*
- LP 1239 - Dave Myers & Surftones - *Hangin' Twenty*
- LP 1228 - Centurians - *Surfer's Pajama Party*
- LP 1235 - V.A. - *KFWB's Battle of the Surfin' Bands* (includes Bruce Johnston, Lively Ones, Sentinals, Jim Waller & Deltas, Rhythm Kings, Dave Myers & Surftones, Soul Kings, Impacts, Challengers, Biscaynes, and Charades. Also printed as KEWB, KPOI.)

SHEPHERD LABEL
- LP 1300 - V.A. - *Surf War* (includes Dave Myers & Surftones, Centurians, Jim Waller & Deltas, Bob Vaught & Renegaids, and Impacts)

GNP LABEL
- LP 83 - Bob Vaught & Renegaids - *Surf Crazy*
- LP 84 - V.A. - *Original Surfin' Hits* (includes Sentinals, Rhythm Kings, Soul Kings, Jim Waller & Deltas, Bob Vaught & Renegaids, Breakers, Dave Myers & Surftones)
- LP 85 - V.A. - *Surf Battle* (includes Rhythm Kings, Dave Myers & Surftones, Lil' Ray)

GSP LABEL
- LP 6901 - V.A. - *George Sherwood Presents* (includes Surf Bunnies, Charades, Sentinals, Surfaris, Dave Kinzie, Breakers, Revels, Sanford & Sandies, Judy Russell, Gary Paxton)

ALMOR LABEL
- LP 108 - V.A. - *The World of Surfin'* (includes Dick Dale, Fireballs, Surfaris, Surfteens, Dimensions)

CALIFORNIA SURF INSTRUMENTALS
A Selective Discography

MISCELLANEOUS SURF-RELATED ALBUMS
(Instrumental & Vocal)

Adrian & Sunsets - *Breakthrough* -Sunset 601 (ex-Rumblers)
Aki Aleong & Nobles - *Come Surf With Me* - VJ 1060
Mike Adams & Red Jackets - *Surfers Beat* - Crown 312
Richie Allen & Pacific Surfers - *The Rising Surf* - Imperial 9229
Richie Allen - *Surfers Slide* - Imperial 9243
Astronauts - *Surfin' With* - RCA 2760
Astronauts - *Everything is A-Okay* - RCA 2782
Astronauts - *Competition Coupe* - RCA 2858
Astronauts - *Astronauts Orbit Campus* - RCA 2903
Astronauts - *For You—From Us* - RCA 3359
Astronauts - *Down the Line* - RCA 3454
Astronauts - *Travelin' Men* - RCA 3733
Astronauts - *Go.....Go.....Go!* - RCA 3307
Astronauts - *Rockin' With* - RCA PRM-183
Avalanches - *Ski Surfin'* - Warner Bros 1525
Blasters - *Sound of the Drags* - Crown 392
Al Casey - *Surfin' Hootenanny* - Stacy 100
Catalinas - *Fun Fun Fun* - RIC 1006
Challengers - *Surfbeat* - Vault 100
Challengers - *Surfin' With the Challengers* - Vault 101A
Challengers - *On the Move* - Vault 102
Challengers - *K-39* - Vault 107
Challengers - *Surf's Up* - Vault 109
Challengers - *Challengers A Go-Go* - Vault 110
Challengers - *Greatest Hits* - Vault 111
Challengers - *At the Teenage Fair* - GNP 2010
Challengers - *The Man From U.N.C.L.E.* - GNP 2018
Challengers - *California Kicks* - GNP 2025
Challengers - *& Billy Strange* - GNP 2030
Challengers - *Wipe Out* - GNP 2031
Challengers - *Light My Fire With Classical Gas* - GNP 2045
Challengers - *Vanilla Funk* - GNP 2056
Challengers - *Greatest Hits* - GNP 609
Challengers - *Go Sidewalk Surfin'* - Triumph 100
Challengers - *Where Were YOU in the Summer of '62?* - Fantasy 9443
Chantays - *Pipeline* - Dot 3516
Chantays - *Two Sides* - Dot 3771
Jerry Cole & Spacemen - *Outer Limits* - Capitol 2044
Jerry Cole & Spacemen - *Hot Rod Dance Party* - Capitol 2061
Jerry Cole & Spacemen - *Surf Age* - Capitol 2112
Cornells - *Beach Bound* - Garex 100
Calvin Cool & Surf-Knobs - *Surfer's Beat* - Charter 103
Dan Dailey - *Surf Stompin'* - Crown 314
Dartells - *Hot Pastrami* - Dot 3522
Deadly Ones - *It's Monster Surfing Time* - VJ 1090
Jim Waller & Deltas - *Surfin' Wild* - Arvee 432
Deuce Coupes - *The Shut Downs* - Crown 393
Duals - *Stick Shift* - Sue 2002
Fantastic Baggys - *Tell 'Em I'm Surfin'* - Imperial 12270
Johnny Fortune - *Soul Surfer* - Park Ave. 1301
Mr. Gasser & Weirdos - *Hot Rod Hootenanny* - Capitol 2010
Mr. Gasser & Weirdos - *Rods n' Ratfinks* - Capitol 2057
Mr. Gasser & Weirdos - *Sufink!* - Capitol 2114
Good Guys (Challengers) - *Sidewalk Surfing* - GNP 2001
Hondells - *Go Little Honda* - Mercury 20940
Hondells - *The Hondells* - Mercury
Hot Doggers - *Hot-Doggers* - Epic 24054
Hot Rodders - *Big Hot Rod* - Crown 378
Bruce Johnston - *Surfin' Round the World* - Columbia 8857
Knights - *Hot Rod High* - Capitol 2189
Jerry Kole & Strokers - *Hot Rod Alley* - Crown 5385
Kustom Kings - *Kustom City USA* - Smash 27051
Marketts - *Take to Wheels* - Warner Bros 1509
Marketts - *Out of Limits* - Warner Bros. 1537
Marketts - *Sun Power* - WB 1870
Marketts - *Surfing Scene*
Marketts - *Surfers Stomp* - Liberty 3226
Jim Messina & Jesters - *The Dragsters* - Audio Fidelity 7037
Mustangs - *Dartell Stomp* - Providence 001
Dave Myers Effect - *Greatest Racing Themes* - Carole 8002
New Dimensions - *Deuces and Eights* - Sutton 331
New Dimensions -*Surf'n'Bongos* - Sutton 332
New Dimensions - *Soul Surf* - Sutton 336
Persuaders - *Surfer's Nightmare* - Saturn 5000
Pyramids - *Penetration* - Best 1001
Bob Vaught & Renegaids - *Surf Crazy* - GNP 83
Revels - *On a Rampage* - Impact 1
Rhythm Rockers - *Soul Surfin'* - Challenge 617
Rincon Surfside Band - *Surfing Songbook* - Dunhill 50001
Rip Chords - *Three Window Coupe* - Columbia 9016
Rip Chords - *Hey Little Cobra* - Columbia 8951
Risers - *She's a Bad Motorcycle* - Imperial 9269
Rivieras - *California Sun* - USA 102
Rivieras - *Campus Party* - Riviera 701
Road RUnners - *The New Mustang* - London 5381
Rod & Cobras - *Drag Race at Surf City* - Somerset 20500
Ronny & Daytonas - *GTO* - Mala 4001
Ronny & Daytonas - *Sandy* - Mala 4002
Routers - *Let's Go* - Warner Bros. 1490
Routers - *1963's Great Instrumental Hits* - Warner Bros 1524
Routers - *Play the Chuck Berry Songbook* - W.B. 1595
Routers - *Super Bird* - Mercury 682
Rumblers - *Boss!* - Downey 1001 (also Dot 3509)
Sandells - *Scrambler!* - World-Pacific 1818
Sandals - *Endless Summer* - World Pacific 1832
Scramblers - *Cycle Psychos* - Crown 5384
Scramblers - *Little Honda* - Wyncote 9048
Sentinels - *Vegas-A-Go-Go* - Sutton 338
Silly Surfers - *Sounds Of* - Mercury 60977
Spinners - *Party—My Pad! After Surfin'* - Time 52092
Sunrays - *Andrea* - Tower 5017
Super Stocks - *Thunder Road* - Capitol 2060
SUper Stocks - *Surf Route 101* - Capitol 2113
Super Stocks - *School is a Drag* - Capitol 2190
John Severson (presents) - *Sunset Surf* - Capitol 1915
Surf Riders - *Surf Beat* - Vault 105
Surf Teens - *Surf Mania* - Sutton 339
Surfaris - *Wheels* - Diplomat 2309
Surfaris - *Wipe Out/Surfer Joe* - Dot 25535
Surfaris - *Play* - Decca 4470
Surfaris - *Hit City '64* - Decca 4487
Surfaris - *Fun City, USA* - Decca 4560
Surfaris - *Hit City '65* - Decca 4614
Surfaris - *It Ain't Me Babe* - Decca - 4683
Tides - *Surf City/Surfin' USA* - Wing 12265
Tokens - *Wheels* - RCA 2886
Tornadoes - *Bustin' Surfboards* - Josie 4005
Torques - *Zoom* - (local label, Princeton, NJ)
Trashmen - *Surfin' Bird* - Garrett
Wave Crests - *Surftime USA* - Viking 606
Wedges - *Hang Ten* - Time 2090
Weird-Ohs - *Sounds of the Silly Surfers* - Hairy 101
Burt Wheels & Speedsters - *Sounds of the Big Racers* - Coronet 216
Winners - *Checkered Flag* - Crown 5394
Woofers - *Dragsville* - Wyncote 9011
Zip-Codes - *Mustang!* - Liberty 3367

LATE ADDITIONS

Buddies - *Go-Go* - Wing 16306
Buddies - & Comets - Wing 16293
Competitors - *Little Deuce Coupe/409* - Dot 25542
De-Fenders - *Play the Big Ones* - World-Pacific 1810
Preston Epps - *Surfin' Bongos* - Original Sound 5009
Ghouls - *Dracula's Deuce* - Capitol 2215
Go-Gos - *Swim With* - RCA 2930
Kickstands - *Black Boots & Bikes* - Capitol 2078
Nep-Tunes - *Surfer's Holiday* - Family 552
Risers - *She's a Bad Motorcycle* - Imperial 9269
Squiddly Diddly - *Surfin' Surfari* - HBR 2043
Sunsets - *Surfing* - Palace 752

VARIOUS ARTIST SURFING ALBUMS

Beach Party - GSP 6901: Dave Kinzie, Kenny & Sultans, Surf Bunnies, Sentinals, Charades, Surfaris, Breakers, Revels, Sandford & Sandies, Judy Russell, Gary Paxton
Shake! Shout! & Soul - Impact 2: Dave Myers & Surftones, New Dimensions, Steve Korey, Surfaris, Lil Ray, Virtue Four
Surf's Up! at Banzai-Pipeline - Northridge 101: Soul Kings, Dave Myers & Surftones, Surfaris, Neal Nissenson, Jim Waller & Deltas, Dug Hume, Biscaynes, Bob Vaught & Renegaids, Bob Hafner (also issued on Reprise 6094, with the addition on side 2 of Surfaris, Coast Continentals
Surf War - Shepherd 1300: Dave Myers & Surftones, Jim Waller & Deltas, Centurians, Bob Vaught & Renegaids, Impacts
Original Surfing Hits - GNP 84: Sentinels, Rhythm Kings, Soul Kings, Jim Waller & Deltas, Breakers, Dave Myers & Surftones
Surf Battle! - GNP 85: Rhythm Kings, Dave Myers & Surftones
Hot Rod City - Vault 104: Grand Prix, Customs, Quads
Hot Rod Rally - Capitol 1997: Super Stocks, Roger Christian, Steve Douglas
Oldies, Goodies & Woodies - Vault 103: Busy Bodies, Beach Girls, Tom Starr & Galaxies, Challengers, Gladiators, Vibrants
Battle of the Bands - Star 101 (Hawaii) Frolic Five, Rivals, Lepricons, Escort, Arcades, Duplex, Thunderbird, Kona Casuals, Statics, Renegades, Raiders, Dimensions, Impacts, Majestics, Star Lighters, Checkmates, Adventures, Sensations, Royal Malads, Infasions
Shut Down - Capitol 1918
Surfing's Greatest Hits - Capitol 1995
Draggin' and Surfin' - Modern Sound 536
Dick Dale, Surfaris, Fireballs - Almor 109
My Son the Surf Nut - Capitol 1939

DEL-FI ALBUMS

1226 Lively Ones - *Surf Rider*
1228 Bruce Johnston Surfing Band - *Surfer's Pajama Party*
1228 Centurians - *Surfers Pajama Party*
1231 Lively Ones - *Surf Drums*
1232 Sentinals - *Big Surf*
1234 Impacts - *Wipe Out*
1235 V.A. - *KFWB's Battle of the Surfing Bands*
1236 Surf Stompers - *The Original Surfer Stomp*
1237 Lively Ones - *Surf City*
1238 Lively Ones - Great Surf Hits
1239 Dave Myers & Surftones - *Hangin' Twenty*
1240 Lively Ones & Surf Mariachis - *Surfin' South of the Border*
1241 Sentinals - *Surfer Girl*
1242 De-fenders - *Drag Beat*
1243 Deuce Coupes - *Hotrodders' Choice*
1244 Darts - *Hollywood Drag*

LIBERTY ALBUMS - "Action SOund Series"

7346 T-Bones - *Boss Drag*
7348 Hornets (Jerry Cole) - *Motorcycles U.S.A.*
7363 T-Bones - *Boss Drag at the Beach*
7364 Hornets (Jerry Cole) - *Bg Drag Boats U.S.A.*
7365 V.A. - *Shut Downs and Hill Climbs*

MISCELLANEOUS SURF-RELATED SINGLES
(Instrumental only)

DOWNEY RECORDS

101 Pastel Six - Twitchin'/Wino Stomp
101 Pastel Six - Open House at the Cinder/Twitchin'
102
103 Rumblers - Boss/I Don't Need You No More (also Dot 16421)
104 Chantays - Pipeline/Move It (also Dot 16440)
105
106 Rumblers - Boss Strikes Back/Sorry (also Dot 16455)
107 Rumblers - Angry Sea(Waimea)/Bugged (also Dot 16480)
108 Chantays - Monsoon/Scotch High's
109
110 Ginny & Gallions - Hava Nagila/pt 2
111 Rumblers - It's a Gass/Tootenanny (also Dot 18292)
112
113
114 Rumblers - Night Scene/High Octane
115 Jessie Hill - Chip Chop/Woodshed
116 Chantays - Space Probe/Continental Missile
117
118 Hustlers - Inertia/Eight Ball
119 Rumblers - Riot in Cell Block #9/The Hustler
120 Chantays - Only If You Care/Love Can Be Cruel
121 Richard Ward & Hustlers - The Well of Loneliness/Topless Bathing Suit
122 Pat & Californians - Be Billy/Bad
123 Revels - Intoxica/Commanche
124 Jessie Hill - Never Thought/T.V. Guide
125
126 Chantays - Beyond/I'll Be Back Someday
127 Rumblers - Soulful Jerk/Hey-Did-a-Da-Da
128
129 Sunday Group - Edge of Nowhere/Pink Grapes
130
131 Sir Frog & Toads - The Frog/Mustang
132 Margaret Williams - My Love/Baby Please
133 Rumblers - Boss Soul/Till Always
134
135 Slipped Discs - Smokey Places/If I Had Your Love
136
137
138
139 Pat Powdrill - I Can't Hear You/Do It

ADEN RECORDS
(Downey subsidiary)

101 Riviares - The Bug/Mocolotion

X-P-A-N-D-E-D SOUND RECORDS
(Downey subsidiary)

101
102 Kicks - Tell Me Why/Oh My Baby
103 Leaping Ferns(Chantays)-It NeverWorks OutForMe/Mavbe Baby

AERTAUN RECORDS

100 Tornadoes - Bustin' Surfboards/Beyond the Surf
101 Hollywood Tornadoes - The Gremmie/pt.2
102
103 Tornados - Phantom Surfer/Lightnin'
103 Tornados - Phantom Surfer/Shootin' Beavers

ARLEN RECORDS

506 Sonny Gee & Standels - Tidal Wave/Ingrid
509 Dartells - Hot Pastrami/Dartell Stomp
511 Custons - Because of Love/Earthquake
513 Dartells - The Scoobie Song/Dance,Everybody,Dance
514 Billy & Fleet - Power Shift/Nobody Wants to Give Me What I Want
515 Larry Reed & Shado's- Little Miss Surfer/Bread n' Butter
516 Jeff Bradley - Little Bit of Heaven/Tired of Running
517 La Rays - A Woman Like You/Yesterday & You Around
1014 Lester Rose - Wino Blues/Alimony Blues

GOLIATH RECORDS

1348 Vulcanes - Stomp Sign/Public Record #1
1351 Leggeriors - Flame of Love/Justine
1352 Surf Bunnies - Surf Bunny Beach/Our Surfer Boys (also Dot 16523)
1353 Surf Bunnies - Surf City/Met the Boy I Adore
1355 Silvertones - Bathsheba/Get It
1357 Sea Shells - Love Those Beach Boys/Close to Jimmy

UNION RECORDS

501 Mar-Kets - Surfer's Stomp/Start
502 Denels - Here Come the Ho-Dads/Massacre Stomp
503
504 Marketts - Balboa Blue/Stompede
505 Continentals - Coffee House/Lord Douglas Byron - Big Bad Ho-Dad
506
507 Marketts - Canadian Sunset/Stompin' Room Only

LUCKY TOKEN RECORDS

107 Bel-Aires - Baggies/Charlie Chan
108 Resonics - I'm Really in Love/Think Right
112 Crossfires - One Potato Two Potato/That'll Be the Day
1003 Col. Splendid - Emperor Hudson/Blue-Eyed Blast
1006 Col. Splendid - Emperor Nelson/Cavendish Caper

VAULT RECORDS

900 Challengers - Torquay/Bulldog
901 Bruno & Gladiators - Istambul/Warm is the Sun
902 Challengers - Moondawg/Tidal Wave
903 Sonny Patterson & Pastel Six -Troubles/GoneSoLong
905 Beach Girls - He's My Surfin' Guy/
906 Grand Prix - Candy Apple Buggy/'41 Ford
907 Quads - Little Queenie/Surfin' Hearse
910 Challengers - Hot Rod Hootenanny/Maybelling
911 Travelers - She's Got the Blues/Spanish Moon (orig. on Princess 52)

(Plus many later, non-surf releases.....)

(turn to page 46)

The Weird World of BEATLE NOVELTIES

SURF INSTRUMENTALS

ASSORTED SURF INSTRUMENTALS (from page 10)
Alpines - Shush-Boomer/Skier's Melody - Challenge 59230
Aquanauts - Rumble on the Docks/Bombora - Safari 1005
Johnny Barakat&Vestells - Dell Star 103
Blue Bells - Atlantis/Moccasin - Last Chance 1
Baymen - Bonzai/Daybreak - Merri 6000
Bel Airs - Mr. Moto/Little Brown Jug - Arvee 5034
Bonnevilles - Bonnevilles Stomp/Knock Around - Question
Breakers-Kami-Kaze/Surf Breakers-Vrana 1001 Mark 103
Breakers - Say You're Mine/Once More - Moxie 103 (Tucson)
Buddies - Pulsebeat/The Beatle - Swan 4170
Busters - Bust Out/Austronauts - Arlen 735
Busters - All American Surfer/Pine Tree Hop - Arlen 740
Catalinas - Bail Out/Bulletin - Slmms 134
Catalinas - Safari/Pretty Little Nashville Girl - 20th 299
Challengers - Pipeline/Asphalt Spinner - Triumph DJ 1/2
 (also many on Vault)
Chan-Dells - Sand Surfer/Louie Louie - ARC 8101
Chevelles - Let There be Surf/Riptide - Chevelle 101
Clee Shays - Dynamite/Man from Uncle - Triumph 65
Conrad & Hurricane Strings - Hurricane/Sweet Love-Daytone
Cornells - Agua Caliente/Malibu Surf -Garex 102   6401
Cornells - Do the Slauson/Surf Fever - Garex 206
Chiyo & Crescents - Pink Dominos/Devil Surf-Breakout 3/4
Crescents - Pink Dominos/Breakout - Era 3116
Currents - Night Run/Riff Raff - Laurie 3205
Defiants - Surfer's Twist/Twistin n Stompin - Baronet 5
Denels - Here Come the HoDads/Massacre Stomp - Union 502
Diaboliques - Bubbles/Blackout - Merri 6005
Dave & Customs - Ali Baba/Shortnin Bread - DAC 500
Drag Kings - Nitro/Bearing Burners - UA 676
Du-Kanes - Our Star/Shock Treatment - HSH 501
Duvals - The Last Surfer/Roast - Prelude 110
Ebb Tides - Low Tide/Ballad of Jed Clampett - R&R 303
Ebbtones - Ram InductioN/Rockin' on the Range - Part 70026
Eddie & Showmen - Toes on the Nose/Border Town - Liberty 55566
Eddie & Showmen - We are the Young/Young & Lonely - Liberty 55720
Embers - Moonlight Surf/Little "D" Special - Moonglow 232
Emeralds - Little "D" Special/Search for Love - Riviera 714
Embers - I'm Goin' surfin'/Why am I so Blue - SUemi 4553 (TX)
Esquires - What a Burn/Flashin Red - Durco 1001
Fabulous Continentals - Undertow/Return to Me - CB 5003
Fairlanes - Surf Train/Lonely Weeksnds -Reprise 20213
Fender IV - Everybody Up/Malibu Run - Imperial 66098
Fender IV - You Better Tell Me Now - Imperial 66061
Johnny Fisher - Tan Dan/Every Time You Cty - Park Ave 125
Johnny Fortune - Surfers Trip/Soul Traveler - Park Ave 103
Johnny Fortune - Soul Surfer/Midnight Surf - Park Ave 110
Johnny Fortune - Dragster/Siboney - Park Ave 130
Frogmen - Underwater/Mad Rush - Candix 314
Frogmen - Seahorse Flats/Tioga - Scott 101
Gamblers - Moon Dawg/LSD 25 - World Pacific 815
Gestics - Invasion/Rockin' Fury - Surfer 114
Gene Gray & Stingrays - Surf Bunney/SurfersMood-Linda 110
Greenstreet - Moon Shot/Locust Raid - Corsair 400
Jimmy Hayes & Soul Surfers - Summer Surfin/Down to the Beach - Imperial 5986
Ray Holland - Surfboard Stag/My Summer Baby - Margo 101
Hong Kongs - Surfin in the China Sea/Popeye-Melody Mill 303
Hollywood Persuaders - Grunion Run/Tijuana - Orig.Sound 39
Hollywood Persuaders - Drums-a-go-go/Agua Caliente-OS 50
Hornets - Runt/Breakfast in Bed - Emerald 5014
Irridescents - Bali Ha'i/Swamp Nation - Hawk 4001
Jesters - Tiger Tail/Panther Pounce - Feature 101 (J.Messina)
Jimmy & Illusions - Undertow/Karen - Julynn 36
Joiairs - Count Line/Ralphie's Tune - Delmar 101

Hial King - Malibu Sunset/War-Path - MBK 104
Walt Lawrence - Cascade/Twilight Adrift - Hollywood Int. 2/3
Legends - Surf's Up/Dance with the Drummer Man-Doc Holiday 107
Lively Ones - Night & Day/Hey Scrounge - Smash 1880
Losers - Snake Eyes/Balboa Party - Parley 711
Manuel & Renegades - Woody Wagon/Surf Walk - Piper 7000
Manuel & Renegades - Rev Up/Trans Miss Yen - Piper 7001
Marksmen - Night Run/Scratch - Blue Horison 6052
Aston Martin & Moon Discs - Fallout/Moonbeat - Del Rio 230
Gerry McGee - Moonlight Surfin/Cajun Guitar - A&M 771
Jim Messina & Jesters-Breeze&l/StrangeMan-Audio Fid. 98
Moongooners - Moongoon Twist/Willie&HandJive-Esar 1007
Moongooners - Moongoon Stomp/The Long Trip - Candix 335
Jim Musil Combo - Grunion Run/North Beach - JayEmm 423
Dave Myers & Surftones-Let the Good Times Roll/Gear! - Wickwire 13008
Newport Nomads - Blue Mallard/Harem Belles - Prince 6304
Pagents - Big Daddy/Enchanted Surf - IKE 631
Patents - Jumpin In/Blue Surf - Hart-Van 127
Perfidians - WHiplash/La Paz - Husky 1
Piermen - Piermen Stomp/Nancy - Jesse 1000
Polaras - Cricket/Breaker - Pharos 100
Rancheros - Linda's Tune/Little Linda - Dot 16572
Rangers - Mogul Monster/Snow Skiing - Challenge 9196
Rangers - Justine/Reputation - Challenge 59239   59229
Revels - Six Pak/Good Grief - Lynn 1302, Swingin 620
Sam Eddy & Revels - Skip to My Lou/Lonely Walk - Dayco 702
Larry Reed & Shado's - Little Miss Surfer/Bread n Butter - Arlen 515
Rhythm Rockers - Foot Cruising/Get it On - Wipeout 102
Rhythm Rockers - Rendezvous Stomp/The Slide - Chall.9196
Rhythm Surfers - Big City Surfer/502 - Daytona 6301
Richie & Saxons - Bottom of the Barrel/Easy Now -Tip 1020
Road Runners - Quasimoto/Road RUnner - Felsted 8692
Rip Tides - Hanky Panky - Challenge 9062
Royals - Christmas Party/White Xmas - Vagabond 134
Royals - Surfin' Lagoon/Wild Safari - Vagabond 444
Sandals - 6 Pak/Endless Summer - WP 415, WP 77840
Sandells - Scrambler/Out Front - World Pacific 405
Sandells - Cloudy/House of PaintedGlass - WP 77867
Scuba Crowns - Scuba Dive/Concentration - Chall. 9204
Scavengers - Devil's Reef/Little Annie - Stars of Hollywood 1212
Sharks - Big Surf/Spookareno - Sapien 1003
Skyliters - Tidal Wave/Schroeder Walk - Scotte 2666
Sentinals - Tell Me/Hit the Road - Westco 14
Snow Men - Ski Storm/pt. 2 - Challenge 59227
Marlo Stewart - Sky Surfin/Rip Tide - Souvenir 102
Starfires - Billy's Blues/Chartreuse Caboose - Pama 117
Starfires - Space Needle/Jordan Stomp - Round 1016
Surfaris - Surfari/Bombora - Del-Fi 4219 (many others)
Jeff Hamman & Surf Teens - Moment of Truth/Moonshine - Westco 9 (Morro Bay, CA)
Surf Men - Malibu Run/El Toro - Titan 1727
Surfmen - Ghost Hop/Paradise Cove - Titan 1723
Surfers - Widget/Stompin at the Surfside - DRA 318
Temptations - Blue Surf/Egyptian Surf - P&L 1001
Torquays - Surfers Cry/Escondido - Gee Gee Cee 1009
Trademarks - Baha Ree Ba/pt. 2 - Jubal 91
Tuffs - Surfer Stomp/pt 2 - Dot 15304
Viceroys - Dartell Stomp/Granny Medley - Bolo 743
Vince & Waikiki Rumblers - Waikiki RUmble/Pacifica - Big Ben 1003
Vibrants - Scorpion/Wild Fire - Triumph 101
Vistas - Surfer's Minuet/Ghost Wave-Venpro 101,Rebel 77755
Wailers - We're Goin Surfin/Shakedown - Etiquette 6
White Caps - Fender Vender/Hi Roll - Blue River 201
Woody's - The Saints(Go Surfin In)/Red River Valley-Calif 304
Wow-Wows - Richmond Rally/Countdown - Titanic 59046
Charles Wright & Malibus - Latinia/Runky - Titanic 5003
Dave York - Let's Have a Beach Party/I Wanna Go Surfin - PKM 6700
Johnny "Z" - Midnight Beach Party/Beach Bum - Dore 667

BEATLE NOVELTY ADDS
CLIVE BALDWIN - Now It's Paul McCartney Stevie Wonder Alice Cooper Elton John - Mercury 73680
BEAGLES - Deep in the Heart of Texas - Era 3132
BEATLES - The Girl I Love - Quest 101
BOCKY & VISIONS - The Spirit of '64 - Philips 40224
CHUBBY CHECKER - Do the Freddie - Parkway 949
JIMMY CROSS - I Want My Baby Back - Tollie 9039
RONNY DAVIS - Let's Beetle in the Rocket - Sheridan 573
DEFENDERS - Beatles, We Want Our Girls Back — Now - Realm 001
JACK DORSEY BIG BAND - Ringo's Dog/March of the Gonks - Parkway 938
JERRY FOSTER - I Ain't No Beatle - Spar 30014
FOUR SISTERS - I Want Ringo for Christmas - Hermatage 822
KEITH GREEN - Sgt. Pepper's Epitaph - Happy Tiger
JOHNNY GUARNIER - To Kill a Beatle - Magnifique 18
DAVE HAMILTON - Beatle Walk - Fortune
CONNIE HOLIDAY - Mrs. James I'm Mrs. Brown's Daughter/ Old Friend - Capitol 5447
RUPERT HOLMES - I Don't Want to Hold Your Hand - Epic 50096
HOMER & JETHRO - I Want to Hold Your Hand/She Loves You - RCA 8345
CHRISTINE HUNTER - Santa, Bring Me Ringo - Roulette 4589
INNER CITY MISSION - Get Back John - Kama Sutra 510
JAPANESE BEATLES - The Beatle Song(Japanese Style)/pt2 Golden Crest 584
LENORE KING & TOMMY ANDERSON - The Beatles is Back (Yea Yea Yea) - Her Majesty 101
FRANKIE LEHMAN - A Long Days Fight - VJM Russ 4424
FREDDIE LENNON - That's My Life/Next Time You Feel Important - Jeden 792
LIVERPOOL LADS - Scowser City - Lloyds
AL MARTIN SIX - Baby Beatle Walk/Prego - Bell 605
ZEKE MULLINS - Beatle Fan/Worried Man - Timber
DICK PILLAR & ORCH - Beatle Song/Johnny's Polka - Steljo 602
REAL ORIGINAL BEETLES - The Beetle Song/pt 2 - Dot 16655
GARY RHAMY - Invasion of the Bagels
BILLY SHEARS & ALL-AMERICANS - Brother Paul/Message to Seymour - Silver Fox 12 + 1
TRACY STEELE - A Letter to Paul/Your Ring - Delaware 1705
JUDY STEWART & HER BEATLE BUDDIES - Who Can I Believe/I'll Take You Back Again - Diplomat 0101
TWILIGHTERS - My Beatle Haircut/Sweet Lips-Roulette4546

BEATLE NOVELTY ALBUMS
Louise Harrison Caldwell - *All About the Beatles* - Recar 2012
1966 American Tour - Beatle-Views 1966
Beatles Blast in Stadium - Audio Journal 1
The American Tour With Ed Rudy -Radio PulsebeatNews #11
1965 Talk Album - Radio Pulsebeat News #3
Al Fisher & Lou Marks - *It's a Beatle World* - Swan 514
A Hard Day's Night & Others - Wyncote 9037
Liverpools - *Beatle Mania in the USA* - Wyncote 9001
Liverpools - *The Hit Sounds From England* - Wyncote 9061
Weasels - *The Liverpool Beat* - Wing 12282
Buggs - *The Beetle Beat* - Coronet 212
Beat-A-Mania - Design 172
Schoolboys - *Beatle Mania* - Palace 778
The Original Liverpool Beat - 20th Century 3144
Bearcuts - *Beatlemania* - Somerset 20800
Liverpool Kids - *Beatle Mash* - Palace 777
Beats - *The Merseyside Sound* - Design 170 (same as above)
B.Brock & Sultans - *Do the Beetle* - Crown 399
Manchesters - *Beatlerama Vol. 2* - Diplomat 2310
Sparrows - *That Mersey Sound!* - Elkay 3009
Charles River Valley Boys - *Beatle Country* - Elektra 74006
Beatlerama Vol. 1 - Guest Star 2307 (also Diplomat 2307)
Ed Rudy - *Open End Album* (unverified)
Mersey Beats of Liverpool - *Mersey Hits* - Arc (Canadian)
Billy Pepper & Pepperpots - *Merseymania*

INTRODUC ROCK fea Q65, The Blue

The following article cannot by any stretch of the imagination be considered definitive. Call it an introduction of sorts. After all, my conception of Dutch rock up to a year or so ago wasn't much advanced over the average guy's notion that it was exemplified by "Tiptoe Through the Tulips", and that "Dutch" Holland was a cute name for a DJ. I remembered the hits from the "Dutch Invasion" of 1970, by the Shocking Blue, Tee Set, and George Baker Selection, and that was about it. But a growing fanaticism for the former group spurred me to investigate further, leading to the personal discovery of one of the most exciting mid-60's rock scenes anywhere.

As in Australia/New Zealand, Germany, and Scandinavia, Holland was heavily influenced by Merseybeat. There was also apparently a thriving Shadows-derived instrumental scene (Z.Z. & the Maskers, Willy & His Giants, the Jumping Jewels) previously and simultaneously, again as in other countries. Besides the usual British hit influences, a major catalyst was the arrival of the Scorpions. Like the Renegades and the Deejays in Scandinavia, the Scorpions were a British (Scottish?) band who struck out to Europe in search of greater fame and fortune. They had a smash hit in Holland and elsewhere in March 1965 with a Fendermen/Huey Smith-style version of "Hello Josephine" (similar to the Danish (?) Rockin' Ghosts' "Don't Ha Ha", another contemporary smash. Their album is full of Merseybeat/R&B standards like "Under the Boardwalk", "Rip It Up", "Not Fade Away" and good versions of "Some Other Guy" and "Ain't That Just Like Me," but also contains an early cover of "Gloria" and the mysterious European staple "Balla Balla," a nonsensical, almost bubblegum, dance tune once covered by Chubby Checker with ZZ & the Maskers (in Holland only) and originally a hit by the Rainbows (issued on both Epic and Jamie in the US, with Sam the Sham's "Ju Ju Hand" on the flip).

Anyway, the Scorpions' follow-ups (including the millionth rock update of "Greensleeves") weren't hits, but Dutch bands like the Jay Jays ("Bald Headed Woman") and the Phantoms ("I'll Go Crazy") had similar chartbusters (the Phantoms had a pretty good album as well).

Space limitations, lack of records, and/or relative mediocrity (take your choice) forbids more detailed coverage of these groups and others through the years, like the Shoes, the Rod-y-s (reportedly excellent), the Scamps, Bintangs, Rob Hoeke R&B group, the Swingin' Soul Machine, Tremors, Hunters, Clungels, Johnny & His Cellar Rockers (including Jan Akkerman of Focus fame—his first group), the In Crowd, the impressive Zipps, Cuby & the Blizzards (quite raucous in their early days), the Tee Set (also more of a Mod/punk band before their "Ma Belle Amie" days), Eddy Jones, the Haigs (pretty good), the Cats, Kannibal Komix, Earth & Fire, the Buffoons, F.J. King & Smash (who perpetrated the intriguing feat of recording Jr. Walker's "Pucker Up Buttercup" with organ, guitar, and *no* sax, an achievement comparable to cutting "96 Tears" without organ, or "Rockin' Pneumonia" *sans* piano, as the Shocking Blue actually dared on their first album), Boo & the Boo Boos, Sandy Coast (a long-lived and fairly good group whose version of the Small Faces' "Sorry She's Mine" is meritorious), or Linda van Dyck, whose "Stengun" is a marvelously tough gangster rocker.

A word should be devoted to the Golden Earrings, who date back to 1965 and have almost always been a high-quality band (hopefully we'll have a complete and long-overdue article on them in an upcoming issue). Their early hits ("Please Go", "That Day" and others) have a strong melodic Beatlish flavor, and their *Greatest Hits Vol. 1* compilation (Dutch, but available through Jem, etc.) is highly recommended.

A minor group of interest are Les Baroques, whose "Such a Cad" was a hit in April 1966. The record, true to the group's name, is an odd combination of baroque and garage-rock, woodwinds mingling with fuzz guitar and a smarmy vocal which reminds me of the nasal Changin' Times. Good disk, as is the pretty flip side, "Summerbeach." A follow-up, "I Know" followed the same stylistic guidelines but sounds less inspired;

Ken Barnes

WHO PUT THE BOMP

...TION TO DUTCH
...uring The Outsiders,
...Motions, & Shocking

however a later record, "Love is the Sun" is a classic flower-power item. Limned as a dream "in the land of love", it contains references to flowers and San Francisco and all, plus lines like "Burnt banana, it was lots of fun" and "Yellow, red and purple/Let me in their circle." Attractive tune too, and a real mindblower.

Aside from Merseybeat again, one of the strongest influences on Dutch rock was the Pretty Things. Much bigger in Holland than in England, with "Road Runner" a major hit (it wasn't even a single elsewhere), their Bo Diddley beat, shrill harmonies and raw vocals were adapted by the best Dutch bands with astonishing fervor. "Don't Bring Me Down" seemed to be the primary stylistic model—"You Mistreat Me" by the Outsiders, one of my three favorite mid-60's Dutch groups, is a dead ringer. It's an early track, found on a compilation album called *Outsiders or Insiders* with three other first-rate tunes, including another Pretty Things-type called "Feel Like I Wanted to Cry."

These were early singles; the group later moved to the Relax label and had at least five big hits, all of which are on an album called *Story 16* or another, *Songbook*. They retained vestiges of their raw rocking days, in brilliant ravers like "That's Your Problem and "Thinking About Today," but were mutating towards a softer sound. The hit "Touch" is a bridge of sorts, with that Pretty Things harp mingled with delicate, romantic interludes; a superb single. "Lying All the Time" is a fine Byrds-style number, and "Summer Is Here" sounds something like what you'd imagine the Gene Clark Group of 1966 (which never recorded) would have turned out. Both of these were hits, but others ("Monkey On Your Back", "Summer is Here") were a trifle anemic. Still, *Story 16* is an indispensable album—the Outsiders at their best were brilliant.

Just as good were Q65, a quintet presumably formed in 1965. Their first hit was "You're the Victor" in February, 1966, another tremendous "Don't Bring Me Down" variant. They had four other chart hits through 1967, but probably gained even more fame from their album *Revolution*, apparently the classic party album of the era and the first homegrown LP to make a significant impact. It's led off by another big hit, "The Life I Live," a brooding rocker with the atmosphere of the Shadows of Knight's great "Bad Little Woman" (originally a British release by the Wheels, actually) and similar vocals, too, courtesy of Willem Dieler, perhaps Holland's top rock singer of the time. There are more powerful originals, like "I Got Nightmares" and "Sour Wine," and a number of blues-rockers, including a masterfully crude "Spoonful", "I'm a Man", and "Down at the Bottom." It's topped off by a 13:45 version of "Bring It On Home", not the Sam Cooke song but a Willie Dixon tune learned from a Sonny Boy Williamson rendition. The performance is a classic in the extended, post-"Goin' Home" genre, and most of it holds up well.

Revolution obviously deserved its landmark status, but even better in terms of playability is *Q65's Greatest Hits*, covering 1966-69. "Life I Live" and "Victor" are included, with other hits like the melodic "From Above" and the slightly-languid "World of Birds." "I Despise You"/"Ann" was a double-sided hit, the B-side a charming ballad and the top deck yet another killer rocker, with stinging guitar and an impact comparable to the best American rockers of 1966. "Ridin' On a Slow Train," a later track, is spectacularly haunting with intonations and intimations of the Velvet Underground, while "I Was Young" pulses with more Shadows of Knight feedback. There are a few lesser numbers, but there's also Q65's all-time classic, "Cry in the Night" (B-side of "The Life I Live"). With a Shadows of Knight vocal, this storming rocker is, with one exception, the best Dutch record I've heard and qualifies for the uppermost echelons in world-class ranks.

Q65 split in 1969 or so, came back in 1970 for a couple albums and at least one reasonably good single, "I Just Can't Wait." Another breakup, a partial reformation as Kjoo, and further fissionings followed but a legendary reputation has endured.

The last early Dutch titans in my trinity were the Motions, a quartet featuring Rob van Leeuwen (later to form the Shocking Blue) as guitarist and chief composer. While many Dutch bands were fearfully under-recorded (especially bass), the Outsiders foremost among them, the Motions had a ferocious, diamond-hard instrumental sound, raw like the Pretty Things-influenced bands but considerably heavier, akin to the early Who. Many of their songs, paradoxically, were light and melodic, so often there was an odd effect not unlike a heavy Searchers—difficult to define but most attractive.

"It's Gone", the first Motions single (I think), features that light-melody/heavy-instrumental dichotomy, and is an electrifying record. The follow-up, "You Bother Me", is even heavier, inspiring possible comparisons to Ron Wood's Birds, and its flip, "We Fell In Love" is a mostly-instrumental number reminiscent of the Searchers' "Someday We're Gonna Love Again" (but again, heavier). An odd stylistic shift marked the third release; "Wasted Words" is a naive, pessimistic protest number about American civil rights, with a light, appealing folk tune. Its flip, "I'll Follow the Sun," is a folky plaint done better by the Shocking Blue later, but not much to speak of on any account.

Their first album, *Introducing the Motions*, is a knockout. "You Bother Me" and "It's Gone" are represented, plus prime cuts like "Love Won't Stop" (resembling hard-rock Everlys), "Be the Woman I Need" (Pretty Things-ish), and "I've Waited So Long" (Mojos-style). Three highly melodic originals also sparkle, and the LP is, yet again, indispensable.

Yet the Motions topped it on their next single. The A-side, "There's No Place to Hide" is an American composition which sounded very English, like a good Mindbenders record. But the B-side, "Everything (That's Mine)" is a mad Who/Creation-style raver, with an impassioned vocal, thunderous backing and a fabulous feedback break straight out of "Anyway Anyhow Anywhere"—*the* most stunning individual Dutch record (the picture sleeve's total resemblance to the Who's American *My Generation* cover only adds to the impact).

The next pair of singles ("Why Don't You Take It" and "Every Step I Take") epitomized the Motions' light/heavy juxtapositions, and are very strong. Van Leeuwen got production credits for the following disk, a well-produced cover of the Four Tops' "Same Old Song" which was a sizable hit but a qualitative comedown (December 1966). Shortly afterward van Leeuwen departed, but the Motions persevered. The first post-van Leeuwen record I have, "I Want You I Need You," is marred by horns but is a creditable pounding beat number not unlike the Equals. Then they hooked up with British producer/writer Peter Lee Stirling (now Daniel Boone) for a delightful flower-pop ditty called "Nellie the Horse" and a last-gasp psychedelic hard-rocker, "Make It Legal," which is one of their best. My last Dutch single, "Try to Make You Happy" is horn-ridden and only fair.

The Motions had four Dutch albums (two were compilations of hits). *Motions Songbook*, the only one I've heard besides *Introducing*, has singles spanning the early days ("Wasted Words") and, mostly, the post-van Leeuwen period (including a solo single by singer Rudy Bennett). It's chiefly notable for interviews in Dutch with the group and in English with Stirling, and for a real oddity, the MC5's "Ramblin' Rose." The motions also had one album released on American Philips, *Electric Baby*, only intermittently interesting.

Back to Robby van Leeuwen. He formeed Shocking Blue in 1967 sometime, with the initial single, the pleasant rocker "Love is in the Air", failing to hit. Lead singer at the time was a male vocalist, unnamed on the first album. It's quite a mystery to me actually, since my copy is actually autographed—by the other three members of the group. Interestingly, Barry Hay, an Englishman later to become Golden Earring's lead singer, co-wrote two of the tracks, and someone named Dimitri co-wrote three. Information, anyone?

Anyway, the first album is quite weak considering van Leeuwen's work with the Motions and subsequent Shocking Blue recordings. At first I thought it was perfectly dismal, but later listenings revealed it's really a pleasant '67-68 rock album, but without significant impact and rather lightly recorded. There's a lot of American influence;they do the recycled folk song "Little Maggie" (first of several van Leeuwen was to adapt), the previously-cited "Rockin' Pneumonia", a creditable "That's All Right Mama" and a little Dutch rockabilly with Gene Vincent's "Hold Me Hug Me Rock Me" (not too hot, actually).

The difference between the first album and "Venus," released in July 1969, is staggering. The loose, rambling feel of the album gave way to a crisp, economical tightness on this classic radio rocker. It's a brilliant rock track, and the alien, mechanical vocal of Mariska Veres (at the time, I didn't know the singer was a girl for months) adds the final chilling touches. "Venus" hit in Holland and Europe through late '69, and hit #1 in America in early 1970. (The flip, "Hot Sand" is a non-LP track and a neat rocker).

"Mighty Joe" followed, again huge in Europe and Top 50 here, a deliberate, mesmerizing number with a savage chorus, but not quite up to "Venus" standards. The next American single, "Long and Lonesome Road," was a pulsating rocker with all the hit's successful elements, but sadly not a hit itself.

"Venus" justified the release of an American album by Colossus Records (an MGM affiliate run by longtime producer Jerry Ross, who'd also snapped up the Tee Set, George Baker Selection, and Kannibal Komix, with albums by each), their one and only. Like all their albums, it's spotty, with a trendy/boring sitar instrumental, a track spoiled by both sitar and atrocious horns ("Butterfly & I"), and other dispensables ("Poor Boy" for half its length is a modal instrumental straight out of San Francisco's second division, and sounds like It's A Beautiful Day on the other half—yet is still not unpleasant in certain moods, as when staring at old Fillmore posters and smoking incense).

Nonetheless, it's a (you guessed it) indispensable album, for the three singles discussed above, for their idiosyncratic hard-rock "Bool Weevil," for the super-kinetic break in the "Venus"-like "California Here I Come," and for "Send Me a Postcard," an explosive, viciously powerful, speedy hard-rock gem which tops the set.

As far as I can tell, the next Dutch album was *Scorpio's Dance*, partially recorded in New York in 1970. There's a lot of mystical piffle on the LP, and van Leeuwen again gives way to his unfortunate weakness for sitar drones, but the last three tracks pick up, especially "Keep It If You Want It" and "Water Boy."

The third album, titled *3rd LP*, came out in early 1971, has a couple fine singles, the old Motions song "I'll Follow the Sun", some more average material and two new standouts. "I Saw Your Face," not written by van Leeuwen but sung by him, is a mysterious modal drone with neat harmonies and good guitar work. "The Bird of Paradise" ("flew up on my nose") bears no discernible relation to Little Jimmy Dickens, but is a brooding rocker with a marvelous guitar tone to it. A solid improvement.

The last album I have, *Eve and the Apple*, from late 1972, is the most concise and consistent—12 songs all 3 minutes or under. Highlights, besides two singles (to be discussed later), are the rocking "The Devil and the Angel," Robby's "Don't Let Your Right Hand Know," a 2:05 raver, and "Broken Heart," with electrifying guitar chords. About other albums, there's one recent LP called *Good Times* (I think without van Leeuwen, who reportedly left in 1974)), a live package, an LP called *Inkpot* from 1972, and a greatest hits collection, none of which (except the latter) I've heard. Maybe others, too.

But albums were never the Shocking Blue's real strong point. It was as a singles group that they excelled—certainly "Venus" approaches 45 perfection, and several others are in the same league. Their achievements were all the more to be treasured when considered against the backdrop of their era—1969-1971 was a deathly time for singles groups. The hitmakers of the immediate past either faded or spaced out their releases (in more ways than one), and new acts either didn't try or weren't allowed (by restrictive radio policies) to fill the gap, Creedence Clearwater Revival of course excepted. Shocking Blue maintained their hit string only in Holland, but the quality of their singles was uniformly high, and they deserve the warmest accolades.

In America they followed "Long & Lonesome Road" with "Never Marry a Railroad Man" in early 1971. On the lighter side, pretty but still rocking, it did nothing here;likewise "Bool Weevil", the followup. Buddah somehow got into the picture, and issued a track off the third album, "Serenade," a mystic all-is-one routine but very appealing. It was never a Dutch single and might as well not have been an American one for all the action it aroused. And that was it, save for three MGM and Polydor pickups from their international parent company in 1972-73.

Dutch singles were legion, and I'm quite sure I won't be covering them all. At any rate, "Hello Darkness" probably dates from 1970, slow and bluesy but melodic with a great heavy Duane Eddy guitar tone.

Its flip, "Pickin' Tomatoes," a subject of universal concern, is even more attractive, especially its guitar line, and ranks as one of the best.

"Shocking You" is on the third album, and is a theme song of sorts ("We're shocking you until you turn to blue"). It starts out like the Leaves' "Too Many People" crossed with "Bits & Pieces," and proceeds into hard-rock high gear. The flip, "Waterloo" is notable for a midway "Do It Again" ripoff, but is overall an affecting slow number (no relation to Abba). "Blossom Lady" was a hit in Autumn 1971; it's very simple and straightforward pop, not a raving rocker, but somehow appealing far beyond its intrinsic qualities. "Is It a Dream" on the back side is mysterious, opens with heavy breathing, and is one of the group's most compelling songs ever.

"Out of Sight Out of Mind" continued the band's blithe new pop direction, was a hit again, and reminds me a bit of Abba; an irresistible song. A curiosity on the flip, an unadorned, rather girl-groupish ditty called "I Like You", quite charming. "Inkpot" followed shortly, a chunky tune full of "shoobie doowah"'s and thoroughly hypnotic despite one of the less inspired erotic metaphors extant ("put the ink in the inkpot").

My chronology gets shaky here, but I think the next single was "Eve and the Apple" from the album of the same name. It returned the group to rock, a relentless pounder in the "Venus"/"Long & Lonesome Road" mold. Fairly dismal B-side, though ("When I Was a Girl", not on the LP). "Rock in the Sea" was on the album, another of van Leeuwen's folk adaptations (the verse quoted by Greil Marcus in his *Basement Tapes* liner notes, about the mole in the ground tearing the mountain down, is present). It's a simple sing-along affair, but oddly enchanting, plus it has the album's best (or close to it) track on the flip, "Broken Heart."

"Oh Lord" came out in early 1973 or thereabouts, sounding much like "Iko Iko" with an added Bo Diddley beat and a fine vocal, a topnotch single once again. Flip was yet *another* van Leeuwen folk update, this time the blues "In My Time of Dying", most familiar to rock audiences as performed by Dylan and Led Zeppelin. This one's a good ominous version. MGM in the States coupled "Inkpot" and "Oh Lord" as a '73 release, this after releasing "Eve & the Apple" intact in late 1972.

"Let Me Carry Your Bag" was overly melodramatic, insufficiently tuneful and one of their worst, but was released at the end of 1973 by Polydor, the last US Shocking Blue release. "I Saw You In June," the flip, was unimpressive as well. The last van Leeuwen single I have is a 1974 release called "Dream On Dreamer." It's a big improvement on "Bag", a simple melodic, hook-filled rocker, with a stately, attractive B-side called "Where the Pick-Nick Was."

The last two singles were co-produced with Fred Haayen of Golden Earring fame. The next one (if my time-sense hasn't evaporated) does not seem to feature van Leeuwen anywhere, but is produced by Rudy Bennett, the Motions' ex-lead singer. In keeping with the old-home-week atmosphere, the B-side, a mostly excellent tune called "Come My Way" with a driving old Small Faces intro, was written by one M. van Dijk, who also wrote Les Baroques' "Love is the Sun." The A-side, interestingly, is that often-cut Vanda—Young rocker "Good Times" ("Gonna Have a Good Time"). Shocking Blue render one of the best performances, a strong rocking vocal. It's the most recent of many versions of the never-hit song, at least until Paul Revere & the Raiders put it out in mid-1975 (flip of "Your Love.").

And that's where it stands—van Leeuwen almost certainly out of the band (wonder what he's doing.....), Mariska Veres still leading them, and their current activities unknown. In any case, lovers of simple, concise rock & roll are sure to wax ecstatic over these wonderful records, and the Shocking Blue should garner some sort of recognition for their accomplishments.

I hope to be able to write more about the Dutch rock scene, surely one of the most exciting, as more data comes in—all info is eagerly sought, naturally. Let the above prolixities serve as an introduction, though, along with the following woefully incomplete but intriguing discography.

(turn page for listings)

• Two of Shocking Blue's later albums. Wish we could show 'em to you in color, but you can probably guess what the colors were.....

DISCOGRAPHY of Dutch Rock

(All records listed are Dutch releases except as noted.)

OUTSIDERS

	You Mistreat Me/Sun's Going Down -	Muziek Express 1003
	Felt Like I Wanted to Cry/I Love Her Still	Musiek Express 1006
7-66	Lying Sll the Time/Thinking About Today	Relax 45004
10-66	Keep on Trying/That's Your Problem	Relax 45006
12-66	Touch/Ballad of John B	Relax 45016
3-67	Monkey on Your Back/What's Wrong With You	Relax 45025
6-67	Summer is Here/Teach Me to Forget You	Relax 45048
	I've Been Loving You So Long/I'm Only Trying to Proof to Myself	
	..That I'm Not Like Everybody Else	Relax 45058
	Don't Worry About Me/Bird in a Cage	Relax 45068
	Strange Things are Happening/Cup of Hot Coffee	Relax

Outsiders - Relax 30007
Songbook - APLP 102
Story 16 - Imperial
CQ - Polydor 236 803

Q 65

2-66	You're the Victor/And Your Kind	Decca AT 10189
5-66	The Life I Live/Cry in the Night	Decca AT 10210
10-66	I Despise You/Ann	Decca AT 10224
1-67	From Above/I Was Young	Decca AT 10248
4-67	World of Birds/It Came to Me	Decca AT 10263
9-67	So High I've Been So Down I Must Fall/Where's the Key	Decca AT 10286
7-68	Ann/	Decca AT 10336
?-69	Sexy Legs/	
?-70	I Just Can't Wait/We're Gonna Make It	Negram NG 230

Revolution - Decca PL 625 363 - 10-66
Greatest Hits - Decca 6454 409 - 1969
Revival - Decca XBY 846515 - 4-69
Afghanistan - Negram NELP 075 - 1970

MOTIONS

3-65	It's Gone/I've Got Misery	Havoc SH 105
6-65	You Bother Me/We Fell in Love	Havoc SH 107
9-65	For Another Man/	Havoc SH 108
11-65	Love Wont Stop/No Matter Where you Run	Havoc SH 110
12-65	Wasted Words/I Follow the Sun	Havoc SH 111
4-66	There's No Place to Hide/Everything (That's Mine)	Havoc SH 114
7-66	Why Don't You Take It/My Love is Growing	Havoc SH 116
10-66	Every Step I Take/Stop Your Crying	Havoc SH 121
12-66	It's the Same Old Song/Someday Child	Havoc SH 122
	I Want You I Need You/Suzie Baby	Havoc SH 130
	Nellie the Horse/Make It Legal	Havoc SH 137
	Tonight Will Be Stoned/One Million Red Balloons	Havoc SH 139
1-68	You're My Choice/Hey Conductorman	Havoc SH 142
4-68	Take Your Time/Make It Legal	Havoc SH 146
5-68	Miracle Man/Something	Decca AT 10.327
7-68	I Aint Got Time/Fantasy Club	Decca AT 10.337
12-68	Take the Fast Train/Hamburg City	Decca 10.361
3-69	It's Alright/Hey Everybody	Decca AT 10.374
4-69	Take the Fast Train	Negram NG 195
6-69	Freedom/What's Your Name — Little Boys Life	Decca AT 10.382; Philips 40624 (A)
	Nellie the Horse/Wonderful Impressions	

Every Step I Take/Hard Time Blues/Stop Your Crying/Everything (That's Mine)
  INT 18097-EP

(Rudy Bennett solo singles)

	How Can We Hang on to a Dream/Reason to Believe	Havoc SH 124
	Amy/Goodnight Sleep Tight	Havoc SH 129
	I'm So Proud	Havoc SH

Introduction to the Motions - Havoc HJH 2
Their Own Way - Havoc HLP 2
Motions Greatest Hits - Havoc HJH 136
Motions Songbook - Artist Promotion Teenbeat APLP 101
Electric Baby - Philips PHS 600-317 (A)
Live - Marble Arch 201

SHOCKING BLUE

?-67	Love is in the Air/	
	Lucy Brown is Back in Town/	
7-69	Venus/Hot Sand	Pink Elephant
12-69	Mighty Joe/	Pink Elephant
?-70	Hello Darkness/Pickin' Tomatoes	Pink Elephant 22.045
?-70	Never Marry a Railroad Man/	Pink Elephant
?-71	Shocking You/Waterloo	Pink Elephant 22.050
9-71	Blossom Lady/Is This a Dream	Pink Elephant 22.053
1-72	Out of Sight Out of Mind/I Like You	Pink Elephant 22.055
4-72	Inkpot/	Pink Elephant
9-72	Rock in the Sea/Broken Heart	Pink Elephant 22.059
11-72	Eve and the Apple/When I Was a Girl	Pink Elephant
?-73	Oh Lord/In My Time of Dying	Pink Elephant
10-73	Let Me Carry Your Bag/I Saw You in June	Pink Elephant
?-74	Dream On Dreamer/Where the Pick-Nick Was	Pink Elephant
?-74	Good Times/Come My Way	Pink Elephant 22.846
	Send Me a Postcard/Harley-Davidson	Pink Elephant
	Loveis in the Air/What You Gonna Do?	Polydor

At Home (Dutch/British equivalent to American LP, one different track) - Pink Elephant PELS 500 (Holland)/Penny Farthing PE 888.001 (England)
Scorpio's Dance - Pink Elephant PELS 510/Penny Farthing PE 877002

3rd Album - /Penny Farthing PE 877010 (called *Shocking You* in UK)
Eve and the Apple
Live
Good Times - Pink Elephant PE 877.069
Shocking Blue's Best - Pink Elephant 877.???/basically equivalent to *Hello Darkness*, Penny Farthing PE 888007
Inkpot - Pink Elephant/Penny Farthing PE 877018

(American releases)

12-69	Venus/Hot Sand	Colossus 108
3-70	Mighty Joe/I'm a Woman	Colossus 111
5-70	Long and Lonesome Road/Acka Ragh	Colossus 116
12-70	Never Marry a Railroad Man/Hear My Song*	Colossus 123
2-71	Bool Weevil/Long and Lonesome Road	Colossus 141
	The Butterfly and I/Acka Ragh/Send Me a Postcard	Colossus PB 1000†
10-71	Serenade	Buddah 258
11-72	Eve and the Apple/When I Was a Girl	MGM 14481
4-73	Inkpot/Oh Lord	MGM 14543
11-73	Let Me Carry Your Bag	Polydor 15084

*same track as "California Here I Come" on LP
†Special radio promotional EP

DELTA Label (affiliated with Decca/Negram/Havoc, somehow or other)
(prefix DS)

1158	Roek Williams & Fighting Cats - I'll Cry/Any Bad News
1158	Sandy Coast - Subject of My Thoughts/I'm A Fool
1167	Selfkick - Gosh I'm Your Woman/Blues for Strawinsky
1171	Roek Williams & Fighting Cats - Please Don't Go Away/Always
1172	Explosions - Explosion/10:32
1173	Sandy Coast - That Girl Was Mine/I Lost a Dream
1175	Triffits - Monkey Business/Stay
1179	White Comets - Tell Me Baby/Pretty Little Girl
1180	Tremors - Dont You Fret/Put Me Down
1183	N.V. Groep '65 - Pipe and Love Is It/Lost
1187	Selfkick - Zo is het trevalling/Blues for Us by Us
1189	Triks & Paramounts - Doe Maar Net Zoals Ik/Kam II Op Je Bouwe
1192	Sandy Coast - We'll Meet Again/Coming Home
1193	Roek Williams & Fighting Cats - Take your Time/Scarlet Ribbons
1194	Tee Set - Early in the Morning/Nothing can ever change this love
1197	Mokumbeat 5 - Trouw Nooit/Wat Scheel Je Nou
1204	Tee Set - Believe What I Say/Dont Mess With Cupid
1206	Ronnies - Boem Boem Is Ho/Dear In De Wildernis
1208	Insect - Pitch Me Out/Be Good and Go
1209	Roek Williams & Fighting Cats - I Dont Believe You/All My Dreams
1210	Sandy Coast-Sorry Shes Mine/Make Me Belong to You
1211	Prop - It's Too Late/A Bit of String
1216	Explosions - I Try to Find/Russian Love
1217	Hamlets - Looking in your Eyes/It's Autumn
1221	Hangmen - We're the Hangmen/Seasons
1227	Sandy Coast - Sing Before Breakfast
1232	Mokumbeat 5 - She was Gone/Apologize
1236	Rhythms - Girl I Left Behind Me/Sugar Blues
1237	Ronnie & Ronnies - Beasties/Suzy
1241	Peter & Blizzards - He Can Laugh/Foolish Inside
1243	Groovys - Stop, Get a Ticket/That's My Trouble Now
1245	Double Dutch - You're Out of Sight/Double Cross
1248	Wheels - Come on Down the Roof/I Despise You
1249	Hague Sound Boys - Whiter Shade of Pale/First Time
1254	Roek Williams & Fighting Cats - Jean Mr. Kellygan/Now You're Mine

ASSORTED DUTCH SINGLES, 1965-68

Adjeef - leek, I'm a Freak/Squafrech Leman Comes Back - Action 1003
Adam's Recital - Theres no place for Lonely People/NY City - Barclay
After Tea - Not just a Flower in your Hair/Time is Right - Decca AT 10.288
After Tea - We Will be There After Tea/Lemon Colored Honey Tree - Decca
After Tea - Snowflakes on Amsterdam/The Cotton Blossom Floating Palace Showboat - Decca
Alligators - I Feel Like Crying/I'm on the Run - Decca AT 10.243
Artificial Ear - Bolderman/Wietjes - Bust AB 003
Attention - I Must go on Without You/Change Your Mind - Decca AT 10.227
Attention - I Cant Help Myself/Picture Me, Fool! - Decca AT 10.277
Les Baroques - Sch a Cad/Summerbeach - Europhon P 5010
Les Baroques - I Know/She's Mine - Whamm PS 006
Les Baroques - I'll Send you to the Moon/Troubles - Wamm PS 008
Les Baroques - Working on a Tsjing-Tsjang/Dreammaker - Basart PS 011
Les Baroques - Bottle Party/Bread - Whamm PS 016
Les Baroques - Love is the Sun/Dreamed My Dreams Away - Wamm 022
Les Baroques - Indication/When You're Feelin Good - Whamm
Les Baroques - LP: *Barbarians with Love* - Whamm Int. PS 10.003
Eric Bender & Jets - Het Strandfast (hot rod record)
Bintangs - Riding on the L&M
Bintangs - Splendid Sight/$60 Boxx - Yep 1012
Bintangs - Pileworks/See Me Waiting Girl - Injection 61003
Bintangs - Please Do Listen/No Blame - CNR
Bintangs LP: *Blues on the Ceiling*
Blues Dimension - Think of Me/Emergency ggg - Havoc SH 131
Blues Dimension - You Cant Leave the Past Behind/End of the Battle - HJavoc SH 136
Blues Dmension - Like a Mistake Machine/Chains - Havoc
Blues Dimension - Baby I Need Your Lovin/Double Deal - Decca
Blues Group 5 - Come & See/But on the other hand Baby - CBS 2698
Budhi - Preacher/Embryo - Polydor S 1228
Buffoons - My World Fell Down/Tomorrow is another day - Imnperial 744
Buffoons - It's the End/Maria - Imperial
Bumble Bees - Maybe Someday/Girl of my Kind - Philips JF 333.677
Cats - What a Crazy Life/Hopelessly - Imperial 709
Cats - Viva l'amour/But Tomorrow - Imperial 726
Cats - Sure He's a Cat/Without your Love - Imperial 733
Cats - What the World is Coming to/How could I be so Blind - Imp. 759
Cats LP: *Cats as Can Can* - Imperial 8002
Chapter II - East of my Place/She sends me Away - Philips JF 333.616
Chapter II - We'll be Friends again/Heyday - Philips JF 333.676
Check - Let me be Happy/Free Time Spending - Tania
Clungels - Have you ever had the Blues/Do the Dog - Artone 25.452
Clungels - Someone Cried/Make Noise - CNR 61011
Condors - Tomorrow/It Was a Lie - RCA 47-9735
Condors - Set me Free/Wanted - Tania BG 6730
Coopers - Didn't I/Not a Bit - Philips JF 333.683
Counts - It's Allright/I Can't Go On - Polydor PS 1240
Counts - I Should be Better Off Without You/Stay With Me - Philips

(turn to page 37)

BLEIB ALIEN SIGHTED IN N. HOLLYWOOD!
"I am an alien..." ROKY ERICKSON TELLS OF MARTIAN TAKEOVER IN EXCLUSIVE BOMP INTERVIEW

"The beginning of this sounds really far out—like a spaceship takin' off or something......."

The voice at the mike stopped and the audience seemed rather stunned, or at least confused. The stage light focused on Roky Erickson (aka the Rev. Roger Roky Kynard Erickson) as he hit the first chords of "Red Temple Prayer (Two Headed Dog)." It sounded like an unholy sunthesis of Black Sabbath and "Gimme Shelter" at 115 decibels, when Erickson cut loose with lyrics that seemed to erupt and somehow keep pace with the hysterical tempo. "Two headed dog, two headed dog; I've been working in the Kremlin with a two headed dog," he screamed maniacally. That was enough for the few unsuspecting fans of the Thirteenth Floor Elevators, who had come merely expecting to see the Sir Douglas Quintet. By the time the song had ended, after some twenty outraged cowboys headed out the front door of the Palomino Club in North Hollywood, it was obvious to these devoted fans that Roky Erickson had returned from whatever limbo he'd been in since the Elevators disbanded.

To backtrack slightly, Roky's recent history is as follows. He's currently involved with a new group, known as BLEIB ALIEN. They've been together a few months, playing locally in clubs around Austin. Roky has composed a considerable amount of new material, and a 45 should be out by the time you read this. Doug Sahm has apparently played a key role in Roky's rehabilitation (so to speak). They've been friends for some time, and so has Craig Luckin of Tornado Management in San Francisco, who (at his own expense) paid for Roky to come to LA and join Sir Doug for three nights at the Palomino.

But there are still a lot of unanswered questions. Like, where has Roky been all these years? Where's Lelan Rogers? And what was the real story behind International Artists, the demented label that put out the four Elevators LPs, which have become some of the most avidly sought collectors items of the '70s?

To get the answers to these questions while I had the opportunity, I made an appointment to interview Roky, who eagerly consented to rap about the old times. Steve Besser and Howard Kromholtz, fellow Elevators fans, accompanied me to Roky's room, armed with their own set of questions. The following, in as unedited a state as possible, are Roky Erickson's answers.

BY GREG TURNER

ROKY ERICKSON MEDICAL HISTORY

Name: Roger Erickson
Born: July 15, 1947

2/22/69	Arrested for possession of marijuana
3/12/69	Sent to Austin State Hospital for examination
3/14/69	Erwin Taboada, M.D. certified Erickson as mentally ill: "Schizophrenia acute, undifferentiated"
5/23/69	Escaped from hospital
8/15/69	Arrested in Austin
7/29/69	Discharged from Austin State Hospital and transferred to Rusk State Hospital
10-8-69	Ruled insane 147th Judicial District, Court of Travis County, Texas
11/28/69	Ruled sane by Austin District Court, and released from hospital
7/7/72	Dr. J.A. Hunter at Rusk: "Patient was felt to be floridly psychotic at the time of his admission here— psychosis on a toxic basis, due to multiple drug abuse. After admission he had a number of frequent visitors, including his mother, his attorney, and his girl friend, along with members of his musical group. Following these visits his psychosis became much worse and we began to suspect his visitors were smuggling drugs to him... Erickson is legally sane, but I feel he still requires hospitalization for the welfare and protection of himself and others. J. Grady Baskin, M.D.: "Recommend dismissal from hospital."

"THE MARTIANS PLAN TO THROW A DANCE FOR ALL THE HUMAN RACE....."

GT: *Prior to formation of the Elevators, you were with the Spades, right?*
RE: Right.
GT: *What about the other members of the Elevators, were they with another band too?*
RE: Yeah...(long pause).....Lingsmen, Linksmen....I think....
GT: *How old were you when you were in the Spades?*
RE: Seventeen.
GT: *You were still in high school?*
RE: I quit high school and joined the Spades.
GT: *Did the Spades ever tour around Texas, or just play locally in Austin?*
RE: We were gonna tour; we thought we would make it big with this record [referring to "You're Gonna Miss Me"/"We Sell Soul"]. But it wasn't a hit; they played it on KROD but it didn't really go. Soon after that I joined the Elevators. But they didn't really push it. The manager of the Spades told me later, when the Elevators got busted, that I had gotten with the wrong crowd and that I should've stuck with the Spades.
GT: *How long was it before the Elevators got a recording contract?*
RE: About a year.
GT: *On all the albums except Bull of the Woods, Lelan Rogers is credited as producer. What exactly did he do? Besides owning the label, I mean....*
RE: He just... well, let's see, I dunno. He said he was a friend, but I don't know if he was because they never gave us any money for anything.
GT: *What was the first song you wrote with Tommy Hall [the lyricist on most of the Elevators' tunes]?*
RE: I think it was "Reverberation"...no, it was "Roller Coaster," then "Fire Engine." The way we wrote was, I'd have all these tunes and he'd take the ones he liked and put lyrics to 'em... "Slip Inside This House" was like that....
GT: *Did that song get a lot of airplay?*
RE: It gets airplay all the time on FM stations in Texas, still.
GT: *What groups or individuals have influenced you?*
RE: You know it's funny, I liked Led Zeppelin a lot and apparently Robert Plant said that he was influenced by me. Not that he copied anything of mine but, either he said he liked my singing or that y'know I would learn something from him and he would learn something from me.
SB: *Were the Elevators very close friends or just business associates?*
RE: [emphatically] We were VERY close friends. We lived in a world where there were no mistakes. Anything that was in our way, we could think it out and have a solution.
SB: *Would they ever gig if you weren't with them?*
RE: No. We'd never perform if anyone was absent.
GT: *Did Lelan ever give you trouble about performances?*
RE: No, he never did really. He'd say, "could you boys speed it up a little bit—we're payin' for the time" or something like that. And I'd say, "who is this *weird* man with the white hair?" He was weird looking, his head was red as a beet.
GT: *Did he rip off all his artists? all the other groups on the label like Lost & Found, Bubble Puppy, Power Plant, Red Krayola, etc.?*
RE: I Don't know, man. We certainly got ripped off. I don't know if it was Lelan, but *somebody* was responsible.
GT: *The story I've heard is that Lelan panicked when IA was headed toward bankruptcy, and at that time he gave all the label's rights to his lawyer. Now, supposedly, Lelan's living secluded on a farm with his mother. Nobody seems to know exactly where he is except for his brother, Kenny Rogers. But Kenny isn't talking.....*
SB: *To change the subject for a moment, I'd like to know about the liner notes on the back of your first album that supposedly explain the meaning of all the songs. That whole rap about Aristotle, etc. Who wrote it?*
RE: Tommy Hall.

GT: *Was he really serious with the explanations he gave?*
RE: Sure...Yeah, sure he was.....I didn't really agree with what he said about "You're Gonna Miss Me", though. I think it means "you are gonna miss a Martian E", that's what I was really aiming at. I've been pushed, or should I say rudely awakened, to believe that I am an alien...
GT: *From outer space??*
RE: Like from Mars, y'know... I've even had it notarized. A Notary Public had me swear it was true, so tht I wouldn't be threatened by anyone who would think I was an alien and trying to hide it, thereby making it illegal. So it's like it's not *my* decision, it's someone else saying they're sure of it....
GT: *How long have people believed you were an alien from Mars?*
RE: Well my mother and father believe it. And Doug's pretty sure of it. And I'm getting to be pretty sure of it...
GT: *But I'm still not exactly sure how all this ties in with "You're Gonna Miss Me".*
RE: Well, that song may have been an ESP from Mars, saying —it sounds far out, but just sayin'—"You're gonna miss a Martian E." Some kind of a message.... If I was an alien it would be a very terrifying thought to think that you'd miss knowing it. To me it would. I know so much about aliens, their minds, that if I didn't be one, didn't know one, I'd feel like I missed out on half my life.
GT: *Who was the leader of the Thirteenth Floor Elevators?*
RE: There was no leader... One time Dick Clark asked us who was the head of the band, and we said "we're *all* heads".....and his face turned so red!
HK: *You were on American Bandstand?*
RE: Yeah. We did "You're Gonna Miss Me."
SB: *Did you wear your cape?*
RE: And Paul Revere & the Raiders were there. I liked them, I liked some of their songs. There's one [stops to think]
HK: *"Kicks"?*
RE: Yeah, I think it was that one.
HK: *Do you listen to much of the new music that's popular today?*
RE: I don't really get a chance to. Our house burned down and took our record player with it.
GT: *How many times have you been busted?*
RE: Twice. The first time we got acquited and Tommy got probation. Second time I got sent away to the mental hospital. Three years. Y'see they were gonna send me to jail and I told them I was crazy... I told them I was seeing things on the wall and hearing voices so that they'd send me away, and they did. Y'know I was such a good actor, I'm as good an actor as I am a singer.
GT: *So then the whole time you faked it?*
RE: Yeah. You know Mick Jagger said "I'm always hearing voices on the street" and maybe that's what he meant: let him out... My lawyer said "Be sure and don't tell them you think Mick Jagger wrote you a song, otherwise they'd never let you out!"
GT: *Okay, enough of the past. For the record, what's the name of your new band?*
RE: BLEIB ALIEN.
GT: *How long have yhou been together?*
RE: It's been about a year, I guess. No, about half a year.
GT: *How many songs have you written since you were with the Elevators?*
RE: I've written about a hundred and seventy.
GT: *How many of these do BLEIB ALIEN perform?*
RE: Well, we do a song called "Starry Eyes." We do "Red Temple Prayer (Two Headed Dog)" and "Don't Slander Me" and "Don't Shake Me Lucifer" and "You're Gonna Miss Me". And we do "Song to Abe Lincoln", "Hide Behind the Sun", "I Am Her Hero, She Is My Heroin", "Are You Going to Bermuda", "Stand For the Fire Demon"...
GT: *Do you get requests from the audience for Elevators songs?*
RE: Yeah, but it's like when I was with the Elevators in the beginning, our audience would always request "Louie Louie". But when they heard *our* songs, they started requesting *them*. Now if they give us—BLEIB ALIEN—a chance to play our songs, they'll start requesting them also. Like they request "Two Headed Dog" and "Starry Eyes" all the time.
GT: *What exactly is the significance of the name, BLEIB ALIEN? Specifically BLEIB. What is it besides a scrambled spelling of BIBLE?*
RE: BLEIB is kinda like communication between God and the Devil... It's in the Bible, the word BLEIB is in the Bible, but I've never read what it means. I've got a new song that I've written, it's called "The Beast is Comin'" and it's really far out! It's a blues song and goes:
"The beast is comin' to your world
The beast is comin' to your world"

And it goes on and says how you'd be a beast too with fangs and everything!

• Mayo Thompson, mastermind of the Red Krayola.

The classic first Elevators LP

• Mayo Thompson's rare local solo album.

INTERNATIONAL ARTISTS

The International Artists label, based in Austin, Texas and owned by Lelan Rogers, is (along with Dunwich) the most important label to collectors of '60s punk. Asthetically, however, it has more in common with Chicory, in Colorado. Both labels had their quota of ordinary rock and country records, but seemed to specialize in a certain kind of dementia. In IA's case, a psychedelic vision of interplanetary profundity infected everything from the obviously-deranged 13th Floor Elevators to blues singers like Lightnin' Hopkins or hillbilly singers like Sonny Hall who fell under the weird spell of what was happening at IA. According to Chet Flippo (*PRM*, 2-74), this tendency to freak out (also seen in the Legendary Stardust Cowboy and many other Texas rockers of the '60s) stems from the traditionally repressive nature of Texan culture. That's as good an explanation as any, but it still falls short of accounting for some of the extremes of bizarreness that came out of Texas in this era.

We'll have a full report on the Texas punk scene in an upcoming issue. In general, however, the IA records stand above the rest of Texas rock, in a category uniquely their own. Besides the craziness, there was also a lot of merely great music on IA, in particular the Chayns, a greatly under-appreciated punk band whose version of the Strangeloves' "Night Time" is by far the best I've heard.

Further information on International Artists can be obtained from the International Aritsts Fan Club, c/o Greg Turner, 4857 Beeman Ave, N. Hollywood, CA 91607, and from Doug Hanners, whose fanzine *Not Fade Away* is devoted to Texas punk and the IA artists in particular.

SINGLES
101
102 Ray Brooks - You Done Me Wrong/Because You're a
103 Johnny Williams - Honey Child/Another Love Man
104 The She's - The Fool/Ah Gee! Maurie
105
106 Tom Harvey - So Ah In Ah Love/My Heart is There
107 13th Floor Elevators - You're Gonna Miss Me/Tried to
108 Sterling Damon - Rejected/My Last Letter Hide
109 Disciples of Shaftesbury - My Cup is Full/Times gone by
110 Thursday's Children - Air Conditioned Man/Dominoes
111 13th Floor Elevators - Reverberation/Fire Engine
112 Frankie & Johnny - Sweet Thang/Music Track - Times Gone By
113 13th Floor Elevators - Levitation/Before You Accuse Me
114 Chayns - Night Time/Live With the Moon
115
116 Billy Wade McKnight - I Need Your Lovin'/Trouble's Comin' On
117 Frankie & Johnny - Right String Baby/A Present of the Past
118
119 Chayns - There's Something Wrong/See it Thru'
120 Lost & Found - Forever Lasting Plastic Words/Every-
121 13th Floor Elevators - She Lives/Baby Blue body's Here
122 13th Floor Elevators - Slip Inside This House/Splash 1
123 Beauregard - Mama Never Taught Me How to Jelly Roll/Popcorn Popper
124 Rubayyat - If I Were a Carpenter/Ever Ever Land
125 Lost & Found - When Will You Come Through/Professor Black
126 13th Floor Elevators - I'm Gonna Love You Too/May the Circle Remain Unbroken
127 Lightnin' Hopkins - Baby Child/Mr. Charlie
128 Bubble Puppy - Hot Smoke & Sasafrass/Lonely
129 Endle St. Cloud in the Rain - Tell Me One More Time/Quest For Beauty
130 13th Floor Elevators - Livin' On/Scarlet and Gold
131 Sonny Hall - The Battle of the Moon/Poor Planet Earth
132
133 Bubble Puppy - Beginning/If I Had a Reason
134
135
136 Bubble Puppy - Days of Our Time/
137 Shayde - A Profitable Dream/Third Number
138 Bubble Puppy - What Do You See/
139 Endle - She Wears It Like a Badge/Laughter
140
141 Arnim & Hamilton - Pepperman/
142 Ginger Valley - Ginger/Country Life

ALBUMS
1 13th Floor Elevators - *Psychedelic Sounds Of*
2 Red Crayola - *Parable of the Arable Land*
3 Lost & Found - *Everybody's Here*
4 Golden Dawn - *Power Plant*
5 13th Floor Elevators - *Easter Everywhere*
6 Lightnin' Hopkins - *Free Form Patterns*
7 Red Krayola - *God Bless*
8 13th Floor Elevators - *Live*
9 13th Floor Elevators - *Bull of the Woods*
10 Bubble Puppy - *A Gathering of Promises*
11 Dave Allen - *Color Blind*
12 Endle St. Cloud - *Thank You All Very Much*

RELATED
Spades - You're Gonna Miss Me/We Sell Soul - Zero 10002
13th Floor Elevators - You're Gonna Miss Me/Tried to Hide - Contact
Demian - *Demian* - ABC 718
Beauregard - Sound Productions
Potter St. Cloud - *Potter St. Cloud* - Mediarts 41-7
Mayo Thompson - *Corky's Debt to His Father* - Texas Revolution 2270

• IA album #11, one of the hardest to find.

• IA album #6: Even Lightnin' Hopkins got a bit freaky...

• IA album #4 — more psychedelia.....

SOUNDS of the SIXTIES

Part Three: BOSTON & New England

A CONTINUING SERIES EXAMINING REGIONAL MUSIC SCENES OF THE MID-LATE SIXTIES. IN PARTS ONE AND TWO, WE COVERED SAN FRANCISCO AND MICHIGAN. NOW IT'S TIME TO LOOK AT

BOSSTOWN IN THE GLORY YEARS

A GENERAL SURVEY OF BOSTON ROCK

BY DAVID JOHNSON

IT ALL STARTED WITH THE REMAINS

In the beginning, there were the Remains. This premier Boston-Based group set a standard for New England that wasn't matched until the success of the J. Geils Band a half dozen years later. Bobby Hebb, composer of the pop standard "Sunny" and now a resident of Salem, Mass., recalls the Remains well from the 1966 tour when they both opened shows for the Beatles. "They were really good. I think they would have made it big if they hadn't broken up." But, as Hebb went on to say, a group's staying power is one of the vital ingredients of success, and Barry Tashian, Vern Miller and company had gone their separate ways even before the release of their first and only album.

•The Remains: N.D., Briggs, Vern & Barry.

The impact of the album, and the group's frequent live appearances prior to that, are significant forces in the development of New England rock. On the one hand was a bluesy-folksy tradition which remains a dominant motif on the New England musical landscape. On the other hand is the natural desire of almost every rock band of the '60s to copycat the new energy and power-rock which was being imported from Britain. By all recorded and written evidence, the Remains leaned heavily to the Anglo side of this picture; but it is important to note that one of the most powerful cuts on their album was the then-obscure Charlie Rich's "Lonely Weekends."

Another outstanding cut, "Don't Look Back," has a marvelous voice-over-drums-&-bass break that is as much gospel as anything else. So the Remains were, in what was to become a tradition in New England bands, eclectic. They took their music from many sources: country, black, English and what have you. The reverse side of this eclecticism was the debilitating trait of being simply derivative — that is, sopping up the sources, but failing to stamp any originality or character on them. This, as well as lack of musical maturity, may have been the fatal flaw in the much-heralded Bosstown Sound cooked up by MGM Records in 1968. The Remains had character. So has the J. Geils Band. Many lesser-known New England bands have also had character, while some of the better-known names failed badly to develop any recognizable musical style. Other bands or individual performers simply had staying power.

NORTH SHORE, SOUTH SHORE

Like Caesar's Gaul, the Boston-area rock scene of the early and mid Sixties was divided up into three parts: the South Shore, the city of Boston itself, and the North Shore. To get the picture geographically, Boston's South Shore is a string of suburbs extending 15-20 miles down from the city toward Cape Cod, while the North Shore stretches north of the city about the same distance. Both shores are mostly seacoast areas, with many small towns and a lot of history. Although small in territory relative to the rest of New England, these three areas were by far the biggest contributors to regional rock & roll.

Active on the South Shore at the Surf Nantasket Ballroom were the Rockin' Ramrods, who released singles under that name and finally made an album under the name Puff during the Bosstown period. The Ramrods reigned supreme in mainstream rock, receiving numerous plugs from Arnie Ginsberg on Boston's WMEX, and when the Rolling Stones first visited Boston in 1965, the Ramrods opened the show. At that time they were a four-man group clad in white Levis and matching jackets, with a repertoire based heavily on the Kingsmen.

While we are still speaking in geographical terms, it might be a good time to mention the Barbarians, because this group occupies a unique position, both musically and geographically, in the history of New England rock. Based as they were in Provincetown, the Barbarians' launching pad toward a brief but highly visible career was the outermost extremity of the Massachusetts peninsula called Cape Cod. And since Provincetown was the location of the state's only identifiable gay community in the mid-Sixties, the Barbarians' smash hit "Are You a Boy Or Are You a Girl?" carried a lot more overtones in the minds of New Englanders than it may have elsewhere. Regionally, the hit was heard as a direct reference to the Provincetown subculture, rather than as a punk discourse on the subject of long hair.

Regardless of the interpretation, "Are You a Boy?" remains *the* hit from New England during the Sixties; and if the Barbarians had been able to hold their act together for any length of time, their influence might have been substantial. As it was, local groups fell enough under their spell to attempt to do the follow-up hit, "Moulty," with a bent coat-hanger dangling in a grotesque imitation of the Barbarians' drummer's missing limb. Such was fame for a group from the far reaches of New England's seacoast — now back to the mainland.

The North Shore equivalent of the Ramrods was Teddy & the Pandas. That is, the Pandas occupied a similar popularity slot, but their approach leaned more toward punkish anarchy than matching-outfit mainstream. The group's self-penned "Sunnyside Up", a rude and arrogant song, became a sort of anthem for younger North Shore groups.

The group did finally produce an album, but as with the Remains, their best days were behind them when the album, *Basic Magnetism* was released. "Once Upon a Time" was a moderately successful single, but the flip, "Out the Window" was more typical of where the group was at. Again, a similarity to the Remains, whose hit "Diddy Wah Diddy" was not that representative of the bulk of their work. Group name-sake and lead guitarist Teddy Dewart is merely listed as guest artist on the Pandas' album, having renounced rock for college. Without Teddy, the group disintegrated fast.

As a sidelight to the Pandas' saga, bassist Bill Corelle of Beverly, Mass. has carried through a number of North Shore groups, and Pandas producer Bruce Patch did an independent album for one of them, Dr. Feelgood. Corelle told me at the time of the album's release in 1971 that he was hoping for a major company to pick up on it. This never came to pass, and Bill is now with another line-up of veteran North Shore rockers

called the Cleaner Brothers.

Recording success never came for one of the most interesting of the North Shore and regional rock groups, called variously Presence, Genesis and the Underground Garage. Signed to Atco in 1968, the group cut several potential album tracks at the Hit Factory in New York but was released from its contract after Jerry Schoenbaum (the group's angel at Atco) left the company to head up the American division of Polydor.

From the western part of Massachusetts came Bold, who made a brief debut in Boston in 1969 and later released an album which I have only glimpsed once. There was also the Ft. Mudge Memorial Dump, who recorded an album for Mercury and are best forgotten.

BOSSTOWN

This capsule survey of the suburbs clears the path for a consideration of Boston. Most infamously, Boston rock came to equal Bosstown. Ah, Bosstown..... Down the proverbial tube went the talents of such units as the Beacon Street Union, Ultimate Spinach, Ill Wind, Orpheus, Phluph (not to be confused with Puff), and, on the periphery, Eden's Children and Listening. Connie Devanney, who sang beautifully for Ill Wind, recalled the era well when she told me about a new, more stylish group she is in: "We're all a bunch of dropouts, really, from bands tht we hated. You know, Bosstown bands.... Ill Wind, Ultimate Spinach..... There were so many of us. We were almost interchangeable back then." They weren't interchangeable, really, at least for the many loyal fans who thought that Boston was becoming the new San Francisco.

The Beacon Street Union were the true punkers, with a lot of stage presence and one fine melodramatic album to their credit. The follow-up album, *A Clown Died in Marvin Gardens*, features the group's frenetic stage showpiece version of "Baby Please Don't Go." Out of this union of Boston University and Boston College students came bassist Wayne Ulaky, who later played (along with 3 other BSU members) with a one-album group called Eagle, and singer John Lincoln Wright, who is currently fronting New England's hottest country and western band, the Sourmash Boys.

The BSU were the best of the worst, so to speak. The New England bands of the Bosstown era simply didn't have the talent to compete successfully on the national market, and MGM lost a lot of money before realizing this. One excellent single was produced in this era ("I Can't Find the Time to Tell You" by Orpheus) and all the groups were capable of some exciting live sets. But it was the groups who avoided the Bosstown hype, for one reason or another, who eventually went on to the big time.

The best example is the Hallucinations. Maybe they simply weren't good enough back then (my esteemed friend Prof. Gerald Priesing tells me they were terrible in an early stage appearance in Boston), but charter members Peter Wolf and Stephen Bladd survived to form the nucleus of the J. Geils Band.

The Orphans, now known simply as Orphan, were ably managed by Peter Casperson, who used to run the group all over New England in order to keep them working. There should be a few Orphans singles kicking around, as they were regional hits in Maine and Rhode Island. Casperson now manages a classy musical stable, Castle Music, which includes Jonathan Edwards (who was lured to Boston from Ohio by rumors of Bosstown gold) and Martin Mull.

Lost in the shuffle somewhere was a group known as exactly that: The Lost. They had a reunion at the Boston Tea Party concert room in the late '60s, along with the Remains. They also had a legendary single, "Blue Velvet Gown." In their prime, they had certainly been among the best, as evidenced by this quote from budding Bosstown impresario Ray Paret in January, 1969:

"I came to Boston as a freshman at MIT," Ray told *Vibrations* magazine. "I was almost immediately involved in the music scene that was happening—the Remains and the Lost. I saw the Lost, one of the best groups around, go through wringers. Boston can destroy anything it creates." These words, spoken about an earlier Boston scene, proved all too prophetic in the cases of several Bosstown groups which Paret later managed.

CAMBRIDGE

Cambridge, across the Charles River from Boston, was always something of a separate scene, due to the influence of Harvard University and the Harvard Square mystique, which seemed to attract a lot of musicians (mostly folk) and some of the earliest of that questionable breed known as rock critics (the original *Crawdaddy!*, the first modern rock magazine, was born there). Strangely, the very inner sanctum of folk music, the Club 47, became a once-a-week home during the mid-60's for one of the area's only true punk-rock bands, the Trolls.

The Trolls' lead singer Tom Flanders graduated to the early Blues Project, and when he returned to Cambridge in late 1965 with the Al Kooper-Danny Kalb aggregation, he demonstrated a remarkable ability to do full Jagger-like splits on the Club 47's tiny stage. The Blues Project wasn't very well known at the time, so when Tom asked the audience if anyone remembered the Trolls, it was amazing that at least three out of the fifteen people there applauded in recognition. As a nod toward rock, the Blues Project then launched into the Searchers' hit, "Ain't That Just Like Me?" These Trolls, by the way, are not to be confused with the Chicago group on USA and ABC.

Little more in a rock vein was heard from the Cambridge side of the river until 1967, when two moderately successful groups broke up to form a third, which eventually made it onto record. The parent groups were Grass Menagerie and Streetchoir. Menagerie had been active in Boston, while Streetchoir was turning Harvard dances into mini-concerts as increasing numbers of the audience just stood and watched the musicians. The merger of the two groups was called Listening, with guitarist Peter Malick, who now plays a tasty lead for the James Montgomery Band, and organist Michael Tschudin, who had started his career by writing the music for a Harvard Hasty Pudding Club show.

This unusual combination of talents and ages (Malick was only 16 at the time) enjoyed one of its finest moments when Cream was delayed for several hours before appearing at Brandeis University in Waltham, Mass. Listening was called in at the last moment, Malick recalls, and the group managed to keep a packed auditorium relatively tranquil until the main event finally arrived at 2am.

Another Peter, Peter Ivers, had been the original front man for Streetchoir, playing a virtuoso harp, and he occasionally sat in with Listening. Ivers has since released two albums under his own name.

A final Harvard-based group from the same era was Bead Game, who used to borrow Listening's equipment to practice in a run-down building in East Cambridge. Never making it onto record, but appearing on national TV because of their show business connections, were the members of Central Park Zoo, which included Peter Gabel (son of the actor Martin Gabel) and Jonathan Cerf (son of Random House's former main man, Bennett Cerf).

COUNTRY ROOTS

While these city folk were busy exchanging personnel and equipment, Peter Rowan from westerly Wayland, Mass., was serving a country apprenticeship with bluegrass giant Bill Monroe in Nashville. Rowan soon brought his talents to bear on the Boston scene with Earth Opera and later Seatrain, and two younger brothers, Chris and Loren, signed with Columbia and were the subject of much press not so long ago. Back in Bosstown times, Loren had been part of a two-man group named after the family dog, Boswell. Peter Rowan reflected the country roots which frequently surfaced in New England and now represent almost the dominant strain. "I've always loved country music," Peter told me during the Seatrain years. "I heard it when I was a kid." Eric Lilljequist of the Orphans (now Orphan, as noted) was another Bostonian who says he felt the country influence while quite young.

A genuine country boy was the late Gram Parsons from Florida, who spent a semester at Harvard in 1965 before dropping out to join a succession of bands, notably the Byrds and Flying Burrito Brothers. In one of those bizarre musical connections which sometimes make keeping track of group scenes akin to tracing the genealogy of a family with multiple marriages, Barry Tashian of Remains fame returned to Boston in the spring of 1969 with a band called Flying Burrito Brothers East. Barry said he had permission to use the name because he had been jamming with the original Burritos on the West Coast. Any doubts about Barry's claim were put to rest with the release of Gram Parsons' first solo album, which featured Barry as a sideman. Perhaps it was Tashian who persuaded Gram to do the J. Geils Band's "Cry One More Time For You", a song totally out of character with the rest of that fine album.

BARBARIANS INVADE NEW YORK

by Trivia S. Tappe

Don't get nervous, it was only the Barbarians' group and they didn't really invade; they just went zapping around to places like Song Hits and Ondine.

"BLANGGG!!!"

And the Barbarians make - absolutely FORCE - all the people to get up and dance all night. But they don't like New York - think it's far behind Boston, the South and the West Coast musically - and they especially don't like playing club dates. During a break one Barbarian said to me, "See that guy? He's a millionaire, right?"

"Wrong. He's a menswear buyer on Seventh Avenue and he's in debt up to his ears." But he still wasn't convinced.

The Barbarians are from Massachusetts, and although their records - "What the New Breed Say," "Are You A Boy or a Girl?" - and the fact that their album is among the top ten in New England - mean they have to come to New York occasionally, they're really much happier in Bos'on and on the Cape.

GERARD JOSEPH CAUSI

At first glance you'd think The Barbarians are the most far-out group ever, particularly Moulty, who has longer-than-shoulder length hair. But they're not, in fact, they themselves say, "We hate beatniks. We hate hippy people, especially New York hippies who wear John Lennon hats and Benjamin Franklin bird glasses. We hate 14-year-old girls from the Bronx who go to the mod shops and say, 'What can we get that's English to walk around the Village in today?' And at eleven they have to take off their John Lennon hats and go home...."

They like: James Brown. Mitch Ryder. Cape Cod. The Beatles and Stones. The Spoonful. The M.F.Q. The Remains. Room Service - and four single rooms ("Yeah!"). Walker's Riding Apparel in Boston, where they get their clothes. America ("We really like it - except for New York. We're not alienated from American life; this is our part of American life").

Besides Moulty, who is 21, the Barbarians consist of Geoff Morris 22, Jerry 22, and Bruce Benson, 19. "We started the band two summers ago, in Provincetown," they tell me, "and two months after the band had come into existence we went on the Tom Show. We've played clubs all over the country and in Canada. We can't stand 'em though - won't go back."

If they weren't The Barbarians?

Geoff: "I'd be in college."

Bruce: "I'd be stuffing chairs."

Jerry: "I'd be in the Coast Guard."

Moulty: "I'd be playing drums somewhere."

"It was so simple...we just kind of fell into it. But there's nothing else we'd rather be doing. We kind of scorn work.

Hobbies: Skin diving. Motorcycles. "Wimmin."

Goals for the future: To escape from working, be rich enough to travel without any hangups.

Place they'd like to consider home: "Boston!" "And," one says, "an island by myself in the Pacific." "Yeah," everybody choruses, "islands in the Pacific - four singles!"

Marriage: "That scares us." "Who's scared; we're smart, that's all."

MOULTY MOLTEN

JEFF MACKAY MORRIS

BRUCE BENSON

Embarrassing experiences: "Well, a lot of times we just play half a song or so, and the whole audience is on stage. That happened in Buffalo. All the kids got excited. We said, 'You better hold those kids back.' The cops said, 'Noooo, that won't happen here.' Then - wow: they started coming; we left. We had to climb over the stage to get away!

"The first time that happened we just stood there and let 'em get us...after that we never did it anymore. The police escort us now.

"One time in Provincetown a girl in the crowd had a pair of scissors..."

What do you think of girls who chase you that way? "If they don't we're in trouble. If it weren't for them we wouldn't be anywhere. As long as you can find out how to get away if you need to. If there's a couple hundred, and they're coming right at you, it's terrifying."

Any parting words? "Buy Barbarian records."

"And thank them all for being interested in us."

"They don't even have to buy our records - they can just send us money." □

THE NEW ENGLAND SCENE

By JOEL BERNSTEIN

The return of Barry Tashian to Boston brings us more or less full circle in this quick trip through the last half decade. Tex Loman, a veteran equipment man at the Ark/Boston Tea Party club, had looked forward to Tashian's reappearance with an emphatic: "He's the most exciting rock performer ever to come out of Boston." But time, age, and perhaps a touch of West Coast lassitude had gotten to Barry. Still a precision guitar picker, though looking bald and relatively middle-aged in the Boston club crowd, he failed to display any of that emotionally-charged guitar thrust or vocal power that was so evident on the Remains' one and only album. The Remains were better off a legend.

THE FINAL ANALYSIS

The reality, for Boston and New England in general, was that the region hadn't produced a single nationally successful group during one of the most fertile periods in American music. The Remains came closest to the pinnacle, but couldn't hold it together. Orpheus had the potential, with years of folk experience, but couldn't break nationally even with a superior single. The Beacon Street Union had all the moves and flash, but lacked a strong lead voice and were also reportedly hampered by their production contract with Wes Farrell.

A group like the Colwell-Winfield Blues Band had such a wealth of instrumental talent that, in retrospect, it's hard to believe they couldn't even make a regional dent—let alone national—with their album. Reedman Collin Tilton and Jack Schroer later helped Van Morrison create his early Warner Brothers classics, while Chuck Purro is singing, writing and drumming for the James Montgomery Band. Ill Wind kept going for years as local favorites. Quill looked for a time like an intense art-rock group on the way up. Ultimate Spinach even had a hit with a remake of "Just Like Romeo and Juliet." But that was it.

All these groups were scenes in a musical movie which never came to a logical ending, at least by the end of the decade. To find true national success, one has to look to the emergence of the J. Geils Band in late 1970, followed by Jonathan Edwards' smash hit "Sunshine." Ironically, in light of the Bosstown hype, New England is now bursting with talent, and there's a pattern here that might help explain much of what happened.

With the exception of the Remains and possibly the Beacon Street Union, the New England bands simply weren't *defiant* enough to meet the standards of the middle and late Sixties. The region had a tradition of .....well.....tradition—and that is why the bands and performers who have been able to succeed are firmly based in either blues or folk. When it comes right down to it, Tom Rush has been the region's single most consistent star through all the years we've talked about. Others, like Jon Edwards, never could make it until they reverted from rock to rock-folkie (although Jon's original group, Sugar Creek, did manage to get an album out), and J. Geils and James Montgomery are deeply seated in the traditions of bar-band blues and soul.

Too often, New England was imitative and derivative—a region with a great ear but a lack of conviction, except when solidly based on the bedrock of tradition. It's interesting to note that New England has generally been more successful in the production of critics than performers in the rock field, and maybe that's the key to the whole thing: Academic New England was just too damn educated to be punk.

There's more to Boston's rock past than the Barbarians, the Remains, and a crock of hype. Plenty of good and/or popular groups were around in the mid-60's, and while a lot of them made it onto vinyl I'd be surprised if the percentage isn't much lower than in a lot of other cities. Or maybe it's just that Boston groups couldn't get their records played on the radio; in researching this article I was amazed to find how few local records actually got any meaningful airplay here, especially in comparison to their counterparts in Cleveland and Chicago. In he latter cities it seemed there were always at least a half-dozen local records getting played in a given week, while in Boston it was rare to have two at a time. Now I like Bocky & the Visions as much as anyone, but I don't think their records were really any better than the Rockin' Ramrods, not to mention the Remains or the Lost. Needless to say, if a group couldn't get a hit in its own hometown, its chances of national fame were sharply reduced.

RADIO

Boston radio in the '60s consisted of three major forces—WMEX, WBZ, and Arnie Ginsberg. Ginsberg was WMEX's top DJ, but he was actually a power of his own. He wasn't bound by the same restrictions as his fellow jocks—he had virtually unlimited freedom to play, or not play, whatever he chose. Many a hit was broken nationally on his show. However he was not, as some people think, completely all-powerful. He played a lot of new records as they came out, but most were dropped after a few days, and a lot of these eventually became hits elsewhere and returned to Boston radio to soar into the Top Ten. The point of all this is that even though Ginsberg did play most of the local releases as they came out, his support was too brief to have much effect unless there was other local play to back it up. There was no likelihood of a local record returning to Boston radio via the national breakout route. For all intents and purposes, it never had a chance.

Meanwhile, neither WBZ nor the rest of WMEX paid any attention at all to most new local releases. Any TV actor who made a record, no matter how unsuccessful nationally, was assured of a hit in Boston (remember those smashes by Jerry Mathers and Vince Edwards?). Ginsberg was busy making novelties into national chartbusters ("Does Your Chewing Gum Lose Its Flavor", "My Boomerang Won't Come Back"). Perhaps what it all means is that Boston's musical inferiority complex, though by many to be a result of the Bosstown fiasco, actually existed all the time.

THE ROCKIN' RAMRODS

Who were these groups whose records were ignored? Well, how about the Rockin' Ramrods. They led the pack with eight (plus one that actually became a hit), and in fact their longevity gives them the distinction of having the largest record legacy of any pre-Bosstown local group, an item which must come as a surprise to almost everyone. And if you count their subsequent efforts under the name Puff, there's no contest. No one would claim that they (or their records) were the best the area had to offer. In fact, they were a highly derivative outfit who played to an audience that was hardly punk at all. Their major gig through the years was as regulars at Arnie Ginsberg's Saturday hops at The Surf at Nantasket Beach south of Boston (this is also where Freddie Cannon rose to stardom, and you may soon realize this is no mere coincidence). While their later records show considerably more imagination than the early efforts, it's their longevity, and the many twists it entails, that makes them so interesting.

Although the Ramrods are generally thought of as a South Shore group (because of their Surf gigs, and because their later releases were on a label from the same area) they actually hail from Newton, a well-to-do suburb adjacent to Boston on the West. Bill Linnane was the original leader, but it was two other members—Vin Campisi and his younger brother Ronn—who give the group its place in history. (The Rockin' prefix prefix presumably resulted from the existence of another Ramrods who recorded for Amy in the early '60s. According to Ronn, the group always hated it and was glad to be able to drop it on their last two records.) The group was wailing away as a typical high school band when a momentous event occurred—they were seen by Freddy Cannon's mother. She soon brought her famous son around, and he was impressed enough to finance a record.

"Jungle Call" is lost to posterity, but it is known that both sides were instrumentals (the accepted norm

• The Rockin' Ramrods: Ron, Vin, Lenny, Bob.

for pre-Beatles local rock records) and it's not hard to imagine what it sounds like (one can even surmise that it began with a Tarzan yell or something similar). This was the beginning and end of the Explosive label, but Freddy, with a different partner, tried again on the equally short-lived Bon Bon label. "She Lied" is a crude record which rocks nicely, but the raw vocals have not yet been turned into an asset, as they will be later. They were soon passed on to Cannon's producer Frank Slay, for whom they made several records. In between, they put out one on their own—a pair of Lennon-McCartney tunes which capture the energy (if not the talent) of the early Beatles. This is also the only local-group record known to have come with a picture sleeve.

The Slay period marked the group's national phase. Not only were their records on labels with more than local distribution, but they wre also on tour with the Rolling Stones and in a schlock movie (*East is East*) which also featured Peter & Gordon and the Applejacks (This movie is reportedly one of the all-time turkeys, but its local promotion was impressive. When it opened in downtown Boston, the Ramrods appeared live the first three days, with a different headliner each day.) This was also the group's Kingsmen phase; "Fumanchu" and "Play It" were especially in that vein. "Fumanchu" was almost a national hit, getting heavy play in several major cities, but surprisingly it too was ignored in Boston. This is especially ironic in that around the same time the Kingsmen themselves enjoyed major hits in Boston with two records that bombed nationally. The group's association with Slay ended with a total of seven records (one an uncredited back-up stint on the movie's title song) and nothing close to a local hit.

Amazingly, the group persevered. Linnane was gone by this time, and Ronn Campisi's increasing interest in writing and producing made him the group's leader. After tapes produced by Strangelove Jerry Goldstein failed to find an interested label, Campisi's new talents had a chance to reach full bloom. Reactivating their Plymouth label, the group turned to a whole new sound. From Kingsmen raw to flower-power light, the group was actually in on the beginning of a trend for the first time. With its light bounciness, lilting harmonies, and its title, "Bright Lit, Blue Skies," released in June of '66, was a perfect summer record. And rewarded they were—#16 on WMEX, #17 on WBZ, and similar success in Providence—despite poor distribution and anti-local prejudice. (#16 may not seem like much to folks in other cities, but in Boston only the Barbarians and Teddy & the Pandas ever did better. Oh yeah, and Tony Conigliaro. See what I mean?). "Flowers in My Mind" did less well, and it's certainly too gimmicky for my extremely simple tastes.

By now it was Bosstown time. Alan Lorber nabbed the group, changed their name to Puff, and out finally came their album. It was as successful as the other Bosstown albums. (Ronn Campisi had left the group before this record, but did write all the songs.) And so at last ended the career of the Rockin' Ramrods—gone and quickly forgotten.

THE LOST

Durability is certainly not what makes the Lost interesting. They came and went faster than any other popular local group. But their brief career was sheer brilliance, and if the Remains were Boston's greatest tragedy, the Lost was not far behind. They were the true punks of the local scene, and their sloppy, druggy image was not conducive to success in 1965. At first, however, it seemed they would make it big despite their image. Formed in 1964 at Goddard College in Vermont by Willie Alexander and Ted Myers, the group gigged in the north country for several months before moving to Boston in December. In a relatively short time, they were signed to Capitol, and seemed to be on their way. But it wasn't to be.

The rock scene in Boston was just developing at this time, and venues were still very limited. Many of the teen clubs were non-alcoholic, and some required coats and ties on weekends. Obviously a scruffy, dirty, stoned outfit like the Lost was not as well received as the ordinary group. Only their superb performances enabled them to get work at all. As the group became forced to take more and more gigs in Western Mass. and upstate New York, the first traces of self-destructive bitterness set in. But in '65 they were still playing primarily the limited Boston scene, and they fell in with Remains leader Barry Tashian, whose group played the same circuit. A Tashian-produced demo was made and was a major factor in the group's being brought to the attention of Capitol. (According to Willie Alexander, this demo was perhaps the best recording the Lost ever made. This is particularly interesting in that a Tashian-produced demo of the Remains is generally regarded by the few who have heard it as the best-ever by that group.)

The first Lost single was "Maybe More Than You," and it burst onto the scene in the Fall of 1965 with a torrent of radio play. However, by the time it staggered to #30 on WBZ several weeks later, it had already died. a shame indeed, because this rocker was one of the very finest Boston singles—sort of Bob Dylan punk as sung with perfect nasality by Alexander (Myers normally sang lead). It did somewhat better in the western part of the state and in upper New York, and the group began spending as much time in Albany or Buffalo as in Boston. When they toured the Northeast with the Beach Boys in 1966 they were mobbed in Worcester. In most places it took them a while to win over the surf crowd (bear in mind the tremendous difference in the images of the two groups) but they were always successful. But disintegration was already in motion, as the group distrusted their agent, their manager, and eventually each other.

Their next release was "Violet Gown," but Capitol yanked it off the market almost immediately and brought in Jerry ("Here Comes Summer") Keller to produce a new version. This makes "Mean Motorcycle," the flip of version one, the rarest Lost record (it's also the weakest). The group, already on the verge of breaking up, became thoroughly chagrined as Keller insisted on playing tambourines himself and generally dominating the session completely. There isn't all that much difference between the two versions—either is a lovely ballad which makes a great disc but is not at all representative of the group. The flip of version two, a semi-instrumental called "No Reason Why" is much more indicative of their rawness. Plenty of other stuff was recorded for Capitol, more than enough for an album. According to Alexander, the unreleased material includes some real killers (one of these tunes, "Everybody Knows" was re-recorded by Willie's later group Bagatelle).

In 1967, the Lost was no more. Ironically, the breakup came at a time when their 1965 image was just becoming fashionable. Like so many who are ahead of their time, this group had suffered for it. All the members were still to be heard from, however. Lee Mason had left the Lost several months before the end to form what became a popular soul-rock group, Bagatelle. Ted Myers joined Ultimate Spinach in time for their last album, then on to the short-lived Chameleon Church (which lasted long enough to churn out an album). He then moved to the West Coast and became a songwriter (landing the B-side of a Three Dog Night single). Kyle Garrahan was with Chameleon Church and then pursued a solo career, managing to get one single released, and was last heard from on the legitimate stage in France.

Willie and Walter Powers moved to Grass Menagerie, which also included Doug Yule. When that group broke up, Walter went to Listening and Willie (after a cameo appearance on that album as Willie Loco) joined Bagatelle. When Lou Reed exited the Velvet Underground, first Powers, then Alexander were summoned by Yule to join him and Maureen Tucker in that group's final days. Bringing things up to date, Willie Alexander has just released a new record on the local Garage label. "Kerouac" and "Mass. Ave." are two of the best cuts I've heard on a new 45 in a long time. It won't be a hit (radio stations are giving it the same reaction they gave "Maybe More Than You" in 1965: "too raw") so don't tarry if you want a copy. Send $1.25 to Garage Records, Box 308, Newtonville, Mass. 02160.

BANDS IN BOSTON

So much for the legends. Now it's time to make some (and maybe break a few as well). There were plenty of other bands around town with substantial followings, but as our Lost story indicated, truly crude bands had a tough time finding gigs in Boston. Hence the bands that became poular enough to record tended tobe more like the Ramrods than the Lost. There were punk bands galore; virtually every city or town had its high school band. However, any with aspirations were forced into the mainstream. If a cruder band wanted a disc, they had to do it themselves, and not everyone can afford that. Hence, the relative blandness of Boston's recorded legacy. (If you want to read about really obscure groups, find old issues of New England Teen Scene; one in particular covers almost every group in the area, with the Lost a conspicuous absentee. *Ed. Note:* Bomp *will pay top price for any and all issues of this magazine!!*).

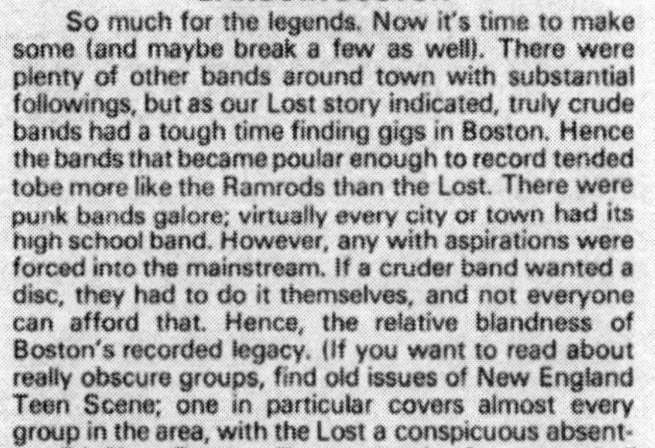

•The Ones.

The Improper Bostonians had four records, a couple of them moderately successful, in 1966-67. Pretty much a mainstream group, their records never impressed me much. They seemed to be caught somewhere between punk and pop, with a bit of folk-rock thrown in. Perhaps the most significant comment on their place in history is that neither I nor anyone who helped me with this article could remember anything substantial about them.

Teddy & the Pandas, whose singles were dismissed rather abruptly by David Johnson, were the only group to hit the local Top Ten with two consecutive releases. "Once Upon a Time" was also the only record to be picked up by a national label after breaking in Boston on a local label. "We Can't Go On This Way" was the group's biggest hit, but despite making it in several other cities, such as Washington and Miami, it never achieved the national success it deserved. The tune was covered a few years later by the Unchained Mynds from Milwaukee, whose Buddah release also enjoyed regional success. The Pandas' Musicor hits weren't punk, merely excellent pop, but the flips showed their rawer side, including "Sunnyside Up," the flip of the third and last Musicor release. Before landing onTower, they had an obscure release on the Timbri label.

The Pandoras would be an oddity even today, but in 1966 a female group that played their own instruments was a definite freak. They played regularly at the Rathskellar, the club that "made" the Remains and the Lost, and their first single "About My Baby" was fairly successful in the area. It's one for the girl-group fans, while the flip was a rather ordinary piece of folk-rock. The Pandoras were handled by Boston's biggest booking agency, and while one of the girls became its secretary, another wound up marrying the head of the agency. Only in America.....

And there were lots more. The Rondels had several instrumental releases on Amy in the early '60s, including one national hit. Their vocal version of Ritchie Valens' "C'mon Let's Go" was an attempt to adjust to changing times. It was weak. The Trophies were actually from Western Mass., but their only known record was a hit in Boston, so I'll include them here. Their versions of "Walking the Dog" and Eddie Cochran's "Somethin' Else" are energetic and enjoyable, but surprisingly no followup is known to exist. The Pilgrims were a popular South Shore group containing several future members of Sha Na Na. There are rumors of a disc entitled "Bad Apple" and I know of the existence of a record called "Plymouth Rock" by a group called the Pilgrims, but as I heard it on a Detroit station it may not be the same group.

The Talismen were a good punk group who managed one disc on their own label; a Rolling Stones cover backed with a Beatles-inspired original. Said to be a worthwhile disc. And let's not forget the Ones, an excellent punk group who survived into the Bosstown era and couldn't be bothered putting out a single. They released an album, with tunes like "Can't Explain", "Hang On Sloopy", and "Diddy Wah Diddy." To put it mildly, it's hard to find, and worth trying. That goes double for the Rising Storm, a group of students from Phillips Academy in Andover, Mass., whose album includes Love's "Message to Pretty", plus covers of the Remains' "Don't Look Back" and the Ramrods' "Bright Lit Blue Skies. Another oddity is the Knights, who released two albums, one in 1966 and one in '67, including covers of popular British and soul hits of the time.

There are also records without groups—no one seems to know who Monday's Mondos were, but both sides of the record are superb, especially "Crying" which is pure energy in the Kingsmen style, but without that group's R&B trappings. One of Boston's few punk classics. The Cobras record was brought to me in 1967 when I was a college radio DJ in upstate NY. It was said to be from a Boston suburb, but I can't remember which one, and no one in Boston knows about it. It's an excellent Zombies-styled disc, and deserved to be played by more than just me. But probably wasn't.

And there was Georgie Porgie & the Cry Babys, whose reputation was made in nonmusical fashion. Georgie was booted out of school for having his hair too long (he said he needed long hair for his musical career). After hearing his records, I can only hope he got his diploma. Before ending our Boston coverage, mention must be made of one group that deserves to be remembered although they definitely never recorded. They played at bars in Boston's Combat Zone, and each member of the band had his hair dyed a different color, hence the group's name: the Rainbows.

RHODE ISLAND

Californians have a warped sense of geography. Greg, at least, seems to think that the whole East Coast is one big "New England Scene", while Bostonians, on the other hand, consider anything beyond Route 128 (about 10 miles) to be a foreign country. What all this means is that coverage of the rest of New England is going to be very sketchy, and we're counting on readers in these areas to write and fill in the blanks in future issues.

Providence was blessed with something that Boston has never had: an "angel" willing to send virtually any halfway decent local talent into the studio and onto vinyl. There were two, actually, but the Super label (whose releases I've never heard) was apparently more into Rascals-styled groups (*Ed. note: they had some good folk-rockers too...*), while Planet had a great variety of releases. (See *TRM #7*, page 30, for info on Super) The Malibus' "Leave Me Alone" is the only one known to have received significant local airplay; both sides could have been classics (in a Zombies style, the top side featuring an outrageously blatant plagiarism from "Leave Me Be") were it not for the extremely poor vocal. There are two records on Planet I regard as real gems. "Hootenanny Baby" was "discovered" for me by a rockabilly fan who couldn't believe how late the record was (1965), showing once again that punk is just

the rockabilly of the '60s. Despite the Buddy Holly style hiccup vocals, it's definitely punk, but moves fast enough to keep anybody happy. Then there's Planet 59; the A-side, by John Broughton, is deathly slow with heavy organ, muddy vocal, and it really works; the B-side uses the same formula, but it's a frantic rocker sung unintelligibly by the intriguingly-named Shawkey Se'au. This record is a classic from top to bottom, and certainly one you'd never have expected to hear on the radio. There are other decent relases on Planet, but minor league compared to the ones above.

It's really amazing when you think about how many Providence groups got records out as compared to Boston (which undoubtedly had many more groups in its Metro than did Providence). It goes to show that quality and/or on-stage popularity are less important in determining who gets to record than is financial backing. It's a problem that always has and always will continue to plague acts in a city which, like Boston, has no local entrepeneur willing to provide backing.

CONNECTICUT

Now we're really getting far away. Hartford and New Haven both had thriving scenes, and many of the groups recorded, but only the Wildweeds are at all known in Boston. This group from Hartford had four singles on Cadet which reign as major collectors' items, and also had a stage act that was as popular with fans of the Rascals-styled groups as it was with fans of punk and mainstream rock. In other words, they were big. Their first record, "No Good to Cry" was the group's smash. It made it to Boston and several other cities, but somehow failed to get above #88 on the national chats. The next two Wildweeds records were almost as good, but the fourth delved into a more progressive bag which I find less satisfying. They moved to Vanguard for an album, but like Teddy & the Pandas, they were a completely different group by the time they got onto a 12-incher. Al Anderson, who wrote and sang almost all their material, is now with NRBQ, which plays regularly in the same areas in which the Wildweeds were big, thus keeping the legend alive.

The other big groups in Connecticut were the Shags and the North Atlantic Invasion Force, both from the Hamden-New Haven area. The Shags were the post-British Invasion biggies, dressing in British style and doing lots of songs made famous by the Beatles and their countrymen. One of the group's many singles was "I Call Your Name," and one Kayden release had the group's name lettered old-fashioned British style. Two Kayden discs are all I have by the group; interestingly, each has one punk side and one side in a rickytick style. They don't impress me, but since they're probably late records they're probably not valid criteria for judging the group's merits. NAIF came along a bit later; they had four records beginning in 1967 with "Blue and Green Gown", an excellent, bouncy punk platter. Likewise is their third disc and reportedly biggest hit (a giant in New Haven, I'm told), "Black on White." Their second release, "Sweet Bird of Love," had a problem that seemed to be very common with local Connecticut records—the hole was printed off-center.

There was also a Hartford group who recorded on three different labels under three different names. The Bluebeats and the #1 were two of their names; the third escapes me. The #1 record is the only one I'm familiar with. It's an eerie Sonny Curtis song on one side, and a good Jay & Americans styled tune on the flip. Big local record, I believe. There were a lot of Rascals-styled groups like the Van Dykes and the Chosen Few (who had the big local version of "Hey Joe"—and doesn't it say something about Boston that we never had a local hit on either this song or "Midnight Hour," maybe the only city in America that can make that claim.) to round out the Connecticut scene.

MYSTERIES & MISCELLANIES

The big cities obviously had the lion's share of the groups, but you may have noticed in reading so far,

most of them were somewhat, if not entirely, mainstream. And it stands to reason; after all, if you're going to compete in the big cities with lots of other groups, you've got to be fairly commercial and not too far out. To paraphrase Greg, punk rock is not the music of big cities—it's the music of the suburbs. It stands to reason that the best truly punk bands in New England existed in the areas that I haven't covered because they had no scene per se. But any bands that did exist in the small towns of Western Mass. and northern New England were probably hard-core punks. If they were good enough or ambitious enough for the big time, they'd have moved to Boston or some other metropolis. Since reputations didn't travel any further than the groups themselves, these true punks are unknown to anyone who didn't see them, unless they made a record. And if there is a record then, assuming you can find it, you still don't know exactly where it came from. Presumably some or all of our "mystery records" such as Monday's Mondos, came from this kind of environment. Let's hope some readers can help solve these mysteries and provide info on other legendary small-town punks.

Two superb punk records which appear to be from somewhere in New England are those by the Stonemen and the Royale Coachmen. Punk classics with not a clue as to origin. The Kingtones record would be in the same category except that there is a Derry in New Hampshire, so maybe that's where the record is from. There was also an excellent record by a group called the Warlocks. It got onto Decca but is definitely from somewhere in New England.

Some less mysterious miscellanies exist. The Shillings had a couple of records, including a regional hit called "Lying and Trying," and I think they were from Vermont. (There was a Boston group with that name who quickly added the hit to their repertoire and did nothing to discourage people from thinking it was theirs, although it wasn't.) The Minets record got a lot of local play in '64, and although they tried to pass themselves off as British, I'm pretty sure they weren't. The Blue Echoes were a Worcester group with an instrumental release on a Pittsburgh label, while Cory and the Knightsmen were also from Western Mass. and had a nice, folkish single (and thank goodness for a local record that actually tells you where it's from: Agawam, Mass.) And don't forget the Trophies, who were mentioned in the Boston section, but were actually from Greenfield, Mass., in the Berkshires, and the only mystery here is how they got so much Boston airplay with such a crude record (not being from Boston undoubtedly helped....).

So much, for now, for New England. Hopefully, as readers send in details of more obscure local records, some of the smaller local scenes will begin to take on shape—although, due to the nature of things as discussed above, the totality of New England rock will probably never be fully known.

ROCKIN' RAMRODS

?-63 Jungle Call/Indian Giver - Explosive
?-64 She Lied/Girl Cant Help It - Bon-Bon 1315
1-65 I Wanna Be Your Man/I'll Be On My Way - Plymouth 2961/62
7-65 Wild About You/Cry in MyRoom-SouthernSound205
9-65 Dont Fool with Fumanchu/Tears Melt the Dtones Claridge 301
?-66 Play It/Got My Mojo Working - Claridge 317
6-66 Bright Lit, Blue Skies/Mister Wind - Plymouth 2963/64
Flowers in my Mind/Mary, Mary - Plymouth 2965/66
(on last two Plymouth releases, group was "The Ramrods")
(as PUFF)
Looking in my Window/Rainy Day - MGM 14040
as uncredited backup to Casey Paxton:
East is East/Baby Baby Go Go - Claridge 308

BARBARIANS

?-65 Hey Little Bird/You've got to Understand - Joy 290
6-65 Are you a Boy or are you a Girl/Take it or Leave it Laurie 3308
10-65 What the New Breed Say/Susie Q - Laurie 3321
1-66 Moulty/I'll Keep on Seeing You - Laurie 3326

REMAINS

3-65 Why Do I Cry/My Babe - Epic 9783
12-65 I Cant Get Away/But I Aint Got You - Epic 9842
2-66 Diddy Wah Diddy/Once Before - Epic 10001
8-66 Dont Look Back/Me About You - Epic 10060

TEDDY & THE PANDAS

2-66 Once Upon a Time/Out the Window - Coristine 574 & Musicor 1176; Musicor LP 2101 *The Gene Pitney Show*
7-66 We Cant Go On This Way/Smokey Fire - Musicor 1190
Searchin' for the Good Times/Sunnyside Up - Musicor 1212
The Lovelight/Day in the City - Timbri 101
8-68 Childhood Friends/68 Days 'Til Sept. - Tower 433

LOST

10-65 Maybe More than YHou/Back Door Blues - Cap.5519
Violet Gown/Mean Motorcycle - Capitol 5708
8-66 Violet Gown/No Reason Why - Capitol 5725
(Kyle Garrahan solo)
I Shall Be Released/? - Janus 109
(Willie Alexander solo)
Kerouac/Mass. Ave. - Garage 505

IMPROPER BOSTONIANS

9-66 How Many Tears/I Still Love You - Minuteman 207
1-67 Set you Free this Time/Come to me Baby - Minuteman 208
Out of my Mind/You made me a Giant-Minuteman209
Gee I'm Gonna Miss You/Victim of Environment - Coral 62543

BEACON STREET UNION

South End Incident/Speed Kills - MGM 13865
Blue Suede Shoes/Four Hundfred & Five - MGM 13935
Mayola/May I Light your Cigarette - MGM 14012
Lord Why is it so Hard/Cant Find my Fingers - RTP 10011/12
(as Eagle)
Kickin' it Back to You/? - Janus 113
(as John Lincoln Wright & Sourmash Boys)
?-75 EP: Too Much Water/Try to Win me Over/Wrong Place Wrong Time/Sweet Montana

ORPHEUS

Cant Find the Time/Lesley's World - MGM 13882
Brown Arms in Houston/I CanMake theSunRise-MGM 14022
I've Never Seen a Love Like This/? - MGM
I'll Fly/?

MISCELLANEOUS

Prince & Paupers - Dont Wake Up/No Shame to Hide - Clarity 115
Tinkers - You're Just Like all the rest/Love lights - Stop 106
Tinkers - You're Making me Sad/My lost Love - Stop 107
Listening - Hello You/Life Stories - Vanguard 35094
Richie's Renegades - Baby it's Me - Polaris ('65)
Bugs - Pretty Girl/Slide - Polaris 0001
Little John & Sherwoods - Rag Bag/Long Hair-Fleetwood 001
Brent & Spectras - Oh Darling/Patricia - Spectras
Steve Colt & the 45's - Dynamite/Take Away - Big Beat 1006
Steve Colt & the 45's - Hey Girl, How Ya Gonna Act/I've Been Loving You - Big Beat 1001
Steve Colt & the 45's - Just a Little Bit of Soul/So Far Away - RCA 8913
Swallow - Yes I'll Say It/Aches & Pains - WB 7613
Urban Renewal - Love Eyes/People - St.George Int. 7-702,271
Garden of Eden - Flower Man/Samantha - Verve 10541
Bead Game - Sweet Medusa - Avco-Embassy 4539
Travis Pike's Tea Party - The Likes of You/If I Didn't Love You Girl - ALma
Wild Thing - Weird Hot Nights (Suffer Baby)/Don't Fool with My Girl - SPQR 1003
Wild Thing - Next to Me/Old Lady - Elektra 45672
Bonnie Floyd & Orig. Untouchables - I'm Just a Poor Boy/? - Bright Yellow 1067
Velvet Seed - Sharon Patterson/Flim Flam Man - MAI 201
Quarry - Mockinbird Hill/We're all going to Leave this World SOmeday - Berkshire Harmony 0001
Buss - Too Young to Understand/Woman - Onyx 7008
Monday's Mondo's - Minnie Ha-Ha/(I'm) Crying - Columbia 1041
Georgie Porgie & Cry Babies - Sad Kid/Hurt - Georgie Porgie 96281/82
Georgie Porgie & Cry Babies - He's Just Like That/Holdin On - Jubilee 5578
Georgie Porgie & Cry Rabis - The Lake/Enter Sunshine - Jubilee 5597
Georgie Porgie & Cry Babies - Crocodile?
Rondels - C'mon Let's Go Sweetheart - Nota 4001
Minets - Secret of Love/Together - Rock It 200,054/055
Minets of England - Wake Up/My Love is Yours - DCP 1129
Talismen - Little By Little/You Dont Care About Me - Taily
Pandiras - About My Baby/New Day - Liberty 55954
Pandoras - Games/Don't Bother - Liberty 55999
Orphans - There's No Flowers in my Garden/One Sponen Word - Epic 10288
Orphans - This is the Time/Deserted - Epic 10348

RHODE ISLAND

PLANET label (selected releases)
54 Ray Gee & Counts - Hootenanny Baby/Arabic Jazz
57 Monterays - Blast Off/You Never Cared
58 Malibus - Leave Me Alone/Cry
59 John Broughton - Walk Alone/Shawkey Se'au - Just One More Time
65 Jan-Ells - Last Walk TOnight/Love is a Place
76 Essex St. Journal - Walk On/Progression 256
'66 '66

SUPER Label
101 Cal Raye - You're My Lovin Baby/My Tears Start to Fall
102 Ascots - Monkey See—Monkey Do/You Cant Do That
103 Ascots - Midnight Hour/pt. 2
104 Ascots - Put Your Arms Around Me/Sookie-Sookie
106 American Rebels - Rebel Song/Rebel Theme

Spektrum - I Was a Fool/Confetti - Somethin Groovy 500
Out of Order - Lonely Sentry/It's Alright - Lauren 2930
Cowsills - All I Really Wanta Be is Me/And the Next Day Too - Joda 103

CONNECTICUT

WILDWEEDS

No Good to Cry/Never Mind - Cadet 5561 (4-67)
Someday Mornin'/Cant You See that I'm Lonely - Cadet 5572
It Was Fun (while it lasted)/Sorrow's Anthem - Cadet 5586
I'm Dreaming/Happiness is Just an Illusion - Cadet Concept 7004

NORTH ATLANTIC INVASION FORCE

Blue and Green Gown/Fire,Wind & Rain - Congressional 999
Sweet Bird of Love/Elephant in my Tambourine - Majestic
Black on White/The Orange Patch - Mr. G 808
Rainmaker/Elephant in My Tambourine - Mr. G

SHAGS

As Long as I Have You/Tell Me - Kayden 407
Breathe in my Ear/Easy Street - Kayden 408
Hey Little Girl/Dont Press Your Luck - ? (5-66)
I Call Your Name/Hide Away - Laurie 3353

The Insane - I Can't Prove It/Someone Like You - Allen Associates 201,347 (Plymouth, CT)
The #1 - The Cllector/Cracks in the Sidewalk - Kapp 824

MISCELLANEOUS NEW ENGLAND AND POSSIBLE BOSTON

Stonemen - No More/Where did our love go -Big Topper 107
Royale Coachmen - Killer of Men/Standing over There - Jowar 103
Warlocks - Temper Tantrum/I'll Go Crazy - Decca 31806 5-65
Trophies - Walkin the Dog/Somethin' Else - Nork 79907 6-64
Cobras - Come on Back/Summertime - Feature 201,264/5
Kingtones - Twins/Have Good Faith - Derry 101
Blue Echoes - Blue Belle Bounce/Tiger Talk - Itzy 11
Cory & Knightsmen - Sittin in a Railway Station/Bulldog WG 40231
Sillings - Lying and Trying/Children and Flowers - 3 Rivers 701
SHillings - Goodbye My Lady/The World could Stop - 3 Rivers 6778/79
Delrays Inc - I'm a Lovin/Billy's Beat - Salen 002
Pilgrims - Bad Apple?
Pilgrims - Plymouth Rock?
Tidal Waves - You Name It/So I Guess - Strafford 6503
Falcons - There's a Tear/I Gotta See Her - Strafford 6504 (both Durham, N.H.)
Sean & Sheas - Spiders/Hi Diddle - Yorkshire 004
Dick Moorehead & Paramounts - Spanish Batman/Mommie & Daddy's Doing the Latest Dance - Cloud 508
Boston Hitesmen - My Babe - MTA 104
DMZ - Somewhere in Between - MTA 135

BOSTON ALBUMS

Apple Pie Motherhood Band - Atlantic SD 8189
Apple Pie Motherhood Band - *Apple Pie* - Atlantic SD 8233
Art of Lovin' - Mainstream 6113
Bagatelle - *11PM Saturday* - ABC 646
Barbarians - Laurie 2033
Bead Game - *Welcome* - Avco-Embassy 33009
Beacon St. Union - *Eyes of* - MGM 4517
Beacon St. Union - *Clown Died in Marvin Gardens*-MGM 4568
Black Pearl - Atlantic SD 8220
Black- *Live* - Prophecy 1001
Brother Fox & Tar Baby - Oracle 703; Capitol
Chameleon Church - MGM 4574
Tmothy Clover - *Cambridge Concepts* - Tower 5114
Colwell-Winfield & Friends - *Live Bust* - Za-Zoo 1
Colwell-Winfield Blues Band - *Cold Wind Blues* - Verve-Vorecast 3056
Country Funk - Polydor 4020
Dirty John's Hot Dog Stand with Kenny Paulson - *Return From the Dead* - Amsterdam 12004
Eagle - Janus 3011
Earth Opera - Elektra 74016
Earth Opera -*The Great American Eagle Tragedy*-Elektra74038
Eden's Children - ABC - 624
Eden's Children - *Sure Looks Real* - ABC
Far Cry - Vanguard Apostolic 6510
Flat Earth Society - *Waleeco* - Fleetwood 3027
Freeborne - *Free Impressions* - Monitor 607
Ford Theatre - *Trilogy for the Masses* - ABC 658
Ford Theatre - *Time Changes* - ABC 681
Fort Mudge Memorial Dump - Mercury 61256
Ill Wind - *Flashes* - ABC 641
Kangaroo - MGM 4586
Listening - Vanguard 6504
Orpheus - MGM 4524
Orpheus - *Ascending* - MGM 4569
Orpheus - *Joyful* - MGM 4599
Orpheus - Bell 6061
Phluph - Verve 5054
Puff - MGM 4622
Quill - Cotillion 9017
Remains - Epic 26214
Swallow - *Out of the Next* - WB 2606
Sugar Creek - *Please Tell a Friend* - Metromedia 1020
Tangerine Zoo - Mainstream 6107
Teddy & Pandas - *Basic Magnetism* - Tower 5125
Ultimate Spinach - MGM 4518
Ultimate Spinach - *Behold and See* - MGM 4570
Ultimate Spinach - MGM 4600
Wild Thing - *Partyin'* - Elektra 74059

LOCAL ALBUMS

The Ones - *Vol. 1* - Ashwood House 1105
Shaggs - *Philosophy of the World* - Third World 3001
Dr. Feelgood - *Something to Take Up Time* - Number One
Knights - *Across the Board* - MG22,854
Knights - *1967* - MG 201,302 (Mt. Herman, MA)
The Rising Storm - *Calm Before* - Remnant 3571 (Andover)
Moonlighters - *An Evening With* - Century 29132
Ha'Pennys - *Love is Not the Same* - Fersch 1110
V.A. - *Connecticut's Greatest Hits* (New Haven) Van Dykes, Chosen Few, Majenics, Leo & Duets, Tony IV, Pearlean Gray & Passengers, Fred Parris) Co-Op 101

Dutch Rock

(continued from page 18)

Les Cruches - I'm Gonna be a Father/Walkin & Strollin
'les Cruches - Keep Off/I Try to Find - CBS 2425
Les Cruches - It's Always Me/Nose for Trouble - CBS 2560
Les Cruches-Will you always love me/Mum&Dad -CBS 2766
Clarks - All the Time/Spanish Fly - Tania
Caz - Shala-La/I Feel Alright - Philips JF 333.608
Crash - Last Week/One Rainy Day - Philips
C-Sounds - Reasons/Claudette - Decca AT 25.006
Cuby & Blizzards - Back Home/Sweet Marie - Philips 333.506 (many other 45's and LPs)
Daddy's Act - Eight Days a Week/Gonna Get You - CNR 61006
Dimitri - I Got a dog named Sally/Strange in the Grass-Polydor
Dirty - John the Rainmaker/Bad Merchandise - Decca
Dragonfly - Celestial Dreams/Desert of Almond - Philips
Eddy & Eddysons - Oh Susannah/Oh So Wrong - Heinsma
Elements - You won the score/The loves Ihad before-Relax047
Fallouts - I'm Sick of Living/I've been Waiting-Funckler 25.532
Fashions - There Goes my Baby/All Aone - CNR 9895
First Move - My Love has Gone/A Hard Days Fight - Decca 285
First Move - He looks like a Swina/There is More - Decca
Frogs Ltd. - Man on the Cloud/Playgirl - Polydor S 1239
Flesh Point 6 - Sweet Sally/Reading - Negram
Driftin' 5 - A Long Time/Hard Headed Baby - RCA 47-9754
Full House - Do it Right/Still feel the same way - Barclay 60.815
Fun of It - Make me Happy/Never will a girl look better-Decca
G Bros - Let me find a sun/She - Dureco
Groep 1850- Misty Night/Look Around
Groep 1850- I Want More/I Know - Philips JF 333.035
Groep 1850 - Mother No-head/Ever, Ever Green - Philips
Group Reza - It's a Shame/From Here - Yep 1015
Fun of It - Silly Baby/Drollery - Yep 1011
John Hatton & Devotions - I'm Gonna Stay/I SHould beAfraid
Haigs - Never Die - Funkler Havoc 118
Haigs - Separated/Where to Run? - Funckler
Haigs - From Now On/Hey Baby - Polydor 1220
Haigs - Saturday Night/You've Got It - Polydor 1230
Haigs - Roly, Poly Martha/Out of Life - Polydor
Rob Hoeke R&B Group - Rain,Snow,Misery/When People Talk - Philips JF 333.592
Rob Hoeke R&B Group - What IsSoul/DownHere-Philips 833
Rob Hoeke R&B Group - DOnt Ask Me What I Say/Baby Dont Go - Philips JF 333.865
Honest Men - In My Room/I've Been Wrong - Havoc SH 127
Honest Men - Mister Mister/The Trouble - Havoc SH 135
Honest Men - It's too late to turn around/New York's My Home - Delta
Hu & Hilltops - Cry Me a River - Polydor
Hu & Hilltops - Cant you Hear Me/I'll Follow You - Polydor
Hu & Hilltops-Touchin You/Ella May - Polydor 1241
In Crowd - Stay/Summertime - Relax 45054
In Crowd - I'll make it all up to you/When people talk - Polydor 1206
In Crowd - Cwong/I'll Keep you Happy-Polydor 1215
Indiscrimination-Wishful Thinking/Harp Blowing Blues - Decca AT. 25.008
Incredible - Upstairs Downstairs/She Died - CNR 61007
Ivo & Furies - Mountain of Love/Dady's Classical Emotion -
Jay-Jays - Bald Headed Wman/So Mystifying CBS 2498
Jay-Jays - Waauw/A Distant Place - Philips JF 333.615
Jay-Jays - Are you a Woman/Cause you're Mine - Philips 615
Jay-Jays - Respect/Cool Jerk - Philips JF 333.832
Jenny & Rascals - That's a Man's Way/Baby You Know You Ain't Right - Artone WS 25.519
Jets - If I Could Start My Life Again/The Worker in the Night Fontana YF 278-131
Jets - Please send me a letter/Love Love Love - Fontana
Jumping Pop-In - If you Like/Silly Chap - Decca AT 10.252
Johnny Kendall & Heralds - Girl/Do You Remember-RCA 9654
Johnny Kendall Selection - I Realized too Late/Cryin - Havoc
Johnny & Cellar Rockers-ILoveYouYes I Do/Why-Decca 106
Key - I See Your Image/Play Vivaldi - Yep 1010
F.J. King & Smash - Pucker Up Buttercup/Hold What You've Got - Relax 45036
Ronnie Lake - Higgledy-Piggledy/Dont you Know - Philips 617
Lazy Bones - I'm Driftin/Big Boss Man - Op.Bibl.RC166
Mack-All my hope is gone/Its gonna work out fine-Havoc 126
Mack-Do it another/LittleLovelyHoney - Teeset Records
Maskers -3's a Crowd/Living in the Past - Artone 25343
Maskers - Batman Theme/The Saint - Artone 25376
Maskers - Come on boy,join the Army/He Cursed Him - Artone 25430
Maskers - Georgia on my mind/Unchain my heart - Artone 497
Maskers - Shame on you/Hold of me - Artone 25.546
Maskers - Annabelle/Baby Don't Do It - Artone 25.290
Marquees - Tribute to THem; Call My Name/Last Night - Relax 45.033
James Mean - James Blues/What can I Do - TSR
Met & Zonder - Now I Know/Afterbirth of a Dream - Fontana
Mec-op Singers - Dies Irae/Peppils - Artone HE 25.469
Midnight Packet - Keep Lovin me Babe/Worried Man Blues-CNR 61002
Mods - Dont Bring Me Down/Baby Please Dont Go - Decca
Moody Sect-Mockingbird/Ballad of a Waitingman - Decca 009
Moan - Flowers Everywhere/Everyday is just the same - Philips
Moan - Ruby/A Servant's Dream - Polydor 2050 120
Mother's Love - Highway to Heaven/Lady from the Ballroom Havoc SH 132
Mother's Love - Raise the Sails/Saint without Glory - Havoc
Nicky & Shouts - Tears Inside/Guilty Man - CNR 9834
Nicky & Souts - Think/Everytime a new surprise - CNR 9897
Names & Faces - You're an old leaf/Keep smiling - Fontana
Nicols - Lord, I've Been Thinkin/I Cant Forget Her - CNR 61001
Nicols - Delighted to see you/It's easy to stay - Philips
Maskers - Heatwave/Death - Artone
Penny Wise - Silver Girl/Jacky's S.S.S - Imperial IH 739
Peter & Blizzards - Sittin in my Room - MuZiek Expr.
Peter & Blizzards - It Happens Everyday/Cold as Ice - Yep 1014
Price John - Little Indian/I Told Her - Philips
Phantoms - I'll Go Crazy
Phantoms LP: *The Phantoms* - Dureco 51.036
Ro-d-ys - You better take care of yourself/Wheels,Wheels, Wheels - Philips JF 333.645
Ro-d-ys - Take Her Home/Only One Week - Philips 333.830
Ro-d-ys - Just fancy/Gods of Evil - Philips JF 333.855
Ro-d-ys - Anytime/Dr. Sipher - Philips
St. John & Crew - I'm a Man/You belong to Me - Whamm 009
Sandy Coast - And her name is.../Anyway you want me - Relax 45.212
Sandy Coast - Milk&Tranquilizers/Working my way back to You - Havoc 1240
Sandy Coast LP: *There Name Is* - Marble Arch 202
Sandy Soul Set - Mean Talk/Banana Disease 1967 - Relax 063
Scandals - What Will TOmorrow Bring?/Are youMyMan-CBS
Scorpions - Hello Josephine - CNR
Scorpions - Greensleeves/Hey Honeyh - CNR UH 9767
Scorpions LP: *Hello Josephine* - CNR GA 5000
Scorpions LP: *Hello Josephine* - Polydor 623 012 (first LP listed has 12 tracks, 4 not on Polydor LP. Second album listed has 14 tracks, 6 not on CNR LP,& is a reissue.)
Shane - Lady Bountiful/Got to hold on - Decca AT 10.253
Sharons - I Cant Leave/Handle with Care - Decca AT 10.1230
Sharons - It's a Wonder/Weekend on the wood - Decca 10278
Sharks & Me - Let the good times in/Buses - Tania
Short '66 - Another Man
Short '66 - Steal your heart away/4 men's sadness-Relax 212
Short '66 - Every moment/People Gotta Go - Decca AT 10.266
Short '66-Hard to get up in the morning/I'L'N'doubleU-Decca
Short '66 - Going my way/Come the day - Decca
Shoes - Standing&Staring/Ask my mother - Polydor 1210
Shoes - Na Na Na/Listen - Polydor 1219
Shoes - Peace&Privacy/Once Again - Polydor 1237
Shoes - Farewell in the Rain/What in the world is love-Polydor 1249
Shoes - Man's Life
Shoes - Don't You Cry For a Girl
Shoes - End of the Line
Six Young Riders - Let the circle be unbroken/Count Down Havoc SH 128
Sound Magics - Whatever you do/Just for You - Philips 658
Stew - It's Alright/Somebody's gotta do it - Basart Park
Static - What you gonna do to my heart/I Love you Girl
Frankie Sue Selection - Are you sincere/No Make Believe - RCA 47-15014
Sweet Nothing - Just keepin it up/Thinkin of you - CBS 2629
Teckels - Mabel/Save Our Souls - Relax 45033
Tee Set - Now's the Time/Bring a Little Sunshine - TSR 12512 (many other 45's & LPs)
Test - I walk through the gates/Please give me the key-Philips
Tielman Bros - Nina Dont Go/Maria My Love - CNR
Tielman Bros - Goodbye Mama/Cant Help Falling in Love - Negram
Tielman Bros - Hello Caterina/Say you're mine - Decca 276
Tielman Bros - Wandere Ohne Zeil/Viel Zu Spat - Decca 898
Timebreakers - Look at my baby/Now Time Has Come - Decca AT 10.245
Twilight Kids - A wondering Man/It's Your Fault - CNR
Tykes - Double crossin Time/Hey Girl - Polydor 1242
Tielman Bros - My Little Bird/Gone for Good - Delta
Un'beat'able - Even the bad times are good/Changing Times Philips JF 333.850
Zen - You better Start Running Away from Me/I've Been Drowned - Philips JF 333.858
Zen - Dont Try Reincarnation/Sad Song - Philips
Zipps - Highway Gambler/ - Muziek Expr.
Zipps - Kicks & Chicks/Hipsterism - Relax 45015
Zipps - Dutch Milk/Maria Juana - Relax 024-M

VARIOUS ARTIST ALBUMS

Beat From Holland - CNR (Gamblers/Entertainers/Beatniks/Marks/Cuby & Blizzards/Losers)
Beat Met Eeen Zachte G - Relax 30.565 (Go-Gos/Pandora's Box/Mental Bats/Heating/Chums/Fairytale)

We'll save the Golden Earrings for a later date.

Thanks for material aid to Cornelius Brinkerink, Julian Hardstone, Archie Barneveld, and especially Arnold De Reus and Gerard Davelaar.

FINAL NOTE: I've just started to get into much of this music, and though I was able to borrow many of these records, still have woeful gaps in my own collection. I'm actively seeking to buy or trade for a great many of the records on this list, and of course any not listed. Let me know what you have (see address in *Reverberations* column. —Ken Barnes.

(Ed. Note: I also need a lot of these records, also information and/or discs relating to '60s recordings by any groups from the Continent, Scandinavia, Asia, Africa, etc. for future articles. In particular, Sweden and Australia/New Zealand, which we hope to do next.—Greg Shaw)

JUKE BOX JURY JUNIOR

BY GREG SHAW

ROKY ERICSON & BLEIBALIEN - "Red Temple Prayer (Two Headed Dog)"/"Starry Eyes" - Mars 1000 9-75

Released after our feature article was finished, this single presents Roky's new group doing two of their strongest songs. "Red Temple Prayer" sounds a little like "Gimme Shelter" if it had been written by the Stooges, and recorded in Ron Weiser's swimming pool. The sound, mixing and pressing are so technically bad, it's hard to believe this didn't come out in 1966. Fortunately, though, the material lends itself to this primitive treatment, and the record is a must. Produced by Doug Sahm, the record can be obtained from Doug Hanners, 1316 Kenwood, Austin, TX, 78704

DAVID PEEL - "Bring Back the Beatles"/"Imagine" - Orange 1001 '75

This is David's first new record in quite awhile, and as you might expect, it's about as bad as every other Beatle novelty, though actually a bit better than most of Peel's stuff. Copies should still be available from 1126 Boylston, Boston, MA 02215.

OUTCASTS - "I'm In Pittsburgh(and it's Raining)" -Askel 102 '66

By far the most outstanding punker I've found in months, this Texas relic comes on like some weird hybrid of the Yardbirds and the Pretty Things. Even weirder is the flip, "Price of Victory," which is one of those offbeat pro-war statements like Bob Seger's "Yellow Berets" or Jan Berry's "Universal Coward."

HARUMI - "Talk About It"- Verve-Fore. 5086 '68

Harumi was that Japanese hippie whose double-album was full of Samurai freakouts and is worth picking up. This is the best cut on it, but it sounds better on a 45. If you like heavily overdone phasing and trippy studio effects (like "Pictures of Matchstick Men") you'll find an overdose here. And if you can wade through the soup, there's a good tune underneath.

LYDIA MARCELLE - "The Girl He Needs"/"Come On and Get It" - Manhattan 805

Manhattan was New Orleans' closest thing to a teenage label in the '60s. They had a couple of good punk-rockers, but my favorite so far is this female vocal, which sounds like Jackie DeShannon backed by the Byrds, or perhaps the Squires. Really dynamic, with a strong British flavor as well, this is one to look for. Flip is a Marvelettes-like ballad.

THE FREE - "Decision for Lost Soul Blue" Marquee 448

Here's a Detroit record that came out somewhat late for our Sounds of the Sixties survey, but should be in every collection just the same. It's got a driving Spencer Davis beat, resounding folk-rock guitar chords, and an electrifying punk-psychedelic solo at the end. The record was apparently a regional hit, and came out nationally on Atco.

THIRD BARDO - "I'm Five Years Ahead of My Time" - Roulette 4742 5-67

I don't know where this classic is from, and I can hardly believe it was produced by Teddy Randazzo. It's as thunderously raw as the Music Machine at their best, and features a mysterioso organ out of early H.P. Lovecraft, and overfuzz-feedback raga-rock guitar, with the addition of quaintly smug lyrics that capture perfectly the punk approach to early psychedelic visionary philosophies.

SPARKLES - "The U.T."/"He Can't Love You" - Caron 94 '62

Somehow, I began collecting "UT" records. There were a whole bunch of them, on various odd LA labels, many with Kim Fowley involvement. Most were dumb instrumentals. From the name, I thought this might be a girl group. It turned out to be an astonishingly tough late rockabilly mutation — the singer sounds like Eddie Cochran, the band like the Rock-a-Teens. A restrained, yet powerful recording. The flip reminds me of Ral Donner.

BRYAN & THE BRUNELLES - "Jacqueline" - HMV 1394 (E) 2-65

Only known release by this obscure British group is a surprisingly well-conceived song in the melodic, understated Zombies/Searchers vein, building to climaxes at each chorus, where the hard-rock backing comes forth. Rather infectious. Flip is a fair version of "Louie Louie."

SCOTT MORGAN - "Take a Look"-Detroit 1000 '75

Morgan, formerly of the Rationals, has been working with some ex-MC5 members and other Detroit locals, and this limited release is the first tangible product of the revived Detroit scene. Though badly produced, the song itself is pretty good, having a lot in common with the Flamin' Groovies' legendary "Slow Death." Morgan's voice is still in fine shape, and in the right hands he could make good records again.

WHEELS - "Gloria"/"Don't You Know" - Columbia DB 7682 (E) '65
WHEELS - "Bad Little Woman"/"Road Block" - Columbia DB 7827 (E) '66

Here's where rock history starts getting really bizarre. Neither of these records came out in the US or was a hit in England; they were about as obscure as, for instance, the Sons of Adam were here. Yet somehow the Shadows of Knight must have got hold of their records (they had another, "Kicks"/"Call My Name"). I always assumed "Gloria" came from Them, but there's no other explanation for "Bad Little Woman" (and this is definitely the original;, besides which the Wheels had a real Them fixation — "Road Block" is "Mystic Eyes" punked-over, and "Call My Name" is probably the Morrison song too. They were an excellent, raunchy band, and it's easy to see where the Shads got their inspiration.

SENSATIONS - "Yes Sir That's My Baby" - Atco 6056 11-55
HALE & THE HUSHABYES - same - Reprise 0299 8-64
THE DATE WITH SOUL - same - York 408 9-67

Three rock versions of a song you wouldn't think much could be done with. The Sensations, way back in '55, slowed it down and funked it up in the standard doo-wop manner, applying a proto-girl group vocal that set the stage for Jack Nitzsche's 1964 production, almost certainly done at Gold Star during the Phil Spector days, and in all probability a Spector-produced out-take. There's no mistaking that sound, and I'd swear only Darlene Love could be singing it. The male bass part in the Sensations record is also present, and could even be Bobby Sheen. This makes me wonder about another record, "Cause I Love Him" by Alder Ray (Liberty 55715) which, to my ears, could only be a Spector track, though his name appears nowhere on it. Maybe he made deals to unload tracks he had spent money on and then couldn't use... The Date With Soul disc is identical to the Hale & Hushabyes, no doubt reissued by Greene & Stone when they were working with Nitzsche later on.

RAVE-ONS - "Love Pill" - Twin Town 710 '65

Few local records out of Minneapolis were as polished or effective as this one. The song (not about The Pill, though it should've been — somebody ought to do one) has a good melody, a great hook, solid harmonies and British-influenced vocals. Not sensational, but the kind of record one can learn to love.

TONY & SIEGRID - "Long Hair" - RCA 8981 8-66

Fans of producer Tony Visconti (T.Rex,etc) won't want to miss this early waxing, on which he waxes poetic in a Sonny Bono vein. Along with the Barbarians, one of the great stupid protest records. ("You know Benjamin Franklin and George Washington/They both had long hair but they got their jobs done...")

VINCE TAYLOR - "Do You Wanna Rock n' Roll" Rockhouse 7503 (Dutch) '75

Taylor, a legendary leather-jacket rocker of British and European fame, is making his comeback with the help of Rockhouse (Bert Rockhuizen's active and promising new operation). This disc, which comes with a nice picture sleeve, ain't exactly savage rockabilly, but it's something for the collector. Order from Bob Morris, Box 3285, Midland, TX 79701. Bob also has other neat European imports for sale, so ask him...

WAYS & MEANS - "Breaking Up a Dream" - Trend 1005 (E) '68

If you loved the Easybeats for their unfailing kineticism and pop harmonies, this is a record to obtain at any price. A classic of its type, it's a fast-paced, driving rocker with Hollies vocals and tasty guitar.

WIMPLE WINCH - "Rumble On Mersey Square South" - Fontana TF 781 (E) '67

We'll close with a real mystery. From the title, I expected an instrumental, instead finding a long (over four minutes), convoluted experiment, ranging from a simple tale of Mods/Rockers confrontation to 10cc-like harmonic interludes. There's more happening in this record than I could possibly sort out, and most of it comes off exceedingly well. I'd love to know who was behind this...any info would be appreciated.

QUICK SPINS: The Beach Boys' hopelessly obscure first record, "Barbie"/"What Is a Young Girl Made Of" (under the name Kenny & the Cadets, on Randy 422) has now been reproduced and is available from International Artists (see ad on p. 45)... Before breaking up, Ducks Deluxe put out a live EP through Skydog (Box 421, Amsterdam) that includes "I Fought the Law" and 3 other hot rockers... Tom King, one of the original Outsiders, has produced a new version of "Time Won't Let Me" by J.C. Messina on his own label. Pretty good...

Does anybody know anything about a record "Fortune Teller"/"Poison Ivy" by the Teen Tones on the Don and Mira label out of South Bend, Indiana? It sounds a lot like the Rivieras ("California Sun") who later recorded "Fortune Teller" in a similar arrangement, and I read somewhere that the group made a record back in Indiana before joining up with Bill Dobslaw and moving to Michigan, under some dumb name that might well have been the Teen Tones. Can anyone verify? It's a good record, in any case.....

A couple of interesting things on British UA: "Yesterday's Hero" by Jeff Phillips (UP 35893) is a Vanda-Young song about faded popstars making comebacks. It's a solid, kinetic pop-rocker with a catchy melody hook. Better than most recent V-Y songs. Also "I Am An Aminal" (sic) by an anonymous group called Tiger (UP 35848) is a typically simple British pube-glitter tune that's a surprise to see on UA and not RAK. A good two-chord romp. Also from England, a strange, very

(turn to page 42)

JUKE BOX JURY, JR.

(continued from page 28)

intense thing called "Rave 'N' Rock" by Daddy Maxfield (Pye 7n 45266, '73) that shouldn't go unheard.

Fans of early '60s high school pud rock should pick up on "You Made Me Cry" by the Small-Fries (Mutual 501), apparently the first release on the label that later had the Chartbusters. This sounds like Lesley Gore if she had recorded for Chancellor, in a garage. Rather primitive for this usually-polished style, which makes it a rare example of its type, but the melody and some of the production touches are very strong, and it's a nice female vocal. "Here Comes School Again" by Tony Ray (Dot 17301) was produced by Ray Ruff (of Texas punk fame) and Jack Nitzsche, and is a powerful, Eddie Cochran-like rocker with a vocal reminiscent of early Bob Seger. Definitely worth finding. An unusual and surprisingly unknown record is "Everybody's Gone Into April" by the Bone (Poison Ring 712). Good power chording and a good melody back a singer who sounds unnervingly like Ray Davies. Very nice. Willie Alexander's "Mass Ave."/"Kerouac" is reviewed elsewhere, but I just wanted to add that it's a great neo-punk sound, not unlike the early Velvets. Order from Garage Records, Box 308, Newtonville, MA 02060, $1.25. Willie, of course, was formerly with the Lost, and also Doug Yule's Velvet Underground, so I guess it makes some kind of sense.....

Greg Shaw's ERRATA & ADDENDA

(Thanks to George Tweedy, Dick Rosemont, Joel Bernstein, Vic Figlar, Joe Sicurella, Bob Westfall, Don Huff, Fred Masotti, Al Quaglieri, Tony Arioli, Ed Engel, Jim Santa, Kevin Walsh, John Blair, Mad Peck, Bill Smart, Tom Elligett, Steve Kolanjian)

BAY AREA
Diplomacy 3 - Jim Doval & Gauchos - Scrub/Donna
Diplomacy 3* - Jim Doval & Gauchos - Scrub/Barracuda
Diplomacy 21 - Stepping Stones - Pills/So Tough
Diplomacy 15- Stepping Stons - Little Girl of Mine/I Only Want to Dance With You
Diplomacy 30 - Brymers - I Want to Tell You/Sacrifice
Diplomacy ? - April Silva - Under My Thumb
Jimmy Holiday -- "The New Breed" (dip. 20) & "I Can't Stand It" (Dip. 23) were combined on Kent 482

South Bay 101 - Darryle Gentry & Januarys - Lonely Am I/There Is a Ship
The Wildwood - Free Ride/Wildwood County - Magnum 421
Merced Blue Notes - Rufus/Your Tender Lips - Accept
Bethlehem Exit - Walk Me Out/Blues Concerning My Girl - Jabberwock 110 (Walnut Creek)
Rhythm Rockers - Does She Love Me/Sail On - Chance
Trolls - Walkin' Shoes/How Do You Expect Me to Trust You?/ - Peatlore 23267 (both sides written by Jim McPherson of People; great Brummels-like folk-rock.)
Batwing 1001 - Gotham City Crime Fighters - Who Stole the Batmobile/That's Life

HANNA-BARBERA RECORDS
443 - Billy Bossman - Up the Road/same, instr.
480 - Epics - Blue Turns to Grey/Goes to Show (Sloan-Barri)
489 - Ronnie & Robyn - Cradle of Love/Dreamin'
492 - 13th Floor Elevators - You'reGonnaMissMe/Tried to Hide
512 - Rainy Day People - Junior Executive/I'm Telling It to You

KNICKERBOCKERS
Jimmy Walker - Chop on Wood/Feel the Warm - Columbia 4-45181

SEEDS
Psych-Out Soundtrack - Tower 5913: Two Fingers Pointing at You

FLAMIN' GROOVIES
Played on Roger Ruskin Spear's Electric Shocks: Mattress Man

Mike 4007 - Attic Sounds/Shadows/Let Us Pray
Enith 1266 - Tri-Lites - You're Looking atMyGuy/Oowee, Oowe
Enith 1268 - Spats - Gator Tails&Monkey Ribs/The Roach
Enith 715 - Danny Weldon - Surf Dreamin'
Cameo 456 - Demotrons - Beg, Borrow & Steal/Midnight in NY
Cameo 104 - Tommy Ferguson Trio - Mary Anne/Jus Squeeze Me

MICHIGAN REVISITED

Our history of Michigan rock in #13 generated a large and much-appreciated response. There are undoubtedly many more local discs to be discovered, and we thank all those who sent in these additional listings.

MICHIGAN ADDENDA

IMPACT RECORDS
1002 Mickey Denton - Mi Amore/Aint Love Grand
1010 Tartans - I Need You/Nothing But Love
1012 Classmen - Everything's Alright
1016 Nick & Dino - Wish I Was a Kid Again/Boy
1017 Volumes - Trouble I've Seen/That Same Old Feeling
1020 Sincerely Yours - Shady Lane/Little Girl
1027 Patti & Mickey - My Guy, My Girl/

PALMER RECORDS
5000 Tobi Lark - I'll Steal Your Heart/Talk to An Angel
5002 Tim Tam & Turn-Ons - Wait a Minute/Opelia
5003 Tim Tam & Turn-Ons - Cheryl Ann/Seal it With a Kiss
5007 Me & Dem Guys - Black Cloud/Come On Little Sweetheart
5010 Shaggs - The Way I Care/RingAround theRosie
5017 Canadian Rogues - Ooh-Poo-Pa-Doo/Deep in Touch
5018 Trademarks - I Need You/If I Was Gone
5022 Ronnie Gaylord & Burt Holiday - A Place to Hideaway/Love (Where Have You Gone?)
5032 Joey Welz - The Mini Rock 'n Roll Revival/A Rose and a Baby Ruth
5034 Joey Welz- Return to Me/Pretty is as Pretty
5036 Joey Welz - Runaway/Come Go With Me Does
5038 EP: Joey Welz - medley of oldies

LUCKY ELEVEN RECORDS
227 Bossmen - Wait and See/You're the Girl for Me
234 Chuck Slaughter - You Got Me Cryin/Tightrope
??? Bossmen - Easy Way Out/Say What You Think
??? Bossmen - Listen Now Girl/I Cannot Stop You

DETROIT SOUND RECORDS
222 Wanted - Here to Stay/Teen World
223 Wanted - Midnight Hour/Here to Stay (also A&M 844)
225 Michael John - Goodbye Babe/You Had My Love
226 Little Sisters - Summer Rain/Just a Boy
229 Little Sisters - First You Break My Heart/Just a Boy
230 Wanted - Lots More Where You Came From/Knock on Wood
232 Wanted - Sad Situation/East Side Story
233 York Mills Trio - Sockit to 'em Tigers
??? Robt. Walker & Night Riders - Keep on Runnin/Everything's Alright

Detroit Sound was headed by promoter Erv Steiner, whose son was Chip Steiner of the Wanted.

REFLECTIONS
GW 12 Like Columbus Did/Lonely Girl
GW 22 Wheelin' Dealin'/Deborah Ann
GW 29 Girl in the Candy Store/Your Kind of Love
ABC 10822 Long Cigarette/Gotta Find Out

Reflections LP was Golden World 300, not 301.

JAMIE COE
Addison 15001 - Summertime Symphony/There's Gonna Be a Day (first record, ca. '59
ABC 10120 Goodbye My Love/There's Never Been a
ABC 10149 Jesse James/Say You Night
Enterprise 5050 I Cried on My Pillow/My Girl

MITCH RYDER
New Voice 830 Ruby Baby & Peaches on a Cherry Tree/You Get Your Kicks
Mitch Ryder's Greatest Hits - Virgo 12001 ('72)

(as Billy Lee & Rivieras)
Hyland 3016 Won't You Dance With Me/You Know

(as The Motivations)
Dynovoice ??? Slow Fizz/?
(as Detroit)
Paramount 0133 - Rock & Roll/A Box of Old Roses

MISCELLANEOUS LISTINGS
Fenton 1004 JuJus - You Treat Me Bad/Hey Little Girl (fantastic punk rocker)
Fenton 2016 - Saharas - I'm Free/The Mornin'
Panik 5112 - Only Ones- You're the Reason/Find a Way
CAMEL DRIVERS - You Made a Believer of Me/Give It a Try - Top Dog 200 (It's Gonna Rain is #100, not 200)
DOUG BROWN - Swingin' Sue/Blue Night - Checker 1001 (early '62)
DEBUTANTES - On Broadway/Little Latin Lupe Lou - Gail & Rice 101

FABULOUS PACK - Tears Come Rollin'/Color of Our Love - Wingate 007
FABULOUS PEPS - I Can't Get Right/Why are You Blowing My Mind - Premium Stuff #1
GIGOLO'S - Dont You Just Know It/Movin' Out - Enterprise 5000
TERRY KNIGHT & PACK - You Lie/Kids Will Be the Same - A&M 769
LAZY EGGS - I'm Gonna Love You/As Long as I Have You - Enterprise 5060
LENNY & THUNDERTONES - Thunder Express/Alabamy Bound - COmma 444
ME & DEM GUYS - Black Cloud/Dont You Just Know IT - Dearborn 550
NEW ERA - We Ain't Got Time/Won't You Please Be My Friend - Great Lakes 2532
ONLY ONES - You're the Reason/Find a Way - Panik 5002
ONES - As Long as I've Got You?/? - Rare Earth 5018
ONES - You Haven't Seen My Love - Motown 1117
PLAGUES - Why Cant You Be True/Through This World - Quarantined 2020
PLEASURE SEEKERS - Good Kind of Hurt/Light of Love - Mercury 72800
? & MYSTERIANS - Make You Mine/I Love You Baby - Capitol 2126 (great!)
? & MYSTERIANTS - Hot 'n Groovy/Funky Lady - Luv 159 '72
LINDA RAE - I Don't See My Baby/I'll Always Remember - Meadowbrook (no #)
RAINY DAYS - Turn On Your Lovelight/Go On & Cry - Panik 7542
RAINY DAYS - I Can Only Give You Everything/Go On & Cry - Panik 7566
BOB SEGER - Heavy Music, Persecution Smith, and East Side Story all re-released on Abkco.
SHY GUYS - Payin' My Dues/? - Shamley 44001
SUNLINERS - Hit It/The Islander - Hercules 183
DANNY ZELLA & HIS ZELL ROCKS - Wicked Ruby - Fox 10057 (perhaps Detroit's first real rocker)

MICHIGAN ERRATA

The Yorkshires' "Tossed Aside" was typoed as "Tossed Salad" (p.37) ... The mention of Frost evolvint into Bossmen was, of course, reversed; the Bossmen became Frost ... Under the A-Square listing, the asterisk should say Cameo, not Capitol ... Hideout 1004, by the Underdogs, was mistakenly listed under the Shy Guys ... Under Bob Seger, "Ramblin' Gamblin' Man" was preceded (not followed) by "2 + 2, although the former was actually recorded earlier at Cameo ... The name of the group on SVR 1008 was The Unknown ... And obviously, there were more than 2 releases on Coconut Groove (as reported in the Flint section), since the accompanying label listing included 8 ... And, an interesting theory, but it makes sense: the Westchester label apparently used Hideout numbers............

"Black Cloud" by Me & Dem Guys is Palmer 5007 as well as on Coral Gables. A different version of "Black Cloud" came out on Dearborn 550, also by Me & Dem Guys... Glenn Frey, Doug Brown & Davy Whitehouse (Underdogs) sang background vocals on "Heavy Music." Frey also sang on "Ramblin' Gamblin' Man"...

(Readers are encouraged to write to this column with questions concerning any aspect of record collecting or rock history—our staff of experts is ready and waiting to take on all comers! One of the functions of this column is to discuss subjects too limited for feature coverage, so please, send your information, queries and comments, and we'll respond as best we can. —Ed.)

EQUAL SPACE FOR SPACE

Your editorial this time was truly superb. You obviously gave considerable thought to the matter of cycles in rock—and I don't mean Hondas and Harley-Davidsons either. You substantiated your claims very well and I really think it is a piece that should get much wider distribution. Very well wrought and quite thought-provoking. There are some areas that I think missed your attention but perhaps they don't really fit into the scheme after all. I was going to mention groups like Dan Hicks & His Hot Licks, Maria Muldaur, and the David Bromberg Band, but I guess they are not really compatible with your discussion of teen music, for their audiences tend to be older freaks, not the teenyboppers who do indeed set the rock trends. I think you did overlook the whole space rock set, however. I think Hawkwind was the first of that school I ever heard. Didn't care much for them and the others but they are a real sector of the rock scene. Even though I don't care for it I do think it is a cycle that should not be ignored. But it can easily be placed onto your chart and in no way interferes with the validity of your comments.

—Terry Hughes
Arlington, VA

BACK TO PUNKHEAD?

Everyone who's read the latest *WPTB* has been thoroughly impressed. Jerry Rubin, the music director of W4, thought it the best thing he's seen. I also was informed that John Sinclair, Ted Lucas, and Jerry Patton were all in a state of awe over the Michigan history. Sinclair has since gone straight, no doubt as a result of *WPTB*. In fact, I've heard of some Krishna people pushing *WPTB* instead of the infamous *Back to Godhead* fanzine.

—Pat Murphy
Detroit, Mich.

IF IT'S NOT ALREADY....

I was in England not long ago and got to see some of the British groups the way they are today, and many of them have really changed. Did you know that Freddie of Freddie & the Dreamers has his own TV show? I would say it would be England's answer to our "Wonderama" that's on Sunday mornings here in the East. I also saw the Hollies, Dave Clark Five, the Rolling Stones, the Bee Gees, and I even got to see Lulu who has her own show every week on ITV which is England's Independent TV station. Peter Noone was a guest on the show. He also has changed, he sure isn't the innocent little Herman we used to know! Any idea when he'll have a new record out?

Your magazine is really far out by the way. I believe that it should really be one of the biggest selling mags in the country if it's not already.

—Mame Reinmann
Parsippany, NJ

[Peter Noone now lives in California much of the time, and has just released his second single on Casablanca. The Hermits are apparently doing well on their own, playing clubs and campuses in the East and the South.]

MEMORIES OF JOY PLEASURE SHOP

The Detroit history was excellent. I remember being a rock & roll teenager buying 45's from Dan Bourgoise at his store "Joy Pleasure Shop" (the best white record store in Detroit). He once told me how embarrassed he was about calling his company "Bimas Music." Don't forget the importance of Terry Knight in Detroit. He *was* the Sixth Rolling Stone. He once played "It's All Over Now" for one hour continuously on CKLW.

—A. Trentacosta
Menlo Park, CA

LOOSE ENDS

Diplomacy was a Tulare label, if anything, co-owned by Al Verissimo and Bill Silva. This pair sold Jim Doval & the Gauchos masters to ABC and one to Dot. Enith 1268 was "Gator Tails & Monkey Ribs"/"The Roach" by the Spats (before ABC). Can you locate the Johnson Brothers? There was another (San Jose) Chance release. "Does She Love Me"/"Sail On" by the Rhythm Rockers featuring the elusive Troyce Key on vocals. The Rhythm Kings on Tollie, both sides are previously released surf instrumentals, with overdubbed vocals. The Brogues were from Merced, I guess everybody knows that. They played Fresno lots (along with the Cindermen, the Roadrunners, the Ebonites, Jesters and others).

—Bill Smart
Fresno, CA

[What to you know about the Johnson Bros.? I just found their version of "Casting My Spell" on Valor, which I guess is the original, but who were they and how did this obscure record come to be done by so many English groups?]

PILLS

The editorials look sane, sound sane, and taste sane. Well, anyway.... your analysis of the rock cycles struck me as basically true, although I could quibble with your idea of "a general climate of optimism has returned to America" now that Nixon has gone. I think that there is a certain relief on everyone's part now, but in view of the continuing sagas of Rockefeller, the CIA and Middle-East crises, the current mood of the country may perhaps be likened to mild catatonia following sensory overload. Which helps sell crisp but shallow records to a freaked-out populace, but doesn't really equal "optimism." As for a new generation coming along to change the music to their own ends—I'm sure something will occur when they finally take all those so-called "hyper-active" school children off of downers—most likely a new era of 30-second long songs to fit the fractured attention spans of our post-literate generation of former junkies.

—Jay Kinney
San Francisco, CA

[Well, perhaps I was being a bit prematurely optimistic, if you'll pardon the expression. I think the process itself is inevitable, but as you correctly point out, there are so many tangential factors that effect the evolution of pop, things we're just beginning to understand, that can seriously influence the "natural" progression of things... but hope springs eternal, and all I know is there sure are a hell of a lot more great records coming out these days than a couple of years ago, and I think kids are changing a lot faster than people realize. I mean, when sidewalk surfing becomes a national craze in 1975.....]

USZNIEWICZ-TONES IDENTIFIED

In regard to your review of "Surfin School" by King Uszniewicz and the Uszniewiscz-Tones, the lead singer was Mike Patterson, *aka* "Lurch" (not the same Mike Patterson as in Mike Patterson & the Fugitives, famous for the single "Jerky"/"Cookin' Beans"). Mike is a roadie for Brownsville Station and the guitar is played by Cub Koda, while the lead is shared by Patterson. I learned from Patterson that there are only 100 copies of this disc. I also heard another tune from the same session, a cover of the Novas' "The Crusher." Also, the so-called kazoo solo on "Surfin School" was Cub Koda on sax.

—Leo G. Whitehouse II
Destroyed, Mich.

MORE TRIVIA

In reference to Sal Valentino: he recorded at least one solo record prior to his involvement with the Brummels. This was "I Wanna Twist"/"Lisa Marie" ON Falco 306, a San Francisco label which also released the great "Candy Apple Red Impala" by Little "E" & the Mello-tone Three. Also a member of Stoneground was John Blakely who did a lot of gigging around the Riverside area in the '60s. He was the lead guitar for a group called the Sandals (*Endless Summer* soundtrack). The Sandals released several 45s and 2 LPs on the World Pacific label.

—John Blair
Riverside, CA

THE REAL POOP

Some random info and memories concerning the subjects of the last two *Bomps*:

Seeds: I have vivid recollections of the Seeds showing up hours late for a gig at the Thousand Oaks Recreation Center wherein hundreds of screaming teenies were packed to the rafters. I wasn't a Seeds fan (their musical ineptitude appalled me) but I *was* curious about "big time" band backstage activities. It was there that I discovered what I rather remotely suspected about the band. They were re-learning their material because they had forgotten how to play it! They were nice people, though, and it was as funny to them as it was to me. They proceeded to play 3 songs and then split!

Beau Brummels: *Triangle* was described by *Playboy* in its record review section as the "best rock album of the year." I disagree with Bill Small's description of "One Too Many Mornings"—I still find the Brummels' version appealing and a lot of other people in the Ventura County area did also, where it was a small regional hit. No mention was made of the incredibly rotten sound quality on *Bradley's Barn*. The Beau Brummels were also in a film (*Wild Wild Winter* or some such teen-a-go-go type flick) in which they did a vocal version of their instrumental "Woman" (from *Vol. Two*). They also did a remixed (or re-recorded) version of another of their songs, the title of which escapes me right now.

Hollywood Stars: According to the wife of the drummer in Adrian, Adrian never made an album; however Adrian (the bloke the band was named after) recorded an album with a group of his called the Tangerine Zoo (which did *not* contain any members of the band Adrian, particularly Scott Phares. The band was Boston-based).

—William Stout
Hollywood, CA

[They made two albums, in fact: Mainstream 6107 and 6116.]

THE WIGAN SOUND

Comparing the similarities of "Glitter rock 72/73" with the '65 Mod period was interesting, tho I have different ideas. Glitter rock (i.e. Roxy, Gary, Slade, Sweet) were to me just flabby, ageing rockers camping it up in a last desperate bid for the big time. I agree they brought "fun" back & made 45's respectable (well a bit) again, but if you compare the main exponents of glitter to the Mod stars of the mid-60s, I can't see it. The only one who really fits your analogy is Bowie, and this is where I suspect you draw most of your opinion from.: What was more or just as comparable to '65 was the follow-up fad in England, "Northern Soul", which started to emerge nationally in mid-73, just on the fall of Glitter rock. This latest cult had no leaders, just as Mod in '63, yet kids were dictating what discs were to be heard & what clothes to be worn—as with Mod. Most of all, dancing became "in" again. By late '74 the writing was on the wall for England's most promising teen trend since '67.

Northern Soul was essentially a Midlands-based cult, especially Wigan, and the center of all the action was the Wigan Casino. The discs were mainly just old soul stuff from '67-70 that never made it at the time. Worst of all came a disc, the ultimate in hype by--get this! Wigan's Chosen Few, called "Skiing in the Snow." The group was featured on *Top of the Pops* with the "top dancers from Wigan" doing their latest thing. As an attempt for respectability and mass following, the whole thing failed dismally.: One who could have emerged as a leader was of course Bowie, who had his ear close to the ground when he suddenly took up "soul" again. The trouble was, he was too big and established in his own role at the time. If he had emerged *with* Northern Soul, i.e. through the clubs, and was more in tune with their thoughts, perhaps this particular teen dream would have been fulfilled.

The plain fact is that all what was laid down during the '60s just ain't gonna happen in the '70s. What have kids today got to be expressive, aggressive or even revolutionary about? We've had the satisfaction of seeing our dreams of greater freedom for young people come true, and now we're paying the price with today's apathetic younger generation and the bland music they accept.

—Don Hughes
Hanworth, Middlesex
-England

BEAU BRUMMELS BROUHAHA

There was a Beau Brummels album you missed in your discography: *The Beau Brummels Sing* on the Post label. Is this the rarest Brummels album? A rare records store in Scranton, PA had 2 sealed copies and over 74 bids came in on them. Top bid was $145.00.... There are cuts on it that were not on any of their albums on Vault, Autumn or Warner Bros. Can somebody please clear up the origin and true value of this album? The other Post albums (Crests, etc) seem to be pretty common.

—Jim Flanik
Ambridge, PA

MICHIGAN GRAFFITI

The only Michigan group I saw live in the mid-60s was the Lourds. It was at our 1965 Spring Fling and they crashed the place. We had already paid another band but halfway through the dance the Lourds came in with their equipment while the other band took a break.. There were five Lourds and every one had picked a Rolling Stone to copy. John Drake had Jagger's every move down pat. Also, to answer a question of yours, Ted Nugent was in the Lourds. In fact, I still have the group's business card with their names on it. But it wasn't a progression from Lourds to Dukes. It went from the Lourds to the Gang in early '66 to the Amboy Dukes.

—Danny Ray
Hollywood, CA

BOMP RECORDS

("Yesterday's Sound Today!")

INTRODUCES

BRINGING MERSEYBEAT TO THE SEVENTIES AS YOU HAVEN'T HEARD IT IN YEARS!

NO MERE NOSTALGIA MONGERS, THE POPPEES ARE A NEW, EXCITING, CREATIVE GROUP WITH ROOTS IN LIVERPOOL, A SOUND AS FRESH AS ANYTHING OUT TODAY, AND NEW SONGS THAT RANK WITH THE CLASSICS OF THE SIXTIES.

THE POPPEES' DEBUT SINGLE IS AVAILABLE NOW ON BOMP RECORDS. IT WAS RECORDED IN NEW YORK, IN THE SAME STUDIO USED BY THE McCOYS AND THE STRANGELOVES, PRODUCED BY GREG SHAW AND CRAIG LEON.

"IF SHE CRIES" is a raving original, with all the spirit of the early Mersey groups, destined to become a classic of its type

"LOVE OF THE LOVED" is a 1963 Lennon-McCartney song, written for Cilla Black, heard here for the first time as the Beatles themselves might have done it!

"IF SHE CRIES"/"LOVE OF THE LOVED" by THE POPPEES - BOMP 103

LIMITED PRESSING
$2.00

BOMP RECORDS, P.O. BOX 7112, BURBANK, CALIFORNIA 91510

Rock History & Trivia · Jukebox Jury · International Rock News

WHO PUT THE BOMP!

Spring '76 $1.50 / 75p

Gala Girl Issue

THE RUNAWAYS
Jailbait Rock

LEADERS OF THE PACK:
Jackie DeShannon
Lesley Gore
Shangri-Las

DAVE EDMUNDS
The Rockfield Rebel

Plus:

Liverpool Today

Flamin' Groovies:
new LP!

Chicago rock
in the '60s

British Rock
Encyclopedia

...and much more!

THE BEAT
Editorial by Greg Shaw

Well, here we are again. A little late as usual, but closer to being on schedule than ever before; we'll get there yet! We've got a fun issue for you this time. Besides the survey of Chicago rock that you've been clamoring for for so long, and a new installment of our monumental British Rock Encyclopedia, this issue features the story of Dave Edmunds, the man Phil Spector regards as the best producer around today and whose career is documented here exclusively for the first time anywhere, along with the inside story on Rockfield Studios, which many consider to be the most important studio in the world today, and certainly the only one that can be said to have a "Sound" in the classic sense of labels like Sun and Philles. In addition to that, we've got informative, thought-provoking stories on three of my favorite, and too often unsung, female artistes: Lesley Gore, Jackie DeShannon, and the sublime Shangri-Las. Who could ask for anything more?

The Rockfield story is, of course, a result of my visit to England during September and October of last year. It was my first time over, and quite a thrill. As expected, I found London to be virtually bereft of old records, and about as "swinging" as San Diego. And yet, beneath the surface, there's a lot going on. The pub scene is still active, only instead of country-rock groups the pubs are full of bands influenced by Dr. Feelgood and, yes, the Flamin' Groovies. I saw a group called the Snakes (featuring guitarist Nick Garvey of Ducks Deluxe fame) who did a set consisting of 4 Groovies tunes and the rest Chuck Berry songs. Chicago blues/R&B seems more popular than at any time since 1965. A group called the Count Bishops (great name!), soon to have an EP out, do strict interpretations of electric blues, and several others that I heard about but wasn't able to see are apparently equally promising. One other group I saw, Eddy & the Hot Rods, were (don't laugh!) like some weird combination of the Chocolate Watchband and the N.Y. Dolls; they did crude, teenage punk music, with a couple of good originals, and a lot of posturing. Their manager, who stood beside me in the pub while a full crowd danced, turned out to be a BOMP reader. With the growing number of fan-oriented labels and entrepeneurs springing up, hopefully a lot of these groups will be recorded soon—and you can be sure that when they are, we'll let you know.

CONVENTIONAL THOUGHTS

It was great seeing so many of you at the ECHO '75 convention in New York last October. Suzy and I had a marvelous time, and I think we all owe Mark Zakarin a hand for his pioneering effort in organizing the con. Rock fandom has reached a point now where such conventions are feasible at least once a year, and regional cons (west coast, east coast, midwest) might even be practical. The main obstacle seems to be that nobody in rock fandom has any experience in organizing cons—for there are myriad problems that have to be dealt with before one can be put on. But ECHO set a high level of professionalism, and if we can learn from the few mistakes (confused scheduling, over-crowding, other minor things), rock cons will be a source of much fun for us all in times to come.

• The BOMP editorial board meets at ECHO '75. L-R: Alan Betrock, Greg Shaw, Ken Barnes.

The fact that so many people turned up at this con, despite rain and other factors, is but a further indication of what direction we can expect rock fandom to go in over the next couple of years. Most of the attendees were not hard-core collectors; a lot of them were looking only for records by Bowie or Elton John. But we have to realize that contemporary records are now a big part of the collecting scene, which of course is healthy. The more removed we become from that old attitude of "oldies" vs. "new" music, the more aware we'll all be. Young people who start by collecting new records soon learn to develop an interest in the roots, going back to discover what they've missed. Thus rock fandom as a whole undergoes a steady process of enlargement as successive waves of participants start at the fringes and work their way deeper.

The result of this will be a rock fandom many times larger than anything we've seen, as more and more average record buyers realize that there's an organized outlet for their interests. And the type of fandom that will develop is one based on taste and musical quality, rather than nostalgia. This is something I've always felt was of supreme importance, that we not turn the '60s into a travesty as the fans of '50s rock did to their decade, almost to a point beyond repair. It's vital for the mass body of rock fans to be educated enough about all phases of rock history to respect and encourage valid revivals and reworkings of past styles, to avoid the sort of "oldies" prejudice that has proved fatal to so many artists whose only crime was not fading away, and to have the musical awareness and grounding necessary to develop good taste—the ultimate result of which will be better music for all of us, and less garbage thrust on us by the tastes of ignorant buyers.

The role of rock fandom is to nurture the educational process; to make available, through gatherings like ECHO and magazines like BOMP the information, the records, and their sources, for those who want to learn more about the music.

One of the most valuable projects toward this end is the *Record Collectors' Price Guide* just published by Jerry Osborne and Bruce Hamilton. Every major collecting field, from baseball cards to comic books, relies on this sort of volume to set a standard for the field, making it easier for the novice to become acquainted with the ground rules and feel at home among other collectors. This volume, which is being widely advertised in mass magazines and on TV, will have the effect of swelling the ranks of fans enormously, and as time goes by I think we will see record collecting take its place as one of the great hobbies of our time, rivalling stamp and coin collecting. If rock music is the most far-reaching cultural movement of this period in history (which few would deny) then the collecting of records as a national pastime seems inevitable.

MEET THE POPPEES

Another great thing about the ECHO con was seeing the Poppees and the Marbles perform. The whole New York scene has become very active again, and these two groups are among the more interesting. The Marbles are managed by our old friend Alan Betrock, contributing editor to BOMP and former publisher of *TRM*. Naturally a chap of Alan's refined taste wouldn't become involved with any group that wasn't young and talented and in some way influenced by the rock classics of the '60s, which the Marbles are. They do all original songs, have a fresh, engaging stage manner, and should make it. If you're a record company A&R man, take heed.

By now many of you have heard the Poppees' debut single on Bomp Records, and don't need to be told that they're the closest thing to an authentic Liverpool group that's been seen on these shores since the last Gerry & the Pacemakers tour. They also happen to be fine songwriters and masters of English-style harmony singing, and I believe they have a big future; that's why they were the first, and so far the only, act signed to Bomp Records, and the next recordings we do should be a lot more indicative of the full range of their talents.

• The Poppees: Arthur, Pat and Bob (holding guitars) and their ex-drummer. New drummer, Jett Harris, will be seen on the group's upcoming EP cover.

However, it's as a live band that they come across best, which is why I so enjoyed seeing them in New York, since it was the first time I'd had a chance to observe them in concert. They only do one Beatles song, "Love of the Loved"; the rest of their set consists of the kind of material all the Liverpool/Hamburg groups were doing in 1961 and '62, and they've got the style, look and attitude down cold. It's not as obvious as some of the Beatle Revival groups making the rounds, but it's a concept any reader of BOMP should delight in. If you're in or around New York, I strongly advise you to check them out; they play regularly at various NY clubs such as CBGB's.

This column's a bit cramped (as John Denver, who has such a remarkable way with words, says, we're all "looking for space" this issue), so the usual random ramblings are truncated—none of the enthralling concert reviews, trendy gossip and trenchant commentary which have impelled thousands of Bomp readers to turn immediately to the discographies. Before quickly moving to the record section ("I had the impression that Reverberations started out as a regular column and degenerated into a record review," writes one satisfied customer, in a touching testimonial), I thought I'd list a few faves of this past year, as a helpful outline of my current tastes and incidentally as proof I don't live in 1966 *all* the time).

•The best single of 1975? Ken Barnes thinks so.... you got any better ideas?

Top Single of 1975 (non-hit division): "You Were So Warm"—Dwight Twilley Band (even better than "I'm on Fire")
Top Hit Single: "Love Hurts"—Nazareth
Top Albums: Simultaneously too many and not enough—no single standout, but *Beserkley Chartbusters* is as good a candidate as any (especially Jonathan Richman—can't wait for their Modern Lovers LP!)
Top Live Band: Hunter-Ronson (real staying power, too)
Top Airplay Irritant: "Feelings"—Morris Albert
Top New Fanzine: *Back Door Man*—the fanzine future is in their hands.
Top Publication: *New Musical Express*, hands down. NME invariably comes up with a product that for literary elan, critical vision, humor and general outrage puts everyone else to shame—and they do it *every* week.
Top Tip For Liverpool of 1976: San Diego—right, Alan?

Well, that's a representative sample. Leader of the pack so far for '76, singles division, is Patti Smith's "Gloria," an incomparable rock & roll rush on a 45 and a remarkable tribute to a classic anthem. (Parenthetical rambling reminiscence: Them's version only reached #93 nationally, but up and down California it was #1 and without doubt the most popular rock band staple of the midsixties. Everybody did it—in fact, rummaging through my tape box, I unearthed a 30-minute extemporaneous "Gloria" medley from 1966 performed by an embryonic version of the Savage Cabbage, the notorious band I was in. It poses no threat to Patti & Group). The live, non-LP "My Generation" on the flip is brash and crude, and I like it the same way I like earlier covers of the song by the Bards, the Rovin' Kind, and others—and I hope Lenny Kaye, for one, will take that as the compliment it is.

Dick Campbell Sings Where It's At—Mercury SR 61060/MG 21060—
A major exhumation here. The site was Chicago, and carbon dating establishes the time as late 1965/early 1966. Wedged in a rock formation known as "igneous" or "blues-folk," it is a perfectly preserved fossil, a facile carbon copy of Dylan's "Like A Rolling Stone" style, which precedes Mouse & the Traps and other inspired imitations. Campbell can't really sing, but the backing is raucous blues/folk-rock, with Mike Bloomfield supplying the same guitar licks he bestowed upon Dylan. Other session notables include Peter Cetera, later with Chicago; Marty Grebb (Buckinghams), and two-thirds of the Paul Butterfield Blues Band—all for some highly amusing period protest songs (titles: "The Blues Peddlers," "The People Planners"—these made up a single, Mercury 72511—"Despairs Cafeteria," "Girls Named Misery," "Object of Derision," and "Approximately Four Minutes of Feeling Sorry For D.C."). And you thought P.F. Sloan and Bruce Springsteen were heavy....There's also a genuinely pretty tune, "Where Were You," later covered by Ian & the Zodiacs (in which configuration I raved about it a few Reverbs back). Scour the drugstores for this one!

ADAM SAYLOR - "I Will Go Away" - Original Sound 57 - '66
More protest, one of the earlier explicit anti-draft numbers, fraught with throbbing conviction, as passionate as Bob Seger's classic "2+2," which it slightly resembles. Real anguish in the chorus:
"I've been drinkin' thinkin' all night long
Are the leaders right or are they wrong
The answer to the question I don't know
But if they call me I will go...
Away—even if it's to stay"
One odd couplet: "If I had a degree I'd be an advertiser/But now I'm gonna be another Viet adviser".

•The Count Bishops bring Pretty Things consciousness back to the London pub scene (and motorbikes too....).

COUNT BISHOPS - *Speedball* - Chiswick 1 (EP)
Finally, a new one—this four-track EP dates from last year but you'd swear it was 1965 as the Bishops power through vintage Londonized R&B with as much velocity and as little regard for the original nuances as the Rolling Stones or Pretty Things in their prime. Every bit as good as Dr. Feelgood, with "Beautiful Delilah" perhaps the standout (other tracks: "Route 66," "I Ain't Got You," and "Teenage Letter").

SATANS - "Makin' Deals"/"Lines & Squares"— Manhattan 801 '66
The label's distributed by Dover out of New Orleans, but the record's from L.A., produced by Bob Summers (a Mike Curb crony with interesting credits). Well before "Sympathy for the Devil" Lucifer (who's got a terrific Standells-style delivery, by the way) was makin' deals for souls and asking "Can you guess my name?" The Satans' tough hard-rock sound is unbeatable. Flip's an odd folk-rock version of "The Bears" (the Quicksilver/Fastest Group Alive novelty), best I've heard.

NOVAS - "William,Jr."/"And It's Time" - S.T.A.R. 001 '66
This is from Texas (the label initials stand for Southwestern Talent and Recording), extremely polished 5 Americans-style folk-rock, possibly even better than that fine group. Lyrical content unexceptional, but both sides are musically superb.

NEW GENERATION - "Sadie & Her Magic Mr. Galahad" - Spark 1000(E) '68
Iain Sutherland's early groups first record, as good as the previously-cited "She's a Soldier Boy" (Imperial 66317). Lovely bit of pop-rock, again up there with the best latter-day Sutherlands/Quiver material.

TINTERN ABBEY - "Beeside"/"Vacuum Cleaner" - Deram 169(E) '67
Heavy British acid-pop (1967-69) is becoming a consuming interest of mine, and this oddly-mixed obscurity is one of my favorites. The flip sounds not unlike the Creation, with a feedback that in truth suggests an amplified vacuum cleaner; while "Beeside" (the A-side) sounds like 1969 Pink Floyd as played by a real rock band, and is most mysterious and fascinating.

ELIPSIS SWEET AS CANDY
Lots of other good records were spaced out this time, but some new stuff merits a plug—Roky Erickson's "Two Headed Dog" (Mars 1000), of course, since that alienated alien supplied this column's title...And a whole raft of stuff from Boston—Marc Thor's "Holiday Fire"/"Boystown Boize" (Indy 141) rocks solidly—I like the B-side best...A group called Fate, who made a fair cover of "Darlin'" a year or so back, have come up with one of the most startling Beach Boys cops yet—"How Long" (Rocky Coast 19753, 21 Jacob Way Reading, MA 01867) sounds just like "Feel Flows" or any of those elaborate modern Beach Boys extravaganzas, and melodic too...And Willie Alexander's "Kerouac/Mass Ave.", which just missed last column's deadline, but is nonetheless worthy of a belated but enthusiastic mention...And speaking of the Lost and Boston in general, Ted Myers, who wrote the Lost singles, was later part of a fairly good art-rock group called Chamaeleon Church (on MGM), whose organist was none other than Chevy Chase, star of NBC's fab *Saturday Night*. With Marcia "Flower Children" Strassman costarring on *Welcome Back Kotter*, TV may be the latest refuge for faded rock artists. If only Sky Saxon had capitalized on his *Mothers-In-Law* exposure....

Also in the Beach Boys vein is a killer Flash Cadillac-style harmony rocker called "Good Time Music," by one Jack "Stack-a-Track" (nee Grochmal, I think, on Hot Lix 4001, from 1975). Watch out for more stylized delights from this wizard engineer and friends (pending record deals), including bubblegum, Searchers, and more surf remakes....Small print correction: The One-hit Wonders record last column should have been dated 1972, not 1965...Small print appeal (Part IV): Response to earlier solicitations for overseas (Europe, Australia, Japan, etc.) record-trading correspondences has been somewhat less than totally gratifying. Still anxious to deal here at P.O. Box 7195, Burbank, CA 91510...Small print credits: Fervent thanks to all who sent records and suggestions for this column—maybe someday we'll have space to print actual name-checks....

Final tip: Reliable industry sources indicate the Next Big Thing for 1976 will be horse racing, off-track betting music, spearheaded by Patti Smith's *Horses*, Dylan's *Blood on the Tracks*, and other pioneering "race" records. Already legions of musicians are jockeying for position, but the morning line tabs as early odds-on favorites Bahaman superstars Perry Mutuel and the Wagers. Sporting hair-styles (the famous "fetlocks") and already spurring audiences to foaming frenzies with their high-energy "bookie" jams, they're a cinch to be awarded best-of-breed honors, if they're not saddled with a "too-ethnic" handicap. The reign of Race Music is about to begin, it's sure to stirrup some action. You read it here first....

THE SHANGRI-LAS
Psychodrama In the Suburbs

by Mitch Cohen

At this point in the rock continuum, considering the current media obsession with feminine imagery in rock and our culture at large, it seems appropriate to delve into the life and times of one of the most extreme manifestations of the female figure in rock, the immortal Shangri-Las.

These three Long Island teens were heiresses to a great tradition in girl groupdom, and indeed in rock lore in general—that is, a reputation and a career based on perhaps a half-dozen singles (about ten, really, but why quibble); a total of maybe a half-hour of recorded music. Each one of these hot-selling 45's then had to be a perfect pop statement, gripping yet ephemeral, very much rooted in its time and hence immediately nostalgia-producing. The middle ranks of Billboard's Hot 100 are swarming with similarly-styled groups of the era that couldn't pull it together the second time out: Reparata & the Delrons, Candy & the Kisses, the Jelly Beans. Why then the Shangri-Las, instant myth-makers, subject of penetrating critical analyses, object of disproportionate devotion? The answer, one is tempted to assert, was Shadow Morton, not so much producer as creator, synthesizer. As Spector was to the Ronettes, as Brian Wilson was to American Spring, so was Shadow to the Shangs, though without benefit of marriage, and of course with the indispensible contribution of Ellie Greenwich & Jeff Barry. But it was Shadow, that mysterious pseudo-Spector who earned his monicker by such habits as leaving a meeting for a drink of water and never returning, who posed blatantly in shades and tried to desperately to fulfill the image of what he wanted to be that indeed one can only marvel that he succeeded so well, it was this Shadow Morton who takes the credit for packaging pomp and sentiment into street-corner schmaltz in a way none before or since has been able to approach.

Just picture them. The cover of *Golden Hits of the Shangri-Las* will serve as illustration. They're doing some arcane version of the shing-a-ling, dressed in contrasting pastel pedal-pushers, hoop earrings and white, sleeveless scoop-necked blouses. Check out the one on the far right, the lead singer. Long strands of red Veronica Lake hair, the ends of which cover and curl around her perky little breasts. Unlike the other two, who have both hands flung toward the sky, this peppy number (Mary) has one palm curved against the inside thigh of her pink hip-huggers. Her mouth is wide open. Get the picture? The other two Shangs are her supporting cast, but much more crucial image-wise than the two practically anonymous Vandellas, for

• The Shangs: ladies in waiting to a virgin queen

example.

The Shadow knew that Betty and Mary were the record-buying public, the girls who flanked the head cheerleader hoping for a few cast-offs, jealously ruminating and pumping our heroine for the sordid details as to what transpired behind the bleachers during half-time. Ladies in waiting to a virgin queen. So, on the records, Mary got the action, her inquisitive (or warning, or sympathizing) buddies got their vicarious thrills, and Mary ended up guilt-ridden, seduced and/or abandoned. Nothing like an adolescent martyr. Maryann and Betty, with their taunting cries of "Remember!" or "Yeah? Well I hear he's bad", were the voice of wallflower America. Add to this subliminal message Shadow's montage of threatening strings, sound effects and celestial choruses and there is the crux of the Shangs' short but spiritually enduring career, and the secret of their appeal. They didn't just speak to the "bad" girls out there, they reached every girl who was tempted to sin but wanted to be convinced that her worst fears were well grounded. And their appeal to the boys was obvious.

Some of their best singles, "Leader of the Pack", "Out in the Streets", "Give Him a Great Big Kiss", were composed in whole or part by Jeff Barry and Ellie Geeenwich, among the most prolific of the Brill Building style husband-wife teams. Two solid writers, having a gift for teen drama and realism that was not to be found in their rivals Goffin-King or even Mann-Weil, Barry & Greenwich were a staple of the Spector stock company and free-lance hit makers, and the backbone of Leiber & Stoller's publishing arm Trio Music at the time they formed Red Bird Records (in fact, it could be said that Red Bird was intended as a vehicle for B&G's talents as much as Dimension was for Goffin & King's). They could probably have produced the Shangri-Las almost as well on their own, but as the man who discovered them languishing on such short-sighted labels as Smash and Spokane, seeing their potential and bringing them rightly to Red Bird as the best possible outlet for what they had to offer, of course his involvement was, fortunately, ensured. And beyond the mere greatness of the records, it was his vision of how the group should be packaged and presented that made the Shangri-Las something more than just another great girl group.

A shorter version of this article appeared in Let It Rock *in 1975.*

"Leader of the Pack" is, of course, a legend. Suffice it to add that this serio-comic masterpiece enjoyed the great distinction of being featured on *I've Got a Secret* (Betsy Palmer and Kitty Carlisle or somebody acted it out and the panel had to guess what it was—they couldn't) and also the honor of inspiring a follow-up parody record, "Leader of the Laundromat" by the Detergents and honorable mention in other novelties of the time including Jimmy Cross's classic "I Want My Baby Back" ("I Can Never Go Home Anymore" was also lampooned by the Detergents, less inspiredly, as "I Can Never Eat Home Anymore"). And when the Shangs were appearing at a swanky charity benefit with the Beatles at the Paramount in N.Y. (Oct. '64), the Shadow himself roared onto the stage on a motorcycle and conducted the orchestra in denims, shades and a wild-one leather jacket. The impact on high society was not inconsiderable.

"Out in the Streets" might well be a sequel to "He's a Rebel." Mary has hooked and reformed her hoodlum boyfriend, only to be disappointed by the result, i.e. he's become too damned respectable; the reason she wants him is also the reason she can't possess him. He belongs with the gang, she (with assistance from the envious yentas who chime in on the chorus) concludes. It ain't exactly on a par with the writings of Sophocles, but it's undeniable high tragedy in realistic teenage terms. The elements of classical tragedy recur in all the best Shangri-Las songs; noble souls, brought down by the Achilles heels of their mortal emotions, and doomed by the inexorable finalities of Fate. Never, except on "Great Big Kiss" (which of course could merely be the prelude to the anguish of "Never Go Home Anymore") are the Shangri-Las allowed to experience the simple bliss enjoyed by most other girl groups with their Chapels of Love. We must empathize with the pangs of guilt felt by the semi-suburban slut who took her man out of his element. Barry & Greenwich's cosmopolitan savvy endowed "Streets" with a kind of smirky charm, emphasized by Shadow's dense production. And the bridge ("He grew up on the sidewalks...") is pure N.Y. bop, a piece of churning beauty.

The death of the young lovers in "Give Us Your Blessings" is the quintessence of the Shangri-Las' talent for piling up one wave of emotion over another, culminating in the final tragedy. They didn't see the sign that said Detour because they were crying over the fact that they had to elope due to their parents' misunderstanding and disapproval of their relationship. This Barry-Greenwich heartbreaker is historically notable primarily for the double death. Traditionally, in "Teen Angel", "Tell Laura", "Last Kiss" etc., there is one of the pair left to despair over the loss of the other. Here, only the parents are left to take the blame and grieve. The formula, then, is death as an ultimate act of defiance, and the Shangs brought it to life with far greater mastery than Ray Peterson's histrionic original.

While we're on the subject of parents, it might here be noted that Shadow went on to produce the records of one Janis Ian, a whining kvetch now attempting a comeback with basically the same formula. The fact is that Janis Ian was merely a turned-on, intellectual Shangri-La, and while we really can't see her black stud of "Society's Child" ramming his bike into a tree, the tearful sacrifice is very nearly identical, as are the reactions of each girl's schoolmates. Only the Shangs were a lot more fun. Ol' sensitive Janis, furthermore, for all her posturing would never have been able to pull off "I Can Never Go Home Anymore", an hysterical tour-de-force that turns the tables on "Give Us Your Blessings." On this one the child abandons the mother, sort of like "I'm Living in Shame", and dear mom dies of loneliness, leaving a contrite daughter weeping. With the dual themes of parental conflict and thwarted sexual relationships filling those Red Bird grooves, the diary-scribbling female market was a wrap-up. For awhile, anyway.

The commercial success of the Shangri-Las began and ended on the beach. One can only assume that the swain who used and abused the protagonist of "Remember (Walking in the Sand)" is the cause of her defensive frigidity in "Past, Present and Future," where she warns a boy who walks with her along the shore, "Don't try to touch me, 'cause that will never happen again." These two records were among the oddest single releases of the mid-Sixties, the first a monstrous end-of-summer smash replete with ominous piano chords and squalling seagulls, the second a triumph of sustained dramatic mood and a relative chart disaster, utilizing strains of Beethoven (a precursor to Shadow's involvement with Vanilla Fudge) and an eerie spoken narration, oblique in its sexual references. By that time the particular brand of histrionics Shadow concocted for the Shangs had begun to seem remote from an audience ready, it seemed, for a different type of honesty and maturity. Sadly, few of the new breed came even close to the crude, overblown gut-level greatness of the Shangri-Las.

The Shangri-Las had a deadly, exact sense of our inflated notions of life—however absurd their little melodramas, they were no less so than the daily excesses of awakening emotion among their

adolescent purchasers. What Shadow Morton and the Shangri-Las attempted to do was deal out a stacked deck to people who had to believe that a returned I.D. was a gesture of heroic proportions, that mommy and daddy could never possibly comprehend the depth of their feelings. It was a pre-fab exercise in under-the-streetlights and behind-the-bushes sociology, and the main characters were instantly recognizable whether we wanted to get into their pants or participate second-hand in their soap opera tragedies. If the Ronettes were the queens of the fire escape, the Shangs were back seat debs with their own keys to daddy's car.

But when the jivey, candy-store chatter of "Give Him a Great Big Kiss" and the wise sass of "Right Now and Not Later" gave way to the don't-sit-under-the-appletree tripe of "Long Live Our Love", with its solemn rendering of "When Johnny Comes Marching Home" and vague references to "trouble in the world" and "fighting overseas", the concept was finished. We wanted gang fights under the El, not guerrila warfare. The Shangri-Las delivered, then faded, but while they had it...well, you shoulda heard 'em do "Twist and Shout", that's all.

[turn to next page for discography]

*On stage with Freddie Tieken (see article in upcoming issue of BOMP!) doin' the Shingaling.

SHANGRI-LAS DISCOGRAPHY

SINGLES

12-63	Simon Says/Simon Speaks (both sides live)	Smash 1866
?-64	Wishing Well/Hate to Say I Told You So	Spokane 4006
8-64	Remember (Walking in the Sand)/It's Easier to Cry	Red Bird 008
10-64	Leader of the Pack/What is Love?	Red Bird 014
12-64	Give Him a Great Big Kiss/Twist and Shout	Red Bird 018
12-64	Maybe/Shout	Red Bird 019
1-65	Wishing Well/Hate to Say I Told You So	Scepter 1291
4-65	Out in the Streets/The Boy	Red Bird 025
5-65	Give Us Your Blessings/Heaven Only Knows	Red Bird 030
10-65	Right Now and Not Later/The Train From Kansas City	Red Bird 036
11-65	I Can Never Go Home Anymore/Bull Dog	Red Bird 043
2-66	Long Live Our Love/Sophisticated Boom Boom	Red Bird 048
4-66	He Cried/Dressed in Black	Red Bird 053
6-66	Past, Present and Future/Paradise	Red Bird 068
6-66	Past, Present and Future/Love You More Than Yesterday	Red Bird 068
1-67	Sweet Sounds of Summer/I'll Never Learn	Mercury 72645
5-67	Take the Time/Footsteps On the Roof	Mercury 72670

ALBUMS

2-65 *Leader of the Pack* - Red Bird 101
  Give Him a Great Big Kiss/Leader of the Pack/Bull Dog/It's Easier to Cry/What is Love/Remember (Walking in the Sand)/Twist and Shout/Maybe/So Much in Love/Shout/Goodnight, My Love/You Can't Sit Down(side 2 live)

11-65 *I Can Never Go Home Anymore* - Red Bird 104
  Right Now and Not Later/Never Again/Give Us Your Blessings/Sophisticated Boom Boom/I'm Blue/Heaven Only Knows/I Can Never Go Home Anymore/Train From Kansas City/Out in the Streets/What's a Girl Supposed to Do/You Cheated, You Lied/The Boy
  (issued with at least 2 different back covers, some with liner notes)
  (originally issued as *Shangri-Las — 65!*, with "The Dum Dum Ditty" in place of "I Can Never Go Home Anymore")

?-67 *Golden Hits* - Mercury SR 61099 (original Red Bird recordings)
  Leader of the Pack/Past, Present and Future/Train From Kansas City/Heaven Only Knows/Remember (Walking in the Sand)/Out in the Streets/I Can Never Go Home Anymore/Give Him a Great Big Kiss/Long Live Our Love/Give Us Your Blessings/Sophisticated Boom Boom/What Is Love?

POSSIBLE SHANGRI-LAS

These records are often represented as Shangri-Las recordings. The Nu-Luvs is a Shadow Morton production, sounding very much like the Shangs, though no moreso than the Whyte Boots. The Bon Bons have the same sound as well, and could be authentic, although it's improbable.

?-64	Bon Bons - What's Wrong With Ringo?/Come On Baby	Coral 62402
?-64	Bon Bons - Everybody Wants My Boy Friend/Each Time	Coral 62435
4-66	Nu-Luvs - So Soft, So Warm/Take My Advice	Mercury 72569

1st. TIME EVER now-defunct MODERN LOVERS RECORD available by mail order Only from Home of the Hits

Ernie Brooks, Jerry Harrison, Jonathan Richman and David Robinson were the Modern Lovers. They appeared primarily in the Boston area at high school dances and college mixers. They became the most sought-after band in the entertainment business. They were hot. During this period 16 track demo tapes were produced by the finest upandcomers and widely circulated in the industry. These demo tapes are now available in LP form for anyone interested.
—Matthew Kaufman

$3.99

also available 17"×22" Poster $3.00 (SHOWN HERE ½ ACTUAL SIZE)

and 8 TRACK and CASSETTE TAPES $4.99

Make checks payable to "Home of the Hits" and Add 50¢ Postage & Handling

Order from: Home of the Hits
PO BOX 589-F BERKELEY, CA. 94701
© 1976 HOME OF THE HITS

WHEN IN SAN FRANCISCO...REMEMBER IT'S

AQUARIUS RECORDS

"WE PAY FOR THE RECORDS YOU DON'T PLAY"

NEW & USED LP'S
ROCK & ROCK IMPORTS, JAZZ, CLASSICS, etc.

MON.-SAT.: 10-7
SUNDAY: 12-5

524 CASTRO
863-6467

SAWYER & BURTON
THE GLYCERINE QUEENS OF MASCARA ROCK

By KEN BARNES

Lori Burton & Pam Sawyer were one of those writing teams I would see on singles every now and then, often enough to interest me—especially since they were one of the few female writing/producing teams of the day. Some of their credits were noteworthy—they deserve honorable mention in the Songwriters Hall of Fame for composing "I Ain't Gonna Eat Out My Heart Any More," the Rascals' finest hour, an unforgettable image (to say the least), and a memorable rock tune covered countless times. I liked other Sawyer/Burton songs, too—the ballad "Baby Let's Wait," a Rascals LP cut which the Royal Guardsmen hit with in late 1968, and the Vacels' "You're My Baby," Kama Sutra's first release, co-authored by Sawyer.

Of the team's antecedents, origins, circumstances of meeting, circumstances of parting, and present whereabouts I knew nothing, and today know little more. But I did recently happen upon Lori Burton's mid-1967 Mercury album, Breakout, and it is definitely worthy of note.

The cover itself deserves a comment or two. The front shows a sultry Ms. Burton peeking out of a torn-paper tent, bangs completely obliterating her forehead, wearing enough eye makeup for any 10 girls (or any three Dusty Springfields). The back spotlights a torn photocopy of a 1967 Billboard Hot 100 chart with "Windy" at #1 and the Choir's "It's Cold Outside" mired at #68, discernible in the right-hand corner. The whole concept is supposed to represent the "Breakout" of the title, an inspired conception all the way around.

All 10 songs were written and produced by the Sawyer/Burton team, with Lori of course singing. Most of the songs seem designed to be covered, and were probably demos polished up for public consumption. They're very interesting songs, mostly big beat ballads with a lot of rock and soul influence. Burton sings in the Dusty Springfield mode, with a huskier voice, less polished and less skilled but not unappealing.

A few of the songs, notably "Since I Lost Your Lovin'," employ a dramatic crescendo effect strongly based on Lorraine Ellison's sublime "Stay With Me Baby"—an admirable model even if quite difficult to match. Three of the songs on the first side have a strong Motown stamp. "Love Was" employs a muted variant of the Pretty Things' "Midnight to Six Man" riff, an attractive ballad all in all. "Only Your Love" could have been a big hit for Cher; it's got a definite Bono folk-rock waltz sound to it. And "Bye Bye Charlie" is pure Neil Diamond sound-wise, a tough putdown number full of nasty chuckles and whatnot.

Breakout is one of the more interesting female-vocalist albums of the mid-sixties, wort' picking up for the aforementioned songs alone. But it also has "Nightmare." You probably read about "Nightmare," if you've been conscientious, in Greg's review in Bomp, the single by the Whyte Boots on Philips. To recap briefly, it's one of the most bizarre extensions of the Shangri-Las' grand melodrama genre, in which the female protagonist is egged into a fight with the girl who stole her boyfriend, accidentally knocks her head on the sidewalk and kills her, and is carted away by the cops protesting numbly that she "didn't want to fight," all related in starkly classic girl-group form.

Sawyer and Burton produced and of course wrote the Whyte Boots version, which came out a few months before the Burton LP. Although the record was a substantial stiff, the Whyte Boots actually got some coverage in New York's pop tabloid GO which is fairly amusing to read now. Ronda Copland, Page Miller and Kathy Francis were friends studying at the American Music and Drama Academy in New York. According to Ronda, "One of our teachers told us we had what it takes for a recording session. He got in touch with producers Pam Sawyer and Lori Burton...The song 'Nightmare' is a great number and it gave us the opportunity to project some of our acting techniques into music."

The group name, by the way, came about accidentally. "At first, we decided on the Red Boots, but when we went out to get Mod blouses, skirts and boots, we couldn't find anything red. Everything was white. We could have dyed things red, but the overall effect when we were dressed in white seemed to be much better." (Red overalls would have been a bit much).

GO also ran a "Diary of the Whyte Boots", describing a hectic fortnight of record hops, radio station visits, and a bit of recreation: "Threw a huge happening at our apartment. Guests showed up in some wayout gear!". "Heard the good news that the disc has been picked as a 'Breakout' on the West Coast." (There's that word again). "Took all our Mod clothes with us—real handsome photographer—had us doing some groovy things." We can imagine.

Interestingly, the Lori Burton version is identical to the Whyte Boots', leaving the trio and their "acting techniques" in a rather dubious position. Not that such fictional groups were all that unusual (GO's Whyte Boots hype was neatly juxtaposed next tc an editorial castigating the Monkees for not playing their instruments). Anyway, whatever it did for the Whyte Boots' credibility, the inclusion of "Nightmare" on Lori Burtons' album makes it a must-buy for dedicated girl-group fans.

Shortly afterward, Burton & Sawyer split up. Sawyer went to Motown as a staff writer, getting co-credits on "Love Chile," "My Mistake" by Marvin Gaye & Diana Ross, Martha & the Vandellas' antiwar single "I Should Be Proud," and David Ruffin's superb "My Whole World Ended." Burton was heard from less—she co-produced "The Letter" by the Arbors, and cut a single on Columbia, a fairly slushy version of Randy Newman's "I'll Be Home", in April 1971.

As a team they cut quite a few forgettable soul records, and they hardly rank in the Greenwich/King/Weil league. But for "Ain't Gonna Eat Out," "Nightmare," and Breakout, Lori Burton and Pam Sawyer deserve their due degree of celebration. As the liner notes to her album admirably put it, "That many talents belonging to the same person should constitute a record. And, as a matter of fact, they do. It's time you listened to it."

SONGOGRAPHY

Lori Burton:

Yeh Yeh Yeh/	Roulette 4609
The Hurt Won't Go Away/Bye Bye Charlie	Mercury 72663
I'll Be Home/Missing You Today	Columbia 45359
Breakout (Mercury SR 61136/MG 21136)	

SAWYER/BURTON COMPOSITIONS

Ain't Gonna Eat Out My Heart Anymore — Young Rascals (Atlantic 2312) Loose Ends (UK-Decca 12437) New York Public Library (UK-Puppets (Red Rooster 311) Resumes (Sho-Time 69)
All Or Nothing — Patti Labelle & Blue Belles (Atlantic 2311)
Baby Let's Wait — Royal Guardsmen (Laurie 3461) Sweet Slice of Life (Pi 35415) Rascals (LP)
Bye Bye Charlie — Lori Burton (LP)
Forget About Me — Denny Belline (Columbia 45123)
Gotta Get Over You — Lori Burton (LP)
Gotta Make You Love Me — Lori Burton (LP)
I Give In — Lazy Susans (KAPP 741)
If I Had You Babe — Millionaires (Philips 40477)
If You Love Me — Lazy Susans (KAPP 741)
It Won't Hurt — O'Jays (Imperial 66145)
I've Got My Needs/Your Love is My Love — No Deposit No Return (Philips 40451)
Let No One Come Between Us — Lori Burton LP
Love Was — Lori Burton (LP)
Nightmare — Lori Burton (LP) Whyte Boots (Philips 40422)
Only Your Love — Lori Burton (LP)
Since I Lost Your Lovin' — Lori Burton (LP)
Slow Fizz — Sapphires (ABC 10778)
The Hurt Won't Go Away — Lori Burton (LP)
There Is No Way(To Stop Lovin' You) — Lori Burton (LP)
Together — Candy & Kisses (Scepter 12106)
Try to Understand — Cindy Malone (Capitol 5734) Lulu (Parrot 9791)

PAM SAWYER (CO)-COMPOSITIONS

Are You Proud — Jan Tanzy (Columbia 43219)
Bill When Are You Coming Home — Supremes (Motown 1162)
For Better Or Worse — Supremes (Motown 1153)
Gotta Hold On To This Feeling — Jr. Walker (Soul 35070)
Happy — Supremes (Motown 1182)
His Loss Is My Gain — Carl Dobkins Jr. (Colpix 762)
I Should Be Proud — Martha & Vandellas (Gordy 7098)
(I Thought It) Took A Little Time — Stephen Scharf (WB 8124)
I Wore Out Our Record — Dodie Stevens (Dolton 83)
If I Ever Lose This Heaven — Average White Band (Atlantic 3285)
If I Were Your Woman — Gladys Knight & Pips (Soul 35078)
I'm Living in Shame — Supremes (Motown 1139)
Is There Anything Love Can't Do — Chuck Jackson (VIP 25029)
Just Like A Little Bitty Baby — Opals (Laurie 3288)
Just Seven Numbers — Four Tops (Motown 1125)
Love Chile — Supremes (Motown 1135)
My Mistake — Marvin Gaye & Diana Ross (Motown 1269)
My Whole World Ended — David Ruffin (Motown 1140)
— Kiki Dee (LP)
The Day Will Come Between Sunday & Monday — Kiki Dee (LP)
This is the Story — Supremes (Motown 1196)
Tonight Tonight — Exciters (Roulette 4591)
You're My Baby — Vacels (Kama Sutra 200)

Lori Burton co-productions:
Living Without You — Denny Belline (Columbia 45123)
The Letter — Arbors (Date 1638)

JUKE BOX JURY JUNIOR

BY GREG SHAW

I'd like to devote the main part of this issue's column to a survey of some recent British releases of particular merit. England has been a very hot source of pop singles in recent months; there are a lot of new labels, many of them run by producers or songwriters or groups of interest, and a lot of odd, one-shot studio groups have appeared, making the sort of records Bomp readers love. It's not easy to keep up with them all, but you can subscribe to a handy weekly guide called "The New Singles" (Francis Antony Ltd, Frenance Mill, Blowinghouse Hill, St. Austell, Cornwall, PL25 5AH) which will at least tell you what's out, and then take your chances ordering them from whatever source you can find. Most of the best ones won't ever come out here, and only stay around a short while in England, making them prime collectors items.

THE ROLLETTES - "We Love You Rollers" - GTO 19 (E)
This is the first Roller novelty that's come to my attention, and there's been at least one more since which I haven't heard. Such records are the kind of tribute money can't buy, and the most convincing evidence that anybody really does care about this so-called phenomenon. This happens to be an excellent record, with a strong, Roller-like beat, a good melody, hotly produced, and sung by a bevy of British cheerleaders. All the Roller hits are woven into the lyrics, of course. If you like Roller-rock, as I do, you'll get a kick out of this.

SUGAR CANDY - "Mummy, I Want to Go to the Discotheque" - EMI 2285(E)
From the title, I expected something like Ricky Wilde, instead getting something more like Claudine Clark's "Party Lights". The names have been changed, and the production is mod, but I'd know that whining voice anywhere. What an amazing throwback...

WARWICK - "Let's Get the Party Going" - RAK 211(E)
There's nothing unique anymore about attempts to recreate the Spector Sound, but for those who like to have them all, this is one well worth getting. Produced by Chinn & Chapman, it has a bit of Sweet dynamics and the vocals are male glam, but the track is pure "Be My Baby" and the overall effect quite enchanting.

BEANO - "Little Cinderella"/"Bye and Bye" - Deram 427 (E)
BEANO - "Candy Baby"/"Rock and Roll (Gonna Save Your Soul)" - Deram 424 (E)
A similar feel pervades the records of Beano, particularly "Cinderella" which is a girl-group sound with Sweet energy and a sort of lightweight Rubettes arrangement. Far more than the Rollers or any of them, the Rubettes are the kings of that resurrected Four Seasons harmony pop, and once you accept the limpness of the vocals, it's a very pleasant little genre. "Bye and Bye" is Elvis adapted to the reggae of "Young Americans", and "Candy Baby" (belatedly issued here on London 20085) is even more like "Be My Baby" than the above record, with breathy vocals and a teenage triangle set at a high school dance.

HELLO - "Game's Up" - Bell 1406(E)
These guys have been churning out a lot of interesting, Mike-Leander-produced 45's starting with "Tell Him" (Bell 1377) back in '74. They're a bit like the Rollers, and while this one isn't their best, all their records are worth getting if only for their obscurity value.

THE ALLENS - "High Tide"/"California Music" - Mowest 3029(E)
Since it was produced by Michael Lloyd, this must have been released here, but I haven't seen it. In any case, no neo-surfer should be without this fine beach revival, sounding a bit like Flash Cadillac though with that insistently bouncy beat that at first fooled me into thinking this might be an English production. Both sides abound with harmonies and are equally sterling examples of '70s summer music.

THE RUBETTES - "Fore-Dee-O-Dee - State 71(E)
While others imitate their early sugar-candy-kisses style, the Rubettes have moved on to a sound that, while still pleasingly synthetic, relies on a heavily rocking beat and the kind of pseudo-50s vocals the various RAK artists like Mud have been failing so abysmally with. "I Can Do It" was one of the year's hottest rockers, and this, the follow-up, is in the same vein. For my money, the Rubettes are the best English pop group going.

MATCHBOX - "Rock 'n' Roll Band" - Dawn 1104(E)
This anonymous record also rocks out quite nicely, in the style of Earl Vince & the Valiants' "Somebody's Gonna Get Their Head Kicked In Tonight" but without the parody aspect. It's good ersatz English rock, predictable but fun.

LIGHT FANTASTIC - "We are the Song" - Blue Jean 704(E)
A solid, Glitter Band-style thumping chant with good fuzzy guitar work, again mainly of interest as a minor artifact of an all-too-ephemeral trend. One other interesting thing, the song was written by Keith Locke, possibly the same one who had a gigantic hit in Malaysia with "Push Push" almost ten years ago. Can anyone shed light on this person's identity and history?

PAUL DA VINCI - "If You Get Hurt" - Penny Farthing 852(E)
Paul's the one who sang those incredible falsetto parts on the early Rubettes hits, and since leaving he's done 3 or 4 equally charming discs on his own. This latest is strongly reminiscent of Gene Pitney, still pure formula, but good for what it is.

ROCKIN' BERRIES - "Rock-a-bye Nursery Rhyme" - Pye 45394(E)
Their years in cabaret have been put to good use in this delightful effort, a pastiche in the tradition of the Barron Knights' "Call Up the Groups" and the Four Preps' "More Money For You and Me" medley. Artists here parodied include Bryan Ferry the Rubettes, and the Bay City Rollers, as the Berries render various nursery rhymes in the style of each. Interestingly, novelty kings Vance & Pockriss are listed as co-authors.

The next few are among the best discoveries of my recent trip to England:

SOUTHERN SOUND - "Just the Same as You"/"I Don't Wanna Go" - Columbia 7982(E) '66
Fans of Who/Creation style mod-rock don't need to be told about the Sorrows' "Take a Heart"—it's a classic in that style, and so is "Just the Same as You", with the same kind of throbbing beat and blistering guitar. That alone would be enough to ensure this record's importance, but there's more. The flip side is a demented, pounding raver, with
[turn to page 30]

The Southern Sound

SURF ROOTS

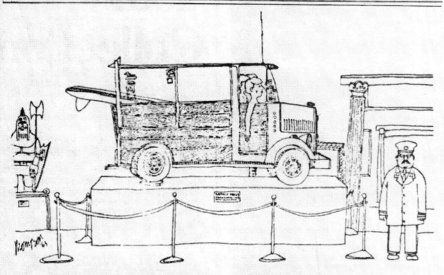

[Last issue we published a large list of instrumental surfing records, as distinguished from the more common vocal variety. Though admitting that no such list could ever be complete, we have since obtained listings for a number of others that are of special interest to the collector and surf music fan. In addition, we have a few more listings for surf-oriented LPs, a genre we feel has now been almost completely catalogued. Incidentally, the editors would like to obtain copies of most of the LPs listed here; if you can supply any, let us know...]

Downey 108 - also issued on Dot 16492.
Downey 128 - Bel Canto's - Feel Sw Right, pt. I & 2
Downey 142 - E.S.P. Unlimited - Cry Baby
Agates - Rumble at Newport Beach/Last Call for Dinner - Dore 681
Johnny Baraka & Vestelis - Long Ride/Happy Time - Dell 103
Blazers - Bangalore/Sound of Mecca - Acree 102
Catalinas - Bonzai Washout - Rik 113
Cornelis - Mama's Little Baby/Wak-a-Cha - Garex 100
Creations - Crash/Chickie Darlin - Top Hat 1003(NY)
Esquires - What a burn!/Flashin'Red - Durco 1001
Kenny Hinkle - Over You/The Bee - Westco 5
Hong Kongs - Surfin in the China Sea - Counsel 050
Jesters - Drag Bike/A-Rab - Ultima 705(JimMessina)
Kenny Karter - Blue Booze/Surfing with Bony Moronie - Westco 8
Knight Trains - Beach Head/Surfin' on the Rocks - Hart-Van 126

•The above cartoon, by John Thompson, was originally done in 1963—somewhat ahead of its time!

Newporters - Loose Board - Scotchtown 500
Nova-Tones - Walk on the Surf Side - Rosco 417
Opposite Six - Church Key,pt.68/Continental Surf - South Shore 721
Pendletons - Board Party - Dot 16511
Premiers - Frantic - Sahara 103
Rip-Tides - Machine Gun - Challenge 59058
Rondells - On the Run/Far Horizon - Dot 16593
Roulettes - Surfer's Charge - Angle 1001
Sentinal Six - Infinity/Encinada - Era 3117
Sentinals - The Bee/Over You - Point 5100
Sentinals - Blue Booze/Bony Maronie - Point 5101
Sentinals - Sunset Beach/Big Surf - Del-Fi 4197
Sentinals - Tor-Chula/Latin'ia - WCEB 23
Sentinals - I've Been Blue/Hit the Road - Westco 12
Sharks - Big Surf/Spookareno - Sapien 1003
Surfaris - Psych-Out/Tor-Chula - Felsted 8688
Surfaris - Wipeout/Surfer Joe - Princess
Velvetones - Static/Doheny Run - Glenn 309
Vibrents - Fuel Injection/Breeze & I - Bay Towne 409
Vulcanes - Cozimotto/Last Prom - Goliath 1350

ALBUMS

Glaciers - *From Sea to Ski* - Mercury 20895
Vaughn Monroe - *Surfers Stomp* - Dot 2419
Jack Nitzsche - *The Lonely Surfer* - Reprise 6101
Sandals - *The Last of the Ski Bums* - World-Pacific 21884
Ruby Short & Dragsters - *Hot Rodders Battle Rock and Roll* - Palace 776
Sunsets - *Surfin' With* - Palace
Surf Knobs - *Surfer's Beat* - Charter 103
Tom & Jerry - *Surfin' Hootenanny* - Merc. 60842
Ricky Vale & His Surfers - *Everybody's Surfin'* - Strand 1104
Vettes - *Rev Up* - MGM 4193
Kai Winding - *Soul Surfin'* - Verve 8551
Willie & Wheels - *Surfin' Songbook*-RCA 70044(Gr?)
V.A. - *Big Hot Rod Hits* - Capitol 2024
V.A. - *Surfin' on Wave Nine* - King 855

[Advertisement]

JAY KINNEY is available for illustration, cartooning and design at 1786 Fell, San Francisco, 94117. (415) 567-9159

JUKEBOX JURY (continued from page 26)

berserk drumming, guitar as staccato and kinetic as Townshend at his best, and a weird, intense production sound that makes it seem as though the very grooves are about to shake apart. Simply awesome.

EQUALS - "I Can See But You Don't Know" - President 303(E) '70
Everything I said about the above record applies to this one. I've never understood how the Equals, with 6 albums, piles of great singles, and at least a dozen songs that I'd place in the first ranks of English rock, seem to be remembered only for their early hit "Baby Come Back"—later on they tackled mod rock and anticipated glitter rock, experimented with Spector-sounds, and so much more that should be common knowledge but regretfully isn't. This is by far their classic performance. It's the equal of anything by Creation...need I say more?

NIGHTRIDERS - "It's Only the Dog" - Polydor 56116(E) '66
Move fans prize this record for its Mike Sheridan connections (the Nightriders were his ex-backing group) but now that I've heard it, I think it should be in equal demand among punk-rock enthusiasts, being one of the few genuine English punkers extant. It's got a sort of fractured "Louie Louie" sound, with shades of the Raiders, the Music Machine, and even Mouse & the Traps.

CHIP FISHER - "An Ordinary Guy" - CBS 202010(E) '65
All I knew about Chip Fisher is that his father was in the fish & chips business, which makes this bizarre record all the more intriguing. Always a fan of novelty records, you can imagine my joy when I discovered that Chip was a singer of anti-protest folk rock, taking off on Barry McGuire and criticizing the excesses of Dylan, Paul Simon, Sonny & Cher, P.F. Sloan ("gone out on his own..."), Donovan, and other noted protestors of the day.

AMERICAN ROCK.

BOB & SHERI - "The Surfer Moon"/"What Is a Young Girl Made Of"
The "first Beach Boys record" controversy rages on. This '61 disc, written & produced by Brian, with his home address on the label, features a couple of neighborhood kids neither of whom are known, and involvement by any other B.Boys is doubtful, but it is probably Brian's first recording... Incidentally,there is only one known copy and it recently sold for$200.

PATRICK & PAUL - "You and I Are Gonna Say Goodbye" - Mercury 72792
This duo had at least one other 45, on Uni, but nothing to equal their Mercury outing. I guess you'd call it bubblegum, but really it sounds more like Paul Revere & the Raiders imitating the Archies, and it rocks quite savagely in addition to having a fine melody and excellent harmony vocals.

NEW LEGION ROCK SPECTACULAR - "Second Cousin"/"Wild One" - Spectacular 11075
Readers of PRM will already have seen my rave on this record, but in case you missed it, be advised that this oldies band from Milwaukee has come up with a thoroughly electrifying treatment of one of the Flamin Groovies' best old rockers, complete with a faithful parody of Roy Loney's affected vocals. There's a looseness, vigor, and sloppy energy in this record that belies the group's categorization as a mere oldies band, and it's evident on the fine Jerry Lee Lewis inspired flip too. A must for diehard rockers (available from Bomp at $2 a shot).

DAVE EDMUNDS
THE ROCKFIELD REBEL

Phil Spector singled him out, in a recent interview, as the producer he most respects in the world today. Many people (including Eric Carmen, who told me he thought Edmunds should have been asked to join the Stones when Mick Taylor left) consider him one of the best guitarists alive. Musicians, critics, people in the music business generally, have such enormous regard for him that the slightest news concerning his activities is enough to arouse keen excitement.

And yet, what does anyone really know about Dave Edmunds? He remains a shadowy figure, a name that people who notice such things connect with some of the most wondrous records of the past few years, and that AM radio listeners with long memories might recall as the one-hit artist of "I Hear You Knockin", a Top 10 entry in late 1970. And that's about all; not exactly the plethora of well-known achievements one might expect of a man widely regarded as one of the true legends of his time.

The fact is, Dave Edmunds has never sought the easy road to fame.

After "I Hear You Knockin", he could have put together a band and done a world tour. He could have moved to London and joined the trendy in-crowd with their private clubs, super-session albums and jet-set parties. The reason he did none of these things, resisting the efforts of those who would make him a "star", has a lot to do with why he became a legend instead.

When I speak of Edmunds as a legend, I mean more than the mere fact that his accomplishments are fabled. Beyond this, there is a deeper, transcendent quality that can be discerned in all his work. Few individuals in the history of rock & roll have possessed the qualities of consistent genius, perfect refinement and utter, natural economy in their art, and that precise combination of inspiration from the roots and vision toward the future of the music that seem to be the primary attributes of rock's truly mythic figures. In such company, among Phil Spector, Brian Wilson, Buddy Holly, John Fogerty, Lennon & McCartney at their peak, and very few others, do I rank Dave Edmunds.

* * *

Edmunds was born in 1946 and grew up in Cardiff, S. Wales. When rock & roll hit the British Isles in 1955, Edmunds was much younger than the Teddy Boys who were demolishing theatres to the tune of "Rock Around the Clock", but he was entranced by the wild sounds nonetheless. He took up guitar and practiced until he could duplicate anything on record.

As a rebel, young Edmunds was a serious artist. He dressed hip, acted cool, played the rocker although his energy found its outlet in music rather than violence. His natural shyness became the moody detachment of the loner; his quick intelligence, instead of impelling him to his studies, drove him to seek after the hidden mysteries of rock & roll. After spending time in his brother's skiffle group, the 99ers, he formed a group of his own, called the Raiders.

For years, the Raiders were one of Cardiff's more popular local bands, playing the same sort of hard-hitting rock & roll that the Beatles specialized in at this time, around 1962. By the mid-60s, Wales boasted a number of other fine beat groups, such as the Bystanders, the Jets, Amen Corner, the Blackjacks, Eyes of Blue, and the Iveys. Edmunds was getting older, the Raiders weren't getting anywhere, so they packed it in and Edmunds entered a government trade school, where he was trained to be a motor mechanic. He stayed there three years, playing on the side in a trio called the Image, doing mostly Stax material.

In 1967, flower power was exploding in London, attracting many young Britons, including Dave Edmunds. He spent most of the year there, dressed in paisley and beads like everyone else, soaking up the underground scene and watching dozens of groups achieve success with nothing more than a timely gimmick. It was time, he decided, to get another group together.

Back in Cardiff, he rounded up Tommy Riley (from the Sons of Adam, later in the Grease Band) and John Williams to form the Human Beans. He also began dropping in at Rockfield, a few hours drive from Cardiff, where a lot of Welsh bands had begun taking advantage of the recording facilities. A single was cut and released on Columbia, following which Riley left the band and the name was changed to Love Sculpture, with Edmunds on guitar, Williams on bass, and Bob 'Congo' Jones on drums. A song written by Charles Ward, "River to Another Day" was cut and placed by the Wards on Parlophone.

Love Sculpture had got off to a strong start locally, with a modernized approach to the same rock standards, plus interpretations of Beatles songs and a few flash-fingered renditions of classical motifs, featuring Edmunds. John Peel, England's most influential DJ, had spun "River" a few times and liked the group. After they played a gig with the Nice in Cardiff, Lee Jackson mentioned them to Peel, who then asked them to come on his show. They showed up with a tape of "Sabre Dance," a lightning-speed rave-up of Khatchaturian's well-known classic, and played it on the air. Peel was deluged with letters, Parlophone rushed out the record, and Gordon Mills, the powerful manager of Tom Jones, signed Love Sculpture to his management firm.

In America, "Sabre Dance" was not a hit, though it received tremendous airplay on FM radio and made enough of an impact to justify a US tour for the group. In England, though, it was a Top Ten smash. The group moved to London, taking a flat together in Dulwich. Along with fame came charges of fake, from critics who just couldn't believe anyone could play guitar that fast. Actually, Edmunds was playing no faster than Alvin Lee or Eric Clapton were doing at the time, although the number of difficult changes and the virtuosity with which he played around Khatchaturian's melody make it a very impressive recording. One of the record's strongest features is the use of echo as counterpoint, a tricky effect that instantly identifies it as a Rockfield production.

Interviewed at the time, Edmunds made several prophetic remarks. "I've always dreamed of having a record in the charts. Now that it's happened I don't know what the next goal is for us. My main ambition is to own a recording studio. I've always been interested in recording and have been playing around with tape recorders for years." Asked how he felt about groups using electronic effects for recordings and not being able to reproduce them on stage, he replied, "I don't think it matters really. As long as the finished product turns out well I don't see why people should object."

Despite steady popularity in concert, Love Sculpture was never able to follow-up their hit. Determined not to be typecast, they put the similar-sounding adaptation of Bizet's "Farandole" on the back side of "Seagull," a vaguely Procol Harumish vocal ballad, meanwhile releasing an album consisting mostly of old blues workouts. One of the group's chief drawbacks was that none of them could write songs, though Edmunds' "In the Land of the Few" was an exception.

Besides confusion in their public image, there were problems with their internal self-image. "I was never satisfied with the group," says Edmunds today. For one thing, although he was unavoidably the front man, he disliked that role and would have much preferred to remain in the background. Still the cocky rocker, yet no less the shy introvert, Edmunds was emerging as a rather complex character. The brilliance of "Sabre Dance" lay as much in the imagination that spawned it as in the speed and technique with which it was executed, and in his attempts to apply the same imagination, the same stretching and reworking of form, to blues, pop, and straight rock, Edmunds was fighting against the limitations of categorized music, seeking a dimension where all that mattered were the basic elements of beat, riffs, dynamics, and pure sound. Within those parameters, in Edmunds' hands, anything could become classic rock & roll.

When it reached a point where the limitations of being in a group outweighed the advantages, and following a brief second lineup without Jones and with the addition of Terry Williams and Mickey Gee, Love Sculpture broke up. Now that he had a little money, Edmunds was anxious to realize his long-time ambition of building his own studio. It happened that Kingsley and Charles Ward were then in the process of expanding Rockfield, having just got their first 8-track, so Edmunds joined with them in turning the old stable into a full-fledged recording studio. They built and installed all the equipment by hand, designing the place from the point of view of the sound they wanted to get out of it.

Together with John Williams, Edmunds spent several months in the studio, trying to reconstruct the classic Sun Records sound. You might think it no great difficulty to match on modern equipment the sounds made in a primitive Memphis back-room studio in 1955, yet countless attempts by others had never even come close. Edmunds finished a number of tracks that had visitors gaping and swearing they couldn't tell them from the original Presley masters. This was the first evidence of Edmunds' uncanny skill at mimicry, later exhibited on "Promised Land" (on which his voice sounds more like Berry's than Chuck himself ever did) and his many renowned Spector recreations. These tapes have sadly been lost, but may yet turn up amidst the clutter.

With that Sun sound as a reference point, Edmunds (in the words of an old bio) "expanded on to original and constantly metamorphic genres." Which is to say that, having mastered the Sun sound, he proceeded to improve on it, or at least to give it the benefit of modern technology, its own wall-of-sound impact, while remaining faithful to the intrinsic dynamics of the music. The first example of this was also the first big hit to come out of the new Rockfield studio, "I Hear You Knockin'," with all the funky rhythm of Smiley Lewis' original, the biting echoed guitar force of anything in modern rock, and an overall richness of sound that proved irresistible to record buyers all over the world. Released on Mills' new MAM label, it hit #1 in England, #4 in America, and similar positions in most countries.

Its success caught Edmunds unprepared; there was no band to tour in support of the single, and

• Love Sculpture: John Williams, Bob Jones, Dave

not even a follow-up in the can. His method of recording was to lay down a basic track with himself on drums and Williams on bass, then go back and spend weeks overdubbing guitars, keyboards, other instruments (all played by himself) and vocals until the track was finished. It was over a year before he had enough finished tracks for an album. In the meantime he had released two more singles, "I'm Coming Home", a flat-out rocker much valued by his fans but only barely denting the charts, backed by "Country Roll", an odd sort of Celtic hoedown with droning guitars, a weird hybrid style Edmunds later returned to with "Pick Axe Rag." Thinking perhaps another Domino type song would do the trick, he next released "Blue Monday," which however flopped even worse. (An interesting parallel can be drawn with Jerry Jaye, a Nashville country singer who began his career with a hard-rocking, very Edmunds-sounding version of "Hello Josephine" which made the Top 30 in 1967, followed by a flop with "Let the Four Winds Blow" and a return to country.)

Edmunds however was far from discouraged. Delighted with the money that was pouring in and the initial success of his experiments, he threw himself into work on the album. When it came out, it proved to be a stunning representation of Edmunds' abilities. Besides "I Hear You Knockin'"

(its B-side and the other 4 single sides were left off and are now collectors items), it included a couple of taut, electrifying Chuck Berry tunes, and fascinating arrangements of such varied material as Ron Davies' "It Ain't Easy" and Dylan's "Outlaw Blues."

The album's primary focus is guitars—guitars that sound like banjos, pianos, voices, an "electric guitar salad" as one reviewer put it; guitar on guitar, all phased and distorted in special ways that only Rockfield studios could accomplish. The most complex use of this approach is on "Egg or the Hen", on which Andy Fairweather Low of Amen Corner assists, providing a solid base while Edmunds' multi-tracked guitars swoop and scream like some four-dimensional kaleidoscopic "Layla."

Although a critical favorite, the album was a belated anticlimax, coming more than a year after the hit, and there were no singles released from it. Edmunds, who had used his "I Hear You Knockin'" money to buy a beautiful old house in Monmouth (which can been seen on the cover of his album) and also to become a partner in Rockfield, settled into a comfortable lifestyle, "being basically a very lazy person," in his own words. When he felt the urge, he'd drop into Rockfield and putter, sometimes spending months on one song.

In 1972 he also began a second career, that of producer. He'd got a taste of it in 1970, during his Sun sessions, when he produced an LP by Shakin' Stevens & the Sunsets, a '50s revival group from Penarth, a Cardiff suburb. As their subsequent albums proved, they were no better than the Wild Angels or any of the oldies groups then popular in England, but their one LP with Edmunds is a triumph, and ranks in my mind with the very best of American rockabilly. The sound is taut, kinetic, exciting, with the perfect blend of echo and presence, and Edmunds' blistering guitar clearly evident on most cuts.

The first thing he produced for an "outside" (non-local) group was Foghat's debut album, including the hit single "I Just Want to Make Love to You." Again the characteristic Edmunds/Rockfield sound is there, a raw tension almost tangible in its intensity. It must also have been around this time that an album was recorded which came out as Warren Phillips & the Rockets, with no information on the sleeve, consisting entirely of '50s rockers. It wasn't very good, and while the recording quality is very Sun-like, it doesn't really bear the telltale stamp of a Rockfield production. Still, the group has been variously reputed to be Foghat, Savoy Brown, or some brief reincarnation of Love Sculpture, so there could be some Edmunds involvement.

Other 1972 productions included 7 tracks with the Flamin' Groovies, and portions of Man's *Be Good to Yourself* album. Man, another Welsh group whose history goes back to 1963 when they started as the Bystanders, have gone through countless personnel changes and spinoffs, many of which involved Edmunds. He also played guitar on two of their other albums, although most of the recording

[turn to page 22]

"SOUND ON SOUND"

THE ROCKFIELD STORY

OR

"How to Turn an Old Farm Into a Famous Recording Studio in Your Spare Time"

As a rule, recording studios are pretty dull stuff. They represent one of the most tedious aspects of the process of making rock & roll. Every studio boasts some different combination of equipment, acoustics, ambience and personnel, so in theory, each one ought to have its own unique, recognizable sound. Maybe they do, to a trained ear, but to us fans the products of one studio sound pretty much like any other. They all seem to be striving for the same textbook sound—clean, evenly balanced, free from distortion or rough edges. How few studios, in rock's 20 year history, have made any contribution to our appreciation of *sound* as a prime ingredient in rock & roll recording? One could name the Sun Records studio in Memphis, Cosimo's in New Orleans, Gold Star in Los Angeles during Spector's tenure there, and that's about it. It could be argued that the 'sound' linked to these studios was mainly the product of the people using them, but that's a moot point, one that in no way changes the fact that since the early '60s only one studio has come along to add its name to that illustrious triumvirate—Rockfield, with the unlikely location of Monmouthshire, South Wales.

Monmouth is a small, quaint farming town, noted for being the birthplace of Admiral Nelson, and the nearby ruins of Tintern Abby. Until recently. In the last 3 years, Rockfield Studio has attracted enough musicians to foster a sizable tourist trade in the town, and put the place on the maps of music fans the world over.

It's not easy to find the first time out. The town of Rockfield, a mile or so down the road, consists of just a store, a telephone box, and a few houses. You have to find your way back to the modest stone gates, through which a road leads to a typical-looking farm, with no sign posted except "Amberley Court." With cows in the field, tractors plowing, sheep grazing, etc., you'd never know you'd arrived at any sort of pop mecca, unless someone happened to open the door of the stable, emitting an unexpected scream of electric guitars into the pastoral silence outside.

This initial sense of incongruity proves to set the tone for everything to do with Rockfield. If the most modern sounds in the world are being made in an ancient stable built with stones the Romans left behind, why shouldn't the most professionally crafted records be made by a crew of wild-eyed farmers with a tendency to babble? Once you accept the reality of the place, it all begins to make a weird kind of sense.

Indeed, when you begin hearing some of the stories told by and about the resident loonies, like the one about the mad uncle in the house on the hill who hasn't come down in 15 years (ever since his dog was shotgunned in retaliation for eating Kingsley Ward's chickens) or the time someone tried to land an airplane in the orchard, you realize that most ordinary representatives of the recording industry would be painfully out of place here. Yet

•Kingsley Ward, the Madman of Monmouth.

somehow, just as the greatest truths are always couched in paradox, the Monty Python mentality surrounding Rockfield disguises a discipline and expertise second to none. Because they don't give a damn about doing things the 'right' way, they're able to make their own rules, thereby achieving the extraordinary on a regular basis.

* * *

Fifteen years ago, Rockfield was merely a farm like many others in the area. It had been there for hundreds of years, producing a steady crop of grain and vegetables. Three generations of the Ward family lived on the land and worked the fields. The premises included four houses, two stables, and a large square courtyard surrounded by a series of connected old stone buildings. Not all these facilities were being used at full capacity, though the farm was still a commercial business.

The two young brothers, Kingsley and Charles, went through their teens in the '50s, and like so many of their generation, were rock & roll fanatics. With a long series of bands, they played rock shows all over South Wales, starting in 1958. Kingsley: "Charles bought an electric guitar, but he didn't realize that you had to have amplification. We went for this audition at Abergevenny, and walked on, Charles with his guitar and no amp, the drummer's cymbal held up with a milk bottle top and me, drunk out of me head, on keyboards." Already the Rockfield method was taking shape.

This group, the Infernos, lasted until 1960, working constantly. "Sometimes we wouldn't get back until 4 or 5 in the morning and then we'd have to get up at 7 to milk the cows. We were working 90 hours a week!" The next group was the Charles Kingsley Combo, which backed stars like Ricky Valance on their Welsh tours, often booked by the Wards themselves.

They made their first tape in 1962, in the hallway of their house. After being turned down by George Martin at EMI and a lot of other people, they took it to Joe Meek, the crackpot producer whose seances and dreams of outer space spawned a studio sound that was the most advanced of its day, and is still worshipped by many English fans. Meek had a giant hit at the time with "Telstar" by the Tornados, and when he heard the Wards' tape he flipped. They had the identical sound, but recorded two years before! He helped them get a song from their tape, "Lost Planet" released in America under the name the Thunderbolts, though declining to make further records with them. He encouraged them to continue recording, though, little dreaming they'd carry on his tradition so successfully after his death.

Back at Rockfield, they bought a couple of old EMI Ferrograph recorders, and installed them in the attic, using them to record some of the local groups. One of these, the Interns, were signed to Parlophone as a result, and two singles were made at Rockfield. Soon other groups like Amen Corner, from nearby Cardiff, were using the facilities. The Charles Kingsley Combo became the Charles Kingsley Creation in 1965 and had a single released.

In 1967, things finally began taking shape at

Rockfield. They'd added an 8-track recorder, and a lot of the Cardiff groups were hanging around, including Dave Edmunds, with a group tentatively called the Human Beans, for whom the Wards got a single released on Columbia that summer. This group presently became Love Sculpture, and with a song written by Charles, "River to Another Day" came to the attention of John Peel and the London underground. Love Sculpture's next record, "Sabre Dance" was a huge hit, inspiring the Wards to pack in their own band and concentrate on making records.

The 16-track studio in the stable, where Edmunds does all his recording, was built in 1968 by Charles and Kingsley, between shifts in the fields and milking the cows. The Studer board, the same kind used by the Beatles, was fitted with a custom-designed mixing console, which partially accounts for the sounds achieved there. The solid stone walls, over a foot thick, didn't hurt either. The first thing cut in that studio was Dave Edmunds' "I Hear You Knockin'," and from then on it's all been magic.

It took awhile for the English record industry to acknowledge Rockfield. At first they only laughed, saying it would never work because all the best session men were in London and London studios were the best. Their first support came from United Artists, who with Man and Deke Leonard had become champions of Welsh rock anyway. UA acts like Brinsley Schwarz, Help Yourself, the Neutrons, the Flamin' Groovies, even Hawkwind began making the 300-mile trek to Rockfield, to 'get it together in the country.'

Cliche though it is, there's a lot of truth in that oft-heard phrase. Recording is never comfortable in a professional studio where everyone's watching the clock and the engineers punch out at 6:00. At Rockfield, a group books the studio for a week or whatever, and works at their own pace, all night if they want, without pressure or interruptions, and the rest of the time they relax in one of the farmhouses, eating fresh farm food and enjoying the bucolic way of life.

It soon became apparent that for every group that was intrigued by the "Rockfield Sound" there were a dozen others who liked the place simply because it was so pleasant to work there. Demand became so heavy that a 24-track studio was installed in part of the old courtyard. Currently a second 24-track console is being put in the stable, with the old 16-track moving to another converted barn up on the hill, near the guest house. Though Rockfield is still thought of more as a "studio in the country" than the home of a revolutionary sound, that's changing fast.

The growth of the Rockfield legend was spurred by the debut of Rockfield Records in 1972. RCA offered Rockfield their own label if they could come up with product, and it happened that Dave Edmunds' contract with MAM had just ended, so they issued "Born to Be With You" and had a Top 10 hit with the first Rockfield release. The RCA deal

[turn to next page]

DAVE EDMUNDS DISCOGRAPHY

HUMAN BEANS (early version of LOVE SCULPTURE)
7-67   Morning Dew/It's a Wonder - Columbia 8230 (E)

LOVE SCULPTURE
2-68   River to Another Day/Brand New Woman - Parlophone R 5664 (E)
9-68   Wang Dang Doodle/The Stumble - Parlophone R 5731 (E)
11-68 Sabre Dance/Think of Love - Parlophone R 5744 (E) Parrot 335 (A)
2-69   Seagull/Farandole - Parlophone R 5807 (E)
2-70   In the Land of the Few/Farandole - Parlophone R 5831 (E) Parrot 342 (A)

LP: *Blues Helping* Rare Earth RS 505 (A) Parlophone PCS 7059(E) 12-68
    The Stumble/3 O'Clock Blues/I Believe To My Soul/So Unkind/Summertime/
    On the Road Again/Don't Answer the Door/Wang Dang Doodle/Come Back
    Baby/Shake Your Hips/Blues Helping

LP: *Forms and Feelings* - Parrot PAS 71035 (A) Parlophone PCS 7090(E) 1-70
    In the Land of the Few/Seagull/Nobody's Talking/Why (How-Now)/Farandole/You Can't Catch Me/People People/Mars/Sabre Dance

(unreleased)
15-minute Chipmunks-style version of "Hey Jude" made on home tape machine

DAVE EDMUNDS
First Rockfield sessions: the legendary rockabilly reconstructions.
Baby Let's Play House/My Baby Left Me/Good Rockin' Tonight/etc.

12-70 I Hear You Knocking/Black Bill - MAM 1 (E) MAM 3601 (A)
3-71   I'm Coming Home/Country Roll - Regal Zonophone 3032 (E) MAM 3608(A)
7-71   Blue Monday/I'll Get Along - Regal Zonophone 3037 (E) MAM 3611 (A)
7-72   Down, Down, Down/It Ain't Easy - Regal Zonophone 3059(E)

LP: *Rockpile* - MAM 3 (A) 1-72
    Down Down Down/I Hear You Knocking/Hell of a Pain/It Ain't Easy/Promised Land/Dance Dance Dance/I'm a Lover Not a Fighter/Egg or the Hen/Sweet Little Rock & Roller/Outlaw Blues

2-73   *Live at the Patti* (10-inch 2-LP set) United Artists UDX 205/6 (E)
       Includes Edmunds playing with Man on "Life on the Road"/"Shuffle", and with Martin Ace, Terry Williams, & Mickey Gee as Plum Crazy, on "Jingle Bells" and "Run Run Rudolph"

12-72 Baby I Love You/Maybe - Rockfield ROC 1 (E) RCA 74-0882 (A)
6-73   Born to Be With You/Pick Axe Rag - Rockfield ROC 2(E) RCA 5000 (A)
?-74   Need a Shot of Rhythm & Blues - Rockfield ROC 4(E)RCA
7-75   I Ain't Never/Some Other Guy - Rockfield ROC 6 (E)   RCA JB-10118(A)
3-76   London's a Lonely Town/   RCA (E)

LP: *Stardust* soundtrack - Arista 5000
    When Will I Be Loved/Need a Shot of Rhythm & Blues/Make Me Good/You Kept Me Waiting/Let It Be Me/Some Other Guy/Take It Away/Americana Stray Cat Blues/C'mon Little Dixie/Dea Sancta/Da Doo Ron Ron

LP: *Subtle as a Flying Mallet* - Rockfield RRL 101)e) RCA 5003 (A)
    Shot of Rhythm & Blues/Billy the Kid/Born to Be With You/She's My Baby/I Ain't Never/Let It Rock/Baby I Love You/Leave My Woman Alone/Maybe Da Doo Ron Ron/Let It Be Me/No Money Down

LP: *Dave Edmunds & Love Sculpture — The Classic Tracks* -One-Up 2047(E)
    I Hear You Knocking/You Can't Catch Me/In the Land of the Few/Farandole/Summertime/Blues Helping/The Stumble/Down,Down,Down/Seagull/Sabre Dance/Outlaw Blues/Promised Land

(unreleased)
1972: Sweet Little Rock & Roller, The Joke
1975: Ju Ju Man, New York's a Lonely Town

RECORDS PRODUCED BY DAVE EDMUNDS

WARREN PHILLIPS & THE ROCKETS
1969   LP: *Rocked Out!* - Parrot 71044 (A) *The World of Rock & Roll* - Decca SPA 43 (E) (uncredited, unconfirmed)
SHAKIN' STEVENS & THE SUNSETS
1970   LP: *A Legend* - Parlophone 7112 (E) (Edmunds also played guitar & bass)
FOGHAT
1972   LP: *Foghat* - Bearsville 2077 (A)
FLAMIN' GROOVIES
1972   Slow Death/Tallahassie Lassie - UA 35392 (E)
1972   Married Woman/Get a Shot of Rhythm & Blues - UA 35464 (E)
1972   (also recorded) Shake Some Action*, You Tore Me Down*, Little Queenie
       *released 1976 on Sire LP 7521 (A)
1975   LP: *Shake Some Action* - Sire 7521 (A) Edmunds plays piano on "St. Louis Blues", and 4th guitar on "Let the Boy Rock & Roll"
       (also recorded) Sweet Little Sixteen, I Got Mine
BRINSLEY SCHWARZ
1974   LP: *New Favourites* - UA 29641 (E)
MAN
Edmunds plays guitar on 3 of their LPs:
       Do You Like It Here Now - UA 29236 (E) 1971
       Back Into the Future - UA 60053/4 (E) 1973
       Be Good to Yourself - UA 077 (A) 1973
DEKE LEONARD
1973   *A Hard Way to Live* - UA 359 (A)
DUCKS DELUXE
1974   LP: *Taxi to the Terminal Zone* - RCA SF 8402 (E) Edmunds plays guitar on 2 tracks
DEL SHANNON
1974   And the Music Plays On - UA 35740 (E)
MOTORHEAD
1975   Various unreleased tracks
DISCO BROTHERS
1976   Let's Go to the Disco/Everybody Dance - UA UP 36057
PETE DUNTON
1974   Taking Time/Still Confused - Rockfield 4(E) RCA 0262(A)

ROCKFIELD DISCOGRAPHY

THUNDERBOLTS
?-64   March of the Spacemen/Lost Planet - Dot 16496 (A)
CHARLES KINGSLEY CREATION
?-65   Summer Without Sun/Still in Love With You - Columbia DB 7758(E)
INTERNS
7-66   Is It Really What You Want/Just Like Me - Parlophone R 5479 (E)
?-??   Ray of Sunshine/? - Parlophone

ROCKFIELD RECORDS
1   Dave Edmunds - Baby I Love You/Maybe
2   Dave Edmunds - Born to Be With You/Pick Axe Rag
3   Dave Edmunds - Need a Shot of Rhythm & Blues/Let It Be Me
4   Pete Dunton - Taking Time/Still Confused
5   Rockfield Chorale - Evensong/Amberley
6   Dave Edmunds - SOme Other Guy/I Ain't Never
7   Chuck Bedford - Ray of Sunshine/?

ROCKFIELD/UA
UP 36068 - Pennies - Juliet/Stuck on the Ground
UP 36071 - Bryn Yenn - Wasted Days & Wasted Nights/It's You
LP: UAS 28908 - Barry Melton - *The Fish*
LP: UAS 28909 - Hobo

Scheduled: Ray Martinez, Shikane

PARTIAL LIST OF GROUPS WHO'VE RECORDED AT ROCKFIELD
Man, Brinsley Schwarz, Help Yourself, Deke Leonard, Shakin' Stevens &the Sunsets, Flamin' Groovies, Ducks Deluxe, Hawkwind, Tim Rose, Van Der Graaf Generator, Neutrons, Horslips, Barry Melton, Ace, Stackridge, Arthur Brown, Gypsy, Albert Lee, Roy Young, Del Shannon, Brotherly Love, Queen, Budgie, Sassafras, Dr. Feelgood, Be Bop Deluxe, Prelude, Mr. Big, Elephants Memory, Andy Fairweather Low, Home, Starry Eyed & Laughing, Frankie Miller, Judas Priest, Black Sabbath, Hobo, Tyler Gang, Alkatraz, Shanghai, Clive John, Memfis Band, Solution, Bintangs, Alquin, Hustler, Bees Make Honey

DAVE EDMUNDS
[Continued from page 19]

• Studio A, where Edmunds does his thing.

recently expired, and besides Edmunds there haven't been any further hit acts, but a new distribution deal with UA will give Rockfield an outlet for a lot of the odd tracks that are always being recorded. While I was visiting, Kingsley was producing a Spector-like Christmas record that I thought was sensational. I asked him who the artist was. "Oh, just a couple of guys who work in the fields."

Among the first few things out under the new deal are a remake of "Juliet" by former members of the Four Pennies (who had a #1 hit with the song in 1964), "Wasted Days and Wasted Nights" by Bryn Yenn, a Welsh singer remembered by a handful of discographers as having fronted Yem & the Yemen, a short-lived 1966 beat group. There will also be albums by Barry Melton, of Country Joe & the Fish, and a group called Hobo, made up of Rockfield personnel, who for the last couple of years have played pub dates frequently around South Wales.

• Kingsley Ward, master technician.

Rockfield has attracted a small but impressive staff. Fritz Fryer, once of the Four Pennies, is always around producing or recording something. Pat Moran has been there 4 years as engineer, part time member of the studio band, and a promising producer (from the crazed look his eyes sometimes take on, I suspect he'll produce great records someday). Kingsley himself has become such an accomplished producer that he can duplicate the Dave Edmunds sound with no apparent effort. Indeed, as he stands in the control room, eyes bulging wildly from their sockets, shrieking "knobs? what knobs??!" or some such nonsense while unearthly echoed castanets tumble from the monstrous studio monitors, one gets the feeling that Kingsley Ward is the real spirit behind Rockfield.

Meanwhile Charles Ward, a little older and saner (but just barely) continues to work the fields and keep things under control. Their parents live on in the old Georgian master farmhouse, the wives manage the daily affairs of the place, the mad uncle stays up on his hill, the children play with the horses, and, amidst a million or so quid worth of space-age electronic gear and a growing stream of incredulous musicians, life at Amberley Court goes on.

took place in London.

United Artists, Man's label, began using Rockfield extensively, being among the first to recognize the extraordinary potential of the studio's sound. Edmunds was hired to produce a Brinsley Schwarz album, a Del Shannon single, and Deke Leonard's great "A Hard Way to Live", which with the names changed could easily be an Edmunds track.

In the course of all this producing, studio time permitting, Edmunds was working on a series of tracks aiming at a modern application of Phil Spector's overpowering 'wall of sound.' He cut "Baby I Love You", "Maybe" and "Born to Be With You" plus a version of "Da Doo Ron Ron" which later turned up on the Stardust soundtrack. His contract with Gordon Mills had expired, and he had no outlet for his records, but Rockfield had just done a label deal with RCA, so they put out "Baby I Love You" at the tail end of 1972.

With Edmunds' first-time luck, it jumped into the British Top 10, encouraging him to release "Born to Be With You", which became an even bigger hit. The depth and power of these records were simply breath-taking. He was using all Spector's techniques, but in his own style, with his phased-out guitars and the 'Rockfield Sound' that was fast becoming as recognizable as that of Motown, Philles or Sun. "Born to Be With You" also renewed his practice of dredging up forgotten, obscure songs that fit his style perfectly; the song had been done often before, by the Chordettes and Sonny James among others, but always as a breezy, hummable pop ditty. Edmunds slowed it down, drenched it with Ronettes sauce, and made it a modern classic.

To those who might have stereotyped him as just another Fifties-obsessed ex-rocker, Edmunds was rapidly proving his command of a wide array of musical influences. The same ear that picked up the rock & roll potential in "Sabre Dance" was listening to everything and contriving new ways to expand the definition of rock & roll without leaving behind the basic qualities that the music depends on. While going through his so-called Phil Spector period, Edmunds was also working on tracks derived from the Everly Brothers ("When Will I Be Loved"), Webb Pierce ("I Ain't Never") and the early Liverpool era ("Some Other Guy").

One of his most classic recordings is an unreleased 1972 track called "The Joke," a slow folk blues in which sharp-edged guitars bite in and out like a whiplash as Edmunds whines a series of humorous tall tales out of American folklore.
Sample verse:
> They say that Wyatt Earp rode a horse
> But that's not so; he drove a car
> They say that Jesse James had a gang
> But he really had a ragtime band....

While other English rockers were buying lurex sox and miming Jerry Lee Lewis records, Edmunds was reaching back to the wellsprings of American culture, like John Fogerty returning to the bayou, for a strength and inspiration to match the power of his music.

In 1973, then, Edmunds was becoming recognized as an extraordinary talent. The makers of That'll Be the Day, a very successful film dealing with England's American Graffiti days, asked Edmunds to help with the sequel, Stardust. One of the truly essential rock films, it dealt with the rise of a scruffy English bar band to the heights of world popdom, loosely modeled on the Beatles' career. Edmunds was cast as the group's lead guitarist, and though it wasn't widely publicized, he provided all the music heard in the film. In addition to giving them whatever odd tracks were lying around the studio, he did several new songs including "Make Me Good", "You Kept Me Waiting", "C'mon Little Dixie" and "Americana Stray Cat Blues." He also did a version of "Dea Sancta", the excessive production number that climaxes star Jim Maclaine's career, but because David Essex insisted on singing that one himself, Edmunds' magnificent version was never heard.

Although he didn't get proper credit, Stardust did serve to establish Edmunds further in the awareness of the British music industry and inspired a repackage of Love Sculpture and early solo tracks, and the release of his second solo album, Subtle as a Flying Mallet, which combined a few old tracks with some unheard gems such as "Leave My Woman Alone", "Billy the Kid" and the fantastic live recordings of "No Money Down" and "Let It Rock", probably taped sometime in 1973, but much better than his brief live appearance on the Christmas at the Patti album.

I first met Dave Edmunds in October, 1975, when I made the trek to Rockfield with the Flamin' Groovies to cut an album with him as producer. I found him to be a somewhat enigmatic character—bright, full of life, with wide blue eyes; obviously very aware of his talents and dedicated to his music, yet more restrained in his outward personality than any rock star I'd ever encountered. More than just shy, he exudes a modesty that borders on humility. He only really opened up late at night, in the studio, when an after-hours jam session found him exulting at the discovery of a new variation on one of Chuck Berry's old riffs, in a bizarre tuning of his own invention. The band got behind him and they played on for an hour or more, and when they came back in the booth Edmunds was more alive than I saw him at any other time in the week I spent there.

His style in the studio was far from what I expected. Instead of being hyper-active, twisting knobs like mad, calling out a constant stream of commands, he just sat quietly at the console, saying nothing except "how d'you like it?" at the end. At times he'd get an idea for a guitar part, plugging right into the mixing board and playing along (most of the guitars on his records were played this way too, right in the control room). His real effort came in the mixing, when suddenly the room was full of tape loops spinning at weird speeds, black boxes doing indescribable things to the sound, and echoes the like of which I'd never heard in a studio before.

In February, Edmunds made a promotional trip to the US, spending 2 weeks in Los Angeles. He brought with him a tape of "New York's a Lonely Town", which he ended up redoing completely at RCA studios, with Bruce Johnston producing and various others including Gary Usher and Curt Boetcher adding backup vocals. While in LA he met his two idols, Phil Spector and Brian Wilson, and also began to realize what a tremendous following he has here among press and radio. Although Rockfield's contract with RCA has expired, Edmunds will most likely stay with them. With any luck, now that the momentum of his reputation is finally overtaking him, and his own confidence is growing, the time will be right for Dave Edmunds to emerge as one of the true giants of rock & roll in our time.

• Dave Edmunds at the control board, adding a guitar part to one of his songs.

SOUNDS of the SIXTIES

Part Three: CHICAGO

By Cary Baker & Jeff Lind

A CONTINUING SERIES EXAMINING REGIONAL MUSIC SCENES OF THE MID-LATE SIXTIES. PREVIOUS INSTALLMENTS HAVE INCLUDED BOSTON, DETROIT AND SAN FRANCISCO.

CHICAGO ROCK: A CAPSULE HISTORY
BY JEFF LIND

The city of Chicago borrowed heavily from many sources in attempting to forge its own musical identity in the '60s. Thanks to these influences (East Coast R&B, West Coast experimental sounds, the British Invasion, and particularly Chicago blues—plus the abundance of independent recording firms, producers, and talented groups, Chicago was able to fashion a highly individual and commercially viable sound, even if the local scene never outwardly reflected it to the extent that scenes in Detroit and other areas were seen to flourish.

Let's examine those influences as they applied to Chicago rock. Though the Windy City has been known since the mid-'50s as one of the nation's most fruitful R&B centers (thanks mainly to the efforts of Curtis Mayfield, Jerry Butler and Gene Chandler), the smooth, one might even say sophisticated sound they created, in contrast to the rough R&B of Memphis, Detroit and LA, was a direct outgrowth of the pioneering New York groups and producers, such as Leiber & Stoller and, in particular, their work with the Drifters. While never as popular with the white teenage groups as funkier James Brown type sounds, this Chicago style of R&B helped build the city into a recording center. Mercury, one of the largest record companies, is based there, and usually picked up the better local groups for national exposure. Chess, one of the country's most successful independent labels since the early '50s, was also based there. And literally hundreds of small, blues or R&B-oriented labels supported an extensive system of recording studios, mastering labs, pressing plants, and night clubs.

The British Invasion and the West Coast scene (which introduced surfing in '63, hotrod music in '64, folk-rock in '65, and acid rock in '66) were a double-barreled influence that dominated rock in the '60s, especially in the Midwest where countless bands appeared, offering endless combinations and permutations of these influences.

But if any factor could be said to define Chicago rock in the '60s, and to set it apart from that of other cities, it was Chicago blues. The importance of local scenes is that they took these same influences (British and West Coast rock) and combined them with local culture to cause a proliferation of new styles and ideas in rock. In Chicago, blues was such a powerful influence that it eventually permeated all of '60s rock.

The importance of Chicago as a blues center needs no reiteration in these pages. Throughout the '40s and '50s, Chicago was the blues capitol of the world, with such legendaries as Muddy Waters, Willie Dixon, Howlin' Wolf, Chuck Berry and others. Most of these had brought the Mississippi Delta blues up with them and revolutionized the form by adding electric guitars, drums, and creating in effect the direct source of modern rock & roll. Most of the Chicago punk groups depended heavily on a blues/R&B repertoire—even the Shadows of Knight, the punkiest of them all, filled their LPs with Willie Dixon songs. Paradoxically, however, since nearly all the teen bands were based in the suburbs and the blues scene was restricted to the treacherous South Side where few parents would allow their offspring to go, there was little direct contact. The songs were known to the groups from airplay on local radio, but the blues scene itself was another world. Only a few local kids such as Paul Butterfield, Mike Bloomfield, Elvin Bishop, Barry Goldberg, Corky Siegel and Jim Schwall got involved in the South Side scene, but it was their influence, along with others like Nick Gravenitis, that made the blues such an integral part of American rock from 1967 onward. It's even been said that, by drawing away the most "hip" and innovative young musicians, the local blues scene kept the Chicago rock scene from realizing its full potential.

At the same time, it should be noted that the blues influence, though it came from the South Side, reached many white teenage musicians via the English groups like the Stones and Animals who were more aware of the rich musical traditions in their own back yard than the local kids themselves!

In the early '60s, the forerunners of Chicago rock began to appear. Ral Donner, one of the better Presley imitators, had several fine national hits. Ronnie Rice was a young Chicagoan with a Bobby Veeish voice whose best early effort was "Come Back Little Girl", an answer to Steve Lawrence's "Go Away Little Girl." His solo career never got off the ground, but he later emerged as songwriter and performer with the New Colony Six. Ann-Margaret might have gone far in music had she never gone to Hollywood. As a local girl from Winnetka she had two fair-sized hits on RCA. Then of course there was the abortive recording career of the controversial Chicago DJ Dick Biondi whose novelty hit "The Pizza Song" provided a few chuckles back in '61. His main contribution was in promoting local artists.

Mention should also be made of Bobby Whiteside and George Edwards. Whiteside had a regional hit in '65 with "Say it Softly" but has since done well with songwriting and producing, tho still recording R&B for a variety of labels. Edwards was into folk blues and cut a couple of sides with friends including Steve Miller and Maurice McKinley for Dunwich. But of them all, it was the Shadows of Knight who were the messiahs of Chicago rock.

THE SHADOWS OF KNIGHT

They went through three main incarnations. 1965-mid'67 they were Jim Sohns (leader), Tom Schiffour, Joe Kelley, Warren Rodgers, Jerry McGeorge, Norm Gotsch, & Dave Wolinski. In mid-67 they became Sohns, Kenny Turkin, Dan Baughman, Woody Woodruff, & John Fisher. Then in early '71 they returned with Sohns, Bob Harper, Charlie Hess, Eric Blomquist, & Jack Daniel (later replaced by Gary Levin.)

The Shadows were straight-forward, defiant, and sexual in their approach. Their music was raw, powerful rock & roll with a punky flavor. It was this garage punk feeling that turned out to be such an inspiration for other local groups, and also the fact that they were the first to break through onto the national charts.

Jim Sohns formed the band after graduating from Prospect High School in 1965. For 9 months the group played gigs and parties locally. They soon became the de facto house band at a new Arlington Heights teen club, the Cellar, owned by Paul Sampson, an independent music promoter who also managed a local booking agency. Sampson was one of many independent promoters in the area, and he dealt with the many local record firms in the suburbs as well as Chicago proper. Many of these promoters and producers were dedicated to the development of a "Chicago Sound", among them Bill Traut, Bob Monaco, Jim Guercio, George Badonsky, Jim Golden, Ray Peck, Mike Considine and Frank Rand. Also instrumental in helping local groups were DJs like Clark Weber, Art Roberts, Barney Pip, Joel Sebastian and Dick Biondi. The two major rock stations, WLS and WCFL competed to see who could play more local records, after the Shadows of Knight became the focal point of a strong local audience.

Jim Sohns didn't even want to record "Gloria" at first since the song had been a flop for Them, but Paul Sampson (now their manager) insisted, and they cut it in 35 minutes. Released on January 31, 1966, it immediately began drawing heavy requests on WLS and CFL. The group's fanclub, the Shadows' Shadows, organized a phone-in during Art Roberts' Top Three Request Show one night, and WLS was deluged with calls. The song eventually became Top 5 nationally.

The subsequent records, however, failed to click and by mid-1967 Johns broke up the group and formed a new band, who hooked up with the Team label, run by Katz & Kasenetz of future bubblegum fame. This resulted in their second and last national hit, "Shake." This also proved to be a dead end, however. Today, the Shadows of Knight survive playing heavy metal glitter rock at local bars. But no one in Chicago will ever forget their importance in launching the local scene, nor the greatness of their early records as attested to by a growing cult of collector enthusiasts who pay $30 or more for their Dunwich albums....

SATURDAY'S CHILDREN

They were the esoteric counterparts of the Shadows, important not so much for their recording efforts, which were limited, but because of their influence on other local groups like the Cryan' Shames, Shady Daze, etc. The Children were the second group to be managed by Paul Sampson, and their sound was heavily influenced by the Beatles, as evidenced by their compositon "You Don't Know Better." Though they remained unknown outside the city, they were one of the most talented Chicago bands.

THE LITTLE BOY BLUES

Led by the multi-talented Ray Levin (organ, piano, harpsichord, flute &bass) this group started out playing old Chicago blues standards, later branching out into jazz-flavored tunes, even experimenting with the 12 tone scale and classical music on their long-awaited LP, released in '69. Still, they are best remembered for their single "The Great Train Robbery" on Ronco, and their wild version of "I Can Only Give You Everything" on IRC, two of the all-time classics of Chicago punk.

THE NEW COLONY SIX

They actually broke onto the local and national charts before the Shadows, hitting in December '65 with "I Confess". They played basic British-flavored blues, mainly their own compositions, but had no real hits of any consequence until Ronnie Rice joined and started composing soft ballads. With Rice, they had two national hits, "I Will Always Think About You" and "Things I'd Like to Say." After these, in 1968, their career stalled, but they kept recording steadily and in 1974 signed with the powerful MCA Records, with the promise of better things ahead for these 10-year veterans.

THE BUCKINGHAMS

Named after Chicago's famous fountain, this group thoroughly dominated the charts in 1967 due to the writing talents of Jim Guercio, Jim Holvay and Gary Beisber (the latter two being also members of another local group, the Mob). Behind Dennis Tufano's smooth crooning, they struck gold with their fourth release, "Kind of a Drag" which became #1 across the nation. Four other hits, plus 2 LPs, followed that year. By 1968, however, popular tastes had passed them by. All members are still active, notably Jim Guercio who went on to manage Chicago, the Beach Boys, and Caribou Studios.

THE MAUDS

Another band managed by Paul Sampson, they got their start on the North Side. Jimmy Hodgers, their leader, was dedicated to R&B, and his vocals were tinged with gospel excitement. Curtis Mayfield was impressed with the way the Mauds did his songs, and their live concerts were legendary. By remaining true to R&B, though, they gave up their chances of wider appeal, and their career had reached a standstill by 1968. Their two big hits, "Hold On" and "Soul Drippin'" are still capable of creating a frenzy, almost 8 years after their release.

THE AMERICAN BREED

The Breed paid their dues for several years as Gary & the Nite Lites, and were also deeply steeped in rhythm & blues. Like the Mauds, they were capable of tremendous live shows, but it was in the studio that they really shone. Thanks to Eddie Higgins' tasteful brass arrangements, and the group's own unusual 4-part harmonies, they put together the original sound later known as "brass rock." Their records, such as their first hit "Step Out of Your Mind" were always driving and dynamic. Their biggest success was in 1968 with "Bend Me Shape Me" which sold a million, though it was all downhill from there. With several personnel changes, they are back on the charts today as Rufus.

ROTARY CONNECTION

This group was originally Marshall Chess's pet project in his attempt to 'psychedelicize' the image of Chess Records, but public response to their first LP was so overwhelming that he had to put together a touring group to promote the album. Their most distinctive feature was the lofty, lilting voice of young Minnie Riperton. Their overall sound was too far from the mainstream, however, and they finally gave up the ghost after 5 years, with only one minor hit, "Want You to Know" to show for it. Minnie of course is now a star of some repute.

SPANKY & OUR GANG

Elaine MacFarland put her gang of musicians together in the mid-'60s to play what was called "good time music." Their early career was spent in small clubs around Coconut Grove, Florida, where they mixed with such folk heroes as Fred Neil and John Sebastian. With Spanky's voice and Malcolm Hale's vocal arrangements they put together some beautiful vocal stylings, reminiscent of the Mamas & Papas, especially on songs like "Sunday Will Never Be the Same" and "Like to Get to Know You." All this took place after they returned to their home town, Chicago. After the release of the controversial "Give a Damn" the group found itself shunned by radio stations and promoters alike. From here their fortunes declined, culminating in Malcolm Hale's death in 1969, which brought about the dissolution of the band. Recently, Spanky got together with the original gang member Nigel Pickering to release a new album on Columbia. It's good to have her back.

THE FLOCK

This most innovative of all Chicago groups began its career with a string of not-so-successful singles on Destination & USA, the most notable of which were "Take Me Back" and "What Would You Do if the Sun Died?" Starting out as a basically an R&B band, the Flock successfully synthesized elements of jazz, blues, rock and country idioms into their own style. Essential in their sound was the imaginative violin playing of Jerry Goodman. The band should have been more popular nationally than they were, but they did have a successful European tour. Their lack of commercial success eventually broke them apart, but they reformed in 1972. Goodman, in the meantime, had gone on to fame in the much-acclaimed Mahavishnu Orchestra.

BANGOR FLYING CIRCUS

One of the first Chicago 'supergroups', they combined jazz-like swing with rock & roll into a brand of music that was years ahead of their time. They later changed their name to Madura, though it didn't help. They remain one of the best and most under-rated Chicago bands.

H.P. LOVECRAFT

They named themselves (in line with Bill Traut's Lovecraft/Dunwich obsession) after the legendary writer of horror stories, and the name was not inappropriate. They were a bizarre band whose music was the ultimate in progrossive rock for its time, and today, more than 7 years later, it still sounds timeless. Dave Michaels and George Edwards formed the band, and from folk-rock they branched out into eerie, spacey tunes, often with classical overtones and electronic segments. Their *H.P. Lovecraft II* album is still a classic among heavy, heady rock masterpieces, and even the spaced-out Ken Nordine made a brief appearance on it.

The group was largely ignored in Chicago for being too eclectic and perhaps too esoteric, but they won critical acclaim throughout the rest of the country, which they toured several times. They never had a real hit single, though, and eventually faded away. Mike Tegza reformed the group in 1970 and again in 1975, though there was little similarity to their original sound.

THE TROLLS

The Trolls added humor to Chicago rock with their energetic recording "Every Day and Every Night" which concerned the trials and tribulations of a local rock star being pursued by the 300+ lb. fire chief's daughter. They also had a fine punk sound with a folk-rock flavor, and their records rank among the best of Chicago garage bands.

BABY HUEY & THE BABYSITTERS

Baby Huey was 300 pounds of joy, and his Babysitters were a few tons more. He was popular in the same way as Jimi Hendrix, with the then-novel approach of black progressive blues aimed at white audiences. They were at the top of the heap among club bands for many years, until Baby Huey died tragically in 1970.

THE MOB

Two of their members were Jimmy Holvay & Gary Beisber, authors of all the Buckinghams' big hits. Too bad they didn't save some for themselves, for the Mob had none. They could never capture on record the excitement they generated in concert. They continued recording though, and their 1975 LP on Private Stock was a strong comeback.

[Turn to page 36]

USA RECORDS

USA started as a blues label but soon became one of Chicago's most prolific punk labels.Period covered here is roughly 1961-69. A 100-gospel series is still active.

714 - Adam & Eva - Need You/Lonely
715 - Tobin Matthews - Oh Julie/Pretty Sue
716 - Tobin Matthews - Groanin'/Slippin' & Slidin'
718 - Tobin Matthews - Think it Over/LoveHasFunnyWays
723 - Don Bailey - Be My Own/Wedding Day
729 - Oscar Boyd - Twist with Ossie Lee/She's My Baby
733 - Cory Wade - Not for a Penny
934 - Joey Madrid - Mr. Lucky/See Saw
735 - Willie Mabon - Just Got Some/That's No Big Thing
736 - Junior Wells - Ev'ry Goodbye Ain't Gone/I'll Get You Too
737 - Geraldine Hunt - Sneak Around/It Never Happened Before
738 - Jessie Fortune - Too Many Cooks/Heavy Heartbeat
739 - TV Slim - You Cant Love Me/Hold Me Close to Your Heart
741 - Willie Mabon - I'm the Fixer/TooHotToHandle
742 - Junior Wells - WHen the Cat's Gone the Mice Play/ She's a Sweet One
744 - JB Lenoir - I Feel So Good/I Sing Um the Way I Feel
745 - Koko Taylor - Like Heaven to Me/Honky Tonky
746 - Homesick James - My Baby'S Sweet/Crossroads
747 - Jessie Fortune - Good Things/God's Gift to Man
748 - Perk Lee - The Docks/Peanut Butter Sandwich
749 - Jay Johnson - Karen/Married to Sherri
750 - Willie Mabon - I'm Hungry/Ruby's Monkey
751 - Billy Emerson - Hotspring/I Get That Feeling
753 - Four Uniques - Endlessly/Maybe Next Summer
759 - Willie Mabon - Some More/New Orleans Blues
760 - Al Perkins - Kuz'n Bill/She's Alright
761 - Vice-Roys - Liverpool/Tonk
765 - Al Perkins - You Left Me/Love Me Baby
767 - Willie Mabon - Harmonica Special/SOmebody Gotta Pay
772 - Chick & Nobles - I Cry/Island for Two
776 - Mona Thomas - There He Goes/Just In Between
778 -Andrew Brown - You Better Stop
779 - Ricky Allen - Going or Coming/Little by Little
786 - Al Perkins - Step it Up/Nothing but the Pure of Heart
787 - Willie Mabon - Sometime I Wonder/Lonesome Blues
788 - Nobles - That Special One/Marlene
789 - Lonnie Brooks - I'm Not Going Home/Figure Head
790 - Junior Wells - Lovey Dovey Lovey One/Come On In This House
793 - Wiley Terry - Follow the Leader, 1&2
801 - Baby Huey - Messin' With the Kid/Just Being Careful
814 - Detroit Jr. - The Way I Feel/Call My Job
822 - Al Perkins - So Long/I Feel All Right
833 - Gary & Knight Lites - I Dont Need Your Help/Big Bad Wolf
834 - Mary Crystal - Dont Tell on Me/Who Are They
835 - Crestones - My Girl/The Chopper
837 - Phil Orsi & Little Kings - Sorry/Whoever He May Be
844 - Buckinghams - I'll Go Crazy/I Don't Wanna Cry
848 - Buckinghams - I Call Your Name/Makin' Up & Breakin' Up
??? - Daughters of Eve - Hey Lover/Stand By Me
??? - Carl Bonafede - Good Old Days/St.Louie Here I Come
850 - Cambridge Five - Heads I Win/Floatin'
851 - Oscar & Majestics - I Cant Explain/My Girl is Waiting
853 - Buckinghams - I've Been Wrong/Love Ain't Enough
854 - Carole Waller - Say Say Chicken Man
857 - Lord & the Flies - Come What May/Echoes
860 - Buckinghams - Kind of a Drag/You Make Me Feel So Good
861 - Mighty Joe Young - Nobody Home
866 - Michael & Messengers - Midnight Hour/Up Til News
869 - Buckinghams - I Call Your Name/Lawdy Miss Clawdy
871 - Good Griefs - Shy Girl/Oop-Oop-Pah-Doo
873 - Buckinghams - Summertime/Don't Want to Cry
874 - Michael & Messengers - Romeo & Juliet/Lifs
875 - Cambridge Five - I Hate to Laugh Alone/Keep On Running
876 - Alan Gari - Too Bad it Didn't Work Out/Good Lovin' Woman
880 - Skopes - She's Got Bad Breath/Tears in Your Eyes
881 - Lost Agency - Time to Dream/One Girl Man
882 - Five Bucks - Without Love
883 - Shady Daze - I'll Make You Pay/Love is a Beautiful Thing
886 - Family - So Much to Remember/Face the Autumn
887 - Bondsmen - Shotgun/Patricia Anne
891 - Daughters of Eve-SymphonyOfMySoul/HelpMeBoy
892 - Carnival of Slush - I Can't Remember
893 - Martinis - Holiday Cheer/Bullseye
894 - Family - San Francisco Waits/Without You
895 - Cherry Slush - I Cannot Stop You/Don't Walk Wway Don't Walk Away
897 - Michael & Messengers - Gotta Take It Easy/I Need Her Here
898 - Chicago Fire - Candy & Me/Come See What I Got
900 - Sonny WIlliams - Sweetest Little Girl in Town/ You Didn't Find Her That Way
902 - Invaders - Flower Song/With a Tear
905 - Trolls - I Got to Have You/Don't Come Around
907 - McKinley Sandifer - Sweet Little Woman/Get Up
909 - Hermie - The Littlest Flower/Hermie's Prayer
910 - Flock - Magical Wings/What Would You Do if the Sun Died?
922 - Factory - High Blood Pressure/Lonely Path
1213 - Nobelmen - Thunder Wagon/Dragon Walk
1221 - Von Gayels - Twirl/Loneliness

The Ides of March & The Cryan Shames
By Mike Thom

Of all the Chicago bands who took a shot at the big time following the Shadows of Knight's success with "Gloria" in March, 1966, two of the most worthy (and unfairly overlooked by rock historians thus far) were the Ides of March and the Cryan' Shames.

Most bands of this era, drenched in the excitement of the British Invasion, were content with either imitating the English groups or covering their material. In a sense, the Ides of March started in the former category and the Cryan' Shames in the latter. (The Cryan' Shames, incidentally, should not be confused with the British group the Cryin' Shames, who had a minor hit with "Please Stay".)

As time went on, many Chicago groups realized that it wasn't enough to assimilate English rock. They started developing their own styles that reflected more on the American outlook, and it is here, I think, that "Punk Rock" as a true genre was born. The English Mods were rebellious enough, and records by the Stones and the Who were as tough as you could please, but American high-schoolers might well have had trouble trying to put themselves into the situations described in the songs; they had to be satisfied with identifying with the image and basic attitude of the groups. Punk rock employed typically American imagery, slang, and settings. While based on the British instrumental sound and structural breakthroughs, it generally downplayed certain elements, such as harmony, while emphasizing others, such as the use of organ, bass, certain guitar techniques, and an overall crudeness that was implied in English records but taken much further by the Americans.

Most Chicago groups took little time to start developing their own style. The Shadows of Knight ditched the British approach right after "Gloria", and returned to their R&B roots so fast that "Gloria" sounds rather out of place on the group's first album, which featured three Willie Dixon songs in a row.

THE IDES OF MARCH

For the Ides of March, the transition came slower. The group stayed with their English-influenced approach for at least a year until their better-known brass sound began creeping in, on "My Foolish Pride."

Their first release was "You Wouldn't Listen." The group wrote the song, but it could easily have been written by Gerry Marsden. It peaked at #42 in August, 1966. The flip, "I'll Keep Searching" was in the same vein, and another original.

The follow-up, "Roller Coaster" (written by lead singer Jim Peterik) was much better. It surges with great Byrds-like rhythm guitar and harmonies, and the production is amazingly full with just the right amount of rawness; it's definitely one of the classics of its era. It charted for one week at #92 and then flopped. For their next single, Peterik wrote "You Need Love," a decent riff song but in no way abandoning the English influence – as is obvious from the flip, a cover of the Small Faces' "Sha-La-La-La-Lee." This too was a commercial stiff.

Sometime in 1967 they released "My Foolish Pride." Although the flip was much like previous recordings, this song, as noted previously, introduced horns – a step that would prove as wise commercially as it was disastrous aesthetically.

Surprisingly, after so many failures, Parrot saw fit to release one last single. "Hole in My Soul" was much like the Cryan' Shames' "Sugar and Spice" and "Girls Don't Grow On Trees" was a great cop from "Last Train to Clarksville."

After being dropped by Parrot and picked up by Warner Bros., the Ides chose to go with a softer approach, perhaps because of the success of their home town rivals the New Colony Six. "One Woman Man" is a powerful ballad that should've been a monster hit. Peterik was disappointed but hadn't given up yet. Looking around to see who else was making it, he observed the great and overnight success of groups like Chicago and Chase with big, brassy rock raunchers.

The next Ides of March release was a perfect imitation of that sound. "Vehicle", released in early 1970, made it to #2. Their first album was released around this time.

By now the Ides of March were unrecognizable to fans of their early work. They followed "Vehicle" with a carbon-copy called "Superman", which got no higher than #64. Next they tried the MOR approach with "Melody" (fairly obscure since it wasn't a hit and was never on an album). It was a nice idea, but didn't quite come off. But the same approach worked the next time out with "L.A. Goodbye", their second biggest hit. It sounded more like the Association because it substituted vocals for brass.

Following this, the *Common Bond* album was released. Its highlight was an 11½-minute epic called "Tie-Dye Princess", with a blend of vocals, brass, percussion and strings that was quite exceptional. An edited version of this song was their next single. It never made the charts, nor did "Giddy-Up Ride Me", a return to the "Vehicle" formula.

The next step was to drop the brass sound. On RCA now, they cut their next album (like its predecessors, in Chicago), and it was much like *Common Bond* in its contrasts of material, but with brass on only one cut. Again there was no hit single. The next, and to date last, album was *Midnight Oil*. It's a rather weak attempt at turning the Ides into a country-rock band.

Since then, nothing has been released by the Ides of March. It's doubtful that they're still together. However, Peterik and Frank Rand (who co-produced all 4 of the group's albums) are currently working with a new group, Essence, whose first single is "Sweet Fools", a soul record. It appears that Jim Peterik is determined to continue his policy of pursuing hit records by adapting whatever current trends seem hottest, and while as a result his music has always lacked a certain quality of personality or individuality, no doubt we haven't heard the last of him.

THE CRYAN' SHAMES

The Cryan Shames cashed in on the Chicago punk rock boom when their version of "Sugar and Spice" climbed to #49 in the summer of 1966. For them, the English influence was more pronounced, as "Sugar and Spice" had previously been recorded by the Searchers. The record came out on Destination, a local label; when Columbia (who picked up several Chicago groups, including the Buckinghams, Illinois Speed Press, and Chicago), saw that it was becoming a hit, they signed the group.

Their first album was rather uneven; "Heat Wave" and a faked live "We Gotta Get Out of This Place" were pretty poor, but they did nice versions of the Byrds' "She Don't Care About Time" and "We'll Meet Again" and most of the originals are well done. The next single, "I Wanna Meet You" was lead guitarist Jim Fairs' ode to the magazine model. Like all their subsequent 45s, it failed to burn up the charts, peaking at #85.

In the summer of 1967 a second album came out, with a single, "It Could Be We're in Love" which stayed on the charts for eight weeks yet failed to get any higher than its predecessor. The album was fairly bland, but included a number of fine originals; this move toward group compositions was to prove significant on their next album.

Prior to that, the group released a fairly obscure single called "Georgia". Two other singles from the album failed as well. Their next effort was a new song, written by William Swofford (aka Oliver), which made it to #99.

In October 1968, the Cryan Shames (having deleted the apostrophe) released a fantastic album called *Synthesis*. Like *Sgt. Pepper*, it was a concept album without any real concept, but featuring some really powerful songs, mostly originals, and unbelievably complex orchestral arrangements. In my opinion this album was, along with *Aorta*, one of the two best albums from the Chicago era.

However, when a single of "First Train" from the album flopped, Columbia apparently gave up on promoting it. By early 1970, the group had decided to call it quits.

Lenny Kerley contacted former Cryan' Shames drummer Dennis Conroy (who'd played on the first 2 LPs) and with Dave Curtis and Jan Knopek, formed a short-lived group called Possum River. Meanwhile Isaac Guillory made the trek to England to record solo. He made a drastic change of direction and began writing folk songs. Jim Fairs helped Guillory cut a solo LP which was released last year on Atlantic.

• The Ides of March

IDES OF MARCH		
6-66	You Wouldn't Listen/I'll Keep Searching	Parrot 304
9-66	Roller Coaster/Things Arent Always What They Seem	Parrot 310
11-66	You Need Love/Sha-la-la-la-Lee	Parrot 312
?-67	My Foolish Pride/Give Your Mind Wings	Parrot 321
?-67	Hole in my Soul/Girls dont Grow on Trees	Parrot 326
12-69	One Woman Man/High on a Hillside	WB 7334
3-70	Vehicle/Lead Me Home, Gently	WB 7378
7-70	Superman/Home	WB 7403
11-70	Melody/The Sky is Falling	WB 7426
1-71	LA Goodbye/Mrs. Grayson's Farm	WB 7466
5-71	Tie-Dye Princess/Friends of Feeling	WB 7507
10-71	Giddy-Up Ride Me/Freedom Sweet	WB 7526
9-72	Mother America/Landlady	RCA 74-0850
?-73	Hot Water/?	RCA
ALBUMS		
4-70	*Vehicle* - WB 1863	
2-71	*Common Bond* - WB 1896	
9-72	*World Woven* - RCA 4812	
7-73	*Midnight Oil* - RCA 0143	

CRYAN' SHAMES		
7-66	Sugar & Spice/BenFranklin'sAlmanac	Destination 624
11-66	I Wanna Meet You/We Could Be Happy	Col. 43836
3-67	Georgia/Mr. Unreliable	Columbia 44037
8-67	It Could Be We're in Love/I Was Lonely When	Columbia 44191
4-68	Up on the Roof/?	Columbia 44457
6-68	Young Birds Fly/Sunshine Psalm	Columbia 44545
9-68	The Warm/Greenburg, Glickstein, Charles, David Smith & Jones	Columbia 44638
7-69	First Train to California/A Master's Fool	Columbia
1-70	Rainmaker/Bits & Pieces	Columbia 45027
ALBUMS		
9-66	*Sugar and Spice* - Columbia 9389	
8-67	*A Scratch in the Sky* - Columbia 9586	
10-68	*Synthesis* - Columbia 9719	

An early version of the group appears on the LP *Early Chicago* (Happy Tiger 1017) doing "You're Gonna Lose That Girl."

RELATED
Possum River (Kerley, Conroy, Dave Curtis, Jan Knopek)
| ?-71 | *Possum River* - Ovation LP 14-14 |
| ?-74 | Isaac Guillory - Atlantic LP 7307 |

The Dunwich Story

By CARY BAKER and JEFF LIND

Despite the traditional difficulties of local record companies in the midwest, one man has kept Chicago rock alive on vinyl come hell or high water. Producing sessions for a gamut of labels, and issuing records under his own Amboy, Dunwich and Wooden Nickel banners, Bill Traut's been at it since he was 14. He's now old enough to boast a son, Ross, who's a successful Chicago jazz musician. Meanwhile, the old man is still supporting Chicago rock and remains a progressive thinker.

Traut, orphaned at age 12, got his start in music as a polka musician in his native Fon du Lac, Wisconsin during World War II, playing trumpet, trombone, keyboards and reed instruments. Many dance bands had taken on teenage musicians to replace players drafted into the service. When Traut turned a wordly 16, big band leader Les Brown came through Fon du Lac and his tenor sax man was called away on a family emergency. Traut filled in, and was thereafter asked to tour with the band. Following years saw him touring with Stan Kenton, Sonny Dunham and Johnny (Scat) Davis, all of this prior to Traut's 18th birthday.

Then, at 18, Traut left music behind, suffering a complete physical breakdown. Late nights playing, and moreover, excessive drinking ("I was a lush at 18," he says) were the causes.

He entered the University of Wisconsin, Madison, to "straighten out and sober up" and stayed clear of the music scene. In time, he played occasional dates, and booked prom bands from his dorm room. By the time he graduated, Traut had no particular plans, so he enrolled in the Wisconsin law school, inspired by one professor, the daughter of Justice Brandeis. All the while, Traut played in local groups, and worked as a record store clerk. At this point, he was sure that he wanted to enter the record business. He remembers his uncle telling him he'd one day be president of RCA.

A position almost materialized at Am-Par Records, predecessor to the latter-day ABC-Paramount. Of 50 applicants for A&R chief, Traut and Creed Taylor were the prime contendors. Taylor got the job, but Traut was promptly offered a position as A&R man and liner-note writer for the Contemporary label. He commuted weekends between Oregon and Los Angeles, and produced early sessions by John Coltrane, Sonny Rollins and Phineas Newborn.

A few years later, Traut worked as a background music programmer for the Seeburg Co., which took him from San Francisco to L.A. to Chicago. His office in Chicago was in the same building as both Universal Studios and 50,000-watt AM monster WLS. Traut met up with jazzman Eddie Higgins in '61, then a daytime studio engineer at Universal, and a top nightclub entertainer by night. Traut and Higgins kept in close contact.

In 1964, while dining at Eli's in Chicago, Traut, Higgins, and East Coast producer George Badonsky pondered the formation of their own record label. Traut and Higgins had previously produced two jazz LP's for Atlantic. They had unlimited free studio privileges at Universal.

The name Dunwich was taken from an H.P. Lovecraft novel. Traut and Higgins shared an affinity for the author, and had several contacts in the industry who also admired Lovecraft's work, notably Atlantic exec Jerry Wexler, and reedman Charles Lloyd, who signed his letters "H. P. Lovecraft." Badonsky, the third partner in the new firm, objected to the name, contending it sounded too much like Dunhill, but the name stuck. Subsidiary firms, Yuggoth Music (BMI) and Arkham Artists, were likewise culled from Lovecraft.

The threesome's initial jazz productions drew marginal profits. They were aware that rock & roll was happening all over, and the Chicago area rock market was virtually untapped. Unfortunately, neither of the three knew anything about it. Higgins adamantly opposed it, Badonsky was merely ignorant of it. But for purely commercial gain, they auditioned two rock bands, the Shadows of Knight and the Ted Nugent Group. Paul Sampson, owner of a club out in Arlington Heights called the Cellar, had been trying to sell Traut on the Shadows of Knight for some time.

When they arrived at the Cellar, the Shadows of Knight were onstage and cooking. They played some punk-tinged blues and some Chuck Berry oldies. But when they broke into a cover of Van Morrison & Them's "Gloria," the crowds went wild. The teenage clientele squealed with delight, got loose, got dancing, got shouting "G-L-O-R-I-A."

The Them recording of "Gloria" had hit in Texas

•Bill Traut, 1976: the man who gave us "Gloria".

and Florida. Clark Weber, music director at WLS, had played it one morning over the air and greeted three complaints from mothers who objected to its suggestive subject matter. "Gloria" by Them contained a line about "I go up to a room/And roll around/And have a lot of fun." All three mothers said they'd forbid their offspring to be exposed to such vulgarity.

Traut met Weber one day over breakfast at the Stone Container Bldg. on Michigan Avenue. Weber was well familiar with the Shadows from sock hops he'd emceed. He assured Traut that if he recorded a "clean" version of the tune, he'd give it a spin. Weber was not only convinced that the Shadows were clearly the hottest rock band in Chicago, but that "Gloria" had the makings of a popular demand record.

"THERE WERE A FEW PROBLEMS—LIKE A PIANO DROPPED FROM A 23rd FLOOR WINDOW...THE SHADOWS OF KNIGHT WERE REAL PUNKS!!"

Weber premiered the record on the Art Roberts program the day he received it. The lines flooded with requests. A group of kids at the Cellar had taken to the pay phones to request it endlessly, but calls were coming in from the 40-some states WLS reaches; It was no fluke. The industry had hit on something huge. Traut pressed an additional 15,000 copies and Chicago's Royal Disc Distributors wholesales them in a week. "Gloria" had become a full-fledged monster. Traut wasn't sure he could handle it, so he turned to fellow Lovecraft enthusiast Jerry Wexler. A distribution agreement was formed between Dunwich and Atlantic over the phone. There was never a written agreement.

"Gloria" sold 950,000 records in its first incarnation. "Gloria '69," a sequel with Hendrix-like guitar dubbed on by Jim Vincent, brought sales to a million, Atlantic, however, lost count, and there is no gold record.

By '66, Dunwich had become the hub of midwest rock & roll. Its competition consisted of Sentar Records (distributed by Cameo) with the New Colony Six, and Paul Glass' USA label (the Buckinghams, Cryan Shames, Flock) whose stock was widely held by Leonard Chess. Subsequent Dunwich releases by the Del-Vettes, Sounds Unltd., Half Dozen, Omens, George Edwards, Rovin' Kind, Little Boy Blues, Pride & Joy, Trolls and Saturday's Children were met with varied degrees of success. In many cases, WLS and competitor WCFL would throw them against the wall and see if they stuck. But for the most part, things were anti-climatic after "Gloria." The Shadows' "Willie Jean" was a hit, as was the Del-Vettes' "Last Time Around," a crusher punk single. Unfortunately, "Last Time Around" proved true to its title for the Del-Vettes and their later incarnation, the Pride & Joy.

Traut assumed managership of the Shadows, a role that caught him off guard. First, he had to deal with the suburban piety of the band members' parents. Second, the members' own punk narcissism. Third, a piano reportedly dropped from a 23rd floor window. Fourth, pillows and sheets stolen from hotel rooms. Yes, the Shadows were true punks. But the kids loved them, and they needed solid management and direction.

Then there were bizarre complications. One early Shadow was axed from the band when he was caught in bed with the acclaimed male lead singer of a popular punk group. And there was no keeping vocalist Jim Sohns away from the little girls, two or three a night sometimes! This, in turn, was giving guitarist Joe Kelley all sort of inferiority problems. Traut was father, mentor, producer and businessman.

A corporate split occured in '68. Traut and Badonsky were at odds with one another and divided the Dunwich holdings right down the middle. Traut retained the name Dunwich and two acts, the Nazz and the American Breed. Badonsky made off with the Shadows of Knight, the Mauds, and the group H.P. Lovecraft. Badonsky is now a successful Chicago restauranteur. Paul Sampson, the Cellar entrepreneur brought into the Dunwich group to handle Arkham Artists, was having serious family problems which necessitated that he leave show business all together. Then, a rift between Traut and Wexler occurred. Dunwich folded. Buddah (Super-K) got the Shadows of Knight, who soo n returned to Chicago, "pissed as hell," after one album and a hit, "Shake."

Traut continued to produce records for other labels. The American Breed, who had recorded for Chuck Colbert's Nike/Cool label as Gary & the Night Lights and the Light Nights, signed to Acta, a short-lived venture instigated by former Mercury sales v.p., Kenny Myers. Originally, Traut had submitted their "I Don't Think You Know Me" as the final Dunwich/Atlantic collaboration, only to be met with a Wexler veto. Wexler, hot on Aretha's career, wanted black music out of Dunwich. Traut felt firmly that Curtis Mayfield, Carl Davis and Johnny Pate were better equipped to handle the black Chicago market.

Acta's Meyers was detained in Chicago during "The Big Snow" of '67 when no flights left O' Hare. Traut arrived at Myers' hotel room with a Gary & the Night Lights tape. Meyers was ecstatic and immediately signed them under two provisions: they add horns and they change the gawdawful name. The one they chose was just as awful, the American Breed. Their first 45, "Step Out Of Your Mind," was a mid-chart hit, but "Bend Me, Shape Me" catapulted them to the top, until it was evident that the band could produce no follow-up. Several members diffused into Ask Rufus, now simply Rufus (with Chaka Khan).

Traut produced the Mauds for Mercury, and had two hits in Hayes-Porter's "Hold-On", and "Soul Dripping,"an original. A young singer from suburban Crystal Lake, Megan McDonough, cut a single for Mercury under Traut's auspices, "Blue Eyed Soul," which bombed, her career saved by four subsequent Wooden Nickel LP's. Meanwhile, Traut recorded ex-Friend & Lover vocalist Jim Post, now of DeKalb, Illinois, under the name of The Last Cowboy for Tallent (#1118). Simultaneously, he had the Troys (Tower Records; leader was Randy Curlee, now of Zazu), who later became Magic and Pendragon; the Byzantine Empire on Any; the Rumbles Ltd. and Keith Everett on Mercury; the Castaways on Fontana; Raintree (formerly Family & Virginia's Wolves) and Crow on Amaret; the Will-O-Bees on Date; the Idle Few on Soma; Aorta (one 45), Eddie Higgins, the Enchanters and the New World Congregation on Atlantic; Bobby Whiteside on USA; and Chad Mitchell, on his final throes, on Amy. He also recorded Coven's first LP, and singed Mason Proffit (Two Hangmen," "Hope") to the Happy Tiger label, which also released a Dunwich punk anthology, *Early Chicago*, compiled by Traut.

It was a lucrative but time-consuming period for Traut. But rock was changing at a rate so fast that one man couldn't keep up. Many of his acts crumbled, changed members, changed names, or left him. He retained on Mason Proffit and Megan McDonough, and acquired Siegel-Schwall.

"Singer Bobby Whiteside was a huge *rumor*-monger. I told him USA and Dunwich were soon to merge," Traut said, "And sure enough he spread the rumor. I got a phone call from USA president Jim Golden relaying the 'rumor'. But we got to talking about it and it didn't seem like half a bad idea." Traut and USA's Jim Golden and Bob Monaco became partners at a luncheon that day.

"There were changes in the operation," he added,

For one thing, I had always developed my own talent. USA used to purchase masters. They purchased the Buckinghams. Golden brought that element into the company."

It was then that Traut, Monaco and Golden ventured to L.A. to talk with Jerry Weintraub about forming a new label. According to Traut, Jerry got on the phone and made three phone calls. Capitol wasn't interested in Chicago "shoppers." Clive Davis of Columbia wanted only one Traut act, String Cheese. RCA offered them their own label. And so it became a four-way partnership, with Weintraub now a member. The new label was Wooden Nickel, distributed by RCA. They signed Siegel-Schwall, Wolfman Jack, Styx (formerly TW4, and whose "Lady" was a number one hit for Traut last year) Bazu, and Megan McDonough. When Styx left for A&M (owing Traut one more album), RCA lost interest, and Wooden Nickel, as an RCA affiliate, was over. Traut was too busy to mourn the loss, engrossed in a reformed Love Craft (minus the H.P.) who he was grooming for Mercury.

With Wooden Nickel now an idle property, Traut has returned to law, defending the Ohio Players at present, and hard at work amassing a new artist roster (jazz pianist Judy Roberts, the Balls, and Capitol artist Natalie Cole at present). Mercury has evicted Love Craft but another major seems interested at time of writing, with a more pragmatic approach toward production.

The Shadows of Knight, by the way, are still kicking dust around the Chicago area. They've played the Alley in suburban Highwood and the Train Station in Mount Prospect, two "meet your meat" bars. It's not anticipated that they'll record again.

DUNWICH RECORDS

- 6 - Shadows of Knight - Gloria/Dark Side
- 7 - George Edwards - Norwegian Woods/I'm Freezing
- 11 - Luv'd Ones - I'm Leaving You/Walking the Dog
- 12 - Shadows of Knight - Oh Yeah/Light Bulb Blues
- 13 - Ken Nordine - Bachman/Crimson & Olive
- 14 - Things to Come - I'm Not Talkin/Til the End
- 15 - Del-Vetts - Last Time Around/Every Time
- 18 - Shadows of Knight - Bad Little Woman/Gospel Zone
- 19 - Banshees - Project Blue/Free
- 20 - Luv'd Ones - Stand Tall/Come Back
- 21 - Warner Bros - The Same Without Her/Lonely
- 22 - Curley Barrix - A World You Destroyed/Big Blue Monster
- 24 - Half Dozen - Angels Listened In/Another Day
- 25 - Wanderin' Kind - Wynken, Blynken & Nod/Something I Can't Buy
- 26 - Luv'd Ones - Dance Kid Dance/I'm Leavin You
- 27 - Curley Barrix - Blue Ribbon Clown/I Talk in my Sleep
- 29 - Saturday's Children - You Dont Know Better/Born on Saturday
- 30 - Amanda Ambrose - Door Swings Both Ways/Why Do I Choose You
- 31 - Shadows of Knight - I'm Gonna Make You Mine/I'll Make You Sorry
- 32 - Del-Vetts - I Call My Baby STP/That's the Way It Is
- 34 - Saturday's Children - Deck Five/Christmas Song
- 36 - Rovin' Kind - My Generation/Girl
- 37 - Knaves - Leave Me Alone/Girl I Threw Away
- 49 - Light Nites - One, Two, Boogaloo/Same Old Thing
- 51 - Shadows of Knight - Willie Jean/Behemoth
- 52 - Pride & Joy - Girl/If You're Ready
- 54 - Rovin' Kind - She/Didnt Wanna Have to Do It
- 56 - Saturday's Children - Leave that Baby Alone/I Hardly Know Her
- 57 - Sounds Unlimited - Little Brother/Girl as Sweet As You
- 59 - Space Band - Winchester Cathedral/Tic Toc
- 60 - Mauds - Hold On/
- 67 - Shadows of Knight - Someone Like Me/Three For Love

DUNWICH PRODUCTIONS

- Acta 817 - Pride & Joy - That's the Way it Is/We Got a Long Way to Go
- Acta 821 - American Breed - Dont it Make You Cry/Green Light
- Acta 833 - American Breed - Enter Her Majesty/Hunky Funky
- Acta 836 - American Breed - Walls/Room at the Top
- Acta 837 - American Breed - Cool It/The Brain
- Acta 2247 - American Breed - Keep the Faith/Private Zoo
- Amaret 100 - Ginny Tiu & the Few - Let Me Get Thru to You Baby/I've Got to Get you off my Mind
- Amaret 106 - Crow - Time to Make a Turn/Busy Day
- Amaret 119 - Crow - Slow Down/Cottage Cheese
- Amaret 129 - Crow - Watching Can Waste Up the Time/Yellow Dawg
- Amaret 132 - Rochelle - I Want to Give You My Everything/Blue-Eyed Soul
- Amboy 115 - Univacs - BBC Theme/Silver Thumb
- Amy 11,018 - Byzantine Empire - Snow Queen/Girl In the Courtyard
- Amy 11,043 - Chad Mitchell - For What It's Worth/
- Amy 11,046 - Byzantine Empire - Shadows & Reflections/You
- Amy 11,054 - Chad Mitchell - Bus Song/What's That Got to Do With Me?
- Atco 6443 - Boys Next Door - One Face in the Crowd/Mandy
- Atco 6455 - Boys Next Door - Christmas Kiss/The Wildest Christmas
- Atco 6477 - Boys Next Door - See the Way She's Mine/Begone Girl
- Atco 6604 - World Column - Lantern Gospel/Midnight Thoughts
- Atco 6634 - Shadows of Knight - Gloria '69/Spaniard At My Door
- Atco 6667 - New World Congregation - Day Tripper/My World is Empty Without You
- Atco 6676 - Shadows of Knight - I Am the Hunter/Warwick Court Affair
- Atco 6775 - Enchanters - Winds and Sea/The Struggler
- Atlantic 2545 - Aorta - Strange/Shape of Things to Come
- Atlantic 2597 - Brim - There Must Be/She's No Good For You
- Bell 790 - Sonny Cox - Chocolate Candy/The Choking Kind
- Beverly Hills 9340 - Geneva Convention/Something Beautiful/Call My Name
- Columbia 44870 - Aorta - Strange/Ode to Missy Mtfzspklk
- Date 1515 - Will-O-Bees - The World I Used to Know
- Date 1543 - Will-O-Bees - Shades of Gray/If You're Ready
- Date 1583 - Will-O-Bees - It's Not Easy/Looking Glass
- Fontana 1615 - Castaways - Walking in Different Circles
- Fontana 1626 - Castaways - What Kind of Face/Lavender Popcorn
- Fontana 1666 - Golden Horizon - Love is the Only Answer/Dear Emily
- Fontana 1671 - Bazooka Company - Cant Make It Without You/When I'm With You
- Happy Tiger 545 - Mason Proffit - Voice of Change/A Rectangle Picture
- Happy Tiger 552 - Mason Proffit - Sweet Lady Love/Two Hangmen
- Happy Tiger 567 - Aorta - Willie Jean/Sandcastles
- Happy Tiger 570 - Mason Proffit - Good Friend of Mary's/Hard Luck Woman
- Mercury 72690 - Rumbles, Ltd. - Out of Harmony
- Mercury 72694 - Mauds - Hold On/It'll Be Alright
- Mercury 72723 - Rumbles, Ltd. - Jezebel/
- Mercury 72815 - Rumbles, Ltd. - 99% Sure/Every-day Kind of Love
- Mercury 72854 - Keith Everett - The Chant/Light Bulb
- Mercury 72904 - Megan McDonough - Blue-Eyed Soul/Don't Jump to Conclusions
- Mercury 72973 - Coven - Wicked Woman/White Witch of Rose Hall
- Paramount 0040 - American Breed - When I'm With You/Can't Make It Without You
- Philips 40464 - HP Lovecraft - Anyway That You Want Me/It's All Over For You
- Philips 40491 - HP Lovecraft - Wayfaring Stranger/The Time Machine
- Philips 40506 - HP Lovecraft - White Ship/
- RCA - 0228 - Hardy Boys - Love and Let Love/Sink Or Swim
- SGC 002 - Will-O-Bees - Listen to the Music/Make Your Own Kind of Music
- SGC 007 - Will-O-Bees - It's Getting Better/November Monday
- Smash 2149 - Hudson Bay Co. - I See Her Face/
- Soma 1457 - Idle Few -
- Tallent 118 - Last Cowboy - Singing on the Front Porch/Jim Tucker
- Tower 406 - Troys - Gotta Fit You Into My Life/Take Care

ALBUMS

- Mauds - *Hold On* - Mercury 21135
- American Breed - Acta 38002
- American Breed - *Bend Me, Shape Me* - Acta 38003
- American Breed - *Pumpkin, Powder, Scarlet & Green* - Acta 38006
- American Breed - *Lonely Side of the City* - Acta 38008
- Shadows of Knight - *Gloria* - Dunwich 666
- Shadows of Knight - *Back Door Men* - Dunwich 667
- Aorta - Columbia 9785
- Aorta - *II* - Happy Tiger 1010
- The Troll - *Animated Music* - Smash 67114
- Mason Proffit - Happy Tiger 1009
- Mason Proffit - *Movin' Toward Happiness* - Happy Tiger 1019
- Coven - *Witchcraft* - Mercury 61239
- Siegal Schwall - *Siegal Schwall '70* - Vanguard 6562
- HP Lovecraft - Philips 600-252
- HP Lovecraft - *II* - Philips 600-279
- Hardy Boys - *Here Come The* - RCA 4217
- Hardy Boys - *Wheels* - RCA 4315
- Crow -
- Crow -
- Crow -
- Crow -
- V.A. - *Early Chicago* - Happy Tiger 1017

CHICAGO ROCK: AN EPILOGUE

The years 1966-68 were the heyday of Chicago rock. By mid-'68, one could see signs of the scene beginning to dry up. Progressive music was replacing punk rock, and the happy-time music of the Chicago bands just didn't fill the bill.

Chicago's AM stations, faced with stiff competition from newly-emerged FM radio, began tightening up their playlists, with the result that local artists were now denied exposure. Regional music was a dying trend—all eyes were on the coasts and England. Soon the most talented musicians were leaving Chicago en masse to seek their fortunes.

Ironically, one of the bands that left in 1968 returned in 1970 to become the city's biggest hitmakers ever, with what has since become popularly accepted as the "Chicago sound." Tey called themselves Chicago, but it really wasn't the same.

In recent months, there has been a strong upsurge of interest in Chicago's roots. Kiderian Records and other local indies like Dharma are recording actively, and producers like Traut and Peck are talking about reissuing the classic punk records of Chicago. The musicians themselves are turning up again: Ronnie Rice has a new band, the Flock, Spanky & Our Gang, and HP Lovecraft have LPs out on major labels, and new groups like the Eddie Boy Band are becoming popular nationally with music that doesn't rely on horns. There are several fine local music papers: *Illinois Entertainer, Interphase, Spotlight*, and there's talk of a Chicago rock fanzine being started. The *Entertainer* has done a marvelous 12-part series (by Jeff Lind) tracing the history of Chicago rock in much greater detail than we have been able to do here, and on the whole it seems that the glory of its past is not altogether forgotten in Chicago.

[*Thanks to Rod Heiden, Ken Voss, Ray Peck, Bill Traut, and Perry Johnson for their help in preparing this article.*]

KIDERIAN RECORDS

45111 - Night Shift - I Call Your Name/She
45112 - Nobody's Children - Girl I Need You
45113 - Ray Peck & Placy Anatra - You Must Believe Me/Makin' Up and Breakin' Up
45114 - Conquest - Is It Right?/Look at Me
45115 - Mourning Dayze - Fly My Paper Airplane/Sad Man's Dayze
45116 - Donn & Delighters - Pretty Black Girl/Fighting for My Baby
45117 - Roy Manning - I've Got My Thing
45118 - Dottie Marie - Did I Ever Care/Burning Bridges
45119 - Roy Manning - Pride
45120 - Gollum - Prayer of Despair/Desert Heat
45121 - Creme Soda - Keep It Heavy/And That Is That
45122 - Creme Soda - I'm Chewin Gum/Roses All Around
45123 - Diana Frazier & Crosstalk - Just Another Day/Come Walk With Me
45124 - Geoffrey Kafitz - Harder to Do
45127 - Sonic Prism - Your Time is Going to Come/Situation
45129 - Rick Karas - Sun Up—Me Down
45131 - Damrod - Twelve Hour Man/Once Again
887 - Bondsmen - Shotgun/Patricia Anne
1001 - Facts of Life - Joy of Loving You

NEW COLONY SIX

3-66	I Confess/Dawn is Breaking	Centaur 1201
6-66	I Lie Awake/At the River's Edge	Centaur 1202
9-66	Cadillac/Sunshine	Sentaur 1203
12-66	Ballad of the Wingbat Mamaduke/Power of Love	Sentar 1204
12-66	Love You So Much/Let Me Love You	Sentar 1205
3-67	You're Gonna be Mine/Women	Sentar 1206
6-67	I'm Just Waiting Anticipating For Her to Show Up/Hello Lonely	Sentar 1207
12-67	Treat Her Groovy/Rap-a-Tap	Mercury 72737
2-68	I Will Always Think About You/Hold Me With Your Eyes	Mercury 72775
6-68	Can't You See Me Cry/Summertime's Another Name For Love	Mercury 72817
10-68	Things I'd Like to Say/Come and Give Your Love To Me	Mercury 72858
5-69	I Could Never Lie to You/Just Feel Worse	Mercury 72920
8-69	I Want You to Know/Free	Mercury 72961
12-69	Barbara I Love You/Prairie Grey	Mercury 73004
4-70	People & Me/	Mercury 73063
7-70	Close Your Eyes/Little Girl	Mercury 73093
8-71	Roll On/If You Could See	Sunlight 1001
11-71	LongTimeToBeAlone/NeverBeLonely	Sunlight 1004
2-72	Someone SOmetime/Come on Down	Sunlight 1005
3-74	Never be Lonely/LongTimeToBeAlone	MCA 40215
9-74	I Dont Really Want to Go/Rain	MCA 40288

ALBUMS
6-66 *Breakthrough* - Sentar 101
6-67 *Colonization* - Sentar 3001
6-68 *Revelations* - Mercury 61165
10-69 *Attacking a Straw Man* - Mercury 61228

IRC RECORDS

6917 - Ronnie Rice - Come Back Little Girl/Who's the New Girl
6918 - Buddy & Citations - Juvenile Delinquent/?
6928 - Little Boy Blues - Look at the Sun/Love for a Day
6931 - Ronnie Rice - Tell Her/I Want You,I Need You
6935 - Danny's Reasons - Little Diane/Believe Me
6936 - Little Boy Blues - I'm Ready/Little Boy Blues' Blues
6939 - Little Boy Blues - I Can Only Give You Everything/You Don't Love Me
6943 - Tamara's New Generation - Just Flowers/Traffic

TMP-Ting RECORDS

115 - Syl Johnson - Falling in Love Again/I've Got to Get Over
117 - Barry Goldberg-YouGotMeCrying/Aunt Lilly
118 - Keith Everett - Conscientious Objector/DontYouKnow
119 - Bobby Jones - I Loved and Lost/Slow Down
120 - Seeds of Euphoria - Let's Send Batman to Vietnam
121- Keith Everett - She's the One Who Loved You/Lookin' So Fine

DESTINATION RECORDS

601 - L.C. Cooke - Do You Wanna Dance/I'll Wait for You
603 - Bobby Whiteside - Say it Softly/I'll Never Get Away
606 - Bobby Whiteside - You Give MeStrength/theSummit
607 - Kane & Abel - A Man Aint Supposed to Cry/Twist it Back
612 - Warner Bros - Please Mr.Sullivan/I'm GoingYourWay
617 - Warner Bros - Little Darlin/I'm Going Your Way '65
621 - Sheffields - Do You Still Love Me/Nothing I Can Do
624 - Cryan Shames - Sugar & Spice/Ben Franklin's Almanac
628 - Flock - Can't You See/Hold on to my Mind
629 - Ricochettes - I Don't Want You/Find Another Boy
630 - Boyz - Come with Me/Never be Lonely
631 - Flock - I Like You/Are You the Kind
633 - What For - We Could be Happy
635 - Flock - Each Day is a Lonely Night/Take me Back
636 - Young Chicagoans - Summertime Blues/Bad Boy
637 - Next Five - Little Black Egg/He Stole My Love
638 - Destinations (Robbs) - Hello Girl/With You
7719-01 - Boyz - Hard Times All Over

QUILL RECORDS

104 - Malibus - I'm Crying/Runaway
109 - Proper Strangers - Joyce/One in a Million
110 - Fabulous Flippers - Woman Aint Good for Me/Dry My Eyes
111 - Fabulous Flippers - Harlem Shuffle/I Don't Want to Cry (also Cameo 439)
112 - Original Royals - I Wanna Do It/Heart is Made of Many THings
114 - Exceptions - As Far as I Can See/GIrl from NewYork

SEEBURG JUKEBOX RECORDS

3010 - Seeburg Spotlite Band - Slow Down/Jolly Roger
3013 - Curiosities - Money/Sunset Strip
3014 - Curiosities - Twist & Shout/Big "J"
3015 - Curiosities - Johnny B. Goode/The Memphis Style
3016 - Gary & Nitelights - Sweet Little 16/Take Me Back
3017 - Gary & Nitelights - Bony Moronie/Glad You're Mine
3018 - Del-Vetts - Little Latin Lupe Lu/Ram Charger
3019 - Sweethearts - Come and Go With Me/It Only Hurts When I Laugh
3020 - Sweethearts - Love is Like a Heatwave/Understand

CHICAGO ALBUMS

Buckinghams - *Kind of a Drag* - USA 107
Buckinghams - *Time and Charges* - Columbia 9469
Buckinghams - *In One Ear and Gone Tomorrow* - Col. 9703
Buckinghams - *Made in Chicago* - Columbia 33333
Shadows of Knight - Super-K 6002
Illinois Speed Press - Columbia 9792
Illinois Speed Press - *Duet* - Columbia 9976
Fabulous Flippers - *Something Tangible* - Veritas 2570
Flock - Columbia 9911
Flock - *Dinosaur Swamps* - Columbia 30007
Flock - *Rock & Roll*
Little Boy Blues - *In the Woodland of Weir* - Fontana67578
Second Coming - Mercury 61299
Bangor Flying Circus - Dunhill 50069 (became Madura)
Baroques - Chess 1516
Not listed: Rotary Connection, Rufus, Fabulous Rhinestones, Siegel-Schwall, Chicago, & many other non-60s, non-punk albums.

MISCELLANEOUS CHICAGO SINGLES

All Night Workers - Why Dont You Smile - Round Sound 1
All Night Workers - Honey and Wine - Cameo 420
Angelo's Angels-I DontBelieveIt/ShimmyJimmy-Ermine 59
Bangor Flying Circus - Come On People/A Change in Our Lives - Dunhill 4220
Bondsmen - I've Tried and Tried/You Must Believe Me - Orlyn 8140
Boston Tea Party - Don't Leave Me Alone/Is It Love-Fona 311
Blue Nite - Lonely Soul/Am I the Man - Cha Cha 759
Buckinghams - Sweets for my Sweet/Beginners Love - Spectra-Sound 003
Capes of Good Hope - Shades/Lady Margaret -Round 1001
Centuries (Buckinghams) - I Love You No More/It's Alright - Spectra-Sound 641
Chicago Loop - She Comes to Me/This Must be the Place - DynoVoice 226
Chicago Loop - Cant Find the Words/Saved - Merc.72755
Chicago Loop - Technicolor Thursday/Beginning at the End - Mercury 72802
Chips - Break it Gently/Mixed Up Girl - Philips 40520
Chips - Country Fair
Clann - Hey,Baby/Tall Towers - GAP 109
Crestones - She's a Bad Motorcycle/The Grasshopper Dance - Markie 117
Crestones - I've Had It/Little Girl of Mine - Markie 123
Daughters of Eve - Social Tragedy/A Thousand Stars - Cadet 5600
Daughters of Eve - He Cried/Dont Waste My Time - Spectra-Sound 920
Kal David & Exceptions - Searchin/Daydreaming of You - Tollie 9007
Denny Davis & Glades - Sally Go Round the Sunshine/I Love You - Age 29121
Delights - Long Green/Find Me a Woman - Delaware 1712
Deights - Every Minute,Moment,Hour/Just Out of Reach - Smash 2072
Exceptions - You Dont Know Like I Know/You Always Hurt Me - Capitol 2120
Exceptions - Rock & Roll Mass (EP) - Flair 810
Dirty Wurds - Takin My Blues Away/Why - Marina 502
Fabulous Flippers - Women Aint Good For Me/West Side Story - Fona 312
Fabulous Flippers - Turn On Your Lovelight/Shout - Cameo 454
Fabulous Flippers - Harlem Shuffle/I Don't Want to Cry - Cameo 439
Falling Pebbles (Buckinghams) - Lawdy Miss Clawdy/Virginia Wolf - Alley Cat 201
Few - Why/How Much Longer - Skokie 451
Flock - Tired of Waiting/Store Bought Store Thought Columbia 45021
Holocaust - Savage Affection/Tutti Frutti - Red Robb 2025
Hudson Bay Co. - I See Her Face/You - Smash 2149
Huns - WInning Ticket/Destination Lonely - Rock'n'Jazz 8668
Id - Stop & Look/Come to Me - Hand-Di 7007
Infinities - Thousand Tears/Heidi - Ka-Hill 6060
Intruders - World You've Created/Bringin Me Down - Claremont 665
Illinois Tollway - Candy & Me/Another Summer to Remember - Spectra-Sound 101
Hatful of Rain - Peculiar Situation/Have You Ever Loved Somebody - Sentar 1208
Bobby Jones - A Certain Feeling/Sugar Baby - VJ 672
Knaves - Leave Me Alone/Girl I Threw Away - Glen 8303
Lincoln Park Zoo - Love Theme From Haight St/If You Gotta Go (Go Now) - Mercury 72708
Little Boy Blues - Season of the Witch/The Great Train Robbery - Ronko 6996
Little Boy Blues - It's Only You/Is Love? - Fontana 1623
Dave Major & Minors - You Are All I Need/She Doesn't Know - BC 4503
Males - Kiddie a Go go/same - Fibra 4776
Mass - Hear Me Out/I'll Meet You in My Dream - Neil 001
Mauds - Soul Drippin'/Forever Gone - Mercury 72832
Mauds - Man Without a Dream/Forget It,I've Got It - RCA 74-0377
Holly Maxwell - Only When You're Lonely-Constellation162
Medallions - Leave Me Alone
Raymond John Michael (New Colony Six) - Let There Be Love/Feel Free - London 136
Raymond John Michael - Rich Kid Blues/Hitch-Hiker - London 145
Missing Links - Get Ready/Under My Thumb - Marek 676
Omes - Searching/Girl Get Away - Cody
One-Eyed Jacks - Love/Sun So High - White Cliffs 265
One-Eyed Jacks - Sky of my Mind/Getting in a Groove - Roulette 7035
One-Eyed Jacks - Together We're in Love - Roulette
Osgood -Everybody Sing - Golden Voice 834
Outsiders - Go Go Ferrari/Big Boy Pete - Cha Cha 724
Paegans - I Can Only Give You Everything/Good Day Sunshine - Rampro 122
Perpetual Motion - You Hurt Me/Sally Brown -Rock'n'Jazz 9188
Princetons - Killer Joe/Georgianna - Colpix 793
Poorboys - Think of Living/Julie Julie - Flame 8199
Barney Pip (WCFL dj) & the Rovin' Kind - You Turn Me On/Can't Sit Down - Smash 2102
PC Limited (Purple Cucumber) - Sunny was a Fool/Here We Come - Fontana 1643
PC Limited - Sunshine Superman/Carnival - Ivanhoe 1800
Purple Cucumber - SOme Kind of Magic/Green Eyed Song Smash 2163
Revelles - Something Good About Living/Little Girl - Jim-Ko 106
Riddles - Sweets For My Sweet/It's One Thing to Say - Mercury 72669
Robin Hoods - Baby Let Your Hair Down/Everything's Al'right - Mercury 72526
Robin Hoods - Wait for the Dawn/LoveYouSo-Merc.72445
Rovin' Kind - Everybody/Bound to Roam -Contrapoint 9006
Rovin' Kind - Night People/Right on Time - Roulette 4687
Royal Flairs - Suicide - Marina
Shadows of Knight - Shake/From Way Out to Way Under Team 520
Shadows of Knight - Potato Chip - Columbia Special Products (5" cardboard disc,NR in any other form)
Same - Sunshine,Flowers & Rain/If You Love Me - Barrington 5004
Satyrs - Marie/Yesterday's Hero - Spectrum 2668
Shy Guys - Rockin Pneumonia & Boogaloo Flu/YouAre My Sunshine - Rampro 122
Society's Children - Mr. Genie Man/Slippin Away - ChaCha
Sonics - You Make Me Feel so Good - Cha Cha
Summits - Sophisticated Lady/Lets Love Now-Lasalle 504
Tabs - Dance Party/All By Myself - VJ 418
Thunderbirds - Your Ma Said You Cried/Before It's Too Late - Delaware 5635
Trolls - Are You the One?/Every Day and Every Night - ABC 10823
Trolls - Something Inside Here/Laughing All the Way - -ABC 10884
Trolls - There Was a Time/They Don't Know - ABC 10916
Trolls - Who Was That Boy?/Baby,What You Ain't Got - ABC 10952
Vectors - It's Been a Day or Two/What in the World - Analysis 4323
Warner Bros - Three Little Fishes/Mairzy Doats-Everest2043
Warner Bros - Study Hall/Centipede - Kandy Kane 408
Warner Bros - 3 Cheers/Lost - Ballance 2002
Wet Paint - At the Rivers Edge/Shame-RoyalHollywood101
Wylde Heard - Take it on Home/Stop it Girl - Philips 40454

FEEDBACKKKKKKKKKkk
letters
SUNN
Kinney

BOSSTOWN REVISITED

Here's some stuff to fill a few gaps in the Boston article. First let me stress the delight I have in looking back on my copies of *New England Teen Scene* magazine (later taken over by Barry Glovsky who changed it to *Fusion*). The '67 issues were predominantly New England-oriented with only local groups mentioned. In 1968 they switched to the San Francisco Sound, the only local stuff being coverage of Boston as the "next San Francisco." I can't believe anyone ever fell for the Myth of the Boston Sound, but they did. The magazine also had a tight connection with Come On Strong beverages, a youth-oriented soft drink company with flavors like Tamerindo, chinoto, and guanabama. I might also note that it was probably the only magazine ever to review the Faine Jade LP!

Concerning radio, Joel forgot to mention Carl de Suze's Soliloquoy on the Twist on WBZ records. The Lost were great. I remember seeing them and the Remains together at the Boston Tea Party. I know there must be tapes around as the Tea Party taped almost everything. Ted Myers and Kyle Garrahan went to Chameleon Church from the Lost before Myers went to Ultimate Spinach, not after. Also in CHameleon Church was Chevy Chase, later of the National Lampoon LPs and now a regular on *Saturday Night Live* (the NBC 11:30 Sat show, not Howard Cosell's). Grass Menagerie, as mentioned, included a couple of Losts and Doug Yule later of the Velvets. Yule started out in a group called Thee Argo (formerly Argonauts) who were fine and included Bill Colby who later went on to play bass for Jay & the Americans.

The Improper Bostonians had another single, "We're Gonna Make It"/"You Made Me a Giant", label unknown. The Pandoras were mentioned as an all-girl group who played their own instruments. Don't forget Borogroves Ltd, and the Peppermint Conspiracy who were also all-girl configurations. Regarding Connecticut, one cannot forget the Shandells, whose record of "Stop Your Cryin' " on the Music Town label wasn't bad if I remember correctly. Also the Bluebeats single is dynamite. The Tidal Waves were from York Beach, Maine. To back up for a minute, Ultimate Spinach had Jeff Skunk Baxter as a member for awhile, coming from a group called Faith that also gave us Jimmy Thompson of Butter. Butter was one of those three-man trios (compare the name with Cream) that had a black guitarist styled after Hendrix.

New Hampshire gave us the Spirit of Now who had a single called "Sun Also Rises." The What Four had two singles on Fleetwood: "Don't Laugh"/"Marshmallow Dream" and "Basement Walls"/?. Universal Sounds had "Eileen"/"Wild" on the New York based Nola label. The Shadows Four had a single of "I'm Begging You." Tony Conigliari had three or four singles, mostly backed by Lloyd Baskin (later of Seatrain) and some members of the Myddle Class. The Bagatelle had four guys from a black gospel group called the Mandrell who returned to that name as a soul group after the Bagatelle broke up. The Bagatelle also was to do the soundtrack to an Allen Gitten (who?) movie called *Parachute to Paradise* according to *Crawdaddy!* at that time.

Joel is right when he says the Bostonians were quite forgettable. The only real thing I know about them is that they were the house band for a club of the same name for awhile. There were also a couple of singles on Seville by the Ragamuffins, who if memory serves were formerly The Lords and the Ladies.

Many collectors search desperately for the Frumious Bandersnatch EP from Berkeley. There was also a Frumious Bandersnatch from MIT that had a single out at the same time.

—Frank Brandon
Eureka, CA

ROOTS OF LELAN ROGERS

I was interested to see your story on Roky Erickson. As you know, I was running Hanna-Barbera records in 1966, and I made a deal in Houston to pick up "You're Gonna Miss Me" from the Contact label, and sign the group to HBR. I really believed in the group, and had convinced Hanna & Barbera to do an all-out push on them. I was so into it that we made the deal on the spot, on a Saturday when we can't get a lawyer. So it was a handshake deal and I called LA and had them make a master off the Contact record and rush it over to the pressing plant. We kept the plant going all weekend on that record, just to get it out in a hurry.

You made one mistake in the story, and that was in saying that Lelan Rogers owned IA. The real owner was a guy named Ken Skinner, who represented a group of oil men. Lelan had lived in Texas, but at the time he was in LA, working for A&M. They'd hired him to start a new subsidiary label specializing in R&B, but he fouled it up somehow and got fired. After we'd gone and pressed up all those records, Skinner showed up in my office with Rogers, and told me that unless I hired Lelan as my national promotion man, the deal was off. I already had a good promo man and I didn't like the way they did business, so I called the deal off. We called the records back, the only place the HBR pressings got out was Florida. After that it came out on International Artists, and apparently Lelan went back to Texas with Skinner and ended up running IA. I used to get calls all the time from the guys in the Elevators, wanting me to get them out of the deal, but there was nothing I could do. I don't know where Lelan is now, but after he left IA he went to work for Shelby Singleton in Nashville. Shelby put him in charge of a new label called Silver Fox. The label was named for Lelan, who as Roky says in your story, had silver hair which he wore in a big pompadour.

—Tom Ayers
Hollywood, CA

WHEELS ORIGINS

I can provide some info on the Wheels. Two of the members, Demick and Armstrong, put out an LP in England 3 years ago on A&M, called *Looking Through*. Both are originally from Belfast but I'm not sure if the Wheels were Irish. At any rate, they played clubs mainly in the north of England.

—Bernard Watts
Springfield, MO

THE FINAL WORD ON KING USZNIEWICZ

To clear up the great 'snevitch controversy once & for all, let me start by saying whoever Leo G. Graphouse III is, he sure didn't get his facts straight. As president of the 1-Shot/Police family of labels (home of such finely honed artists as King Uszniewicz, Logjam Lurch & the Turkeynecks, Dr. Earwax & His Blues Surgeons, the Bops Rabbit Revue, Keen Steve & the Teens, Sagebrush Phil & the Wild Dogs of Kentucky, Rick Kay & the Shades of Today, and of course our resident party record comedian, the Howlin' Banana) I feel it my duty to furnish the following personnel listing for both sides of 1-Shot 175:

SURFIN' SCHOOL: King Uszniewicz (lead guitar & tenor sax) Logjam Lurch Patterson (lead guitar &backup vocal) Jay Frey (rhythm guitar) Doctor Earwax (bass & backup vocal) Bob Nalli (drums).
CRY ON MY SHOULDER: King Uszniewicz (lead vocal & tenor sax) Logjam Lurch Patterson (lead guitar & com-ments) Jay Frey (rhythm guitar) Billy Lee Small (electric piano) Randy 'Jazzbo' Ackley (bass & tailend comment) Shub Blootz (drums).

I hope this clears up most of the questions for your readers, and by the way, yes only 100 copies were pressed, which have been distributed thru the 1-Shot Record Club members & dropped off at selected Goodwills and Salvation Army thrift stores across the US.

—Cub Koda
Manchester, MI

[See "Juke Box Jury Jr" for a full report on the activities of 1-Shot/Police Records, a truly exciting new company, whose releases incidentally are all available thru BOMP]

SOONER OR LATER THEY ALL TURN UP....

Noticed your review of the Swedish group Svenne & Lotta. I suppose you know this is Svenne Hedlund, former lead singer of the Hep Stars, and Charlotte, one of the girls in the Sherrys (of '62 "Pop-Pop-Popeye" fame) who stayed on in Sweden after a tour and married Svenne?

-- Anders Ek
Karlstad, Sweden

FROM THE HORSE'S MOUTH

Some comments on your last issue: The Aztecs were *not* Billy Thorpe's group, they were the house band at the Ad Lib club. Megan Davies of the Applejacks was not Ray's sister. The Johnson Brothers were identical Negro twins, they still write songs in LA. Alonzo Willis of the Spats wrote "Mr. Peppermint Man"; he also wrote "The Roach" by Gene & Wendell. The Sons of Adam were named by me. The picture you ran with the San Joaquin story was actually taken in LA, the band included Michael Lloyd and John Paul Jones.

—Kim Fowley
Hollywood, CA

OUR MISTAKE

After reading my article (*Songs They Never Sang*, BOMP 14) I was surprised to find you'd mentioned "Love of the Loved" as being a radio station promo; I thought I'd mentioned that it was a bootleg, not an official demo.

Chris Fonvielle
Wilmington, NC

NERVOUS ON THE ROAD

I just picked up a copy of the latest BOMP in the dressing room of the Smiling Dog Saloon here in Cleveland, where I'm undergoing various depths of misery and joy as manager of Starry Eyed & Laughing. Gluttonously devouring every word, cover to cover as usual, I came across a reference to the single by Bryan & the Brunelles. If you're interested in some useless information about them, here you are:

They came from Luton in Bedfordshire, which, in view of Vauxhall Motors, is a sort of mini-Detroit, which spawned many bands—contemporaries being the Avengers with Mick Abrahams, the Warriors with Clive Bunker, the Raving Cannibals with Graham Waller, etc.

Bryan was Brian Burke, who I know from Luton Grammar School, and the group was formerly known as Bryan & the Hangmen, which HMV changed to a more 'tasteful' name. Lead guitarist was a bloke called Snip Turner who lived near me in Cutenhoe Rd, Luton, but I can't remember the others.

They were managed by Bryan's dad, and were very popular in local youth clubs and the Dolphin Coffer Bar in Waller St—the 'in' place of late '64-early '65. I used to run my folk club there and people like Donovan would come & play, also the Supremes dropped in to see where the local action was when they came to the Odeon on a package tour in Spring '65.

"Jacqueline" was written by two local songwriters who had high opinions of themselves, and used to sweep into the Dolphin, swaggering and stuff, even tho "Jacqueline" was the only thing they ever got onto record. The local paper made them stars. When the single failed, a lot of local pride & hopes went down the drain with it. It predated a lot of other failures by locals like Orange Bicycle, Sweet Slagg, etc, etc. I guess Luton never made it—though Jethro Tull were ¾ Luton and ¼ Blackpool.

—Pete Frame
Cleveland, OH, Oct. '75

[Thanks a bunch, Pete! It's a rare treat these days to hear from you. For anyone who isn't already aware, Pete is somewhat a legend for having founded Zigzag magazine and kept it alive against all odds, and in his current capacity as manager of Starry Eyed is responsible for one of England's most delightful bands. Any BOMP reader who doesn't own both their albums should be ashamed. By the way, Pete, is there anybody in England you didn't go to school with???]

SURF THEORY FOR THE SEVENTIES

More info on the surfing instrumental scene: Norman Knowles in Morro Bay had Westco Records, in some form of partnership with Hilder. It was primarily a demonstration label for airplay and sales to larger record companies, and was in operation from approx. '62-'65. Knowles produced a number of records on Westco and other labels, including GNP. Westco material was released on Del-Fi albums. Their groups included the Sentinals (including Knowles; Kenny Hinkle, who also sang as Kenny Karter and possibly Kenny Hill, now in LA and signed to RCA; Tom Numes, now working with Hinkle in LA; John Barbata, later with the Turtles, CSNY, Starship, etc.); the Revels, the Continentals, and possibly the Impacts.

Most of the recording was done in Watts in an independent non-union garage-studio also used by the Platters, the Moonglows and similar groups. "Church Key" by the Revels was used in a documentary film on Indians living in LA, called *The Exiles*, which won a prize at Cannes.

For some reason Westco material seems to have had regional popularity in Pittsburg, including "Over You" by Kenny Hinkle-Karter-Hill. Most of these bands played at the Rendezvous Ballroom in Balboa—locally the scene was the Rose Garden (previously the Peppermint Twist) in Pismo Beach, which used to bring in unknown British bands (like the Missing Links) on weeknights, turning the weekends over to the surfers. Later, after the surfing scene was dormant, they occasionally brought in bands like Quicksilver and the Sons of Champlin.

I was stimulated, if not particularly encouraged, by Lisa Fancher's guest editorial. The current crop of mid- late-teenagers (14-19) sometimes appear to me to have been quite cruelly cheated—generally too young to have experienced the '60s when they were fresh, ill-prepared (although not neces-

more FEEDBACK

sarily too old) for whatever revitalization the late '70s may or may not bring. On the other hand, maybe they're having a better time than we ever did—after all, if something was lost, we're the ones who lost it; if there's something missing, we're the ones who miss it. Indeed, we may be missing some great enjoyment that is to be found in these apparently quite dull years just passed. Who knows? Fancher's assessment of her peers has the ring of uncomfortable truth about it; I look forward to further observations from her.

Those '60s revivals are starting to seem a bit eerie; Dylan's Rolling Thunder Revue, the Golden Hits of the Monkees tour, Rock Scene magazine, the Troggs' comeback, the still-theoretical punk revival, etc.—no matter how fresh, genuine, spontaneous, substantial, and well-received these things may be, so often the guiding force behind them seems to be senior-junior citizens (mid-20s thru mid-30s) who, whether truly enthusiastic or merely nostalgic, or both, are looking for the Good Old Days. It almost looks as if we are trying to guide teenagers into following the paths that we traveled, as if we are trying to entice them into recreating the Sixties. (It also seems—occasionally—that we are trying to convince ourselves that we are still young. The implications of that are too damn awful to contemplate...)

While we shouldn't even try to sell the high-schoolers a used decade, we certainly might inspire them to create an era worthy of the name before both generations contract an unnecessary case of terminal respectability. The Monkees tour may be a healthy, if ironic step in the right direction. Dolenz, Jones, Boyce & Hart played at Santa Maria High School recently to an audience of less than 500. There may have been no more than a dozen non-teenagers in the audience; there was a surprising number of junior-high-age kids. The crowd was one with virtually no direct experience of teenage life in the Sixties. These very gratifyingly uncool kids screamed throughout the show, grabbed at DJB&H's clothes, tried to pull them off the stage, danced, cheered, laughed, and generally put most audiences of 12,000 to shame. It appears that, among 12 and 13-year-olds at least, the two ex-Monkees—and possibly even moreso the two songwriters—are once again teenage heartthrobs.

The show itself was quite good. Boyce & Hart filled in quite well on background vocals; their solo and duet material was good too. Dolenz and Jones were visibly older—Mickey looked tired, sad, perhaps bitter; after all, the way that our "free and tolerant nation of youth" has continually given him and others the shaft must turn his stomach at least as much as it does mine; Davy had a 5 o'clock shadow and a rather fine face. Tired or not, they sang their asses off. Between the singers, the backup band (Boyce & Hart played acoustic guitars and keyboards, Mickey used did some drumming) and the audience, it was one of the best concerts in my memory; the equal of the Beach Boys tour of a few years ago. And to top it all off, the backup band's lead guitarist, who bore a strong resemblance to Paul McCartney, turned out to be none other than Keith Allison! He was introduced and sang "Where the Action Is." Les neiges d'antan, ces sont ici! (at least it seems that way sometimes).

—Michael Churchman
Santa Maria, CA

[I too have been heartened and somewhat bemused by the current popularity of the Monkees. Their TV show, which is on weekdays here and probably other parts of the country, is much better than I remember it having been, and no doubt has an effect on the teens who are flocking to the revival concerts. The relevance of this to the issue you raise concerning the recycling of the '60s bears further examination. My belief is that today's kids are removed enough from the prejudice that surrounded groups like the Monkees, Raiders, and even the Beach Boys in the late '60s to be able to appreciate the music on its own terms. I also believe that a lot of kids today, having heard constantly how fabulous the '60s were, are developing a natural inclination to acquaint themselves with the era—all of which, including even most of the Beatles' work before "Hey Jude", is pretty much unknown to anyone under the age of 20 who hasn't consciously tried to educate himself. I'm sure most of us who grew up in the mid-60s wouldn't mind spending the rest of our lives there—in almost every sense, it was a better world than we are likely to see again. But that nostalgia factor should be kept separate from efforts to study the music of the '60s and, most important, acquaint today's generation with it and point to ways in which the underlying values [as opposed to the temporal trappings] that worked to make the era's music as transcendently great as it was, can be applied to contemporary music in a manner that can only be beneficial. I think the current popularity of the more memorable artists of the '60s reflects the desire of today's kids to find out what they were all about, and represents a transitional phase following which, having familiarized themselves with it, these kids will in turn be inspired by the classics of the past to create classics of their own. I see this as a wholly separate and purely healthy process, entirely removed from the cramming of '60s culture down the throats of early teens in the late '60s and early '70s, a period that resulted in practically nothing of musical worth and a generation of dispirited neo-hippies. If things continue as they've been going, I think we may be back on the right track at last. What about the rest of you readers, any comments? It would be nice to hear from an actual teenager who attended the Monkees show...]

Gyrodub's ERRATA & ADDENDA

BEATLE NOVELTIES

Phaetons - Beatle Walk - Sahara 103
Jamells - Beatle March/Tears of Joy - Crosley
Zacherias & the Tree People - We're All Paul Bearers - Viking
Col. Whithedge & Marmaduke Druid - Liverpool Landing - Counsel 050
K. Young & English Muffins - Mrs. Green's Ugly Daughter - Diamond 183
LP: *Beatle Buddies* - Diplomat 2313
LP: *Mersey Beats* - Int. Award 237 (same as Design 170)

INTERNATIONAL ARTISTS

136 - B-side: Thinkin' About Thinkin'
138 - B-side: Hurry Sundown
141 - B-side: Walkin' Midnight Coffee Break
104 - also issued as: Frankie Lee - Another Love/I Love the Go Go Girls
Contact 5269 - You're Gonna Miss Me/Tried to Hide

MICHIGAN

Four Sharps - Doin' the Roostertail/U-44 - Gale 801
Soul Benders - Petals/7 & 7 Is - Phantom 2568
? and Mysterians - Talk is Cheap/She Goes to Church on Sunday - Chicory 410
Semi-Colons (? & Mysterians) - Beachcomber/Set Aside - Cameo 468
Jamie Coe - The One Who Really Loves You/A Long Time Ago - Enterprise 5070
Sheffields - Do You Still Love Me/Nothing I Can Do - Destination 621
Bel-Aires - If You Love Me/Ya Ha Be Be - Discotheque 1004
Ronnie Fray & Reptiles - Wastin' Your Time/I Am No One - Cineman 1635
Soul Benders - Hey Joe/I Can't Believe in Love
Rock Garden - Johnny's Music Machine/Love is a Good Foundation - Capitol 2806
Garden - Winds of South Chicago/First Day of My Life - Capitol 2919
(same as Rock Garden; David Geddes was a member. Released singles previously as Frederic on the Phantasm label)
Smoke - Half Past End/My Mama - Smoke 1316
JoJo's - Do You Understand Me/I'm Really Sorry - United 121569
Tempests - Look Away/Carousel Blues - Fujino 6946
Jay Hawkers - To Have a Love/Send Her Back - Deltron 1228
Troyes - Rainbow Chaser - Space 7001
Troyes - Love Comes, Love Dies/Help Me Find Myself - Space 7002
Princetons Five - Roll Over Beethoven/Passing By
J&B Rare - Open your Eyes/Little Children - Colortronics 5204
Tornados - Let Me Be Your Man/Alone - Phalanx 1004
Tino & Revlons - Lotta Lotta Lovin'/Red Sails in the Sunset - Dearborn 540
Impact 1012: - Classmen - Everything's Alright/Susie Jones
Palmer 5025 - Grifs - Northbound/Keep Dreaming
Ludky-11 108 - Sebastian Shane - That's What She Said/Hey Everybody

FENTON LABEL

945 - Renegades IV - Autumn Night/Greensleeves
948 - Sue & Dynamics - Go Tell it on a Mountain/Love in My Eyes
987 - Scavengers - Oasis/Curfew
2032 - Quests - Scream Loud/Psychic
2040 - Lyn & Invaders - Secretly/Boy is Gone
2064 - Don Hanke & Echo Men - You Put a Tiger in My Tank/You Are the One
2086 - Quests - Shadows in the Night/Tempted
2101 - Pedestrians - Think Twice/Snyder's Swamp
2118 - Sheffields - Fool Minus a Heart/Blowin in the Wind
2174 - Quests - Shadows in the Night/What Can I Do
2188 - Ray Hummel III - Fine Day/Gentle Rain
2226 - Pedestrians - You Aren't Going to Say/Un..ect Little Miss Kinsy
2512 - Legends - I'm Just a Guy/I'll Come Again
2522 - 4 U and Him - Back Door Man/Travl'n Light
(2101 was a huge Grand Rapids hit, displacing "I'm a Believer" at #1 in the local charts. 2226 was also Top 20 locally. 2188 is a great punk sound. 2032 is a Beach Boys style record. 2086 is also a tremendous punker.)

BOSTON

(Lost)
Kyle Garrahan - I Shall Be Released/Shame - Janus 109
Kyle - Virginia Traveler/The Reason - Paramount 0100
Kyle LP: *Times that Try a Man's Soul* - Paramount 6006

(Beacon Street Union)
Eagle - Kickin' It Back to You/Come In, It's All for Free - Janus 113
Eagle - Working Man/Brown Hair - Janus 135

(Orpheus)
I've Never Seen Love Like This/Congress Alley - MGM
By the Size of my Shoes/Joyful - MGM 14139 13947
Big Green Pearl/Sweet Life - Bell 45,128

(Wildweeds)
And When She Smiles/Paint and Powder Ladies - LP: Vanguard 6552 Vanguard 35134

MISC. BOSTON

Richie's Renegades - Dont Cry/Baby, It's Me - Polaris 002
Renegades - Waiting for You/Tell Me What to Say - Polaris 501
Swallow - Rockin' Shoes - WB 7713
Bead Game - Sweet Medusa/Country Girls - Avco 4539
Pandoras - All About Jim/Hey Ah - Imperial 66029
Pandoras - About My Baby/New Day - Liberty 55954
Apple Pie Motherhood Band - Long Live Apple Pie/Flight Path - Atlantic 2477
Art of Lovin' - You've Got the Power/Good Times - Mainstream 687
Bagatelle - Such a Fuss About Sunday/What Can I Do - ABC 11063
Peter Ivers Group - Aint That Peculiar/Clarence O'Day - Epic 10681
Bold - LP on RCA
Monday's Mondos - on Columbus, not Columbia
Just Us - Can't Grow Peaches - also released on Colpix 803
Chameleon Church - Camilla is Changing/Your Golden Love - MGM 13929
Earth Opera - American Eagle Tragedy/When You Were Full of Wonder - Elektra 45636
Earth Opera - Home to You/Alfie Finney - Elektra 45650
Ford Theatre - From a Back Door Window/Theme for the Masses - ABC 11118
Ford Theatre - I've Got the Fever/Jefferson Airplane - ABC 11227
Kangaroo - Such a Long Long Time/Never Tell Me Twice - MGM 13960
Barbara Keith with Kangaroo - Daydream Stallion/The Only Thing I Had - MGM 13961
Barbara Keith - Fisherman King/Good Lovin' Man - Verve-Forecast 5108
Barbara Keith - All Along the Watchtower - Reprise 1144
Phluph - Doctor Mind/Another Day - Verve 10564
Shags - Crying/You're a Loser - Jo-Jo 101
Georgie Porgie - Love You Girl Always/You Could Love Me - GP 96401/02
Latterday Pendulum - Let the Flowers Grow/Boston Common - Pillar 001

MISC. CONNECTICUT

Bram Rigg Set - I Can Only Give You Everything/Take the Time - Kayden 112
Bluebeats - extra Girl/She's the One - Columbia 43760
Boss Blues - Before the Dawn/So, Go - Direction 101
Count Down & the Moonsters - Hindu on a Honda/Shimmy-Shimmy Shake-Shake - Pocono 801
Connecticut Vibrations - It's Love/Go-Go - Carolyn 100

MISC. NEW ENGLAND

The Last Resort - I Want to Know/I'm Trying - Demco 1007 (Laconia, NH)
The Morning After - Things You Do/If You Love - Tam 201,369/70
Original Sinners - You'll Never Know/I'll Be Home - Discotech 1001
Thunderchicken - Wabash Cannonball/Fresh and New Love - Big Yellow 65 (Portland, ME)
Esquires - Shake a Tail Feather/Down the Track - Salem 003 (Framingham, MA)
Citations - Take Me/Phantom Freighter - University 101
Rite of Spring - The King in Your City/Happy Feet - La Fra
Black Ravens - Young Love/Wipe Those Teardrops - B&R 201
Sabres - Gnna Leave/It's All in Your Mind - Prince 101
Troupe of Love - Raining in the North End/Running Away From Love - Empach 001

MISC. ADDENDA

Mike 4010 - Linda Rae - The Time to Love is Now/Mid Summer Night's Dream
HBR 512 - Rainy Day People - Junior Executive/I'm Telling It To You
HBR 516 - Time Stoppers - I Need Love

(Bay Area records)
Twilight 401 - Billy Lane - Little Boys and Girls/All of the
Twilight 409 - Lance Hill - What Have I/Swiss Chalet Time
Scorpio 406 - B side: I Never Really Knew
Tom Thumb & Casuals - I Don't Want Much/I Should Know - Verve 10478
Duane 103 - Roy Montague - What's Holding/Revenue Man
Duane 109 - Roy Montague - Shadow of a Wall/pt.2
People - Ashes of Me/Apple Cider - Capitol 2251

THANKS

Vic Figlar, Danny Benair, Steve Kolanjian, Richard Vancil, Kevin Walsh, Bob Geden, Alan Betrock, Dave Goodrich, Richard Riegel, Don Colonna, b Wagenaar, Bruce Edelson, Barry Margolis, Don Huff, Joel Bernstein, Mike Thom, Bob Dalrymple, and anybody we left out.....

THE BEAT
Editorial by Greg Shaw

Something about this magazine seems to make people want to express their innermost feelings about rock & roll and what it means in their lives. Nothing strange about it; BOMP is written by and for people who take the music seriously and relate to it on a deeper, more emotional level than, say, your average Kraftwerk fan. What's strange is that we seem to be a minority. If BOMP appears at times to be more concerned with events 10 years ago than with today, it's only because some of us remember a time when rock & roll mattered to everybody (or at least everybody we knew). The music elicited such a strong sense of involvement from its fans that it became an integral part of our existence, and the involvement was only intensified by the thriving pop culture that surrounded rock & roll in its better days. Small wonder that some of us have maintained that attitude and given our full support only to artists and trends capable of leading us back to that state of grace.

Anyway, our readers get pretty intense. They write us long unbelievably personal missives, and bare their souls as if finding a kindred spirit were some kind of minor miracle. And in a sense I suppose it is. Five years ago, the tone of our mail was often bitter or desperate; everyone wanted to relive the past, seeing no hope in the future. But lately, in the last year or so, all that has changed. Now the letter-writers are telling us excitedly about new groups, new records and new scenes—often in their own home towns. Defeat and apathy yielded to guarded skepticism and then gave way to unbridled enthusiasm. It's pretty clear to everyone now that the renaissance is at hand and we're all gonna have a lot of fun.

I've found it particularly gratifying to observe this process in some of my friends. For instance Gene Sculatti, whose guest editorial appears on the opposite page. Gene's one of my oldest friends; we started writing for a lot of the same magazines in 1966, and since then have had frequent long discussions about pop culture and rock history. If I was premature in predicting a pop revival back in 1972, Gene has only lately come to acknowledge it. Gene's editorial makes a strong case for how much improvement there's been in the records of this last year or so. What Gene doesn't mention, and what I'd like to explore, is the state of pop culture, beyond what's on record.

First, though, a slight digression. When I speak of Gene being among the last to recognize the fundamental change coming over rock, naturally I mean of us hard-core fans. What I'm wondering now is, what's the matter with everyone else? I can excuse the millions of kids still buying Deep Purple and Rick Wakeman; after all, they're at the mercy of whatever's pushed on them by record stores, radio stations and *Rolling Stone*. But what about these latter parties? Retail ignorance can be excused for obvious reasons, and the problems with radio are too deep-rooted to even begin investigating here. At the very least, though, one would expect the press, that elite corps of trained trend-spotters and the entrusted arbiters of our collective taste, to have a little more on the ball.

My contempt for most 'professional' rock writers is no secret. The majority of them are glorified male groupies, gossip queens and cocktail leeches, whose lack of writing ability is exceeded only by their lack of critical judgment. They churn out reams of rehashed bios and blind reportage of things seen and heard, without ever invoking the use of their brains. How they pass as 'critics' is beyond me. But let's overlook these people, because it isn't really their fault the record industry encourages this sort of parasitism.

- Pop
- Not Pop

We're still left with a good number of people whose intelligence and training makes them qualified, respected rock critics/journalists, the ones you see most often in national publications. Of these, there are about a dozen who've consistently shown any sensitivity to changing trends, who have embraced a large enough perspective to evaluate events in any sort of historical context. The others display a kind of persistent blindness that I fear will bring ridicule upon them when their time is over.

In the main, they suffer from the same malady they accuse us rock & roll addicts of: becoming habituated by their tastes, taken in by hype, and limited by their own nostalgia. The difference is, they don't see it in themselves. Of course we love hype; a really good, attention-grabbing, razzle-dazzle campaign is in the best tradition of rock & roll, and is no more to be feared than television (though it seems many of the same people who fear hype also live in morbid dread of TV). But those who claim abhorrence of hype fall victim to the more subtle hype of anti-hype, echoing "far out, man" to every low-key FM come-on. And as for nostalgia, I can't see how waiting for the next Dylan or Buffalo Springfield is any different from waiting for the next Beatles. Except that these people think of themselves as being hip. We think of them as being hippies.

To get more directly to the point. Most of these people have no business writing about rock & roll. Jon Landau said as much in his last *Rolling Stone* column. He pointed out that rock writers are hung up on words, place undue emphasis on lyrics, when they are after all only an incidental factor in the greatest rock & roll recordings. These college grad intellectuals would be better off reviewing films or books—as in fact most of them would prefer doing anyway. I can think

- Mod
- Not Mod

of no better explanation for the fact that so many rock critics continue touting the same tired old artists that were big 6 years ago, and grovelling at the feet of any spinoff from the Woodstock Nation that happens to form a new group. All the forces of the music industry may be behind such artists, but the thrust of history has passed them by. They're yesterday's heroes. And anyone who can't distinguish yesterday from today from tomorrow should not be writing about teenage music.

Actually, this hasn't been that much of a digression. The rock press is a vital element in pop culture, and the fact that it's reflecting yesterday's culture is as good a starting place as any to launch our ruminations on this sticky subject. It isn't only what they write about—really, I see nothing wrong with their continued coverage of artists who are, after all, selling millions of records—but the style in which they write and the format in which they present their articles does have a bearing.

The point to be grasped here is that boring subject matter naturally tends to be presented in a boring format (*Rolling Stone*) just as psychedelic writing used to appear in rainbow-washed sheets of hand-drawn newsprint. On the other hand, if the subject is exciting, it should be displayed in an exciting fashion. *16* may be crude, but it gets the message across to its readers: there's a lot happening here. *Hit Parader* had the same cheesy layouts in the mid-60s, and yet it was the most relevant and intelligently-edited magazine of its kind.

There's great excitement in the new rock & roll—the teeming clubs of New York and Boston with their stark, staring, leather-clad groups—and who wouldn't rather see a few pages of Blondie clutching her thigh or Richard Hell biting his guitar than a 4-page color spread on Jethro Tull? Imagination, even amateurishness, is more effective in presenting this material than the staid magazine layouts commonly employed. That's why magazines like *Back Door Man* and *New York Rocker* have more to do with today's pop scene than anything else around.

Television has a bit of catching up to do, too. *Midnight Special* and *Rock Concert* are mired in a worn-out concept of presenting bands as if the viewer were at a mini-rock festival. The camera is here, the stage is there, the audience is over there, and it's all separate, all cleanly engineered and professionally filmed by the same union crews who do the *Carol Burnett Show*, so that any sense of involvement is negated. The viewer of *Midnight Special* is as detached as the reader of *Rolling Stone*; he's simply not part of any process of excitement that might otherwise be generated.

The exceptions come when a group makes their own film under controlled conditions. The few I've seen (I must confess rarely tuning in these days), notably the Bay City Rollers special—have often approached the excitation level of *Shindig* or even the TAMI Show. It's a lot easier to film rock & roll correctly than to re-educate studio engineers to record it properly. What's wrong is simply the *concept* of how the music is presented—they're still laboring under the delusion we want to sit in our homes pretending to be at the Fillmore, when we'd really rather be at CBGB. Still, it's improving. Some fine video-taped concerts have been shown on UHF in New York, capturing the scene in all its kinetic splendor. Now if only they'd show *The Blank Generation* on national TV.

Any discussion of pop culture must come round eventually to fashion. It's all fashion, ultimately, but clothes are the most obvious and yet the most subtle indication of changing modes of thought. I have no intention of competing with "Eleganza", but in recent months my travels to France, England and various cities of the USA have revealed, even to these unobservant eyes, a startling influx of new trends among the most pop-conscious young people.

We're all aware of the death of hippie culture, even though the streets are still littered with its more stubborn trash. Long hair, beards, sloppy clothes, all that stuff is definitely out. So's glitter. So, in fact, is the fake Art Deco chic of Bryan Ferry and his ilk. Everyone now is conscious of their clothes, and dressing I think more neatly. But at the lunatic fringes of fashion, what do we find bu—nouveau Mod! Yes, guys in early '60s dark suits, white shirts, even the dreaded *narrow black ties*! A lot of the groups in New York and London appear on stage and on the street that way, with Beatles '65 haircuts. Girls are growing bangs, letting their Betty Boop bobs grow out to Sandie Shaw cuts, donning black knee-length boots, and yes you'll find the odd mini-skirt creeping in.

This isn't '60s revival, though. In the '60s we wore that stuff because we had little choice. Now, with every choice, it's done to achieve an effect, and the effect fits well with that of the music surrounding this scene, a music based just as casually on '60s Mod.

In England, incidentally, the papers are full of reports of a Mod revival, in fact there was a huge gathering of Mods held not long ago.

Greg Shaw and Bob Wayman of the Poppees, 1975.
(Photo: Ida Langsam)

[continued from p. 5]

Rockers are back too, they held a demonstration recently, and at its extreme the British anti-hippie backlash has produced groups like the Sex Pistols whose growing legion of fans sport rudely butchered short hair, deliberately slashed and blood-stained working class clothes, and other things not so easily described.

Suits, ties, short hair, Mods & Rockers, and a general sense of alienation and protest—these are the real signs that something big is brewing. Far more indicative than the records. Every year has had its good records, and if we've got more this year than we've had since 1967, it means little in itself. But the existence of an audience looking for a style and a stance of its own is the most crucial thing we've been missing these many years, and now we see it forming.

It's no coincidence that the inspiration in fashion, like the inspiration in music, has come from the mid-'60s. That was the last great pop era, as no reader of BOMP needs to be told, and we must pick up from there in order to go forward. Only now it's not rock theory, not my opinion or Ken's or Alan Betrock's. These kids are doing it because it *feels right*, and historically, it is right.

Where it goes from here is anybody's guess. This whole scene may yet fizzle out before it can spread to the teenage masses. It's very disturbing to see how readily they all respond to the ersatz excitement of bands like Aerosmith and Starz and, even though I like them, Kiss. The kids in England are equally conditioned to accept the phony. Watching *Supersonic* (a British TV rock show now being syndicated in the US) has been an education. Week after week acts like Gary Glitter, Alvin Stardust, David Essex, Mud, etc., etc. appear with the most artificial staging you could imagine, until they begin to seem interchangeable.

All I keep seeing is the manipulators—the managers, agents, publishers, etc.—perched somewhere in the rafters, pulling the strings. Larry Parnes and Jack Good would be proud. In fact it's *exactly* like what was happening in 1962. What's the difference between David Essex and Adam Faith? The Glitter Band and the Shadows? Alvin Stardust and Shane Fenton!

So much of what we accept as rock/rock culture is phony and dishonest. Is this the same music that was founded on defiance and rejection of hypocrisy? At one time we all knew what the enemy was, and that rock was youth's best weapon against it. So we grew out hair long like the groups, spent all our money on their records and concerts, and called ourselves hip, because we knew what was real and most people didn't. Now everyone has long hair, nothing is real, and the rock stars have so much money they identify more with Rockefeller than with the kids who gave them credence. Somewhere along the line, people stopped being concerned with what was real, and assumed they could just keep the long hair and still go on calling themselves hip. What a joke!

This pseudo-hip/hippie culture, if you can call it that (at one time it was; now it's nothing more than a set of hackneyed cliches) is the major impediment to the spread of a '70s pop culture. Like the 'critics' who are aesthetically stuck in the period of Crosby, Stills & Nash's first album, we're afflicted with FM djs who think it's hip to play Moody Blues and Ten Years After (I'm not making this up, I actually hear it, day after day, on both of LA's top FM stations). What makes them think it's hip or happening in any sense? Well, gosh, weren't these groups at Woodstock? Didn't you see 'em in *Rolling Stone*? Didn't their former members unveil their new solo albums at Carnegie Hall? What else do you want?

These people aren't aware of how foolish they are, because they're not aware of anything. Thankfully, the new generation is. There are enough people supporting the 'street band' scene, and in England the 'nouveau punk' scene, that these scenes will grow, and kids will have the choice between something real and the phony crap that's all around. It's hard for a mere teenager to reject a whole culture, especially one that calls itself 'hip', without an alternative. Now the alternative exists, and that simple fact is our best hope for the survival of rock & roll and the vital new pop culture that's waiting, just waiting for its chance to explode.

Reverberations
By Ken Barnes

Welcome back to my corner of the world's only semiannual quarterly. It's a momentous occasion for *Reverberations* this issue—we graduate, I'm told, to larger print, which means half the word length for me but you can put away the magnifying glass. Whether legibility will improve this column has yet to be determined.

It's been a good summer for live rock, with Dr. Feelgood, Fleetwood Mac (surprisingly rocking in person) and a Flamin' Groovies/Ramones bill blowing into town, but the supreme moment is still Tommy James performing "Crimson & Clover" at the Troubadour. I ranted about Tommy's great act at great length in the August *Phonograph Record*, so I won't run it into the ground here, but don't miss him if he comes around. Don't miss *PRM* either (commercial break), because they've got Mark Shipper's *Pipeline* back and it's still, as it was the first time around in 1973, the funniest rock writing around (and not just because it's practically the *only* funny rock writing around, a situation calling for skillful repair).

Anyway, aside from Tommy, the top 60's act in recent months was that old reliable Paul Revere with his ever-changing Raiders (minus Mark Lindsay, sadly; Mark's busy with his solo career, cutting Tastee-Freez commercials and singles for Greedy Records). The Raiders had graduated from the amusement park circuit to the Playboy Club, which lost them their rabid subteen audience (gaining a rabbit post-teen crowd instead) but enabled Revere to tell a lot of dirty jokes, which he clearly enjoyed. They still ably performed an amazing number of hits, and even the Lindsay-less vocals sounded fine. Apparently Revere and his rotating Raiders will be able to go on forever.

Owing to spacial concerns I'll hold the Singles Spotlights to three. The Rogues' "You Better Look Now"/"Train Kept a Rolling" (Audition 6110) is the leading obscure mid-60's rocker discovery, an enthralling folk-rocker featuring an uncanny Jim McGuinn imitation on the top side, and an ear-frying outing on the familiar B-side rocker that some say outstrips the Yardbirds (I'm inclined to agree). Sharon Tandy was a South African emigre to England, where she cut a number of records including the astonishing "Hold On" (Atlantic 584219—UK, 1967). The Fleur De Lys, a mildly legendary outfit, backed her up and consummated manic marriage of psychedelia and hard-rocking R&B, with a mad, searing, unforgettable guitar solo. Classic time.

Finally, a record so bizarre I couldn't leave it out. Mike Condello was a fairly well-known Arizona figure with an album on Scepter in 1969. Some time before (I think) he cut an EP called "Commodore Condello's Salt River Navy Band Makes a Comeback", on Blitz Cheap 006. Titles include "Gerald of Sunnybrook Farm", "The Time Machine," and "Sonic Boom," but when you play the first two they turn out to be near-letter-perfect musical copies of two songs from the first Bee Gees album, with different, original lyrics. "Sonic Boom" is a thunderous "Purple Haze" carbon copy, with nifty new lyrics like "Sonic boom all in my ears/Breaks my windows and chandeliers/Blasts my house, it shakes the ground/Who needs...jet planes faster than sound" and "Got me scared so I can't sleep/Is it just practice or World War III?"

To top it off there's a terribly paranoid tune called "Soggy Cereal" (more or less to the tune of "Those Were the Days") which uncovers such a perfidious plot that it deserves quoting in full:

> Soggy cereal [*three times*]
> You drop it in the bowl/The milk goes on
> The telephone rings and for a moment you're gone
> And when you get back your temper grows hot
> For you've just discovered a Communist plot
> Commie cereal, soggy cereal
> They're one and the same/Oh who is to blame
> It seems such a shame/It's unAmerican
> What will you do/About all that goo
> Probably Fu Manchu is behind this too
> Uncle Sam wants you/Bo hoo boo hoo
> Tippecanoe and Tyler too
> It's an American dream, includes Indians too
> I can't go on...

It's that last deft quotation from the collected works of Eric Burdon that cinches Condello's status as unheralded genius for me. One of the Tubes played with Condello on his album, and you can certainly see some form of genesis on this record...

Dots & Pickups: Last column I was awaiting with bated breath a Modern Lovers LP—by now there are two on Beserkley, and the earlier one is as brilliant an album as I've heard in years, both for the great crypto-Velvets music and Jonathan Richman's strikingly original sensibility. The new one is almost all sensibility, but it's still wonderful... Tons of homegrown records spring up all over, too many to list addresses (see October issue of Warner Bros. *Waxpaper* [*or for that matter this issue's Jukebox Jury Jr. column—Ed.*] for details) and really too many to list, but my recent favorites include the six-song EP from Sneakers (Chapel Hill, NC), Pere Ubu's "Final Solution" (Cleveland;, "Call Me" by the Hounds (NY), and "Cry Uncle" by Amnesia (Tampa). All highly recommended, as is an older Reddy Teddy record (Boston) I just got, "Novelty Shoes", and especially the upcoming Droogs single, "Overnight Success," the best rocker yet from this talented L.A. foursome. It's a tribute of sorts to Sky Saxon, and much more... Speaking of Sky, his new single "Universal Star" sounds pretty good (wish I could dig up a copy), and one of the rarest Seeds 45's, "Shuckin' & Jivin'/You Took Me By Surprise" has been pressed up by the folks at International Artists (see ad this issue); definitely worth having.

Fashion note: For all those appalled (as was I) by the trendy modified Eno hairstyle I sported on page 4 last issue, you'll be thrilled to learn it's been replaced by a modish styling created exclusively by Little Joe's Institute of Trichology (the study of hair's foibles and

• Is this Ken's new haircut, or an old picture of Jonathan Richman?

follicles) in Hollywood (they promised me a sizable discount if I plugged them in print). A number (two) of famous rock writers frequent the joint, and it's a great place for a haircut—even if they don't succeed, they give it the old Trichology try... Finally, the original subtitle for my Monkees piece this issue was "Colgems Time Again." Anyone guessing the complex and devious derivation of this title wins a free single, while they last. Entries to PO Box 7195, Burbank, CA 91510.

Venus & the Razorblades?

HOLLYWOOD—"The Runaways are finished," says Kim Fowley, the man who created them. There was a recent falling-out between Kim and the girls, he has given up his contract and washed his hands of all interest in the Runaways. He's got something better. "Venus & the Razorblades," he enthuses, "are much better. There have been all girl bands before, but this is a *mixed* group—Venus," he confides, after cautioning us to tell no one yet) *is a guy!* And so what if the Runaways are 16; the girl guitarist in this band is *14!*

"The Runaways are scared!" Kim continues. "Joan and Cheri came down and spied on our rehearsal last weekend. They know their trip is finished without me, and they also know I'll have to come up with something better to prove they weren't an accident. This is it."

Further developments as they unfold.

The ARRANGER As SUPERMAN

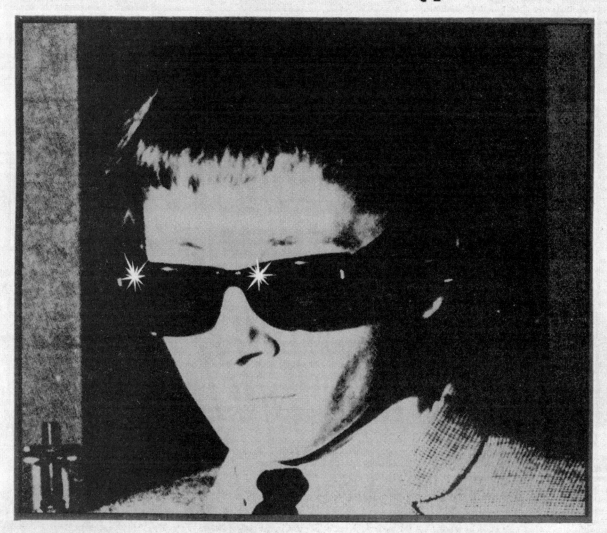

a Nitzschean View of Pop History
(THE JACK NITZSCHE STORY)
By Ken Barnes

Jack Nitzsche is one of the most crucial "back-room" figures in rock annals, as producer, arranger, and writer of over 50 hit records, many of them true classics. He's also one of the most mysterious personalities, infrequently interviewed, rarely stepping into the spotlight, remaining (perhaps by choice) a shadowy figure, seldom photographed, occasionally visible hunched over a piano backing Neil Young from time to time.

Nitzsche's career is a microcosm of L.A. rock & roll. Starting with Specialty Records in the late 50's (A&R chief: Sonny Bono), he worked with Lee Hazelwood, Lou Adler, Lester Sill, Terry Melcher, Nik Venet, and other pioneers of the West Coast record industry. Arranging nearly every Philles record, he translated Phil Spector's grandiose concepts into thunderous musical monuments, and a significant portion of the credit for all those beloved Crystals, Ronettes, and Righteous Brothers records is due him. Spector, never noted for sharing the honors, asserted that Nitzsche was merely a musical secretary, taking down Spector's ideas, but Nitzsche's track record as a producer/arranger apart from Phil demonstrates his mastery of that marvelous production style. Here, according to Nitzsche (as told to *Crawdaddy*, is how it works:

"Four guitars play 8th notes; four pianos hit it when he says roll; the drum is on 2 and 4 on tom-toms, no snare, two sticks—heavy sticks—at least five percussionists." Now go ahead and try it.

Nitzsche was also a gifted songwriter (the classic "Needles and Pins" is his), and over the years has worked with artists as varied as the Rolling Stones, Jackie DeShannon, Neil Young, the Turtles, Ringo Starr and the Tubes. He scored several movies, including the memorable *Performance* soundtrack and *One Flew Over The Cuckoo's Nest*, not to mention orchestrating the legendary *Tami Show*.

Through it all he's remained unknown to the public at large, and has acquired a reputation for moodiness and inaccessibility. On the occasion of this interview, Nitzsche, accompanied by managerial reps (and noteworthy record biz figures in their own rights) Denny Bruce and Dan Bourgoise, proved charming, humorous, and frighteningly knowledgeable (further interviews would doubtless shed light on vast areas of rock history not covered here).

For the interview, I brought along as many noteworthy Nitzsche records as I could dig up, and recorded his comments. Here, then, is the edited transcript, arranged and produced by Ken Barnes (egotism running rampant), with discographical assistance from Greg Shaw, Dan Bourgoise, and Jack Nitzsche.

PART ONE

(roughly 1960 to early 1964)

THE BEGINNING: FINDING A NICHE

?-60	Kerri Lynn—Summer Days/ (Auburn)(Arr.)
8-60	Preston Epps—Bongo Bongo Bongo/ (Original Sound 9)(Arr.)
?-60	Daniel A. Stone—(title & label unkn.)(Arr.)

[*How did you start?*] Kerri Lynn, the record was called "Summer Days" and it was on the Auburn label. That was the first string arrangement I ever did...1960, 1961? You don't have that one, right?

I joined the union through Nik Venet, with an artist called Albert Stone, whom Nik "nick-named" Daniel A. Stone, because of Ben E. King. I got a union card from that one. Preston Epps wasn't union. That was when I was sweeping floors. Preston Epps was before that.

The first time I worked in records was when Sonny Bono was A&R at Specialty (in the late 50's). I would play him songs that he thought were almost but not quite there. He let me hang around him...I started doing lead sheets for him, Don & Dewey's lead sheets, then he'd give me the chance to arrange something. I did voices for Larry Williams, some horns...

A MYSTERIOUS APPEARANCE OF A BOMP SUPER HERO

Denny Bruce: There was another guy hanging around at that time, from Salt Lake City....

Sky Saxon! He was one that Sonny was thinking of recording. At that time he was sounding like Dee Clark, "Just Keep It Up." He was Richard Marsh then, that's right. The next time I saw him he asked me if I'd play on the Seeds' sessions and produce. I told him I didn't want to do that, and he ended up telling me he'd pay me just to come down and be at the sessions.

DAYS WITH TERRY DAY

6-62	Terry Day—That's All I Want/I Waited Too Long (Columbia 42427)(Arr.)
1-63	Terry Day—Be a Soldier/I Love You Betty (Columbia 42678)(Arr.)
4-63	Frankie Laine—Don't Make My Baby Blue/ (Columbia 42767)(Arr.)
10-63	Frankie Laine—Take Her/I'm Gonna Be Strong (Columbia 42884)(Arr.)
12-62	Eddie Hodges—Seein' Is Believin' (Columbia 42649)(Arr.)
2-63	Eddie Hodges—Too Soon to Know/Would You Come Back (Columbia 42697)(Arr.)
6-63	Eddie Hodges—Halfway/ (Columbia 62811)(Arr.)
2-63	Rip Chords—Here I Stand/Karen (Columbia 42687)(Arr.)

Terry Day was the alias employed by Terry Melcher of Ripchords, Bruce & Terry, and Doris Day kinship fame, during a two-single recording stint with Columbia prior to becoming a staff producer there].

The first Terry Day record was a guy named Al Hazan, who wrote these two songs. He used to hang around Argyle, El Centro, all that record business area. His songs always sounded like hits but they never were. Ali Hassan was his name on the Philles record (103). After that Terry wanted Phil Spector (who produced "Be A Soldier") and he'd do anything. He told him he'd let him score his mother's next movie....

Frankie Laine, he was great. "Muletrain" was one of my favorite records. When Terry Melcher was hired as producer at Columbia, there were certain acts he could do. That was a good record ("Don't Make.."). (The version of "I'm Gonna Be Strong" by Laine preceded Gene Pitney's hit by a year; the A-side is an early Randy Newman song).

Bruce & Terry were on there ("Here I Stand"). There were also two guys who were early Christians, going to a seminary. Bruce & Terry sang on that record, they made it sound the way it did.

DAYS WITH DORIS DAY

| | Doris Day—Move Over Darling/ (Columbia) |
| ?-63 | Doris Day—Let the Little Girl Limbo (unreleased)(Arr.) |

That was a legitimate session. We (Terry Melcher and Jack) made some good records with Doris Day, but Marty Melcher thought they were bad for her image, so they never came out. "Let The Little Girl Limbo" was one, that never came out.

[*On the heels of "Blame It On The Bossa Nova?"*]

Yeah, it was. Barry Mann and Cynthia Weil wrote it, and I think it could've been a hit for her.

DAYS WITH BOBBY DAY

| 2-63 | Bobby Day—Another Country Another World/I Know It All (RCA 8133)(Arr.) |

I don't have a copy of this. "Another Country, Another World." I'd like to hear that. Crystals song, Phil Spector/Doc Pomus. That was a good record. Gracia (Nitzsche, Jack's wife) and the Blossoms singing. I thought he was so good! I did about three other records with him on RCA. Later I heard he went to Australia as the Hollywood Flames, Bobby Day, and Bob & Earl. All three of them were the same thing in Australia! Marty Cooper produced? Olympia. He's the voice on the Olympia Beer commercials. I used to do lead sheets for him. He never came up with anything worthwhile till the Olympia Beer commercial.

REPRISE COURSE

4-63	Jimmy Griffin—What Kind of Girl Are You/A Little Like Lovin' You (Reprise 20,161)(Arr.)
11-63	Jimmy Griffin—Marie is Moving/Little Miss Cool (Reprise 20,221)(Arr.)
4-64	Jimmy Griffin—My Baby Made Me Cry (Reprise 0268)(Arr.)
9-63	Jimmy Griffin—*Summer Holiday* LP (Reprise R9-6091)(Arr. — "Ooh, what a bad one!")
6-63	Soupy Sales—Hilly Billy Ding Dong.../ (Reprise 20,189)(Arr.)
6-63	Dorsey Burnette—Invisible Chains/Pebbles (wr.David Gates)(Reprise 20,177)(Arr.)
9-63	Dorsey Burnette—Where's the Girl/One of the Lonely (Reprise 20,208)(Arr)
3-64	Thurston Harris—Dance on Little Girl (Reprise 0255)(Arr. – "Trying to remake his hit.")
4-64	Billy Ford—My Girl/This is Worth Fighting For (Reprise 0265)(Arr.) (A-side written by Nitzsche & Jackie DeShannon)
5-64	Lifeguards—Swimtime USA(wr.Sloan-Barri)/Swim Party (Reprise 0277)(Arr.)

[*Nitzsche did a great deal of arranging for Reprise between 1963 and 1965, thanks to label production head Jimmy Bowen, who had a high respect for his services. Nitzsche on the whole is not presently enamored of much of this work, though it generally sounds fine for the period.*]

"Hilly Billy Ding Dong Choo Choo." It was fun. My son was just a little boy, and he got to come to the session, so it was worth it. It was also fun to hear Soupy swear.

"Where's The Girl" I like. That was good. It was a Jerry Butler demo, it was really good. Leiber & Stoller (its writers) were so pissed off *we* made the record...

THE "WHO IS PAT POWDRILL" MYSTERY REMAINS UNSOLVED

| 4-63 | Pat Powdrill—I Only Came to Dance With You (wr.PJ Proby)/Fell by the Wayside (wr. Joe South)(Reprise 20,166)(Arr.) |
| 8-63 | Pat Powdrill—Happy Anniversary (co-wr. Ellie Greenwich)/I Forgot More Than You'll Ever Know (Reprise 20,204)(Arr.) |

Oh this is awful stuff. I've got copies of all these. Everybody was just trying to imitate Phil Spector. It was good but no one did the right thing in the booth, no one used Gold Star.

[*Was Gold Star the secret?*]

Oh, yeah. The echo chamber. There's no echo chamber like that in town. I want to use it. That chamber's still there.

[*Nietzsche's disclaimer notwithstanding, "Happy Anniversary" is a lovely little Chiffons soundalike—almost uncannily so. So who WAS Pat Powdrill?*]

I don't know, somebody Jimmy Bowen found. Token black at Reprise...

WILDCAT SESSIONS!

| 2-64 | Wildcats—What Are We Gonna Do in '64/3625 Groovy Street (Reprise 0253)(co-prod) |

Lee Hazelwood (*writer, co-producer*). That's the Blossoms. They were singing behind Duane Eddy, and they figured if he was having hits because of them, which was kind of true on his comeback ("Boss Guitar," "Dance With The Guitar Man"), that they could have them on their own. That's all that was. What are we going to do in '64? The same thing we did in '63 obviously.

[*The Blossoms, by the way, were L.A.'s top session singers, and cut records on their own from the late 50's through to the early 70's. Personnel included Darlene Love, Fanita James [also one of Bob B. Soxx's Bluejeans, as was Darlene, who was also an occasional Crystal—gets confusing, doesn't it], Jean King [who had a solo album on HBR Records in '65], and sometimes Gracia Nitzsche]*

FOUR ON THE FEMME SIDE

?-62	Judy Hart—That's Enough/Didn't He Ramble (Staccatto 101)(Prod)
4-63	Toni Jones—Dear (Here Comes My Baby)(wr.P. Spector)/Love is Strange (Smash 1814)(Arr.)(uncredited)
?-63	Ramona King—Soul Mate/Oriental Garden (Eden 3)(Arr.)
?-63	Marry Clayton (sic)—The Doorbell Rings (Teldisc 501)(Co-prod., arr.)
6-63	Merry Clayton—It's In His Kiss/Magic of Romance (wr.Jeff Barry)(Capitol 4984)(Arr.)

That's obscure. Judy Hart is Judy Henske. H.B. Barnum and I went into business and both started labels. That's just a takeoff on the Gospel Harmonettes record. Just a lyrical change, that's horrible.

Toni Jones, produced by Steve Douglas, "Teenage" Steve. That was a pretty good record, that's one of the few I don't have. "Puddin' Tain," thank you.

[*Spector had nothing to do with this?*]

No, just the influence.

That's a good one, this is (*Ramona King*). There was a time when I shared an office with Lee Hazelwood and we had a deal. This was his first label—Era distributed it. I like this one....

[*Was this before she did "It's In His Kiss?"*]

This is before that. Did Ramona King do that? I didn't do it, did I? No.

I don't even remember this one (*Merry Clayton*). Russ Regan and Joe Saraceno wrote it?

Denny Bruce: Russ Regan was an artist, too, as Davey Summers.

I like this. This was before "It's In His Kiss."

[*Note: The Merry Clayton version of It's In*

"The first time I met the Stones, it was in '64 and they weren't making it too well. Brian Jones told me he was ready to leave the group if I could get him on some sessions as a professional harmonica player... I had to talk them into doing the TAMI Show; they were afraid to play in America!"

His Kiss" was the first, months ahead of both Ramona King's and Betty Everett's (the hit)].

FOR THE ROSES: BOBBY DARIN

5-63   Bobby Darin—18 Yellow Roses/Not for Me (Capitol 4970)(Arr.)

Bobby called me. My wife sang with the Blossoms, and they worked some of his dates. He always appreciated that high-powered thing that Spector was doing, but he liked Donny Kirshner better, he thought that was where it was at. He hired me for "18 Yellow Roses" and we became friends.

WONDER BREAD ON THE SIDE

2-64   Stevie Wonder—Castles in the Sand (Tamla 54090)(Arr.)

String overdubs. I really didn't have much to do with that.
I'd done stuff with Brenda Holloway before she was Brenda Holloway, on Era—Brenda and Patrice. Hal Davis did that, so when he went to Motown that was one of the first things he got to do something with, so he gave it to me to do strings on.

A CREDIT LOSS PLAYING THE MARKETTS

11-63   Marketts—Out of Limits (WB 5391)(uncr.)

It credits Ray Pohlman. I came in and did that arrangement—it was called "Outer Limits" at that time, after the TV show—but they wanted to add something to the record, so they took my chart—I couldn't make the next date—and gave it to Ray Pohlman and he added a French horn or something, and they credited him for the record. I don't really give a shit, but I did at the time.

THE LONELY SURFER—JACK AS SOLO ARTIST

7-63   The Lonely Surfer/Song for a Summer Night (Reprise 20,202)
11-63   Rumble/Theme for a Broken Heart (Reprise 20,225)
4-65   Puerto Vallarta/Senorita from Detroit (Reprise 0364)
1-76   theme from *One Flew Over the Cuckoo's Nest*/The Last Dance (Fantasy 760)
10-63   *The Lonely Surfer* (Reprise 6101)
?-66   *Dance to the Hits of the Beatles* Reprise
?-66   *Chopan '66* (Reprise 6200) 6115
?-73   *St. Giles Cripplegate* (Reprise MS 2092)

It all came about because of all those Spector hits and all that arranging. Jimmy Bowen said, "you want to do an instrumental?"—I did a lot of stuff. It was fun. I was never thinking of making hit records though, I was just playing with the orchestras. I never had a chance to do that so I did it.

[Nonetheless, "Lonely Surfer", with its novel French-horn dominated arrangement, was the first easy-listening surfing hit, and "Rumble" was an interesting orchestral treatment of the Link Wray classic. St. Giles Cripplegate is a rather fascinating neoclassical orchestral LP]

EARLY-60'S WRAP-UP

4-63   Davey Summers—Calling All Cars/ (Vim 101 & Zen 107)(Arr.)
2-62   Gary Crosby—That's Alright Baby/Who (Gregmark 11)(Arr.)(A-side wr. by P. Spector)
   Jamie Horton—Oh Love/Go Shout It From a Mountain (Joy 269)(Arr.& Con.)
   Jamie Horton—Only Forever/ (Joy)(Arr.)
   Brenda & Patrice—?/? (Era)(Arr.)
   Castells—?/? (Era)(Arr.)
1-63   Moments—Walk Right In/ (Era)(Arr.)
   Billy Storm—I Can't Help It/Educated Fool (Infinity 023)(Arr.)
   Greensleeves—Like Greensleeves/Horse Opera (Capella 502)(Arr.)
2-63   Joel Hill—I Ran/Secret Love (Monogram 510)(Arr.)
   Dorothy Berry—The Girl Who Stopped the Duke of Earl/I'm Determined (BNH 11)(Arr.)
   ("Richard Berry's wife," recalls Jack. Richard of course wrote "Louie Louie";
   Dorothy was a brilliant singer who made excellent records with David Gates later)
   Yolanda & the Castanets—What About Me/Meet Me After School (Tandem 7002)(Arr.)
10-62   Yolanda & Charmanes—There Oughta be a Law/Hootchy Cootchy Girl (Smash 1777 (Arr;uncr.)
   [last two entries probably same group]
12-63   Nino Tempo & April Stevens—Whispering (Atco 6281)(Arr.)
2-64   Nino Tempo & April Stevens—Stardust (Atco 6286)(Arr.)(uncredited on both)
2-64   Escorts—No City Folks Allowed/The Hurt (RCA 8327)(A-side Arr.)
   Bobby Crawford—Please Wake Up Joan/ (?)(Arr.)

Gary Crosby, "Who"? That was Lee Hazelwood, that was before I met Phil Spector. Did he write that? ("That's Alright Baby"). I didn't even know that.
The Moments—the same as the Shacklefords (Marty Cooper's longterm, generally unsuccessful folk group), without Lee Hazelwood and Marty Cooper. My wife Gracia, that was her, and Albert Stone, that was all the same people on all those records. The only singers in town...who would work without a contract!

[Other wrap-up notes: the Joel Hill is the same guy who later joined Canned Heat and the Flying Burritos. It's conceivable that the unknown Bobby Crawford (Johnny's brother) record is the same Chip Taylor song Little Eva cut in 1965 as "Wake Up John," in which case it would definitely be one to seek out].

REBEL-ROUSING WITH SPECTOR

[Nitzsche arranged the following Philles records, 1962-1964 (early)

9-62   106 Crystals—He's a Rebel*
11-62 107 Bob B. Soxx & Blue Jeans—Zip a Dee Doo Dah
12-62 108 Alley Cats—Puddin N' Tain
12-62 109 Crystals—He's Sure the Boy I Love
2-63   110 Bob B. Soxx—Why Do Lovers Break Each Other's Hearts/Dr.Kaplan's Office
3-63   111 Darlene Love—The Boy I'm Gonna Marry
4-63   112 Crystals—Da Doo Ron Ron
5-63   113 Bob B. Soxx—Not Too Young to Get Married
7-63   114 Darlene Love—Wait Til My Bobby Gets Home
8-63   115 Crystals—Then He Kissed Me
8-63   116 Ronettes—Be My Baby
10-63 117 Darlene Love—A Fine Fine Boy
12-63 118 Ronettes—Baby I Love You*
12-63 119 Darlene Love—Christmas*
1-64   119x Crystals—Little Boy
2-64   London 9852 (UK) Crystals—I Wonder
3-63   Philles LP 4001 Crystals—*He's a Rebel*
?-63   Philles LP 4002 Bob B. Soxx & Blue Jeans—*Zip-a-Dee-Doo-Dah*
?-63   Philles LP 4003 Crystals—*Sing the Greatest Hits*
?-63   Philles LP 4004 V.A.—*Today's Hits*
12-63 Philles LP 4005 V.A.—*A Christmas Gift*
* = uncredited

(Nitzsche relates the circumstances of his meeting Phil Spector)

Lester Sill and Lee Hazelwood were partners, and I was working with them. Then Lee split from Sill and made a deal with me, and that was when Eden Records happened. I'd just do all the arranging, wouldn't have to pay for an office, and if a record was a hit I'd get so much percentage, but I wouldn't get paid for the arrangement. I'd just get the office. It was all right, I got to ride in Lee's Cadillac and all that. Then Lester got an office right upstairs...6515 Sunset, I think, the first record building (in L.A.). One day Lester Sill called down—he and Lee were really enemies by now—and said that Phil Spector wanted to talk to me, and that was that. "He's A Rebel" was the first, written by Gene Pitney.

[Spector and Nitzsche rushed out their version, demolishing a competing rendition by Vikki Carr on Liberty, and the partnership was underway....]

PLEASE MR. POSTMAN

Philles 108 *(see above listing)*

The Alley Cats...Lou Adler brought them in, a guy named Brice Caufield. Remember an album called *Music From Lil' Brown* by Africa (Ode)? That was them. Brice Caufield—Phil would spend 12 or 15 hours on vocals, and so he had the Alley Cats in there all night long recording, like five in the morning, and Brice Caufield started complaining just a little bit. He was a mailman, he had to leave the session and go walk that beat...

SPECTOR PUTS THE SCREW TO EX-PARTNERS

Philles 111 - Crystals—(Let's Dance) The Screw *(withdrawn)*

Lester Sill and Harry Finfer were Phil's partners in Philles Records. And all of a sudden Phil couldn't figure out why he needed *them*...They ended up with a contract saying they would have a piece of the next two Crystals records, and it was too late to stop "Then He Kissed Me." So they had a piece of that, but the follow-up...they sent 50 copies to each distributor...it was just handclaps and a bass, and every time they'd stop, Phil's attorney would go "Do The Screw." That's what it was.

PART TWO

(approximately 1964-69)

ON NEEDLES AND PINS

5-63   Needles & Pins (wr. Nitzsche/Bono)—Jackie DeShannon (Liberty 55563)
[Also recorded by the Searchers, ELiminators, Bobby Vee, Del Shannon, Gary Lewis, Little John & the Monks, Cher, Love & Tears, and doubtless many more...]

We (Sonny Bono & Nitzsche) were all hanging out with her (Jackie DeShannon), I had that riff for a long time.

[The riff, a true classic, was an early folk-rock precursor and doubtless a major influence on the Byrds, as I ventured to say....]

Yeah? You think so? That isn't a 12-string guitar either, it's a lot of guitars played in unison...Sonny always used to try to take credit for it. We had to keep the tape recorder running when we were recording that, and at one point Sonny says, "You taught me a whole new way to write songs tonight." I want to clip that little piece out...

BREAKING IT UP ON THE DeSHANNON DISCOGRAPHY

[Nitzsche wrote "Should I Cry," "Be Good Baby," and "I Keep Wanting You" with Jackie, who recorded all of them. He worked

on the following Jackie DeShannon records:]

5-63	Needles & Pins/Did He Call Today Mama (Liberty 55563)(Arr.)	
7-63	Little Yellow Roses/Oh Sweet Chariot (Liberty 55602) (Arr.)	
11-63	When You Walk in the Room/Till You Say You'll Be Mine (Liberty 55645)(Arr.)	
2-64	Oh Boy (Liberty 55678)(Arr. uncredited)	
6-64	Hold Your Head High/She Don't Understand Him Like I Do (Liberty 55705)(Arr. uncr.)	
10-64	He's Got the Whole World in His Hands/It's Love Baby (Liberty 55730)(Arr.)	
2-68	I Keep Wanting You/Me About You (Imperial 66281)(Prod., Arr.)	
7-63	Jackie DeShannon (Liberty LRP 3320)(Arr.)	
7-64	Breaking It Up on the Beatles Tour (Liberty LRP 3390)(Arr.)(reissued as You Won't Forget Me (Imperial LP 9294)	

ANOTHER REPRISE

3-65	Peter James—You Won't Forget Me (Reprise 0357) (Arr.)	
4-65	Donnie Brooks—If I Never Get to Love You (Reprise 0363) (Arr.)	
6-65	Joni Lyman—I Just Don't Know What to Do With Myself/Happy Birthday Blue (Reprise 0378)(Prod/Arr)("Oh God, learning how to produce records…")	
8-65	Dino Desi & Billy—Chimes of Freedom (Reprise 0401)(Arr.)("Forget that!")	
11-65	Caesar & Cleo—Love is Strange/Let the Good Times Roll (Reprise 0419) (Arr.)	
12-65	Regents—When I Die Don't You Cry/She's Got Her Own Way of Lovin' (Reprise 430)(prod,arr)	
4-66	Gas Company—You're All Alone/You'll Need Love (Reprise 0464) (Prod.)	
9-66	Paris Sisters—It's My Party/My Good Friend (Reprise 0511)(Prod./Arr.) ("Please don't remind me of them!")	
9-66	Gas Company—Get Out of my Life/We Need a Lot More of Jesus (Reprise 0512)(Prod/Arr)	
1-67	Paris Sisters—Some of your Lovin'/(wr. King/Goffin)/ (Reprise 0548)(Prod./Arr.)	
3-67	Judy Henske—Dolphins in the Sea (Reprise 0567)(Arr.)	
7-67	Judy Henske—Road to Nowhere (Reprise 0585)(Arr.)	
6-67	Gail Martin—After Loving You (Reprise 0585)(Arr.)	
9-65	Dino Desi & Billy—I'm a Fool (Reprise R-6176)(Arr, some tracks)	
8-67	Paris Sisters—Sing Everything Under the Sun (Reprise R-6259)(Co-prod.)	

[The Jimmy Bowen connection continued at Reprise, and Nitzsche began to produce records for the label as well, for which he seems to retain little affection]

Donnie Brooks. I bet this must be horrible. Oh God—"Crocodile Rock!"
[The vocal chorus in fact is a dead ringer for Elton's opus…]
Denny Bruce: Elton probably has it, that's where he got the lick.
No, it came from something else. "Little Darlin'…"
[Or "Cry Myself To Sleep" by Del Shannon…]
My God, I don't even know who they (the Regents) are! Can I hear that one? They played at It's Boss (primordial Hollywood rock spot)?
Got it!
Denny Bruce: They played on The Dating Game, too.

Thank you, Byrds [laughs at stereotypical folk-rock riffing]. I remember them now. Boy were they lame! They were terrible. No one knew what to do. It was all those Jimmy Bowen contacts with club owners, the owner of PJ's, etc…

Caesar & Cleo. This one was recorded in '64 or '65. It was after "Baby Don't Go," really, in terms of recording. "Baby Don't Go" was the same time as Hale & the Hushabyes [see below].

That was a good record [Judy Henske]. I liked the first one better. It was done at the same session—"Road to Nowhere."

[Note: Mike McDonald of the Regents later gained fame in Steely Dan and currently the Doobie Bros. Caesar & Cleo were of course our old friends Sonny & Cher in Roman/Egyptian drag.]

THE EMINENT DOMAIN OF BOB KRASNOW

4-64	Round Robin—Kick That Little Foot Sally Ann (wr. Sloan/Barri) (Domain 1404)(Arr.)	

Bob Krasnow's label. I never got paid for it. Every time I'd go in to get my check, he'd say, "Goddamn, those partners of mine ran off with all the money. Those bastards! They didn't pay you either?

GIRL TALK

6-65	What Four—Anything for a Laugh/Baby Can't you Hear Me Call Your Name (Capitol 5449)(Arr.)	
12-65	Donna Loren—Call Me (Capitol 5548)(Arr) ("The friendly Pepper-Upper")	
8-64	Fashions—Baby That's Me (Cameo 331 (co-wrote)	
9-65	Karen Verros—You Just Gotta Know My Mind/Karen's Theme (Dot 16780)(Arr.)	
7-65	Karen Verros—Little Boy/I Can't Remember Ever Loving You (Dot 16815)(Arr.)	
5-66	Satisfactions—Daddy You Gotta Let Him In/Bring It All Down (Imperial 66170)(Prod/Arr)	
9-67	Cake—Baby That's Me (Decca 32179)	

Steve Douglas. These [What Four] are four girls, right? Well, one of them was real pretty. What for the What Four? Well, one of them was real pretty!
Is that "Little Boy"?
[No, it was the other Karen Verros record, a Donovan song, but was that the same Crystals tune, and did it come out?]
Yeah, on Dot. It sounded exactly like the Crystals except for her. We did four tunes in one session, three hours. She was awful!
It [The Satisfactions] wasn't done well. This one's embarrassing because I should've done this at Gold Star.
The Cake. I don't know a whole lot of stories about them. It was just Charlie and B Brian [Greene & Stone] as far as I was concerned. I wrote it a long time ago. All I know about is the Lesley Gore and the Cake. I don't know the Fashions. Greene & Stone had the demo. We were all friends—all incestuous stuff.
[Note: Despite Nitzsche's demurrals, the Satisfactions record is a highly enjoyable Crystals-meet-Shangri-Las motorpsycho extravaganza, and the Karen Verros record has a great instrumental track. The Donna Loren reference above, which might seem a bit cryptic, alludes to her lucrative gig as the Dr. Pepper girl in mid-60's TV commercials.]

WHAT AM I GONNA DO WITH YOU (HEY BABY)—WITH LESLEY GORE

	Lesley Gore—No Matter What You Do (Mercury 72513)(Arr.)	
	Lesley Gore—Off and Running (Merc.72580)(Arr.)	
	Lesley Gore—You Sent Me Silver Bells (Mercury 72892)(Arr.)	
	Lesley Gore—My Town My Guy and Me (Mercury MG 21042)(Baby That's Me; A Girl in Love ;What Am I Gonna Do With You)(Arr.)	

I don't have this ["Off and Running"] either. There was a better one on the date, that was on her album. I don't remember the song, it wasn't "Baby That's Me." Russ Titelman and Gerry Goffin wrote it, and that was a pretty one…
[The song was "What Am I Gonna Do With You (Hey Baby)," a moody masterpiece as done by the Chiffons, excellent by Lesley as well and covered rather ably by Skeeter Davis, too. "Off and Running" is a stirring Merseyish rocker, also done by the Mindbenders, and one of Lesley's better late recordings.]

A DATE WITH SUPERSTARS

8-64	Hale & Hushabyes—Yes Sir That's My Baby/Jack's Theme (Reprise 0299) (Arr/Co-Prod.)	
7-67	Date With Soul—Yes Sir That's My Baby/Bee Side Soul (York 408) (Arr./Co-prod.)	

[In 1964 Nitzsche assembled an all-star cast in the studio as a favor for his temporarily-destitute friends Charlie Greene & Brian Stone, notorious LA managers/manipulators who masterminded Sonny & Cher, the Troggs (in America), the Cake, and Buffalo Springfield at different times. The record was an awesome, stately Spectorian renovation of the Gus Kahn chestnut; the story behind it is rather intriguing as well.]

This [the York reissue as Date With Soul] is the third one. There's one on Reprise as Hale & the Hushabyes and one before that on another label [Apogee]. That's an all-star group, that one—that's Brian Wilson singing falsetto, with Sonny & Cher and the Blossoms and Albert Stone. The guy singing bass is someone who was in the lobby. Honest to God, a black guy was in the lobby and I went out there and said, "Do you sing bass?" He said yeah, and I said, "Come in and sing it." That's Edna Wright singing lead, singer of the Honey Cone. Darlene Love's singing background. Jackie DeShannon's on there. It was good.

That was also the session where I met the Rolling Stones. Andrew Oldham called me and asked if they could come. All these people were in the studio recording and the Stones walked in. Wow…but nobody cared.

First Terry Melcher did this ["Yes Sir"] with a guy named Little E [a legendary Bay Area R&B/rock pioneer noted for his "Candy Apple Red Impala" in the early 60's—see the BOMP Bay Area special in #12]. So we did this at Columbia but it never came out. I thought it was a good idea…Charlie and Brian didn't have any money, so we went to RCA and just recorded it, because we were so sure of it—and nobody got paid. Sold it to Reprise. I got the people. Charlie and Brian just sat there and smiled.

CAR TALK WITH LOU CHRISTIE—THE GYPSY TRIED

8-66	Lou Christie—If My Car Could Only Talk/Song of Lita (MGM 13576) (Prod/Arr)	
10-66	Lou Christie—Wild Life's in Season (MGM 13623)(Prod./Arr.)	

[I intro'd "If My Car" as one of my personal favorites…]
Me too! The Gypsy—Twyla [the middle-aged Romany type who's been Christie's collaborator forever—today,too]. I thought they were good. Lulu and Twyla. He was really a pro at what he did.
I was with Bob Marcucci [Christie's manager]. We were supposed to do a production thing, and he wanted to rewrite "La Boheme" and he used to say I was his Puccini. Then I realized the whole office was gay. I liked him though. "Wild Life's in Season" we did on the same date.

RETURN OF EDDIE HODGES

10-65	Eddie Hodges—Love Minus Zero/The Water is Over My Head (Aurora 156) (Arr.)	

That's Crazy Horse singing behind him on that record. I didn't even know them. I think they were the Rockets by then.
[Apparently early 60's child film star Eddie was in pretty shaky shape by this time, and in truth little has been heard from him since. Nice record though.]

BRIAN W. MEETS PHIL S.—BIG TROUBLE

	Ronettes—Don't Hurt My Little Sister (unrel.)(Arr.)	
	Blossoms—Things Are Changing (Equal Opportunity T-4LM-81721)(Arr.)	

I remember that. I bet Gracia was on that. I think I did do it. That's great!
[At this point I am struck by the Blossoms track's distinct resemblance to the Beach Boys' Today track "Don't Hurt My Little Sister". Recalling a rumor I'sd heard I ask if Brian Wilson had ever worked with Phil Spector.]

"I always told Neil Young he should make solo records. Stills didn't want him to sing, 'He's got that funny shaky thing in his voice' he'd say. I said, 'That's the thing I think is interesting!'"

Yeah. He did a song that Phil was gonna record with the Ronettes called "Please Don't Hurt My Little Sister." Brian wrote the song and came to the session, and I thought it was a real good session, but Phil never released that one because he didn't...share in it, the writing. During that date Leon Russell was playing piano and he got so drunk he couldn't play any more ... he was drinking gin and Pepsi Cola, and he stood up on the piano and started preaching for real, and Phil had to ask him to stop playing piano, so Brian played it.
[*Apparently some remnants of the track were salvaged to make the Blossoms' Equal Opportunity record.*]

THE DOG REMEMBERS—P.J. PROBY AND THE WALKER BROTHERS

5-65	Walker Bros.—Love Her/The Seventh Dawn (Smash 1976)	(Arr.)
6-63	P.J. Proby—So Do I/I Can't Take It Like You Can (Liberty 55588)	(Arr.)
10-66	P.J. Proby—I Can't Make It Alone/If I Ruled the World (Liberty 55915)	(Prod.)
2-67	P.J. Proby—You Make Me Feel Like Someone (on *Enigma* LP, Liberty LST 7497)	(Arr.)

I like that one [*Walkers*]. It's a good song. Was it done in L.A.? Yeah.
([*Nitzsche and Nik Venet cut the record, a 1963 Everly Bros. single, with the Walkers while they were still in Hollywood, appearing in beach movies and as residents on the Hollywood A-Go-Go TV show, just before they emigrated to England and became stars. Although their catalog is full of brilliant productions, you'd be hard-pressed to find a better Walkers record than this majestic, heartbreaking disk.*]
That [*"I Can't Make It" by P.J.*] was when he came back here from England. That was a good song too.
[*Had he worked with Proby earlier, before he emigrated to England and became a star?*]
Yeah, demos. When he thought he was Johnny Cash. "(The Dog Remembers and) So Do I..." He was always drunk, but he was...I've always liked him a lot. He deserved to be a lot more than he was; ver talented. He could sing like anybody. Gene Pitney and Johnny Cash...
[*Or, in the case of "I Can't Make It Alone", like the Righteous Bros.—it's a masterful production ballad, great song, great performance, too...*]

FEAR AND TREMBLING: ON FOLLOWING JAMES BROWN (THE *TAMI SHOW*)

I put the band together for *The TAMI Show* [*the justly legendary 1964 film which captured most of the reigning rock royalty of the time in memorable live performances*], did all the arrangements, tried to make it sound like the records. I don't know if it did or not. The Four Seasons were supposed to be on that show. They asked for more money than anybody on the show (including the Beach Boys and Rolling Stones), so they were cancelled. I think they asked for $45,000 —that's for being there two days, and then they wanted limos... so Bill Sargent [*producer*] showed them...
Denny Bruce: The Stones insisted on closing the show, which makes a good story...
They didn't. I really thought they should. They had been on tour before, and they'd played a rodeo in San Antonio and no one liked them; *Hollywood Palace*, with Dean Martin, it was horrible. So they didn't feel like coming back to America, at least very soon. When I went to England, I told Bill Sargent I thought they were going to be big...it was pretty easy to see, don't you think? When I asked them to do *The TAMI Show*, Mick said, 'What, and play for a bunch of fuckin' cows?' Anyway, I said they should close the show. Bill Sargent said, "I can't, James Brown's going to close the show." Of course the Stones *wanted* to close the show, but they'd never seen James Brown before. It was one of the only times I've ever seen Jagger crack. We all stood at the side of the stage watching James Brown do his act, and after it was over Mick said, "We'll go on first. Any place on the show—we can't follow that." But they did well. Everyone's standing on their chairs screaming for James Brown, and the Stones come out and all the girls are crying—it was a new reaction, I thought.
Denny Bruce: It was a landmark show...the Billy J. Kramers, though...

NEIL YOUNG MEETS THE CASCADES

6-67	Cascades—Flying on the Ground (Wr: Neil Young)/Main Street (Smash 2101)	(Arr.)

Oh yeah, I never heard that record! Andy Di Martino [*noted San Diego area entrepeneur, later Captain Beefheart's manager/collaborator*] was making the engineer crazy by grabbing the dials. Is the other side "Out of My Mind"? That was on the same date. I think Neil even played guitar on this record.

THE FIRST SUPERGROUP—THE MERCURIAL CAREER OF THE PHILISTINES

There was going to be a group once, that Phil was gonna play guitar in, I was going to play piano, Sonny Bono—I don't know what *he* was gonna play, but we were all gonna make a group and it was going to be called The Philistines.

THE ELUSIVE PRODUCER CREDIT—WITH BOB LIND

All by Bob Lind:
1-66	Elusive Butterfly/Cheryl's Goin' Home (World Pacific 77808)	(Arr/Prod; uncred.)
4-66	Remember the Rain/Truly Julie's Blues (World Pacific 77822)	(Prod./Arr.)
7-66	I Just Let it Take Me/We've Never Spoken (World Pacific 77830)	(Prod./Arr.)
10-66	San Francisco Woman/Oh Babe Take Me Home (World Pacific 77839)	(Prod./Arr.)
4-66	*Don't Be Concerned* (World Pacific WP 1841)	(Prod./Arr.)

"Elusive Butterfly" says 'Produced by Richard Bock' and he wasn't even on the date! They just had him [*Lind*] down at Liberty. He's got some new material. I think he could be a funky John Denver again. His new stuff—he's grown a bit. Looking for a deal. I want to make a record with him again, at least one...

NITZSCHE RATES THE GAS COMPANY

10-65	Gas Company—Blow Your Mind/Your Time's Up (Mirwood 5501)	(Prod.)

[*See ANOTHER REPRISE section above for later Nitzsche/Gas Co. collaborations*]

It's awful, please don't play that.
[*Greg Dempsey, the songwriter here, later produced Kathi Dalton*]
Yeah, that's them together on this record.
Denny Bruce: He's co-writer of Leon Russell's "Roll Away the Stone," I think. He gets about one a year, and she gets deals...

STONES UNTURNED

Nitzsche played on the following Rolling Stones albums, sometimes contributing arrangements:

12x5; Rolling Stones Now; Out of Our Heads; December's Children; Aftermath; Between the Buttons; Flowers; Let It Bleed; Sticky Fingers.

Andrew [*Oldham*] called me and said we've met Phil Spector and we want to meet you...I said I was doing a session if you want to bring everybody down. They walked in looking so weird, putting everyone on, of course. Hal Blaine had to take pictures, he didn't know who they were but they looked so strange, and he put his light meter up, and Charlie Watts leans over it like it was a microphone and says, "I like it very much in America," and then he continued to tell me forever he thought it was a mike. Brian Jones was the only one dressed up in a three-piece suit and tie. He told me he wanted to leave the Stones 'cause he thought he could be a professional harmonica player. "If I came to LA, would you get me on a lot of dates?" They weren't making it too well...
I went in the studio with them and played piano. Oldham wanted to be a genius, but I don't think he had that much to do with anything. I arranged "Can't Always Get What You Want", "Standing in the Shadows", there was another one. That was a funny time. That was when I decided I didn't want to do this shit anymore. It was a whole new way of approaching records. Instead of trying to get four records in a three-hour date, you'd book the studio for two weeks for 24 hours and do whatever you wanted to, and if you didn't get anything in those two weeks, screw it. Or if a tune didn't work one way try it as a tango, try it as this, try it as that. I just took a lot of time after that!

GOOD TIMES MUSIC

3-67	Don & Goodtimes—I Could Be So Good to You (Epic 10145)	(Prod, co-wrote)
4-67	Don & Goodtimes—*So Good* (Epic LN/BN 24311/26311)	(Prod,co-arr.)

Don "Goodtime" Gallucci. That's the Don who was the leader of the group who was fired before they did this record. That was awful, that thing. The record [*"I Could Be So Good"*] I liked all right, but they just hated me from the top, and didn't like anything I was doing, till they heard it on the radio, I think on KHJ. [*This was the same DonGallucci, incidentally, who later produced Crabby Appleton and the Stooges as an Elektra staffer.*]
I tried to make a follow-up to this which they really hated. You know a Neil Young song called "Whisky Boot Hill" [*it turns out to be the first segment of Young's "Country Girl" suite on Deja Vu as well as the instrumental prelude to Young's first solo album*]? I made a real good record on them with that and they thought it was too far out. How could they sing that when their album cover was...an ice cream truck? The Goodtimes. They had a *good time* on stage, they couldn't sing that stuff...
Denny Bruce: They were always fond of saying, "You know, up in the Northwest we blow Paul Revere & the Raiders off the stage!"
[*The Goodtimes, who joined the Raiders as regulars on* Where the Action Is *in 1967, also served as a sort of farm team for Revere—whenever)as frequently happened) a backup Raider would get restless, Revere would grab a Goodtime to replace him.*]

AN UNEXPECTED BOUQUET FOR GARRY BONNER—KOPPELMAN-RUBIN DAYS

10-67	Garry Bonner—The Heart of Juliet Jones/ Me About You (Columbia 44306)	(Prod/Arr)
8-67	Gary Lewis & Playboys—Jill/ (Liberty 55985)	(Arr.)

[*continued on p. 58*]

THE WORLD OF UNDERGROUND ROCK

OFFERING THE BEST OF NEW-WAVE RECORDS FROM EVERY COUNTRY AT LOW PRICES, EXCLUSIVELY FOR BOMP READERS.

Wayne County - Max's Kansas City (PC) $2	Del Shannon - Tell Her No/Restless $2.50
Thundertrain - Hot for Teacher (great PC) $2	Del Shannon - Cry Baby Cry [co-wr. Jeff Lynne]/ In My Arms Again $2.50 [These 2 Island singles will never be on an LP and are already rare!]
Sneakers EP: 5 songs (great PC) $2.50	
Loose Gravel - Frisco Band (PC) (lim. ed.) $2.50	
Wildman Fisher - Go to Rhino Records [his most recent; weird] $2	Ramones - Blitzkrieg Bop [British import] $1.50
New Legion Rock Spectacular - Second Cousin/Wild One (torrid 2-sider!) $2	Flamin' Groovies - EP: Shake Some Action +2 [British import] $2
Jan Berry [of JAN & DEAN] - Sing Sang a Song [his last, not released to public] $3.50	Legendary Masked Surfers [Jan, Dean, Brian, Rog, Christian, Leon, Bruce & Terry, others] Gonna Hustle You/Summertime $2
Creme Soda - Keep it Heavy [Tommy James style bubble-punk] $2	Seeds - Shuckin' and Jiving [private re-pressing of their rarest record] $3
Creme Soda - Chewin Gum [wild rockapunk] $2	Kenny & Cadets - Barbie [private re-pressing of the first Beach Boys disc] $3
Boyz - Laughs on Me - Kiderian (Chicago folk-rock/punk) $2	Spades - You're Gonna Miss Me - Zero [private re-pressing of original version of 13th Floor Elevators hit, featuring Roky Erickson A wild punk rocker] $3
The Boys - She's All Mine - Outrave [great Anglo-punk from Nebraska] $2.50	
The Count - EP: 4 great songs [like Velvets, Mod. Lovers, etc. many pix & inserts] $3.50	Eddie & Hot Rods - Live at Marquee EP $3.25
Slickee Boys- EP: Manganese Android Puppies, Psycho Daisies +2, full color cover $3	SIRE BOOKS - Greg-Shaw-edited series, full of rare pix, complete discographies, a must for every fan. Only $4.95 each. Titles include Beach Boys (Ken Barnes), Elton (Greg Shaw), Carole King, Rod Stewart, Allman Bros. These are substantial, 9x12 volumes...you'll love 'em!
Vince Taylor - Do You Wanna Rock & Roll Rockhouse [Dutch import] $1.75	
Blondie - X-Offender - [Spector-style] $2.25	
Gizmos - EP: 4 songs [fabulous—like Iggy, Dolls, Reed, Dictators; see review] (PC) $3.50	
Primitives - EP: Sneaky Pete, Cycle Annie +2 [Lou Reed, John Cale pre-Velvets. Private re-pressing of rare tracks, with PC] $3.25	ALSO TRY US FOR THE LATEST UNDERGROUND RECORDS AS THEY COME OUT. WE CARRY THE BEST AT LOWEST PRICES. (Add postage .25 first record, .05 each extra) [Canada & overseas: .25 & .10]
Dave Edmunds - Here Comes the Weekend [British import, rocks like crazy!] $2.50	
Beatles - Live at Shea '64 - 2 EPs [privately pressed, Dutch import. Taken from the original '64 EP, every rare] Both records $15	

ORDER FROM P.O. BOX 7112, BURBANK CALIF. 91510 USA
(Overseas orders welcome)

BACK ISSUES

#10-11: British Invasion. Special double issue, articles & pix on scores of groups...
#12: Punk Rock. Seeds, Standells, Brummels, San Francisco punk.
#13: Flamin' Groovies, Detroit, Beatle novelties, Rockabilly, Cameo, H'wood Stars
#14: Surf roots, Dutch rock, Beatle songs, Boston, British rock encyclopedia, more
#15: Girl groups (Runaways, Lesley Gore, Jackie DeShannon, Shangri-Las), Dave Edmunds, Liverpool, Chicago, British Rock encyclopedia, more

```
BOMP Back Issue Dept. PO Box 7112, Burbank, CA

Dear sirs:
Please send me the following back issues, for $1.50
each [US & Canada; overseas add 50 cents per issue]
  □ #10-11  □ #12  □ #13  □ #14  □ #15
Total amount enclosed:

Name _____
Address _____
State _____ Zip _____

Please allow up to 4 weeks for delivery.
```

The ARRANGER As SUPERMAN

[continued from p. 30]

11-67	Gary Lewis & Playboys—Has She Got the Nicest Eyes/Happiness (Liberty 56011) (Arr.)
10-67	Zal Yanovsky—As Long as You're Here (Buddah 12) (Prod/Arr.)
6-67	Turtles—She'd Rather Be With Me (White Whale 249) (Arr. horns)
8-67	Petula Clark—Cat in the Window/Fancy Dancin' Man (Warner Bros 7073) (Arr.)

[Jackie DeShannon's previously cited "I Keep Wanting You" falls into this period as well.]

[Charles Koppelman and Don Rubin supervised a talented stable of writers and producers) Artie Kornfield and Steve Duboff, Joe Wissert, and ex-Magicians Alan Gordon and Garry Bonner among them), and had hits like "If I Were a Carpenter" with Bobby Darin and "Happy Together" with the Turtles. Nitzsche worked with K&R for a time, and apparently did not relish the experience, except for working with Garry Bonner...]

The best. The best white soul singer ever. I did a record with him called "Juliet Jones." That was really good, I think, that one holds up. Garry Bonner, the White Tornado. The best. I did a record with Bobby Hatfield called "I'm Free," which was a really good record, but they never released it, 'cause he couldn't sing it. The reason he couldn't sing it was he came in and he wasn't making it on the vocals, so Garry Bonner came up to the microphone and said, "Let me sing it one time for you," and he sang it. Hatfield walked out and said, "Why don't you do it, I can't do that!" What a singer!

RUFF TIMES

9-69	Tony Ray—Here Comes School Again/ Lonely Weekends (Dot 17301) (Arr.)
?-70	Them—Lonely Weekends/I Am Waiting (Jagger/Richard) (Happy Tiger 525) (Arr.)

Oh my God. Well, I didn't do that one [Tony Ray]. Oh my God! Is it the same track ["Lonely Weekends"]? Has to be. "I Am Waiting." I don't remember doing that. Sometimes they put the name on both sides of the record, but that doesn't mean I did it. I was asleep during these. I was chewing tobacco and spitting into a can. Ray Ruff. Weird! I wondered what he was doing in the studio. Yeah, it's probably mine. I don't remember that one at all.

[Ray Ruff, a Buddy Holly-ish rocker in the early 60's and producer of the Blue Things, apparently wigged out a bit in the later 60's when he was a staff producer for Dot and Happy Tiger, and recently he surfaced with a ridiculously grandiose rock opera telling the story of the Bible called Truth of Truths) Oak Records) and in 1976 with a no-less-modest Bicentennial rock tribute album Happy Birthday USA on 20th Century [featuring Paul Revere & the Raiders on one cut]. Actually, the near-identical arrangements of "Lonely Weekends" are both good rockers and Tony Ray's A-side is a nifty Eddie Cochran adaptation. The Them in question is a highly dubious post-Van Morrison aggregation.]

AN ADDED PHILIP: MORE ON SPECTOR

[Nitzsche arranged these latter-day Philles records]

3-64	120 - Ronettes—Breakin' Up
4-64	121 - Ronettes—Do I Love You
5-64	122 - Crystals—All Grown Up
9-64	123 - Darlene Love—Stumble & Fall/Quiet Guy [withdrawn]

10-64	123	Ronettes—Walking in the Rain/How Does It Feel
12-64	125	Darlene Love—Christmas/Winter Wonderland
1-65	126	Ronettes—Born to Be Together
3-65	127	Righteous Bros—Just Once in my Life
5-65	128	Ronettes—Is This What I Get
5-65	129	Righteous Bros—Hung On You
11-65	130	Righteous Bros—I Love You For Sentimental Reasons
4-66	131	Ike & Tina Turner - River Deep Mountain High
9-66	133	Ronettes—When I Saw You [uncr.]
5-67	135	Ike & Tina Turner—I'll Never Need More Than This
?-67	136	Ike & Tina Turner—A Love Like Yours
?-64	Phil Spector 1	Veronica—So Young
?-64	Phil Spector 2	Veronica—Why Don't They Let Us Fall in Love
8-76	Warner-Spector 0409	Ronnie Spector—Paradise
12-64	Philles LP4006	*Presenting the Fabulous Ronettes*
6-69	A&M SP 4178	Ike & Tina Turner—*River Deep Mountain High* (some tracks)

[and the following newly-released Philles vault tracks]
Darlene Love—Run Run Run Runaway; Strange Love; Long Way to Be Happy
Ronettes—Soldier Baby; Girls Can Tell; Woman in Love; Here I Sit; Keep On Dancing; Everything Under the Sun/Wish I Never Saw the Sunshine
April Stevens—Why Can't a Boy and Girl Just Stay In Love
Crystals—Heartbreaker
Bob B. Soxx—But You Don't Love Me
Modern Folk Quartet—This Could Be the Night

[*We were talking about the Bonnie & the Treasures record "Home of the Brave," and its credited producer, Jerry Riopelle*...]

Phil really took him [*Riopelle*] under his wing. He was gonna be his new writer. It came to the point where Phil...it was all his conception, those records, but as soon as he got a press agent he would say that he wrote 'em, arranged them, produced them, and told the singers how to sing them. Everybody started to feel a little funny about that—and then Jeff [*Barry*] and Ellie [*Greenwich*] went and recorded "Chapel of Love" with the Dixie Cups and it had been recorded with both the Crystals and the Ronettes before and none of 'em came out, so they went and did that. I went to New York one time, my wife and I, and I ran into Jeff Barry and he invited me over. So I told Phil, I'm going to dinner at Jeff Barry's and he said [*growls*] "What are you gonna do, listen to the *Dixie Cups* record?" He said, "I really wish you wouldn't do that," and I said, "Why, we're still friends." He said, "I'd like to create the illusion there are 'separate camps'."

After all these writers were saying one after another that he's taking all the credit, then he started working with people like Jerry Riopelle. Bonnie & the Treasures...Ronnie sang on that.

THE PHILLES EPITAPH

Philles 135 [*see listing above*]

[*Although it's commonly accepted that Phil Spector, mortally offended by American rejection of "River Deep Mountain High," immediately quit the record business, in truth the Philles label lasted for five more issues, not to mention limited pressings of the Ike & Tina Turner album and a Lenny Bruce LP. The last record was a track from the Ike & Tina LP, "A Love Like Yours," but the real last hurrah was an all-stops-out Ike & Tina single recorded after the album, Spector's one last irresistible stab at grabbing the gold ring again; "I'll Never Need More than This".*]

That was after "River Deep." I never heard that. That was the last attempt, I think that was the last one he and I ever did together. This is going to be sad. I think that song would be fun to do again. It's so good. I can see why it wasn't a hit, though. A little too 'pop'-oriented [*presumably in the sense of MOR-pop*], isn't it?

MID-60'S WRAP-UP

7-64	Concords—Should I Cry (Epic 9697)(Co-wr)
3-65	Jerry Cole—Every Window in the City/Come on Over to My Place (Capitol 5394)(Arr.)
4-64	Righteous Bros—Try to Find Another Man/I Still Love You (Moonglow 231)(Arr; pre-Spector)
9-65	Bobby Vee—Run Like the Devil/Take a Look Around Me (Liberty 55828)(Arr.)
?-65	Explosions—?/? (Liberty) (Arr.)
?-65	Gene McDaniels—?/? (Liberty) (Arr.)
?-67	Suzi Jane Hokom—Same Old Songs (LHI 19) (Arr.)
9-65	Palace Guard—All Night Long/Playgirl (Orange Empire 331)(Arr.)[*"Forget it"*]
3-66	MFQ(Mod.Folk Quartet)—Night Time Girl/Lifetime (Dunhill 4025) (Prod./Arr.)
1-67	Gentle Soul—Tell Me Love (Columbia 43952)(Arr.)(Prod. T. Melcher)
9-68	Monkees—Porpoise Song (Colgems 1031) (Arr.) [*"I love that one!"*]
10-66	Tim Buckley—*Tim Buckley* (Elektra EKL-4004) (Arr. strings)

I don't remember that one [*Jerry Cole*]. I do remember he came into a session with a submachine gun once. He's really into guns.

Done on the same session with the Explosions and Gene McDaniels, all on one date [*Bobby Vee*]. All Joe Saraceno hits.

I liked that one [*MFQ*], sort of. I don't like that mix—I didn't do that mix, Lou Adler did.

Don't have this one [*Gentle Soul*] either. I don't even remember it. Ry Cooder played on a lot of these. I was on that. The Beatles Baroque.

PART THREE
Modern Times

YOUNG UPSIDE DOWN

1-67	Buffalo Springfield—Expecting to Fly (Atco 6545) (Co-prod; co-arr.)
1-69	Neil Young—*Neil Young* (Reprise 6317) (Wr;arr. "String Quartet From Whiskey Boot Hill", worked on some other tracks)
2-72	Neil Young—*Harvest* (Reprise MS 2032) (Prod/Arr.'A Man Needs a Maid','There's a World')

I met Neil through Charlie & Brian. [*Was "Expecting to Fly" intended as a Neil Young solo single?*]

Yeah, I was the evil one in that. Stephen never wanted Neil to sing and I thought Neil could do it by himself. Stephen would say, "He's got that funny shaky thing in his voice." I said, "That's the thing I think is interesting."

I loved that record [*Young's first and in some ways best solo LP*].

I set that up with Warners for him to be a solo singer. He asked Denny [*Bruce*] once when I was going to do the record and Denny said I had the name down in my book, and he said, "I'm not a name in a book, I'm Neil Young!" Neil wanted to be a star.

CRAZY HORSE

4-71	Downtown/ (Reprise 1007) (Co-prod.)
7-71	Dance Dance Dance/ (Reprise 1025)(co-or.)
9-71	Dirty Dirty/Beggar's Day (Reprise 1046)
3-71	Crazy Horse (Reprise RS 6438) (Co-prod)

[*Nitzsche played in Neil Young's back-up band Crazy Horse in early 1970, and was prevailed upon to join the group when they got a solo deal with Reprise. Their first album (1971), with any number of brilliant Danny Whitten songs, guest Nils Lofgren's chilling "Beggar's Day," and two remarkable songs by Nitzsche and Russ Titelman ("Gone Dead Train," a distrubing rocker earlier cut by Randy Newman for the Performance soundtrack, and a delightful girl-group-styled ditty called "Carolay" which is ripe for recutting), holds up extremely well today and is one of the best rock & roll albums of the fallow early 70's.*]

Neil was working with them and he asked me to play piano. Did you really see that tour [*a fairly legendary series of warm-up gigs at small California junior colleges, my occasion being a brilliant show at Palomar JC 30 miles north of San Diego*]? That was a good tour, that one. The last one [*ca. 1974*] was horrible.

From there they wanted to make an album of their own. Elliott Roberts became my manager and Neil's, and they said if I produced it [*Crazy Horse*] and became part of the group, that it would work, and I did that, for one album... They're not really musicians—they'll give anyone the faith to become musicians. That album was okay. I don't like any of the Nils Lofgren stuff on the album. He's another of them that wants to be a star so bad...

FINAGLING WITH THE TUBES

?-71	Ron Nagle—*Bad Rice* (WB 1902)(Prod.)
6-76	Tubes—Don't Touch Me There (A&M 1826) (Arr.)

Ron Nable—that's the best undiscovered talent around [*an opinion shared by a number of rock writers*]. He's super. He's real good at making records.

Nagle brought me in [*on the Tubes session; Nagle having written the song, a satirical girl-group number*]. They did miss the point on that record. It's just an imitation, a bad one. Not just the singing [*is off*], but the whole thing. They wanted that sound as a put-on, but they didn't understand it at all. It'd be a lot funnier if they were more serious.

MODERN TIMES WRAP-UP

5-69	Marianne Faithfull—Sister Morphine/Something Better (London 1022) (Arr.)
9-70	Randy Newman—Gone Dead Train (Reprise 0945) (Prod/co-wrote)
4-70	Randy Newman—*12 Songs* (Reprise 6373) (Co-prod "Let's Burn Down the Cornfield")
?-72	Buffy Ste. Marie—*She Useta Wanna Be a Ballerina* (Vanguard VSD 79311) (Co-prod)
4-74	Mac Davis—Stop & Smell the Roses (Columbia 10018) (Arr.)
8-74	Mac Davis—Rock & Roll (Columbia 10070)
4-75	Mac Davis—If You Add All the Love in the World (Columbia 10111) (Arr.)
9-73	Ringo Starr—Photograph (Apple 1865)(Arr)

Nitzsche also did the music (produced and arranged) for *Performance* and *One Flew Over the Cuckoo's Next*, and worked on the music for many other films including *Candy*, *Greaser's Palace*, *Sticks and Bones*, and *The Exorcist*.

[*In recent years Nitzsche has been involved in a number of varied projects, many of which he has not enjoyed—he had little to say about working with Mac Davis, for example, and did not seem especially enthusiastic about Cuckoo's Nest.*]

[*His future plans seem unsettled...*]

I don't have any. There's a movie that I think is going to be real good. Bob Downey's new movie called *Jive*.

[*Nitzsche has scored that film. He would also like to work with Ronnie Spector again, and at press time there seems to be at least a slight hope that it could happen. Jack Nitzsche is obviously an independent type, one who had and probably will again have trouble fitting smoothly into the banal everyday record biz routine and its prevailing attitudes. The unimaginative souls who account [in more ways than one] for a large proportion of the industry today have trouble pigeonholing Nitzsche, which in part explains his rather patternless track record of the past few years. But looking over the record of his accomplishments from 1960 to 1976, it's impossible not to be awed, and it seems a certainty that this supremely gifted man will continue to create musical monuments in the future.*]

PUNK ROCK of MEXICO!

By Phast Phreddie

My initiation into the collecting of Punk-Rock of Mexico (hereafter abbreviated PROM) came in a greasy restaurant in Carson California. I had just bought a pile of records at the local Salvation Army and I had hardly put them down when Emanuel, the busboy, came by and dropped an additional 45 atop the other discs and said "Para Usted, Amigo".[1] I checked it out and saw that he had given me a copy of "Hey Lupe"[2] by Los Rockin' Devils, which turned out to be a much sought after item among PROM enthusiasts, at least as good as "Watcher of the Skies" by Genesis and twice as rare.

From then on I've been making regular excursions into East LA and even Tijuana, to find the records I so desperately need for my collection. Believe me, it's a lot cheaper to take the short drive across the Rio Grande than to sell your stereo, TV and car and go to Europe, only to find all the Focus singles were already bought up by a guy from Japan.

The main PROM band is Los Rockin' Devils. So far seven 45's, an EP and three LPs have turned up in California. Their debut single was "Juego de Amor"[3] on the formidable Orfeon label. According to Emanuel, "Juego" bombed in most of the markets in Mexico, except the city of Oaxaca where it received minor airplay. When a DJ in Mexico City started playing the flip side, "Todos Queremos a Lupe"[4], the record shot up to the top of Las Cartas[5] in early 1965 and Los Rockin' Devils became big stuff.

This hit was followed by a wild version of James Brown's "Soy Feliz"[5] which bashed its way up to "El Numero Uno" position on Las Cartas late that summer. As "Soy Feliz" descended Las Cartas, the long-awaited LP was released, to "mucho albanzo"[7] by the fans, but "Los Criticos"[8] hated it. And with good reason. Exitos A Go Go is awful, comprised for the most part of popular tunes from the US charts, like "You Soy Enrique VIII", "Los Pajaros y Las abejas"[9] and "Hey Lupe." The main reason Los Criticos hated the LP was because one song, "Todo El Dia y Toda la Noche"[10] was sung in English instead of Spanish. You must understand that Los Criticos of Mexico are devout purists and would even object to eating at Taco Bell.

Nonetheless, Exitos A Go Go did quite well and another 45 was let loose. "Sigue Asi"[11] was the biggest selling single in the state of Chihuahua in 1966.[12] There was a huge promotion campaign featuring the distribution of cardboard *tortillas* with photos of Los Rockin' Devils on them.[13]

A tour was set up which took the band to key Mexican cities such as Merida, Vera Cruz, Pachuca, Monterey and reaching as far north as Mexicali. While in Mexicali, the drummer (Jengibre Pastelero) crossed the border into the USA where he was arrested as an illegal alien near San Clemente. Disillusioned, Los Rockin' Devils returned to Mexico City to find a new drummer.

Later in 1966, they recorded their second LP. The new drummer, Alphonso Robles, proved to be a gifted translator of songs into Spanish, and every BOMP reader should recognize tunes like "Chichardos Dulces", "Caperucita Roja", "La Patita" and "Regressas a Mi."[14]

The single pulled from the LP was "Gorda A Go Go"[15] which flopped. The flip was "La Pequena Lupe Lu"[16], a fine rocker which now fetches from 90 to 125 pesos from the collectors who invade Tijuana every

---

1. Translation: For you, friend.
2. "Hang On Sloopy."
3. "Game of Love"
4. "Everybody Do the Sloopy."
5. The charts.
6. "I Got You."
7. Much praise.
8. The critics.
9. "I'm Henry the Eighth", "The Birds & the Bees."
10. "All Day and All of the Night."
11. "Go Ahead On", written by Chris Montez
12. According to Miguel Jimenez of Chico's Car Wash in San Pedro.
13. These items are quite rare now and fetch from 45 to 80 pesos each.
14. "Sweet Pea", "Little Red Riding Hood", "The Duck" and "Together Again."
15. "It's Going to Rain."
16. "Little Latin Lupe Lu."

record season.

From 1967 until 1973, the band remained fairly inactive, except for a 1971 single done by Robles, lead singer Jose Martinez and a group of studio musicians in Tijuana. "Mujer de Honky Tonk"[17] was released late that year as a Los Rockin' Devils 45. The percussion intro sounds like a monkey beating on stale taco shells and Joe's voice fails to match his earlier high standards. The *gatos estudios*[18] failed to measure up to the former Devils sound. Of course it was a big hit anyway, topping Las Cartas in Durengo, La Paz, Toluca, Guadalajara and even the jukebox in Hombre Facil, a popular burrito palace in East LA, known for its generous portions of Montezuma's Revenge.

They went on to release another album featuring the vocals of Elena Palma, and several singles, the last-known being their 1974 "Gritos", a rocker in true Question Mark & Mysterians style, which had moderate success throughout Mexico.[19]

Another Mexico City band was Los X-5 who had a more Anglo sound. On their album *Al Compas de la Nueva Ola* they perform 3 Beatle songs, 3 Dave Clark Five songs, some originals sounding like Gerry & the Pacemakers on reds, and a sped-up version of "Apache."

When Jengibre Pasterlero, Los Rockin' Devils' old drummer, got out of jail in San Diego, he went straight to Tijuana where he formed Los Babys. Although Los Babys have released many albums, the only one worth mentioning is *Sabor Ritmo y Sentimeinto*. It has one killer song called "Esos Ojitos Negros", a psychedelic rave-up much like the third Chocolate Watchband LP run through hot sauce.

From Oaxaca came Los Freddys. Their first LP is classic, but after that they sort of gave up. Their three follow-up LPs consisted of Mexican folk-songs; no rock & roll. But that first one was boss. It contained a couple Beatle songs, "Tengo un Corazon", "Dime Que Quieras"[20] and two Gary Lewis & Playboys tunes—all done up with a certain ineptitude that, well, if you like the Ramones..

One of my favorite PROM bands is Los Hitters who have a firecracker of an LP on the Primvox label. The songs include "Por Tu Amore", "Tratala Bien" and "Ven a Mi."[21] Also of note is a version of Travis Wammack's "Scratchy" and a surf instrumental called "Mary y Juana"—now THAT's *punk*.

The Los Hitters LP came out in 1966. In 1967, they broke up due to an excessive amount of drug overdoses among the band members, as well as roadies, las sanguijuelas[22] and management.

Chihuahua is the home of Los Apson. Although they made 3 albums, only the second, *Satisfaccion* can be considered a true PROM record. The outstanding feature of the first album was the fact that the keyboard player had no legs[23] and was pictured on the cover with a pair of synthetic legs, sitting on a railroad track as the bass player and drummer help him up, while the two guitarists mimic him by clowning with fake crutches. The second LP featured a great fuzz-tone revamp of the Stones classic "Satisfaccion." Somehow they screwed up the lyrics and lines like "Yo tengo solo cinco pesos yella quere seis"[24] were added with spectacular results. And on "Croscopio Bikini"[25] they prove themselves to be as capable as Hermans Hermits.

But the real Standells of Mexico is Los Ovnis. I don't know how they're set for singles, but I've got three monster albums by them. The first features "Muchacha", "Repitelo Repitelo", and "Un Hombre Respetable"[26], each having been a sizable hit down home. Even the cover was a classic in the Punk Rock mold: a black & white photo of the five Ovnis, each wearing a pin-striped long-sleeve shirt with buttoned collar and black vest.

Los Ovnis got a great sound out of their obviously Woolworths amplifiers and Emeny guitars, too. Their sense of humor is aptly portrayed in their version of "Sacudiendo Todo"[27], doing the German band The Lords one better by singing the entire song in Spanish.

The real gem is their odd rendition of "Baby Please Don't Go" (here called "El Ovni"[28]). They must have been very knowledgeable rock fans; in the middle of this song they break into Jimi Hendrix' "Third Stone From the Sun", strange voices and all.

A second and third LP were released by Los Ovnis, but both were relatively disappointing, although still better than the vast majority of PROM. A fourth album is rumored to exist. The story on that is that by the time Los Ovnis were in the recording studio for their third try, the ECO label decided to drop them, and the fourth LP was pressed only in small promotional quantities. Entitled *Boracho*, the LP received minor airplay on an Army base radio station in Fresnillo and never touched Las Cartas. Disillusioned, Los Ovnis went their separate ways in 1968.

I hope to be writing more about the Punk Rock of Mexico as more data comes in—all info is eagerly sought, naturally. Let the above serve as an introduction only, along with the following incomplete yet eccentric discography.

Thanks for material aid to Emanuel, Miguel Jimenez, Juan Llescas, Julio Bendejo, Ricardo Ovideo, Jose Manon and Los Mermanos at Hombre Facil.

DISCOGRAPHY OF MEXICAN PUNK ROCK

LOS ROCKIN DEVILS
Orfeon 45's
1803 Juego de Amor/Todos Queremos a Lupe
1807 Soy Feliz/Dime
1876 Sigue Asi/Otro Amor
1906 Gorda a Go Go/La Pequena Lupe Lu
???? *Mujer de Honky Tonk/Azucar, Azucar*
2038 Georgina/Chula Tu (Sugar, Sugar)
2309 Estos Fueron Los Dias/Gitos
Orfeon EP 843 - Estos Fueron Los Dias/Un Paso al Amor/Gritos/Pilotos

Orfeon LP 472 - *Exitos a Go Go*
Dimsa LPs (subsidiary of Orfeon)
1021 - *Nuevos Exitos Con*
1061 - *Esos Fueron Las Dias*
Also of note: Orfeon 2017 - *Los Grande Anos de Rock 'n' Roll Vol. 1* (various artists) includes "Diablo con Vestido Azul 7 la Plaga"

Other noteworthy PROM LPs:
X-5 - *Al Compas de la Nueva Ola* (Kristal 2020)
Los Hitters - *Hey Lucy* (Primovox 030)

THE ECO LABEL
The ECO label is the largest independent record company in Mexico. They dealt with a variety of Mexican noises, therefore only the rock & roll LPs will receive mention.
388 Los Aspen - *Por Eso Estamos Como Estamos*
400 Los Aspen - *Satisfaccion*
453 Los Ovnis
493 Los Ovnis - *Somos Amantes*
522 Los-Freddys
601 Los Babys - *Sabor Ritmo Y Sentimento*
798 Los Aspen - *El Compadre Vadilador*
895 Los Freddys - *Sin Tu Amor*
921 Los Babys - *Carino*

---

17. "Honky Tonk Women."
18. Studio cats.
19. According to Juan Llescas, "Gritos" was number one in Peru for 18 months in a row in 1974-75, selling a total of 523 copies.
20. "Heart Full of Soul", "My Girl."
21. "For Your Love", "Treat Her Right", "Stand by Me."
22. The groupies.
23. Take that, Moulty.
24. "I only have five pesos and she wants six."
25. "Dizzy Miss Lizzy."
26. "Girl", "Over and Over" and "A Well Respected Man."
27. "Shakin' All Over"
28. I don't know what the hell this means.

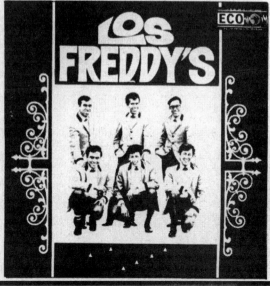

SOUNDS of the SIXTIES

Part Four: SWEDEN

By Greg Shaw & Lennart Persson

Our survey of Dutch rock (BOMP 14) brought out the fact that many countries besides the US and England spawned prolific local music scenes during the beat era (1964-67). Having got past the initial impulse to write these scenes off as unimportant, with the exception of what few worldwide hits they produced, one soon realizes that quite a few countries managed to come up with groups the equal of many now worshipped by collectors, and occasional classic records that belong in the front ranks of international pop greatness. While we rave about the Pretty Things, Creation, Move, etc., equally superb groups such as the Motions and Q65 in Holland, the Rokes in Italy, Masters Apprentices in Australia, and many others, languish unrecognized. Sweden, one of the greatest pop hotbeds of the '60s, produced groups such as the Tages, Ola & the Janglers, the Lee Kings, the Shanes, and the Lee Riders, whose work I would consider essential to any collection of '60s rock. Recently, the success of Abba has served to remind us that something of worldwide importance can arise from one of these forgotten national scenes.

With the help of Lennart Persson, one of Sweden's top pop journalists/Historians, we have put together an introductory survey of Swedish rock in the '60s. As with our similar Dutch survey (BOMP 14), this article reveals only the tip of a vast iceberg; its purpose is not to be a definitive history, only an overdue acknowledgement of a scene that produced an impressive amount of fine music.

BACKGROUND NOTES

By LENNART PERSSON

It happened in the years 1963-68; as in America and England, the golden years were 1964-66. Before that, the Swedish rock scene consisted of very bad copies of English and American hit records. Some of the big names were Rock-Ragge, Little Gerhard, and Jerry Williams. Williams (real name Erik Fernstrom) was the only one with any kind of talent, voice and originality, and when he got decent material his records were worth listening to. He made quite a few, with and without the Violents, right through the '60s.

In Sweden, as in many other countries, the appearance of the Beatles in 1964 brought a reaction against the stagnant music scene of previous years. Literally thousands of pop groups appeared from nowhere. The inspiration in music and appearance was clearly the British beat groups. Some Swedish bands (Gonks, Steampacket) even borrowed names from English groups. Such was the demand for beat music that many British groups, including the Deejays, Red Squares, Renegades and others, moved to Sweden and became much bigger stars than they could have back home. Instruments, amps and PA's were still small—the Beatles played *schools* in Sweden in 1963 with 30 watt amps!—and anybody with small hips, a passable voice or a three-chord knowledge of electric guitar could be a real pop star. At least in your own school or on your own block....

The centres of activity were Stockholm (the capitol, population about one million), Goteborg (Sweden's second largest city, about ½ million) and Malmo (third largest). There were hundreds and hundreds of pop clubs with live entertainment scattered all over the country. The groups played for peanuts—all the money went into the pockets of managers and agents. Nearly every English group also played these places. Stones, Who, Small Faces, Pretty Things, Troggs, Them, Hollies, Moody Blues, Searchers, Swinging Blue Jeans, etc.

A lot of groups made records, but very few of them sold more than to the group's families and friends. You didn't sell records by having your pic in *Bildjournalen*, the most important magazine. The most crucial step on the way towards success was "Tio i topp", a weekly radio program that went on the air live every Saturday afternoon. It was a program where 200 teenagers voted for the ten most popular single records. The program was sent from a different place in Sweden each week and many groups made "coups" to get their record on the list. The Shanes once drove to the town the program was being sent from and handed out pictures of themselves in the town square to all the town's teenagers and encouraged them to vote for their record—which they did. The Lee Kings played for free at a school dance the night before the program was broadcast from the same town.

There were lots of incidents like these and they all added a bit of fun to the proceedings, but there were nevertheless few Swedish records in the Top Ten and correspondingly not many were sold. The man behind "Tio i topp" and all of Swedish radio's pop coverage at that time was Klas Burling, a young guy who had toured with the Beatles in England before "Love Me Do" and had seen the light. He was very important in the scene. The biggest and most successful groups were the Hep Stars, Tages, Ola & the Janglers, and Shanes. The second division consisted of Mascots, Lee Kings, Hounds, Jackpots, Lucas, Slamcreepers, Shakers, Gonks, Namelosers, Maniacs, Annabee-Nox, Caretakers, Fabulous Four, Merrymen, Shamrocks, etc., etc.

THE BEST OF SWEDISH BEAT

By GREG SHAW & LENNART PERSSON

Most of the groups mentioned above, like the best punk and beat groups of any country, made some excellent records, although it was a rare exception when any of them showed the strength or imagination of the British groups who were their inspiration. But there are enough such exceptions to torment the serious fan with curiosity as to what treasures may yet remain undiscovered. And by the same token, what collector doesn't derive a slight thrill from hearing some group who never got beyond a high school in Goteborg doing a primitive version of one of his favorite Who or Kinks songs, hearing them mispronounce the lyrics, and gazing at the strangely evocative picture covers, wondering what it all must have been like?

Herewith, then, a guide to the major groups, and some of the more exciting records that came out of Sweden in the '60s.

SPOTNICKS

The Spotnicks predated the Beat era, and were in fact a Swedish response to the

Shadows era of British rock. Before Joe Meek and the Tornadoes, the Spotnicks unveiled a weird, 'spacey' sound, augmented with their use of space-suits as stage costumes, and their invention of remote-controlled stereo guitars and other technological breakthroughs. They were undoubtedly ahead of their time, thanks mainly to Bo Wimberg, an electronics genius and leader of the group. Other members were Bob Lander, Bjorn Thalin, and Ove Johansson (two of whom were replaced by Englishmen in 1963, after their decline had begun). They exploited the space image to the hit.It; one of their early hits was called "Rocket Man". Most of their material was instrumental, and during the height of the instrumental boom they toured England a couple of times, and had several hits.

Even after falling off in England, the Spotnicks remained popular elsewhere, doing a world tour that took them to Japan, Hong Kong, Mexico, Turkey and most of Europe. On this tour, they took along new member Jimmy Nicol, former replacement drummer for the Beatles. By 1970, Winberg was the only original member left, though the group was (and is) still going strong. To date, they have released over 22 albums.

(all on Karusell label)

- 340 The Old Spinning Wheel/Riders in the Sky
- 347 Orange Blossom Special/Spotnicks Theme
- 362 Rocket Man/Galloping Guitars ('62)
- 369 Old Clock at Home/Endless Walk
- 384 Ol' Man River/My Old Kentucky Home
- 405 Hey, Good Lookin'/What'd I Say
- 424 Highflying Scotsman/Thundernest
- 464 Have Nagila/Johnny Guitar
- 465 Mt Bobbie/Midnight Special
- 498 Amapola/I'm Going Home
- 510 Just Listen to my Heart/Pony Express ('63)
- LKPs: 1012 - *Out-a Space*
- 1014 - *In Paris*
- 123 - *Live in Japan*
- 125 - *In Stockholm*
- 127 - *In Winterland*
- 136 - *In Berlin*
- 137 - *In Acapulco*
- 138 - *Hey Hey, Here is the Spotnicks*
- 155 - *Psst, Baby Spotnicks are Calling*
- 157 - *By Request*
- 33 - *At Home in Gothenburg*
- 38 - *In Tokyo*
- 42 - *Around the World*

(many releases on various Dutch & British labels)

HEP STARS

Lennart is puzzled by the attention given the Hep Stars by American fans. "Most of their records are trash, and not even good trash," he says, "and worse yet, they had no *style* whatsoever. They were ugly, fat old rockers who had let their hair grow, and they had no taste in clothes. Their audience consisted of girls in their pre-teens and the lead singer was even a cripple!" True, all true. But the Hep Stars were the first Swedish group I discovered, some 5 years ago, and I thought their live album was just amazingly good. I was impressed that any Swedish group could do a live LP full of songs like "Bald Headed Woman", "If You Need Me", "Surfin' Bird", "So Mystifying" and "Farmer John", to name only a few of the highlights. There is a tremendous live atmosphere on the album, one of the best ever captured on wax.

Unfortunately, the remainder of their work fails to match this pinnacle. Most of the songs on the live album were among their early hits, but the studio versions were exceedingly lame. Best is their "Tribute to Buddy Holly", which hardly compares to Mike Berry's original. Their hit period ran thru '66, after which they made progressive records, laid-back records, added a girl singer

(with whom they had an LP released in Canada) and finally broke up. They did have one particularly odd record, a version of Curt Boettcher's "Musty Dusty" produced by Steve Clark and released on an obscure L.A. label. They also had their own label, Hep House, releasing records by many Swedish groups. But their chief claim to historical fame is having produced Benny Andersson, who began writing songs with Bjorn Ulvaeus while still in the Hep Stars, then left to start Abba. The Hep Stars made one LP without him, then disbanded.

- 65 Kana Kapila/I Got a Woman - Olga 03
- 65 Tribute to Buddy Holly/Bird Dog - Olga 04
- 65 Summertime Blues/If You Need Me - Olga 05
- 65 Farmer John/Donna - Olga 06
- 65 Cadillac/Mashed Potatoes - Olga 09
- 65 Bald Headed Woman/Lonesome Town - Olga 11
- 65 No Response/Rented Tuxedo - Olga 12
- 66 Young and Beautiful/So Mystifying - Olga 13
- 66 Should I/I'll Never Get Over You - Olga 17
- 66 Sunny Girl/Hawaii - Olga 21
- 66 Sunny Girl/When Mt Blue Moon Turns to Gold Again - Olga 25
- 67 I Natt Jag Dromde/Jag Vet - Olga 29
- 67 Don't/Consolation - Olga 33
- 67 Malaika/It's Nice to be Back - Olga 38
- 67 Mot okänt Mal/Nagonting Har Hant - Olga 49
- 68 Like You Used to Do/She Will Love You - Olga 50
- 68 Let it Be Me/Groovy Summertime - Olga 64
- 68 Tanda Pa Varann/Sagans Land - Olga 72
- 69 Spelman/Precis Som Alla Andra - Olga 87
- 69 Little Band of Gold/Another Day - Olga 93
- 69 Musty Dusty/It's Been a Long Long Time - Cupol 226
- 69 Musty Dusty/It's Now Winter's Day - Charmaker 414 (A)
- 69 Speedy Gonzales
- LPs: *Hep Stars On Stage* - Olga LPO 02
- *The Hep Stars* - Olga LPO 04
- *Golden Hits* - Olga LPO 05
- *Songs We Sang* - Olga LPO 07
- *How It All Started* - Efel 003
- *California Maiden* - Philips 6316 013

SHANES

The Shanes, on the other hand, were consistently good throughout their long career. In 1965, they were a good imitation of the Pretty Things, with a raw R&B sound. "Roadrunner" "I Don't Care Babe" and "People Don't Like Me" are among the wildest Swedish recordings. By '67 they had become more polished, and "Chris Craft #9" became a hit throughout Europe, with a sound reminiscent of the Hollies and Herman's Hermits at their best. They developed strong harmonies and continued recording in a pop vein. In 1968 they had their last hit with "Cara Mia" and then faded away.

- 64 Gunfight Saloon/The Ripper - Odeon SD 5939
- 64 Pistoleros/Oh, Wow - SD 5950
- 64 Gun Rider/Banzai - SD 5961
- 64 Keep a Knockin'/Come on Sally - SD 5968
- 64 Let Me Show You Who I Am/Say You Want Me - SD 5969
- 65 Georgia's Back in Town/My Lover Baby - Columbia DS 2256
- 65 I Don't Want Your Love/Sweet Little Rock & Roller - DS 2264
- 65 I Don't Want Your Love/New Orleans - Columbia 7601 (E)
- 65 Crazy Country Hop/My New Yorker - DS 2271
- 65 Skinny Minnie/It's All Right Baby - DS 2278
- 65 People Don't Like Me
- 65 Blue Feeling - DS 2295
- 66 I Don't Care Babe/I Like to Know - DS 2302
- 66 Hi Lili Hi Lo/Leavin' - DS 2319
- 66 Can I Trust You/Like Before - DS 2327
- 67 Chris Craft # 9/Time - DS 2339
- 67 Chris Craft # 9/Time - Capitol 5963 (A)
- 67 Drip Drop/One Way to Love - DS 2346
- 67 Cara Mia - DS 2355
- 67 No Nox/Extra Kick Theme Gulf I (promo)
- 68 Save the Last Dance For Me - DS 2359
- 68 Friday Kind of Monday/Bound for Nowhere - DS 2397
- EPs: Shanes & Moonlighters—Live! - Columbia 138: Marshall Clayton/Roadrunner
- Columbia 147: Let Me Tell Yah/You Gotta Tell Me/Too Much For Me/I Wanna Go Bowlin'

- LPs: *The Shanes* - Columbia SGLP 528
- *Let Us Show You* - Columbia SSX 1011
- *The Shane Gang* - Columbia SSX 1020
- *Shanes Again* - Columbia SSX 1022
- *Sssshanes! Explosive* - Columbia SSX 1026
- *Shanes VI* - Columbia SSX 1030

TAGES

Widely regarded by such American connoisseurs as Alan Betrock as the premier Swedish group, the Tages began by imitating the Beatles, and in fact were voted "the Beatles of the west coast" in 1963. They dressed sharp and mod, and guitarist Tommy Blom was a veritable teen idol. Besides Liverpudlian harmonies and bouncy songs ("I Should Be Glad", "The One For You"), the early Tages also had their raunch sound, as "Bloodhound" proves. By their second album, they were writing sophisticated, melodic rock ballads of the type found on *Rubber Soul*, in addition to the more straight-ahead rockers, and songs like "Guess who" combined with the best of both approached in a way that ranks with the best of the early Kinks. The Kinks were also a big influence on the raving "I'm Mad." Then again, "Understanding" on their third album is a great tribute to the early Small Faces, and their cover of "Friday On My Mind" on the same LP is super.

Their 1966 hit "Crazy Bout My Baby", a brisk, double-timed R&B harmony number, made some noise in England, and from then on their best records were on a par with the best British groups, as the Tages came to be regarded as an impending sensation. "I'm Going Out", "Every Raindrop Means A Lot" and the sublime "Treat Her Like A Lady" stand as timeless pop production classics, and they even excelled at Angloid psychedelia, as witness "Fuzzy Patterns."

They experimented, got heavy, had more hits, wrote more great songs, and lived up more than ever to their reputation as Sweden's own Beatles (every country had to have one...). Their version of the Herd's "Halcyon Days", produced in England, was even released in America, sounding a bit like "Penny Lane." Then, for whatever reason, they broke up. Two of them immediately resurfaced as a group called Blond, whose only LP was released here on Fontana, and is a fine example of late '60s European pop. Today, Blom is a scientology priest in Stockholm, and Goran Lagerberg is still playing—until recently, with a group called Kebnekaise.

```
64  Donna/Forget Him - Platina 101
64  Sleep Little Girl/Tell Me You're Mine - Platina 102
65  I Should Be Glad/I Cry - Platina 103
65  Don't Turn Your Back/Hound Dog - Platina 104
65  The One For You/I Got My Mojo Working - Platina 105
65  Bloodhound/Whatcha Gonna Do About It Platina 109
66  So Many Girls/I'm Mad - Platina 115
66  I'll Be Doggone/Hitch Hike - Platina 121
66  In My Dreams/Leaving Here - Platina 122
66  Crazy Bout My Baby/Go - Platina 125
66  Miss Mac Baren/Get Up an Get Goin - Platina 130
67  Secret Room/Friday on My Mind - Platina 131
67  Gone Too Far/Understanding - Platina 134
67  One Red, One Yellow, One Blue/True Fine Woman - Platina 139
67  Dancing in the Streets/Those Rumors - Platina 141
67  Mohair Sam/Ride Your Pony - Platina 145
67  Dr. Feelgood/Dimples - Platina 149
67  Every Raindrop Means a Lot/Look What You Get - Parlophone SD 6004
67  I'm Going Out/Fuzzy Patterns - SD 6005
67  She's Having a Baby Now/Sister's Got a Boyfriend - SD 6009
67  Treat Her Like a Lady/Wanting - SD 6011
68  There's an Old Man Playing Fiddle in the Street/Like a Woman - SD 6024
68  Fantasy Island/To Be Free - SD 6036
68  I Read You Like an Open Book/Halycon Days - SD 6054/Verve 10626 (A)
    EPs: Platina 2001: Don't Turn Your Back/Forget Him/Donna/Hound Dog
         Hits Vol 1 - Platina 2005: Sleep Little Girl/I Should Be Glad/Don't Turn Your Back/The One For You
         Hits Vol 2 - Platina 2006: In My Dreams/Bloodhound/So Many Girls/I'll Be Doggone
         Hits Vol 3 - Platina 2007: Miss Mac Baren/Crazy Bout My Baby/Secret Room/Gone Too Far
    LPs: Tages - Platina 3001
         Tages 2 - Platina 3002
         Extra Extra - Platina 3003
         Best of Tages - Platina 3005
         Forget Him - Platina 3007
         Contrast - Parlophone 313
         Studio - Parlophone 316
         Good Old Tages - Odeon 577 (Parlophone material)

(as BLOND)

68  I Wake Up and Call/The Girl I Once Had - Fontana 271 281
63  The Lilac Years/Six White Horses - Fontana 271 282
    LP: The Lilac Years - Fontana 881 015/Fontana 67607 (A)
```

OLA & THE JANGLERS

Led by Claes of Geijerstam, this group was among the most professional in Sweden, but were never as influential as the Shanes or Tages because of their reliance on British songs. Most of their early records were covers of things by the Stones, Kinks, Who, and Zombies. They recorded for Sonet, and most of their records—9 albums, plus two solo LPs by Ola Hakansson—are still in print. They did creditable versions of "Leave Me Be", "Surprise, Surprise", "We Got a Good Thing Goin'", and "She's Not There". Though most of their hits were in '65 and '66, as late as 1969 they made the American charts with "Let's Dance", prompting the release of a generally worthless album on these shores. Ola now leads a ballroom band, while Claes recently toured America with his group Rocket, and is a successful producer (Svenne & Lotta, etc.).

```
65  No No No
65  She's Not There
65  Land of 1,000 Dances/Thinking of You - Gazell 167
65  Surprise, Surprise/It's All Right - Gazell 172
66  Love Was On Your Mind/Stop Your Sobbing - Gazell 175
66  Donna Donna/Come and Stay With Me - Gazell 180
66  La La La/Can't You Feel - Gazell 183
66  Poetry in Motion/We've Got a Groovy Thing Goin' - Gazell 186
66  Alex is the Man/Now I Like Her - Gazell 190
67  Bird's Eye View of You/No One Knows What Happens - Gazell 191
67  Strolling Along/Story of Glory - Gazell 197
67  Runaway/Teardrops - Gazell 200
68  Juliet/This Ring - Gazell 202
68  I Can Wait/Eeny Meeny Miny Moe - Gazell 204
68  I Can Wait - London 20034 (A)
68  Julia/Desertoren - Gazell 206
68  What I Heard Today/Under the Ground - Gazell 208
68  What a Way to Die/Oh What a Lovely Day - Gazell 212
68  Tracks of my Tears/Farewell My Love - Gazell 219
68  Let's Dance/Hear Me - Gazell 220
69  Let's Dance - GNP 423 (A)
69  California Sun - GNP 432
    LPs: Surprise, Surprise - Sonet GP 9928
         12 Big Hits - Sonet GP 9939
         Discotheque Number One - Sonet GP 9949
         Patterns - Sonet GMG 1204
         Limelight - Sonet GMG 1205
         Pictures & Sounds - Sonet GMG 1208
         Underground - Sonet GMG 1211
         Let's Dance - Sonet GMG 1214/GNP 2050 (A)
         Happily Together - Sonet GMG 1217
(Claes of Geijerstam)
    LP: Out of My Hair - Sonet SLP 2518
```

LEE KINGS

The Lee Kings, also known as Lenne & the Lee Kings, had a large hit with the pulsing "L.O.D.", released two very interesting albums, and also made (in my opinion) the hands-down greatest Swedish record ever. "On My Way" takes its inspiration from "My Generation" and "Anyway Anyhow Anywhere" but moves ahead with stunning originality to carve its own niche in the rave-up/distortion hall of fame. I can't even begin to do this record justice; it's simply devasting.

Of their two albums, the one on Sonet contains predictable covers of "Like a Rolling Stone" and other familiar songs, but the one on RCA is one of the best all-round LPs by any Swedish group. There's a strong Byrds influence, 12-strings and harmonies, with "It's Not Right" and "Smile For Me" being special standouts. "Why Why Why" even reminds me of the Monkees. What higher praise could there be?

```
66  L.O.D./It's Rainin' - Gazell 173
66  Stop the Music - Gazell
    Sticks and Stones - Jukebox EP 5548
    Always & Ever - Jukebox EP 5559
    On My Way
    Concrete and Clay/Outside - RCA 755
67  Smile for Me/Take a Message to Mary - RCA 786
67  Hot Dogs/Come on Home - RCA 788
    LPs: Bingo - RCA 10106
         Stop the Music - Sonet GP 9911
         Beat Hits 65/66 - Sonet GP 9907: Like a Rolling Stone
```

MASCOTS

The Mascots are also special favorites of mine, primarily due to "Words Enough to Tell You", which I find as essential to life itself as my very favorite Hollies records such as "Yes I Will", in the same vein. It's a classic of Liverpool-style pop, with beautiful harmonies and even authentic-sounding scouse accents. Most of their records were a little rougher, more in the Swingin' Blue Jeans style, such as "Baby Baby" and "Stones Fell". I'm particularly fond of "The Girl That You Are", a driving, insistent rocker whose picture cover depicts the group standing on their amps with nooses around their necks. Swedish picture covers, incidentally, are among the best-designed of any I've seen, and a large part of the pleasure in collecting these records. Getting back to the Mascots, the one album by them I've found doesn't seem to have any of their singles on it, although it does contain some marvelous material.

```
65  A Sad Boy - Decca
65  Baby, Baby/Call Me Your Love - Decca 44420
65  Stones Fell/From My Love - Decca 44442
66  Woman/Meet Me - Decca 44512
66  I Want to Live/Different Mind - Decca 44518
66  Things are Turning Out/The Girl That You Are - Decca 44521
66  Words Enough to Tell You - Decca
67  If I Had a ship/Everyone Knows for Sure - Polydor 59748
69  You're Never Gonna Find Me/A Life Like That - Parlophone 6064
    LP: Elpee - Decca SKL 4806
```

LEA RIDERS GROUP

Not much is known about this group, but from the evidence of the 3 singles I've found, they must have been Sweden's weirdest bunch of maniacs, their country's own Mothers or Deviants. Their earliest record, "Got *No* Woman!" is a garage-primitive R&B tune. Next time out they had "Ain't It Strange?", for which they take composer credit, although it's identical to a rather sickly demented record called "History Repeats Itself", done by Buddy Starcher on the Boone label in April of '66. The idea of the song is to catalogue the similarities in the circumstances of the assassinations of Lincoln and Kennedy. I find this perfectly straight rendition, by a Swedish mod group, just slightly inexplicable.

The capper, though is "Dom Kallar Oss Mods". The B-side of "The Forgotten Generation" (whose lyrics are printed in English on the sleeve), it's from a film of the same title that must have been the mod classic of Sweden. Although I called "I'm On My Way" by the Lee Kings the best Swedish record, this must certainly be the most advanced. I'd say honestly it's the most successful record by anyone, anywhere, trying to capture the sensation of being drugged and psychedelicized. It's nothing like Pink Floyd or the Strawberry Alarm Clock or anything obvious like that; I really don't know how to describe it. It's a long record, over 4 minutes, and one of the most intense recording I've ever heard. The lyrics, about being a confused, dope-addled teenage failure, are right up there with the best of Townshend, and the delivery is inspired—demented, yet completely controlled. I get dizzy just listening to it. Never in any Hollywood exploitation movie was a bad trip so graphically or successfully dramatized. It's an astonishingly vivid record by a group (and from a film) that really ought to have been exposed outside Sweden.

66 Got *No* Woman!/But I Am, and Who Cares? - Philips 350 297
66 Ain't It Strange/Beloved Baby - Philips 350 313
67 The Forgotten Generation/Dom Kallar Oss Mods - Philips 350 334

LOOSE ENDS

I have yet to hear more than a sampling of the more obscure Swedish groups, so without trying to be comprehensive, I'll just mention a few of my favorites. The Renegades weren't obscure, of course, having scored one of the biggest domestic hits with "Cadillac", that old warhorse of a tune that was done by just about every Scandinavian group. Their other records weren't nearly as good. Similarly, the Jackpots were quite popular in Sweden, and even had records released in the U.S., but although they sported gorgeous falsetto harmonies (and were even produced at one time by Perry Ford of the Ivy League), the same fans who gobble up groups like Harmony Grass seem unaware of how delightful the Jackpots were. They covered material by the 4 Seasons, Beach Boys, the Tokens, the Shirelles and others, and their LPs, which can occasionally be found, are well worth the investment.

A lot of groups never recorded much, yet had one or two outstanding songs. One wonders why some made it and others didn't.

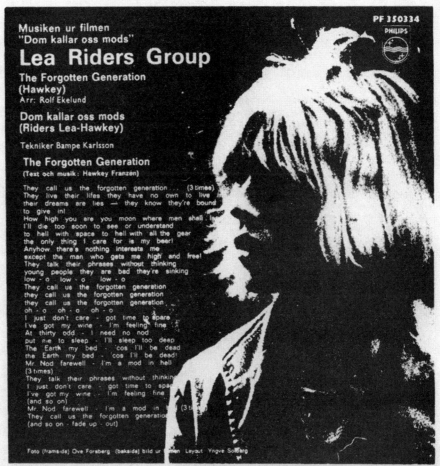

• Freaking out on the Fjords: The protest generation in Sweden had problems Sonny & Cher never dreamed of!

The Shamrocks, for instance, were as good as the early Shanes, in fact as good as any English Marquee Club group. Their "Midnight Train" raves out like Cyril Davies' "Country Line Special", one of the alltime primo R&B sizzlers, or anything by the early Yardbirds. Or how about the Namelosers, whose "Do-ao" is a high voltage masterpiece in the same vein. Their other stuff, especially "Night of a Thousand Dances" is equally raw and exciting.

The Shivers did a fine cover of the Sorrows' "No No No No". "Take Her Any Time" by Steampacket is a nicely-fuzzed rocker. "Mister Mystified" by the Evil Eyes is another Who cop, somewhere between "My Generation" and "Happy Jack". "Ann-Louise" by the Nashmen is a charming (though low-keyed) effort in the early Searchers style. "I Could Hear Her Cry" by the Flippers reminds me of the Kinks doing "Long Tall Shorty." "She Lied to Me" by Jean Lundens could have been by any one of your favorite English groups—a polished sound. "Hard to Forget" by the Moderations is an intriguing record that sounds like Peter Noone backed by the McCoys, with the Larks on backing vocals.

And we mustn't forget Tom & Mick & the Maniacs, who had all kinds of hit records together and separately, and were apparently the Paul & Barry Ryan of Sweden. Their "Instant Sorrow" and "Pandemonium" should not be missed.

Some groups arouse interest with their names alone, or the names of their songs. It's a well-known fact that some pretty deviated stuff tends to develop in the musical backwaters. What would you expect, for instance, from a group called the Slam Creepers doing "Mister Personality Man"/"Cash Box Ladies Behavious"? Or how about a group with a name like the He-Goats? Only in Sweden!

We realize, naturally, that unless you have a friend in Sweden, few of the records discussed in this article are ever likely to come your way. But fortunately, there is an album entitled *Swedish Graffutu* containing 32 representative hits by almost everyone mentioned here. Not in every case the songs I would have chosen, but a solid introduction along the lines of *Hard-Up Heroes*, with great liner notes (in Swedish, unfortunately), lots of photos, etc. It's put out by Sonet, who also keep most of their old material in print, and might send you a catalog if you write to Sonet Records, Hornsbruksgaten 3A, 117 34 Stockholm, Sweden.

THE BEAT BOOM ENDS

Sometime around 1969 there was a change. By that time all the groups had folded or badly compromised in their music—witness for example the Hep Stars' "Speleman", which by the way was one of the first Bjorn/Benny collaborations. The Tages was the one example among the big groups who didn't try to change their music to appeal to the kind of middle-aged audience the Hep Stars were after.

A new kind of group began appearing as part of the worldwide reaction to the Beatles-inspired pop wave. Yes, the nemisis we know as "progressive rock" had raised its boring head. The heroes changed from Hollies and Kinks to Zappa and John McLaughlin, as groups got more political, more "serious", more concerned with its lyrics and jazz influences. The progressive scene has grown in Sweden and is today quite strong with groups like Hoola Bandoola Band selling more records than the Tages ever dreamed of. Only one of these groups, Nationalteatern, is much good, and none of them can compete with Abba—whose music, by the way, they all loathe and call reactionary crap. The real curse of Swedish rock today is the incorporation of influences from Swedish folk music, rather than from British and American rock and R&B, an approach which brought out the best in Swedish musicians during the golden years we've been discussing.

For a less biased view of modern Swedish rock, we present the following short survey by a man who actually listens to progressive rock(!):

PROGRESSIVE MUSIC IN SWEDEN

By TOM LONG

Since the late '60s progressive rock has been knocking on the doors of almost every country on the glove. Sweden, in particular, boasts one of the most progressive scenes around. Many fine groups are now plugging their way through Scandinavia playing jazz rock or redoing traditional folk songs of Swedish origin.

Groups like Kebnaijse and Flasket Brinner whose roots go back to such mid-and late-'60s groups as Blond and the Mecki Mark Men are typical of where Swedish progressive rock is at today. Bo Hansson (late of Hansson and Carlson group), Janne Schaffet (who records with Abba), George Wadenuis (late of Made In Sweden and BS&T) were all members of some of Sweden's short-lived '60s bands. Some of these artists are turning out some of the best music in the western world, and deserve to be better known.

For those that have never heard of this stuff, here is a short discography of current Swedish groups:

Kebnekaijse - Resa mot okant mal
　　　　　Kebnaiaijse 2
　　　　　Kebnekaijse 3
Flasket Brinner - Flasket Dbl. LP
　　　　　Flasket Brinner
Janne Schaffer - Janne Schaffer
　　　　　Andra LP
　　　　　Pop Workshop Vol 1 & Vol 2
Bo Hansson - Sogan om Ringer
　　　　　Urtrollkarlens Hat
　　　　　Mellanvasen
Nature - Nature
　　　　　Earth Mover
　　　　　Nature #3
November - En Ny Tid an Har
　　　　　6:E November
　　　　　2:a November
Sage - Saga

Here are some shops who sell these and many other LPs by mail order:

　　Musikens Makt
　　Sam Distribution
　　Fack 185 00
　　Varholm, Sweden

　　Nick Strom
　　Olivedalsgaten 27
　　413 10 Goteberg, Sweden

　　Lars Ake Hjort
　　Lundbergsgatan 5
　　217 51 Malmo, Sweden

SWEDISH ROCK DISCOGRAPHY
(all Swedish releases unless otherwise noted)

ANNABEE-NOX
66　Jump Right Down/The Kids Are Alright - Columbia DS 2304
67　Ain't Gonna Let You Be/Silverspoon - Columbia DS 2348
67　Playboy on the Run/Corinna, Corrina - Columbia DS 2367

CARETAKERS
66　The End of the World/Whitsand Bay - SweDisc 1151
66　Lost Someone/Hey - SweDisc 1169
66　Unchained Melody/All You Got To Do - SweDisc 1178
　　Lenhovda City - Juke Box EP 5559
　　Secret Love - Jukebox EP 5562
　　LP: *Have a Ball With* - SweDisc 51

DEEJAYS
65　Long Tall Shorty/I Can Tell - Polydor 10980
65　Farmer John/I Just Can't Go to Sleep - Polydor 10983
65　Blackeyed Woman - Polydor
65　Coming on Strong/Dimples - Polydor 56034 (E)
　　Dum Dum/Picture of You - Hep House 01
　　Somewhere, My Love/It's Gonna Work Out Fine - Hep House 06
　　I'll Never Get Over You/Baby Talk - Hep House 07
　　Working Out Fine/Love Me - Hep House 26
　　LP: *The Deejays* - Polydor LPHM 46254

FABULOUS FOUR
　　Anita Change Your Mind/Sitting in the Grass - Hep House 19
　　Brown Eyed Girl/Life is Fab - Hep House 27
66　Puff the Magic Dragon - Hep House
67　Don't Go Out Into the Rain
67　Island in the Sun
67　Rhythm of the Rain
　　Quello Con Gli Occhiali (Get out of My Life Woman)/Fatti il Segno Della Croce - Fontana TF 268013 (It.) (sung in Italian)

GONKS
　　Keep Your Big Mouth Shut/I Believe in Your Love - Nashville 846
66　Words - on sampler LP *Package of Sound* - PRO 5001
67　Loppan/No Doubt - Tommo TPS 2
　　Things I Give to You/Happy Crowd - TPS 4
　　We're Still Happy/Four or Five Times - TPS 8
　　Happy Crowd/St. Louis Blues - TPS 13
　　Georgia on my Mind/Work Song - GP GPS 1003
　　In a Persian Market/Going Round - GP GPS 1005

HOUNDS
67　Short Days, Long Nights - Jukebox EP 5566
67　The Lion Sleeps Tonight - Gazell
67　Exodus
67　A Summer Song
67　Sealed With a Kiss
68　The Gypsy Cried
　　Can't Grow Peaches on a Cherry Tree/The Office Girl - CSL 102(A)
　　LP: *The Lion Sleeps Tonight* - Sonet GP 9941
　　　　Beat Hits 66/67 - Sonet GP 9914: Barbara Ann/Sloop John B/Til the End of the Day

JACKPOTS
66　Younger Girl
67　Funny How Love Can Be - Jukebox EP 5566
67　Walk Like a Man
67　Tiny Goddess
68　Back to the City
　　Jack in the Box/Henbanes Sacrifice - Sire 4113 (A)
　　LPs: *Tic Tac Toe* - Sonet SLP 57
　　　　Jack in the Box - Sonet SLP 68

LOLLIPOPS
　　Words Ain't Enough/Who Cares About Me - Vault 926(A)
　　Do You Know/There Was a Time - Karusell 573
　　Lollipops Shake/Look at the Boy - Karusell 581
65　Little Bad Boy/Don't Matter What You Do - Karusell 603
66　Birthday Party - Jukebox EP 5535
66　Words Ain't Enough/Who Cares About Me - Polydor 59711
67　Naked When You Come/Little Cat Lost - Polydor 59724
67　Another Girl/You Don't Have to Go - Polydor 59730
67　I Can't Live Without Your Loving/Swing and Sway - Polydor 59737
　　Sussy Moore/Love - Fontana 271 603
　　EP: Karusell 3322: Lollipops Boogie/Speedy Gonzalez/Birthday Party/All My Loving

MANIACS
66　Don't Worry Baby/Someone to Care - Columbia DS 2329
　　Dear Mr. Jones
　　(Tom & Mick Maniacs)
67　Somebody's Taken Maria Away/I Got the Feelin' - DS 2361
67　Can I Get to Know You Better/Free - DS 2368
68　I(Who Have Nothing) - DS 2376
68　24 Hours From Tulsa/Koko Joe - Sonet 7731
　　LPs: *Tom & Mick Maniacs* - Columbia SSX 1029
　　　　Someone's Taken Maria Away - Sonet GP 9968

NAMELOSERS
65　New Orleans/What'd I Say - Columbia DS 2255
65　The Dog/But I'm So Blue - DS 2261
65　Night of 1,000 Dances/Suzie Q - DS 2286
　　EP: Viking label: New Orleans/Bama Lama Bama Loo/What'd I Say/Around and Around

NEW GENERATION
68　Two Faces Have I - Gazell
69　Peaches and Cream - Jukebox EP 5589
　　Candy/Just Give it to Me - Sonet 7728

RENEGADES
65　Cadillac/Every Minute of the Day - Polydor 56508 (E)
65　Cadillac/Matelot - Congress 241 (A)
　　Thirteen Women/Walking Down the Street - Polar/President 106 (E)
　　Take a Heart - Polar
　　Take a Message/Second Thoughts - Parlophone 5592 (E)
　　LP: *Cadillac* - Scandia 600
　　(rumored to be 3 LPs in Finland)

SHAMROCKS
65　Cadillac/Easy Rider - Karusell 608
66　Smokerings/I'm on the Outside Looking In - Karusell 691
66　Travellin' Man/Gypsy Lullabye - Karusell 727
66　Crossbow/Midnight Train - Hansa 19186 (Gr)
　　EP: Polydor Intl. 60 124(Fr): Don't Say/Days/Smoke Rings/How the Flies
　　EP: Polydor Intl. 60 122(Fr): Cadillac/Easy Rider/Thing Will Turn Out Right TOmorrow/Balla Balla

STREAPLERS
63　Diggiti Doggety - Columbia
63　Sakkijarven Polka
64　Mule Skinner Blues
65　Rockin' Robin
　　Get It
68　For Dig Jag Kanner Just Ingenting - Columbia 2357

SUZIE (Married to Lee Kings bassist Mike Watson)
63　Johnny Loves Me - Sonet
　　Don't Let It Happen Again - Jukebox EP 5548
70　Walking Back to Happiness

SVENNE & LOTTA
　　Bang-a-Boomerang
　　Dance - MGM 14779 (A)
　　LPs: *Oldies But Goodies* - Polar 251
　　　　Svenne & Lotta/2 - Polar 258

(continued on p. 57)

FEEDBACKKKKKKK
letters

JUST A KISS AWAY

Does the word "Entmoot" mean anything to you? That question and others of the same variety have been going through my mind for some time now. I mean, names like Jay Kinney, Tom Dupree, Lenny Kaye, and of course Paul Williams keep popping up in the rock press and it finally registered: science fiction fandom grew up and became rock & roll fandom!

I suppose I first started suspecting things when I saw words like fanzine and fandom in Rolling Stone and being aghast at the fact that my secret organization was suddenly common knowledge... Great Ghu!! Fanzine reviews and a lettercol to boot, in a rock & roll magazine yet!!

At one point in my life, sci-fi fandom was all I lived for. But something happened. I started a band and my ego was being satiated far more than it had ever been. Since that time ('69 or '70) I've been in this band, and I've gotten to see the world and all the rest of that, but I always did miss the fanzines. And you've done it Shaw: managed to combine the best of two worlds.

Some suggestions: how about a piece on the Music Machine (the influence of those leather gloves had much to do with Kiss, as did their "Talk, Talk") and one on the Easybeats too, please!!

I don't herald the coming of the Runaways (as I do that of the Silver Surfer, for instance) but I do think their existence is essential to all future girl bands. A respectable first step, say I. If you don't like their record, you can always hang out backstage and try to make it with them—something I intend on doing, purely as a religious experience, you understand.......

—Gene Simmons
c/o Rock Steady Management
New York, NY

[Thanks for your letter Gene. We haven't written about your group yet, but in another 5 years the history of blitzkrieg rock in the mid '70s will make a great story. It's a real surprise to find a fellow former SF fan in such an unlikely place, but I'm glad you can appreciate some of BOMP's more subtle aspects. By the way, we've got an interview with Vanda & Young and a complete Easybeats history coming up very shortly—Ed.]

CHICAGO

New issue was great, your best yet. The Chicago section turned out quite well. Allow me, however, to correct a few things. Bill Traut of Dunwich claims that "Gloria" sold only 750,000, while Shadows of Knight lead singer Jim Sohns said recently that cumulative sales are over a million and a quarter. The list of Dunwich productions are not all Traut efforts. Jim Golden produced Keith Everett, Ken Nordine and the New World Congregation. Bob Monaco produced Crow. Also, Traut is not producing Natalie Cole as reported.

I caught the Shadows of Knight twice recently, and they were great. Fans might like to know that they do a 30-minute version of "Gloria" with riffs stolen from everyone from Dick Dale to Lenny Kaye (Sohns loves Patti Smith's version of the song).

Apparently Mike Thom wasn't aware that the Ides of March and the Cryan Shames were merged for a short while last year as the Ides-Shames Union. Peterik's Shy Rhythm Section has an album in the can for Epic, and the Shames have reunited sans Fairs and Guillory.

—Cary Baker
Wilmette, Ill.

FAVE RAVES

The new issue of BOMP is a stunner! I was particularly enchanted with Greg Shaw's Flamin' Groovies review. Obviously, the LP is brilliant, but the review is just as strong in its own right. The passages on adapting past songs, and the final paragraph on what separates good from great songs, are incredible. Robert Christgau should be forced to read the review until he finally understands what rock & roll is about.

—Stephen Neill
Carson, CA

CHICAGO II

I have a few comments on the Chicago survey. The Dunwich story brings up an interesting point that bears further examination: censorship. Clark Weber, as program director of WLS, was reluctant to put anything even remotely off-color on the air. The "Gloria" thing was a setup, where he played the record, deplored the 'suggestive' lyrics, and asked for opinions from listeners. WLS censored many records during this period, including "Rhapsody in the Rain" by Lou Christie, which they flatly refused to play. Meanwhile, CFL was playing it to death. When "Hold On" by the Mauds came out in the spring of '67, WLS refused to play it due to the lyrics "Hold on, I'm coming..." The group had to provide WLS with a special version where they sang "Hold on, don't you worry". Incidentally, about that time Van Morrison's "Brown Eyed Girl" was also censored, with the line "Makin' love in the green grass behind the stadium" altered to "Laughin' and a-runnin' behind the stadium" and this version actually showed up on the mono version of the album. It all seems silly now, doesn't it?

The Baker-Lind story states the Shadows of Knight's "Willie Jean" was a hit, which it wasn't, making an anemic #26 on CFL's top 30 for one week only. Also, you might note that "Oh Yeah" on the first Shadows LP is not the same version of "Oh Yeah" released on the single. The 45 version is in true stereo on the Nuggets album.

Unfortunately, it seems the people doing the stories on the New Colony Six and the Cryan Shames had only the Whitburn book of national charts to go on. Actually these two groups were much more successful in Chicago than is reflected in the Billboard Top 100.

Mike Thom's story on the Cryan Shames contains one glaring goof: "Georgia" was hardly "a fairly obscure single" since the flip was actually the A side: "Mr. Unreliable" was a top 10 record in Chicago, in April '67. "I Wanna Meet You", which Thom notes "failed to burn up the charts, peaking at #85" was also top 10 locally.

As for the New Colony Six, the national charts do not reflect their hometown impact either. "I Confess" and "I Love You So Much" were monsters, making #3 and #2 respectively, and many of their other 45's did reasonably well.

—Mike Callahan
Falls Church, VA

HOT COMBS AND BON BONS

I've been collecting records since 1959, when I was turned onto it by my then-best friend, Lenny Kaye. Our earliest Flatbush, Brooklyn singing group consisted of Lenny, myself and one Harvey Citrin, who was later the lead singer/guitarist for the Rick Brand (ex-Left Banke) managed group, Life. We did killer versions of the Passions' "I Only Want You" and the Visions' "Teenager's Life."

At any rate, in 1965 the aforementioned Harvey Citrin and myself were pushing a demo we had made called "The Mouse" to cash in on the popularity of Soupy Sales and the mouse dance that he did. In our travels up and down Broadway we met one slick agent named Ron Schubert.

To sum up Ron in one sentence, he was the first person I know that used a hot comb. He took interest in our song and tried to push it for us. Quite naturally, he would tell us about other acts he was working with. One of these acts was a female group that used to do demos for the songs subsequently recorded by the Shangri-Las. I believe this group was the Bon Bons, mentioned as Shangs sound-alikes in the last BOMP.

—Stephen Bennett
Brooklyn, NY

About the Shangri-Las: remember an Ellie Greenwich quote concerning the death of the girls? Is this true? Also, I vaguely recall seeing the Shangs at one time having 3 girls in the backup rather than the classic 2. Any idea?

—Tim Doherty
Pacific Palisades, CA

[At one time, there were indeed 4 Shangri-Las, but I don't know the exact story. I have heard though that Ellie Greenwich is putting together or writing songs for a "new" group of Shangs, and that Shadow Morton is somehow involved. Further reports as they come in....]

WELL YOU HEARD ABOUT THE BOSTON...

I'm writing concerning the Boston/New England article in BOMP #14. There were two important areas which the article didn't touch. The first was AAA Recording Studios, located just outside the Combat Zone (Boston's adult entertainment district). In the following discography of Boston singles, some are listed as being recorded at AAA, and the rest seem to follow a pattern of matrix numbers:

Tallysmen - "Little By Little"/"You Don't Care About Me - Tally 200,688/9
Head & the Hares - "I Won't Come Back"/"One Against the World" - H&H 200,891/2
Twin Della - "Nancy"/"Love Em and Leave Em - Twin-Dells Records 201, 022/3
No Mads - "Breaking Free"/"Liverpool Lover" - Battle of the Bands 201,353/4
Chain Reactions - "What Am I Supposed to Do"/"Life" - Francais 201, 436/7
Violets of Dawn - "Violets of Dawn"/"Wind is Wind" - Vecchia 201, 449/50
The Collage - "Best Friend"/"Girl Don't Tell Me" - Coliseum 201, 468/9
Whirlwinds - "Let Her Know"/"Any Old Time" - Parsay 2002

Also possibly connected are these already listed in your article:
Minets - "Secret of Love"/"Together" - Rock It 200, 054/5
Cobras - "Come On Back/Summertime - Feature 201, 264/5

Also, no mention of Minuteman Records except for Improper Bostonians releases. I have 3 earlier releases, and it appears Chip Taylor and Al Gorgoni were involved in all 3:
200 - Don Thomas - "Turn Her Around"/"Do You Wanna Know"
203 - Just Us - "I Can't Grow Peaches"/"I Can Save You"
205 - The Doorway Through - "Springtime"/"Keep Talking River"

Don Thomas played guitar on Just Us LP on Kapp. Just Us were of course Gorgoni and Taylor, "Peaches" was a big hit in Jan '66, and picked up nationally by Colpix (803), hitting #55 in Cashbox 4/16/66. The Doorway Through had a girl singer, both sides are quiet folk rock.

—Ed Bangs
Charlestown, MA

WHATEVER HAPPENED TO FESTIVALS?

Regarding the Pop Festival of 6-3-63 at Hayes mentioned under Ray Anton in your British Encyclopedia, I was there and still have the programme! You may like to know the order in which the acts appeared: Blue Diamonds; Ray Anton; Mickie Most; the Golli Golli Boys; Jimmy Crawford & the Raven; Johnny, Mike & the

DAVE EDMUNDS SEZ:

I HEAR YOU KNOCKIN' BUT YOU CAN'T COME IN — UNLESS YOU'RE WEARIN' A BOMP T-SHIRT!

```
SEND CASH, CHECK OR MONEY ORDER
MAIL TO:
BOMP, PO Box 7112, Burbank, CA 91510

Please send me ☐ BOMP T-shirts at $3.50 ea.

Size: ☐ Sm  ☐ Med  ☐ Lg  ☐ X-lg.

All shirts high quality white with blue trim
```

[Add postage: .35 (US&Can.)/.80 (overseas)]

Join the fabulous FLAMIN' GROOVIES Fan Club!

YOU GET:
* Membership card
* Newsletters
* Special book
* 2-color lapel button, large
* Press kit with photo, bio, etc.

Send $7 to P.O. Box 7112, Burbank, CA 91510

MILK & COOKIES FAN CLUB
729 Arbuckle
Woodmere, NY 11598

more FEEDBACK

Shades; Jackie Lynton & the Teenbeats; the Cresters; Robb Storme & the Whispers; Del Shannon; Cherry Rolland; Cliff bennett & the Rebel Rousers; Screaming Lord Sutch & His Savages; Billy J. Kramer & the Dakotas; Tony Holland & the Packabeats; Vince Taylor & the Playboys; Freddie & the Dreamers; Brian Poole & the Tremeloes; Eden Kane. Each act played from ten minutes to a half hour. Mickie Most had just returned from S. Africa after 11 #1s of Buddy Holly covers. He was pretty bad.

—Dave Germardi
Middlesex, UK

IN MEMORY OF KEITH RELF

Remember the Yardbirds—all of them. In my area it takes a long time to confirm outside obscurities and the death of Keith Relf seems to be just that, just as his career was obscured by circumstance. Besides giving one of the new rock poets the opportunity to say something typically (in)appropriate, the article that gave me the pre-mortem opinions made much mention of guitarists. While the Big 3 are all fine technicians and Jeff Beck has gone beyond the limitations of rock & blues progressions, it's about time Relf got some credit, at least in his own obituary.

In 1964, when everybody from over there hit over here, they all came on like Junior Jr. Parkers. Keith Yardbird had like most British bruiser-bluesers vocal limitations; not much range, power, etc. But he came up with a style totally unique. A master of off-key intonation, incredibly strange phrasing, a nasal-slur, with just a hint of Slim Harpo and equally creative harp playing.

Along with Phil May, he was the main prototype for American punk-rock. Count 5's singer wins the all-time Relf-resemblance-riff for the howl between the 1st and 2nd verses of "Teeny Bopper, Teeny Bopper".

When fame came to the guitar alumni, 'Kent' Relf was written off with other misspelled band members (who could ever forget S. Smith-McCartney and good ole Ereja/Drega) as "picking up the odds & ends in the background".

In the eyes of many he was "Mr. Zero". In Sept. '71, I and a few friends asked 74 college students if they knew who he was. 3 did. Perhaps he himself didn't conceive his better side, and while Renaissance is lovely, Armageddon was just that after a wait of half a decade.

For Keith Relf, his present fame may lie in being a kind of king of those shooting stars of the '60s the public has forgotten, never known or understood. Roky Erickson, Tommy Hall, Syd Barrett, Arthur Lee, Sean Bonniwell, Mayo Thompson, Sky Saxon and on into the deep. Thank you for reminding us of our roots, as deep as some of them go.

—Brent Hosier
Richmond, VA

NOTHING ESCAPES OUR READERS

In case you haven't turned it up yet, Cynthia Weil's early solo record was "The Toddle"/"Miss Prim's Theme" by Miss Prim & the Classroom Kids, on Amy 872. Both sides Mann-Weil-Mike Anthony, produced by Barry Mann. Good novelty disc—even has a few token "bomps" thrown in for good measure!

—David Gnerre
Fontana, CA

HELP ANYONE?

Seeing that 1966 hit list for WBZ Radio reminded me of my desire to locate old surveys from stations in LA where I grew up. Can you help me locate these? I need KRJ lists from #1 (mid-1965, I think) through 1969, and KRLA from as far back as 1963, to its discontinuation in the early '70s.

—Michael Devich
Box 659, Lake Isabella, CA

DANDELION WILL MAKE YOU WISE...

I was really pleased to read, in BOMP 15, praise for some of the stuff Mike Hart recorded for Dandelion. It's most frustrating to work on records you believe to have some real merit only to see them ignored by the folks lining up for the newie from Purple or the Zeps. Mike Hart Bleeds sold, I think, about 800 copies, and the single fared even worse.

I wonder if any of your corps of loony readers ever managed to get into Stack Waddy (or Stackwaddy—we were never sure which) who made two tempestuous LPs for us?

I am, I'm afraid, an irregular reader of BOMP—not because there is anything wrong with it, but because reading it makes me fretful, over-anxious and envious. How can there be so many fine records which have contrived over the years to avoid my acquisitive clutches?

Finally, can anyone help me find a record by an Oklahoma band, Dann Uankee & the Carpetbaggers? I used to work with them a lot in the mid-'60s when I was John Ravencroft and working for KOMA. They only made one single and I can't remember what label it was on. Titles were "Roll Over Beethoven" and "If You Gotta Go, Go Now."

—John Peel
London, England

[Appreciate the comments, John, and if it's any consolation, we don't have all the records written about in BOMP either; not by any means. Nobody ever will, I'm afraid. As for the Carpetbaggers, that's one I never heard, but rest assured the second copy that comes my way will be instantly forwarded to you! I'm sure many of our readers are familiar with Stackwaddy, but for any who aren't, their two British-only LPs are a must. They were like a heavy metal, punk version of Dr. Feelgood, 5 years ago. Their songs included "You Really Got Me", "Rosalyn", "It's All Over now", "I'm a Lover Not a Fighter", "Long Tall Shorty", "Bring It to Jerome", "Mystic Eyes" and "The Girl From Ipanema"....]

WHOSE PARTY?

It was great seeing an article on Lesley Gore. I'd like to make a few comments: According to an interview Lesley did a couple years ago, she did not "sing at her best friend's 16th birthday party." At that time she was into jazz. She had a cousin who played drums and was in a group. One day she was present when the group's vocalist called and told the cousin she couldn't make it to some Italian wedding they were supposed to do in Queens. Her cousin asked Lesley to come and join them, and this was the first time she sang publicly.

She worked with the group awhile and one night Quincy Jones heard them. That was the beginning of "It's My Party." Lesley mentioned that she heard the "birthday party" story before and believes it was some kind of Mercury promotion gimmick. The fact was that Quincy and she sat down and listened to about 200 demos after they had already decided to record. "It's My Party" was among the songs they decided to cut.

Also, as a point of interest, two of her biggest hits were written by a fellow who has recently become quite famous: Marvin Hamlisch. He co-wrote "Sunshine, Lollipops and Rainbows" and "California Nights."

—Suzanne Dreyfus
Bronx, NY

Dear Ann Landers,

Last night I had a party for my fifteenth birthday, so naturally I invited my boyfriend Johnny. Well, after a little while nobody knew where he'd gone, but my best friend Judy had left the same time. When they finally came back an hour and a half later, they were holding hands and Judy was wearing his ring! I was so upset I just sat down and cried my eyes out. My friends tell me that that was a foolish thing to do, but I say that it's my party and I should be able to cry if I want to. Who is right?

Leslie

Dear Leslie,

I can understand how you felt, but it wasn't proper for you to cry just then. A hostess should conceal her feelings and make sure that her guests are having a good time. I hope you will be big-hearted about this and not let it come between you and your girlfriend. Good luck and thanks for writing.

Ann Landers.

THE BON BONS—and did you ever see such four living, breathing, singing, dancing DOLLS. Come on, Baby, their first recording on the Coral label, skyrocketed them to overnight fame. You'll be hearing lots about these teens.

THE REAL BON BONS!

Concerning the Shangri-Las/Bon Bons rumor, this photo appeared in the Aug. '64 issue of *Teen Life*. A bogus group of Shangri-Las recently played a nearby club doing disco versions of the hits. A few years ago, the real group (Mary at least) looked and sounded great at a Murray the K tribute show. Aside from being on 2 of his live albums, they also appear on a Gus Gossert album which includes the lines: "Is he picking you up after the show tonight?" "No, he's dead."

—Billy Miller
Carle Place, NY

ON GETTING TOGETHER

I recently tried ordering the book *All Together Now* from a book store, and was told I had to write directly to the publisher. I did so, and received a note saying they were completely sold out and wouldn't have more copies for at least 5 weeks. But if anyone else is interested in obtaining the book [*with its nearly complete Beatle recording data, as reviewed in BOMP #15*], they should write to Pierian Press, 5000 Washtenaw Ave, Ann Arbor, MI 48104. It costs $14.95, cloth bound.

—Mike Schaalma
Fond du Lac, WI

PICKY PICKY

While admiring the efforts in assembling a 'complete' Encyclopedia of British Rock—a painstaking work for which you are to be congratulated —it must be said that some of the information in your listings is sadly inaccurate.

The assumption, for instance, that Irish-born B.P. (Bernard Patrock) Fallon was in any way involved in the Anglos 45 from 1965 is fanciful, as he didn't come to England until 1966—to work in a bakery. No, the record was arranged, conducted, co-written and produced by one Larry Fallon. Though I know nothing else about the gent in question, he did crop up on former Uglys singer Steve Gibbons' solo LP *Short Stories* (Wizard 1971) playhing brass & flutes on one track.

Another peculiarity was in attributing the Graham Bell single on Polydor to his namesake in Skip Bifferty. I can understand the mixup as the record was made in '66 and Bifferty wasn't formed until a year later, but the fact is it's another G.B.

—Pontus von Tell
Sweden

[*Thanks for the corrections. We don't claim to be perfect, but with the help of triviologists like yourself we should be able to plug most of the gaps eventually.*]

TEEN TONES THEORY DEBUNKED

In the Fall '75 issue you asked if the Rivieras had anything to do with "Fortune Teller" by the Teen Tones. Well I remember the Teen Tones and I also talked to Bill Dobslaw's wife who said he didn't think there was any connection. By the way, Dobslaw now writes a 'conservative' column for a local paper, and sings in a barbershop harmony group!

—Ron Trowbridge
South Bend, IND

[*Thanks to everyone else who wrote; sorry we couldn't squeeze in all your letters, but don't let that discourage you from commenting on every issue. We read them all carefully and are greatly interested in what you have to say. Send all letters to P.O. Box 7112, Burbank, CA. 91510.*]

SWEDISH ROCK
(continued from p. 32)

TROUBLEMAKERS
- 66 Funny Man/Blow the Horn - Hep House 12
- 66 A Lay-About's Lament/Sally - Hep House 22
- 67 Always Something There to Remind Anyhow - Tommo 5
- 68 Rock Around the Clock/Mary Ann with the Shaky Hands - Tommo 9
- 68 Juliette/You'll Be Fine - Tommo 10
- 68 In the Mood/Waiting for Recording Engineer Stan - Tommo 11

JERRY WILLIAMS & VIOLENTS
The Wanderer/Runaround Sue - Laurie 3339(A)
- LPs: *Live at the Star Club* - Sonet GP 9913
- *Feelin' Blue* - Sonet GP 9919
- *Alpen Ros* - Sonet GP 9926
- *Rock & Roll Time* - Sonet GP 9938
- *String Time* - Sonet SLP 34
- *Mr. Dynamite* - Sonet SLP 35
- *More Dynamite* - Sonet SLP 40
- *Action* - Sonet SLP 55
- *Power of Soul* - Sonet SLP 61
- *Dr. Williams & Mr. Dynamite* - Sonet SLP 2502
- *Leader of the Pack* - Sonet SLP 2511
- *Live!* - Sonet GP 10010

MISCELLANEOUS GROUPS
- BEATCHERS - EP (same as Namelosers)
- BEST - LP: *Beat Hits 65/66* - Sonet GP 9907: Get Off My Cloud/Hang On Sloopy
- CADS - Don't Know My Tomorrow/Get out of my Life Woman - Sweden 4505 (68)
- CHICKS - Christmas Present/My Song and You - SweDisc 1006
- EVIL EYES - Mister Mystified/Moving Around - Decca 44524
- FEW - Hum-a-Zoo/Once I Had a Dream - Mercury 131400
  - They Won't Go/Seeing is Believing (67)
  - Time and Tide/So Long (68)
- FLIPPERS - The Children/I Could Hear Her Cry - Karusell 621
- "14" - Im Krankhaus/Meet Mr. Edgar - Olga 39
- FRIENDS - He's in Town/Joe McCartney - Karusell 666
- GIANTS - LP: *Live*
- HI-BALLS - Cause I Want to Know/Look at Me - Karusell 656
  - LP: *Beat Hits 66/67* - Sonet GP 9914: I'm a Boy/Hi Lili, Hi-lo
- ICECREAM - Mohair Sam/I've Been Lovin' You - Platina 182
- INSIDE LOOKING OUT - Make Love/Love Potion - Polydor 2053013
- JOKERS - Broken Engagement/I Won't Untie You - SweDisc 1147
- LADY KATE 6 - LP: *Beat Hits 65/66* - Sonet GP 9907: Eve of Destruction/Midnight Hour
- LORDS - There's No Other/Walkin' Talkin' - Record 2002
- LUCAS
- JEAN LUNDENS - She Lied to Me/She Has Gone Away - Gazell 169
- MERRYMEN - Walking Down Lonesome Road/Spider - Karusell 617
  - In Vain (65)
- MICHAEL & PLAYMATES - LP: *Beat Hits 65/66* - op 9907: Yesterday Man/It's My Life
- MODERATIONS - Hard to Forget/Shake - G&P 1009
- MODS INC - First Woman/Yes I Want - Carnival 101
- MOONLIGHTERS' - Today is the Day/Cave of Gold - Interdisc 1187
  - Hi Lili, Hi-Lo (66)
- EP: Shanes & Moonlighters Live - Columbia 138: Shot of R&B/I Can't Stand It
  - LP: *Pop Nonstop* - Sonet 9904
- NASHMEN - Ann-Louise/Carol - SweDisc 1063
- NORTHERN LITES - (called Hootenanny Singers in Sweden; Included Bjorn Ulvaeus)
- LP: *Gabrielle* - UA Intl. 14507 (A)
- PANTHERS - EP: Polydor Intl. 60 118(Fr): Baby/I Just Wanna Make Love to You/I'll Be Pleased/Hey Woman
  - Don't You Know Why/Halfway to Paradise - Sunset 6
  - LP: *Beat Hits 66/67* - Sonet GP 9914:
- PLOMMONS - Are You Sure   Very Last Day
- POPSIDERS - Somewhere/Dancing in the Street - Sunset 9 (66)
- ST. MICHAELS SECT - And Most of All/I Can't See - Sweden 4506
- SECRETS - Michelle - Jukebox EP 5548
- SHELTONES - A Little Bit Me, a Little Bit You - Jukebox EP 5562
  - Stewball - Jukebox EP 5562
- SHAKERS - Tracks Remain/I've Been Loving You Too Long - Fontana 271275
  - All I Want it My Baby/The Sun is Shining - Odeon 5985 (66)
  - Too Much Monkey Business - Columbia

- SHIVERS - I Don't Mind/No No No No - Gazell 194
  - LP: *Zingo Toppem 2511*: Baby It's Too Late
  - LP: *Beat Hits 66/67* - Sonet GP 9914: Just Like a Woman
- RED SQUARES - Sherry - Columbia DS 2328 (67)
  - Turning Around - DS 2341 (67)
  - Lollipop - DS 2358 (68)
- SLAMCREEPERS - Cross a Million Mountains/I've a Way of My Own - Bill 110
  - Mr. Personality Man/Cash Box Ladies Behavious - Bill 126
  - It's Saturday (68)
  - Land of Love (68)
- SLEEPSTONES - My Little Girl (65)
  - Good Morning Little Schoolgirl (66)
- SPREADERS - LP: *Beat Hits 66/67* - Sonet GP 9914: With a Girl Like You

- STEAMPACKET - Take Her Any Time/Only in Her Home Town - Polydor 59725 (66)
  - Baby, You've Got It/She's Down Knappupp 4600
  - Viva L'Amour (67)
- STRANGERS - Trust Me (65)
  - Certain Girl (66)
  - You Can't Sit Down (66)
- SUNSPOTS - Sonet LP 9911: To Feel and Hold/Romance/She Said That She Loves Me
  - LP: *Beat Hits 65/66* - Sonet GP 9907: My Generation
- TEENAGERS - Girl on a Swing/I Never Found You - Columbia DS 2335 (67)
- TRONICS - Burn That Candle (65)
- VAT 66 - The Birds in the Sky/The Square of the Won Fights - Olga 34
  - Lady Lady/I'll Better Be Alone - Olga 41
- WIZARDS - Well All Right/That She Does - Scan-Disc 1019

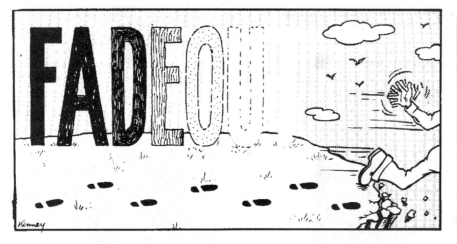

You can expect a lot of changes in 1977, as far as BOMP is concerned. The appearance and quality will continue to improve, of course, and we also hope to be able to announce national distribution and a much more frequent schedule — bi-monthly if possible. There will also be big news in the coming months from BOMP Records, and plenty of surprises. So stay tuned, and tell your friends: this is where it's happening.

As you can tell, we're still experimenting heavily with the format. Although BOMP will always be concerned with rock history, there is less historical trivia and more coverage of current events. My policy has been that we would never write about anything new unless it was as good as the old records we all love, and I couldn't be more delighted that music of that caliber is once again being made. If there is indeed to be a worldwide resurgence of the rock & roll spirit, I'd like BOMP to serve as its focal point. So keep sending those letters, let us know what's going on in your part of the world, share those local records with us, and of course we always welcome your suggestions.

Greg Shaw's ERRATA & ADDENDA

CHICAGO ROCK

DUNWICH PRODUCTIONS
Shadows of Knight - My Fire Dept. Needs a Fireman /Taurus - Super K 8
LP: *Blackwood Apology* - *House of Leather* - Fontana 67591
Dunwich 164 - Knaves - Inside Outside/Your Stuff
DESTINATION RECORDS
607 - Kane & Abel
611 - Sweet Nothings - Cry Baby Cry/Baby Please
618 - Valiants - Tell Me Tell Me
627 - Boyz - Hard Times All Over
QUILL RECORDS
106 - Ronnie Rice & Gents - La-Do-Da-Da/Warm Baby
113 - Ralph Marterie - Masquerade
USA RECORDS
713 - Frankie Gem - Crystal Rock
890 - Trafalgar Square - Til the End of the Day/It's a Shame Girl
901 - Affluents - Get Ready/Tom's Song
IRC RECORDS
6904 - Dick Biondi - Knock Knock/Pizza Song
6910 - Ronnie Rice - Over the Mountain/T.N.T.
MISC. CHICAGO RECORDS
Angelo's Angels - Spring Cleaning/Tomorrow - Ermine 55 (local top 20 hit)
Blue Angels - Shake a Tail Feather/Dance With Me Lynda - Cap 077
Buckinghams - LP: *Portraits* - Col. CS 9598
Cave Dwellers - Run Around/You Know Why - Jim-Ko 41085
Cryan Shames - Up on the Roof/The Sailing Ship - Columbia 44457
Flock - Mermaid/Crabfoot - Columbia 45295
Ides of March - Nobody Loves Me/Strawberry Sunday - Kapp 992
Ides of March - Hot Water/Heavy on the Country - RCA 0052
Mauds - Hold On/C'mon and Move - Merc. 72694
Mauds - You Must Believe Me/He Will Break Your Heart - Mercury 72760
Mauds - You Made Me Feel Bad - Merc. 72720
Mauds - Only Love Can Save You/Sgt. Sunshine
New Colony Six - People & Me/Ride the Wicked Wind - Mercury 73063
Oscar & Majestics - Top Eliminator - Score 1005
Ronnie Rice - I Know/Who's the New Girl - MGM 13153
Seeds of Reason - I'm Your True Love/Somewhere There's a Girl - Lakeside 1982
Turfits - Losin' One/If It's Love You Want - Capitol 2018

LESLEY GORE
Immortality/Give it to Me Sweet Thing - A&M 1510
Sometimes/Give it to Me, Sweet Thing - A&M 1829
That's the Way Boys Are/That's the Way the Ball Bounces - Mercury 72259

"Consolation Prize" issued in limited quantities to fan club members
LP: *Love Me By Name* - A&M 1464
Note: on *Greatest Hits* several songs are different versions than on the 45's

MICHIGAN
Doug Brown - Swingin' Sue/Blue Night - Checker 1001

SAWYER & BURTON
Bad Apple/You Satisfy Me - Pilgrimage - Mercury 72631
Light Bulb - The Five Kings - Columbia 43060
Ain't Gonna Eat Out my Heart Anymore - NY Public Library - Columbia 7684(E)
Lori Burton - Yeh Yeh Yeh/Who Are You? - Roulette 4609

BEATLE NOVELTIES
Bob Moline - Beatle Stomp - Charger 100
LP: Blue Beats - *The Beatle Beat* - A.A. 133
LP: Mersey Boys - *15 Beatle Songs* - Vee Jay 1101

JACKIE DE SHANNON
(as Jackie Dee)
8-58 Buddy/Strolypso Dance — Liberty 55148
How Wrong Was I/I'll Be True — Gone 5008
(as Jackie Shannon & the Cajuns)
?-59 Just Another Lie/Cajun Blues — Sage 290 Dot 15928, Fraternity 836
?-59 Trouble/Lies — Sand 330, Dot 15980
(as Jackie DeShannon)
9-72 Sweet Sixteen/Speak Out to Me Atlantic 2919
12-73 You're Still Gonna Be My Star/Your Baby is a Lady - Atlantic 2994
LP: *Songs of Jackie DeShannon, Jimmy Holiday & Eddie Reeves* - UAMG 108 (publishers demo)
6-75 LP: *Very Best of* - United Artists UA-LA-434 (possible Jackie DeShannon records)
Sharon Lee - No Deposit, No Return/Kissing Game Rendezvous 401
Sherry Lee Myers - releases on Glenn, Marvel (songs written by Jackie DeShannon)
Too Far Out - also done by the Impac - CBS (E) (with Jimmy Page)
In My Time of Sorrow/I Know You're Missing Her - Gay Shingleton - Reprise 0385
(with Sharon Sheeley)
Dream of the Year -, Jimmy Elledge - RCA 8355
Don't Put Your Heart in His Hand - Ral Donner - Reprise 20,176
Carrying a Torch - Wynona Carr - Reprise 20,201
Jimmy Baby; I Shook the World - Bob B. Soxx & Blue Jeans - Philles LP 4002

MANN & WEIL
BARRY MANN RECORDINGS
7-76 The Princess and the Punk - Arista 0194
CYNTHIA WEIL RECORDINGS
(as Miss Prim & the Classroom Kids)
1-63 The Toddle/Miss Prim's Theme - Amy 872 [Mann-Weil-Anthony]
MANN COMPOSITIONS WITHOUT WEIL
1-60 In the Fall - Brooks Arthur - Carlton 526
?-61 Movie Star [Mann-Hunter] Donnie Dean Apt 25082
? I Play the Part of a Fool [Mann-Hunter] Rocky Hart - GLO 5216
MANN-WEIL SONGS - additional cover versions
7-62 Before I Loved Her - Johnny Maestro-UA 474
Soul & Inspiration - Pigeons - Wand LP 687
?-65 She's Sure the Girl I Love - Fortunes - Decca LP 4597(E)
?-66 Looking Through the Eyes of Love - Fortunes - Press LP 83002
10-67 Where Have You Been - Villagers - Atco 6517
?-70 Feelings - Fortunes - WP-LP 21904
?-76 We're Over - Sheri Jarrell - Private Stock 048

BOSTON ROCK
Royal Aircoach - Wondering Why/Web of Love - Flying Machine Records 8868
Trans-Atlantic Subway - Servant of the People/Winter Snow - Lightfoot 100,333/4
Rogues - Next Guy/Faves on the Wall - Waverly 108
Lost Legend - Love Flight/Yes I'm Ready - Onyx 6901
Children of the Night - World of Tears/Don't Cry Little Girl - Bella 101 (Saybrook, CT)
The 5: PM - Auburn Red/How Many Days - Ace 179
Alan Burns & the Ushers - Whirlpool/Lion in Love - Tuesday 11/12
Psychopaths - Till the Stroke of Dawn/See the Girl - David Lloyd Presents 201,438/9
Ascots - I Need You/Knock on Wood - Super 105
LP: Swallow - *Out of the Nest* - WB 2606 (Vern Miller of the Remains)

MISCELLANEOUS
SEEDS
Little Ritchie Marsh - Goodby/Crying Inside My Heart - Ava 122 ('62?)
INTERNATIONAL ARTISTS
105 - Kathy Clarke - My Summer Prayer/Little Girl Called Sad
JUKEBOX JURY JR.
Bob & Sheri (first Brian Wilson record) B-side is "Humpty Dumpty", not "Young Girl" as listed
DUTCH ROCK
Motions - It's Gone - Congress 237 (A)

[Thanks to Jeff Lemlich, Chris Peake, Lee Wood, Jim Duffey, Steve Bennett, Ed Bangs, Bernie, Dave Germardi, Mark Ddick, Bruce Edelson, Brian Hogg, Doug Hinman, Danny Benair, Gary Tibbs, Brent Hosier, Crescenzo Capece, Gary Reese, David Shelby, Paul Bezanker, Wolfgang Weissbrodt, Kevin Walsh, Nick Duruta, Jack Fitzpatrick, Bob Westfall, Doug Kibble, George Praetzmann, George Maier]

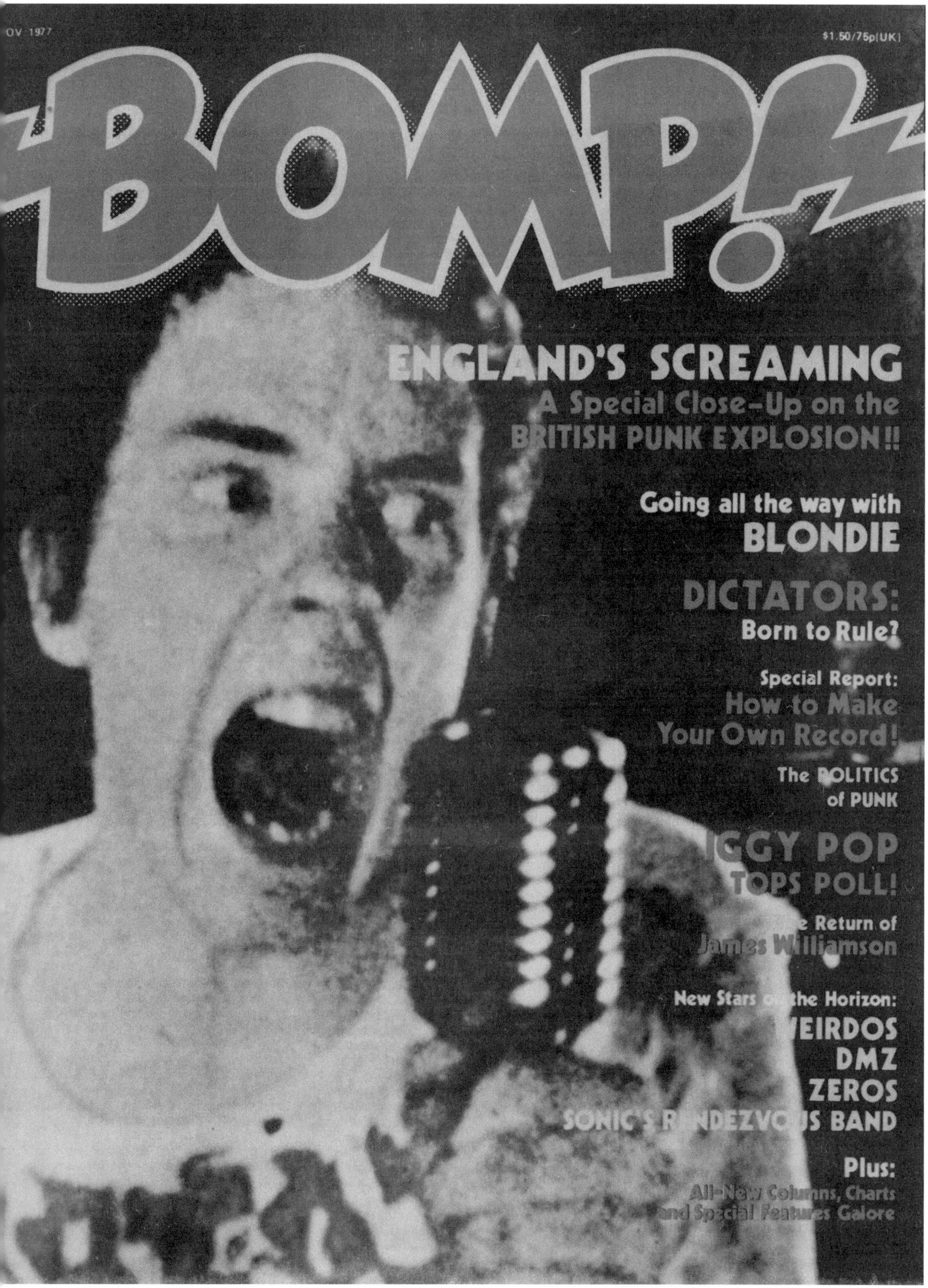

BOMP!

NOV 1977 $1.50/75p(UK)

ENGLAND'S SCREAMING
A Special Close-Up on the
BRITISH PUNK EXPLOSION!!

Going all the way with
BLONDIE

DICTATORS:
Born to Rule?

Special Report:
How to Make Your Own Record!

The POLITICS of PUNK

IGGY POP TOPS POLL!

The Return of
James Williamson

New Stars on the Horizon:
**WEIRDOS
DMZ
ZEROS
SONIC'S RENDEZVOUS BAND**

Plus:
All-New Columns, Charts
and Special Features Galore

Welcome back to my little corner of the world's only *annual* quarterly. Just kidding, of course folks; with the infusion of dynamic new editorial blood [*the Rh factor—!*] into **BOMP**'s masthead, I think you'll be seeing this fine publication on your newsstands much more frequently—every ten months on the dot.

But enough of this pleasant japery; I should have saved it for the April issue—as the French say, there's nothing like japery in the springtime. Anyway, as I was about to say before I was waylaid by a severe attack of second-rate monologorrhea, it seems like forever since I last pontificated in this space. For one thing, an entire British rock revolution has transpired since **BOMP**'s last issue, with impressive strides registered for the American new wave as well.

For another, not unrelated, thing, I've noticed my personal attitude towards rock and rock history (the prime concerns of this magazine as originally conceived by Greg in 1949) changing. Before this year, while I was of course ever on the lookout for good new music, my orientation was towards the 50's and (mostly) the 60's.

•Teenage girls greet the news of Ken's flagging interest in rock history with unbridled hysteria.

Despairing of the present and future, I eagerly looted the past. It was the same reaction to disturbing conditions, I imagine, that caused Mark Shipper to create the bargain-bin cult around *Flash* magazine in 1972; the same impulse that impelled Lester Bangs to codify his crucial punk-rock esthetic (ex)postulations in "Carburetor Dung" (*Creem*, June 1971); the same reason, in fact, that **BOMP** began.

It was a noble impulse, but one that may have served most of its purpose. It got a lot of people through a lot of lean years, but now it seems

like another example of the Bob Seger Syndrome (good name for a band): "Too many people lookin' back." Right now there's so much exciting new music around that there seems to be almost no need to bother with the past. The good new stuff is coming out of the mainstream (Fleetwood Mac, Tom Petty, Bryan Ferry, Heart, Piper), the American New Wave (unforgivable imprecise term encompassing Television, the Rubinoos, the Dictators, Reddy Teddy, Blondie and so many more), and most of all out of England, where even to someone as sound-saturated as I've become it's almost as exciting as discovering the Who, Them, the Zombies, the Yardbirds and that lot. The Jam are just about my favorite group in the world now, and the pleasure of walking into one of L.A.'s hepper record stores and buying the latest London groove hot off the plane from the Clash, Nick Lowe, the Sex Pistols, Elvis Costello, and all *that* lot is indescribably sublime. I moved in May and didn't start to unpack my singles collection for two solid months, existing quite happily on new acquisitions only—and *that's* a change.

Nick Lowe said it: Pure Pop for Now People is what's happening. Realistically, it's not, of course; New Wave music (and a disheartening proportion of worthwhile mainstream material) is having the devil of a time securing radio airplay and sales success (except, in terms of sales at least, in England). But at least the music is out there, fairly readily available, with an acceptably-sized cult audience to support it, and it's more than enough to sustain the addiction that practically everyone reading this must certainly have developed.

On my part, I'm not planning to forsake rock history, archive fun, or whatever you want to call it. There's still a lot to cover, this magazine is one of a disturbingly few places where it's covered with any balanced combination of accuracy and style, and I'm sure I'll still find out my share. Right now, though, for the first time in years, what's new is finally more exciting than what's old again, and though I'm not the first to feel it (note Alan Betrock's directional change from *The Rock Marketplace* to *New York Rocker*, or Greg's own multifarious New Wave enterprises).

RAVES FOR FAVES

Now that I've reached the frontiers of my manifesto destiny, I ought to try to catch up on nearly a year's worth of recorded events. No trouble at all. Just give me ten more pages to reverberate in and we'll be up to date in a jiffy. Lacking that, I'll briefly run over a few of my current favorites and let you take it from there.

New tips for the top include "All Around the World" by the Jam (great guitar break) and Chris Stamey's intense "Summer Sun". I'm listening to the Table's "Do The

•Doing the 'Standing Still' with THE TABLE.

Standing Still" because it's so bizarre; the Ring's "I Wanna Be Free" because it's delightfully dumb; Michael Stanley's "Nothing is Gonna Change My Mind" because it's surprisingly stellar power-pop. Walter Egan's "Only the Lucky" and "When I Get My Wheels" singles are diverting mainstream pop-rockers; Heart's "Barracuda" and Abba's "Knowing Me Knowing You" rule the radio. Jan Berry's cut his best record in years with "That's the Way It Is" (B-side of his current "Little Queenie"). Van Morrison's cut his *weirdest*—"Mechanical Bliss," the non-LP B-side of "Joyous Sound" and a surreal slice of strangeness that gives me more hope for the future than all of *A Period of Transition* put together.

Goldmine ERRATA & ADDENDA

MANN/WEIL:
LP: *Solid Gold* - Screen Gems CPL 712 (song demo LP issued by publishing co.)
On Broadway - The Crusaders-World Pacific 401
JACK NITZSCHE:
Gary Lewis & the Playboys - Jill (arr..)
Soupy Sales - Santa is Coming to Town/Santa is Surfing to Town - Reprise 244
Young Jesse - Mary Lou/You Were Meant For Me - Mercury 72146
LP: *Listen* - Gary Lewis & Playboys)
SURF ALBUMS:
Woofers - *Dragsville* - Wyncote 9011
Nep-Tunes - *Surfers Holiday* - Family 552
CHICAGO:
Nu-Tones - Fell in Love/Sharon Lee - ChaCha 716
Gary & Knight Lites-Will You Go Steady/Can't Love You ANy More - Prima 106
American Breed - Take Me/Ready Willing & Able - Acta 825
MICHIGAN
Precisions - Wy Girl/What I Want - Drew 1002
SAN JOSE
Mourning Reign - Our Fate/Satisfaction Guaranteed - Link MR1(PS)

---

swedish rock

ABBA:
Mamma Mia/Tropical Loveland - Atlantic 3315
Fermando/Rock Me - Atlantic 3346(A)
Knowing Me, Knowing You - Atlantic 3372(A)
BLUESQUALITY:
67 Rock Me/Gamblers Blues - SweDisc 1199
RICK BROWN & HI LITES:
True Love/Yes - SweDisc 1131
CARETAKERS:
66 Woods/All of Me - SweDisc
67 Bless This House/Lies - SweDisc
DEEJAYS:
  I Can Tell/Long Tall Shorty - Polydor 10980
67 Zip-a-dee-doo-dah/Bama-lama-lou-Polydor
67 Hey Baby/Fever - Polydor
  LP: Hep House
DORIS:
69 Wouldn't That Be Groovy/One Fine Day - Columbia 2423
70 Did You Give the World Some Love Today, Baby?/Don't - Odeon E006 34194
FABULOUS FOUR:
Puff the Magic Dragon/This Land is Your Land
Dont Go Out into the Rain/Gnny COme Lately Hep House 23
Island in the Sun/For You & Me - Hep House
Rhythm of the Rain/I Still Love You
Rotten Rats/Goodbye My Love - Fontana
After All/Sheila - Fontana
LP: *That's All* (soundtrack from film)
FRIENDS:
He's in Town/Joe McCartney - Karusell 666
GONKS:
In a Persian Market/Going Round - G&P 1005
HEP STARS:
66 The Music Bow/Wedding - Olga 24
67 Jingle Bells/Christmas on My Mind-Olga 47
69 Holiday for Clowns/A Flower in My Garden Olga 80
68 Sagen Om Lilla Sofi/Det Finns En Stad - Cupol 232
69 Speedy Gonzales/ Ar Det Inte Karlek,Sag - Olga 91
70 Venus/Boy - Strike
70 Blue Suede Shoes/Nere pa hornet - Strike
LP: *Hep Stars Bastra* - Efel LPE 005
LP: *Hep Stars pa svenska* - Efel LPE 012
Sunny Girl/No Response - Olga 21
Save Your Heart for Me/Aldus m'n horoscoop - Olga 32

Komm Little Tom/Die Spieluhr (in German) (re-releases) - Olga 05
LP: *Songs We Sang* - Efel LPE 015
LP: *On Stage* - Efel LPE 013
LP: *We and Our Cadillac* - Efel
BENGET HJORD (the Swedish Bob Dylan)
It's Just a Song/That's Why I'm Here-Bill 101
LEE KINGS
65 Sticks and Stones/Que Sera Sera - Gazell
65 Stop the Music/Always and Ever-Gazell 158
66 WHy WHy Why/Give Me Just Another Beer - RCA 760
66 La La Lies/I Just Wanna Make Love to You
67 GonnaKeep Searchin/Smile for Me-RCA 768
67 The Trees are Talking/Orient Express-RCA
67 I Can't Go On Living Without You/They May Forget -RCA
68 DayTripper/Coming from the Ground - RCA
LOLLIPOPS:
67 Susy Moore/Love is a Game for Two - Fontana 271603
  Little Bad Boy/Dont Matter What You Do - Karusell 603
  I'll Stay By Your Side/That's All-Karusell 607
  EP: Lollipop Lips/Hey Sing Dey Dee Doo Daa/Movin ghe Shoes/Shakin All Over-Karusell 3313
  LP:Polydor
LORDS:
Walkin Talkin/There's No Other (Like My Baby) - Record 2002
LUCAS:
67 Hymn to the Sun/Antisocial Season-Polar
MASCOTS:
65 Goodbye/For Him - Decca 44500
66 Woman/Meet Me - Decca 44512
66 Nobody Crying/We Should Realize-Decca 44514
66 I Want to Live /A Different Mind-Decca 44518
67 So Sad About Us/Stewball-Hep House 09
67 You Could Be My Friend/Dave's Idea-Hep House 11
  Tell Me Lady/Aaah, I Love You-HepHouse 15
LP: *Your Mascots* - Decca LK 4704
66 Since You Broke My Heart/Droopy Drops - Decca 44525
68 Baby You Are So Wrong/Moreer Parlophone
68 Whooee/Black and White-Parlophone
MOONJACKS:
You Dont Love Me at All/It Ain't Me Babe - Decca 44513
NASHMEN:
Bom Bom/Tenderly and Closely - Swedisc 1110
NEW GENERATION:
68 Candy/Just Give It to Me - Sonet 7728
ANNABEE NOX:
65 Where Have You Been/Move It Baby-Col.
66 I'm Not Talking/My Baby Don't Care - Columbia 2298
NURSERY RHYMES:
67 We're Gonna Hate Ourselves in the Morning /Jiving Teen - Polydor 59743
OLA & THE JANGLERS:
No No No/In Vain - Gazell
California Sun/Baby Baby Baby - Gazell
EP: Land of 1000 Dances/Leave Me Be/Thinkin' of You/Tomorrow's on Our Side - Gazell
OUTSIDERS:
67 Kinda Dead/So You're My Sister s Boyfriend - Nashville 860
PALMES:
67 This Little Bird/The Nazz Are Blue-Col.2356
PETE PROUD:
69 Crying All Night/Ba-ba-do-da-Polydor 59772
PUSSYCATS:
Purdy Patsy/Just a Little Teardrop - Nor-Disc
Ebb Tide/Cadillac - Karusell 613

RENEGADES:
(as Joe Dunnett & the New Renegades)
76 Cadillac/Lay Down - Philips 6003 571(Gr)
SCIENCE POPTION:
Monica/? - Glasyra 45v (w/PS made of *straw!*]
SHAKERS:
68 Sing This All Together/Summertime Blues- Mallwax 5002
SHAMROCKS:
65 La La La/And I Need You - Karusell
66 Balla Balla/Things will Turn Out Right-Karu.
SHANES:
  Blue Feeling/Breakdown
68 Faces,Faces/It's No Use - Columbia 2383
  Crazy Country Hop/My New Yorker - COl. 2271
  I Don't Care Babe/I Like to Know - Col. 2302

STEAMPACKET:
Viva L'amour/Trouble&Tea-Polydor 59733
STRANGERS:
EP: Peanuts Butter/A Shot of Rhythm & Blues/You Dont Love Me Anymore/Get on the Right Track Baby - Philips 433 466
STREAPLERS:
66 Bad Tough Luck Girl/Untie Me - COl. 2300
65 Making Love/I'm Coming Home - Col. 2284
T-BOONES (sounded like Stooges!: other discs
67 I Want You/Mr. James - Decca
TROLLS:
Alone/To My Second Home - Philips 350317
JERRY WILLIAMS & VIOLENTS:
73 Til I Cant Take it Anymore/ Jungle Hop-Sonet 7909

NOTES
LEIF WIVATT: The band pictured above the Tages was in fact the Fabulous Four. The Lotta in Svenne & Lotta is Charlotte Walker, former member of the Sherrys from Philadelphia ("Pop-Pop-Popeye"). The Deejays were English although based in Sweden. The Caretakers had a very good English lead singer named Mike Wallace. The Renegades were English and the Lollipops came from Denmark. The RedSquares (a Four Seasons modeled group) were Englishmen based in Denmark, and the Wizards were Norwegian.

[Special thanks to the follwoing people for supplying information: Kevin Walsh, Doug Hinman, L.R. Piekutowski, Klaas Westra, Doc Gonzo, Dave Goodrich, Rob Eastman, Chris Savory, Leif Wivatt, Lennart Boberg, Roland COoper, Tony Pavick, Mike Thom, Dave Schulps, Fred Velez, Iggy Emoar, Mike Callahan, Jim Henkel, Doug Grant. Apologies to any we left out!!

FADEOUT

Well friends, the long hiatus is over, and **BOMP** is back—with the first of our new series of bi-monthly issues. I've learned not to make rash promises, but now that we've got our own typesetting and production equipment, with a fully-equipped studio & staff to put it all together, I'm feeling very hopeful about our prospects for staying on a tight schedule and perhaps even going monthly before too long. Who knows...

It's taken a lot longer than we'd hoped to get to this point, and I regret that we haven't been able to chronicle the countless dramatic and significant events of the past year, but you can consider this issue a sort of catching-up, and when #18 hits the streets you'll find **BOMP** right up to the minute, anticipating and exploring future trends to a greater extent than ever before. Incidentally, I want to reassure our veteran readers who may interpret the almost complete absence of rock history & discographies in this issue as an indication of **BOMP**'s abandoning this area. Not true. As I said, we had a lot of catching up to do this time, and in the months ahead we'll be continuing all the historical features **BOMP** has been known for, and launching new ones as well, for with a more frequent schedule we can present more rock history yet in a more reasonable proportion to our coverage of current and future events, which not only tie in thematically but make **BOMP** more accessible to the new readers who will become the fans & collectors of tomorrow...

I'd like to take this opportunity to welcome Gary Sperrazza! to the **BOMP** team. Gary comes to us from Buffalo where he once edited the legendary zine *Shakin' Street Gazette*. As Managing Editor, Gary will be handling many of the day-to-day operations of the magazine, as well as taking over the fanzine and letter columns.

A final word of appreciation to the thousands of loyal subscribers who've stood by without a word of complaint while we've been struggling to prepare **BOMP** for this giant step forward. We like to think it's always been worth the wait, but of course there are limits, and you've all been very kind in letting us stretch them... Rest assured we're working with superhuman determination to make **BOMP** a successful venture without sacrificing any of the quality that you value it for.

One last thing. As many of you already know, we now put out another sheet, the *Bomp Newsletter*, designed to spread current information as fast as possible—the *BN*, issued several times monthly, costs only $3 for 12 issues, and is heartily recommended to all who thrive on the kind of news, gossip, trivia and outrageous rumors even a monthly magazine can't keep up with.

That's it for now. See ya in two months...
— Greg Shaw

The Vanda-Young Story

Sometime during 1963, at a hostel in Sydney, Australia, a diminutive Scot and a young lanky Dutchman were drawn together, informally beginning one of the most productive partnerships in the history of pop music.

Harry Vanda and George Young, along with Stevie Wright, Dick Diamonde and Snowy Fleet became Australia's best loved rock sons—The EASYBEATS. For 2 years they swept thru Australian rock as unrivalled champions before leaving for England where they scored an almost immediate international Top 5 hit with the stunning "Friday on My Mind." Despite the lack of comparable follow-up singles, the EASYBEATS remained a major force in the rock world until their eventual demise in 1970.

Recognition of their talent as professional songwriters began, rightfully enough, in Australia where acts like Johnny Young, the Valentines, Larry's Rebels and the Soul Agents covered EASYBEATS songs. However the move to England exposed their works to a larger market and covers of their songs soon appeared by such diverse artists as The Shadows and Los Bravos.

Once the EASYBEATS became accepted into the very tight English rock scene, Vanda/Young songs were eagerly sought by major chart acts. Amen Corner, Marmalade, Shocking Blue, Tremeloes, Joe Dolan and Gary Walker all recorded their songs during the late '60s.

Back in 1969, after 3 albums and endless management problems, the EASYBEATS made a final tour of Australia and went their own ways. Harry and George returned to England and production/songwriting. A variety of artists continued to record their songs and they played on so many sessions they can't begin to remember them all. Other efforts were issued under a variety of group names.

In 1973, they returned to Australia. Working out of independent Albert Productions, they began writing and/or producing hits for a staggering array of artists including Stevie Wright, AC/DC, John Paul Young, William Shakespeare, Ted Mulry, Johnny O'Keefe, Ray Burgess, Johnny Farham and others. So successful were they that at one time they had 5 records in the Top 40 at once!

International interest in their material began to ignite again, David Bowie chose "Friday on My Mind" for Pin-Ups and Rod Stewart recorded "Hard Road."

Interviewed in Australia, George Young talks warmly of the EASYBEATS, Vanda & Young, the launching of AC/DC and gives a hint of the potential still left in what has been described as "the last great songwriting team of the sixties."

THE GEORGE YOUNG STORY
1963-1976

I came out to Australia in 1963 from Scotland with my family. Glascow was one of the centers for blues music in Britain, and it wasn't till I came to Australia that I started playing rock music.

That's where all the EASYBEATS got together. We were all living at the Villawood Migrant Youth Hostel. Stevie had been in Australia and he'd come through the ranks of local clubs and talent shows. He was only a kid of 12 or 13—I was about 16. Dick and Harry came from Holland and Snowy from England, where he played in the MOJOS. He came up with the name "EASYBEATS." We had a guy singing with us in the begining called John Bell, but he was a bit shy and we wanted a singer with get up and go, so we picked Stevie. John later became leader of THE THROB.

We did the usual auditions around Sydney then a friend of ours got us various auditions. Eventually we went out on our own, after being kicked out of one pub for being too loud and filthy. Because of a Dutch friend we soon became the resident band at Beatle Village.

That was 1964. We were scruffy long hairs then, but compared to nowadays, we looked tidy and neat. Australia, at the time wasn't very fashion conscious. But in England, where we had come from, fashions were taking off, so we got into it, wearing matching suits and other gear like that.

At one of our gigs, Mike Vaughn approached us and asked if he could be our manager. He had good connections with Ted Albert at J. Albert and Sons, and he organized an audition. Ted liked it and we were on our way. We laid down 3 or 4 tracks at that session, "For My Woman," "Please Say That You're Mine"—that's all I can remember. They weren't demos, they were actual masters. Alberts were quite happy, and they put out "For My Woman" as a single. It didn't do that good—they had trouble getting stations

to play it—the old reluctance to get in deep with an Australian band.

The record company was pleased, tho, because it was the first time apart from Billy Thorpe, that they had managed to get a local act off the ground with original material. Stevie and I were doing most of the writing then. Harry could barely spell English, so he worked on the music and really got into writing later on. We kept playing and went back into the studio and put down "She's So Fine." In those days, recording was a real drag. The equipment was so terrible. Such a long, tedious operation to get a half decent cymbal sound. Anyway, after a lot of carry on, we got the 45 down. That came out and just took off—it was our first national #1. The money got better, the responsibilities got heavier, and the spin-off was that the first record became a hit. It was pretty pleasing. Then the fan hysteria thing

by Glenn A. Baker

"We could've gone on stage and picked our noses, it wouldn't have made any difference..."

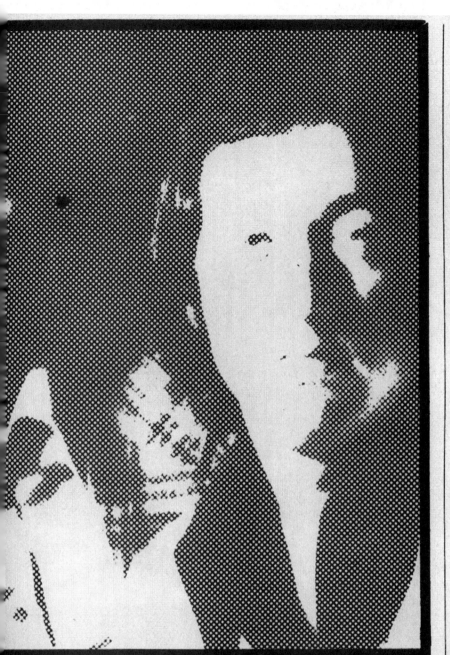

started. Only Normie Rowe was happening really big at the time. He was a good mate of ours, there was friendly rivalry between us.

Anyway, with a #1 record, that's where all the bullshit started. We weren't really playing anymore, we were trying to satisfy demand, trying to please the record company, promoters, record stores, radio station, fan magazines, here there everywhere. It took all the enjoyment out of actually playing. We went out and did one half-hour, nobody could hear, we could have gone out and picked our noses, it wouldn't have made any difference.

After "She's So Fine" came "Wedding Ring," not #1, but top 3. But early as it was, we went through that musicians' phase where we tried to get clever. You can try to prove that you're more than just a 3-chord rock 'n' roll band. With that track we tried to be commercial, but at the same time, be a bit different. It paid off, but wasn't as big a hit as we thought it could have been. We decided **then** that we wanted to get out of Australia. The next single was "Sad and Lonely and Blue"—a bit of a bomb for us, but I think it made the top 10. Again, it was an extension of being clever.

But after seeing the records progressively going down, we thought "Bugger it! Let's go back", so we gave up all pretensions and gave the kids what they wanted—to dance and sing to good, happy choruses. So we knocked out this thing in 10 minutes called "Woman." By that time we had realized that all the little girls were going for Stevie. So we wrote this tear-jerker for Stevie, "In My Book" for the B-side. We did it on TV, Stevie would have tears rolling down his cheeks, by turning around and rubbing an onion in his eyes just before he started singing. Occasionally he'd do it without the onion—just stick his fingers in his eyes. Anyway, it was a double A-side hit.

By this time, we'd made our second visit to Melbourne, and we were taken by our record co. to the plush Windsor Hotel, across the road from the Parliament House, so all the politicians drank there. We met all the DJ's from the nearby radio station and we were supposed to be nice and generally get them to play our records. In the pub at lunchtime there were a whole bunch of labourers and of course the long hair thing came up and they started laughing at us, calling us poofs and abusing the shit out of us. Eventually one of them called us "English bastards" or something. So fuck it, we tore into these guys and started beating the shit out of them- disc jockey, politician, we didn't give a shit. Of course we got a hiding in the end, but it was worth it—you can only take so much. When we left the pub, after we came to, we all felt depressed. But we got word back later from the DJ's that it was the most enjoyable lunch they'd ever had, and they put the record on the air the same day.

By this time, we were being heavily managed, not musically, but business-wise and personal-wise. We had everything done for us, we practically had our arses wiped. The management excuse was that we were so busy being the **EASYBEATS**, we had no time for anything else. But musically, it was all our control,

The Role of the Producer in Powerpop

By GREG SHAW

If you could condense the essence of Powerpop down to two key elements, they would have to be (1)Style, and (2)Sound. There is a definite sound that one identifies with Powerpop, so definite that even the forms that come closest to it can be distinguished clearly— the pop-rock of **Badfinger** from the Powerpop of the **Raspberries**, for instance. This sound and its elements have been amply described elsewhere in this issue; what concerns us immediately is the role of the producer in creating and developing the sound.

Many groups have evolved their own sound, by themselves or with a producer whose primary function was to develop their ideas— as Jimmy Ienner with the **Raspberries**, one assumes from hearing his other productions. In other cases, the subtle aspects of recording and production technique that elevate a record from mere pop to Powerpop can be ascribed either wholly (the Phil Spector style) or partially to an individual producer. It happens that in the realm of Powerpop, there are four producers whose influence has been strong enough to attach their names to a style.

The first name that leaps to mind is that of Shel Talmy. The mere fact of his having worked with the **Kinks**, **Who**, **Easybeats** and **Creation** is enough to make him a key figure in the evolution of Powerpop. The ears detect strong similarities in the approach of the latter three— from things you can put your finger on easily like the recurrence of upfront, single-note bass patterns to the more subtle matter of dynamics and kinetic energy, hard to define but even harder to miss when (all too rarely) achieved in the studio. Undoubtedly, Talmy's ideas have made their mark on all these acts, although both he and the groups, when asked, deny that any special style was being consciously attempted.

It's impossible to say what of his own he actually contributed to any of these groups' sound, especially considering the **Easybeats'** best recording were made before him, and many of the **Who's** afterward, but certainly in the **Creation** we hear the merger of structured power and pop immediacy that make this group, for many, the definitive Powerpop band. On the other hand, it's even more

• Harry Vanda and George Young at the control board: the best of all Powerpop pro

difficult to ascribe a particular style to Larry Page, although again he cropped up in the background with many groups and has had a hand in innumerable classic records from pure pop to hard pop-rock and every shade inbetween.

The most clearly identifiable sound belongs to Chinn and Chapman, and if we accept Glitter as a form of halfbreed Powerpop, then they deserve credit for having reduced the art of generating pop power within the limits of a brief, ultra-commercial single to an exact, replicable science. At the same time, even their best records lack the element of spontaneous, explosive urgency one associates with the real classics; ultimately, C&C (along with cohort and **Sweet** producer Phil Wainman) are to be remembered for having created an entire oeuvre which was immensely successful and extremely influential on the young listeners who comprise today's Powerpop generation.

Which brings us to the fourth and, to me, most important force in the development of the sound known as Powerpop: Vanda and Young. As the article which follows will detail, they have been making music since 1963, and have never once faltered from the ideal of Powerpop. A case could be made that they created the form, in fact, since they were almost certainly doing something comparable before the **Who** released their first record, and even the earliest **Easybeats'** records were, down to the last detail, solid Powerpop at its most exhilarating. Nobody has yet surpassed their sense of dynamics, and what's more impressive, with the passage of time their music has lost none of its forcefulness. Listen to the "yah yah yah" chorus in "Sorry"(1966), next to the guitar chords opening "Natural Man"(1973) or the original "Can I Sit Next to You Girl?"(1975) and it's there, unchanged: the energy that Townshend had, and lost; that Roy

THE EASYBEATS

[continued from page 41]

although we were still meeting other people's demands. "Come and See Her" was another record put out to keep interest up. Another #1 hit!!

At first we took a lot of notice of overseas trends in groups, but then it became apparent to us that it was all just a money game and it didn't mean so much. We weren't making any money at the time because of high overheads and lack of exploitation on the management side. As a #1 band, the group should have been making tons of money, but it wasn't. We never questioned the management. The manager to us was father and God rolled into one. Nobody questioned him, there was no reason to question him, never any mistrust. About this time, we decided we were going to England. The record co. wanted an LP, so we gave them one. Out of the album came the *Easyfever* EP, which reached #1 just as we left. We put down another single for release after we left called "Sorry" and that didn't do too bad either.

Then to London late in 1966, just prior to the Flower Children thing, which was really a drag for us, being hostel boys. The first thing we laid down in England was four tracks: "Friday on My Mind," "Made My Bed," and a re-recording of "Pretty Girl" and "Remember Sam." The first single was "Friday," really working class rock 'n' roll. Being hostel boys that's what you dream about. Friday! It was practically a repetition of the same situation with our first record in Australia, not many people were interested. But then the pirate radio stations, who had Australian DJ's would slip in the

•Little Stevie shouting the blues.

record even tho it wasn't programmed. It went #1 and it was one-in-the-eye to everyone who thought it wouldn't make it. It didn't take long before we were back in the old scene.

The record went into the U.S. Top 10, so we did one tour of the East Coast of America.

We toured for about 2 months, with the Buckinghams, Happenings, Music Explosion, and other top American groups.

•The Easybeats in England with Tony Cahill, 1968.

Wood knew, and forgot.

Those lucky enough to have access to more than a few of the great many records these two have written, produced and performed on since (let alone with) the **Easybeats**, will see a complete understanding of and lifelong dedication to the kind of sound that is Powerpop. They discovered it, and to their everlasting credit, know full well its worth.

Listen to the best **Easybeats** sides: "Sorry", "Friday", "Pretty Girl", "Good Times", "Easy as Can Be", "Can't Find Love" and too many more to name. Listen to "Natural Man", "Yesterday's Hero". Listen closely — note how they start the excitement building from the first ringing chords of the guitar, then steadily build it until by the song's climax you can't stop your flesh from tingling (or feeling actual chills!) as the energy sweeps over you. That's Powerpop, and nobody does it better than Harry Vanda and George Young.

That was when the rot set in. We were under a lot of pressure to come up with another "Friday", which was pretty much impossible. All you've got to do is look at the history of rock to see that if you ever get a particularly good track, there is no way you can duplicate it style-wise or musically and achieve the same success. American bands have been known to use the same backing track for a follow-up single but we are different. We had done a trip back to Australia prior to the American and Snowy decided o stay on there. We got Tony Cahill from the Purple Hearts and he came to the States with us. We did a recording session in the States. It was in an old studio in NY that was no longer operating. We laid down "Falling Off the Edge of the World" there.

By that time the band was stoned off their nuts most of the time and we had been at it for a fair while. When everybody else was getting into it, we were trying to get out of it. Although we never took anything in Australia, funnily enough. The general lethargy of the band was due to the dope thing, plus there were contractual hassles popping up and we *still* weren't making any money. Then we found ourselves *exclusively* signed to more than one record company! To this day, we're still involved in lawsuits over it. Mike Vaughan obviously didn't do it on purpose, but he was small fry over there and the first Australian manager to bring an act to England.

The next single became "Who'll Be the One" which was rubbish, but it *seemed* to satisfy most people. Shel Talmy produced it, a hell of a good producer in the classic American traditions of a follow-up record sounding like a first hit. "Who'll Be the One" wasn't in the same league as "Friday" — it wasn't even on the same planet! But it seemed to satisfy the demand — there was a basic similarity of styles, but it flopped anyway.

Then the "Heaven and Hell" "Pretty girl" single slipped out and it didn't seem to do much either. "Heaven and Hell" lacked a strong melody, we tried to cram a lot of musical experimentation into a three minute commercial single; it didn't work, it never does. Often, if a band tries to reflect their present awareness into a hit single, it flops, you need a lot more time than three minutes. But it really was a good record, produced by Glyn Johns.One of the reasons it didn't do well on the charts was the title — some thought there were drug connotations and other reports from America said they wouldn't play it because of its title.

It all comes back to the dope thing. If you go back to the nitty gritty, the **Easybeats** were a rock 'n' roll band, a three chord band who liked to rock. We made the same mistakes as we did in Australia — tried to get too clever. We brought out this thing called "Music Goes Round in My Head", which everybody in the business thought was great. We were into a blue beat, reggae thing — the album that influenced me was "Ska '67"

By then things had really deteriorated overall — dope, disinterest and not least of all, nobody was making any money out of it. A lot o money was being earned, but it al seemed to go on expenses, bills, etc That's when the squabbles started with the management and we eventually moved on from it.

The flower power thing eased off Big ballads came in — Humperdinck Tom Jones etc. — and again we still hadn't learned, so we decided to take on these guys with a big ballad of ou own — "Hello, How Are You". Again the people in the industry dug it and i skidded in and out of the Top 20. But i was a classic mistake from our point o view, we were a rock 'n' roll band and what was a rock band doing with thi cornball schmaltz shit? We shouldn' have done it. I think after that the *Vig* LP came out, and by this tim everybody in the band was pretty jacked off, so we dug out this thing recorded sometime previous called "Good Times" for the nex single."Good Times" was REALLY rock 'n' roll but it was the same thing then as it is now — bands have to have some sort of musical identity. By tha time, the **Easybeats** had blown it a an identity thing. What with "Friday" a good rocker, "Who'll Be the One" load of rubbish, "Heaven and Hell" complicated self-indulgence, "Musi Goes Round" reggae flower power "Hello" Tom Jonesy, "Good Times" a screaming rocker, people didn' know what to make of us. It was shame that "Good Times" didn' follow "Friday" — it would have bee the ideal thing. It didn't make th charts, but it got an incredibl reaction, like McCartney jumping ou of his car to ring the BBC and all tha carry-on. Stevie Marriot did most o the background singing on it too.

After doing a few cover songs as relief ("Hound Dog", "Hit the Road Jack", "See Line Woman", "I Can't Stand It"), we finally decided to pack it in. We did another tour of Australia, which was reasonably successful, but by then, even Australia was into the flowery musical thing and we were back into what we were before: a rock band. So they just didn't think we had even progressed. Australia sees us as this brash, couldn't-give-a-shit rock & roll band coming along and spoiling all their beautiful flower thing, which had of course died in England by that time. So *we* died a death twice.

The band more or less split up in Australia. Tony Cahill joined Python Lee Jackson. Dick got religion bad, dope bad, generally went off the deep end. We had a strange piece of news the other day, that Snowy had died. Snowy used to write regularly, but hasn't for awhile. We tried to find him, but no luck.

Before we left London, we laid down a few tracks, which became the basis for the last LP, *Friends*. That actually wasn't an album. Polydor got hold of some demo tapes we had done for other artists and put them out as an LP. It wasn't even an **Easybeats** LP per se, just Harry and I with Stevie on some vocals. "St. Louis" was our last single, the only thing on the album that was laid down in a real studio.

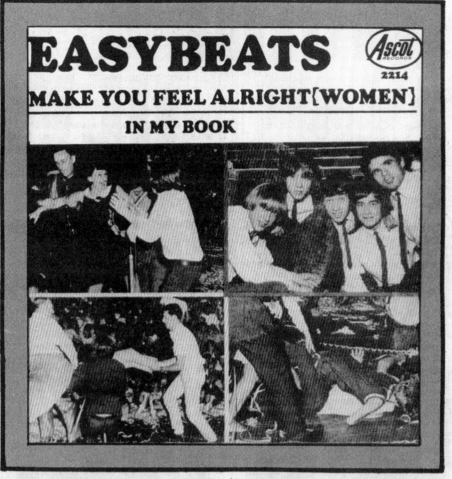

"The Easybeats were a rock & roll band. When flower power came in, it killed us."

So Harry and I went back to England, flat broke, hoping to produce some records. Thru friends with studios, we did this thing called "Get Ready For Lovin'," which got out under the name **Paintbox**, written by Alex. On the B-side was a song Harry and I wrote called "Vietnam Rose," which meant a dose of the clap. Young Blood Records liked it and put it out again as an A-side, calling the band **Tramp**. It was sung by Ian Campbell, an amazing singer. Then Alem's band **Grapefruit** had all but broken up, so we went in the studio with him and cut the final Grapefruit 45, called "'ha Sha." And then a whisky company was bringing out a new blend called Haffy's Whisky Sour. Now to me, that name conjures up a southern American moonshine image. Well, we went in the studio and laid down this track called "Shot in the Head")which later turned up on the **Marcus Hook** LP in a different version). Campbell sang it, it was one of my favourite tracks—very down home dirty. Savoy Brown covered it really nice. Around this time a lot of our songs were being covered by small time English bands like Mosaic, Jennifer's Friends, Rag Dolls, Terry & the Trixons, Popper, Worth, Fluff and lots more. There was one guy called Phil Pickett, who is now in Sailor, who took a liking to our songs. He recorded "Pasadena" under the name of Buster and "Beautiful and Black" as Heavy Feather.

We also did these things called "Lazy River" and "Free and Easy" which were put out under the name of **Moondance**, although I think in Australia they just came out as Vanda & Young. Then we did some tracks for Decca under the name of **Band of Hope**.

The last part of our four year binge was the **Marcus Hook Roll Band**. When EMI finally released the album they called it *Tales of Old Grandaddy* and on the cover they had a drawing of an old man sitting in a rocking chair, which was complete bullshit. It should've shown a bottle of Old Grandaddy bourbon, that's what it was all about. The story of **Marcus Hook** was that there was this friend of ours called Wally Allen who used to play in the Pretty things. He was

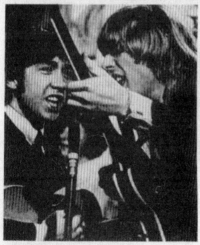

*The early days of Easyfever.

producing at EMI then and thought it would be fun to get us down to Abbey Road to cut some tracks and then call it some group. He would supply the booze, we'd supply the music. So we rounded up the boys, went down there and knocked out about 4 or 5 tracks on the spur of the moment. Apparently it got a lot of interest in America, especially "Natural Man" which became the single. After returning home, we got word from the US that they were hot on this Marcus Hook

[continued on p. 64]

The Vanda-Young Story

[continued from page 45]

Roll Band, which we thought was hilarious— it was just a joke to us. We weren't interested in finishing off an album, so they came to us. We went into EMI-Sydney for a month and Wall supplied all the booze. We had Harry, myself and my kid brothers Malcolm and Angus. We all got rotten, 'cept for Angus, who was too young, and we spent a month in there boozing it up every night. That was the first thing that Malcolm and Angus did before AC/DC. We didn't take it very seriously, so we thought we'd include them to give them an idea of what recording was all about. The American company asked us time and time agian if we'd promote it, but we didn't want to go thru *that* again, and because of that they didn't promote it. It didn't do a real lot, but it got released in America, England and Australia.

So we were back in Australia and we just carried on where we left off. But we decided to get back into some serious work, so the first thing we got into was the Stevie Wright album. At that time, there were a few attempts to get a live thing back together with the **Easybeats**, so we did 3 heavily promoted shows with Stevie. There was a lot of pressure to reform the band, we didn't want to know about it. That was all history.

Then we started to take producing seriously: John Miles, Les Kirsh, Willian Shakespeare. Harry and I have thousands of songs, but we haven't got around to writing anything together for about 18 months, except for that **Flash in the Pan** single. We're going thru a bit of lack of interest, but AC/DC are a part of building up that interest again. To us, helping to get them off the ground in such a short time, getting them off to England, and also getting them a good deal was another exercise.

Having David Bowie and Rod Steward record our song was great because they picked them out of the blue. I've only heard Bowie's "Friday on My Mind" and Stewart's "Hard Road" once, but I wasn't really impressed. The best cover of one of our songs was "Superman" by Allison McCallum because it was so *different*.

The future? I don't really know. We've done the production things and that's appealed to us. There are a lot of songs which just have to be put down on tape. It's just getting the energy and shaking ourselves out of the lethargy of our petty, bourgouise existence. Ha!!

Special thanks to Harry Vanda, George Young, and J. Albert & Sons for their cooperation.

THE BOMP NEWSLETTER

Have you subscribed yet? If not, you're missing out on lots of great news, gossip, opinion and information designed to supplement what you read in these pages and provide an ongoing document of the New Wave scene. Inclueded are news items and special reports from all over the world, discussions of trends in records, local scenes, etc, and the hottest rumors that come over the wire... at the ridiculously low price of 12 issues for $3 (overseas $5 for 12, airmail) you can't afford not to join the hundreds of hep cats who, by sending us local news and reading the BOMP Newsletter, are an active part of today's lively, vital music scene. Simply write to BOMP Newsletter, P.O. Box 7112, Burbank, CA 91510. USA.

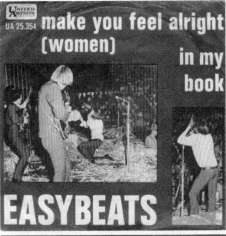

The Vanda-Young Discography
by Glenn Baker and Ken Barnes

EASYBEATS   AUST.   US.   UK
- 3-65 For My Woman/Say That You're Mine — Parl. 8146 NR / NR
- 5-65 She's So Fine/Old Oak Tree — Parl. 8157 NR / NR
- 8-65 Wedding Ring/Me or You — Parl. 8168 NR / NR
- 11-65 Sad Lonely & Blue/Easy as Can Be — Parl. 8171 NR / NR
- 1-66 Women/In My Book — Parl. 8186 NR / NR
- 4-66 Come & See Her/I Can See — Parl. 8200 NR / NR
- 7-66 Come & See Her/Women — NR / NR / UA 1144
- 8-66 Women/In My Book — NR / Ascot 2214 / NR
- 10-66 Sorry/Funny Feeling — Parl. 8224 NR / NR
- 10-66 Friday on My Mind/Made My Bed — Parl. 8234 / UA 50106 / UA 1157
- 3-67 Who'll Be the One/Saturday Night — NR / UA 1175
- 4-67 Who'll be the One/Do You Have a Soul — Parl. 8251 NR / NR
- 6-67 Pretty Girl/Heaven & Hell — Parl. 8255 / UA 50187 / UA 1183
- 11-67 Music Goes Round My Head/Come In You'll Get Pneumonia — NR / NR / UA 1201
- 1-68 Music Goes Round My Head/Good Times (German UA 67-111)
- 12-67 Falling Off the Edge of the World/Remember Sam — NR / UA 50206 / UA 2209
- 3-68 Hello How Are You/Come In You'll Get Pneumonia — UA 50289 (German UA 67-116)
- 6-68 Land of Make Believe/We All Live Happily — NR / NR / UA 2219
- 7-68 Good Times/Land of Make Believe (reissued in Australia 7-76)
- 9-68 Good Times/Lay Me Down & Die/See Line Woman
- Good Times/Lay Me Down & Die — UA 50488
- 6-69 St. Louis/Can't Find Love — Rare Earth 5009 / Polydor 56-335
- 9-69 Peculiar Hole in the Sky/H.P. Man — Parl. 8892 NR
- 5-70 Who Are My Friends/Rock & Roll Boogie — NR NR / Polydor 2001-028

AUSTRALIAN EP's
- 11-65 She's So Fine/Say That You're Mine/The Old Oak Tree/For My Woman - Parl. GEPO 70024
- 4-66 Easy as Can Be/Sad Lonely & Blue/Me or You/Wedding Ring - Parl. GEPO 70028
- 8-66 *Easyfever*: Too Much/I'll Make You Happy/A Very Special Man/Tryin' So Hard - Parl. GEPO 70032
- 9-67 Friday on My Mind/Sorry/Who'll Be the One/Made My Bed - Parl. GEPO 70041
- 11-67 Heaven & Hell/Women/Come & See Her/Pretty Girl - Parl. GEPO 70046
- 1-68 *Easyfever Vol. 2*: Happy is the Man/Saturday Nite/All Gone Boy/You, Me, We Love - Parl. GEPO 70048

AUSTRALIAN LP's
- 9-65 *Easy* - Parlophone 9484
  It's So Easy/I'm a Madman/I Wonder/She Said Alright/I'm Gonna Tell Everybody/Hey Girl/She's So Fine/You Got It Off Me/CryCry Cry/A Letter/Easy Beat/You'll Come Back Again/Girl on My Mind/You Cant Do That
- 3-66 *It's Too Easy* - Parlophone
  Let Me Be/You Are the Light/Women/Come & See Her/I'll Find Somebody/Someway, Somewhere/Easy as Can Be/I Can See/Sad Lonely & Blue/Somethin' Wrong/In My Book/What About Our Love/Then I'll Tell You Goodbye/Wedding Ring
- 11-66 *Volume 3* - Parlophone 7537
  Sorry/Funny Feeling/Say You Want Me/You Said That/Goin Out of My Mind/Not in Love with You/Promised Things/The Last Day of May/Today/My My My/Dance of the Lovers/What Do You Want Babe/Can't You Leave Her
- 6-67 *Best of the Easybeats + Pretty Girl* - Parlophone 9958
  For My Woman/She's So Fine/Wedding Ring/Sad Lonely & Blue/Easy As Can Be/In My Book/Women/Pretty Girl/Come & See Her/I'll Make You Happy/Too Much/Sorry/Made My Bed/Friday on My Mind
  (reissued 1969 as Best of the Easybeats Featuring Stevie Wright, Drum 8119)
- 10-68 *Vigil* - Parlophone 7551
  Good Times/See Saw/Fancy Seeing You Here/Sha La La Leeh/What in the World/Bring a Little Lovin'/Land of Make Believe/We All Live Happily/Falling off the Edge of the World/The Music Goes Round My Head/Come In You'll Ger Pneumonia/Hello How Are You
- 8-69 *Friends* - Parlophone
  St. Louis/Can't Find Love/Friends/Holding On/I Love Marie/Watching the World Go By/Rock & Roll Boogie/Tell Your Mother/The Train Song/What Becomes of You My Love/Woman You're on my Mind
- 10-69 *Best of the Easybeats, Vol. 2* - Drum 8151
  Peculiar Hole in the Sky/H.P. Man/My Old Man's a Groovy Old Man/Such a Lovely Day/Good Times/Down to the Last 500/Hello How Are You/Heaven & Hell/Come In You'll Get Pneumonia/Lay Me Down & Die/Do You Have a Soul/Land of Make Believe
- 1-77 LP: *The Shame Just Drained: The Vanda/Young Collection Vol.*
  Albert Productions APLP 026: Little Queenie/Baby I'm a Comin' Lisa/I'm on Fire/Wait a Minute/We'll Make it Together/Peter/Me & My Machine/The Shame Just Drained/Mr. Riley/Kelly/Where Old Men Go/Johnny No-One/Amanda Storey/Station of Third Ave.

AMERICAN ALBUMS
- 7-67 *Friday on My Mind* - United Artists UAS 3588
  Friday on my Mind/River Deep, Mountain High/Do You Have Soul/Saturday Night/You, Me, We Love/Pretty Girl/Happy is the Man/Women/Who'll Be the One/Made My Bed/Remember Sam/See Line Woman
- 12-68 *Falling Off the Edge of the World* - United Artists UAS 6667
  (same as Vigil, omits "Sha La La La Leah" & "We All Live Happily")

BRITISH ALBUMS
- 5-67 *Good Friday*
  (same as US *Friday*, omits "Women", includes "Hound Dog")
- 6-68 *Vigil* (same as Australian *Vigil*, includes "Can't Take My Eyes Of You", "Hit the Road Jack", "I Can't Stand It", omits "Bring a Little Lovin'")
- 11-70 *Friends* (same as Australian *Friends*) Polydor 2482 010

RELATED
STEVIE WRIGHT
- ?-74 LP: *Hard Road* - Albert Prod. APL-005 (prod. by Vanda & Young)

VANDA & YOUNG
- 2-69 I Love Marie/Gonna Make It — Polydor 56357
- 11-71 Lazy River/Free and Easy — Albert Prod. 9710 NR NR

VANDA & YOUNG UNDER VARIOUS ASSUMED NAMES
PAINTBOX
Get Ready for Love/Can I Get to Know You - Young Blood 1013(E)
Get Ready for Love/Vietnam Rose
Come on Round/Take It From Here - President 384(E)
TRAMP
Vietnam Rose/Each Day - Young Blood 1014(E)
HAFFY'S WHISKY SOUR
Shot in the Head/Bye Bye Bluebird - Deram 345
GRAPEFRUIT
Sha Sha/Universal Party - Deram 343(E)
MOONDANCE
Lazy River/Free & Easy
BAND OF HOPE
Working Class People/Stay on My Side - Decca(E)
MARCUS HOOK ROLL BAND
Natural Man/Boogalooing is for Wooing - RZ 3061(E)/Cap. 3505(A)
Louisiana Lady/Hoochie Koochie Har Kau - RZ 3072(E)/Cap. 3560(A)
LP: *Tales of Old Grand-Daddy* - Albert (Aust.)
Can't Stand the Heat/Goodbye Jane/Quick Reaction/Silver Shoes/Watch Her Do It Now/People & the Power/Red Revolution/Shot in the Head/Ape Man/Cry For Me
FLASH & THE PAN
St. Peter/Walking in the Rain - Albert 11224(Au)/Ensign(E)/Midland(A

- 10-77 LP: *The Vanda-Young Story* - Drum 8132
  Lady River/Superman (Vanda & Young) Falling in Love Again/Ain't It Nice (Ted Mulry) Pasadena/Love Game (John Paul Young) Yesterday (Mark Williams) Can't Stop Myself from Loving You/My Little Angel (William Shakespeare) Things to Do/One Minute Every Hour (Johnny Farnham) Workin My Way Back to You (Bobbi Marchini) Love (Jackie Christian & Target) Evie (Stevie Wright)

UNRELEASED EASYBEATS SONGS KNOWN TO EXIST
(Australia, 1965-66)
I Who Have Nothing; Skinny Minnie; The Bells; I'm in Love With You; No One Knows; Good Evening Girl; I Know Something; Keep Your Hands Off My Baby; I'm Happy; Hold Me; Anyway with the Wind; Mean Old Lovin' You Talk Too Much; Lindy; Insight; Oh No No No; Everynight; I Believe in You; Steady On; Just to Be Free; Hey Babe; Mama; Goin' Out of My Mind; Woe is Me; I Don't Agree; I Can Still See the Sun; Yes You Did; Nothing in Particular; HowYou Doin' Today; Farewell; Everything You Got Babe Crowded City; Need a Little Bit of Love; Paradise; So Many Things Anytime; Shut Your House Down; Her; Not in Here With You; Memories Some Other Guy's Gonna See My Baby
(England, 1967-68)
Sweet Jenny Brown is Swinging; Little Red Bucket; Lori; Mother; Fly With Me; Walking & Talking; Got Until Morning; Monkey See Monkey Do Mandy; Where Did You Go Last Night; Watch Me Burn; Look Out I'm on the Way Down; I'm Just Trying; You Don't Care No More; You Don Know; I'm Gonna Be Somebody; St. Peter.
[1969] Party's Over; Can't Wait for September

We'd like to list all the Vanda-Young productions, but there are too many to even start. In recent years some of their biggest hits have been with John Paul Young, AC/DC, Ted Mulry, William Shakespeare. Some of the best of these can be heard on the 1977 LP *The Vanda Young Story*, and still more can be found on an Australian sampler called *Rocka* (Albert SCA 006) which includes Marcus Hook, AC/DC, Stevie Wright, the Angels, Little River Band, John Paul Young, Ted Mulry and others

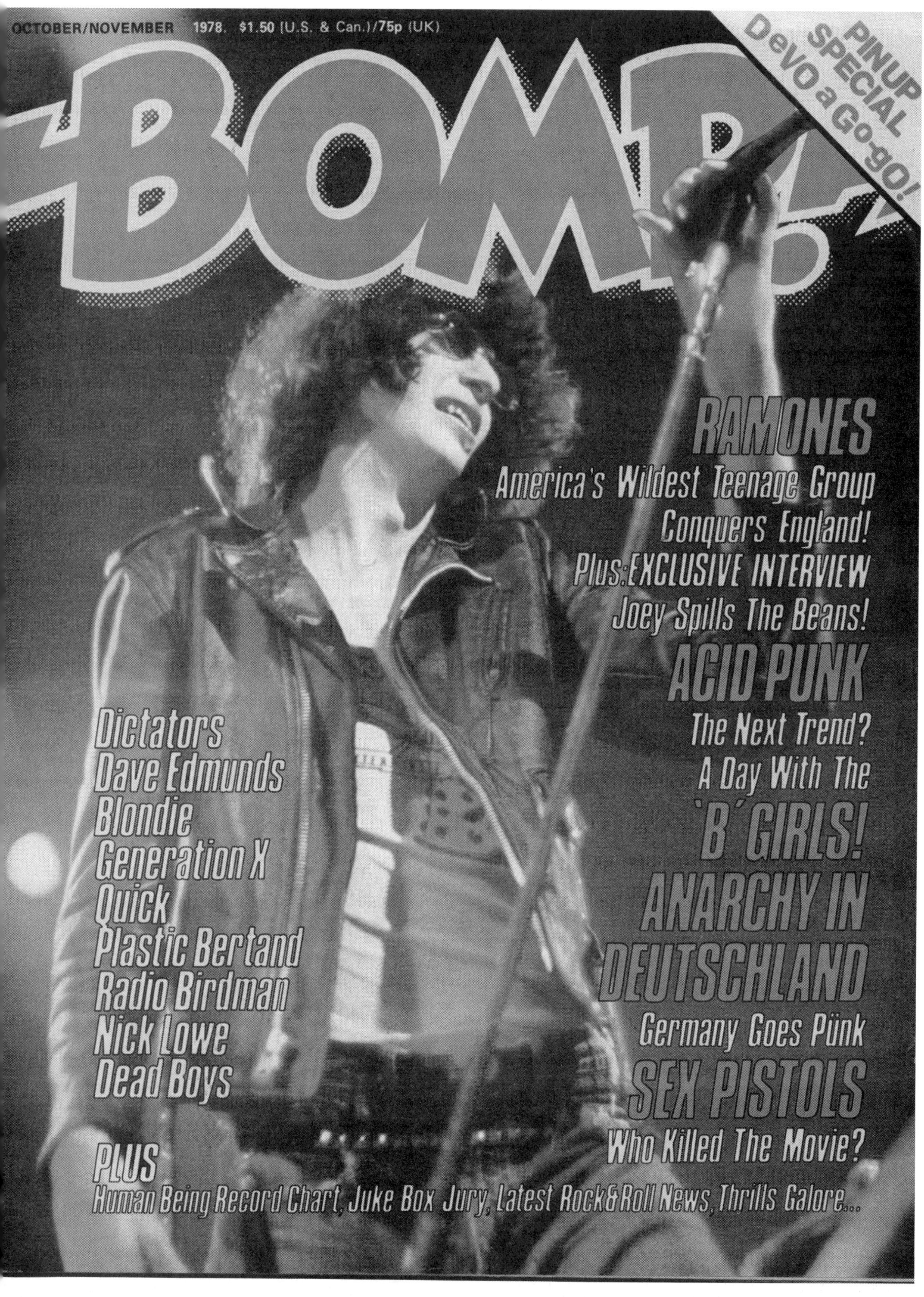

OCTOBER/NOVEMBER 1978. $1.50 (U.S. & Can.)/75p (UK)

BOMP!

PINUP SPECIAL DeVo a Go go!

RAMONES
America's Wildest Teenage Group Conquers England!
Plus: EXCLUSIVE INTERVIEW
Joey Spills The Beans!

ACID PUNK
The Next Trend?
A Day With The
'B' GIRLS!

ANARCHY IN DEUTSCHLAND
Germany Goes Pünk

SEX PISTOLS
Who Killed The Movie?

Dictators
Dave Edmunds
Blondie
Generation X
Quick
Plastic Bertand
Radio Birdman
Nick Lowe
Dead Boys

PLUS
Human Being Record Chart, Juke Box Jury, Latest Rock & Roll News, Thrills Galore...

THE BEAT — Greg Shaw EDITORIAL

PURE NOW FOR POP PEOPLE

A number of people have suggested that this would be an opportune time for me to issue some kind of manifesto for what **BOMP** is and why, now that we're reaching a lot of readers who've had no previous exposure to **BOMP** or rock fandom. Here it is then: if not an actual manifesto, at least a statement of purpose as we enter what seems to be a new era.

BOMP is quite purposely unlike other rock magazines. We write about what we feel is important, not what is popular. We make no pretense of being 'objective', on the contrary we are openly biased towards music that advances the highest standards of rock & roll, by our definitions, and unafraid to criticize or ignore that which does otherwise. We've been called "elitist," and I guess we are, but the elite for whom we write is one we'd like someday to include everyone.

To us, rock fandom is the important thing. It s growth is the reality of which the "New Wave" is but a symptom. **BOMP** was started in 1970 when no such thing as rock fandom existed. Through ceaseless campaigning and editorializing we have, over the years, helped encourage thousands of people to start fanzines, form bands, and promote the idea that rock & roll can be as real and honest and exciting today as it has been in the past. That's the concept behind **BOMP**, the magazine and the record label and every other aspect of what we do.

We realize **BOMP** is a confusing magazine. Many of our readers came aboard when it was devoted to music of the 50's and 60's, others think it's a Punk Rock magazine, and after our last issue the punks dont know what to think of it! It's simple: We're a magazine that reflects the interests of its editors, tries to make sense of the chaos of music and media that surrounds us, and always with one eye on the past and the other on the future. We're historians helping to make history, if you will.

We believe that **BOMP** is the kind of magazine whose time has come. Any magazine that matters must have a purpose or reason to exist, otherwise it's just so much wasted effort. When *Crawdaddy* started in 1966 it was the first intellectual rock zine. When *Rolling Stone* started in 1967 it was the first journalistic rock paper. When *Creem* went national in 1972 it was the first to capture the zany, irreverent fun of rock and roll in print. All these magazines have either worn out or sold out their claim to relevance. Today's emerging rock culture is a direct outgrowth of fandom, whose power is the specialized cults and their commitment to the music that matters. Today's audience is better educated, more historically minded, more aware, and more theoretically inclined than any we've known before. It is for this audience that we produce **BOMP**, a magazine for today because it encompasses yesterday and tomorrow.

Eventually our concept will become dated and somebody else will come along with something better. For right now, we're here and we've got a lot we want to say.

BEYOND TRENDS

A lot of people missed the point of our Powerpop issue last time, unfortunately. It's a shame that we can't make use of labels and categories to what they are, namely convenient guideposts to help us make sense of the bewildering pop landscape. If we don't understand what "punk" is, what "pop" is, what "progressive rock" is, etc., and if we dont share common definitions of these terms, all the writing and arguing and expostulating we do will lead us only deeper into semantic confusion. A state in which many otherwise sane people now seem to find themselves.

A common misconception has been that, with Powerpop, I have picked up on a new "cause" with which I can now be expected to bore everyone for the next three years. Primarily, of course, among people who haven't followed **BOMP** through the years and thus dont realize how broad our aesthetic base really is.

The problem for me has been not to defend my position (because that would be boring too, and time will prove what's what in the end anyway), but what to follow with in this issue. Should I annouce *another* new trend this time and keep doing the same every issue until the point is sufficiently made, or should I do a send-up editorial on why "Power Polka" is the Next Big Thing, or what? So I started thinking about what really *was* on the horizon, and decided to play it straight once again, since the possibilities seem so much more intriguing.

For starters, "Powerpop" as a rallying cry for the New Wave is clearly dead, killed off mainly by the greedy British record industry, who fell all over themselves to push lame, wimpy pop mannequins onto the market in the name of "powerpop", with such blatant avarice that it made all the real fans sorry they'd ever heard the word. Our notion of "powerpop" as an ideal to inspire the efforts of New Wave groups currently responding to the need for more depth and structure in the music, while still a potent force among the newer generation of bands, never had the chance to result in any classic recordings before all the offensive publicity killed its effectiveness. People run around condemning the whole idea of "Powerpop" because they don't like Shaun Cassidy, never realizing how much they'd love '70's Powerpop if any were being made. When a band with as much guts and energy and commitment as the **Sex Pistols** comes along playing power chords or Rickenbacker guitars and songs with melody, harmonies, and minor chord progressions, then maybe Powerpop will be a reality. The **Jam, Generation X, Rich Kids**, etc are as close to the ideal as **Freddie & the Dreamers** were to the **Beatles** - hell, none of these bands has even matched the energy of the 1966 **Who**, let alone surpass it. But try telling that to a punk who can only think of Donny and Marie when he hears the word "pop".

So why waste our time. It was a nice idea, but it won't be the first good thing to be corrupted by the media, right gang? Consider punk for instance. When the most boring members of society pick up on something, it's time for us to have moved onto something else, and it's reaching that point. Anybody who calls himself a "punk" today is like the kids who became "hippies" in 1968. When they're selling safety pins in the punk boutique on Love Street, forget it...

Which brings us back to where we started: What next? As far as I can see, the New Wave seems to be splintering musically into a plethora of trends and hybrids thereof, while the New Wave audience itself continues the process of growth and unification. The more people come in, the more time goes by, the more new ideas will be grafted onto the corpus of New Wave rock, and that's a good thing, as long as it doesnt divide the audience. In this issue, we talk about such developments as "Acid Punk", and "Reggae Punk", which are but two of the trends currently gaining vogue, some of the others being "New Musik", (**Pere Ubu, Devo, Throbbing Gristle**, etc), Rockabilly, Art Punk(**Talking Heads, Patti Smith, Wire, Dishes, Snatch,** etc) Merseybeat (not to be confused, as the British have, with Powerpop), girl-groups, the pub-rock revival (Stiff & co), and the various outgrowths of Powerpop, such as Progressive Pop, Art Pop etc. These will lead to others, like Bubblepunk, Bubblepop, Acid Reggae, etc, and a host of new, unpredictable innovations once some of the more unbalanced minds of our time are turned loose in studios with larger budgets than have been available to New Wave talent heretofore.

All of the above is likely to happen in 1978, making this the year of all trends, and therefore, no trends. And note that all of this happens simultaneously. It isn't one fad replacing another. Powerpop didn't 'replace' punk, it expanded its scope. None of these stylistic possibilities are likely to disappear from the New wave vocabulary until they have been exhausted, which they are unlikely to be because as times change, new interpretations of the basic forms are always possible.

This is something I've always maintained, that what the New Wave has done is not to retreat into the past, but rather to draw inspiration from the past, to unearth every idea and approach that has been of value in rock's 30-year history, and see which of them work in today's context. As it turns out, they all do, because in rock & roll, a good idea is always good. If it was cool once, *it will always be cool.* I believe that, strongly. That's why rockabilly has as much (or more) importance today as in the '50s. And ditto for all this stuff. The reason rock & roll will never die (if we accept that old dictum) is that its basic, implicit message is timeless. A million different ways have been tried to express that message, and some have worked. Most haven't. We're now learning to figure out the difference. That's why all these apparent "trends", as one after another great idea, lost in the ignorance of the past, is discovered and redefined in today's terms.

A year from now, this whole discussion will (I hope) seem academic. It seems that way to me now, in fact it's so basic it ought to be taught in junior high schools. I, for one, will be thankful when all the smoke clears and we can get down to the serious business of enjoying the '80s pop culture we've created.

THE AESTHETICS OF PSYCHEDELIC MUSIC

By PHAST PHREDDIE

Leave your cares behind
Come with us and find
The pleasures of a journey to the center of your Mind
Come along if you care
Come along if you dare
Take a ride to the land inside of your Mind... [1]

In the summer of 1968 I was fourteen years old. My father took the family to spend a week at Big Sur National Park. There were a lot of hippies there. I remember my parents being quite disgusted with them. I also remember walking to the market with my mother when a beat-up Ford Econoline van pulled up and stopped. The hippies inside opened the back doors and played *Wheels of Fire* by **Cream** at an extremely high volume. The hippies wore a lot of brown leather and beads and joked about drugs while one of them went into the market for wine. My mother was not amused. I had *Wheels of Fire* at home. I wanted to run away from home to be with the hippies and take all sorts of drugs. I thought it was romantic

What does this all have to do with Psychedelic music? Plenty! Hippies and Psychedelic music go hand in hand. Who else but the hippies could come up with music that celebrated the joys of smoking joints and dropping acid while living free in the country? The **Beatles** and others of that ilk were mere pretenders. They were too rich and successful to relate to hippies and Psychedelia. Whenever they made an attempt to record Psychedelic music, they were caught with their stash down. They never took the chance of being laughed at as did the less successful casualties of Psychedelia such as **Fifty Foot Hose**, the **L.A. Smog**, and **Group Axis**. Where else but in Psychedelia could you find albums such as Fifty Foot Hose's *Cauldron* listing the following instruments: Audio Generators, Echolette, Squeaky Box, Siren, Ringing Oscillator Circuits, Theremin, Microphone, and Speakers. That is true acid dementia.

THE VANILLA FUDGE SYNDROME

In the late '60s, when Psychedelia was in full bloom, a favorite thing to do was to take a normal song and Psychedelicize it. The **Vanilla Fudge** did it more than anyone else. Their first and biggest hit was the **Supremes'** "You Keep Me Hanging On." They followed it up with a cover of "Take Me For A Little While," a minor hit for the **Bluebelles**. They weren't the only ones, though. **Deep Purple** scored with **Joe South's** "Hush," then covered "Kentucky Woman" and "River Deep Mountain High." **Blue Cheer** made history with "Summertime Blues." An early single by **Yes** (who always reminded me of **Vanilla Fudge**) was a reworking of **Simon and Garfunkel's** "America". The list goes on.

Anyway, these new interpretations were interesting enough. In 1968, the Fudge's second album was released. I used to read *Rolling Stone* back then and they reviewed the album by noting that *The Beat Goes On* was the most pretentious album of the year. Without looking up the definition, I went out and bought the album. It had a Psychedelic medley of Beethoven's "Fur Elise" and "Moonlight Sonata." On subsequent albums the **Fudge** executed **Donovans'** "Season of the Witch" and **Nancy and Lees'** "Some Velvet Morning," among others. I sincerely believe that if the **Vanilla Fudge** were from England instead of Long Island, they would be playing in huge arenas. Hell, what they did back then, ELP and Yes are making a mint with today

Another group of wackos who meant a lot to the Psychedelic Revolution was **Lothar and the Hand People**. About all I can remember about them is their single, "Looking At The World Through Rose Colored Glasses," a contest in *Hit Parader* or some other magazine in which the prize was a date with Lothar and the Hand People, and presumably a hand job in the process, and of course their unforgettable version of the Woody Woodpecker theme song. I have no idea where this group went after this was all over, but a deep sense of gratitude is owed them. They stuck their necks out all for the love of Psychedelic music.

Of course there are literally tons of good Psychedelic albums. There were records by the **Blues Magoos**, **Kaleidoscope**, the **Seeds**, **Bob Seger**, the **Pretty Things**, the **Amboy Dukes**, **Quicksilver Messenger Service**, **Autosalvage**, **Grateful Dead**, **Steppenwolf**, **Clear Light**, **Electric Prunes**, and of course **Kim Fowley**.

You may also want to check out the more advanced sounds of LSD, such as **Terry Riley**, **John Coltrane**, **Cecil Taylor**, **John Cage**, and certain Stravinsky works. Also, give a listen to the lawn mower, garbage disposal, door knob, Red Crayola, or most any record played at 16 RPM (I suggest **Ginger Baker** drum solos, but to each his own).

If you do happen to get into Psychedelia so much that you find yourself never getting enough, please don't contact me and tell me what joys you find with this new discovery. Leave me alone. I've got enough problems trying to figure out how to play records on a cassette deck rebuilt to fit four-track cartridges.

Now my journey is ended
And I'm back where I belong
And I've seen things beyond your wildest dreams
As I've searched the Soul of Man
Though I die unknown and unrecognized
I'm glad that I've found the time
To take the journey to the center,
To the center of my Mind [2]

1. *From the song "Journey to the Center of Your Mind" by the* **Amboy Dukes***, written by* Ted Nugent *and* Steve Farmer.
2. *From the song "Conclusion" by the* **Amboy Dukes***. Written by* Ted Nugent *and* Steve Farmer.

FEEDBACK

A MAN CALLED SHAW

I just wanted to let you know how much I liked the new issue. I honestly don't know of another magazine I read so ravenously from cover to cover, or another magazine that contains as much information and thought. The reactions I feel while reading Greg Shaw's column, or the Twilley/Ramones piece is that I'm not thinking hard enough about what's going on. Only that you and a handful of others are doing all of my work for me and I'm too lazy to do more than sit back and enjoy. It's so neat to be able to cover the oldies front and still be so in line with the powerpop theme. This is of course where BOMP excels, the multi-dimensional overview. And that's why the editorials are so important, to establish perspective for the various other features/foci. I guess the big question is whether the average non-BOMP reader is interested – or can he/she be made to be interested – in the movements and art/trend manifestations of rock. Do they only want to deal with rock at its basic level (not that we don't demand gut reactions in and to our music) and not think about it? Still, it's important to reach non-BOMPers, otherwise the audience is too limited for the crusading feeling I get while reading the magazine. Do you only want to influence those trendsetters who have probably been reading BOMP all along? Certain things, like the graphics and features may help bridge the gap. Rephrased: we love charts and lists, but how many other people care what your all time favorite pop records are? (I'm being intentionally cruel because as I'm sure you well know, many people feel that Greg Shaw is some kind of egocentric forcing his opinions and prophecies on an insular group of people). I don't get that impression from Shaw's writing. He is remarkably kind, patient, open-minded and his enthusiasm comes thru nicely, but let's face it, when people go down the table of contents and see that he wrote 50% of the copy they can't help but think they aren't going to get a balanced picture. Does BOMP intend to try to give each issue a theme? After a certain point it will seem artificial and reflect badly on the magazine. I do not think Shaw is trendy or a scenester but that is one impression that will continue to grow if he does more theme oriented or trend oriented issues and keeps making up labels for this and for that type music. Powerpop is certainly a legit musical distinction, and one more discernable than punk/new wave, but the fact that it follows so closely on the heels of the punk thing makes it seem to many people like just one in an unending series of movement/fads. True the nature of anything that is called "popular" suggests its eventual fading away and replacement by yet another "popular" thing. But some kind of stability and unchanging criteria may be necessary if we are to get adults to relate to rock as it exists in 1978. I think the opening editorial and the powerpop story establishing archetypes really helps people get a handle on the historical aspects which are certainly complex enough. I see one of the big steps in getting BOMP to a wider audience is making the factual history stories less dry. Perhaps as your audience grows your feature writers (me included) will stop taking their readers general interest in the subject matter for granted. It seems to me that it is possible to make your story interesting reading without compromising the music by shifting to "personality" type interviews. But, like I said, BOMP is really getting up there now, and the big circulation is no longer a pipe dream.

– Teri Morris
Felton, CA 95018

[Thanks, Teri; yours is the kind of well-meant criticism that is most valuable to me. I too am concerned about the 'image' of BOMP and its potential for being misunderstood by the new or casual reader (see The Beat and Fadeout this issue) and you can probably tell from the radical changes in this, and previous BOMPs, that we're still seeking the ideal format, and the right blend of history/propaganda/and objective reportage. I wish I could get away with writing less, but aside from yourself and a few others, I'm at a loss to find writers whose critical perspective and sense of overview correspond to the standard BOMP is known for... Besides, we never pretended to present a 'balanced' or unbiased picture of anything. There are plenty of magazines that try to be 'all things to all people' and that approach never appealed to me. BOMP represents a definite point of view, mine, but one I feel is shared by most of our readers. We could probably reach a lot more people by being less rigid, but then it wouldn't be BOMP, would it? —G.S.]

POWERPOP PETERS OUT

With every issue you've been getting more and more ridiculous, but this Powerpop-Mods revival thing takes the cake!! I can certainly see it coming musically, new and improved of course, but...so what? Why make a trend out of it? Pleeze, not again...no more idiocy...if I ever hear that word again...oy vey...let's just listen to the f.....g music, okay? Enough of the early '60s, of labels, comparisons, historical cycles, blahblah...Strictly rockers here, okay? Okay!! Awright, already!! This is the Modern World!!!

– One tortured soul from the Heart of the Midwest

[...Okay...you...win!!...We...get!!!...your message...!!!]

ANOTHER BLACK WORLD

I have read the new BOMP and after digesting it all day, I had to write. I enjoyed Greg Shaw's editorial (he seems to have a fetish for philosophizing, but I don't mind since he echoes my sentiments 100%) and the piece on 20/20 (who sound very promising), but I've really got to hand it to Gary Sperrazza for the excellent "Oh Yeah?" he wrote on the sick state of soul in '78. This has been a pet peeve of mine for quite some time now. I get so GODDAMNED MAD I'M READY TO BEAT THE LIVING PISS OUT OF THE NEXT MOTHER WHO SAYS THAT ANYBODY WHO HATES DISCO IS A BIGOT. Damnit, the f.....g Bee Gees make disco, and I hate their white asses more than anybody!! There – now that I got that occasional outburst of non-academia out of the way, I just want to say that I agree that soul music has been wiped out by the putrid, empty contrived disco sludge that has seen an all time low in the integrity and credibility of black culture. If I were a black man, I'd be embarrassed to death to be associated with the low intelligence state of my musical culture. Hell, soul died with Otis Redding, and those who survived (Wilson Pickett, Sam and Dave) have been forced into hiding. You must have

been reading my mind though.

– Mike McDowell, *Ballroom Blitz*
P.O. Box 279
Dearborn Heights, MI 48127

[*This man is obviously a bigot. No further comments. All joking aside, Wilson Pickett is actually in charge of his own label and is once again putting out singles. Let's cross our fingers and hope that the Wicked Pickett is back. Concerning your contention that he was driven into hiding, tho, we must disagree. If you recall, Pickett released some abysmal pseudo soul/lounge/MOR albums during the time of the great soul decline, such as Miz Lena's Boy and You've Got Pickett in the Pocket, so in essence he created his own exile. Aside from that, we agree with you completely!*]

SURFBOARDS & BOLOGNA SANDWICHES

I'm at the beach in Southern California, it's a sunny day in February, warm in a wintry way. I'm playing a tape given to me, one of old surf sounds, a scene described well in a book by Tom Wolfe, *The Pump House Gang*, a crazed time in which groups of surfers attended the Watts riots like it was a homecoming football game against their rival school. On the same tape between the surf songs was some music from a new scene, a new wave, The Ramones. "Sheena is a Punk Rocker", after "Little Honda", followed by "Be True to Your School", into "Rockaway Beach". People like Phil Spector, Johnny Rotten, Brian Wilson, and the Ramones are all commentators, articulating what is happening, capturing with their lyrics the essences of the social scenes. I feel that punk rock is a negative stand with positive musical energy reflecting the seventies. They are right on or if you're a punk rocker, right off. the titles - wow! Like "Teenage Lobotomy" and "Beat on the Brat", and back then there was Jan & Dean's "Horace the Swinging Bus Driver", Dave Myers and the Surftones "Frog Walk" articulating the fifties stigmata of easy living, as compared to our now self-indulgent greed. The violence of pent-up horrors is finding its outlet in music, always the truest common denominators of the times. Music always reflects what is happening. It's not pretty, it's rock & roll. Maybe the relationship between the scenes is so parallel because both of these periods have an absence of pressure (except that we now seem to have a dying economy). They are both in between times - fillers. Who knows? I feel that the Beach Boys, Jan & Dean, the Ramones, Dave Myers & the Surftones, the Sex Pistols, Tremors, Dick Dale – all surf bands, all New Wave and Punk bands are statements. Some will lead, some will follow, but they are all catalysts for tomorrow. The music is always a vehicle for expressing the art. The forms of dance-expressing the movement - like the Surfers Stomp, the Pogo Bouncem the Graham Parker New YorkShuffle. If you've seen them you know what I mean. The sun, the tape, the herb all push me on to deeper introspections, but I thought discussing punk rock and surf music in a thousand words or less would do. "Martha, would you make me a bologna sandwich on white bread, plain, and pass the surfboard please!"

-Organic Bertrand

[*It's comforting to know that people still read Richard Brautigan...*]

THE BLACKS CAME BACK

I think I am really going to enjoy reading BOMP now that Gary Sperrazza started writing for you. I first knew he had good taste when he recognized Cheap Trick (my favorite band) as the best rock band since the DC5. But when he had the balls to do an article on black music while everyone else is talking Ramones and Stooges, well he's ok in my book. I too was disappointed when Motown went Las Vegas. What disturbs me is that black people accept disco as their music, even though most disco is made by white people, in Germany, or on synthesizers yet!

– Mark Michel
St. Louis, Missouri 63143

WHAT YEAR IS THIS?

We are a libertarian anarchist collective and we feel that rock & roll, especially new wave punk rock is the truest cultural expression of the emerging post industrial anarchist social revolution i.e. grass roots control of (Sun, Moon, Wind) energy base. Certainly, this is only our opinion but this is the way that we see it. We have each written several song lyrics e.g. "Rock & Roll the Rulers," "Cry Me A River To Liberty," and "All Cracked Up on Militia Hill" to name just a few. None of us are performing musicians and we would like to send our lyrics to Patti Smith and Johnny Rotten (Sex Pistols). We understand that the Sex Pistols have split up but we are hoping that they will get back together again. Could you send us their mailing addresses or information on how to get our lyrics to them. We feel that a cultural correspondence between like-minded groups will strengthen the new wave.

– Black Chain
Arlington, MASS. 02174

[*We can't help you with Rotten. He left no mailing address since moving to Texas and rooming with Dean Coryl, but if all else fails, buy yourself some beads, get a ticket for Trans-Love Airways and contact Eric Burden. He's always looking for people like you...*]

[*continued on page 53*]

Mark Lee Productions Proudly Announces the Return of

KENNY AND THE KASUALS

The Legendary Punk Rock Kings of the 60's

A Special Re-Release
Mono LP5000/Mark Records

It's one of the best live LP's . . . maybe the best one from the 60's
NOT FADE AWAY MAG
August, 1977

. . . probably the rarest punk LP of the 60's
BOMP MAG
Nov. 1977

. . . a landmark in punk nostalgia . . . the most sought after esoteric punk album in existence.
CREEM MAG
Feb. 1978

. . . a great year for Texas Rock, highlighted by the re-issue of Kenny and the Kasuals, Live at the Studio Club.
ROLLING STONE MAG
Rock and Roll Awards '77
Jan. 1978

THIS IS THE REAL THING!
ORDER NOW: $6.50 plus 1.00 Post & Hndlg.
MLP/P.O. BOX 57093/Dallas, Tx. 75207

STILL THE BEST SOUND AROUND!

FADEOUT

Looking back over the ideas and themes covered in this issue, I can't help reflecting on the state of today's music scene, and how dramatically it continues to change. A few months ago it seemed significant that most of the major record companies had picked up a NW act. Now it seems those acts are turning into major attractions. **Blondie** has had a worldwide #1 hit, **Elvis Costello** has gold records, **Patti Smith** has penetrated to the heart of Top 40 land, **Tom Petty** is rapidly becoming a star, and the **Ramones** seem destined to follow in the footsteps of **Kiss** into the center ring of the grand arena. Hundreds of NW records are coming out every month, and major labels are signing them as a matter of course. The reality has bypassed the rhetoric completely: the struggle to promote New Wave seems, on close examination, academic.

Granted, a lot of people — the lowest mass level to which any cultural trend must ultimately filter down — are still grappling with the meaningless question of whether the "violence and lack of musicianship in punk music" can appeal to more than a cult, and unfortunately this squarest segment of society happens to include most of the people in the radio industry today, but so what? The facts speak for themselves. It's been demonstrated that this new music can find acceptance with a broad audience, and the truth seems to be that, once exposed to it directly, most rock & roll fans are quickly won over. With every day that passes, more people have accepted the new music, and at concerts you see younger and younger kids, and average people of all kinds, compared to the cult audience of a few months ago.

The last phase of the "struggle" is now underway, and that is to bring into this expanding pop culture the kids of the **Kiss** generation, the 10 - 16 year olds who will transform this country into a teenage utopia. All these kids will form bands, and from there there'll be no turning back. When millions of kids want to hear this music, the radio stations will have to play it, and once again the best rock & roll will be the most popular music, as it was in the 50's and the 60's. At least, that's how it's supposed to work. Nothing is ever certain, but things seem to be moving so steadily in that direction that I have few complaints.

We've discussed elsewhere the effectiveness of labels, catagories, classifications. In the sense that I'm a historian of pop, I can't overlook the value of having an overview, and of isolating the factors that make up musical styles and trends. It's the only way to get a grip on what's happening and why. How can we compare what's going on today in England, or in Detroit for that matter, with the way it was before unless we can refer to statistics, and determine how much room for growth there still is? And needless to say, if today's bands weren't fully conscious of what punk rock in the 60's was all about, their music would not remotely resemble its present form.

But just as clearly, we must weigh the usefulness of this kind of analysis against its damaging effects when picked up by the fad-happy media or even music fans without the background to place it in proper perspective. So "punk rock" started as a fanzine term reflecting the link between the **Standells** and the **Ramones**, but ended up as a media term whose repercussions, at first positive (solidifying the new generation) then negative (scaring the public, putting bands out of work, inciting anti-punk violence) were discussed in my "Politics of Punk" essay in #17. Today, the word "punk" has become merely a millstone around the neck of the new music, keeping alive false stereotypes of the music's crude early days, and holding back the commercial success it now merits. And again with "powerpop", a term coined and popularized by fans as an idealization of what pop, at its best, should be, and then quickly bastardized by would-be profiteers, and just as quickly rejected by the paranoid protectors of a (mythical) punk power structure. So what good does it do us to analyze events to the point where we understand why things are happening, if that knowledge is going to be abused to the extent that it damages the very things it was meant to expedite?

These kind of labels are useful, to be sure, but we must be careful not to attach too much weight or emotion to them, or identify with them to the point of fanaticism. They are guideposts to understanding, and once we've understood, it may be best to discard them, to keep arriving at new evaluations and frontiers. The built-in obsolescence of pop music should extend to its critical body. Thus, if "acid punk" is a trend right now, we must assume it will metamorphose into something else by the time the squares read about it in *Rolling Stone*, and stay 2 steps ahead by figuring out where it can go from there.

When we write about trends in **BOMP**, it's with the understanding that we're *not* in a position to lead the blind consumers into yet another deceptive hype. We like to assume our readers are too aware to be hyped. We think of you as the trend-setters, the people who are spearheading the new developments in music, forming bands, editing fanzines, and supporting your local scenes as actively as you can. We assume that you share our interest in the more subtle aspects of rock history and theory and can make use of this information in your own creative activities.

Perhaps **BOMP** has grown to the point where this is no longer true of the majority of our readers, but it is certainly true of the core that has grown with us over the years, and when we lapse into esoterica or start building Kantian "castles in the sky", it's for the sake of those most dedicated of our readers. If **BOMP** is to remain a forum for these kind of ideas, we must accept that this approach is implicitly, like Hesse's Magic Theatre, "not for everyone."

Personally, I think we've reached the stage where even the term "New Wave" has outdated itself. It still seems necessary in any kind of comparative discussion, but in terms of how this music is promoted and presented to the general public, and what the music itself has now become, it might be best to simply begin thinking of it as "rock & roll", if we define rock & roll as a sort of music and cultural catalyst that we haven't had any of since 1967. It's a rock & roll renaissance as well as a "New Wave", just as the Liverpool groups represented a renaissance of traditional rock & roll values as well as a fad known as the "British Invasion." What the New Wave has brought is actually that, a return of real rock & roll, and real pop music, as well as a host of other, related phenomena that give us more possibilities for an exciting music scene than we've ever had before. But it's still basically that, and maybe it's about time we started applying some minimalism in the critical assessment of the whole thing, as well as in the music.

There is no longer any need to persuade anyone to join a cultish backlash against disco and pompous rock music, so terms and concepts that serve to divide and polarize are no longer useful. The NW scene is well enough entrenched that its survival is not in doubt. If we start thinking of it as just good music, the rock & roll music of today, I think we'll do more to spread its growth than by dwelling on its esoteric ideological aspects. I invite your thoughts on this subject...

—*Greg Shaw*

JANUARY, 1979 — $1.50 (U.S. & Canada)/ 75p (UK)

BOMP!

Ramones
DEVO
Wire
Syl Sylvain
Australian New Wave
Throbbing Gristle

NICK LOWE
Insults Everybody
An Outrageous Interview

DETROIT
The New Motor City Sound

Staying Ahead of the Majors:
Sire, Stiff Lead the New Indies

New Wave in Trouble
A Probing Editorial

PLUS
Human Being Record Chart, Juke Box Jury, Latest Rock & Roll News, Thrills Galore...

THE BEAT — Greg Shaw
EDITORIAL

So here we are again, another issue of America's magazine of teenage music, rock & roll mania, pop theory, future history, and fandom. Not quite as fancy as last issue, you'll note, but we thought you'd rather have it in more modest form for awhile than not at all, and all that extra color costs a lot more than we can afford right now. Like a lot of people who have become deeply involved in the struggle for new music over the last couple of years, BOMP has been feeling the crunch of late....

This issue's editorial has not been an easy one to write. I've done two already, set in type and everything, before deciding they weren't right and starting this one. The problem has been putting my finger on exactly what it is that I, and everyone else involved heavily in the New Wave scene these days, is feeling about the cultural climate coming out of the summer of '78 and heading into a winter that may be as symbolic as it is literal. A spirit of disenchantment is certainly in the air, and for a lot of valid reasons. I was going to go into some of this, but better yet, those who care should pick up the latest issue of *New York Rocker* with its extensive analysis of the New Wave recession, including some of my thoughts on the economic factors.

The fact is, it has happened. What started as a year of unbridled optimism is ending in confusion and doubt for a lot of people. Even as recently as the last issue of BOMP, I as speaking of a permanent, expanding New Wave scene as an accomplished fact. The change must seem abrupt to readers who have not kept their gaze riveted on the front battle lines the last few months, but it did happen rather suddenly (though the signs were there to see, if we wanted to see them—which of course we didn't!). What actually happened, I guess, was that the momentum pushing everyone along just sort of collapsed as more and more people realized they weren't getting anywhere. It got harder and harder to believe that this scene would explode when people finally got exposed to it, after the mass audience had every opportunity for exposure and still remained apathetic.

Alan Betrock, in *NYR*, has a very depressing editorial in which he talks about the decline of culture (meaning chiefly rock & roll/pop culture) and the public's unwillingness to do anything about it, even when given the means. He's right in a way; as the entertainment industry which projects our mass culture becomes truly sophisticated in its method of achieving high profits at low risk (a sophistication which has only begun in the last few years and still, frighteningly enough, has a long way to go), we've seen the disappearance of individuality in all the arts, and a nation of people content to become cultural modules with Farrah hairdos, Travolta suits, and hypnotized by discos, McDonalds-like "self-awareness" cults and slick voyeuristic films, books, magazines, etc., disguised as "sexual freedom" propaganda to believe the world is one big carefree party where all you have to do to be in with the in-crowd is buy all the most heavily advertised products... It's a nightmare right out of all those "Mad. Ave. run amok" books sci-fi writers like Frederick Pohl and C.M. Kornbluth were writing in the '50s, or Philip K. Dick at his most paranoid. But all the other dangerous visions of 20 years ago seem to be coming true all of a sudden; we think nothing of cloned babies, cities in space, picture phones, video discs, home computer systems, bionics, etc., why should we be surprised at the arrival of the kind of synthetic, mass-produced, soulless culture that science fiction writers have, almost without exception, always seen ahead for us?

It's not hard to fall into a kind of gloom thinking about the inexorable "progress" of our civilization and all the wonderful, unique forms of human expression that have vanished, never to return. But then again, the ancient Greeks were saying the same thing, as has every generation since. No doubt our kids will look around one day at the world they've made and long for the simple times when robots couldn't run for public office or join major league football teams, and you could have sex without wondering whether your partner came out of a womb or a laboratory...

I don't think people or their nature have changed that much in the last 10,000 years, or that in the last 10 years they've become so stupid they'll let their lives be dictated without a whimper. People have *always* been stupid; what changes sometimes is the ability of the smarter ones to con them for their own purposes. Given an understanding of mass psychology, you can always manipulate the public with a good hustle. Maybe the golden ages of culture occur when some form of individuality breaks through that's so strong it kindles the spirit in everyone—until the manipulators learn to harness and synthesize it, at which point it dries up until some new breakthrough comes along.

Rock & roll is (I'm reluctant to say "was") the most potent expresssion of individual, humanistic art to emerge in modern times, and it took some 20 years for the controllers to master it. Their first attempts in 1959 were briefly successful, until the Beatles and their generation asserted themselves. The prospect today is certainly more foreboding, but at least we ought to be able to isolate the enemy and recognize his tactics. That's why I found the other comments in *NYR* more encouraging than Alan's remarks. The suggestion of rock & roll as a permanent, self-supporting and self-protective microcosm within the overall rock industry has the ring of reality to it; the industry is too powerful, the public too gullible, for rock & roll to take over completely the way it did in the late '60s. That was, as Lenny Kaye says, probably a fluke. It isn't that the public was any hipper or smarter when good music dominated our culture—they were just being exposed to the media manipulation of people who were more in tune with our standards of good taste than those pulling the strings today. From Brian Epstein to Robert Stigwood, Gloria Stavers to Jann Wenner, Phil Spector to Richard Perry, Andrew Loog Oldham to Dee Anthony; That's the real story of the last 10 years. The public is not to blame: they have no choice but to buy what they are told is the correct product.

I feel like Elvis Costello in "Radio Radio" where he says "I want to bite the hand that feeds me". The radio has helped make him a star, but he's still embarrassed and disgusted to be a part of such a corrupt industry, one that's out to destroy everything he values. It's the same with the record industry. If anything is responsible for the failure of New Wave to get anywhere, it's the industry's basic attitude about musical values and profits. Sure, they gave it a year to prove itself—against impossible odds—and then withdrew their support when they didn't see sales in the half-million range overnight. If the only music allowed to survive is that which returns the highest profits for the industry, the future will be very grim.

It comes down to the need for us to strengthen the underground culture on which rock & roll depends, to act as watchdogs and offer alternatives to the industry. In a sense we must become protectors of an endangered life form. Rock & roll still has the power to break through the crap and ignite our culture again, but its attempt to do so through New Wave failed. Maybe somewhere down the line, in some other form, it will succeed. But the only chance for that is if people like us maintain the standards we know it's possible to apply, to use whatever influence we have with the industry and the public to keep the best music of the past in print and in the hands of as many people as possible, and to prove that industry and culture can both thrive on a common diet of music and art with some substance to it. We know it can work on a limited scale; they believe it can't work on a mass scale. If we believe differently, our only course is to expand those limits until they can see it.

The sophisticated music industry that has become the nemesis of new music will not go away just because we'd like it to. "Radio Radio" won't make Bill Drake retire in shame. But by being on the radio, Elvis Costello may acquire the power to get some of the changes he wants, and by being aware of the industry's dangers and its weak points, maybe the survivors of New Wave will someday be able to give us more of what we want as well.

I'd like to second all of the 8 recommendations made in *New York Rocker*. We desperately need sound programs, realistic goals, to replace the utopian rhetoric. Some of these goals, such as requiring the record industry to keep back catalog in print at budget prices, lowering list prices on new releases, and setting a limit on their own freebie allowance, are totally unrealistic and directly opposed to current trends. But it doesn't hurt to state them anyway, because their intent is valid. These measures *would* improve things, if the industry would go to the trouble and expense. A public boycott of overhyped garbage would be a good idea, not to mention industry's attempts to pervert and milk our natural fannish enthusiasm by means of colored vinyl and other over-exploited gimmicks. But who among us would refuse to own the Blondie picture disc or anything else on principle alone? Not enough to make a difference.

The most realistic proposal I've seen is for the establishment of a rock & roll archive that would make our history and the fruits of our culture accessible to anybody. **Jerry Wexler** made the excellent observation that in other forms of art—literature, painting, sculpture, whatever—each generation goes back to the beginning and studies all that has gone before prior to defining its own contemporary style. In pop music this is impossible because the sources (records, magazines, etc.) are in the hands of a few private collectors and the industry has no interest in making back catalog available on more than a haphazard basis.

What I'm wondering is why the back-patting industry, including **Wexler** and other so-called "renaissance men" like **Clive Davis**, don't take some of the millions of dollars they contribute annually to non-music related charities or jive foundations and set up some kind of society for the preservation of pop culture? Someone in **Wexler's** position could easily propose and probably succeed in organizing such a thing. All the companies, everyone with a share of history to take pride in, would surely contribute, especially since it would be tax-deductable. Such a foundation could even be self-supporting by means of releasing a series of records, books, etc., with licensing rights donated by the membership companies.

This foundation could be controlled by a panel of the most enlightened industry veterans—people like **Wexler, John Hammond, Seymour Stein, Andrew Lauder**, tied in with an advisory committee made up of representatives from fandom, leading collectors, organizations like the Bowling Green University Popular Culture Dept. and **Johnny Otis'** small independent rock & roll archive, who would have power in determining what projects the foundation would engage in. In order for it not to turn into another sham like the Grammy Awards, its goals and purposes could be set out in a charter that would have to be signed by the entire governing body, and an initial funding budget guaranteed by sponsoring companies that would allow for the assembling of the revenue-generating projects mentioned above.

The primary goal would be the collection, on tape and microfilm, of a definitive library of music, film, video, and printed history of pop music, starting with today and working backwards into the early years of the century, eventually linking up with other organizations dedicated to preserving the history of jazz, folk music, etc. But first taking care of rock & roll. At the rate the cybernetic revolution is progressing, by the time this could be done every school, library, and maybe even home, in America would probably be able to have direct access to all this material. Imagine 20 years from now, if every teenager could sit in his bedroom with a computer screen and terminal (with stereo speakers attached) and call up anything he wanted, from **Billy Ward & the Dominoes** to **Ed Banger & the Nosebleeds**—see what they looked like, read extracts from fanzines and historians who wrote about them, cross-referenced to other artists and sources, and above all hear the music, and maybe even see film footage if any exists. All of this is feasible with the technology of today and the next couple years. Its effect would be to create a lasting rampart against the danger of gigantic industry brainwashing the public and eliminating all roots, all variety from our culture. Even disregarding that, it would be a worthwhile effort from the standpoint of preserving a huge chunk of American culture. I wouldn't be surprised if certain industry execs who are known to be chummy with **Jimmy Carter** (not to mention the many other strong ties between today's record industry and high level politics) were able to arrange grants or some other form of outside funding. The possibilities are practically endless.

The one problem would be that some people would have to spend a lot of time and energy to make it happen. Even though the fan consultants would probably be willing to do most of the work, and some full-time workers could be paid salaries, even the advisory time spent by executives would amount to a substantial contribution, the kind nobody likes to make except to self-serving enterprises like the RIAA (which could easily have tackled, or at least proposed, something like this by now if it were really the kind of music industry Academy it professes to be). But it could be done.

I, for one, will start the ball by freely offering my time, the use of my collection, and anything else I can do. But unfortunately it's not within my power to do more than that. Someone who has the ear of the "big money" boys in the record industry will have to convince them it's time to throw some bread back on the water. If something like this could be accomplished, it could make up for a lot of the wrongs committed by the record industry, and do more for the future of rock & roll in the long run than the New Wave ever had a chance of doing....

*We invite your thoughts, comments, etc., on the views expressed in this column. Send all feedback to FEEDBACK, c/o **BOMP**, P.O. Box 7112, Burbank, CA. 91510.*

Photo: Ann Summa

FANZINES

by Gary Sperrazza!

October 1978: no catalogue listings/reviews this issue. Because the process of condensing 150-200 various fanzine issues per **BOMP** leaves little room for conjecture and general commentary, the next few installments of **Fanzines** will cover the more specific markets I feel have been neglected in this column over the past two years. But first, a few opinions, some predictions and a general overview.

It is of course no surprise that the virtual deluge of punk fanzines this year has dwindled considerably. The few that have survived don't seem to really matter much in the scheme of things. Why? Well, for one, the punk scene has largely become the very antithesis of its founding principles: to have fun, celebrate a reaction to the past and crank out some more great 3-chord rockers. Many of last year's punk fanzines recreated the same crude and loveable qualities: spontaneous, immediate journalism quickly thrown together and often simply xeroxed or mimeographed. These zines were entirely dependent on the freshness of the music. But how long is a 16 yr. old from Decateur or Port-au-Prince raving about the return of rock 'n' roll going to keep an audience captivated? We *know* it's back, schmuck, we've been fighting for its return for upwards of 7 years!

This brings up the point that the punk fanzines were largely divorced from the fan mainstream, anyway. Implicitly, it was their own decision to alienate themselves from that mainstream, on the surface their goals mirrored the music's. Take *Slash Magazine*, whose first issue editorial made claims to covering 'rebel music.' You mean rebel music, like **Gene Vincent** to the **Stooges** to the **Pistols** to U. Roy? Fine! But no, as the punk scene grew increasingly stereotyped and 'safe', suburban punk bands worked their way into the true rebel pockets, and *Slash* prefabricated a microcosm that only hurt them in the end as their own audience got bored and moved on to other magazines (or back to the TV). Now, *Slash* are in a position whereby continuing to review local punk bands will sell maybe ten papers at best. Expect a big change in *Slash* as they return to the stance set by their first issue, redefine their goals, raise their cover price and expand their coverage just enough to attract outside readers again. They'll do alright, once they jettison the punk wallflowers (as boring as hippies two years after 1967, in fact they're cut from the same mold, anyway).

One thing *Slash* always had going for it was the 50 cents cover price. In a scene where fanzines become increasingly star-struck, like raising cover prices to $1.50 and more, some ended up pricing themselves right out of their market and had to fold. For example, why pay $1 or more for a British punk zine like the defunct *Sniffin' Glue* when a weekly staple like *The New Musical Express* covers the punk scene so thoroughly and still manages to dispense the news about everything else occurring in today's fluctual music scene? *NME's* perspective and abundance of great (oftentimes unbeatable!) writers enabled them to cover the punk scene much better, I think, than most fanzines could. Despite this, there are a few UK fanzines worth searching for, and I'll run those down in a later installment of this column.

Here in the States, it's been interesting to watch the front line fanzines jockeying for position in the wide-scale distribution markets. *Trouser Press* are now serious contenders for the position once held by *Creem*; that is, the most widely read of American rock 'n' roll fanzines now growing out of their adolescnece. *Creem* is of course not the bastion of lunacy we once enjoyed under the tutelage of **Lester Bangs** and its current blandness may be the essential quality in the success of *Trouser Press*. However, *TP* seems a bit more like this decades' *Zoo World* than anything else. Many people complain of *TP's* general lifelessness and surmise they'll make it because they won't go over the heads of the rock fan in, say, North Dakota. When they do attempt entertainment/humor, it seems forced and rarely is it ever wry or implicit in their writing, as it should be.

However, there *does* exist a demand and desire for a national magazine that is at once comprehensive/factual and entertaining/silly, in the tradition of the best rock 'n' roll (and if any moneybags want to throw some money my way, we'll set the magazine world on its ear!). I think *Trouser Press* will make it into the realm of stereo and cigarette ads, but whether it forces its way in guns a-blazin' or pleads meekly for an invitation is anyone's guess.

BOMP, on the other hand doesn't have much strength in terms of 'straight' journalism nor does it expect inroads into the mass market. Instead, it seeks to supply a broad perspective that gets overlooked in the rush of events. Its major strenghts lie in the critical moxie of contributors; after all, they (I speak as an outsider now) *are* heavily opinionated. And in a world where Jann Wenner devotes pages in *Rolling Stone* to retract statements made by his *own* writers (hence earning him the Suckass Award of the Year; but then again, would you buy *RS* even if the toilet paper industry went bankrupt?), that doesn't bode well for **BOMP's** mass-market success. Future **BOMP's** promise less concentration on trends, more ongoing coverage of everything (both past and present). With a smaller format moving towards regular publication, there will be less need for major statements and summaries.

Becoming Front Line material are two excellent fanzines, *Blitz* and *L.A. Beat*. *Blitz* is out of the Detroit area (formerly *Ballroom Blitz*) and editor Mike McDowell knows more obscure facts than just about anyone I've ever encountered. His magazine is a clear, concise rundown of all the latest in rock 'n' roll/new wave coupled with fascinating articles on 60's pop and soul. Issue #27 in particular has the most powerful interview I've read in ages, with **Sam Moore** of **Sam & Dave**. "I just do not understand this disco," says Sam, "and I can't support it. I know for a fact that there is a growing underground movement in Soul music of people who are out to do something about this disco nonsense." You won't see *this* kind of talk in any national publication and it's the lively, *important* interviews combined with McDowell's hard-hitting, impassioned writing and editing that makes *Blitz* the special magazine that it is.

L.A. Beat is a digest-sized fanzine packed with stories about *pop* bands related in an honest, straightforward format. It eschews much of the trendiness and bullshit associated with similar publications and editor Steven Zepeda writes with a flair and perception in the tradition of fanzines past. There are two issues out and tho he doesn't publish as regularly as some others, letters and subscriptions on your part will help *Beat* to come out on a regular basis.

Probably the most interesting development in the fanzine world these days is a more concentrated attempt on the part of active fanzine writers to organize their talents into a single unit. R 'n' R fandom is so far behind science fiction and comic fandom in terms of development and solidarity. For example, the comics/SF scene has an organization called *United Fanzine Organization* run by Jay Zilber, who puts out a monthly newsletter with a checklist of all recent fanzines and contributions from fanzine editors and writers. Something like this is sorely needed in r 'n' r, but previous attempts at organization (1972's Memphis Convention sponsored by Ardent Records; 1974's Buffalo Convention sponsored by *The Shakin' Street Gazette*) have been ridiculed by the very writers an orgnization would be formed to help. So don't expect anything wide-scale yet in this department, although John Koenig's *Cowabunge* (where has it been?) and Suzanne Newman's *Rockin' in the Fourth Estate* are doing their part to organize a section of fanzine regulars and interested freelancers who grew up with r 'n' r fandom. I think all you pampered 'rockcritics' with your cushy jobs and mailing lists and groupies (with faces like Picasso paintings) are sealing your own fate by NOT getting involved. *Rockin'* is a slick little newsletter giving information and advice to writers, like a consumer guide to freelancing in the rock nationals, fanzine listings, reviews of reference books, editorials on aspects of rock 'n' roll fandom, etc. Suzanne's got herself a smashing little fanzine, and I for one am going to do what I can to help support it.

The next few installments of this column will spotlight specific genres: soul/r'n'b fanzines, the collectors magazines, British punk fanzines, and more. I am particularly interested in receiving a good cross-section of soul/r'n'b 'zines because it's an area that needs some developing and could benefit from some exposure now that there's a definite rumbling of a rhythm 'n' pop revival (NOTE: this is the first reported usage of the term 'rhythm 'n' pop'. Keep that in mind once this trend goes thru the same laundering as 'power pop', etc.).

Lastly, thanks to all the fanzine people who keep in close touch with this column, contributing ideas and criticism, sending their issues persistently, and generally keeping this column alive. Whether you've received praise or pans in this column, keep in mind that simply by making the effort to put together a fanzine, you're better and COOLER than the fans who do naught but complain. Granted, that knowledge and $1.50 will get you a copy of *Billboard*....

FEEDBACK

THE FINAL WORD

Since I finally found the original **Pete Townshend** quote about Powerpop, I figured you might want to print it as the actual opener (and perfect closer) to the Gary Sperrazza! story in **BOMP** #19.

"Powerpop is what we play, what the **Small Faces** used to play, and the kind of pop the **Beach Boys** used to play in the days of "Fun Fun Fun"." (from the paperback *Rock and Other Four Letter Words*).

Congratulations on #19; you turned in your usual great job putting things in perspective and Sperrazza! consolidates his position as the best smartass-but-sincere pop music writer in the marketplace. His story on the **Pistols** movie was well-received. Despite all the brouhaha over the film, I don't think anyone else gave the scoop on the actual *content* of the movie and why it would've been important. *Crib Death* is still the most interesting new column you have introduced over the past two years—who else is so maniacally review-minded to actually critique demo tapes?!?!? Overall, **BOMP** still makes every other magazine look anemic by comparison.

— Stewart Pid
Watertown, MA

MORE CRIB NOTES

Just a note to let your mag know the latest of Seattle's #1 group. Thanks to the *Crib Death* column for the status of "Pick hit"! It's really nice to get some recognition for a lot of work. The **Lewd**'s single is due to be released any day now, on Scratched Records, a new independent out of Seattle with us as the first artist signed. Best wishes to America's best rock mag. You've got the real eye on today's and tomorrow's music.

— The Lewd
Seattle, WA

THEY DON'T ALL LOVE US...

It's time you took a long hard look at what you're doing. As regards most matters, you seem to be a member of the "I know, but..." school of reaction to outside criticism. You're smart enough to know where problems exist, but you're all too ready to brush that knowledge aside and pretend everything's all right. The two prominent examples that I have in mind are (1) your admission that **BOMP**'s audience has grown beyond the realm of the committed few crusading record collectors, and your subsequent decision that you'll continue directing **BOMP** towards those few. At first thought it seems inspiring that someone in a position of some power and influence is willing to stick to his guns; to deliberately refrain from stooping to the level of the "ignorant masses". What you don't appear to realize is that there exists a very large group of people who are neither diehard collectors nor ignorant slobs, who possess a modicum of intelligence and interested about rock and its history, who are not being reached by **BOMP**.

[*But that's exactly who is buying all those copies of **BOMP** these days, and exactly the kind of readers I always hoped we'd attract with growth. That's why there's less "hard" history, more current coverage & analysis in **BOMP** these days. But although the proportions have shifted, my statement was meant as an assurance that there would always be something meaty for the hard-core fans in **BOMP** as well as more accessible fodder for non-fanatics... — Ed.*]

The second issue about which I think you should reconsider is your use of labels. I understand how necessary categorization must be in any attempt to come to terms with mass quantities of information, however categories can never be more than general compartments. It follows, then, that any compartment is going to contain as much or more disparate and even conflicting information as elements held in common. It is one of the primary failings of contemporary arts criticism that the act of categorization has become more than just a handy reference tool, that it has in fact supplanted the development of large overviews of materials as a critical maneuver.

Continuing in this grand tradition is **BOMP**, which is frequently molded around themes, and which often spends its pages doing such things as terming the **Residents** an "acid punk" band! We need help if this nebulous thing called "the scene" is ever to be comprehended to any degree. For **BOMP** to devote so much of its energy toward cultivating an awareness of similarities and trends is a very useful thing, but you're leading us astray if you don't spend as much time discussing the differences between and the uniqueness inherent in our greatest art.

I don't think **BOMP** is a great magazine yet (I must admit to never having seen your early issues) but I'm convinced you're a very good one. You're consistently more informative than any fanzine I've seen, and much more satisfying than *Trouser Press*. However you've really got to listen hard to letters like mine and who knows how many others. I like **BOMP** too much for its potential, and for sometimes living up to that potential, and I want you to accept this letter in that light.

— George Romansic
Seattle, WA

[*Okay, I'm listening, but it's really not clear to me what you're suggesting. Of course I realize the silliness of lumping the **Residents** in with the **13th Floor Elevators**—look at the intro to the "Top Ten of Acid Punk" page, not to mention the tongue-in-cheek tone of the whole "acid punk" section, which incidentally was a deliberate spoof of many people's humorless reaction to our "powerpop" issue. Some people take things far too seriously, above all pop music, and to me that's one of the major pitfalls to be avoided. I will always find it useful, instructive, and imagination-stretching to point out similarities, cross-influences or whatever among seemingly disparate events, and if I can perceive enough evidence of similar thought-processes evolving on the fringes of musical evolution, I'll always deem it the place of **BOMP** to suggest a trend in the works. What's wrong with that? The balancing factor, as you say, is an exploration of what makes individual artists unique in relation to one or more trends to which they may be conceptually linked, and this is done in feature articles on said artists, though admittedly not as much as I'd like to see. **BOMP** still doesn't have enough writers we can depend on to hit the nail on the head. The real overview emerges from the two approaches, to be sure, but you must admit that plenty of other magazines, even Rolling Stone, offer perceptive profiles of artists, while none concern themselves with analysis. So as long as **BOMP** has to be unbalanced, I'd rather it be in this direction. It's a pity you haven't seen more earlier issues, because you'd see how radically we've changed, not only from year to year, but from issue to issue. The present product is not the ultimate design. There's still a long way to grow... — Ed.*]

A DECIDEDLY BELATED RESPONSE

I've been reading your British Invasion issue for about the 3,000,000th time today and was thinking it was one of the greatest buys ever. I've finally received my British UA copies of the *Mersey Beat*, and for the first time am able to hear some songs you talk about. I'm most surprised by your dismissal of **Rory Storm** as a singer. "I Can Tell" sounds quite good to my ears, certainly a change from its usual treatment. After spending good $ on **Ian & the Zodiacs** after your recommendation I was a bit disappointed, but I think the issue was seminal in its completeness and insight. Your assessment of the Liverpool "style" was excellent to the extent that it mirrors my own feelings. I would have much preferred you to that asshole **Lester Bangs** to prepare a section for the *Rolling Stone Illustrated* thing.

— Paul Money
Boone, N.C.

SUBSOIL ERRATUM

Enjoyed your article on psychedelic rock, since I'm an avid Texas punk fan. I thought I would relay some information about one of the records you listed. **Sagamore Subsoil & the Psychoceramics**, I'm sorry to say, is not a punk record. It came out in late 1962 on Sound Tex Records #621215. Titles are "Build Yourself a Girl"/"Shame of it All". A popular San Antonio DJ at the time put it out as a comedy/novelty. It became a local semi-hit reaching #20 before sinking into oblivion. It's definitely a must for novelty collectors. Also, I've heard that the **Crystal Chandlier** 45 "Suicidal Flowers" is from Texas and came out in '69. Can you relay any additional information such as label, city, producer, etc?

— David Shutt
Austin, TX

[*Crystal was indeed a Texas boy, tho I don't know what city. He has other records floating around. "Suicidal Flowers" was on a Buddah subsidiary called Cobblestone and should be possible to find, I would think. — Ed.*]

THE NEW PSYCHEDELIA

Since Christgau, fans have organized their records in separate and unrelated groups—Jazz, Soul, Heavy Metal, etc. The main emphasis in his system of storing knowledge has been on the identification of individual artists and their work rather than on the relationship between people and music, or the process by which music can help mold our thinking and our lives, especially while we're young.

Had we fans been able to see past this hypnotic way of thinking (as did Lenny Kaye), we would now enjoy the perfect sanity which comes from relating to the outside world through a pop music and a pop culture by means of which a clear vision of truth may be sustained, maintained and focused. Instead, we find ourselves in a world splintered, fragmented, rife with confusion and bereft of meaning. Something has gone amiss; it's high time we set things right.

Recently, it has become possible for man to consciously alter his mental state and thus alter his point of view (that is, his own basic relation with the outside world which determines how he assembles and stores his record collection). He can then restructure his tastes and change his buying habits so that music bears more relation to his life, allowing him therefore to approach it more sanely.

COMPLETE CONTROL

explains the difference between the old and the new systems. The old record industry, which was preoccupied with manufacturing superstars, appears to us today as artistically insane. The new system involves a major evolutionary step, in which record buyers have a new consciousness of how the business works. The new fan views the old men who still go to Grateful Dead concerts in much the same way as Jerry Garcia must view the Monkees.

ROLLER COASTER

describes the discovery of the new direction and purpose to rock fans' lives, the movement toward ultimate self-determination, the dizzying peak of total artistic freedom achieved at last—and then the immediate descent to greater conformity than ever before.

I'VE SEEN YOUR FACE BEFORE

characterizes a meeting between an enlightened pop fan and a typical new wave zombie whose passive acceptance of corporate-packaged trends is reminiscent of a darker age.

REVERBERATION

is the root of all inability to find one's own values. Torn between conflicting ideas of what constitutes valid music, one experiences doubt, which reverberates and hampers clear thinking. If a person learns and organizes his knowledge of rock history in the right way, evolving a permanent value system and personal set of standards, he need not experience doubt when confronted with something new. He'll know intuitively whether or not it's cool.

JOURNEY TO THE CENTER OF THE MIND

is the message of the new psychedelia. Seeing the futility of negativity, the enlightened one rejects the temptation to react to an ugly world by surrounding himself with ugly art. The best minds of today are accepting the challenge to ennoble man and his world through visionary art, daring to trust the inner voice of optimism.

THE NEW PSYCHEDELIA

rejects the naive hippie ethos of the '60s while recognizing the fundamentally higher nature of celebratory art. The abrupt change in fashion modes from violence to violets signals the passing of the present-day culture adhered to by those who, for the sake of appearance, took on the superficial aspects of the quest but lacked the courage to follow through to its ultimate conclusion. The dismissal of such persons is long overdue...

PRETTY VACANT

describes those who forgot punk rock's dream of ending illusion. Today's illusion is the myth of hopelessness.

THE KINGDOM OF ROCK & ROLL IS WITHIN YOU

Many BOMP Editorials have stated that our only salvation lies in reinterpreting the pure essence of rock & roll, the true liberating force of our age. With its power, we fans can rebuild our world as we've already remade the record business. The New Psychedelia, then, is a sign that some have found a vision worthy of the inner eye. It is this quest for pure sanity that underlies the new BOMP.

GARAGE BAND NATION

In these pages we'll be sharing with you portions of our ongoing research work, and soliciting your help with various projects. *Garage Band Nation* is the working title for our planned book of local band histories. We're working on it intensively these days, and will be publishing more segments in this magazine, but new information and records are turning up every day, and there's a tremendous amount of data needed that only you can help us find.

We're looking for experts who can fill in some of the gaps in our knowledge of various local/regional scenes of the '60s, particularly these: Ohio, Texas, Phoenix, Albuquerque, Colorado, Minneapolis, Wisconsin, New York, Iowa, Atlanta, Memphis, Florida, and Canada. Needed are listings of local records (write first and we'll send you a list of what we already have), interviews with key people, reminiscences and narrative histories similar to what you've seen in **BOMP**'s past "Sounds of the Cities" articles, and any photos of local bands.

You may be more of an expert than you think. We need the help of all fandom in order to make this book the definitive work it should be.

We'll also be asking everyone's help in various problem areas. So many questions keep coming up that we can't be sure of the answers to. For instance: Has anyone actually seen the Bobby Fuller Four "Civil Defense" LP? Does anyone have a copy of the Human Beinz' *Live in Japan* LP? Does anyone have the Pastel Six album on Zen? The Tino & Revlons LP on Dearborn? The Weekenders LP? The collection of local bands released by the Newman Center of Marin (near San Francisco) in 1966?

Origins of groups is another problem. Where were the Knickerbockers **really** from? Were Angelo's Angels from Chicago or Milwaukee? Where were the Fabulous Flippers really based? Were the Volumes on Impact and American Arts the same group who had "I Love You" on Chex? Does anybody know anything about the Warner Bros. *Was* there an Allusions record on Laurie or any other label?

One of the greatest requirements is lore on local labels. We'll be running lists in this column of numbers missing from our collection – if the sequences hold true, there are thousands of 45s that have never turned up on any auction list and are unknown to us or any of our experts. Sometimes the questions that arise from researching local labels are more puzzling than those concerned with the artists.

Who ran the Chicory label and why did it have so many bizarre releases? What's the story behind Frog Death Records? What exactly was Pa Go Go records, why did it have as many Michigan releases as Texas bands, and what were the 10 or more numbers we're missing? It's hard to even pin down the location of some labels. Freeport, which had both Chicago and Florida groups is an example. Why was Manhattan, an LA label, distributed by a New Orleans company? Why did Danny's Reasons, a Minneapolis group, put out a record on IRC, a Chicago label, when there were dozens of labels in their own home town? How could a label like IGL, out in the wilds of Iowa, apparently release 100 or more outstanding records by local bands, all unknown and practically impossible to find? and so on.

There are the hundreds of records about which we have no clue whatsoever – where they came from, who they were, or if they have any connection with records by groups on other labels with the same names. Some of these groups and their labels are listed here in case anyone out there can help:

American Beetles (Roulette)
Antiques (Hi)
Attic Sounds (Mike)
Avantis (Argo)
B.C. & Cavemen (Stone Age)
Bad Medicine (Orbit)
Barons (SRO)
Baroque Bros (Backbeat)
Beets (Dial)
Black Ravens (B&R)
Bristols (Audio Dynamics)
Bronze Locomotive (Overland)
Bruthers (RCA)
Buffaloes (GMC)
Bugs (Astor)
Byron & Mortals (Preshun)
Canticle (Century)
Caravelles (Onacrest)
Cavemen (20th)
Characters (Vitron)
Checkerlads (RCA)
Children (Sweet Smoke)
Claytons (M)
Coachmen (Roulette)
Counts IV (Date)
Larry Coverdale (Snap)
Cult (20th)
Custer & Survivors (Golden State)
Dangs (RBP)
Danny & Sessions (Saligo)
Destination (Northland)
Dave & Orbits (American Arts)
Davey & Dolphins (20th)
December's Children (Col.)
Dearly Beloveds (Col.)
Day Bros. (Col.)
Dicky Dee & Revenues (Action)
Deltas (EMP)
Demotrons (Scepter)
Dino & Suspicions (Busy Bee)
D-Men (Kapp, Veep)
Distortions (Sea, Capitol, Smash, Malcolm Z. Dirge)
DMZ (MTA)
Dick Domani & Demons (UA)
Druids (Select)
Dynasty (Westchester)
Electric Elves (MGM)
Emperors (Wickwire)
Enfields (Richie)
English Setters (Jubilee, Glad Hamp)
Ernie & Emperors (Reprise)
Esquires (Dot)
Fabulous Fakes (Col.)
Fabulous Thunder (Tight)
Fallen Angels (Laurie)
Fenians (Dee Gee)
Fifth Order (Laurie)
Five Bucs (Omnibus)
Five Hungry Men (Melmar)
Floor Traders (MTA)
Friday & Week Ends (Dynamic Sound)
Front Page News (Dial)
Furlongs (CRS)
Fyre (Courtn)
Gents (Normandy)
Go-Betweens (Cheer)
Good Feelins (Liberty)
Great Scots (Epic)
Great Scots (Triumph)
Green Men (Kapp)
Greg & Unknowns (Vicki)
Grim Reapers (Chalon)
Grodes (Splitsound)
Guise (Musicland USA)
Hallmarks (Smash)
Cal Hayes (d'oro)
Head Lyters (Wand)
Heros (M-Gee)
Holidays Combo (Dixie)
Hysterics (Bing, TOttenham)
id (Jolly Roger)
Ill Winds (Reprise)
Impacts VI (Lampliter)
The "IN" (Hickory)
Inmates (Col.)
In-Ovations (Ascot)
Inn Crowd (20th)
Invaders (Capitol)
Invictas (Rama Rama)
Jagged Edge (Twirl)
Jagged Edge (Gallant)
Jagged Edge (RCA)
James Boys (Col.)
Jay Walkers (Wisteria)
Jerry & Catalinas (Veroona)
Jim & Kay & Chaunteys (Keye)
Johnny & Thunderbirds (Ric)
Junior & Classics (Magic Touch)
Keepers (Brabura)
Keytones (Chelsea)
King Charles & Counts (Crusader)
Knight Kaps (Ricky)
Kords (Laurie)
Lancers (Lawn)
Larry & Gents (Delaware)
Larry & Paper Prophets (Epic)
Lawrence & Arabians (Hem)
Liverpool Set (Col.)
Living End (DiVenus)
Lloyd & Village Squirds (Jubilee)
London & Bridges (Date)
London Dri (Yobo)
London Knights (Mike)
Long Bros (Jubilee)
Lords (Kris)
Fax (Trans-Action)
Madcaps (Unca)
Luke & Apostles (Bounty)
Lost Chords (Vaugn-Ltd)
Magic Reign (Jamie)
Marauders (Banyan)
Marauders (Almo)
Mark 4's (Bonus)
Menn (Mod)
Michael & French-Canadians (Danco)
Midnight Angels (Apex)
Mistics (Wide Art)
Mods (Peck)
Monacles (Monacles)
Moptops (Teen)
Morning After (Tam)
Morticians (Roulette)
Morticians (Mortician)
Motormen (Momentum)
The Mumy (Mumy)
Musics (Col.)
Mustangs (Capitol)
Mynt Julep (Ty)
Napoleonic Wars (20th)
Noblemen (CJL)
Nobody's Children (Bullet)
Nocturnals (Embassy)
Nomads (Tornado)
Only Onz (Time)
Other Four (PLAY)
Others (Mercury, Jubilee)
Outlaw Blues (Era)
Oxfords (ABC)

Pageboys (Seville)
Paniks (20th)
Peepl (Roaring)
Peter & Wolves (Tidal)
Plymouth Rock (LBL)
Prophets (Shell)
Randy & the Rest- (Jade)
Raves (Smash)
Raving Madd (Golstar)
Reactions (Mutual)
Red Coats (Laurie)
Restless Feelin's (UA)
Riders of the Mark (20th)
Rites (Decca)
Rock-a-Go-Gos (Flower Power)
Rockers (Audio Fidelity)
Rockin Rebellions (Vaughn-Ltd)
Rockin Royals (Lebam)
Royale Coachmen (Jowar)
RPMs (Ambassador)
Runarounds (Capitol)
Sangralads (Whap)
Sants (Format)
Saturday Knights (Nocturne)
Scepters (MOC)
Scotland Yardleys (Smash)
Scoundrels (ABC)
Sean & Sheas (Yorkshire)
17th Ave Exits (Modern)
Shades (Cadet)
Shags (Jo-Jo)
Shan Dels (Showcase)
Shanes (Hoshi)
Shapes of Things (Laurie)
Shadden & King Lears (Arbel)
Silvertones (Goliath)
Sir Richard & Knights (American)
Sir Winston & Commons (Nauseating Butterfly)
Skunks (Mercury)
Society (Mark VII)
Some Other Animal (Cypher)
Soul Inc (Laurie)
Soul Trippers (Providence)
Sound Effect- (Love)
Spades (Ace)
Squires (Ateo)
Stains (Lotus)
Starfires (Yardbird, GI)
Statesiders (Providence)
Sticks & Stones (Coral)
Sting Rays (Lawn)
Sting Rays of Newburgh (Col.)
Stone Wall (Free and Easy)
Strangers in Town (Date)
Sundowners (Filmways)
Sur Royal Da Count (Villa-Yore)
Dave T & Del-Rays (Carousel)
TJ & Fourmations (Liberty)
TR4 (Velvet Tone)
Teemates (Audio Fidelity, Idle)
Teenmakers (Jamie)
Thee Insight (Three Guys)
Third Bardo (Roulette)

13th Hour Glass (Prestige Prod)
Don Thomas (Coral)
Tomorrow's People (Col.)
Tormentors (Royal)
Torquays (Colpix)
Traveling Salesmen (RCA)
Tumblers (Pocono)
Tweeds (Coral)
Twigs (Dot)
Uncalled For (Dollie, Laurie)
Un-Four Given (Dot)
Unluv'd (True Love, MGM)
Urban Roots (RCA)
U.S.Six (Ascot)
J.M. VanEaton & Untouchables

Varatones (kay)
Van Ruden (Ivanhoe)

Waphphle (Elektra)
Warden & Fugitives (Bing)
George Washington & Cherry Bombs (MGM)
Wayne & Mustangs (Kingston)
Weads (Duane)
Weathervane (Plamie)
What's Happening (Coreco)
Wig/Wags (Sama)
Ed Wool & Nomads (RCA)
Wrench (Dore)
Yesterday's Children (Showcase)
Yorkshire Puddin (Dellwood)
Young Ideas (Date)
Young Ones (Col.)
Yo Yo's (Coral)
Yo Yo's (Goldwax)

Silver Fleet (Uni)
Robin & Three Hoods (Hollywood)
Descendants (MTA)
Four Fifths (Col.)

Mersey Beats USA (Top Dog)
Skeptics (Showboat)
Beethoven's Fifth (MGM)
Dee & Tee (Coral)
Stumps (Boyd)
Foggy Notions (Ginny)
Hysterical Society (UA)
Ichabod & Cranes (Coral)
Powers of BLue (MTA)
20th Century Zoo (Caz)
Clockwork Orange (Rust)
Sean & Brandywines (Decca)
Barking Spyders (Audio Precision)
Embers (Liberty)
Evil "I" (Bridge Society)
Swingin Yo Yos (Jubilee)
Unwanted Children (Murbo)
Chains (Linpoint)
Green Gang (Bragg)
Lost Generation (Bofuz)
Mo Shuns (20th)
Vikings (Viking)
Zekes (BH)
Jaybees (RCA)
Bare Facts (Jubilee)
Knights Bridge (See Ell)
Quadrangle (Philips)
Druids (NMO)
Eccentrics (Applause)
One of Hours (Chetwyd)
Hysterical BOys Society (EBR)
Countdowns (Link)
Rogues (Living Legend)
Grotesque Mommies (Piece)
Piggy Bank (Lavette)
Third Evolution-(Dawn)
Undertakers (PH)
Squires (Crestline)
Psychos (Tiki)
Arturo Pat & Invaders (Pharoah)
Dickens (Format)
Boston Tea Party (Vogue Intl)
Answers (Blue Boy)
Cavaliers (Crisis)
Branded "X" (Lauren)
Run-a-Rounds (Tarheel)
H.M. Royals (ABC)
Milan (Flower)
Living CHildren (MTA)
Lords of Tonk (Jamie)
Cherokees (Gary)
Fads (Mercury)
Union (Radel)
Lord Alan & Sir RIchard (Cannon)
Outcasts (Prince)
Aldermen (Sir Graham)
Time of Your Life (Ionic)
Four Rogu-es (Philtown)

Casualeers (Roulette)
Bedford Set (RCA)
Count Vict-ors (Coral)
Bad Seeds (Col.)
Victor & Spoils (PHilips)
Page Boys (Camelot)
Children (New York)
News (MV)
Venturie 5 (Venturie)
Chic & Diplomats (Ivanhoe)
Mushroom Farm (Gigantic)
Ravin' Blue (Monument)
Cobras (Big Beat)
Omegas (UA)
Act of Creation (Capitol)
Aerial Landscape (RCA)
Agents (Rally)
Baytowners (Smash)
Bedford Incident (Kapp)
Birth of Spring (Mercury)
TJ Black (Jubilee)
Bright Image (Amigo)
William Bonny *(Mercury)
Care Package (Jubilee)
Catamorands (DGMR)
Flower Power (Tune-Kel)
Furnacemen (Jubilee)
Harbingers (Col.)
Hinge (Highland)
Hungry IV (Era)
Industrial Image (Epic)
Jamie & Blackhawks (MGM)
Law Firm (Imperial)
Mor-Loks (Decca)
Don Norman & Other Four (MGM)
Now (Embassy)
Outcasts (Decca)
Plastic People (Kapp)
Don Ray (RCA)
Rusty Gaytz (Trend)
Sapians (Mercury)
Sidewinders (Look)
Skunks (World Pacific)
Spindrift (Scepter)
Striders (Delta)
Sweet Smoke (Amy)
Tiffany System (Minaret)
Trips (Score)
Truths (Circle)
Webster's New Word (Col.)
Wildlife (Col.)
Words of Luv (Hickory)
Yankee Dollar (Dot)

Kavaliers (Morgan)
Koffee Beans (Format)
Regis Mull (Verve)
Jay Daye & 4 Knights (C Flat)
Motifs (Selsom)
Black River Circus (MRC)
Squiremen Four (Squire)
West Minist'r (Magic)
Warlock (Ex-plo)
Plague (Epidemic)
Spontaneous Combustion (Rod)
Trademarques (Reginald)
Loved Ones (Ambassador)
Stark Reality (Big Yellow)
Jades (Denim)
Malcontents (Gems)
Shags (Golden Voice)
Inner Depths (Hotline)
Magid Triplets (Kef)

Mascots (ABC)
Todds (Todd)
Gladiators (British Lion)
Thorns (Piper)
Marvells (Butane)
She (Kent)
Steve & Pharoahs (Best)

Dick Wadson 5 (UI)
Pleasures (Catch)
Lost Tribe (UA)
Off-Set *Jubilee)
Best Things (UA)
Buzzsaw (RCI)
Younger Brothers (Scepter)
Liverpool Lads (Lloyds)
Pilgrimage (Mercury)
Vandals (Tiara)
Knights of Dey (Col., Tower)
Mal-T's (Lady Luck)
Fanatics (Gina)
Velvets (Monument)
Ronnie Dean & Bedford Set (Dean)
Ides of Love (Talmu)
Roads End (Brahma)
Plague (Wright)
Minets of England (DCP)
13th Hour (J udge)
Chosen Few (Power Intl)
Hatful of Rain (Sentar)
Thrillers (Pageant)
Jerry & Landslides (PPX)
The Spirit (Roulette)
Emperors (Sabra)
Jolly Green Giants (Redcoat)
Troyce Key (WB)
Len Weinrib (Capitol)
Front End (Smash)
Twilights (Capitol)
Boston Hitesmen (MTA)
Carriage Trade (Filmways)
Bitter Sweets (Hype)
Psychopaths (D.L.P.)
Conception (Perfection)
Glory Rhodes (U-Doe)
Danny & Other Guys (CP)
Shades (Ercore)
Akoustiks (Markus)
Missing Lynx (Donovoice)

.........Whew! That's quite list, but it's only the start. Obviously, it's impossible to find out who all these groups were, but every little bit helps. We have names/listings for thousands more groups, by the way, and there are no doubt many more yet to be discovered. If you have any knowledge of obscure groups of the '60s, or know someone who was in such a group, please get in touch with us. We're inviting you to participate in what we feel is the most exciting project BOMP's ever undertaken.

Speaking of big projects, many of you have been asking about the Encyclopedia of British Rock. It's nearing completion now, needing only a few hundred hours of re-typing and maybe a year of production, at which time we hope to publish it in book form. We don't need any more discographical help, but we do need people who can write short histories of some of the groups, especially the lesser-known ones. If this appeals to you, get in touch.

Actually, come to think of it, there are two things we could use to get it out faster. (1) Someone in the L.A. area who would volunteer to help with those hundreds of hours of typing--but it must be someone who understands discographies, knows something about British rock of the '60s, and has an orderly, methodical mind, capable of coping with mountains of information and putting it in cogent form.

And (2), someone with lots of spare cash who wants to finance publication of the book!!! Speaking of books, by the way, we've heard from a publisher in Germany who's interested in putting out a book of selections from BOMP --it would be translated into German, of course. We'll let you know if anything comes of it.

We're planning some pretty interesting stuff for future issues--most of it discographical, but there will also be articles on groups, interviews, and articles on aspects of rock history, rock culture, etc., that strike us as interesting. We welcome your contributions, especially interviews with obscure artists of the '60s, or producers, label owners, etc.

We're also open to suggestions for things you'd like to see, and if you've got questions of your own relating to collecting lore, our letter column is there for you.

Some of the things in the works for future issues include:

Instrumentals. An overview of the field, styles & trends within it, its role as the stylistic link between rockabilly and (continued on p. 44)

THE ORB STORY

according to Kim Fowley

It all started with a studio in San Gabriel, California, owned by Harold Schock, an old guy about 85, and another old man whose name began with "L." The place was S&L Recorders, and I cut some of my best stuff there. We cut "Sharon" by the Raiders, the flip of their first single on Gardena, "Ski Storm" by the Snowmen, which was some of the Sunrays, "Worse Record Ever Made" by Althea & the Memories, and "Comedy and Tragedy" by the Murmaids, all those were cut there. I liked the studio because the guy was so old, you could make any kind of noise or weird distortion and he wouldn't correct it because he was hard of hearing I think.

Anyway, Schock died eventually and the studio was taken over by a karate instructor named Denny Hardesty. His partner, who he knew from the service, was a guy named Steve Waltner, up in Corvalis, Oregon. They got this weird arrangement going where Hardesty would cut records in San Gabriel and Waltner, who changed his name to Wilson, would press and distribute them in Oregon. The idea being that the people in Oregon would accept them as local records, and the major labels would assume these were valid local recordings, which would make it easier to sell any of the masters that started getting action.

Wilson had a record out on Corby, and he also had one on GNP-Crescendo (348, "Pretty Little Angel"/"When Will I Learn Not to Cry"). He had a lot of spare time up there in Oregon, so he'd take the records around in the trunk of his car and distribute them. The label was named after a farmer in Portland who put up the money for the pressings, although he'd only pay for 500 of each.

"Pretty Little Angel" was a #1 record in Corvalis and even got on the charts in Portland. I went up there with Michael Lloyd and a bunch of people when we cut "The Trip", which was a minor hit in Oregon and L.A. before it was covered by Godfrey, a local DJ, on the Cee-Jam label. This was a spinoff of Them that I produced in Ireland, had a Northwest hit with "Secret Police", which was "The Trip" with a few things changed.

S&L Recorders was one of the happening studios for awhile. Tim Hardin recorded an album of unreleased Hank Williams songs there, in the nude, with James Hendricks' wife watching. We cut "Vaquero Stomp" by the Vaqueros (on Vaquero Records) there, that was the Blendells. And there was a record of "Buzz Buzz Buzz" by Dante on Challenge, which was me. Then they moved to a new studio in Arcadia – the old place became a Christmas tree warehouse – and continued to cut lots of records. I did a few things there, "Superfox" by the Hound Dog Clowns, which came out on Living Legend and was sold to Uni; "Heavy Love" by the Doll House on Living Legend, which was the Beach Girls who recorded on other labels.

They put out a few records on Corby from the Arcadia studio, but it wasn't the same, and not as many people wanted to record there. They eventually went out of business.

CORBY DISCOGRAPHY

#	Artist	Title
200	Chancellors	Weird/Jam
201	Jim Hunter	Sweet Lovin'/Just Being Young
202	Steve Wilson	Out L.A. Way/Feelin' Blue
203	Steve Wilson	Pretty Little Angel (5-65)
204	Navarros	Ikie/Moses
205		
206	Kim Fowley	The Trip/Big Sur, Bear Mountain, Ciros, Flip Side, Protest Song
207		
208	Steve Wilson	Where Did My Baby Go/
209	Ralph Geddes	Give Me Peace Feelin' Blue
210		
211	Deuces Wild	Keep On/Keep On Sing-a-Long
212	Carol Hughes	Let's Get Together Again/Don't Turn Your Back (5-66)
213		
214		
215	Solid City	Chinese Checkers/Fat Mama
216	Giant Crab	Listen Girl/Soft Summer Breezes
217	Giant Crab	Kind of Funny/Day By Day
218	Morning Sun	Someday/Hold Fast Your Dreams
219	Lenny Roybal	By the Time I Get to Phoenix/Wishing Well
220	The Midnight Snack	Mister Time/Jenny Adaire (6-69)
221	Giant Crab	It Started With a Kiss/The Answer Is No
222	J.C. Horton	Why Why Why/Overly Lonely
223		
224		
225		
226		
227	Ronnie McFarlin	Too Sweet To Be Forgotten/Forty Days
228		
229	Ronnie McFarlin	The Promised Land/Mean World (PS)

MARGINAL JOTTINGS...

One of the biggest mysteries in the field of garage band research is the identy and locale of the many small labels that were active, and the vast amount of unknown releases implied by gaps between the numbers of what is known.

We know that some of the most prolific regional labels of the '60s, especially in the midwest, were offshoots of recording studios or pressing plants, with many releases of no interest--country, polka, etc. But how can we be sure which ones?

Labels like NWI (Northwest), Band Box (Colorado), Soma, Studio City (Mpls), Fenton (Mich) are examples of this, with hundreds of numbers unknown to collectors. Of course there's always the chance they never issued the missing numbers, and again, some labels had such bizarre number sequences it's impossible to tell. Consider these:

```
ORLYNN (Chicago): we have 8140-8843,
 8140-2553, 8140-6020, and 66312.
FULLER (Fla): we have 0031, 2597, 2684
BEV-MAR (Pgh): we have 401, 402, 419, 575,
 605, 960, 1001, 1601
ST. CLAIR (Pgh): we have 777, 07, 009, 69,
 3333
AMBER (S.F.): we have 101, 3352, 3537, 4086,
 6657
GOLDEN STATE (S.F.): we have 501, 653, 657,
 1721
```

In many cases these numbers no doubt tie in to master numbers arbitrarily assigned at studios or plants, but to trace them would be difficult if not impossible.

Just as vexing are the local labels whose numbering leaves no doubt that a certain number of records were released or scheduled for release, and that we can safely assume were in the vein of the label's other releases. Now that so much warehouse stock of '60s punk is coming onto the market, many of these gaps can be filled, but the only sure method is for research-minded fans to track down people with first-hand knowledge of these labels. In the meantime, we invite you to share with us any additional info you have. Since what we have at this point is so far from complete, we present it not as discographies, but merely as work in progress that maybe, someday, will be more complete.

To start with, a random selection of labels whose gaps have proven as provocative as their known releases.

DELAWARE: Somehow I don't think this label was based in Delaware. At least 3 of these groups are known to have been from Chicago. Does anyone out there know for sure?

```
1700 LARRY/GENTS-Little Queenie/CantYou Tell
1703 FOUR WHEELS-Sneaky Little Sleeper/Ratchet
1705 TRACY STEEL-Letter to Paul/Your Ring
1707 - Dead Ends - Poor Thing/
1710 THUNDERBIRDS-Your Ma Said You Cried/
      Before It's Too Late
1712 DELIGHTS-Find Me a Woman/Long Green
50051 A.J. & THE SAVAGES - Long Long Time/
      Farmer John
```

SHOWCASE: A subsidiery of Pickwick, Int'l, this label had the rare Beachnuts (Lou Reed) single and some great punk records.

9810 HENRY THE IX - Dont Take Me Back Oh, No!
9811 LOST IN SOUND - You Can Destroy My Mind/ Stubborn Kind of Fellow
9812 YESTERDAY'S CHILDREN - Wanna Be With You/ Feelings

9902 BEACHNUTS - Iconoclastic Life

We also need info on the related label, PICKWICK CITY (any besides Primitives & Tran-Sisters)

MINUTEMAN: This Boston label seems to have been folk-rock oriented, and in the case of both Don Thomas and the Improper Bostonians, records were leased nationally to Coral. But what were its other releases?

202 CADALINAS - Bad Girl/Back in Town
203 JUST US - Cant Grow Peaches on a Cherry Tree/I Can Save You
205 THE DOORWAY THROUGH - Springtime/ Keep on Talking River
207 IMPROPER BOSTONIANS - I Still Love You/ How Many Tears
208 IMPROPER BOSTONIANS - Set You Free This Time/Come toMe Baby
??? DON THOMAS - Turn Her Around/Do You Wanna Know
810 THIRTEENTH COMMITTEE - You Really Got a Hold on Me/Sha La La

KANWIC: I'm told the Blue Banana were a Colorado group, and the guy who produced their record (Don Clyne) also produced the King Midas record listed here. However there is another record by King Midas/Mufflers, which I don't have, on Chrome, which is said to be from Kansas. Can anyone clarify? And what other Kanwics are there??

143 KING MIDAS/MUFFLERS - Mellow Moonlight/ Tramp
152 BLUE BANANA - Spicks and Specks/My Luv

THREE RIVERS: The label says "New York", but the Shillings are said to be a Boston band, although some identify them with the band of the same name that was active in Pittsburg. The erratic number system makes it impossible to speculate how many other records exist on this label. Please help!

701 SHILLINGS - Lying and Trying/Children and Flowers
6778/9 SHILLINGS - Goodbye My Lady/The World Could Stop
7427 EDDIE HAZELL - The Lonely World of Jennie Jones/The Telephone Song

RALLY: Other listings needed.
501 BILLY QUARLES - Bring Up What I've Done Wrong/Little Archie (by BILLY & THE AR-KETS)
502 BEVERLY NOBLE - Love of My Life/Better Off Without You
504 AGENTS - Gotta Help Me/Calling an Angel
505 GRODES - Love Is a Sad Song
1601 - RICO/RAVENS - Don't You Know
66507 - PERPETUAL MOTION WORKSHOP - Won't Come Down

WICKWIRE: An L.A. label, evidently active for a short time around '64, it either started with 007 and we are missing one release, or there were 6 before the Emperors that we don't know. Anyone?

13007 EMPERORS - Laughin' Linda/Blue Day
13008 DAVE MYERS/SURFTONES - Gear!/Let the Good Times Roll
13010 LADYBIRDS - To Know Him is to Love Him/Girl Without a Boy

AUDITION: Some great records on this label, yet little is known about it. Was it a demo label, an offshoot of some studio? Evidently based in or near Rochester, NY, they had two monster punk discs by the Heard and the Rogues-- both of whom I once thought to be L.A. bands. And nobody seems to know much about the early releases. Greg Prevost--how about a story?

6102 VAQUEROS - Echo/Desert Wind
6104 VITRONES - Linda/London Fog
6107 HEARD - Stop it Baby/Laugh with the Wind
6109 ROGUES - Train Kept A-Rollin'/You Better Look Now
6110 HUMANS - Warning/Take a Taxi

APOGEE: There must be a story behind this label. Brian Wilson sang on 2 of its releases, including the legendary Hale & Hushabyes session (featuring Sonny & Cher, Darlene Love, Jackie DeShannon, Jack Nitzsche--see BOMP 16), produced by Nitzsche as a favor to Green & Stone, on whose York label it later appeared. But how did it come to be on Apogee? And how the Basil Swift happen to come out on Apogee prior to its national release on Mercury? Perhaps this was a demo label belonging to or used by some hot L.A. producer, agent, or manager of the era? David Gates was involved in 106, and 101 featured Pat & Lolly Vegas, go-go perennials in their pre-Redbone days.

101 PAT & LOLLY VEGAS - The Robot Walk/Don't You Remember
102 LINDA GAYE SCOTT - Joey's Last Big Game/ The Spark That Flamed the Fire
103 RICKY ALLEN - It's Love Baby
104 HALE & HUSHABYES - Yes Sire, That's My Baby/900 Quetzals
105 SCOTT DOUGLAS - The Beatles' Barber/ The Wall Paper Song
106 DAVE HILL - New Orleans/The Only Boy on the Beach
108 BASIL SWIFT & SEAGRAMS - Farmer's Daughter

CHICORY: Although many Colorado groups appeared on it, Chicory was based in L.A. and run by Frank Slay, former manager of Freddy Cannon and partner of Bob Crewe. Slay moved around a lot in the '60s and it's hard to say for sure, but his Claridge/Southern Sound labels were going around the same time, recording mostly East Coast groups. But Lady Wilde, Monocles, Rainy Daze, Boenzee Cryque and Higher Elevation were definitely Colorado-based, and Slay parlayed "Acapulco GOld" into a national hit with Uni Records, who also picked up Boenzee Cryque and other Slay groups like the Strawberry ALarm Clock (nee Sixpence) for whom Slay imported John Carter, author of "Gold", to write "Incense & Peppermints" and others. But the Colorado connection has never been fully explained, and what's more, the 1600-series, initiating a London distribution deal, seems to consist of NY recordings, with the first 3 produced by Charlie Calello, an old Crewe sidekick. The remaining questions include: how did Question Mark/Mysterians come to be on Chicory, and who on earth were Chess and Checker with the bizarre "Chicken in the Logo" and indeed, why did Chicory have so many strange, freaky releases (ie 407,408,401,1603)??

400 LADY WILDE - Noise of Sound/Poor Kid
401 CHIP TYLER - Because I Love You
402 PAT BANNISTER - Mad-Mod-Miniskirt/ One Too Many Mornings
404 RAINY DAZE - That Acapulco Gold/In My Mind Lives a Forest
405 DARIUS D'PAUL - Beauty/Challenge of Youth
406 BOENZEE CRYQUE - Still in Love With You Baby/Sky Gone Gray
407 MONOCLES - Spider and the Fly/On the Other Side of Happiness
408 HIGHER ELEVATION - Diamond Mine/Crazy Bicycle
410 QUESTION MARK/MYSTERIANS - She Goes to Church on Sunday/Talk is Cheap
1600 RENAULTS - Two Face/Ten Questions
1601 SHONA & PARTY LIGHTS - Miracle Maker/ Nice Guy
1602 JIM ELLER - It's as Simple as That/ For Adults Only
1603 CHESS AND CHECKER - Chicken in the Logo/Babycakes

There's also the possibility that the 1600 series came before the 400's. In fact, considering the dates, it's probable. In that case "Chicken in the Logo" may be called the transitional record to all the weirdness that followed. Frank Slay, if you're out there: care to clear things up for us?

DUANE: Not to be confused with the San Jose label of the same name, this is a label apparently based in Bermuda, with some kind of New York connection. We know of 2 singles:

1042 - Weads - Today/Don't Call My Name
? - Gents - If You DOn't Come Back/?

and one LP: THE SAVAGES - Live & Wild

HIGHLAND: We're looking for any listings at all on this L.A. label, which may have had as many as a couple hundred 45s in the early-mid '60s, including the classic "Security" by the In-Be-Tween (pre-Slade) and lots of weird surf novelties, Fowley/Paxton productions, etc.

HYPE: We need any and all listings for any and all labels using this name (send xerox of label if you can).

INVICTA: Any listings besides what we have here, for this label that seems to have been run by Skip Battyn. Also any info...

9001 - Skip & Hustlers - In the Soup
9004 - Babs Cooper - Little Echo

MUSICLAND: Another confusing number series, and ambiguous geography. Best known as the label of Bob Kuban & the In-Men, a St. Louis group, the label also had singles by the Ohio group Fully Assembled, and some by the Klassmen (with and without Gayle McCormick), and a lot of missing numbers. It was distributed nationally by Bell, but the details of who ran it, where it was based, and what else was released, we don't know.

20001 - Bob Kuban - The Cheater
20003 - Bob Kuban - The Pretzel/Pretzel Party
20006 - Bob Kuban - The Teaser
20007 - Bob Kuban - Drive My Car
20011 - The GUise - Long Haired Music/When You're Sorry
20015 - The Guise - Chumpy McGee/Half a Man
20016 - Klassmen - Can't You Hear the Music
118 - Gayle McCormick & Klassmen - Wondrous Time/Mr. Loveman
1112 - Fully Assembled - The Cheater/Feel It

Incidentally, both sides of 118 were written by Keith Colley, an L.A. songwriter who also penned songs for the Knickerbockers.

NOTE: I know we've left out some obvious ones, but the BOMP collection isn't fully cross-indexed yet, so bear with us, and send in whatever additional listings you may have...

TOWER RECORDS

Until the recent publication of the final edition of the Stack-o-Wax books, we were planning to run a discography of this label, one of the truly important singles labels of the '60s. So much for that. However there are still some gaps to be filled, and it occurs to me that some of the missing numbers may have been given out by Capitol (the parent label) when it did custom pressing jobs. For instance, Hand 496, by the Oxford Watchband, has what could be a Tower number, and it's even got the same typeface. I throw this out as a mere hypothesis, but if anyone out there can suggest other numbers that tie-in, maybe we can solve this question...

Well that's enough questions for this time. I realize magazines are supposed to answer questions, and we've been asking an awful lot, but it should be evident that the story behind all the thousands of odd records of the '60s can only be pieced together with the cooperation of us all, from each part of the country, and that it will take years. This is the purpose to which the new BOMP Magazine is devoted, so get ready for plenty more puzzlers in the issues to come. And as the pieces come together, the answers will appear......

FEEDBACKKKKKK letters

ATTACK OF THE GARAGE BANDS

You deserve a medal for remaining true to your convictions throughout **BOMP**'s sordid history, which I've witnessed since issue #3. Although the music and artists have changed, you've managed to focus on the pure *fun* of rock 'n' roll in both today's and yesterday's life. Great stuff!

It seems to me that in much of the new rock journalism I sense an enshrinement of '60s garage bands as representing America's last honest rock 'n' roll; it deserves mention that garage bands played that way because they didn't know any better and we enjoyed their fresh spirit because we didn't *have* any better. The people who made that music either dead-ended and wound up selling shoes, or progressed in their musical knowledge & sophistication and made the music we've loved/hated over the past dozen or so years. The latter artists have at least realized that junior-high lyrics and pure energy alone do not make great music. Today, the musical proficiency of people like Lowe, Costello, the Knack, the Cars, the Records, etc., combines with the raw power to make for some terrible music, music that couldn't be performed by people who didn't know their instruments. The *spirit* of garage bands was untouchable — let's emulate that energy, not the shoddy musicianship of the '60s. There's no excuse for bad playing anymore!

— Al Quaglieri
Albany, NY

[*I'm not sure about that one...in some of the new punk bands, early Pistols for instance, lack of musicianship was more than compensated by energy and attitude, an important factor you overlook. The garage bands you mention had an attitude of naive arrogance that may in fact be timeless. Without an attitude worth identifying with no amount of proficiency can make a band interesting. Just ask Rick Wakeman. Anyway not all '60s garage records were badly played. Most of the legendary ones were, I think, a lot better than the general run of today's punk attempts.* —ed.]

CLASH COURSE REQUIRED

Do you know of where I can get the lyrics to the Clash's "White Man in Hammersmith Palais?" I want them for my high school class I teach in English, but I can't make out all the words of the song.

— Gary Brown
Orlando, FL

[*The words are in English already.* —Ed.]

BERLIN DIARY

I'm afraid I won't be able to write a full story for you on the Berlin beat scene, simply for time problems. This project would need many interviews, and a comprehensive approach. Having been around, having seen most of them and known a few members would not be enough, though I will continue to share with you what springs to mind when I am writing letters. Like:

The Hound Dogs and the Boots were two of the major groups in Berlin as far as a steady following goes. The Hound Dogs covered the North of the city, whereas the Boots were from the South and playing the clubs there, especially the Top Ten in Berlin-Rudow, now called the Top Disco. An interesting note about the Hound Dogs is that they played "House of the Rising Sun" in 1963, before the Animals had it on record. The Hound Dogs were asked to record it, but refused, later they started recording, without much success. "House of the Rising Sun" never appeared by them. When the Who came to Berlin to appear at the Sportpalast (now torn down) in '66, both the Hound Dogs and the Boots were among the support bands. It was a "Battle of the Bands." Also among the support acts were the Summer Set, who were close on harmonies and sounded somewhat like the Beach Boys. Their organist was none other than Les Humphries, who became extremely famous in the 70s with his choir, the Les Humphries Singers.

Making records wasn't very profitable for bands in the 60s. It was mostly singles and they sold in low numbers. German bands didn't mean much in their own country; except the Rattles and the Lords, none of them recorded prolifically.

Perusing **BOMP**'s Star Club listing (certainly a label that had to catch your eye as it is the only coherent German beat label), I want to make some points about the Odd Persons (STC 148551). They were originally known as Dietmar & the Beat Boys when they were still amateurs. I heard Dietmar's band several times in '64 at a youth club called The Flamingo Club in Berlin-Schoeneberg. The club was a ramshackle house that burnt down at least twice in its history and was notorious for trouble in the late '60s. Dietmar and the Beat Boys had a large following in their district and were a vigorous, sweaty band who could really whoop it up. Their lead guitarist Ingo Kramer was the son of a famous radio orchestra guitarist and is now a session-man. Their drummer tended to undress from the waist up during shows, which is now very common, but in '64 was pretty wild doing! When they went professional they changed their name to Odd Persons. You will most likely have seen the write-up about them in Star Club News, just after the name change.

The other Berlin groups on Star Club were the Team Beats Berlin (natch!) and the Ones (148593), who came rather late and had a young white boy with a soulful voice as their vocalist, something like Berlin's own Stevie Winwood.

About Drafi Deutscher: his career took a serious slump when he was tried and convicted of posing naked at his window in front of a girl child. At the time he lived in Berlin Hansaviertel, a nice quarter of apartments that were all built in '56 during the Interbau exhibition. After this incident he faded from the scene and started a business selling goods on local markets. He tried a comeback some time ago, but never became as hot again as he was in '64-66.

On the subject of **BOMP**, I'm very thankful that you are changing it back to something resembling the old format. I didn't have much illusion about the new wave scene in the first place, so it comes as no surprise to me that you're getting disillusioned with it now. I believe that in a time when "big money" is waiting for any band capable of holding their instruments and hopping on a bandwagon, a strong musical scene cannot develop long enough in a grass roots environment. As long as the sound stays in certain clubs, pubs or collectors circles without surfacing, only the good and true examples can gain any value. But once it's out to the public, any music is bound to get watered down by monetary influences and by the need to compromise for a bigger audience.

Some musical scenes that lasted for quite some time before they got caught by the money machine are British R&B and Northern Soul (popularized mainly by clubs and collectors), British pub rock, and rockabilly.

— Wolfgang Weissbrod
Berlin, W. German

PARLAIZ-VOUS FRANCOISE?

Finally somebody does a piece on Francois Hardy! It was a half-assed job but anything on her is welcome. However the history had gaping holes in it. The discography was pathetically inadequate and there was no mention of her current activities.

Francoise has comfortably settled into middle age with a low-key Carly Simon type image, although she's better at it than Carly. She released an LP, *Star*, which was finally released in the U.S. by Peters last year. She has recently had a hit single in France and just released a new LP, although I've yet to hear it. She was recently photographed in a Ramones-style jacket with the same hairstyle she fancied in the mid-60's. She looks older but she can still share a bottle of wine with me anytime.

I would much rather have seen a color picture of her than the Go-Go's. But thanks anyway for the effort. Why don't you con those clowns at *Trouser Press* into doing something more elaborate on her? She was a hell of a lot more fun than Dire Straits anyday.

— M. Monko
San Francisco, CA

[*But not as commercial, eh wot? Anyway, don't blame Andy Simons for the gaps in his article — we sat on his story for a couple of years before it was published. As for the discography, we'd love to print any addenda you or others would care to send.* —Ed.]

BETTER LATE THAN NEVER

Dear Greg Shaw:

I just want to say that I'm a fan of your magazine and your courage to speak your mind way back in 1973 when I believe you spoke about a revival of 1960's type music which led to your getting fired from *Creem*. They thought you were crazy or bizarre because you thought the Standells were better than the Allman Brothers, but you weren't. I'm glad you turned out to be right. I hope your magazine is still in existence and you plan to still write columns and produce records because God knows we need people like you. I know that it has become more and more difficult to make profit from this passion called rock & roll. But still we need the free-enterprise system and I'd like to say thanks for being a good American.

My brother Robert is the drummer of 2 bands in Southeast Wisconsin. He's in a band called the Orbits, one of Milwaukee's finest, and also in the Phones, out of my hometown, Elkhorn. The Phones even do a Flamin' Groovies song. The Orbits do "A Quick One" so us Midwest cats certainly aren't stupid.

Me, I'm in the army. I certainly don't want to go to war but I'd love to go over to Iran to blow somebody away. If you're shy of death you shouldn't come in.

— James L. Wren
HAAF, Georgia

UGLY THINGS magazine

"Ugly Things continues to be the best fanzine ever" - Greg Shaw

Since 1983 UGLY THINGS MAGAZINE has brought its readers unparalleled coverage of WILD SOUNDS FROM PAST DIMENSIONS: the best lost, unknown and overlooked music of the 1960s and beyond. Published twice a year, each issue features around 200 pages of in-depth features, exclusive interviews, rare photos and more, including a massive review section sifting through hundreds of CD and vinyl reissues as well as music-related books and DVDs. UGLY THINGS is not a hobbyist publication for trainspotting elitists, it is a high energy magazine about music and the stories of the people that made it happen.

Bands and artists we have covered include: The Misunderstood, The Belfast Gypsies, The Move, The Monks, The Creation, The Yardbirds, The Seeds, The Sons of Adam, Love, The Music Machine, The Phantom Brothers, Kim Fowley, The Missing Links, The Shangri-La's, The Chocolate Watchband, The MC5, Screaming Lord Sutch, The Downliners Sect, The Real Kids, The Dave Clark Five, The Damnation of Adam Blessing, The Outsiders, and The Pretty Things.

"Why don't you call it Ugly & Beautiful Things?" - Sky Saxon

www.ugly-things.com